ISBN 978-0-656-34798-8
PIBN 10798879

THE
POETICAL WORKS
OF
ROBERT MONTGOMERY, M.A. OXON.

COLLECTED AND REVISED BY THE AUTHOR.

LONDON:
CHAPMAN AND HALL, 193, PICCADILLY.
1854.

LONDON:
BRADBURY AND EVANS, PRINTERS, WHITEFRIARS.

GENERAL PREFACE.

"God Himself is Truth; in propagating which, as men display a greater integrity and zeal, they approach nearer to the similitude of God, and possess a greater portion of His love."—JOHN MILTON.

"Lux crescit indies: per adversa ad victoriam enititur veritas: multis de rebus posteritas aliter judicabit. O Deus! Tuô judiciô stat caditve, quicquid stat vel cadit: quod per me operari dignatus es, tuere: lectorum et mei miserere. Tibi est gloria, et esto in perpetuum!"—BENGEL.

SEVERAL works of the author's having been for some period out of print, an opportunity offered itself for publishing a collected edition of his poetical works in one volume, and the result is now before the public in the present volume. The different poems of which this edition consists, for several reasons, are not arranged in chronological order; they commence with "The Omnipresence of the Deity," which was written in the author's nineteenth year; and are followed by "The Christian Life," his latest production in a lengthened form. Each poem has been diligently revised; and that one ("Luther") which, from its peculiar difficulties, seemed to require the most elaborate revision, has been extensively corrected; and, in many places, re-written and newly arranged.

"Commenta opinionum delet dies; Naturæ judicia confirmat," is a Ciceronian maxim equally useful for authors and readers to recollect and apply: and since a long preface is an infliction few people like to endure, the writer will be as brief as decorum will allow, on the present occasion. Each of the works contained in this volume is accompanied by the Preface which originally introduced it to the world, and is best calculated to explain the nature and design of what is there attempted. Hence, a few general remarks are all which shall now be obtruded on the reader.

The late accomplished scholar and critic, Kerchever Arnold,* in

* In his "Theological Critic."

a comment on "The Christian Life," said that, "with the exception of Wordsworth, few writers had experienced extremes of criticism equally with the author of that volume." How far or not this was correct, others will decide; but if the reader desires to have *one* illustration of what Arnold meant, he has only to compare the criticisms on Poems which appeared more than twenty years ago, from the pen of Professor Wilson in the pages of "Blackwood's Magazine," with reviews on the same works, in its Northern cotemporary. One thing is undeniable, viz., to a vast extent the history of Criticism abounds with examples of condemnations reversed, and approvals unconfirmed. The proper effect of this fact is, not to provoke sardonic triumph on the one hand, or splenetic ill-humour on the other: but, modesty of mind; diffidence in pronouncing our opinions; and that genial state of heart which prompts us rather to encourage effort than depress it,—these are among the moral benefits which this contrast between individual strictures and popular decisions, is calculated to produce.

Some of the poems which this volume contains, have stood the test of nearly a quarter of a century; and under the protection of this fact, an author can scarcely be accused of unseemly confidence in expressing his hope, that such productions cannot have entirely failed in finding a welcome in the catholic sentiments, and a home in the common heart, of Mankind. Differ as we may in our standards of individual taste,* it will

* A true critic is an intellectual benefactor to mankind; and in the priesthood of Letters, no function ought to be considered more sacred than that of conscientious criticism. But it cannot be denied, something more than intellectual power, correct taste, dialectic skill, and classical erudition, are required for the constitution of such a critic; and that is—a principle of moral elevation and sacred rectitude, which lifts them above what is conventional, into the pure region of ideal Beauty and abstract Truth. Meanwhile, all who appreciate mental culture lament to see Criticism lose its legitimate influence; and to hear, when works are eulogised, the ordinary question—"Who is the *friend?*" when they censure—"Who is the *foe?*" Many palliations may be offered for such a state of things; among them, not the least would be, the ever-recurring novelties in the world of publication, which defy the energy of the most honest reviewer to overtake their number, and appreciate their claims. Let it be also remembered, we are living not only at a period of great intellectual excitement, but when the deepest Problems and most difficult Questions of our common Humanity, are being analysed around us. Hence, there are few volumes which can be discussed simply and exclusively on the basis of their own isolate merits. They impinge upon a myriad associations; and the critic, with every desire, perhaps, to be impartial, is *unconsciously* swayed by one-sided influences derived from political bias, personal feeling, or sectarian prejudice. Meanwhile, looking to our common nature; remembering our Fatherhood in God, our Brotherhood in Christ, and His Mystical Body the Church, our safest excess is on the side of charity, when we pronounce a critical judgment upon the writings of others. It is easy to be severe; but always noble to

be admitted by the varied schools of Criticism, that, after all, *Public Appreciation* is the ultimate Judge by whose decisions writers, whether in prose or verse, are permanently affected. Every author must be

be just. We may think it right to chastise arrogance and expose pretension; but let it never be forgotten, he who *wilfully* commits intellectual injustice, is a moral criminal. He writes, indeed, behind the Press; but he acts before his God; and is, therefore, as truly responsible for the influence he exercises in printed words, as he is for the example he exhibits by personal character.

Much, perhaps, of what now appears arbitrary and capricious in criticism upon the Fine Arts, would be removed, if the Judgment to which they are submitted were better trained for the office it attempts to fulfil. But, unfortunately, a profound work on the Principles of Taste and the Philosophy of Criticism, is a boon yet to be conferred on English Literature. At present, there seems to be no common standard, no decisive test, unto which a final appeal can be made. All seems to be accidental preference; or individual caprice. Of course, we are not unmindful of Lord Kaimes' "Elements of Criticism," "Blair's Lectures," &c.; but neither of these works approaches to the philosophy of Criticism and Taste.

Thus, in the present state of diffused literature, a youthful reader, who has a modest fear of his own powers, and desires to have the taste disciplined and judgment guided by our leading Reviews, finds himself in a frequent dilemma; that is to say, he perceives the *same* work which is eulogised as a masterpiece of intellect by one critic, denounced as the perfection of imbecility by another! and, in either case, he is ingenuous enough to believe, that these contrasted judgments are pronounced with candour and discrimination. Now, at this point of intellectual experience, a comprehensive Treatise on the true Principles and Philosophy of Criticism would be a refuge to which he might resort, for guidance and instruction. But the limitation of a mere note will not allow us to proceed; we will, therefore, terminate it by adducing one or two extracts bearing upon the general subject from writers of acknowledged authority.

Dugald Stewart, in his "Philosophical Essay," (p. 428, &c.,) observes, "Although, in ancient languages, the word 'Taste' was certainly not employed in that metaphysical acceptation which has now become so familiar to the ear, it is evident that the analogy which led to the metaphor did not entirely escape the ancient critics. Quintilian, in particular, speaking of this very power, observes, '*that it is not to be communicated by instruction any more than the sense of taste or smell.*' (?) And with respect to some of its objects, he tells us, '*they are perceived by a latent judgment of the mind, resembling the decision of the palate.*' 'Quod sentitur latente judiciô, velut palatô.'" The same delightful Essayist, also, quotes a curious passage from the "Theætetus" of Plato. "There is no question," says Socrates in this Dialogue, "*concerning that which is agreeable to each person, but concerning what will in time to come be agreeable, of which all men are not equally judges. You and the cook may judge of the dish on the table equally well; but while the dish is making the cook can better foretell what will ensue from this or that manner of composing it.*" How exactly does this coincide with that remarkable expression which Lord Chatham applied to the taste displayed in landscape gardening, when he spoke of its "*prophetic eye.*" Again, Stewart thus alludes to morbid fastidiousness and one-sided individualism, in criticisms on the Fine Arts: "'The tragedy of Douglas (says Gray in one of his letters) has infinite faults; but there is one scene (that between Matilda and the old peasant) *which strikes me blind to all the defects.*' * * * Such also was the feeling which dictated a memorable precept of La Bruyère, of which I will not impair the force by attempting a translation. 'Quand une lecture vous élève l'esprit, et qu'elle vous inspire des sentimens nobles et courageux, ne cherchez pas une autre règle pour juger de l'ouvrage; il est bon, et fait de main de Ouvrier.' How different both sentiments, from that fastidiousness of Taste, by an affectation of which it is usual for little

inwardly conscious how far or not his aims are noble, his inspirations pure, and his mental endowments consecrated to the sacred function of glorifying their Divine Original, by promoting the real elevation of mankind. If indeed "*whatsoever things are lovely and of good report*" (Phil. iv. 8) actuate his energies, and inspire his faculties, then may he boldly endeavour to fulfil the Mission of mind unto which he conceives himself called. Under the banner of those sublime words, "None of us liveth *to himself*" (Rom. xiv. 7), let him be faithful to his Conscience and his Creed; and leave the issues with *Him* in whose hands our destinies both for time and eternity repose.

> Nam pro jucundis aptissima quæque dabunt Dî
> Carior est illis homo quam sibi;
> Permittes ipsis expendere numinibus, quid
> Conveniat nobis, rebusque sit utile nostris.*

minds to court the reputation of superior refinement!" (p. 464). In producing, however, this fastidiousness, whether affected or real, various *moral* causes, such as jealousy, rivalship, personal dislike, or the spleen of conscious inferiority, may conspire with the *intellectual* defects which have been mentioned; nay, the same moral causes may be conceived to be so powerful in their influence as to produce this unfortunate effect in spite of every intellectual gift which nature and education can bestow. It is observed by Shenstone, that "*good taste and good nature are inseparably united;*" and although the observation is by no means true when thus stated as an unqualified proposition, it will be found to have a sufficient foundation in fact to deserve the attention of those who have a pleasure in studying the varieties of human character. One thing is certain, "*that as habitual deficiency in good humour is sufficient to warp the decisions of the soundest taste, so the taste of an individual, in proportion as it appears to be free from capricious biases, affords a strong presumption that the temper is unsuspicious, open, and generous.*" (p. 465.)

On the difficult subject, whether Taste be an ultimate principle, and as to what constitutes its absolute Standard, Blair speaks with much truthful discrimination in the following passage. ("Lectures," vol. i.)—"Taste is ultimately founded on an internal sense of beauty, which is natural to man, and which, in its application to particular objects, is capable of being guided and enlightened by reason. Now, were there any one person who possessed in full perfection all the powers of human nature, whose internal senses were in every instance exquisite and just, whose reason was unerring and sure, the determination of such a person concerning beauty, would be a perfect standard for the taste of all others. But as there is no such living standard, no one person to whom all mankind will allow such submission to be due, what is there of sufficient authority to be the standard of the various and opposite tastes of men? *Most certainly there is nothing but the Taste, as far as it can be gathered, of Human Nature. That which men concur the most in admiring, must be held to be beautiful. His taste must be held to be just and true, which coincides with the general sentiments of men. In this standard we must rest. To the sense of mankind the ultimate appeal must ever lie in works of taste.* If any one should maintain that sugar was bitter and tobacco sweet, no reasoning could avail to prove it. The taste of such a person would infallibly be held to be diseased, merely because it differed so widely from the taste of the species to which he belongs. In like manner, with regard to the objects of sentiment, or internal taste, the common feelings of men carry the same authority, and have a title to regulate the taste of every individual."—(pp. 38, 39.)

* Juv. Sat. 10.

If, in the pursuance of such hallowed purpose, he awakens abiding echoes in the heart of Humanity, he will be grateful unto the Supreme Author of good. If, on the contrary, he finds he has overrated his powers, and does not reach the goal where he hoped to arrive, he must endure the result with Christian resignation. Although he has not succeeded in procuring fame, let him remember no public career is a failure, if the Intellect has been trained, and the Will disciplined, by purifying labour and elevated effort. Indeed, compared with the spiritual expansion of a man's own nature, how worthless is mere reputation, were it possible to be wide as the universe, and lasting as eternity! Constituted as our fallen world is, the proud achievements of intellect, apart from all moral consideration, will never cease to fix and fascinate the regards of mankind. But, He who "*made himself of no reputation*," has revealed unto mankind a "*more excellent way*" in those awful words, which prophetic Conscience reverberates: "*What shall it profit a man, if he shall gain the whole world, and lose his own soul?*"

One point remains, unto which the author may now be permitted to refer. In a series of poems extending from the verge of boyhood unto mature life, it must be expected, during so long a period, a writer's sentiments and opinions on themes of vital interest will undergo various modifications, and exhibit corresponding developments. In the present instance, it would be uncandid not to confess, that the catholic Attributes of the Church, and her Sacramental connections with the One Almighty Head of His Mystical Body, when the author published his early poems, were almost doctrinally ignored and popularly forgot. Hence, between his first and last production, a theological reader will detect expressions and thoughts which attest the power and presence of those Spiritual Influences awakened around him, during the period referred to. But surely, it would be a harsh injustice to brand all modifications of religious Sentiment as apostacies! Supposing them to be a conscientious growth of our spiritual and intellectual Being, and controlled by those supernatural aids, obtained by all who seek them in faith and prayer,—no honourable mind will condemn them as mere inconsistencies. More or less, such variations in mental and moral life are almost inevitable. Again: no author who compares what he wrote at nineteen, with what he has published at forty, can realize the comparison without a feeling of self-correction. If he be a devout man, he will at once confess, that had *some* of those high and hallowed Themes to which his youthful powers were consecrated, been deferred to a later period of life, he would have discussed them with more reverence, fullness, and depth, than his earlier pages now exhibit. But, perhaps, it may be replied, although this regret is, in a moral respect, a sound one, it is both useless and unphilosophical. According to the will of Providence, a man can no more forestall his intellectual development, than he can anticipate his physical vigour. Each is analogically subject unto time and experience; and depends upon those gradational laws by which mind and body are changed and controlled.

The writer will now conclude these imperfect remarks by appending a letter from the poet Wordsworth,* in relation unto that manly spirit of mental independence an author should exhibit towards his own productions. It was addressed unto him nearly twenty years since, in reply to an epistle written under extreme dejection; and will be found full of dignity, sobriety, and good sense. The eulogistic paragraphs on "The Omnipresence," &c., are omitted; and those portions alone retained which may be as suggestive to some of his youthful contemporaries, as the author trusts they proved unto himself. The Preface unto which Wordsworth alludes, will be found in the present volume; and serves to introduce an edition of "The Omnipresence of the Deity," published in 1835.

From "Memoirs of Wordsworth," vol. ii. p. 294.

"*February*, 1835.

"In your letter, for which also I thank you, you allude to your Preface, and desire to know if my opinion concurs with yours on the subject of sacred poetry. That Preface has been read to me, and I can answer in the affirmative; but, at the same time, allow me frankly to tell you, what *most* pleased me in that able composition is to be found in the few concluding paragraphs, beginning,—'It is now seven years since,' &c. . . . .

"I cannot conclude without one word of literary advice, which I hope you will deem my advanced age entitles me to give. Do not, my dear sir, be anxious about any individual's opinion concerning your writings, however highly you may think of his genius, or rate his judgment. Be a severe critic to yourself, and depend upon it no person's decision upon the merit of your work will bear comparison in point of value with your own. You must be conscious from what feeling they have flowed; and how far they may, or may not, be allowed to claim, on that account, permanent respect. Above all, I would remind you, with a view to tranquillize and steady your mind, that no man takes the trouble of surveying and pondering another man's writing with a hundredth part of the care which an author of sense and genius will have bestowed upon his own. Add to this reflection another, which I press upon you, as it has supported me through life, viz., that posterity will settle all accounts justly; and that works which deserve to last will last; and if undeserving this fate, the sooner they perish the better.

"Believe me to be faithfully,

"Your much obliged

"W. WORDSWORTH."

For the able and accurate Index which accompanies this edition of his collected Poems, the author is entirely indebted to the taste and judgment of the Rev. JOHN TWYCROSS, A.M., &c.

CONTENTS.

THE CHRISTIAN LIFE—*continued.*

MISCELLANEOUS POEMS—*continued.*

ALPHABETICAL LIST OF FIRST LINES TO CHRISTIAN LIFE.

THE

OMNIPRESENCE OF THE DEITY.

"Whither shall I go from Thy Spirit? or whither shall I flee from Thy presence?—If I ascend up into heaven, Thou art there: if I make my bed in hell, behold Thou art there. If I take the wings of the morning, and dwell in the uttermost parts of the sea; even there shall Thy hand lead me, and Thy right hand shall hold me."—*Psalm* cxxxix. 7—10.

"Thou sole Transcendency! and deep Abyss
From whence the universe of life was drawn,
Unutter'd is Thy nature—to Thyself alone
The fathom'd, proved, and comprehended God!"

THE

OMNIPRESENCE OF THE DEITY.

PREFACE

TO

THE TWENTY-FIFTH EDITION.

(1848.)

THE present Edition of the following poem is accompanied by some descriptive lines entitled "*Scarborough*,"* which appear for the first time, in their enlarged form, among the miscellanies contained in the volume. In addition to this, a few other poems of a meditative character have also been transferred to the position they now occupy. Beyond this brief notification, little requires to be said. However, it may not be obtrusive for the Author to refer to a theological difficulty almost inseparable from a metrical work which endeavours to celebrate the Omnipresence of God in a simple and popular form. What he means will be understood, perhaps, by the following considerations.

Revelation is not absolute, but relative; that is to say, the language of the Bible, though inspired, is necessarily finite, and *refers* not to what the Godhead may be in Its Divine Essence *absolutely considered*, but rather unto those mutual relations which subsist between the perfect Creator and the imperfect creature; consequently, all the knowledge which we possess of the Divine Nature must be analogical; or, in other terms, a knowledge of *relations* existing under a presumed resemblance. This necessary view of the Deity has been powerfully treated in Dr. King's celebrated "Discourse on Predestination," which speaks as follows on this subject:—

"It is in effect agreed on all hands, that the nature of God, as it is in itself, is incomprehensible by human understanding: and not His nature, but likewise His powers and faculties, and the ways and methods in which He exercises them, are so far beyond our reach, that we are utterly incapable of forming exact notions of them." * * * "We ought to remember that the descriptions which we frame to ourselves of God, or of the Divine attributes, are not taken from any direct or immediate perceptions that we have of Him or them; but from some observation we have made of His works, and from the consideration of these qualifications, that *we conceive would enable us to perform the like*." * * * * "Thus our reason teaches us to ascribe these attributes to God, *by way of resemblance and analogy* to such qualities and powers as we find most valuable and perfect in ourselves. If we look into the Holy Scriptures, and consider the representations given us there of God or His attributes, we shall find them generally of the same nature, and plainly borrowed from some resemblance to things with which we are acquainted by our senses." * * * "And this brings me to the second head, which I proposed to myself in this discourse, which was to show you why God and heavenly things are, after this manner, presented to us in Holy Scripture. And the first reason I shall offer is, that we must be either content to know them this way, or not at all. I have already told you, and I believe every considering man is assured, *that the nature and perfections of God as He is in Himself, are such that it is impossible we should comprehend them*, especially in the present state of imperfection, ignorance, and corruption, in which this world lies. He is the object of none of our senses by which we receive all our direct and immediate perception of things: and therefore if we know anything of Him at all, it must be by the deductions of reason, by analogy, by resembling Him to something that we do know, and are acquainted with."—"This analogical knowledge of God's Nature and Attributes, is all of which we are capable at present; and we must be either contented to know Him thus, or sit down with an entire neglect and ignorance of God, and finally despair of future happiness!"

* This Poem will be found among the Miscellaneous Subjects at the end of the volume.

So far, then, as the use of analogical terms is involved, a poem on The Omnipresence is intimately connected with forms of language, partaking of analogy and moral resemblance, presumed to exist between the relations which men bear to men, and God bears to all mankind; thence a danger arises of our humanising the Idea of Divine Omnipresence, as though God were present by local diffusion, and a kind of infinite expansion. This, of course, is not correct, because it would be more accurate to assert that *all place is present unto God*, than to affirm that *God is present to all place*. In order, then, to protect the reader from this erroneous conception of the Omnipresent nature of Deity, the following propositions, from one of the noblest of our divines, are worthy our deepest consideration:—"Our knowledge of God is mostly withdrawing from Him, or denying to Him, in our conception, any weaknesses or imperfections in the creature. As the infinity of God is a denial of limitation of being, so immensity or omnipresence is a denial of limitation of space: and when we say God is *totus* in every place, we must understand it thus,—that He is not everywhere by parts, as bodies are, as light and air are; He is everywhere; that is, His nature hath no bounds; He is not tied to any place, as the creature is, who, when he is present in one place, is absent from another. As no place can be without God, so no place can compass and contain Him." * * * "The essential presence of God is *without any division* of Himself." "*I fill heaven and earth*," not part in heaven and part in earth; I fill one as well as the other. One part of His essence is not in one place, and another part of His essence in another place; He would then be changeable; for the part of His essence which were new in this place, He might alter to another; *but He is undivided everywhere.* As His eternity is one individual point, though in our conception we divide it into past, present, and to come, so the whole world is as a point to Him in regard of place;" &c. &c.

In a deeper strain, and with more fulness of doctrinal significance, the religious metaphysics of Coleridge have been brought to bear on the popular notion of Christ's omnipresence, as realised by the worshipping faculties of our nature. In his "IDEA OF CHURCH AND STATE," (4th Ed. p. 129,) he thus writes: "'Where two or three are gathered together in my name, there am I in the midst of them.' The true import of these gracious, soul-awing words, is too generally overlooked. It is not the comments or harangues of unlearned and fanatical preachers that I have in my mind, but sermons of great and deserved celebrity, and divines whose learning, well-regulated zeal, and sacred Scriptural views, are as honourable to the Church as their piety, beneficence, and blameless life are to the Christian name, when I say that passages occur, which might almost lead you to conjecture that the author had found the words, '*I will come and join you*,' instead of '*I am in the midst of you*:' passages from which it is difficult not to infer, that they had interpreted the promise as of a *corporal co-presence*, instead of a Spiritual immanence (ὅτι μένει ἐν ἡμῖν); as of an individual coming in, or down, and taking a place, as soon as the required number of petitioners was completed; as if, in short, this presence, this actuation of the I AM (εἰμὶ ἐν μέσω αὐτῶν) were an after consequence, an accidental and separate result and reward of the contemporaneous and contiguous worshipping; and not the total act itself, of which the spiritual Christ (one and the same in all the faithful,) is the originating and perfective unity. Even as the physical life is in each limb and organ of the body, all in every part, but is manifested as life, by being one in all, and thus making one all; even so with Christ, our spiritual life. He is in each true believer, in his solitary prayer, and during his silent communion in the watches of the night, no less than in the congregation of the faithful: but He manifests His indwelling presence more characteristically, with especial evidence, when many, convened by His name, whether for prayer or for counsel, do through Him become one."

Such are some of the aspects under which theological Science would have us contemplate the omnipresence of Divine Personality. But let it not be forgotten, that unto us, the baptised and believing members of Christ's Church, pure and apostolical,—THE INCARNATION is both the centre and circumference of the manifested Jehovah; and since the Humanity of the Redeemer is literally related unto the limiting conditions of space and time, we are not heretical in associating our ideas of God in practical connexion with the local and the temporal. After all, however, dogmatic severity of statement, and metaphysical acuteness, are neither necessary nor suitable in a poem that mainly addresses itself to the sacredness of the *religious sentiments*, and which is designed, not to feed the intellect with doctrinal truth, but rather to reach the conscience, and radiate through the character, by means of the *beautiful, and good*, as emotionally perceived. Nor let us hesitate to remark, God is not revealed unto us in Scripture in that cold, stiff, and scientific manner, in which scholastic theology delights to consider Him; but rather, in His adorable Personality, as a reconciled Father in Jesus Christ, abundant in mercy, clothed with the mysterious tenderness of the Incarnation, and commending His Attributes unto our moral affections, far more than unto our intellectual faculties. For this reason, the creed of a God-taught peasant, whose religious life moves onward with patriarchal simplicity, is approved in Heaven, prized by angels, and more in accordance with what our Church teaches,—than all which barren Metaphysics inculcate touching the omnipresence of Deity.

R. M.

51, TORRINGTON SQUARE,
August 27th, 1848.

PREFACE

TO

THE THIRTEENTH EDITION.

(1834.)

Ἴσασιν οἱ μεμυημένοι—St. Chrys. Hom.

"Si ipsius Poeseos ultima origo quæratur, ad *religionem* omnino videtur referenda. Hujusce originis non obscura indicia etiamnum præ. se fert Poesis, eo quod sacram et celestem materiam veluti parentem suam et educatricem ardentissimo affectu semper amplectatur; huc veluti ad germanam patriam amet recurrere, ibique et lubentissime versetur et maxime vigeat."—Lowth's Prælec. i. pp. 20, 21.

The Author cannot permit a revised edition of this Poem to appear, without a grateful retrospect of the reception it has obtained from the public. Many thousand copies have circulated in this country, and various foreign editions have also been published. To seem ungratified by such success would be an affected insensibility. And should the reader imagine he detects a vanity in this confession, the Author can assure him that it is subdued by a recollection of the vast disproportion which may exist between the popularity, and the merit, of any production.

The present edition has undergone a careful revision; the suggestions of critics, both hostile and friendly, have been duly regarded; and many passages which savoured of exaggeration, or obscurity, have been omitted or amended. The additional lines that accompany it, will be found, perhaps, not discordant with the general tone and tenour of the work; while the sentiments which now conclude the first part, may remove an objection which has existed against the deficiency of Christian allusion in those passages of the poem illustrative of nature, and its effects on a contemplative mind.*

A preface is an infliction which most readers deem superfluous; yet the author will venture to brave their repugnance, and to proffer some remarks on the present occasion, however unimportant they may appear.

A love for the IDEAL is enthroned in every reflective mind; and though there may be periods, when a perception of the Beautiful and the Unseen appears to slumber, or be palled,—this earthly dimness which overclouds the bright instincts of the soul, soon passes away. All that concentrates itself round the thought of man's Eternity may be referred, more or less, to a passion for the Ideal; and Religion, while eminently practical in its lofty influence, is ever attracting our Spirit to contemplate that paradise which blooms in the regions of hereafter. What is there noble in the records of Mind, to which the Ideal is entirely unrelated?—The crown which the eyes of the Martyr miniatured as he closed them in flames; the divine imitation which Meekness and Righteousness picture before them in the war of life; the grand discoveries which the prophetic dreams of Science anticipate, when she contemplates the worlds of air, or fastens her gaze on the wonders of earth; and, finally, that faultless Model which Genius ever images, in her toils and pains,—all these, in a great degree, arise from that dominion which the Ideal exercises over mankind. To assert, therefore, that this no longer exists, libels the character of the human Soul.

Now, it is the privilege of Poetry to adumbrate in language that glory, loveliness, and sublimity, which the creative eye of Imagination beholds. The living and the actual are neither perverted nor forgotten; and while the truth and sternness, the passions, principles, and working-day realities of life are described with severe fidelity, the yearnings of the soul for perfection, and its deep sense of the infinite and the immortal—may be interpreted and described. The Ideal and the Actual thus move hand in hand along the page of poesy, each lending the other its native influence; as light and shadow over a landscape contribute a divided charm, and blend with the beauty of the whole.

To the minds of those who think the art of converting pence into pounds the noblest objects of human pursuit,—observations on the benign influence of poetry will sound like the mere

---

* A mere poetical belief of a Divine Presence in the glories and harmonies of nature, if unaccompanied by a deep recollection of God's *moral attributes*, forms but a false and perilous theology. Pope's "Essay on Man," exquisite and sublime as many portions are, tends (according to Bishop Horne and other ethical critics) to an imaginative Deism; and those who have analyzed the spirit of their writings, will find that Shelley, with his system of "plastic nature," and Lord Byron, in his references to the Deity,—differ very little from the Lucretian doctrine, by which we are taught,

"Omnis enim per se Divum natura necesse est
Immortali ævo summa cum pace fruatur
Semota a nostris rebus, sejunctaque longe."
Lucret. lib. i.

To such a cold and sterile system, Clarke thus alludes, (Evid. of Nat. and Rev. Relig.)—"How handsomely soever these men may seem to speak of the *natural* attributes of God, of His knowledge, wisdom, and power; yet neither can this opinion be settled on any certain principles, nor defended by a consistent reasoning; nor can the natural attributes of God be so separated from the *moral* but that he who denies the latter may be reduced to a necessity of denying the former likewise:—he who denies the justice and goodness of God, or which is all one, denies the exercise of those attributes *in inspecting and regarding the moral actions of men*, must also deny either His wisdom, or His power, or both; and consequently must needs be driven into downright Atheism."—This opinion may be paralleled by a maxim of Tertullian.—"Deum negat auferendo quod Dei est."—Adv. Marc. c. 3.

prattle of puerile enthusiasm. And yet, though it may harmonise with the doctrines of an utilitarian to decry poetry, and to shed the mildew of his irony over every work which attempts to reveal it,—he is as tasteless, as he is unphilosophical; and, while professing to triumph over the dreams of Sentimentalism, proves himself to be the wildest of all visionaries : for, is he not so, who thinks and writes as though "profit and loss" were the be-all and the end-all of Man's existence; and considers him only as a creature for time, while the instincts of Eternity already throb in his bosom? Now, next to the renovating power of Religion, true Poetry confronts this worldly epicureanism with a sacred defiance; and, viewing man in his twofold responsibility, for time and for eternity,—appeals to him with a voice that is echoed from the depths of his intellectual being.

Lord Bacon has defined poetry to be "feigned history;" * thereby shewing what may be termed the spiritual REALITY of the poetical Ideal. Fallen from its first estate, and sullied though it be, the Soul yet retains some lineaments of the Divine Impress; and when the beautiful and good are presented for its approval, they are at once recognised as pertaining to those primeval attractions which God intended to form its chief delight.

If it were not so, what has made the visions of Milton immortal?—It is the antetype which they have found in imaginative souls, that accounts for their immortality. Divinity moves within and around us; and over the chaos of our troubled minds there often broods the calming breath of the Almighty. And as the earth, though the living bloom of Eden no longer arrays its surface, to the gaze of true Sentiment presents dream-like traces of a Paradise no more,—so, to the eye of poetical Faith, does the soul reveal faint but sublime reflections of the original brightness it had, when man walked with God, and conversed with angels, without fear.†

With reference to sacred poetry, as the writer has been favoured with much critical admonition, it will be but courteous in him to offer a few candid remarks in return.

Encouraged by the reception of his first work, the author presumed to proceed in the composition of kindred poems, intended to embody and portray whatever was allied to the Imaginative in natural and revealed religion. But, in the meantime, there rushed forth a wild flood of what was called, "Religious poetry:" the consequence might easily be anticipated : a tempest of severe censure arose, and voices of sarcasm rang loudly in the ears of the public. But the storm has long subsided : and those "bubbles" which rise from time to time in the streams of our periodical journalism have broken, burst, and died. Far be it, therefore, from the author to interfere with the privileges of oblivion; or revive for a moment that which has long since been forgotten. Still, he may be allowed, perhaps, without the slightest acerbity, to protest against certain doctrines which were then promulgated. It is quite right to lash what is arrogant, profane, or impiously absurd; and good taste will discriminate between him whose devout song arises from an adoring heart, and one who struts into the Holy of Holies, and shouts an Εὕρηκα! over the ark of divine Mystery. But there is a vast difference between correct taste and false censure; and if, on the one hand, a perversion of sacred poetry has disgusted our feelings, the rashness of erroneous condemnation, on the other, has equally offended a sound judgment.

From numerous fallacies frequently ventured on this subject, let the following be selected;—themes of religious grandeur are not adapted for poetical treatment, *because they can receive no additional glory from the pen of the poet.* Now, this *dictum*, if it contain anything, involves the supposition,—*that nothing but what poetry can intrinsically elevate or magnify, is fit to be poetically described*—which amounts to palpable absurdity. Did it never occur to the critic, that poetry can be glorified *by* a subject, though it may be inadequate to impart any glory *to* it?—Can poetical description always equal what it describes?—The brightness of the sunbeam, the tenderness of moonlight, the hues and harmonies of twilight, the sublimity of ocean, the terror of a storm, or the pastoral loveliness of an English landscape,—have perhaps never been vied by representations in verse; nay, how much is there in the meanest cottage flower, which the descriptions of language can never equal! And thus, analogically, with sacred Poetry. It is conversant with the Sublime, the Beautiful, and the Holy, in their most perfect combination; it dreams on the verge of Heaven, and is permitted, ever and anon, to have a faint view of the thrones

* "The use of this feigned history hath been to give some shadow of satisfaction to the mind of man in those points wherein the nature of things doth deny it, the world being in proportion inferior to the soul, by reason whereof there is, agreeable to the spirit of man, a more ample greatness, a more exact goodness, and a more absolute variety, than can be found in the nature of things. * * * And therefore it (viz. poesy) was ever thought to have some participation of divineness, because it doth raise and erect the mind, by submitting the shows of things to the desires of the mind; whereas Reason doth truckle and bow the mind unto the nature of things."—*Vide* ADV. LEARN. b. ii.

† "Hence in all the ages and countries of civilization, Religion has been the parent and fosterer of the fine arts—as of poetry, music, painting, and the like, the common essence of which consists in a similar union of the universal and the individual. In this union, moreover, is contained the true sense of the ideal. Under the old law, the altars, the curtains, the priestly vestments, and whatever else was to represent the beauty of holiness, had an ideal character; and the temple itself was a masterpiece of ideal beauty."—COLERIDGE.

and veiled Seraphim, and haply to drink in, with unsated ear, the melodies which are wafted from the songs of the redeemed.

Now, poetry cannot increase the vastness or sublimity of those objects and emotions which the Bible contains and excites; but, in the contemplation of them, as they exist with reference to our own destiny,—it derives an elevating purity which no other sources of inspiration can supply.* In fact, taken in the full and philosophical meaning of the words, sacred poetry comprehends whatever is sublime in Religion, grand in Morals, holy in Man, or attractive in Nature: and, as it is possible for a poem under a sacred title to be utterly profane, so it is certain, that where its true characteristics exist,—there the elements of the loftiest inspiration abound. Passion in its utmost intensity, and pathos in its profoundest effects, may also be comprehended within its scope; so that, when a writer decries sacred poetry, he must either be the victim of tasteless delusion; or, be petrified into apathy with regard to all that is great and good.

And what a range is there for a writer, thoroughly impressed with Eternity, and convinced that Revelation is a Voice from out its deep,—in subjects of sacred magnificence! Man is no longer regarded as the mere slave of impulse, but the heir of an immortal destiny; the material world is not only viewed as a visible Symbol of that Beauty which is behind the veil, but the full meaning of an awful passage,† where St. Paul describes the whole creation groaning with unutterable pangs for deliverance from the CURSE of SIN—is exemplified and illustrated: and, finally, God is not only recognised as the great I AM on the throne of eternity, but as a PARENT reconciling the world to Himself, through the sacrifice of His adorable Son.

True, poetry on sacred themes is liable to egregious imperfections. While we are in this bodily frame, the obstructions of sense will cloud our dreams of what is spiritual and impalpable.‡ Turgidity of expression, dimness of meaning, and false elevation, will inevitably occur; and it is an author's duty to be perpetually alive to these imperfections. A critic, however, who is noble in mind as well as cultivated in taste, will not detach his view from all that may otherwise merit approbation, to fix it on such errors; no more than a man who enters a garden, would neglect the fruits and flowers, to search for insects, or examine grubs.

But it is time to terminate a preface which has expanded far beyond the writer's original purpose; and as it may be many years before he intrudes on public attention again,—he cannot take his prefatory farewell, without acknowledging the forbearance with which his imperfect writings have been received. Whatever the sceptic in an author's modesty may imagine,—of the varied imperfections crowded in his pages, no one has been more conscious than he who had the greatest reason to regret them; and it is hoped, that in the new editions of his poems which are about successively to appear, the revision they have each undergone, will manifest the sincerity of this avowal.

It is nearly seven years since this poem was published; and how much he has been indebted to it, for the personal friendship and sympathy it has gained him in hearts and homes, where, but for its introduction, he had been a stranger,—can only be understood and appreciated by those who have had the same reasons to be grateful. But this recollection is not unmingled with melancholy: for in our retrospect of a few years, how much is there that the sigh of memory would in vain recal!—Many who greeted his first attempts have gone to their rest; and many a voice that counselled and cheered him in his onward path, has been hushed in the grave. Alas for our affections, if *this* life were all!—we should indeed be of all men "most miserable."

But the hope of Immortality makes the dawning heaven of our earth; and he who clings to this, will alone be enabled to speculate rightly on life and conduct, and on that which is to be revealed beyond the grave. In the flush of youth, an exciting love of reputation is too apt to domineer over the mind; but the experience of a few years cools this down to its proper state, and more and more are we inclined to feel,

> "La Nominanza e color d'erba,
> Che viene e va; e quei discolora,
> Per cui vien fuori della terra acerba."

The appreciation of fame is laudable under certain moral limitations; but our *motives* of action should ascend to a far higher source.—And, would that a deeper view of what forms the true greatness and glory of the mind more thoroughly pervaded our literature! How much that is low, would then be exalted; how much that is servile, made free; and, where now envy and malice strut their miserable hour, how soon would magnanimity and genius, hand in hand, complete their bright career! But in the war of emulation the noble aims of mental exertion

* "I can truly affirm of myself, that my studies have been profitable and availing to me, only so far as I have endeavoured to use all my other knowledge as a glass, enabling me to receive more light in a wider field of vision from the Word of God. * * * Digress for a few moments to another book, likewise a revelation of God—the great book of His servant, nature. That, in its obvious sense and literal interpretation, it declares the being and attributes (?) of the Almighty Father, none but the fool in heart has ever dared gainsay; but it has been the music of gentle and pious minds in all ages; it is the poetry of all human nature, to read it likewise in a figurative sense, and to find therein correspondencies and symbols of the spiritual world."—COLERIDGE.

† *Πᾶσα ἡ κτίσις συστενάζει καὶ συνωδίνει ἄχρι τοῦ νῦν, κ. τ. λ.*—Rom. viii. 22

‡ *Οὕτως ἀμηχάνον τοῖς ἐν σώματι, δίχα τῶν σωματικῶν πάντη γενέσθαι μετὰ τῶν νοουμένων.*—GREG. NAZ. Disc. 34.

soon evaporate; the noise, and not the power, of reputation alone is prized; and under a mania for literary prominence on the public stage, ambition darkens into envy, and disappointment is soured into rivalrous contempt.

Yet may the eye of the contemplatist repose on a more attractive scene; and behold in the varied ranks of learning, science, and taste, men who stand apart from the emulations around them,—silently building their monument of fame; or, from time to time sending forth streams of thought that refresh and invigorate the world of truth. And yet, to those who estimate fame by the talk of the tongue, rather than by the homage of the mind, the works of such men seem to languish in unappreciated excellence; * but it is far otherwise: the noble thought, the wise reflection, or the beautiful idea,—each has its hour and scene of influence; though often, like a trackless angel on some errand of love,—acting silent, secret, and unobserved.

Let it never be forgotten, that as good and evil are the two antagonistic Influences at war in the world, so every writer, whatever his intellectual rank, ranges himself on one side or the other:—it is a glorious reflection that he co-operates, however humbly, with the former; and infinitely awful to be found, however triumphantly, with the latter!

When the paleness of death was on him, and his hand shook with almost its last tremor, Coleridge wrote, as it were, under the very gaze of the Almighty,—"It is the most ennobling of all privileges to be a Christian."† With meek but fervent sincerity does the writer of these lines echo the sentiment of that eloquent man; and if, in the seclusion of his after life, he may venture to think he has brightened a mental dream, or afforded a ray of pure enjoyment, it will form one of the few pleasures which time can neither weaken nor destroy.

STRAND ON THE GREEN, KEW.
28th August, 1834.

---

* The biographer of Wordsworth tells us that the first edition of "The Excursion" occupied five years in being sold, and the second edition an equal period; and thus ten years were required to exhaust 1000 copies of "the Excursion," the two editions being each only 500! Such was the appreciation which Wordsworth *then* received; But, "tempora mutantur" now.

† In the spirit of a deep and sublime philosophy, he observes, in one of the admirable notes appended to his Essays on Church and State:—"Christian love is the last and divinest birth, the harmony, and unity, and godlike transfiguration of all the vital, intellectual, and moral powers. Now it manifests itself as the sparkling and ebullient spring of well-doing, in gifts and in labours; and now as a silent fountain of patience and long-suffering, the fulness of which no hatred or persecution can exhaust or diminish."

"By day the present, but at night, the past
Prevails: a moonlight tenderness o'er things
Departed, sheds a fond and dream-like gloom."

'TIS dreaming midnight: from unnumber'd spires
Funereal wails for the departed Day
Arise, as from a host of yawning tombs;
Awhile the wafted echoes float around,
Then faintly ebb upon the spectral air,
And melt to muteness through the starry skies.

There is a voiceless melancholy that wakes
The heart's mysterious chords, until they stir
Like air by music charm'd, when on the verge
Of time's unfathom'd gulf the dying Hours
Drop into dark eternity.—A Day
Is dead! and, with it, many a breathing Shape
Of life shall breathe no longer. Many an eye
That smil'd upon the morn, is film'd and cold;
And many a heart that leap'd with living joy,
Lies spiritless, and still;—a solemn thought,
Truth-born and deep: but Life o'ershadows death
Beneath her giant wings; and day from day,
And hour from hour recedes; yet, unappall'd,
We dream and dance along life's varied road
Till death arrests us, and our graves are dug,
And o'er us hangs oblivion's moveless pall:
Then, some dark thinkers, when they pause and hear
A dusky steeple moaning to the clouds,
Will sigh, and say, "Another day is dead!"—
And thus rolls on the sea of human fate,
In ruthless havoc over hearts and souls.

'Tis midnight; and before me lies outspread
A sleeping City, with its towers and domes
All shapeless and sublime; or, darkly girt
With funeral air, save where the casement sheds
Its lambent smile around: And here, alone,
With few to bless, and bless'd by few, I dream
And muse, until Imagination grasp
The universe; and trace in every isle
That gems the sea, and every land which blooms
Beneath the sun, the sleepless power of God,
Who with a veil of love invests the world.

But see! the Moon unrobes, and from her face
Beauty goes forth, and fills the heavens with light,
Till the vast concave blossoms out in stars.
At such an hour, while day-worn Nature sleeps,
And Silence walks the world, pervading God!
Awe-smote, before Thy vision'd Throne I lay
A lowly gift of unaffected song,
Though meritless, sincere.—But who shall paint,
Or mirror forth thy majesty supreme,
Almighty, vast, and terrible UNKNOWN,
Whom dread Eternity itself adores!
And yet, on earth some faint reflections fall,
From Thine infinity of brightness shed;
And poetry, the heart's true seraph, finds
Creation's glory in Thy shadow seen.

If aught, then, of the mind's devotion warm
The page, where feelings from the fountain-soul
Gush into glowing verse, from Thee deriv'd,
Direct them, God! and may they glide the world
Around, and win to Heaven harmonious Mind.

BATH, *March 2nd*, 1828.

PART I.

ANALYSIS OF PART I.

THE Poem opens with an apostrophe to the DEITY—He was, ere Time began—Vision of the Creation—We cannot escape the Omnipresent God—He pervades all things—Allusion to His appearance on Mount Sinai—The Red Sea—Nature attests the presence of her Architect—The impossibility of perfectly tracing the Deity's influence: we can only select those scenes which impressively demonstrate it—The thunder—the ocean-tempest—The Presence of the Deity felt in the repose of Nature—The calm which succeeds a storm — Aspirations awakened by a view of the setting sun.

The hand of God is next traced in a rapid view of the Seasons :—Spring—Mountains—Sacred feelings kindled by the sight of an august ruin—The Convalescent—The Heavens—A moonlight walk—The soul conscious of its celestial origin—Every clime an object of the Deity's care — Condensed view of His providence—Not only nature, but human life, in all its diversified forms, regulated by Him. But there is a far sublimer sense in which a Christian enjoys a Divine Presence in creation, and therefore, this part of the poem is concluded by a consideration of the doctrine which Christianity reveals, by whose light the glory of nature is rendered more glorious, and all the beauty of outward things becomes a symbol of that which is unseen.

THOU UNCREATE, UNSEEN, and UNDEFINED,
Source of all life, and fountain of the mind;
Pervading SPIRIT, whom no eye can trace,
Felt through all time, and working in all space,
Imagination cannot paint that spot,
Around, above, beneath, where Thou art not!

Before the glad stars hymn'd to new-born earth,
Or young creation revell'd in its birth,
Thy Spirit moved upon the pregnant deep,
Unchain'd the waveless waters from their sleep,
Bade Time's majestic wings to be unfurl'd,
And out of darkness drew the breathing World.

Priméval Power! before Thy thunder rang,
And Nature from eternity outsprang;
Ere matter form'd at Thy creative tone,
Thou wert; Almighty, Endless, and Alone:
In Thine own Essence, all that was to be,—
Sublime, unfathomable Deity:
Thou saidst—and lo! a universe was born,
And Light flash'd from Thee, for her birth-day morn.

The Earth unshrouded all her beauty now;
The kingly mountain bared his awful brow,
Flowers, fruits, and trees felt instantaneous life:—
But, hark, creation trembles with the strife
Of roaring waves in wild commotion hurl'd,—
'Tis Ocean winding round the rocking world!

And next, triumphant o'er the green-clad earth,
The universal Sun burst into birth,
And dash'd from off his altitude sublime
The first dread ray that mark'd commencing time!
Last, came the Moon upon the wings of light,
And sat in glory on the throne of night,
While, young and fresh, a radiant host of stars
Wheel'd round the heavens upon their burning cars.

But all was dismal as a world of dead,
Till the great Deep her living swarms outspread:
Forth from her teeming bosom, sudden came
Uncounted monsters,—mighty, without name;
Then, thick as dews upon a twilight green,
The living creatures rose upon the scene.

Creation's master-piece! a breath of God,
Ray of His glory, quicken'd at His nod,
Immortal Man came next, divinely grand,
Glorious and perfect from his Maker's hand;
Last, softly beautiful as Music's close,
Angelic Woman into being rose.

And now, the gorgeous universe was rife,
Full, fair, and glowing with created life;
And when th' Eternal, from His starry height,
Beheld the young world basking in His light,
And breathing incense of deep gratitude,
He bless'd it,—for His mercy made it good.

And thus, THOU wert, and art, the FOUNTAIN SOUL,
And countless worlds around Thee live and roll;
In sun and shade, in ocean and in air
Diffused, yet undiminish'd—everywhere:

All life and motion from Thy source began,
From worlds to atoms, Angels down to Man.

Lord of all being! where can Fancy fly,
To what far realms, unmeasur'd by Thine eye?
Where can we hide beneath Thy blazing sun,
Where dwell'st THOU not, the boundless, viewless One?
Shall Guilt couch down within the cavern's gloom,
And quiv'ring, groaning, meditate her doom?
Or scale the mountains, where the whirlwinds rest,
And in the night-blast cool her fiery breast?—
Within the cavern-gloom Thine eye can see,
The sky-clad mountains lift their heads to Thee;
Thy Spirit rides upon the thunder-storms,
Dark'ning the skies into terrific forms!
Beams in the lightning, rocks upon the seas,
Roars in the blast, and whispers in the breeze;
In calm and storm, in Heaven and Earth Thou art,
Trace but Thy works—they bring Thee to the heart!

The fulness of Thy Presence who can see?
Man cannot live, great God! and look on Thee;
Around Thy path the quenchless lightnings glow,—
Thy Voice appals the shudd'ring world below.

Oh, Egypt felt Thee, when, by signs unscared,
To mock Thy might the rebel monarch dared:
Thou look'dst—and Ocean sever'd at the glance!
Undaunted, still the charioteers advance;
Thou look'dst again—she clash'd her howling waves,
And Storms in triumph revell'd o'er their graves!

On Sinai's mountain when Thy glory came
In rolls of thunder, and in clouds of flame;
There, while volcanic smoke Thy throne o'ercast,
And the mount shrunk beneath the trumpet-blast,
How did thy Symbol blind all Israel's eye,
How dreadful were the gleams of Deity!

There is a voiceless eloquence on Earth,
Telling of Him who gave her wonders birth;
And long may I remain th' adoring child
Of Nature's majesty, sublime or wild;
Hill, flood, and forest, mountain, rock, and sea,
All take their terrors, or their charms from Thee,
From Thee, whose hidden but supreme control
Moves through the world—a universal Soul.

But who could trace Thine unrestricted course,
Though fancy followed with immortal force?
There's not a blossom fondled by the breeze,
There's not a fruit that beautifies the trees,
There's not a particle in sea or air
But Nature owns Thy plastic influence there!
With gaze devout still be it mine to see
How all is fill'd and vivified by Thee;
On the vast scene of earth's majestic view,
To paint Thy glories, and to feel them too.

Ye giant Winds! that from your gloomy sleep
Rise in your wrath, and revel on the deep;
Lightnings! which are the mystic gleams of God,
That glanced when on the sacred mount he trod;
And ye, black Thunders! that begird His form,
Pealing your loud hosannahs o'er the storm;
Around me rally in concentred might,
And strike my being with a dread delight;
Sublimely musing, let me pause and see,
And pour my awe-struck soul, O God! to Thee.

A thunder-storm!—the eloquence of heaven,
When the thick clouds, like airy walls are riven,
Who hath not paused beneath its hollow groan,
And felt omnipotence around him thrown?
With what a gloom the ush'ring Scene appears!
The leaves all fluttering with instinctive fears,
The waters curling with a fellow dread,
A breezeless fervour round creation spread,
And, last, the heavy rain's reluctant shower,
With big drops patt'ring on the tree and bower,
While wizard shapes the bowing sky deform,—
All mark the coming of a Thunder-storm.

Oh, now to be alone, on some vast height,
Where heaven's black curtains terrify the sight,
And watch the clouds together meet and clash,
While fierce-wing'd lightnings from their conflict flash;
To see the caverns of the sky disclose
The buried flames that in their wombs repose,
And mark the lurid meteors fall and rise,
In dizzy chase along the rattling skies,—
How quakes the Spirit while the echoes roll,
And God, in thunder, speaks from pole to pole!

And thou, weird Ocean! on whose awful face
Time's iron feet can print no ruin-trace,
By breezes lull'd, or by the storm-blasts driven,
Thy tow'ring waves uplift the mind to heaven.

Tremendous art Thou! in thy tempest-ire,
When the mad surges to the clouds respire,
And like new Apennines from out the sea,
Thy waves march on in mountain-majesty.
Oh! never can the dark-souled ATHEIST stand,
And watch the breakers boiling on the strand,
Nor feel RELIGION from the sea arise,
And preach to conscience what his WILL denies;

His heart is wiser than his head would be,
And awe instinctive tells, O God, of Thee!
He hears Him in the wind-heav'd ocean's roar,
Hurling her billowy crags upon the shore;
He hears Him in the horror of the blast,
And shakes while rush the raving whirlwinds past!

But not alone, when waves and whirlwinds rise,
And wing their voices through the startled skies;
Not in the storm, the thunder, or the sea,
Alone we feel thy dread ubiquity:
In calmer scenes, and the unruffled hour,
Our still'd hearts own Thine omnipresent power.

List! now the cradled winds have hush'd their roar,
And infant waves curl gamb'ling to the shore,
While Nature seems to wake up fresh and clear
As Hope emerging from the gloom of fear,
And the bright dew-bead on the verdure lies,
Like liquid rapture upon beauty's eyes,—
How heavenly 'tis to take our pensive range,
And mark 'tween storm and calm the lovely change!

First comes the sun, unveiling half its face,
Like a coy virgin, with reluctant grace,
While dark clouds skirted with a slanting ray
Roll, one by one, in azure depths away,
Till pearly shapes, like molten billows, lie
Along the tinted bosom of the sky:
Next, breezes murmur with harmonious charm,
Panting and wild, like orphans of the storm;
Now sipping flowers, now making blossoms shake,
Or weaving ripples on the grass-green lake;
And thus, the Tempest dies: and soft, and still,
The rainbow drops upon the distant hill:
But now, while bloom and breeze their charms unite,
And all is glowing with a rich delight,
God! who can tread upon the breathing ground,
Nor feel Thee present, where Thy smiles abound?

When Day hath glided to his rosy bower,
And twilight comes—the Poet's witching hour,
And dream-like language from the soft-toned wind
With pensive cadence charms the list'ning mind,
Then nature's beauty, clothed with dewy light,
Melts on the heart like music through the night.

And not in vain, voluptuous Eventide,
Thy dappled clouds along th' horizon glide;
For oh! while heaven and earth grow dumb with bliss
In homage to an hour divine as this,
How sweet, upon yon mountain's azure brow,
While ruddy sun-beams gild the crags below,
To stand, and mark with meditative view,
Where the far ocean faints in hazy blue,
While on the bosom of the midway deep
The emerald waves in dimpling splendour leap;
Here, as we view the gorgeous Priest of time,
Wrapp'd in a shroud of glory, sink sublime,
Thoughts of ethereal beauty spring to birth,
And waft the soul beyond the dreams of earth.

And who hath gazed upon the bright-wing'd Morn,
Breezy and fresh, from out the ocean born;
Her rich-wove cloud-wreaths, and the rainbow hues
From heaven reflected on creation's views;
Or mark'd the wonders of a day depart,
Nor felt a heaven-caught influence at his heart?
Through all the seasons' varying course of love,
Who hath not traced the Spirit from above?
The howl of Winter in the leafless wood;
The ice-bound torrent, and the whelming flood;
Or Summer's flush, or Autumn, robed in grey,
Whirling the red leaves round her bleak-worn way,—
All tell one tale of Heaven. But thou, young Spring!
Glad as the wild bee on his glossy wing,
Bedeck'd with bloom, and breathing life around,
Within thy breast Elysian charms abound.

The mercy-fountains of Divinity
Now stream through all, with vigour full and free;
As if unloosen'd from their living source,
To carry with them spring's creative force.
The sky is garlanded with waves of blue,
Like ocean dawning on the distant view;
The sun lies mirror'd on the radiant streams,
The sea-waves gambol in his noontide beams,
The boughs hang glitt'ring in their locks of green,
And airy poets carol to the scene;
While sea, and sky, and land, and fragrant Earth
With her rich promise budding into birth,—
Seem, like a heart o'erfill'd with sacred love,
Glowing with gratitude to Him above.

Terrific giants that o'erlook the sea,
Enormous masses of sublimity,
Ye mountain-piles! Earth's monuments to Heaven,
Around whose brows the reeling storms are driven,

Whether in climes where 'bove the ice-chain'd deep
Ye rise in piles magnificently steep,
Or where in living bloom your bosoms swell,
And fierce and far the headlong torrents yell,—
Where snow-drifts whiten, or where sunbeams warm,
Your brows are girdled with almighty charm!

When drops the sun in yonder western deep,
The waves unruffled, and the winds asleep;
And isles of beauty float the brilliant sky,
While Fancy muses with enamour'd eye;
Then comes the hour to fascinate the sight,
Where the wild mountain rears its massy height.
There, as we gaze, mysterious thoughts begin
To stir th' immortal spark that burns within;
Till Wonder starts with a bewild'ring fear,
As if the advent of our God were near!

And where, beneath the stern decree of time,
Columns and temples sink in age sublime;
Where by the ruin'd battlements are heard
The wailing sorrows of some midnight bird,
While low winds mutter through the roofless halls,
And ivy-boughs bend weeping o'er the walls,
Imagination loves to stand and dream,
And mark yon ruin in the moonlight gleam,
Till summon'd Ages startle from their sleep,
And plaintive Mem'ry turns aside to weep!—
Or view, when sunset drinks the forest-breeze,
Where some grey abbey glimmers through the trees,
And on the turrets evening's pallid rays
Gleam like the glory of departed days,
How soon the cloister'd stillness of the spot*
Brings heaven around us, till the world's forgot;
While Retrospection draws the moral sigh,
And dreams embodied move before her eye.

Great Architect of worlds! whose forming power
Presided o'er creation's natal hour,
Stamp'd man Thy miniature, and bade him run
A race of glory, till his goal be won;

When wan Disease exhales her withering breath,
And dims his beauty with the damp of death;
At some still hour the holy sigh will swell,
The gushing tear of gratitude will tell
That Thou art by, to temper and to tame
The trembling anguish of the fever'd frame.

But oh! when heal'd by love and heaven, we rise,
With radiant cheek, and re-illumin'd eyes,
Bright as a new-born sun, all nature beams,
And through the spirit darts immortal dreams.
Now for the bracing hills, and healthful plains,
And pensive ramble when the noontide wanes;
Now for the walk beside some haunted wood,
And fancy-music of a distant flood;
While far and wide, the wand'ring eye surveys,
And the heart pants to pour away its praise!

But, turn from earth to yonder glorious sky,
Th' imagin'd dwelling-place of Deity.
Ye quenchless Stars! so eloquently bright,
Ye radiant Watchers of reposing night,
While half the world is lapp'd in blissful dreams
And round the lattice creep your fairy beams,
How sweet to gaze upon your placid eyes,
In lambent beauty looking from the skies!

And when, oblivious of the world, we stray
At dead of night along some noiseless way,
How the Heart mingles with a moon-lit hour,
And feels from heaven a sympathetic power!—
See, not a cloud careers yon pathless deep
Of molten azure,—mute as lovely sleep;
Full in her pallid light the Moon presides,
Shrined in a halo, mellowing as she rides;
And far around, the forest and the stream
Wear the rich garment of her silver beam.
The lull'd Winds, too, are sleeping in their caves,
No stormy prelude rolls upon the waves;
Nature is hush'd, as if her works adored
The night-felt presence of creation's Lord.

And now, while through the ocean-mantling haze
A mournful lustre tremulously plays,
And glimm'ring loveliness hath veil'd the land,
Go, stranger, muse thou by the wave-worn strand:
Cent'ries have glided o'er the balanced earth,
Myriads have bless'd, and myriads curs'd their birth;
Still, beauteously yon starry watchers glare,
Unsullied as the God who throned them there!
Though moral earthquakes heave th' astounded world,
And king and kingdom from their pride are hurl'd,

* In Mr. Charles Butler's Life of De Rancè, there is a passage which may be quoted as illustrative of that feeling of awe inspired by a venerable ruin. Speaking of the Abbey de la Trappe, he writes—"All travellers who have given a description of it agree that the monastery and its environs present a scene which even the strongest mind cannot view without a sentiment of awe. At a small distance from the monastery, a dark forest encircles it on every side; and eleven lakes, the water of which is always of a dismal hue, and always stagnant, form around it, in two circles, a double moat. The solemn stillness of the scenery completes its horror."

Intensely calm, *they* hold their bright career,
Unheedful of the storms and changes here:—
We want no hymn to hear, nor pomp to see,
For all around is felt divinity!
The wing'd heart flutters to ascend above
To HIM whose nature and whose name are Love.
And if revered ones, from their hallow'd sphere,
May witness warm Affection's faithful tear,
At this deep hour they hear the mourner's sigh,
And waft a blessing from their homes on high.

Stupendous God! how shrinks our bounded sense
To track the triumphs of Omnipotence;
From sky-clad mountain, to the deepest den,
From the mean insects, to immortal men;
Bless'd with Thy brightest smile, dare we confine
Paternal Providence, supreme as thine?
Far as the fancy flies, or life-stream flows,
From Georgia's desert to the Greenland snows,
Where space exists, Thine eyes of mercy see,—
Creation lives, and moves, and breathes *in Thee!*
Unseen, but felt, Thine interfused Control
Works in each atom, and pervades the whole;
Expands the blossom, and erects the tree,*
Conducts each vapour, and commands each sea;
The Laws of Nature Thy decree fulfil,
And all Her powers but realise Thy will.

E'en now, while tragic Midnight walks the land,
And spreads the wings of darkness with her wand,
What scenes are witness'd by Thy watchful eye,
What millions waft to Thee the prayer and sigh!
Some gaily vanish to an unfear'd grave,
Fleet as the sun-flash o'er a summer-wave;
Some wear out life in smiles, and some in tears,
Some dare with hope, while others droop with fears;
The vagrant's roaming in his tatter'd vest,
The babe is sleeping on its mother's breast;
The captive mutt'ring o'er his rust-worn chain,
The widow weeping for her lord again,
While many a Mourner shuts his languid eye,
To dream of heaven, and view it ere he die,—
And yet, no sigh can swell, no tear-drop fall,
But Thou wilt see, and guide, and solace all!

And thus, a Preacher of eternal might,
Sublime in darkness, or array'd in light,
In each wild change of glory, gloom, and storm,
The starry magic, and the mountain-form,
Art thou,—dread Universe of love and power!
But, higher still the Muse's wing may tower,
And track the myst'ry of almighty ways,
Through paths that glitter with the solemn rays
The awful noon of revelation shed
From Calv'ry,—when the God Incarnate bled.

For what is Nature,* though religion seems
To lend a tone to all her winds and streams;
To whisper, God! when night and darkness creep
Round the dim trances of Creation's sleep;
To teach a prayer when twilight hush descends,
And the mute bough in adoration bends;
Or bid the woods a leafy anthem raise
When the rich verdure shines with emerald rays:
Or spring, the Angel of the seasons, pours
A tide of beauty round exulting shores:

---

* "Glows in the stars, and blossoms in the trees—
Lives through all life—extends through all extent—
Spreads undivided—operates unspent."—POPE.

* In reference to the boasted, but unreal, connexion between certain facts of physical science, and the truths of God's moral government, Dr. Chalmers ably and eloquently observes:—"It is all true that this is a very enlightened age; but on what field has it acquired so flattering a distinction? On the field of experiment. The human mind owes all its progress to the confinement of its efforts within the safe and certain limits of observation, and to the severe restraints which it has imposed upon its speculative tendencies. Go beyond these limits, and the human mind has not advanced a single inch by its own independent exercises. All the philosophy which has been reared by the labour of successive ages, is the philosophy of facts, reduced to general laws, or brought under a general description from observed points of resemblance." * * * * "Tell us a single discovery which has thrown a particle of light on the details of the Divine administration,—tell us a single truth in the whole field of experimental science, which can bring us to the moral government of the Almighty by any other road than His own Revelation. Astronomy has taken millions of suns and systems within its ample domain; but the *ways of God to man* stand at a distance as inaccessible as ever; nor has it shed so much as a glimmering over the counsels of that mighty and invisible Being, who sits in high authority over all worlds. The boasted discoveries of modern science are all confined to that field within which the senses of man can expatiate,—they all serve to exalt the Deity, but they do not contribute a single iota to the explanation of His purposes,—they make Him greater, but they do not make Him more comprehensible. He is more shrouded in mystery than ever. It is not Himself whom we see, but His workmanship; and every new addition to its grandeur or variety, which philosophy opens to our contemplation, throws our understanding at a greater distance than before from the mind and conception of the sublime Architect,—every new triumph, which the mind of man achieves in the field of discovery, binds us more firmly to our Bible; and, by the very proportion in which philosophy multiplies the wonders of God, do we prize that book, on which the evidence of history has stamped the character of His authentic communication."

Say, what is meant?—a soft mysterious glow,
A breath too pure to live on earth below,
An evanescent luxury of thought,
Cull'd from the feast Imagination brought,—
But, frail and feeble, as the charm that dies,
When the dead waken upon mem'ry's eyes.*

When lived the Age, or where the clime so rude,
What island-nursed in billowy solitude,
Where dreams of God were never known to shine
Round a dark soul, with imagery divine?
The Heathen through his cloud of error saw,
A faint reflection of celestial Law;
E'en the grim savage, when his eye commands
A broad extent of green-apparel'd lands,
Or views the Tempest wave his cloudy wing
In sultry darkness o'er the world of spring,
Can hail the image of some dreamt Unknown,—
A sceptred BEING on his boundless throne.
Then boast not thou, whose spell-bound eye can see
In nature's glass reflected Deity;
From whence does moral elevation flow,
What pang is mute, what balm prepared for wo,
Though ocean, mountain, sky, and air impress
Full on the soul a felt Almightiness?
Can Ocean teach magnificence of mind?
Is truth made vocal by the deep-voiced Wind?
Can flowers their bloom of innocence impart,
Or tempt one weed of vileness from the heart?
Can thy benevolence, all bounteous Sun,
Thou burning Shadow of the brightest ONE!
Array our souls with emulative beam
Like thine, to glad life's universal stream?
From yon pale stars does purity descend,
And their chaste beauty with our spirit blend?—
Alas, oh, God! if Thou *alone* art found
When most creation with Thy smile is crown'd;
Rather in blindness let this outward eye
Be dead to nature, than Thy throne deny,
Raised on the pillars of Redemption's might,
And dazzling angels with too deep a light!

There is a PRESENCE spiritually vast
Around Thy Church, arisen Saviour! cast;
A holy Effluence, an unspoken Awe,
A Sanctity which carnal eye ne'er saw,
A pure, impalpable, almighty Sense
Of peace, by reconciled Omnipotence,
Which hallows, haunts, and makes a Christian mind
Rich in all grace, celestially refined:
Mere Nature's worshippers can never feel
The fulness of that high seraphic zeal
Which veileth all things with religious light,
And works unwearied in Jehovah's sight:
Thought, dream, and action,—ev'ry pulse of soul
The awe of Christ will solemnly control;
Girt by THE SPIRIT, wheresoe'er we rove,
True Faith is feeding on His word of love.
Nature is now a more than nature far;
Each miracle of sun, or moon, or star,
Each sight, and sense, and sound of outward things,
Seems haunted by august imaginings;
A dream of Calvary around her floats,
And oft the dew of those delicious notes
By angels once in Bethlehem's valley pour'd
Descends, with all their melody restored,
Till peace on earth! to pardon'd man good will!
With tones of heaven the ear of fancy fill.*

* The sum is, that Divine truths are not immediate objects of the understanding; for then we should be able to have a full idea, knowledge, or apprehension of them. But they are mediately so by communication, and what therefore we can have no apprehension or notion of, but as they are communicated or represented to us. It is this gives act to that capacity of the mind, which was only potential before; for as objects are visible to the natural eye, but not without the interposition of light, *so neither are heavenly objects to the intellect, but by the intervention of some agent, which can be only God.*—(Ellis on Knowledge of Divine Things, p. 130.)

* As a fuller and more thoughtful development of the Divine Spirit's work and office in the Church, and consciousness of our redeemed Humanity, the author ventures to append the following extract from a poem written in maturer life —

Mysterious Spirit of the ceaseless mind!
Heart of the Church, as Christ the only Head;
Soul of our souls, in supernat'ral light;
Unbounded, deathless, and transforming Grace
And Love, and Wisdom!—Thee I now invoke;
And to Thyself presume to consecrate
Pages,—that whatsoe'er of hallow'd power
They have, from Thee alone their truth receive
And virtue. Oh! thou Sempiternal Life,
Breathe o'er this effort, and with force array
Whate'er is feeble; and with heavenly touch
And tone their meaning so affect and fill,
That onward to the inner mind of man,
Or Central being, where high Conscience holds
Her seat august, and faith's dominion acts,—
What truths they carry may be safely borne
Beyond the heartless, and above the vain
To warp, or weaken. Here beneath the arch
Of midnight, solemn, deep, intensely calm,
Thy presence would I realise; and lift
Mine awe-struck nature to the heights unseen
Of Essence uncreate,—where Thou art third
In Godhead, where the Fountain Sire is first,
Second, the Filial Word, and All supreme
In One co-equal, co-eternal Three
The God tripersonal and true, complete.

Descend, pure Spirit! light and life and love
Without Thee, are not: poetry is Thine,
Reason, and science, and majestic arts,
The heaven-born virtues, intellectual powers

PART II.

"Of finer mould, and far sublimer view,
Whate'er his lot; on Fortune's envied mount
High-throned, or lost in the secluded vales
Of lowliness, is he whose hopes are built
In Heaven:——
Not all the pomp and pageantry of worlds
Reflects such glory on the Eye Supreme,
As the meek virtue of one holy man!—
For even doth his angel from the face
Divine, beatitude and wisdom draw."

ANALYSIS OF PART II.

The second part of the Poem is devoted to a consideration of the Presence of the Deity, as influencing Human Life—In our journey through the world, we cannot but admit an overruling Power—The paternal care of the Deity—Consolation thence derived in scenes of woe—Pictures of a street-wanderer and an exiled captive—The hopes imparted to the soldier, by his confidence in the presence of God—The Sailor—Storm and wreck described—His consciousness of Preserving Providence.

As misfortune is observed by God, so, in like manner, the crimes of the wicked cannot escape Him—Picture of a murderer—Darkness; its varied influence depicted—Penitence—The young convict—The maniac boy—The arctic traveller—The missionary.

The Sabbath—Feelings excited by the tones of an organ swelling through a cathedral—The village christening—Rapid survey of the common lot.

As God has been defined "Love," we may be assured that He eminently favours virtuous affection—The marriage scene—Raptures arising from the retrospections of the virtuous—Picture of a grandsire, sitting by his winter fire, and retracing the scenes of his life—Friendship.

Death—Apostrophe—Picture of a dying old man, attended by his daughter—The Funeral—The Almighty Presence.

Along the barren world as doom'd we roam
By devious paths to one pèrennial Home,
In tears or smiles we own the o'erruling Hand
That beckons on to that celestial Land,
Where, harbour'd all, life's billows sink away,
And the bright spirits bask in heaven's immortal ray.
And happy thou! through all the change of time,
Whom sorrow cannot burden with a crime;
Whose joyless heart and never-lighten'd care
Can nobly scorn the refuge of despair.

With all pre-eminence of grace or gifts,—
Are but as glances from Thy glory cast,
And caught by Mind. But, who Thy sway can tell?
For at the first, the heavens and all their host,
Moon, stars, and planets,—from Thy hand derived
Their radiance, from Thy wisdom learn'd thy paths.—
And Earth is thine; her elementary laws,
Her motions, harmonies, and living hues
And beauty, are but emanated powers
From Thee, great Beauty's archetypal Seal!
While Man himself, (that miracle of forms)
Into his mould was copied from Thy cast
Ethereal; and the whole of truths inspired,
Prophetic Utt'rance, or mirac'lous Deed,
Which was, or is, or shall be,—are but rays
Sent from Thine Essence to created mind.

Without Thee, more than night Egyptian reigns;
Duty sublime would stern distraction be,
Commanding what our impotence alarms,—
To love that Holy which our hearts abhor
By nature: but Thy promised aid attends,
Arches our being, like the roof of heaven,
Where'er we wander; and to Will perverse
Such power imparteth, that the precept takes
Thy Presence with it in each task assign'd.

Thou teachest God; and Man himself abides
In fact unfathom'd, till thy light reveal
The two eternities of coming truth
Within Him folded,—like a double germ
Soon to expand in heaven or hell complete.
And hence our Nature grows an awful thing;
We thrill eternity in touching Man;
For, from the eye-balls of his living head
Outlooks the Everlasting!—though eclipsed;
While every heart-pulse in the life of faith
Throbs with Thy Spirit, Inspiration's Lord.

And now, O Spirit! at the noon of night,
Under the arch of this poetic sky
While all around me breathes the hush of heaven,
Thee I invoke, this erring strain to crown:
Without Thee,—'tis but vanity and voice
And mere vexation, into language thrown;
But with Thee, weakness is itself made strong,
While nature's darkness turns to light divine.
And if with me one aspiration dwell
For truths, beyond philosophy to preach
Or master; if one thought this perill'd mind
Inspire, where Thou, O God of grace, art seen,
Prevenient Spirit! 'tis from Thee derived.
And oh, if life with all its loneliness,
The glow of youth hath still in heart retain'd;
If all the waste, the fever, and the fret
Of buried pangs beyond the world to know
From boyhood in its bleakness; e'en till now,
Have not untuned me; but a tone have left
In concord with the beautiful and bright;
If nature thrill me, with as keen a joy
As in the poetry of pensive youth
It ever did; if such for bliss remain,
Blent with far deeper things, by suff'ring taught,
And faith transmuted for the life within,
As onward through a bleak and heartless world
My pathway windeth to the waiting tomb,—
Spirit of Glory! take my gratitude,
And sanctify the closing strain I sing:
Bear with my soul; Thy blessing o'er it breathe,
And all who love the Master whom I serve.
Divine Emmanuel! peace may all thy Church possess,
Till faith shall in sublime fruition end,
All symbols cease, all sacraments retire,
And earthly Sabbaths into heavenly melt
For men, and angels; where the host redeem'd
Shall in the Temple of pure Godhead keep
The sabbath endless of almighty love.

Luther, 6th Ed., 1852.

Like ocean's wand'rer guided by his star,
Thy heaven-taught spirit looks to him afar.

Say, ye whose hearts unburden'd can enjoy
The bliss of life, without the world's alloy;
What can illume their melancholy way,
Where Want begins, and Mis'ry crowns the day?
When bow'd by woe, and bleach'd by with'ring age,
Alone Life's orphan treads the world's cold stage;
His fortune wreck'd, his friends beneath the sod,
Where shall he fly, but to the arms of God?
Blest be yon viewless Spirit thron'd on high,
No heart's too wretched to attract His eye;
No lot too lowly to engage His love,
And win the smile of Mercy from above!
He gazes on the sleepless couch of wo,
And bids the dying light of hope to glow,
Unarms the peril, heals the wounded mind,
And charms each feeling home, to fate resign'd.

At wintry eve, when savage night-winds blow,
Pierce his cold cheek, and drift his locks of snow,
As oft the vagrant shivers through the street,
No voice to pity, and no hand to greet,
With many a pause he marks that window-pane,
Whose flick'ring blaze recalls his home again!
The friend and face, the music and the mirth,
And social magic of his evening-hearth,
Awaked by mem'ry, warm his widow'd heart,
Till real woes in fancied bliss depart;
And one by one, as happier days appear,
To each he pays the homage of a tear;
Though homeless, still he loves home's joyous glare,
Looks up to heaven, and feels *his* home is there!

Within a dungeon, mildew'd by the night,
Barr'd from salubrious air and cheering light,
Lo! the pale captive pines in hostile lands,
Chain'd to his doom by adamantine bands.
Oh, how he pants to face the fresh-wing'd breeze,
And hear the voices of the summer trees:
To breathe, and live, and move, and be as free
As Nature is, and Man was made to be!
And when at night, upon his flinty bed,
Silent and sad, he lays his grief-worn head,
There as the dungeon-bell, with dismal sound,
Tolls midnight through the sleeping air around,
Remembrance wafts him to paternal climes,
And frames a fairy world of happier times.
The woodland haunts around his native scene,
The village dance upon the festive green,
His sloping garden where he lov'd to ply,
And smiled as peeping flower-buds hail'd his eye,
His beauteous partner and her blue-eyed boy,
Who prattled, played, and fed his soul with joy,—
By thought created, crowd around his heart,
And force the pangs of fond regret to start;
Each soft delusion claims a genial sigh,
Each dream of happiness bedims his eye;
Till, warm'd by Heaven, his home-wed bosom glows
With hopes that triumph o'er remember'd woes;
And far away the chainless spirit flies,
To vision'd realms of rest beyond the skies.

Spirit of Light and Life! when Battle rears
His fiery brow amid terrific spears;
When deathful cannons to the clouds uproar,
And gasping hosts sleep shrouded in their gore,
E'en then, th' intrepid Heart that nobly glows
To face the fury of invading foes,
May look to Thee for mercy and for power,
To brave the peril of the carnage-hour;
Or, doom'd to fall amid the furious din,
While battle storms without, may find a peace within.

List! war-peals thunder on the battle-field;
And many a hand grasps firm the glitt'ring shield,
As on, with helm and plume, the warriors come,
And the glad hills repeat the stormy drum!

And now are seen the youthful and the grey,
With bosoms burning to partake the fray:
The first, with hearts that consecrate the deed,
All eager rush to vanquish or to bleed;
Like young waves racing in the morning sun,
That rear and leap with reckless fury on!
But, see that scar-worn man, who looks on high
With musing valour mirror'd in his eye;
Not all the bleeding revels of the day
Can fright the vision of his home away;
The home of love, and its attractive smiles,
His wife's endearment, and his baby's wiles:—
Fights he less brave through recollected bliss,
With step retreating, or with sword remiss?
Ah no! remember'd home's the warrior's charm,
Speed to his sword, and vigour to his arm;
For this he supplicates the God afar,
Fronts the steel'd foe, and mingles in the war.

The cannon's hush'd!—nor drum nor clarion sound;
Helmet and hauberk mingle on the ground;
Horseman and horse lie welt'ring in their gore;
Patriots are dead, and heroes dare no more;
While solemnly the moonlight shrouds the plain,
And lights the lurid features of the slain.

And see! where swift the banner'd coursers past,
A battle-steed beneath his rider cast;
Oh! never more he'll rear with fierce delight,
Roll his large eyes, and rally for the fight;
Pale on that bleeding corse a warrior lies,
While from the ruffled lids his white-swell'd eyes
Ghastly and grimly stare upon the skies!

But who, upon the battle-wasted plain,
Shall count the faint, the gasping, and the slain?
Angel of Mercy! ere the blood-fount chill,
And the brave heart be spiritless and still,
Amid the havoc Thou art hov'ring nigh,
To calm each groan, and close each dying eye,
And waft the spirit to that halcyon shore,
Where war's loud thunders lash the winds no more.

And on Thy deep, the girdle of the world,
When the fierce Hurricanoes have unfurl'd
Their thousand wings, to battle and to rave,
Sweep down the rock and scourge the yelling wave;
When skies in tempest-agonies outgroan,
And the mad elements seem left alone,
Lord of the Storm! oh, Thou art present there,
In the loud thunder, and the lightning-glare,
While from the rollings of unfathom'd sea
A mariner's last sigh ascends to Thee.

Lo! to the yellow beach a maiden hies,
Love at her heart, and sorrow in her eyes.
Warm down her cheek impassion'd drops of woe,
Through fearful omens, for her lover flow:
Oh will he, far by faithless ocean borne,
Dream of his lonely maid who lives to mourn?
Will he, whene'er by palmy streams he roams,
Muse on their twilight-walks and woodbine homes,
And that first spring, when in the cowslip dale
She blush'd an answer to his wooing tale?

The beach is won; before her moans a sea,
In all its dim and dread immensity!
Wide o'er the wave a wistful glance she throws,
Till the fond lover smiles away her woes;
Voiceless awhile he clasps his dark-eyed maid,
Then looks the promise love has often said;
But, ere his vessel, in the horizon's blue
Veil'd by the mist, hath vanish'd from her view,
Sweet mourner! heavenward hope uplifts her mind
To Him who wings the storm, and walks the wind.

Thrice has the sun upon his green-wave bed,
'Mid rosy clouds, his vesper radiance shed;
And thrice the moon from out the ocean rose,
Like pale-eyed beauty waking from repose;
While rock'd beneath, the melancholy wave
Sang like a mermaid o'er the seaman's grave.

The morn is up: and in her mellow ray
Millions of youthful billows pant and play;
Greeting the stately vessels as they glide
In sail-wing'd triumph o'er the breezy tide.

But, lo! around the marsh'lling clouds unite,
Like thick battalions halting for the fight;
The sun retires, and rending whirlwinds sweep
Fierce through the air, and flutter on the deep;
Forth from their caverns rush the fatal blasts,
Tear the loose sails, and split the creaking masts,
And the lash'd billows, rolling in a train,
Rear their white heads, and race along the main.

And, see! hurl'd backward from a hidden rock,
A shatter'd vessel reeling with the shock,
Like one appall'd by an unearthly sight,
Who stands, and shivers with convulsive fright:
There, in a den of waves, she heaves awhile,
Till on her deck the howling surges pile;
Then struggling sinks beneath the water's leap,
Like a huge monster wrestling with the deep.

Borne like a sunbeam on the bounding waves,
Behold! a mariner the tempest braves;
Home, life, and love, and near-imagin'd death,
Nerve the stout limb, and lengthen out his breath:
A rock is reach'd, dash'd on a wave-worn peak
Lies the wreck'd sailor, shiv'ring, wan, and weak;
With livid face, and looks of ghastly dread,
And locks, like sea-weeds streaming from his head;
Unmoved the lips, but with his upturn'd eyes,
He shadows forth a Saviour in the skies;
Visions a viewless temple in the air,
Feels God around, and silence is his prayer!

Can Guilt, though hidden from the gaze of earth,
Fly from *His* view, who gave all being birth?
From her first shadow on the yielding soul,
To the dark hour when all her terrors roll,
His sleepless eye detects each buried plan,
And bares the bosom-secret of the man.
Yes! oft He locks the weapon in his hand,
And makes the murd'rer for his capture stand;
Or, when the flood of years has roll'd away
The darksome horrors of the blood-curs'd day,—
His vengeance frowns upon the felon's sleep,
Forcing his haggard eye to wake, and weep!

Upon the midnight-heath, where fierce winds growl,
Like famish'd wolves careering as they howl,
While cloudy billows darkly swell and rise
As if an ocean brooded in the skies,
Aghast and quaking, see the murd'rer stand,
Shrink from himself, and clench his crimson hand;
Unearthly terrors freeze his shudd'ring frame,
While conscience writhes upon the rack of shame:
Beneath him gasps the victim of his deed,
In that faint struggle ere the spirit's freed;
One piteous gaze—his languid eyelids close,
And life and torture sink to dead repose.

Why stands the murd'rer fetter'd to the spot,
Life, fame, and judgment in his guilt forgot?
Chain'd by his crime, he cannot—dare not fly,
A Spirit seems to grasp him from the sky!
And though no human eye the murder sees,
A curse from heaven comes mutter'd in each breeze.

Though Crime entomb herself within the heart,
And veil her anguish with dissembling art;
Though 'mid the glare of day, and dazzling strife
That flashes o'er the shadowy stream of life,
She move as merry as the morning air,
Unmarr'd by grief, unsorrow'd by a care,—
Darkness shall bear the burden of her sin,
And fan the hell of thought that flames within!

At deep dead night, when not an earthly sound
Jars on the brooding air that sleeps around;
When the coarse raptures of a Christless day,
Touch'd by the wand of Truth, dissolve away,
Unhallow'd Guilt shall in her bosom feel
A rack too fierce for language to reveal;
A sense unutt'rable within the soul
Of Him pervading—living through the whole:
On ev'ry limb shall creeping terror come,
Lock the white lips, and strike cold anguish dumb;
Vengeance shall utter an imagin'd yell,
And Fancy flutter round the gulph of Hell.

Not so comes darkness to the good man's breast,
When Night brings on the lulling hour of rest;
Tired of the day, a pillow laps his head,
While heavenly vigils watch around the bed;
His spirit bosom'd on the God of all,—
Peace to the hour! whate'er the night befal:
Then, pleasing Memory unrolls her chart,
To raise, refine, and regulate the heart;
Exulting Boyhood, and its host of smiles,
Next, busy Manhood battling with its toils,
Delights and dreams that made the heart run o'er,
The love forgotten, and the friends no more—
The panorama of past life appears,
Warms his pure mind, and melts it into tears!
Till, like a shutting flower, the senses close,
And on him lies the beauty of repose.

Yes! in the dark, Imagination seems
Girt with a shadowy brood of awful Dreams,
Which round her in appalling visions fly,
Dread as the phantoms on a thunder-sky;
And Guilt starts back, by gloomy horror driven,
But Virtue braves them with a smile from Heaven.

'Tis night: and sternly comes the mutt'ring wind,
While cloud-battalions slowly march behind;
Alone the way-worn pilgrim winds his track,
His wallet resting on his weary back;
Though dark the path, and dreary grows the night,
And not a heaven-lamp yields its holy light,
Firm o'er the starless wild he moves his way,
For HE pervades the night, who form'd the day!
Thus on he roams beneath the brooding sky,
Till, lo, a lattice twinkles on his eye,
And merrily from out his woodland dome,
His babes bound forth, and hail the wand'rer home.

When Conscience darts her stings into the mind,
And heart-broke Folly turns to look behind,
Then, righteous Heaven, without Thy hopeful ray,
What fell despair would lower on our way!
Where shall we light the burden of our woes?
How should we lull our anguish to repose?—
But, when the rebel Heart has ceas'd to roam,
And yearns o'er visions of forsaken home,
Thy love will hail the chasten'd wand'rer there,
And hush to peace the tempest of despair.

And not more beautiful beneath the ray
Of risen morn, night-shades dissolve away,
And the unmantled world, embathed in light,
Awakes in orient glory, clear and bright,—
Than do the sinful mists that shroud the soul
Melt off beneath religion's mild control,
Till the full impress of our God appears,
Made pure and perfect by repentant tears.
Now, day by day, celestial feelings rise
Fresh from the heart, and reach th' immortal skies:

Now comes the hour, when rambling all unseen,
Except by stars, upon the dusky green;
When winds are voiceless, and the breezes still,
Save truant ones, which rove some wooded hill,
Eternal glories dawn upon the heart,
Till tears ecstatic from the soul-fount start;
And sorrow, bursting from ideal gloom,
Soars after Christ, and triumphs o'er the tomb.

But when the erring heart at Passion's shrine
Hath basely sacrificed each trait divine:
When Guilt hath stain'd it with her deepest dye,
And blood for blood is Nature's dreadful cry,
Angel of Mercy! thy becalming power
Alone can tame the terrors of the hour;
Thine is the charm that bids the heart unbind,
Mount on the wings of Faith, and leave Despair behind;
Thine is the voice that soothes the dying breath,
And breathes a halo round the brow of Death.

And hark! the midnight bars have ceas'd to sound,
The dungeon guard has paced his clanking round,
And all is lone, and dismal as the deep
When weary Storms sink mutt'ring into sleep;
But one there is, in yonder glimm'ring cell,
Whose young heart wept, and wonder'd while it fell;
A wreck of crime upon his stony bed,
With eye wild-rolling and bewilder'd head.
'Tis not the chain that clinks upon his straw,
'Tis not the blow of violated law,—
But racking thoughts which rive his shudd'ring heart,
And make each fibre of the bosom start.
Yes! they have borne him to his native streams,
Where young-eyed Fancy wove her fairy dreams;
To each wild glade where Boyhood loved to roam,
Till twilight came, and call'd the truant home:
And where is she who rock'd him to repose,
And sang, and smiled, to lull his infant woes?
And he who greeted with paternal joy
The dawning virtues of his darling boy?
Afar, beneath the trampled sod they sleep,
He neither heard them sigh, nor saw them weep!—
That wasted eye and palpitating cheek,
Those wringing hands, and that delirious shriek,
Oh, these betray the burning load of pain
Remembrance piles upon his phrensied brain:
Till Faith descend upon her wings of Love,
And show the Mercy-seat unveil'd above;
Then, firm his glance, hush'd every groan and cry,
And hypocrites might shake to view a felon die!

'Tis sad to see the eye forget its ray,
And sorrow sit where smiles were wont to play;
'Tis sad, when youth is fresh, and fair, and warm,
And life is fraught with every sweeter charm,
To see it close the lip, and droop the head,
Wane from this earth, and mingle with the dead;
But, oh! nor death, nor wo, can ever seem
So heart-appalling as that wild'ring dream.
That life in death—a desolated Mind,
Around whose wreck the weeds of madness wind.

Down yon romantic dale, where hamlets few
Arrest the summer pilgrim's frequent view,
The village wonder, and the widow's joy,
Dwells the poor, mindless, pale-faced maniac boy:
He lives, and breathes, and rolls his vacant eye
To greet the glowing fancies of the Sky;
But on his cheek unmeaning shades of wo
Reveal the wither'd thoughts that sleep below.—
A soulless Thing, a haunter of the woods,
He holds wild fellowship with fields and floods;
Sometimes along the woodland's winding glade,
He starts, and smiles upon his pallid shade;
Or scolds with idiot threat the roaming wind,—
But rebel music to that ruin'd mind!
Or on the shell-strewn beach delighted strays,
Playing his fingers in the noontide-rays;
And when the sea-waves swell their hollow roar,
He counts the billows plunging to the shore;
And oft, beneath the glimmer of the moon,
He chaunts some wild and melancholy tune,
Till o'er his soft'ning features seems to play
A flick'ring gleam of mind's recover'd sway.

Thus, like a living Dream, apart from men,
From morn to eve he haunts the wood and glen;
But round him, near him, wheresoe'er he rove,
A shielding Angel tracks him from above;
Nor harm from flood or fen shall e'er destroy
The lonesome wand'rings of that maniac boy.

But lo, in pale sublimity of forms
The arctic billows glare like frozen storms!
For thus, in terrible array, are seen
Mountains of ice where never man hath been,
Where not a sound, nor motion dares advance
To violate their everlasting trance;
Save when the riven glaciers downward crush
Themselves to water, with chaotic rush;
Or Silence trembles, like a thing aghast,
When o'er her waste the wolfish echo pass'd;—

E'en here beneath the wings Almighty roam
The brave sea-warriors from their English home,
And find amid such wilderness of waves
An Eye that watches, and a Hand that saves.

Behold ! yon Vessel with heroic prow
Through a white realm of ice advancing now,
Her cables stiffen'd into chains of frost,
And the proud bearing of her beauty lost,—
The prey of ocean, will she not descend,
Tomb'd in dead ice, with none to mark her end?
No ! faith and valour, and inviolate hope,
With danger in its deepest midnight cope;
And Home shall listen yet, with pausing breath,
To tales of ruin—the romance of Death,
When frowning o'er her, like a Fiend he stood,
And mutter'd, "Sink in ghastly solitude !
And may the corpses of thy crew be seen
To freeze and whiten where thy sails have been !"

Victors of Nature in her dreadest might !
Dauntless as winds that roam with free delight,
When once again the rocks of England rise
In tow'ring welcome on your dazzled eyes,
As round the hearth young household-voices ring,
Like the glad melodies of jocund spring,
What records with your laden hearts unroll?
Where is the painter, on whose gorgeous soul
Visions of undepicted beauty rose,
Like them that glitter'd on irradiant snows?
Bright as the Palace John of Patmos view'd,
What ice-domes flash'd in frozen solitude !
What rocks of ruby glare,* when sunset came
Full on their whiteness, like a wingèd flame !
And while the crimson of declining day
Lit the cold fretwork of the crystal spray,
How oft a seaman with ecstatic eyes
Drank the rich magic of celestial dyes,
Blent like a rainbow's, when the waters heave
And tremble, while the braided colours weave.—
But there was beauty that outdazzled this,
Making the air one fairy-clime of bliss,
When moonlight flung a robe of silver haze
Athwart the mountains that received its rays,
Till the stain'd welkin by reflection shone,
Like floating emerald, or a verdant sun,
So brightly green, so exquisite the glow !—
And then, what meteors did pale twilight throw
O'er the chill air, in wild electric play !
Sublimely fierce, or delicately gay,
The Borealis like a creature spread
Its length of living glory o'er their head,
And seem'd exulting with victorious light,
To mock the darkness with its radiant might.
But, oh, the silence !—dream-like, cold, and vast,
As though the day of awful doom had pass'd,
And Earth remain'd to wither, dead and lone,
A blighted rebel, by her God unknown !
So mute and soundless must that hour have been,
When, gazing round on nature's ghastly scene
Of crag and ice interminably piled,
A frozen chaos, a sepulchral wild,—
The seaman ponder'd till a thought of death
Check'd the cold murmur of his faintest breath:
Nature and God alone were reigning now:
And the high meaning of his dauntless brow
Dethroned by awe, dissolved and waned away,
For Silence, like a spirit, seem'd to pray,
Till the blood listen'd in his breathless frame,
And, small and still, the voice Almighty came !

Exhaustless Mercy ! like that pilgrim brook,
That never once the marching hosts forsook,
When through the scorching wastes of Egypt's land,
The cloud-led Israel steer'd by God's command,
Thy stream, along the herbless path of life,
Makes verdure smile, with bloom celestial rife:
But if there be, round whom with holier might
Dwells the deep sense of Heaven's o'erwatching light,
Soldiers of Christ ! whose banner faith unrolls,
The true schechinah of protected souls
'Tis theirs to witness, when through clime and zone
Where the grim idol mounts Jehovah's throne,
And Man, degraded as the trampled clod,
Bleeds at the shrine of some barbaric god,
Wild as the torrent in its desperate fall,
Whom blood, nor death, nor agonies appal,
With spirit blighted, and with reason blind,—
Who can rebuild his desolated mind?

"Go forth and teach"—and ye have gone, and done
Deeds that will shine, when thou art dark, O Sun !
Heroes, whose crowns with gems of glory shine,
Dug from the depths of heaven's eternal mine,
Oh, what a conquest hath the Cross obtain'd !
E'en where of old a hell of darkness reign'd,
And Crime and Havoc, fiend-begotten pair,
In mortal bosoms made their savage lair,
And issued thence to riot, rage, or kill,
Like incarnations of a demon's will,
The peace that passeth understanding grows,
And Earth seems born again, without her woes;
So wondrously the spell divine descends,
And man with nature in communion blends:

* See Parry's Voyage, and others, to explain some local allusions in this polar sketch.

The isles have seen HIM! and the deserts raise
Anthems that thrill the halls of heaven with praise;
Crouching and tame the tiger Passions lie,
Hush'd by the gaze of God's subduing eye:
Temples and homes of sacred truth abound,
Where Satan once with all his fiends was found:
And, hark! at sunset while the shaded calm
Of forest coolness floats on wings of balm,
As roams the pilgrim in that dying glare,
From a lone hamlet winds the voice of prayer,—
Breath of the soul by Jesu taught to rise
And blend with music heard beyond the skies!
Ecstatic thought! the zenith of our dreams,
Error has died in Truth's victorious beams:
And where the savage round his altar fed
On the warm fragments of the limbless dead,
Cots which an English heart delights to hail
Deck the green wilds of many a foreign dale,
And, turn'd by Piety's familiar hand,
Religion sees her tear-worn Bibles stand.

"Thy kingdom come!" prophetic voices throng
In choral harmony, and chant, "How long,
How long, O beatific King of kings,
Till ransom'd earth with gospel-music rings?
How long a period ere that Sun arise
Which glitter'd on Isaiah's holy eyes,
And clad the cedar'd hills of Palestine
With veils of glory, wove from sheen divine?"

Oh for that day, beyond what poets dream,
Deck'd by Imagination's crystal beam,
When vanquish'd Sin shall leave Messiah's throne
To rise in full transcendancy alone:
Hate, War, and Tumult, all the brood of crime,
Shall then be banish'd from the scene of time;
Evil be dead, Corruption breathe no more,
And Peace, the seraph, smile from shore to shore,
While round her Prince sublime hosannahs swell,—
"Thy truth has wither'd all the thrones of Hell!
For ever and for ever live and reign,
Till earth be purified to heaven again!"

Thou unimagined God! though every hour,
And every day speak Thy mysterious power;
Upon the seventh, creation's work was crown'd:
Upon the seventh, ten thousand worlds wheel'd round!
And ever hallow'd be Thy chosen day,
Till Nature die, and Time shall roll away.

Sweet Sabbath morn! from childhood's dimpled prime
I lov'd to hail thy calm-renewing time;
Soft steal thy bells upon the tranced mind,*
In fairy cadence floating on the wind,
Telling of friends and times long flown away.
And pensive hopes harmonious with the day.

On thy still dawn, while holy music peals,
And far around the ling'ring echo steals,
What Heart communes not with the day's repose,
And, lull'd by angel-dreams, forgets its woes?
Who, in His temple, gives to God a prayer,
Nor feels an image of bright heaven is there?
The pleading stillness of the vaulted pile,
Where gather'd hearts their homage breathe awhile,
The mingled burst of penitential sighs,
The choral anthem pealing to the skies,
Exalt the soul to energies sublime,
And thoughts that reach beyond the realm of time.

Emblem of peace! upon the village plain
Thou dawn'st a blessing to the toil-worn swain:
Soon as thy smiles along the upland play,
His bosom kindles to salute the day;
Humble and happy, to his lot resign'd,
He owns the inward sabbath of the mind.

And when, with low-drawn sighs of love and fear,
His suppliant vows have sought Jehovah's ear,
Serene the thoughts which o'er his bosom steal,
As home he wanders for the sabbath meal:
There shall kind Plenty wear her sweetest smiles;
There shall his ruddy children play their wiles;
While the fond mother, lapp'd in worldless joy,
Fondles with frequent kiss her infant boy.
At noon, a ramble round the burial-ground,
A moral tear on some lamented mound;
Or breezy walk along the green expanse,
Where endless verdure charms the ling'ring glance,—
These are the wonted blessings of the day,
Which all his weekly toils and woes repay.
And when the shroud of night hath veil'd the view,
And star-gleams twinkle on the meadow-dew,
Some elder boy beside his father's knee
Shall stand and read the Eternal History:

* It is instructive to find that the most tempestuous minds can be tranquillised into a holy state of feeling by the simple peal of church bells. Buonaparte is recorded to have said,—"Last Sunday evening, in the general silence of Nature, as I was walking in these grounds [of Malmaison], the sound of the church bell of Ruel fell on my ear, and renewed all the impressions of my youth; I was profoundly affected. Such is the effect of early habit and associations."

Or household-prayer, or chanted hymn shall close
The hour that charms him to a sweet repose.

And Melody,—an echo breathed from heaven!
By her ineffable delight is given;
Whether she melt a passion from the mind,
Or with Æolian languish lull the wind;
Whether she madden in the mingled roar
Of Alpine billows bounding to the shore;
Or on the elfin pinions of a breeze
Float o'er the flowers, and woo the vernal trees,—
Alike divine! But, deeper in the soul
Sinks melody's omnipotent control.
When from the fluted organ, full and deep
Billows of music through the dim aisles sweep!
Ear, eye, and heart, confess the awful spell,
While soul and being with the magic swell,
And as the spiral echoes upward wind,
Die off—and scarcely leave the man behind.

And now, while faintly-ebbing murmurs roll
Entrancing music o'er the prostrate soul,
Religion loves to linger in some aisle,
Where through emblazon'd panes a vesper smile
With pallid radiance quivers in the gloom,
Or crowns, like seraph-light, th' inspiring tomb;
The thrilling echoes of sepulchral ground,
The monumental awe suffused around,
The fretted arch with its gigantic sweep,
The world's great Spirits throned in marble sleep,—
Subdue each earthly passion into fear,
As though the resurrection-hour drew near!

But not alone the vast and vaulted pile,
An echoing cloister, or the pillar'd aisle,
Hallow the mind: for humblest fanes impart
A holy magic to the feeling heart.

And see, down where yon arches shed their gloom,
And mottoes speak from many a time-worn tomb,
There, where the Font uprears its marble brow,
The village sponsors breathe their sacred vow,
While timidly a mother, young and mild,
To Heaven presents her dedicated child:
And oft she gazes on the sleeping boy,
Lock'd to her breast with all a mother's joy;
Fearful and fond, and twining for repose,
Like a young bud around the parent rose.

But who shall paint her meditative eye,
Her look of love and heaven-appealing sigh,
When on the cherub brow, with hope divine,
The holy preacher prints the liquid sign?
Joy, doubt, and fear in mingled passion rise,
Gush through her heart, and glitter in her eyes.

Whene'er I gaze upon a sinless child,
Tossing its merry head of ringlets wild,
Lip, cheek, and eye, all in that lovely glow
Young spirits feel, as yet unchill'd by wo,
A voiceless wonder animates each sense,
To think how Mercy watches innocence!

Survey the scene of life: in yonder room,
Pillow'd in beauty 'mid the cradle gloom,
While o'er its features plays an angel-smile,
A breathing cherub slumbers for a while:
Those budding lips, the faintly-fringèd eye,
That placid cheek, and uncomplaining sigh,
The rounded limbs in soft embrace entwined,
Like flower-leaves folded from the sev'ring wind,—
All by their tender charms her babe endear,
And feed the lux'ry of a mother's fear.

Next, mark her infant raised to childhood's stage,
Bound in the bloom of that delightful age,
With heart as light as wavelets on the deep,
And eye that Wo has scarcely taught to weep:—
The tip-toe gaze, the pertinacious ken,
Each rival attribute of mimick'd men,
The prompt decision, and presuming way,
Now picture forth his yet auspicious day.

Whether at noon he waft his tiny boat
By winding streams, and woody bank remote,
Or climb the meadow-tree, or trail the kite,
And thinks that heaven ne'er match'd that moving sight!
Or roam the haunted wood at dying day,
To list with spell-bound ear the cuckoo's lay,—
A Hand above o'er-rules the vent'rous boy,
And draws the daily circle of his joy.

And thus, when manhood brings its weight of care,
To chain the soul, and curb the giddy air,
The father, friend, the patriot, and the man,
Share in the love of Heaven's parental plan;
Till age o'ersteal his mellow'd form at last,
And wintry locks tell summer youth is past;
Then, like the sun slow-wheeling to the wave,
He sinks in glory to a welcome grave.

Lord of the Universe! enthron'd sublime
In secret glory over Space and Time,
Though oft the red-wing'd lightnings sear the sky,
And mutt'ring thunders mark Thy track on high,
One omnipresent, ever sleepless Love
Pervades what issues from Thy power above:

When from Thy hands primeval earth out-sprang,
And starry music o'er the launch'd world rang,
Thine emblem, God, was Love! nor eye can see
Where love is not the master-trait of Thee.

And since that time, when first in Eden's bower
The stainless Adam bent to beauty's power,
Have Souls commingled in affection's flame,
In weal unsever'd, and in wo the same.

Young, chaste, and lovely—pleased, yet half afraid,
Before yon altar droops a plighted maid,
Clad in her bridal robes of taintless white,
Dumb with the scene, and dazzled with delight.
Around her hymeneal guardians stand,
Each with devoted look, and feeling bland;
And oft she turns her soul-expressing eye,
Dimm'd with a tear for happiness gone by!
Then coyly views, in youth's commanding pride,
Her own betroth'd one kneeling by her side:
Like lilies bending from the noon-tide blaze,
Her bashful eyelids droop beneath his gaze;
While love and homage blend their blissful power,
And shed a halo round his marriage-hour.

What though this chance-abounding life ordain
A path of anguish and corrective pain;
By want or wo, where'er compell'd he rove,
A cot's a palace by the light of love!
There beats *one* heart, which until death will be
A fountain-source of fondest sympathy;
One frownless eye to kindle with his own,
One changeless friend, when other friends are flown:
Oh, sanction Thou the love-united pair,
Author of love! for Thou art present there.

There be some heart-entwining hours of life,
With uncontrollable sensation rife;
When mellow'd thoughts, like music on the ear,
Thrill through the soul, and revel in a tear.
And, such are they, when, tranquil and alone
We sit and ponder on long periods flown;
And, charm'd by Fancy's retrospective gaze,
Live in an atmosphere of other days;
Till friends and faces, flashing on the mind,
Conceal the havoc time has left behind.

Yon aged man,—with what a musing eye
He dreams and lingers o'er the days fled by,
When pensive, sitting by his evening-fire,
To Mem'ry's peaceful glade his thoughts retire,
While cherub grandsons pat his willing knee,
Shake their bright curls, and prattle off their glee.
Now gently fleet back joy-wing'd days of old,
When Hope led forward, and the eye look'd bold:
With holy calm he thinks of place and time,
Beloved when left, unblotted with a crime;
Cold friendship's smiles are re-illumined now,
And gleams of fancy lighten on his brow!
What Hand puissant gave to life each form,
Scatter'd the cloud and piloted the storm?
Guided him onward through his thorny road,
Bestow'd each joy, and brighten'd each abode?
Ah! see the pious tear of mem'ry roll
In welling rapture from his grateful soul,
That trembles like the waking pulse of joy,
To feel, Heaven raised the man, and rear'd the boy!

Chain'd to the car of Time, as on we roll
Through cloud and sunshine to th' Eternal goal,
How favour'd he, whose soul, through Grace refined,
Meets by the way some all-partaking mind,
Some feeling friend, by Nature mark'd our own,
And moulded true to every tender tone!
Let fortune frown, congenial scenes depart,
And "farewell" rive the fetters of the heart,—
'Tis sweet, when roaming by a wave-girt strand,
To weave fond visions of our own far Land;
Or dream, while faintly chimes the convent-bell,
Of distant friends, and each domestic spell,
And feel one Spirit tracks our lone career
And dwells in every heart to Friendship dear.

And if brief absence in our chequer'd life
Wake in fond bosoms sympathetic strife,
How deep the wo when death's terrific hand
Tears a loved victim to a shadowy land!—
Oh Death! thou dreadless Vanquisher of earth.
The elements shrunk blasted at thy birth;
Thine is the conquest of untold mankind,
Victims before, and carnage strewn behind!

And say, when thoughtful on our couch we lie,
And scan the future with uncheated eye,
How fancy dreads to realise the tomb,
Shrinks into awe, and shudders at its doom;
What shapes of horror glide around our bed,
Damp from the ghastly regions of the dead,
While nature hovers o'er that fearful brink,
Where Faith turns wild, and Thought too weak to think;
Trembling and startling, like a shade in sleep,
Or a lone vessel on the surging deep,—
Till Revelation's heaven-directed beam
Melts every doubt in some celestial dream;
Oh, then no more convulsing terrors roll;
Then, then, the hallelujah of the soul!

Wing'd on the hope of heaven, it speeds away
To the bright source of beatific Day.

Lo! on a shaded couch, with pillow'd head,
And pallid limbs in dewy languor spread,
The dying parent, like a wailing breeze,
Moans in the feverish grasp of wan Disease;
While sad and watching, with a sleepless eye,
A lovely daughter sits and muses by:
So Gabriel sat within the Saviour's tomb,
When his pure spirit walk'd th' Eternal gloom.

There, as some ancient abbey's muffled bell
Tolls o'er the drowsing world the day's farewell,
Frequent she glances at his wrinkled brow,
And those dear eyes, so dim and deathful now,
Till all his love and all his care returns,
And memory through her brain and bosom burns!—
That drooping hand, so delicately weak,
How often had it smooth'd her infant cheek;
Or danced her, lightly tripping by his side,
And prattling sweetly with delighted pride;
Or pluck'd the baby flower that charm'd her age,
Or gently oped Instruction's pictured page,
Or pointed to some mild and mournful star,
That throned its beauty in the sky afar.

And see, no more the arrowy throes of pain
Pierce his bound head, or force the plaintive strain;
Slumber hath heal'd them with its holy balm,
And chain'd the senses in oblivion's calm;
Pleased at his quiet mien, with timid breath,
She stirs to see—alas! the sleep of Death;
Pulseless and pale, beneath the taper's glow,
Lies her loved parent, but a lifeless show!

She shook not, shriek'd not, raised no maniac cry,
Nor wrung her hand, nor heaved one heart-deep sigh;
But stood aghast, too awful for relief,
Mute, stiff, and white,—a monument of grief!

To hear a dying lip's last accent speak,
And watch the death-chill on a sunken cheek;
Or see the flaming eye-ball fiercely roll,
As if it wrestled with a parting soul;
Or, hear the last clod crumble on the bed,
And thrill some hollow mansion of the dead,
This, this is wo!—but deeper far the gloom
That haunts us, when we pace the desert room,
And shadow forth an image of our love,
Rapt to Elysian realms of light above;
'Tis now, while low and long the heavy knell
Pours on the breeze a parted soul's farewell,
Despair and anguish curtain round our view,
And all but sorrow seems to be untrue.
How sadly vacant turns the frequent gaze,
To where a mourn'd one smiled in other days!
The eye that glitter'd with each gen'rous thought;
The glowing mind with worth and wisdom [fraught;
The twilight walk by some romantic stream,
Where Friendship warm'd, while Fancy wove her dream;
The smile, and wit,—all, all the feeling heart
Delights to trace on mem'ry's faithful chart
Return upon us; Omnipresent Power!
'Tis Thine to lull this agonising hour;
To charm the burden from the soul, and be
A Saviour-God in more than sympathy.

PART III.

"In the wild mystery of earth and air,
Sun, moon, and star, and the unslumb'ring sea,—
There is a meaning and a power, commix'd
For thought, and for undying fancy tuned.
And by thy panting for the unattain'd
On earth; by longings which no language speak:
By the dread torture of o'ermast'ring doubt;
By thirst for Beauty, such as eye ne'er saw,
And yet is ever mirror'd on the mind;
By Love in her rich heavenliness array'd;
By Guilt and Conscience,—that terrific pair,
Who make the dead to mutter from their tombs,
And colour nature with the hues of hell!—
By Revelation's everlasting truths,—O Man,
Thou art immortal as thy Maker is!"

ANALYSIS OF PART III.

If there be no God, the former parts of this Poem are moulded from dreams of superstitious fiction;—But can we observe the wonders of Creation, and deem Chance their origin?—The consequences that accrue from this distempered doctrine:—By a natural, but melancholy digression, we are here led to glance at Atheism—as partially influencing the horrors of the French Revolution—Marie Antoinette—Her appearance on the balcony during the tumults at Versailles.

Return to a consideration of Atheism—It is a sorry boast to triumph over a belief of man's immortality—If the soul be not immortal, how are we to account for those aspirations which are never satisfied with the highest attainment of earthly enjoyment? The dismal doctrine of believing all ties of love eternally severed by death:—when we reflect on the master-spirits of gone time, can we imagine them eternally quenched?—Consolations derived from a belief in a future state—Pictures of a deathbed of a Sceptic and a Christian—The Poem concludes with a description of the final Doom.

Now, while the stars in meekest beauty rise,
And gaze on earth, like Heaven's maternal eyes,

Oh, let sublime Imagination soar,
And tread the region Milton trod before,
Ride on the deep, or travel with the sun
Far as creation smiles, or time has run,
So shall her eagle eye divinely see
A universe that glows with Deity,—
In every wave and wind, and fruit and flower,
The glory, truth, and terror of His power.

Who hung yon planet in its airy shrine,
And dash'd the sunbeam from its burning mine?
Who bade the ocean-mountains swell and leap,
And thunder rattle from the skyey deep?
Through hill and dale who twined the healthful stream,
Made rain for nurture, and the fruit to teem?
Who charm'd the clod into a breathing shrine,
And call'd it Man, a miniature divine?—
Lord of Creation, Love, and Life, and Light,
Arise, and vindicate Thine awful right!

And dare men dream that dismal Chance has framed
All that the eye perceives, or tongue has named,
The spacious world, and all its wonders, born
Designless, self-created, and forlorn?
That no First Builder plied His plastic force,
Gave to each object form, to motion course?
Then may Religion, Morals, Truth, and Worth,
Perish from out this atheistic earth!
Why should the orphans of the world who roam
O'er earth's bleak waste, without a friend, a home,
With *resignation* mark their fellow clay
Bask in the sunshine of a better day?
Why should the vagrant shiver at the door,
Nor crush the miser for his treasured ore,
Save Faith's sweet music harmonised the mind,
Whisper'd of Heaven, and bade it be resign'd?

And here let Mem'ry turn her tearful glance
On the grim horrors of tumultuous France;
When blood and blasphemy defiled her land,
And fierce Rebellion raised her savage hand,
While women flung their female hearts away,
Rear'd the red pike, and butcher'd for their pay.*

No more the Tocsin for the carnage tolls,
No dead-piled tumbril from the slaughter rolls;
The blood has dried upon each wither'd plain,
And brave La Vendée blooms in peace again;
Still may we paint an image of the times,
And draw a moral from a Nation's crimes.

Ill-fated Land! did godless wisdom pour
The light of liberty from shore to shore?
Ah no, perverted freedom cursed the day
With nameless deeds of horror and dismay;
Virtue was death-struck, Vice alone had power,
And Fiends saw hell on earth, in that black hour!

Let streets of blood, let dungeons choked with dead,
The tortured brave, the royal Hearts who bled;
Let plunder'd cities, and polluted fanes,
The butcher'd thousands piled upon the plains,
Let the foul orgies of stupendous crime
Witness the raging havoc of that time,
When leagued Rebellion march'd to kindle Man,
Fright in her rear, and Murder at her van.

And thou, sweet flower of Austria! slaughter'd queen,
How oft will Hist'ry in thy dreadful scene
Sigh to relate, what once a woman saw,
Whose very look had *been* a nation's law;
When all high chivalries of heart were fled,
And Treason's dagger pierced the monarch's bed.
But thou wast fearless 'mid the savage yell
When Murder hooted, as the hatchet fell.
Queen to the last! methinks I see thee stand,
With infants clasping thy maternal hand,
And face unmoved the murd'rous throng who came
A deed to do which Earth might shrink to name.

Unmann'd of men! whose thankless eyes can glance
On all around, and deem it born of Chance;
Self-martyr'd victims to appalling doom,
Your life a vision, and your heart a tomb,—
The source and end of Being in the ground,
Where all is silent, and *your* goal is found!

* This revolting scene is thus described by Sir Walter Scott, in his Sketch of the French Revolution, prefixed to his Life of Napoleon:—"The outside of the palace was still besieged by the infuriated mob, who demanded with hideous cries, and acclamations the most barbarous and obscene, the Austrian, as they called the Queen. The unfortunate Princess appeared on the balcony, with one of her children in each hand. A voice from below called out 'No children!' as if on purpose to deprive the mother of that appeal to humanity which might move the hardest heart. Marie Antoinette, with a force of mind worthy Maria Theresa, her mother, pushed her children back into the room, and turning her face to the tumultuous multitude, which tossed and roared beneath, brandishing their pikes and guns with the wildest attitudes of rage, the reviled, persecuted, and denounced queen stood before them, her arms folded on her bosom, with a noble air of courageous resolution."

How charmless time must stream away with you,
To struggle, wish, and weep, and then—Adieu!
Ye cannot stifle Sorrow at her birth,
By hopes prevailing o'er the woes of earth,
Nor soothe the passions which besiege the soul
By immortality's divine control,
Share with the majesty of earth and sky,
Mount on a thought, and talk with Deity!

Boast not of wisdom, if her precepts say
Th' Immortal Essence mingles with the clay;
In polar isles, where wisdom's mellow beam
Ne'er chasten'd beauty's glance, or rapture's dream,
E'en there a Deity pervades the mind,
Speaks in the storm, and travels on the wind.*

And shall the Soul, the fount of reason, die,
When dust and darkness round its temple lie?
Did God breathe in it no ethereal fire,
Burning and quenchless, though the breath expire?
Then, why were godlike aspirations given,
That, scorning earth, so often frame a heaven?
Why does the ever-craving wish arise
For better, nobler, than the world supplies?
Ah, no! it cannot be that men were sent
To moulder in ethereal discontent,
That soul was fashion'd for betrayful trust,
To think like God, and perish like the dust!

If Death for ever doom us to the clod,
And earth-born pleasure be our only god,
Remorseless time shall bury all we love,
Nor leave one hope to reunite above;
No more the voice of friendship shall beguile,
No more the mother on her infant smile,
But vanishing, like rain upon the deep,
Nature is,—Nothing, in eternal sleep!

Monarchs of mind! and spirits of the just,
Are ye entomb'd in everlasting dust?
Shall ye, whose names undimm'd by ages shine,
Bright as the flame that mark'd ye for divine,
For ever slumber,—never meet again,
Too pure for sorrow, too sublime for pain?
Ah, no! celestial Fancy loves to fly
With eager pinion, and prophetic eye,
To radiant dwellings of immortal Bliss,
Far from a world so wo-begone as this;
There, as the choral melodies career,
And wind and warble through heaven's mystic sphere,
In perfect forms you all again unite,
And worship Godhead on His throne of Light.

When friends have vanish'd to the spirit-home,
And we are left companionless to roam,
Oh, what can cheer our melancholy way,
But hopes of union in the land of Day?
Soul-loved! companions of our greener years,
Warm'd at our joys, and weeping at our tears,
How oft descriptive mem'ry paints each hour,
When friendship triumph'd, and the heart had power!
Yes, hallow'd are those visions of the brain,
When Heaven unveils, and lov'd ones smile again.

And Thou, for ever fond, for ever true,
Beneath whose smile the boy to manhood grew;
To sorrow piteous, and to error mild,
Has Death for ever torn thee from thy child?
Thy voice that counsell'd, charm'd, consol'd, and bless'd,
Thy deep solicitude which found no rest
But in completion of some pure design,
To make *my* happiness the spring of *thine;*
Thy boundless love, whose providential gaze
Pour'd light and tenderness round all my ways;
Those myriad fascinations felt and known
Of truth maternal to be borne alone.
(Too coldly prized while we can call them ours,
And feel them gladden the unduteous hours,
But, oh! how worshipp'd, magically dear,
When woke to life by mem'ry's votive tear!)
Though these have perish'd, Love in deathless bloom
Outlives the torpor of the wintry tomb.
There is a clime where sorrow never came,
There is a peace perennially the same;
There rolls a world where sever'd Hearts renew
Bright sympathies, the exquisite and true!
But chasten'd, calm, exalted, and refined
To each pure tone of beatific mind.
There may we meet, departed Spirit! there,
The home of bliss, the paradise of prayer:
A few more pangs, a few more tears to shed,
And I shall mingle with the faded dead;
A few fleet years, and this tried heart must brave
The damp oblivion of the dreamless grave;
When, true as thine, may resignation close
These eyes for glory in their last repose.

And if the Dead on this dull world may gaze
To breathe a blessing round our guarded ways;
If by some ministry, to man unknown,
They still can make a human wish their own,
And wander round, ineffably serene,
That unforgotten home, where life has been,—
Spirit maternal! often gaze on me,
And soothe the pang that so remembers thee!
Hover around me when I mourn, or pray,
Cheer the lone night, and consecrate the day:

* "Lo the poor Indian, whose untutor'd mind
Sees God in clouds, and hears him in the wind."

When temper kindles, or when passion dares,
Renew thy warning, and recall thy cares,—
Bid thy past love like inspiration rise,
And plead for Virtue with a mother's sighs!

But say! how will the sceptic brave the hour
Of crushing death's inexorable power,
When all this gorgeous world shall glide away,
Like painted dreams before the breath of day?
See, how he shudders at a glance of death;
What doubt and horror hang upon his breath;
The gibb'ring teeth, glazed eye, and marble limb,—
Shades from the tomb stalk out, and stare on him!

Lo, there, in yonder spectre-haunted room,
What mutter'd curses trembled through the gloom,
When pale and shiv'ring, and bedew'd with fear,
The dying sceptic felt his hour draw near!
As the last throes of death convuls'd his cheek,
He gnash'd, and scowl'd, and raised a hideous shriek,
Rounded his eyes into a ghastly glare,
Lock'd his white lips—and all was mute despair.

Go, child of Darkness! see a christian die;
No horror pales his lip, or dims his eye;
No fiend-shaped phantoms of destruction start
The hope religion pillows on his heart,
When with a falt'ring hand he waves adieu,
From Hearts as tender as their tears are true;
Meek as an infant to the mother's breast
Turns, fondly longing for its wonted rest,
So to his God the yielding soul retires,
And in one sigh of sainted peace expires.

But what is death or danger, storm or sea,
What are the loudest thunders launch'd by Thee,
Thou dread Jehovah! to a blazing world,—
Creation from its huge foundation hurl'd?
Then, then will reign Thine unimagin'd power,
And Earth in flames expect her funeral hour.

Ages has awful Time been trav'lling on,
And all his children to one tomb have gone;
The varied wonders of the peopled earth,
In equal turn, have gloried in their birth;
We live and toil, we triumph and decay,—
Thus age on age rolls unperceived away;
And thus 'twill be, till Heaven's last thunders roar,
And Man and Nature shall exist no more.

Oh! say, what Fancy, though endow'd sublime,
Can picture truly that sepulchral time,
When the last sun shall blaze upon the sea,
And Time be buried in eternity?
A cloudy mantle will enwrap that Sun
Whose face so many worlds have gazed upon;
The placid Moon, beneath whose pensive beam
We all have loved to wander, and to dream,
Dyed into blood, shall glare from pole to pole,
And tinge the gloomy tempests as they roll;
And those sweet Stars, that like familiar eyes,
Are wont to smile a welcome from the skies,
No more shall fascinate our dreaming sight,
But quench their beauty in perpetual night.—
And, hark! how wildly on the ruin'd shore
Expiring Ocean pants in hollow roar,
While earth's abysses echo back the groan,
And startle Nature on her secret throne!

But ere creation's everlasting pall
Unfold its darkness, and envelop all,
The tombs shall burst, the cited dead arise,
And gaze on Godhead with unblasted eyes.

Hark! from the deep of heaven a trumpet-sound
Thunders the dizzy universe around;
From north to south, from east to west it rolls
A blast which summons all created souls;
And swift as ripples form upon the deep
The dead awaken from their dismal sleep!
The Sea has heard it; coiling up with dread,—
Myriads of mortals flash from out her bed,
The graves fly open, and with awful strife
The dust of Ages startles into life!

All who have breathed, or moved, or seen, or felt;
All they around whose cradles Kingdoms knelt;
Tyrants and warriors, who were throned in blood;
The great and mean, the glorious and the good,
Are raised from every isle, and land, and tomb,
To hear the changeless, and eternal doom!

But, while the universe is wrapt in fire,
Ere yet the splendid ruin shall expire,
Beneath a canopy of flame behold,
With shining banners at his feet unroll'd,
Earth's Judge! round Whom seraphic minstrels throng,
And chant o'er golden harps celestial song.—
But, let the hush of holy silence now
Brood o'er the heart, and more than words avow,
While the huge fabric of the world gives way,
And shrieking myriads to the mountains pray,
"Descend upon us! Oh, conceal that sight,
The Lamb encompass'd with consuming light!"

Behold a burning Chaos hath begun,
The moon is crimson'd, and how black the sun!

While cloud-flames, welt'ring in confusion dire,
Flash like a firmament of sea on fire;
Yea, all the billows of the main have fled,*
And nought appears but ocean's waveless bed,
Whose cavern'd bosom with tremendous gloom
Yawns on the world like dead Creation's tomb!

But lo! the breathing harvest of the earth
Reap'd from their graves to share a second birth;
Millions of eyes with one deep dreadful stare
Gaze upward through the flaming scene of air,
In pierced Immanuel their own Judge to see,
And hear him sentence man's Eternity!
Wing'd like bright angels, warbling hymns of love,
The saints are soaring unto Christ above;

* There was *no more sea.*—Rev. xxi. 1.

Still as they mount increasing splendours play,
And light the progress of their hallow'd way.
Yet, hark! what horrid yells beneath him rise
From perish'd Souls, who lift their guilty cries,
And by the brink of sin's awarded Hell
Shriek unto God and man their wild farewell!

But here, let silence our religion be,
And prayer become the Muse's poetry;
Nor must the power of meditative song
Grasp the high secrets which to God belong.
Struck with due awe, let Fancy then retire,
And faith divine the dreaming soul inspire,
Under the shade of that almighty Throne
From whose dread face the Universe hath flown!*

* See Revelation.

THE CHRISTIAN LIFE.

TO THE QUEEN'S MOST EXCELLENT MAJESTY.

MADAM,

IN accordance with your Majesty's gracious permission, I have the honour to submit the following pages to your Majesty's notice, in the respectful hope and religious belief that they contain nothing but what is consistent with the pure Word of God, and the catholic teaching of England's Church.

That your Majesty may long be spared to reign over a free, because a Christian, people, is the heart-breathed prayer of,

MADAM,

Your Majesty's most dutiful and humble Servant and Subject,

ROBERT MONTGOMERY.

LONDON, 51, TORRINGTON SQUARE,
November, 1848.

PREFACE

TO THE FIRST EDITION.

(1848.)

"Sing victorious agonies of saints and martyrs, the deeds and triumphs of just and pious nations, doing valiantly against the enemies of Christ; lastly, whatever in religion is holy and sublime, in virtue amiable or grave . . . . to inbreed and cherish in a people the seeds of virtue and public civility, allay the perturbations of the mind, set the affections in right tune, and to celebrate in glorious and lofty hymns the Throne and Equipage of God's almightiness."—*Milton.*

"I can truly affirm of myself, that my studies have been profitable and available to me, only so far as I have endeavoured to use all my other knowledge as a glass, enabling me to receive more light in a wider field of vision FROM THE WORD OF GOD. I digress to another book, likewise a revelation of God,—the great book of His servant—Nature. It has been the music of pious and gentle minds in all ages; it is the poetry of all human nature, to read it likewise in a figurative sense, and to find therein correspondences and symbols of the spiritual world."—*S. T. Coleridge.*

THE Christian Life hath its ultimate origin in the Mind of the Almighty; its perfect embodiment was realised by the incarnate glories of the Son of God, and from Him, as the supreme Archetype and spiritual Head of the Church,—the whole mystical Body of the faithful derive their principle of grace now, and their promise of glory for hereafter.

It is in allusion to these fundamental truths, that the author has ventured to condense the spirit of the following pages into the title, "Christian Life," because all they contain is, directly or indirectly, related to their dignity, grandeur, and importance. As to the theological character which these pages develope, the writer firmly believes them to be in doctrinal accordance with all which a loyal Churchman should believe and profess,—being that which is sanctioned by divine Scripture, canonized by the teaching of our own Apostolical Communion, and maintained by the catholic fathers of the christian Church in every age. More than grateful will he be, if aught of the calm purity, chastened majesty, and loving gentleness of that best comment on the Bible, our English Prayer-Book, have breathed its hallowing control over the present volume. It is a sincere, but inadequate effort, to portray in a poetical form, somewhat of the creed and character, the duties and dangers, the hopes and fears, the faults, privileges, and final destinies of a believer in the religion of Christ. Moreover, the Divinity, Personality, and Operation of the Spirit, the sacramental privileges of the Church, the due subordination of the lower and sensuous understanding to the higher and holier law of a spiritualised conscience—are not the least of those sacred themes the author would ever desire to propound, and revere. Let the pride of Rationalism speculate as it may, Christianity and the Church, are those two miracles of permanence which constitute the centre of political history, and the circumference of moral destiny, in this, and in all other nations. A scientific arrangement of such a work would, obviously, be unfit, and throw a cold air of repulsive formalism over pages, where religion is mainly contemplated in connexion with the poetry of the affections, the fancy, and the heart. Hence, the divine omniscience of Scripture, as applied by God to unfold and feed man's spiritual life, has been allowed to display its own deep wonderfulness,—by the simple plan of selecting those leading texts, which associate inspired truth with the glories of nature, the wisdom of providence, and the mysteries of grace.

Nearly seven years have elapsed since the writer last intruded on the public; and some twenty years have passed since he published his first poem, "The Omnipresence of the Deity," &c. Solemn as human life must ever appear, when estimated by a religious conscience and a thankful heart, seldom ought its responsibility to be more deeply pondered, than when an author renews his connexion with the mind of others, through the medium of the press; however transient such connexion may presume to be.

For his own part, when he reverts to the experience of vanished years, he hopes he can say, with Christian truthfulness, two feelings predominate. The first is one of sincere *humility*, arising from the painful consciousness that his writings, whether in prose or verse, are so distant from that Ideal he has ever tried to set before him. At the age of eighteen or nineteen, the mind is but partially developed, and the taste imperfect; hence the large circulation, and continued hold on popular favour which "The Omnipresence of the Deity" has been so fortunate as to command, may be ascribed to other reasons than those purely of a mental character. That this humbling sense of an unreached Idea is not a mock confession, merely paraded for a prefatory purpose, is proved by the fact that "The Omnipresence," as now published, has been corrected almost into a *new poem*, when compared with the early editions. This appears to be unknown, or forgotten by certain writers. Hence, a sarcasm which appeared some sixteen years ago in the "Edinburgh Review," and since republished with Mr. Macaulay's name, only serves to perpetuate verbal errors and defective lines *which no longer exist, except in his criticism*. Doubtless, as one who professes to love truth, candour, and integrity of disposition, that successful writer will not republish his assault without some reference to the circumstance here stated. As the "Essay," now stands, it is merely a sarcastic exaggeration of defects which have long been removed, and gives an untruthful representation of the Poem's real character.

The second feeling the author desires to realise, is that of *gratitude*. However coldly others may talk of literature, depreciate its inspirations, and revert to its pursuits, he cannot regard it altogether in the light of false dreams, fading hopes, and feverish solicitudes: nor could he, without a most graceless discontent, swell the querulous cry of disappointment. On the contrary, he has to thank Literature for the mental intimacy and moral esteem of many of the good and great in England, and other countries; and also for pleasures, and privileges of a pure and an abiding character. Among the last, let him record some Christian friendships, whose broken links in time, he fondly hopes and believes will be readjusted in eternity. Most truly can he add, too, that the cultivation of literary pursuits, when rightly indulged and religiously watched, will only serve to endear to a spiritual student, that Book which contains the revealings of Heaven in the language of God,—even the Scriptures of human salvation. So far, indeed, as poetry is concerned, in the words of one who first encouraged him to think his way down to the roots of his own inward being, let him be permitted to say, "Poetry has been to me its *own* 'exceeding great reward;' it has soothed my afflictions; it has multiplied and refined my enjoyments; it has endeared solitude; it has given me the habit of wishing to discover the good and the beautiful in all that meets and surrounds me." In addition to this, an author may be allowed to render public thanks to the Great Inspirer of all virtue, that he has been preserved from penning a line, a word, or thought, that could stain the vestal purity of religious principle, or tinge with a demoralising hue the imagination of a single reader. So far as a superficial acquaintance with his own heart can authorise him to speak, his ruling desire has ever been,—to realise and extend the dominion of the Holy, the Beautiful, and the True, in that world which a beneficent God created, redeemed man inhabits, and Incarnated Deity has visited and rescued.

But, with this expression of gratitude, he may also blend a feeling remembrance of the social past. Will not *some*, then, who may chance to peruse these pages, be interested in learning, that the author's first effort in poetic literature owed not a little of its success to the generous welcome of veterans, whose genius has contributed so much to the intellectual wealth and moral progress of this country? Among those who actively helped to circulate "The Omnipresence of the Deity," was the poet Crabbe, and the venerable Lisle Bowles, now on the very brink of the better land. Southey too, and Wordsworth, welcomed his appearance in public with noble encouragement; and, not a little was this first effort advanced into public estimation, by a long and eloquent criticism from the pen of Professor Wilson. But, above all those whom he is bound to commemorate in this retrospective glance, let the author be permitted to add the venerated name of Sharon Turner,—England's Anglo-Saxon and sacred historian. His counsels and criticisms were invaluable: and long as memory retains its consciousness, will he revere the intellectual worth, and strive to profit by the Christian wisdom, of his earliest and unforgotten friend.*

Twenty years form an awful portion in our human career; and, when we connect their progress with the history of some of the great and good who have preceded us into the spirit-world, reflections, deeper than imperfect words can disclose, seem to inspire the mind of a serious man. *Two* are insufficient to form a pure and perfect friendship; there must be a *Third*, and He is divine! But when such friendships are

* The Poem entitled "Power of the Dead" relates to the feelings here expressed.

indeed consecrated by their alliance with that Redeemer, Who is the uniter of hearts on earth, may we not believe that, under some glorious modification, they will be perpetuated in heaven, and prolonged through the ages of coming glory?

But *where*, and *what*, are the sons of genius and song *now?* Eternalised in human praise below, can we be such grovelling materialists as to think, the sainted Minds which rule and reign over us, are not, in some blissful section of God's universe, as conscious, and as individual, as ever? Yes; if they dedicated the high gifts which Heaven bestowed, to the sublime priesthood of glorifying God, and the purification of human nature, we may righteously conclude that the master spirits of our world are "ἰσάγγελοι" (Luke xx. 36), being redeemed unto God, and etherealised into "just men made perfect," (Heb. xii. 23). Could they disclose the veiled secrets of Eternity from their calm homes of purity and bliss, perhaps, it might be found that, what we call the mere dreams of lofty Idealism, are but pale shadows cast from the substance of infinite Glories to come? Thus, the poetry of spiritual minds on earth, would be proved unconscious prediction of diviner Mysteries yet to be unfolded in heaven.

But, all this is mental suggestion, and nothing more. We must patiently abide "until the daybreak, and the shadows flee away" (Cant. ii. 17). Meanwhile, be this our prayer, that each in his own orbit, and according to his relative gift, strive to remember and realise his baptismal consecration unto Him, who died for us once, that we might live for ever. Let the world sneer as it may, after nearly six thousand years of experience, The Christian is the highest style of man: and blessed, beyond mortal speech to declare, is the condition of him, who can say with his lip, what he echoes by his life, "To live is Christ, and to die is Gain," (Phil. i. 21.)

RAYNERS, PENN, BUCKS,
October 24th, 1848.

THE IDEA OF GOD.

"In the beginning God."—*Gen.* i. 1.

ENTHRONED in vast eternity
How awful, God! to muse on Thee,
Voiceless and viewless, First and Last,*
The All in All, without a past!†

When thus to Thee our minds would mount,
And trace pure Being to its fount,
O'erawed they shrink abash'd and dim,
Like glory-dazzled Cherubim.

For, once Thou wast the dread Alone,
No universe around Thee thrown,
No choral worlds to chant Thy praise,
No spirits basking in Thy blaze;

But in Thyself, that sacred Three,*
Whose name is Love, and Mystery,—
In trinal grandeur thus enshrined,
Unheard, unfelt, and undivined.

Thou didst not, then, the worlds create,
Because Thy glories fail'd to be
Whate'er of infinitely great
Belongs to full-orb'd Deity:

But, from Thine Essence freely came
Creative power, and light, and love,
And all which men or Angels name,
Of bright below, or blest above.

And hence yon worlds, with all they hold
Of perfect, pure, serene, or grand,
The purpose of Thy will unfold,
And fill the hollow of Thy hand.†

From Thee our thoughts their grace derive,
Chaste hearts receive celestial glow;
And vainly would the sceptic strive
Without Thee, e'en to think below.

The mind which cannot God discern
Grows day by day more weak, and vile,
Must soon its very self unlearn,—
Absorb'd in sin, and sunk in guile.

Eternal Light! and Law of mind!
If in Thy beams calm angels see
A lustre that would strike them blind
Were they to think they fathom'd Thee;‡

Let insects like ourselves beware
What majesties to Heaven belong!—
Our science is believing prayer,
And flesh is weak, when faith is strong.§

Most glorious God! while thus we scan
Earth, air, and ocean through their bounds,
And yearn to trace the measured plan
Of Wisdom in her mystic rounds;

Be ours the humbling thought, that all
Of form and function, life or sense,
Which men sublime and wondrous call,—
Is nothing to Omnipotence!

* Rev. i. 11; 2 Pet. iii. 18. † Exod. xiii. 14.

* 1 John v. 7; Col. ii. 2. † Isa. xl. 12. ‡ 1 Pet. i. 12. § Matt. xxvi. 41.

It was not once; it would not be,
If Thy dread fiat said, Depart!
For then, the universe would flee,
And leave Thee, Godhead as Thou art.

GOD CREATES.

"God created."—*Gen.* i. 1.

THERE is religion in the common earth,
 A creed of beauty in the open sky;
And shower and sunbeam prove a sacred birth,
 When fancy views them with a feeling eye.

What men call Nature, is a Thought divine,
 The Infinite in forms of finite grace,
Where all conditions, seen in God, combine
 To make this earth a consecrated place.

Th' unwritten bible of the woods and fields
 By love perused, and ponder'd o'er by prayer,
A second gospel to the poet yields,
 Who walks creation, knowing Christ* is there.

Nothing is mean, by Power celestial made,
 And nought is worthless, by His wisdom plann'd,
Who fashion'd all, that Faith may find display'd
 The holy impress of God's master-hand.

Oh, could we hail the Element divine
 That circles round whatever lives, or moves,
A mystic radiance would o'er all things shine,
 And teach the coldest how the Godhead loves!

One vast cathedral, with its roof of sky,
 The earth becomes to reverential souls,
When deepen'd by such felt divinity,
 Our heart-breathed hymn of ceaseless worship rolls.

But like a cloud doth sensual dimness hide
 The heaven-born glories that around us gleam,
While min'string angels to and fro may glide,
 And yet not wake us from our worldly dream.

Alas! for men, when thus creation grows
 An orphan'd scene, where God moves undiscern'd;
While for the bliss His gracious hand bestows,
 Our thankless hearts, how seldom have they burn'd!†

This canker-worm of atheistic sin,
 Thrice Holy One! do Thou by grace destroy;
Breathe o'er the deadness of the mind within,
 And brighten nature with religious joy.

May the hush'd feeling, Thou art ever nigh,
 God in the creatures, Life and Law of all,
Unveil pure Edens to our purgèd eye,
 And free the spirit from degrading thrall.

Then will a spell of solemn beauty grace
 The humblest object which the senses scan,
A temple rise in every cloister'd place,
 And all cry, "Worship!" to believing man.

Mountain or forest, wood, or wild, or shore,
 Roam where we choose, whatever scene be trod,
The reign of mindless solitude is o'er,
 For now, like Enoch, conscience walks with God.†

And, thus companion'd by His love and word,
 Each man as brother, faith delights to own;
Peasant and prince, from each alike is heard
 "Our Father!" warbled to creation's Throne.

Were but this creed by loving hearts enjoy'd,
 And God paternal by the soul embraced,
How much of dark'ning self would be destroy'd,
 And beauty live, where now breathes moral waste!

Our common life would seem a holy thing,
 The lone creation be with God allied,
And not an hour but would some anthem sing,
 To praise the Fountain which our stream supplied.

Around, above, beneath, 'tis all divine,
 When faith the grand Original can see,
And, while Sense worships in the outer-shrine,
 Know the vast world was once a thought in Thee.

Lord! may Thy Spirit to our spirit lend
 A princely heart of innocence and prayer,
Whose unction shall the sacred feeling send,
 That proves, at every pulse, our God is there.

Radiant his soul, though dark the sense-bound doom
 Terrestrial changes for its home supply,
Who feels, before his dust descend the tomb,
 That all is christian to the christian eye.

* Col. i. 13, 14, 16. † Luke xxiv. 32.

* Gen. v. 24.

OUR DUTY IS OUR GLORY.

"Whatsoever ye do, do all to the glory of God."
1 *Cor.* x. 31.

Beauteous words ! with glory burning,
Guide and guardian of our days,
Let us be for ever learning
Wisdom from their wealth to raise :
In them hides a heavenly power
Which may hallow scene and hour,
Touching all we hear, or see,
With soft rays of Deity !

He who call'd us into being,
Each created for some plan;
And, by prescience all foreseeing,
So equipp'd the soul of man,
That unless the sleepless Mind
Love itself in all mankind,
Whatsoe'er bright scenes present,—
Dark life grows a discontent.

Yet, apart from Revelation,
Wisdom no true motive found,
That with perfect inspiration
Could for *all* alike abound:
Pleasure, gain, or mental force,
Palms which crown Ambition's course,—
Sages found some lofty name,
Thus to fix the final aim.

But, where exists in heathen story
Bard, or sage, who could descry
Such a path for peaceful glory
While we live, or when we die,
As this text of heaven-breathed truth
Here unfolds for age and youth,—
"Whatsoe'er ye think, or do,
Be your God the goal in view ! "

'Twas Thine own celestial motive,
Lord, when Thou on earth didst live;
So, with spirit pure and votive
Let us vow ourselves to give
Back to Thee !—in woe or weal,
Let our lives be one long zeal
Never from Thy Church to roam,
Faith's delight, and Feeling's home !

None can reach a blissful centre
Where the reas'ning mind can rest,
Save by fellowship they enter
On the pathway God hath blest:
Great and glorious as may seem
All which gilds an earth-born dream,
Self can frame no heaven for sin,
But it works a hell within !

Blest is he who thus resigneth
Soul and body unto Him,
From Whose words whoe'er declineth,
Martyr, saint, or seraphim,
Must in darkness, death, and woe,
Downward to perdition go,
Reaping from self-will a curse,
That would fire the universe.

Sons of Heaven ! be this your glory,
Christ as motive so to feel,
That life nor death shall set before ye
What can daunt, or dim your zeal:
Rich, or poor, or small, or great,
Nought to you is outward state:
God and grace within you dwell,
And your mercies who can tell?

Happy, happy is the feeling,
Life *belongs* to Him who died,
By atonement thus revealing
Love incarnate, crucified.
Duty, danger, toil, and time,
Now are touch'd by truth sublime;
All we have to faith appears,
Sacred to His blood and tears.

With such motive deeply glowing,
Sin and self we learn to shun,
So on heaven our hearts bestowing,
That the angel * seems begun;
While more purely we can pray,
And our creed of glory say,
"Thou art worthy ! Thou alone !
Be our hearts Thy hallow'd throne ! "

Needs no rank, nor wealth, nor learning,
When our sainted wills incline
With a passion ever burning
To pursue the path divine :
Humble care and cottage-scene
To the Lord's elect have been
Little Edens, where they found
Angels camping all around !

Though thy station be but lowly,
Christ is there, the soul to bless;
Though thou seem'st forgotten wholly,
Left to toil in loneliness,
Eyes through heaven are peering down,
In thy cross to see thy crown :—
Let thy task in prayer be done,
And thy glories are begun !

Tell me not, in gloom and anguish,
Lone and needy thou art left;
Faith can ne'er for duty languish,
Love and Hope are not bereft,

* Matt. vi. 10; xxii. 30.

If thy soul can truly say,
At the close of each calm day,
"Father! do Thy gracious will,
Let my life Thy law fulfil!"

Hast thou cheer'd the broken-hearted
With a look of genial love?
As the dying breath departed
Didst thou point to worlds above?
Hast thou sought the peasant's door,
Soothed the sick, or cheer'd the poor,
Lighted up the widow's eye,
Or relieved an orphan's sigh?

Fameless, then, though Earth deny thee
Wealth and grandeur, power and place,
More than worlds could e'er supply thee
'Tis to love the human race!
Like some instrument of sound
Changing with all airs around,
Hearts of heaven can sympathise
With whate'er a spirit tries.

Read we then in hallow'd story
With a swell of wordless joy,
Duty forms divinest glory,
When our lives for God employ
Feeling, faculty, and power,
Home and heart, and scene and hour,
As one sacrifice of soul,
Due to Him who gave the whole!

THE FIRST MAN.

"Let us make man."—*Gen.* i. 26.

Now, Heaven and Earth in finish'd beauty rise,
And Ocean peals her new-born harmonies;
And lo! awaking into life
With stainless glory rich and rife,
Under the breath of God's creative word,
The realms of Being into bliss are stirr'd.

Oh! to have gazed on glorious earth and sea,
When, like the Infant of eternity,
Our breathing World began to smile;
Or, like some list'ning heart awhile,
In mute suspension waited for a Soul
To greet her glories, and command the whole.

For, how could dumb magnificence display,
Or this blank world as reasonless, portray
The higher attributes of God,
Till earth by human feet was trod;
And young creation gain'd some priestly Mind
To offer incense, pure as God design'd?

But, hark! within the deeps of that Recess
Where God enshrines His awful consciousness,
Three Persons speak, Three Minds commune,
A Council holds the dread Triune; *
And "Let Us make" him, symbols forth to man
The outward meaning of Their inward Plan.

And thus, obedient to that forming call,
Emerges Man, the blissful lord of all;
Soft lustres o'er his features play,
And brow and bearing both display
That regal air, God's image ought to show
As priest and monarch of His world below.

Hosannah! now ye choral planets sing;
Poetic winds and waters, hail your king!
Wake Sympathies! through earth and air
Your genial motion everywhere;
God's labours now their sabbath-haven reach, †
And silence echoes with the charm of speech.

O happy vision! O celestial scene!
What Heaven beheld, what sinless Earth hath been,
When Paradise and perfect bliss
Hallow'd a world sublime as this;
Wing'd angels quiver'd over Eden's bowers,
And Eve look'd fairer than the vestal flowers.

Departed glory!—back to earth it seems
At times recall'd, in those seraphic dreams
When round us steals the witching sense
Of man's unblotted innocence,
And o'er the harp-strings of entrancèd soul
Fragments of forfeit Eden's music roll.

But, never let our joyless gloom repine,
Blest Lord! as though there breathed not hopes divine,
That earth may boast a nobler doom
Than Paradise in perfect bloom;
For Thou hast purchased, by atoning blood,
A world transcending what was once the "good."

And may the Spirit of Thy grace ‡ descend,
Our feelings hallow, and our hearts amend;
Inspire us, O Creative Three,
To image forth the Trinity,
Till man shall witness more than Eden saw,
His heart Thy temple, and Thy truth his law.

---

* Gen. i. 26. † Gen. ii. 2. ‡ Eph. ii. 8.

MIND OF LITTLE CHILDREN.

"Who is the greatest in the kingdom of heaven? And Jesus called a little child."—*Matt.* xviii. 1, 2.

Men call it wisdom, when they grow
Less and less like a child;
But let the harsh and haughty know
Such wisdom is defiled;
The cold perfection of a cautious man,
Who gains by cunning,—what the Serpent can!

He, whose all-meas'ring Soul perceived
The heights and depths of mind,
A nobler creed would have believed
When present with mankind,
Who said, with Infancy beside His knee,
"He that is greatest, like a child must be."

Heaven to a child comes nearer far
Than in maturer age,
When passion's brunt and blighting war
Their ceaseless battle wage
Against those young simplicities which dwell
Deep in the bosom, like a guardian-spell.

Oh! for a reverential eye
To Childhood which pertains,
That sees religion in the sky,
And poetry in plains;
To whom a rainbow like a rapture glows,
And all is marvel which th' Almighty shows.

Blest age of Wonder! when a flower,
A blossom, fruit, or tree,
Gives a new zest to each new hour
Which gladdens home with glee:
When like a lisping stream life rolls along
In happy murmurs of unconscious song.

It smiles on that, and speaks to this,
As if each object knew
A child exulted in the bliss
Of all that charms its view:
Personified the whole creation seems
Into a heart that mirrors back its dreams.

Life looks a fairy landscape spread
Before the untaught gaze,
As on the infant Soul is led
To meet its vernal days,
Where pure-eyed Innocence may well discern
A deeper beauty than the wise can learn.*

* Matt. xi. 25.

Fresh from the hands of God they come
These infants of His grace,
And something of celestial home
Yet lingers in their face;
Strange to the world, no worldliness defiles
The little history of their tears and smiles.

Candid and curious, how they seek
All truth to know and scan;
And, ere the budding mind can speak,
Begin to study Man!
Confiding sweetness colours all they say,
And Angels listen, when they try to pray.*

More playful than the birds of spring,
Ingenuous, warm, sincere,
Like meadow-bees upon the wing
They roam without a fear;
And breathe their thoughts on all who round them live,
As Light sheds beams, or flowers their perfume give.

And how the Church o'erawes their sense,
With rite and ritual graced!
Whose creed is loving innocence,
Which time hath not effaced;
And would that those, who Manhood's paths have trod,
Like infants trembled at the name of God!

Mysterious age! the type of heaven,
By Jesu's blessing crown'd,
To thee a purity is given
Grey hairs have never found;
The arms of Christ do yet encircle thee
Like a soft halo which the Heart can see.

Mere knowledge makes us keen and cold,
And cunning dwarfs the mind,
As more and more the heart grows old
With feelings base and blind;
Our light is clearer, but our love is less,
And few the bosoms which our own can bless!

Spirit of Grace! we learn from Thee
This noble truth, at length,—
That wisdom is simplicity,
Simplicity is strength;
A Child-man, could the world a model find,
Would be a living type for human-kind.

* Matt. xviii. 10.

SOOTHING CHARM OF TIME.

"No chastening for the present seemeth to be joyous, but grievous: nevertheless afterward it yieldeth the peaceable fruit of righteousness."—*Heb.* xii. 11.

When Time shall lay his lenient hand
On this large grief of ours,
The burden'd Heart will understand
The mystery of past hours;
But now, so thick a tear bedims the moisten'd eye
That earth looks sever'd off from yonder loving sky.

Mere fragment of a mighty Whole,
How little man can see,
While sin contracts the clouded soul,
Of plans becoming Thee,
Who didst by wisdom deep, from Thine all-boundless mind,
In heaven forecast the lot for human souls design'd.

To two eternities relate
The pangs endured on earth;
And all which marks our mortal fate
In sickness, death, or birth,
In awful depths of God before all time was plann'd,*
And carries with it more than sin can understand.

Yet, when the cloud of woe hath burst
Upon our hearts and homes,
And Guilt appears by God accursed,
The wistful Spirit roams
From earth to heaven, in hope that some dear light will dart
A ray of guiding truth, to cheer the chasten'd heart!

Then, crowded o'er with sumless graves
This blighted world appears;
O'er each young joy the cypress waves,
The eye seems made for tears;
Calm mercies which remain in darkness now recede,
And boding Fancy dreams, that Life was born to bleed!

Unwise, unholy, and unjust
We mourners then are found,
Who, in bereavement, cannot trust
Those Arms encircled round

* Luke xii. 7; Rom. viii. 28.

All sorrow, time, and change, whate'er the trial be,
To girdle man with strength, if Faith those Arms would see.

Afflictions should be sacred things;
Some drops that overflow *
From that great Cup the Saviour brings
Of anguish, grief, or woe,
To each disciple here, who bears his Master's cross,
And, when he calls him, "Lord!" doth count the gainful loss.

How can the sainted child of God
Resemble Christ, unless
His upward path of life be trod
Through shades of stern distress?
The Lord of bleeding love, oh, lived He not alone,
Unecho'd by a heart that understood his groan?

And think, bereaved one! in that hour
When ruin'd hopes lie cold,
While death and darkness overpower
Whate'er thine eyes behold,
Of Him, who had not where to rest His gracious head,
Weeping with stricken heart, when Love "forsook and fled!"

Dejection now may cast
A dimming veil round all
Which brighten'd o'er thy youthful past;
While underneath the pall
That seems to overshroud whate'er we love below,
Thy creedless heart detects no sight but death and woe.—

Still, when the Dove of Peace divine
Shall o'er thy spirit brood,
And with His calm thy love combine,
The soul will say, 'Twas "good;—†
Affliction with its flame hath purified the dross,
And deeper in my soul enstamp'd a Saviour's cross."

And thus, the nerveless Mind will gain
New force, and faith to meet
Each rising swell of future pain,
And lay it at His feet;
As sunk the billows down along their placid sea,
When Christ in calmness walk'd the waves of Galilee.

* Matt. xx. 23; Col. i. 24. † Psalm cxix. 71.

Eternal Soother of the soul!
True Paraclete for all
Who yield to Thy serene control,
On Thee for aid we call;
Anguish, and gloom, and grave, can make the mourner sigh,
But, ah, we shall not sink,—The Comforter is nigh!

Perfect through suffering!—'tis the plan
Mysterious Love decrees;
And Christ, who was The sinless Man,
From this found no release:*
His life was living prayer, with every pang combined,
Where men and angels see a perfect Will resign'd.

We seek not, Lord, a pangless life
In homes and haunts of bliss;
But, only that our mental strife
May ne'er Thy presence miss:—
Not starless is the night, when radiant truths arise,
And point each promise forth that beacons to the skies! †

* Heb. ii. 10. † John xiv. 1, 2.

CHRIST THE GRAND REFUGE.

"Lord, to whom shall we go? Thou hast the words of eternal life."—*John* vi. 68. "There is none other name under heaven given among men whereby we must be saved."—*Acts* iv. 12.

Lord, and whither shall we go?
Thou alone hast words of life:
In our stormful griefs below
Who, but Thou, can heal the strife
Sin and sorrow round us bring,
In life's vale, while wandering?

What can mortal Wisdom teach
If o'er graves it cannot soar?
How can rest the conscience reach
If it leaves us as before?
Guilty shades will haunt us yet,
Making life one long regret!

Poet! shall we come to thee,
Harping forth some noble strain,—
Songs of fire, which tell the free
Never to be slaves again,
Till they echo back thy word
As by trumpet-music stirr'd?

Son of Science! shall we soar
Through yon starry worlds, to find
Burning secrets which before
Never glanced on human mind,—
Orbs of myst'ry, as they roll
Preaching God to sense and soul?

Man of Learning! may we dare
From *thine* oracle to draw
Truths which tell us what we are,
Or, that hush the dreadful Law,
Thund'ring forth from earth and sea,
"Render what thou ow'st to me?" *

Can you ease a burden'd soul
From the crushing weight of sin,
When it feels some fierce control
Like a throbbing hell within?
Can you cry to wearied Breast,
"Hither! here is holy rest?"

Have your words a healing skill,
If applied with perfect art,
To renew the rebel Will
Till it take the better part,†
Bidding ev'ry wing'd desire
Upward to the heavens aspire?

God and man can ye unite
In such bonds of sacred peace,
That the blood-wash'd heart is white
By Atonement's blest release?
Can ye show a radiant Heaven
Smiling o'er the soul forgiven?

Foolish all false wisdom is,
If to such attempts it rise;
Would we claim a power like this?—
Seek it, then, beyond the skies:
Man at most can human be;
What we want, is Deity!

Blessed Christ! embodied Word!
Thou alone art Life and Light;
Saints who have Thy truth preferr'd
Walk in peace, and worship right;
Thou alone to sin canst say,
"I am Love, the Living Way."

Sun of Grace! oh, ever shine
Round our paths, where'er they lead;
Midnight feels a ray divine
Breaking through the darkest need,
If we hear, when most dismay'd,
"It is I! be not afraid!"

* Matt. xviii. 28. † Luke x. 42.

Pardon, peace, and purity,
  Gifts without, and grace within,
Love and light, which set us free
  From the curse and chain of sin,—
These, Emanuel! Thou canst give,
While upon Thy words we live.

Not a want, Thou canst not fill;
  Not a fear, Thou wilt not tame;
If, indeed, repentance will
  Rest upon Thy glorious name,
High o'er every guilt and grave
Shall Redemption's banner wave!

Lord, then whither shall we go,
  Save to Thee, our Refuge sure?
Balm to each bereaving woe,—
  Who alone the heart canst cure,
Turning sickness into health,
And, to want, becoming wealth.

Well of Comfort! Vital Spring!
  Other source we dare not seek;
Broken cisterns only bring
  Mocking draughts which make us weak:
If our souls would slake their thirst,
They must die, or seek Thee first!

Saviour! be our Polar Star
  Shaded by no sinful night;
Shed upon us from afar
  Living beams of holy light:—
When we reach our radiant home,
We shall know the way we come.*

POWER OF THE DEAD.

"I praised the dead which are already dead, more than the living which are yet alive."—*Eccles.* iv. 2.
"Blessed are the dead which die in the Lord, from thenceforth . . . . They rest from their labours."—*Rev.* xiv. 13.

My thoughts are with the dear and dead,
  Who wake the inward sigh,
And here an atmosphere have spread
  Breathed from the days gone by.

Then do not mock the mental gloom
  That o'er my brow is stealing;
For, *could* I walk this well-known room
  Without an ancient feeling?

What genial hours of mirth and glee
  Have here those bright friends known,
Who since to hush'd eternity
  Like living Dreams have flown!

And think not that a stoic chill
  Is o'er my present cast;
But, something more than mem'ry will
  Untomb the buried past.

What, though these walls no longer now
  Present that household grace,—
A pictured father's pensive brow,
  A mother's beaming face,

Yet, I can almost hear them speak,
  And wake each cheerful tone,
And catch the gladness of her cheek
  That lighted up my own.

Oh, here has swell'd the choral song,
  And music's charm hath been,
While mellow'd feelings moved along
  Like waves in moonlight seen.

And kindly words of love and truth
  From lips now cold in death,
Come wafted from the days of youth,
  Like resurrection-breath!

So full the present fills the past
  With tenderness and tears,
Time seems by some fond Angel cast
  Back into buried years.

I think of her whose azure eyes
  Were motherly and mild,
Clear as the morn's cerulean skies,
  In sweetness when they smiled:

Gentle in tone, and graceful, too,
  In motion, mind, and mien,
How warm the social ray she threw
  O'er each domestic scene!

As mother, wife, and peerless friend,
  In all her ways appear'd
A beauteous Soul, in whom did blend
  The graces love revered.

And he whose world-wide fame is wed
  To History and to Man,
Though number'd with th' immortal dead,
  How high a course he ran!

I see him now, his fervid gaze
  Illumined keen with thought,
And glow beneath the flashing rays
  From his bright wisdom caught.

With heavenly truth historic lore
  His works have nobly blent,
And Time, who keeps our mental store,
  Shall make his monument.

---

* Deut. viii. 2.

Can I forget that hoary sage,
   The generous, pure, and good,
Who counsell'd oft my unripe age
   As only Virtue could?

And, when I dared to strike the lyre
   In loneliness and fear,
Who bade me as the Bard aspire,
   And woke my grateful tear!

But, like a vision all are gone
   To join the world unseen,
And when these walls I gaze upon,
   I ask,—if such have been?

Mysterious Charm! Oh, solemn Past,
   How deeply felt art thou!
Beyond the scenes around us cast,
   The world exciting now.

The touching thought—no more! no more!
   Doth sanctify the room,
Where blending Hearts embraced of yore,
   Now pulseless in the tomb.

But, why and whence, we cannot tell,
   A living moment fails
To rule us with that inward spell
   Which from the past prevails.

The perish'd bloom of boyhood's prime
   How beautiful it seems,
When, tinged with melancholy time,
   It dawns upon our dreams!

Forth from the heart there went a hue
   Which made the world romance;
But ah, how changed and chill the view
   As riper years advance!

Rank, wealth, and reputation, all
   Must leave the breast a void,
Whene'er our yearning hearts recall
   What vanish'd youth enjoy'd.

Eternity familiar reads
   To Faith's perusing eye,
As spirit after spirit speeds
   To populate the sky.

Each added year *that* Home commends
   Where Souls unbodied dwell,
To all, who feel how parted friends
   Retain their living spell:

For while we tread the room they trod
   And haunt the scene they chose,
We love to think they dwell in God,
   All rapture, and repose!

BODILY SUFFERING.

"Always bearing about in the body, the dying of the Lord Jesus."—2 *Cor.* iv. 10. "I bear in my body the marks of the Lord Jesus."—*Gal.* vi. 17. "Christ shall be magnified in my body."—*Phil.* i. 20. "This sickness is not unto death, but for the glory of God."—*John* xi. 4.

Who can explain the living dust we bear?
   That breathing miracle of pain or bliss,
Incarnate Soul, what science can declare?—
   Yet, did we ponder on a truth like this,
Each pulse of being would proclaim our God,
And preach His wisdom wheresoe'er we trod.

But health with such pure harmony of ease
   The inward play of wonted life preserves,
That not till flesh be pierced with sharp disease,
   Or pang convulsive all the frame unnerves,
Are men awaken'd from their godless dream,
To mark what mercies in the body teem.

Tis now, while throbbing fires of fever burn,
   Or the vexed life-blood mantles brow and brain,
And on his couch, with many a wearied turn,
   Moans the pale martyr of mysterious pain,—
Oft is the soul by lingering sickness taught,
A deeper love than health-days ever brought.

Oh! how we pine for Nature's freshness now,
   For wood and wild, and many-voicèd stream,
And long to feel upon the wasted brow
   The quivering gladness of her sun-warm beam,
When pining Languor, with dejected eye,
Through half-veil'd window sees the orient sky.

And blessings, which in hours of heedless calm
   Were lightly view'd, or out of God partaken,
Now they have vanish'd, with remember'd balm
   Rebuke some thankless Heart they have forsaken;
While forms and faces, which indifferent were,
Throng round the soul, and thrill it into prayer.

The stern seem mild, the harsh attemper'd down
   To childhood's softness, or to woman's tear,
And the false gildings of ambition's crown
   Grow dimly pale before one righteous fear:
Life drops the mask, and all Earth's painted show
Melts into gloom, and looks one shaded woe.

Soon, conscience wakes; and sin and guilt are seen
In the deep blackness of their dismal truth;
Clear on the soul, though flesh-veils intervene,
Remembrance visions both our age and youth;
And faith sees God's detective eyebeams dart
Their piercing brightness through the naked heart!

O, Thou incarnate Sympathy for all!
On earth a Saviour, and in heaven the same,
Now to the sick those precious truths recal,
Which crown the wonders of Emanuel's name;
Calm the wild conscience with a word of peace,
And in Thy Merit show the soul's release.

For though no malady by Thee was felt,
Nor sickness by Thy sacred flesh endured,
Ne'er did the music of compassion melt
With softer tones, than when some pang was cured;
Anguish and grief in Thy pure breast were known,
And suffering raised Thee to yon glory-Throne!

Then, doubt not, Child of sickness and of woe,
When through sad vigils of the wakeful night
Thy cup of trial seems to overflow,
Till earth be tomb-like to thy weaken'd sight,
That Jesu numbers all dark moments bring
To harrow Flesh with untold suffering.

Heavy, and lone, and long the night-hours wear,
And minutes seem with leaden pace to move,
But o'er thy couch, when riseth low-breathed prayer,
Throbs the pure heart of that almighty Love
In Christ embodied, when for man He died,
By friends deserted, and by foes denied.

Pains are dread mysteries! not from God they came
By pure creation, when man's perfect mould
Of outward beauty to the inward frame
Of innocence did fine proportion hold:—
From sin and self, all pangs and pains begun,
That since the Fall their withering course have run.

But mercies hover o'er a sick man's bed,
Wing'd for descent, on lenient plumes of love,
And virtues oft from frail disease are bred,
Which ripen souls for sainted bliss above:
Health needs a cross, whose Christ-like touch shall thrill
The fainting treason of our palsied will.

And but for sickness, health would rarely be
What by dread contrast Trial lives to know,—
From God direct, a pure gratuity
Sent from His heart and hand, to Whom we owe
Not grace alone our forfeit souls to save,
But all pure mercies which precede the grave.

And, ah! what purity from pain hath sprung,
That in the turbid rush of healthful joys
Seems lost, and leaves wild passion warm and young,
To Earth's delirium, and her base alloys;
For sufferings oft etherealize the heart,
Till false emotions into faith depart.

Silence and solitude a lull beget,
Or tame Life's pulses into hallow'd rest,
Chasten the mind, and calm that secret fret
Man's harsher world-life chafes within the breast,
As rivers, tranced by some Canadian frost,
Have turn'd to lakes, and all defilement lost.

Thus may pale sickness prove a blessed Thing,
And pain achieve, what pleasure never can,—
Teach the gay heart, beneath th' Almighty wing,
To learn the mystery of redemption's plan,—
How faith by suffering must to glory soar,
And drink the cup her Master drank before.

GOD'S IMAGE.

"God created man in His Own image, in the image of God created He him."—*Gen.* i. 27.

As Lord of this terrestrial sphere,
Semblance divine did Man appear;
Just moulded by the hand of God,
The soil of virgin earth he trod,
And when through his mysterious frame
In gushes of pure rapture came
Bright feelings born of innocence,
And sanction'd by Omnipotence,
O God! Thine Image was enshrined *
In the clear depths of his calm mind.

"Man in Our Image,"—mighty thought!
With more than human meaning fraught;
For, how can sinner's filmèd eye
The glories of that Speech descry?
How can the soil'd and earth-bound soul
Itself release from blind control,
And thus, from passion nobly free,
Hail the crown'd work of Deity,—

* Psalm cxxxix. 14.

Perfection in the dust began,*
God's "image" in the soul of man?

Alas! the words beyond us soar;
Dead Paradise revives no more;
For in the soil where thorns abound
God's curse still preaches from the ground,†
And Labour, with its sunken brow
Of weariness, fulfils it now;
And in the soul, lo! all is sin;
Darkness and death prevail within,
Where Self is like a Satan throned,
A hell preferr'd, and God disown'd!

God's "image," is it seen below
In this sad world of blight and woe?
Where can we view its peerless grace,
And look upon that perfect face
Which lightens up with Deity,
Till Angels their own likeness see,
And transcripts of such glory shine,
That they reflect the looks Divine?
In priest, or poet, saint, or sage,
In parted years, or present age?

Go! search mankind from pole to pole,
The archives of the past unroll,
Consult the chart of history,
As read in hoar antiquity,
Select, combine, and concentrate
The models of our good and great,
The paramounts of man and mind,
The lords and lights of human Kind,—
And, then we challenge each and all,
To make God's "image," since the fall!

In human light a darkness lies;
All human love a hate supplies;
Our human wisdom folly stains;
O'er human strength a weakness reigns;
To human virtue baseness clings;
And Glory mounts on sullied wings;
Love, Truth, and Wisdom, Virtue, all
Our wav'ring creeds perfection call,
What are they, in God's balance weigh'd,
But sin, by gilded self array'd?

Thus, imperfection mars and maims
What Nature for her noblest claims;
The upas-blight, the poisoning breath
Of inward guilt and moral death,
Lurks in the soul of whatsoe'er
Men laurel as the bright and fair.—
"God's image," then, oh! where on earth
Can Faith behold its beauteous worth?
Where can we sun our hearts awhile
In virtues which no stains defile?

* Gen. ii. 7. † Gen. iii. 17—19.

Thou Third in Godhead! Holy Ghost,
The Christian's life, the Church's boast,
Pure Helper of the heart's distress,
And Cheerer of lone weariness,
The inward Sun of heaven-born souls,
Who all their prayer and praise controls,
To Thee, true Paraclete! we owe
The all of God that lives below,—
What broken fragments yet may shine
Of that whole "Image" once Divine.

There is a sacramental birth,
A promise of baptismal worth,
A life from heaven to earth sent down,
A jewel dropt from Jesu's crown,
A power that with celestial art
Can renovate the ruin'd heart;
Unheard, unseen, unscann'd, unknown,*
This wonder-work is all Thine own;
The power is felt, 'tis born of Thee,
Yet who, dread Spirit! grace can see?

But, let God's image be restored,
Let guilt be wash'd, and sin deplored,
And saintly virtues, meek and mild,
Will shadow forth God's chosen child;
Without, within, by faith and prayer
Will breathe that reverential air,
That shows the world what Christ hath done,
The trophies which the Cross hath won
In winning back what Adam lost,—
A forfeit Soul, at such a cost!

But oh, blest Lord! if men would see
The perfect type of Deity,
Then, from the Church's child of grace
We turn, to look on Thy sad face,
O Man of Sorrows! Son of God!
As o'er the world Thy way was trod,
Each living impress of Thy love
To man below shows God above,
While in Thy doctrine, death, and tears,
Jehovah in our flesh appears.†

THE DYING GIRL.

[INSCRIBED TO PHILIP ROSE, ESQ., THE FOUNDER OF THE HOSPITAL FOR CONSUMPTION.]

"Her sun is gone down while it was yet day."
Jer. xv. 9.

CONSUMPTION.

A BEAUTY clothes the hectic cheek,
A radiance fills the sunken eye,
But when her mellow'd accents speak,
They make the sadden'd hearer sigh;

* John iii. 7, 8. † 1 Tim. iii. 16.

For, softer sink they in their cadence far
Than Autumn's dying tone, beneath some mournful star.

They bore her to that healthful Isle
Whose rocks of terraced verdure rise
And catch the Morn's celestial smile,
Responsive to the greeting skies;
And vainly prophesied, the island-breeze
Would freshen her white cheek, and waft away disease.

But there she sicken'd, day by day,
In shrinking paleness, like a flower,
Yet from her glance there flash'd a ray
Of almost supernat'ral power;—
So bright the lustre of her eye-beam fell,
It touch'd the tender mind with more than woman's spell.

For mother too, and far-off home,
Her plaintive heart in secret cried;
And backward long'd her soul to roam,—
Since in the churchyard, side by side
Under the green turf, where loved sisters lay,
She hoped her dust might wait the awful Judgment-day.

And, there behold her once again
In her own room with placid brow,—
So pale, you see each azure vein
Meander through her beauty now;
Yet, like a pulse of rosy light at even,
Oft to her faded cheek a crimson flush is given.

Seldom she sighs, but veils within
Much that would grieve fond Love to know,
And when some pensive tears begin,
She tries to check their overflow;
Safe in the arms of Jesu rests her soul,
Nor does the early grave with gloom the mind control.

Not for herself, but for the heart
Of Love maternal, she could weep;
And often in young dreams will start,
As girlish days through mem'ry sweep,
While faintly through her lips there steals a word,—
And, "Oh! my mother dear!" is like low music heard.

She dies,—as Beauty ever dies
When sad consumption finds a tomb;
With brilliance in her deep-set eyes,
And on her face a healthless bloom;
No harsh transition, but a soft decay,
Like dream-born tones of night, which melt by dawn away.

They wheel her round each garden-walk
Where oft her lisping childhood play'd,
And loved to hear the old nurse talk
And soothe her when she seem'd afraid,
While danced her ringlets as she prattled on,
More playful than the birds she loved to gaze upon.

She looks, as they alone, who feel
The *last* of earth before them lies,
While o'er them soften'd mem'ries steal
Which melt the heart into the eyes,—
For, tree and turret, woods and uplands, all
Back to the dying girl her childish past recall!

Dream-like the hush of twilight floats,
Veiling the lilac-bowers around;
While in the air melodious notes
Of soft dejection sweetly sound:
The Landscape, like a conscious mourner, seems
To lie in brooding shade, and sadden as it dreams.

Now, to her chamber home return'd,
Before the casement there reclined,
Just as the broad horizon burn'd
With the last blush Day left behind,
Her eye reposed upon the dying sun,
Fading like feeble youth, before life's course is run.

Hush'd is the breezeless air, and deep
The awe around each mourner stealing;
Bend o'er her form, but do not weep,—
Death is too grand for outward feeling!
As sinks the sun beneath yon golden sea,
So ebbs her spirit back to God's eternity.*

THE HOSPITAL.

She dies, as countless martyrs die
Beneath the blast of that Disease,†
Which summons to th' immortal sky
All ages for their blest release:—
Not for the dead, but for the living mourn,
And childless mothers' hearts, and homes bereaved and lorn!

---

* Eccles. xii. 7.

† The sad eloquence of the following statistics will commend itself to every feeling heart:—Of the 60,000 deaths which occur every year in England and Wales,

But oh, unlike that beauteous maid
Who died in mercy, truth, and prayer,
Millions expire on damp stones laid
With none to watch them wither there;
Creedless and hopeless, fever'd, sad, and lone,
Their life an anguish seems, their death a muffled groan!

Compassion! 'tis for such we plead;
Open thine hand, protect the poor,
And Christ, who soothed Creation's need,
Shall bless thy basket and thy store;
Counting all mercies to the orphan shown,
As done unto Himself, when Earth beholds His Throne.*

And Thou, on Whom disease and health
Alike for stay and hope depend,
A godlike heart bestow on Wealth,
And let the strong the weak defend;
Till charity in perfect type appear,
And leave the glow of heaven on this benighted sphere.

Guard then, O Lord! that sacred pile
Whose walls o'ershade the sick and poor,
For there, Thine own benignant smile
Descends to gild each opening door;
And where the pale ones in consumption lie,
Some gracious beams bestow of Thine o'er-watching eye!

The Saviour in the poor man lives
Reflected through his pain and grief;
And he who to the wretched gives,
To Christ himself imparts relief.†
And therefore, Shrine of Hope! we hail thy walls,
Where true compassion works what God on earth recalls.

And faith from out this calm disease
May waft to heaven its holy breath,
Ere the last sigh hath brought release,
And smile away the gloom of death;
For wan consumption lets the spirit pray,
And leaves the mind to act amid serene decay.

When fever-throbs of fiery pain
Beat through the blood with burning start,
How can sublime religion gain
A sainted hold upon the heart?
To human sense, a ruin man appears,
All blacken'd with despair, and blind with hideous fears.

But, Mercy! thou canst cheer the bed
Where gradual weakness gently dies,
As o'er the life past sin hath led
Repentance heaves accepted sighs;
And that which careless Health had never taught,
Some hallow'd Sickness oft to erring souls has brought.

And, Lord, this blissful hope we nurse,
That many a wild and wand'ring Soul
Who reap'd in crime Thy dooming curse,
And heard its coming thunders roll,
Here, in this guardian home of peace and love,
May shed the precious tears glad Angels greet above.*

SOCIAL, AND YET ALONE.

"It is not good that man should be ALONE; I will make him an help meet for him."—*Gen.* ii. 18.

"IT is not good for man to be alone,"
Thus spake the Godhead from his viewless Throne;
And yet, if ever Soul might be
In solitude divinely free,
'Twas when emotion through the young earth ran,
As the first sunbeam fell on perfect man.

Though all without was beautiful and bright,
And grace within made intellectual light,
While sinless heart and loyal will
Harmoniously did each fulfil
The law of love, by wisdom round them thrown,—
It seem'd not good that man should be alone.

---

from slow and lingering diseases, about 36,000 are probably due to Pulmonary Consumption. One-ninth, therefore, of the total mortality of all ages, and more than one-fifth of the mortality of adults, is due to this cause! and as the duration of the disease, taking one case with another, is about two years, it follows that about 72,000 persons are constantly suffering from Consumption, being at the rate of four persons in every thousand of all ages, and eight in every thousand adults!

Again, of the 45,000 deaths occurring every year in the metropolis, about 5,600, or one-eighth of the total mortality of the metropolis at all ages, and little less than one-fifth of the mortality of adults, arises from this fatal disease; and upwards of 11,000 persons, being about one in 170 of the entire population of the metropolis, and more than one per cent. of the adults, are constantly wasting away under the attacks of this lingering malady.

* Matt. xxv. 40. † Matt. xxv. 35, 36.

* Luke xv. 10.

It is not "good!" for That most awful Three
Whose name is Love, whose shrine, Eternity,
In plural bliss for aye commune;*
Their Godhead is a blest Triune,
Eternal One in Three, and Three in One,
Unfathom'd, Infinite, and Unbegun!

But erring, sinful, branded as we are,
How little each another's heart can share!
How much within us, none can know;
What feelings Words might blush to show,
Hid from the fondest eye which ever gazed
Under the shroud confiding friendship raised!

And tones are felt of individual heart
We cannot, if we would, by breath impart,—
So deep, so delicate they glide
Under the soul's mysterious tide;
Blent with those shifting thoughts that form and die,
Too faint for words, too subtle for a sigh.

And who has not, in those ideal hours
When Nature marshals her majestic powers
Which mountain, sky and ocean yield,
Tempests awake, or torrents wield,—
Within him felt, what speech has not convey'd,
And soft tears only to the sense display'd?

Or, when a sun-burst of entrancing good
Gladdens our being into gratitude,
And thoughts emotionally bright
Leap in the heart like waves of light,
How have our quiv'ring lips refused to speak
What flush'd its meaning through our raptured cheek!

And often too, when sorrow's milder gloom
Shades the still bosom into memory's tomb,
When buried friends of boyish days
Deep yearnings in our spirit raise,
How vain the effort to unwind the zone
Which girds the heart, and keeps it all alone!

And thou, Religion!—who can half unfold
The spells divine thy deeper graces hold?
Before mute conscience lies a screen
That hides from human words, I ween,
Those loving secrets and those solemn fears
Which God interprets through our spirits' tears.

And thus, a sense there is, in which alone
We must be,—for the soul cannot be shown;
And hence, all life is loneliness;
Our highest moods are echoless;
Single we live, in solitude we die,
For each heart only can itself descry.

But still, what self-born dangers e'er infest
The man, who cloisters in monastic breast
Feelings and hopes, which God intends
As living cords, to fasten friends
In that sweet bond of amity and love
Form'd by the angels, when they sing above!

Sternly alone, forbid us, Lord! to be;
Warm our chill minds, and centre them on Thee;
Bought by one price, Thy precious Blood!
And in Thy church, a brotherhood,
With God's elected may we ever meet
In mystic oneness at Thy mercy-seat.

For what, though morbid Sentiment may dream
That nought so like a bosom'd heaven can seem,
That man himself from man should hide,
And soul by soul be undescried,—
The heart collapses into coldness, when
We nurse no feeling for our fellow-men.

Social in essence is the christian's God;
Social in life, the scene our Saviour trod;
And selfish chains contract the mind,
That should encircle human kind,
Reflecting Him, who veils His awful throne,
And dwells in Glory that is not *alone*.*

* 1 John v. 7.

* John i. 1, 18.

GREAT UNTRUTH.

"Ye shall not surely die."—*Gen.* iii. 4.

"Ye shall not surely die,"
Dark speech! that dared defy
The God of Glory, Who created man,
And, save yon mystic tree,
Heaven's garden left him free,
Where rich the streams of primal music ran.†

A love was in that law
Beyond what Reason saw,
Whereby obedience would have hallow'd bliss:
It typed a truth divine,—
That man, oh God! was Thine,
And should have learnt it by a law like this.

A ruin'd Angel came;
Yet not on wings of flame,
With lustres wreath'd around his kingly brow;
But, in a serpent-form
Conceal'd his venom'd charm,
And poison'd Man to what we see him now!

† Gen. ii. 10,

Oh ! deep as dread the spell
The Arch-fiend wove so well,
Who whisper'd treason* unto creatures fair,
Which, pure from guilt and guile,
Beneath God's holy smile
Bright Priest and Priestess of creation were.

Tremendous was their fall !
And dark the fiendish thrall
Which so encompass'd with corrupting power
Both soul and body then,
That on the race of men
Came death,—the penance of that dooming hour !

And doth the Tempter cease?
Hath Earth obtain'd release
From all the blighted Seraph can employ,—
That stains our yielded soul,
And, by undreamt control,
Heaven's inward light may darken or destroy?

The wide world answers, No !
For, still he reigns below,
And syllables in spirit o'er again
The magic of that word
Primeval woman heard;
"Ye shall not die,"—*yet* sounds that impious strain !

" Ye shall not surely die ! "
Men listen to the Lie
That so enchains them to the serpent's doom,
For passion, pride, and will
To God act treason still,
Nor heed what thunders roll beyond the tomb.

O ! Virtue, Love, and Truth,
Array'd in vernal youth
With life before ye, like a long romance,
Why not to Grace retreat,
Who from the Mercy-seat
Lifts o'er your perill'd ways her watching glance?

Believe that sin *is* death,
That poison taints its breath,
Nor ever by the grave-stone thoughtless be;
For sepulchres can preach,
And pallid conscience reach
With sermons on sin-hating Deity.

Unweave that serpent-lie
" Ye shall not surely die,"
Spirit of grace ! within these hearts of ours;
And by Truth's cheering ray
Disperse sad doubts away,
And seal with holiness† men's ransom'd powers.

* Gen. iii. 11. † Eph. i. 13.

And thus, though tombs remain,
And still the loathèd chain
Of sin and sorrow bind us to the earth,
When once the fight is o'er,
Emanuel ! we shall soar
To share Thy kingdom of the second birth.

THE WEEPING CHRIST.

" Jesus wept."—*John* xi. 35.

There is a mute but mighty voice in tears,—
Words of the eyes, that passionately weep.
A liquid eloquence, which Pity hears
Gush from the heart's unfathomable deep.

Whether soft teardrops, like a starry dew,
Bedim the eyeballs of some beauteous child,
Till the soul glistens through their heaven of blue
Mournfully bright, or exquisitely wild;

Or, drawn from depths where burning silence glows,
From passion-fountains, or, from feeling's soul
When like a heart-rain, inward grief o'erflows,
And down pale woman's cheek the rich tears roll;

Or, if in shaded walk, or crowded street,
Some iron visage where cold harshness dwells,
Melted and mild, in tears we chance to meet,—
How are we moved by all sad contrast tells !

Yet Painting, Poetry, nor Pathos can
Touch the pure mind with such majestic pain,
As when from eyelids of the Son of Man
Roll'd human tears, untinged by human stain!

But, with that pain a blissful feeling blends,
Born of this thought,—our Lord beside the grave,
True to our nature, was sublime of Friends,
And sympathized with those He came to save.

Awfully veil'd a God in Flesh appears !
But, Faith is challenged to a deeper awe
When she beholds Him with subduing tears
Hallow the scene delighted Angels saw.

And to that grave-scene, turn thee, mortal, now;
Where Jesu wept, true hearts will often be,—
And while we gaze upon His awful brow
Come, Holy Ghost ! and let us learn from Thee

How no immunities divine remove
  Incarnate Mercy from our common doom;
Down to our tears descends His mortal love
  With eyes which moisten'd to behold a tomb!

And may Suggestion, with a sacred awe,
  Dream that He wept the cited dead should come
Forth from those glories which the spirit saw
  In the bright region of its boundless home?

If to this lovely creed the heart may cling,
  Then, O pale weeper! for the loved and gone,
Ne'er wilt thou yearn once more on earth to bring
  Back to life's gloom, some dead, but glorious one.

Emanuel wept!—enough *this* truth to know;
  Lord of our spirit, let Thy tear-drops fall
Full on sad hearts, till faith's responsive glow
  Warm the cold breast to cry, "My All in All!"

Religion, Friendship, Feeling, Love, and Truth,
  All in Thy tears a consecration find,
To soothe worn age, or sanctify wild youth,
  And haunt the temple of each tender mind.

And when bereaved ones o'er the coffin bend
  To hear the earth-clod with an echoing heart,
Saviour, who wept for Thine unrisen friend,
  Breathe o'er the soul the sympathy Thou art!

VANITY OF ALL CREATED GOOD.

"Vanity of vanities, saith the preacher, vanity of vanities, all is vanity."—*Eccles.* i. 2. "The creature was made subject to vanity."—*Rom.* viii. 20. "Arise and depart, for this is not your rest."—*Micah* ii. 10.

There is no rest for man below,
  Soil'd earth is not our home;
The sigh must heave, the tear must flow,
  Howe'er for bliss we roam.

The hollowness of human things,
  The wear of fev'rish thought,
Each to the heart a shadow brings
  From tombs of mem'ry brought.

A broken cistern ev'rywhere
  Proves nature's purest joy;
Though fresh the draught imagined there,
  How soon we taste alloy!

Yet still, prophetic youth believes
  Bright Edens must abound;
And fairy Hope fond visions weaves,
  As o'er enchanted ground.

But soon dark years instruction bring,
  And teach the lesson grave,
That over earth's most radiant thing
  The cypress-banners wave.

The burden and the mystery
  Of Life will soon be felt,
As truths beyond cold Sense to see,
  Will through our being melt:

Upon thee, like an inward weight
  Eternity will lie,
And conscience bow beneath the freight
  Of thoughts which never die.

The poet's wreath, the warrior's plume,
  And hero's envied bays,—
They cannot hide the haunting tomb,
  Nor lengthen out thy days.

The cankerworm of coming death
  Begnaws the core of all
Blithe youth, with its impassion'd breath,
  Would fain perfection call.

And yet 'tis hard, when vernal health
  Glows brightly on the cheek,
When Learning, Beauty, Wit, and Wealth
  Their wonted homage seek;

When life a lovely Poem seems,
  Whose ev'ry line appears
Descriptive of those sunny dreams
  That dazzle future years,

'Tis hard to think of grave and gloom,
  In such glad hour as this,
And pile, in thought, the distant tomb
  That shall contain our bliss!

But oh, believer young and bright,
  With heart and hope awake,
Come hither! and with soul aright
  Truth's sober lesson take.

Were this vast world, with all its joy,
  Its glories, crowns, and charms,
Secured from change and sad alloy,
  At once within thine arms,

E'en then, thy heart would hunger still,
  And oft in secret pine;
The universe would fail to fill
  A spirit vast as thine!

Christ, or despair! *—behold thy fate
To that sole choice is bound;
And blest are they, who not too late
Their heaven in God have found.

For, such will learn to look on all
Bewilder'd passions love,
As Sin and Satan's blinding thrall
To keep us from above.

And yet, that Book which thus reveals
Life's baseless dream below,
And on the heaven false worldlings feel,
Writes words of death and woe,

Say, is it not the page profound
Which opens realms divine,
And, where no pangs nor pains abound,
Cries, "Christian! *they* are thine?"

Then, bids thee, eagle-like, to soar
Right upward for the sun,
And not this gilded world deplore
Where peace is never won?

Thy home is yonder pangless clime
Where saints and martyrs meet,
And with this choral-burst sublime
Anthem the mercy-seat,

"Worthy the Lamb! for sinners slain,
Who once the wine-press trod,†
Eternity shall be His reign,
Who ransom'd men for God!"

VOICE OF GOD IN THE COOL OF THE DAY.

"They heard the VOICE of the Lord God walking in the garden in the cool of the day."—*Gen.* iii. 8.

How soothing, when the noise of day is o'er
And fever'd heart-cares sink, becalm'd and cool,
To wind the bay of some receding shore,
And bathe our spirit in the beautiful!

Creation is no mute unconscious mass
Of pregnant matter, into being plann'd,
For, when behind the outer-veil we pass,
Faith hears it speaking of Emanuel's hand.‡

* Acts iv. 12. † Isa. lxiii. 3.
‡ Prov. vii. 27, 29; John i. 3.

The blood-priced earth's a Sacrament of Him
Whose regal glories make man's All in All,
Under Whose throne both saints and seraphim,
Inflamed with burning adoration, fall.

There *was* a time when Eve and Adam heard
His voice almighty through soft twilight roll,
And, like glad waters by deep music stirr'd,
They felt it echo'd by responsive soul.

But, when dark Treason like a hell-cloud rose
And guilt between them and His glory came,
The full warm current of affection froze,
And Conscience shudder'd at Jehovah's name!

"I heard Thy voice, and hid myself, afraid,
For naked horrors scared the inward eye,
And while my ruin'd soul was thus display'd,
The ground beneath me mutter'd, 'Thou shalt die!'"

Oh! dread confession of our fallen doom,
That men are exiles from their God, afar,
That souls are pall'd with atheistic gloom,
And, but for grace, would perish as they are.

For like as Adam shrunk behind a tree,
And paled with cowardice to look on God,
Revolting hearts the Holy Presence flee,
And tread the path that first transgressor trod.

But, Lord of heaven! when Thy relenting hand
The ruin'd soul hath reconciled with Blood,
And Thy blest will, by holiness preferr'd,
Becomes at once our glory and our good,

Then, unlike Adam, by dark guilt appall'd,
We shrink no longer from the Voice Divine,
But love to hear it in our hearts recall'd,
And see creation * with redemption shine.

The challenge dread, "Where art thou?" booms no more,
But, "Here are we," anticipates the cry;
For Sinai's thunders hush their penal roar,
And sound as gently as Emanuel's sigh.

Where shall we hie to hear that mystic tone?
To halls of Splendour, or to homes of Sin?
Not there, my brother! can The Voice be known
Whose breath is music heard from God within!

But if thine ear be tender, clear, and true,
And sensual clay no longer clog the mind,
Then may thy soul His hidden glory view,
And hear Christ vocal in the wave and wind.

* Rom. viii. 21.

Whether, if cherub Morn her wings unfold,
And drops of balm each glade and glen array,
Thou lov'st to mark the orient mists uproll'd,
While ope the eyelids of commencing Day.

Or, on the marble sea, at noon entranced,
In breezeless glory rock'd to living rest,
From some lone cliff thy pensive eye has glanced,
Till ocean's calm lay mirror'd on thy breast;

Or, thou hast mused at sunset, sad and pale,
By pebbled shore where plaintive waters meet,
Till gradual Twilight dropt her dewy veil,
And dark the seaweed slumber'd at thy feet,—

Alike in all a saintly mind can hear
Some tone celestial, like a spirit glide,
And breathe to Nature that her God is near,
And all her spell-work by His hand supplied.

And thus, dear Lord! in what we do, or dare,
Be Thy meek virtues our most glorious choice;
From sea and mountain may we lift our prayer,
And hear creation echo'd with Thy Voice.

In the cool evening of life's calm decay
Soft o'er the soul may lulling whispers fall,
And Wisdom teach our filial hearts to pray
"Father in Heaven! for home prepare us all."

GOD'S CURSE UPON THE GROUND.

"Cursed is the ground for thy sake . . . . Thorns, also, and thistles, shall it bring forth to thee."—*Gen.* iii. 17, 18.

THOUGH sumless mercies teem around
In ocean, earth, and air,
Mysterious vengeance haunts the ground,—
A curse is cleaving there!
The thorn which mars our blighted fields,
The thistle that appears,
Each to our soul a lesson yields
Becoming thoughtful fears.

And, add to this the weariness
On Manhood's sunken brow,
The burden and the bitterness
Which darken Labour now,
Together with the barren soil
That gives a stern reply,
To hearts that tend and hands which toil
Beneath a threatful sky,—

These unrelenting symbols tell,
O'er this sad World of ours
The frownings of Jehovah fell,
And blighted all her bowers!
Unbeautified and bare they seem
Her landscapes, scenes, and all
Which once surpass'd the Muse's dream,
And men Elysium call.

The curse of sin's avenging God
Hath sear'd the blasted earth,
And glooms of His judicial rod
Hang o'er us from our birth:—
Yet, with the curse Compassion weaved
A mystery of love,
And Angels o'er the past who grieved,
Sang wonder-hymns above

To see while Godhead in His wrath
The gates of Eden closed,
Calm o'er the exiled sinner's path
A ray of Christ reposed! *—
Light in our darkness yet remains,
Flowers bloom among our weeds;
And Grace unbinds the loathèd chains
With which tried Nature bleeds.

And Thou art branded, fiendish One!
Who tempted man to sin,
A hell in hell † thy crime hath won,
To blast despair within.
And ye! the guilty heirs of dust
Who fain from earth would fly, ‡
Stand, and be doom'd by heaven ye must,—
Can God Himself deny?

But good shall out of evil spring,
And love with judgment blend,
For, round the curse God's ransom'd sing,
"Our Father! and our Friend!"
And though pale mothers here may read
Of birth-pangs, and their woes, §
Yet is not Christ the woman's seed,
Whom earth to mother owes?

And if round spousal love there winds
A thorny wreath of care,
Myriads of married Hearts and Minds
Prove wedlock pure and fair:
Men are not tyrants, though they rule, ||
If christian lords they be;
And women by subjection school
Their love for liberty.

---

* Gen. iii. 15. † Matt. viii. 29; James ii. 19.
‡ Gen. iii. 8. § Gen. iii. 16. || Gen. iii. 16.

And never be this truth forgot,
That Wedlock is a sign,
The Church endures no widow'd lot,
Her Husband is divine!
And though cold Earth reluctant now
Brings forth her fruits and flowers,
While sweating anguish damps the brow
By work, and wearied hours,

Yet in that toil emotions lurk
To keep the heart awake;—
Where is our wisdom, if no work
Our laggard dreams can break?
And from the soil we plough and turn
With labour's ceaseless hand,
Religion may her Bible learn,
And think of God's command!

Thus, though the sentence, "Dust thou art,"
And low in dust shalt be,
Booms like a knell within the heart
When wrung by memory,
Yet may the trump of Easter sound
O'er each sepulchral sod,
"Awake! thou sleeper, from the ground,
And gaze upon thy God!"

WEEP NOT FOR THE DEAD.

"Weep not for the dead, neither bemoan him."
Jer. xxii. 10.

Oh, weep not for the holy dead
Embosom'd in their God,
But rather that high pathway tread
Their sainted virtues trod:

Their home is now the tearless clime
Where sins nor sorrows reign,
And all the pure they lost in time
True Hearts embrace again.

The Lord who came our souls to save
Dead Laz'rus did not mourn,
But His sublime compassion gave
To sisters left forlorn.

It must be so; for ponder well,
When God's award is given,
Love cannot rescue vice from hell,
Nor pity saints in heaven.

'Tis true, as thoughtful years advance
We muse with sadden'd mind,
When mem'ry throws a tearful glance
On scenes long left behind!

Where have they fled, the brave and dear,
The brightest of the throng,
Who gladden'd home's delighted sphere
With sunshine and with song?

'Twere vain to tell us not to weep,
When Mem'ry opes that tomb
Where buried Joys in darkness sleep,
That fill'd young life with bloom.

For often in some bleak distress
The dead upon us rise,
As though they knew our loneliness,
And echo'd back our sighs.

'Tis then the heart-dew riseth fast,
And moisten'd eye-beams tell
Our Souls are with the solemn past,
And feel its mighty spell!

And will not gentle Bosoms weep,
To think what pangs we gave
To friends above whose dreamless sleep
Funereal banners wave?—

How often might some healing word,
Or tone of kindness spoken,
With love's divinest thrill have stirr'd
A heart that seem'd half broken!

GLORY OF DEPARTED SAINTS.

"Absent from the body—present with the Lord."
2 *Cor.* v. 8.

Hail to the bright and blissful Choir
Who wreathe the Saviour's throne!
Eternity hath strung their lyre,
And Glory gives the tone:

We mourn them not, we mourn them not,
Who crowd the halls of Heaven,
For theirs is now the pangless lot,
The smile of saints forgiven.

Through shades of wintry loneliness
While here our pathways wind
As orphans in the soul's distress
We seek some answ'ring mind,

Yet, proves it like some balmy dream
From heaven just floating down,
When round our yearning fancies beam
The lustres of their crown!

On this bad earth, like us, they knew
The with'ring curse of sin;
Or shudder'd o'er some hideous view
Of dawning hell within:

The wingèd thoughts which bravely soar'd
Beyond the realms of time,
Those deepest prayers that once ador'd
The King of Kings sublime,

What were they, in their rapt delight
Outsoaring all we feel,—
But bird-wings broken in their flight,
When storm-blasts round them wheel?

Upward and upward did they rise
From earth's pollution free,
Those Eagles of the Lord, whose eyes
Glow'd with eternity!

But oh, at best, they did but scan
Far off that living Sun,
By whose rich glory rescued Man
From darkness hath been won.

But now, the coil of earth removed,
No sins their conscience stain;
We call them dead,—but Their Beloved
Becomes a deathless gain.*

They sun their souls in living rays,
His Form of glory darts,
While swells of superhuman praise
Heave from their burning hearts.

Then, who would call them back to earth
These holy Dead, on high?
No! rather let their peerless worth
Attract us to the sky:

Their task is o'er, their toil is done,
Embower'd in bliss they dwell,
And would we wear the crown they won?—
Then, let us fight † as well!

Far better this, than mourn the dead
By selfish grief inspired;
Their path to glory may we tread,
By pure example fired:

So shall we reach our home at last,
Whate'er the wilds we trod,
And find the dead from earth who pass'd
Were still our friends in God.

* "To live is Christ, and to die is gain."
† 2 Tim. iv. 7, 8.

THE RELIGION OF SOLITUDE.

"Surely the Lord is in this place, and I knew it not . . . this is none other but the house of God, and this is the gate of heaven."—*Gen.* xxviii. 16, 17.

Lone nature is no loneliness to me,
Her solitude makes my society,
For there I listen to a Voice that seems
Like heaven-tones heard by prophets in their dreams.

Serenely awful o'er my trancèd soul
I hear the music of th' Almighty roll,
And each deep cadence oft appears to tell,—
"My Hand o'ershades thee, though invisible!"

Thus have I felt, in regions wild and lone
Where Nature loves to rear her rocky throne,
Where nought intrudes to mar the tranquil mind,
And nothing murmurs but the mountain-wind,

Or, happy brooks which down the hillocks play
And sing, like birds in sunbeams far away,
Or, glancing bees that o'er the wood-born flowers
Whirl their gay dance, and hum away the hours.

Yet, perfect solitude there cannot be,
Since all around us acts Divinity;
Like space to body, so is God to soul,
Who all created, and contains the whole.

The hush of Nature may be holy calm
Breathed by blest Angels, when they spread the balm
Of beauteous quiet o'er the heart of things,
And veil the landscape with their viewless wings.

When wearied Jacob, pillow'd on the stone,
Slumber'd at dewy night, he seem'd alone;
What Sense beheld, no sacred token found
That Haran's desert was a haunted ground:

But, when a dream-power purified his glance,
His eye unseal'd, survey'd in wondrous trance
Angels ascending and descending there,
And when he woke—he trembled into prayer!*

And so, round us may guardian Spirits move
To ply unseen soft ministries of love,
While we walk careless o'er the greenwood sod,
Nor rev'rence nature as instinct with God.

* Gen. xxviii. 17.

Then read creation with religious eye,
If God and angels thou wouldst there descry,
To which alone the Patriarch's dream is given,—
A mystic ladder linking earth with heaven.

FIRST EXILES.

"The Lord God sent him forth from the garden of Eden."—*Gen.* iii. 23.

Though earth abounds with choral streams,
And sunny gladness smiles and gleams
O'er forest glade and woodland-flower,
Yet man has lost his fairest bower!

With arching glory bright and blue
Though heaven attract the minstrel's view,
And bird and breeze, upon the wing,
Their lyric strain in concert sing,

Yet may each pure poetic spot
Where grief and guilt are most forgot,
Faint shadows of our exile feel
Around it, like dark memory, steal.

For, there intrudes an aching thought,
A feeling with dejection fraught,
An under-tone of discontent
With our serenest rapture blent.

The whence, and why, we cannot tell,—
But girt we are with such a spell;
A zone mysterious which can bind
And oft enclose the calmest mind.

Who hath not felt such worldless mood
When cloister'd in green solitude,
With nothing near, but earth and sky,
And none to read him, but God's eye!

And oft, too, when we cease to roam
Amid the heaven of virtuous home,
With leisure, books, and wedded love,
And peace and pureness from above,

E'en then, a craving thirst will rise
For more than present bliss supplies;
Soft yearnings through the spirit melt,
And seek what soul hath never felt.

Whence come these moods? we vainly ask:—
"Oh! why is life a wearied task,
Where unreposing trials speak,
The world is sad, and nature weak?"

Is it, because no being can
The inward deeps of deathless man
With such a rich contentment fill,
As leaves the conscience lull'd, and still?

Or, shall we find the felt unrest
That haunts the hour most deeply blest,
In man's indwelling plague of sin,—
The venom'd fire that burns within?

Yea, these, and more than we divine,
May round these perill'd hearts combine,
To darken with unearthly hues
Our radiant hours, and richest views.

And when we know, that Adam's fall
O'er bright creation drew a pall,
And over man and nature cast
The shadow of a ruin'd past,

Behold! the myst'ry half unwinds,
Why sadness dims some holy minds,
And mild dejection inly sighs
For brighter scenes, and bluer skies.

It is because, like exiles we,
When roaming on a foreign sea,
While pilgrim waves approach the strand,
Are dreaming of our own far land;

And thus to realms of gracious thought
Are mystic recollections brought
Of vanish'd Eden, and the bowers,
Where God and innocence were ours.

As exiled ones, a branded race
Whom sin and self alike disgrace,
Say, ought we not, where'er we roam,
By faith to see our forfeit home?

And never, oh! Thou Source of Light,
Let this cold earth become too bright;
Lest, world-enamour'd we may grow,
And root our hearts in bliss below.

Rather on high, ascended Lord!
Lift we our souls on Thy loved word,
And through God's Eden yearn to rove
That blooms and brightens with Thy Love.

MODERATION.

"Give me neither poverty nor riches."—*Prov.* xxx. 8.

I will not sigh for vast domains,
For festive halls and homes of pleasure,
Nor do I seek redundant gains
To heap my huge and hoarded treasure;
But this I dare to ask,—a placid mind
In every pulse of thought to heaven resign'd.

There is a wealth in calm desires,
In chaste content and holy feeling,
Beyond their reach whom gold inspires,
But madly from themselves are stealing
That more than jewel'd mines those hearts possess,
Which beat secure in God's almightiness.

Extremes are not what man endures
Unless by heavenly wisdom guided;
And Gain the heart to guilt allures,
When once a soul becomes divided
Between what God and duty only claim
From all baptised into Emanuel's name.

Thus, riches prove a deadly gift
Which oft corrupt each calmer blessing,
And to such height the mind uplift,
That soon it shrinks from e'er confessing
How all we have, and are, or hope to be,
Flows from the fountain-grace of Deity.

'Tis sad to think how gilded clay
Hath tempted man from God, and glory!
And lured him on the broad bad way
Which Christ reveals in warning story;*
That path whose breadth doth equal Passion's will,
And widens ever to increase the ill.

But there is wealth for all whose eyes
Can hail true charms around them glowing,
And more than mines in those supplies
Creation's scenes are e'er bestowing,
Would men but love them with congenial mind
And seek pure riches, such as God design'd.

Here is an heritage for all,
A patrimonial bliss unbounded,
The ruin'd orphans of the world may call
Their own, howe'er by want surrounded:—
Of Nature's glories none but Hearts complain
Whose coldness feels their inspiration vain.

Then, bless we God for this bright world,
Its majesty of form and motion,
For all the beams by Light unfurl'd
Which grace the earth, or gild the ocean;
For the mild lisp of each melodious breeze
And word-like whisper of those conscious trees!

Nor be forgot the seasons' change
In rounds of restless life recurring,
Through which the poet's eye can range,
And feel his lyric bosom stirring,
When oft he views in vestal skies afar
The dream-like radiance of some throbbing star.

And are there not, apart from gold
And haughty Grandeur's sumptuous dwelling,
True mercies, which the pure behold
With silent hymns of gladness swelling,—
Health, food, and raiment, and the countless store
Of blessings, that enwreath some cottage door?

Bright homes of bliss, and hearths of joy
With Love's glad face upon us beaming,
And genial friends, whose smiles destroy
Autumnal shades, when doubt lies dreaming;
The infant's prattle, and the mother's tone
Whose wedded heart seems throbbing through our own!

Yes, these are more than gold can gain,
And often fly the haunts of splendour,
Whose pomp excites ambitious pain
And leaves the selfish heart untender,—
Dead to its God, and cold to all who plead,
When doom'd to lie like Lazarus in his need.

And add to this, that Book Divine!—
The God in language manifested,
Where glory streams from each true line
By earth and heaven for aye attested;
Ah! none are poor who call such volume theirs,
And of its promises are heaven-born heirs.

And we have sacraments and rites
The holy Church to all presenteth,
With peaceful hopes and pure delights
To each whose tearful soul repenteth,—
Prayers, hymns, and chants, and hallelujahs deep
Whose choral thunders round the dim aisles sweep.

Nor let us, with unloving mind,
Forget what art and science granteth,
What music yields to ears refined
When harps resound, or Woman chanteth;
True are such pleasures, innocently loved,
By reason sanction'd and by heaven approved.

* Matt. vii. 13.

Then seek we not for vast domains,
For sumptuous halls and homes of pleasure;
He more than royal Crœsus gains
Who finds in God his gold and treasure:—
With Him the destitute have boundless store,
But, oh, without Him, Wealth itself is poor!

Our noblest wealth is heaven-born grace
From out the Spirit's heart descending,
Which leaves in men a living trace
Of holy truth, their hearts amending:
Here are deep riches, fit for realms divine,
Gems of pure gold from God's eternal mine.

INFANCY IN HEAVEN.

"Of such is the Kingdom of Heaven."—*Matt.* xix. 14.

Thou beauteous Morn of sainted rest!
Breathing like balm along the troubled breast,
Now while the sacred chimes are pealing
Floats o'er my soul a soften'd feeling,
That springeth not from earth alone;—
My heaven-gone babe! I think of thee,
Who in thy young eternity
A sabbath *first* wilt call thine own.

But one week since, and thou wert here
Tender as Morning's crystal tear,
A little flutt'ring shape of life
Too frail to bear the breath of strife,—
We almost fear'd on thee to gaze!
While something like prophetic sighs
Did from parental hearts arise,
When dreaming o'er thine unborn days.

Calm innocent! whose helpless charms
Lay nestled in thy nurse's arms,
We loved to watch each dawning gleam
That from thy soul began to beam,
And half believed it long'd to smile;
And though unlisp'd thy thought expired
Within mysterious depths retired,—
Thy lip seem'd eloquent the while!

'Twas beautiful in sleep to view
The radiance of a rose-like hue
Bloom softly o'er thy rounded cheek,—
As though some Angel did bespeak
Thy spirit with an unvoiced spell;
Since more than beauty then array'd
Thy features, while their flush betray'd
What earth-breathed tones can never tell.

How often, when no eye could see,
I breathed a father's prayer o'er thee!
And where thy little cradle stood
Besought the Source of heavenly good
Thy life to overshade with love;
How did I mark with doating gaze
Thy baby wiles and winsome ways,
And blest for thee my God above!

Such wert thou, ere the Voice Divine,
"The first-born, ere it sin, 'tis mine," *
Roll'd through our hearts its awful cry!
And, softer than aërial sigh,
To heaven return'd thine infant-breath;
Like a dead lily wert thou laid
Ere sin had cast its poison-shade
Around thee, white in lovely death.

We wept, as *they* can weep alone
Who first a parent's grief have known;
And felt as though a life-chord broke
At spectral dawn, when Day awoke,
And all was breathless in thy room!
Oh, there the hush of graves did brood,
And awful seem'd the solitude
That was to wrap thine early tomb.

One last, and long, and clinging look
Of thy dead face and form I took,
And into memory did receive
An image, that shall never leave
My soul, while time and truth remain!—
Seldom has Death more beauty hid
Under a coffin's tiny lid,
Than thine, within the churchyard lain.

All this thou wast; but what, and where
Thy spirit now, can none declare:
For, born in sin, baptised and seal'd
With grace divine, God bid thee yield
Thine innocence to Him on high;
Back, like a heaven-bird to its home,
Borne by blest Angels, didst thou roam,
And vanish'd to thy genial sky.

Oh, wond'rous change!—the purest word
By mental wisdom breathed, or heard,
The brightest dream that can entrance
A raptured saint, or martyr's glance,
Are all too weak and worthless things
E'er to unfold what thou must feel,
To whom Heaven's glories now reveal
More than the harp of David sings!

A nursling wert thou, wan and weak;
A sigh was all thy soul could speak;

* Exod. xiii. 2.

Frailer than new-born lambs which feed
When dropp'd upon the sunny mead,—
We only trembled, while we gazed,
To think that such a cradled form
Could weather out life's wasting storm,
That must around thy lot be raised.

A watch-tick would have been to thee
The height of human mystery;
A tone, a sunbeam, or a flower
Have all surpass'd thy mental power,
And rapt thee in amazement deep;
But *now*,—beyond what Saints believe
Thy faculties in heaven receive,
And neither sin, nor weep!

Yes, in a moment, vast the change
That must around thy spirit's range
Have circled its divine excess
Of all which can the glorious bless!
While o'er thy manumitted soul,
Transcending all the Church hath known
Since Christ ascended to His throne,—
Voices and visions grandly stole.

Baptismal grace and purity,
Far more than time, befitted thee
For scenes of splendour, which await
Bright Spirits in their perfect state,—
The sacramental Host in heaven:
What lofty minds but half presage,
To thee is now an open page
Beyond the glance in scripture given.

And oh, what bliss, which baffles thought!
To think that upward thou art caught
To some chaste realm of cloudless joy,
Before the touch of earth's alloy
Had stain'd the virgin soul with sin;
Ere passion, or polluted deed
Had caused the harrow'd mind to bleed,—
Heaven oped its doors, and let thee in!

Thus while yon pensive chimes are pealing
Floats o'er my soul a sacred feeling,
Mournful, but mild, and full of prayer,—
A thought beyond what creeds declare,
That thou, sweet babe! art shrined in glory,
'Mid saints and prophets, priests and kings,
A Spirit graced with star-bright wings,
With innocents who died before thee.

Here, in this vale of time and tears
While we fulfil our fated years,
'Twill oft refresh my heart to dream
What living splendours round thee beam,
That issue from The Lamb who died;
While lisping cherubs, like to thee,
Warble before the Deity
Soft anthems to The Crucified.

DIVINE WALK.

"Enoch walked with God."—*Gen.* v. 24.

And didst thou choose the narrow path
Which sainted feet have ever trod,
And know the peace high Virtue hath
When pillow'd on the breast of God?

Though all around thee crime and sin
Their moral desert made and threw,
Was thy religion felt within,
And outwardly embodied, too?

Primeval saint! seraphic man!
By ardent grace so fill'd and fired,
Thy blest eternity began
Before the common age expired.

No spectral glooms, no pangs of death,
No hollow cheek, no sunken eye,
Nor pallid swoon, nor panting breath
Betray'd the King of Terrors nigh:

Bright trophy of atoning Blood!
Thy doom escaped them, one and all;
As if thou wert for earth too good
Thy native heaven did thee recall.

At once to glory upward soar'd
Thy being, with unwav'ring flight;
No kindred heart thy death deplored,
No grave inhumed thee out of sight.

Thou wert not!—this seems all we know
Of thine unview'd ascent to bliss;*
What more relates to thee below,
Belongs not to a state like this.

In flaming cars with steeds of fire
Rapt in a whirlwind, didst thou rise,
To mingle with that harping Choir
Who worship God with wing-veil'd eyes?

Or, did some mission'd angel-bands
Speed from the bowers of blissful love,
To waft thee with encircling hands
To thy pure home prepared above?

In vain of this and more we dream,
Nor *how* can sainted fancy tell
Thy soar outwing'd the solar beam,
And vanish'd through the visible!

Yet, could we, like an Enoch walk
And closely with our God commune,
With more than angels men might talk,
And earth itself to heaven attune.

* Gen. v. 24.

We should not seek for temple-roof
  To overarch our heads in prayer,
But find in ev'ry scene a proof
  Jehovah was enshrouded there.

The poet's walk through pensive scenes
  Companion'd with God's love would be,
When doubt, nor darkness, intervenes
  To hide his heart from Deity.

All beauty would more beauteous grow,
  All music more melodious sound,
Did moral hues of heaven below
  More freshly in our ways abound.

It is because the Cain-like heart
  To selfish pride retreats alone,
That God and glory dwell apart
  From that cold bliss we call our own.

But when, like Enoch, men can muse,
  And with our Maker's smile array
The path of life they rightly choose,
  What gleams from heaven adorn their way!

Jehovah's will, Jehovah's word,
  Within, without, rules everywhere;
And conscience is obey'd and heard
  Till man becomes incarnate prayer.

Abroad, at home, in sun, or shade,
  By rocky shore, or mountain-stream,
Divinest thoughts the soul invade,
  And nowhere can we orphans seem;

Since Faith *applies* vast providence
  To each peculiar grief and groan,
And grasps believed omnipotence
  As though it ruled for Her alone.

Awake, and sing then, christian soul!
  If, like yon saint before the flood,
Under the Spirit's true control
  A frowning world thou hast withstood.

Enoch was not;—to God he soar'd,
  Left a low earth defiled like this,
Sought the bright Parent he adored
  And melted in almighty bliss!

Thus, more and more to yonder fount
  Of perfect glory thou may'st glide;
And nearer still like Enoch mount
  To regions ne'er by sin descried.

As He was not, thou shalt not be
  Discern'd by what the world calls sense—
Thy dwelling-place is Deity,*
  And simple Faith thy sure defence.

* Ps. xc. 1.

STRIVE NOT WITH THE SPIRIT.

"My Spirit shall not always strive with man."
Gen. vi. 3.

Most awful booms that word
  Rolling its cadence deep,
Till the roused heart is inly stirr'd
  From out its iron sleep,
When God "repents" He e'er created man,*
Since like one giant sin, the earth to ruin ran!

Can mortal accent tell
  How heaves th' Eternal Mind,
When these divine emotions swell,
  Commoved by human kind,—
"With man My Spirit shall not always strive,
For it repents Me now, that such I made alive?"

In this the harvest see
  By Adam's sin first sown!
All vices reign, all virtues flee,
  And from His watching Throne
When scans the Godhead our apostate race,
No hallow'd feature there can His omniscience trace.†

For not one thrill of thought
  Which plays within the soul
That is not with rebellion fraught,
  Now sin hath seized the whole
Our flesh and spirit, heart and will include,
With utter hate of God, and dread ingratitude!

Evil, and nothing more,
  Behold, man's nature now:—
Blest Angels! did ye not deplore,
  When Earth her wither'd brow
Lifted beneath you, in yon spheres of light,
And show'd her branded front, of old so pure and bright?

But, lo! the hour of wrath,
  Commission'd from above,
Stern vengeance o'er the sinners' path,
  With whom the Spirit strove,
Shall roll in ruin; and the godless world
See thunderbolts of death from His fierce anger hurl'd!

Insect, and man, and beast,
  Whatever lives and moves,
The lofty sinner, and the least
  Who madly crime approves,—
The broken fountains of the deep shall burst,
And sweep them into gloom, like things by God accurst!

* Gen. vi. 6. † Ps. xiv. 2, 3.

And is the record dead,
Which here unveils to man
The ruin early vice had bred,
When lawless will began
Reason and Conscience both at once to sway,
Till, like embosom'd fiends, bad passions had their play?

No! judgment never dies,
But lives as long as sin
The law of love and truth defies,
And renders Man within
A jarring discord, out of tune with heaven,
A wreck of sinful woe, by darkest vices driven.

Go, Rebel! take thy stand
On some steep rock, which frown'd
In fearful gloom above the land
By God's vast deluge drown'd,—
As if thou heard'st the desolating roar
Of billows when they lash'd th' uncoffin'd dead they bore,

And there, let Conscience learn
A lesson for all time,—
That God must aye with anger burn
O'er unrepenting crime:
He cannot, will not, on the sinner look,
Until the weeping Heart hath guilt for grace forsook.

Come, then, celestial Grace!
Like dew of Hermon steal
O'er the dry souls of our sad race,
Until they pray and feel;
That so Thy Spirit, when He plies His love,
May not, by us aggrieved, return to Thee above.

For His deep coming, watch
With list'ning heart of prayer!
And ever lift the inward latch
That yields him entrance there;
So less and less His strivings will be known,
And God's bright Spirit seem commingled with our own.*

Then, like a temple built
By some celestial Hand,
No more shall gloom and dreadless guilt
Benignant grace withstand,
But each pure Soul a living shrine will be,
Where Angels view enthroned the awful Trinity.

* 1 Cor. vi. 17.

A BELIEVER'S WISH.

"To depart and to be with Christ—is far better."
Phil. i. 23.

I WISH I lived where Jesu reigns
In yonder sinless world above,
Where not a pang the bosom pains
And all is light, for all is love.

There, with rapt Seraphims, how sweet
Anthems of choral bliss to blend,
And thus with white-robed * myriads greet,
In Glory's form, the sinner's Friend.

No self will there the soul defile,
No shadows o'er remembrance steal,
But conscience, purged from guilt and guile,
Shall all the heaven of virtue feel.

Those fever-dreams of sense and time
Which now profane our purest bliss,
Shall not infest that hallow'd Clime
With stains which mar a world like this.

Oh! bright excess, beyond all thought,
When saints have reach'd that radiant goal
Where Man, to full perfection brought,
In God shall ark his wearied soul!

For, what can sense-born pleasure give
When most the world itself imparts,
But bribes to let base passions live
Like serpents in our selfish hearts?

The chastest scene, the calmest home
By poet hymn'd, or reason blest,—
Who has not felt his fancy roam,
And image forth a finer rest?

Our dream for some diviner world
Can never pause in realms of time,
When hope's fair wings, by faith unfurl'd,
Would waft us to that pangless clime.

Safe in the shadow of Thy throne,
Reveal'd Almighty! let us dwell,
And in yon circling rainbow † own
The hues which our redemption tell.

Thou art, O Christ! the sinner's heaven;
Without Thee, man is death and gloom,
And only with that word, "forgiven,"
Can hearts approach the dismal tomb.

* Rev. xix. 8. † Rev. iv. 3; v. 6.

Be Thou the vital sun and shield
  To light our path, and guide our souls;
Nor let our tempted bosoms yield
  Except to what Thy will controls.

Life of our life! be all our bliss;
  Torn from Thy truth, since none are blest;
Without Thee, men and angels miss
  That centre where the creatures rest.

And can we doubt, if Godhead find
  Complacency * in Christ the Lord,
That He excels whate'er the mind
  Creates in thought, or calls by word?

Ye heavens! though bright your splendour be,
  Emanuel forms your living fount,
And none can rise to Deity
  Who do not through His merit mount.

Then, hail the hour! that summons Man
  Beyond our sullied earth to soar
To Him, Whose finite heaven began †
  When first for sin the cross he bore.

* Isa. xlii. 1. † John iv. 34; Ps. xl. 8.

HERE WE HAVE NO ABIDING HOME.

"Here we have no continuing city, but we seek one to come."—*Heb.* xiii. 14. "They that say such things declare plainly that they seek a country."—*Heb.* xi. 14.

Since all we love on earth must die,
And swift as hues of morning fly
    The hopes young bosoms store,
Oh, softly let thy feelings twine
Round the rich heart thou callest thine,—
    For soon 'twill beat no more!

When first our virgin senses wake
And of fair Earth a prospect take,
    Her treasures, homes, and smiles,—
A false eternity arrays
The scene that mocks our dazzled gaze
    With its ambitious wiles.

And yet, might reason's colder truth
Unveil dark facts to wayward youth,
    Creation doth not hold
A perfect semblance to her past;
But everywhere dim shades are cast
    On what she was of old.

The clouds of heaven for ever change;
The tints of earth and ocean range
    Through colour's varied gleam;
And all which eyes enamour'd view,
Reflect on man that restless hue
    Which hints our life a dream!

The sweetest notes bland music brings
To vibrate o'er those moral strings
    Which make the heart a lyre,—
E'en while we listen, lo! they die
In lulls of languish, like the sigh
    Some Angel might respire.

And, look upon the face we love!
More eloquent than skies above
    When clothed with chastest light,—
Its spell of beauty is the change
Expressions leave, as there they range
    And fascinate our sight.

Thus, all we view of scene or sound
With sad instruction doth abound,
    And preach,—"Prepare to part!"
For souls can have no resting-place
Where sin hath left a with'ring trace,
    And shadow on the heart.

Too many tears our eyelids wet,
Too many graves are open'd yet,
    To leave the mind at peace;
And, where the soul, without a thorn *
To probe it, till it bleeds forlorn,
    And yearns for heaven's release?

And blest are they whom Grace hath brought
To bow content before the thought,—
    Earth's dearest ties are frail;
These will not, in the rending hour
When Death unveils his darksome power,
    Like unbelievers, quail!

But woe! to wistful hearts that cling
To whatsoe'er wild passions bring
    Of fulness, fire, and force,
Till idols mount the bosom-throne,
Where God and grace should rule alone
    The soul's most secret course.

And, woe! to young Affection's eye
Which half adores what soon must die,
    And melt in mortal clay;
Eternal beauty dwells not here,
And ill becomes that tainted sphere
    Where Death demands his prey.

But did we, like the saints of old,
Hereafter through this Now behold,

* 2 Cor. xii. 7, 8.

What pangs our hearts would save!
Eternity our home would seem,
And life become a brilliant dream
Dissolving o'er the grave.

Wild heart of wasteful Youth! begin
At once to cool the thirst of sin
For ever here to bide;
Life, love, and earth can flatter thee,
But cannot thy salvation be,
Nor death, nor judgment hide.

Ah! wert thou touch'd with heavenly love,
Did Christ, thy magnet, far above
Attract thy veering eyes,
How would the wing'd affections mount
And flutter near that blissful Fount
Who all our heaven supplies!

Unwav'ring Souls which pant for bliss,
Will feel their perfect treasure is
Where nothing false is found;
And since in heaven Messiah dwells,
They will not dread those bleak farewells
With which dark years abound.

"Gone to prepare a place for you,"—*
Hosannah to that promise true!
It opens heaven for prayer;
If in our souls one pulse there beat
Of Godhead, at the mercy-seat,
They long to worship there!

For heaven is not a desert cold
Which cannot human feelings hold,
Where Christ as Man is seen;
Since they adorn that region bright
From earth redeem'd, array'd in white,
Who once like us have been.

OUR TRUE COMPANION.

"Abide with us, for it is toward evening, and the day is far spent."—*Luke* xxiv. 29.

Abide with us! sustaining Lord, abide;
Without Thee, vain is all the world beside:
When Thou art vanish'd, nought true Souls can see
But the sad loneliness that sighs for Thee.

The life we bear is oft a burden'd thing
Fill'd with a load of varied suffering,
Though, mask'd with smiles, the forehead seems to say
"My heart is sunshine in its golden play."

A thousand shadows from the soul arise
Casting a tinge o'er all young natures prize;
E'en from the centre of consummate bliss
We inly murmur, "breathes there truth in this?"

Without, works mystery; within, the same;
And truths, profounder than mere words can name,
Float through the mind, like seraph-whispers sent
From the far glories of God's firmament.

Lofty but low, abased and yet sublime,
With hearts eternal in a home of time,
Sinful, but sainted, doom'd on earth to walk,
And yet with Seraphim in spirit talk,—

Extremes of contrast! such our being rule;
And fever'd Life, with contradiction full,
Can echo the beseeching twain who cried,
"Lord of our souls, for ever with us bide!"

The beautiful and bright, creation yields
From rock and dale, from forest and from fields,
Lacking Thy presence, want that master-grace
Which decks the earth with each diviner trace.

Oft o'er yon heav'ns when strays the poet's eye
While soundless evening steals along the sky,
That Afterward, to which no after comes,
Seems to salute him from ideal homes,

Which pale and pensive, from each pilgrim star
Gleam through the air, and glisten from afar:
And then, dear Lord! amid the vast and lone
Faith can discern Thee on creation's throne.

Thy solemn grandeurs, Thy nocturnal scenes,—
How oft 'tween us and them there intervenes
A troubled shadow, which our guilt must throw
On all which manifests dread power below!

But oh, amid the struggle, toil, and tears,
And blighting anguish of our baffled years,
The hush'd religion of a grief-worn heart
How does it love Thee, Healer as Thou art!

But when life's wearied days are spent and gone,
And calm eternity is coming on,
Ere the wing'd soul shall take its awful flight,
Abide with us! and death will be delight.

---

* John xiv. 2.

OUR MORROWS BELONG TO GOD.

"Take therefore no thought for the morrow; for the morrow shall take thought for the things of itself. Sufficient unto the day is the evil thereof."—*Matt.* vi. 34.

Our morrows unto God belong;
This day can be our own,
If on the Stronger than the strong
We lean our hearts alone,
Casting on Christ our grief and care,
By constant power of heaven-breathed prayer.

But, Gentiles with a Christian name
We gravitate to earth,
And by our heathen darkness shame
The glories of our birth;
If sons who God their Father call,—
To Him why trust not all in all?

Oh, could we like the Saviour be,
Whose "meat and drink" it made
Heaven's will alone in life to see
In all He did, or said!
No longer would base Mammon find
A temple in our care-worn mind.

Behold! creation's world of sense
Rebukes the carking race,
Whose creedless hearts of Providence
Discern no living trace,
Though earth and sky and choral sea
Are throbbing with divinity.

The fowls which populate the air,
The lilies of the field,
Fed and adorn'd without a care,
Divine instruction yield;
They teach us what wise Nature can,—
The arms of God environ man.

And vain, too, each prophetic thought
Whereby the fretted soul,
With fever-visions overwrought,
Man's future would control;
Our being's age and body's growth,—
The Lord alone predestines both.*

Why, for mere raiment, meat and drink,
Our future so forecast,
As though, like Pagans, we could think
This life were first and last?
Forgetful, that one thought sublime
Outweighs a world of sense and time!

* Matt. vi. 27.

Our little faith,—alas! 'tis less
Than what the least should prove,
Making our scene a wilderness
Which might be one of love:
Like orphan'd souls in solitude,
Denying Him we call The Good.

Gaze upward, soul! on God the true;
Each burden cast on Him,
Believe Jehovah cares for *you*
Not less than seraphim:
The very hairs of men are number'd,
Why then with woes be overcumber'd?

But still these boding hearts, like Seers
On whom the future lowers,
Project themselves o'er unborn years,
And crowd the coming hours
With destinies that haunt the mind,
Till weaken'd faith grow wan and blind.

Condemn'd be such unhallow'd care,
Which lets to-morrow's weight
O'erburden with a gaunt despair
What cheers our present state;
As if each day on life's dull road
Were harness'd with too light a load!

Sufficient for the Day when born
Is each new pang that sighs;
Let those who will not sink forlorn,
In Jesù's name arise:
Since ye belong to Heaven's control,
Foreseen to-morrows! quit the soul.

Simplicity is wisdom when
Our yielding minds obey
The law which God ordains for men,—
Our duty is to-day!
Our burden too, *that* cross to bear,
And not forecast imagined care.

And let thy teaching grace, oh Lord,
Such perfect sway impart,
That faith may hear this haunting word
Like music in the heart,—
Sufficient is the moment given,
And thy to-morrow safe in heaven.

SILENT PRAYER.

"Now Hannah, she spake in her heart; only her lips moved, but her voice was not heard."—1 *Sam.* i. 13.

We do not pray, because we move
Our lips in oral speech,
For depths abound of deeper love
Than words can ever reach.

Nor is it prayer, when utter'd thought
With ardent feeling glows,
As though th' excited breast were fraught
With flame that overflows:

For words may flow from fluent powers,
And prove a dubious sign;
'Tis only when the truth is ours,
The heart, oh Lord, is Thine!

The raptured tongue whose tones arise
Like sparks of mental fire,
Not ever breathes those contrite sighs
Deep thoughts of sin inspire.

And oft when o'er moved fancy rolls
Soft melody of speech,
No inward awe the mind controls
With truths words cannot reach.

True prayer is that mysterious breath
The Spirit from above
Breathes through the heart in life, and death,
And is the pulse of Love!

'Tis God within, imparting grace,
'Tis heaven come down to earth,
That man may look in Mercy's face,
And feel his second birth;

A sense of want, of woe, and sin,
A creed that Christ is all,
A faith whose filial voice within
Can God "My Father!" call;

Reliance on atoning Blood,
Convictions true and deep,
Attesting that the Lord is good
Who bids us smile, or weep;

With aspirations pure and high
That souls, like saints, may be
Both while we live, and when we die,
From guilt and Satan free,—

Behold a Prayer! a breath divine,
Whose sacred throb and thrill,
Believer, can that heart of thine
With unvoiced worship fill.

In such high mood of heavenliness,
Upon thy spirit's chords
Devotion feels a magic stress
Beyond translating words:

But He, benign Interpreter!
Who hears an inward groan,
In heaven perceives the voiceless stir
Of souls He calls His own.

Unbreathed, unspoke a prayer may be,
Nor vocal lips proclaim
What God alone can hear and see,
When Love adores His name.

Then, cheer thee! sad but sainted Heart
That pines for spoken prayer;
Be sure, if child of God thou art,
More love than lips declare

Dwells in thy depths of being still,—
Howe'er some baffled word
Break down beneath those thoughts which fill
The soul where God is heard.

And thus when dying voice decays,
And pulse and motion cease,
Heaven marks the speaking eye that prays
For mercy's last release.

True Christians live beyond their speech,
And faith is more sublime
Than syllables of breath can reach,
Framed out of sense and time.

MUSIC AND THE EVIL SPIRIT.

"Seek out a man who is a cunning player on a harp: and it shall come to pass, when the Evil Spirit from God is upon thee, that he shall play with his hand, and thou shalt be well."—1 *Sam.* xvi. 16.

Two worlds around us act and move,
Though one alone we hear, or see;
And they whose souls are born above,
Will not repulse that Mystery
Which binds them both by one harmonious law,
Deeper than earth-framed science ever saw.

The world of sense is fair to sight,
Though touch'd all o'er with taints of sin;
Gay morn, and noon, and magic night
Accost the charmèd soul within,
And, like faint beams on Memnon's fabled stone,
Draw from our spirit some responsive tone.

Mountain, and field, and forest wide
With their green coronal of trees,
And Ocean, with his billowy tide
Rolling in wave-born ecstasies,
Cities, and hamlets, and the high-wall'd town,
And sculptured marbles, breathing dead renown,—

In each and all there reigns and lives
Far more than sensual eye beholds;
A Presence which no token gives
Of what the heart of things enfolds,—

Save to deep Souls whose inward eye can see
Symbols that charm the faithful, and the free.

Another and a holier sphere,
A viewless world, unheard, unknown,
More awful than religion's fear,
Around embodied minds is thrown;
And while the earth-bound walk by sense and sight,
That orb engirdles them by day and night!

Angels, and Spirits of the blest,
Stern Attributes, and sacred Powers
Nature and Providence invest,
And circle this vex'd life of ours;—
While voiceless mysteries, whence we cannot tell,
Throb through the flesh, did we but mark them well.

And thou, deep charm of sevenfold grace,
Sweet Music! Thou art more than sound;
For melodies from God's bright place
Within thy blissful spell abound,
Like broken echoes, that have thus o'erran
Angelic lyres, and trembled down to man!

Oh! call not music by a word
Terrestrial minds alone approve,
For in it more than tone is heard,—
A something deep as Spirits love;
Painting, and poetry of sound are there,
Blent with the lulling pause of secret prayer.

Such was the minstrel's art divine
When David struck his chorded lyre,
Where earth and heaven in one combine,
And by commingled sway inspire
Soft airs, before whose superhuman spell
The Fiend shrunk wither'd to his native hell!*

And He, the dread and dauntless seer,†
Whose word could seal and open skies,
The awe of music did revere,
And bow'd beneath those harmonies
That gush'd around him, soft, serene, or grand,
Like air-chords thrill'd by some celestial hand.

MAKE THEE AN ARK.

"Make thee an Ark . . . Behold! I, even I, do bring a flood of waters upon the earth . . . Come thou and all thy house into the Ark."—*Gen.* vi. 14, 17; vii. 1.

THOUGH youth's bright world looks fresh and fair,
And proud the pulse of feeling there,

* 1 Sam. xvi. 23. † Elishah.

While syren hope sings everywhere
Of promised bliss to come,
Yet signs exist of sternest woe
Which tell young Hearts that all below
May yet the primal ruin show,
And prove earth not our home!

Deep, dark, and cold the cruel grave,
When big and burning tear-drops lave
The cheeks of Love, which mourns the brave
And beautiful who fly!
The bloom and breath of dawning Life
Are each with slow consumption rife,
And mark how soon the parting strife
May close the sunken eye!

Scarce dies a day, but rings the knell
O'er something which we love too well,
Or cherish with so close a spell
That when it droops, we bleed;
While pride and passion round us throng,
And pleasures with voluptuous song
Entice warm souls the way along
Which ends in wrath decreed.

Hence, life is peril; and how blest
The minds that in some ark can rest,
Secured and safe, howe'er distrest,
From final wreck and woe!
The storm may rise, the surges roll,
Rude whirlwinds seem to rend the soul
No mortal wisdom can control,
Yet none that ark o'erthrow!

"Make thee an Ark," of old was heard;
And, true as echo to the word,
His heart with pure allegiance stirr'd
The hand which Heaven obey'd:
To Noah, God believed was law,
O'erruling all he felt, or saw,
With that serene and soothing awe
Which keeps man undismay'd.

And thus, when sea and sky were blent,
While raged the roaring element
Until each Vial's wrath was spent,
Safe o'er the storm he rode;
Around him cries and corpses were,
And oft was yell'd man's howling prayer,
Mix'd with the wild beast's in his lair,
When furious waves o'erflow'd.

And so with saints of Light 'twill be,
When taught, oh God! by grace and Thee,
At once to that retreat they flee
Where shelt'ring mercies bide;
No ark they need to frame, or form,
To shield them from each rushing storm
Round life and death that spreads alarm,—
For that Thy truth supplied.

And dost thou seek, where stands the Ark,
That, when wild tempests, stern and dark,
Engulph and wreck each human bark,
May waft thee safely on?
Behold it, in the Church of grace,*
Prepared for each believing race
Who there may find, with contrite face,
The shelter Jesu won.

Here babes, besprent with sacred dew
Ere sin and sorrow yet they rue,
Baptismally a nature new
From God's own Spirit gain;
On their white brows a mystic sign,
Behold it tell this truth divine,—
Yon infant, Christ! is sealed for Thine,
Blood-wash'd from guilty stain.

And onward as progressive life
Encircles man with clashing strife,
Howe'er the world with sin be rife,
And dangers round us roll,
Ark'd in Thy founded Church, O Lord!
Thy promisèd Grace, Thy precious Word,
If by our prostrate will preferr'd,
Shall keep unwreck'd the soul.

Safe in the Ark by Jesus built,
Beyond the flooding waves of guilt
We float, and, through the blood He spilt
On Calvary's deathful tree,—
Victoriously our spirits ride
Over the sad and surging tide
That welters o'er the world beside,
Unanchor'd, God, in thee.

And blest are they, with minds unskill'd
By rebel pride to plan, or build
An ark no present Christ hath fill'd
With sacramental love;
Who in the Church can sweetly rest,
Till peace divine becalm their breast,
And, howsoe'er by storms distress'd,
A haven reach above.

OH THAT I HAD WINGS!

"I said, Oh that I had wings like a dove! for then would I fly away, and be at rest."—*Ps.* lv. 6.

Bird of beauty! upward soaring
On thy plumes of lustre white,
Far beyond the tempest roaring
And the gloom of gath'ring night,
While they watch thee speed away
Where no awful lightnings play,
Many an earth-chain'd Heart will sigh,
"Lend me wings, and let me fly!"

"Dove-like let me, proudly rising
Out of sin, and woe, and crime,
Feel my wingèd soul despising
Fetters wove from earth and time;
And by faith ascend to see
Shrines that glow with Deity,
And in bowers of glory find
Bliss of heart, and calm of mind."

Men, whose hearts by grace enlighten'd
Once for heaven in concord beat,
Have their taste by truth so heighten'd
That no more in earth's retreat
They contentment can perceive,
But for ever pine to leave
Scenes where passion's fires abound,
And, like fiends, our faith surround.

Not by creedless foe and stranger
Are disciples wrong'd alone,
But apostate friends endanger
Those they once have loved, and known,—
Who amid the morn of youth
Both pursued and pray'd for truth,
And along Time's ancient road,
Calmly sought the house of God.

Keen beyond all pangs distressing
Is the piercing one that finds
Friends of old in faith caressing,
Chill'd in heart, and changed in mind;
Each to each an alien grown,
All fond smiles of welcome flown,—
Heart-breathed wish and household word,
Never more in union heard!

Not again behold them taking
Counsel sweet and sacred talk,
But their holy Church forsaking
For some wild sectarian walk:—
Who can mark such sever'd friends
When their love in loathing ends,
Nor, like David, long to soar
Where the saved are gone before?

He whose heart true light discerneth
In Thy beams, Incarnate Love!
At Thy footstool deeply learneth
Lessons that will last above;
Nor amid such bleak distress,
Sighs he for lone wilderness,
But in prayer true solace finds,
Opening heaven to sainted minds.

---

* 1 Pet. iii. 20, 21.

Wearied, worn, and oft benighted,
Want and weakness round us reign,
Yet the Dove on Christ who lighted
Thus prolongs that healing strain,—
"Cast thy burden on My breast,
Where the weary drop to rest;
Harass'd pilgrim, hope and pray,
Learn of Me, and love the way!"

THE ARKLESS DOVE.

"The dove found no rest for the sole of her foot, and she returned unto him into the ark."—*Gen.* viii. 9.

The ghastliness and gloom of death
Cover creation like a pall,
Without a pulse, without a breath,—
Sepulchral waters bury all;
Like a huge corse the dead Earth lies
A floating mass beneath the skies!

It must have been a wild'ring sight
Which roll'd his palsied heart-tide back,
When Noah for the raven's flight
Open'd the ark, and in yon track
Where the wild deluge spread its wave
Beheld but one stupendous grave!

But, hark! a mild and gracious breeze
Like a wing'd mercy floats along;
The music of poetic trees
Has never shed so sweet a song;
For where its fresh enchantments play
The floods decrease, and die away.

The fountains of the Deep are closed,
The windows shut of wrathful heaven,
And, safe on Ararat reposed,
The ark of life to Noah given;
Judgment is o'er, and grace seems nigh,
And green earth soon shall hail the sky.

He sends the raven, and on wings
Of fierce delight it hurries forth,
Yet, ah! no olive-branch it brings,
But east, and west, and south, and north,
Flutters about by night and day,
And banquets on vile carrion-prey.

True emblem of those Belial hearts
And canker'd minds, debased and dead,
Who feed on what foul Earth imparts
Of loathsome passion born, and bred;
For, raven-like, they haunt the scene
And revel most where vice hath been.

But thou, sweet dove of radiant white!
Methinks I watch thee in the beam
Wave thy fair wings with free delight,
And glisten in that snowy gleam
Which round about thee glances mild,
Decking thy plumage undefiled.

Hither and thither wing'd the dove,
And sought in vain some verdant tree;
The waves beneath, the sky above
Were all its vestal eyes could see;
So, backward to the ark it flew
And nestled in that shelter true.

And, trace we not a symbol here
Of that unrest the holy feel,
When doom'd to haunt some alien sphere
Where nothing reigns but carnal zeal;
Where all looks selfish, low, and base,
And time and sense our God displace?

Oh! how they yearn for lone retreat,
Some temple where religion dwells,
While, sitting low at Jesu's feet,
Their bosom with his doctrine swells;
For Christ is their celestial Ark
Which lifts them o'er life's ocean dark.

Dovelike, amid the haunts of sin
Howe'er the Saints are forced to roam,
There is a pure unrest within
That pants for some more perfect home;
And *that* the Saviour's Church hath proved
To God's elect, by angels loved.

And e'en as once the dove brought back
To Noah's hand, at twilight-hour,
The branch of peace, that on its track
Was pluck'd from some diluvian bower,—
The soul of saints on earth may see
Tokens of tender Deity:

And as that bird, when once again
The flooded soil began to rise,
Till green apparel robed the plain
And crystal sunlight clad the skies,
No ark required, but in wide air
Found a pure freedom ev'rywhere,—

So, when this ruin'd earth recedes,
Our perfect spirits will not ask
A local church, where sorrow pleads
For shelter from life's whelming task;
Since heaven will prove one church of praise,
And each true soul a temple raise.

But ye unblest! of men deceived,
Who think this world a good imparts
Beyond what martyr'd saints believed,
And welcomed in their wounded hearts,

Of this be sure,—ye cannot find,
From heaven apart, the peaceful mind!

Go, child of Sin! pursue each path
That opens on thy restless view;
Prove all which gain, or glory, hath,
Admire, enjoy, exhaust them too,
But, still unreach'd is that repose
That sainted virtue only knows!

Ambition, pleasure, pride, or pelf,
What gilded fame, or fortune gives,
Feeds but the gnawing worm of Self
Which on contentment preys and lives;
Remote is that ideal rest
Whose home becomes a hallow'd breast.

Man was not made for finite good,
The Infinite to Him pertains;
Heaven's manna forms his genial food,
Though unbelief from such refrains:
O, that in Mercy's ark of peace
The erring mind would seek release!

Return unto thy rest, return
Thou arkless soul of sinful man!
For, until chaste affections burn
With ardour pure as spirits can,
Thy life will be a discontent,
In fitful dreams of folly spent.

Deep Spirit of divinest calm!
Descend, and soothe unquiet hearts;
Breathe o'er each ruffled mind the balm
Thy perfect nobleness imparts,
And then, oh Lord! Thy saints will be
Sublimely ark'd in heaven and Thee.

THE BOW OF PROMISE.

"The bow shall be in the cloud; I will look upon it that I may remember the everlasting Covenant."
Gen. ix. 16.

Thou liquid bow of beauty and of grace
Arching the rain-cloud with a bended way,
Religion cannot mark thy gleaming trace
And muse not, how the mighty God did say

That when yon sacramental arch should span
The hills beneath, or paint the heavens above,
He would recall His covenant with Man,
And feel the vastness of forgiving love.

Summer, and seed-time, harvest, winter, spring,
Whate'er the seasons in their mercy bear,
Each unto ransom'd Earth should ever bring
Tokens of peace and God's paternal care.

And thus, a symbol art thou, and a sign
Of what no wisdom in the schools could teach;
A sacred emblem, preaching truths divine
More eloquent of Christ than angel-speech.

'Tis not alone that Childhood's greeting eyes
When first thine arching loveliness they see,
Gladden beneath it with entranced surprise
And hail the miracle of hues in thee!

Nor is it, that our Priests of earth and heaven
Who at the altar of the Muses stand,
To whom the glorious privilege is given
To summon beauty when they wave their wand,

The gem-like radiance of thy form admire,
And liquid blending of thy rain-born hues,
Or, oft to hymn thee, strike the hallow'd lyre
And into words thine opal gleams transfuse.

Still less can Science, with her colder gaze,
Suggest what thy prismatic splendours mean,
When dim and delicate with tearful rays
She marks thee outlined in the storm-veil'd scene.

'Tis Faith alone thy full enchantment feels
Mild grace and glory of the firmament!
When o'er the heart remember'd judgment steals,
And grateful love with tender awe is blent.

Since, not a pulse of life in earth, or sea,
That should not in thy graceful symbol find
A token which our God express'd by thee,—
His curse has roll'd away from wreck'd mankind!

Pure arch of triumph! wove through Nature's tears
In fairy gems reflected as they fall,
Bright may thy bow, beyond our mortal fears,
Preach the vast mercy which encloseth all!

And, deeply touching to the soul made wise
Is the great truth primeval words declare,—
That when a rainbow consecrates the skies
Both God and man commingle glances there.

Mercy The One in that soft omen sees,
View'd in the promise which of old He swore,
That earth should witness what His will decrees,
And not be deluged as she was of yore.

And man, the monument of matchless love,
When he beholds yon bow of beauty form,
Saint if he be, recalls the Christ above
Who rescued Nature from her ruin-storm.

But, high o'er heaven's purpureal ether mount
To that sunn'd region where no storms prevail,
And even *there*, at mercy's crystal fount
The rainbow of our human past we hail! *

Round the white Throne where sits the Prince of Light,—
Glory beyond all glories to express!
Lo, the same rainbow gleams like emerald bright,
And girdles Him with awful loveliness.

And oh, believer! does not this declare
That covenants divine abide the same?
How saints of old, as living Christians are,
Were rescued by the one redeeming Name?

Lord of our souls! Thou Saviour ever dear,
Be still our rainbow in the clouds of life;
In Thy chaste sunlight melt each rising tear,
And arch with triumph scenes of darkest strife.

Radiant with mercy, calm the sinking heart,
And beam through sorrow's night and suff'ring's gloom,
A deathless Iris, that will ne'er depart,
But shine immortal o'er our destined tomb!

CHRIST IN COMMUNION WITH THE SOUL.

"Abide with us."—*Luke* xxiv. 29.

Abide with us, dear Lord! abide;
No hearts can beat, and be untried
By pangful woe or care;
But, if Thy shielding arm o'ershade
The creature which Thy love hath made
Hell cannot harm a hair.†

Around us Powers of evil throng
Who fain would hurry souls along
The wilds of sin and gloom;
And principles within us rage
In vernal youth, or wintry age,
Which haunt us to the tomb.

But Thou, abiding Lord of peace!
Art light, and liberty's release
To all meek sons of faith,
Thy word divine who e'er attend,
And listen to the sinner's Friend
Though dark the truth He saith.

The sinful Earth looks sad and lone,
And guilty hearts around us moan,
And graves, how fast they rise!
As added years their record bring
Of havoc, change, and suffering,—
What sadness loads our sighs!

But should Thy presence be supplied,
What calming powers of truth abide!
Our cross is meekly borne;
Though spent the noon, and night appears
To darken through our spirit's tears,
Life will not be forlorn.

When sickness shades the soul with dread,
And Fever moans with throbbing head
Till wild the pulses play,
Abide with us! blest Lord, and be
A balm beyond all sympathy
To awe the Fiend away.

Or, should it be our lot to keep
Night-watch beside the guarded sleep
Of parent, child, or friend,
There, as we note each ebbing breath
And scan the chill of coming death,
Thy dews of mercy send.

Or, when the churchyard-gloom we pace,
And oft with tearful silence trace
The tombs of friends no more,
Abide with us! that Hope and Prayer
May warble words of glory there,
Which back the dead restore.

But oh, blest Lord! of all the wounds
With which man's wearied life abounds,
Not death, nor sickness, they
Which most disease the mind with pain,
Or bid us view the world as vain,
Where grief and anguish sway;

But, hollow tongues and heartless smiles,
And glozing friends who were but wiles
Of falsehood lightly drest,—
These melt us into more than tears,
And make us feel our martyr'd years
A burden on the breast.

---

* Rev. iv. 3. † Matt. x. 20.

O then, abide with us! and calm
Our spirit with that sacred balm
Pure grace alone imparts;
Thy Presence like a heaven will be,
When all the false ones fade and flee,
And soothe our sunken hearts.

Abide with us!—why pray we so,
As if disciples did not glow
With Thine own promise sure?
"Lo! I am with you, till the chime
Of Ages sounds the last of time,
While earth and man endure."

Yes, Thou art "with us" in Thy word;
Thy Voice in sacraments is heard,
And prayer and praise reveal
How through the soul Thy blessings glide,
As o'er the heart's most gloomy tide
Thy radiant comforts steal.

Dejection oft, but not despair,
In this tried world of woe and care
It may be ours to face;
Only, be Thou the sleepless guide,
Morn, noon, and night with us abide
Till we complete our race.

We ask not blissful calms to dwell
Around us with unbroken spell,
Nor seek a pangless lot;
But, by the breathing of Thy word
Be our faint bosoms freshly stirr'd,
Nor sigh, as if forgot!

DEPARTED, NOT DEAD.

[C. H. E. M., BORN MAY 4, 1848: DIED JUNE 8, 1848.]

"As one in bitterness for his first-born."—*Zech.* xii. 10.
"Redeemed from among men, being the first-fruits unto God and to the Lamb."—*Rev.* xiv. 4.

Thou art not dead, my vanish'd one!
But living in the light
Of some pure world, beyond the sun,
Where death creates no night,
And sumless babes are smiling now
As bright and beautiful as thou.

When first I saw thy baby-form
With eyes of tearful love,
I little thought a hidden storm
Was looming from above,
So soon to blast my May-born flower
Beneath the blight of deathful power.

The Lord who gives, hath ta'en away,
And blest be His high name!
Oh, that with calm I this could say
And feel God's hallow'd claim:—
Cease, rebel heart! be calm and still,
And bow beneath a Father's will.

Pale relic! now enrobed for death,
Nurseling of hopes and fears,
How did I watch each ebbing breath
And kiss thine infant tears,
When throbs of suff'ring o'er thee came
Thy wordless tongue could never name.

Departed babe! how many a dream
Brighten'd thy father's heart,
When like a vision thou didst seem
In life to take such part,
That o'er his hours there breathed a spell
More exquisite than tones can tell.

With thy soft features round me glowing
Amid the world I went,
And with a heart to heaven o'erflowing
Bless'd thee, bright innocent!
And felt, howe'er my path should roam,
My little star-beam reign'd at home.

Already Hope's prophetic eye
Beheld some future spot,
And underneath life's vernal sky,
Pictured thy maiden lot,
Where truth and grace would be thy guide,
And all thy wants by heaven supplied.

I dream'd, if God thy life should spare,
How blessèd it would be
To hear thy budding lips declare
Young words of Deity;
To watch thy spirit, day by day,
Rise into speech, and learn to pray.

I fancied how my hand would lead
Thy tiny feet along,
By placid shore, or sunny mead
Where brooklets sing their song,
While gay-wing'd breezes round thee flew
And clad thy cheeks with vermeil hue.

And oh! I dared, through Him, to hope,
To Whose baptismal arms
I gave thee,—that thy mind would ope
Each year, with sacred charms;
As more and more The Spirit taught
Thy gentle soul what Jesu wrought.

But thou art pale, a perish'd flower,
  A blossom on Life's tree,
Nipp'd in the bud, before the power
  Of sin corrupted thee:—
Wash'd in the blood of Jesu white,
Babe, art not thou in glory bright?

Cold, cold, my child! I view thee now
  Like Sleep in marble lying,
With paleness on thy placid brow
  Which sets my heart a-sighing;
And round thy lips there linger still
Dead smiles that shall remembrance fill.

My first-born! God has call'd thee back,
  His gift He doth resume,
But o'er thy father's blighted track
  Darkens thine early tomb,—
A haunting shade of more than grief
To which man's world brings no relief.

From room to room I wander on
  Where thou hast been of yore,
And all mine eyes can gaze upon
  Recalls a child no more;
As though each object would declare
Thy darling glances rested there.

Beloved and beauteous wreck of all
  That warm'd this aching breast
With hopes, that when the funeral pall
  Should o'er thy parent rest,
There still might be a loving one
To think of him, whose course was run,—

Farewell! farewell! departed child,
  Sweet darling of the soul,
Gone to the grave, ere sin defiled
  Thy conscience with control;
I mourn, my babe! but not for thee
Becalm'd in Christ's eternity.

Before me lies a perill'd way
  Of trial, change, and tears;
If short or long, life's future day,
  Rests with the God of years,
Who measures our appointed span,
And deals the thread of time to man.

Yet I shall smile, and act, and speak,
  As though thou ne'er hadst been;
And they who scan the brow and cheek
  And judge by outward mien,
Can little dream how much we hide
Under the heart's unwitness'd tide!

The purest thoughts lone spirits bear
  Are marr'd by being spoken,
And more than deepest words declare
  Lives in some heart half-broken;
A transient grief light tongues may tell,
But cloister'd Anguish keeps her cell.

A thousand things must wake the sigh
  That shall remember thee,
And raise before the mental eye
  Those tombs of memory,
Which o'er the churchyard of the heart
Cast inward shades, which ne'er depart.

The beam, the bud, the blooming grace
  Of some infantile flower
Which smiles into a poet's face
  In Nature's conscious hour,
Oh! each and all will oft restore,
A mental gleam of her no more.

But melody, beyond all charms,
  The buried past regains;
And oft the spoiling tomb disarms
  By resurrection-strains,
In whose rapt tones the dead revive,
And untomb'd years appear alive.

Thus will thy sylph-like features float
  Before mine inward gaze,
Call'd into life by some sweet note
  The harp of feeling plays;
Across my soul thy shape will beam,
And smile like some incarnate dream.

Farewell, my child! but not farewell
  For ever;—we shall meet
When sounds creation's dooming knell
  Before the judgment-seat;
And I shall know thy little face
Amid the world's assembled race.

Thrice happy babe! thou beauteous Soul
  To some bright world ascended,
How glorious that celestial goal
  Where thy brief course is ended!—
And most divine that hour will be
That bids me mount, and follow thee.

June 8th, 1848.

PREVAILING INTERCESSION.

"I will speak, yet but this once: Peradventure ten shall be found there. And He said, I will not destroy it for ten's sake," (*Gen.* xviii. 32,) compared with, "Ye shall go and pray unto me, and I will hearken unto you."—*Jer.* xxix. 12.

Thou dost, O God! transcend the All
Creative thought can into vision call,
  When most enrapt and raisèd Mind
Darts through the regions of the undefined,

Conceiving there the beautiful and bright
In the deep centre of Ideal light;
Eternal! Thou art perfect good,—
Such glory, who but Thou, hast understood?

And yet, may soul-breathed prayer ascend
And with those anthems of Thy worship blend,
Which round that secret Glory dwell
Where Thou art shrined in shades invisible:
Not dearer to Thine ear of love
The hymns and hallelujahs heard above,
Than is the contrite sinner's cry,
The broken cadence of his burden'd sigh.

O mystery! fathomless to thought,
With truths august how infinitely fraught!
That He, The Essence Uncreate
Throned in the blaze of His almighty state,
Should bend to hear the falt'ring praise
We sinful earth-worms to the Godhead raise,
And so in Christ should condescend
To call the Dust of woman born, His "Friend!" *

Hence, prayer becomes a pious wing
By which we soar to where crown'd Angels sing,
Ensphered in realms surmounting time.—
Through the dread vastness of the heavens sublime
Souls cleave their flight, until they see
The mercy-shrine of prayer-moved Deity;
There, entering in behind the veil,
Our suppliant hearts may breathe their sorrowing tale.

And, what a privilege for those
Foundlings of grace, o'erwhelm'd by frequent woes,
Whose faith-wing'd souls with seraph-zeal
Rise to *That* Heart in heaven, which learn'd to feel
In this rude world where sorrows reign,
The direst throbbing of terrestrial pain!—
Who, though on high He weeps no more,
In bliss remembers what on earth He bore.

Yes! Sympathy beyond the skies
Reigns, feels and acts for souls renew'd, which rise
And with adoring boldness ask
Due strength to aid them in life's weary task:
There Christ, our elder Brother, lives,
And echoes back whate'er the suppliant gives
Of low-breathed sigh, or sorrow's tone,
As though the Church's trial were His own.

* 2 Chron. xx. 7.

Hence meekly wise, the heaven-taught Mind
By prayerless reason grows not base and blind;
For God is honour'd when we pray:
In the rich glories of their guardian sway
His Attributes we then confess,
Alone can blast us, or supremely bless;
A sigh, or look, or breath of prayer
Brings Heaven to earth, and proves God ev'ry where.

Arm'd with the strength true prayer bestows,
How fearless martyrs triumph'd o'er their woes!
The sworded despot, fire and chain,
The dungeon-midnight, and the exile's pain,
With all tyrannic horrors press'd
Through the deep gloom of some o'ertortured breast,—
Melted, like shades, before the sense
That prayer on earth was man's omnipotence.

Devotion guides the soul to God
By the same pathway blest Emmanuel trod;
Its power may range all nature through,
And in the dark of providence can view
Soft tokens of celestial light,
Calm spots of glory, which allay the night;
And grasp, while griefs around them stand,
The feeling guidance of their Father's hand.

Who lives on this lone earth of graves,
Will find bare wisdom nought from ruin saves:
Sorrow and sin encompass all
Which men of flesh their finest rapture call,
Without,—delusive spells abound,
And Fiends unview'd our holiest shrines surround;
Within,—behold the traitor's will!
With some dark lust that dares besiege us still.

In vain will unanointed eyes
Seek for a halcyon bower below the skies:
Gay inexperience soon will find
The ruin'd conscience, and the restless mind,
And marvel, as swift years advance,
How many a tombstone hails its tearful glance;
While busy Homes, once bright with glee,
Th' eclipsing shadow of their dead will see!

More blest are they, whom Christ hath taught
To seek that Home true saints have ever sought,
E'en that pure orb of perfect rest
Where sin nor sorrow clouds the aching breast:—
And, who are these, but men of prayer
Who unto God committed grief and care,
And on the heart of Jesu laid
Each burden down, which lighten'd as they pray'd?

They knew, that saints alone are strong,
Who mourn what weakness must to saints belong,
And to the last corruption feel
Like a slow plague-spot o'er sick nature steal:
Their wisdom was themselves to know,
Whose guiding law was God revered below;
Their lives were liturgies of love,
And Christ the loadstar they obey'd above.

And so with us 'twill ever be,
If true to heaven our hearts beat loyally.
What souls to living bodies are,
To faith heaven-born becomes the pulse of Prayer,—
The spirit's life that throbs within,
And gently masters each embosom'd sin,
Reigning victorious over all
Which back to earth the mounting soul would call.

True prayer is thus Religion's breath,
That hallows life, and haunts her until death;
Without it, holiness expires,
Dark grow our hopes, and sensual our desires;—
Since, not a grace the Gospel gives
But in the power of prayer it moves, and lives,
And Christ His perfect image sees,
When He beholds him on adoring knees.*

LIFE IS A FADING LEAF.

"We all do fade as a leaf."—*Isa.* lxiv. 6.

Chill o'er yon heath autumnal shadows fall,
The dusky twilight reigns with deeper sway,
While soft dejection seems to mantle all,
Like nature mourning for the death of day.

As hectic hues on pale consumption's form,
Red tints of ruin deck the flower and tree,
And low winds murmur like a wailing storm,
Or dirges o'er the dead entomb'd at sea.

Where is the flush, by vernal radiance clad,
That late o'er all the glowing landscape smiled,
Making the heart of hoary age as glad
As though 'twere backward into youth beguiled?

'Tis gone, that bright and beauteous glow,
Which o'er the teeming breast of nature threw
A charm that bad the bleakest mind o'erflow
With feelings exquisite, and fancies new.

* Luke xxii. 41.

There is a deadness, clothed by wintry awe,
Encircling now what then with bloom was bright;
And where the freshness of young spring we saw,
Floats the chill moisture of the coming blight.

Here as we roam adown yon woodland-dell,
The stricken leaves in yellow showers descend,
And each one seems to sigh a sad farewell,
Like love-tones murmur'd o'er a dying friend.

Meet emblem this of transient life's decay,
How all things perish which we prize below;
Where, like sear'd foliage, youth soon fades away,
And wither'd hopes bestrew the path of woe.

We learn mortality where'er we look,
The dust we tread subserves a moral plan,
And when aright we read creation's book,
Lo! all its pages are address'd to man.

Summer and winter, autumn and mild spring,
May each instruct us by their beauteous lore;
Each to our soul a sacred lesson bring,
And buried warnings into life restore.

In some high mood of melancholy thought
Nature herself doth almost human grow,
And mirror back what Mind to her hath brought,
And leave men wiser than mere sages know.

And well it tempers with a sober hue
The gayest scenes that youthful passions find,
To cast o'er coming death a pensive view,
And breathe the quiet of a prayerful mind.

Dejection makes the autumn of the soul,—
But let autumnal feelings have their sway,
And, shrink not, Christian! from their just control,
But grasp their blessing, ere they glide away.

Yet may not wintry skies, nor leafless bower
Oppress the spirit with too damp a gloom;
For in man's being lurks a vital power,
By Christ obtain'd, victorious o'er the tomb.

Thus, though man wither like an orphan leaf
Which lies forgotten in the lonely dust,
His dead corruption is a moment brief,—
For, hark the trumpet! and arise he must.

'Tis here the parable of nature's death
Fails to adumbrate what our doom shall be;
Life does not perish with corporeal breath,
But live once more to look on Deity!

Earth, air, and ocean, wood and wildest shore,—
Sleep in the dust where mortal embers may,
When rings the trumpet, each shall back restore
The deathless atoms of departed clay.

Creation finds an everlasting grave;
Where fall the dead leaves, they for ever lie,
No resurrection-winds shall o'er them wave,
And show their beauty to a new-born sky:

But, Man shall triumph o'er an endless tomb;
When God's loud clarion wakes his sleeping frame,
A dread eternity *must* be his doom,
In heaven immortal, or in hell, the same!

A FOUNTAIN IN THE DESERT.

"God opened her eyes, and she saw a well of water."
Gen. xxii. 19.

Under the burning eye of heaven
Breathless and bright as noon can be,
Mother and child,—behold them driven
O'er the hot wild in agony;
While each heart throbs that fearful prayer,
"Relieve me, Death! from black despair."

Beersheba's desert, lone and dun,
Around them both lies grimly spread;
No veiling cloud-shade hides the sun,
And underneath, as on they tread,
The fierceness of its flaming heat
Doth blister their unsandall'd feet.

O, for the music of one breeze
To warble through the windless air!
Or, cooling breath from some chance trees
To mitigate the savage glare,
Which reddens like a furnace-glow
O'er sky and herbless soil below.

But still untamed, the eastern noon
Burns round them in a breezeless trance;
And, yellower than the harvest-moon
Yon wither'd heath which meets their glance;
Above, below, where'er they gaze,
'Tis cruel heat, and cloudless blaze!

No bird-wings break the hush intense,
No murmurs fall from leafy bough;
The very insects in suspense
Refrain their tiny descant now:
So dead the stillness reigning round
A man might hear his heart-beat sound.

Yon haggard mother lifts her eyes,
Around the scene they wildly roll,
And who can list the choking sighs
Which heave from out her riven soul,
And not believe, intenser pain
Could never cleave a heart in twain!

Foodless and fainting lags her child,
Its bleeding feet can hardly stand;
Yet, fired with thirst, along the wild
She guides it with a fev'rish hand:—
The water spent, along her frame
The shudderings deep of horror came!

In vain her sunken eyes survey'd
The arid heath and desert bare,
To see if one lone streamlet stray'd
In flow of mercy lingering there;
For neither gushing well, nor brook
Replied to her despairing look.

Oh, sad Egyptian! outcast one,
By Sarah hurl'd from all thy bliss,
Ten thousand deaths have now begun
To mingle in a death like this;
Methinks I mark thee, Hagar wild,
Shudder to view thy sobbing child!

Fainter and fainter moves each limb,
The parchèd mouth no more can speak;
And when thy tears descend on him,
They burn upon his hollow cheek;
The swoon of death is coming fast,—
The child beneath yon shrub is cast.

Parental Love! 'tis now the hour
To testify how deep thou art;
Replete with superhuman power,
Thy fountain is a mother's heart:
Though fathom'd seas their depths unfold,
The deeps of love *what* tongue hath told?

From God a mother's feelings rise,
A fount divine is their high source,
And, purer than our thoughts surmise,
They stream through life their endless course;
Outlasting all we love to see,—
They blend with soul's eternity!

And this was hers, who could not dare
Behold her gasping child depart,
But laid him down in mute despair,
Then turn'd her eyes, but not her heart
From that dread sight:—behind a tree
She shrunk, and wept, how bitterly!

And as she wail'd, what sobs and sighs
  Along her quivering heart-strings came!
While closed her boy his fainting eyes,
  And scorching thirst subdued his frame:
She dared not see, but how she *felt*
His throbs of anguish through her melt!

But God is nigh, oh, mother wild!
  Behold a mission'd angel's wings
Arch their rich glory o'er the child,
  And, hark! the mercy that he brings,—
"Hagar arise, God hears thy prayer,
Go, drink yon well which warbles there."

Her eyes were open'd; from the ground
  She saw the crystal water rise,
And then, as though from death unbound,
  Outburst a mother's ecstasies!—
She gave her child that cooling stream,
And stood entranced, as in a dream.

And God be thank'd! for this deep tale
  Where grief and grace so finely blend;
And ne'er may such high story fail
  Our own chill'd hearts to warm, and mend;
For much it holds, if right we read,
To soothe us in dejection's need.

Not from the bond-maid are we born,
  But children of the Church, and free;
Yet, oft vex'd life appears forlorn
  As though forgot by Deity;
Cains of the heart, we rove accurst
Till life becomes one aching thirst.

But in the gloom of this rack'd hour
  When all around looks bleak and bare,
Betake thee to yon gracious Power
  Who listen'd to the weeping prayer
Lone Hagar lifted in the wild,
And brought down Godhead to her child.

For, have we not a Living Well
  Of consolations deep as pure?
Nor are its waves invisible
  If love and faith our hearts assure;
Since Christ is our celestial Spring,
Whom prayer to earth can ever bring.

And minor wells from Him may flow
  Of comfort, joy, and heaven-like peace,
Which calm the fever'd heart of woe,
  And grant the mind a fresh release;
And such are found in His blest Word
When God by faith is seen, and heard.

There crystal wells of grace abound,—
  The promises, which man console,
And cool life's arid desert round
  With streams that freshen as they roll;
And seraph heart and saintly mind
Can ever such refreshment find.

Thou Light of reason! Lord of grace,
  Heaven's Paraclete, by Christ obtain'd,
Descend, and from our souls displace
  Whatever throne the world hath gain'd;
Dark eyes unscale, and let them see
Our everlasting Well in Thee!

MEDITATION AT EVENTIDE.

"Isaac went out to meditate in the field at eventide."
Gen. xxiv. 63.

I LOVE the still romance of lonely fields,
  When shading twilight like a Spirit-wing
Broods o'er the landscape, and the air-tone yields
  To the charm'd mind a pensive murmuring.

There, unbeheld by man's intrusive eye,
  Let the lone pilgrim wind some willow'd path,
And in the silence of the years gone by,
  Feel the soft bliss a sacred memory hath.

When the rude passion of the roaring winds
  Louder and louder swells along the sea,
Their voice is echo'd by tempestuous Minds
  Who love reflections of themselves to see:

Or, climb some rock where cloud-born anthems peal
  And hymning thunders all around thee roll,
And, throned in darkness, thou may'st learn to feel
  The dread foundations of the human soul.

But, wisdom most with tenderness doth dwell;
  And silent eve, and solitary spot,
Will clothe remembrance with a lasting spell
  When stern magnificence is all forgot.

So have they felt, who roam'd thy realm sublime,
  Heroic fatherland of Tell the free!—
Helvetia, while they trod that haunted clime,
  And drank the magic which inspireth thee.

There the huge mountains lift their billowy forms,
  And glaciers whiten by the gorge's steep,
O'er rocks of icy gloom resound the storms,
  And pine-trees rend, as on the whirlwind sweep:

And I have heard the Alpine thunder groan
Blent with the avalanche's crushing roar,
As though the Lord of nature left His throne
For chaos to resume its reign once more.

Darkness, and thunder, crag, ravine, and rock,
And precipice that strikes the pilgrim chill,
Send to the o'erawed mind a secret shock
And with terrific glories mem'ry fill.

But, oh! how often when the stern and wild
Die into sadness, like a tragic dream,
The loved impressions of some landscape mild
In fresh reality still glow, and gleam.

The lyric cadence of each choral breeze
Mix'd with the tinkling cow-bells' pensive tone,
The grazing herd, the chalets bower'd in trees,
And mellow calm upon the mountains thrown,

With deep-valed haunts, whose matchless beauty made
The heart o'erflow with loveliness profound,
While pine-woods round the curving shores display'd
Their forest-grace with leafy grandeur crown'd,—

Say, have not these beyond dread storms impress'd
On pure remembrance what the past hath been,
And left a magic that serenes the breast
Like thy hush'd vale, thou unforgot Orsine?*

'Tis thus, the calm of beauty most appeals
To finer moods when sainted feeling reigns,
Which downward to the root of mem'ry steals,
And all the softness of our spirit gains.

And oft when ruder life with stormful grief
Rocks the torn heart, till inward tempests rise,
Ideal landscapes lend a soft relief
And smile upon us, like subduing eyes!

So felt the patriarch, when he wisely chose
The lulling hour of loneliness and shade,
To drink the freshness of that pure repose
A quiet evening round the meadows made.

* A valley of exquisite wildness and softness, between Martigny and Chamouni, near the hamlet of Couteraie.

He went to meditate, to muse, and dream,
Where nought broke stillness but the vesper song
Of some gay insect, bird, or babbling stream
Which feels half conscious as it flows along.

Perchance, he mused on nature, man, and God,
Creation's wreck, and ruin'd innocence,
On fortune's sunshine, or affliction's rod,
And all which Grace and Goodness here dispense.

Floated the hymns of angels on his ear,
As once they warbled over Eden's bower?
Or, did he vision, through a rising tear,
The star maternal of his childish hour?

Time has not told: but yet, like him, we may
Wander at eve to meditate and muse,
Far from the hum of crowds and cities stray,
And nature's quiet o'er the heart suffuse.

They cannot nurse nobility within
Who ne'er the solitudes of nature thread,
And, far removed from man's tumultuous din,
Recall the vanish'd, and revive the dead.

There is a wisdom in the wood and field,
A sacred meaning in the silent flower,
And shrines of loneliness instruction yield,
Did we but haunt them in a genial hour.

Cities of men and mortal baseness preach;
But sylvan dales, like holy things, impart
A healing quiet, which may conscience reach,
And bring God closer to an alien heart.

The open vastness of yon vaulted sky
When o'er our heads we view its arching sweep,—
There should we learn to lift a thoughtful eye,
And muse on mercy, till remembrance weep.

And thus, disciple of that Lonely One!
Who through the night-watch often wept, and pray'd,
Do thou, like Isaac, when the day is done,
With God converse, and seek Him in the shade.

There will Emmanuel to thy soul draw near
And bid thee more for saving glories yearn,
As on "the way" He soothed disciples' fear,
And reason'd with them, till their hearts did burn!

One pensive hour with nature, God, and prayer,
While the dusk Evening wraps her dewy veil,
Cools the hot fever on each brow of care,
And cheers the soul when brighter prospects fail.

There, in that hush of meditation lone,
The still small accents of the Spirit speak
Truths, in the whirl of life how rarely known,
And by dead conscience heard, as dull and weak!

Believer, thus to silence yield the soul,
Be thy calm mind to musing loneness given,
Till secret earth-clouds from thy vision roll
And show thee glimpses of a Saviour's heaven.

MORAL POWER OF HARMONY.

"The rest were chosen to give thanks unto the Lord .... with musical instruments of God."—1 *Chron.* xvi. 41, 42.

I LOVE to hear the wizard tones
Of thunder, storm, and booming sea,
The wave-voiced winds, and tragic groans
Which make creation's minstrelsy,—
When Art and Genius such a triumph gain
That all seem blended in some master-strain.

And Harmony can also bring
What mental visions love to view,
Pictures, beyond what poets sing,
When most they make the world untrue,—
Landscapes of beauty, isles of bloom and balm,
Elysian verdure, and ambrosial calm.

But, Music wields a nobler spell
Than nature can alone impart;
And with far more than tones can tell
She oft inspires the echoing heart:
To her belongs Association's power,
Which haunts remembrance in its purest hour.

Melodious counterparts of mind
How often do some chords impress,
When Genius, with a hand refined,
Creates the sounds we inly bless!—
All passions, hopes, all principles and fears
Melt into music, and entrance our ears.

Thus, harmony to man may seem
A soul in sound, express'd and heard,
Or like an Angel in our dream
Who whispers some celestial word,
Till minds o'erfraught with feeling's warmest glow
Thrill into tears, and softly overflow.

And oh, ye dead! who never die,—
For though removed from outward gaze,
Your resurrection is the sigh
Pure memory unto virtue pays,—
Though unbeheld, how oft in music's strain
Your deep eyes look into our hearts again!

Yes, chords are touch'd, whose tones awake
And strike the soul's electric string,
Which vibrates till it seems to break
With those intense appeals that bring
Youth, home and childhood, fields, and faces dear
Back to the Heart, which bathes them with a tear.

Thus music, like religion, oft
May elevate the heaven-wing'd mind,
By wafting it to worlds aloft
For peace and purity design'd:
'Tis inspiration, though mere sound it seems,
Prompting the good to more than Glory dreams.

We praise Thee, God! for this fine spell
Pervading harmony can wield:
But, teach us to employ it well,
That it may grace and grandeur yield,
Whether by organ-chant, or choral hymn
Which rolls and deepens down cathedrals dim.

And when congenial hearts delight
In homes of quiet bliss to hear
Soft household-strains, which make the night
To memory as to music dear,
Like silver drops of some melodious shower
Heard in the dewy hush of twilight hour,—

Music seems more than common air
Through chorded instrument awaking,
And oft resembles dying prayer,
Or sighs from lonely hearts half-breaking:
Thus none can dream whence harmonies descend,
Or how their spirit with our own can blend.

Hence music proves a sacred thing,
A power no mortal words can tell;
A heaven of sound it seems to bring
On earth awhile to float and dwell,—
A breaking forth of melodies above,
A speech of seraphim, on lips of Love!

And oft, methinks, the tones which die
And soundless grow to mortal ear,
May re-ascend their mystic Sky,
From whence they sank to our low sphere,—
Like that bright Choir who soar'd from Judah's plain,
To chant in heaven what earth ne'er heard again.*

THE REDEEMER'S SIGH.

"And looking up to Heaven, He sighed."
Mark vii. 34.

And did The gentle Saviour sigh,
As once He wept a tear,
When sorrow dimm'd His mournful eye
Drawn from a mortal sphere?

Then let the Church this breathing sign
Of Christ's unutter'd thought,
With all that spoken love combine
With which each word was fraught.

For, oh, it proves a symbol deep
Beyond what language tells
When most true Pathos bids us weep
Beneath her moving spells—

How Christ in sorrow, pangs, and tears,
Though social, stood alone,
Since while He wept for others' fears,
He chiefly sigh'd His own.

And in that hour, when doing good,
While making dumbness speak,
Dark meanings fill'd His solitude,
And shaded brow and cheek.

When sinful men a boon bestow,
Bright gladness marks the hour;
They do not sigh, but only glow
To feel their gracious power;

But such the cup of anguish quaff'd
Emmanuel in His gloom,—
He wept and sigh'd, but never laugh'd,
From manger to the tomb!

His life was one celestial pain,
A martyrdom of care;
Denial had its perfect reign
In each perfection there.

Through all some crucifixion ran,
The Cross became His will,
Where God beheld a faultless man,
And cries, "Behold him!" still.*

MAN'S HEART, DECEITFUL ABOVE ALL THINGS.

"The heart is deceitful above all things, and desperately wicked: who can know it? I the Lord search the heart."—*Jer.* xvii. 9, 10.

As Christ was God in flesh array'd,
So God in language is that Word
Where man is inwardly portray'd,
As though his copied heart were heard.

For not a single throb of thought
Vibrates within his viewless mind,
That is not to conviction brought
By heaven's dread Book, which reads mankind!

And is not this a crushing tone,
An avalanche of stern rebuke,
A thunder-peal from His high throne
Before whose glance Creation shook,—

That Man becomes incarnate lie,
A living mass of low deceit,
Baffling the search of mortal eye
To scan the guiles which in him meet?

Beyond *all* creatures, and above
What sin and Satan can unfold,
The venom'd coil around him wove,—
The serpent-depths no tongue has told!

And desperate too, if finite cure
Be *all* our hopes pretend to find,
Those fell deceits which men allure
And leave the conscience dead and blind.

We grant there are distinctions true
Between degrees of social worth;
For, some are tender, warm, and true,
And others, iced as frozen earth:

And some we hail, whose hearts expand
Like bounding waves beneath the sun;
While these, with shut and selfish hand
A vile career of passion run.

* Luke ii. 13, 15.

* Zech. vi. 12.

Gradations thus 'tween man and man
When measured by our moral test,
Are undenied; and reason can
Perceive them in the human breast.

But still, if heavenward we ascend,
And by the law of love divine
Discern how far our natures tend,
Apart from Thee, oh God! and Thine,

Then, hear a thunder-peal like this
From out the clouds of Scripture roll,—
"Deceitful and most desperate is
The life of unconverted soul!"

And can we dare this truth deny,
How nature marks her hate with smiles,
And loves the most enamell'd lie
Which polishes her venal wiles?

And if, alas! *ourselves* we scan,
Deceitful prove we, to the core!
The child doth prophesy the man,
The man repeats the child before:

All, all, in youth, and age alike,
Abroad, at home, for word or thought
The bosom may with anguish strike,*
And be with full contrition fraught,

If but an hour we search, and see
What broken vows condemn our ways,
How fairest resolutions flee,
And we are charm'd by cheating praise!

The very sins men weep at morn
And at the mercy-seat confess,
Again before the night, are born,
And stain them with new loathsomeness!

Well may we hang the head, and mourn,
Nor doubt that piercing Word is true
Which saith, no Hearts to heaven return
Except by mercy, born anew.

Faith heeds not how false worldlings smile;
God's truth can ne'er be sneer'd away;
The heart is one abyss of guile
Whose throbs, like Judas, Christ betray.

And in us all by nature lurk
The germs of unimagined crime,
Which often dares the Demon's work
And crimsons o'er the cheek of Time.

* Luke xviii. 13.

Yes, Adam, Cain, and Peter's lie,
Herod and David in their sin,—
Let candour search, and so descry
Their secret prototypes within.

Come, Holy Spirit! mystic Dove,
Thine innocence from heaven impart;
Our hate transform to heavenly love,
And build Thy temple in our heart.

The purest soul pleased Earth admires,
Who to the centre scans it all?
The highest Angel back retires,
And prostrate worlds in silence fall.

Who knows it? Echo answers, "Who?"
Created minds are bow'd and dumb:—
"Jehovah,* I can search it through,
And enter where no creatures come."

Tremendous thought! that God and man
By contrast both should searchless be;
The last too vile for thought to scan,
The First, unfathom'd Deity!

* Jer. xvii. 10.

EXPRESSIVE NIGHT.

"Night unto night showeth knowledge."—*Ps.* xix. 2.
"Even the night shall be light about me."—*Ps.* cxxxix. 11.

SHADES of the soft and stealing night!
More eloquent than joyous light
Is your dark magic, deep and still
Descending over bower and hill.

There is a hush, a holy spell
Breathed o'er dim earth by day's farewell;
A calm more chaste than words define,
A feeling that is half divine.

I love to watch the quiv'ring gleams
Of twilight, when they braid the streams,
Or with slant radiance hue the flowers,
Which close their lids in garden-bowers.

Now, cold and mute Creation grows,
As drops her curtain of repose;
The birds are songless, and the air
Seems hallow'd into silent prayer.

Like Music's death, serene and slow,
Pale twilight yields a pensive glow,
And soon will turret, tree, and spire,
All viewless into gloom retire.

Now is the witching time for thought,
Th' elect of heaven have ever sought;
By patriarch, saint, and poet found
With high-breathed instincts to abound.

Angelic choirs may now descend
And with our souls serenely blend,
Hover around where'er we stray,
And thrill, when Thought begins to pray.

Thus, when the fev'rish day was o'er,
Rapt Jesu sought the quiet shore;
Or, on loved Hermon, lone and still,
Breathed, "Oh, my Father! do Thy will."

So, Christian, while the prayerless throng
Whirl time away in feast and song,
Be thine the pure and placid spell
Which night and nature weave so well.

Creation, providence, and grace,
Let each assume its hallow'd place
In thought serene,—by Heaven bestow'd
On all who trace the narrow road.

Night is the time when buried days
Rise from their tomb, and dim our gaze
With tearful shades, from scenes of yore,
And loving hearts which throb no more.

So rules the Past, that faint and far
As fancy eyes each vestal star,
Young poets dream how there abide
The deathless ones, on earth who died.

Night for the present, too, creates
A charm which oft the mind elates,—
A lone, but still a lofty dream
That men are *more* than yet they seem.

And on thy future let such hour
Look like a prophet in his power,
Predicting much that God and grace
Reveal to guide our erring race.

Nor be forgot, in heaven Thou art
A Priest, oh Christ! whose boundless heart
Thrills to each cry, which all may dare
To utter forth in fervid prayer.

Now in the hush of holy night
Claim we, blest Lord! the glorious right
Before Thy Throne of grace to bring
All forms of human suffering:—

A Husband to the widow be; *
A Sire may orphans find in Thee;

* Isa. liv. 5.

And to Thy sad and stricken poor
Let heaven unfold its waiting door;

And where dejected hearts incline
To question, Lord, the Will divine,
The Blood of sprinkling let it fall,
And while it cleanses, calm them all.

For church, for country, and for child,
A mother dear, or sister mild,
For all true souls and social ties
Now let entreating prayer arise.

And, cradled on maternal breast,
May each sweet babe in slumber rest,
And round pale captives in their cells
Hover dear homes, and native dells.

Morn, noon, and night, O God! are Thine,
In whom their blended charms combine;
Nor is there scene, or spot, or hour
Untouch'd by Thy mysterious power.

Yet, faith and feeling both declare
That hour belongs to Thee and prayer,
When stillness to the soul is given,—
For night, not day, seems nearest heaven.

THE PRAYERLESS.

"Thou restrainest prayer before God."—*Job* xv. 4.
"If thou knewest the gift of God . . . . thou wouldest have asked of Him, and He would have given thee living water."—*John* iv. 10.

"My heart is cold, I cannot pray,"
Methinks I hear the worldling say;—
But is not this blind nature's sin?
Thou graceless outcast! lift thine eyes
To where man's home of glory lies,
And thou may'st hear the God within.

Did we but fathom more and more
Our inward deeps, we should deplore
Those unborn sins which there abide:
With truthful anguish might we plead
For God to help our sinful need,
And cast us on The Crucified!

Who does not pray, our God unthrones,
His word rejects, His will disowns,
Till life becomes one guilty sigh;
Pure Reason from her shrine is hurl'd,
And earth appears an orphan'd world,
Whose Maker is no more on high.

O, creed of death ! and cold despair,
Which thus repels the power of prayer,
By peerless saints and martyrs loved ;
Since faith and reason both unite
To vindicate God's awful right,
By prayer to have His throne approved.

The very Power to whom we pray
Is He who prompteth what to say,—*
'Tis spirit, more than spoken word ;
For thought is speech, and heard on high
The sadness of some low-breathed sigh,
When penitence by love is stirr'd.

Alas ! for thee, thou prayerless one,
Thy living hell is now begun
In passion blind, and base desire;
The torment of apostate will
Must ever make thy chosen ill,
And fill thee with perdition's fire.

Could vain men see how vile they are,
Sublime would beat the pulse of prayer
In temple, home, or twilight-field ;
Believing thus with loving thought
What strength to Christ Himself it brought,—
Pure bliss would high devotion yield.

But, dost thou mourn thy heart is cold,
And rev'rence truth divinely bold ?
Then, undevout one, here it lies,—
Th' unfeeling soul, and faithless mind,
Oh, *these* are they which render blind
When upward gaze thy restless eyes.

This world is far too closely coil'd
Around a heart by pleasure soil'd,
Where sin, desire, and Satan dwell ;
Ambition's guilt and lust of gain
Within thee hold infernal reign,
And triumph with a wizard spell.

But wouldst thou taste the bliss of prayer,
Breathing on earth celestial air ?
Then, burst thy Belial chains away !
Each wand'ring thought to God call home,
And ponder on the world to-come
Till conscience prompt thee how to pray.

Go, learn it of that martyr'd host
Who bled for Christ, and pray'd the most
Because they loved Him unto death ;
Hark ! how their wingèd raptures rise,
And catch the lustre of their eyes
Who praised Him with departing breath.

Or, rather That pure Spirit seek,
Whose love can so uplift the weak
When dull they seem, and dead they grow,
Till oft with mental groans unheard
Their souls by unbreathed prayer are stirr'd,
And with devotion overflow.

Incarnate God ! while here we live,
Be this our prayer, "Forgive ! forgive !"—
But, who can fathom *all* we mean ?
Eternity itself will prove
A paraphrase of pardoning love,
And teach Heaven * what the Cross hath been !

* Rom. viii. 26, 27.

* 1 Pet. i. 12.

DREAD SACRIFICE.

"Take now thy son, thine only son, Isaac, whom thou lovest, and offer him for a burnt-offering."—*Gen.* xxii. 2.

And must a father slay his only child ?
Dark thought in which ten thousand deaths abide !
Was ever parent with such blood defiled,
Or such a victim to a God supplied ?

And Isaac too ! the promised heir of age,
The child of covenant, by heaven bestow'd
To cheer the sire in his sad pilgrimage,
At whose glad birth his full heart overflow'd.—

'Tis thus, whate'er in living depths of love
Haunts the pure heart, parental as profound,
Might well have shudder'd at the Voice above,
"Let Isaac for my human lamb be bound !"

If dies the son, then how shall Abram's seed
Inherit Canaan's heaven-distinguish'd land ?
Or, if the child must by the parent bleed,
How can the covenant in Isaac stand ?

Reason and conscience, shall they both arise,
And shrinking heart-blood grow with terror pale
When looks the patriarch in loved Sara's eyes,
And on his lip expires the awful tale ?

The savage heathen, will they not abhor
A God of blood, and call the deed profane
Beyond the fury of the fiercest war,
That strews a battle-field with tombless slain ?

And thus, if nature be the *only* guide
  Of what a patriarch in such hour should be,
Rebellion had the tempting God denied,
  And back recoiled from vocal Deity.

But faith the hoary friend of God inspired,
  And mortal Will before a Voice divine
Fell like a sacrifice, by love attired
  And offer'd freely on Religion's shrine.

Obedience absolute, submission's law,
  On this alone the patriarch's eye was bent,
And God was greater than the grief he saw,
  Whose Hand recall'd the mercy He had lent.

Perchance, 'twas in the hush of holy night
  The dread command to offer Isaac came,
E'en while the father, lull'd with fond delight,
  In dreams parental murmur'd Isaac's name.

For, soon as Morning o'er the orient hills
  Shook the bright dewdrops from her beaming hair,
Behold, the sire his sacred work fulfils,
  Strong with resolve, and sanctified by prayer.

But ah! forgive him, if from Sara's eye
  His shrinking heart refused to take farewell;
He could not trust the cadence of a sigh
  Which might have hinted, what he dared not *tell*.

Three days they travell'd on, that son and sire,
  And sought together Christ's prophetic hill,
Where *this* must bleed in sacrificial fire,
  And *that* His own devoted offspring kill.

It was indeed a spectacle profound
  And touch'd with majesty, and truth how meek!
When the hoar'd Patriarch on bland Isaac bound
  The wood for sacrifice,—and did not speak.

Part II.

THE MORAL.

But when at length a signal cloud reposed
  On the lone hill, where God would have the deed,
Did not the hand which then a knife enclosed
  Tremble, and all the father in him bleed?

And, hark, how piercing, like a thrill of death,
  Clave through his soul one simple cry of love,
"My father!"—in the fondness of that breath
  How did the patriarch seek for strength above!

"My father!" and he answer'd, "Here I am;"
  "The wood behold, and here the needed fire,
But where is found the sacrificial lamb
  Which God ordain'd should in the flame expire?"

"God will provide!"—'twas all he dared to speak;
  So went the pilgrims to their awful task,
The blood grew paler on the patriarch's cheek,
  But no deliv'rance did cold reason ask.

The Lord had spoken! He who cannot err,
  His fiat issued, "Slay thy son for Me;"
True to his God,—rebellion shall not stir,
  But Faith adore Him on submissive knee.

And ne'er did infant with its clinging form
  And tiny limbs of tenderness, embrace
The fondling circle of a mother's arms,
  When she enclasps it,—with a blander grace,

Than did calm Isaac to the cordage yield
  His frame for havoc on the burning pile;
Not once outcried he at the coming death,
  But gazed on Slaughter with religious smile.

His limbs are bound, and on the altar laid
  Behold the parent sees an only son!
And now, both hand and heart display'd
  A faith unparagon'd, since time begun.

But God is mercy: hark! like thunder mild
  From clouds of golden beauty rolls the cry,
"Friend of Jehovah! spare thine offer'd child,
  And mark yon victim, in the thicket nigh."

Believer! Christ was in that angel-voice,
  And His atonement typed in all the scene,—
Child of Jehovah's everlasting choice
  Who hath the Isaac of salvation been.

But would we in some lower range of truth
  Search for the holy spells our hearts require?
Then may we trace them on that sainted youth,
  And see them mirror'd in his matchless sire.

By large devotion of our loving will,
  Like the meek Isaac's let our spirit bend,
And with unreas'ning faith at once fulfil
  Whate'er the fiat of our God may send:

To live, or die, be healthy, sick, or sad,
  In wealth to bask, or poverty to bleed,
In gloom to perish, or in peace be glad,—
  Let God decide, who understands our need.

And ye, who clasp with such intense desire
 Of fond retention in life's vale below,
The breathing Idols whom your souls admire,
 Think of the Patriarch in some night of woe!

The fondest heart, round which affection twines,
 Is most obtain'd when most in God enjoy'd,
And happiness with sacred lustre shines,
 When not by shades of selfish will alloy'd.

Disciples must not, like the godless, cleave
 To aught created in this world of sense;
Nor round the ruins of the present grieve,
 As though the future had no Providence!

The cherish'd Isaacs of our heart and creed
 Like a pure holocaust of grace must fall,
And on Love's altar, while we inly bleed,
 To heaven and duty Faith must offer all.

The dearest sacrifice is aye the best,
 And let us yield it, though severe the rod;
For on this truth may bleeding Anguish rest,—
 We lose an idol, but we gain a God.

PERFECT PEACE.

"Thou wilt keep him in perfect peace, whose mind is stayed on thee."—*Isa.* xxvi. 3.

Humility doth mark
The child of heaven within salvation's ark:
Through all his hallow'd ways
He harps the hymn of ever-deep'ning praise,
For mercies which surpass
The power of numbers to recount, or class;—
Yet, sins as sumless claim a constant tear,
That God, by prayer invoked, may hush all guilty fear!

But humble though the hearts
Of God's own children, this their creed imparts,—
A boldness to believe
That Christ is near them, when His chosen grieve:
Though each an atom seem
Lost in vast glories which around Him stream,
Each individual heart and lonely mind
In Christ a Brother clasps, and bears its doom resign'd.

No mere Abstractions dead,
By science out of arid reason bred,
And call'd creation's laws,
Which Sense adoreth as presiding Cause,—
A faith divine can own;
But o'er all life perceives the Saviour's throne:
A God tripersonal believers love,
And in Emmanuel's name seek all they find above.

Though moral earthquakes shock
The Systems round us, till they reel and rock;
While mad Opinion rules,
And Satan out of pride begets dark schools
Of sentiment, or sin,
Which scorn without, and stifle Truth within.—
A more than halcyon in his bosom reigns,
Who hath a Heart in heaven which echoes all his pains.

Unstable is weak earth;
And nothing which in space, or time, has birth,
A resting-place can give
To Souls who on this tearful world must live;
Since wayward passions will
Haunt the vex'd world, and never leave it still;—
The gnawing fever of some inward pain
Is all unchristian hearts from their false life obtain.

But, there is peace divine,
A calm unrippled, which, O God! is Thine;
A rest of saintly thought
From out the deeps of heaven by mercy brought;
It droppeth like a dew
The Hermon of the heart distilling through,
And, 'mid the restless change time undergoes,
That peace remains unmarr'd, above convulsive woes.

Salvation rears the walls *
Of that truth-keeping race whom Jesu calls;
Under His shielding arms
The burden'd mind escapes from sinful harms;
And while transgressors roam
Abroad unrestful, and the same at home,
No dread concussion in the realms of Time
Can rob believing souls of this their calm sublime.

Descend then, Prince of Peace!
And with thy Spirit bring worn minds release;
When skies and seas depart
Serene eternity of truth Thou art,

* Isa. lx. 18.

Lord of celestial life!
Beyond our sorrows, and above our strife;—
Yet so benignant, that Thine eye can see
Each pulse of loving prayer which throbs the heart to Thee.

STARRY DREAMS.

"Tell the stars if thou be able to number them."—*Gen.* xv. 5. "He telleth the number of the stars: he calleth them all by their names."—*Ps.* cxlvii. 4. "We have seen his Star in the East."—*Matt.* ii. 2.

THEIR names and numbers who can tell,
Yon quiv'ring gems of mystic light!
That throb with such irradiant spell
And fascinate our dreaming sight;

So countless looks their burning throng
No finite thought their sum can hold;
For, like a secret, they belong*
To One by numbers uncontroll'd.

How beautiful their lustres are!
Whether on infant-eyes they gleam,
Which often, like some pensive star,
Glance moisten'd with a mournful beam:

Or, when in elder life we gaze
On each faint pulse of throbbing fire,
Till feeling hearts reflect the rays
And mirror back what they inspire.

So fair to each and all they shine,
Stars often seem responsive Eyes
That greet us from their calm divine,
And answer our ascending sighs.

Attracted out of earth and time
The starry vault of air we roam,
And dream the poetry sublime,
Which makes each orb a spirit's home:

A home, perchance, where, bright and blest,
The loved, but not the lost, remain,
Whom there embower'd in blissful rest
Our souls may clasp in heaven again.

Ye dead! whose tombs are loving hearts,
Whose epitaphs, memorial tears,
Whose image from no scene departs,
But shades the colour of our years,

Not seldom, when the noise of day
Beneath the trance of dewy night
Is hush'd, and meekly dies away
The last wan smile of waning light,

Lone martyrs of dejection steal
From the harsh scene of crowd and care,
Religion in the stars to feel
As though enshrined in glory there.

How eloquent that voiceless hour!
Holy, as if creation knelt,—
Or mute before her Maker's power
Thrill'd Earth some adoration felt.

Yet, would that in primeval days
These orbs of speaking light had known
No worship which mere wonder pays,
And orient verse hath often shown;

For oh! their beauty, radiance, power,
Which seem'd oracularly bright,
Such myst'ry wove at midnight hour
That gods they grew to heathen sight.

Yet not by us, in Christ renew'd,
Pure members of His Body made,
Are heaven's bright miracles so view'd,
Though dazzling be their spell display'd.

We love them! for indeed they look
So placid, mournful, pale and mild,
That when we read Night's starry book,
We spell it, like a lisping child.

Like gleaming Apparitions sent,
They beckon man on high, to see
His home ensphères yon firmament,
That shines in starr'd eternity.

And tears will often through the eyes
Distill the heart, and make us seem
As though we sail'd cerulean skies,
Unbodied in some astral dream!

But more than sentiment and song
The host of heaven from hearts excite,
Who feel that to such orbs belong
Deep lustres which excel the light.

For, can we not pure incense bring
To Him, the bright and Morning Star?
Some anthems round His cradle sing,
Surpassing eastern magi far?

Though jewell'd mines we cannot give,
Not ours, but us, Emmanuel claims;
And if on Him by love we live,
His breastplate bears our chosen names.

---

* Deut. xxix. 29.

Be ours the incense of a soul,
  Through faith and fellowship divine
Rising beyond where planets roll,—
  And richer than Arabia's mine.

True sacrifice is love alone:
  And worship from unwav'ring Hearts,
To Him Who wields creation's throne
  A throb of finite bliss imparts.*

Without it, vile are myrrh and gold,
  And vain the swell of soaring word,—
For He who can our thought behold,
  A loveless prayer has never heard.

So may the church to Christ present
  Our body, spirit, soul, and all,
That truth and grace omnipotent
  May us elected children call.

Such worship will be hail'd on high
  Where uncreated glories shine,
When heavenward soars the wafted sigh
  Which meekly warbles, "Christ is mine.

"In life and death, my Lord, Thou art,
  Celestial Prophet, Priest, and King!
True incense is a grateful heart,
  And this makes all my love can bring."

CHRIST OUR PORTION.

"There is none on earth I desire besides thee."—*Ps.* lxxiii. 25. "The Lord is the portion of mine inheritance."—*Ps.* xvi. 5. "Your life is hid with Christ in God."—*Colos.* iii. 3.

Whom have I in the heavens but Thee
Adoring faith desires to see,
Divinely pure and perfect fair
Whom all Thy works and words declare?

The heavenliness of heaven art Thou,
Who bor'st the curse upon Thy brow;
And round the Throne no glories shine
Which issue not from Thee, or Thine.

Imbruted Minds, that think, nor pray,
Basking in pleasure's sensual ray,—
No cloud appears to shade their sky,
And nothing tells them Sin must die!

Yet, soon the lying spell recedes,
The worm awakes, and conscience bleeds
When sickness chokes the ebbing breath,
And life is darken'd into death.

Oh, in that hour of shudd'ring prayer
Eternity from God may glare,
And luridly emerge from hell
Secrets, and Shapes, no tongue can tell!

Lord of true bliss, in joy and health
Be Thou our wisdom, hope, and wealth;
Without Thee, vain are creatures all!—
A universe we nothing call

If center'd not in this high creed,
That God alone can help our need;
Christ in the creature is the goal
Of all which should attract the soul.

The Lord our true perfection is,
Both law of Being, and the bliss;
Dark, dead, and cold, creation seems,
If not enrobed with sacred gleams

Caught from the Presence, and the power
Of Christ, who hallows scene and hour,
Matter and mind, and makes them good,
By showing each with heaven imbued.

Friendship and love, though pure and deep,
Can echo not lone cares which sleep
Unsyllabled within the mind,
And shun the gaze of mortal kind.

And shifting hues there play of thought,
And feelings with devotion fraught,
Dejected hours, and voiceless moods
When souls are thinking solitudes,—

Sigh, tear, nor language then reveals
The awful gloom pale conscience feels,
When man's o'erburden'd heart within
Bows with eternity, and sin.

Alone we live, alone we die,
Unfathom'd by no human eye,
But search'd by Him, whose wisdom can
Peruse the depths of inward man.

Thus, orphan'd Souls who cannot see
On earth one source of sympathy,
Whose hearts unecho'd pray and beat,
Are answer'd at the Mercy-Seat,

Where Heaven's incarnate Love replies
To each mysterious heart that sighs,
And while unwitness'd tear-drops fall,
In grace descends, and dries them all.

God in the mind makes glory there,
The spring of thought, the source of prayer;
From Whom adoring saints derive
Stern grace against themselves to strive.

* Isa. liii. 11.

Let God then thy religion be,
And not religion, God to thee:
Without Him, worlds would leave us poor,
And with Him, who can want for more?

ANGELS.

"Of the Angels he saith, Who maketh his Angels spirits, and his ministers a flame of fire."—*Heb.* i. 7.
"Some have entertained Angels unawares."—*Heb.* xiii. 2.

Ye bright-wing'd Choir! who in the rays
Which beautify yon realm of glory,
Delight to read in rich amaze,
The archives of redemption's story,—
More magical your lustres seem
Than ever crowded poet's dream.

Before the countless stars began
To glisten through the dewy air,
Or Heaven perceived adoring man
Ascend her crystal height with prayer,
Your beaming Shapes, around the Throne,
Ages of wordless joy had known.

Serene, and passionless, and pure,
Unshaded by the hue of sin,
No discord can the will allure
To mar each moral tone within,—
That melody of sainted love,
The pulse of bliss which beats above.

Dread Angels! who excel in strength,
And sung creation's birthday song,
Or, through the world's unmeasured length
In viewless splendour wing'd along,—
When God commands them, glide and go,
With speed that proves the lightning slow!

Stern ministers of sacred wrath,
How often their avenging hands
Emptied God's vials o'er the path
Of guilt, and atheistic lands,
When blood and blasphemy began
To render earth a hell for man.

Yon cities, cinder'd by the burst
Of red destruction's rolling flame;
The myriads by the plague accurst,
Whose ruin darken'd David's name;
And banner'd hosts, which in one night
Were blasted by resistless blight,—

Oh! these reveal how dread and vast
In bodiless and bright array
Such Angels are, who have not cast
Their crowns of innocence away;
But ranged before the Godhead, still,
Brighten as each obeys His will.

And when we turn to that high Word
Where Christ, and church, and christian meet,
Are not emotions deeply stirr'd,
To mark above the Mercy-Seat
How studious Angels bend and strain,
To see what truths its depths contain?

Confirm'd, tho' not redeem'd by Him,
Lord of the radiant hosts above,
Legions of loyal seraphim
In Christ concenter all their love;
Thus saints and angels both combine
To chant the praise of Blood Divine.

And bless'd as beautiful the thought,
That when man's rebel-heart they see
Repent for sin the soul hath wrought,
They arch their wings in ecstasy;
While louder, louder swells the tone
These harpers chant around the Throne!

And is not earth the haunt and home
Of mysteries more than sense descries,
Where viewless Spirits round us roam,
Unvisioned by embodied eyes?—
Hence that which science never saw,
Seems more an angel than a law.

The motions of material things
So wonderful, involved, and vast,
Each hue and harmony that brings
Expression, where our looks are cast,
Serene, or exquisite, or grand,—
Some working angel may have plann'd.

And, when amid the flushing noon
Faith wanders forth in woods, or fields,
Or hearkens to the breezy tune
A choral landscape round her yields,
And thus with calm contentful eye
Drinks the deep spell of earth and sky,—

Then, dream not that impassive laws
Can e'er achieve what *mind* must do;
If each effect presumes a cause,
Let Nature have her master too;
Till all her work, beneath the sun
Seems duty, by an Angel done.

The meanest object man can view,
A herb, a pebble, or a ray
Which tints the grass with golden hue,
Might prompt poetic mind to pray;
And Faith can nothing coldly see,
If there angelic spell-work be.

And, oh ! how solemn grows the scene
  When not beheld as dumb and dead,
But one where spirits intervene,
  And such a consecration shed,
That, like a temple, common air
Inspires religion every-where !

As features in some lovely face
  Express the soul, eye cannot see,
And shadow forth with speaking grace
  Each line of sorrow, hope, or glee,—
Moved elements may oft reveal
What angels from cold sense conceal.

Thus, sun and air, and cloud-graced heaven,
  The lisping wave, or laughing wind,
With whatsoe'er to earth is given
  Attuned to man's accordant mind,
Should make us dream, where'er we stray,
Unvision'd angels throng the way.

The sunbeam in its happy toil,
  The breeze that fans an infant flower,
Those dew-falls which refresh the soil
  Or beautify a sylvan bower,—
Pure Minds with peaceful wonder fill,
Who trace them to angelic skill.

The motion of mysterious storms
  That glance and play with hectic gleam,
May be the flutter of their forms,
  The glory which their garments beam,
When, summon'd by their vast control,
The fiery tempests flash and roll !

RELIGION AND THE SEA.

"Fear God, and worship him that made the sea."—*Rev.* xiv. 7. "Jesus went unto them, walking on the sea."—*Matt.* xiv. 25.

Eternity of waters ! there Thou art,
Dear to the eye, and glorious to the heart;
Bounding in brightness as they plunge on shore,
I greet thy waves, and gladden in their roar.

Alone in grandeur, ever-living Sea !
Thou swelling anthem sung to Deity,
When thy deep thunders with a dying fall
Roll like Hosannahs to the Lord of All.

Religion only to thy power replies
And echoes back the solemn harmonies,
Which seem to tell with supernatural tone,—
Here God is reigning on His ocean-throne !

And ever, O thou Element of might !
Hast thou administer'd a dread delight
To all who heard thy loud pulsations beat,
Till shores embay'd seem'd throbbing at their feet.

Before the birth of billow, or of wind,
Thou rolledst through the Everlasting Mind
In waves hereafter destined to expand,
And bathe the shores of many a famous land.

Man rules the earth, but God upon the sea
By vast distinction doth appear to be,
Whose swelling glories baffle change and time,
And awe the conscience, like a creed sublime.

Kindred with man, deep Ocean ! movest thou,
Baring to heaven thine ever-dauntless brow;
In all the murmurs of thy mighty heart
A mystic echo of his mind thou art.*

Passion intense, and sentiment profound
In thee some answer to such moods resound;
While haunted Sadness, tender, deep, and lone,
Thrills to the pathos of thy pensive tone.

Genius and Glory, both in thee delight,
Heard in gay morn, or through the hush of night,
When, like a psalm, thy billowy tongues proclaim
How nature murmurs with her Maker's name.

And has not Painting from thy myriad views
Of liquid grace, and oceanic hues,
An inspiration for her colours caught,
Making immortal what thy spell has wrought ?

The Poet, too, in ev'ry age hath been
A solemn haunter of thy wizard scene;
In breeze, or blast, rich noon, or balmy eve,
To him thy waves cathedral-anthems weave.

He can interpret thine impassion'd mood,
And sympathise with sea-made solitude;
By rock and bay, or sanded beach can roam
And feel immensity his proper home.

Nor need we tell how Commerce hath supplied
An empire's storehouse from the wafting tide,
Since on thy waters, far as winds can flee,
Her boundless treasures are attain'd by Thee.

Still less doth Valour need victorious lyres
To sing how Britain's heart the sea inspires :—
The Isle of Freedom is the friend of waves,
That field of battle where the world she braves !

---

* Isa. lvii. 20.

And will not heroes of the Cross who roam,
Far from the spells which bind the heart to home,
To tell the heathen how the Lord is King,
Chants of true glory to old Ocean bring?—

Majestic, lone, and melancholy Sea!
Sprung from thy God in dread immensity,
For aye art thou to reverential mind
A floating wonder by no words defined.

A vast eternity in endless flow
Thine image wears; and in thy depths below
How sleep the young, the beautiful, and brave,
Till the last trumpet shall unclose their grave!

Farewell! thou symbol of almighty grace,
Whose deeps adumbrate * what for our lost race
Mercy provides, when pardon's hush'd abyss
Engulphs the guilt which loads a world like this.

Eternal seem'st thou till th' Archangel rings
A blast that summons all created things;
Then rise the dead from out thy dismal roar,
And Time shall gaze upon the sea no more! †

* Micah vii. 19. † Rev. xx. 1.

IDOLS IN THE HEART.

"These men set up their idols in their heart."—*Ezek.* xiv. 3. "Little children, keep yourselves from idols."—1 *John* v. 21.

THERE was a time, in ages dead,
When temples huge and vile
Their lowering fronts of darkness spread
O'er Albion's sea-wall'd isle.

But Christ by His apostles came
To preach the word divine,
And, lo! before truth's living flame
Dissolved each idol-shrine.

And now, a Church maternal opes
Her arms of christian love,
Embracing with their new-born hopes
Bright children for above.

And by her sacraments and rites,
Her discipline and care,
Calm vigil, fast, and chaste delights,
And pure diurnal prayer,

With whatsoe'er of secret grace
The Lord to her commits,
She strives to rear a heavenly race,
And each for glory fits.

But oh, these hearts we poorly scan
If idols none are seen;
Their temple is that inner man
Where God's own gaze hath been!

Eye cannot pierce, nor ear perceive
What buried thoughts avow;
Yet souls, who dare the Spirit grieve,
Must to some idol bow.

We shudder when Christ's heroes find
Myriads in pagan gloom,
With poison'd heart, and palsied mind,
And conscience like a tomb:

Such tale when holy Mission tells,
Demands the Church's tear;
And who can hear of demon-spells
Nor throb with sacred fear?

But, are not souls baptised a home
For God enshrined within? *
Father and Spirit, do they come
To reign o'er self and sin?

Yet, what if our base idol be
Desire, instead of God?
Proud will,—a strong divinity
That rules us with a rod?

Say, are we not, before the eye
Of Him who fathoms thought,
Idolators, whose hearts deny
The God our fathers sought?

We need not by the stumbling-block
Of wood, or stone, or gold,
Discerning reason madly shock
With shapes which men behold;

Idolatry depraves the Will,
Our idols are desires,
When once our breast some passion fills
Which aught, save God, inspires.

It may be, that the crown of praise,
The wreath proud genius wears,
A warrior's plume, or poet's bays
Excite ambition's prayers;

* John xiv. 23.

Or, forms of love, whose grace becomes
The bloom and breath of all
We value in these earthly homes,—
May weave our inward thrall;

A husband in the wife may see
A heaven of human charms;
Or, he to her, life's angel be,
A shield from daily harms;

Or infant beauty, like a ray
From her own being sent,
To mother's love, may night and day
Impart too deep content:

Whate'er the guise, or winning name
Our bosom-idols take,
Strange incense with our altar-flame
Is blent, when we forsake

That God who claims the heart alone
For His peculiar shrine:—
A creature must not mount the Throne
Where rules a Love divine.

Heirs of the Spirit, are we not
Anointed sons of grace?
Alas! if our celestial lot
By treason we efface.

To some base darling of desire,
Some earth-made god of sin,
Shall censers hold unhallow'd fire,
By passion breathed within?

Oh, better far that love and life,
With hope, and peace, and joy,
Howe'er with seeming mercy rife,
Some blast from heaven destroy;

Better be friendless, aidless, lone,
With none to weep our woes,
Than let some idol seize that throne
Sworn faith to Jesu owes.

For what is there, on this side hell,
Which so like hell appears?—
A doom of dooms! no tongue can tell,
Thus rolling on our ears,

"Ephraim * to idols hath his heart
From God and glory turn'd,—
Let him alone, and be his part
The solitude he earn'd!"

* Hos. iv. 17.

INFANTS AND INFANCY.

"Out of the mouths of babes and sucklings thou hast perfected praise."—*Matt.* xxi. 16.

The dew-drop, in whose mirror lies
A miniature of morning skies;
The violet-bud which blooms in spring,
The flower-bee on its fairy wing,
The broken lisp of some shy brook
That babbles in a shady nook,

All that is fragile, coy, and fair,
As types of beauty, may declare
The cherub-loveliness that seems
To mantle those embodied dreams,
Sweet infants! when their baby forms
Come forth to face life's gloomy storms.

Oh! I can watch, and almost weep
To view some angel-child asleep;
To mark the alabaster brow
Where sinless calm is brooding now,
Or see the silken fringe that lies
And covers its innocuous eyes.

So have I stood, and heard each breath
Like music in melodious death,
And soft and slow it swells and heaves,
And at each fall such cadence leaves,
As may to pious fancy seem
A sigh for Glory in its dream.

There is a purity which plays
In the quick gleam of infant's gaze,
That innocence of heaven-born light
Which beams for vulgar sense too bright,—
A lustrous depth whose dazzling spells
Are richer than the blue gazelle's.

'Tis now the budding dawn of mind,
Ere the worn heart grows weak and blind;
The orient blush of radiant thought
Ere life is with those shadows fraught
Experience unto manhood brings,
Or sorrow round cold memory flings!

To see them in glad sunbeams play
As bounding and as bright as they,
Or, like young wavelets laugh and sing,
Or romp like breezes wild of wing
Exulting over fields and flowers,
When May-time leads the lovely hours,—

Oh, this can melt the heart, and make
Maturer life new colours take,
A sentiment of vernal hue,
Which softens down each sterner view

Till Age becomes a child again,
Encircled by some infant train !

But yet, a holier chain there is,
The glory of maternal bliss,
When first the blossom'd mind is heard,
In pretty lisp and prattled word,
While, peering through a curious eye,
It longs to measure earth and sky.

And, beautiful beyond compare
An infant kneeling down to prayer !
When, lifting up its little hands,
The soul beyond the age expands,
And, touch'd by God's baptismal grace,
Adores bright Mercy face to face.

And Infancy hath inward speech,
A mental life, man cannot reach ;
For, intercourse of grace may be
Between a babe and Deity,
Too rapt and raised for oral sign,
And deeper than our thoughts divine.

There's something holy in a child,
Ere yet by darken'd years defiled,
When lip, and brow, and cheek declare
'Tis fit for Jesu's arms in prayer ;
And when to God and glory given,
Though born on earth, it breathes of heaven.

PARADISE OF THE DEAD.

"He is not a God of the dead, but of the living; for all live unto him."—*Luke* xx. 38. "Absent from the body, present with the Lord."—2 *Cor.* v. 8. "This day shalt thou be with me in Paradise."—*Luke* xxiii. 43. "The general assembly of the first-born—the spirits of just men made perfect."—*Heb.* xii. 23.

The dead in body are in soul alive ;
Distinct locality to them belongs ;
No more, like us, with sin and woe they strive,
But in those bowers, where rest the white-robed throng
With garments by atoning Blood made clean,—*
Behold ! pure Spirits who on earth have been.

In years departed, Superstition dared
That veil to ruffle with irrev'rent hand,
Behind whose folds lie undeclared
Secrets no bodied nature understands ;
For there in awful shades, our God alone
Wields His dread sceptre, and holds back His throne !

* Rev. vii. 14.

But we are sense-blind, and too much adore
The painted dreams which time and space befall ;
Full seldom do our hearts the dead restore,
Or back their features into life recall ;
Their tombs like portals to oblivion were,
That closed upon us, when we laid them there.

Material life the sad horizon makes
Of half a worldling's creed pronounces true ;
In soul a Sadducee, his reason takes
No holier vision and no higher view,
Than poor realities, which Flesh discerns,
And earth-sprung feeling into glory turns.

But Minds exist to whom the dead are dear ;
Still in warm memory lives th' unburied past :
Their grief is something nobler than the tear
Impassion'd Feeling on their coffin cast;—
The disembodied to the heart and home,
Oft in pale dreams of resurrection come.

Shame on our souls ! if narrow earth enclose
Spirits which have eternity to range ;
If ne'er beyond the tomb a Christian throws
A thought which images their blest exchange,
Who neither bound, nor barr'd by blinding sense,
Reap in rapt bliss what Light and Love dispense.

A conscious portion of the Church are they
Who speed before us to the realm unknown ;
Although no longer in the beams of day
They lift their brow, and call this life their own,
Yet do they all to that One Christ pertain,
Who out of dust shall rear their forms again.

Nor, let the worshipper of sense, who binds
To this base world an eagle-spirit down,
And only in the realm of Epicurus finds
His grandest sceptre and his brightest crown,—
Reflect on Hades, where the dead repose,
As whelm'd with darkness in a land of woes :

'Tis worse than pitiful, when men presume
Our God to limit to this world of crime ;
Who call it vacancy beyond the tomb,
And make eternity succumb to time !
Whereas the Spirit, when unearth'd and free,
Is far diviner than this life can be.

Think on the numbers who to Christ have fled,
From babes too beautiful on earth to stay,
To those departing with a hoary head,
Beside whose couch 'twas heaven to watch and pray;—
Myriads which no created mind can count,*
Complete the glory of that great amount.

And could we gaze beyond an earth-bound screen,
No barren solitude our eyes would view;
But, all empeopled with a host serene
The world of spirits would emerge as true,
And far more vital, glowing quick with mind,
Than this dull orb the Dead have left behind.

And oh! bethink thee, pilgrim, sad and lone,
Musing through capitals, where Ages dead
Lie sepulchred, and riven arch and stone
Reveal what desolation's curse hath bred,—
That all who throng'd some immemorial street,
Are mingled souls which now in Hades meet.

So, when thou linger'st on some battle-plain
Dyed by red carnage once, where Nations fell,
While banner'd thousands heard the iron rain
Of death-shot round about them roar, and swell,—
The spirits who that crimson light did face,
Are yet alive, and fill their destined place,†

And in the churchyard, where some grassy mound
In trampled ruin all unweeded stands,
Or sculptured aisles, where marble tombs abound
And memory ponders while the mind expands,

* Rev. vii. 9.

† As the Author finds he has here unconsciously copied from himself, he ventures to append an extract, which may be probably unknown to the general reader.

"But, deep the thought! momentously sublime,
To think,—that not one pulse of conscious mind
A Will Divine hath ever caused to play
In human being, hath a single rest
Experienced, since its primal throb began.
The spirit-people of the Land Unseen,
Millions on millions though their number be,
Are conscious,—more than when by flesh encased,
And clogg'd in action: not a Soul's extinct!
Still Adam thinks; still Alexander feels;
Cæsar hath being; Cleopatra lives;
And those crown'd butchers whom the world calls brave,
Are feeling more than when they battles fought:
Yes, all who *have* been,—great, or good, or vile,
Patriarchs, prophets, and the lords of mind,
Heroes and warriors, and those laurell'd priests
Of truth, the poets of eternity," &c. &c.

"LUTHER," *Sixth Edition.*

Till saints and warriors, heroes, martyrs, all
Speak out of stone, and to the living call,—

Forget not, while the vaulted nave is trod,
That each unbodied is a thinking Soul
Under the blessing or the ban of God,
Replete with life, as when their felt control
By sceptred majesty, or moving speech,
The heart of empires and of men did reach.

Thus should we speculate on parted Mind,
And speak with tones of reverential truth,
Whene'er the screening veil of sense behind
Religion enters, and on age and youth
Dreams with pale awe, and hails the sumless host
Who still are loved, and not to faith the lost.

Yes, be our epitaphs of brighter cast,
And take our elegies a purer tone,
Nor speak, as if corporeal life surpass'd
The consciousness a spirit calls its own:—
Mere flesh can moulder, yet the Soul survives,
And in that thought there breathe immortal lives!

SUBLIME OF PRAYER.

"I beseech thee, show me thy glory."
Exod. xxxiii. 18.

Heroic guide of Judah's race
Who saw Jehovah face to face,
Sublime of men!—behold him now,
As there enshrined, within the cloud
Which wraps him like a burning shroud,
He boldly breathes the prayer, "O God, unveil Thy brow.

"Eternal! in the flaming sign
What though I saw dread beams combine,
When Sinai's bush was clothed with fire,
Or on Thy cloudy pillar gazed,—
Yet when the riven mountain blazed
With Thy descending pomp, I dared for more aspire!

"And I have fasted, pray'd, and felt
For forty days my being melt
With wand'ring awe, as Thou didst trace
That 'Pattern' whose mysterious plan
O'erveil'd the future Christ for man,
And prophesied in types, the hidden truths of grace.

"And I have heard that thunder-tone
Which thrills high angels round the throne,—

The rollings of celestial Voice;
And seen unearthly lightnings play,
Which lit me up that rocky way
When Thy dread law decreed for life, or death, the choice.

"And now, I would no symbol see,
But gaze on full-orb'd Deity;
Thy glory let me witness now:
God of my soul! before I die,
Centre on Thee my thirsting eye,
And let Thy lustres bright through all my being flow!"

So prayed the meek, but yet the bold
Giant of grace, who would behold
The Self Eternal!—God reveal'd
Not in the shadow, nor the sign,
But in deep radiance all-divine,
Where dwells the viewless God, all gloriously conceal'd.

It was, indeed, a prayer sublime
Surpassing all conceived in time,
Or nature,—scaling that dread height
Where Attributes are searchless things,
And Seraphim reverse their wings,
And shrink, and shudder back, before Essential Light.

Yet, God is moved by mighty prayer;
And Moses found his answer there,
When ark'd within the cloven side
Of Horeb's sacramental rock,—
Jehovah "passed" him, while the shock
Of glory shook the soul, till awed Convulsion cried.*

But we, who with reverted gaze
Can rend the veil of typic days,
May in the Church a glory view
Outshining far what Moses saw,
When God in thunder gave the law,
And lightnings red and fierce around Mount Tabor flew.

And is not this the prayer intense
Of all, who soar above what sense
And self and sin combine to claim,—
That more and more meek hearts may rise
To vision with prophetic eyes
What hidden splendours haunt Jehovah's hallowed name?

Divine ambition must be ours;
And faith so form the mental powers
Under Emmanuel's teaching grace,
That love in earth, and sea, and air,
May find reflected ev'ry-where
The glories which effulged before great Moses' face.

And how seraphic proves the spell
In those deep hearts, which love to dwell
Within the inner shrine of things!—
Who can all scenes in Christ behold,
And see, as in bright trance unroll'd,
The charms He there unveils, beyond what poet sings.

Standard and type for all who pray,
Be this the liturgy we say
To Him who hears the spirit cry,
"Thy deeper glories, God! unshroud;
Break, I beseech Thee, break the cloud,
And on Thyself unveil'd, oh, let me rest mine eye."

The highest saint who heavenward soar'd,
Prophet, or priest, who God adored,
In this vast prayer their motto find:
Such Hearts will hunger, Lord of grace!
To look upon Thy perfect face,
And in that light supreme to love all human kind.

REPENTANCE.

"Repent ye, for the kingdom of heaven is at hand."
Matt. iii. 2.

Wake, power divine, awake!
Arm of the Lord! arise,
And from our spirit take
The mist which round it lies;
Each blinding shade of self dispel
That veils the sin we love so well.

Stern Preacher of the wild!
Enrobed with camel-hair,
Convince cold hearts defiled,
And melt them into prayer;
Through conscience be thy thunder sent,—
"Arise! cold sleeper, and repent."

Bold lightnings of reproof
Through each dead conscience dart,
Till we no more aloof
From heaven shall hide the heart:
E'en as of old, Judéa heard,
Be all our souls with anguish stirr'd.

---

* Exod. xxxiv. 5, 8.

Lift, brave Elijah, now
  That voice of dauntless truth!
Till shame upon each brow
  Of weeping age and youth
Shall print the scarlet blush that tells
What pang in deep repentance dwells.

Thine axe,* Conviction, lay
  Down to the roots of thought,
Until Remorse shall pray
  O'er all vile sin hath wrought:
For that which love doth not inspire
Must perish in God's penal fire.

And let repentance prove
  Its vigour by the fruit;
That cannot spring from love
  Which doth not bud, and shoot,
And by a life of tears and prayers
Attest the change God's will declares.

Thy fan, O Spirit! wield,
  And purge the chaff-strewn floor,
Until the garner yield
  Of wheat a precious store;
Baptised with fire, so let us be,
And bid our hearts resemble Thee.

"Repent ye!"—'tis the cry
  By conscience echoed back;
From earth and vaulted sky
  Along our sin-worn track,
We hear its awful cadence roll
Like thunder through our warnèd soul.

Nor let religious pride
  On fruitless names repose;
For heaven hath aye denied
  A faith of forms and shows,
And, rather than rank falsehood own,
Will raise a seed from out the stone.†

"Repent!"—again we hear
  That cry of just alarm;
And let it shake the soul with fear,
  To rouse the opiate charm
Which lulls the hypocrite to death,
And cheats him to his latest breath.

Repentance!—what is life
  But matter fit for tears?
Since, all we are is rife
  With worse than what appears:
If tried without, men are but sin;
Yet God discerns the heart within!

* Matt. iii. 10. † Matt. iii. 9.

Our virtues oft are self,
  In bland disguise conceal'd;
Our charities to pelf
  Some wretched incense yield,
And holy graces are at best
But weakness by religion dress'd.

Repent we then!—yet, where?
  Not as Iscariot did;
But by the Cross in prayer
  Be our deep anguish hid:
On Jesus gaze we,* till the sight
Shall melt our hearts, and make them white.

Repentance stern and true
  Exceeds all common woe:
Despair for crime may rue
  And scalding tear-drops flow,
But Self in this alone abounds,—
Repentance rests on nobler grounds.

What is it but a change
  By Godhead work'd within?
A principle whose range
  Subdues the love of sin?
'Tis man renew'd, and heaven resought,
With hate for what our guilt has wrought.

And what can *this* create?
  Not all the powers of earth;
The perfect forms of good and great
  In wisdom, truth, or worth;—
Not heaven with glory, hell with pain
Could sinful man for God regain!

The faintest sin defies
  A universe to crush
The strength which in it lies;
  And so, 'twill madly rush
Downward to face th' infernal deep
Where blasted spirits burn and weep.

But, oh, there is a Power
  This granite of the heart
To soften, in that hour
  Ere conscience may depart,—
Atoning Love, through guilt forgiven,
The rescued heart can raise to heaven!

Such pure contrition springs
  From Mercy's bleeding charm,
Whose soft compulsion wrings
  The soul with safe alarm;
And thus, when wrought by Christ above
Repentance works by weeping love.†

* Zech. xii. 10. † Gal. v. 6.

HEARTS WHICH HAVE NO ECHOES.

"The heart knoweth his own bitterness; and a stranger doth not intermeddle with his joy."—*Prov.* xiv. 10.

Some hearts lie wither'd in their transient spring
Long ere the yellow leaf of change began;
Seldom to them may human summer bring
A beaming welcome from the soul of man.

Cinctured as by a preternatural spell,
Languid their pulse of low dejection beats;
Yet none who mark their smile-clad face, could tell
How dark the mood which back from man retreats!

And what, though circumstance may seem
To gladden life with fortune's envied glow,
Or on their brow some bright delusion beam,
Hiding the haunted gloom that reigns below,—

They bear a burden language could not speak,
They feel depression too profound for tears,
And blush to fancy a betrayful cheek
Should wear the paleness of their inward fears.

Yet, say not such sad martyrs of the mind
Are fever'd by ambition's vulgar fret;
Nor think they loathe the love of human kind,
Or hate warm hours when echoing souls are met.

But in them dwells the hush'd and voiceless thought,
How all which reigns without, or rules within,
With grave-like hollowness is ever fraught,
Or, canker'd through with selfishness and sin.

And oft the bitterness of secret pride
Rankles beneath the play of baffled will,
While Feeling, wounded by some fate denied,
Bleeds at the root, though all without look still.

And moods they cherish, passionate as deep,
And wing'd desires that eagle-like would soar,
Which never waken from their wordless sleep,
But prey upon the spirit more and more.

And when quick minds, electrically strung
As though each chord of feeling moved on fire,
Some pang would tell,—how oft the fearful tongue
Has felt each accent on the lip expire!

And thus there is a loneliness of heart,
In all deep souls a never-enter'd shrine,
Where neither love nor friendship takes a part,
Which no eyes witness, but, Jehovah! Thine.

But shall we mourn, that each is circled round
With veiling mystery from the ken of man?
That waters deep within the soul abound
No word has fathom'd, and no wisdom can?

No, rather let such merciful disguise
Move the just thinker unto grateful prayer;
For who could live beneath terrestrial eyes,
If such could witness *all* secreted there!

And if no mantle by our God were thrown
Round fallen souls, to hide man's world within,
How should we hate, what now we love to own,
And cry for darkness to conceal our sin!

None are so chaste, unselfish, and sincere,
As not to feel the taint of Adam's fall;
So, heaven in mercy hides that inmost sphere
Where each dreads each, and all would censure all.

Yet beats One Heart all other hearts above,
Whose sympathy no human errors tire,
E'en Thine, pure Lord of uncreated love,
Incarnate Semblance of The heavenly Sire!

There, may we prove deep tenderness divine,
And yet, so human that it wept and sigh'd;
And when to coldness burden'd hearts incline,
Haste we to Him, who loved us till He died.

There is no self in that almighty Heart,
No changing motion in the casual will,
For Thou, Lord Christ! celestial mercy art,
And though we shun Thee, Thou art gracious still.

O balmy thought! which, like nocturnal dews
Whose silver freshness stars the herbless plain,
When worse than midnight shades our mental views
Recalls Emmanuel to the mind again.

Others may gaze with half-averted eyes,
Coldly may spurn, or scan the woe we feel,
But o'er His heart are breathed our inward sighs,*
And through His breast our veil'd emotions steal.

* Isa. lxiii. 9.

Nor can one shade of sorrow clothe the cheek,
Nor tear-drop from the spirit-fountain roll,
But He interprets what no tongue can speak,
And reads the thinking volume of our soul.

Here boast the saints, what no bright seraph can,—
That they have sympathy upon the Throne;
Christ loves the Angel, but he feels for man,
Whose very nature hath become his Own.

No hearts beat echoless, if they believe
A more than Brother * in yon heavens is theirs,
Who loves them most when all alone they grieve;
And with His incense can perfume their prayers.

His love is greater than our heart, and knows
What secret burden loads the inward sigh;
And wordless pangs to Him are open woes,
Clear as the glories which emblaze the sky.

Dear Lord! be ever thus our Friend divine,
Our Anchor sure while rocking tempests roll,
And when departing into hands like Thine,
Relume Thy promise,† and receive the Soul.

INSPIRATION OF THE PAST.

"Your fathers, where are they? And the prophets, do they live for ever?"—*Zech.* i. 5. "God . . . . in time past, spake unto the fathers."—*Heb.* i. 1.

OUR fathers, where are they,
The prophets of the past?—
Like solemn dreams, long flown away,
And with th' eternal class'd!

Those patriarchs of the soul
Of lion heart and mien,
Scorning the world's depraved control,
They hallow'd history's scene;

Heroes of faith and prayer,
They fought salvation's fight,
Ready to do, and boldly dare,
When God reveal'd the right.

* Heb. ii. 11. † Ps. xxiii. 4.

Such were those mental sires
Who made our English mind,
Whose page the saintly heart inspires,
Whose words entrance mankind.

Yes! they, indeed, were men
Of loftiness divine;
And not till such shall breathe again,
Will British glory shine.

We want majestic hearts
Like those which burn'd and bled,
When Rome, with her resistless arts,
Denied the Church's Head.

The dungeon, steel, and stake,
A bloody doom, or block,
Not one of these their vow could break,
When summon'd to the shock.

Peaceful as lambs, as lions brave,
The saints of hoary time,—
Still may we hear them from the grave
Preach with a voice sublime.

Their tongues are tipp'd with fire,
Their accent sounds the free,
And into us such men inspire
Their own eternity.

RELIGION OF THE YOUNG.

"Remember now thy Creator, in the days of thy youth, while the evil days come not."—*Eccles.* xii. 1.

AND wilt thou bring a virgin heart,
And lay it on the shrine
Of holy Love, that so the part
Of Mary may be thine?—
Retreat beneath the Saviour's eye,
And to His tones of heaven reply,
While outward breath, or inward sigh
Adores Him as divine.

Then may thy youth securely rest
On more than earth bestows;
Eternity within thy breast
Already throbs, and glows;
Thou hast, ere sin the breast alloy,
That colour of celestial joy
Which brighten'd o'er the sainted boy,
Whose cry, "Speak, Lord!" arose.*

* 1 Sam. iii. 10.

He, to the Temple when a child
By his dear mother brought,
Ere manhood's guilt the heart defiled
With years of sinful thought,
Like a young priest his ephod wore;
And on his girdled form he bore
The truth of all meek Hannah swore,*
When she the Lord besought.

Thus, in the vernal prime of youth
How blest are they who bring
Their souls a sacrifice for truth,
And round Christ's altar sing!
Ere shades of evil darkness fall,
Like folds of that primeval pall
Which, soon or late, envelops all
On earth now wandering.

Age has not loosed the silver cord,
Nor at the fountain-head
Doth Weariness pronounce the word,
"My pleasant things are fled!"
For still around, hope's morning dews
Fall freshly on thy fairy views,
And Nature wears those lust'rous hues
O'er life by feeling spread.

In youth there breathes a vital bloom,
A buoyancy and glow
Which seem to triumph o'er the tomb
And gladden off dull woe;
Elate as lofty, swells the hope
That longs with dangers firm to cope,
And ever round some daring scope
An eager glance to throw.

When years have cast their blighting frown
And wither'd prospects pine,
While on the head Time's hoary crown
Betrays old age is thine,
Then, sinner! 'tis a rueful sight,
To view thee through thy heart's deep night
In horror seek that saving light
Which flows from truth divine.

It is not, that a dread "too late!"
By mortal dare be sigh'd;
For never to a brother's fate
Be hope of heaven denied:
But, oh! methinks when harrowing fears
Haunt the dark mind, and bitter tears
Like drops of anguish damp the years
Of those who God defied;

When memory's weak, and conscience quails,
And life's gay tone is dead,
While hideous doubts the heart assail
By base experience bred,
'Tis awful on Death's couch to find
Some ruin'd Shape of woe reclined,
Sick of the world, but unresign'd
In dust to lay his head.

Divinest Spirit! truthful Lord,
May youth remember Thee,
And gladly in Thy glorious word
A bright hereafter see:—
There, bloom the Canaans of the young,
There, fields with hallow'd fruitage hung,
Richer than God's own poets sung
Should wave in Galilee.*

Thy grace bestow, that vestal hearts
May more and more be given
To Thee and Thine, ere youth departs
From God,—by passion driven
Along that dark and dismal way
Where virtues into vices stray,
Which tempt polluted souls to say
"Earth makes my only heaven!"

* 1 Sam. i 11; ii. 18.

* Isa. lxv. 17.

SYMPATHY OF CHRIST.

"Cast thy burden upon the Lord, and he shall sustain thee."—*Ps.* lv. 22.

Go, cast thy burden on the Lord,
Thou laden Bosom! dark and lone;
Nor deem thyself by Him unheard
Whose heart beats human on the Throne.

A Man of sorrows and of tears
The Saviour once was like to thee,
And learn'd to face those mortal fears
Which pierced His soul with sympathy.

'Tis thus we mark Him, homeless, sad,
A Pilgrim whose mysterious lot
Was shunn'd by all the gay and glad,
Unfelt, unpitied, and forgot.

Yet learnt He thus from finite woe
What heaven's calm glories could not teach,—
For there, no tides of anguish flow,
And no dark cares that kingdom reach.

And is it not a whelming thought,
That Christ should leave His heavenly throne
To be on earth affliction taught,
And suffer more than flesh hath shown!

Oh, had He in yon realm of bliss
But simply fathom'd what we feel,
Could mortals from their sad abyss
To Him as brother now appeal?

But when we read His matchless life
That wept, and sigh'd, and sorrow'd o'er
The heavy pangs of human strife,
And all which burning conscience bore,

Such life becomes a lovely proof
That into His deep bosom pass'd
Experience, which can ne'er aloof
From pilgrims now on earth be class'd.

Nor deem, that when on high He soar'd
And o'er the radiant heavens retired,
By chanting hosts to be adored
Whose hymns are by His Blood inspired,

What here below as Man He felt,
Is now engulph'd in bliss eterne;—
Still through His heart emotions melt,
And in Him pure affections burn.

His regal crown is all divine,
And glory-flames engird Him now,
But Faith beholds Him still the same,
For human feelings line His brow.

And thus, O weary, wand'ring soul,
By tempest worn, and toss'd, and tried,
Though surging waves around thee roll,
Thine anchor is The Crucified!

Thy sin confess, each sorrow tell,
Bold on His love thy burden cast,
In heaven Who yet remembers well
The storms through which on earth He pass'd.

A mother may her babe forget,
An exile ne'er his home recall,
Nor orphan'd child the hour regret
Which reft him of parental all:

But, oh, whate'er the scene or clime,
Devotion may Emmanuel see,
Whose heart expands o'er man, and time,
Who bled for our eternity!

Yes, sympathies intense and deep
Surpassing all our souls contain,
Still through His breast in glory sweep,
And shall for ever glow and reign.

A sinless Lord, yet touch'd in heart
With all which blighted moments bear,
In heaven, O Priest divine! Thou art
A man-God, with our feelings,* there!

By gentleness, by grief, and grace,
By depth of sigh, and tears profound,
Faith views Thee to our fallen race
In links of loving union bound.

Both heaven and earth in Thee combine
In Whom that mystic wound † appears,
Which gash'd in death Thy Form divine,
And crimson'd it with gory tears.

Then, lay thy burden on the Lord
Child of dejection! pale and lone;
Thou canst not sigh by Him unheard,
Whose heart throbs human on His throne.

NO PEACE FOR THE WICKED.

"There is no peace, saith my God, to the wicked."
Isa. lvii. 21.

How like a spirit shrieks the startled Wind,
As though the air to agony were torn,
When conscience hears it with a haunted mind,
Waking at midnight, fearful and forlorn!

No peace apart from purity abides,
Deep in the heart some dark unrest will be;
Though calmest azure gild the ocean-tides,
Stern are the currents which no eye can see.

What, if the world, that sees by sense alone,
Seldom below the surface of our smiles
Surveys the secrets which to God are shown,
Believes mock gladness which the truth beguiles;

Resounding bursts of Bacchanalian joy
Oft though they ring from out the Belial mind,—
Be sure there lurks some unbetray'd alloy
Of sad rebuke, yon gilded face behind!

The peace of sinners is the trance of death,
The putrid stillness of a stagnant tomb;
Or like the pause before some parting breath
Which shakes and shudders o'er eternal doom.

---

* Heb. iv. 15. † Rev. i. 7; v. 6.

But oft this lulling opiate of the heart,
By passion drunk while principle expires,
Fails in some hour to do its deadly part,
When Vengeance lights her agonising fires.

And thus the wicked have no vital peace,
Nothing which reason, truth, or knowledge makes;
The "Blood of Sprinkling" hath not brought release,
Nor calm'd the tempest which dark conscience shakes.

In vain may riches, rank, and power, and pride,
Fawn round the creedless heart and lawless will,
There is no heaven but in bad self denied,
And less than Godhead can no bosom fill.

Man's peace is grounded on majestic truth,
Enlightened conscience, hope, and faith-breathed prayer,
And they who seek it in hoar'd age, or youth,
Yearn for God's Holy One to guide them there.

Cold gnaws the worm which on pale conscience feeds,—
A darksome pang of dreariness within;
And oft in silence sad remembrance bleeds
O'er bosom'd stores of unrepented sin.

The grave! the grave! its horrent gloom appals
The craven souls which no atonement seek,
And from hereafter comes the hell that calls
The blood of gladness from a blooming cheek.

To guilt eternity a dread appears,
And God Himself is vision'd as a foe;
And how the Throne dark retribution rears,
Shades a bright present with prophetic woe!

Martyr in soul! with all thy painted smiles,
Hie thee at once to free salvation's ark,
And shun the snare of those satanic wiles
Which dazzle myriads into regions dark.

Lo, where The Church with mild maternal tone
Thy soul invites to share mysterious peace,*
Pure as Emmanuel once proclaim'd His own,—
Born of The Blood which purchased man's release.

* John xiv. 27.

Such is the rest, divinely rich and deep,
Beyond tempestuous waves of woe to break;
Soft as the trances of that blissful sleep
Which lull'd the Saviour on the storm-rent lake.

Let but the Spirit of the Lord descend
And o'er our bosom brood with dovelike sway,
Then shall Jehovah be our guardian friend,
Point to glad Zion, and protect the way.

So will that hollow rest poor worldlings love,
No longer o'er the cheated bosom reign;
But Peace, descending from her Prince above,
Becalm our conscience like His breath again.*

* John xx. 21, 22.

INFANT DEATH.

"Rachel, weeping for her children."—*Matt.* ii. 18.
"Thus saith the Lord, Refrain thy voice from weeping, and thine eyes from tears . . . . they shall come again from the land of the enemy."—*Jer.* xxxi. 16.

Pale mother! art thou weeping
Beside yon cradled form,
Which now reclines unsleeping
In fever's raging storm?
Fair mourner, let me feel for thee,
Engulph'd in such an agony.

Thine eyes are red with sorrow,
And sunken back with woe;
Or ever dawns to-morrow,
Thy heart will overflow,
While tears of burning anguish lave
The victim of an early grave.

Such death seems like the rushing
All sudden, fierce, and strong,
Of chainless whirlwind, crushing
The forest-boughs along;
As onward sweeps that rending blast,
Wild ruins tell its wings have pass'd.

Yet, mother! when caressing
Thy darling in thine arms,
While brooding o'er the blessing
So treasured in its charms,
Did not this dream thy soul appal,—
"Perchance my living flower must fall?"

And often, when surveying
Its mournful depth of eye,
A something seem'd arraying
Those features for the sky,—
A pensive meaning, sad and mild,
Too earthless for an earth-doom'd child.

But since the Soul hath parted,
Above that baby face
Thou bendest, broken-hearted;
For, cold as sculptured grace,
The whiteness of that cherub brow
Maternal tear-drops moisten now!

Yet be not thou repining,
And nurse the pang unmeet,
Because, no longer shining
Thy glow of love to greet,
Infantile charms and elfin ways
Are welcomed by thy doting gaze.

Like cherubim surrounding
The Throne where Jesu reigns,
With more than bliss abounding,
And touch'd by no earth-stains,—
Unbodied infants, in the blaze
Of Godhead, lisp their perfect* lays.

Nor dream, because unspoken
In flesh, the word of grace,
Thy darling had no token
Of God's paternal face;
Baptismal wonders oft infold
A germ of Christ no creeds have told.

Think not, that when translated
To realms of hallow'd bliss,
An infant can be rated
By such base world as this:
In heaven transform'd, its mind expands,
And more than scripture understands.

Then, cheer thee! stricken mother,
Let praise ennoble tears;
Thy babe has found a Brother
In yonder heaven-bright spheres;
For God's Elect, the Undefiled,
Was once on earth a cradled Child.

Though now enshrined in glory,
What here below He felt
As read in awful story,
Doth still remembrance melt;
As if the babe His bosom press'd,
For ever thrill'd That gracious Breast.

Though viewless, yet not banish'd,
Thine infant, conscious now,
From this cold world hath vanish'd
In heaven to lift its brow,
Where babes redeem'd, in radiant white
Girdle the Throne, with angels bright.

* Matt. xxi. 16.

A PERFECT WILL.

"Then cometh Jesus . . . to be baptized . . . Thus it becometh us to fulfil all righteousness."—*Matt.* iii. 13, 15.

Thou, who didst rend the heavens to be
The Man, in whom God's eye should see
A human Archetype of all
His wisdom could perfection call,
From Thy sad manger to the tomb
Through shades of grief, and storms of gloom,
Implicitly Thy passive will
Each dictate of the law did lovingly fulfil.

When Peter's rude and reinless zeal
Would fain have bade Thee scorn to feel
The pangs a felon's death must bear,
What did the Prince of Peace declare?—
"Get thee behind me, Satan! thou
Of man, not God, dost savour now;
Disciple if thou dar'st to be,
Martyr thy human will, and meekly follow me!"

The dauntless Eremite who saw
His Lord obey baptismal law,
And meekly as a lamb descend
Beneath a sacrament to bend,
And in God's mystic waters lave
A Form which came the world to save,—
At once recoil'd with holy dread,
And, gazing on the Lord, aloud in wonder said:

"Wilt Thou, by God and angels prized,
Prince of all peace! be thus baptized
By one like me, whose atom worth
Is but a speck of sinful earth?
Rather baptize me with that fire
Of holiness Thou dost respire;
Too abject am I here to stand,
Or on Thy sandall'd feet to lay my soilèd hand."

So spake th' Elijah of the wild;
But He, of woman born, and mild
As moon-lit water, when a breeze
Tones the soft accent of the seas,

Bent o'er the Baptist His meek brow,
And answer'd, "It becomes us now;"
And lo! at once the laving stream
Shed o'er His awful face its sacramental gleam.

And as He rose from that green bank,
Yon heavens the scene of wonder drank
Into their depths, which saw their King
To God such ritual glory bring!
Obedience then received a crown
Surpassing all sublime renown,
The Law obtains from perfect will
Bodied by angels forth, who all His work fulfil.*

But while by yon enraptured Heaven
Peals of divine applause are given,
And downward on His wings of love
Descends the everlasting Dove,
And ere that thunder-voice hath ceased
Proclaiming how The Father's "pleased,"
Let the saved Church a truth discern,
And man's o'er-reas'ning heart a lofty science learn.

Subjection is our love divine;
Believer! let its law be thine:
"All righteousness," however small
Cold reason may its canons call,
Compliant Faith will yearn to do,
Finding in Christ her model true;
Nor dare to dream men suffer loss
When duty points the way, and God provides the Cross.

And, wouldst thou like thy Master be?
Go, find him near that ancient sea,
Where the awed Baptist on His head
The sacramental water spread;
There, as thou wander'st, seek a will
Which can all rectitude fulfil,
And consecrate thine inmost soul
To that unfathom'd Law no reason can control.

And then may He, whose glory came
On mystic plumes of dovelike flame,†
That Spirit, who on Christ did pour
The sevenfold grace His priesthood bore,—
Some drops of saving unction give
By which believing martyrs live;
Till thou, in all thy works and ways,
Shall unto God devote the priesthood of thy days.

---

* Ps. ciii. 20. † Matt. iii. 16.

CHIEF OF SINNERS.

"Jesus came to save sinners, of whom I am chief."
1 *Tim.* i. 15.

Low in the dust, oh! let me lie,
And heavenward lift my asking eye,
Till Christ becalm with lenient gaze
The pang which on my conscience preys.

The more I think, the more I feel
This heart hath proved in woe and weal
A Cain-like rebel to my God,
Whate'er the path experience trod.

My past appears one blended crime,
Extending through all scene and time,
And well may conscience quail to see
How Self dethroned the Deity!

Ay, Self has proved the spring of all
Enamour'd eyes perfection call;
Thought, will and motive, deed and word,
In each vile Self has been preferr'd.

Here is the Upas-blast of sin!
The poison-blight which burns within,
The venom'd source of vicious life,
With treason to the Godhead rife.

'Tis Self by whose defiling breath
The soul deserves eternal death;
A taint whose omnipresent power
Contaminates man's purest hour.

It matters not, what form it takes,
When human will our God forsakes:—
The essence of all sin we find,
Not in the flesh, but in the mind.

When passions nurse their lava-fires,
Or Belial lust the blood inspires,
Or vice, and vulgar riot reign,
There Self reveals its coarser stain.

But may not sin defile that soul
Where bland refinement wields control,
While art, and taste, and beauty dwell,
And Culture charms with graceful spell?

Yes, there while nature's glories rise
To fascinate our partial eyes,
And painting, poetry, and speech,
A throne of regal magic reach,

While private zeal, or public worth
Adorns the land which gives them birth,
Believe not, in this bright display,
That Sin and Self have died away!

Yea, rather may refinement shroud
A godless will beneath a cloud,
And lull the conscience, till it fail
To know if God, or man, prevail.

Thus, "chief of sinners!" forms the cry
Of all who see with inward eye
That self is sin, howe'er disguised,
And by approving falsehood prized.

On these Heaven's perfect law will dart
Those searching beams which bare the heart,
Till each fine chord of feeling there
Thrills into dread, and throbs with prayer.

DIVINE THIRST.

"My soul thirsteth for God."—*Ps.* xlii. 20.

As pants the hart for living brooks
So pines my soul for Thee;
Away from this lone earth it looks,
And longs Thy face to see.

Thrice Holy One! athirst I am
From man's false world to fly,
And on the glories of the Lamb
To feast my fasting eye.

'Tis here a bleak and barren land
Where hearts and hopes are vain;
But Faith perceives at Thy right hand,
Supernal wonders reign.

There pleasures bloom which cannot lead
Compliant souls to sin;
And all celestial Love decreed
Victorious martyrs win.*

No shades of guilt or sorrow now
Athwart remembrance roll;
Eternity unveils its brow,
And God énshrines the soul.

Those pulses of ethereal bliss
Which here so feebly play,
Shall throb within a realm like this,
Divine beyond decay!

At length we find our purest dreams
Of finite rapture flown,
When saints are basking in the beams
Which glorify Thy Throne.

* Rev. ii. 10.

The Past will not return in sighs,
The Future ne'er appal,
The present charm celestial eyes*
With Christ, the All in All.

And dared men like rapt David feel,
Our frigid hearts would be
On fire with archangelic zeal,
That heaven of Heavens to see!

* 1 John iii. 2.

THE HEART'S TREASURE.

"Lay up for yourselves treasures in heaven . . . for where your treasure is, there will your heart be also."—*Matt.* vi. 19, 21.

Men of faith's heroic mould!
Who your birthright have not sold,
But the heirship of God's truth
Have preserved to age from youth,
Let the freedom of your soul
No debasement draw from earth,
But the Law of heaven control
What you deem of peerless worth.

"Let not earth your treasure be,
Ne'er from rust and robber free;
But in heaven behold a mine
Where the gold is all divine;
That which mortal love doth measure
As of time the truest spell,
Aye becomes a witching treasure
Where false hearts delight to dwell."

Miser! with thy golden heap
Glaring through perturbèd sleep,
In thy wealth no wisdom lies;
Yet thy soul doth sacrifice
Heaven and hope, with all the bliss
Which on high the pure await;
Gilded clay thy treasure is,
And how cursed thine envied state!

Worldling! who for earth-prized gain
Creed and conscience both wilt strain;
Fill'd, and fever'd o'er with cares,
Doom'd to be but Sorrow's heirs,
Dwarf'd and mean thy nature grows,
Day by day intensely vile;
Deeper far than virtue knows,
Coils the serpent in thy smile!

Patriot! in whose haughty plan
Looks reveal'd a heaven for man,
Madly dreaming time and sense
All in all for man dispense,

Brain may work, and genius build
Schemes of most colossal name,
But o'er visions unfulfill'd
Thou shalt sing the dirge of shame.

Student! cloister'd in the cell
Haunted with some hoary spell
Books of sages and of seers
Breathe from immemorial years,—
Rich and radiant are the hopes
Round thy soul that beam and play,
But ambition with thee copes,
And of this thou art the prey.

Poet! thou art priest of song;
Heaven and earth to thee belong;
Beauty, grandeur, love and grace
Circle round the bardic race;
Seize thy harp, and sweep the chords
Till they glow with mental fire,
And like oracles, rich words
Roll from thy melodious lyre;

But if gold, or gain intrude
On thy soul in solitude,
If mere passion for renown
Should assail thy minstrel-crown,
Should thy chant, debauch'd and base,
E'er for sordid end be sung,
Angels blush for thy disgrace,—
Would thy harp were never strung!

Lord! and will affections be
Fill'd with dust, and dead to Thee,
If around one heart they twine,
With a passion half divine?
Teach us, then, no creature can
Saint, or seraph-heart enchain,
But it mars the mighty plan,—
God alone as God must reign!

Mother! 'tis a beauteous sight
When thou watchest day and night
Fondly round some elfin creature
Budding with maternal feature,
Oft in cradled slumber rock'd,
Flush'd with fascination's dreams,
While each baby hand enlock'd
Clasp'd in adoration seems;

But if love should Christ betray,
And devotion steal away
From the God of babes, and men,
Wilt thou not be chasten'd then?
Or perchance, when fever'd breath
From thy little one is heaving,
Thou wilt learn by infant's death
That thy soul has God been leaving!

If upon thy sailor-boy,
Star of home and social joy,
Far amid the wild sea-waves
Where his head the tempest braves,
Thou art dreaming, when thy prayer
Heavenward should in faith be swelling,
Canst thou hope thy God is there,
If no grace be in thee dwelling?

Wife, and parent, husband, child,
Let not feeling be defiled
By a worship that withdraws
Love from those celestial Laws
Which in creatures claim the heart;—
There the Lord erects a throne
In whose glories none have part,
Where He reigns, and reigns alone!

Hide our treasure, Lord, in Thee!
And regenerate hearts will be,
Like the ransom'd, more and more
When they scan their radiant store,
Bliss seraphic taught to feel
While around the Lamb they bend,
Chanting with impassion'd zeal,—
"Glory's fount! and sinner's Friend!"*

WISDOM OF PRAYER.

"O Thou that hearest prayer, unto Thee shall all flesh come."—*Ps.* lxv. 2.

Why should the reas'ning sceptic dare
To stand between the Godhead and our prayer?
A mental antichrist, too oft
Madly presuming mind will soar aloft,
And from Jehovah's nature draw
A reason why we should reject his law,—
That all who would Heaven's pardon claim
Must clasp that mercy in Emmanuel's name.

God is not changed by hearing prayer,
But would be changed, if our petitions were
By Him unheard; Whose page inspired
Hath said, "For this My Throne shall be enquired."†
Thus, end and means together meet
When bows the sinner at Heaven's mercy-seat:
To this God's changeless purpose tends,
And with His glory our salvation blends.

---

* Rev. v. 9. † Ezek. xxxvi. 37.

Avaunt! ye hell-breathed doubts, away!
Morn, noon, and night, let true adorers pray;
Precept, and promise, doctrine,—all
To this vast privilege our being call.
No saint in earth, or heaven is found,
Who did not in such glorious work abound;
His prayer, whatever path he trod,
Drew God to man, and lifted man to God.

Prayer conquers scene, and space, and time,
Entreats no temple, and demands no clime,
But, like an omnipresent charm
Can shield the saints from all corrupting harm;
Howe'er remote from genial home
The surging waves of life may bid them roam.
Oft riven Friendships pray afar,
Each thrilling each, beneath some alien star.

Elijah, Moses, Jonah, pray'd;
And how those heroes of The Spirit sway'd
Nature, and Providence, and Man!—
As though the movements of almighty plan,
However fathomless they were,
Hung on the breathings of a human prayer;
Or else, that He whose will is law,
Were sway'd in heaven, by what on earth he saw.*

And mark, thou prayerless Thing of dust!
If doubt thy God, and reason be thy trust,
How Abram, that Elect of heaven
To whom the Church's promises were given,
With sixfold intercession bent
Before His wrath, Th' enthroned Omnipotent!
And, when the bolt was almost hurl'd,
By prayer held back His thunders from the world.

But oh! if pure example can
Melt the cold mind of antichristian man,
Behold it, in the Saviour mild,
The God in flesh, the manhood undefiled:
For He, by whom the worlds were made,
In the hush'd midnight on the mountains pray'd,
And wintry stars from their high spheres
Blent their cold radiance with His awful tears!†

Here let us pause: His finite will
Before the Infinite of heaven did fall;
Though spotless, Christ was human still,
And ceased not on His Father-God to call.
And what but heartless sin will dare
To doubt that He is moved by mighty prayer?—
My Saviour wept, and watch'd, and pray'd;
Be each unhallow'd thought by that o'ersway'd.

And this, when worlds shall disappear,
Will rock to slumber each tempestuous fear;
All pangs without, all pains within
Yield to its spell; and each tyrannic sin
Is vanquish'd by believing prayer,
Which proves God greater than our greatest care!
And deep will be his hallow'd rest
Who drops his burden on Emmanuel's breast.

* Gen. xviii. 23—33. † Heb. v. 7.

CONVICTION, AND CONFESSION.

"He will reprove the world of sin . . . because they believe not on me."—*John* xvi. 8, 9. "O wretched man that I am, who shall deliver me?"—*Rom.* vii. 24. "Wretched, and miserable, and poor, and blind, and naked."—*Rev.* iii. 17.

There was a time, when earth appear'd
From each cold mist of sorrow clear'd,
A landscape clothed with calm and grace,
Whose flowers conceal'd the serpent's trace.

Then Nature seem'd a fairy world
Where beauty all its wings unfurl'd,
Till soil, and sea, and sun, and sky
Entranced me with their poetry.

Brightness and bloom o'er objects threw
The witchery of that wond'rous hue,
Which makes the very ground to glow
With gladness beaming hearts bestow.

And as with Nature, so with life,—
It seem'd with radiant magic rife,
Where hearts, and homes, and friends, and smiles,
Around me group'd their dearest wiles.

I did not hear the booming knell,
Nor let the tomb its wisdom tell;
Sickness and sorrow, change and grief,
Appear'd too dark for my belief.

And when from Heaven's most awful book
My blinded heart some utt'rance took,
The God I worshipp'd was my own,
Without a sceptre, law, or throne!

And thus, Religion's peerless claim
A sentimental lie became:
It touch'd the fancy—but the heart
From ruling grace beat all apart.

Till He, who bowed the heavens in love,
Beheld me from His shrine above,
And so my sensual trance awoke,
With legal Sinai's lightning-stroke.

Then, dread conviction through me burst,
And I sank down, accurst! accurst!
No more I lived, but seem'd to die *
Like those who dare their God defy.

Both heart and brain with horror felt
Vengeance divine my being melt:
The pleasure loved, grew loathsome now,
And stamp'd, like Cain's, my branded brow.

Creation's glories ceased to shine
Upon a heart depress'd as mine;
And round her fairest landscape stole
The blight and blackness of my soul.

Where'er I went, whate'er I saw,
The haunting curse of holy law
Came like my shadow;—dread and deep
It quiver'd o'er my harrow'd sleep.

Matter and mind, and time and space,
Sun, air, and sea, with heaven's bright face,
Whate'er I saw, or felt, or heard,
Echoed The Law's condemning word.

"Oh wretched man!" (thus breathed my groan)
"The body of this death to own;
As though the corpse from out its grave
Were fasten'd to some living slave,†

I bear without, and drag within
The clinging weight of woful sin!—
Who can deliver, and my soul
Rescue from this abhorr'd control?"

My virtues, now, to vices turn'd,
As more enlighten'd reason learn'd
The pureness of that perfect Law,
Which sees what Conscience never saw.

Eager with light from God's own eye
It can the shades of sin descry:
Nor could one pulse of feeling play
That throbs not in its searching ray.

And thus, gay sinner! down to dust
Be all thy tow'ring virtues thrust;
The law of God is legal death
By guilt inhaled at every breath.‡

Go, cultivate a grief divine;
A noble wretchedness be thine;
A heaven-born pang, like Paul's profound,—
The bleeding of the spirit's wound.

* Rom. vii. 9. † Rom. vii. 24. ‡ Rom. vii. 10.

Nor fancy, as we Godward rise
And grace soars nearer to the skies,
Our sainted calm will deeper grow,
As if we found true heaven below.

Insatiate conscience, strong and stern
Will evermore this wisdom learn,
That our perfection is to prove
Imperfect reigns man's purest love.

Oh! bless we God, for gracious tears,
For sunken hopes, and shadowy fears;
Those Hearts are not for glory meant
Who feel no glorious discontent:

Enough for souls this truth to gain,—
In Christ alone we live and reign;
And all who would perfection find
Must seek it in the Saviour's mind.

BELIEVER'S DESTINED WORK.

"Ye are the salt of the earth . . . ye are the light of the world . . . let your light so shine before men, that they may see your good works, and glorify your Father which is in heaven."—*Matt.* v. 13, 14, 16.

The World exults to crucify
The truth it loathes to feel;
And thus, all time repeats the Cross,
And Christians must through shame and loss
Maintain a martyr-zeal.

They cannot on this impious earth
Expect a brighter doom
Than that the Prince of Glory bore,
When He rebuked the world of yore,
And gain'd a borrow'd tomb.

But not for this, with craven hearts
And love of selfish ease
Shrink they from conflict, or the crowd,
And in dull cloister bent and bow'd
Enjoy a bad release.

Alas! for their religious mock
Whose creed is Self disguised;
Our sacrament of second birth
Anoints us to contend with earth;—
Have we our unction prized?

The heavenliness of blissful calm
In some poetic shade,
Where nature is the nurse of thought,
And all seems with religion fraught
And for devotion made;

For this indeed, mild spirits yearn,
And long for dove-like wings
Away to flee, and be at rest
With God and angels purely blest
Above terrestrial things.

Hence, most divine to musing hearts
When sick of toil and strife,
Monastic bowers of peace and prayer
Where time intrudes no fev'rish care
To fret the saintly life.

But, where is then the martyr's will?—
That oath by which we vow'd
Under Christ's banner, in His name,
To battle for His crown and claim
Amid earth's warring crowd?

Mistaken victims of themselves!
Who violate their creed
And fly with recreant heart and will,
Instead of facing stern and still
The front of battle's need;

'Tis not by flight or fear we gain
The jewell'd crown of bliss;
But by enduring unto death,
And battling to our latest breath,
We claim reward like this.

The world is dark, the world is dead,
Corruption broods in all;
Those painted splendours which appear
Glitter like spangles on a bier,
And worse than gloom appal.

Hero for heaven, baptised and brave,
The vow is on thee,—fight!
Full at the Fiend, the flesh, and world
Be all thy weapon'd graces hurl'd,
And God shall guard the right.

Or, if thou wilt the mystic words
Of "light" and "salt" translate,—
Then, shine by contrast in the dark,
And by correction probe and mark
The evils of our state.

We live in evil times; and tongues
Against the truth contend;
When Motive, Principle, and Power,
Around us in rebellion tower
And loud their challenge send.

Then, soldier, put thine armour on
And wield thy weapons bright;
With spear and breastplate, sword and shield,
Thus panoplied,—go, take the field
And foremost fall, or fight!

How can we "shine," unless we face
A world of guilt and gloom?
Or, be like salt's corrective force,
By hallow'd deed, or high discourse,
If life itself entomb?

Earth needs the grace, and wants the beams
Embodied grace imparts,
When worldlings view a valiant band
Maintain with hope and heart and hand
The creed of sainted hearts.

A cloister's gloom, a cowl, and cell
May oft a mind conceal,
Where rancour, pride, and envy reign,
While Passion gnaws a viler chain
Than fettered world-slaves feel.

Lord of the Church! of creeds, and souls,
Thy wisdom make our own,
Not *of*, but in, this world to be,
And hear the summons, "Follow me,"
From manger to the throne.

Contention with a godless world,—
Here is our law of life:
The salt must spread, the light must shine,
Unless we cross the will divine
And sink from duteous strife.

'Tis easy when the flesh-born will
In solitude retires,
To choose the calm of constant prayer,
And thus avoid the fretting care
A public fate inspires.

But, social is the cause of God;
And Christ demands a creed
That shall not seek monastic shade
Of all but righteous self afraid,—
But front the dreadest need.

True salt and sunlight make us, Lord!
Thy Spirit forms them both;
So may we best Thy word obey,
And rev'rence thus by night and day
Our sacramental oath.

The crowded world Thy Sceptre rules;
And Thou not less art there,
Than in the lull of lone retreat;
And saints may thy pure guidance meet
In duties ev'ry-where.

But while we seek to shine and act,
In all our words and ways
Thy veil, Humility! bestow,
And over us protection throw,
Lest we aspire for praise.

The work, but not the worker, seen,—
Behold! a heaven-drawn plan*
For saints to lead their life in God;
Such path a Saviour's virtue trod
And made it bright for man.

SACREDNESS OF FLOWERS.

"Consider the lilies."—*Matt.* vi. 28. "Glorious beauty is a fading flower."—*Isa.* xxviii. 1. "All flesh is as grass, and all the glory of man as the flower of grass."—1 *Pet.* i. 24.

YE silent poems! which from nature's book
Warble of Eden to our inward ear,
Filling the thoughtful eyes that on ye look
With the soft mystery of a sacred tear,

Not the chaste stars, whose placid eyes salute
The musing gaze of man's poetic mind,
Throned in their skyey radiance,—dare dispute
The spell ye wield o'er every heart refined.

Since God, from Whose ideal wealth of thought
All that is bright, or beautiful, or fair,
By shaping wisdom into form was wrought
And thus committed unto sun and air,

Made the wild flowers like earth-sprung stars to shine
With gleams of almost sacramental power,—†
Dull is the heart which hails no tone divine
When these accost him from their vernal bower!

Nor dream, that He who marks a sparrow's flight
Forgets the dew-fed darlings of the Spring;
Angels are not more surely in His sight
Than the soft flowers which breeze and brightness bring.

For such adjustment doth His hand ordain
Amid all forms and faculties to be,
That 'tween the snow-drop and vast earth must reign
Proportions pure as Science loves to see.

Were the huge world one atom more or less
In majesty, from centre to the pole,
The flowers might lose their bending loveliness,
Like living sympathies with nature's Whole.

And in man's world, where sin and woe prevail,
Harshness, and heat, and hurry so abound,
How sweet the hush of some sequester'd dale
Where slaves grow freemen upon nature's ground!

There can we hold communion meek and mild
With flowers, which deck some grove, or vernal wood,
And guard their innocence as undefiled
As when their greeting Maker call'd them "good."

Orphans of Eden, their parental soil
Has long been wither'd, and by weeds o'errun;
While burden'd Manhood, with a brow of toil,
Endures the desert, and outworks the sun;

But these, like babes whose mother we deplore,
Still do their budding features love to keep
A soft sad trace of paradise no more,
And waken memories that well may weep.

Of old, before the God Incarnate came,
Oft did high song, and sentiment, and art
Borrow from flowers an ever-beauteous fame
Which feeds the mind, and purifies the heart.

But since the hour a lily blush'd, and bow'd
Its head of grace beneath Emmanuel's smile,
Divine and deep associations crowd
The dreaming soul which o'er them bends awhile.

"Behold the lilies of the field, and learn
From their sweet lives, who neither toil, nor spin,"—
Well may such consecrating words return,
And waken truths whose echoes sleep within!

And might we shape one hallow'd dream of Him
Whose life was pure, mysterious, deep, and lone,
Whose glory to the wing-veil'd Seraphim
Beamed from the Cross, more wondrous than His Throne,—

Thought may imagine hours of worldless calm,
When all unwatch'd, Messiah's human soul
Found in far meads a meditative balm,
And in bright flowers some beautiful control.

As God, He made them, and as Man, admired
The blooming product of His lovely power;
And oft may genius, by their grace inspired,
Read silent poems in a sacred flower.

---

* Matt. vi. 16. † Matt. vi. 28, 29.

INGRATITUDE TO ANGELS.

"He shall give His angels charge over thee, to keep thee in all thy ways."—*Ps.* xci. 11.

AND must we, now the God-man reigns
In regions where no senses roam,
Refuse to hear angelic strains
Float through the heart, and fill our home?
Have Seraphim quite ceased to walk
Man's world, and with man's spirit talk?

'Tis true indeed, nor eye nor ear
Their shapes discern, nor know their voice;
But still they haunt a human sphere,
To make elected souls their choice;
And round them may bright Angels be,
Though nothing but blind earth they see.

Oh! never till the clouds of time
Are rent by awful death from man,
And he from yonder heaven sublime
Shall look back where dark life began,
Will gather'd saints in glory know
What blessings men to angels owe.

This earth is but a thorny wild,
A tangled maze where griefs abound,
By sorrow vex'd, by sin defiled,
Where foes and fiends our walks surround;
But does not dread Jehovah say,
Angelic guardians line the way?

It is not when gigantic woe,
Or crisis unforeseen assails
Our earthly doom, that most we glow
To feel heroic faith prevails,
When perill'd by the bitter shower
Temptation pours in sorrow's hour.

The precipice men rarely find;
On us no avalanche may fall;
But petty woes distract the mind
And take sweet temper from us all;
As some by thickets are o'erthrown,
Whose feet escaped the crushing stone.

Mean trifles our true dangers make,
Weak'ning the spirit unawares;
And tiny griefs would often break
The heart unbow'd by pond'rous cares,
Did not our guardian angels glide,
And watch, unseen, the naked side.

Some pebble in our daily path,
The little stone we scarce behold
A world of secret ruin hath,
O'er which might trip the brave and bold,—
Should not blest angels' saving arms
Upbear the soul from sudden harms.

And moods are felt no words define,
When earth and heaven appear to meet,
While faith half hears a tone divine
From out yon orbs of Glory greet
Each praying heart, and placid soul
Which echoes to such sweet control.

When gracious beams of holy light
From spheres of radiance seem to play,
And from lone hours of suff'ring night
Melt half their haunted gloom away,—
Our perill'd souls prompt Angels see
And hover by the bended knee.

Sickness and sorrow, too, may have
Ethereal Hosts whom none perceive,
Whose golden wings around us wave
When all alone men seem to grieve;
And while we sigh, or shed the tear,
Their sympathies may flutter near.

Or, by some law to man unknown,
Their spells may o'er us act and steal,
And strengthen Faith upon her throne,
When fury-passions make us feel
How Self and Sin would monarchs be,
And give the law to Deity!

Thus, human Life from them may take
Some moral tinge, or mental hue,
Which not till dust the soul forsake
Elected saints will value true:—
Before God's throne, and only then
These guardians will be thank'd by men.

FOLLOW CHRIST.

"Jesus saith unto them, Follow me; and . . . . they followed Him."—*Matt.* iv. 18—20.

THE sheep who know the shepherd's tone
Delight to hear his voice;
His guiding way becomes their own,
His wish their willing choice:
So is it with regenerate Souls,
Whose love the law of grace controls;
Let but the Shepherd of the Spirit call,—
Like echoes they reply, and leave their noblest all!

So was it in the Church of old
When, walking by the sea,
The Lord of Mercy did behold
The twin elect of Galilee,

Two fishers there, who cast the net
The produce of the lake to get;
But when that "Follow Me!" from Christ was heard,
The laden ships they left, responsive to His word.

So is it now; if Hearts be true
To Him whose shepherd-cry
Will never cause that soul to rue
Which dares itself deny,
And lives for Christ, where'er it roam;—
Serene abroad, resign'd at home,
By crowded mart, or in resounding street
Where all the mingled tides of sin and struggle meet.

Life need not seek monastic cell,
Nor yearn for cloister'd shades;
Nor sigh for some Arcadian dell,
And green poetic glades
Where blissful Quiet can enjoy
The bower of peace without alloy;
But rather rest where Providence doth say,
"Move in thine orbit here, for Wisdom chose the way."

They are not meek who fretful ask,
Or pine for distant spheres;
Let heaven be view'd in ev'ry task
And *that* will soothe our fears!
We should not e'en by thought rebel;
For God works all things wise and well,
And for each being doth unroll the plan
Eternity decreed, before the hills began.

To sigh for some romantic spot
Of solitude and peace,
And clasp in dreams a perfect lot
Where care and sorrow cease,—
To God must breathe of discontent,
Howe'er with sainted feeling blent;
Our proper sphere in providence must be
Where Christ in spirit comes, and utters, "Follow Me!"

Localities alone confine
The gilded mocks of earth;
But they who bear a charm divine
Which seals our second birth,
High o'er the world's bewilder'd sphere
The still small voice of Christ can hear:
And so, when Mammon tempts, or Belial reigns,
Bound at the Master's voice, and burst their venal chains.

Thus to the publican there came
A "Follow Me," which drew
His heart to hear That holy Name
Which heaven proclaim'd the true;
All circumstance, and scene, and lot,
The den, the dungeon, or the cot,—
Let but the voice of duty call us there,
And Faith may hallow each by watchfulness and prayer.

And hence may those who dwell
Far from the hurried mart,
Where sylvan homes with quiet spell
Attune some thinking heart,
When haply through harsh cities loud
They wind amid the toiling crowd,
Or through damp courts and dusky lanes of woe
See haggard Want and Age, with shrunken features go,—

Oh! let them not presume to say
That there, 'mid vexing strife,
No saintly Minds can muse or pray,
Or consecrate a life
To heaven-born cares, and hopes of bliss
Which lift them o'er a doom like this:—
For though the heart in rustic dreams will roam,
It glories in the truth, that Faith can find a home

Wherever love and prayer abide:
And hence, dear Lord, may we
Remember that calm Voice which cried,
To Levi,—"Follow Me!"
Whate'er the pathway life must tread,
Around us be Thy graces spread,
And thus no time, nor toil, nor space, nor scene
To hide Thy Word from us will ever intervene.

If such Thy will, by wooded streams,
Or vales of blissful calm,
Where the deep hush of holy dreams
Inspires unearthly balm,
Where from green hills the gladden'd eyes
Look speechless hymns beyond the skies,—
If there embower'd, Thou doom'st our lot to be,
Lord of the landscape fair! we glow to "follow" Thee.

Or, if Thy regal Word decide,
That cities throng'd and loud
Which billow with the restless tide
Of life's tumultuous crowd,
Should be our peopled deserts, where
Unechoed hearts conceal each care,—
Still may our souls by meek compliance find,
The ever-present Christ an anchor for the mind.

Love need not quit the humblest call,
But calmly work and wait;
For safety dwells where duties all
Attend our mortal state;—

Messiah did not die to give
Each heart the choice where faith would live;
But this He grants to all who seek for grace,—
The guidance of His truth, and glory of His face.*

Yes, "Follow Me!" be this the word,
The motto of our lives;
Morn, noon, and night, let such be heard,
When Sin or Satan strives;
Should Passion rage, or Pride begin,
Or treason-banners rise within,
In all we feel, or fancy, do or dare,
Let Thy mild "Follow Me," pursue us every where,

Great Captain of the meek and good!
Whose crimson guilt and stain
Shall never, through Thine awful blood,
Assail their souls again,
In self-denial, grief, or loss,
In all we have of care and cross,
Thy hand of mercy out of heaven bestow,
And let us feel its grasp, where'er our footsteps go.

Thy path was one of pain and grief,
A sacrifice of love;
Nor God, nor angel brought relief
From bowers of bliss above;
We ask not then poetic fields
Where life all bloom and brightness yields;
But this we seek,—a soul from murmurs free,
Whose heaven on earth it proves, in all to follow Thee.

NAME WITHOUT NATURE.

"Thou hast a name that thou livest, and art dead."—*Rev.* iii. 1. "Many will say unto me, in that day, Lord! Lord! have we not prophesied in Thy name? . . . Then will I profess unto them, I never knew you."—*Matt.* vii. 22, 23.

When plaintive knells peal sadness o'er the wind,
And echoes haunt the mind
With thoughts, whose voiceless depths of awe infold
Meanings which are not told,
Dark fears from hush'd eternity arise
Too deep, except for sighs:
Men dare not speak it, but they ponder this,
Where wings the parted Soul?—to agony, or bliss?

And solemn terrors, blent with truths profound,
In these vast words abound,
Which tell what imitation's power achieves,
When formal man believes.
That he in Christ by nature, as by name,
His own can truly claim,—
While far as earth from heaven his spirit lives
On that base food alone, the power of pleasure gives.

And marvel we, such midnight error can
So darken over man,
That he a hollow lie for truth mistakes,
And life for death forsakes?
And thus, while dead in selfishness and sin,
Doth never gaze within
The deeper fountains of his soul to prove,
Whether from earth they rise, or stream from grace above?

The mystery may here its web unwind,—
Self-love deludes the blind;
And in the blindness of bad hearts they see
A shade of miscall'd deity;
And, like their god, a false religion seems
Reflecting back their dreams;
And so, from year to year they live, and die,
Feeling their souls secure as angels in the sky!

Void of all grace, perceptive reason can
So educate the man,
And unto plastic mind and morals give
Those forms, by which men live
In seeming concord with what Heaven requires:
Yet God alone inspires
Life from The Spirit, and that sacred love
Whereby all saints on earth, are yet in soul, above.

Thus can the outworks of religious grace
Impress their lovely trace
On creed and conduct, character, and all
The world-slaves "nature" call;
Reason and Sentiment may both forbear
To doubt what texts declare;
And ritual zeal so mechanise the soul
That much the Church decrees, may wield a due control.

The beauty of unblemish'd morals, too,
May guard its vestal hue,
Nor vulgar passions by their vicious reign
Cast o'er the law a stain;
And thus complete in all mere sense admires,
Who doubts, that faith inspires
So fair a specimen of social truth
Beheld in wintry age, or seen in vernal youth?

---

* Ps. iv. 6, 7.

Love will not criticise a brother-soul;
And when the death-knells roll
Their dirge-like cadence, while the living sigh
To think, how soon we die!
Oh, marvel not, blind Charity conceives
That he who this world leaves
With such a sanctity around him spread,
Hath up to Glory's throne by angel-bands been led.

Still, dare we not Truth's warning tone forget,
For, ah! 'tis needed yet:
"Lord," on our lips most orthodox may be,
And none our danger see;
And yet not Christ, but our own will preside
O'er passion's inward tide,
O'er thought and feeling, motive and desire
Which from the outer-sense to secret life retire.

Yes, we may prophesy and preach,
And high distinction reach;
O'er our mute dust pale monuments arise,
Or throne us in the skies,
While the loud trumpet of a world-wide fame
Rings through all hearts our name;
And when rapt eyes our sculptured praises read,
They glisten with the thought,—here lies a saint indeed!

And yet our soul's eternity, the while,
Unlit by glory's smile,
Though canonising Praise adorns our tomb,
May be immersed in gloom;
And realms of horror round that darkness burn,
Where hypocrites must learn
How vast a gulf between profession lies
And that celestial life which moulds us for the skies!

But, Lord, while we in self-abasement lie
Beneath Thy searching eye,
Home to the centre bare the soul within
Where hides a bosom-sin,
Which oft amid pure seemliness of life
With secret lust is rife:
Yea, some, professing to uphold Thy throne,
Have cast all devils out, except their spirit's own! *

From such delusion, God! our conscience save,
Which to the very grave

* Matt. vii. 22.

And e'en beyond it,—to the Judge on high *
Extends the cheating lie!—
That spell of Satan, whence a worldling dreams
He is the all he seems,
And dares not search his own deluded heart,
Till Christ shall rend the veil, by that dread word, "Depart!"

* Matt. vii. 22.

THE HOMELESS ONE.

"The Son of Man hath not where to lay his head."
Matt. viii. 20.

Could Fancy, in some dream sublime,
With circumstance have clothed the time
When God incarnate should appear,
To roll the curse from earth's dark sphere,

With what a pomp of heaven-bright rays
Would she have circled round His ways!—
Angel, and harp, and seraphim
Would all have been foretold for Him.

Sun, moon, and star, and sky and sea,
Would each have felt a sympathy:
Some impulse, like a throbbing awe,
Through Earth had thrill'd, when Christ she saw.

But, not in Glory's pall He came;
Nor did an earthquake's throb proclaim
The world's Creator was a child,
Born in our flesh, but undefiled.

No fameless offspring of the poor
On mountain bleak, or barren moor,
Was ever rock'd on mother's breast,
To outward sense, so little blest

As yonder Babe Divine appears,
Baptised by Mary's virgin tears,—
Those pearl-drops of the heart which flow
While mothers o'er a first-born glow.

And as the inns no room afford
To cradle earth's infantine Lord,
But in the manger's welcome cold
The Virgin must her Child enfold,—

In this, prophetic shades we find
Of that dark lot, by heaven design'd
Hereafter to o'ershade The Man,
In working out redemption's plan.

Grandeurs, indeed, to Christ belong;
But shine they not in bardic song,
Such as the lyric choirs of earth
Are wont to chant for Hero's worth.

Ne'er did our world such meekness view,
Such self-oblivion, vast and true;
His very majesty was mild,—
The Man of Sorrows never smiled.

The fox his cave, the bird his nest,
But where His glorious head to rest
My Saviour had not!—doom'd to roam
From earth to heaven without a home.

Oh, miracle! which dazzles thought,—
With all the wealth of Godhead fraught
That He, who died the world to save,
Was buried in a borrow'd grave!

And yet, beneath that bland disguise
What glory in suspension lies!—
Jehovah, in our manhood shrined,
Is mock'd by unappall'd mankind.

But He, by whom yon worlds were made,
Whose will their huge foundations laid,
Though matter, motion, time, and sense
Were slaves to His omnipotence,

Repress'd His Godhead; nor allow'd
Full beams to flash from out the cloud;
For at the glance of one dread ray
The Universe had shrunk away!

For Him no monuments arise;
No motto'd pillars seek the skies;
Unlike the earth-gods fame admires,
His awful life no World inspires.

Alone, beyond all loneliness,
Which e'er a burden'd soul could press,
Emmanuel's heart through toil and tears
Went beating on its destined years.

Martyrs are found, whose bosoms bleed,
When by mysterious Heaven decreed
In the hush'd depths of their lone heart
To bear untold some venom'd dart;

But neither saint, nor angel could
Uncurtain that veil'd solitude
Where Christ alone,* unstain'd by sin,
Baffled the powers of Hell, within.

* Isa. lxiii. 3.

And thus, eternity nor time,
Nor sorrowing earth, nor heaven sublime,
Except in Christ,—did ever see
A Soul without a sympathy,

And wilt thou, ere thy course be run,
Betake thee to the Homeless one?
Then, sinner, count the mighty cost!—
To thee the world is blind and lost;

Not rashly bear His awful name;
Nor dream that fortune, bliss, or fame,
Or aught that hero-worship loves,
The Lord of meekness e'er approves.

In fasting, solitude, and fears,
Through buried pangs, and hidden tears,
Unecho'd, and by most, unknown,
Prepare, like Christ, to live alone.

Yet oh, within thee, dark and deep
When thy crush'd thought retires to weep,
And harshly cold, its iron heart
The world presents to all thou art,

Then, think of Him! and back recall
The Homeless, Who was Lord of all;
A God with angels round the throne,
Too poor to call the grave His own.

Pillow in prayer thine aching breast
On Him, who had not where to rest
His head on earth; but Who in heaven
Can feel thy heart, and cry—forgiven!

FIRST SOUL IN HEAVEN.*

"By faith Abel . . . obtained witness that he was righteous, God testifying of his gifts: he being dead, yet speaketh."—*Heb.* xi. 4. "No man could learn that song but . . . the redeemed."—*Rev.* xiv. 3.

In hush'd eternity alone
  Before all creatures were,
Jehovah held His awful throne
  Unworshipp'd by a prayer.

There was no space, nor scene, nor time,
  Nor aught by names we call;
But, center'd in Himself sublime
  Was God, the All in All!

* In this, and other portions of the volume, the word "heaven" is used in a popular and poetical sense, rather than in the strict and theological one.

But through eternity there ran
A thrill of coming change,
And lustrous Shapes of life began
Around His Throne to range.

Radiant with rapture, pure as bright,
Angelic myriads rise,
And glow and glisten in the light
Of God's approving eyes.

In volumed waves of golden sound
Roll from celestial lyres
Those swelling chants, which peal around
From new-created choirs.

But, hark ! amid the shining throng
Of Shapes who arch their wings,
A single Voice another song
With mortal cadence sings :

Alone he seems, and chants apart
In unexpected notes
A music, where the grateful heart
In strains of feeling floats :

A beauteous Soul ! whose seraph brow
Is bright with glory's hue,—
Lo, Angels pause to hear him now
Their harping praise outdo.

Their choral rapture swell'd as deep
As purity could pour;
But they, who have not learn'd to weep,
May never God adore

With such a burst of whelming love
As Earth's first martyr sang,
When, glory to the Lord above !
The voice of Abel rang.

Angelic harps their key-note found
In God, as great and good:
But Abel's life-pulse beat and bound
As only sinner's could.

"Worthy the Lamb ! who shall be slain;
Redemption crowns my song:
Ye seraphim ! your notes retain,
But these to me belong."

Thus might the primal Soul who came
Forth from its bleeding clay,
Kindle the heavens with His bright name,
Who is our Truth, and Way.

And with that blissful song he blent
A humbling depth of tone,
Which to the ransom'd harper lent
A music all its own.

Angels for bliss and being sang
Their ecstasies on high;
But how the heavens with wonder rang
When Man awoke the sky

With that new song, Redemption gave
To Abel's pardon'd soul!
Till angels ceased their wings to wave,
Nor let their chorus roll,

But listen'd with entrancèd ears
To that bright martyr's strain,
Whose notes were born of banish'd fears
And breathed of ended pain.

But from the hour when rescued man
Enter'd within the veil,
And heaven's delighted host began
To list Redemption's tale,

Myriads of blood-wash'd souls have flown
Where the first spirit went
Till he, who once hymn'd Christ alone,
Is now with numbers blent.

Each nation, kindred, home, and clime
Helps to increase the throng,
Making the heavens grow more sublime
With Earth's redemption-song.

Each minute, guardian angels mount
With some new soul on high,
And hear it, close to Glory's fount,
Deepen that endless cry,—

"Salvation ! through the bleeding grace
Of God's incarnate Son,
Whose merit for a banded race
A more than Eden won."

And louder, louder, yet will grow
That song before the Throne,
As added saints set free from woe
Shall make the strain their own.

Lord ! grant that we on earth begin
To tune the heart's deep lyre,
And by prophetic notes within
Anticipate the choir,

Who ever round Thee chant, and sing
The song no angels can,—
"Hail ! Prophet, Priest, and destined King
Before the world began,

"Prostrate beneath Thy face to fall
And cast our crowns before Thee,
Oh Thou, The Everlasting All,
Be this our brightest glory !"

GUILTY FEARS.

"O thou of little faith! wherefore didst thou doubt."
Matt. xiv. 31.

Around us moves this magic world
With all appeals of blended power;
And o'er our heads unfurl'd
The heavens, which change each hour.

Above, beneath, where'er we gaze
On sky, or soil, or living sea,
Some chord is touch'd, which plays
And thrills, O God! from Thee.

Divine as deep the eloquence
Through form and fact creation wields,
When through the veil of sense
A solemn vision yields

Stern truths,—which teach the soul to pray,
And ponder them with deepest awe;
Till conscience own the sway
Of heaven's interior law.

For though in calm, the poet sees
Rich Beauty reigning like a queen,
And grace from flowers and trees
Bedecks some fairy scene;

Yet Nature hath her moods of ire,
Deep thunders of prophetic tone,
Lightnings of ghastly fire,
And winds with conscious moan.

Darkness and thunder, wave and wind,—
Amid them let the godless think,
And soon the awe-struck mind
Will in dejection sink.

For, oh, that echo faint and broken
Of God, the holy and the just,
Within us like a token
Awaken will,—and must!

And then, judicial conscience yearns
To know where God and man can meet?
And with this question burns,
"Is there a mercy seat?"

But what can mere creation preach?
Is mercy mirror'd on the sky?
Can all earth's glories reach
The source of one deep sigh?

Is there a grace to heal our sin,
Atonement for the guilt-stain'd hearts?—
Around, above, within,
No answer earth imparts.

In health, and hours of reckless glee,
We mould a god from mortal smiles,
And thus, from judgment free,
Enjoy our transient wiles.

Still conscience is not murder'd quite;
But in some gloom of anguish rolls
Its challenge for God's right
Athwart our echoing souls.

Then, to the root of moral life
Our being rocks with more than fear;
And in that harrowing strife
The Judge seems drawing near!

Hence, like disciples on the deep
When yawning billows o'er them swept,
While lapp'd in lovely sleep
The Lord calm slumber kept,

Our souls are in tempestuous fright,
Our bark of hope is sinking fast,
And death's eternal night
Seems all around us cast.

Then, fear we, Lord! and learn at length
What saints must feel before they die,—
A sinner has no strength
Except to grace he fly.

"Oh, little faith;"—alas, how true!
Our pagan fears in calm and storm
Darken from love's own view
Thy Mercy's present form.

And thus, 'mid promises divine,
And with the wealth of Godhead stored,
Like orphans, Christians pine,
As if they had no Lord!

Shame on our sunken hearts, and base,
That men like creedless orphans live,
Though God redeem'd our race
With all a God could give.

Oh, had we faith, though earth and sky
To second chaos were confounded,
Christ would not hear the cry,—*
"By death are we surrounded!"

But, calm, as was the Saviour's brow
Who slept amid the thund'ring wave,
Each soul would prove him now
Mighty to shield and save.

---

* Matt. viii. 25.

Rebuke then, Lord! not waves and winds,
But rather raise our blush of shame,
That men with heathen minds
Can bear Thy blessed Name.

Anchor of Souls! in life and death
Though loud the storms of anguish be,
May Love, with latest breath,
Her haven seek in Thee.

JESUS TEMPTED.

"Then was Jesus led up of the spirit into the wilderness, to be tempted of the devil."—*Matt.* iv. 1.

And wert Thou by the prompting Spirit led
Through desert lone, to face Satanic power,
Oh second Adam! our anointed Head,—
To balk the demon in his blackest hour?

One moment, by baptismal waves we hear
From opening skies deep melody descend,
And drink that Voice with reverential fear
Which hail'd Thee, Son of God, whom Grace did send:

The next,—and Thou art in yon homeless wild
Fasting and foodless, with no eye to see
How the lost angel tempts Thine undefiled
Manhood, to break the bond of Deity.

'Twas even so: and if when Satan threw
A fiendish shade of subtlety and hate,
By tempting wickedness of words untrue
Into the heart of man's primeval state,

A mystery darkens round the deepest mind
Which ponders o'er that scene with prayerful thought,
How can we dream (unless by sin struck blind)
A tempted Christ, with less of mystery fraught?

Thus doth our Athanasian symbol teach
A truth sublime which deep in Godhead dwells,
Something beyond a soaring thought to reach,
Surmounting all that wingèd reason tells,—

How in Emmanuel God and Man unite
Both natures true, in properties and powers;
The first retain'd its uncreated light,
The second, sin except, was weak as ours.

In act quiescent, though by Godhead there,
Divinity did not the man withdraw;
And thus obedient down to weeping prayer
The Infinite became, by finite law.

So may we read, with simple hearts and pure,
How thus between the Darkness and the Light
A conflict reign'd; nor let cold science lure
Our souls from faith in that mysterious fight.

No dream it was; no parable, no trance;
Nor mental ecstasy, which rapt the soul
Beyond the bounds where time and space advance
Their true conditions, or their just control:

Close to the record simply may we cleave;
Then, each temptation will to man impart
Wonders that whelm no reason to believe,
And awing wisdom which improves the heart.

Tempted by Satan, lo, the Adam first
Yielded, and fell beneath a boundless lie;
And by his fall condemn'd mankind were curst,
In whose one death all generations die!

But when again the Prince of Evil would
A second Adam likewise have assail'd,—
Based on eternity, our Rock * withstood
And humanly o'er sin and hell prevail'd.

Vainly to crush Him thrice the Tempter brought
The magic fulness of infernal skill;
Nothing which sense or inward feeling wrought,
Assail'd the Holy One with shade of ill.

Far o'er the fiercest hunger faith arose;
No pride of life His meekness could o'erwhelm;
And Kingdoms of the world, as painted shows,
His heart rejected from its holy realm.

He came to suffer, long before He reign'd,
And home to God our human will to bring;
Thus, no temptation from the demon stain'd
That perfect Virtue, saints and angels sing.

Hail, Son of Mary! Arch-Elect † of heaven,
Victim Divine, whose blood redeem'd our fall,
Conquer'd by grace, to Thee the world is given,—
Wield Thy love-sceptre, and subdue it all!

---

* 2 Sam. xxii. 32. † Isa. xlii. 1.

VOICE OF THOSE NO MORE.

"He being dead, yet speaketh."—*Heb.* xi. 4.

Our Fathers, where be they,
The guides of vernal youth,
Who taught our infant lips to pray,
And vow'd the heart to truth?

The Prophets, who foretold
What life's worn scene would be,
And bade us in our God behold
The hopes which make us free?

All fleeted by, and fled
To orbs of bliss unknown;
Their dust is with the countless dead,
And we,—must walk alone.

But in time's weary track
Of sorrow, change, and care,
How oft their words come rolling back,
And breathe us into prayer!

Oh, little did we think
When their hoar'd wisdom spake,
How soon our lofty hopes would sink,
And life's gay bubble break!

We call'd them gloomy seers,
Too boding, dull, and sad;
And when their eyes were dimm'd with tears,
Our own smiled ever glad.

They warn'd us of the world,
Gave to each rose its thorn,
And when false hopes their wings unfurl'd,
Spake words which seem'd forlorn.

They bade us walk with God,
And, Christ-like, bear the cross,
Learning true wisdom in the rod,*
And love from earthly loss.

And have our lives gainsay'd
The warning truth and word
Which once, ere Time these hearts betray'd,
Approving conscience stirr'd?

Ah, no!—in grief and gloom,
Their counsels and their cares
Accost us from their distant tomb,
And show the truth was theirs.

Though mortal was their breath,
Immortal breathes the mind;
For how can That be sunk in death,
Whose wisdom rules mankind?

Dead prophets, then, seem nigh,
And round us dwell and reign;
And all who in the Saviour die,
Shall hear those seers again.

* Rev. iii. 19.

SINFULNESS OF SIN.

"Sin, that it might appear sin, working death in me by that which is good; that sin by the commandment might become exceeding sinful."
Rom. vii. 13.

Sin colours all we do and prize,
And, like our shadow, ne'er departs;
E'en when we sleep, its blackness lies
In spirit brooding o'er our hearts.

The cleansing grace of Blood Divine
Alone can wash the stain away,
"So let it bathe this heart of mine!"—
Believers thus for ever pray.

Sin struck the moral root of Man
And poison'd there the branches too;
From Adam down to us it ran,
And venoms all we think and do.

Still, not in earth, but heaven above
Rebellion first its flag unfurl'd,
When God's bright Angel left his love,
A fiend became, and sought our world.

O mystery! too deep for all
Except for Truth's omniscient eye,
That one in heaven from faith might fall,
Whom nothing from *without* could try.

Yet refuge in this thought we find,
That sin no perfect substance is;
But mere negation, bad and blind,
Which cankers man and mortal bliss.

Dark paradox of will perverse,
Self-worship forms the secret ground
Where Sin begets that boundless curse,
Hearts without God have ever found.

Self-pref'rence frames a hell within,
Eternity in seed is there;
And death and darkness thence begin
The torment souls undone must share.

How sin commenced, vain reason tries
  To speculate, till thought grows wild;
But modest faith this truth can prize,—
  That God is pure, though man defiled.

Sole Teacher of all saving truth!
  Divine Convincer of our need,
Guardian of age, and Guide of youth,
  Under the Cross we learn our creed:

Sin blasted with primeval blight
  Our first estate in Eden's bowers,
Cover'd creation o'er with night,
  And crush'd her prospects, and her powers.

And since that most stupendous fall,
  Matter and mind, with secret groan
Have ceased not for their God to call,
  Like orphans left to sigh alone.

All pangs, and penalties, and pains,
  Sickness and sorrow, grief and care,
Where ruin frowns, or anguish reigns,—
  The sinfulness of sin is there.

The babe who dies; the tomb which opes
  For buried joys, or broken hearts;
Each leaf that falls from wither'd hopes
  As friend on friend from earth departs,—

What prove they all, but seal and sign,
  How sin hath havock'd earth and man,
And, as the foe of law divine,
  Merits an everlasting ban?

But seek we this sad truth to know
  How sin by virtual root can be
A deicide, who strikes a blow
  Which aims at awful Deity?

Then, look we to supernal Grace,
  Almighty Love in flesh unveil'd,
Whose worth restored our sunken race
  To heights beyond what thought hath scaled.

Did grateful awe His form attend?
  Or, round Him adorations fall,
And with encrowning anthem blend
  In one loud burst,—"Hail! Lord of all!"

Alas! the world an atheist proved;
  His life became embodied woe,
And He whom God supremely loved
  Was hated, worse than fiends below.*

Sin nail'd Him to the felon's tree,
  Marr'd His meek face, and spear'd His side;
Nor was one sigh of sympathy
  Breathed o'er Him, when the Man-God died!

Well might Creation feel affright,
  And her dread anguish seem to say
The sun could not endure that sight,
  But veil'd its brow, and look'd away.

Yet man, the sinner, does not shake,
  Recoil nor shudder, groan nor weep;
And while the very dead awake,
  His heart retains its iron sleep!

Lord of the soul! while thus we find
  Ourselves in all the Past hath done,
Teach the bad conscience of the blind,
  Of spirits all Thou art the Sun.

In Thy pure lustre, sin appears
  A contrast fell to man and God;
And makes us tremble at the tears
  Which gush'd where bleeding Mercy trod.

Religion thus atonement brings
  When faith and fear in one combine;
While purity from pardon springs,
  And proves them both indeed divine.

WORLD OF SPIRITS.

"Give place: the maid is not dead, but sleepeth."—*Matt.* ix. 24. "God is not the God of the dead, but of the living."—*Matt.* xxii. 32. "To-day shalt thou be with me in paradise."—*Luke* xxiii. 43.

Men are not dead because they die,
    From outward sense receding,
  But where extends no mortal eye
    A spirit-life are leading:
In some vast orb, whose unveil'd glories shine,
They wait the pealing of the trump divine.

  What, though the slaves of tyrant sense,
    Wild Hearts, with sorrow blind,
  Dare catechise Omnipotence
    As though it mock'd mankind,
And tempt some daring Sadducee to say
"On life unseen can Reason dart her ray?"

  Yet, just as reason sense can lift
    Into some higher sphere,
  So can pure faith, heaven's peerless gift,
    O'er reason's known career

---

* John viii. 42, 44.

Soar on wing'd thoughts,—and bid rapt feelings roam
In dreams immortal round the Spirit's home.

That spirit-home ! that clime of Souls,
The palace of the Blest,
Where neither storm nor shadow rolls
Athwart the halcyon breast,
Oh, there embower'd, unbodied saints repose,
And each pure heart with placid virtue glows.

They are not dead, whose bodies die,
Commingling with cold earth;
For soul is man's eternity
And hath such godlike worth,
That no corruption makes its pulse to pause;
Nor can mere death arrest its mighty laws.

Created once, it lives, and lives
For ever, and for ever !
The God of souls a fiat gives
That flesh from it may sever,
But round itself no trance sepulchral steals,
And when unearth'd, diviner impulse feels.

The life men touch, and see, and taste,
Is but organic show;
And onward as wing'd moments fleet
Our organs weaker grow;
But character enfolds eternal doom,
Bearing a life which breathes beyond the tomb.

And might some parted soul return
Back from the viewless state,
Our yearning minds would meekly learn
What voiceless wonders wait
The flesh-deliver'd, who, from bondage free,
Fly to that Hades God proclaims to be.

Secrets of glory might disclose
Their rich contents to man;
And truths beyond what Learning knows
Or Science ever can,—
Might then illuminate with earthless gleams
Darkness which makes us tremble in our dreams !

But He, who is of life and death
Puissant Lord and King,
And portions out all human breath,
Forbids the Dead to bring
Intelligence from that far world unknown,
To whose veil'd wonders countless souls have flown.

Six thousand years have almost roll'd
Their human waves along,
Since Death, the uncontroll'd,
Hath triumph'd o'er the strong,
The weak and bad, the beautiful and brave,
And made the earth-scene one enormous grave.

And yet, of all our sumless dead
Not one hath back return'd
To soothe some heart which inly bled,
And for this secret burn'd,—
To understand, how Spirits think and act,
And what the glories which the dead attract?

In vain may restless minds intreat,
Or for such knowledge groan;
Silence before the Mercy-seat
Befits the faith we own,
When Hearts bereaved a parted soul pursue,
And seek to learn what martyrs never knew:

Oft in the hush of holy night,
In shades of solemn grief
When bow'd beneath some awful blight,
With none to bring relief,
How have we sigh'd to see that viewless State
Where dead Immortals for their glory wait !

But, ah, the Universe is dumb
To each high-breathed prayer;
From earth and heaven no answers come,
But echo murmurs "Where?"
When lonesome Thinkers in the churchyard cry,
"Where rest the souls whose bodies round us lie?"

But, calm thee, riven Heart ! lie still;
Nor wise beyond The Word
Attempt to prove, lest haughty will
To Christ should be preferr'd;
Enough to know, that all in heaven who trust
God shall awaken from sepulchral dust.

They "are not dead, but sleeping,"—
Bright words of balm and grace !
To Anguish worn, and weeping
Above some marble face,
When placid death has closed the silken lid
And from our hearts the soulless glances hid.

But in that hour of deepest trance
While bend we o'er the dead,
And into realms of thought advance
Where Scripture hath not led,
The calm seraphic each white feature wears
Seems to embody what The Lord declares

When death a transient "sleep" He calls;
And thus from hearts half-breaking
Rolls back the cloud which flesh appals,
And prophesies the waking
Soon to begin !—when Time's last trumpet rolls
The blast that summons bodies back to souls.

Meanwhile, though "earth to earth"
Be o'er their temples cried,
The souls who shared a second birth
No dust and darkness hide:
Wafted by angels to immortal bowers,
They muse in Paradise, with conscious powers.

Beyond such creed faith dares not go,
Nor speculate on more;
True wisdom loves her sphere to know,
Nor lets the heart run o'er
In aimless dreams, which cannot love inspire,
But mock the fancy with a lurid fire.

When Laz'rus back to life was brought,
He breathed not what he saw;
As though oblivion's spell had wrought,
Or some celestial law
The lip restrain'd, and lock'd in silence all
The shrouded wonders which the dead befall.

And that young maid of Judah's race
Whom Christ to earth restored,
When life's glad bloom inspired her face,
And she whom Love deplored,
Clasp'd in a mother's arms, again was prest
Heart close to heart, and breast to echoing breast,—

No whisper gave she of the scene
To which her spirit fled;
Nor conscious look'd her soul had been
Communing with the dead,—
Glory and Music *might* have seen and heard,
For which on earth we find no sign, or word.

O Thou! Whose sceptre life and death
By equal law obey,
The grace to consecrate each breath
To Thee, our Truth and Way,
Be ours to prize; and then, both dooms will be
Soothed with the thought, that each is sway'd by Thee.

GLORY OF THE MOUNTAINS.

"The Lord called to him out of the mountain."—*Exod.* xix. 3. "The glory of the Lord stood on the mountain."—*Ezek.* xi. 23.

How glorious are the mountain-Kings! who overawe the soul,
And lift us into fellowship with their sublime control.
An era forms it in the hearts which first beneath them bow'd,
When haughtily some Alpine-peak out-soar'd the highest cloud.

They are not what the dull believe, a mass of speechless earth,
But with embodied eloquence proclaim their regal birth;
Like anthems mute but magical, to inward thought they praise
That Infinite of Architects, Who their foundation lays.

Be glory to the mountains! then,—what poetry they make
When canopied by lucid air, or mirror'd on the lake;
Or when the ravish'd pilgrim cries, from off some wooded brow,
"Three hundred cloven summits lift their ice-bound foreheads now!"

The throned Archangels who in bliss on seats of glory rest,
And through eternity behold the landscapes of the blest,
Can scarce, to our imperfect dream, sublimer views enjoy,
Than what these Alpine monarchs form,—the mountains of Savoy.

The magic of their whiteness seems miraculously pure,
And upward their ascending snows our lifted hearts allure;
And radiant are the icy spells their soaring masses wield,
When seventy leagues cannot o'ershade the dazzling sight they yield.

All glory to the ancient hills! which to the godless preach
Sermons of more stupendous power, than erring man can reach;
Dumb orators to sense they look, but how divinely grand
The deep significance they bear, to hearts that understand!

The stillness of their frozen trance is more than thunder's tone,
Resembling that celestial hush which deepen'd round the Throne
When silence through the heaven of heavens for half an hour there reign'd,
And seraphim before their God eternity sustain'd!

It is not that the clouds array with myriad-tinted hues
Those peaks of alabaster ice which pinnacle our views;

Nor is it, that our sateless eyes are spell-bound by the scene
Of rocky scalps ten thousand feet above some black ravine:

Nor is it, that the glaciers lift their crags of gleaming snow
And move down in a noiseless march to meet the vale below;
Nor all the dreadful joy that chills the soul of him who braves
Montânvert! from thy summit vast, the ever-frozen waves:

Far more than this do mountain-spells to echoing minds impart
When through the veil of outer sense, they reach the central heart,—
There enter with mysterious power, like purities to reign,
And over all its hidden springs a moral influence gain.

Thus oft amid the crowded street, or some contracted room,
Or in that hour of mystic sway when all things wear a gloom,
The Alpine monarchs lift their peaks, and in remembrance rise,
And elevate our sunken hearts through their bewitching skies!

They cause our very souls to blush, to think how base and weak
Are half the fancied woes we feel, or morbidly would speak;
Until their awful summits seem to lift the rallied mind,
And bid it soar to peerless heights above depress'd mankind.

But what a sacred loftiness do regal mountains claim,
When we connect their giant forms with that undying fame
Which clings and cleaves to each and all celestial archives bring,—
The truths, that martyr'd seers foretell, or sainted harpers sing!

Then, glory to the sacred Hills! which rose in childhood's years,
And by their ever-awing names inspired our faith and fears,—
Moriah's mount, and Amalek, Gilboa and the scene
Of Hermon and of Horeb too, where God of old has been.

How Gilead and Gerizim's forms, with Lebanon, appeal,
And Ebal's, whence the curse roll'd down, to man's religious zeal,
And make us through believing awe invest a mountain's brow
With magic and with deathless might, beyond what lips avow.

And, who but recreant hearts forget, how much sublime event
Hath to the hills of Palestine a solemn beauty lent?
Behold the peaks of Ararat! for there the Ark did ride
And floated o'er a deluged world, which then our God denied.

And were not earth's primeval shrines upon lone mountains built?
Upon them rose the altars green, where offer'd blood was spilt;
There sacrifice from votive hearts, with incense-prayer was given,
And who forgets Moriah's hill, and Abram's crown from heaven!

And did not in deep thunder-tones the Decalogue descend
From Sinai's brow of burning gloom, and with dark conscience blend
Such horrors of unearthly sound, that pallid hosts must cry,
"Oh, let not God directly speak, or we the death must die!"

But neither what dread Moses saw, nor hoary Tishbite heard,
Hath ever man's responsive mind with such emotion stirr'd
As have those hills and heights divine, where Jesu pray'd and trod,
Who by the priesthood of His grace brings pardon'd man to God.

'Twas on some mountain where He met the Demon in that hour
When all the gather'd crafts of Hell combined their gloomy power;
And thus on hills of loneliness, in lofty hush afar
Emmanuel kept His midnight-watch, and pray'd beneath the star.

And when His form transfigured grew, with glory more than bright,
Which dazzled into dim eclipse the powers of mortal sight,

'Twas Horeb in its soaring grace that witness'd what appear'd,
When God Himself unclosed the Heavens, and pale disciples fear'd.

But ah! of mountains all which speak to ears of list'ning Time
With tones of superhuman truth and eloquence sublime,
Dread mountain of The Crucified! in faith we turn to Thee,
And echo, with revering hearts, the name of "Calvary!"

And next to this eternal Mount, be that where Jesus taught
His sermon on Beatitude, with grace and glory fraught,—
Those lessons which divinely tell how pure that Heart must be,
Which hopes to hymn the Lamb above, and gaze on Deity!

So, when the Lord of light arose from out this world of gloom,
And re-ascended back to God, His splendour to assume,
Thy mountain, Olives! was the spot from whence He upward soar'd,
While underneath a cloudy shrine the prostrate band adored.

Then, glory to the mountain-Kings! they charm the brave and free,
Like monuments to God uprear'd, proclaiming liberty;
Religion, Law, and Grace combine, around their form to cast
A lofty spell of more than earth, while time and being last.

Lord of the Everlasting Hills! Thou life of nature's scene,
Whene'er upon some mountain-brow our musing steps have been,
Not seldom have such heights become, for mental sacrifice,
Like altars which from earth to heaven in lonely grandeur rise:

There in the hush of twilight-hour, oh, teach us how to pray,
And 'mid their sainted calm of scene adore the Truth and Way;
Till what begins in poesy, shall end in deepest prayer,
The Mountains into temples turn, and God be hallow'd there.

OUR PATTERN IN TEMPTATION.

"We have not a high priest which cannot be touched with the feeling of our infirmities; but was in all points tempted like as we are."—*Heb.* iv. 15.

Come to the desert where sad Jesu went
Lone sinner!—there, as in God's mirror, see
Reflected truths, by gracious wisdom meant
To balk the arch-Fiend when he tempteth thee.

Prophetic actions, typically deep,
Forecasting all the future Church should feel
When blasting trials round her bulwarks sweep,
And fiend and foe combine against her weal

Were those dark trials, when by grace upheld
The fasting Saviour with a Demon fought,
And by His word the powers of darkness fell'd
And back to perfect heaven our Nature brought.

Unknown, the virtue which is never tried;
And principle by keen temptation proves
How much for God and glory is denied
The earth-born will our ruin'd manhood loves.

The triple* force of this perverted world
Aims at our heart a threefold blow of sin:
And souls that would not from their faith be hurl'd,
By providence without and prayer within

Defence must find;—from these apart, they fail
The world, the devil, and the flesh to fight;
Darkness and doubt will o'er their creed prevail
And, Cain-like, plunge them in disastrous night.

How did Emmanuel each infernal dart
Repulse, unwounded, from His perfect soul?—
By words divine! those bucklers of the heart,
Temper'd by Heaven against the Fiend's control.

Alas! for souls, if in their perill'd hour
When sin and self, those Satans of the mind,
Besiege our graces with commingled power,
Staid reason prove the only shield we find.

---

* 1 John ii. 16.

Nor let the righteous who to Love belong,
Dream that temptation will not dog their path;
When saints are weak, alone they seem the strong,
And self-mistrust a true foundation hath.

E'en in pure ecstasies of prayer and praise
When nearest round the Throne of bliss they move,
Visions from hell may float before their gaze,
And hide the glories of the heaven they love.

Here is our wisdom,—with a wakeful mind
The sense to watch, and pray down each desire
Which tempts the conscience to be base, or blind,
By fanning embers of unhallow'd fire.

And oh, what deeps of consolation ope,
Like heavens of comfort, in this creed divine,—
That not alone with Darkness thou wilt cope,
For in temptation Christ believed is thine.

He left His Throne, The stricken Man to be,
Tempted and tried, by anguish spent and worn,
And drew from earth that boundless sympathy
By which He lives,* to succour the forlorn.

Then cheer thee! O thou troubled, toss'd, and tried;
Orphan'd in spirit, dream not of despair,
Open yon heavens, and lo! The Crucified
Echoes thy heart in beating concord,† there.

Thy Lord beseech, by all on earth He knew,
Facing the Demon in his dreadest hours;
Whose soul remains as tender and as true
As when it wept o'er Judah's fated towers.

A mother *may* her new-born child forget,
And exiled hearts their fatherland forego,
But Christ in heaven eternalizes yet
Each tone of Manhood He obtain'd below.

E'en there, behold our sympathising Priest
In feeling human as in form divine;
And seraphs listen, when of saints the least
May boldly cry,—"Incarnate Love is mine!"

* Heb. vii. 25. † Isa. lxiii. 9.

REASON AND DEATH.

"The righteous perisheth, and no man layeth it to heart . . . none considering that the righteous is taken away from the evil to come."—*Isa.* lvii. 1.

The noblest wealth our world contains
Is holiness of heart;
All other gold it gets, or gains,
But proves the meanest part.

Most regal is that glorious will
Enslaved to God alone,
Which finds it freedom to fulfil
Each mandate of His throne;

Blest Angels by a law like this
Partake their perfect heaven,
And could not feel consummate bliss
If other law were given.

Obedience is adoring joy,
Rebellion brings despair,
And would the heaven of heavens destroy
If Self-will triumph'd there!

Yet holiness may not avoid
The doom corruption brought;
Since Adam fell, by sin destroy'd,
Hath death his carnage wrought.

The sting, but not the stroke, of death
The Lord from man removed;
And they who draw the briefest breath
Are oft the most beloved,—

Beloved by God, and angels too,
And thus from grief and pain
Rapt far above our sense-bound view,
With Christ in heaven to reign.

But oh! how cold the world becomes
As saint on saint departs,
To brighten in elysian homes
With pure and perfect hearts.

As if from out yon starry choir
Which chant around the sun,
Some choral planet quench'd his fire
Which we were gazing on,

Impov'rish'd seems our orphan'd earth
When good men pass away;
Time cannot spare their solemn worth,
But needs it, day by day.

But still, for them we dare not grieve
The christian path who trod,
If early call'd this life to leave
For glory, and for God.

To them the gain, to us the loss
High providence assigns;
And so appoints a deeper cross
Than mortal thought divines.

Genius, and worth, and wisdom, all
From God alone arise;
And when He wills the same recall,
They seek their natal skies.

Then hush thee, murm'ring Heart! and let
Profound bereavements teach
Lessons more pure than pale regret
By discontent can reach.

The righteous die, but still they live
A life of soul in bliss;
And what Eternity can give,
Outweighs a world like this!

Men would not marvel, could they see
The lustres round The Throne,
Why saints and martyrs yearn'd to be
Where all the Just have flown.

Sorrow, and sin, and change no more
In heaven their love alloy;
The fever of harsh time is o'er,
And Christ their perfect joy.

We talk and think, as if *our* world
Were all Jehovah made,
And when from some false mountain* hurl'd,
Tremble, as tho' betray'd:

Yet, earth is but a point in space,
Our being, scarce a breath;
And he who will not life disgrace
Must die before his death.†

The booming knell, the opening grave,
The vacant room and chair
Should summon us to hopes which save
The mind from meaner care.

Hereafter is the home of soul,
The paradise of thought,
And with its unsubdued control,
Lord! be our bosom fraught.

* Psalm xxx. 6, 7. † 1 Cor. xv. 31.

As friend on friend, revered and wise,
Leave wither'd hearts alone,
Lift our low dreams beyond the skies
Around Thine argent throne!

Weaker and weaker grows the spell
Which binds the soul below,
When more than burning numbers tell
By grace begins to glow

Deep in those hearts, which death has fill'd
With placid grief profound;
Where every pang is lull'd and still'd
By Him who gave the wound.

Thus with the dead the living hold
Communion grave and high;
Their bodies are but pulseless mould,
But spirits claim the sky.

Thy church, O Christ! is unconfined
By what men hear, or see,
Since all who own a saintly mind
Are in eternity

By hope and faith,—from whence they draw
Breathings of praise and prayer;
While He, Whom martyr'd Stephen saw,*
Becomes their Magnet, there.

* Acts vii. 56.

THE POETRY OF SPRING.

"Lo the winter is past, the rain is over and gone; the flowers appear on the earth; the time of the singing of birds is come."—*Cant.* ii. 11, 12. "Bless the Lord, O my soul . . . He sendeth the springs into the valleys—watereth the hills from his chambers—causeth the grass to grow—appointeth the moon for seasons . . . O Lord, how manifold are thy works! in wisdom hast thou made them all: the earth is full of thy riches."—*Ps.* civ. *passim.*

Hark! breezy anthems from the new-born spring,
Like hymning air-birds on exultant wing;
Wide o'er the fields a flushing radiance glows,
And vernal gladness through each woodland flows.

A seeming consciousness inspires the earth
As though the soil were blooming into mirth,
And, like rich blood in some glad creature's veins,
New tides of life are mantling through her plains.

Music and motion haunt each choral bough,
Like living spirits fill'd with joyance now;
Here, lyric tones, there, wave-like murmurs rise,
And there, the cadence of contented sighs.

Swift o'er the pebbles haste the hill-born streams,
And lisp and laugh, like infants in their dreams;
Or else, make liquid music as they run,
In fairy stanzas warbled to the sun.

The stainless magic of each new-born flower
Mirrors the charm of Heaven's creative power;
Beauty comes forth, like melody from lyres
Swept by some hand which Poesy inspires.

Look where you may, expressive gleams of youth
Dart through the conscience this celestial truth,—
That Christ is working resurrection-life,
Till earth grows radiant and with fulness rife.

The silken azure of yon ruffled sea,
The wing'd emotions of each bird, and bee,
Blent with a chorus of yon festal streams,—
All sway the sense, and beautify our dreams.

And when Morn reddens, until soft and soon,
The golden brightness of unbreathing noon
O'erveils the landscape with a slumb'rous light,
Still shall creation yield intense delight.

Let but the heart be spiritually clear,
Let but our soul this God-made earth revere,
Then will poetic eyes religion greet,
From stars on high, to insects at our feet.

For what is Nature, but a Book divine
Where Godhead dictates each material line,
Where each pure object proves almighty Thought
Forth from its viewless depths to vision brought?

Alas! for Souls, if men baptized can find
Nothing in nature to accost the mind,
Since all around them, did they read it well,
Bears the high meaning of some holy spell.

Sense cannot see them, but bright Angels may
Direct the sunbeams which adorn the Day,
Entone the breeze, and oft at vesper-hour,
Close the bent eyelid of each baby flower.

Cold Science worships philosophic Cause,
And for its God reveres vicarious laws,
Orphans creation of Jehovah's care,
And longs to silence what her scenes declare;

But Thou! by Whom all seasons reign and rule,
Fount of the fresh, the fair, and beautiful!
For ever may Thine angel-spring impart
This glorious symbol to each saintly heart,—

As wintry Earth Her floral garb assumes,
So will the dead, when summon'd from their tombs,
Rise at Thy voice, in resurrection-dress,
And beam with everlasting loveliness.

Beatitudes.

POOR IN SPIRIT.

FIRST BEATITUDE.

"Blessed are the poor in spirit, for theirs is the kingdom of heaven."—*Matt.* v. 3.

WITH awful gloom when Moses brought
The law of fire and flame,
Eternal Duty then was taught
In dread Jehovah's name.

But radiantly descendeth now
Deep wisdom from above;
For mildness clothes His gracious brow
Whose ev'ry line is love.

It was not thus the Type of old
Imperial Law declared,
When round Him pealing thunders roll'd
And red-wing'd lightnings glared.

The people shudder'd, like a leaf,
Amid their black'ning gloom;
And Conscience saw no just relief
Beyond, or in, the tomb.

But bright the contrast now appears,
When the mild Lord of grace
From you green Mount dispels all fears,
By His benignant face.

The breeze, soft lyrist of the spring,
Was harping o'er the flowers;
And humming bees upon the wing
Enjoy'd their golden hours;

A vernal radiance threw its gleam
Of gladness o'er the hills;
While, rich as love-tones in a dream,
The gushing of the rills.

And like the season, so the Word
Was mild as mercy's breath;
No curse was in His counsel heard,
Nor doom of legal death.

That Christ, who came the lost to save,
With blessing did begin;
And thus from guilt, and death, and grave
Redeem'd the heart within.

Humility and meekness were
The groundwork Jesu laid;
And He, whose life was living prayer,
Their perfect types display'd.

All mental grace, all moral gift,
Whate'er men seek, or find,
Is blasted,— if it proudly lift
Or bloat the conscious mind.

Contingent, finite, from the dust,
What Nothings are we all!
For in the tomb the proudest must
A worm his brother call.

All pride becomes a fiendish spark
Of hell, within the soul;
And He who dreads that region dark,
Abhors its least control.

The poor in spirit, blest are they
Above the world who live;
Their wisdom is to watch and pray,
And, like their Lord, forgive.

Nor seek they for ambition's wealth,
Or sigh for world-applause;
But, calm in sickness as in health,
To Heaven commit their cause.

True meekness is that master-grace
Which saints and martyrs wore;—
Behold, who led proud Judah's race,*
How mild a mien He bore!

We cannot back to God return
From the base depths of sin,
Until beneath the Cross we learn
To form the Christ within.†

* Numb. xii. 3. † Gal. iv. 19.

And was He not, of worlds the Lord,
In meekness all divine,
Who with each high and heavenly word
A lowly grace did twine?

A passion for imperfect good,—
Behold, what fosters pride;
While God Himself is thus withstood
No idols are denied.

But mortal, wouldst thou blessèd be?
From finite good retire;
And in the depths of Deity
Thy soaring thoughts inspire.

In humbleness of mind believe
A true contentment reigns,—
Desires which no compunction leave,
And joys that bring no pains.

Then turn thee, O earth-fever'd Soul!
From broken cisterns fly;
For couldst thou drink their blissful whole
They still would leave thee dry.

The utmost in all creatures fails
An inward lull to bring,
Since, when our purest dream prevails,
Unrest keeps murmuring.

Low as some weanèd child to lie
Before Emmanuel's feet,
And in the guidance of His eye
To find a safe retreat,

Like Him to crucify the will,
As merciful and meek,
And each just orb of duty fill
Whene'er we act, or speak,—

Be this, disciple of the Cross!
The glory of thine aim;
And though on earth thou reap the loss,
In heaven perceive thy gain.

But, saith He not, that here below
Beatitudes begin,
For all whose hearts by meekness grow
Above the self of sin?

A kingdom of the mind is theirs
While yet on earth they bide;*
And heaven seems dawning through the prayers
God's Spirit hath supplied.

* Matt. v. 3.

Celestial Dove of grace ! descend,
Thy gentleness impart;
Till Faith shall build the "Sinner's friend"
A temple in her heart.

THEY THAT MOURN.

SECOND BEATITUDE.

"Blessed are they that mourn, for they shall be comforted."—*Matt.* v. 4.

Oh, paradox divine, as deep !—
The blest are those who wail and weep,
And bear that burden which no hearts allay:
With rose-buds though the World be crown'd
While rubied wine-cups circle round,
In fev'rish gloom her false dreams melt away.

The Man of Sorrows, in Whose tear
The Church can type her own career,
The God-man, whose profound extremes combined
Whate'er of glory and of gloom
His awful Person could assume,—
On Mourners stamp'd the name of blest mankind.

But not o'er all sad minds, which mourn
Like orphans in a world forlorn,
Have lips Almighty thus pronounced the "bless'd;"
For grief is oft a selfish chord,
Whose earth-tones can no proof afford
That God and grace have e'er the will impress.

The mourners who "about the streets"*
Of thronging life a stranger meets,
Full often are they but proud Sin in tears;
'Tis worldly sorrow working death
Which now intones their anguish'd breath,
And fetters them with darkness, and with fears.

Spent Minds, like these, none dare believe
Are purely blest, because they grieve,
Or pine that earth no more their heaven supplies;
But blest are *they* who mourn within
The rankling wound of venom'd sin,
Waking, beyond all woe, their soul-heaved sighs.

* Eccles. xii. 5.

For, sin is that stupendous grief
Which out of God finds no relief,—
A tainting curse which cleaves to flesh and soul;
And so abhorr'd around The Throne,
The very heavens * appear to groan
And bow dejected at its dread control !

'Tis true, bland Nature's tear-drops flow
To mark cold earth a churchyard grow,
While tombs rise countless as the waves at sea;
Sickness and sorrow, change and care,
And pale-worn features ev'ry where
Reveal the hollowness vain life must be.

But Zion's mourners grieve and pine,
To think that law and love divine
O'er caitiff man can wield such transient sway,—
How all the Trinity of grace
One bosom-sin will oft displace,
And give to passion's dream its boundless play !

Such weepers mourn before The Lamb,
And cry, "Oh ! wretched that I am !
Who shall deliver me, and burst my chain?"
Their hearts are crush'd, and inly rent
To find what base alloy is blent
With that "fine gold" where virtue feels no stain.

For this they blush, and burden'd lie,
In self-abhorrence shrink, and sigh;
And when they muse on Jesu's awful groans,
And how the garden soil was wet
And crimson'd with His bloody sweat,—
Their hearts beat prayer, which Godhead hears alone !

'Tis here a grief sublime appears:
And rays of glory light the tears
Of Souls, which mourn for heaven's almighty wrong:
Oh ! then descends the Paraclete
And calms them with mild comfort meet,
And turns their sadness to victorious song.

Dejected Minds, who thus are blest
By sealing grace, are more impress'd,
And bland and meek as charity become:
Reflective awe and deep'ning prayer
The growing work of God declare,
And bid them pant for heaven's unclouded Home.

* Jer. ii. 12, 13.

So, when these days of darkness cease,
And holy death shall bring release
From sorrow's gloom, and sin's intense alloy,
How will they glory in that God
Who said, while earth's bleak wilds they trod,
That they who sow in tears, shall reap in joy!

MEEKNESS.

THIRD BEATITUDE.

"Blessed are the meek, for they shall inherit the earth."—*Matt.* v. 5.

Thy ways, O Lord, are unlike ours,
Thy Thoughts surpass our own; *
And angels, when they scan their powers,
Fall wing-veil'd-round the Throne.

Eternity Thine eyes peruse,
Omniscient is Thy mind;
And whatsoe'er Thy wisdom choose
Is perfect in its kind.

But we, by pride and passion stain'd,
Our good no longer know,
And when we dream the goal is gain'd,
Have reach'd intenser woe.

Ay, Good and Evil, Pain and Bliss
In vain blind heathens thought
To image in a world like this
Those models which they sought.

Our Centre true they could not see
In aught the creatures bring;
But Christ, who show'd us Deity,
Unveils that holy Thing.

But yet a paradox this wears
To men who walk by sense,
Which deep humility declares
The heart's sublime defence.

Resistance seems a noble gift
To reason's haughty view;
And passions that proud self uplift
Re-echo it as true.

But He whose will was crucified
Throughout His sad career;
Whom earth abhorr'd, and man denied
One sympathetic tear,

By bearing outrage, wrong, and hate,
This heaven-born lesson taught,—
That souls are not divinely great
Except with meekness fraught.

Submission tender, mild, and deep,
Not sullen, stern, or sad,
But gentle as when Angels weep
While they o'erwatch the bad,

Such the chaste virtue Christ commends,
Believer! as divine;
And if thy heart its Master bends,
That lovely grace is thine.

And who with such a just appeal
To injured souls could cry,
"Like Me must true disciples feel
If doom'd to live or die?"

In Christ the Lamb and Lion met,
Their graces were combined;
And blest are those who follow yet
The path He left behind.

Whether before the Council placed,
Or girt with savage yell,
Or else, by fiendish mock disgraced
Whose accent came from hell;

Or, nail'd upon the wrenching Cross
In one incarnate pang,
While foes beneath Him rage and toss,
And impious gibings rang,—*

However tried, 'tis patience all!
From Him no wrath-tones roll;
To God ascends each dying call
Which rent His yielded soul.†

And who can keep a Christlike heart,
Except his moral tone,
When call'd to bear life's bitter part,
Recall the Saviour's own?

Yet deem not that in stoic frost
Warm feelings must be chill'd;
Or that impassion'd minds are lost
When thus by patience still'd.

Perturb'd emotions, strong and keen,
When pure Religion's cause
Demands a Hero for her scene,
Infringe no hallow'd laws:

---

* Isa. lv. 8.

* Matt. xxvii. 39. † Luke xxiii. 46.

But, guard thee well! lest temper stain
    And poison glorious zeal,
Till selfish anger's secret reign
    Proves all the god we feel.

Meek charity, that master-grace
    The peerless type of heaven,
Oh, let it from thy creed displace
    What cannot say, "forgiven!"

Nor ever let the sun go down
    Upon our inward ire;
They cannot wear a Saviour's crown
    Whom love doth not inspire.

Pure Lord of lowliness, and love!
    Thus make Thy model dear
To all who live for thrones above,
    By bearing crosses here.

Thy meekness hath its own reward,
    Calm blessings line its path;
Without, it keeps celestial guard,
    Within, true peace it hath!

The proud are poor, 'mid all the gold
    Ambition's pride obtains;
The meek are rich, though none behold
    The beauty of their gains.

No acres may to them belong,
    No scenes of garish pleasure;
But yet they chant a mental song
    O'er Truth's divinest treasure.

Then, Lord of Gentleness! be Thou
    For ever at our side;
And when we mark Thy wounded brow,
    Abhorr'd be human pride!

We are not Thine, unless we bear
    Thy yoke upon our souls,
And welcome in each cross and care
    The Hand which All controls.

Disciples true the Christ reflect,
    And must His shadows be;
And none but craven souls reject
    The watchword,—"Follow Me!"

Yes, "follow Thee;" Lord, grant the will,
    And Love at once agrees
Their heaven to taste, whose hearts fulfil
    What Thy calm word decrees.

In life and death such spirits burn
    To hear Thy Voice divine,
And glorify each grace they learn
    By using it as Thine.

RIGHTEOUSNESS.

FOURTH BEATITUDE.

"Blessed are they which do hunger and thirst after righteousness, for they shall be filled."—*Matt.* v. 6.

The hand of Him who framed the earth
    Hath fill'd it with harmonious grace,
That men, who boast immortal birth,
    In each created thing may trace
How wondrously celestial Art,
    From all without which meets the eye,
Appeals to our most inward heart,
    And proves two worlds in harmony.

The world we see, and what we are,
    Illustrates that accordance due
Which reigns from insect up to star,
    And hallows all we feel, or do,—
If thus our hearts delight to prove
    How faculties their objects find,
And render Life a hymn of love
    To Him who hath both worlds combined.

But still there is a craving force
    In appetites to sense allied,
Which nature in its noblest course
    Hath never to the brim supplied;
Though charm'd and fed, they are not fill'd,
    But fever'd oft with discontent;
The cry for "more!" no joy hath still'd,—
    Unrest is with fruition blent.

Though sumless orbs of beauty roll
    In burning magic through the sky,
When mortal gaze commands the whole,
    For brighter longs the asking eye!
And when we hear the tones which make
    The sweetest heaven that sound can bring,
Melodious thirst they do not slake
    For some diviner murmuring.

But while both eye and ear demand
    What no imperfect Sense enjoys,
Spirits who under grace expand
    A bliss partake which never cloys,—
The bliss of hung'ring more and more
    That "righteousness" may still dispense
To sainted hearts an added store
    Of purer calm, and innocence:

Behold! a hunger, and a thirst
    Which God Himself will soothe and
        slake,—
Ambition by no fever cursed,
    A hope no blighting sorrows break;

For all those wingèd dreams that rise
  And flutter round a World divine,
When heaven unveils its hidden prize,
  Will find far more than dreams combine.

Perennial glories there surpass
  All which seraphic Minds desire,
Whom angels with themselves may class,
  With fervid hearts for God on fire;
Of finite good who only drinks,
  Such water will be found in vain;
A deeper want than passion thinks,
  Will soon enkindle thirst again.*

The man who lives by sensual dross,
  May banquet on some hollow bliss;
But yet this truth his mind will cross,—
  I was not made for food like this!
Hunger and thirst, they make the all
  Which carnal wisdom can create,
Whate'er encrowning words may call
  The glories which enwreathe the great.

From joy to joy the jaded Sense
  Pursues each worn and wearied path;
Though big may be this world's pretence,
  The mind eternal hunger hath;
Within, what flaming thirst there burns
  Which all polluting draughts excite,
As passion and supply by turns
  Fever the day, and fret the night!

But Grace forms those, to whom is given
  A glorious passion fix'd on God,
Who breathe on earth the air of heaven,
  And tread the ground Emmanuel trod;
Their creed and conduct are combined
  In unity of peace and power,
And mirror forth a saintly mind
  When darkness clouds the drearest hour.

They must be tranquil, who are made
  By God, the guardian of the blest,
Of neither Hell nor Earth afraid,
  While panting for elysian rest:
Their hunger is a holy thing,
  Their bosom-thirst a painful bliss;
And lauding Seraphs shake their wing
  Of rapture o'er unrest like this!

What is it?—but to nobly pine
  More Christlike in true love to be,
Or body forth the will divine,
  And heaven in all things ever see:
Till rectitude a nature grow,
  And holiness the spirit's breath,
And faith alike in weal or woe
  Adorn our life, and vanquish death.

* John iv. 13.

But if indeed the hunger'd mind
  And thirsting heart for Jesu long,
Then will they not meet nurture find
  To nurse and make religion strong?
Incarnate God! such mystic food
  Thine own ordaining words supplied,
Which in Thy Body and Thy Blood
  A Banquet for the soul provide.*

Thy sacred Flesh, oh! let us eat,
  And drink the awful Wine-blood there,
Where faith Thy bleeding Form can greet
  'Mid swells of sacrificial prayer:
The blasting spells of unbelief
  Must sure those famish'd Hearts infect,
Who feel no pang of boundless grief
  When they such angel-food neglect.

Soul of our souls! almighty Grace,
  A sacramental life impart,
And by some inward power erase
  Whatever dulls the deaden'd heart:
For holiness a hunger give,
  And yearnings of intenser love
That we on Christ may learn to live,
  Like daily Manna from above.

In heaven we need no sacrament;
  Nor signs nor symbols there are found,
When glory with its full content
  Shall each elected Saint have crown'd;
Adorn'd in robes of radiant white
  They neither thirst, nor hunger more,
But bask in beams of pure delight
  With all their toils and trials o'er.

Around the Throne in rich array
  Perfect and sinless are they now,
And in God's temple night and day
  Before the shrine of Glory bow;
The Lamb Himself their food supplies,
  And on His fulness they can feed,
Who follow Him with tearless eyes
  Where paths to living fountains lead.†

BE MERCIFUL.

FIFTH BEATITUDE.

"Blessed are the merciful, for they shall obtain mercy."—*Matt.* v. 7.

When God to man His awful Image gave
  In pure creation's primal bliss,
The Wisdom, Who hereafter came to save
  A sinful world so vile as this,

* John vi. 54. † See Rev. xiv. 4, &c. &c.

The brightest feature of the Godhead drew
By deep impression on his soul,
And bade compassion most divinely true
Reign o'er his breast with unsubdued control.

Our mix'd emotions may be good, or vile,
They govern by ambiguous laws;
But mercy is of nobler cast and style,
And rooted in no selfish cause;—
How godlike, let Emmanuel's life declare!
Whose heart with such compassion beat,
That His pure soul to each sad tone and prayer
On earth became an echoing mercy-seat.

Let stoic Schools from other creeds erect
An iron system, cold and dead,
That would from God-created souls reject
Emotions out of pity bred;
Men are half-monsters, if no heart be left
To throb with pathos, and to feel
Like Jesus, when He saw a home bereft,
And down His cheek compassion's tear did steal.

Thus mercy forms the Saviour's darling grace,
And in Him took a shape divine;
In word and deed, behold its beaming trace
Throughout th' Incarnate Myst'ry shine!
His heart replied to each pale Woe that wept,
Or echo'd back man's deeper sigh;
And by the grave, no icy grandeur kept
The tear of Manhood from His sacred eye.

The haughty coldness of inhuman creeds
May scorn Compassion shedding tears,
And blandly pouring over Sorrow's needs
Those genial tones which soften fears;
And Science may to selfishness ascribe
What soft-eyed Pity for the wretched feels;
But, heaven-born Virtue bears the heathen gibe,
Nor checks the tear which from compassion steals.

Of Men the wisest, bravest, and the best,
The lofty-hearted, firm, and free,
On whose proud name an empire's glories rest,
Who guide the land and guard our sea,—
No leaden calm of unimpassion'd mind
Their boast has been, or proved them brave;
But all pure links, connecting kind with kind,
They deem'd them holy, as beyond the grave!

Men are not wise because they cannot weep,
Nor basely soft because they sigh;
For there are fountains in the heart that sleep
Which moisten oft the sternest eye;
The sainted heroes, canonised by time,
And martyr'd hosts, who burn'd or bled,—
The wide earth doth not deem them less sublime
Because they soothed the sad, or mourn'd the dead!

The perfect God, though passionless as pure,
Hath symbolised His awful Name
By deep emotions, which the heart allure,
And bend the will before His claim:
He speaks not only in the whirlwind's tone,
But with the calm of cooling eve: *
And oft holds back the thunders of His Throne,
That dreadless Minds may love Him, and believe.

But Thou, blest Archetype of love divine!
In whom the Trinity express
Whate'er by union God and man combine
Of moral grace, and loveliness,
Thy Soul was tender as thy Flesh was true,
And throbb'd with thrills of deepest power;
Unmoved in Godhead, yet a living hue
Of warm emotion tinged Thy farewell-hour.†

And art Thou now, embodied Lord of love!
In such deep calm of bliss enthroned
That to the Priesthood of Thy grace above,
Though deep the sigh by anguish groan'd,—
It cannot ripple into feeling there
Thy heart of tenderness, and truth?
Oh, is it echoless to high-breathed prayer,
Utter'd by sin and woe, from age, or youth?

That creed reject! 'tis infidel and wrong;
The Church adores a Priest in heaven
To Whom compassions most intense belong,
By which He feels for man forgiven;
And He is touch'd with sympathies that thrill
Through the rich glories round His Throne;
Since all those splendours leave Messiah still
The weeper's refuge, and the widow's own.‡

Fountain of mercy! whose melodious word
Peals in the soul like pity's voice,
Be each chaste heart by such compassion stirr'd
As makes Thy love its peerless choice;
For if with mercy for their fallen clay
Men are not melted, nor commoved,
How will they shrink from that awarding Day
When barren creeds by Christ are unapproved!

---

* Gen. iii. 8. † Matt. xxvii 46.
‡ Heb. iv. 15; Isa. liv. 5.

Souls cannot love, unless like Him they feel
For human sorrows, hopes, and fears;
And learn to soften with benignant zeal
The bitter gush of orphan tears:
For God is Love; compassions wreathe His name;
And children of pure Grace are we
When, like His echoes, we become the same,
And Love on earth reflects her Deity.

PURE IN HEART.

SIXTH BEATITUDE.

"Blessed are the pure in heart, for they shall see God."—*Matt.* v. 8.

How blessèd are the pure in heart!
And none are blest beside;
For nought of heaven can grace impart
If pureness be denied.

Can sightless eyeballs see the Sun,
Though Earth lie bathed in beams,
And o'er each hill he shinès upon
A ray of rapture gleams?

No more can tainted spirits gaze
On glories round the Throne:
Mere darkness would become That blaze
Pure hearts can bear alone.

The Moon cannot her image glass
On restless waves which rise,
For when the storm-winds o'er them pass,
Her broken semblance dies;

And so, where passion's lurid fires
The love of truth erase,
No sight of God the soul inspires,
But all grows blind and base.

By heavenly likeness Hearts discern
The secrets most divine; *
Just as we live, so much we learn
Of Thee, O God! and Thine.

Those inward eyes of purity
By which the mind beholds
Ideal truths Sin cannot see,
That God Himself unfolds,—

Unless we have them, vain is all
The science stored within;
Our creed the world may holy call,
But such proud wealth is sin.

* Ps. xxv. 14.

And here, behold that peerless Law
Proving the Gospel's worth,
Beyond what sage or poet saw,
When most he soar'd from earth:

That law is purity intense,
A chastity divine,
A sacred glow of innocence,
Which keeps the heart a shrine,—

A shrine of holiness and power
Whence praise and prayer ascend,
To seek what soothes the sternest hour
Which can the Christian bend.

Then, weigh thy heart! disciple, keep
That ceaseless pulse of life;
Which even through innocuous sleep
Can throb with sin, and strife.

Mysterious, ever-active spring
Of central thought, and will!
To which time, sense, and motion bring
Perpetual good, or ill.

By thee we live, and love, and hate,
The inward Man art thou;
Thy nature dooms our final state,
And *that* is forming now!

Oh! watch we then, with jealous eyes,
That world where God alone *
Searches the secret thoughts which rise
Like shades before His Throne.

As local space the body holds,
So God the mind contains;
And who can dare what He enfolds
To mar with sinful stains?

He dwells in us, and we in Him,
The Temple of all souls!
And pure as prostrate seraphim
Be all which He controls.

For if the ground by Moses trod
With sanctity was fill'd,
When erst the flaming bush of God
An o'erawed patriarch still'd,

Sublimer far than thought can trace
Is He, the all-divine,
Who is in Christ our dwelling-place †
And Soul-embracing Shrine.

* Jer. xvii. 10. † Ps. xc. 1; Acts xvii. 28.

Eternal Spring of purity !
Descend, propitious Dove ;
From heart-corruption make us free,
By turning law to love.

The blessèd are the pure, indeed,
And wretched, the defiled ;
In whose dark bosom dwell and breed
Lone passions, fierce and wild.

By likeness only, souls can see
The glories Heaven contains ;
But minds which nurse impurity
Would feel them worse than pains.

For purity is heaven below,
And sin the hell of man,
And all eternity will show;
Will be,—what time began.*

PEACEMAKERS.

SEVENTH BEATITUDE.

"Blessed are the peacemakers, for they shall be called the children of God."—*Matt.* v. 9.

When first rebellion in the Will began
And faith in God to faith in Self was changed,
Wild discord woke within the soul of man,
And headlong impulse o'er his being ranged.

For peace expires where purity is lost,
And purity by love to God begins ;
Who calls him "Father !"—let him count the cost
And pluck the right eye from his bosom-sins.†

And who, with such a God-beseeming grace,
Could weave heaven's garland round the tranquil mind,
As Christ, who purchased for our forfeit-race
The peace divine which lulls heart-torn mankind ?

Lord of our lineage, and of saving calm,
When first from veil'd eternity He came,
A natal anthem o'er night's dewy balm
Sang the rich notes of His melodious name ;

And they breath'd, "Peace on earth ! to man Goodwill !"
And, ere He soar'd to His primeval splendour,
"Peace" was the word that hung soft music still
Round farewell doctrine, so benignly tender.‡

* Rev. xxii. 11; 1 Cor. xv. 53. † Matt. v. 29. ‡ John xx. 19.

The first of blessings, like the last, is found
Thus by our Lord, as deepest and divine ;
And ne'er may calm and confidence abound
Till faith and feeling round this truth combine.

Where low'ring envy, wrath, or secret pride,
Ambition, avarice, and revenge are nursed,
Here can no halcyon from the heavens abide,
But all is chaos, with convulsion cursed.

Base passions are the serpents of our soul,
Which bite, and sting to bitterness the heart,
And where they wield their unsubdued control,
Angels and grace from that foul den depart.

But when these hearts atoning Blood makes white,
Soft o'er our spirit broods the mystic Dove ;
Like the hush'd band who watch'd their sheep by night,
A "peace on earth," replies to peace above.

Then like our Lord, magnanimous and meek,
Move where we may, our end is still the same ;
Firm to our vow, in all we do or speak
We dare embody our baptismal name.

No longer as the Lord of Hosts, and War,
Doth God the glories of His will unfold ;
But radiant as the lull of evening star
As Lord of Peace His pard'ning smile behold.*

And saints on earth resemble Him in heaven,
Who help to circulate the calm of love,
And by imparting what to each is given
Prove their high lineage from the Lord above.

Makers of Peace ! your task divine complete,
Two sever'd hearts in unity restore ;
And bid mild harmonies of friendship meet
To rule in homes where they have reign'd before.

For ah ! how mournful, when two friends depart
Wider and wider into distance stern,
While each one holds the arrow at his heart,
And, but for pride, would lovingly return.

And more than beauteous is a god-like word
Breathing soft balm o'er that tempestuous hour,
When some vile Satan of the soul hath stirr'd,
Or maddens nature with demoniac power.

* Isa. xlvii. 4; Exod. xv. 3; 2 Thess. iii. 16.

To stand between like mediating Grace
And make two alienated minds agree,
Sublimes our being, and reveals the trace
Of true adoption into Deity.

And, blest are they who private love promote
In bow'rs domestic, where meek Virtue dwells;
While feelings motherly their aim devote
To people home with tranquillizing spells.

And not unblest are those, who nobly guard
The lofty sacredness of public Weal;
Theirs the rich peace that brings its own reward,
When Empires at the throne of Godhead kneel.

And He, in whom all unities reside,
Celestial Fount from whence communions flow,
Husband of Souls, who took His chosen Bride
And call'd it by the name of Church, below,—

How can we love Him, if we dare to rend
By the rude harshness of sectarian will
That Mystic Body, where all members blend
And by their harmony due office fill?

How can we love Him, if our "Church" we choose
As pride, or reason, and presumption sway?—
Defend us, Grace! from Babylonian views,
And teach us, not to argue, but obey.

Be ours submission, Mary-like and meek,
Who love the path anointed martyrs trod;
Learning to crucify what most we seek
When Self would image a sectarian God.

So shall we have that sabbath peace of mind,
A wealth beyond the golden worlds to buy,—
A boundless heart which beats for all mankind,
As though it throbb'd beneath the Saviour's eye.

True source of harmony, and sacred peace,
Spirit Divine! without Thee all is vain;
Descend, and with Thy lulling power release
The souls which suffer from a selfish chain.

A loving will that leaps at duty's call
Do Thou bestow, whate'er the trial be,
Bearing the cross which heaven provides for all
Whose faith, O Lord, exults to follow Thee.

Unfathom'd peace! my Saviour's final prayer,
Deep in pure Godhead doth thy basis lie;
Reign like a boundless glory everywhere,
And guard us while we live, and when we die.

THE REVILED.

EIGHTH BEATITUDE.

"Blessed are they which are persecuted for righteousness' sake . . . when men shall revile you . . . and shall say all manner of evil against you falsely for my sake: great is your reward in heaven."—*Matt.* v. 10—12.

"My years are in the yellow leaf,
Though few their number found,"—
But, God is greater than thy grief
And knows the deepest wound;
Be this thy balm, in some distemper'd mood
When sad Thoughts sing their dirge in mental solitude.

This world becomes a barren scene
To eyes of sunny Youth,
When vices have victorious been,
And falsehood vanquish'd truth,
Where good men weep, and Virtue droops in shade,
And minds of most heroic mould are blighted and betray'd.

Thus to pale martyrs of the Cross,
Distracted earth appears
An orphan'd realm, where pain and loss
Demand perpetual tears;
And were it all that God for man decreed,
Who would not in despair for widow'd Nature bleed?

But soon will dawn a radiant clime
Where sin nor sorrows reign,
Beyond the clouds of changing time
To shadow, or to stain;
A bright eternity of balm and bliss
Where pangless hearts forget a life so false as this.

And let the full-toned anthem rise
In swells of grateful joy,
That Faith beholds with prescient eyes
What time nor tears destroy,—
A perfect life, compensative of all
Impetuous thoughts presume unworthy heaven to call.

It was not thus ere christian light
Arose on heathen gloom,
For then the soul immersed in night
Found life a living tomb;
Confusion reign'd o'er providence denied,
And when of death it thought, the craven bosom sigh'd.

But now, a beam celestial plays
From out the Page divine;
And round the gloom of grief-worn days
What dawning glories shine!
O'er ruin'd hopes descending to the grave
The banners of the Cross, sublimely do they wave.

And thus what Sense injustice deems,
That saints can suffer wrong,—
No more a fearful problem seems
To souls by faith made strong;
For o'er them, hark! the "blessed" mildly breathed
From Him who round His head the crown of anguish wreathed.

Yea, "blessed" are the souls which bear
For Christ, and His pure laws,
The moral pang and mental wear
Which friend, or foe can cause;
Since all we suffer, if the will be sound,
Hereafter in the Heavens shall to our bliss redound.

And thus when God incarnate taught
Upon the Mount enthroned,
That they should be to glory brought
Whom scorning earth disown'd,
And so enjoy, by His great mercy given,
A crown which shall outshine what seraphs wear in heaven,

A vision then before Him rose
Of all His Church would be,
As doom'd to battle with her woes,
Till death and darkness flee;
And not one heart that since has broke, or sigh'd,
A soothing balm for which He did not then provide.

Hosannah! cry celestial Hearts
Whom persecution brands,
And bear unmoved infernal darts
When hurl'd by godless hands;
'Tis thus the Soldiers of the truth are train'd,—
Those Heroes of the Lord, who heaven's own laurels gain'd.

By love, and patient suffering led,
More Christlike men become;
And meekly while the path we tread
Which leads our spirit home,
Our graces brighten while they vanquish woe,
And saintly virtue springs from soils where trials grow.

And, do we not corruption feel
Our purest dreams assail,
While wounds which grace alone can heal
Make harrow'd conscience pale?
But these are cleansed by consecrated fire,
As persecuted saints more soaringly aspire.

When clothed with age, or clad with youth,
Whate'er life's era be,
Men glorify the force of truth
Who God in anguish see;
And prove what strength His promises impart
Who, high upon His Throne, can hear the fainting heart.

In all things should the Church reflect
Her regal Lord divine;
And ne'er with sin, or change, or sect,
Her vestal charms * combine:
To suffer, is the privilege of love,
In which the saints outsoar what angels do above.

Then wonder not, if sighs or tears,
Or contumelious shame,
Inweave the web of perill'd years,
Nor God's deep wisdom blame;
But rather, in earth's malediction see
A shadow of the Cross endured, O Lord, by Thee.

Those peerless graces hearts require
To fit the Saints for heaven,
Are burnish'd by that sacred fire
To martyr'd anguish given;
Love, faith, and valour, are the three which make
The stature of the Soul her full perfection take.

And, thus conform'd to Thee and Thine,
Seraphic Minds ascend,
Till with Thine image, Lord, they shine
And with Thy glories blend; †
So proud a bliss heroic saints procure
Who with undaunted hearts their giant pangs endure.

SILENCE OF THE SOUL.

"Joseph could not refrain himself . . . Cause every man to go out from me. And there stood no man with him, while Joseph made himself known unto his brethren."—*Gen.* xlv. 1.

The depths of ocean rest unseen
However loud the storm-blasts ride,
Though where some whirlwind's rage hath been
Foam whitens o'er the flashing tide:

* 2 Cor. xi. 2. † 2 Tim. ii. 12.

For underneath in waveless trance
  The spirit of stern Water sleeps,
And thunderbolt and lightning-glance
  Disturb not its unechoing deeps.

But not like this, majestic Souls
  The tempest of the heart betray,
Whom wisdom chastens, or controls
  By principles of regal sway:
Unlike the sea, *their* surface lies
  Becalm'd without; all pale and proud,
Where not a ripple meets the eyes
  Of those who make the vulgar crowd.

And thus the heaven-born Spartan bears
  With mien and manner undisturb'd
Whatever doom his God declares:—
  He by divine restraint hath curb'd
Those passion-bursts, which wildly break
  From mere excitement's maddening hour,
When stormy pangs the bosom shake
  And palsy Reason's noble power.

Who that has heard the gush of woe
  From some wild mourner by the grave,
And mark'd the scalding tear-drop's flow
  A sunken cheek of sorrow lave,
Or thrill'd beneath those harrowing sighs
  Which burst from out a breaking heart,
And felt not, with o'erflooding eyes,
  What giant pangs death-scenes impart?

But grief there is far more sublime,
  Enacted in this world of gloom,
Which haunts us through memorial time
  With shadow deeper than the tomb;—
'Tis when we hear an earth-clod fall
  Upon the coffin's lid of death
With clay-cold accents, which appal
  And half suspend our choking breath,

With stealthy eye we dare to scan
  The face of some bereaved one there.—
And lo! he seems a tearless man,
  Whose pang no outward signs declare?
No shudders through his bosom heave,
  His features with no anguish move;
And worldlings guess he does not grieve,
  And think him all too stern to love!

But, look again! and thou wilt see
  That iron Soul which sheds no tear,
A mass of buried agony
  Though none to outward sense appear:
His very calm is woe congeal'd,
  A pulseless depth of chill despair;
And what no stormful pang reveal'd,
  Felt like a frozen tempest there.

Hush'd are high feelings, when their course
  Springs from the soul's pure fountain-head;
Though language cannot speak their force,
  Yet, far beyond what lips have said,
Down the deep spirit's veil'd recess
  They nurse their harrow'd nature true;
And those mankind for stoics guess
  Bear hidden wounds, which none can view!

The storm-voice of some open grief
  Too often proves a shallow heart;
And there are pangs from earth's relief
  Which proud and pure stand all apart;
Like the stern patriarch's, when he felt
  Fond yearnings of the brother rise,—
The voiceless heart they inly melt,
  And shun the gaze of common eyes.

So dwells there in each virgin mind
  Some bashful Grace, that will not bare
Its beauty unto coarse mankind,
  But comes to God in secret prayer:
The tumult of religious talk,
  Impassion'd tones of Self unveil'd,
With all which crowds life's vulgar walk,—
  Heaven has not for her children hail'd.

Thus Nature hides her "secret things;"
  Her wonder-works,—what eye can see
The plan whereby Perfection brings
  Their essence out of Deity?
All matter, motion, growth, and life
  Are myst'ries here, which man defy,
And work with deeper wisdom rife,
  Than Science reads below the sky.

And He of hearts the saving Light,
  Our living Sun, within Whose rays
A soul can bear the blackest night
  That deepens round misfortune's days,
Alone He was; unseen, unheard,
  In vigil, fast, and awful fears;
Few pangs He breathed through mortal word,
  But spake them by His blood-shed tears!

At midnight, on calm mountains cold
  Awed angels might have heard Him pray;
But not disciples could behold
  What suff'ring in His silence lay!
And He who seeks a sacred heart,
  In solitude must learn to feel;
Nor to the blushless world impart
  Those deeper thoughts the wise conceal.

In lofty silence, sad and meek
  Thy cross confront, and bear it well;
And if thy soul an echo seek,
  To Christ the hidden anguish tell:

In thy lone chamber kneel, and pray
Where none but God, and thou art nigh;
And He who said,—"Our Father say," *
Shall echo back thy deepest sigh.

SENTIMENT OF FLOWERS.

"As a flower of the field, so he flourisheth."
Ps. ciii. 15.

The Lord, who once celestial radiance threw
Round the gay lilies in their regal dress,
Hath long receded from the church's view,
And Earth seems flow'ring in her loneliness:

But still the Saviour's cry, "Behold!" remains
Deep in the ear, and haunts the spring-toned breeze,
Where pilgrim Thought along secluded plains
Roams by the flowers, beneath romantic trees.

Seems it, as though a consecration hung
On the rich bloom of each innocuous flower,
And grace beyond what minstrel Lyres have sung,
Since Christ arrayed them with a teaching power.

And they are beautiful as infant-eyes,
Sparkling, or pale, when pensive, blue, or mild;
Now, softly vocal, while the air-tone sighs,
And then, in breezy motion dancing wild.

And, like fair visions haunting Memory's dream,
So to the serious mind may flowers impart
In pale seclusion by some lisping stream,
A graceful moral to the feeling heart.

For oft like infants nursed on nature's breast
The dawning buds come forth in sun and dew,
Rosy as Childhood in rich beauty drest,
When life enchants it with a fairy hue:

And beaming Girlhood, in its beauteous grace,
Seems like a new-blown flower in bloom to be,
While fancy muses on that vernal face,
And thinks, how soon that spring of heart will flee!

And have not sentiment and soul-breathed song
From flowers a classic inspiration caught?—
Their spells of beauty to the bard belong,
And grace his lines with many a lovely thought.

In hoar'd cathedrals, solemn, huge, and grand,
Where tombs have tongues, and eloquently preach,
Who has not felt the wingèd mind expand
Soaring to realms beyond mere earth to reach?

There has Devotion traced those marble flowers
Which still to fancy wear a stony bloom
That triumphs o'er decay's funereal powers,
On hero's cenotaph, and martyr's tomb.

And since all matter should to mind attest
Deep truths, significant of sacred worth,
Are not the lilies, by their Maker drest,
Types of the pure, unstain'd by sordid earth?

Emblems of those, the gentle and the good,
Plants of the Spirit, who delight to grow,
And in the hush of thinking solitude
Nurse the meek grace His will and word bestow?

There is an air of chastity and calm
Breathed from the pureness of a vestal flower,
Soft as a breath from Eden's bloom and balm
That shames coarse passion in its rudest hour.

And when on couch of languishment there lies
Some pale-worn victim of disease and pain,
Oft can a flower relume the sunken eyes,
As though they gazed on garden-walks again.

Or, when the boy by Circumstance is led
From the green hamlet where young life began,
And 'mid the large loud city round him spread,
For fields and groves, views artificial man,

If some chance-flow'ret near his path should lie,
How does it thrill association's law,
Making the heart for home and country sigh,
And tread the landscape rosy Childhood saw!

So have I mark'd, amid some fever'd court
Crowded with dens where degradations hide,
Where passions vile with poverty resort,
And orphan'd babes have hunger'd, wept, and died,

* Luke xi. 2.

Some lonely window, with a sickly flower
  Pining as pale, still struggling to endure,
And thrill'd to think how Nature's lovely power
  Could thus the heart of wretchedness allure!

Contemn not this: for in bleak haunts of woe
  Undying thoughts of sylvan life remain;
And many a poor man, while his tear-drops flow,
  Hails a sad violet through a broken pane.

We bless Thee, then, Thou Lord of flowers and trees!
  Bought by Whose Blood, the whole creation lives;
Glowing with health, or martyr'd by disease,
  Hail, to each beauty Thine atonement gives!

And when affection seeks the solemn grave
  To sprinkle flowers upon the guarded mould,
Where in chill darkness sleep the perish'd brave
  Whose memories beautify the days of old,

O Thou! the Resurrection and the Life,
  Thy viewless presence grant at this deep hour,
And to sad mourners, with dejection rife,
  Reverse the emblem of that votive flower.

"Behold the lilies!"—Lord, we would obey;
  But still they wither, while their charms delight;
And in the lustre of their rich array
  Lurks the cold shadow of a coming blight:

But thou, believer! not, like flowers, wilt fall
  Ne'er from the dust in blooming grace to rise;
But when for thee, Earth's citing trump shall call,
  Eternal spring shall fascinate thine eyes.

Celestial beauty, undecaying bloom
  Clothes the pure flesh with more than lilies wear;
And thou, transplanted from the wintry tomb,
  Wilt bud in heaven, and flower with glory there.

RECONCILIATION.

"First be reconciled to thy brother, and then come and offer thy gift."—*Matt.* v. 24.

Pure glory of forgiving Love!
Whose archetype exists above
    In God the reconciled;
By nine degrees * of soaring worth
May our wing'd souls ascend from earth
    To Thee, the undefiled.

Bootless are sacramental Forms,
If in our hearts the hectic storms
    Of sullen anger dwell;
Angels in mien, but Cains in mind,
Men dare to dream their God too blind
    To see their bosom-hell!

No mortal hate with love divine
Can ever in one soul combine,—
    Deceit must both deprave;
For love is that seraphic glow
Which cannot chill before a foe,
    But tracks him to the grave.

Proud thoughts create a mental war
Nor let us see the truth we are,
    But hide from Self our sin;
Aloud men cry o'er wrongs they feel,
But all the wrongs they do, conceal
    Like pharisees within.

Could we ourselves as clearly scan
As we unshroud our brother man,
    How humbly might we walk!
And never in the maddest hour
When vile self-worship wields its power,
    Of our meek virtues talk.

Let Conscience learn, the sharpest word
Our ulcerated pride has heard
    Is tender, more than true;
Since all that envious eyes can see,
Is pure to what Divinity
    In man's vain heart can view.

Thy temper soothe, thou ireful one!
Nor ever may the west'ring sun
    Go down upon thy wrath;
Thy brother seek, each fault confess,
And with sad tones of mild distress
    Win all the love he hath.

If by cold word, or thought, or deed
Thy heart has caused his own to bleed,
    Promptly that ill repair;
Nor dream that thus to condescend,
Will one dark hue of meanness blend
    With aught thou feelest there.

---

* In a strain of beautiful inspiration, Chrysostom, when commenting on Matt. v. 44, says, Εἶδες ὅσους ἀνέβη βαθμοὺς, κ. τ. λ. "Do you observe the scale he has ascended, and how he has placed us upon the pinnacle of virtue? &c. &c. The *Ninth* to God for Him. Do you mark the summit of philosophy?"—*Chrysost. Hom.*

But if in soul, a sullen thought
With scowling pride of anger fraught
Toward friend or foe remain,
Presume not, where Christ's altar stands
To offer with polluted hands *
What Heaven must so disdain.

First to a brother give thy heart;
Let bitterness of soul depart,
And then, that meal partake
Where Love Incarnate bleeds and dies
In His memorial sacrifice,
Presented for thy sake.

Fathom thy deeps of sinful mind,
Keen to thyself, to others blind,—
Be this thy noble plan!
Beneath enamell'd smiles and ways
Let Conscience dart her searching rays,
And thou wilt pity man.

Self-ignorance makes the spirit proud,
And o'er clear error casts a cloud
Of flatt'ry's genial power;
But Self-illumed by heaven's own ray
Can melt that painted mist away,
And humble ev'ry hour.

Vain hypocrites, and worse than vile
If passions dark our soul defile
And fiendish thoughts are nursed,
While outwardly in church and creed
We call ourselves a "holy seed,"
By God we are accursed!

Heaven's lineage must heaven's likeness wear,
And not alone by praise and prayer
Authentic worship prove;
When Faith beholds her God of grace,
The brightest Feature she can trace
Is that which glows with love.

Then, grant us, Lord, a heart like Thine
As deep in mercy, as divine,
Celestial, mild, and true;
And learn we all, the more we live,
The godlike must like God forgive †
All daring Wrong can do.

Creation seems instinct with love,
A parable of His above,
Father, and Friend of all;
And not a rain-drop Earth renews
And not a sunbeam lights her hues
Which does not grace recall.‡

* Ps. xxiv. 3, 4. † Matt. v. 48.
‡ Matt. v. 44, 45.

O'er just and unjust, what a shower
Of raining mercies falls each hour,
Bought by atoning Blood!
From Whose vast merit all that is,
Derives each energizing bliss
Which makes our common good.

Two Bibles thus our hearts may teach
A pure sublime of man to reach,
In love for friend and foe,
Since Nature, like the Gospel, pours
O'er "good and evil" all her stores,
That each may Godhead know.

ANGELIC MINISTRY.

"Are they not all ministering spirits, sent forth to minister for them who shall be heirs of salvation?" —*Heb.* i. 14. "He shall give his angels charge over thee, to keep thee in all thy ways."—*Ps.* xci. 11. "The angel of the Lord encampeth round about them that fear him, and delivereth them." —*Ps.* xxxiv. 7.

Say, why do sceptic hearts decline
In nature more than earth to view?
We cannot trace the word divine,
But angel-forms attend us through:
Salvation's heirs they watch and keep
Both when they wake, and while they sleep.

And how could perill'd infants rove
Light as elastic breezes play,
Secure as if in heaven above
They tripp'd along some crystal way,
Unless beloved by angel-powers *
Who hover round their fleeting hours?

All Nature feels a lovely awe
Environing the aidless child;
And fancy dreams her iron law
Before it grows relax'd and mild;
E'en the stern brute a babe will spare;
And why?—some angel watches there.

When shepherds on the midnight-plain
Of Judah kept their flocks at night,
Who hymn'd that heaven-reecho'd strain
At which applauding Worlds grow bright,
But angels, whose ethereal tongue
The glorious Incarnation sung?

And when the Fiend of darkness tried
To wrestle down that perfect will,
By which the Prince of Peace defied
His threefold power of lying ill,

* Matt. xviii. 10.

Behold! yon Seraph leaves his throne
To soothe Him when the fiend had flown.

But, turn to dread Gethsemane;
That garden pall'd with spectral gloom
Where, bow'd with wordless agony
Messiah bled, before his doom,
That bloody sweat,—that crimson dew
Which strain'd His tortured spirit through!

E'en then, from yon bright Host above
A sympathetic angel came,
And o'er him warbled tones of love
Which dropt like balm upon His frame;
For, dread to think!—imputed sin
Convulsed *His* finite soul within.

But when before the radiant morn
The Lord of Resurrection rose,
Winding the grave-clothes Death had worn,
As though just risen from repose,
Two angels watch'd, as guardians meet,
Where lay His awful head and feet.

And like a sunburst from the south
On wings of archangelic sheen,
To roll from that sepulchral mouth
The rocky stone where Christ had been,—
Two Creatures of celestial might
Came speeding down from worlds of light.

So when at length Emmanuel soar'd
And left His loved disciples' view,
While their ascending glance adored
The Lord, who back to heaven withdrew,
What bounding hopes within them burn
When angels say, "He shall return!"

INFANT FELLOWSHIP WITH GOD.

"Hid from the wise and prudent . . . revealed unto babes."—*Matt.* xi. 25.

Mysterious infant! on thy fairy brow
A far-off glory seems reflected now,
A pensive, mild, and melancholy ray
Like the last hue of heaven's most lovely day;

Thou living harebell! 'mong the human flowers
Which bud and blossom in domestic bowers,
The liquid azure of thy placid eye
Gleams like the softness of a vernal sky:

Feeble to sense and sight indeed thou art,
But oh! within thee dwells a mighty Heart,
Capacious of eternity, and God,
E'en now, before the travell'd earth is trod.

Fragile the organs that connect thy soul
With those blent world-scenes, which our own control;
But let not creedless Science this declare,—
That God and angels are unvision'd there.

Souls in pure essence are, like grace, unknown;
For all we hear is but the outward tone,
A broken echo of a voice within
Muffled by earth, and jarr'd by jangling sin:

But if The Spirit must a soul renew
Ere glory open on its blissful view,
Then must the babe unbreathed communion hold
And have with Heaven some intercourse untold.

Sinless in fact, untempted babes depart
To where, O Christ, ensphered in bliss Thou art;
And ere time's language to their lips is known,
They learn The Cross before salvation's throne.

And who remembers not some deep-eyed child,
Unearthly, pale, and exquisitely mild,
Purer than chisell'd alabaster shines
Where sculptured poesy hath traced its lines?

But 'tis not beauty, delicate and bright,
Nor limbs elastic as incarnate light,
Nor that seraphic grace of brow and cheek
More eloquent of mind, than words can speak:

'Tis something finer than all beauty far,
Tender as dreams beneath a twilight-star;
A heaven-like stamp of saintliness which glows
O'er each calm feature in its chaste repose.

And who denies, prophetic babes may see
Secrets and Shapes which throng eternity,
Visions of glory, such as elder man
Has never imaged in the course he ran?

A wordless infant in some mystic hour
May have The Spirit in His deeper power,
Converse with angels, and in God behold
Truths which heroic Saints have never told.

The tearful radiance of a baby's eye,
The pleading music of its pensive sigh,
The looks that seem so spiritually deep
Turn'd on beholders, till they almost weep,

May be the symbols of a faded heaven
To infants in angelic slumber given,
Which leaves them, when they face the world again,
In dim remembrance and in dawning pain.

And none can tell, but hov'ring babes above
To babes on earth may whisper tones of love,
Melodious fragments of cherubic song
On Glory's breeze for ever borne along.

And, childless mother! let a thought like this
Becalm thy bosom with sustaining bliss,—
When thy pale infant heaved the parting sigh
Some Angel bore it to the peopled sky.

Bright from the waters of baptismal life,
Stain'd by no sin, nor touch'd by earth-born strife,
Straight to its God thy sinless babe hath flown
And join'd the myriads which enwreathe His Throne.

THE SINGLE EYE.

"If thine eye be single, thy whole body shall be full of light."—*Matt.* vi. 22.

Though ruin'd, deathless man is noble still,
In whom fair lines and lineaments remain
Of all he was,—ere sin by lawless will
Cast on the glorious Soul a guilty stain;
And not with harsh irreverence should we dare
One trace despise, which Heaven has treasured there.

As round a gloomy shrine, in grand decay
Where crumbling arch and ruin'd pillar fall,
Remnants of beauty yet the pile array
And the dead sculpture into life recall,
When sacred fancy with religious eye
Dreams in the ages of a World gone by,—

So, 'mid the sinful waste of man perverse
Faint hues and harmonies of Eden dwell,
Not all remanded by the righteous curse
Which on the forfeit-state of Adam fell:
Round the sad ruin of his fallen soul
Shadows divine of vanish'd Glory roll.

But if by earth-fed passion, lust, or pride,
Greedy of gain, or gorged with self-esteem,
Majestic reason is just power denied,
The central life becomes a ghastly dream,
Where all our faculties and functions blend
In dread confusion, which can never end.

For then, Incarnate Wisdom so declares,
That which by nature should our light become,
And starlike, lead us through the night of cares
Which deepens round us till we reach our home,
Itself is darkness! and the beam that glows
Is that which Falsehood to blind feeling shows:

How great the "darkness," not e'en Christ hath said!
As though such midnight of the mind surpass'd
Whate'er rebellion of the heart or head
By finite language can be call'd, or class'd:—
"Darkness" that e'en from Him a wonder drew,
To Whom no sight in earth, or hell, was new!

Single the Eye, when jealous conscience guards
Its vestal chastity by prayer and truth,
And not to Reason, but to Grace awards
Those inward laws which hallow age and youth,—
Those godlike principles by which men live,
And the dread Soul to its own Author give.

Resist we, then, the sorceries of sin;
The lust of income and the love of power
Cloud the clear Eye, whose vision acts within
And ought to rule and rectify each hour:
So will our reason, with no jaundiced gaze,
Interpret duty through a blinding haze.

Religious principle and moral code
Diseased by passion, most perversely act;
And Vice, recoiling from heaven's narrow road,
Dares its own decalogue of Self enact:
Our way is hell-ward, though we heed it not,
Sinai renounced, and Calvary forgot.

Oh! better far be reasonless and mad,
Than thus transform the rectifying Guide
Which God ordain'd to govern good and bad,
And legislate on virtue's lovely side;
For, when distorted, conscience proves a curse
Whose cruel wisdom makes condition worse.

As though the needle in its compass were
Reversely guiding o'er a sea of gloom
The storm-heaved ship, while lurid tempests glare,
And ocean blackens like a billowy tomb;—
Her wreck is fated though she proudly rides
In foaming triumph o'er the furious tides!

Nor dream that when by damning vice depraved,
The central light of reas'ning conscience fails
To warn the victim of desires enslaved,
Corrective Wisdom o'er such doom prevails:—
An Archimedes in the world of mind
Who fix'd his lever and hath raised mankind,

If not with him the single eye and pure
For sacred guardianship of soul remain,—
His teachings prove but spell-words to allure
The hearts which hear them, into vice and pain:
The rays of Genius, when to darkness turn'd,
What fiendish laurels have they found, and earn'd!

Spirit of wisdom! pure and perfect Light,
Come from Thy region of celestial grace,
Through the bad gloom of unbelieving night
Dart the mild beams of Thy majestic face:
By loving Thee, saints learn to grow divine,
And as they live, resemble Thee, and Thine.

That single Eye, which God and glory views,
Whose seeing power by holiness is keen,
And doth o'er all things Christ supremely choose,—
Be this our wisdom in life's perill'd scene;
So shall we vanquish, by enduring, ill,
And find it heaven to do our Father's will.

MY FIRST-BORN.

"The Lord spake, Sanctify unto me all the first-born; it is mine."—*Exod.* xiii. 2.

[C. H. E. M. BORN MAY 4TH, 1848.]

My first-born! when I heard thy faint low cry,
Home to the heart was echoing nature stirr'd
With more than man can tell by tear, or sigh,
Or Fondness image through a shaping word;
For Life is deeper than our language far,
And dimly mirrors but the half we are.

The fountains in the inward deep of soul
Seem'd broken up with preternat'ral start,
And onward gush'd with sweetest uncontrol
The new-born raptures of a parent's heart:
Each chord of feeling trembled like a tone
Which haunts the harpstring, when the hand is flown.

How shall I doat upon thy dawning smile
When conscious reason first begins to play!
And watch the beauty of each dimpling wile
Clothing thy cheek with what the lip would say,
Were but the gladness of thy spirit heard
In the lisp'd cadence of some little word.

Holy is childhood! through that lovely age
Incarnate Mercy did not shun to live,
And thereby circled life's commencing stage
With halo pure as innocence could give,—
A charm which consecrates an infant now,
When the first Sacrament bedews its brow.

Nor doubt, the infant Christ at mother's knee
The priceless volume of celestial Love
Conn'd day by day,—that parents hence might see
How lisping babes ascend to truth above;
Nurtur'd for heaven as their young spirits grow,
By wisdom strengthen'd in this world of woe.

Nor let some Cain-like reason coldly ask
How with the mind of some unspeaking child
Regenerate Love can ply its living task,
And to the heart teach lessons undefiled?—
Baptismal grace exceeds what eyes discern,
And more than Science dreams, a babe may learn.

Think how Emmanuel, when man's world He walk'd,
Stoop'd to those little ones, who round Him came;
And when of more than angels knew He talk'd,
Anthem'd with high-toned joy God's mystic name,*
Because what hoary Sages oft refuse,
That for some nursling God's free-will doth choose.

So with a sacredness from heaven decreed
My first-born! by the Church environ'd round,
May the blest Spirit help thy dawning need
From hallow'd stores, which in His breast abound,
Who e'en in glory can remember still
How on sad earth He felt each infant thrill.

Lamb of the flock! within thy Saviour's fold
Calm may'st thou roam, by living pastures green
'Mid waters bright,—with footstep never bold,
Follow The Shepherd through life's destined scene;
Thou wilt not want, if He become thy guide.
With rod of love and staff of grace supplied.

---

* Luke x. 21.

Coil'd in the secret of His purpose vast
Firstling of Hope ! thine unread future lies,
But should thy doom for ripening years be cast
And thou be spared to light enamour'd eyes,
How will maternal Fondness round thee twine,
And my heart gladden when it dreams of thine !

To aid thy lip Christ's glorious name to speak,
And hear thy sweet mouth lisp its little prayer;
To watch emotions mirror'd on thy cheek
When first religion is reflected there,
While with lock'd hands of reverential love
Thou kneel'st to ask a blessing from above,—

By soft degrees to view thee conscious grow
Of God and nature, mind, and scene, and man,
Gently to chide each fault, and calm each woe
As only echoing hearts of parents can,—
Delights like these will anxious toil repay,
And sun my spirit with perpetual ray.

And should my darling add to loveliness
A frame responsive to those fine appeals,
Which earth's dumb eloquence doth aye impress
On each who nature's living poem feels,
With sacred rapture shall I watch thee try
To read God's epic, in the glorious sky !

But oh, of joys the brightest, purest, best
Will that be found,—when first thy budding mind
Words of redeeming grace and truth arrest
And glorify thy love for human kind;
Or when thy broken accents would explain
What Childhood feels for God's incarnate pain.*

But these are dreams :—and voiceless omens creep
Round my chill'd Spirit, when it looks on thee,
Making the moist eye almost bend and weep
O'er the veil'd depths of hush'd futurity ;
For soft dejection in thine infant-gaze,
Like dim prediction, seems to tell thy days.

God shield thee, darling !—like a dewdrop now,
In radiant freshness on the tree of Life
Trembles thy being ; but with prescient brow
I darkly ponder, lest disease and strife
Crush thy soft nature, now so fair and frail,
And bid thee into death at once exhale.

* "I learn to believe in God the Son, who hath redeemed me."—*Catechism of Church of England.*

Mysterious God ! should this deep trial come
And thou, my first-born, find the infant's grave,
Long ere thy sire, shouldst thou be summon'd home
And heaven remand the treasure that it gave,
Oh ! teach me, Lord, this awful prayer to say,—
"Blest be His name, who gives, and takes away !"

JUDGE NOT.

"Judge not, that ye be not judged. For with what judgment ye judge, ye shall be judged; and with what measure ye mete, it shall be measured to you again."—*Matt.* vii. 1.

Eye of the Lord ! in whose omniscient ray
Our motives play,
Like motes in sunbeams, each distinctly bare,
Can sinners dare
Rash judgment o'er that secret heart to strain,
Where Thou dost reign

Alone,—from Whom no buried thoughts are hid?
Men are forbid
To scan a brother with censorious eye ;
Or sternly cry,
"Let me the mote from out thy vision draw,"
As though they saw

With holy clearness of unclouded view
The pure and true :
While in their eye-glance dwells one sinful beam
Men little deem,
How all who virtue love, will strive to be
From sin set free.

A flagging will, a feeble mind
To Glory dead and Wisdom blind ;
A neutral cowardice of heart
That shrinks from taking noble part,
When Christ, and Church and Creed demand
The prowess true of heart and hand,—
Lord ! not for these Thy words assign
The guerdon Faith believes divine,
When Thou dost bid each duteous mind
Abstain from judging mortal kind.

The truth must e'er the falsehood fight,
While wrong pursues the hated right ;
And they are craven to the Cross
Who quail for dread of earthly loss ;
Or else, because the coward Will
Recoils from rude oppressive ill,

Refrain from branding sin and crime;
And so caress the vassal time
That vice and virtue, false and true
Become the heart's chameleon hue!

Avaunt! such antinomian Ease,
Whose gospel is self-will to please.
But, come ye Inspirations given
Fresh from the heart of Christ in heaven!
Mild Charity, and modest Thought,
And Meekness with Devotion fraught;
With radiant Candour, rich in love,
And motherly, as born above,
Which, mindful of Redemption's plan,
Embraces universal man.

The perfect Judge is God alone;
And he usurps His legal Throne
Who rashly dares to pierce and scan
Those spirit-fibres of the man.—
Motives! which are of acts the soul,
And subject to Divine Control:
By man unprobed, in all their change
They move within His mental range,
By Whom is mark'd the embryo sin,
Ere yet 'tis born the soul within.

But e'en when action, motive, thought
Are into clear exposure brought,
And all which meets our human gaze
Harrows the soul with stern amaze,
Man must not wield the judge's rod,
Or make himself the bar of God.
Love in that light, oh! let there be
By which our hearts a brother see;
Since, blind and partial are we, when
Hurt feelings try our fellow-men.

Be merciful! for sinners all
Are they, who Christ their glory call;
Such Minds can weep where others frown,
To see how soon we wander down
Those sad descents of worldly sin
Which tempt without, and try within.—
The holy are the humble, too;
Rather in silence will they rue
The faults and failings brethren show,
Nor be the first a stone to throw.

Their sin we view; but not the strife
Or writhings of that inward-life
Where passion, conscience, and desire
In some convulsive mood conspire:
Nor can we measure with just mind
How circumstance with choice combined;
Or mad temptation, swift and wild,
Tore like a fiend the heart defiled;

Or, how resistance unto prayer
Fought with the Crime which conquer'd
  there.

O God! before Whose perfect eye
Are cloud-stains on the crystal sky,*
Were we but judged by those degrees
By which malign Suspicion sees
A brother in his conduct fail,—
E'en martyrs would the Judgment wail.
Rather, through love's kind error, be
Victim of fond credulity,
Than like some cold and cutting blast
Which near the frozen Sea hath past,
Breathe o'er thy brother words that wring
The soul with unvoiced suffering.

Come then, celestial Archetype for all,
  To Thee we call;
And ere the bolt of Censure can descend
  On foe, or friend,
Oh, introvert the spirit's eye, to scan
  Our inward man.

For thus, what boundless error should we see
  In us to be!
The arm reversed would then no censure throw
  On friend, or foe;
But, as dark evils which deserve a stone,
  Would brand our own.

AWFULNESS OF SPEECH.

"By thy words shalt thou be justified."—*Matt.* xii. 37.

We ought to dread what Speech can do,
  And mortal words have done,
As vain or vile, or false or true,
  Since Language first begun:

For speech the soul can so empower,
  For fiends', or angels' work,
That Death, or Life, each dawning hour,
  Within some tone may lurk.†

A speechless thought innocuous seems
  To all except the Mind,
Through whose vague depths it acts, or dreams
  For self, or for mankind;

But when abroad, by speech, or press,
  Our Thoughts their course begin,
Conception cannot dare to guess
  What conquest they may win.

---

* Job xv. 15. † Prov. xviii. 21.

Through regions, empires, heart and home,
A trackless Thing it hies,
And through eternity will roam,—
For Influence never dies.

To counsel, flatter, charm, or cheer,
How potent human speech!
To summon smiles, or mould a tear,
To pray, rebuke, or preach,—

Thus life and death within the spell
Of living words reside,
And blest are they, who wield them well,
Rememb'ring Him who "sighed!"

And why? Because the Saviour knew
That since our primal Fall
No tongues are to their glory true,
Except on God they call.

Eye, Ear, and Speech, each organ may
A ban or blessing prove,
According as we learn to lay
Their service out in love.

Thus did Emmanuel sigh to know,
That when Compassion gave
To dumbness power the mind to show,
From sin it would not save,

But might hereafter frequent tempt
His tongue to many a crime,
That, but for speech, had proved exempt
In silence half sublime.

He mark'd the victim, mute and sad
Who thus before Him stood;
And cried "Be open," not "Be glad,"
Though speech itself were good.

And so with us: 'twere better far
As dumb and deaf to be,
Unless in spoken life we are
From worded vileness free.

And never may we speak, or write
A word which others know,
Unless 'twill bear His searching light,
From whom all speech doth flow.

Let that deep sigh the God-man drew,
Around us swell and heave,
And when we utter words untrue
That sigh will make us grieve.

LET US PRAY.

"If ye, then, being evil, know how to give good gifts unto your children, how much more shall your Father which is in heaven give good things to them that ask him?"—*Matt.* vii. 11.

All that of Eden now remains
Lives in the lovely page of God,
Where o'er green earth a beauty reigns
As when by Christ at evening trod;*
Oh! were it not for this pure story,
Our hearts might scarce conceive the glory
Which still that paradise of words arrays
With all those hues of heaven, which spell-bound Adam's gaze.

The weed, the thistle, and the thorn,
And stooping Labour's moisten'd brow,
Are types and tokens men are born
Under the primal ruin now;
The kingly mind of innocence
Seems crush'd by sin's omnipotence;
And riper passions round our virtues prey,
And with envenom'd tooth begnaw their strength away.

But still beneath man's ruin lives
One feeling, which survived the Fall,—
That which parental fondness gives
To those who hear their children call:
Men are not fiends, but still reply
Like echoes, to each filial cry
A son puts forth in some beseeching hour,
When lisping Childhood yearns for parent's guardian power.

Divine emotion! deep as pure;
Without thee, Scripture breathes a tone
Which could not alien hearts allure
To bend before the Mercy-throne:
But when "Our Father!" thence is heard,
Dead feelings in their tomb are stirr'd;
And like the ladder joining earth and skies,†
They form attractive steps, by which to heaven we rise.

And thus hath Christ affections used
When pleading oft with prayerless mind,
And shown that, though by sin abused,
There is a law that wields mankind,
By which parental natures prove
The throbbings of eternal Love,
When Hunger seeks them with dejected cry,—
"Food for thy famish'd child! or he must die."

* Gen. iii. 8. † Gen. xxviii. 12.

And, Lord, if thus the sin-worn heart
So much of paradise retain,
Why dare we doubt in heaven Thou art
Responsive to each prayer-breathed strain?
Did Faith but ask, and knock, and seek,
What giants would become the weak!
And Conscience realise Thy love as true
As when its death-gasp groan'd, "Forgive them what they do."

Could men but feel, how constant prayer
Sustains the most heroic Mind,
Their life would be one holy care
A Father-God in heaven to find;
Not as a Judge, with iron brow,
Before Him would they bend and vow;
But from the deeps of man's parental heart
Gather some loving gleams of what, O God! Thou art.

Saviour of souls! our Truth and Way,
Bread for the famish'd hearts which pine,
Instruct us like Thyself to pray
"Father! Thy will be done, not mine."—
Tender has been the tearful thought
A babe-cry to some mother brought; *
But far more tender is The Heart above
Whose echoing depths repeat the name of holy "Love." †

DIVINE FAITHFULNESS.

"The mountains shall depart, and the hills be removed; but my kindness shall not depart from thee."—*Isa.* liv. 10.

The mountains shall from earth depart,
The hills may be removed,
But thou of God elected art
And as a "bride" beloved;
Our God as soon might cease to be,
As break His covenant with thee.

Election flows from no high worth
In fallen souls foreseen;
For where is good on this bad earth
Which free grace hath not been?
Did God demand prevenient love,
Heaven would not shrine one soul above.

Thou barren Heart! which hast not borne
The hopes that make thee sing, ‡
Oh, dream not thou art left forlorn
In widow'd suffering:

* Isa. xlix. 15. † 1 John iii. 16.
‡ Isa. liv. 1.

For like a wife in youth forsaken,
Back to thy Lord shalt thou be taken.

Though toss'd on life's tempestuous sea
Affliction's waves run high,
For one small moment Heaven from thee
Averts its loving eye,—
Yet, soon will mercy's overflow
Around thine anguish brightly glow.

No crisis can our God subdue,
No change His will surprise;
Close to His ancient counsel true
His grace for ever lies;
The "Lord of Hosts" reveals His name
In love eternal, and the same.

He does not find a lovely thing
And love what He discerns;
But His pure love becomes the spring
Of what in martyrs burns
Of holy passion, zeal, and prayer
By God's own Spirit kindled there.

Then, courage! torn and troubled Mind,
The Glorious One appears;
Nor let Dejection leave thee blind
With her impassion'd tears:
Soon shall thy blest Redeemer come
And guide thee safe to Glory's home.

No weapon'd hand its deadly wound
Shall in thy spirit make;
Nor all the raging tongues around
That bond of goodness break
Which God in Christ for thee doth hold,
And His deep heart of grace enfold.

With sapphires thy foundations fair *
Shall soon by Him be laid;
Nor shall oppressive Wrong be there,
As though thou wert betray'd: †
Terrors themselves shall learn to fear
A kingly saint to Godhead dear.

The Spirit's love, a love divine
Though earth and heaven decay,
Is true, O Lord! to Thee and Thine
Though worlds dissolve away;
Had Souls true faith, they could not dread
The deepest midnight round them spread.

A dying world for dying men
For saints hath Heaven decreed,
And wisely plans the where, and when,
Each burden'd heart must bleed;

* Isa. liv. 11. † Isa. xliv. 11.

But, Love this truth can understand,—
Each blow is from a Father's hand.

And thus, if fortune, home, and friend,
And social bliss, no more
Around us their rich magic blend
As they were wont of yore,—
Reflected on our falling tears
The iris of God's love appears.

Timeless and changeless is the plan
Before all worlds begun,
From whence that mercy reacheth man
Incarnate Merit won:—
Though toss'd, and by the tempest shaken,
Believer, thou art unforsaken!

REVERE THE DEAD.

"Blessed are the dead who die in the Lord."
Rev. xiv. 13.

Pity the dead!—nay, rather mourn for those
Who battle on through Life's harsh scene of care,
In whose grieved breast the thorn of trial grows,
While in the crowd all echoless they are:
Bearing some poison'd shaft within the heart
They feel, bad World! the hollowness thou art.

Pity the dead!—no, rather weep for them
Who on vex'd earth must suffer, toil, and sin,
And pray, their passion's burning tide to stem
And keep close watch o'er waywardness within;
Who hour by hour repentance must renew,
And mourn how little for their Lord they do.

But oh! the dead, the justified and saved,
Children of glory, wrapt in Jesu's arms,
The darkness of the sepulchre they braved
And there are shielded safe from Earth's alarms;
Pure in the brightness of ethereal bliss,
They would not change it for a scene like this!

The spirits of the Just, made perfect now,
Have each in heaven their beatific calm;
Serenity arrays each kingly Brow,
And through each Heart distils celestial balm;
Their hope as cloudless as the peace divine,—
Seraphic visions round them reign, and shine.

And He is there! the kingdom's Light and Lord,
Who out of time and toil has call'd them home,
And now fulfils each wise and glorious word
True faith believed, when doom'd on earth to roam,—
E'en Christ, who beautifies the Spirit-throngs,
'Mid their deep worship of adoring songs.

But, ah! fond Nature, in thy bosom yearn
Feelings which oft our passive faith o'erflow;
And with such flame intense affections burn
That time, nor truth, can quench their secret glow;
Down the deep heart some unvoiced thoughts remain,
And bid us sigh to see our Dead again.

"My beautiful, my bright, my darling child!
Her smile was eloquent with soul to me;"
Thus the wan mother in her anguish wild
Echoes the regions of eternity,
When round the heart-strings thrills the seeming breath
Of some loved daughter, tomb'd in early death.

"And thou, my dead, my unforgotten boy!
Prop of our home, and pillar of our race,
Genius was thine, and brow of princely joy,
And more than beauty clothed thy classic face;
How did I dote, and for thy future build
Schemes which parental hearts alone have fill'd."—

So grieves a sire, when Love's ideal hours
Roll their sad cadence o'er his dreaming brain,
When the dead Past resumes a living power
And with such resurrection smiles again,
That hand in hand his child he seems to hold,
And hear the Voice that lull'd him so of old.

And thou, lone sister! who pale watch didst keep
Night after night, around some fairy child,
Marking each dimple which in rosy sleep
Sunn'd the pure face, as though an angel smiled,
When Death withdrew it to th' unseen abode,
Thy heart to madness almost overflow'd.

But, peace! fond mourners: calm your souls to rest,
The Dead you weep are still alive to Him,
Lord of those mansions, where the bright and blest
Are pure and peaceful as the seraphim;

No sin infects, nor sorrow clouds that scene
Where the saved dead since Adam's death have
been.

Here, while we travel through the dust of time
Dark imperfections oft the soul defile;
Whate'er the circumstance, or change, or clime,
Creation's noblest is but vain and vile:
What are our woods and fields, our mountains,
glens, and streams,
To God's bright landscape, which in glory
beams?

Then, hush thy moan, Affection! curb thy will;
Think of the dead as to perfection brought,
In heart all holy, as the conscience still
Feels the rich calm the "Blood of Sprinkling" wrought:—
No cloud to tinge the colour of their days,
They harp the anthem of redemption's praise.

Dead though their forms in dust sepulchral lie,
Ecstatic faith the spirit loves to view,
And longs to vision with prophetic eye
What awful raptures must pervade it through,
As more and more eternity unfolds
Secrets of Glory, vast as heaven beholds.

POWER OF THE REDEEMER'S EYE.

"The Lord *looked* . . . and Peter went out and wept bitterly!"—*Luke* xxii. 61, 62.

NOT poet's lyre, nor painter's line
Could e'er express that look of Thine,
Saviour of men! on craven Peter cast:—
Eternity was in Thy gaze,
And through dark conscience darted rays
Which lighten'd into truth his present, and
his past.

Deep eloquence was there,
Beyond the lightning-glare
Red with the fierceness of the flaming storm;
Nor might loud hurricanes which sweep
In thund'ring air-tones o'er the deep
Till the rent ocean heaves like agonizing forms,

So terribly the soul appal
As that one gaze in Pilate's hall
Shook to his moral root a recreant man!
Apostate as he there denied
That Lord, to Whom his worship cried,
"Though all desert Thee, Christ! my spirit
never can."

Dungeon, nor death, nor chains,
Nor all which persecution gains,
Should tempt him from The Truth to fly;
Though all betray'd Him, he would stand
Faithful among a faithless band,
And boldly for His Lord exult to bleed, or die!

Resolve then reign'd in ardent power;
And feeling hued that full-toned hour
With the rich colour hearts delight to show,
In some rapt mood when men appear
Sublimed above unhallow'd fear,
And with celestial warmth reflect an angel's
glow.

In such high noon of seraph-zeal,
Our breasts an inspiration feel
Lifting us far beyond each low-born aim;
Wing'd thoughts surmount the walls of
time,
And waft us to that world sublime
Where Heaven's clear arches ring with Christ's
resounded name.

But He, to Whom all hearts lie bared,
In that flush'd moment then declared
How thrice, e'er yet the wakeful bird would
crow,
The saint who seem'd so nobly fired
As if by heaven's own warmth inspired,
Vanquish'd by shameful dread,—would all his
vows forego!

And more or less than Man were he
Unmoved who in this hour could see
A brave Apostle from His banner fly:
Assaulted by Satanic power
And sifted in that searching hour,
Thrice did his caitiff mouth the Lord of Love
deny!

If mortal pain could mar the rest
Which broods within an angel's breast,
Sure might St. Peter's crime have drawn his
tear,—
Who swore with ireful oath untrue
He ne'er the blest Redeemer knew,
And sacrificed his vow upon the shrine of
fear.

But, while a third denial hung
With impious accent on his tongue,
Behold! the crowing of the cock began;
And back with its reverted gaze
Bedimm'd with more than tearful haze,
Look'd the calm Eye of Christ on that apostate
man!

He "look'd,"—oh, what a look was there
Of pity, love, rebuke, and prayer!
Angelic, human, and divine the spell
Wielded by Christ in that dread gaze
Which then on Peter poured its rays,
Till down his weeping heart before it writhed, and fell!

'Twas but a glance, and yet it cleaved
The veil asunder, which had weaved
A hiding darkness round that trait'rous heart:
It open'd each vile gulf within
Where lurk the powers of latent sin,
And made him from himself to shudder back, and start.

By day, by night, where'er he went,
As o'er his head the firmament,
Thus o'er his heart with holiness and light
That piercing glance of Jesu cast
Celestial power, where'er he pass'd,
And overarch'd his soul with meaning, and with might.

'Twas with him, when he watch'd or wept,
Or fasted, toil'd, or woke, or slept;
Hunger'd and roofless, wearied, rack'd and worn,—
By shore, or sea, abroad, at home,
Where'er his pilgrim zeal could roam,
Here was the guiding Star, that watch'd him, though forlorn.

In prison, and o'er chains, it threw
A glory which that angel knew,
Who saw his features radiant in repose,
When calm as cradled infant's breath
He slept upon the brink of death,*
In some fond dream of Christ, forgetful of his woes.

And will not fond Devotion say,
That when his form inverted lay
In bleeding anguish on the cross oppress'd,
That still the gaze from Jesu's eye
Beam'd on his soul, till life's last sigh
Wafted the spirit home to its loved Saviour's breast?

But in this page of man may we,
As in some truthful mirror see
Reflected warnings, which may well o'erawe
The boldest, who believe they stand
Like rocks of faith, in self-command,
As did Saint Peter once, before his heart he saw.

---

* Acts xii. 6.

There while he weeps a bitter shower
Of anguish in this rueful hour,
Lord of our spirits! may his teardrops fall
In healthful virtue o'er each heart,
That little dreams how Satan's art
To more than Peter's crime may soon betray us all.

Yea, doth not our baptismal vow
Bend o'er us like a burden now,
And crush pale conscience into sacred tears?
For, leagued with flesh, and fiend, and world,
Oh, have we not to nothing hurl'd
The awful promise made,—that God should have our years?

For gold, or pride, or pomp, and pleasure
As though they form'd divinest treasure,
How basely have we barter'd mind and will!
Betraying our predestined cross,
That we should count our life a loss,
Except for Christ we lived, self-crucified and still.

Sole Healer of the wounded heart!
Who now ensphered in glory art,
When Peter-like, our prostrate vows we break,
Let no red lightnings of Thy wrath
Flash their dread fury o'er our path,
Nor regal thunder-tones Thy terrors o'er us wake,—

But turn Thee with subduing eye,
And from Thy bliss beyond the sky
Look, as Thou didst on Thine apostle's fears:
So melt us into anguish true,
Till Penitence our treason rue
And bathe Thy mercy-seat with love's remorseful tears.

THE GATES OF LIFE.

"Wide is the gate and broad is the way that leadeth to destruction . . . strait is the gate and narrow is the way that leadeth unto life."—*Matt.* vii. 13, 14.

Grief, more than revelation tells,
Shaded The Lord of Glory's heart,
Where slept within its aching cells
Deep woes no earth-breathed words impart;
Pure is the Bible, and a perfect book,—
But Christ had depths where Language could not look!

All echoless by worded sign
Some buried pangs there must have been;
And saint, nor angel can divine
What pass'd behind that mental screen
Where in dread myst'ry, voiceless, lone, and deep,
Pale thoughts of Christ did o'er man's future weep.

Tongue cannot speak, nor soul conceive
The gloom which blacken'd o'er His mind,
When thoughts prophetic bade him grieve
O'er sinful wrecks of sad mankind;
Sorrow like this might soften hearts of stone,
But, ah! how infinite His pangs unknown!

For each lost soul the bloody sweat
And crimson tide of anguish flow'd,
And in His righteous spirit met
All penal claims to justice owed,
For sins beyond what mortal numbers count,—
So vast the myriads of their vile amount!

But more He felt, who bled for man,
When from His cross uprear'd on earth
His Prescience saw that sacred plan
By angels deem'd of priceless worth,
Attract but "few," for whom His Mercy died,
To bear the cross, and love the Crucified.

Of all dark burdens which oppress
And crush warm spirits into woe,
Ingratitude from those we bless
Outweighs the direst hearts can know;
Fiends may abhor, but never can betray
The Souls which trust, and for them toil and pray.

But how did uncreated Love
A sacrifice divine achieve!
When God emerged from light above,
Around His awful head to weave
A thorny crown, this forfeit-world to save,
And roll'd thick darkness from the hideous grave.

Yet, when the unborn Ages rose
Before Him, in His parting breath,
And He beheld what creedless foes
Would still deny His priestly death,
A deeper sadness must have pierced His heart,
Than all which sacrificial pangs impart.

Two paths He saw, two gates appear'd,
Contracted one, the other wide;
Along the last, unfelt, unfear'd,
What myriads rush'd, for whom He died!—
Broad as their wills, and wild as Passion's law
The way of ruin which for them He saw.

But o'er that strict and narrow way
So wisely hemm'd by holy Truth,
He mark'd a sainted number stray,
Faithful as few, to age from youth;
Such are the souls, who count this World no loss
When they have nail'd it to th' atoning cross.

So is it now, to saints who read
The moral scenes of tempted man,
By that pure light blest angels need *
Before they learn the mystic plan,
Whereby the wisdom of God's secret Will
Winds its clear way through vice, and virtue still,

Ambition's fretting pride of thought,
The Hero's falsely-worshipp'd fame,
With all that mock Renown hath wrought
To gild the nothing of a name,—
Are baseless dreams, unsanctified and vile,
And only blast the victims they beguile.

Learning, and Art, and lofty Mind,
Unless beneath the Cross they grow,
Prove but mere forms of Self refined,
Whose "broad way" leads to final woe;
Sin changes not, howe'er by spells array'd,
And out of Christ, what are we, but betray'd?

"Broad is the way,"—oh, crushing thought!
Which must have made Emmanuel sigh,
To see the Soul His anguish bought
- But live to sin, and love to die,—
Enter the "wide gate" with a maniac glee,
And quench bad mirth in glooms of agony!

"Narrow the path,"—but, yet it leads
To Life's consummate goal of bliss;
And though their self-denial bleeds,
Children of light will enter this;
Though few in number, round their heavenward ways
Hover the glorious Dead of elder days.

O'er such high path decreed by God,
Led by The Spirit, let me roam;
For where my Saviour's feet have trod
Bright footprints point me to His home,—
That City clothed with more than crystal rays,
Her gates salvation, and whose walls are praise.

Patriarch and prophet, priest and saint,
Denial's road to heaven preferr'd;
And when their sunken hearts grew faint,
They listen'd for that living Word
Which warbled round them in the deepest night,
"My yoke is easy, and my burden light!"

---

* Eph. iii. 10.

SPIRITUAL DECLINE.

"Oh that I were as in months past, as in the days when God preserved me; when his candle shined upon my head . . . when the secret of God was upon my tabernacle."—*Job* xxix. ii. 2—4.

"OH! that with me, as in the months of yore,
My heart were basking in the smile of God,
When all I saw the sweet impression bore
His eye o'erwatch'd me through the way I trod.

"Then did the candle of Jehovah beam
With loving radiance o'er my rising hours,
And life roll'd onward like a happy stream
Which carols music to the list'ning flowers.

"Bright with the dews of pure devotion, lay
My spirit open to each breath from heaven;
And all who saw me, in their hearts might say,—
Dead paradise re-blooms in sin forgiven!

"Precious was Christ! beyond angelic speech
In might or melody to e'er reveal;
Nor could the songs of sainted rapture reach
All His incarnate glories made me feel.

"Dear was the temple, and the hour of prayer,
And dear the spirit of that ritual Whole
When all my faculties were hallow'd there,
And heaven seem'd dawning on my inmost soul.

"And when the emblems of embodied Love
Bleeding for man, to my awed sense were brought,
Like Stephen, view'd I in the world above
The Christ, by whom a sacrament is wrought."—

Thus moans in secret many a voiceless heart
Heavy with gloom, and harrow'd by distress;
Dull, cold, or dead, as grace and gift depart
And leave the sad One to his loneliness.

Yet, dark believer! may such woeful strain
Issue from shades of cowardice and sin;
And what thou dreamest a majestic pain,
May prove the sign of hollowness within!

There is a trinity in mortal time
By past, by present, and by future made;
And, Conscience wields a potency sublime
When each before her stands, in truth array'd.

Then must we feel how time's divisions mould
One character, in which our fate will rest;
Eternity in seed we thus behold
As heaven, or hell, now ripens in the breast!

Oh, then, not idly, with a weak lament
Sigh o'er some privilege, which breathes no more;
Religion scorns a laggard discontent
That feebly sickens in pale dreams of yore.

Not grace from thee, but thou from God hast gone,
By cold illapse declining day by day;
Or from the paths which lead true virtue on
Turn'd into tracks which tempt the soul away.

Cold in thy prayer, in praise reluctant grown,
Seldom at church, the Eucharist forgot,
Thy creed, self-will, no master but thine own,—
Behold! the secret which explains thy lot.

Obedience is religion's breath of life;
Constant and pure denials must we bear;
Each day should be with crucifixion rife,
Each hour be hallowed with the soul of prayer.

Saints learn by loving, and by love they live;
Who walk with God, must from themselves depart;
And Peace descends not from her Prince above,
Except for God faith purify the heart.

Mourners in Zion oft are minds which fail
To hold their Master's cross supreme in view;
Or let some lust o'er discipline prevail
That renders them to church, and creed untrue.

Thus, like a secret rust the world begins
Eating its way, until our hearts corrode;
Pleasure and profit veil their inward sins,
And wide as passion seems the "narrow" road.

From virgin youthfulness the Soul declines
When from both God and grace it dares to roam,
And can no longer through the Word Divine
Shelter the heart, in true affection's home.

"Oh! that with me as in pure moments past
My God were present,"—vain such cry, indeed,
Unless Repentance thy worn spirit cast
Low at the mercy-seat to lie, and bleed.

Leave sigh and sentiment for Duty's cross,
Haste thee to works of sacrifice and prayer;
Count a gain'd world to be a gloomy loss
And prize hereafter as thy holy care:

So may the smile of Godhead back return
Effulging o'er thee, as in days of old;
Dead in thyself, to live in Jesu learn,
And round His throne God's covenant * behold.

Earth, sense, and time will more and more recede,
Conscience be cleansed, and childlike prayer arise;
Eternity will grow thy grandest need,
God be thy goal, and heaven thy genial prize.

GUIDING TENDERNESS OF GOD.

"I will instruct thee . . . I will guide thee with mine eye."—*Ps.* xxxii. 8.

By gentleness, O God,
Thou wouldst Thy children lead
O'er perill'd ways, by martyrs trod,
Or through life's verdant mead:
Not the stern rod of discipline to wield
Does Thy pure Grace, apart from sin, incline;
But when reluctant hearts refuse to yield
Some iron law instructs the spirit that is Thine.

Yet were we like a child
Loving, and pliant too,
Thy perfect guidance pure as mild
Would guard Life's opening view;
E'en as a glance by some fond parent turn'd
On her frail little one, who waits to see
Those looks where young affection's lore is learn'd,—
So would one gleam of grace attract our souls to Thee.

Oh, for a watchful heart!
A waiting mind of prayer,
To view Thee, gracious as Thou art,
"Our Father!" everywhere.

* Rev. iv. 3; v. 6

Orphan'd in soul, nor friendless, should we seem,
Did but the mind a sacred vigil keep;
For ever would Thy guardian eye-glance beam,—
Star of our troubled life, both when we smile, or weep!

Unless we watch that "Eye,"
Thy Will we cannot read;
For, softer than a vernal sky
It dawns on human need
In gleam and glance, no prayerless hearts discern,
And Love's unwatchful gaze may oft forego:—
Only by looking upward, can we learn
Wisdom divinely bland, to chasten weal and woe.

Bend, pride of Reason! bend,
Become a little child;
And heaven to thee will condescend
In wisdom undefiled;
Oft where the haughty Scribes of learning fail
God to discern in truth's unerring page,
Infants of grace by simple love prevail,
Wing'd by the Spirit's power to heights beyond their age.

Then grant us, gracious Lord!
In Thy blest page to see
The faintest beam a heaven-bright word
Imparts from truth, and Thee;
Mild as the radiance of celestial love,
So will each promise, threat, and precept dart
Glances of truth,—as if God's eye above
Were gazing through them, to inspire the heart.

POETRY OF CLOUDS AND SKIES.

"Number the clouds in wisdom."—*Job.* xxxviii. 37. "God rideth in his excellency on the sky."—*Deut.* xxxiii. 26. "The firmament showeth his handy-work."—*Ps.* xix. 1.

A speaking magic in poetic skies
Affects the soul, and fascinates the eyes;
Look where we may, some cloud-born grace we find
To shade the mirror of responsive mind.

And why did God thus beauteously array
Calm noon, chaste eve, and re-commencing day,
But that our echoing minds should inly feel
How heaven and poetry to man appeal?

Lord of the woods, and waves, and living air!
All lead to Thee when purified by prayer;
Connecting thus with beauty, colour, grace,
The dying mercy which redeem'd our race.

Let but Thy merit through creation shine,
And what was common, now becomes divine;
The beautiful on earth, the bright above,
Are open sacraments which preach Thy love.

How rich the consecrated dome of heaven,
When to some priest at Nature's shrine is given
The power, in all ethereal forms to see
Symbols and signs of present Deity!

The skies have meanings; and emotion seems
Oft to array them with impassion'd gleams,—
Colours intense, as if a conscious hue
Blush'd o'er its birth, and brighten'd at our view.

Painters and poets from the skies have brought
Fancies and feelings, to inspire their thought:
Beauty is there; and sentiment can rise
To noble pathos in the naked skies.

Home of the seasons! and the haunt of storms,
Now fierce with gloom, now fair with opal forms,
Dark in thy strength, or smiling in thy play,
I love thy magic, and revere its sway.

But most I hail thee, golden, calm, and deep,
When isles of radiance on thy bosom sleep;
Or robe-like clouds in rich confusion lie,
As though veil'd angels floated up the sky

Garb'd in the vesture of thy woven sheen,
And left an outline where their veils had been:—
So exquisitely touch'd the tinted air,
Seraphic creatures might be mansion'd there.

And who can tell, since first the heavens have spann'd
Their arching glories over sea and land,
What vast impressions from yon varied skies
Have soothed man's spirit, while it charm'd his eyes?

When to the captive, through his dungeon-bar
Gleams of blue heaven come glancing from afar,
Through fields of childhood Fancy seems to roam
And wind the pathway freedom wound at home.

And think how Sickness, when the pulse renews
Its beat of vigour, hails yon skyey views,
While with new gush of health each glance of love
Seems to be answer'd, when it looks above.

There memory, too, and meditation find
Symbolic hues to mirror forth the mind;
Sky and the soul like sympathies can meet,
Till what our hearts express, the clouds repeat.

And when, pure Lord of loneliness and woe!
We dream Thy pilgrimage of pain below,
Faith may conceive, full oft Thine harass'd eye
Drank the deep quiet of congenial sky.

And as ascending to Thy throne of light
A cloud receiv'd Thee from the spell-bound sight
Of those sad watchers, who beheld Thee soar
Back to the bliss where Thou wert throned before,

So when our hearts the sweep of heaven survey
And solemn fancies o'er its surface play,
Let not religion this true thought disdain,—
A cloud * shall waft Thee to our world again.

TWILIGHT OF OUR BEING.

"One day, known to the Lord, not day, nor night."—*Zech.* xiv. 7. "Jesus said, What I do thou knowest not now, but thou shalt know hereafter."—*John* xiii. 7.

"Though what I do ye know not now
Hereafter sainted hearts shall see,"
Saviour! before that will we bow
And learn our cross by loving Thee:
Grant to our souls the grace on God to live,
And clasp the counsel which Thy precepts give.

Such partial light and shade become
The vexèd life our bosoms feel;
For, could we clearly view the home
Which yonder shrines in heaven conceal,
How should we turn with loathing sense away
From those stern duties, which demand each day!

---

* Rev. i. 7.

All light would make our hearts presume,
All darkness end in black despair;
But God has so arranged the gloom
As best becomes the cross we bear:—
An ampler vision might elate the mind,
And deeper shadows would eclipse mankind.

"We know in part," and part of this
How weakly can the wisest know!
Our purest heavens of hallow'd bliss
Are tinged with soiling earth below:
Put into language, oft doth wisdom seem
The broken semblance of a baseless dream.

Such clouds and darkness round the path
Of God to man encircled lie,
That he who heavenly science hath
This awful truth will scarce deny,—
That earth seems moist with melancholy tears
Dropt from the eyelids of some thousand Years.

Yet sorrow is the penal bane
Attemper'd to a world of sin;
For where our God hath ceased to reign
Darkness and death must enter in;
And saintly eyes should learn to see by prayer
Truths which transcend what mortal lips declare.

THE BLESSED VIRGIN.

"Hail, thou that art highly favoured, the Lord is with thee: blessed art thou among women."—*Luke* i. 28.

Ave Maria! blest o'er women all
Who e'er on earth embodiment have found,
Maiden and mother, both in thee we call
With peerless favour by Jehovah crown'd.

Ave Maria! virgin meek and mild,
Unstain'd by passion's soul-polluting fires,
Faith cannot view thee with thine awful Child,
Nor thrill with more than sentiment inspires.

Ave Maria! since thy sex began,
Woman presents no type to rival thee;
Nor can the feelings of a fallen man
Echo thy thoughts of inward purity.

Ave Maria! o'er the Babe Divine
Bending with awe, maternally entranced,
How must have throbb'd that vestal heart of thine,
On Jesu's forehead when thy fond eyes glanced!

Pure are the fountains of parental love
Whose depths of bliss ineffable remain;
Not the deep ravishment of lyres above
Could e'er attune it with too sweet a strain:

But thou, o'ershadow'd with The Spirit's power,
By heaven's bright herald hail'd supremely blest,
What hallowing mystery clothed that sacred hour
When hung the Child-God on thy virgin breast!

Boundless eternity and breathing time
Blend in communion at thine awful bliss,
And bid us wonder, in a trance sublime,
That earth was hallow'd by a scene like this.

The purest image saintly Thought can see
Of maiden calm, with motherhood combined,
Becomes too earth-born when compared with thee,
Nursing The Babe whose Blood redeem'd mankind.

Well may the poet's harp, and painter's hue,
With all that Sculpture's marble-dreams express,
Become ethereal, when they bring to view
Outlines which hint thy solemn loveliness.

Yet can chaste minds, beyond all visual show,
By thought create what reverence demands,
Ave Maria! when our hearts o'erflow
To see the God-Babe in thy vestal hands.

Feeling and Faith, with poesy and prayer,
Mingle their charms to make one beauteous spell,
And what no melodies, nor hues declare,
Our hush'd emotions unto Godhead tell.

MARIOLATRY.

"Jesus saith unto her, Woman! what have I to do with thee? Mine hour is not yet come."—*John* ii. 4. "I fell at his feet to worship him: and he said unto me, See thou do it not! I am thy fellow-servant:—worship God."—*Rev.* xix. 10.

And yet, forbid it, reason, faith, and love,
Both mortal powers, and Attributes divine,
Ave Maria! that as Queen above,
The worship due to God should ere be thine.

Honour'd and holy, blest indeed wert thou,—
To be the mother of His mortal frame
Before Whose face the universe shall bow
While rapt eternity resounds His name!

The stain, that tempted Eve on woman brought,
Ave Maria! is by thee reversed,—
Mother of Him whose dying merit wrought
A ransom for the race by Sin accursed.

So to the Church's heart be ever dear,
Anointed Virgin! 'mong all women blest;
High o'er thy sex, we none like thee revere
Within whose womb incarnate God could rest.

But ah! we dare not, from the Lord of Lords
Rob the due glory which to God pertains;
Nor crown a creature with adoring words,
And echo "Queen of Heaven!" with impious strains.*

Not sinless wert thou, in the sight of Him
From whose dread gaze the blushing heavens retire,†
While round His Throne the o'erawed seraphim
Prostrate their crowns, and cast their quiv'ring lyre.

They tell us, how all deeps of tender grace
Fresh in thy heart abide for evermore;
And when the contrite seek thy pitying face,
Those wells are open'd, and the faint restore;

But, blest Redeemer! what is finite love
Though most ideal in sublime excess,
With *that* compared, which drew God from above
To agonise for our dark guiltiness?—

Less than a raindrop to the boundless sea,
The vastest love created souls can feel
When rank'd by His, who clothed Divinity
With flesh, and suffer'd all that man could feel!

Ave Maria! were thy vestal glow
Of pity purer than blind error dreams,
Yet unto Christ dost thou thy nature owe,
And all thy goodness from His spirit streams.

But when they dare this awful dream propound,—
That e'en as mother o'er a son prevails,
So at thy plea all grace and gifts abound
And at thy prayer His goodness never fails!

They say the sunbeam can enrich the sun
From whose bright essence its fair beauty flows!—
By such false creed from blinding fancy won,
Which gives to Mary what to Christ she owes.

Ye pious martyrs of a faith untrue,
Who from the fount of God's unfathom'd heart
Turn to broke cisterns, whence dark Ages drew
Deluding errors that will not depart,

Mercy and Grace in Christ embodied live;
Straight from His love let each repenting Soul
Draw the true pardon He alone can give,
Nor dream that woman can a God control!

That creed is sacrilege which dares deny
The sympathies His bleeding Manhood learn'd,
When Christ from glory came to weep and die,
And back to heaven with human heart return'd.

Away with doubt! men want no Virgin's plea,
No angel, saint, nor martyr's prayer to bring,
To gain the mercy which endures in Thee
Thou of all grace the unexhausted Spring!

Ave Maria! maid and mother blest,
High above woman soar'd thy peerless lot;
And with due rev'rence on thy name we rest,
But shrink to credit what thy truth is not.

And oh, in yonder beatific light
Could thy deep calm be ruffled into care,
As creature, thou might'st shudder at the sight
Of sinners, prostrate at thy throne, in prayer!

* Bishop Bull's sermon will at once recur to the devout memory of every churchman, on the true eminence which the Virgin Mary ought to occupy in his esteem. Moreover, in "A Proposal," &c., drawn up by the non-jurors, Collier, Spinkes, and Campbell, for a union with the Orthodox Greek Church, the distinction between what is, and what is not, due, to the Blessed Virgin, is well put. "Though they call the mother of our Lord Blessed, and magnify the grace of God, which so highly exalted her, yet are they afraid of giving the glory of God to a creature, or to run into any extreme by blessing and magnifying her; and do hence rather choose to bless and magnify God, for the high grace conferred upon her, and for the benefits which we receive by that means."—*Lathbury's Nonjurors*, pp. 315, 316.

† Job xv. 15.

Ave Maria! this dread thought o'erpowers
And awes the suppliant, who might worship thee,—
That Jesus is thy* Saviour too, and ours,
The same in time, as in eternity.†

---

* Luke i. 46, 47.

† On the Assumption and Immaculate Conception of the Virgin Mary.

"Hélas! que pouvoit être la terre pour elle; pour elle, dis-je, qui avoit déja au ciel l'objet de toute sa tendresse? Qui est-ce qui eût été capable de la consoler dans ce lieu d'exil, dans cette vallée de larmes? . . . Elle n'avoit plus rien en ce monde. Jésus l'avoit quittée. Ce n'étoient point les dangers dont elle étoit environnée, ni les persécutions qui souffroit déja l'Eglisse naissante, qui la dégoûtoient de la vie; ce n'étoit point la gloire et le triomphe qui lui étoient préparées au ciel, qui lui faisoient desirer la mort: c'étoit uniquement Jésus-Christ, dont elle ne pouvoit sans douleur se voir separée. Toute sa vie n'étoit, selon les termes de Saint Augustin, qu'un désir perpétuel, qu'un long gémissement."—Fénélon's Works, vol. ii. p. 390, Paris Edition, 1835.

As the object of the "Christian Life" is not to provoke controversial discussion, but rather, under the divine blessing, to deepen and purify spiritual tendencies within, through the sympathies and the sentiments,—the Author of these Lyrics does not introduce dogmatic theology and dubious subjects into them. Meanwhile, as the Roman Church has lately endeavoured to canonise a new article of faith, touching what is termed "the Immaculate Conception;" and since the truth or falsehood of this dogma cannot hold a neutral position in the realm of Christian doctrine, a Churchman will not object to some transient remarks on this subject, in the form of a note.

The Anglican doctrine, then, on the place of reverence which the Blessed Virgin ought to occupy in the Church, is apparent from the services appointed to commemorate what is due to the Mother of Emmanuel. Moreover, an English Churchman of the true Catholic type, will at once recall the admirable sermon of Bishop Bull, in relation to the Virgin Mary. But when, from the English Church, we revert to the doctrine, ritual, and practical worship of the Romish Church,—fearful indeed is the distance between her and ourselves! To illustrate this, the reader who has travelled into Belgium, Italy, Piedmont, and Savoy, needs not to be reminded that the worship of the Virgin has almost absorbed, among the people, the adoration exclusively due to her Divine Son, and so completely subordinated Architecture, Painting, Music, and Poetry, that Mariolatry is the dreadful atmosphere in which the great mass of the people are reared and educated from their very earliest years. Omitting, however, a mere geographical view of this subject, and, assuming it for granted, that no real Catholic, as distinguished from a Romanist, requires to be told neither reason nor revelation sustains the Roman Communion in her doctrines concerning the Virgin, let us look at the subject in a more direct point of view.

The Romish doctrine on the Virgin Mary must, of course, be drawn and described from her own authentic representations. Now, among the most solemn utterances of her practical faith, we may assuredly refer to her ritual service; and if we do so, in relation to the subject before us, we find she dedicates two Feasts unto the honour of the Virgin, in neither of which can the Anglican Church, as truly Catholic, take a part. One of these festivals is entitled "The Feast of the Immaculate Conception," and the other (celebrated annually on the 15th of August,) "The Feast of the Assumption." Of the latter, Alban Butler (vol. viii. p. 173,) says,—"The Assumption of the Virgin Mary is the greatest of all the Festivals which the Church celebrates in her honour. It is the consummation of all the other great mysteries by which her life was rendered most wonderful." And, if we proceed further to examine the Ritual of the Assumption, among other miraculous assertions, we find it again and again stated, either in spirit or in words, "To-day, Mary the Virgin ascended the heavens." "Rejoice because she is reigning with Christ for ever." . . . "Mary the Virgin is taken up into heaven, to the ethereal chamber in which the King of Kings sits upon his starry throne. The Holy Mother of God has been exalted above the choir of Angels to the heavenly realms." And to prevent the possibility of our mistaking such language, as simply implying her "Assumption" in a mystical, or abstract sense, her corporeal, local, and literal ascension unto celestial glories is positively asserted in one of the "Lessons" for the day, in the following manner,—"She returned not to earth, but is seated in the heavenly tabernacles. How could earth devour, how could those below receive? How could corruption invade that Body in which life was received? For it, a direct, plain, and easy path to heaven was prepared!" Such is Romish doctrine according to one of its most solemn standards; but if we proceed to inquire, on what basis this religious Festival of the Virgin's Assumption rests, we shall be led to this irresistible conclusion,—The so-called "Assumption" is a pure fiction, an ecclesiastical fancy, a mere religious creation of a superstitious Church, who, by adopting unwarrantable ceremonies and fearful practices, has deified Creatureship, and been seduced into the awful crime of open and palpable idolatry. Were this the appropriate place for historical discussion, the fearful unreality of this "Assumption," and the utter want of Catholic tradition to sustain its truth, might easily be exposed. Meanwhile let it suffice just to remind the reader of two or three undeniable facts. First, then, neither Scripture, nor apostolical tradition, tells us one word as to the date, scene, time, or circumstances of the Virgin's death. Secondly, the reference in the "Chronicon" of Eusebius (A.D. 315), which is supposed to state that in the year of our Lord 48, "the

OUR TRUE CENTRE.

"Return unto me, for I have redeemed thee."
Isa. xliv. 22.

"And ye shall find rest for your souls."
Jer. vi. 16.

Our centre true is God alone;
In whom man's aching breast
Beneath the shadow of His Throne
Can find a perfect rest;
For less than God enjoy'd, would leave within us still
A fev'rish want of soul, the Finite cannot fill.

Yet ruin'd years must haply roll
In anguish, gloom, or woe
Along the worn and wearied soul,
Before the heart can know
What broken cisterns prove the hollow joys we love,
While hearts forsake The Fount of living bliss above.

This world is wound with fatal spells
Attracting youthful Sense;
And each gay scene some falsehood tells
To mar life's innocence:
Nothing but grace divine can disenchant the Earth
And bid the soul aspire for what becomes its birth.

mother of Jesus was taken up into heaven, as some write that it had been revealed unto them," is admitted by Romish historians themselves to be spurious. The seven manuscripts, for instance, of Eusebius's "Chronicon," in the Vatican, do not contain this passage. The edition of Eusebius, printed in Milan in 1818, does not exhibit it; nor is it to be found in a most careful edition of the same author, published by the monks in the Armenian convent, near Venice. Nor, if we refer to Gregory of Tours, do we find this doctrine of the Virgin's "Assumption" supported by aught which claims the dignity of Catholic tradition. Gregory died in 595 A.D.; and we will quote the words of his own Benedictine editor, which are appended to the following monstrous fable, delivered by the Bishop of Tours:—"At length, the course of this life having been fulfilled by the blessed Mary, when she was now called from the world, all the Apostles were gathered together from every region to her house; and when they heard that she was to be taken from the world, they watched with her together. The Lord Jesus then came with his angels, and receiving her soul, delivered it to Michael the archangel, and withdrew!! At the dawn, the apostles took up her body, with the couch, and placed it in a tomb, and guarded it, waiting for the arrival of the Lord. And behold, again the Lord stood by them, and the holy corpse, taken up in a cloud, He ordered to be carried away into Paradise!!" &c. &c. On this preposterous fiction the Benedictine thus comments:—"What Gregory here relates concerning the death of the Blessed Virgin, and its circumstances, beyond a doubt he drew from that book of the Pseudo-Melito, concerning the removal of the Blessed Virgin, which is classed by Pope Gelasius among the apocryphal books, and published in the "Bibliotheca Patrum." Now, that she died at Ephesus, is the opinion of learned men; but no one, before Gregory of Tours, is found to have asserted, in express words, the resurrection of the Blessed Mary, and the Assumption of her body and her soul into heaven. Nevertheless, this opinion, not long after, prevailed in Gaul, so that it was even introduced into the Liturgy. Yet, the Roman Sacramentary of Gregory contained nothing of the kind." After such historical proof as this, it is almost amusing to hear the eloquent, but credulous Bourdaloue, in one of his sermons, "sur L'Assomption," coolly venturing the following statement: "Il est certain, que Marie, entre tous les élus, a reçu une grace superéminente, en vertu de quelle elle peut intercéder pour nous auprès de Dieu, et, par une conséquence nécessaire, il est certain que nous pouvent saintement et utilement, recourir à elle, et implorer dans nos besoins le secours de sa protection. Cette vérité, qui nous est plus que suffisamment révélée de Dieu, et dont toute la tradition est un authentique temoignage [!!] se trouve d'ailleurs si conforme à tous les principes du bon sens, et de la raison, que cela seul suffiroit pour confendre l'obstination de l'hérésie, qui la rejette, et qui la combat."—(Sermons "Sur les Mystères." Tome Second: A Liège, 1724.)

With reference to "The Immaculate Conception," our remarks, for the present, must be exceedingly limited. Without, then, pausing to develop the many fearful consequences this impious dogma involves, in relation to those peculiarities which distinguish the Redeemer from all other beings, as Incarnated Deity,—let us be permitted to refer unto one heretical fallacy which appears to underlie all Romish statements on this subject; and it seems to be in this fact,—that the advocates for the Immaculate Conception virtually attribute unto the corporeal substance of the Virgin a species of meritorious activity in the awful and ineffable mystery of the Incarnation. Now, if we diligently ponder over the terms of the Angelic Annunciation (Luke ii. 31), it will be found that in the mere act of conception, the Virgin Mary is contemplated simply as passively influenced by the conceiving omnipotence of the Divine Spirit. "The power of the Highest shall overshadow thee; *therefore*, also, that holy thing which shall be born of thee shall be called the Son of God." In these sublime words it is undeniable that the statement of the Incarnation proceeds downward from the creative agency of the Holy Ghost, and does not, in any degree, lift up the Virgin Mary into a common or coequal agency with the Almighty Conceiver. Indeed, the more we contemplate such a dogma, the more repulsive it appears both to human reverence and to Catholic verity. Nor does the Nicene Symbol, as adopted by the Second Œcumenical Synod at Constantinople, neglect to shadow forth the distinction between a creatural organ and an Uncreated Effluent, when the Western Church uses it, with this marked alteration from that of the East, as thus: "was incarnate by the Holy Ghost OF the Virgin Mary," and not "was incarnate by the Holy Ghost AND the Virgin Mary."

Independent, however, of this most significative testimony, we can refer to the language of a writer pre-eminently revered by the Romish Communion as orthodox and Catholic,—we allude to St. Bernard of Clairvieux. In his 174th Epist. (Paris Ed., 1839, 8vo. Vol. i., p. 389), after speaking of the Virgin in these dangerous terms: "Prædica reverendam Angelis, desideratam gentibus, Patriarchis, Prophetisque præcognitam, electam ex omnibus, prælatam omnibus. Magnifica gratiæ inventricem," etc, he nevertheless thus argues: "Cæterum quatenus originale peccatum hæc ipsa sanctificatio valuerit, sive pro ipsâ, sive pro illâ propheta, vel si quis alius simili præventus gratiæ fuerit,—non temere dixerim." Again:—"Propter eandem causam etiam utrique parenti ejus festos honores asserat deferendos? Se de avis et proavis idipsum posset pro simili causâ quilibet flagitare et sic tenderetur in infinitum," &c. &c. Towards the end of this remarkable epistle, the illustrious abbot writes thus, "Ubi erit prærogativa Matris Domini, qua singulariter

A fascinating mist o'erveils
Bewilder'd time, and space,
When passion's demon-power prevails,
And lures a sensual race
To dream polluted earth a paradise can be,
And mould imagined heavens apart from Deity.

The bloom of hope, the bliss of health,
The bounding thoughts of joy,
With all that springs from tyrant wealth,
What myriads they decoy!
Till glory, truth, and grace, and bliss by promise given,
From souls recede away, and let this world seem heaven!

But worst of all base spells that blind
The conscience with deceit,
Is that which makes our God mankind,
And bows us at their feet,
Awaiting till they crown by some awarded praise,
The nothing Fashion gilds with her inglorious rays.

Alas! for those who madly think
Immortal Nature can
From lips of transient homage drink
What truly freshens man,
While deep within the soul a thirsting sense abides
For something nobler far than fame's uncertain tides.

Since what is fame, but second-life
In other spirits led?
A feeling with this impulse rife,—
That our creations spread
Ideal worlds of thought, through which we love to roam,
And find in kindled hearts a false, but fancied home?

But thou, believer, think on this,—
God is our only rest;
And he who worships finite bliss
Will live and die unblest:
The infinitely good man's true proportion makes,
And every gift but Christ the trusting heart forsakes.

'Tis true, the subject World is ours;*
But only when we wave
Heaven's banner o'er its hostile powers,
And for the Truth are brave;
Thus panoplied by grace, and girt by secret prayer,
We face embattled Fiends, and fight them everywhere.

But never be this creed forgot,
That men are exiles here;
And they who seek a heavenly lot
Must love a heav'nly sphere;
And oft in soaring dreams of purity ascend
To yon celestial Home, where saints and martyrs tend.

The Spirit's love breathes now, or never,
When souls for God are train'd
Till mortal vice and evil sever
From bosoms, where they reign'd:
For by this truth intense all mighty Hearts must live,—
Eternity will rue what time doth not forgive.

Hail, vast Relief of souls who love,
Lord of regenerate hearts!
Faith can discern in Thee above
A glory which imparts
Far more than angel-life, to all who seek for rest
And their hereafter lay, like John,† upon Thy breast.

As roll the waters to the wind
A moment lifted high,
So, swelling passion heaves the mind
Upward to meet the sky;
But when the storm declines and waters cease to roar,
The folded waves lie down as level as the shore:

So is it with delirious joy
Where mad excitements reign,
Or, blind emotions man decoy
Some glitt'ring lie to gain;
Raised and enrapt awhile, his heaven seems half begun,
But when the dream resolves, unrest alone is won.

creditur exultare et munere prolis, et integritate carnis, si tantumdem dederis et matrii psius? Non est hoc Virginem honorare, sed honori detrahere." Upon the whole, we affirm the daring charge which Fénélon has brought against the Anglican Churches in one of his sermons for Epiphany, is applicable unto Rome, and not unto ourselves: "Rompant le sacré lien de l'unité, qui peut seul retenir les esprits, s'est livrée à toutes les visions de son cœur."—Tome Deuxième. Paris. 1835.

* 1 Cor. iii. 21, 22.

† John xiii. 23.

MOTHER'S GRIEF.

"Weeping for her children because they are not."—*Jer.* xxxi. 15.

The placid azure of thy pensive eyes
Oh childless mother! like dejected skies,
With such dim tearfulness is overspread,
It softly tells thou dreamest of the dead.

Bereaved thou art of that unfathom'd bliss,
A first-born infant; and a pang like this
Home to the centre hath thy spirit stirr'd,
Too deep for sighs, too sacred for a word.

Cold the wan beauty of thy sunken cheek;
And tones of pathos, when I hear thee speak,
Ring like a knell which haunts sad Memory's ear,
And melts warm feeling into woman's tear.

Alone I view thee o'er the Bible bend,
Till solitude becomes thy sainted friend;
While, rapt in stillness, oft the dreaming soul
Wings its lone flight to where no earth-clouds roll.

But wilt thou, mother, in this trance of gloom
Hover and dream around thine infant's tomb?
Dark Fancy! dars't thou lift the coffin-lid,
And view in anguish what the grave hath hid?

Those dawning gleams of consciousness and grace,
The chisell'd beauty, and the cherub-face,
How oft doth speculation these recall,
And tell thee thy sweet babe possess'd them all!

And when some cry of infancy is heard,
Like sleeping water by wild music stirr'd,
Thy heart-strings vibrate to each plaintive tone
As if that weeper were indeed thine own.

But, lady, there is balm and blessing left,
And healing words for hearts like thine bereft;
No childless orphan can the Church become,
Though Christ hath vanished to His viewless home!

Yet shall the Comforter on thee descend,
And heaven-breathed solace with thy spirit blend;
The Lord surrounds thee, when thou seest Him not,
And God must change, ere grief can be forgot.

Be Grace thy refuge: calmer thoughts will rise
And rays from heaven illume thine inward eyes;
Till in their brightness loss becomes a gain,
While God is thank'd for this mysterious pain.

And now, bethink thee, to thy babe in heaven
How much of glory hath Redemption given!
Worn by no race, at once it reach'd the goal,
Sinless on earth, and now—a perfect Soul.

Think, what a dignity to thee belongs
Thus to have deepen'd the angelic songs,
Thus to enrich with thy departed Gem
The lustre of Emmanuel's diadem!

And feel'st thou not, when God and glory seem
To awe thy Spirit with a solemn dream,
An Infant makes the skies familiar be,
And helps to humanise the heavens for thee?

Nor let harsh murmurs o'er thy doom arise
As though God wrong'd the Saint His wisdom tries;
Sorrow befits a world where Jesu bled,
And dust was borrow'd to receive Him dead.*

In Christ, bereaved one! for profoundest grief
Dwells the pure source of all divine relief;
To minds which echo thee, most dear thou art,
But oh! far dearer to thy Saviour's heart.

That living Flow'ret which thy God hath given
His love transplanted to a bower in heaven;
There, shall each grace to perfect beauty rise,
And bud with glory when it breathes the skies.

DIVINE SECRETS.

"Secret things belong unto God."—*Deut.* xxix. 29.

Above, below, mysterious all
The moral facts our souls would scan;
And when some pageant lifts the pall
Which covers vast Creation's plan,
A thinking Titan with his godless mind
To shudd'ring Angels seems a monster blind.

---

* John xix. 41, 42.

When David read man's glorious frame
Ecstatic awe o'erpower'd his view;
And, hymning forth Jehovah's name,
He trembled into words, how true!—
"How fearful am I, when by Love survey'd,
Moulded by heaven, and wonderfully made."*

Awake, what mysteries we enclose,
And when we dream, more wondrous far!
'Tween life and death our limbs repose,
And none can tell the truth we are;
Time and eternity then blend and meet,
As they will mingle at the judgment-seat.

But when from earth to Heaven we turn,
Pure faith is taught this truth to know,—
Proud wisdom must itself unlearn
By lisping childlike prayer below;
Content in darkness to adore HIS ways
With Whom 'tis glory to conceal their rays.†

All Eye, all Ear, all Presence, Power,
In contact with creation's whole,
Closing the eyelids of each little flower,
Or bidding worlds around Thee roll,—
Essential Deity, Thou dread UNKNOWN,
Angels would shudder to unveil Thy Throne!

And yet, deep mystery proves the light
From whence our reas'ning darkness gains
A lustre, which restores the sight
When blinded by some mental pains:
God is a FACT, from whose unfathom'd ALL
Eternity will not remove the pall.

And as our God alone discerns
Himself in Essence, truth, and will,
So faith from revelation learns
To bow before a mystery still;
For God Incarnate is an awful shade
Within whose depths the Church has mused, and pray'd.

And what Thou doest, Lord, in life,
Is dark indeed to those who roam
Anguish'd, and worn by wasting strife,
Creedless in heart, without a home;—
Each grave that opens, and the friend who dies
Some pang of mystery to the soul supplies.

Why virtue droops, and Vice unveils
A blushless front of gain and glee,
Involves a problem which prevails
O'er sceptic Minds, who cannot see
That mortal life our education is,
And builds up final woe, or future bliss.

* Ps. cxxxix. 14. † Prov. xxv. 2.

THE TWO BOOKS.

"You here have an order for prayer, and for the reading of Holy Scripture, much agreeable to the mind and purpose of the old Fathers; nothing is ordained to be read but the very pure Word of God, the Holy Scriptures, or that which is agreeable to the same."—*Preface to the Book of Common Prayer.*

Two Books we have, all other books above,
Which breathe the wonders of Incarnate love;
Each to Jehovah points the living Way,
And both inspire us to repent, and pray.

Perfect as peerless, pure and most divine,
Where God in language moves through every line,
Where each calm word enrobes celestial Grace
And man and Deity meet face to face,

Is that Shechinah of almighty speech
Where dwells The Spirit, time and souls to teach,
Beneath whatever name 'tis known, or heard,
Scripture, or Bible, or the Sacred Word.

With *this*, comparison must be profane:
Yet, laud we not in too heroic strain
Britannia's liturgy, for matchless power
To guide the conscience through its perill'd hour.

Calm deep and solemn, chaste, and most sublime,
Breathing eternity, yet full of time,
Pure as seraphic lips in heaven desire,
And fervid as the souls of saints on fire

With rapture,—is the Litany we love:
Sickness and sorrow both its blessing prove;
And oft have mourners in the heart's despair
Found a deep refuge for dejection, there.

A healing softness, and a holy balm
That book pervade, like inspiration's calm,—
Subdued intensity and sacred rest,
Which never fail the lonely and distrest.

For, oh, we need not morbid passion's force,
Nor hurried feeling, in its reinless course,
Nor problems dark, for reasoning pride to scan;
But what we need is,—mercy-tones for man.

The sun-bright Angel, who adores and sings,
Covers his brow with reverential wings;
And perfect Saints, who most their God adore,
Sink low in feeling, ere by faith they soar.

The past breathes here the poetry of time,
And thrills the present with a tone sublime,
Till buried ages of the Church's youth
Rise, and re-charm the world with ancient truth.

Thou glorious masterpiece of olden Prayer!
Deeper thy wisdom than cold words declare;
Ever opposing some recurrent sin
States act without, or Churches feel within.

Not light men want, but love,—exceeding all
An Age of idols dares devotion call;
A childlike frame of purity and peace,
Where Christ in conscience works divine release.

And who the archives of thy past can see,
Nor recognise the eye of God o'er thee,
Presiding there with providential gaze
To fit thy teaching for these fallen days?

Creedless and proud, high-cultured, full of self,
Greedy of gain, and worshippers of pelf,—
Our wealth grows pagan as the world gets old,
And none seem heroes, but the bad and bold!

Then, bless we God for prayers where men are taught
Low at the Truth to bow rebellious thought;
Each lawless working of the will to chain,
And yield to God the bosom's throne again.

Repentance, bitter, stern, profound, and true,
Obedient hearts, which yearn to dare and do,
Whate'er the doctrines of the Cross command,—
God send the Church, for this apostate land!

Rather as servants, than as sons we bow
Down at the shrine of awful Godhead now;
Though heirs of grace, in Christ our own we claim,—
How have we barter'd our baptismal name!

Hence sad humility and fear become
The sinful Race who leave their Father's home;
Cries of dejection, more than chants of joy,
Returning prodigals may best employ.

Nor be forgot, that England's Prayer Book gives
Pure, full, and plain, THE WORD by which she lives!
Not dungeon'd in some dead and alien tone,
But where the peasant-boy perceives his own.

There, lisping Childhood, when it longs to learn
Truths for which prophets bled, and martyrs burn,
In such pure liturgy of grace may find
All which can feed the heart, and form the mind.

For common prayer, if catholic and true,
Must not be tinged with individual hue,
But be proportioned to the soul of Man,
In deep accordance with redemption's plan.

Lord of the Church! of sacrament and rite,
In this may all adoring hearts delight,—
"How apostolic is the root of all
Our Church maternal would devotion call!"

The heart of Ages still within them lives,
Takes from the past, and to the present gives
That hoary spell which hallows thought and word,
And wakens feeling in its finest chord,

Since, not from Rome, but ancient Gaul we bring
The choral hymns our Altars chant and sing;
And many a word devotion dwells upon,
Hung on thy lips, thou loved and lone St. John!*

Source of the Church! true Paraclete for all,
Long may such prayers on Christ for mercy call;
No deeper grace can Thy pure wisdom give,—
Than what our lips repeat, our hearts may live.

BAPTISM.

"The washing of regeneration."—*Tit.* iii. 5. "Born of water and of the Spirit."—*John* iii. 5.

THOU little trembler, robed in white,
Nursling of Heaven! sweet neophyte
Before the font arriving,
The birth-dawn of thy spirit-life
With holy fulness be it rife,
While hearts for thee are striving
With God in prayer; that soon thy shielded charms
May rest secure in Christ's baptismal arms.

A silence breathed from God above,
A halcyon of celestial love

---

* See Palmer's "Origines Liturgicæ," for historical proof of this.

Now broods with blest control,
Under the Throne of Him who came
In form as weak as thy young frame,—
Thrilling the inmost soul
Of all, whose unfilm'd eye of faith perceives
More than mere water on the forehead leaves.

Bright students of the ways of God!
Who, since Incarnate Mercy trod
The forfeit earth of man,
Bend your adoring eyes to learn
Truths deeper than your thoughts discern,*
Shrined in redemption's plan,—
Ye viewless Seraphim! this rite attend,
And your calm watch with Christian worship blend.

Thou innocent! with man compared,
Thee hath eternal Truth declared
A child of wrath and sin;
But here, adopted, seal'd, and sign'd
By Him who hath redeem'd mankind,
For thee will now begin
That second Birth renewing grace imparts †
Through this deep sacrament to infant hearts.

Oh, if Emmanuel ne'er had said
"Let children to Mine arms be led,"
Parents might shrink aghast
A creature into life to bring,
Whose soul the curse of God might wring
When time and earth are past!—
But for the promise of baptismal grace,
What sight so fearful as an infant's face?

All that a birth of Flesh can give
What is it,—but a doom to live,
A heritage of woe,
A destiny of guilt and death,
A curse inhaled at every breath
Life breathes from sin below?
By grace uncharm'd, destruction seems to lower
On the sad babe, ere Time can count an hour.

But at the Font where Jesu stands
With greeting heart and gracious hands,
Ready to clasp the child,
Pale infant! there, a breath from heaven
May to thy dawning soul be given
Through Him, the Saviour mild,

* 1 Pet. i. 12.

† "Seeing now that this child *is* regenerate and grafted *into* the Body of Christ's Church."—*Baptismal Service.*

"Seeing now that this child is regenerate . . . . it hath pleased Thee to *regenerate* this infant with Thy Holy Spirit, to receive him for Thine own child by adoption, and to incorporate him into Thy Holy Church."—*Baptismal Service of Church of England.*

Who, while He thunders from His regal Throne,
Loves the sweet age on earth He call'd His Own.

The Root of sacramental grace
Is the new Adam of our race,
The Man Divine who bled;
Hence cometh our celestial birth,
Beyond the parentage of earth,
From our generic Head,—
The Lord from heaven, whose vital Spirit gives
All force by which the mystic Body * lives.

More than our first-born parents knew
Before they proved to God untrue,
Works that celestial gift;
Angels, who on their trial stood,
Exceed not this majestic good
Which may thy soul uplift:
A child of God!—can seraphim aspire
To aught sublimer in their sinless choir?

From thee the curse is roll'd away;
Thy soul's new birth begins to-day;
A cov'nant right to all
Immunities and blessings high,
The heart of Jesus can supply
To those who heed His call:
Now to the stillness of thy soul is given,
Like breezeless water, to reflect a heaven.

A City and a Crown are thine
If thou be true to grace divine,
Bearing thy destined Cross;
Lo! on thy forehead lies the seal
Where symbol both and sign reveal
That Life must gain by loss: †
Firm to thy vow, beneath God's banner fight,
And keep thy panoply of graces bright.

Christ guard thee now, thou little one!
His glory be thy shield and sun
Whate'er thy lot may be;
Incorp'rate with the Church thou art,
To thee may life and love impart
The truth which maketh free;
New prospects ope, new principles and powers
Rise into play, and rule thine unborn hours.

And, if in secret darkness lie
The seeds of heaven which none descry,
Dormant and cold within,
May God's reviving Breath awake,
Till such dark bond of slumber break,
And grace o'ermaster sin:—

* Col. i. 18. † Matt. x. 39.

That latent germ baptismal life bestows
Doth oft in elder hearts its buried power
disclose.

How water, word, and grace combine
To work creative spells divine,
In vain let Reason ask;
Children are awful mysteries,
Within whose depth no spirit sees
But His,—who owns the task
Of overcoming, through celestial birth,
That born corruption, which is bred from earth.

Hence! reas'ning sceptic, harsh and cold;
For never will thine eyes behold
Tokens which sense defy:
Nature in secret works her plan,
Her growth escapes the sight of man;
Then, hush thy heartless cry,—
As if the weakness of the water could
Deprive the soul of sacramental good.

True wisdom loves the word "obey,"
And loving hearts but live to pray,
Believing Christ as true;
Safe in His arms, thou mother mild,
With hope baptismal place thy child,
And doubt not * He will do
A work mysterious for that infant soul,—
Baptising nature with divine control.

Henceforward, as a Priest and King,
Thy babe becomes a sacred thing,
An heir of grace and glory;
Mother! to whom such charge is given,
Now rear it for that throne in heaven
Scripture unveils before thee;
So discipline the dawning mind and will,
That each some priesthood unto God may fill.

"Our Father!" now thy babe may cry,
Whose Elder Brother rules the sky,—
The Man Divine, who came
By bleeding Merit to atone
For all the guilt sad Earth must own,
And give the child a name,
New as the sacramental Birth, which then
Through water and by Spirit dawns in men.

Blest Privilege! both deep and pure,
Which might our trembling hearts assure
That we are Christ's indeed:
Our Robe baptismal,—keep it white,
And never wilt thou lose the right
Which marks the heavenly Seed

* "Doubt ye not therefore, but earnestly believe, that He will likewise favourably receive this present infant," &c.—*Baptismal Service.*

Of all who, grafted into Christ by grace,
Born in the Church, are God's adopted race.

Oh, that on Man's expressive brow
Baptismal pureness beaming now
Maturer life might see!—
How should we bless that rite of heaven
Where grace is felt, and sin forgiven
By mercy, full as free;
And find God's Spirit ne'er that man forsook,
Who kept in age, the vow his childhood took.

But soil'd and stain'd by sin and crime,
Corruption deepens with our time,
And thus our hearts o'erlay
That seed of Heaven, the Spirit granted
When the new Birth was first implanted
On our baptismal day:
Yet not for this, let Souls profanely try
From faith to hide what holy means supply.

Rather, repent we! till the soul
Shall yield to that sublime control
Which heals the broken-hearted,
Who in atoning Blood begin
To bathe the soul, and wash their sin;
Mourning they e'er departed
From that blest Lord, whose interceding love
Reigns on the glory-throne He rules above.

CATECHISM.

"Who gave you this name? My Godfathers and Godmothers in my Baptism."—*The Catechism.*

If they who stand beside the source
Of some famed river's mountain-flow,
And ponder on its trackless course
To meet the far-off waves below,
Can feel a pensive influence born,—
Then how, on each Sabbatic morn,
The men of God must inly feel
A musing depth of voiceless zeal,

When at the fountain-head they stand
Of youthful Life's untraced career,
As round them groups an order'd band
Of earnest children, shy and dear,—
Encircled thus, to hear and speak,
With glist'ning eye, and glowing cheek,
Those Truths baptismal, pure and high,
Which link our being with the sky.

"Go, feed My Lambs," The Saviour cried
To Peter's large and loving heart;
And ever have those words supplied
What cannot from the Church depart,—

A pastoral right to form and feed
God's nurslings, by His grace decreed
To taste the food of heaven, and live
By all His word and wisdom give.

What, though the catechiser teach
Unfathom'd truths, which far outsoar
All raptured saints and seraphs reach
When most their minds a God adore,
Love brings a light that truth explains
Beyond what science ere attains,
As Heaven by intuitions mild
Gleams on the conscience of a child.

If faltering tongues of bashful youth
The careful Priest by welcome bland
Attune to some almighty truth,
Beyond a child to understand,
Is not the most gigantic Soul
Which awes the world by deep control,
A mental babe with lisping mind,
Compared with angels in its kind?

The Gospel o'er the cradle bends,
And gently leads each growing child,
Nor at the Font its mission ends,
But follows it with accent mild;
And so, by her maternal voice
The Church directs the infant choice,
And loves to dream on each white brow
The mystic Cross is mirror'd now.

God shield each lamb, and little one!
For soon the world before it lies;
And cold were he who looked upon
Those cherub lips, and chasten'd eyes,
Nor felt his heart-pulse throb with prayer
That all the Sponsors did declare,
When first the white-robed babe was given
To Jesu's arms for life and heaven,

Hereafter each in faith may keep.—
Alas, the infant-grace departs;
Enough to make mild angels weep
Already stains some youthful hearts!
Wilder'd by many a temper wild
Wilful and vain becomes the child,
Till robes baptismal wear no more
The whiteness at the Font they wore.

Yet, Shepherd of Thy blood-priced fold!
Since Thou didst stand at mother's knee,
And as a spotless Babe behold
The virgin brow, which bent o'er Thee,—
Thy spirit hung on each high word
An echoing conscience loved and heard,
While patriarch, saint, and prophet brought
Lessons to rear Thy human thought.*

* Luke ii. 52.

Lover divine of children dear!
In Whose fond arms an infant lay,
E'en now the Church believes Thee near
To hear their budding accents pray;
And oh! if child-born mem'ries still
Thy depths of sacred Manhood fill,
Look from Thy Mercy-Throne on high,
Hear children lisp, and mothers sigh.

Nor let the stern and sceptic Mind
'Tween Christ and childhood take its stand;
And, reas'ning here with falsehood blind,
Presume to hold His secret Hand
Who works by love's mysterious law
A grace cold reason never saw;
And by His Spirit, present now,
Recalls the child's baptismal vow

Back to the soul, perchance with fear;—
And opes the spring of thought within,
Until religion's vestal tear
Is dropt o'er some remember'd sin:
New hopes awake, and conscience burns
With hallow'd blush, as more it learns,
Who at the font His welcome gave,
Still longs in heaven the child to save.

Lord of simplicity and truth!
A scene like this the oldest need,
To summon back regretted youth
And bid them with compunction bleed:
A babe-like spirit, born of love,—
What purer gift can Grace above
Grant to the Saint, who lives below,
More childlike for the heavens to grow?

CONFIRMATION.

"Do ye here, in the presence of God, and of this congregation, renew the solemn promise and vow that was made in your name at baptism, ratifying and confirming the same?"—*Order of Confirmation.*

Lord of the blissful worlds above,
Incarnate Light, celestial Love!
Send from Thy prayer-moved mercy-seat
The grace of grace, Thy Paraclete.—
A touching sight for solemn tears,
Like prophecies of future years,
Under the aisles of hoary fane
Is now enacted: Faith, and Prayer,
O'er each young conscience come and reign,
And, with The Spirit, bless them there!

Round the rail'd altar humbly kneeling,
On each bow'd form, o'erfraught with feeling,
Anointed Hands will soon be laid;
And righteous prayers be duly pray'd;

Nor doubt we that a Gift divine
Shall with the mitred priest's combine.—
An ancient Rite, replete with glory,
By meek apostles used and loved,
Church of the Lord! is now before thee,
By martyrs blest, and saints approved.

But oh, ere yet that sealing grace
God's death-pang won to bless our race,
In answer to this prayer descend,
"Arise, O Lord! this child defend,
Daily increase that store divine
Of love and light which make him Thine,"—
Member of Christ! thou child of God!
Thy central heart examine now;
The narrow way if thou hast trod
Enquire, and ratify thy vow.

To you baptismal life was given
By virtue of its Source in heaven;
And vow'd ye were, for Christ and Cross
To count the world as painted dross:
The burden now 'tis yours to bear!
And can ye unto Christ declare
That awful vow your spirits bore,
When ye, as helpless babes were brought,
Baptised, and made for evermore
God's own to be, in will and thought?

Thou, of thy feeble Self afraid!
Trembling with truth, a pensive maid,
Through thy fringed lid the tearful gaze
The secret of thy soul betrays;
And through that veil of virgin white
Soft tremors reach thy mother's sight.
Pale candidate! though pure and young,
Thy heart is trepid unto tears,
And with a saintly horror wrung,
Lest sin betray thine unborn years.

"Your promise, can ye here renew?"
That deep reply, "O Lord, we do!"
Oh, is it not an awful word
By God and list'ning Angels heard?
Heaven echoes back the binding vow,
And Fiends abash'd, before it bow;
And writhe in darkness, thus to see
A virgin heart which grace inspires,
So consecrate to Deity
Its faith, its feeling, and its fires.

Yet, at the altar kneel in prayer;
Tremble, but hope, for Christ is there!
He will not fail this burden'd hour
To strengthen thee with loving power;
And when confirming hands are spread
In faith upon thine awe-bow'd head,
Thrill'd into speechless thought, whilst thou
Wilt feel Eternity draw nigh,
The heart of Him who hears thy vow
In heaven responds to every sigh.

He knows thee, loves thee, reads thy soul,
Can circle thee with blest control;
And in return for thy vow'd heart
Himself by gift and grace impart.
But, ah, mistake not; hectic zeal
Is but the flush warm fancies feel:
Of these beware, impassion'd Youth!
Nor heed what thrill'd emotions say;
They only love, who live the truth,
And walk in peace the perfect way.

Poetic thrills may soon depart,
And barren oft, some burning heart;
Emotions in themselves are nought
Except to Christian action brought;
Nor is one glorious promise given
To souls which only sigh for heaven.
High feelings to the sense appear
A creed the world may beauteous call,
But Christ hath made this doctrine clear,—
One daily cross transcends them all!

MARRIAGE.

"An honourable estate, instituted of God in the time of man's innocency, signifying unto us the mystical union that is betwixt Christ and his Church."—*Form of Solemnization of Matrimony.*

Although the birthday of this God-made earth
Seraphic harpers rose to sing,
Whose choral ecstasies proclaim'd its worth
And caused Heaven's crystal arch to ring,
All was imperfect, till a Priest was there
Creation's mouth to be, and mind, and prayer.

Vain seem'd the splendour which no eye could see,
The melody that none could hear;
But when God utter'd, "Let Mine Image be,"
Creation thrill'd, as Man drew near;
And what was meaningless, and mute, and dead,
Warm'd into life, and glow'd beneath his tread.

As man for earth, so Woman was required
The crowning grace of man to form;
Alone, not even Adam was inspired
To feel creation's godlike charm:

And thus, faith hears this fiat from The Throne,
"It is not good for man to be alone."

So ere the fall, a Priest almighty brought
A bridal Eve to Adam's heart;
A living Echo to the love he sought,
A help-meet never to depart,
A true companion for the soul to be,
Fresh from her God, in faultless purity.

Marriage is holy. May no heathen-fire
Around the Christian altar flame;
Impassion'd souls let saintliness inspire
And hallow hymeneal claim:
Belials in sense are minds by flesh o'erruled,
And love is vice, unless by virtue school'd.

How hush'd and holy is yon bridal scene
Before God's altar!—view'd by one
Who e'er in faith to Cana's home hath been,
That marriage-group to gaze upon,
Where the pale water blush'd itself to wine,
Moved by a miracle of grace divine.

Stainless in vesture, as the lilies white,
With flower-buds in her wreathèd hair,
Fearful and trepid, with o'erawed delight
Lo, the young bride is kneeling there,
Her dropping lids in mild dejection bent,
And young heart with a holy conflict rent.

In that pure breast what garner'd feelings play
Like pulses with mysterious beat!
To think sweet Girlhood now hath wing'd away
And Love must quit a calm retreat,
Sacred to thought, by friends and forms no more,
And truths, which made the reeling heart run o'er!

It is not, that a voiceless dread awakes
Suspicion, lest her choice be wrong;
No blighting vision o'er the future breaks
To which both guilt and grave belong:
Yet, sadness looms around her like a spell,
As oft in marriage-chime there seems a knell!

Our life is mystery; and the brightest joy
That flushes round a feeling heart,
Seems coldly shaded by some dim alloy
Doom'd never from man's world to part:
True mirth with mournfulness is oft allied,
As living babes suggest the babes who died.

And she, yon bridal Star of beauty now,
Oh, marvel not, as there she kneels,
That ere the wife can dawn upon her brow
Back to bright girlhood fancy steals;
Dead joys revive in tombs to fancy dear,
Melt through the heart, and mingle with a tear.

Last eve, at halcyon twilight's dreamful hour
When none but God the soul could see,
She pray'd and ponder'd in her girlish bower,
And sigh'd, young Past! her thoughts o'er thee;
Flower, fruit, and pathways, all instinct with truth,
Seem'd to accost her like the spells of youth.

She mused on what her spousal Life might fold
Within its undevelop'd scene;
On wings of love recall'd the times of old,
And wept o'er all bright hearts had been;
And scarce perceived the pensive moonlight throw
Its calm cold lustre on the lake below.

But, maiden! ere thy sacred ring be worn,
Beyond a mother's purest gift
The Church hath up to Heaven's high portals borne
A prayer, which shall thy soul uplift
To heights of bliss, serene as brides attain,
Whose wedded hearts are thrones where Christ will reign.

Souls are espoused by every hallow'd claim,
If wedlock far diviner prove
Than mere clay-throbs, which boast the common name
Of what Flesh means by mortal "love:"—
Christ and the Church* are shadow'd out by this,
And cast heaven's radiance round an earthly bliss.

VISITATION OF THE SICK.

"Bear our heavenly Father's correction; there should be no greater comfort to Christian persons, than to be made like unto Christ, by suffering patiently adversities, troubles, and sicknesses."—*Order for Visitation of the Sick.*

Sermons in sickness heaven can preach,
When pangs and penalties may teach
What custom rarely sees,—
That health is mercy next to grace,
And should inspire a sinful race
The God of health to please.

---

* Eph. v. 31, 32.

Strange! if our hearts be so accursed
That nothing, save a gift reversed,
Can make men prize their good:
Blessings look dim which seem to stay,
But brighten, when they wing away
From souls who Christ withstood.

So is it with the fields of youth,
The shrines of tenderness and truth
And all fresh Boyhood proved,—
When we survey the scene no more,
Or dream to life the dead of yore
Whom once we fondly loved,

Oft does the inward blush arise
To think, how calmly we could prize
Redundant mercies, then!
We marvel, why our love was cold,
And boyishly our past behold
Now we are wither'd men!

Parental bowers of peace and home,
And lanes our truant steps did roam,
Make landscapes in our soul;
While votive tear-drops Truth can shed
O'er imaged graves, where sleep the Dead
Whose eyes our hearts control.

Thus longs atoning love in vain
The past should o'er the present reign,
That what *was* once, might *be;*
But youth, and all young hours possess'd,
In thine abysmal darkness rest
Thou pall'd eternity!

And thus, in sickness when we lie
With languid pulse, and fever'd eye,
Pining, and pale, and lone;
While throes of secret anguish burn,—
Love through each throb would have us learn
The truths we ought to own.

Remember'd blessings round us throng
We valued not, when health bloom'd strong,
Which challenge holy tears;
And if chance-gleams of skyey blue
Some half-unblinded window through
Confront our pallid fears,—

How does the distant landscape seem
Apparell'd by poetic dream!
Till fancy yearns for fields,
Brooklet and forest, bank and wood,
And each green shrine where solitude
Religious silence yields.

But what transcends the all of this,—
On the sad couch of pain we miss
Christ's hallow'd courts of grace;
Where Litanies divinely call
From blending souls, which prostrate fall,
For God's uplifted Face.

Not seldom hath the sainted chime
Of sabbath-bells become sublime,
Yet mild, and melancholy,
When pensive Languor, far away
Has heard their ebbing dream-tones play,
In sickness, sad and lowly.

Like Zion's harping saint it cries*
"To thee, oh Lord! my spirit flies,
And fain before the Shrine
My kneeling heart wonld humbly pour
The chanted praise I hymn'd before,
In courts of grace divine."

But, sacred Mother, bring release;
Come, lift the latch, and with soft "Peace!" †
Enter the sick man's room;
O'er that pale brow Thy cross did seal
Shed the soft dews of balm that heal,
And light each haunted gloom.

Far better thus with Thee to hie
And hear a saintly mourner sigh,
Than run where feastings reign;
Wisdom, beyond the schools to reach,
Thy heaven-breathed words of solace preach
To Hearts subdued by pain.

Counsels divine, in tone serene,
Varied with grave rebukes between,
Thine Office now imparts;
And there beside yon dying bed
The Body and the Blood are spread,
Which feed our famish'd hearts.

Lord Jesus! Thou art present there
Entempled ‡ in each awful prayer;
The room our altar is;
Angel and saint we realise,
And vision with prophetic eyes
Scenes of seraphic bliss.

Go, man of pleasure, sensual Thing!
Whose life-boast is to laugh and sing;
Be ours the chamber lone
Where prayer and musing sickness meet,
And find before the Mercy-Seat,
What health has never known.

---

* Ps. lxxxiv. 2.

† "The minister of the parish coming unto the sick person's house, shall say, 'Peace be to this house!'" —*Order for Visitation of the Sick.*

‡ "Inhabitest."

Here may authentic priests, O Lord,
Thy grace dispense, and soothing word,
Like almoners for heaven;
And teach oblivious hearts a lore
Thy peerless martyrs taught of yore,
When conscience heard, "forgiven."

If health have joy, the sick partake
This boon divine,—for Thy dear sake
To suffer, not complain;
And, ere the sun of life go down,
Beyond their cross to see the crown
Of kings, with thee who reign.*

BURIAL OF THE DEAD.

(VILLAGE FUNERAL.)

"Earth to earth, ashes to ashes, dust to dust, in sure and certain hope of the resurrection to eternal life, through our Lord Jesus Christ."—*Order for the Burial of the Dead.*

The bells are tolling with a dreamy chime
Which melts and mingles with the air around,
Mourning for her who died in vernal prime,
Queen of the village by her virtues crown'd.

Last week she bounded, full of girlish life,
Fleet o'er the turf, elastic as the breeze,
Radiant as morn, with bloom and beauty rife,
Fresh as the wave which gambols on the seas;

But Christ recall'd her for His home on high
To harp in glory God's Incarnate love,
Ere guilt had waken'd one remorseful sigh,
Or earth untuned her for a heaven above.

Oh! gently lay her where the yew-trees wave
Their verdant darkness o'er some grassy tomb,
Where sunbeams learn the language of the grave,
Tinging their brightness with a temper'd gloom.

There shall the daisy rear its infant head,
And fairy wild-flowers drink the dew of spring,
While o'er the turf that greenly wraps the dead,
Autumnal Winds their plaintive descant sing.

'Tis the same spot her rosy girlhood sought
Where fresh from school, with bright companions gay,
In maiden fancy, free from troubling thought,
She work'd her sampler, or retired to play.—

Dear is the quiet village church to me,
Saxon, and simple, touch'd with tender glooms;
Lifting its widow'd form so gracefully
As though 'twere conscious of encircling tombs.

Whatever shade expressive clouds can throw,
Or hills wood-crested may around it cast,
I love to view it in the vale below
Connect the present with our storied past.

Oft have I paused, when lull'd by pensive bliss,
To hear the curfew mellow'd on the wind,
Waft the farewell of Day to scene like this,
Soft to the ear, as soothing to the mind.

But far excelling all chaste morn bestows,
The hush of twilight, or the harvest-moon,
Or what mere landscape to the minstrel shows
When silent thoughts their sanctity attune

Is felt,—when village-funeral winds its train
Slowly and sadly to some churchyard-gate,
And our deep Service* tones its heaven-born strain,
To scatter darkness from bereavement's fate.

Hark! from the woodland floats the forward breeze
A low sweet dirge, yon village-maidens sing,
Whose white robes glisten through the waving trees
As on the dead to her last home they bring.

Nay, sob not, mother! for thy beauteous child,
Though like a tendril from thy heart it grew;
Eternity she felt, ere Time defiled,
Or made her soul untender and untrue.

And thou, hoar'd grandsire! with thy grief-worn face,
Oft did the prattler on thy knee recline,
And hold up features Fancy loved to trace,
Which matrons told thee, in thy youth, were thine;

I see thee now, with tott'ring step advance,
Wan are thy cheeks, and drops of aged woe
Bedew thy visage, and bedim thy glance
As onward to the grave the mourners go.

---

* 2 Tim. ii. 12; Rev. i. 5, 6.

* "The priest, meeting the corpse at the entrance of the church, shall say, 'I am the resurrection and the life.'"—*Order for the Burial of the Dead.*

But ONE is present, whom no eye can see,
Except by faith, and that is Christ the Lord!
And "Weep not,"* childless mother, comes to thee,
If thy heart open to His gracious word.

Thou blessed Ritual! throbs of Jesu's heart
Still in thy tones of thrilling mercy live;
When yawns the tomb, most wonderful thou art,
By echoing all God's inspirations give.

The "Resurrection and the Life†" is near,
By Spirit present, and in love as deep
As when He touch'd the young man's open bier,
And gently bid wild Anguish not to "weep."

As o'er that grave the "dust to dust" awakes
A dismal echo in the bleeding soul,
How the damp earth-clod on the coffin breaks,
Till the deep tides of inward anguish roll!

Yet o'er the tomb heaven's canopy unfolds,
And hark! these words of soothing magic sound,
While Grief looks upward, and by faith beholds
The Lord of life and resurrection crown'd,—

"Blest are the dead, who in the Lord depart:
Yea, saith the Spirit, for their pangs are o'er;
Serene as heaven Christ keeps the sainted Heart,
Whose works are ended, and who weeps no more."

CHURCHING OF WOMEN.

"We give thee humble thanks, for that thou hast vouchsafed to deliver this woman thy servant, from the great pain and peril of childbirth."—*English Prayer Book.*

IN mother's love there hides a spell
Maternal hearts alone can see;
Transcending all that tears may tell,
Or man could be.

Far down within the spirit's deep
Her fountains of affection lie,
Like currents which in darkness sweep,
Nor face the sky.

Tender abyss of peerless love!
To heaven's omniscient eye-glance known,
The WOMAN-BORN, Who reigns above,
Thy claims doth own.

A pillow'd Babe on mother's breast,
Beneath Him throbb'd the Virgin's heart,
And, Woman! thou on HIM canst rest,
Whoe'er thou art.

Oh! magic force of nature, felt
Far as the sun and sea extend;
Beneath whose law all beings melt,
All spirits bend.

The Indian mother, stern and strong,
Cradles her infant on the tree,
And wildly chants her loud wood-song
For lullaby.

And the stern negress, seeking food,
Fastens the babe upon her back,
To roam each rocky solitude
Or lion's track.

Nor scene, nor change, nor earth nor sky
Enfeeble Love's maternal force;
Distance and time before it die,
Whate'er their course.

A passion this, so pure, so deep,
That while bereavèd fathers moan,
Oft wordless mothers only weep
In heart alone.

But why did God such love create
Unquenchably supreme, and pure?—
Because from mothers Spirits date
Their curse, or cure.

Thus saints and martyrs, heroes, all
Whom wond'ring Time delights to praise,
In heaven itself may still recall
Their infant-days,

When learn'd they from maternal lips
Lessons of holy love and prayer,
No clouds hereafter could eclipse,
Nor soul's despair.

Then, pallid mother! draw thee nigh,
Perill'd by pangs, but saved in birth;
And gently lift thy downcast eye,
To heaven from earth.

The virgin whiteness of that veil
Becomes thine inward purity,
And hides upon thy forehead pale
What angels see

Of blissful worship,—deep and mild,
Which mothers for their first-born pay,
And Love, with conscience undefiled,
Offers to-day.

---

* Luke vii. 13. † John xi. 25.

Thou art the parent of a Soul,
The mother of a deathless Mind!
And Christ to thee imparts control
For this design'd.

Self-discipline, and prayer-born love,
And persevering wisdom calm
Breathe, Holy Spirit! from above
With soothing balm;

That from Thine altar she may part
In saintly mood, serene and high,
And worship Christ with yearning heart,
Until she die.

Mothers are more than mines of wealth
If God-devoted Souls they be;
And what makes Empires' moral health
And purity

They guard. For, when do Nations sink
Into dark graves of sin and woe?—
When Church and State no longer think
What debt they owe

To christian mothers; unto whom
Both God and nature have consign'd
Existence, from whose dawning bloom
They nurse mankind.

COMMINATION.

"Is much to be wished . . . to the intent that being admonished of the great indignation of God against sinners, ye may the rather be moved to earnest and true repentance."—*Prayer Book.*

As Time grows old, the earth from heaven recedes
More distant far;
No Conscience bleeds.
To feel the burnings of that inward scar,
Which so discolours o'er with sin
Th' apostate soul we bear within.

A period was, when God and angels came
So near to thought,
The Church's name
With the fine strength of holiness was fraught;
Her frown cast midnight where it fell,—
Her blessing wove a guardian spell.

But now, we boast an intellectual blaze
That scatters all,
Cold Reason says
Before the majesty of Mind should fall!
Dazzled with light, but dark in love,
Sin loathes the truth which looks above.

Sensual and proud, a Belial age is ours
Drunken with pride,
And grasping powers
By which the godless will is gratified;
Greedy of gold, athirst for pelf,
And seeking heaven in worshipp'd Self.

Thou fond admirer of a holy time
When earth touch'd heaven!
And thrills sublime
Were to heroic saints and martyrs given
Of something purer than blind Sense
Can to a coarse rude age dispense,—

Marvel no more that Discipline lies dead;
Self-will reigns now;
Laurels, not ashes, crown the creedless head
And wreathe man's brow:
For sackcloth, singing-robes are worn,
And none but saints now seem forlorn!

When God was fear'd, due fasting calm'd the blood;
With naked feet
Then Penance stood
Low at the porch, the pastoral Band to meet,
Sackclothed by shame, with downcast eyes,
Sprinkled with ashes, heaving sighs:

Severely gracious, thus the Church's rod
Wielded o'er sin
The claim of God,
And o'erawed penitents, to weep within,
Driving them forth with scalding tears
To feel the pangs of righteous fears.

So with mount Ebal's menace Zion's song
Was well combined;
And true as strong
The healing power with which it calm'd the mind:
Indulgence then was not in vogue,
Nor framed its pleasing decalogue!

But with Her holiness, the power departs
A Church can wield
O'er chasten'd hearts,
Led by subduing love themselves to yield
To mild Correction's lawful charm,
Which keeps the soul from sinful harm.

Too oft our "church" is self-election now—
Our creed the will;
And few avow
That Christ is throned in christian temples still,
A Presence and a Glory there
Receiving praise, and hearing prayer.

Awake! awake! thou Arm of God, awake!
Put on thy strength,
Thy fear forsake
Church of our fathers! be Thyself at length;
Bride of The Lord, a Mother kind,
Watchful, but not to error blind.

Spirit divine! in this her trial-hour
Of sinful dread,
Inbreathe a power
That shall to glorious Duty lift her head
Whose panoply is ardent prayer
Which more and more each gift should bear.

And we, as children of our Mother dear,
In evil days
Oh, let us fear;
And in our lentine gloom on Ebal gaze,
And as the tenfold curses roll,
Let each, O God! subdue the soul:

For, art Thou not a sin-consuming Fire,
Awful as pure
In Thy dread ire?
Never may sense our godless mind allure,
To think that hell alone can burn
In fictions, which dark fancies learn.

Mercy, Lord Christ! most infinite Thou art:
But judgment true
Will cleave each Heart
That will not dread Thee in some darker hue,
Before Whom prostrate worlds must fall,
And worship Him who sways them all.

So, when the priestly Comminations roll
In thunders deep,
Till each awed Soul
In the hush'd centre of pale conscience weep,
Our sackcloth let repentance be,
Remorse—the ashes God can see.

So will lost Penance in such hour revive;
Sorrow for sin
In prayer will strive;
Till, wash'd and whiten'd by the Lamb within,
The heart-renew'd God's Word descries
Piercing, and pure as angel-eyes.

Back to the world, in penitence and prayer
Then may we speed:
If wounded there,—
Then look we upward, while our spirits bleed;
For, on The Throne there beats a Heart
In all true grief that takes its part.*

* Isa. lxiii. 9.

PRAYERS AT SEA.

"Glorious Lord God! at whose command the winds blow and lift up the waves of the sea, and who stillest the rage thereof."—*English Prayer Book.*

Fond mother, with thy wakeful ear,
Hark, how the storm-blasts through the welkin roll!
Thunder alarms the breast of guilty Fear,
And arrowy lightnings glance from pole to pole.

Louder and louder sweeps the gale!
Fierce, full, and large, the hissing rain-drops fall;
And midnight Terror, with emotion pale,
Begins in secret on her God to call.

Calm as a flower yon nursling lies,
Rock'd into silence on thy cradling breast;
Yet doth thy bosom heave with unheard sighs
Which move the spirit into sad unrest.

But not for thy domestic bower,
Or those who sleep within its guardian-shade,
Art thou awake at this convulsive hour
To hear the crash wild Elements have made.

Yet rides thy heart the rolling deep,
Toss'd on huge billows in tumultuous swell,
And voiceless tremors through thy bosom creep
For thy lone sea-boy, loved at home so well!

But lately, on thy breast he lay
His head in fondness, parting for the sea,
And would not brush the manly tear away
Which flow'd from boyhood, and which fell on thee.

And now, amid the shrouds aloft,
Perchance he grapples with the creaking mast;
Yet can Remembrance hear a blessing soft,
And feel thine arms maternal round him cast.

Mother! The Church confronts the waves;
Her litanies can lull their angry roar;
And He who watcheth o'er the ocean-graves*
Can make the sea as tranquil as the shore.

Christ on the waters, forms a Home
For all who trust Him in the tempest wild,
Far as the pilgrims of the deep can roam,
Or billows lullaby a sea-born child.

Safe is thy darling in this hour,
Dearer to Heaven, than mother's heart can know;
Calmly entrust him to that sleepless Power,
Deepen thy prayers, but let not doubts o'erflow.

* See Rev. xx. 13.

Mirthful and bright, thy sea-boy ran
Around thee once, though garden, grove, and field;
But now, emerging into ripen'd man,
Conscience and creed their sainted influence wield.

Precious, yon Bible!—'twas thy boon;
And, mother, where thy parting tear-gush fell,
Oft on the deck, beneath the sacred moon
He reads the warnings thou hast scored so well.

And that high book of hallow'd Prayer
A treasured sister gave, with farewell-kiss,
Oft will he clasp it on the ocean there,
And hail the sabbath as a holy bliss.

God of the winds, and waves, and seas!
Whom all the vassal Elements obey,
Whether by palmy shores the placid breeze
Soft as a seraph-wing, descends to play,

Or tempests heave the mountain-surge,
Flashing with foam beneath some lurid glare
While the drench'd mariners the vessel urge,
We thank Thee for our oceanic prayer!

Or, when the booming death-guns pour
Peal after peal, redoubling as they roll,
Or Victory shouts her patriotic roar
Of loud huzzahs from seaman's gallant soul,

Lord of the Deep! by Thee inspired,
Our Church for each some high-breathed prayer imparts;
That they whom Valour hath for conquest fired,
Should have the Prince of Peace to hush their hearts.

Seldom can inland-worship prove
Toned with such tenderness, divine as deep,
Like God's own halcyon calming from above
The wailing Hearts which o'er some lost one weep,

As when beneath the tranced air
While moonbeams like a shroud enrobe the wave,
Soft fall the tones of that funereal Prayer
When parts the billow for a seaman's grave.

Tearful the watching comrades stand,
For round a dead One how intense the spell!—
Brushing large tear-drops with a rough-worn hand,
They *look*, but cannot speak, the word, "farewell."

Peace to the Dead! he waits his hour
When the last trumpet shall untomb yon sea,
And with such life-blast all the waves o'erpower,
That risen dust shall soar to Deity.

GUNPOWDER TREASON.

"We adore the wisdom and justice of thy Providence, who so timely interposed in our extreme danger, and disappointed all the designs of our enemies."
Prayer Book.

Two Wills alone may cause our world to move,
Finite below, or Infinite above;
And all which reason and religion say
Points to the question,—"which should lead the way?"
Science the first, but Faith her God will call
Alpha of each, and Omega of all.

God is in history! an almighty Soul,
A secret Energy, divine Control,
Will of all wills, yet leaving manhood free,
Binding our time with His eternity:
No chance can reign, till His dread promise dies,
And orphan'd Earth for vanish'd mercy cries.

God rules in history! read by this deep plan
Gone ages harmonise their truths for Man;
While he, unconscious of those secret laws
Which link the second with a Primal Cause,
Obeys each bias, acts his perfect will,
And yet leaves God supreme in purpose still.

So grant us, Lord, a providence to trace
Directing all things for Thy chosen race;
Kingdoms and kings, the palace and the cot,
Insect, or seraph,—none can be forgot;
For in the hollow of Thy hand repose
Atoms, and worlds; o'er each Thy goodness flows.

And well, on this day, doth our Church decree
Anthems of love, which heave our hearts to Thee,
Celestial Watcher! Whose soul-reading eye
Did from yon heavens the miscreant-plot descry,
And, by that wisdom saints exult to own,
Forewarn'd the Empire, and preserved a throne.

Ripe was the plan; each purpose deeply laid,
And Treason gloated o'er a Church betray'd;
A helpless Victim, soon to be destroy'd
Look'd Freedom then, to faction overjoy'd;
Sworn was the oath, the sacrament was taken,—
But England was not by her God forsaken!

Praise to the Lord! let choral harpers sound;
Praise to the Lord! yet saints repeat around,
The Angel of Whose presence then was nigh
And bared foul Treason to the open sky,
Blasted her guile, and by protective charms
Shielded our Throne, and saved the Church from harms.

And mix'd with praise, let some remorseful prayer
The darksome burden of our guilt declare;
For what but mercies can outnumber sin?—
Whiten our hearts, atoning Blood! within;
Till, hallow'd by celestial truth, we raise
That living hymn where Life becomes a praise.

THE MARTYR-KING.

"Blessed Lord, we magnify thy name for thine abundant grace, bestowed upon our martyred Sovereign."—*Service for King Charles the Martyr.*

Oh, burning plague-spot on the brow of Time,
The withering curse of regicidal crime!—
Mock'd and betray'd by treason-bands
And massacred by murd'rous hands,
On this day soar'd to endless fame
Ascending in Emmanuel's name
True to his creed, above man's impious charter,
Charles the revered,—the Church's royal martyr!

Who has not read, till heart and brain were fired
With holy wrath against Self-will inspired,
When Loyalty, inert and cold,
Parley'd before the bad and bold;
When faction, treason, falsehood, all
In one combined on heaven to call,
Baptised religion into Murder's cause,
And sanction'd regicide with sacred laws!

Alas! for country, church, and crown, and creed,
When martyr'd Principle must burn and bleed;
Or else, a regal Conscience die
Into a mean and miscreant lie,
Forswearing all the truths that shine
With radiance drawn from truths Divine,
Because Democracy would dare to sing
Her psalm of blood o'er England's sainted king!

Oh! Thou, from Whom both king and kingdom draw
Their source, their wisdom, and undying law,
Now let our Church's sighs and tears
Soften the Empire into hallow'd fears;
For on her rests the curse of crime,
A sacrilege which burden'd time
And tinged our soil with that horrific stain,—
The blood of Monarchs, when by God they reign!

Who sign'd his warrant with an impious glee
Proved how satanic blinded souls can be:
As christian, monarch, husband, friend,
Can time to us a nobler send?
His failings rose from junctures bad
Which might have turn'd an angel mad:
Passion ran high; and lust for lawless power
Raged like a fiend in that chaotic hour.

Ruler Divine! Whom heaven-born souls obey,
At least Thy Church on this remorseful day
That murder'd Prince may well recall,
Who prized her glories more than all;
For whom his royal spirit strove
With anguish of exceeding love:
True to her martyr-king, this day be kept,
And weep for him, who oft for Her had wept.

Nor be forgot, that Crimes historic teach
Warnings profound which may the wisest reach.
Dead Sins are living preachers now;
And weeping hearts of prayer avow
That, God! except Thy grace prevent,
Men still are on some madness bent:
Wisdom they want, and meekness more, to own
The sceptred lordship of Thy boundless Throne.

RESTORATION OF THE ROYAL FAMILY.

"The Great Rebellion, and all the miseries and oppressions consequent thereupon."—*Prayer Book.*

Friend of the friendless! Thou art there
When throbs a soul with silent prayer
In hours of sadness holy;
And viewless Angels hover nigh
With placid brow and pensive eye,
To watch our melancholy.

"Stand still! and your salvation see," *—
Duty and blessing both from Thee,
Lord, here may faith discern;
Submission is that saving power
Which glorifies Earth's darkest hour,
Could Love the secret learn.

The Cup that Jesus bow'd to drink,
Though feeling start, and flesh may shrink,
Disciple! thou must drain;
A suff'ring Head each member thrills;
We conquer, by enduring ills,
And bleed before we reign!

---

* Exod. xiv. 13.

Thus, when dead Ages we untomb
And wander down their peopled gloom
Beholding what hath been,—
A patient mind and quiet heart
Have ever filled the Hero's part
In history's troubled scene.

Submission, passive, deep, and pure,
Alone has proved a matchless cure
For all the Church has borne;
Her watchword was, "Stand still! and see
The unbared arm of Deity,
Since thou art unforlorn."

Thus when apostate Creeds began
To blight the erring mind of man,
How meekly bore his wrong
That five-times banish'd Saint,* who kept
The truth unstain'd, while ruin swept
In Arian blasts along.

Still breathes a theocratic air
In church and creed, if God be there,
As Faith will ne'er deny;
Unweapon'd, save by inward grace,
Believers move with martyr-pace
Beneath the fiercest sky.

The worst of kings seems nobler far
Than mad Rebellion's impious war,
In havoc, blood, and fire;
The sin of witchcraft,†—brand it well,
Its birth-seed is the pride of hell,
By which dark Fiends aspire!

A Nemesis for injured kings
Or soon, or late, atonement brings,—
Dead Empires this declare;
Some thunder-blast of whelming wrath
Will burst upon that Nation's path,
Who robs a kingdom's heirs.

And ever, as this day returns
Oh, Saviour-god! our spirit learns
Where safety true resides;
That not our merit, but Thine arm,
Not foresight, but Thy prescient charm
Our refuge still provides.

In orphanhood the Church may roam,
And crownless monarchs need a home
To exiled anguish lent;
Base faction with Iscariot-breath
May shout for dungeon, rack and death,—
But Faith can be content.

Content to watch, and weep, and wait,
And bear the ban of iron Fate
With uncomplaining heart;
Her patience is a holy strength
Subduing crime with prayer at length,
Which Christ and Grace impart.

Sun of the Church! Thou Saviour bright,
A glory gilds the darkest night
Affliction can endure,
When Thy pure Spirit sheds a ray
On saints who keep the narrow way,
Like angel-paths secure.

---

* St. Athanasius. † 1 Sam. xv. 23.

THE ACCESSION.

"Our Sovereign Lady Queen Victoria as on this day set over us by thy grace and providence, to be our Queen."—*Prayer Book.*

THIS world is like that Creature vast*
The royal dreamer had to face;
Whose head from burnish'd gold was cast,
But when you reach'd the talon'd base
Vile metal there commenced its lower sway,
And slowly crumbled into worthless clay.

And who like monarchs this can know,
At whose accession all things wear
The richness of a regal glow,
And triumphs of that festive glare
A coronation and a crown present,
With all the pomps of shouting Welcome blent?

The spangles on the mourning-dress
Worn for some princely head, which lies
Cold in sepulchral nothingness,
Are scarce removed from courtly eyes,—
Ere happy mourners to another king
Their venal chant of vaunted homage sing.

Alas! for Kings, if state and throne,
If splendour and monarchal pride
Were all that royal minds could own,
Or crowns and fawning courts provide:
A fate like this the soul would overpower,
And harrow princes in their calmest hour.

The kingdom of the mind exceeds
Whatever realms and rank impart,
And oft a monarch inly bleeds
To find himself a friendless Heart,—
In crowded loneliness to speak and smile,
And be unechoed in his thoughts the while.

---

* Dan. ii. 32, 33.

And hollow dreams must oft surround
The pageantries of royal state;
Deceits and dangers there abound
While secret anguish gnaws the great:
Peasants can weep, but Princes dare not show
The aching centre of *their* voiceless woe!

Flatter'd by many, loved by few,
Before them group and gather all
Who seek to veil each covert-view,
Their serpent tongues the "country" call;
Too oft fair loyalty is glozing speech
Gilding the cause cold Self desires to reach.

Hence, Thou for whom a realm is kept
O'er which the sunbeams ne'er go down,
Wider than that the eagles swept,
When Rome became a huge renown,—
The Church anoints thee with her unction now,
And drops the crown upon Thy jewell'd brow.

While thrones descend, and empires shake
'Mid loud convulsion fierce and far,
And strife and civil discord make
Pale Europe rock with coming war,
God of our glories! 'tis in Thee we own
The deep foundations of a christian throne.

Lift we our heart-breathed hymn on high
To That incarnate King of kings!
Under Whose providential eye
A coronation-anthem sings
Each patriot soul, who Church and Crown can see
Reposing grandly, when they rest on Thee.

The life-blood of a loyal heart
Flows bravely through our British veins;
Nor shall this hero-truth depart
From cot and palace, shore and plains,—
That Kings on earth a regal shadow throw
Of Him, to Whom all worlds subjection owe.

ORDINATION.

"The congregation shall be desired, secretly in their prayers, to make their humble supplications to God."—*Rubric for the Ordering of Priests.*

Saviour of spirits! if the burden'd life
Our ransom'd being into action bears,
Be ever with some wordless mystery rife
Which mocks what Adoration's lip declares,

Oh, is it not, when Truth's devoted hour
To Thine Own altar some young Levite leads,
And the high gift of Thine absolving power
Endows the Priesthood for celestial needs?

Yes, long as awed remembrance can remain
Shall I that everlasting moment feel,
When in the silence of St. Asaph-fane
Heart, soul, and conscience did these words o'ersteal,

"Receive Thou, for Thy priestly work divine,
A promised unction from the Holy One;
Anointed be thou at this hallow'd shrine,
Watchman of Zion! lo, thy work begun!

"Absolve for Christ the sin pure grace forgives,
For Him reserve what He himself retains;
Dispense the Food by which the spirit lives,
The ruling Sacrament wherein He reigns."

And when a stillness, thrilling, rapt, profound,
Breathed from the depths of each adoring Soul,
Eternity seem'd closing all around
And shaded conscience with divine control.

With seven-fold gifts a Grace did here descend
Hearts to illumine with celestial Love,
And to each priest below some unction send
Perfumed with incense from The Priest above.

Let Faith believe, and ever hope and pray
Lord of the Temple! Thou wert nigh, to bless
Each Shepherd, vow'd to feed thy flock that day,
And fold them safe in life's vast wilderness.

To guard, premonish, and with truth provide
The Saviour's Body here on earth which roams;
Pure unto death, to preach The Crucified,
And beckon pilgrims to their sainted homes,—

Such was the Charge we messengers received,
Such the high call our stewardship obey'd;
Woe be to us! if truths were unbelieved,
Our bosom prayerless and the Church betray'd.

Thus, living Shepherd of immortal Sheep!
If to our pastoral work the soul was given,
Though for sad errors all must wail and weep,
Still, let us hope there breathed a gift from Heaven.

Years since have roll'd, of trial, change and grief,
But still that Ordination-vow is heard;
And what can soothe us with sublime relief,
"But, "I am with you!" oh, Incarnate Word?

And, blent with awfulness of faith and fear,
For each young watchman then for Christ ordain'd
Prophetic Fancy sketch'd some quiet sphere,
Where souls for Jesu might be sought, and gain'd.

Visions, perchance, of rural cots retired
Hover'd around the priested hearts of those
Who, ne'er by sad ambition inly fired,
Haunt the lone hamlet where the poor repose.

Such was the scene our peerless Herbert loved,
Pictured in quaint and quiet Walton's lines;
Which Hooker sought, and Hammond's taste approved,
In whom the image of a Pastor shines.

Yet, little boots it, what our destined place
In the large vineyard of the Lord may be,
Weave but the spells of Thine ordaining grace,
And Time and Scene are lost, O Lord! in Thee.

Whether in haunts of fever, homes of gloom
Where squalid Woe retreats, and yearns to die,
The toil-worn pastor cheers some tatter'd room,
And calms the anguish of a mourner's sigh;

Or, haply down where greenwood-dales retire
Through hawthorn-lanes he wends his thoughtful way,
What time pale sunset gilds the village-spire,
And seeks the cottage where he comes to pray,

Wherever duty, discipline and care,
Faith, hope, and meekness grace his onward path,
A Shepherd finds his flock, and feeds them there,
And the rich promise of his Master hath.

Spirit of Light, of pastoral love and peace,
Divine Sustainer! send Thine unction now;
And teach the watchman, time gives no release
To light the burden of a priestly vow.

But bear thou up, and bear thou nobly on!
To warn the wicked and the saints to guide,
Till thou be summon'd where the dead have gone,
Who lived for Duty, and for Jesus died.

EUCHARIST.

"The most precious Body and Blood of thy Son, our Saviour, Jesus Christ."—*Communion Office of the Church of England.*

BANQUET of bleeding Love, by Christ prepared,
Feast of all feasts! we turn to thee,
Which dying Grace alone declared
Manna of immortality;
For, when the tomb-call must at length arrive,
The Dead shall feel thee in their dust alive.*

There, sacrifice and zeal in one combine,
With brotherhood of blissful love;
And faith-born feelings, most divine,
Alighting from their Source above:
Creeds and commands, and penitence and prayer,
With purity and pardon,—mingle there.

And who can celebrate the mystic Rite,
Perfect and pure, predestined Lamb! †
Nor feel their glory of delight
Who realise the dread I AM,
And worship Him with tender awe intense
In the deep shade the words "Do this," dispense?

List, now the pealing organ-swell is o'er
And hymnèd chants dissolve away,
And through yon temple's archèd door
Cold worldlings seek the din of day,
Sublime the hush! as though the Dead drew near
On balanced wing, our beating hearts to bear.

Let the stoled Priests their order'd station take;
The Shrine of sacrifice and prayer
Lord Jesus! Thou wilt not forsake,
But be our felt Atonement there;
Renew'd by faith, and realised in love,
While o'er Thine altar broods the Mystic Dove.

Oh! rapt Communion, which can raise the soul
To the clear heights of sin forgiven,
Scatter the spirit-clouds that roll,
And feed us with the food of heaven,—
Thine is the hour, when dead and living meet
In blended homage at one Mercy-seat!

---

* John vi. 54. † Rev. xiii. 8.

Who comes with cold or criticising heart
The outward elements to scan,
In this high Feast can have no part,
Where God comes down to sup * with man;
Seeds of Eternity within it lie,
Which bud on earth, to blossom in the sky.

Though bread look bread, and water water seem
To carnal vision dull and cold,
Yet sacraments outsoar the dream
Of those who nought but sense behold:
Faith is the eye by which believers view
Christ in the tokens of His Presence true.

Thou Nourishment for all baptismal souls,
A food high Angels cannot share,
The vastness of thy charm controls
The hearts which palpitate with prayer
Into an awe profound,—but full of grace,
For God incarnate, bleeding for our race.

Incorporate with Emmanuel's Body all
By sacramental union grow,
Who Christ their Resurrection call;
Though sinful dust they seem below,
Faith more than dying Flesh in Man can see,
And in The Lord's *our* true eternity.†

Soul of all Rites! mysteriously sublime,
By whom the fainting Church is fed,
Though veil'd in garbs of sense and time
We know Him, as he breaks the bread! ‡
When Christ dispenses that almighty food,
"Receive my Body and partake my Blood."

Refreshment, pardon, and renewing grace
God's eucharist to each imparts,
That prints a reverential trace
Of Jesus on their sainted hearts:
And who are they who need no heavenly gift
High o'er the world their sinking hearts to lift?

Humility and hope this Feast inspires,
Chastens the mind, and calms our fear;
And cools the uncontrollèd fires
Of those who fancy heaven is near,
Dreaming they stand on Zion's topmost place
Long ere they learn to wind around the base!

A green oàsis in this herbless life,
This desert lone of dreary hours,
Where Time foregoes each warring strife
And Love renews her languid powers,—
Proves the blest Eucharist, to all who know
The weight of this mysterious life below.

* Rev. iii. 20.
† 2 Cor. vi. 16; 1 Cor. vi. 19. ‡ Luke xx. 34, 35.

Thy strength'ning Presence, Lord! we pilgrims need,
Sinful, and oft with sadness worn;
For here our bosom'd sorrows bleed
Till even pleasures grow forlorn,
And hues sepulchral robe the world around,
Which looks like Lazarus in his grave-clothes wound.

And what a bulwark for The Church hath been
This feast of sacrificial Love!
For time has no dark error seen,
The Bread and Wine could not remove;
Christ and the creatures, matter, grace, and mind,
In these pure symbols meet, to bless Mankind.

Dove of the Church! Thou Paraclete, descend,
And such anointing grace impart,
That round Thine altar each may bend
With chasten'd will, and contrite heart;
Not with a conscience, such as earth-slaves feel,
But touch'd like Peter, with impassion'd zeal.

Thus we adore Thee, Thou almighty Priest!
Prophet of hope, salvation's King;
Here where the lowest and the least
May learn the song of heaven to sing,
"Worthy The Lamb o'er men and worlds to reign,
Who back to God redeem'd lost souls again!"

GOD SAVE THE CHURCH.

"I speak concerning Christ and the Church."
Eph. v. 32.

God save the Church! and guard Her free,
Whom Christ ordain'd on earth to be
A sacramental guide and friend,
Our creed to mould, and heart amend.

God save the Church! from Christ She came,
And proved Her apostolic name
When Rome's Augustine vainly tried
To get her free-born faith denied.*

* Concerning the primitive freedom and Catholic antiquity of the British Church, the following extract from a rare tract by Lloyd, formerly Bishop of St. Asaph, will be reverently appreciated by all churchmen:—"For near a hundred years there was almost no possibility of communication between Rome and Britain, and therefore it was no wonder if there was grown a great strangeness between them. Besides, in that interval of time the Roman Church was much

For long before the Danish clan,
Or Saxon, o'er rent England ran,
The monks of Bangor move in glory
Through the stern page of British story.

God save the Church! sectarian Mind
In prayerless reason bound and blind,
From Her serene repulse hath met,
Whose crown remains unsullied yet.

Science and learning, art and song,
Around Her name and nature throng;
Hero and sage, and saint and martyr
Have gloried in Her heaven-seal'd charter.*

So, when I read th' historic past,
And see how persecution's blast
By rack and dungeon, fire and hate,
In vain besieged her queenly state,

Present and future both appear
Enlink'd with her sublime career;
In whom unchanged by friends or foes
The apostolic life-blood glows.

God save the Church! we challenge all
Who English archives dare recall,
To match her sainted roll of men
Whose lives recall'd St. John again.†

Parochial Watchmen, pure and high
Whose worth and wisdom near'd the sky,—
Eternity enshrines their name
Who won their crowns through fire and flame!

Howe'er ungrateful Time forget
On earth to pay the lauding debt,
Delighted Angels watch'd below
Their counterparts in pureness glow.

God save the Church! whose rites control,
Chasten, subdue, and calm the soul;
Something of earth, but more of heaven
To all Her prayer and praise is given.

Time and eternity appear
To melt the sigh, and move the tear,
As oft her liturgy of love
Lifts man below to God above.

Majestic, too, her haunted shrines,
Where sentiment with stone combines:
Chantry and choir, and arch, and nave
Where lie the buried pure and brave,

Breathe mute, but magic eloquence,
And through the eye to soul dispense
A wordless power of inward prayer,
Born of the creed,—that God is there.

Nor be forgot our ivied fanes
Which crest the hills, and dot the plains;
Where gothic roof and graceful tower
Wield o'er the heart a witching power:

So hush'd and heavenlike seems the spot
That time and turmoil are forgot;
And Nature her lone sabbath keeps
Where child, or village patriarch, sleeps.

altered from what it was formerly. . . . The Britons, whom that Emperor had left to themselves, continuing in their primitive liberty, a hundred and fifty years after this, when Pope Gregory the First would make Austin the Monk their Archbishop, they told him plainly, 'We will not be thy subjects:' they knew of no 'authority he had over them.' . . . . By these instances it sufficiently appears that Rome had made great alterations in other things, and made bold to impose them on other Churches as conditions of her communion. It appears that these Northern Churches were shut out of her communion; they were called the schismatics of Britain and Ireland, for no other reason but only because they would not receive these alterations, nor submit to the authority by which they were imposed. . . . Wheresoever they found the Roman tyranny abetted against them, there indeed they stood upon their terms; and laid the schism upon them who were the cause of it, and would 'no more communicate with them than with Pagans,' as Bede tells us. The Scots of South Ireland stood thus little more than thirty years after Austin came over; all the other Scots and Picts held out nearly a hundred years longer: but the Britons much above two hundred years. And yet, the Churches that stood at this distance from Rome, all the while continued communion with each other, and kept their religion the same in all points that it was when the Roman Empire stood, and the same that was anciently in the purer Roman Church."—Lloyd's "Primitive Church," pp. 64, 65, 69, 70.

* John xv. 7; John xiv. 19; Matt. xxviii. 20; John x. 27, 28.

† "'My hope is that I shall shortly leave this valley of tears, and be free from all fevers and pain; and, which will be a more happy condition, I shall be free from sin, and all the temptations and anxieties that attend it: this being past, I shall dwell in the New Jerusalem, dwell there with just men made perfect; dwell where these eyes shall see my Master and Saviour Jesus; and with him see my mother, and all my dear relations and friends. But I must die, or not come to that happy place; and this is my content, that I am going daily to it. . . . And now, Lord—Lord, receive my soul!' Thus he lived and thus he died like a saint, unspotted of the world, full of alms-deeds, full of humility, and all the examples of a virtuous life, which I cannot conclude better than with this borrowed observation,—

———'All must to their cold graves;
But the religious actions of the just
Smell sweet, and blossom in the dust.'"

See WALTON'S *Account of* HERBERT'S *Death.*

God save the Church ! for rich and poor
Alike expands Her gracious door,
Who from the cradle to the grave
Watches the Souls Christ died to save.

The peerage of the Church are those
In whom the Saviour's image glows;
And in the poorest, grant, that we
God's noblemen by saintship, see.

There, prince and peasant, man and child,
Learn saving wisdom undefiled;
And nought is hid by Godhead spoken
To conscience bruised, or spirit broken.

But, most because the Word of Heaven
Is purely to the people given
In British language, broad and free,
Church of my Fathers ! love I thee.

God save the Church, and save the Queen !
Mitre and Throne have ever been
To weal and woe alike related,
By Truth revered, and Treason hated.

God save the Church ! be this our cry
Both while we live, and when we die;*
For, rail Her foemen as they will,
The Church is England's glory still !

* Ecclesiastical annalists of the Elizabethan period relate, that when that good and great prelate, Archbishop Whitgift, was expiring, the only words he could intelligibly express were, "*Pro ecclesiâ Dei! pro ecclesiâ Dei!*" But, what can rival the saintly glories which encircle the dying bed of the illustrious Hooker, as recorded in the quaint page of Walton? "The doctor had occasion to inquire his present thoughts, to which he replied,—'That he was meditating the nature and number of angels, and their blessed obedience and order, without which peace could not be in heaven; and oh! that it might be so on earth!' After which words he said,—'I have lived to see this world is made up of perturbations; and I have been long preparing to leave it, and gathering comfort for the dreadful hour of making my account with God, which I now apprehend to be near; and though I have, by his grace, loved him in my youth, and feared him in my age, and laboured to have a conscience void of offence to him and to all men, yet, if thou, O Lord! be extreme to mark that I have done amiss, who can abide it? And therefore where I have failed, Lord show mercy to me; for I plead not my righteousness; but the forgiveness of my unrighteousness, for his merits, who died to purchase a pardon for penitent sinners. And since I owe thee a death, Lord let it not be terrible, and then take thine own time: I submit to it! Let not mine, O Lord, but let thy will be done!' With which expressions he fell into a dangerous slumber, dangerous as to his recovery; yet recover he did, but it was to speak only these few words, 'Good doctor, God hath heard my daily petitions; for I am at peace with all men, and He is at peace with me; and from which blessed assurance I feel that inward joy, which this world can neither give nor take from me.' More he would have spoken; but his spirits failed him, and after a short conflict betwixt nature and death, a quiet sigh put a period to his last breath, and so he fell asleep."

LUTHER:

OR,

ROME AND THE REFORMATION.

LUTHER.

JUSTIFICATION BEFORE GOD.

"I, Martin Luther, an unworthy preacher of the Gospel of our Lord Jesus Christ, thus profess and thus believe; that this article, 'That faith alone without works can justify before God,' shall never be overthrown, neither by the emperor, nor by the Turk, nor by the Tartar, nor by the Persian, nor by the Pope, with all his cardinals, bishops, sacrificers, monks, nuns, kings, princes, powers of the world, nor yet by all the devils in hell. This article shall stand fast, whether they will or no. This is the true Gospel. Jesus Christ redeemed us from our sins, and He only. This most firm and certain truth is the voice of Scripture, though the world and all the devils rage and roar. If Christ alone take away our sins, we cannot do this with our works: and as it is impossible to embrace Christ but by faith, it is, therefore, equally impossible to apprehend him by works. If, then, faith alone must apprehend Christ, before works can follow, the conclusion is irrefragable, that faith alone apprehends him, before and without the consideration of works; and this is our justification and deliverance from sin. Then, and not till then, good works follow faith, as its necessary and inseparable fruit. This is the doctrine I teach; and this the Holy Spirit and church of the faithful have delivered. In this will I abide. Amen."

PREFACE

TO THE SIXTH EDITION.

1852.

LUTHER.

(*From* HERDER.)

——"Mächtiger Eichbaum!
Deutschen Stamms! Gottes Kraft!
Droben in Wipfel braust der sturm,
Du stehst mit hundertbogigem Armen
Dem Sturm entgegen und grünst!
Der Sturm braust fort! Es liegen da
Der dürren, armen Aeste
Zehn darnieder gesaust. Du Eichbaum stehst,
Bist Luther!"

IT is recorded in the history of Edward the Sixth's coronation, that when three swords were brought before him as appropriate symbols of the three Kingdoms over which he was called to reign, the monarch observed, one was yet wanting. In reply to the nobles who demanded what his majesty was pleased to require, he replied, it was the Bible. The sacred volume being then placed in the royal hands, the youthful king delivered himself in the following noble strain:—

"That book is the sword of the Spirit, and to be preferred before those swords that ought to govern us, who are then for the people's safety by God's appointment. Without that sword, we are nothing, we can do nothing, we have no power: from that we are what we are this day; from that we receive whatsoever it is that we at this day assume. He that rules without it, is not to be called God's minister, or a king. Under that we ought to live, to fight, to govern the people, and to perform all our affairs. From that alone we obtain all power, virtue, grace, salvation, and whatsoever we have of divine strength."

In the spirit of these sentiments touching the regal power and religious supremacy of the Divine Word, the author has the privilege to commit a Sixth Edition of the following Poem to the press. Under disadvantages of a peculiar character, the work has been enabled to maintain its ground; and it is with no vain egotism, but with a thankful heart, the writer is enabled to state that, not only in his own country, but in America, Germany, and on the continent, a poetical essay on the Reformation has been welcomed as not unworthy the sacred cause to which it is devoted.

As regards this new Edition, the Author has to observe, the poem has undergone a complete and careful revision; and that the chapter, entitled "Jesuits and the Mind of Man," is altogether new.

It now remains for him to add, the decisive language he has used in branding the errors of the Papal system, is by no means on a level with the enormities his work attempts to portray. True, indeed, by those who cultivate a latent sympathy with Romanistic doctrine, the writer has been censured for using indefensible epithets when speaking of what the sectarian Council of Trent has canonised. But, in reply to this, he begs to re-affirm, such language is clearly justified by the dogmatic teaching of his own Church; and that in comparison with what Jewell, Ridley, Latimer, Cranmer, Bramhall, Hall, Jeremy Taylor, Wilson and Bull, and even Laud, have written against the corruptions of Rome,—the severest lines in his poem are almost mild and unmeaning negations. It is easy for those who cannot refute an advocacy, to abuse the advocate; to confound charity towards Persons with attachment to Principles; and when superstition is righteously exposed, to raise a denouncing cry of "irreverence" against a writer who has the manliness to be truthful and sincere. But this injustice is too transparent to prevail over any mind acquainted with catholic verity and primitive discipline. "The truth as it is in Jesus," is one thing; and we recoil with absolute dread from language which approximates to irreverence in respect to what such "truth" reveals: but the falsehood as it is in Rome, is another thing; and we maintain, nothing could be so irreverent, as to leave *such* falsehood uncensured and uncondemned.

The moral realities of Luther's personal character, as unfolded in these pages, have been described by some writers as overdrawn; and others, indeed, have professed astonishment—that such a man could form a possible theme for poetry at all! Instead of any formal discussion, let the author be permitted to quote the words of Coleridge, whose judgment on what constitutes the heroical attributes of Human Nature, few controversialists will be so immodest as to dispute.

"Mr. Coleridge happened to lay his hand upon a little old engraving of Luther with four German verses above it. He said, 'How much better this is than many of the butcher-like portraits of Luther which we commonly see. He is of all men the one whom I especially love and admire.' Pointing to the first words of the German verses, he explained them, 'Luther, the dear hero.' 'It is singular (he said), how all men have agreed in assigning to Luther the heroic character, and indeed it is certainly most just. Luther, however wrong in some of his opinions, was always right in design and spirit. In translating his ideas into conceptions, he always understood something higher and more universal than he had the power of expressing. He did not bestow too much attention on one part of man's nature, to the exclusion of the others; but gave its due place to each; the intellectual, the practical, and so forth. He is great, even where he is wrong; even in the sacramental controversy, the most unhappy in which he engaged; for his idea of Christ's body becoming infinite by its union with the Godhead is entirely wrong.' Some one mentioned Calvin. He said 'Calvin was undoubtedly a man of talent; I have a great respect for him; he had a very logical intellect; but he wanted Luther's powers.'"

But we need not confine ourselves to the testimonies of writers who study the character of Luther through the medium of Protestant feelings. When we are next assailed for over-estimating the noble qualities of the German Reformer, we recommend the objectors first to weigh the following words of Frederick Von Schlegel, *after* his perversion to the Roman Church—

"In the first place, it is evident of itself, that a man who accomplished so mighty a revolution in the human mind, and in his age, could have been endowed with no common powers of intellect, and no ordinary strength of character. Even his writings display an astonishing boldness and energy of thought and language, united with a spirit of impetuous, passionate, and convulsive enthusiasm." . . . "Luther, so far from exciting the rebels, like some of the new gospellers, opposed them with all the powers of his commanding eloquence." . . . "None of the other leaders of the new religious party, had the power, or were in the situation to uphold the Protestant Religion, its present existence is solely and entirely the work and the deed of one man, unequal in his way, and who holds unquestionably a conspicuous place in the history of the world. Much was staked on the soul of that man; and this was in every respect a mighty and critical moment in the annals of mankind, and in the march of time." . . . "When we consider the intellectual endowments of this extraordinary man, solely in themselves, the boldness of his speculations, and the energies of his eloquence, will be found to form an epoch (as is universally acknowledged), not only in the history of the German language, but in the progress of European science, and European culture."—*Philosophy of History*, Lecture 15th.

What will our Romish assailants reply? This, be it remembered, is not the heated enthusiasm of an "irreverent dissenter;" but the calm, cool, and thoughtful appreciation of one of the most philosophic historians of Human Nature, and who was, also, a devoted adherent of the papal communion.

As might have been anticipated, on the attributes of Luther's character, the nature of the Roman Apostasy, and the Unity of the Visible Church as disorganised by the principles of the early Reformation—much has been written, and with different objects, by those who have reviewed the present work. Still, as every author is naturally supposed to over-estimate the charms of his own Hero, and to exaggerate his triumphs, moral or intellectual, we are glad in this edition to offer some evidence on these points from parties whom no candid person will accuse of what certain members of our church are pleased to denominate, "Ultra Protestantism."* Hear, then, what ARCHDEACON MANNING says in his work on the "Unity of the Church"—

"I am bound to say that, on the one hand, the just causes of complaint which made Luther first address the bishops of Brandenberg and Mersberg, and his steady appeals through every gradation of ecclesiastical order to the award of a General Council; and, on the other, the violent and corrupt administration of Leo X., ending in an excommunication against a man whose cause was still unheard, seem effectually to clear both him and those who, for his sake, were driven from the unity of the church, from the guilt of schism."—MANNING *on The Unity of the Church*, pp. 328, 329. London, 1842.

* The Bishop of London, in his late charge, tells his clergy that so far from their being ashamed of the name "Protestants," they ought rather to glory in it. And with much reason; since the consistency of the sound churchman, as well as the orthodoxy of the sincere Christian, is here involved. For, what book

In the second place, let us direct attention to the subsequent quotations from a work, which Dr. Pusey, for some reason or other, has ceased to record among his advertised works. We allude to the "Historical Inquiry into the Probable Causes of the Rationalistic Character lately predominant in the Theology of Germany, &c. &c. By E. B. PUSEY, M.A., Fellow of Oriel College, Oxford. London: Rivington. 1828." Let the reader, then, mark the high terms of admiration and reverence in which Dr. Pusey, in his best production, alludes to the great apostle of the German Reformation. We recommend them to the candid attention of those who denounce Martin Luther as an incarnation of polemical fierceness.

"Much, both in the external and internal circumstances of the German Reformation, occurred to prevent its full and adequate development. Had this been perfected in the spirit in which its great instrument might have completed it, if permitted tranquilly to finish his work, or supported by others, acting on his own principles, and surveying the whole system of revolutions with the comprehensive and discriminating view of his master-mind, the history of the German Church had probably been altogether different," &c.—"The fruitless attempts to satisfy an uneasy and active conscience, by the meritorious performances of a Romish convent, had opened his eyes to a right understanding of the Scripture, in whose doctrine alone it could find rest; and the clear and discerning faith which this correspondence of Scripture with his own experience strengthened in him, gave him that instinctive insight into the nature of Christianity, which enabled him, for the most part, unfailingly to discriminate between essentials and non-essentials, and raised him not only above the assumed authority of the church, and above the might of tradition," &c. pp. 7, 8.—"The number of the noble band, who were actuated by the same spirit as Luther was, diminished, and their agency disturbed by the troubles of the times," &c.—"More fatal than the impediments thus presented to the tranquil development of the principles, were the internal divisions, originating in an imperfect conception of its scheme," &c.—"These had indeed been checked by the commanding spirit of Luther," p. 9.

The following beautiful passage, though not immediately referring to Luther himself, is yet too valuable in itself to be omitted.

"The Reformers, in consistency with their great tenet, that Scripture is the only authoritative source of Christian knowledge, had laid the study of the sacred volume as the foundation of all theological science. In the pursuance of this principle they had established as the rule of interpretation one which, when correctly developed, contains all the elements of right exposition, which have since been gradually vindicated by the combination of several partial efforts. Their, or rather (mark this, reader!) the biblical rule, that 'Scripture is its own interpreter,' includes in itself the religious, historical, grammatical elements, which were imperfectly, because separately, brought forward by Spener, Semler, and Ernesti. For it is obvious that if Scripture is to be understood from itself, those only can rightly and fully understand it, who have a mind kindred to that of its authors; as any human production upon which the mind of its author is impressed will be best understood by him whose intellectual and moral character is most allied to the original which it expresses. The individual is thus placed, as it were, at the centre of the same circle from which the views of the author emanated; and contemplates, therefore, every part in the same order, harmony, and relation, of which they were originally possessed. In religious writing it is plain that the spirit required is a religious spirit: that none can truly understand St. Paul or St. John whose mind has not been brought into harmony with theirs—has not been purified and elevated by the same spirit with which they were filled; and this unquestionably was what the pious Spener meant by his much disputed assertion, that none but the regenerate could understand Holy Scripture," pp. 26, 27. —"No wonder that H. Muller should speak against the four dumb church idols, the font, the pulpit, the confessional, and the communion table," &c.—"Such a system could not endure; it contained within itself the seeds of its own dissolution; a reaction was almost the unavoidable consequence, unless some one, or some succession of men, gifted with Luther's pious and discriminating mind, should establish a separation between this accumulation of mercenary human definitions; and the simple truth should replace, by the influential faith of the heart, the barren contentious scholasticism by which the understanding alone was occupied, or rather was distracted," pp. 49, 50.

Once more we shall venture to select a fine passage from this (unfortunately) now neglected work. In allusion to Ernesti's principles of interpretation, Dr. Pusey favours us with the following deliverance:—

"He forgets that every new religion must form to itself a new language; (query, in what sense is Christianity a 'new religion?') that in order to convey new truths, words already in use must indeed be employed to connect them with the primary ideas of mankind; but that the signification of these words must be modified, that they must be recast, remoulded, in order to receive the stamp of the newly communicated truth. The application of classical language, in its full strictness, to the words of Christianity, could not convert them into a document of mere human speculation. That λογος signified 'reason,' and 'wisdom,' in the classics, was a very superficial as well as entirely mistaken ground for supposing that, in St. John, it meant nothing more than the wisdom of the communications made to man. The effect of this is seen in its full perniciousness in his immediate followers. 'Regeneration' was supposed to signify 'the mere reception into a religious society;' the doctrine of the influence of the Holy Spirit became more or less a certain attaining of praiseworthy qualities with the (often merely external) assistance of God; the ἐν εἶναι with the Father's unity of disposition and will," &c.

"In the school of experience, of Luther, he would

in the universe, next to the Bible, protests against Rome with such doctrinal eloquence and scriptural energy as the Prayer Book of our primitive church? See also an admirable charge by the Bishop of Llandaff.

have learnt the analogy of different parts of the life of most christians, and the different stages of the Law and the Gospel."

Let the preceding passages from Dr. Pusey's "Historical Inquiry" be considered in the spirit of their general significance, and few will say, that our view of Luther's spiritual and intellectual majesty as the Paul of the German Reformation—is exaggerated and overdrawn. But, for a far more impressive vindication of the severe language the following work applies to the Church of Rome, we shall now resort, not to the pages of dissent, nor to the works of "Ultra-Protestants," but to none other writings than those of the Rev. HENRY NEWMAN, B.D., Vicar of St. Mary's the Virgin, "Fellow of Oxen College, Oxford," and author of "Tract 90." Let us hear, then, Mr. Newman himself on the essential characteristics of Trentine Romanism. They are "according to the last accounts" of Mr. Newman, by that gentleman himself—

4. In 1838—

"Their communion is infected with heresy; we are bound to flee it as a pestilence. They have established a lie in the place of God's truth, and, by their claim of immutability in doctrine, cannot undo the sin they have committed."—Tract 20.

5. In 1834—

"The spirit of old Rome has risen again in its former place, and has evidenced its identity by its works. It has possessed the Church there planted, as an evil spirit might seize the demoniacs of primitive times, and makes her speak words which are not her own. In the corrupt Papal system we have the very cruelty, the craft, and the ambition of the Republic; its cruelty in the unsparing sacrifice of the happiness and virtue of individuals to a phantom of public expediency, in its forced celibacy within, and its persecutions without; its craft in its falsehoods, its deceitful deeds and lying wonders; and its grasping ambition in the very structure of its policy, in its assumption of universal dominion; old Rome is still alive; nowhere have its eagles lighted, but it still claims the sovereignty under another pretence. The Roman Church I will not blame, but pity; she is, as I have said, spell-bound, as if by an evil spirit; she is in thraldom."

"In the book of revelations, the sorceress upon the seven hills is not the Church of Rome, as is often taken for granted, but Rome itself, that bad spirit which, in its former shape, was the animating principle of the fourth monarchy. In St. Paul's prophecy, it is not the temple or Church of God, but the Man of Sin in the Temple, the old man or evil principle of the flesh which exalteth itself against God. Certainly it is a mystery of iniquity, and which may well excite our dismay and horror, that in the very heart of the Church, in her highest dignity, in the seat of St. Peter, the evil principle has throned itself, and rules. It seems as if that spirit had gained subtlety by years; Popish Rome had succeeded to Roman Pagan; and would that we had no reason to expect still more crafty developments of Antichrist amid the wreck of institutions and establishments which will attend the fall of the papacy! . . . I deny that the distinction is unmeaning. Is it nothing to be able to look on our mother to whom we owe the blessings of Christianity (!!!) with affection instead of hatred, with pity indeed, nay, and fear, but not with horror? Is it nothing to rescue her from the hard names which interpreters of prophecy have put on her, as an idolatress and an enemy of God, when she is deceived, rather than a deceiver?"

I also say—

"She virtually substitutes an external ritual for moral obedience; penance for penitence, confession for sorrow, profession for faith, the lips for the heart; such at least is her system as understood by the many."

Also I say, in the same paper—

6. "In 1834 I also used of certain doctrines of the Church of Rome, the epithets, 'unscriptural,' 'profane,' 'impious,' 'bold,' 'unwarranted,' 'blasphemous,' 'gross,' 'monstrous,' 'cruel,' 'administering deceitful comfort,' and 'unauthorised,' in Tract 38. I do not mean to say that I had not a definite meaning in every one of these epithets, or that I did not weigh them before I used them."

"With reference to this passage the same monitor had said:"—

7. I said in 1837 of the Church of Rome,—

"In truth she is a Church beside herself, abounding in noble gifts and rightful titles, but unable to use them religiously; crafty, obstinate, wilful, malicious, cruel, unnatural, as mad men are. Or rather, she may be said to resemble a demoniac, possessed with principles, thoughts, and tendencies not her own; in outward form and in outward powers what God made her, but ruled within by an inexorable spirit, who is sovereign in his management over her, and most subtle and most successful in the use of her gifts. Thus, she is her real self only in name, and till God vouchsafe to restore her, we must treat her as if she were that evil one which governs her."

And here let the writer be permitted to say a parting word on some church principles, which occasionally appear in this poem, and the reader shall be released from further intrusion. Need it be said, then, no apology is required for the fact, that the Author of this volume is a Churchman, who venerates the polity, and heartily obeys the teaching, of the Anglican Church? And if such be his character, would he not have been a coward and a sycophant, had he endeavoured to hide his real principles, by not viewing the work of the Reformation from the historical standing-point of his own Communion? No honest dissenter can object to this; and while he hopes and believes nothing in the volume breathes a spirit of intolerance against any sectarian, who conscientiously dissents from the Anglican Church,—he is not ashamed to confess, he has contemplated the Reformation as a loyal member and minister of that ancient Communion in this country, which rightly and scripturally claims to be, "The Church *of* England."

In the words of Coleridge, he will now terminate this introduction. Alluding to Blanco White's "Evidence against Catholicism," (Romanism ?) this great poet and profound thinker states—

"When I contemplate the whole system as it affects the great fundamental principles of morality, the terra firma, as it were, of our humanity, then, trace its operation in the sources and conditions of national strength and well-being; and, lastly, consider its woful influences on the innocence and sanctity of the female mind and imagination, on the faith and happiness, the gentle fragrancy and unnoticed ever-present verdure of domestic life, I can with difficulty avoid applying to it what the Rabbins fable of the fratricide Cain,—that the firm earth trembled wherever he strode, and the grass turned black beneath his feet."—COLERIDGE *on the Idea, &c.*, pp. 131, 132.

NOTE.

The above preface was written under a full impression, that a new edition of this volume would forthwith be published. Upon the whole, however, the author thinks it best to retain these remarks; and has merely to add, all which has since occurred in regard to the Romish controversy in England, amply confirms and justifies the strongest statements respecting our ecclesiastical dangers and difficulties. It is, indeed, with a sorrowing heart, subdued hopes, and many fears, he sends forth the present attempt to uphold catholic truth and scriptural Christianity, seeing with what fearful apostacies and perversions our own Church is now visited. Surely, national repentance before God is required, while men of faith, action and prayer, are bound, by the most awful obligations, to sink their complexional differences, and rally round the central ark of the Redeemer's Church and cause. Let us, in meek dependence upon the sustaining promises of the Gospel, combine our energies in one hallowed league of love; and, thus, purified with the graces of the Divine Spirit, proceed "earnestly" to "contend for the faith once delivered to the saints,"—having this battle-cry of celestial encouragement sounding in our ears, —"Be thou faithful unto death, and I will give thee a crown of life."—*Rev.* ii. 10.

EXTRACT FROM A BIOGRAPHICAL PREFACE TO THE FIRST EDITION.

"The progress of the Reformation in Luther's own mind is a very curious subject. Such were the great talents and qualities of Luther, and such the situation of Europe at the time, that the Reformation, in fact, passed from the mind of the one into the mind of the other."—PROFESSOR SMYTH'S *Lectures on Modern History,* vol i. p. 265, Edit. 1841.

"THE following pages are an attempt to reflect, in a poetical form, some prominent features and prevailing expressions in the life, character, and work of Martin Luther, viewed in historical connexion with the Reformation of the sixteenth century. Though each section be distinct, yet it is hoped, in spirit, the poem will be found to constitute the unity of a moral whole. How far, or not, the writer may have succeeded in a style of thought, and structure of plan, somewhat out of the popular track,—must be left to the candour and criticism of others to decide. Whatever may be the reception of these pages, they are, at least, submitted to the public eye with unaffected deference; and with the entire conviction that, if proved to be meritless, their failure must be ascribed to the incapacity of the author, and not to any deficiency of interest in the subject.

"Luther, in the rugged grandeur of his faith, may well be considered as the Elijah of the Reformation; while his life, by the stern and solemn realities of its experiences, and the almost ideal evolutions of events by which it was accompanied, constitutes the embodied Poem of European Protestantism. But, as with others who make or move the history of mankind, Luther must be contemplated under that double aspect, which is answerable to the twofold region where the moral features of manhood are expressed, or betrayed. In the one, we meet external realities, standing forth conspicuously on the broad surface of biography and history; in the other, we are presented with peculiarities of character, which appertain more to the inward man, and are to be detected chiefly in his Correspondence,—more especially, in Letters written from the Wartburg, where he reveals the darkness and despondency by which he was so often haunted, and perturbed. Luther the Reformer is, after all, but an outward and visible index to the inward and invisible characteristics of Luther the Man: and if in the open light of history, we are struck with the almost miraculous consequences a lonely monk, from the depths of an Augustinian convent, put in motion,—not less are we affected to perceive, how wonderfully and wisely the trials and experiences of his inner nature were providentially overruled, and wrought into experimental connexion with those religious achievements which have made the name of Martin Luther immortal. Indeed, to those who love to enter the secrecies of the human Spirit, and advance even unto the very centre of our spiritual consciousness, the German monk, as he appears behind the scene of public life, beyond most men, is an attraction. At one time, we discover him to be all elate, high-wrought, and far-soaring, mounting upward and heavenward in the golden light of hope and joy; at another, he wails and weeps from the very dust of depression and anguish,—uttering either truths of self-exposure, which startle you like thunder-voices, heard at midnight; or else, sighing forth his restless mind with broken murmurs, faint and mournful as the cadence of a distant sea. He dipped his pen, at all times, in the heart-blood of sincerity, and wrote Himself out in a genuine copy, without seeming, for one instant, to care what might be concluded touching the original! In this respect, perhaps no man has ever been self-revealed with more truthful audacity: and thus, in his correspondence and confessions, we have a revelation of the 'hidden man of the heart,' unshrouded to the very core; and are invited to look into the surging depths of a spirit, adown which the deep eye of Dante would have loved to gaze.

* * * * *

"The vast Creation, as constituting a material autograph of its Maker, in letters of dim magnificence and veiled mystery; the divine symbolism which pervades all nature; the Headship of the exalted Redeemer; his mystical Union with the universal Church; the transforming omnipotence of His Word; the omnipresence of His Spirit; the unfolding drama of Providence in connection with the mysterious Cross; and the predestinated enthronement of Messiah over a redeemed and regenerated world,—truths and themes like unto these, have been, and ever will be, a mock and a mystery to secular taste, and the mere victim of this world; yet, in order to estimate Martin Luther, we must remember such were among the inspiring realities which regulated his heart and ruled his life.

"In him, moreover, we find a superhuman reliance on God, heroic zeal for Christ, a perpetual sympathy with the Spirit's movement, and a sublime conviction that in the Word, personal and written, are to be found all the reason, science, beauty, sublimity and harmony of the universe, in their concentrated essence and perfection. Such a being as this, can never, even in bare idea, much less in his moral reality, be understood without at least a portion of divine enthusiasm for God, and Christ, and that love of Man by which his own spirit was ennobled and actuated. With all his faults, take him as a whole, perhaps our world will never look upon his like again. And while a Papist is instructed by the priest to consider the German monk a Satanic incubus; and the man of literary pursuits and earth-born tastes can rarely allow him more than historical preëminence in the controversies of the church, it is gratifying to think that by those who bear on the forehead of their lives the signature of His cross whom they adore,—Luther is revered as a human battle-axe in the hands of the Almighty, for cleaving asunder that System of sacerdotal imposture which has ever been 'the abomination of desolation,' standing in 'the holy place' of God's truth and man's salvation.

"'I did not learn my divinity all at once, but was constrained to search deeper and deeper, to which my temptations brought me; for no man without temptations can attain to the true understanding of the Holy Scriptures. I had, hanging on my neck, the pope, the universities, all the deeply learned, and with them the Devil himself. These hunted me into the Bible, wherein I diligently read, and at length (God be praised!) attained to the true understanding of them.'

"These are Luther's own broad, bold, and characteristic words; and they form a fitting preface to a fine eulogy on his career, from the pen of the polished Atterbury.

"'Martin Luther's life was a continued warfare; he was engaged against the united forces of the papal world, and he stood the shock of them bravely, both with courage and success. He was a man certainly of high endowments of mind and great virtues: he had a vast understanding, which raised him up to a pitch of learning unknown to the age in which he lived; his knowledge in Scripture was admirable; his elocution manly; and his way of reasoning with all the subtlety that these plain truths he delivered would bear. His thoughts were bent always on great designs, and he had a resolution fitted to go through with them. The assurance of his mind was not to be shaken or surprised, and that παῤῥησία of his (for I know not what else to call it) before the Diet of Worms was such as might have become the days of the apostles. His life was holy, and, when he had leisure for retirement, severe: his virtues chiefly active and homiletical, and not those lazy, sullen ones of the cloister. He had no ambition but in the service of God; for other things, neither his enjoyment or wishes ever went higher than the bare conveniencies of living. He was of a temper peculiarly averse to covetousness or any base sin, and charitable even to a fault, without respect to his occasions. If among this crowd of virtues a failing crept in, we must remember that an apostle himself had not been irreproachable; if, in the body of his doctrine, one flaw is to be seen, yet the greatest lights of the church, in the purest times of it, were, we know, not exact in their opinions. Upon the whole, we have great reason to break out in the phrase of the prophet, and say, "How beautiful upon the mountains are the feet of him that bringeth glad tidings!"'

"The author will now take his leave of the reader, and humbly commit this volume to the protecting love and guidance of that high Being 'from whom all holy desires, all good counsels, and all just works do proceed.' Whatever in this volume is in harmony with His Word, may He condescend to bless; whatever is not so, may He graciously overrule, and pardon the sin of the writer.

"'Satis me vixisse arbitrabor, et officium hominis implesse, si labor meus aliquos homines, ab erroribus liberatos ad iter cœleste direxerit.'—LACTANTIUS.

"That he is indifferent to the critical reception which the volume may have,—would be ludicrous hypocrisy for him to assert. It has caused the author extensive reading, study, and reflection; and he will be more than thankful if, as this work haply winds its way through the world, it may here and there please a good man, attract a wise, or gratify a tasteful one. With all its faults, he hopes and believes it contains truths neither uninteresting to the mere reader of poetry, nor unrevered by those who love to penetrate the hidden sanctuary of their own hearts, and ponder on Things beyond the grave. For the imperfections of the work he cannot be too humble; but for the christian Principles which it attempts to embody, he neither has, nor desires to have, any apology. They are in consonance with the Articles, Homilies, and Creed of His own venerated Church; they are those for which sainted martyrs have died, and which have ever constituted the noblest bulwark of nations, because they are in full accordance with the Word of God."

GLASGOW, 1842.

CENTRE OF REVEALED TRUTH.

FROM everlasting was The Christ of God
Veil'd in the purpose of His love divine.
But, God hath no historian; archives none
His past eternity to us presents:
For, who the motions of His voiceless Will
Can number? Saint and seraph here, alike
Are baffled, and the dread I Am adore
With that religion silent prayer begets,
When mind created on Jehovah dwells.
Enough for man this truth august to know,
Redemption was no after-thought, by sin
Awaken'd from thy depths, celestial Love!
When first Humanity the fiend obey'd:
For, in the councils of almighty grace
Thy Priesthood, oh, Incarnate! was design'd
Before creation out of nothing sprang.
But when, at length, the hour predestined came,
Eternity a form of Time assumed,
And from His throne of perfect glory stoop'd
The Second in the Godhead, and Himself
In mortal limbs and lineaments array'd;
Then did Emmanuel, on this blighted earth
Of sin and suff'ring, body forth such grace
As made our orb a wonder-scene of worlds,
By there achieving what the God Triune
Determined, when His master-work was plann'd,—
The vast Atonement blood divine unveils!

Who can express Thee, O Thou great Profound
Of glory, where all miracles in one converge,
And God Himself in concentration shines
For ever? Thee The Father only knows,
And truly fathoms. Thee the Spirit crowns
Sole Prince of Earth, and Paragon of Heaven
In Whom the counsels of salvation reach
Their glorious summit. Thee bright Angels bend
Around, and ever, with enchanted gaze,
Centre and strain their intellectual eyes
Full on Thy wonders,—dazzled, awed, and dim
With Thine excess of all-exceeding love!
Thus, how shall erring man, begirt and bound
With mental darkness, to the heights of grace
Incarnate, lift one clear and cloudless view?—
For in the secrets of Thy Cross we find
A principle, where God alone on God
Is acting,—where the Heart almighty beats
With mercy, and the pangs of Calv'ry prove
His attributes, in full pulsation met.

Expression dies before a theme like this,
Completely master'd; but, the heart of Faith
Breaks into language with outbursting love,
And, taught by scripture, thus presumes to cry,
"Thou art, O Christ! our intellectual Sun
Throned in the firmament of deathless mind;
The radiant Centre of almighty love,
The mystic Vine of everlasting life,
While the dread Trinity in Thee is hymn'd
By saints and angels, with commingled praise."

And, all we have, and are, or hope to be,
Hangs on Messiah, as the holy source;
Who shades with mercy that consuming fire,
Which else creation would at once have smit
To ashes, when the curse for sin was due.
But in the Cross, and by the Cross perused,
How featured with significance sublime
And beautiful, this breathing World becomes!
Creation, by the plastic charm of faith
Transmuted, like a boundless temple stands,
Where all is eloquent of Christ The Lord.
Lo! the broad earth a solemn area seems,
And the arch'd sky a bended ceiling grows
Whose lamps are planets, in their burning shrines;
Wonder is priestess; and the mingled choir,
The organ-music roll'd from waves and winds,—
While, deep with worship, swells th' unconscious voice
Of Nature, when her blent hosannas rise
To bless the Architect and Source of all.

And say, what merit must The Blood express,
That guilt from God in vindication hides?
Oft in the night, when musing thought awakes,
And well remembers all the world has been;
How Sin hath never yet a sabbath kept,
From the first pulse in man's apostate mind
To the last throb in Treason's bosom now,—
Well may the heart, with big emotion charged,
Empty itself in adoration's tears:

And mind devout, with awed amazement, think
How infinite must Calv'ry's pleadings be
Which soften judgment, and sustain a world!

Thus, every mercy our creation holds,
Born of His merit, bears Emmanuel's name;
And through His rent and riven side descends,
Reaches all hearts, and radiates all homes
With christian brightness. Hence, in Jesu's Cross
We glory; all our creed round That revolves:
For there, to heights of unimagined grace
God's Covenant the wond'ring mind attracts
And welcomes, till the o'erwrought heart succumbs
In mute religion at their mystic base.
And therefore, while in nature God we greet,
And in the wrappings of this outer-world
His garments witness, that from sense infold
A Splendour Infinite, a felt Unseen,—
Yet not o'er these the heart's most epic strain
Lift we of lauding rapture. Though the sun
Burn like a mystery of living beams,
Filling our eyes with reverential light
To watch him; though the moon's poetic brow
Be lovely, arch'd with most celestial grace,
And yonder meek and melancholy stars
Thrill like the pathos of eternity
Our pensive bosom,—not in these we boast,
Though beautiful: nor in the sacred Deep
Who chants his lone and everlasting hymn
Of waters, like the psalmody of waves
In worship; nor in all the wondrous things
Which Nature in her realm of varied life
Concenters, can the God-taught spirit trace
Matter for largest triumph.—Nor can Mind
Such rev'rence claim, as that dread hour demands
When burst thy heart, Emmanuel! into blood
For sin, and back the forfeit-heaven regain'd.

CHRISTIANITY.

Thus, "God forbid!" a rapt Apostle cries,
In aught we glory, but the Cross sublime;
Which, planted in this wilderness of worlds,
Hath bloom'd with second paradise to man.
And think, (unless the terror of that thought
Palsy thy mind, or stop the mental pulse
From beating,) think what Man and Earth had been,
If never from Emmanuel's veins had roll'd
The tide of Merit, our atonement drew!
What but a curse, a prison, and a pang
Had reason, life, and apprehension proved?
Amid the howlings of the Law unkept
Encompass'd ever, like incarnate hells
Men would have lived, have wept, blasphemed, and died!
Then, why not, Priests of sentiment and song,
Yourselves baptized, baptize your pages too?
Oh! let the Cross your admiration deck
With solemn beauty, when o'er nature's types,
Her hues and scenes, poetic fervours rise;
For, all creation is with Christ inspired.—
And ye, who through the world of mind delight
In thought to wander, lo! The Christ is there;
Reason is but a ray from Him derived,
That sparkles only with the light He makes.—
Monarchs who rule! remember, lawless will,
But for His pangs, would rank and order crush;
And ye, who legislate for church, or crown,
From the deep science of Salvation draw
Canons of truth, by creed almighty sign'd;
For there, both law and love together form
A perfect Archetype, in Whom they blend.
Or ye, who in domestic bower enjoy
Heaven's fairest miniature, a virtuous home,—
'Tis from the homeless Man of Grief ye draw
Your sweets of gladness, when the hearth-sides glow.
And Christian! what art thou, but Christ in man,
By creed and conduct, character and life
Envolved, and still envolving? Thou in Him,
And He in thee,—thy life but echoes His;
Thy foremost graces are refracted gleams
Directly from His perfect glory cast.
But, all thou art can faith alone depict:
Experience only is description here,
And that, internal:—since the life of truth
Is learn'd by feeling, and by love acquired:
Mere language only is a dead pretence,
Aping the life which love alone can reach,
Or e'er embody. But, if thus the life
Of faith imperfect, far beyond the soar
Of speech, to altitudes of secret awe
Itself exalteth, who, by climbing words
The Lord of Being in His life of faith
Presumes to follow? There all language ends,
As tenses in eternity are lost!
Be this enough for sinful man to know,
In Christ the sum and substance of all truths
Are met, and manifest; in Him, full-orb'd
Religion ev'ry saving virtue finds:
For, there alone the heart of God unveils
Its vast expression: in the Face Divine
Of Him, the arch-Elect, before all worlds
In secresy of Love divine embraced,
In Christ, the counterpart of Godhead, shines
That moral radiance which Himself repeats
By humanised reflection. There alone,
The fallen Spirit, with an eye unfilm'd
By grace, from sin and sensual darkness freed,

Pardon and peace in God for man can find.
All other media which inventive Pride
Presumes to fashion, are but barren dreams:
Man's deity is only dust refined,
Himself re-cast in some ethereal mould,
A finite into infinite enlarged,
And this dilation for a God mistook!
But Thou, Emmanuel! art the Way we come,
The Truth we know, the endless Life secured,
The all in all of God to us reveal'd,
And us to Him restored.—Creation's book
Lies blotted o'er with sin's perplexing stain,
And no erasure can Thy name detect,
In full divinity of sound and sense
Conspicuous, or complete. And, what can Law,
That dreadful paraphrase of Justice, speak
To lawless Guilt, but condemnation dire?
And, how can Reason in her light resolve
That problem, deep as God, and dark as guilt,
How sin is punish'd and the sinner spared,
When falls the sabre of celestial Wrath,
And in one flash both heaven and hell illumes?
Or say, can conscience, whose rebuking voice
In jealous echoes of the jealous God
Is ever sounding through the soul within,
Can this alarmist, to the shrinking gaze
Of guilt, the trembler, mercy's plan unfold?
Ah! no: in Christ alone we Godhead find;
In Christ alone His character evolves;
On Calv'ry's hill God's attributes were throned,
And reach'd a climax when their Lord expired.

MYSTERY OF SUFFERING.

Throughout the universe of God there reigns
A ruling harmony of love and law;
And thus all worlds, by secret link allied,
Together one melodious system make,
Wherein each orb a fated portion fills
In due relation to the boundless whole.
But here, let Reason stand, where Mary stood,—
Under The Cross; nor catechise the work
The filial Word completed, when in flesh
He suffer'd; and His suffering Body taught
How God on time eternity reflects,
And in the mirror of the church's life
Doth glass the features of a sovereign Will,
Secret, and not to faculties create
In flesh, or spirit, e'er to be reduced.
But still, we rest not; and our reason longs
Madly to question what no finite mind
On earth can answer, when our musing eye
Roves o'er the moral waste the church hath been,
And dares to criticise what God hath done
Or Christ permitted, in this world of ours!
For what, but good and evil, strangely mix'd,
Seems the dark mystery of the church's doom?
Here saint and sinner, grace and nature blend;
Angels and Fiends for blood-earn'd souls combine;
All passions, principles, and powers remote,
(From the high daring of celestial hearts
To the low horrors of consummate guilt,)
All strive with each, and each with all conflicts.
And, who can wind his labyrinthine way
Through shades of providence, like these, profound?
We see in part; but when perfection dawns,
Both part and whole shall then Thy name uplift
Almighty! then, the choir of chanting Worlds
Around salvation, one stupendous tide
Of deepening rapture shall for ever roll,
And God His own great Vindication be.

But here, we lisp the alphabet of grace
Alone, and scarcely that at times pronounce.
Infants of time, we yet have much to learn,
And more to suffer, ere we find resolved
The paradox of wrong the church endures.
If to each pang some purpose we could link,
Patience might sing, where now vexation sighs
For wisdom; but the Vision tarries yet!
Between God's purpose and our pang there lies
An Infinite, where baffled Reason, blind
With gazing, would in vain some landmark see.
But grief, when sanctified, is God to man
Himself imparting, for some end conceal'd
Deep in the core of his eternal plans.
Here may we rest; beyond we cannot rise;
Or, on the infinite Unknown we dash
The mind to madness, and our faith to fears.
Perchance, our World to higher Being proves
A Platform, where the truths of heaven enact
Their natures, and to angels wisdom show.
Or, hearts on earth are moral schools to heaven,
And pangs below are preachers to the skies,
While glory shines around each sainted tear
Which faith, or feeling, in our warfare sheds.

Perfect through suff'ring!—such Emmanuel was;
And can the members of that mystic Head
Refuse to echo what their Master felt?
A suff'ring Image must the church become
If with her archetypal Lord complete
Her oneness prove; and what in pangs the Head
Endured, each member must on earth repeat
By thrilling counterpart in truth, and tone,
Of all He suffer'd. Nor in heaven forgot,
Though there unfelt, Messiah's woes remain;
Still through His splendour point the piercing nails;
There in His glory yet the gash is seen;

E'en on His throne, a sacramental Lamb
Types to eternity the Manhood slain !—
And, like her Bridegroom, must the Bride elect
From suff'ring deep to endless glory climb.

We see by part, but suffer in the whole;
There lies the myst'ry! there our flesh complains,
Hurt feeling staggers, and the heart recoils.
Meanwhile, in vain would Souls their doom avoid,
Or mould, or master: each, in turn, must weep,
Writhe on some rack, or drink the cup of woe
Down to the dregs, if such their God present.
All have their pangs, their penalties, and pains,
Some thorn to fester in the spirit-life,
Or, fret the mind to feebleness, or fear
Unholy. But, the Comforter abides!
And while to sense the church an orphan seems,
The Father pities, and His children find
A secret pasture in the promise left,
Though all look herbless to the eye of men
Carnal, or clouded. Nor will more be felt
Than Wisdom, for some destined rank above
Apportions; cross and crown related are;
The one is suffer'd, as the other shaped,
Responsively. And as the artist's hand
Plastic with genius, to some picture gives
Line after line, and touch on touch repeats,
Till colours image what his mind contains
Of beauty,—so, in faith, experience feels
Pang after pang, till God at length transcribes
That viewless copy of celestial life
His purpose imaged, ere our souls were born.
Or even, as the skill'd refiner bends
O'er his fused metal, in the furnace laid,
And heaps new fire, till back its molten face
His own returneth, by reflection bright,—
So in the flame of hot affliction, man
By Heaven in myst'ry is a while retain'd;
Till, purged of dross, and purified from sin,
At last the metal of the heart is clear,
And back on Deity by love reflects
The radiant image which His glory casts.

WISDOM COMES FROM WOE.

We learn by suff'ring, while by faith we live,
And graces brighten as our griefs expand:
But, where indeed, between the woe endured
And height of glory in a heaven to come
Of being, is the true connection found,—
Baffles our reason, in this cloud of flesh
Now to unfold. Yet this, at least, we learn,
The Head of manhood was a suff'ring Head,
And all His members, by their mystic pangs
But echo back what Thy pure bosom felt,
Eternal Archetype of life and faith,
Whom all things emblem! Here alone, there dawn
Truths which illumine what might else appear
Darkness infernal, deep, and black, and dense
To suffocation. Here, some aims profound,
Whose roots are in eternity's result,
Arrest the tear, and calm to chasten'd awe
Secret rebellions of the soul within.
The good shall suffer; yet, if goodness be
To nature fall'n, but the noble part
Of trial, when by sin-consuming grace
Pure love is deepen'd,—not for this repine
The brave adorers of The Crucified!
They glory rather in the racking fires;
The more of grief, the more of God they have,
And do (what seraphim have never done)
Suffer for Christ!—man's pure distinction this!
His high prerogative, His peerless crown
Appointed. Devils for themselves endure,
And angels, quick as sunbeams, glide and go
At His command, and own Him Liege, and Lord;
But Virtue, by the church's heart reveal'd,
Mounts to a range sublimer, and excels
Beyond the burning Watchers round His throne:
For, she can suffer; and by suff'ring learn
Lessons transcending what the angels teach.

And more than this th' afflicted church evolves.
From Abel's cry, to Luther's convent-groan,
Self was our ruin; into that, direct
From God, creation's first apostate fell;
And out of that, alone can Flesh arise,
By will surrender'd, crucified, and slain,
And by the sovereignties of Will Supreme
Master'd, and moulded. Thus, the saints are train'd
From strength to strength, by educating woes,
To loathe that vampire of creation—Sin!
With hate celestial, and on God to live;
While in that Book, whose promises, like stars,
Rule in the night, a radiant charm they have,
O'er all the dim perplexities of doom
Beaming mild comfort, through the blackest woe
Which palls the christian, or a church portends.

GRIEF AND GLORY.

Glory to grief! when thus for God endured;
'Tis but the pang a Saviour's bosom felt,
Re-echoed, and by peerless faith prolong'd.
The Man of Sorrows forms no men of smiles;
Our hearts must bathe in His baptismal fire,
Or ne'er be whiten'd; Cross and Crown were His:

We grant it; but, in order each He took;
The first He suffer'd, ere the last He wore.
And as the Bridegroom, must the Bride be form'd,—
Repeat His Cross, and then reflect His Crown;
That Like on earth, in heaven alike may prove,
In grief below, in glory, one above!
So, in eternal consciousness to come,
Salvation will be sympathy entire
'Tween Head and Members—unity august!
When Christ in each will Self from all absorb.

Meanwhile, to us, Eternal Spirit! grant
The wisdom meek, which lives on truth divine,
However veil'd; a waiting mind impart;
And in our weakness show our strength to dwell.
Like as of old, a pensive Learner sat
Low at His feet, and listened to her Lord,
Absorb'd and self-renouncing, be our soul
Before the Cross in docile rev'rence bent.
For Thou, O Christ! amid the fires hast been;
And o'er the flames, which on Thy church advanced,
The promise, "with you, till the end of time,"
Breathed like the spell of some almighty breeze,
And cool'd them into impotence, or calm.—
No! never hath the murd'rous hoof of Hell
Trampled the heart from out the church of heaven;
Within her, life, when all seem'd lifeless, glow'd;
Within her, grace, when all seem'd graceless, dwelt;
Within her, truth, when all seem'd truthless, reign'd;
While, ever and anon, amid the gloom
Which Priest, or Tyrant, or the Devil made,
Star after star in radiant grandeur rose
To shame the midnight of the soul away.
But, chief o'er all the galaxy of lights
To stud the firmament of christian fame,
Shone Luther forth,—that miracle of men!
A gospel-hero, who with faith sublime
Fulmined the lightnings of God's flaming Word
Full on the towers of Superstition's home,
Till lo! they crumbled; and his with'ring flash
Yet sears the ruin with victorious play.

But thou, who o'er the church a thoughtful mind
Haply in moods of mournful awe hast bent,
Revere the fact, whose deep foundations lie
Far in the Infinite, beyond the wings
Of faith, though plumed with apostolic strength,
To follow:—Christ hath God with man conjoin'd
By union so unutterably close,
Divine, unfathom'd, and for ever firm,
That sun shall wither, all the stars wax pale,
Mountains depart, the heavens to air dissolve,
And the dread universe itself shall die,
But, this Conjunction shall unweaken'd stand
When Time is dead, and Nature drops extinct
Into her grave eternal. Boundless truth!
Which out of Deity all other dwarfs
To less than littleness, beyond compare.
All unions type it; all connections preach;
Nature, and art, and pure affection's ties
Are fill'd with emblems, shadowy, dim, and faint,
Th' exceeding glory of this bond to tell:
Wherein, by unity of mystic power,
Christ and His Church are into One transform'd
Colossal Person, Spirit, Life, and Frame,
And Fellowship, and Feeling. Let that Church
Suffer a pang—the Saviour feels it too!
Touch but a Member, and you thrill the Head
With shock electric, on his Throne perceived;
And therefore, Tyrants! when ye wound a hair
Of God's anointed, up to heaven your wrong
Ascendeth, and the heart of Jesus strikes!
Rays in the sun are not so brightly close,
Trees to their root are not so firmly knit,
And streams to fountains not so close allied,
Body with breath, and both with soul combined
Together, as the Church and Christ cohere.
Hence Earth, nor Heaven, nor Hell that fights with each,
The Bridegroom from his sainted Bride can tear.
Thy Maker is thy Husband, Church elect!
And rich eternity thy radiant dower.
And thus, we lift the shout, and song of faith
Victorious: for the Oneness is so true
Between the members and their living Head,
In vain creation may be tax'd for types
Or teaching shadows, to portray its power,
Since mere analogy in light is lost;
Upward, and heavenward illustration mounts,
Till, near the throned Almighty, overawed,
Faith cannot soar, but folds her duteous wing,
Backward recoils, and trembles into prayer.

HUMAN NEED, AND DIVINE SUPPLY.

E'EN like an instrument, whose chorded depth
Enwraps the unheard music, but awaits
A master-touch of some awaking hand
To make it vibrate, did the high-strung world
Of truth and feeling for impulsive souls
In solemn hush abide, beneath whose sway
The moral harmonies of ransom'd mind
In mingling swell of holiness, and love,
Once more should waken.—Luther was that soul

Predestined ! he, by grace divinely arm'd,
From the foul grave of papal sin and gloom
The buried Gospel came to disinter.
And let us laurel his intrepid brow
Who faced alone (by all save Heaven unarm'd)
That priestly Giantess of pamper'd sin,
Whose throne was blasphemy by pride upheld;
That brazen Arbitress, whose sceptre robb'd
The King almighty of the soul's domain,
Even papal Rome ! who still her wine-cup drugs
With damning charms, and deadly spells; and dares
Within the heart's pantheon yet to shrine
Dark falsehoods, which redeeming truth bemock,
The soul profane, and parody our God.

Eternal hallelujahs rise ! and ring
That Grace around, which call'd the champion forth,
And with heaven's panoply his spirit clad
For combat. With the energies of hell
To grapple, with incarnate fiends to fight,
Behold him summon'd ! On that lifted brow
Heroic calm indomitably smiles;
And in that lion heart each pulse which beats
Throbs like an echo to the cheer of heaven.
Behold him ! grateful Mem'ry, come and gaze;
See Luther, from eternity decreed,
Rise in the majesty of moral force
From superstition's grave to heave the world,
And bid it look upon the Cross, and live.

And oh ! what marvels did that Mind achieve,
Which in itself a Reformation was.
For cent'ries, deep the night of falsehood reign'd,
Mildew'd the Soul, and manacled her powers
With fett'ring darkness; cloister'd Learning pined
In cell monastic; Science grew extinct;
The Bible moulder'd in scholastic rust;
That Fountain, from the Saviour's wounded side
For sin once ope'd, by sealing lies was shut;
And, 'stead of His bright garb which Mercy wove
Of perfect righteousness, by Jesu wrought,
Spangled with graces, rich as God's own smiles,
The filthy rags of ineffectual works
Clad the cold skeleton of naked souls:
While on his throne of sacerdotal lies,
The arch impostor, Satan's rival, sat
Self-deified, and ripen'd earth for hell.
Then, Luther rose; and Liberty and Light
The soul unbarr'd, and let salvation in.
Hark ! the dead Scriptures, into life recall'd,
Harangue the conscience; lo, the Gospel lives;
Swift from the Cross infernal darkness flies:
Martyrs and Saints, like baffled mock'ries sink
To nothing, by victorious truth dispersed;
O'er fancied merit free redemption reigns;
And in the temple of a soul illumed
No venal priesthood, with parade of lies,
And sacraments of sin, can enter now:
There, Christ Himself by triple office rules,
King, Priest, and Prophet, on the Spirit's throne.

THE SOLITARY MONK.

The solitary Monk, who shook the World
From pagan slumber, when the gospel-trump
Thunder'd its challenge from his dauntless lip
In peals of truth, round hierarchal Rome,
Till mitred Pomp, and cowl'd Imposture quail'd,
And each false priesthood, like a fiend unmask'd
And stripp'd of light fictitiously assumed,
By some detecting Angel, shrunk dismay'd
And shiver'd, in thy vast exposure seen,—
Thee would I image, thou colossal Mind !
For what, though sad humanity's broad taint
Of weakness, here and there thy soul diseased;
Or, harshly quick, or, too severely loud
Some intonations of thy spirit rose;
Yet, in the greatness of thy glorious work
Right nobly art thou, like a second Paul,
Apparent, graced with apostolic zeal;
Waving that banner, on whose blood-stain'd fold
Thy name, Emmanuel ! at each ruffling blast
Of conflict, beams with awful brightness forth.

Thee would I vision, and on Mem'ry's glass
Some traces of thy many-colour'd life
In lines of holy miniature reflect.
For in thy destiny our God we find
Himself expounding, by the truth unveil'd.
Upon thy mind, as some prophetic map,
Almighty love mysteriously engraved
An outline wondrous of the work decreed;
Thy moral Self a Reformation seems;
And in each phasis which thy soul presents,
An imaged counterpart of all we trace
Hereafter, in the world's vast scene evolv'd.
And therefore, Hero of a hundred fights
Celestial ! morning star of Jesus ! rise,
Rise in full radiance; through the cloud of time
Dart the rich beam of evangelic day,
And cause the Church's heart to glow with thee.

But yet, how low, to Reason's carnal eye
Which measures all things by the scale of sense,
The means appointed for the end pursued !
How strangely small those intermitting ways

By which, to great results, God's wisdom moves!
Yet, once a manger did th' Almighty hold,
When first Messiah's human life-pulse beat
For our behoof. And were not they, who hurl'd
Philosophy from off her Babel-throne
To speechless ruin, and our rescued souls
To the rich fountain of celestial Blood
Directed,—were not they, the peerless Twelve,
Whose words like arrows pierced the heart of Hell
With fire and fearlessness, the low and weak,
Of man unlearn'd, but learn'd in much of God?
E'en so, from out a shepherd's mountain-hut
Far in the wilds of Alpine bleakness hid,
The Swiss apostle ran his high career;
And he, who, with the sun-like mind compared
That Luther in his flaming boldness show'd,
Soft as the moon in mellow radiance seem'd,
The mild Melancthon!—from a clanging home,
A martial workshop, dates his lowly birth.
And Thou! the Reformation's mental spring,
The Bible's loved redeemer from the cell
Where monkish falsehood barr'd its glory in,
Not from the loins which heraldry admires
Didst thou proceed; of poor, but pious blood
Wert thou; a simple miner call'd thee son.

PROLOGUE AND PREPARATION.

When God to matter gave the fiat,—Be!
E'en like an echo, heaven and earth arose,
The instant product of creative Will,
And Will alone. But when His hand divine
The great Idea, 'fore all ages form'd
Concerning Manhood, would in shape express,
Lo! in The Godhead consultation moves,
The Persons think, the Attributes confer,
And, "Let us make him!" is the awful Speech
Which symbols out to human sense, how vast
And wond'rous was the master-piece of heaven,
Who imaged forth the Trinity, when Man
Rose on the scene, as lord and light of all.

Thus Reason, here, may with Religion cry,
"Oh, what a Fabric eloquently deck'd
With strength and grace, our regal nature is!"
A mental structure, for whose living walls
Eternity and Truth foundations were.
E'en such is Man, when fully bodied forth
By daring energies of mental worth,
And virtue. Hence, when heroes pure and high
Rounded and finish'd into full-orb'd grace,
On earth at length are destined to alight,
E'en like some new apocalypse from heaven,
Truthful and deep, and most divinely touch'd,
In faculty of heart, and mind, they show
In each high lineament the stamp of God.

And such was he, who burst the jail of thought,
Shaking each fetter from the dungeon'd soul
Of ages; and to 'nighted Faith restored
That creed almighty which the Cross enacts.
But e'en as Luther was through grace confirm'd,
And shaped in secret, by the truth applied
In the lone temple of his God-taught mind,
By man untutor'd,—so, the creedless world
A Hand eternal and an eye unseen
By gradual prelude did prepare, and guide;
That when the true Regenerator came,
A platform might await him; and his Work
Fit audience find, to welcome its advance.

And means there were, successive, stern and slow,
By which, as organs, Providence achieved
Each consummation that His will forecast.
Time after time, some lone Elijah lifts
His wail august for Liberty, and Man;
Truth had a voice; though much unseen remain'd,
Like pearls of beauty in a shell conceal'd.
Soon Dante's hell of poetry began
Full on the Pope to flame a fierce revenge,
For virtue: Petrarch call'd on kings to rise:
Then Genius, with her tongue of many tones,
Learning, and Art, and philosophic Scorn,
At once inspired, their banded forces hurl'd
On the huge vice the Vatican uprear'd.
And, long ere this, the great Arabian Lie
Had rippled into life the stagnant pool
Of priesthood:—foul and faithless at the core,
It yet the unity of God preserved;
And by the scoff of its sarcastic light,
Lurid, and keen upon the monkish cowl
Reflected,—good and gracious work achieved.
Remedial truth all falsehood underlies;
And thus Mahommed's arch imposture did,
Beyond intent, in this high prologue act
A part momentous. Next, from Alpine-homes
The exiled Gospel sent its mountain-cry,
All Europe thrilling. Then, the Schoolmen rose,
And, wiser than their conscious wisdom knew,
Embalm'd each verity their words o'erlaid
In secret amber,—safe from popish tact.
And thus, (so wonderful the links that bind
Thought into thought, along the chain of time!)
From Lombard's heaven-awaken'd breast was thrown
A burning ember of immortal truth
Pure into Wickliffe's; thence, to noble Huss

It glow'd along to Jerome's kindred mind,
And he to Luther did that spark convey:
And so that Bible-spark illumines now
The hearts of England with its holy life
And lustre, though seven hundred years have roll'd
Their tide of darkness o'er the Schoolman's head,
Where first 'twas kindled by a ray from heaven.

Here are the signs, predictive as profound,
That all betoken, with precursive truth,
Some Advent mighty, which an empire's heart
Shall welcome. These are like a Baptist-voice
The earth haranguing, with its glorious swell.
But when that crisis of the world arrives,
How doth a Hand almighty o'er the scene
Move unbeheld, and write the coming doom!
See Reuchlin, by his classic lore inspired,
Utter aloud to God's dead language, "live!"
And hark! the Bible, like a Hebrew seer,
Again may preach and prophesy to man:
While e'en Erasmus, cold and cautious thing!
(A craven neuter in the cause of Christ)
Whose head was light, but in whose heart no love
Was kindled, rose beyond himself at times,
With blasting irony to sear and singe
The monk-born vices: thus, that orphan'd youth
To God his genius and his love inscribed,
And voiced the Bible with a Latin tongue.

Nor dare we to progressive mind alone
The conflux strange of tendencies, and truths
Refer, which just before the battle-voice
Of the brave monk around the Popedom hurl'd
Its dreadless challenge, into force arrived,
And action. Mark, at once, a mental blaze
Beyond all precedent, by Heaven illumed.
And first, that fearful Thing which rules the fate
Of battle, thund'ring over field, or deck,
With havoc wing'd on its resistless roar,
Is now compounded; next the Magnet comes,
With true polarity, that ever points,
Like sterling principle, to where it tends;
And marks old ocean, like a map with lines
Of knowledge, till the wave-toss'd pilgrims roam
And coast all seas, all countries, and all climes,
Far as free commerce wafts them. Nor, the least
In rank, nor last in the resulting power
Thy fall, Byzantium! Though the Turkish flag
Moved in fierce triumph o'er thy crumbled walls,
Yet did the Orient with a gush of mind
Burst from its mounds, and through the arid West
Pour the rich blood of intellectual life
And learning. Next, an unimagined World
For ages cover'd with Atlantic gloom,
Secret of waters by stern ocean kept
Inviolable, at length, her silence breaks,
And lo, America on Europe smiled,
Shaking the heart of nations with delight!

Marvel on marvel!—each with vaster range,
Or new excitement, thus to Man appeal'd;
Heighten'd the tone of morals and of mind
Awaken'd, roused the soul from monkish sleep,
And thrill'd the student in Platonic bower
Or cloister'd umbrage, with electric throes
Of more than rapture:—for the social frame,
From east to west, did vibrate with o'erwrought
Emotion. Seem'd it then, as if the Earth
Again were heaving with prophetic throbs,
Sent to precede her soon descending Lord.
So fast did providence itself expand,
Nature evolve, and kindled genius rise
And forward into fields of glory rush.

Yet, in this prologue of adjusted means
Heaven-moulded, chief and prime of arts immense,
See, Printing rise, a universe of powers!
That bids the Past become perpetual Now,
Gives reason sway, imagination shape,
To time a soul, to thought a substance lends,
And with ubiquity, almost divine,
For living permanence and local power
Each ray of soul immortally endows.

MIGHT OF THE PRESS.

Thou great Embalmer of departed mind!
Thou dread Magician! by whose mental charm,
A mournful, pale, and solitary man
Who pines unheeded, or who thinks unknown,
Long after dust and darkness hide his grave,
Himself can multiply, with magic force
Beyond the reach of language to explore,
And the wide commonwealth of minds may rule
With sway imperial! Who can image Thee,
Whether to heaven uplifting mind and man,
Or hell-ward both seducing, like a fiend?
Boundless in each thine unremember'd sway!
Thine was a voice, whose resurrection-blast
Peal'd through the catacombs where buried Soul
For cent'ries lay, and lo! with living might
The Fathers burst their sepulchres, and breathed;
Dead Intellect from classic tombs came forth

Quicken'd, and into active substance changed
By thy vast potency: and then, was felt
The pith of thought, the marrow of the mind
Itself transfusing, like a second life
The old absorbing, as with heat divine.
And since that moment, have not Books become
Our silent prophets, intellectual kings,
Anointed hierarchs of human thought
To vice, or virtue? Are they not like shrines
For truth? cathedrals, where the chasten'd heart
Can worship, or in tranquil hours retreat
To meet the Spirit of the olden time?
Since there, the drama of the world abides
Yet in full play, immortally perform'd.
Still ride the fleets o'er Actium's foughten waves
Before us; patriots fight, and tyrants fall;
Sparta and Corinth, and the famous Isles
Which fought for freedom, till their blood ran o'er
With brave contention, there convene, and clash
Their forces; still the Roman eagle flies
In full-wing'd triumph o'er the subject world;
Cæsar and Pompey yet the earth alarm,
Or, drag their chariot with the captive East;
Battles are raging; Kingdoms lost or won;
Yea, all the genius of gone time is there
In Books articulate, whose breath is mind.

And, was not Godhead in a work like this,
When the World took a most enormous stride
Forward at once, to freedom, life, and law?
Priestcraft and Falsehood (that terrific pair,
Who murder'd Truth, and made the church become
A dungeon, where imprison'd Thought expired,)
Trembled, as if that dooming blow was struck
Which fell'd them into nothingness, or names
For ever: God indeed was now at work,
Though Man, the organ, was alone reveal'd.

BOOKS AND THE BIBLE.

But, why are Books such half-almighty Things,
Making, or marring, whatsoe'er they touch,
With force internal? Whence their wond'rous spell?
Bethink thee, reader! and the answer comes.
The universe itself was once a Thought,
A thought Divine, in depths creative hid;
And so, whate'er this mortal scene invests
Of human action, is but plastic thought
Itself revealing, in some forms without
Apparent. What is half these eyes behold
Of boundless, beautiful, sublime, or vast,
But thought embodied into outer shape,
Or, answ'ring symbol? Arches, cities, domes
And temples, fleets and armies, trades and towns,
Yea, all the might and moral of mankind
To this significance at length arrives,
And backward into thought may be resolved
By fair reduction. Now, if Books be thought
By printing clothed, and palpably endow'd
For its vocation, whether art, or lore,
Poetic vision, or prosaic truth,
Kingdoms immense, or individual Souls
The aim of its predestined mission be,—
Forth to its work that printed Thought proceeds;
And who shall track it, as it rounds the world?
Who can imagine, when 'tis once abroad,
(However humble was its natal home)
The Work it dares, the wonder it achieves?
Black as a Fiend, or like some Angel bright
That Thought in action, may itself approve;
For printing, like an omnipresence, gives
Its power expansion; far and wide it moves,
Reaches all hearts, a host of minds affects,
And executes what none, save God, controls!
Oh, 'tis enough to harrow breath and blood
With chilling horror, thus to feel, and know,
That when some Thinker, who debauch'd his soul
And put damnation into print for fame,
Is cited to the last and long accompt,
His thought is living! like a demon, still
Haunting the world of passion with its power,
Or poison; breathing a perpetual curse,
And dropping hemlock into sensual hearts
Which love the venom which a lie instils;
And thus, for ever! not perchance to cease,
Till Thought and Thinker shall together stand,
Cursed by their victims, at the bar of God!

So great are Books: and what the Bible, then,
By printing voiced, and through all regions sent
To speak the errand of celestial Love!
Here was the Prologue, in consummate form
Develop'd; here the Prelude looks divine:
That God in words, descending into Man,
And there achieving all its creed affirms
Of goodness, that the Bible thus should have
An Organ ready for its godlike mouth,
Here is the Wisdom which on high o'errules,
Making all hist'ry but her echo'd will!

But now, the world is waiting: prescient Hearts
In mute expectance, big with wonder beat,

Predicting what these powers commingled
mean,
Or, Who from out the heaven of truth shall
come
Mankind to marshal, in this pregnant hour?
Shall Prince, or Potentate, or armèd Force
Girt by the squadrons which the world arrays,
March in the van of Liberty, and Light?
"E'en by my Spirit, saith the Lord of Hosts!"
Again that motto to Almighty ways
Becomes embodied, and to life transform'd:
For lo! the Reformation's human spring,
Unknown, unseen, in cloister'd shade retired,
Is framed and fashion'd by the Hand Eterne:
Here, from the depths of convent-gloom, He
calls
The Man He loves, the instrument He wields,
And moulds him for the mighty Work decreed.
But Him, who now a beacon o'er mankind
Flames in the lustre of his far renown,
The Spirit summons from no royal scene,
From throne, nor palace, nor ancestral hall;
But chooses, in the wisdom of free will,
A fameless Monk, of poverty and prayer,
And leaves the palace for a miner's home.

GOD'S HEROES.

The Kings of mind, who govern from their
graves,
Our thoughts their subjects, and our hearts
their homes
Perennial, when they first in light emerge,
Like new expounders of almighty Will,
Forth from the secresy of truth unveil'd
Glad tidings bring they, of a Glory meant
Yet to awaken, and the world invest.
Their utt'rance, large; their meditation, lone;
By passion for the Infinite o'erpower'd,
They dart their glances into Things to come;
Intense, beyond the teachings of the soul
To reach, or satisfy. But, how received,
These new Avatars, sent on missions high,
To herald forth eternity in truth
For all who love them? Are loud welcomes
rung?
Greetings of head, and jubilees of heart
Do these salute them with applausive joy?
Alas! too holy the vocation far
Of Truth's high Priests, when first behind the
veil
Of outward things themselves presume to
pass,
And bid us follow, with responsive track
Through the rent shroud their faith had first
undrawn.
Time is their justice. When their tombs are
rear'd,
Then, Wonder dares to consecrate their deeds;
Will call them, primates in the church of man,
Great Nature's own episcopate they form,
And rule, like metropolitans of mind.

But, mark the conflict when their voice
emerged!
Struggles within, and all without them, rose.
Their great Impression was the God unseen,
But felt, an Infinite through finite glimpsed;
Yet, how they falter'd! of themselves afraid,
When Thoughts in vain articulation sought;
Or giant Apprehensions, dim and deep,
Scarce ventured forth in intellectual shape
And bodied meaning! Oft, expression fail'd
In form to realise what feeling grasp'd:
Language was only a prismatic mean
But half refracting, with imperfect ray,
The truth essential, which they purely saw
Single, and one, within the soul contain'd.
But when the mind *could* stammer forth its
tones,
Profound, original, and preaching high
On God, and Nature, Science, Man, and
Soul,
No music breathed they to the world's dull ear.
But, harshly strange, and dissonant they
seem'd,
With fruitless paradox, for sense unfit
And reason dang'rous! Such the first salute
Prophetic genius from the world obtains:
And such have earth's regenerators met,
From God-called Moses, to the German monk.

But if to Morals and to Man they bring
Authentic tidings from the Throne of Truth,
Divine, yet most disturbing, scowl and scorn,
Affronting coldness, and condemning fears
Assail them ever, with a shameful wrong,
From all who love the ancient, but the new
Abhor, like treason! Thus the world, self-
blind,
Hath greeted oft how many a regal Soul
That rules her now, with legislative awe!
Wisdom itself seems heresy to fools;
And freedom is but license to the slaves
Who love the fetters, which their languors fit.
Their light is darkness, and their being death,
And rotting silence all the soul admires,
Admits, or sanctions, in that dormant calm
By cent'ries gather'd o'er imprison'd mind.
E'en like a temple, where the owls retreat,
And the bats lodge within long-moulder'd
shrines,
Ope but a window, let a sun-burst in,
And what a screaming anarchy awakes
Where falls the light, or sounding footstep
comes!
So, in the temple of deserted Man

Where sin for ages unmolested breeds,
Or lying Errors long repose enjoy,
If but a day-beam of immortal truth
The gloom dissever; or, a living Thought,
Divine as heaven, original from God,
Down from the skies should suddenly alight,
And walk his spirit with a kingly tread
Majestic, what a host of wild alarms
The priests of Dulness round the stranger raise,
And call it mad, the dead in mind to wake!

MARTYRDOM.

HERE is the doom of Hero, Bard, or King:
The cross of hatred first their hearts endure,
And then, the crown of homage on their heads
Dying, or dead, at last cold Justice puts!
Their crown we witness,—has their cross been weigh'd?
We boast their triumphs,—have we told their tears?
We laud their greatness,—have we felt their gloom,
Their lonesome watchings, and their weepings long,
The fret, the fever, and those wasting pangs
Year after year, which wore the heart of Youth
To sickness, ere the laurell'd moment came
When truth and triumph paid high Merit's due?
Result the many only dare to prize;
But still, the process solemn, stern, and strange,
Through stormful agonies, and griefs, and glooms,
By which a Hero to his great result
Attaineth, why should *this* no homage win?
Luther was great at threat'ning Worms, we grant;
But, greater still in solitude, and tears,
When first he grappled with his fiery heart
And, in the prison of a papal creed,
Panted, and pray'd for evangelic day.

Heroes are martyrs, if their minds be pure
And highly-temper'd; for, the Truth is strange
To men who only by their bodies live,
And to the pageantries and powers of Sense
External yield their sympathies alone;
Or, never down Themselves presume to gaze
With eye reflective: so, when prophets rise,
And utter oracles from deeps of Life
Hidden, and heavenly, from the Flesh remote,
To them they sound like necromantic tones;
Eye, ear, and taste, compose their All in All;
And though around, within, above them moves
And lives, an energising Power Supreme,
Whose vesture is that Visible they love,
They give no credence save to flesh, and form.
Yet, what is genius, but a mouth for God
To speak Himself to Nature, and to Man,
And from the visible and vain of sense
Attract us unto mysteries divine,
But viewless, by external semblance hid?
There, Faith's reality alone is found!
Since all expression which the Outward bears,
Is but a token of God's inner-truth
And purpose. Thus, beneath a veiling shroud
The Infinite an awful Presence robes,
His thought embodies, or reflects its power.

IMPERFECT AT THE BEST.

YET, what is life, but imperfection's breath,
And human Being, but incarnate fault
E'en at the best, howe'er by grace refined?
Moses was anger'd; David's honour fell;
Paul felt a thorn, and Peter proved untrue.
Genius hath faults, and Luther's none o'erveil.
A brave restorer of departed truth,
No hollow semblance, and no heartless shade
Came he on earth to manifest, or preach.
Manful, but rugged, to the centre bold,
His heart beat fiercely; and his blood ran fire
When Right divine, or some disastrous Wrong
Challenged his faith, or forced his feeling out
In action; then, the soul's tornado raged,
And shook the spirit to its moral roots!
Stormful, and strong, and gusty in his moods,
Oft the black whirlwind from some ireful cloud
Roused his rent bosom with disturbing rush,
And hurl'd propriety from off its throne
Amazed, and master'd. His was battle-life;
Great-hearted being! with a lion plunge
Full on the foe, with all his living fire
Leapt his free soul, magnanimous as firm,
And,—no surrender! for the Truth must fight,
And Faith prove conflict, if she stand sincere.

Spirits may be, like flowers from heaven that fall,
Deck'd with fine beauty, clad with mental bloom
Most delicate, but soon earth's tainted soil
Bedims them; trodden in the dust they lie,
Forgotten, faded, or defeatured things,
Ere yet they open'd their immortal buds
Of virtue, or their perfect fragrance gave.
Not such was Luther's: like some burly oak
Whose boughs wave battle with the tearing winds
And bend, but never break,—his fighting heart
Contended with all mutinies, which came
From prince, or pope, from circumstance, or creed,
And wrestled with them; or, with Samson force
Subdued them, or himself with glorious fall

Laid prostrate! Sinful oft, his moody ire
Betray'd him; unadvisèd words he spake;
And sometimes, when the fervid heart grew wild,
Scatter'd both friend and foe with burning force
And tameless fury! Like a soul on fire,
The gentle wonder'd, and the wise condemn'd
To see him thus by evil lightnings rent
And harrow'd: but, how soon the tempest died!
When the broad sunshine of forgiving love
Blazed o'er his spirit, like a summer-noon
Settled and bright. Not always hot and harsh
Did nature find him; playful moods had he;
For oft that smiting earnestness of tone
Which scorn'd the false, and cleaved all fiction through,
Priestly or papal, with a forcing might
That flash'd with fierceness, like a sword's descent,
Melted away; and, like an infant lull'd,
Pathetic Luther all the poet-life
Of purest feeling testified, and taught.
Witness, ye tears! that dropt o'er Tetzel's bed
When reft and dying; and o'er thine which fell,
Beloved, and lost, and beauteous Madaline!
Oft in the granite of a soil unhewn
Full many a flower in secret freshness smiles;
And many a stream, where all looks arid blank,
Lurks in the Horeb of some heart, unknown.
E'en such was Luther, with his rocky front
And jagged features, to the foe display'd:
But sweet affections, sanctified, and soft
As ever water'd human breast with love,
Gush'd into force when Feeling's reign began.

LUTHER, AND THE AGE.

Luther had faults, but can a feeble age
When forms heroic, such as olden life
Admired and moulded, are to faith and fact
No more; when little-hearted Truths prevail;
When Mammon chiefly is the standard used,
And God's own world, where angel-wings yet play
In secret motion o'er the homes of men,
Is made an engine, whose mechanic force
A mill can work, or manufacture sway,
The mighty prowess and majestic heart
Of Luther read, with comprehending love?
Belief hath vanish'd in the vast Unseen;
And earth ungodded, to presiding laws
Is given over with a heartless lie,
Till scarce their unbelief some dare believe!—
But Luther's was a lofty soul, which felt
Beyond the body, life's true secret lay;
While faith in Goodness, God, and Truth reveal'd,
Subdued his being with o'ermastering spell.
And thus, by quick intensity o'ersway'd,
He often stumbled, where the colder stand
Securely guarded, in their frost enshrined.

"Luther had faults!" but, oh, ye little Minds
Less in your faith, and lesser still in deeds
Which make the hero, or the man unfold
In full-soul'd daring, while the outer-life
You ponder, have ye pierced the core within?
A fool can censure where a prophet weeps,
When life is only by its faults and falls
Review'd: but underneath, what noble tears,
What pangs remorseful, penitence, and prayer,
What struggles mute, what passionate regrets!
Deep in the bosom—there begins a fight!
And there the battle-scene 'tween Flesh and Faith
Unfolds its grandeur. All without appears
The moral echo of that inward din,
A mere reflection of internal strife
In fitful shadows thrown on human eyes.
Yet, these are chiefly what adjudging sense
Accredits; character from these is drawn;
And so with Luther: bold as blazing fact,
The failings of his outer-life advance
To catch the censure of prosaic eyes,
And hearts which never with emotion sway'd
Themselves, or others. But, the secret fight
Internal, when his wild and wasted soul
Struggled, and strove, contending with the Fiends
Of darkness, baffled oft, and bleeding faint,
And yet, right upward, through eclipsing gloom,
Through storm and danger, and internal wrong,
From famish'd boyhood e'en to fearless man
Advancing, with a most unconquer'd will
To God and virtue,—who hath laurell'd this
Or wreath'd the record with a just renown?
But, true biography in heaven is writ,
And every heart-beat throbs a record there.

'Tis therefore, by successive falls they rise
Step after step, through stormy grief and gloom,
These Benefactors to the boundless mind,
Patrons of soul, and true philanthropists.
Hail to their glory! Let the sceptic rave;
There's something godlike in the truly great;
They find the lever Archimedes sought,
And fix its fulcrum in the soul of Man
And nobly lift him to our destined skies.
Like parts and portions of the primal True,
Like apparitions from a purer World,
Like human echoes of great Nature's heart,

Whose beat is holy,—fresh from God they come,
And summon man to virtue; or, expound
Our vast relations with the Infinite.
Their words breathe might; oracular and strong,
Direct from deep Reality they roll
Like inspirations: or, with soul array'd,
Their meanings fall with fulminating burst
Full on the battlements of ancient Crime,
And crush them!—thus, their mental tones
Are sleepless echoes to the ears of Mind
For ever; time with them is all attuned.

Yet, though these Spirits bear th' almighty stamp,
And challenge far beyond what earth bestows
Of homage, yet the world is all unwont
Voices from out the solemn deeps of Thought,
Divine as theirs, to rev'rence, or regard.
And Luther, like his fellow-heirs in fame,
A great minority, a glorious One
A while stood forth, unaided and uncheer'd.
But here is greatness,—when by truth possess'd,
Earth, Sense, and Time, alone to face and feel.
And where, save in the armoury of heaven,
Found the brave monk a weapon for his fight?
And that was Faith! in God, in Good, and Truth,
In Beauty, Wisdom, and celestial Worth,
Heaven-rooted Morals, in the deathless Mind,
But chief, in Duty!—dread and awful Thing!
Which o'er relations from Th' Eternal drawn,
Reaches on high, to where God's throne is rear'd,
And downward to Perdition's wailing hell
Extendeth.—That which holds our being fast,
And binds together with uniting band
All facts, and feelings, faculties, desires,
All that we suffer, fancy, dream, or do
From life's first pulse of reason to the last,
This power and principle of Duty makes;
To finite deed gives infinite result,
Calls the dead Past to resurrection-life,
Harangues the guilty, and that hour predicts
When mem'ry into one concenter'd whole
Gone life shall grasp, and startled Conscience hear
How the last trumpet can our thoughts restore.

OMNIPOTENCE OF FAITH.

Faith was the weapon! by it Luther fought,
Conquer'd himself, and then, the world subdued.
And what is That, but God by man applied
Above all reason, sense, and earth, and sin,
In things heroic, heavenly, or sublime?
From Abel's worship, e'en to Samuel's word
Faith was a magic which all wonders did;
Whether the pausing sun its cry obey'd
Or, the Moon hearken'd to its holy spell,
Or, Red Sea parted, by its kingly voice
Cloven, and balanced like a billowy wall
On either side, for heaven's anointed Host,
Scatheless the fire, or mute the lion's mouth
Became,—whatever in the kingdoms three
Of nature, providence, or grace, was done,
Faith was the doer, at whose potent cry
Empires and thrones, and alien armies fell,
Weakness grew strength, the mortal, half divine!

And what, without it, seems this fallen world
But Pandemonium, with a purer name?
Clothed in hell-fire, come any Shape of sin,
Take any form, satanic Guile! but this,
The Infidel!—the fellest blight which falls.
No foul elixir of a fiendish lie
So baneful as the cup, which Unbelief
Drains to the bottom with delirious joy.
Oh! 'tis a wasteful, with'ring, black disease
That to the vitals of all virtuous thought
And wisdom, sends a paralysing shock;
The very life-blood of all goodness dies
Before it; like a heart-fiend, lo! it rules;
All forms of excellence and feeling die,
The Beautiful departs, the Brave expires;
Hope hath no heaven, and fear no hell to face:
All high relations are at once relax'd
With God, and duty; self and passion rage
In the hot furnace of a seething heart
Resistless; men are now but fiends, with flesh
Apparell'd; lust becomes a brutal flame,
And all those moral harmonies, which make
Nature a noble, Man a godlike thing,
Have perish'd! Life is then a form of death;
The heart's insolvent; mind a bankrupt too;
Jehovah in eclipse Himself retires,
Till thus, all ghastliness the earth appears,
Orphan'd of God,—a suicidal world!

Here was thy rock, thy fortress, and thy rest,
A faith intense, beyond mutation firm,
Whose solid basis was th' eternal Heart
Open in scripture, by the Spirit read,
But in the life of Jesus heard to beat
With pulse almighty, in its love for man.
Here was thy spell, thy secret, and thy sway,
Thy lock of strength, unsever'd and unshorn.
Luther! in this thine earthly comment lies.
Here is the key, which all thy soul unlocks,
And lets mute Wonder, with exploring gaze
Each hidden region of thy spirit view.
Faith to thy being sun and shield supplied,
Summon'd the soul, and nerved the noble heart
With zeal untamed, to burn, or bleed, or die,
But tremble never!—Thine was spirit-life,
Whose solemn breathings were from scripture drawn,

And adoration; while, both heart and head
Motives and movements from the world to come
Divinely influenced with inspiring force,
Or sanction. Thus, thy mission was complete,
Thy virtue safe, and thy vocation seal'd.
Whether we mark thee, when that rugged face
Beam'd in bold triumph o'er the flaming Bull;
Or on thy forehead, where intrepid thought
Throned its high meaning in the hall of Worms,
Admiring Hist'ry fix her spell-bound gaze;
Or grateful Fancy, by the gospel led,
Bend o'er thy Bible, when some midnight-lamp
Lighted each feature, as the truths divine
Rose into life, by thy translating touch
Restored, or brighten'd,—still, in all we find
Faith was the secret power, whose shaping charm
Moulded the man, when most he grew sublime.

And, whatsoe'er our rank, degree, or lot,
Giant or dwarf in morals, or in mind,
'Tis faith alone true character can build.
Not as we learn, but as we live, we are;
And as we live, with things divinely pure,
These in their depths, we rightly understand.
Since faith is rooted in eternal life;
And all fair promise in the tree of man
Blossoms from thence, or dies a mocking show
Fruitless, and fragile. Give us faith, O God!
Faith in Thyself, and that will Thee impart;
Chaste will life be, and calm its closing hours,
To them who have Thee, all their hearts and souls
Possessing ever, and by them possess'd.
In Thee, and *by* Thee,—thus they live, and love,
They think, they suffer, what they act, achieve!
In all things, heaven and holiness abound;
Minutest objects Thine hand-writing prove,
And Life becomes one grateful hymn to Thee.
So, when that trump, whose archangelic peal
Shall sound the tocsin of creation's doom,
Thunders its challenge, Faith shall then arise
And, firm as Jesus on The Judgment throne,
Look on thy face, Eternity! and smile.

THE CHILD PROPHESIES THE MAN.

The hand of Jesus on thy heart, O child!
In love was laid; He watch'd its hidden play,
And heard it throbbing with unspoken prayer.
Thou fair inheritor of mortal flesh,
Typing the kingdom of the unattain'd!
Prophet! with mighty revelations mute;
Thou priest! with sacrifice of soul to come;
Thou king! whose monarchy young feeling rules,
Meanings around thee, full of heaven declare
'Tis like religion, when we look on thee.

A deep heart thrilling with the Unavow'd,
A spirit dark'ning with the Undescribed,
And his whole being rock'd, and urged, or rent
With big emotions, beautiful and strong,
On Mansfield plains, behold, that destined Boy,
All that is great in earth, or sky, adore.
Earnest he is, and most intensely true;
Free-hearted, bold, with open forehead graced,
Rude as the wave that roughens in the wind
Resistless; gifted with a fervid soul,
Mirror'd by eyes, where mental radiance beams,
And yet, withal, by sadness mildly touch'd
At being's centre; meditative, lone,
And quiet often, as the placid cloud
Cradled at twilight in the lulling west.

The vernal freshness of life's dewy morn
Bedecks his nature, like a magic bloom,
And mantles all things. Now, with dreadless play
Opens the heart at feeling's lightest touch;
Time hath not barr'd it with those jealous bolts
By Prudence framed, which bid the stranger wait,
And knock for years, before he enters in
To find a welcome. All is bold, and free,
Unguarded; giving forth a quick response
To each appliance from the passing scene;
Promptly as flowers to breezes yield their scent,
Or boughs their music to the playing winds
That bend them: such is youth's excited frame,
And such, though brief the guiding annals be,
Was Luther's. Genius is a glorious one;
And all her children like impression bear
Of their high parent. This, in after-life,
Back on dim boyhood darts explaining gleams,
And proves the child then prophesied the man.
Luther in germ, may *now* in heart be seen;
For, what is manhood, but the child drawn out,
By mere expansion of that moral seed
Which buds and blossoms into perfect man,
Whose ripen'd germ is character full-blown?
And now, fair Beauty, Grandeur, Form, and Grace,
Yea, all the felt significance of life
Inner, and deep, begin their blended reign;
And so inspire him, that material earth
Turns one vast mirror to envisage mind.
And with what boundless, sateless, unsubdued
Young appetite, his spirit thus partakes,
At each fine inlet, all this God-made world
Before him, like an inspiration spread!
E'en as a sail to catch the coming breeze,
So boyhood opens its expectant breast,
Panting for beauty, at each conscious pore.
And hence, in all things youth's poetic faith

Beauty perceives; or, by perception makes
The beautiful, a virgin heart admires.
Thus, flowers are fancies by the Earth produced;
The clouds, emotions of the Tempest born,
The arch of heaven, how eloquently high!
A bright archangel of the burning east
The Sun ariseth, on his wings of light
How watch'd, and welcomed! Then, comes Night august,
A dread magician! with her sybil-stars
Attended; and the twilight Sea is made
Creation's poet, with his billowry lyre
Rolling for ever an unconscious chant,
Or broken swell of oceanic hymns.
Blood, heart, and brain, the beautiful inhale;
Matter and mind a very duel fight
By sweet contention, in some high-wrought mood
Of young entrancement! Forms without, appeal,
And thoughts within, like answ'ring music, play;
Till life itself a lovely poem seems
Tender, but touch'd with most impassion'd tones.
So rapt is youth, and fervidly entranced
When genius fills it with her hallow'd fire,
And all the open Secret of the world
Round a lone heart its earthless magic brings.

Such the boy, Luther; simple, rough, and rude,
A thoughtful earnestness his brow enthrones
Beyond all shrinking. His the cloudless heart;
And men may read it with a ready glance.
Like glass transparent, do his actions show
That hidden wheel-work which the heart involves.

GENIUS, SOLITUDE, AND SYMPATHY.

Genius was thine, thou heaven-commission'd Boy!
But surely, Sorrow was thy guerdon too;
Since ne'er doth greatness in a bosom lodge,
But Sadness thither, like a shade, attends,
Its true companion. In this faded world
Our graves and tears are almost equal, now;
And, e'en at best, light-hearted youth must bear
A burden voiceless, and the pang unbreathed
Of many a dark and undevelop'd mood.
The earth is exile; and for Home we pine
How often! when high visitations come
From whence we know not, and the mind o'erwhelm.
As if some Angel by the flesh immured
Our Spirit were, within whose conscious powers
The sounds and splendours of ethereal life,
In dim remembrance, were at times renew'd.—
And did not he, whose pure vocation was
The Infinite with finite things to join,
Wrestle with thoughts, his yearning boyhood strove
In vain to answer? Felt he oft no thirst,
Like a young Tantalus, by mocking bliss
Encompass'd, melting from the parchèd mind?
And did not Dreams, and Solitude, and Night
Profoundly move him, till prophetic thoughts
Imaged the future? Rapt in speechless awe,
Ponder'd he not on *that* behind the Veil,
When round him, like a belting zone which binds
All time, all scene, all circumstance, all change,
Divine Eternity in shadow came?

We know not this; but, e'en as eagles soar
And sky-ward through the rending storm-cloud mount
With plumes unbaffled, Luther's wingèd soul
Against the blast of Circumstance did beat,
And struggle upward to a destined sphere.
From want and woe his educated will
The glory of its resolution caught;
E'en from the cradle, tears his teachers made,
And suff'ring, hard as adamant, engraved
Lessons which left throughout all time their trace
Instructive. Thus, amid the true and stern,
And keen realities of testing life,
The Boy was rounded into full-orb'd Man
And fitted for his function. Thus, a Soul
Predestined, for its prophet-work was train'd,
And grew heroic: till at length, the world
In full apocalypse of all its powers
Emerging shall behold it act, and speak.
And like the hammer of a christian Thor
Down on the Curse of christendom and man
Descend, with most annihilating crash,
His tones of thunder and his truths of life!

But, in those powers auxiliar, which expand
The young Reformer, feeling play'd its part;
And that, perchance, beyond all others, pure.
His was a mother, from whose heart of love
Sacred and deep, with fine devotion full,
As from a shrine, his lisping boyhood took
Counsels of grace, oracular and fond.
And who can say, how much that Luther show'd
In his high work of majesty and mind,
Which grateful Empires with their homage crown,
Sprang from a look, a warning, or a word,
A mother wielded, when she taught him God?
And ever thus, from love maternal spring
Feelings and powers, which o'er progressive life

Reign with a subtile, secret, holy spell:
And deeds, and darings which have moved the world
A cent'ry forward, from a mother's lip
Caught the first glow whence inspiration came.

Yet, bleak the lot his boyish prime endured!
And sad, indeed, and merciless as dark
The shades of circumstance around him fell;
While yet, no precious dawn of grace appear'd
His soul to lighten through domestic gloom.
But, on his cheek a blanching terror came
When *He* was named, within Whose wreathing arms
Of mercy, once, a folded infant smiled!
Foodless, and friendless, oft the fainting boy
Far from his home, with none, save God, his guide,
In Magdeburgh from house to house was doom'd
A meal to beg; and thus, by Heaven was school'd
To hard experience, when Hereafter came.
"Bread for the love of God!" hark! Luther chants
From door to door, through Eisenach's winding street,
Mix'd with a group, as wan and worn as he
Of students poor. But lo! as once he lay
Beneath the umbrage of a cottage-tree,
Alone and pensive, while the leaf-shades fell
Like soft expressions on his speaking face
Of suff'ring, sad and sweet the hymn he sung;
The very echo of his soul was there,
And, like the fragments of a broken heart,
His shatter'd feelings trembled into song.
But not in vain that plaintive scholar mourn'd;
For on the ear of Ursula they sunk,
Those tones of truth, like tears upon some heart
O'erburden'd, dropt from Friendship's genial eye.
Never again shall that pale youth despond
In Famine's grasp, through days of pining gloom!
At once, both heart and home their shelter ope,
And, like the Shunammite, her all she shares
With him, the homeless boy of sorrow, now.

Blessings be on thee! Cotta's lowly bride,
And praise immortal, for the feeling hand
Which dealt thy substance; and the angel-voice
That, rich as dew-fall on a summer eve
Descending, when the fev'rish earth-sod pines,
Besoothed the world's great benefactor, then!
For here, by want unchill'd, by care unworn,
Bosom'd in calm domestic, Luther builds
By soft degrees, his mental being up.
Science, and Art, and Lore, that lovely trine!
Around him throng, and with their blended smiles
The budding energies of mind attract
Forth into blossoms of expanding force,
And freshness; e'en as sunshine tempts
The hue of flowers, and harmonies of spring
To full expression. Home of halcyon ease!
When the loud roar of his hereafter-life
Deafen'd the heart, how oft did Luther love
That sabbath-haven of the soul to haunt
With mem'ry's eye: and once again recal
The bliss of tranquil being, when the noise
Of man's great world with no disturbing sound
The soul distracted: like the far-off waves
To one who, pensive at his window, dreams,
When twilight o'er the palpitating breast
Of Ocean melts in rosy calm away,—
The soften'd echoes of a distant world
But served to make the hush of home more dear.

And Music, too, her poetry of sound
Evoked: for oft, when Evening's pallid veil
Curtain'd the clouds with beauty; or, the Moon
A mild entrancement from her beam inspired,
Did Luther hymn the golden hours to rest
With deep-toned chants, and melodies divine;
Where voice and lute each other's echo seem'd,
So richly one their combination grew.—
When years had flown, and Europe's grateful hand
Round Luther's name a wreath of glory twined,
And at his feet the heart of Empires bow'd
Admiring, Cotta's home, still unforgot,
Was outlined in his mindful heart of love
Serene as ever; while his voice proclaim'd,
By gallantry and grace at once inspired,
There's nothing sweeter than a woman's soul
When Truth divine erects her temple there!

UNIVERSITY.

"Who prays the most, will study best;" so spake,
In noble answer to official pride,
A young Reformer, when th' unfolding gates
Of Erfurth from his asking eye retired,
As pale he stood, her letter'd walls beside
Intreating entrance there. And now, commenced
The waking myst'ries of his mind within!
Around him, more and more, dread shadows fell,
Which seem'd reflected from Almighty frowns;
While conscience, that pale miniature of God!
In outlines faint, the Holiness Supreme

Began to image. Morning, noon, and night,
With soul intense, and heart of upward gaze,
How oft did Luther on the wings of hope
Rise out of earth, heaven's tearless home depict,
And on Christ's bosom pillow all his cares!
'Twas then, while sensitive at ev'ry pore,
His soul lay open to the pregnant beams
Of truth eternal, from the heavens derived,
That Mercy-seat of everlasting mind,
The Bible!—first on Luther's spirit breathed.
Yet, little thought he, when the dust-worn shelves
Were traced, some intellectual food to find,
How God in language to the conscience speaks
When faith in scripture hears the Spirit there.
And scarce could Seraph wave his wings of light
With ecstasy of more celestial glow,
Than did the student, with his raptured eyes
To heaven upraised, the heart's rich anthem peal
Of thankful wonder, for this costly boon!
That moment was the Reformation's seed;
That Volume, then, the universe outweigh'd
In mental preciousness and moral power!
For in its pages slept those living germs
Of principle, from out whose depth have sprung
The faith, and freedom of a christian world.

FALLEN NATURE IN RELIGIOUS FORMS.

SAY, how can man be justified by God?
Challenged eternity would echo, "how,"
But from The Cross responding grace replies
To this high question: faith in Christ is life,
And love, and righteousness, completely fit
To each vast claim of violated Law.
Thus, conscience finds no compromise involved;
Nor Mercy from the hand of Justice grasps
The sceptre, and her awful head uncrowns;
But there, all Attributes divinely blend
In one rich centre of consummate light,
And God, with most benignant glory, smiles
His goodness forth, o'er ransom'd souls and worlds.

But he, pale thinker! in portentous gloom
Robed by the rags of papal righteousness,
Was shiv'ring yet: around his spirit coil'd
The clankless fetters of condemning law;
And upward, when his heart to gaze presumed
A moment, soon it shrunk, appall'd and dim,
From God's dread eye-glance, flaming with the curse!
Dark wrestler with the pangs of sin untold,
Silence and solitude his haunt became,
Transforming nature, till the soul was typed
In all he witness'd, of the bleak and wild.
Down lonely vales, and paths of soundless gloom,
He loved to meditate, and learn'd to mourn;
But, chief the night-blast, with its hollow yell
Rung from the Tempest's riven heart of sound,
Becharm'd him, when beneath the wat'ry moon
Late roaming. Still, the crisis came at last!—
'Twas summer; and with crimson eye of fire
Full o'er the pine-tree boughs the west'ring Orb
Sunk flaming; like a furnace glow'd the air
In breezeless trance, while not a bird-wing moved;
And forest-leaves, as by some fixing spell
Enchanted, like the lids of slumber, hung
Subdued, and motionless: so deep the hush,
Your very heart-pulse strange and loud appear'd;
When, lo! the blacken'd cope of heaven divides,
And flashes; re-divides, and with one fold
Of sheeted flame the firmament involves.
Hark! peal on peal redoubling, and return'd
With raging echo, till heaven's arches ring
And vibrate; then, in one convulsive burst
The clouds are clash'd to thunder, and descends
Down at his feet, in supernat'ral roar,
A death-bolt!—Harmless as the rain-drop fell
The blasting ruin; Luther, in the shade
Of that great Hand, Whose hollow hides the church
From storming earth and hell, was all secure,
Though death glared round him. What a scene was there!
In kneeling agony, with eyes of awe
To Heaven upturn'd, as if the judgment-pomp
And equipage of heaven's almighty King
Emerged apparent, Luther throbb'd, and pray'd;
And vow'd his after-life to God alone,
If safely rescued from the whelming storm.
So sank a great Apostle, when the blaze
Bright as That form of Glory whence it fell,
Abash'd him into blindness, and he heard
The mournful thunder of Messiah's lip
Rebuke him, till his conscience rock'd and reel'd.

But now, all faithful to his word, sincere
In darkness, to the blinding creed he loved,
Hark! on their hinges grind the massive gates
Of St. Augustine's cold and cloister'd pile,
And in the clang of those reclosing doors,
The knell of Luther's freedom! Darkly bound
By dread theology's remorseless chains
Of monkish falsehood, in the deep of night,
Fresh from the haunt of social youth he comes
Self-exiled, and sincere, in convent-gloom
Amid the graves of unproductive mind,

Where dead religion putrified to fear
And fear to superstition,—there to lift
His soul to God, and fashion it for heaven!
Yet, mark in this eternal Wisdom's plan.
A dungeon'd martyr, on whose haggard limbs
The rust-worn chain its branding trace hath delved,
When free again beneath the skies to walk,
Inhaling liberty from each loved breeze
Which carols round him, chief o'er all can tell
How priceless to the heart pure freedom is!
And thus did Luther, by whose dreadless hand
Of truth, base fetters from the mind were fell'd,
As captive, first by dark experience learn
How deep that dungeon of the spirit was,
Where Roman witchcraft plunged, and plagued mankind!
Yes, he, the champion of Jehovah's cause,
Whose bold harangues, like Alpine thunder-peals
Hereafter shook the Vatican to shame,
Himself once crouch'd, in martyrdom of zeal,
Beneath the lashes of a monk's stern lip
In silence; wound the clock, and swept the floor,
And begg'd, a charter'd mendicant, from house
To house, the bread of blushless charity!

But, found he there the holiness he sought?
Did peace divine in purity descend
Down on his conscience, like the calming Dove?
Ah! no; in vain the convent's round of rites,
The fastings dull, the macerations dire,
The penance long, the midnight-watchings pale,
All the mean clockwork of monastic life,
Wheel within wheel, by superstition turn'd!
From righteous acts no righteous nature flows;
First form the nature, then the acts arise
Spontaneous, free, by fertile love produced,
Not pleading merit, but proclaiming Christ
Within, by transcript of His life without.
For, how in Self can man salvation find,
When self is sin, connat'ral and corrupt?
But, like that Bible, which his sateless eyes
Read oft and oft, with most devouring gaze
Of faith and feeling, Luther wore the chain
Which round the soul rank Superstition binds.
Yet, oft the heavings of his spirit rose
In dark reflection, to his pale-worn face!
While e'en the whisper of that still small Voice
Which cowards all, but christians maketh none,
Beneath the roof of his o'erarching cell
Raged into moral thunder, when stern thoughts
Of God in judgment, tore with tort'ring might
And mystery, the troubled mind within!
Thus, like a spectre, through the cloisters moved
With fruitless sigh, and ineffectual groan,
Day after day, all spirit-crush'd, and worn,
The helpless Luther, till the Cross appear'd:
From holy love then true repentance sprang;
And faith, like Mary, at the feet of Christ
Attending, hung upon His lips, and lived.

REVIVAL.

Celestial love! no self-created sound
In the cold depth of man's corrupted heart,
But rather, a responsive echo, waked
By Love supernal, art Thou, when sincere.
By God's to man, man's love to God begins;
And christianity is Christ received,
The soul possessing, and Himself possess'd.
Then thaws the heart, however iced and dead,
In tears which glow with gratitude divine.
So Luther felt, when Love's almighty voice
Becalm'd him; round the Cross he ever read
The page of heaven, and in that Fountain wash'd
His soul to whiteness, which for sin unclosed
In streaming mercy from our wounded Lord.
Light, peace, and order round his being throng'd
In rich communion; prayer and praise arose,
Like native incense from the soul renew'd;
And holiness, man's paradise regain'd,
No effort now, but second nature seem'd,—
Not labour done, but life itself enjoy'd.
Yet, who can tell, as stern-eyed Law retired
And the mild Gospel o'er his conscience breathed
Like Jesus, when He sigh'd the breath of peace,
How on his heart the Bible's image grew,
Till, like a throbbing counterpart, it beat
In living echo to the truth it loved!
While doctrines now, which once with scowling front
Black as the shades which over Sinai hung,
Appall'd him, soft as Christ's own pity, smiled.
No more the penance vile, with venal aim
To bribe Eternal Justice, was achieved:
In Christ her all-in-all stern Conscience found
And, sprinkled with His blood, her claim withdrew
For ever: penal Law its lightning veil'd;
And when from sickness, pale and purified
The convert of the Cross in health arose,
He clung to Jesus with a clasping soul
Devoted, lifted high o'er legal fears,
And from His wounds saw earth's atonement flow.

PREACHER AND PULPIT.

"Go! stand the living and the dead between,
Take the rich censer of Messiah's grace
And stop the Plague." Such looks the Office high
To him appointed, who the tidings glad
Proclaims of Liberty to souls condemn'd
In the black dungeon of the Curse to writhe,
And weep for ever. Well may dread, sublime
As holy, soften'd o'er with human shades
Of feeling, round some youthful Herald steal,
When *first* the embassy of Pardon rolls
In strains of heart from his excited lip,
Which vibrates, like a chord by music thrill'd,
Master'd by young emotion. What a theme!
God in our Flesh, to save that Flesh, array'd,
The Infinite within the finite lodged,
The form Almighty in a frame all weak,
The dread Creator on the Cross unveil'd
In bleeding glory!—Heaven, and Earth, and Hell,
Eternity and Time, and Sin and Grace,
The choral anthems of the blood-bought Church
Circling the Lamb with coronation-joy;
Or, wild Perdition's cry, in lurid flames
Stretch'd on a rack of self-tormenting ire,—
These are the elements combined to throw
Around a Preacher that commanding spell
Of awe, which makes the earthen Vessel bend,
To think it treasures such a peerless trust!

And, who can dare himself sufficient deem
For work so fearful, where seraphic Minds
May travail in the greatness of their strength,
And yet, not scale its altitude divine?
Oh, Thou! Whose office 'tis the Word to bless
And quicken, till it breathes a living grace,
Thee may we ever prove in presence nigh
As Great Inspirer; Whose anointing power
Alone can tune the "sounding brass" to Heaven's
True note, and bid some "tinkling cymbal" do
In mortal accent, an immortal work!
Whether beneath yon bow'd cathedral roof
Of vastness, while the organ's billowy peals
Roll like a sea of melody and might
Down the dim nave, and long-retreating aisles,
Thy Word is preach'd; or in some Saxon fane,
Where rude simplicities, of ancient mould,
Linger in stone's most exquisite decay;
Wherever on the tide of human breath
Floats a rich argosy of Gospel-truth,
As Christ appointed, may dependence be
The preacher's motto, and the preacher's mode;
Dependence meek on that concurring Grace
Of Him, the Bible's Author, by Whose light
Alone our sermons live, and souls are saved.

FIRST SERMON.

So felt the young Reformer, when he rose
Within thy square, high-fated Wittemberg!
Where the grey walls of St. Augustine's fane
Crumble in low decrepitude, and dust;
And from his pulpit, piled with simple planks,
Blew that loud trumpet of Salvation's truth,
Whose echoes yet the heart of empires stir.
Eye, cheek, and brow, with eloquence array'd
As though pure spirit would incarnate be,
Or mind intense would burn its dazzling way
And be apparent,—like a Saxon Paul
Flaming with truth, the fearless Herald pour'd
Himself in language o'er the list'ning throng
Around him! With a mental torrent ran
The rich discourse; and on that flood of mind
Nearer and nearer to the Lamb's white Throne
The soul was wafted, while for Christ he spake,
And hid himself behind the Cross he raised.

A more than Hercules, to cleanse a church
Where priestly falsehood stabled all its guilt
Through cent'ries dark of domineering crime,
So seem'd he *then*; and in that sermon gave
A noble prelude of the trumpet-blast
Predestined from his daring lip to roll
Hereafter, when from lethargy and lies
He roused the Autocrat of Romish priests
In cruelty, and curses, till there came
An avalanche of everlasting truths
Down on the Popedom, in those thund'rous words
Which crush'd it, like th' apocalyptic Stone
Hurl'd by God's angel through the blood-red sea.*

METROPOLIS OF ANTICHRIST.

To shameless Rome, the capital of sin,
When Crime in canonised pretension smiled,
And Pride and Lust pontifically reign'd,
At length, great Luther comes. The glare of skies
O'er which the mercy of no soothing cloud
Had floated, vainly tried his toil-worn frame;
For still, o'er Alpine crags, by torrents wild,
And hoar ravines, within whose rocky depths
Yell'd the loud streams their everlasting cry,
The Monk of Wittemberg, with eager step
And soul expectant, sought the seven-hill'd Queen
Of cities; till, behold! in glimm'ring haze
Her turrets, towers, and giant temple-spires
At length emerge: and low upon the ground,
In kneeling homage, falls her duteous son,

* See Rev. xviii. 21.

To breathe his blessing o'er maternal Rome,
Mother, and Mistress of the churches all!
But when her pillar'd streets of pomp he trod,
And on those ruins, eloquent and vast
Around him in sublime confusion piled,
Gazed with devotion,—what a gushing sense
Of ancient glory through his being swept!
The past in tow'ring resurrection rose
Bright from the tomb of ages; while the air
Which Peter breathed, and Paul himself inhaled,
Play'd round his temples, like a breeze from heaven
New-wafted! Rome and rapture were combined;
And Luther, in one lofty dream of soul
Enchanted stood, and drank the glorious scene;
As if Religion from the very stones
Was preaching where Apostles once had trod,
And over which the martyr's flame of death
Gleam'd in dread radiance, like a glory now.

But, soon the bandage of imposture fell!
And then, e'en like the Arch-fiend's mystic pomp
Summon'd before Emmanuel's heaven-bright gaze,
So fleetly vanish'd into viewless air
Thy pageantries, thou Babylon of guilt,
And scarlet Lady with the costly blood
Of God's elected, drunken and bedew'd! *
Since, then reveal'd in all thy hideous truth,
He found thee but a leprous church of lies
By ages putrified, in papal form.

Oh, grace divine, and wonderful as deep,
That Rome and Luther should confronted be!
And there, in Superstition's heart, one text
Almighty, like a thunderbolt of truth
Down from the throne of Revelation cast,
Should raise him, while he crouch'd in dismal faith,
Deluded! Thus, the Champion for his cause
Was train'd; and thus from Rome *herself* he drew
Weapons of might, whereby her powers would fall.
Hence, swift recoiling from his task abhorr'd,
Uprose the brave Reformer! free and firm
For ever: "By his faith the just shall live!"—
Thus came a Text from Inspiration's lip;
Religion, then, and Luther's mind arose
Erect; upon the rock of faith alone
Together did they face the frowning Hell,
And bid our spirit in the Lord stand free!

* "The woman drunken with the blood of the saints."—*Rev.* xvii. 6.

INDULGENCES.

"Lo! at yon gate," the Mercuries of sin
Are crying, "Stands the awful Grace of God!"
And, in one moment, like a moral wave
Heaves far and wide the town's excited heart;
Council, and nuns, and priests, and monks advance,
And motley crowds, from ev'ry lane and street
Are rushing, while the festive town-clock peals
A loud hosannah from its lofty spires,
And tapers flash, and greeting cymbals sound,
To meet the great Procession. See! they come,
In robes how costly! There, in cushion'd pomp
The Bull of grace, whereby the Godhead's hands
Are bound, and His dread thunders *must* awake
Or sleep, as priestly conjuration bids!
For now, before a wooden cross uprear'd
Bedeck'd with Leo's blazonry of pride,
The loud-voiced Tetzel takes his stand profane:
Prime vender he! beneath whose venal lip
Heaven's attributes, as in a mart exposed,
Are purchased by Indulgence; Christ is sold
In pardons! Sin itself, before conceived,
Or acted, by the Pope's almighty Bull,
Shall not be damning: whatsoe'er Desire
May dream hereafter, through its charm absolved,
Shall be forgiven!—"Down this cross there flows
A grace like that the Saviour's bleeding side
Dispersed; but hark! from deeps of ghastly woe
Where yelling Spirits clang their chains of fire,
Tormented parents, friends, and children, lift
Their tongues uncool'd, and cry for needed alms
To bring them from that red Abyss of wrath,
Where scorch their souls in purgatorial flames!
Let but your money, with its golden clink,
Yon chest descend, and, lo! at once escaped,
Those dungeon'd Spirits, wing'd by papal grace,
Full into heaven's bright welcome flee!"

So cried that dread impostor; and the souls
Of myriads, by anointed lies seduced,
Imperill'd; Christ himself, in blacker shame
Than once the Cross of Calvary o'erhung,
Was openly to mocking Hell exposed;
Eternity a mart of sin became,
Or, papal auction, where that grace was sold
For filthy lucre, which the costly Blood
Which warm'd Emmanuel's veins, alone procured;
And 'gainst the purity of Heaven's high throne
The breath of human blasphemy arose
From Pope, and priesthood. Seal'd the Bible, then!
And sure, if ever down a Seraph's cheek

Roll'd the rich tear immortal feeling sheds,
It trickled now, when thus religion dared
In words divine God's heart of gracious love
To libel; Christ's own pangs for venal lies
To barter, till the Truth of heaven betray'd,
In priestly suffocation sank, and died.

But, there is mercy in thy myst'ry lodged,
Eternal! Out of darkness cometh light
By Thee evoked; and, while the anarch sin
To mortal judgment, in its clouded gaze,
O'er time and circumstance sole monarch looks
Ascendant, all the waves of human will
In lawless riot though they toss and plunge,
Within the circle of Thy will supreme
Alone are heaving; if they rise, or fall,
'Tis only as Thy secret law ordains.

REFORMATION.

Pale with devotion, wrestling long and lone
With God in prayer, behold! the lion heart
Of Luther beats with supernat'ral pulse,
And throbs for Deity, and great design.
Stung to his very soul with piercing shame
Beneath a lie to see heaven's truth expire,
And trampled Scripture gasping in the dust
Of low venality, and priestly lies,
Upon the door of Wittemberg's dark pile
He fasten'd then, with hand divinely firm,
Ninety and five of those all-fearless truths
Which shook the Popedom, and the World redeem'd
From charms infernal, to the Cross alone.
Faith, hope, and love, upon the Rock of souls
Were founded; Grace in gospel-freedom rose,
From Schools and sophistry at length escaped;
And from the fountain of Emmanuel's Blood
Both peace and pardon in conjunction flow'd,
Free, full, and glorious from the heart of God,—
Giver and gift in amnesty combined!
And yet, what eye save His, before Whose beam
Time, place, and all contingencies retire
As though they were not, in this daring act
Of Luther, heard the Reformation's pulse
Of Life and liberty begin to beat?
Or who, among the crowd that rush'd to read
In tumult wild, upon the church's gate,
Those Words, which dash'd Indulgences to air,
The silent thunder of their strength foretold
Upon thine eve, All-Hallows? Monk and priest
And Pope, and hoary-headed Falsehood, then,
Were death-struck: in those few fine truths
The germs of unexpanded glory slept,
As in the acorn future navies float.
And when at night a lonely cell was sought,
Could the brave Monk his deed of pregnant might
Have measured? In the greatness of the act,
Oh, was he conscious of th' Almighty, there?

JUSTIFYING GRACE.

One truth divine, from deeps of scripture drawn,
And by one heart with burning zeal espoused,
Then, bodied forth in majesty of life,
What miracles that single truth achieves
Which rock an empire, or a world restore!
And hence, when pale in his monastic gloom,
Alone, and pensive, groping after God
Through clouds of error, black with Romish guile,
At length the tortured monk, with tears of praise,
Consummate pardon in the Cross alone
Discover'd, then, a peerless Truth was found
From whence instructed Empires learn to live.
And in that hall, where stood the fearless man
Bulwark'd with principle, beyond all powers
By earth created, or by hell contrived,
He grasp'd a truth which Heaven's eternal creed
Hath canonised, and by the Cross explain'd,—
That Grace is God by God alone applied:
On this, Religion all her fabric rears,
That else, is baseless, as the yielding air.

Hence flow those energies through man and mind,
Which mould our being great, or make it good.
Here, by the pardon of perfective grace,
The anguish'd memory can alone subdue
That dread Gehenna, which our guilt inflames
Oft in remembrance; and, from thence derived,
Pure emanations spring, and feelings act
Which feed with moral life the social frame
Of men, and nations; for the heart is free,
And guarded Conscience on the bosom's throne
Reigns in the sanctity which Christ inspires.

'Tis thus, where dreadless martyrs often fail'd,
And ancient heroes their protesting voice
Lifted in vain, to vindicate The Truth
From all aggression, Luther's prowess smote
The Roman Beast to ruin, nigh to death,—
And that, with principle! 'Twas here he fought,
He grappled with the foe of God, and man.
Swift through the night of man's imprison'd soul

He pour'd the beam of evangelic day;
And where Authority, in mitred sway,
Fetter'd weak conscience with infernal chains,
He throned The Gospel, in the light of Grace
At once the law, and liberty of souls.
But, had he only on a mob of "saints"
Shot his keen arrows of sarcastic truth,
Or, laid the monk's Augéan darkness bare,
In form regen'rate, but with life corrupt,
The Reformation then had toil'd, and died.
But, glory be to Him whose Name we bear!
'Twas grace in principle which Luther taught:
Here is the lever which the world uplifts,—
"A Saviour just, for man unjust hath died!"
Here is a Truth, whose trumpet-voice might preach
The Pope's religion into airy nought;
A truth, which is at once the text of texts,
Making all scripture music to our souls.
The Bible read, is God Himself perused
In pages letter'd with almighty love,
When thus proclaiming what the conscience craves:
While the rich fountain of Emmanuel's Blood
Not barricaded round with priestly walls,
Nor blent with superstition's blackening tide
Of "merits," now its healing flood of grace
Full on the heart in one vast current pours!

He ended, thus, where ancient Minds began;
'Gainst outward vice those murder'd Saints appeal'd,
And perish'd: but for Principle Divine,
Bravely alone the monk of Erfurt fought.
He struck the root,—and then, the branches fell;
He purged the fountain,—then, the stream roll'd pure;
The deep foundation down to hell he shook,
And then—the Roman superstition reel'd:
From centre to circumf'rence, did the soul
Of Luther reason out its lonely way;
Till, lo! at length, by Gospel-light reveal'd,
He saw impostures, in successive types
Each after each more canker'd, and corrupt;
And in the Pope that Antichrist discern'd
Whom Daniel vision'd, and St. John unveils.

GOSPEL ACCORDING TO MAN.

I.—Supremacy.

"Son of the living God! The Christ Thou art!"
So spake, by more than mortal wisdom led,
The bold Apostle, when, through flesh and blood
Divinity within the Form august
Of Jesus, shrined in mortal clay, he saw:
And on the "rock" of this confession, high
In Godhead rear'd, and deep in Manhood based,
Emmanuel built His everlasting Church.
But how hath Sin, from out the promise made
To Peter, in apostleship sublime,
But not supreme, beyond his fellows rank'd,
The Keys of power, the Kingdom, and the Laws
Which bind or loose, as papal nods decree,
Derived!—and thus on earth enthroned
A vile dominion, measureless, and vast
As Guile could plan, or cheering Hell applaud.
Admire we then, let gratitude adore
The Power divine, which hurl'd the Popedom down
From that cursed height of blasphemy and crime,
To which, through ages of gigantic skill
By fell gradation, it at length arose;—
Reigning aloft, stern Arbitress of kings
And thrones; dispensing sceptres with a smile,
Or else dissolving Kingdoms by a frown!
For Peter's shadow, and the Roman name
O'er power and policy together ruled:
Then, the high Past a holy magic breathed;
And the rich lustre of a world's regard
Made Rome the palace of Mankind appear,
The true Metropolis of priestly hearts,
A Temple, with apostleship instinct,
The stones all sacred, and Her dust inspired!
Thus magnified, and with mysterious charms
Endow'd, behold, a miracle of pride
Erect! Supremacy, thy Pope survey,
A Breath of sin on Deity's great throne!
Oh, never in the luxury of lies
Hath Self more wanton'd; never in this world
Hath Adulation's most besotted dream
A foul pretence so hideously assumed,
As then, around some ruffian Pope began;
For, palsied Reason to his sceptre bow'd,
And Blasphemy baptised a monster, "God;"
Disgust, be mute! and horror, speechless stand!
'Tis not in language, though each word be fire,
Or, fang'd with truth's most execrating force,
A Pope to paint, *when* deified by sin.
All right above, beyond all law secured,
In errorless perfection shrined aloft;
Of Peter's royalties sole heir, and king;
Of churches, Judge; of christendom the Lord;
And, such an oracle!—that when his lips
Shall condescend some great response to give,
Virtue is vice, and vice may virtue be,
Or, each be neither, if his nod decide!
Since Truth and Nature are at once transform'd
By him, the world's embodied Fiat, now.
E'en more than this!—to heights of sin beyond
These climbing blasphemies of folly scaled,

And from the temple of Jehovah took
The crown, and from the Hand Eternal robb'd
The sceptre, till from Godhead's self there seem'd
To pass all glory; and, in pontific shape,
A mock almighty was the Pope adored!

II.—Mystery.

Above, beneath, around, where'er we move
Or live, an atmosphere of myst'ry floats;
For ever baffling with its gloom unpierced
The pride of reason's analytic gaze.
E'en like that Pillar, which, of cloud and fire
Contemper'd, to the pilgrim-church bestow'd
A guidance solemn, through untrodden wilds,
So human knowledge, in this world forlorn
By shade and light alternately prevails,
Too dark for pride, too vivid for despair.
And thus, accordant with our state corrupt,
From truth to truth, the educated soul
Through shades of awe is humbled yet advanced;
While noble ignorance, that knows itself,
Kneels in the shadow of a Mercy-seat
And prays the heart to piety, and love.

Yes! all is myst'ry: from that blaze immense
In which pavilion'd dwells the Vast Unseen,
Down to the insect of minutest frame,
Science is mock'd. Within retreating depths
The Cause uncaused, above all causes throned,
Who can describe? Yet, what religion owns,
Plain reason grants,—that He is perfect One
Pervading all things with His presence whole;
Unfelt, unform'd, unheard and undefined,
All Eye, all Ear, all Spirit, and all Power,
His center, Light, and his circumf'rence, Love:
Yet, what reveals Him, Who all else reveals,—
The Unexplain'd, who yet explaineth all?
What sun to systems, God to truth appears;
But still, apart, impenetrably shrined
In secresy of light, for ever veil'd.

Then turn to nature, eloquently touch'd
With living beauty; and in sight and sound
Teeming with all which holy Truth admires:
There, though a shadow of the primal Curse
Dims the soft radiance of a virgin-world,
Traces of Eden, tracks of angel-feet
Still haunt creation with a hallowing charm:
But myst'ry, still, o'er nature's Secret broods,
Beyond philosophy's most daring ken
To master; lock'd in mute reserve it lies.
Since, *what* is Essence, *how* formation acts,
Or life and law reciprocally play,—
Can reason here mount explanation's throne?
Nature herself is thine embodied Will
Almighty! There, at last, the mind has gain'd
An ultimatum which unteaches pride;
While Genius, like a second childhood, stands,
And, rapt in wonder, to Religion turns.

And, does not Providence our life invest
With one horizon of perpetual cloud?
But while to man, his planless life appears
A problem made of paradox, and gloom,
Darkness itself may Deity enshrine
When acting mercy, in deep wisdom, there.

But now, within, profound Logician! gaze;
Down thy deep hell of consciousness descend,
Who o'er Jehovah thus presum'st to wave
The treason-banner of rebellious thought.
Thou, to thyself embodied myst'ry art;
And why? Because unfathomably bad,
And thus, by grace unfathomably heal'd!
"Deceitful, vain, and desperately vile
All things above, the heart of man is found;
And who can know it?—I, the Lord *alone!*"
Thus chants a prophet; and we seem to hear
Round all the regions of created soul
Ring his dread challenge; mute alike remain
Seraph and Angel, and the star-bright Host
Who, nearest to the fountain-source of Mind,
'Mid radiance intellectual, shine and sing:—
To each and all unsearchable abides,
The heart of Nature in the human breast.

Then, turn to grace,—the Trinity express'd
In threefold glory, yet divinely One.
There, all is myst'ry, hung with moral gloom.
Flight after flight, in vain proud Reason takes,
And seeks and soars, and soars, and seeks again,
And more confounded by the search becomes:
Till, all exhausted, like the arkless dove
Back to the shelter of a simple truth
The soul retreats, and learns by faith to live,
And love the more, the less it understands
Of the Great Secret which salvation hides,—
The how, and why, in all of Godhead, there.

And Him, the Paramount of living grace,
The Truth Incarnate, how can words reveal?
Or who by comprehension yearns to grasp
Emmanuel's Person, in our flesh array'd?—
True greatness is to know how small we are,
Who learn divinity by loving God,
And as we love, alone can understand.

III.—Mystery of Iniquity.

And thus, at length, analogy conducts
Our hearts to Thee, the consummation dire
Of myst'ries all by Antichrist sustain'd!
Around it more than twice six hundred years
Have travail'd, in the pride of priestly art;
And now, a very prodigy of mind

Depraved, of truth corrupt, and power abused,
It moulds, and masters all whom it beguiles.
Compact, complete, symmetrically form'd
To fit all hearts, whate'er the sensual frame,
Or oscillate to each exacting move,
Mental or moral, varied life presents,—
This myst'ry plays the Proteus with mankind.
From character it draws responsive tones;
From all condition wins a pleased support;
In circumstance, the very crisis wields,
And of weak conscience takes advantage vile:
Virtue and vice alike its charm obey;
And, forging chains that with no clanking fall
The ear arrest, or rouse the dormant soul;
The heart it manacles with fettering guile,
And binds it down, deluded to the last.

"A myst'ry" was this antichristian spell
In wisdom by prophetic Paul foretold;
Nor aught which infidels have dared, or done
The Lord of souls to crucify again,
Like this imposture hath mankind seduced.
There, falsehood in its open vileness reign'd;
Conspicuous, mark'd, and branded as the bad,
The heart may shun it, and securely keep
Both principle and purity awake.
But here, false Darkness, with a face of Light
Deceptively upon its victim smiles;
And, by the aspect of an angel's love,
Ruins the spirit with a demon's guile.
Here lies the danger, lurks the full deceit,—
Pretension, high as heaven's meridian truth,
Performance, low as hell's absorbing lie!
Religion thus, with suicidal hand
Herself destroys; and into death transmutes
A living zeal, which, else, for God and souls
Like inspiration might the world employ:—
Dilates a precept, or a truth contracts,
Can mould a doctrine, or a creed erect;
And round salvation such a dimness cast
That Christ is hidden, and the Church *alone*
In sacramental mist at length adored.

But yet, how stern, how lofty, how refined,
Thy vast professions, Romanistic creed!
Not Purity itself, is pure as Thou
In strictness, and severity of aim.
From the mix'd world, monastically free,
Our spirit thou would'st fain entice; and cast
Its powers in moulds of superhuman faith;
And thus, from foul entanglements of flesh
The mind deliver, till, to earthless heights
Of dazzling purity at length arrived,
That consummation of the church is reach'd,—
Meekness and martyrdom, in one combined!

The Devil is the parodist of God;
And priestly colours are the paint employ'd
To tinge his counterfeits of Truth divine
With holy semblance; and that flaming zeal
For saintliness, apostate Rome affects,
For Him has wrought satanically well.
Pollution's self on Purity's clear throne
In veil'd enchantment thus hath ruled, and reign'd,
Deceiving others, and itself deceived.
The Roman myst'ry *is* a mask of lies,
While yet thy countenance, celestial Truth!
It borrows; Mercy is the mild pretence,
Justice her theme, and love for God the law,
And zeal for Christ the Church's ardent soul
That makes Her all that miracle she is!—
Satan himself can thus religious seem,
And poison Virtue with her very smile.

Gospel and Grace in this dread system die;
And Love and Light to cruel darkness turn,
Shade upon shade, impenetrably deep,
Investing Godhead with a vile array
Of terrors, forged by sacerdotal guile,
And summon'd forth as guilt, or gain demands.
Where is The Father, in that fiction dread,
That ghastly Something, for a God believed,
Which Popery to the harrow'd Mind presents?
Or, when the ague of a guilty heart
Rages in secret, what paternal voice
From God in Christ subdues it into tears?
Then, not direct through Son and Spirit looks
A soul repentant, from the pleading eye
Of faith, on God reveal'd; but damning frowns,
Blacker than Sinai's legal night of death
To daunt the sinner, are at once evoked,
Hiding the cross with intercepting gloom:
Infinite Cruelty thus God becomes;
His throne all blackness, and His heart begirt
With stern-eyed Saints, who awe the spirit down
Till first their mediatorship is moved,
And God, persuaded by their prayer, relents!
As if by impulse an Almighty moved,
Nor in Himself His own great motive was.

IV.—Sacramental God.

But, see the climax of corrupted truth,
An Incarnation, parodied by priests!
Robed for a melodrame of mutter'd spells
Lo, where the sacerdotal Juggler stands,
Beneath whose touch the sacramental Host
To Body, Blood, Divinity, and Soul
Itself transforms, created into Christ!
Emmanuel there, consummate and complete,
Again must bleed, in Calvary revived!
Oh, horrible, and heartless mock of all
Of God in glory, or of man in grace,
That He, whose Person is the Sum and Soul

Of what in time Eternity shall act
High o'er the senses, or mere reason's grasp,—
Is now in sacramental bread *contain'd*
While the blest wafer turns embodied God.*

And Thou, O Spirit! who alone canst rule
The hearts where pantheistic darkness reigns,
Or carnal gods, by dreaming passion shaped,
Debauch the conscience till its light goes out,

* To justify "Transubstantiation," the following is the evidence afforded to us by the "Catechism of the Council of Trent, published by command of Pope Pius the Fifth," as "Translated into English by the Rev. J. Donovan, Professor, &c., Royal College, Maynooth," p. 230.

A perusal of this will convince the reader that notwithstanding the sternness and sarcasm wherewith the Romish Church has accused "Protestantism" for "rationalising" away the highest mysteries of Faith, she is herself guilty of most daring rationalism in thus daring to theorise concerning the mode of the Real Presence in the Eucharist.

"To explain this mystery in a proper manner is extremely difficult. On the manner of this admirable conversion, the pastor, however, will endeavour to instruct those who are more advanced in the knowledge and contemplation of divine things: those who are yet weak may, it were to be apprehended, be overwhelmed by its greatness. This conversion, then, is so effectuated that the whole substance of the bread and wine is changed by the power of God, into the whole substance of the body of Christ, and the whole substance of the wine, into the whole substance of his blood, and this, without any change in our Lord himself; he is neither begotten, nor changed, nor increased, but remains entirely and substantially the same. This sublime mystery, S. Ambrose thus declares: 'You see how efficacious are the words of Christ; if, then, the word of the Lord Jesus is so powerful as to summon creation into existence, shall it not require a less exercise of power to make that subsist which already has existence, and to change it into another thing?'[1] Many other Fathers, whose authority is too grave to be questioned, have written to the same effect 'We faithfully confess,' says S. Augustine, 'that before consecration it is bread and wine, the produce of nature; but after consecration it is the body and blood of Christ, consecrated by the blessing.'[2] 'The body,' says Damascene, 'is truly united to the divinity, the body assumed of the Virgin; not that the body thus assumed descends from heaven, but that the bread and wine are changed into the body and blood of Christ.'[3] This admirable change, as the Council of Trent teaches, the Catholic church most appropriately expresses by the word 'transubstantiation.'[4] When in the natural order the form of a being is changed, that change may be properly termed 'a transformation;' in like manner, when in the Sacrament of the Eucharist, the whole substance of one thing passes into the whole substance of another, the change our predecessors in the faith wisely and appropriately called 'transubstantiation.' But according to the admonition so frequently repeated by the Holy Fathers, the faithful are to be admonished against the danger of gratifying a prurient curiosity, by searching into the manner in which this change is effected. It mocks the powers of conception, nor can we find any example of it in natural transmutations, nor even in the wide range of creation. The change itself is the object, not of our comprehension, but of our humble faith; and the manner of that change forbids the temerity of a too curious inquiry.[1]

"The same salutary caution should also be observed by the pastor, with regard to the mysterious manner in which the body of our Lord is contained whole and entire under the least particle of the bread.[2] Such inscrutable mysteries should scarcely ever become matter of disquisition. Should Christian charity, however, require a departure from this salutary rule, the pastor will recollect first to prepare and fortify his hearers, by reminding them, that 'no word shall be impossible with God.'[3]

"The pastor will next teach, that our Lord is not in the Sacrament as in a place; place regards things, only inasmuch as they have magnitude; and we do not say that Christ is in the Sacrament, inasmuch as he is great or small, terms which belong to quantity, but inasmuch as he is a substance. The substance of the bread is changed into the substance of Christ, not into magnitude or quantity; and substance, it will be acknowledged, is contained in a small as well as in a large space. The substance of air, for instance, whether in a large or in a small quantity, and that of water, whether confined in a vessel or flowing in a river, must necessarily be the same. As, then, the body of our Lord succeeds to the substance of the bread, we must confess it to be in the Sacrament, after the same manner as the bread was before consecration; whether the substance of the bread was present in greater or less quantity is a matter of entire indifference.

"We now come to the third effect produced by the words of consecration, the existence of the species of bread and wine in the Sacrament without a subject, an effect as stupendous as it is admirable. What has been said in explanation of the two preceding points must facilitate the exposition of this mysterious truth. We have already proved that the body and blood of our Lord are really and truly contained in the Sacrament, to the entire exclusion of the substance of the bread and wine: the accidents cannot inhere in the body and blood of Christ: they must, therefore, contrary to the physical laws, subsist of themselves, inhering in no subject. This has been, at all times, the doctrine of the Catholic Church; and the same authorities by which we have already proved that the substance of the bread and wine ceases to exist in the Eucharist, go to establish its truth. But it becomes the piety of the faithful, omitting subtle disquisitions, to revere and adore, in the simplicity of faith, the majesty of this august sacrament; and with sentiments of gratitude and admiration, to recognise the wisdom of God in the institution of the holy mysteries, under the species of bread and wine. To eat human flesh or to drink human blood, is

[1] D. Ambr. l. 4. de sacr. c. 4.
[2] Citatur de consec. dist. 2. can. "Nos autem," &c.
[3] Lib. iv. de orthod. fid. c. 14.
[4] Trid. sess. 13, c. 4, et can. 2, et de consec. distinct. 2, c. panis.

[1] Eccl. iii. 22.
[2] D. Thom. 3, p. q. 76, Trid. sess. 13, c. 3, et can. 3, et Florent. in decret. Eugen.
[3] Luke i. 37.

With what an aping Liturgy of lies
Hath Romish parody presumed to mock
The might, and glory of Thy work august!
And dared, for living waters freshly drawn
From the deep fountains of eternity
And truth, Herself to substitute, and lift
Her canons vile to revelation's throne.

When thus the life-blood of religion's drain'd
By this fell vampire, what for man is left
But the mere carcass of a ritual show,
A mindless worship, meaningless as false,
Where man is God, and God to man transform'd?

Thou dread Almighty! may we dare repeat
With deep-toned echo, that mysterious Cry
Apocalyptic martyrs lift above,
And chant, "How long shall Grace Eternal be
By juggling Rome dishonour'd, and traduced?
How long shall falsehood wear the saintly dress
Of truth celestial, while the Cross is veil'd,
And He, whose merit is creation's shield,
The church's light, and providence's law,
High o'er His Throne, behold anointed dust
And sainted villains, canonised and cowl'd,
Ascend beyond Him, in their plea for grace!"
'Tis thus, the laurels from the brow of Christ
Are taken, and around the head enwreathed
Of Antichrist, for twice six hundred years,—
That aping monster, who travesties God
And in the glory of his darkness seems
A mimic Satan, on Messiah's throne! *

most revolting to human nature, and therefore has God, in his infinite wisdom, established the administration of the body and blood of Christ, under the forms of bread and wine, the ordinary and agreeable food of man. From its administration under these forms also flow two other important advantages: it obviates the calumnious reproaches of the unbeliever, to which a manducation of the body and blood of our Lord, under human form, must be exposed; whilst by receiving him under a form in which he is impervious to the senses, our faith is augmented, 'which,' as S. Gregory observes, 'has no merit in those things which fall under the jurisdiction of reason.' But what has been hitherto said on this subject demands much prudent precaution in its exposition; and in this the pastor will be guided by the capacity of his hearers, by times and circumstances.

"We therefore confess that the sacrifice of the Mass is one and the same sacrifice with that of the cross: the victim is one and the same, Christ Jesus, who offered himself, once only, a bloody sacrifice on the altar of the cross. The bloody and unbloody victim is still one and the same, and the oblation of the cross is daily renewed in the eucharistic sacrifice, in obedience to the command of our Lord, 'This do for a commemoration of me.' The Priest is also the same, Christ our Lord; the ministers who offer this sacrifice consecrate the holy mysteries, not in their own but in the person of Christ. This the words of consecration declare: the Priest does not say, 'This is the body of Christ,' but 'This is my body;' and thus invested with the character of Christ, he changes the substance of the bread and wine into the substance of his real body and blood. That the holy sacrifice of the Mass, therefore, is not only a sacrifice of praise and thanksgiving, or a commemoration of the sacrifice of the cross, but also a sacrifice of propitiation, by which God is appeased and rendered propitious, the pastor will teach as a dogma, defined by the unerring authority of a General Council of the church.

* As the author has been severely censured, in certain quarters, for thus denouncing the ritual abominations of the Mass, he feels it due, alike to his own position as a catholic churchman, and also to the sacred cause of truth, to vindicate the ground he has taken; and before he does so, he wishes the reader to remember one point, i. e., the quotations which occupy this note are not descriptions from Protestant sources, but the formal utterance and dogmatic teachings of the Romish Church herself, as they are developed in her Canons, and Standards. Nothing is easier than to charge this work with distortions and exaggerations; and yet the writer dares to ask, with what conscientious reverence for scriptural orthodoxy, or, on what principle of loyal adherence to his own Apostolic Church in England, can any man do so, who will diligently read and reflect on the following fearful self-description of the papal communion?

The Romish doctrine of the Mass, is thus stated in the fifth article of the Creed of Pope Pius VII.—

"V. I profess, likewise, that in the Mass there is offered to God a true, proper, and propitiatory sacrifice for the living and the dead; and that in the most holy Sacrament of the Eucharist there are truly, really, and substantially the body and blood, together with the soul and divinity, of our Lord Jesus Christ; and that there is made a conversion of the whole substance of the bread into the body, and of the whole substance of the wine into the blood: which conversion the Catholic Church calls transubstantiation. I also confess, that under either kind alone, Christ is received whole and entire, and a true sacrament!"

With regard to the first point, the Church of Rome teaches, "Council of Trent," Sess. 22, Canon 3:—

"If any one shall say that the sacrifice of the Mass is only a sacrifice of praise and thanksgiving, or a bare commemoration of the sacrifice made upon the cross, and that it is not propitiatory, or that it profits only the receiver, and that it ought not to be offered for the living and the dead for their sins, punishments, satisfactions, and other necessities: let him be accursed."

TRANSUBSTANTIATION.

The Papal Church as to the second point in the fifth Article of the Creed, binds upon her members to believe—

"That in the most holy Sacrament of the Eucharist there are truly, really, and substantially, the body and blood, together with the soul and divinity of our Lord Jesus Christ."

In Canon 1, Session 13, of the Council of Trent (on the Eucharist), the Church of Rome decrees:—

"Whoever shall deny, that in the most holy sacrament of the Eucharist there are truly, really, and substantially, contained the body and blood of our Lord Jesus Christ, together with his soul and divinity,

V.—Moral Root.

But, whence this power, which paralyses men
To dull machines, for priestly hands to work,
That from the Cross all crucifixion takes,
And shuts the fountain in Emmanuel's side,
Whence gush'd atonement for the World's great sin,
Till Christ with closèd wounds remains,
Shorn of those beams, which round His ransom play,
And form a Merit fit for man to plead,
Ample as Justice, Law, and God require?
Whence the dread magic, which so mocks the world,
Soothing pale conscience with Iscariot's kiss?
Look in thy heart! there, reader! there it lies.
As fits the die within the forming mould
So false religion for thy heart is framed.

Thy fountains, Nature! are the fatal spring
Whence Popery all her canker'd life-blood drains,
And drains for ever—for they ever flow!
A moral cast from our corrupted soul
Designing Rome hath taken; and contrived
A feign'd religion, that, with fitting art,
Infernally for each expression finds
Some flatt'ring counterpart, or creed, or charm.
'Tis Man's religion from the root of sin,

---

and, consequently, Christ entire; but shall affirm, that he is present therein only in a sign or figure or by his power; let him be accursed."

Also, in the Catechism of the Council of Trent (p. 226), Rome states as follows:—

"Here the pastor will explain, not only that the true body of Christ, and whatever belongs to the true constitution (rationem) of a body, as the bones and sinews, but also, a whole Christ is contained in this Sacrament; that the word Christ designates the Man-God, that is to say, one person in whom are united the human and divine natures; that the holy Eucharist, therefore, *contains* both, and whatever is included in the idea of both, the divinity and humanity whole and entire, the soul, the body and blood of Christ, with *all their component parts*, all of which faith teaches us are contained in the Sacrament."

But can *that* be the body of Christ, in reference to which the following rule is laid down in the "Roman Missal," on "the Defects of the Mass?"—

"If the priest vomit the Eucharist, and the species appear entire, they must be severally swallowed, unless nausea prevent; and in that case the consecrated species must be cautiously separated from the vomit, and laid by in some sacred place until they be corrupted, and afterwards they are to be thrown into the tabernacle (sacrarium); but if the species do not appear, the vomit must be burned, and the ashes thrown into the tabernacle!!!"

As respects the fourth point in Article V. of the Creed of Pope Pius IV., the Romish communion binds her members to believe as follows:—

"I also confess, that under either kind alone, Christ is received, whole and entire, and a true Sacrament."

In Canon 3, Session 13, of the Council of Trent (on the Eucharist), the Church of Rome decrees as follows:—

"Whosoever shall deny, that Christ entire is contained in the venerable Sacrament of the Eucharist, under each species, and under every part of each species, when they are separated: let him be accursed."

Also in Canon 4 (same session), we read:—

"Whosoever shall affirm, that the body and blood of our Lord Jesus Christ are not present in the admirable Eucharist, as soon as the consecration is performed, but only as it is used and received, and neither before nor after; and that the true body of our Lord does not remain in the hosts or consecrated morsels which are reserved or left after communion; let him be accursed."

The following rule is also enjoined respecting the wine ("Roman Missal," "Defects of the Mass"):—

"If, after the consecration, a gnat, a spider, or any such thing fall into the chalice, and if it produce nausea, to the priest, let him draw it out, and wash it with the wine; and when Mass is concluded, let him burn it, and let him throw the ashes and the washings into a sacred place. But if there is no nausea and he fears none, let him swallow it with the blood!!!

"If in winter the blood be frozen in the cup, put warm cloths about the cup; if that will not do, let it be put into boiling water, near the altar, till it be melted, taking care it does not come into the cup.

"If any of the blood of Christ fall on the ground, or table, by negligence, it must be licked up with the tongue, the place must be thoroughly scraped, and the scrapings burned; but the ashes must be buried in holy ground"!!!

Finally, and to wind up this dreadful, but necessary evidence against Rome, let the reader who venerates the Body and Blood of Christ as Sacramentally present in the Eucharist, read the following, and ask his heart whether the line in "Luther,"

"An Incarnation parodied by Priests,"

has, in the least degree, distorted the truth?

Thus then, the Roman Church teaches (on the defects of the Mass), that the validity of the consecration depends on the following:—

"First. That the bread be of pure wheaten flour.

"Second. That it be not made with distilled water.

"Third. That it be not leavened.

"Fourth. That the wine be not sour or putrid, or be made of bitter or unripe grapes, or be mixed with so much water as to spoil the wine.

"Fifth. Due disposition of soul.

"Sixth. Due adjustment of the body.

"Seventh. Due arrangement of garments.

"Eighth. Due disposition in the service itself, as to those matters which can occur in it.

"Ninth. That the minister intend to consecrate, and not to counterfeit; also, if any wafers remain forgotten on the altar, or if any part of the wine or any wafer lie hid, when he did not intend to consecrate but what he saw; also, if he shall have before him eleven wafers and intended to consecrate but ten only, not determining what ten he meant, in all these cases there is no consecration, because intention is required.

By passion foster'd, and by pride increased,
Deep-grounded, in the under-soil intense
Where guilty nature feels the goading pang,
As conscience prompts, or keen compunction wakes.
Hence, creeds are moulded; hence, all gods are made;
While reason, bribed to superstition, bows,
As sin and penance take relieving turns;
Till man himself his own atonement dreams,
And draws salvation out of sighs, and tears.

And thus, not Mind, whate'er its lofty range
Along the pathless Infinite of thought,
A shielding bulwark round the man can raise,
Safely to keep one Romish error out.
For oft, religion is but God disguised;
And when its nature from the name is torn
Mere sounds and shades for sense and substance act;
And cheated man a human mock adores.
But God is love, by his *Own* love inspired,
As seen the sun, by His own ray reveal'd.

Then, vain those pæans which we loudly ring,
As though the great millennium of the mind
Were coming; or, a mental noon began,
Too searching for the Man of Sin to face.
Philosophy the sting of Death renews
And back the vict'ry to the grave restores.
Whatever prospect soaring mind attain
No good it masters, till in God it rest,
Where peace and pardon, law and love combine,
And Christ and conscience can together dwell.
And why? because *some* creed embrace we must;
From heaven or hell religion must be drawn.
For deep within, prognostications lurk
Of tongueless dread; and boding terrors strike
Their hidden chill; and throbs immortal stir,
Like pulses of eternity, our souls;
While moods are felt, when flames of wrath to come
Prelude damnation, such as Guilt foretells,
Till the grave opens through the banquet's glare
And time's last thunders their rehearsal ring.
Though sin confront it, yet will Conscience speak,
Till sear'd, and branded into senseless nought.
Shrined in the centre of our being, dwells
That voiceless Umpire, on his moral throne
Erect, and pure; whose archetype is God,
In the stern radiance of severest law
Reflected there, for legislative might.
Here, Right and Wrong their true award receive;
And Past and Present for acquittal stand,
Or, condemnation from the bar receive;
Here Man, the ruin, in his ashes keeps
Some righteous embers, which a priest can rake,
Or quench, or quicken, as the crisis needs.

When darkly flatter'd, and when deeply read,
Our hearts become but platforms, where a Priest
Can play the drama of his Church, at will,
And shift the scenes with most consummate guile.
Some charm which echoes our exacting taste,
Some lust respondent to the varied will,
Some lie, to oscillate with pleasing sway
And skill'd vibration, as the mood requires,
Some gulling fiend to take angelic form,
And o'er the pathway which to hell conducts
Weave a rich carpet of seductive woof,—
Let these be organised, or well applied,
And man's religion in their magic proves
How wondrously such adaptation works!
Garb'd in a shroud of theologic guise
Behold the Arch-fiend, with undreaded power
His priesthood guiding; and, with ritual spells
To sooth or sadden, flatter, charm or chain
All which in Man of dust or devil acts,
Gild moral ruin with redemption's smile!
Thus, like a puppet, many-wired and weak,
Our handled nature to each sacred pull
Of Popery moves, with most responsive play.

Art thou a Student, from the pristine wells
Of learning, pleased and proud with classic thirst
To drink rich draughts of undiluted Mind?
Or, is thine ear by intellectual taste
To harmonies of ancient thought attuned?
See! the hoar'd Fathers in their hallow'd shrines,
And pale Philosophy, in pensive state,
Ready to bathe thee in some mental calm,
And soothe thy terrors with ascetic trance.
Or, (to the chariot of the senses chain'd)
Do glare and grandeur, and attractive sheens,
And Pomps, and Festivals, and painted Lies
With false and fatal eloquence, appeal
To the base passion of thine earthly will?
Lo! the drunk Sense with reasonless delight
May find a Ball-room spiritually gay,
A ritual opera, by Rome arranged,
Where the blood dances, where emotion reels
While soft damnation, musical and sweet,
Charms faith to feeling, and each feeling, blind!

VI.—Religious Instinct.

But, most to that religiously-depraved
Self-righteous dream of ever-prompting Pride,—
From earth to heaven to win or work its way,
Adapting Popery, with mimetic art

Her necromance of ritual pomp applies.
A finite Self to infinite transform'd,
Some Trentine god by moral fiction shaped,
Is all that Passion's creed impure desires;
And lo ! in Rome the heart's vile canons meet
Their very echo ! grace and sin conjoin'd,
An outward form for inner-life prepared,
A dead religion where no God remains,—
Here is thy Charm, thou sorceress of souls !
Self-gain'd salvation forms thy secret force :
Hence liturgies, to please corruption plann'd;
Hence creeds, to flatter hope, or bribe a fear,
And all the pantomime of bows, and beads.
Thus perfect in pure falsity, Thou seem'st
By the Great Liar of the world inspired,
To set the Adam of the sensual mind
In motion; feeling, so that nothing's felt,
And working, so that nothing's truly wrought
As Law proclaims, or holy love demands.
Yet, nature, pleased with self-atonement, dares
Blindly to merit what mere Grace bestows,
And parts with all things, sin alone except !

And thus, machines, by blind devotion turn'd
For rites external, Rome's deluded slaves
Become; automatons for priestly guile,
Moving, or motionless, as *that* inspires;
For, each false yearning of self-righteous will
In Popery some pleasing vent can find.
Devout fanatics, passionately wed
To forms, where sense o'er spirit domineers,
May there a sanctimonious refuge gain,
From seeming prayer, to suit a prayerless heart,
Down to the beads dull Superstition counts.
Rome loves the Crucifix, but hates the Cross !
And thus, whatever gull'd Emotion longs
Upon her shrine of selfishness to lay,
Her human gospel cunningly applies;
Cheating the soul with skeletons of truth.
No taste, but here a subtle pleasure finds;
No sentiment, but what some echo meets;
Nor fancy, which no fellowship can find.
There, Painting, with its poetry of hues,
And Music, with its poetry of sound,
And temples, with their poetry of stone,
All, all compose a theologic cheat
That charms the spirit from its saviour-God.

VII.—Sorcery.

But thou ! Imagination's martyr'd fool,
Whose faith is fancy, in religion's dress,
Whose shining virtues are but gilded vice
Seen by the Bible's heart-exploring beam,
For thee the cup of Antichrist is drugg'd
With rapt intoxication's master-spells !
Anthems, which seem to roll from Angel-harps,
And silver chants, that Seraphim might sing;
Paintings, where Beauty's virgin grace
Divinely-mortal, exquisitely smiles;
And sights superb, processions' vast array,
Or cloisters pale, where Pensiveness may roam,
Or perfumed incense, with its spiral clouds
Floating to heaven, before the vested priests,
Whose robes with sacramental meaning wave;
All these, with Churches, where religion stamps
The very stones with symbolising force,
And painted windows, by their colours, preach
Sermons which strike imagination dumb,
Or, melt it in soft martyrdom of sighs,—
Here is the weaving of those spells which bind
Millions to darkness, in the chains of Rome !
Whose mock religion The Almighty veils,
And each fine essence out of saving truth
Evaporates, in Forms which stifle faith,
And from the heart its vital heaven exclude :
For, what is holiness but heaven below ?
Or heaven itself, but holiness above ?

But, in some crisis of mysterious gloom
When frowns almighty round the heart of guilt
Darker than death-shades, dismal as profound,
Hover and hang, the buried past revives
Till dead Hours quicken in their secret graves,
The Infinite a voicely fear becomes,
And all of God to all in man appeals
For vengeance ! Horeb is on fire again,
In thunder preaching its horrific curse.
Now, seems a Sinai in the soul of man !
Erected there by that instinctive law
Which Nature's creed must canonize, and own :
And oft, beneath its altitudes of gloom
Pale terrors, and alarm'd compunctions fall,
By strong enforcement, at its awful base;
Till the bow'd spirit trembles into tears,
While thunder-peals of God-proclaiming truth
Preach to our guilt th' uncompromising Law
Which conscience echoes with responsive groan.
Then doubts, which make a Golgotha of mind,
Madden the sinner with a fest'ring sway :
The wind was sown,—the whirlwind hence is reap'd;
The seed was darkness—and the fruit is death !
And where, now pleasure's silken trance is o'er
And fear'd eternity with curses rings,
Shall the torn spirit some true refuge find ?
Oh, fell imposture ! priestly Fiction comes;
And all its juggl'ry of cheating lies,
Indulgence vain, and penances most vile
Which keep the sinner from the saving Cross,
Again renews; the soul with opium drugs;
Infernal laud'num blinded Conscience drinks,
Till thus, from terror into torpor soothed,
Her sunken witness in stagnation dies;
And the torn Heart, by self-atonement heal'd,
Back to its smiles of sinful peace returns

To drink from pleasure draughts of death once more,
Like a mad infant to its mother's breast,
Though pale, and poison'd by some murd'rous hand.

Here is thy venom, here thy spring of strength,
Thou master-spell of Satan's master-piece!
With all the finish of a fiend contrived
To soothe the conscience, when a rack begins;
To keep the penance and a priest in play;
To hold the sinner, but let loose the sin,
And by Confession to absorb the Cross.
Thus, papal lies to nature's roots descend;
They fix, they fasten in the moral soil
Their foul adjustment. Man is papal born,
And false religion must be papal too;
And his exacting nature nicely fit
In heart, in conscience, and uncertain will.
For sin, when loved, for punishment, when fear'd,
Consummate Rome hath thus for both prepared
A recipé, that 'tween the two can act:
A sop for Conscience—when it pleads with dread,
And sin for Passion—when that dread is o'er:
And thus, beneath the burning eye of Heaven,
No parody of truth like this, deceives;
No spell, by genius of satanic might
Forged in the secrecy of mystic lies,
No miracle of dread imposture, works
Perdition with so masterly success
As when God's will, travestied and transform'd,
To Man becomes religion; and *from* heaven
Beguiles him, while it *seems* to guide him There.

INSPIRATION OF THE IDEAL.

'Tween two eternities each hour is born
Of present Being; in the midst, our mind,
(Through some deep sense of undevelop'd power,
Haunted for ever by the Unattain'd)
Fevers, and frets with intellectual thirst
For more of Perfect, Beautiful, or Pure,
For more of Truth, in majesty and might
Than ever rises on the reaching sense,
Or, seems embodied in the shape of Things.
The Infinite we love, and half adore;
Our heaven of feeling seeks a heaven of fact,—
An outward Image, whose responsive mould
May body forth Imagination's dream.
And hence, enthroned in some ethereal calm,
Conceptive Genius from creation draws
Types of vast truth, and symbols of the soul,
To aid Perception, when its shaping power
Would vision out a universe of Love,
And Ideality in life reveal.

But if, beyond what Nature's world supplies
A yearning soul for moral beauty thirsts,
Creative Thought, by combination frames
From all which heroes of the heart have felt,
Or martyrs of the sleepless mind portray'd,
Or dreamt in prison-gloom, or palace-smiles,
A model of true consummated Man!
And, noble is such discontent of soul
Which leads to Virtue's elevating path;
The mind unprisons; or, from chaining Sense,
That coarsely to the common life of things
Would bind us down in drudgery and death,
To freedom and infinitude allures
The man within. And hence, all dreamings high
And holy; hence, imagination's flight;
And aspirations, fetterless and pure.
For, in this orbit of mysterious Life
The central immortality is Man;
And, greater far than all the greatness seen
One viewless Thought of his observing Mind!
Since what the apprehending sense beholds
Forms but a veil, through which are dimly view'd
Deep intimations of diviner Things,
And preludes faint of far profounder Truth
And Beauty, yet by God to be unveil'd.
'Tis thus, the poetry of heart begins,
The painter's longing, and the sculptor's love,
Which purify from sensual dross and guile
Our inner-life, with sacramental force;
Hence, Homer drew; and solemn Milton drank
The inspirations of a deathless song.
In beautiful transcendencies of thought
From earthly matter into heavenly forms.
They soar'd, for ever; and, by shaping dreams,
Imaged a life above the life they felt
And breathed the immortality they sung.
'Tis thus, by passion for the Infinite,
And glorious longings for some Perfect Good,
The heart's millennium, in all ages, acts:
Hence Liberty her laurell'd hero frames,
Martyr, and saint, and sage their stamp receive,
Religion half her purity obtains,
And the bright paradise of Morals blooms.

Thus Luther, in his lone and lofty zeal
Impetuous, bold, and ardent as sublime,
With feelings vivid like the soul they fired,
Who led the exodus of man and mind
From the vile Egypt of enslaving Rome
To Canaan's borders, in the world of truth,—
E'en like a prophet, o'er predestined scenes
Above the cold, the actual, and the coarse
Mounted aloft; and sleeplessly pursued

Through tears and torture, outrage, grief, and wrong,
Through storm and cloud, convulsion and contempt,
That great Exemplar which his mind conceived.
Beauty and Brightness their ideal thrones
Erected in him; while their magic spell
Temper'd his heart for each ethereal type.
And so, by Pre-conception's purest charm
Master'd and moulded, his frail being grew;
He lived the Poetry which others thought;
And from that hour when friendly capture threw
A shroud of safety round his perill'd head
Where the lone castle of Altenstein frown'd,
To that famed crisis, when from cell and chain
Heaven's cloister'd Principles came forth to breathe,
Pale from the prison of a thousand years,
His passion for the Perfect and the Pure
Nerved him for wonders! Like that mystic Voice,
Which often to the soul of seers reveal'd
Visions of Godhead, vocal and distinct,
Heaven-ward, for plans archangels might have cheer'd,
Pure Inspiration seem'd to guide him on.
Gigantic efforts, flush'd with sacred zeal,
And high endeavours, honourably vast,
Ardours intense, with flames of moral ire,
A mental freedom, or that tameless force
Which grappled ever with imagined Fiends,—
All were expressions of one master-wish;
The indications of a Soul, inspired
To be the great Apostle of mankind
In deeds of glory, for a cause divine.
The sigh of Nature with herself to blend
And bind, in one fond brotherhood of faith,
The feelings and the family of Man;
A New Jerusalem on earth to hail;
A Church redeem'd to apostolic mould;
A reigning Jesus, a rejoicing World,—
To such bright centres of consummate hope
Did Luther, with ideal passion, tend;
These made the goal to which he onward press'd,
The lofty mark, at which his virtue aim'd;
And from the level of a monk's low range
Lifted on high his ever-loving heart,
And bade him, in a sunless age, to shine
A moral saviour o'er eclipsed mankind.

MAMMON AND MATERIALISM.

Oh, for a Luther to inspire us now!
Th' awaking magic of some mind God-taught
To charm the sensual from the Nation's soul;
Our passions dark, our appetites of dust
To brighten, or to banish; till the love
Of whatsoe'er is lofty, and divine,
Of whatsoe'er is glorious, and august,
The throne of public Taste may re-ascend,
Give life to Genius, and a law to thought,
And for the Beautiful true homage gain.
Woe to the Land! whose days are evil now:
Venality in vulgar glory reigns;
Profit and Loss intense inspirers are;
The Arts are pining in neglected gloom,
Sculpture is dead, and Poetry in tears;
And Science mostly for the palate reigns!
Utility, a social god becomes,
And Britain but as Dives, longs to live
In pomp and purple, and in sumptuous joy.
The universe for comfort seems arranged;
The world,—a warehouse for convenience plann'd!
And that Creation, which to faith appears
An outer-court to God's more secret shrine,
Is made a temple, where the Senses may
Adore the Useful, with vile worship now.

Alas! for England when her god is gold,
And nought believed but what coarse passions love;
When all of spirit, found in tasteful lore,
In effort noble, or sublime in aim,
A mock becomes, till principle expires,
And base Expediency's polluted breath
Falls, like a mildew, over minds and men.
Romance is faded; sentiment extinct;
All the fine chivalries of ancient Faith
Are laugh'd away, as meaningless, or vain:
While Dulness prospers in her leaden smiles,
And mediocrity, with damping weight,
Each nobler faculty and sacred power
Darkens, at last, to intellectual death,
And leaves to Manhood little but a name.

Oh, for a spirit of reviving truth,
A resurrection from the grave of Mind!
That soon the harmonies of olden thought,
Like buried music, from the past may rise
In solemn cadence, and our souls becalm.
Let Finite in the Infinite be merged;
Let Fancy dream, Imagination dare,
And Effort triumph in heroic forms
Till Art and Genius glorify the world,
And Science from her dreams of sensual bliss
Turn to the Soul, and there, with rev'rent gaze,
Deep within deep those springs of Nature trace,
Where most the unapparent Spirit works,
And awful Conscience from Her secret throne
Each lawless movement of the soul condemns;
Or like an Oracle is ever found
Approving virtue, and proclaiming heaven.

COVENANT OF HEARTS.

Bound in the links of that ethereal Chain
Which upward, from the insect's tiny pulse
On earth that throbs, to yonder wheeling orbs
Enormous, its unbroken coil extends,
Are all things by the Hand almighty held.
And thus, what chance to vulgar sense appears,
Is veil'd causation, and confirm'd decree.
Nature herself, through each organic change
And form, or function, is but Will supreme,
In might, or beauty, marching to result
Predestined. Not an atom is consumed;
No leaf can vibrate, not a billow laugh,
Nor wild breeze flutter on its fairy wing,
But God o'errules it, with control as nice
As that which belts the planets with a zone
Of harmony, and binds the stars with law.
And though mere chaos, to an eye immersed
In sensual darkness, Life's perturbèd scene
Must ever be, not thus to them who scan
The world's confusion by celestial light
From scripture beaming, does mysterious time
Appear. For then, disorder is but plan
Divinely-working, by arranged degrees
Upward and onward into truth evolved
Through the long maze of labyrinthine wills,
Or human actions. Kings, and slaves, and priests;
Erected monarchies, or crumbled thrones;
The shout of warriors, or an infant's wail;
In life, in faith, in conduct, or in creed
Whate'er be witness'd, God behind the scene
From His high watch-tower of incessant sway
Governs, and guides the blended Whole of man.
Never the Eye omniscient drops its lid,
Or slumbers: whether Virtue's godlike brow
Be laurell'd, and the Church's heart exult;
Or dark temptation, like a Demon come,
Harness the soul, and lash Desire along
To ruin,—in that change, no change exists.
For in the freedom of the foulest will
Venting itself in vanity, or vice;
Or in the soarings of a strong-wing'd faith
That heavenward mounts, and leaves low earth behind,
Around them moves One all-inclusive Will
Which, leaving man responsible and free,
For God retains supremacy and law.

And none, whose souls, by sacred fear made wise,
The lesson of their weakness well have learn'd;
Or rightly weigh'd, how much from ties of love
And charms of social power the moral frame
Impression gathers,—dare to Chance ascribe
A covenant of Hearts, when struck between
Two in the faith, accordant and conjoin'd.
Pure Love our moral gravitation makes;
At once the motion, and the rest of man:
But when, and where, and how electric chains
Are closely fasten'd into Friendship's heart,
Should make us ponder; since for bane, or bliss,
Over man's conscious destiny they cast
A character Eternity will not efface!
Since Love is plastic; and by secret charm
Shapes to resemblance with its moral self
Our yielded bosom; and the yearning heart
Thus takes the likeness of each thing it loves,—
E'en as some insect from the herb derives
A hue responsive to the food it eats.
Hence, only virtue forms a solid base
Rooted, and grounded in the heart of truth,
Where friendship's high and holy structure stands
Bedeck'd, and order'd, by approving Heaven.
Two Finites can no lasting friendship make;
Between them both an Infinite must stand,
And He is God! Without Him, all is mock;
The paint and pageant of a soul's outside
By fancy colour'd, or by feeling tinged;
But, wanting holiness, that All it needs
Which crowns a friendship with undying charm.
Fair Amity! when thus, indeed, the fruit
Of sacred principle, by love inspired,
Thy bloom is fragrant of yon world of bliss
Ethereal, and with fadeless beauty rife.
And such, when Luther and Melancthon's heart
In oneness holy blended their deep powers,
Wert thou; a friendship from the Cross which sprang
In the green fulness of their common faith.
And, in the archives of the past, how few
The feelings, that more lovingly have twined
A wreath of nature round the brow of grace,
Than those, which from the young and verdant breast
Of their twin Manhood, did together rise!

DISTINCT BUT UNDIVIDED.

Distinct in tone, yet undivided, both
Their hearts in melody combined, and met.
But if in nature poesy would find
Their fancied echo, hark! the torrent's fall
In liquid thunder foaming loud and fierce,
From crag to crag precipitous, and bold,—
And there, is Luther; while, along the banks
Tree-shaded, list, yon low and quiet stream,
And mark! the mild Melancthon. Each to each
A grace of contrast, and the charm which glows
Round minds which vary while the hearts embrace,

Imparted: both in one vast work converged;
And oh! what hours of evangelic peace,
What hymns of soul, what praises blent with prayers,
What feelings high amid the haunted woods
Of Wittemberg, were oft by each enjoy'd!
And in the lassitude of lofty cares
When, crush'd beneath his adamantine wrongs,
The soul of Luther lay in bleeding gloom,
How the calm sunshine of Melancthon's face
Around him shed some heart-restoring smile!
But o'er Thy page, Eternal Wisdom! most
Did their high friendship in communion blend;
As truth on truth, from out the classic grave
Of language, where dead meanings were entomb'd,
Started to life in Luther's noble tongue
Till Fatherland its own free bible hail'd,
And God in German to his country spake.
Thus, day by day, that Book of Heaven became
A sabbath-port from earth's tempestuous cares,
Which raged and roll'd around them: scene and time
And circumstance, those mast'ring three in one
That make, or mar the All mere worldlings dream,
To them were shadows, which the radiant Word
Dazzled to nought, as clouds in sunbeams die.
The monarch's palace, or the monk's low cell,
Or chamber dim, from out whose frescoed walls
In massy framework look'd the pictured Dead
Who live in hues immortal,*—'twas alike
To men, who on this world, were *in* the next,
By faith or feeling ever wafted there.

Then, what are base alliances, miscall'd
By friendship's name, but artificial modes,
Or satires on the sacredness and sense
Of this high virtue?—mere enamell'd lies!
Too often are they but a painted show
Of pleased Hypocrisy, whose silken ties
Are light as gossamer, before the storm
Severe affliction round our lot may bring.
Convenience; lucre; folly, pride, or gain;
A ride, a dinner, or a small request;
Or sad communion in the common sin
By passion cherish'd—there, mock friendships reach
A zenith, and their noblest zeal expires.
But when, alas! unbodied, and unveil'd
Of earth's false trappings, in the world of souls
These gay companions of a feast and song
Meet in stern truth, unmantled to the core,
Hideously naked, to the very heart
Discover'd,—how each mask of Self will drop!
And many a cheek, by radiant kindness clothed,
Blacken with hate, with horror, or revenge
Infernal: friendship now is ruin found;
And soft-mouth'd men, who seem'd, in time, so dear,
Will each to each satanical appear
And loathe, like fiends, their lost eternity!

But, cast your friendship into chaster mould;
Let genius, learning, or congenial taste,
Or fellowship like what the Muses love,
Refined as Lælius felt, or Scipio found;
Or, let Parnassus sing how poets loved,
Whose lives and verses did together run
And softly blend, like interwoven streams,
E'en at the best, such earth-born magic dies
Soon as dark shadows of the grave begin
To pall the Present, and its passing joys.
Then, all their sweetness and their strength depart!
Bred from the world, they, with the world, recede;
Friendship and flesh, together in one tomb
They perish; for, each lack'd that saving life
Which makes immortal what we cherish here.

CHRISTIAN FRIENDSHIP.

But there is friendship pure as angels love;
Which trust, and truth, and tenderness create
When two fond Hearts with sacred force embrace,
By union deep, unworldly, and divine.
Then friendship, like a school for mind becomes,
Where act to habit may itself mature;
And Self, denied in little things, advance
To show denial, which a world may bless
And all the Churches with due plaudit hail.
Here, faith with friendship can indeed concur;
Beyond mere temper, and accordant tones;
While reign those Principles whose charm outwears
Sickness and sorrow, death, or cold neglect,
With all the jarring dissonance which tries
The force of feeling, in its wisest hour.
But, whence are these, save from th' Almighty drawn,
And, like Himself, unchangeably sublime!
Here is a friendship, perfect, calm, sincere,
Above mutation, as beyond decay;
A friendship, Lord! whose archetype is Thine;
For, when on earth, Thy mortal life assumed
Manhood, with each consummate trait adorn'd;
And human Feeling may exult to view
Laid on thy breast the much beloved St. John!

* These three lines describe an engraved illustration which accompanied the first edition of this poem.

Oh ! for a Friendship which outlives the sun,
To last, when time hath faded, and when Flesh
With all its burden, is a baseless dream.
It drops a balsam in the wounded breast,
Soothes the torn mind, and soul-dejection heals;
'Tis heart to sympathy and hand to love,
Can charm the wisest, or the feeblest worth
Uphold, and makes the poorest rich indeed.

Man forms the foe, but God alone the friend,
If friend he is, with truthful love endow'd,
And graced with those prerogatives of mind
Religion sanctions. Then, what kindred bliss,
What sweet affinities of thought and taste !
The Janus-temple of a jealous heart
That shuts, or opens, as the door demands,
Is here unwitness'd; all is frank display
Which scorns pretence, and scatters each disguise
By sun-clear verity, whose shining force
Copes with all clouds of accident, or change,
And ever beams on Friendship's cordial brow.
Here is an amity our noblest wants
Delight to welcome, as their true supply:
With active force the intellect it feeds,
The heart enlarges into loftier swell
And, in the counterplay it gives and asks,
Finds equal pleasure, when the echo sounds
Sincere and manly. But affliction most
The high-born friendship of heroic minds
Illustrates: then the sacrifice of Self
Devoted, prompt, impassion'd as sincere,
By sorrow, substance, or by costly life,
How godlike is it ! how resembling Him
The soul's Philanthropist, creation's Friend
The world enriching, by Himself made poor !
Friendship like this, the seal of God confirms,
Who cast our nature into social mould
And bade it seek for brotherly response,
Or bosom-counterparts in bliss, or woe:
And thus, whate'er his rank, or high renown,
Man needs an echo, whose responsive charm
Doubles himself, by feeling's prompt reply;
To rich enjoyment adds a height'ning zest
Untold; and when misfortune's east-wind blows
Or cutting blasts of cold ingratitude
Sweep the lorn bosom, by the world betray'd,
Softer than dews from Hermon's sainted height
The tones of Friendship, dropt in feeling's ear
For comfort ! Mine be thus some heaven-made friend,
And I will clasp him, with the heart's embrace
For ever ! Morning with its radiant blush;
Noon with its glory; Twilight with its trance;
Or balmy Night, with all the stars awake
In beauty walking o'er their midnight-round,
How are they each, when friendship's echoing heart
Throbs near our own, with added charm endow'd !
Yea, all those homilies of love and might
Appealing Nature to the pensive reads
Down winding lanes, or paths of vernal bloom,
Or rustic haunt where rambling Boyhood loves
To stray, and linger,—how some tasteful friend
Can, with ourselves, interpret all their tones
In strains of poetry and inward peace,
When souls are mingled, and Creation greets
The hearts who love her. Nor does faith deny
That, e'en in heaven ethereal friendships bring
Their calm addition to celestial joy:
For Truth is social, in the highest orb
Of her dominion ! God Himself is not alone,
But in deep light, Tripersonally throned,
In plural Godhead His perfection holds.

UNION IN THE CROSS.

So Martin Luther and Melancthon felt.
For them, religion was no lifeless creed,
But living virtue: faith and friendship blent
Their pureness, and together nobly grew
In the rich soil of their congenial breasts.
And when we learn what this rare friendship did,
How gratefully will Faith her God adore,
Who so ordain'd, by councils plann'd above,
That Men like these, in place and time should meet,
Blend their brave hearts, and with united hands
The fabric of the Reformation build
In rising glory ! Each that structure claim'd:
And as some builder first in mind conceives
The mansion, which external Art reveals,
And models only from a type within,
So, from His pattern of eternal thought,
The Architect supreme His will expressed
In that vast work the Reformation rear'd:
And not a stone to form that fabric rose,
Nor human workman there his building hand
Devoted, but from God directly came
Some guiding impulse. Glory, then, to Him !
Who thus in hallow'd unity combined
Two hearts distinct, as those twin Leaders bore
That ransom'd Israel from Egyptian chains.
Their's was a friendship, more than Nature forms,
Fancy begets, or genial tastes preserve:
The one, like thunder ! arm'd by daring soul
Breathing defiance with a lion-voice;
Tempestuous often in that mental storm

Which heaved his temper by o'erflowing
wrath,
With rage unbounded : but the other, mild
And chasten'd, passionless and curb'd ;
A halcyon man of holiness and zeal
Whose heart was quiet in its deepest hour.
Or, Nature's imag'ry may thus depict
Their true distinction, in her world of types ;
Intensely burning, like a tropic noon,
In one the character of heart appears :
The other, like a placid twilight-scene
Bathed in serenity of softest dews,
With stars down looking on the lovely whole.

But yet, through many a shock unmoved
they went,
And stood united, when all else dissolved
Around them. 'Twas The Cross, and that
alone,
Which so cemented with abounding grace
Two Hearts, that else were utterly unlike.
Here was a centre; round this changeless
point
Of God for glory, and of truth for Man,
They met, they mingled, with harmonious love
In concord perfect : but in tones of taste
Agreed to differ with delightful ease.
Contrast with them, like two magnetic poles,
Their hearts attracted, and by secret love
Each into each with soft concernment drew
The closer ; union their distinctness proved.
But more than this, may grateful wonder see ;
For each to God's mysterious cause supplied
Some fitting element, or power defined,
Which, wanting, would have left His work
unsafe,
Or tott'ring. Thus, Melancthon's classic toils
And tasteful culture nourish'd growing minds
In progress ; while, from Luther's boundless
zeal
There went a spirit of sublime attack
That shook the Popedom, like a thunder-blast,
Making it tremble down to falsehood's depths
Of darkness. Thus, two Hands distinct they
were,
Each for his task appointed, and prepared,
And both by Wisdom wielded from on high.

FRIENDS IN HEAVEN.

Their work is done, their deathless toil
complete ;
And they are gather'd to that spirit-realm
Where all things tend, as to their final home,
Which are in time and consciousness reveal'd.
But is that friendship, incorrupt and bright,
Effulging from the radiant fount of Love
Celestial, is it in yon heaven absorb'd,
There swallow'd, in some Infinite of bliss
Which now enfolds them? Are those ties of
heart,
Broken on earth, no more in heaven renew'd?
If here below our fondest cravings prove
Affections make the vowels of the mind,
And, like a consonant, when left alone,
Man without love seems unpronounced and
mute,
Will yearning Manhood in the skies be lone?
Alas ! if nothing save what Earth inspires
By us be worshipp'd ; then, as time concludes,
And from eternity rise spectral Woes,
And shapeless Horrors worse than guilt
forebodes
Hover in view, like flashes in the dark
Our earth-born friendships will at once go out
In blackness ; better had they never been !

But when two Hearts, heroic, brave, and
pure
Like Luther's and Melancthon's, nobly throb
Through years of trial with responsive beat
Unfalt'ring, can we think the upper-World
Where men redeem'd the nearest circle form
Of radiant worshippers, who round The Lamb
Hymn golden numbers from their lyres of
light
For ever, can we think, that Souls like these,
Will ever there in single glory chant
That song, united which on earth they sung?
No ! from a heartless creed, for pagans fit,
Our aspirations, dreams, and wingèd hopes
At once recoil, unsocial heaven reject,
And prove it pagan. If below the bonds
Of sacred amity, by grace refined,
'Mid the dark waste of sin-degraded hours
And all th' exacting selfishness which tires
The bosom, yet themselves inviolate keep,
How will such bonds, from imperfection freed,
Gather new strength, and nobler charms enjoy
In that blest Meeting-place of Minds above !
Then shall each excellence, whose winning
form
Though varied, held the heart's accorded throne
So firmly, shine with far intenser ray
Than earth experienced. Thus, ascending
Thought
May cleave the firmament on wings of faith,
Outsoar the stars, beyond the planets rise
And leave creation far our flight behind,
And there, within the heaven of heavens,
behold
Immortal Friends in one immortal home.
From the same Fount of never-failing bliss
Their blending spirits drink responsive joy
Unspeakable : and there in God embower'd,
What once made prayer, is now with praise
enjoy'd ;

The past of earth in heaven a present forms
And gives eternal Consciousness a theme
For wonder, worship, and augmenting love.

SUBLIME OF HISTORY.

Nothing is little in this world of ours,
Because, whate'er the dim-eyed sceptic dream,
In nothing rarely can we act alone.
Built like that fabled roof, whose finest parts
Each into each by interwoven skill
So exquisitely play, with poised effect,
That touch but one, and lo ! the fabric all
Shakes into movement with recoiling shock,—
So is our world by its Great Builder plann'd.
Thus, the first glance which God's forbidden tree
Drew from the eye of earth's frail Mother, forms
With our last sin a fatal union now !

No fact is isolate, no feeling lone;
Entangled are we by perpetual lines
Of moral net-work, infinite and fine,
With magic influence all around us drawn,
Which makes our conduct endless,—by the thrill
And tone of feeling that it often strikes
On the deep chord of ages, yet to come.
Nothing is little, where a moral lurks :
The last vibration of The Saviour's lip,
Expiring, more of deity involved
Than all the gorgeous universe contains.
Though mean the wood, which then Messiah bore
In bleeding glory, while the planted Cross
Lifted Him up a sacrifice for sin,
That sacramental Type a focus form'd
Where the vast councils of Eternal Love
Concenter'd all their wisdom and their wealth
In action !—though a point in space, The Tree,
From out it, as a salient centre, spring
The hopes immortal of our world redeem'd.
Not might of scene, not magnitude of space,
Nor aught of majesty which Sense admires
Or Time can value by his vulgar hours,
To truth a character, or creed a strength
Can give :-for Principle a glory hath
Beyond the limits of defining man;
Enthroned in sempiternal light, it reigns
The Alpha and The Omega of all
In love stupendous, or in law severe.

Thus round that moment, when the Saxon monk,
Bold as some rock which breasts the main alone,
Lifted his brow, and faced his gather'd foes,
What centuries of undevelop'd truth
And change, were secretly encounter'd, then !
To eye of sense, mere Spectacle it look'd
Of men and minds; or, where a rebel stood
Undaunted : but, Another Form there was !
Sightless amid the loud conclave, Who watch'd
Each word that breathed, and master'd all which moved
And thought, but was Himself unseen, unheard,
And unimagined : lo ! The Lord was there
Supreme Director of that scene august,
Where Luther triumph'd, and the Bible rear'd
Its signal far above all thrones of earth,
Untorn, untarnish'd, and untouch'd by man,
The badge of faith and banner of our souls
To be, beyond the rage of Earth, or Hell
To baffle, or resist ! And we, who gaze
Back from the heights of purer worship now
On that gone period, when th' imperial host
Fierce in the hall of unforgotten Worms
Mutter'd, and raged round Luther's dauntless form,
May well that crisis of the World admire !
And think, how from the crystal walls of heaven
Spirits were gazing; or on balanced wing
Hung o'er the chamber where the host convened,
Viewless; and watch'd each mental shade which cross'd
Thy features, while They drank with blissful ear
Each tone majestic, thine unconquer'd mind
By truth inspired, from scripture then awoke
To perish never,—noble-hearted Monk
Of Wittemberg ! Nor let the mocker doubt,
His yes, or no, the wheel of ages turn'd,
And balanced Europe on a single breath;
Since what he felt, the World is feeling still
In heart eternized; Luther is alive
By influence; and each living word of truth
In Worms that sounded an immortal note,
Intones our Churches with some cadence now.

Oh ! 'twas a scene, where hist'ry grows sublime
And unsurpass'd; save when the fetter'd Paul
Lifted his eyes of light and brow of truth
Before Agrippa, till that prince of lust,
Under the sway of his resistless voice
And bold denouncement, quiver'd, like a tree
Shook by the night-blast. From the hills of Rome
The Vatican in vain its thunders roll'd;
And thy huge palace, dark-wall'd Pleissenburg !
Witness'd the brave defender, when he fell'd
Those Anakims of intellectual might,
The proud Goliaths of theology.
But, now, at length, the very Man of Sin,

And crown'd blasphemer who travesties Christ,
Himself upon his Throne of lies shall start
And shiver! "Pile for pile shall kindle now,
Bull, Law, and Canons, and Clementines, all,
Shall in one sacrifice of flame expire!"
So spake the monk undaunted; and the blaze
Redden'd, and rose beside yon eastern gate
Of Wittemberg, above that papal mass
Of fictions mould'ring, and impostures vile;
While by a shout, which should for ever ring
The heart of Europe with responsive tones,
Applauding thousands that bright witness hail'd
Whose keen reflection scorches Popedom, now.

But, there He stands! in superhuman calm
Concenter'd, and sublime. Around Him pomp
And blaze imperial; haughty eyes, and words
Whose tones breathe tyranny, in vain attempt
The heaven-born quiet of his soul to move.
Crown'd with the grace of everlasting truth
A more than monarch among Kings he stood:
And while without, an ever-deep'ning mass
Of murm'ring thousands, on the windows watch'd
The torchlight gleaming through the crimson'd glass
Of that throng'd Hall, where Truth on trial was,
Seldom on earth did ever sun go down,
Or evening mantle o'er a grander scene.
There Priests, and Barons, Counts and Dukes were met,
Landgraves and Margraves, Earls, Electors, Knights,
And Charles the Splendid, in the glowing pride
Of princely youth, with Empires at his feet;
And there—the miner's son, to match them all!
With black robe belted round his manly waist
Before that bar august he stood serene;
By self-dominion reining down his soul.
Melancthon wept; and Spalatinus gazed
With breathless wonder on that wondrous Man!
While mute and motionless, a grim array
Of priests and monks, in combination dire,
On Luther fasten'd their most blood-hound gaze
Of bigotry; but not one rippling thought disturb'd
The calm of heaven on his commanding face!
Meek but majestic, simple and sublime
In aspect, thus he braved the wrath of Rome
With brow unshrinking; and with eyes that burn'd
As if the spirit in each glance were sheath'd:
And then, with voice which seem'd a soul in sound
Made audible, he pled th' Almighty's cause
In words almighty as the cause he pled,
The Bible's! God's religion, not the Priest's
By craft invented and for Lucre preach'd,
For This, life limb and liberty he vow'd
To sacrifice; though earth and hell might rage,
Not Pope, nor Canon, Council nor Decree
Would shake him! From the throne of that resolve
By fiend, nor angel would his heart be hurl'd;
Truth and his Conscience would together fight,
The world 'gainst them—and they against the world!
And then, with eyes which flash'd celestial fire,
Full in the face of that assembly breath'd
The fearless Monk those ever-famous words,
"God help me! Here I stand alone; Amen!"

MORAL RESULTS.

And let all ages that "Amen" repeat,
For it is worthy. Angels might the word
Have welcomed, and th' Eternal arches rung
An echo, as it roll'd from Luther's lip
Solemn and deep, and with celestial might
Impassion'd, since the Truth was then uplift,
The Cross defended, and the Bible crown'd
With vict'ry, when alone the monk of God
Rallied his spirit into high resolve;
And 'gainst the pope, the devil, and The world,
Terror and time, and man's ingratitude,
Fearless like Stephen, when that martyr stood,
Firm as The Rock on which his faith was built.

But not for this, will Persecution's fang
Be blunted. Hark! beneath that vaulted roof
Of Worms' cathedral, rise the chanted hymns
Round the high Altar, while pale incense-clouds
Float their soft fragrance through the aisles immense
Of yon grey temple. There, at Charles's feet,
Haughty, and with imperious rancour stung,
Vile Alexander, on his knee, presents
An Edict, dooming Faith and Luther's soul
Together, under ban and blast to be
Unceasing! "since the Monk was fiendish man,
And all of heresies by heart conceived,
By Satan loved, or damning falsehood dreamt,
Hath Hell epitomised in him, at last!"

Now drops the curtain on the Drama's view;
Strangely and suddenly the scene's o'erveil'd
By myst'ry; human actors are withdrawn:
Inaudibly, along a darken'd stage
Of wonders, moves the lone Almighty now,
Himself evolving what His love decrees
Inscrutable, by boasting man unshared.
And e'en like Philip to Azotus rapt,

Sightless, or lost, shall Luther for a while
Appear; and safe in castled shade retire,
That God alone may God's true champion be;
Nor finite agency presume to claim
For effort mortal, what the Hand Divine
Shall consummate, in secresy unveil'd.
Yes! Man shall vanish, that the Cause may rest
Ark'd in the wisdom of Jehovah's will,
Shelter'd and safe. But he, the hope of all,
Far in the forest of Thuringa hid,
E'en in that hour when most the dazzled scene
Had hail'd him Hero of all prayer and praise,
At once is banish'd! There shall Luther find
A teaching solitude, where Faith may learn
Meekly to suffer, and with flesh contend;
Or, with some Angel of mysterious gloom
Sternly to wrestle, till the break of day,
The morning-twilight of a better mood
Dawn on his mind, in radiant peace again.
Down his *own* spirit he shall learn to gaze
Through many a pangful grief, and sorrowing prayer;
And, like his Lord, that mystic Ladder climb,
Whose steps are suff'rings, but whose top in heaven
Through glory reaches! Chasten'd thus, and calm'd,
The Monk may gather up his soul for God
And learn that faith he taught the world to love.

SYMPATHIES OF NATURE.

Thy beauty, Nature, hath a chorded spell
Responsively for tones of feeling tuned,
In moments deep of myst'ry and of mind.
How often when the human world looks harsh
And loveless; when no eye reflects the ray
Of sorrow, beaming mildly from our own;
When, darkly girdled by a zone of thought,
Apart, and voiceless in our souls we move,
Thy scenes of calm, thy solitudes profound,
Like mute interpretations, seem to wear
An outward mirror of the mood we feel!
Then silence to the soul of thought appeals
With more than language; thy maternal hush
Upon the heart's strange fever falls, like dew.
Sublime in thy sublimities we grow,
And lose the littleness of earth and man
Amid the vastness of those speaking Forms
Of grace, and Grandeurs which Thy throne surround.
Soon may the mind, by such entrancement, soar,
And from the vileness of this vexing world
Awhile set free, imbibe a nobler life,
Holding dim converse with all shapes and hues
Which body forth the Beautiful and Bright
Within, or image forth the mood we feel.
How eloquent the everlasting Hills
Will oft appear! proclaiming with their peaks
Majestic, Him whose fiat bade them stand
Like monuments to Ages long no more:
Or haply, in the heart's deep-thoughted hours
Musing beside an immemorial Sea
On some poetic shore, while wave on wave
In hollow thunder lisps th' Almighty Name,
How strangely does electric nature thrill
Through forms of matter on the feeling mind!
As though the elements, by love inspired,
Interpret what our mental dream enjoys.

And did not He, a beauteous symbol trace
Between the gladness of his free-born soul
And Nature's jubilee of sun and breeze,
Heaven-guarded Luther! on his homeward track
From that proud Diet, where a miner's son
O'erawed the princes in their Hall of pride,
And sent the arrows of resistless truth
From God's own quiver through the heart of Rome?
The crystal radiance of a vernal noon
Around him deepen'd; hark! from forest-boughs
Amid whose branches play'd the truant breeze,
A quiring populace of birds resound
Their tuneful joy; or, jubilant with life,
Hymn wild hosannahs in Creation's ear;
And, high o'er all, th' imperial Lord of day
Eyes, like a parent, the rejoicing earth
Beneath him basking, in a sleep of smiles.
'Twas thus, the countenance of Nature gave
A beaming welcome, bright to Luther's heart.
All elements his counterpart assumed;
Meadow and tree intelligently wore
An aspect, touch'd with some respondent hue
To all within him. In that mood intense,
His rapture was religion,* while the mind

* "Of the tune, which also is by Luther, we have no copy, and only a second-hand knowledge. To the original words, probably never before printed in English, we subjoin the following translation, which, if it possess the only merit it can pretend to, that of literal adherence to the sense, will not prove unacceptable to our readers. Luther's music is heard daily in our churches, several of our finest psalm-tunes being of his composition. Luther's sentiments also are, or should be, present in many an English heart; the more interesting to us is any of the smallest articulate expression of these." "Luther wrote this song in a time of blackest threatenings, which, however, could in no wise become a time of despair. In those tones, rugged, broken as they are, do we not recognise the accent of that summoned man (summoned not by Charles . . . . but by God Almighty also), who answered his friends' warning not to enter Worms in this wise, 'Were there are as many devils in Worms as there are roof-tiles, I would

Revell'd in radiance, like a lark which sings
In sunshine, or a bee that hums in bloom.

His joy was God experienced; and himself
In heart, was living scripture, for the glow
And gladness felt, were letters turn'd to life,
In calm almighty through the bosom breathed.
Hence his free soul, by cheering grace inspired,
Rose like a sail before the gallant wind;

on:'—of him who, alone in that assemblage, before all emperors, and principalities, and powers, spoke forth these final and for ever memorable words:—'It is neither safe nor prudent to do aught against conscience. Here I stand; I cannot do otherwise. God assist me. Amen.' The song is entitled in German, 'Ein' feste Burg ist unser Gott;' and the writer now quoted observes, that 'it is universally regarded as the best of Luther's Spiritual Songs, and indeed still retains its place and devotional use in the psalmodies of Protestant Germany.' On Luther's love of music some remarks are offered in the sequel, but there are few who will not cordially unite in sentiment with the observations of the able writer above quoted. It is this feature, among others, in his character, which has made him the Hero of the people to this day in Germany. His memory is as much beloved and venerated by his countrymen as it is execrated and anathematised by the papists. But we need not be surprised at the resentments of the latter. He smote the objects of their idolatry 'under the fifth rib;' a peasant—a miner's son—gave them their mortal blow."

ORIGINAL.

"Ein' feste Burg ist unser Gott,
Ein' gute Wehr und Waffen;
Er hilft uns frey aus aller Noth,
Die uns jetzt hat betroffen.
Der alte böse Feind,
Mit Ernst er's jetzt meint;
Gross Macht und viel List
Sein grausam' Rüstzeug ist,
Auf Erd'n ist nicht sein's Gleichen.

"Mit unsrer Macht ist nichts gethan,
Wir sind gar bald verloren:
Es streit't für uns der rechte Mann,
Den Gott selbst hat erkoren.
Fragst du, wer er ist?
Er heisst Jesus Christ,
Der Herre Zebaoth,
Und ist kein ander Gott;
Das Feld muss er behalten.

"Und wenn die Welt voll Teufel wär,
Und wollt' uns gar verschlingen,
So fürchten wir uns nicht so sehr,
Es soll uns doch gelingen.
Der Fürste dieser Welt,
Wie sauer er sich stellt,
Thut er uns doch nichts;
Das macht er ist gericht't.
Ein Wörtlein kann ihn fällen.

"Das Wort sie sollen lassen stahn,
Und keinen Dank dazu haben,
Er ist bey uns wohl auf dem Plan
Mit seinem Geist und Gaben.
Nehmen sie uns den Leib,
Gut', Ehr', Kind, und Weib,
Lass fahren dahin.
Sie haben's kein Gewinn,
Das Reich Gottes muss uns bleiben."

TRANSLATION.

"A safe stronghold our God is still,
A trusty shield and weapon;
He'll help us clear from all the ill
That hath us now o'ertaken.
The ancient prince of hell
Hath risen with purpose fell,
Strong mail of craft and power
He weareth in this hour—
On earth is not his fellow.

"With force of arms we nothing can,
Full soon were we down-ridden;
But for us fights the proper Man,
Whom God himself hath bidden.
Ask ye, Who is this same?
Christ Jesus is his name,
The Lord Zeboath's Son,
He, and no other one,
Shall conquer in the battle.

"And were this world all devils o'er,
And watching to devour us,
We lay it not to heart so sore,
Not that they can o'erpower us.
And let the prince of ill
Look grim as e'er he will,
He harms us not a whit,
For why? His doom is writ,
A word shall quickly slay him.

"God's word, for all their craft and force,
One moment will not linger,
But, spite of hell, shall have its course,
'Tis written by his finger.
And though they take our life,
Goods, houses, children, wife,
Yet is their profit small,
These things shall vanish all,
The city of God remaineth."

"Such is Luther's hymn, written immediately after his noble appearance at the Diet of Worms, and before he left that city. It evinces feelings and dispositions worth a thousand arguments; it shows that religion regulated his conduct, and guided him in his perilous enterprise; it shows, in a word, that he was a truly good as well as a truly great man. There is something in it, whatever may be the opinions formed of it as a poetical composition, 'like the sound of Alpine avalanches, or the first murmur of earthquakes, in the very vastness of which dissonance a higher unison is revealed to us.' How strongly is his character contrasted with his popish enemies! Departing from the Diet to his peaceful habitation at Wittemberg, while he knows that an edict is to be published against him, he says in his native German, 'Ein' feste Burg ist unser Gott'—'A safe stronghold our God is still;' while his adversaries are anxious for his assassination, urging the emperor to violate solemn pledges and declarations. Well might Luther exclaim, while he likened the popedom to the 'ancient prince of hell,'

'On earth is not his fellow.'"

LAWSON'S *Life of Luther*.

Though papal Bloodhounds for his spirit yell'd,
A peace beyond disturbing fiends to mar,
His conscience bosom'd: while the tempest raged,
The swelling purpose of his mind, unmoved,
Daunted each danger; as the perill'd bark
Bounds into harbour through a battling sea
And in calm sunshine dries its dripping sail.

ASSOCIATIONS.

Thus, safe is he, against whose life abhorr'd
The dooming blast of Rome's relentless ire
By fell edict was thunder'd; till at eve,
As dew-drops thicken on Thuringa's boughs,
And bird and breeze, on folded wing retired,
Sit brooding, back to Eis'nach's boyish scene
The Monk is wending. But as near he comes,
His brave heart, softer than a willow bends
Beneath the magic of remember'd days!
For now, that local air again he breathes
Where once, a foodless child of woe, he fought
With iron hardship, and with cruel want,
Bathing the crust reluctant Mercy gave
With drops of anguish, from his harrow'd soul
So often wrung. And now, in dreaming calm,
His true heart echoes what reviving hours
Are back restoring to all scenes, and spots,
What once they took of character or tone,
Of stern, or mild, of melanch'ly or strange;
And so, most gently doth the man subside
Down to the boy. For e'en as infant smiles
Transmute the aged, till their features old
With infantile expression learn to gleam
In softest answer, may experienced mind,
Touch'd by the spirit of life's early scene,
Reply serenely to the haunting charm
Of vernal fancies; or, of vanish'd hours
Which waken round us, when maturer life
Down the green windings of gone youth descends.
Hence, all the poetry of peaceful thought
(For men live poems in their purest hours,
But write them, when the heart-song overflows)
Made holy, lulls him into inward prayer.
Oh, had they seen him in his softer mood
Unmantled what a loving heart was there!
Guileless, as that which throbb'd on Jesu's breast
Those cowl'd automatons of monkish cells
Whose frequent worship was but ritual wires
In heartless, mindless, unimpassion'd play
The man evolving, Luther then had taught
By the fond gushes of this feeling hour,
That true religion was a manful love,
A Godward motion of believing soul
Panting for heaven, but yet with earth at peace,
And not ashamed Life's ruling spell to own.

RETROSPECT.

Thus might we, like the travell'd monk, proceed,
And backward to the home of childhood wend,
How much of elemental heart and mind
Would then return, to whence of old it came,
Helping to fashion the unfolding Man!
For character is combination drawn
From time and scene, from circumstance and spot.
The brooks which prattled in gay Boyhood's ears,
Or on whose wavelets sail'd our tiny boat;
The haunted tree; the path we loved to wind,
The cowslipp'd valley or the hawthorn-bloom;
A widow's cottage, or some thatch'd abode
Where dwelt the vet'ran of our native vale,
Who smoothed our head, or tapp'd our rosy cheeks
With ancient humour,—all, with shaping charm
Secret but sure, that Being help to build
Which Manhood in its moral structure shows.
For, there is nothing which we feel, or see,
Admire, or welcome, but a forming power
From thence proceeds, and moulds the plastic mind.
Sunrise and sea, and solemn-vested night
When mute creation God's cathedral turns
For Nature's worship; with all social things,
The hand you grasp, the hearts your own selects,
The sigh re-echo'd, or the teardrop shed
Responsive,—none wield unavailing sway;
But secretly some inward tone impart,
Hereafter in your complex manhood felt
Or found. And, like as our sepulchral dust
Howe'er transmuted by organic change,
Under the blast of Death's awaking trump
Back to the Person, by attractive law
Shall rally, and a perfect body form,
So, may the structure of our moral frame,
Completely, from such causes manifold,
The after-finish of its Form educe.

But now, from scenes where childhood's dark-wing'd years
Had bleakly wafted his unfriended life
Through many a storm, to Mora's rustic wild,
Onward behold the dauntless trav'ller speed.
In that calm village, where a lowly sire
Drew the first breath, his genial soul partakes
The deep o'erflowings of affection's tide,
Tranquil as tender: placed amid kind hearts
Which beat fond echoes to his faithful own,
What peace he finds! what purified repose!
Not his the bosom cold, or shut, or stern;
Nor mock philanthropy, which makes a World
Its giant fav'rite, while domestic chords

Are unallow'd to vibrate through the breast,
And distant love proves mere neglect at home!
Fresh on his soul the dews of feeling lay,
Lovely and bright, as youth's unwither'd prime
Had witness'd; in the man remain'd the boy:
And they who wonder'd, when the hall of Worms
Erect and moveless saw the Hero stand,
Might here have seen him with a graceful stoop
Bend to the lowly; and with winning smile
Attractive, clasp the humblest child who came,
And all his glory into shade recall.
Simplicity alone was greatness here;
And, in the hush of this ancestral vale,
High on the wings of meditative bliss,
In psalms, and melodies of hymning joy
Mounted his heart beyond the rising gloom
Beneath him, o'er his earthly future spread.
Like some gay bird, which oft at golden noon
Soaring and singing, to the gates of Light
Wings its loved way in ecstasy and song,
Yet soon as earth's low atmosphere it tries
Drops the glad plume, and songless grows again.

FRIENDLY CAPTURE.

But this calm Eden of domestic hours
Is brief, as blest. Again, his forward course
Through the green twilight of Thuringa's woods
Behold the man of God in peace renew,
Under the balmy flush of May inspired;
Till lo! at length old Glisbach's hoary fane
Glooms on the air; and, girt with feudal walls,
Altenstein glimmers from its castled height
Serene, but stern. But see! in golden calm
The Day is gliding down the gorgeous west,
Where the red Sun his farewell-pomp arrays;
While round about him, as for royal sheen,
Banners of crimson lustre wave, and wind,
Till the far clouds, with sympathetic hues
As in the blush of radiant sleep they lie,
Mirror bright meanings, from his burning face
Reflected. Soon the forest-boughs begin,
In the tranced quiet of a sunset-hour
To hush their waving; then, the languid breeze
Drops its gay motion; and the insect-hum
Low in the grass delights a pensive ear;
While the glad wings of home-returning birds
Flap on the air, with audible advance,
Which bids you track them to their pine-built nest
With eye pursuant. But, amid this peace
Of nature, deep as if with conscious depth,
Hark! tramp on tramp! with ringing hoofs that rend
The air before them, while the riven trees
Tremble, as if a sudden whirlwind tore
Their tangled umbrage, horse and horsemen arm'd
Plunge into view, in panoply complete,
And mask'd: then, swift and silent, ere a thought
Can think protection, Luther, from his steed
Dismounted, by some mailèd horseman grasp'd
And cloak'd, and on a charger rudely thrown,
At once is captured, as by Magic chain'd!
And in a second, hark, the sounding hoofs
Ring the deep forest with their hollow clang;
Then onward through its beechen wilds and woods
Plunge the mask'd riders, with a trackless speed;
And, Luther! where is now thy destined home?
Who can forecast what God, or man, intends?
Or, tell what dungeon, stake, or crushing wrong
Awaits thee, when a day of brightest hope
Ends in the shadow of so strange eclipse!

But Night hath deepen'd; and her shrouding veil
Garments the woods, which now with blacker gloom
The mountain-heights of lone Thuringa fringe;
And yet the Horsemen, with a voiceless flight
Hurry their captive through untrodden paths
Till the Moon rises, and her silv'ring gleam
Pale on the fortress of the Wartburg sleeps,
Which yonder dim and melancholy stands,
Calm as the clear cold heavens which o'er it spread
Their arch of silence. There the Horsemen pause,
Wearied and worn; and, list! the bugle sounds
A waking challenge in the warder's ear;
Drawn are the bolts, and down the drawbridge falls;
On iron hinges, ponderous and slow,
Opens a gateway to the midnight-Troop;
And mask'd and mail'd, around thee in yon court,
High-wall'd and barricaded, there they stand,
For, Luther, lo! thy Patmos greets thee now.

NIGHT IN THE WARTBURG.

Deep trance of Night! a mystic power is thine,
Which sanctifies creation with a charm
Beyond what day-beams in their brightest glow
Can emanate, whatever scene they gild.
But oh! if ever into heart of man

The Midnight like a mute religion sent
Her spirit, surely, when the captured monk
Down the dim chambers of the Wartburg paced,
Thy genius, then, in solemn glory reign'd!
There, by his window-turret, lofty, bleak
And lone, unharm'd in holy peace he mused,
The past revolved, and o'er his future pray'd.
But moments rise in this unfathom'd life
Of ours, beyond revealing prose, or rhyme
E'er to unveil; so charged with secret might,
They into voiceless sentiment transform
Our being; like a cloud, we seem to float
In formless dreams, with visionary shapes
Confounded; till at length, calm'd nature feels
By truth replenish'd, and distinctive thoughts
Melt from the heart, pathetic, soft, profound,
Like tears of pity in a good man's eye.
Then, all we *have* been, are, or hope to be,
Blends in wild softness; and the soul o'er-sway'd
Throbs with the spirit of unbreathèd prayer.

All that we have been, yes! the night restores:
Form after Form we loved, or knew, or fear'd,
Moves o'er the platform of a summon'd past;
While dead eyes open, and familiar smiles
Fall on our hearts; or household-voices ring,
Till the soul echoes with remember'd tones
Sweeter than music, in its tranced excess.
And all we *are*, oh! Night can this expound;
And self to self beyond all preachers show
In truthful plainness, making conscience start,
As sin on sin, which cov'ring daylight hides,
From the dim back-ground of our Being comes
To awe conception. Then, the future's doom!
Oh, how the spirit of a midnight-hush
To That, significance and shape imparts,
As depths of possibility untold
Open beneath Imagination's eye,
Fearful, and fathomless, and full of God!
'Tis then we soar ourselves beyond, and reach
The skirts and shadows of a higher State
Yet to be master'd. Or, may Thought presume
Thus to imagine, that as embryo life
Hath latent inlets ere the breath begins,
And dormant senses undeveloped powers,
So may our Spirit in the flesh perceive,
Faintly and feebly, some prelusive state,
Or, preconceptions of Hereafter feel
Which antedate a nobler life to come?

And did not Luther, at this dreaming hour,
His great heart yield to more than words depict?
Bathed in the ether of divinest calm
As there he mused, and from yon window'd tower
Greeted the heavens, with planets jewell'd bright?
A holy calm adown the harrow'd depths
Of his vex'd bosom, solemnly was breathed;
While feelings, tinged with supernat'ral awe,
But tender, round him cast their mingled spell.
Like starry gleams, in evanescent play,
Glances of truth upon his spirit dart
But vanish, ere perceiving sense could grasp
A bright suggestion for the soul to read.
Worldless the hour, but how intense the scene!
For never, since in Roman prison clank'd
The fetter'd Paul his honourable chain,
And haply, through his grated window watch'd
The arch of midnight, hath a finer Soul
Look'd o'er yon sky, than that which gazeth now!
Mute as a cloud, the time-worn Castle stands
Of Wartburg, through the glassy moonlight rear'd
In outline black, colossal and abrupt;
Beneath him, wrapt in motionless array,
Thuringa's forest spreads a gloomy wild
Soundless; and so becalm'd in dewy sleep
That e'en the leaflet, when some quiv'ring air
Throbs for a moment, like a lip in dreams
It vibrates, but no vocal murmur makes.
Creation, hush'd in her most holy trance,
Sinks on the soul like one vast sentiment;
From the high moon and melancholy stars
Around her, to the stirless grass beneath,
How mute is nature! how intensely fill'd
With life, with meaning, and with sentient awe!
As if the Earth were conscious that her God
Commanded silence, and she *felt* it rise
Deeper and deeper, from Creation's heart,
And all things binding with religious spell.

But now, the glory of this moonlit-scene
Melts through his being, till each spirit-chord
Thrills to the magic, with responsive tone.
Lo! the large tear-drop on his eyelid hangs
And quivers, like a half-unspoken prayer
Which on the balance of expression moves.
For God, and Truth, and Luther, now commune;
And Midnight hearkens, as the monk adores
The Christ Eternal, in His glory sphered
High o'er yon heavens, beyond conception raised,
And yet by soaring adoration reach'd
Which climbs that region where His radiance dwells,
And thrills the Saviour on His very throne!

PATMOS.

Sublime of privilege! to be alone,
And hold communion with celestial Grace
In the hush'd temple of a hallow'd mind,
Where thought is worship, and Religion wants
No liturgy, save what the heart inspires.
In pensive solitude our God unveils
Those charms almighty, which a sordid love
Of this vex'd world is all too vain to prize;
Then truth ascends our being's mental throne,
To rule and regulate the life within;
While round us shades of man's Hereafter steal
Till awful conscience, with prophetic eye,
Rehearses what the Judgment-Day will be
To men, and angels. Now, from sense withdrawn,
The pious Soul at length presumes to gaze
Down her own deeps, and there a grandeur finds,
A depth in depth unfathomably retired,
Of consciousness, which makes her more sublime
Than all the gorgeousness of glitt'ring worlds.
A single mind the universe outweighs;
A thought than worlds is more stupendous far;
And yon proud stars, which populate the sky
In dazzling multitudes, are less divine
Than the pale forehead of some pensive man
Beneath them watching, from whose lifted gaze
Outshines divinity; whene'er he thinks!

And this we learn, because in this we live,
When from the perill'd life of passion freed
Within ourselves we dare at last descend:
There, truths unvoiced may thoughtful hearts perceive,
And dread predictions, by no language shaped,
Thrill through our conscience with majestic force
And hint the Being men are doom'd to know.

But, solitude a softer mood enjoys;
The past revives; the tombs of time unlocks,
And in the heart's sad resurrection calls
The dead to life, the dear to love, again!
For when this halcyon o'er the spirit broods,
The chain of life, electrically touch'd,
Link after link unwinds, and leads us back
From manhood, with its false and fretting cares,
To childhood, basking in maternal smiles.
Soothed into softness, now the stern can weep;
And shamed ambition from itself recoils
To think how basely, on the World's false shrine
The hopes and aims, which heaven alone can meet,
Our life hath squander'd, with a fruitless zeal.
Ye dreams of Virtue! oft in vice exhaled;
Ye hopes of Greatness! oft in ruin sunk;
Ye full-wing'd Energies! which cleaved your flight
High o'er the vault of young Ambition's heaven,
Reality, the stubborn, and the true,
To airy nought, hath frown'd ye all away!

Still, may we profitably mourn; and muse,
When Memory o'er tombs of buried time
Bends her pale brow, and placidly recals
The spring-like radiance of exulting youth.
For what, though blasting disappointment sear'd
The buds of promise on our tree of Hope,
And few have actualized the heart's fond dreams,
Yet, contrast is our teacher: and we *know*
The truth, by trial only as we live;
And man who sins, by suff'ring must be saved,
While God, through disappointment, makes him wise.

Then hush'd for aye, let all rebellions be:
But welcome, Solitude, however drear,
And come, Reflection! with thy charms august,
And Mem'ry! oft our deeper yearnings wake;
Be to the husband, all the wife appear'd
In the chaste beauty of her spousal morn;
Be to the orphan, what the mother was
When by her knee he knelt, a dimpled boy
Lisping his little prayer; or, on her breast
Pillow'd his head, as if the world were peace:
Act all within, that life without has been,
And from the grave, where dead and dear ones lie,
People our homes with forms true hearts revere!

SPIRITUAL LONELINESS.

And not unlike, in moods of thought intense
To this, was that experience, which the soul
Of Luther gather'd, while for ten lone months
By friendly capture in his Patmos hid.
Here did he muse; and watch, or weep, or pray,
Enter himself, and down the mind's abyss
Take many a deep and undescribèd gaze;
Till forms of terror, phantoms of despair,
And dread emotions, meaningless, or vast,
Throng'd into power, and haunted him like hell!

Meet was the spot for high-wrought feeling's hour.
Within were chambers, long, and large, and roof'd

With fretted stone-work, dimly worn by years,
Where the glad sunbeam caught a pensive tinge
Paler than twilight; and the tread of feet
Fell like a sound, which ought not there to be:
While from their ancient walls the stern-brow'd Dead
Look'd on the living, as with sad rebuke,
Or solemn warning. From a window-niche
The eye might witness hills of forest-wood
In green confusion, stretching far away
Into wild distance; while to Fancy's ear
The pleasing anthem of perpetual birds
Made the huge Forest with their concert thrill.
And here, in myst'ry and in mournfulness,
Shrined in the solitude of his own soul
How much of Deity might Luther learn!
Ascending oft the mountain-peaks of mind,
The Alps of thought, far up the Godhead ranged,
To talk with his Eternity to come.

How like a poem must his life have read,
Where fiction's self by fact had been surpass'd,
When now, by retrospection's quiet gaze
Unroll'd and re-perused! To boyhood's prime
And young experience, when the miner's cot
Roof'd his sad hours of struggle and of sin,
Down the strange past, through all his soul endured,
Dark conscience felt, or prescient fancy dream'd,
Remembrance flew; and now, in castled pomp
Behold him exiled! far from Rome's dread eye
Which glared with hunger for his mangled form.
And well might he, when thus the past renew'd,
The present acted, and the future brought
Prophetic influence into vivid play,
Seem by intensity transform'd, and fired,
Till Unrealities around him throng'd,
And Phantoms, which derision loves to mock,
Fever'd his life with supernat'ral force
Till Matter's self a form of Mind assumed,
And feeling suffer'd all which fancy shaped.

REACTION.

From vast excitement, to the voiceless depths
Of this weird solitude at once transposed,
Who wonders, that reaction like a curse
Besieged him? or, with arid weight o'erhung
The beatings of his brave and free-born heart?
Till, in such blank and barren waste of things,
He sank, and melted into mindless tears;
Or sigh'd, as if the very soul was worn
And weaken'd down to senselessness, and woe.
Oh! there came moments, when a fiendish gloom
A lurid darkness not of earth begot
Enwrapt him, like a shrouding agony;—
A stifled pain, a suffocating pang,
A grief benumbing with torpedo-touch
All the warm currents of his healthful blood,
Till life itself one long compunction grew!
Thus did he suffer: while the brain o'erboil'd
With madness, and his soul was set on fire;
And then, rebukes from some sarcastic Fiend
Would ring around him with disdainful tone,
To mock the little, and to make it less,
Which He and Truth together did, and dared,
When back recoil'd from their combined assault
Popedom and Pope, with all their banded powers!
Nor let the bond-slave of the senses ask,
Why Luther, tempted in such gloom, believed
That ghastly mockers, bodiless and black,
On soundless wing and immaterial tread
Inaudibly around him came; and cursed
And grinn'd, in all the ghastliness of hell,
To shake his spirit from that throne of trust,—
The Word almighty! Yes, when rolling storms
Yell'd in loud rage; or night-wing'd tempests burst,
And howl'd along the wind-rock'd battlements
Of Wartburg, oft did spectral Forms appear
Shading the room with imag'ry of life
And motion; mutt'ring Fiends his couch besieged,
Till Luther shudder'd out his soul in prayer!
But e'en by day, when black depression came
And, like the nightmare of the mind, o'erhung
All faith and reason, in one fell attack,
No flaming death his Flesh could so appal
As this dark anguish did the blood o'erpower;
The pang, without the peace, of death was there!

TOIL AND THOUGHT.

But, like an eagle from his chain unloosed
Darting aloft to his blue home of skies
And sunshine, soon his panting soul escaped
From this dread bondage into purer life.
He pray'd, and open'd Heaven itself by prayer!
Attracting downward some responsive grace,
Or balm, which heal'd him like the hand of God.
Or haply music, as the lyre of old
Tuned into magic by the sweeping touch
Of David, when he charm'd the fiend from Saul,
Besoothed the spirit; till o'er all his frame
A lulling softness exquisitely crept,
And soul was cradled in the charm of sound.

His exile, now, no barren rock became
Where thought must wither into wintry blight;
But rather, grew a bower of mental peace,
An isle of calm amid the sea of life,
A Patmos, where the harbour'd soul retired
From earth's loud shock, to feel the hush of heaven.
Soon, like a giant from his sleep refresh'd,
Up rose the great Reformer! and awoke
The drooping thousands, whose dejected hearts
Pined for one accent of *his* cheering lips.
But, how he wrought, and with what noble bursts
And outbreaks high of eloquence, and truth,
He pour'd his spirit over man, and mind,
Omniscience only can on high explain;
For, souls like Luther's multiply and make
More change within, and character without,
Than mere chronology to men unfolds.
Down to the roots of conscience dived his words
With daring energy, and drew to light
Those hidden workings, and that dark unrest
Which haunt our being: or, on guilt and gloom
The thunderbolt of just rebuke he hurl'd,
And through the provinces of mind career'd
On bold excursion's theologic wing,
And wafted light, where'er his wisdom came.

But, in thy castle, Wartburg! chief o'er all
The monuments which mind up-builded there,
Let grateful Rev'rence long that work admire,
O'er which a Seraph's wings might shake with joy,
By Luther, with colossal power achieved.
There, was the Word Almighty, from the grave
Of buried language, into breathing life
Summon'd, in sainted glory to arise,
And speak to souls, what souls could understand!
Oh! to have seen him, in that toil august,
Lifting to heaven his meditative eyes
Radiant with wonder, as the words of Truth
Eternal gave their hoary secrets up,
While God's own language into Luther's pass'd
With prompt transition; till, behold, the Voice
Of Jesus out of classic fetters came
And, like its Author, to the poor man preach'd.
Noble, beyond nobility to match,
Hero of heaven! was thine achievement here.
To free the Bible, was thy God to throne
Firm on the conscience of adoring man;
And hence, by this supremacy divine
To limit tyrants, should they dare profane
That seat of awe, where none but Godhead rules.

But, intervals there came of lovely calm,
Mild as the languish of a summer-even
Around the poet, by some dream entranced,
When Nature, like a conscious Meaning, acts,
And through cold matter preaches grace to mind.
Then, student of the Spirit! walk with fear
The halls of nature; nor, with pagan eye,
The meanest of Her solitudes and shrines
Inspect thou: ministries of mind are there,
And more than mere philosophy forebodes
Fills the fine atom which a step destroys.
Angels and Spirits *may* unseen preside,
And nature's beauty be a Seraph's work;
Behind the Veil which meets our sensual view
Myriads of Powers may ply their noiseless hands,
And each live function of this breathing Earth,
Serve but to type a Ministry unknown.

And not ungenial to that high-toned mood
When feeling soars, and poetry is born,
In sun and silence Luther wander'd forth;
Perusing earth, or reading air and sky
As one great manuscript, where God had penn'd
Some letter'd outlines of His secret Name.
For, though creation felt the curse's fang,
And beauty from the beautiful hath fled,
And glory from the glorious,—still, the wreck
Is haunted with magnificence and might,
Making the universe a Temple seem,
Whose priestess is the God-revealing Soul
Of man, and worships Him in earth and sky,
Or in the stars, whose bright pulsations throb
Like thrills of glory trembling through the skies.

And, deep the hour, delicious was the calm
When Luther, in some dream, would oft accost
The speaking loveliness of fruits and flowers
Around him scatter'd, o'er the castled hill.
To him they were with more than beauty touch'd,
And seem'd like orphans of dead Paradise
Which smiled upon him, with a mournful grace.
Thus, hues and harmonies of Eden throng'd,
In sweetest union, round his loneliness,
While faith, by rapt imagination raised,
In prayer for those millennial glories pined,
Which God hath promised, and His poets sung,
When spousal Earth her bridegroom-Lord shall greet
Returning, on Creation's throne to reign,
Till every atom of this world redeem'd
Blooms in His breath, and sparkles by His smile.

But, Nature hath her sad and silent moods,
Her solemn counterparts to serious man.
And oft at sunset, when pale Autumn sigh'd
Like a lone Spirit, wailing through the woods
Of Wartburg, Luther mourn'd 'mid falling leaves,
And flowers dejected, till the dew-fall 'gan
To glisten round him; and his boding mind
Took from the season types of man within.
And thus, at midnight, when the Moon commenced
The inspiration of her pallid beam
O'er plain and mountain, from his harrow'd sleep
The exile rose; and, through the window-grate
Of his high turret, o'er yon dew-white fields
And cold earth, slumb'ring in the glassy air,
Gazed mournfully, through many a sleepless hour;
Or wander'd o'er the skies in prayer and praise,
Till to his dream-wrapt eyé those heavens appeared
A scripture bright, whose oracles are stars
Of promise, beaming with prophetic truth,
And high intelligence for holy man.

DARKNESS IN THE HOUR OF LIGHT.

The saints of thoughts, the seraphim of mind,
The sole archangels of our sinful world
Who make, or magnify the page they fill
With moral prowess, what colossal pangs
Were theirs! and what fierce martyrdom they faced,
In bringing forth those Promethéan fires
Which lighten Centuries with their living ray!
But, never yet hath Truth had monuments,
Whose sculptured immortalities of praise
Could half reveal, what lion Hearts have braved
In the great agony of being great!
For what, though history weave its laureate-words
Around some trophy of consummate toil;
Or chant the glory of those giant thoughts
Which grasp'd all ages, with redeeming force;
Result is praised, but not the process told,
Nor the deep racking of those downcast-hours
When darkness, like a fiendish nightmare, sat
Heavy upon them; till the gasping soul
Grew effortless, as if by doubt struck dumb;
While truths, which once like inspiration nerved
The heart for battle, e'en to blood and flame,
Melt into nought, by spiritless eclipse.
And, when have earth's high Benefactors felt
That martyrdom, beyond all fires to make?
Not when the clash and combat fiercely rang
Around them, and the World its weapons drew
To daunt their progress, or dispel their aims:
For then, that eagle of unstooping mind,
Young Energy! could lift itself for flight,
And mounted bravely through the blackest cloud,
Cleaving all tempest with unbaffled wing.
Danger and death were talismanic sounds,
Which from the heart drew forth a secret fire.
Effort was theirs; and mastery sublime
O'er scene and circumstance their faith evinced,
Till lo! the perill'd cause in safety smiles,
And History for its coronation waits.

But in the gladness, and the glow immense,
When hope's millennium seems at last to bloom;
When the calm jubilee of conscience rings,
And Principle its heaven-toned pæan chants
For peaceful triumph, then, while good men pray,
And great ones, in a hush of wonder, pause;
If, in such hour of golden promise, all
Fades into formless vanity, or vice,
And fell Reverse a sudden ruin frown,—
Alas! the Heroes of the heart are left
Unpraised, unsoothed, unlaurell'd, and unsung,
The rack of racks alone to face, and feel,
When virtue's cause a suicide becomes
And stabs itself to impotence, and shame!

But, such the crisis, that with sudden might
And sweeping darkness round tried Luther's soul
Came, in the very noon of noble hopes,
When the bright future cloudlessly began
To open, and in peace and prayer to reign.
Height after height victoriously was scaled
Of priestly bulwarks, and papistic lies;
The Bible, into living freedom loosed,
From cot to palace circulated truth;
The majesties of buried mind began,
Clothed in the radiance of regen'rate power,
The grave-clothes of the monk to throw away:
While, chief o'er all, that Mammon of the priest,
The aping Mass, where bleeding Love is mock'd,
Was banish'd; and Emmanuel's truth began
As Lord of conscience, from all hearts to hurl
That crown'd Melchisedek, whom Rome anoints
Both head and front of Christendom to be.

When lo, at once the anarchy of change!
And Luther, palsied as by dread alarm,
Around him hears fanatic Madness yell,
And the hot Até of excited hearts

Through flame and fury to rebellion sweep.
And now, the Pang ! the concentrated pang,
Which dire, and dark, expressionless and deep,
Heaved in no sigh, and by no tear pourtray'd,
Sank on his soul with adamantine crush.
For all seem'd ruin, and revulsion here:
While leagued Rebellion, with its brazen throat,
Its blasting eye-glance, and its bloody mien,
And mingled yells for murder raging loud,
From the black forest of Thuringa rush'd;
While He Himself an incarnation seem'd
In principle of all perversion did,
That Madness loved, or Murder long'd to do !
The People cursed him,—for he cursed their cause,
And call'd rebellion but the child of hell.
The Princes cursed him,—for the yoke of Rome
His arm had broken from the nation's mind.
Bereft, in solitude of soul apart,
A ruin among ruins, thus he stood
With heart all bleeding, and with spirit bare,
One living agony of gloom, and tears.
And well might Luther, like his Master, feel
Desertion, in that night of nights profound !
For Heaven's own cause fanatically lay
Trampled, and torn beneath a hoof of lies,
When Munzer, and his host by hell inflamed,
Shouted "The Spirit !" and to blood blasphemed
Both God and Bible, with insanest breath.
Each to himself a Holy Ghost became,
And all his madness to th' Almighty gave !
And He, who was on earth the living Type
Of holy Order, and consummate Law,
Both first of Subjects and the first of Kings,
Upon the banners of Rebellion found
His Cross a symbol of destruction made !
E'en common feeling from the roots was torn;
Till all affections, motherly and mild,
Which form sweet nature's consecrated spring,
Nile of the heart ! whose undiscover'd source
Deep in the bosom of the Godhead lies,—
Were parch'd to nothing in that burning waste;
When heroes mad, for demigods mistook,
Mangled their thousands, by a hellish creed,
And christen'd Murder with the name of Christ !

"But fear thou not !" a Voice within him cries;
"Forward ! for I am with thee, man of God !
On to the rescue of My truth ! and fight
With weapons all resistless, as divine !"
And forward went He; with a burst of zeal
Faith from her cloud of black dejection breaks,
And Luther is himself, in soul, again !
While hope, that rainbow of the weeping mind,
The Iris out of tears by passion wove,
Smiles through the sunshine of prophetic calm,
And his heart palpitates with silent prayer.

MENTAL RESURRECTION.

True liberty, O God ! Thy Spirit makes;
For, the vast doctrine of redeeming Love
Holds in itself the majesties of man.
Freedom and faith our twin inspirers are,
The healthful source from which pure greatness springs:
All fine immunities of sense, and soul,
All deeper actings of divinest thought,
All morals, motives, aims, and bold designs,
And aspirations for the Good unseen
In man's free conscience find their perfect root.
For liberty within, forms light without,
And grace the spirit of salvation is.
Whate'er of polity just freedom lauds,
Whate'er of life domestic love reveres,
Whate'er of mind heroic wisdom haunts,
Or, in the temple of essential Truth,
All which our adorations prove divine,
From grace, in principle, directly flow.

The Reformation thus the Mind redeem'd;
The swathing bands which superstition cast
Round the chain'd spirit, were at once dissolved;
And, lo ! a mental resurrection smiled:
A golden dawn of intellectual day
Already round the clear horizon glow'd,
And faintly shined on Europe's rising heart.
See Luther, and Melancthon, all inflamed
Ardent as eagles, in their sunward flight,
From truth to truth victoriously advance !
Instead of Masses, mark the Holy Feast,
The mystic Supper of Incarnate Love
Dispensed with beauty, primitive and plain.
The Visible its hallow'd claim advanced,
And Ideality a form assumed;
While the young Church her pristine features wore.
Thus, rites external, for external sense,
And truths internal, for internal soul,
By fitness due the wants of nature met;
Since, mere Abstractions angels may perceive,
But men embodied must by Forms be led,
And rites are reasons, when by God approved.

Still, not o'er temple-rites alone was breathed
That order Principle from Scripture draws;
But through the heart, by reformation clear'd
From papal mist, the common mind was touch'd,

And the pure founts of intellect unseal'd
From lofty plans see Education stoop
To ply the humblest with appropriate skill;
While cloister'd Learning, from her cells escaped,
Comes to the peasant-home, the people's heart;
Till mind is no monopoly for priests,
And classic Thought in sacerdotal rust
No more lies with'ring; but, at Luther's word,
Walks through the world of feeling, and of faith;
And ye, the symbols of our inner sense,
Types of the Beautiful we cannot reach;
Ye adumbrations of diviner Grace
Than ever seen, when most Invention lifts
Her glad Eureka! round enraptured souls,
Ye Arts! which make imagination's heaven,
By shape, or hue, or melody reveal'd,
Soon from the sacred Reformation caught
A new intensity of noblest power.
For Music rose, seraphical, and pure,
And revell'd in a paradise of sound,
To hymn the Prince of glory, and of peace.
And Painting, from Apostles imaged forth
Forms of fair virtue, in sublimest mould:
While Piety and Painting blent their powers,
Taking a cast from Beauty's very soul
In lines of love, and lineaments of heaven.
And She, the charmer of celestial moods,
High Poetry, the heart's young Priestess, came,
And on the altar of melodious hours
Laid the soft incense of devoutest song.

IDEAL RAPTURES.

And hence, amid the harmony of things,
Awhile, as on the brink of heaven restored,
Rejoiced the grateful Luther. Who can tell,
The Promised Land of hope's perpetual dream
How greenly-bright before him, then, it smiled!
The passion and the principle of song,
With full intensity his being fired:
'Twas thus, the poetry of peace and joy
Each fine pulsation of his nature thrill'd;
And all without, from life internal, took
Some answ'ring tone of sympathetic love.
Through walks, and woods of Wittemberg he roam'd;
Or gave his spirit to the mountain-breeze;
And in the carol of rejoicing streams,
The leafy warble of the forest-boughs,
Or lyric echoes of the laughing wave,
In sound, or scene, and all which nature show'd,
A charm responsive to himself he found.
Nature and man in fine accordance met:
Their smiles and tones reciprocally play'd;
Her forms of matter to his shaping mind
Embodied meaning; and a moral grace
From all Her symmetries appear'd to flow.
Now was the halcyon of the heart; awhile
Bosom'd in peace, the bright-soul'd Monk was blest.
The past was praise, for all that vict'ry won;
The present prayer, for all which Mercy gives;
And o'er the future his prophetic heart
Glow'd with entrancement, as Isaiah did,
When his lyre trembled with exulting tones
Millennial over crown'd Messiah's reign:
Till oft, in rapt Imagination's dream,
Amid the universe of happy worlds
This earth appear'd creation's loved St. John,—
Safe on the bosom of redemption's Lord
Reclining there in glory, and in rest.

And, like th' apostle of a church reform'd,
Who has not, in the harmony and heaven
Of some high mood of meditative calm,
As opes the flower its scented breast of bloom
To welcome there each beautifying ray,—
Yielded his spirit with expanding joy
To Nature, in her eloquence of scene,
As if to consciousness he then appeal'd?
Till all creation grew personified,
And the touch'd earth, to fancy's tender dream,
His living counterpart of joy became.

As by some harp, when exquisitely strung,
A vulgar breeze to music's voice is turn'd
When o'er its chords the airy tremor floats,
In subtile magic, so, to mind intense,
The coarse realities of sense and time
Change, as they touch the intellectual powers,
To meanings beautiful, and mental types.
The prose of earth to poetry of heaven
Is thus transform'd, for faith's perusal, there;
And oh, ye scenes, ye splendours, and rich sounds,
Like inspirations, lo! at once ye act:
All sacramental charms of earth, and air,
All signs and symbols of redeeming grace
Steal into view, with eloquent surprise!
Till the pure eye of sainted Thought conceives
The dust to overflow with teeming spells,
While all things, into sacredness refined,
Make parables which prove redemption's plan.

Thrice happy they, who thus, by heav'n empower'd,
Can find a gospel in the flowers, and leaves!
Creation's book then fancy's bible forms;
And faith poetic, by the Spirit led,
All nature calls a comment on the Cross.
In this let holy Love our teacher be!

A love perpetual,—for in *that* supreme,
The sabbath's God Himself no sabbath keeps.
And then, what great proprietors we are!
E'en on His throne the Uncreate is ours
By covenant, from everlasting made;
And under it entire creation works
All good and glory for the church redeem'd.

Many have much, yet all desire a more;
But less than infinite, to man is nought:
The more must be almighty, or 'tis none!
But who hath Christ, has God by God bestow'd,
And vast Eternity becomes his friend.
Then still, thou Sun! Emmanuel's image be,
And like a shadow of His glory burn;
Thou Moon! His mystic bride on earth, reflect;
Planets! that with prophetic radiance gleam;
Thou paragon of elemental powers,
Myst'ry of waters, never-slumbering Sea!
Impassion'd Orator! with lip sublime,
Whose waves are arguments which prove a God;
Ye Woods! that with tempestuous anthems ring;
Ye Winds! whose allelujahs tongue the storm
With music's deep magnificence of tone;
Ye Mountain-altars! which from earth to heaven
Serenely lift your consecrated steps,
While the soft grandeur of the silent hills
Sinks on the heart like music low, and sad,—
Long in your magic each, and all, abide,
Some teaching mystery of Christ to show:
That hence, in all things, with an eye of praise
And heart of prayer, true Faith may ever find
By nature, as by grace, her God express'd;
And in the temple of creation greet
Perpetual glories which His Name enshrine.

AFFECTIONS MADE FREE.

If ever, since the pulse of feeling play'd
In the quick breast of God-created man,
Companionless, in isolation pure,
The full revealings of his nature might
Themselves in moral harmony have shown,
'Twas when the young creation heard him crown'd
Her living monarch; while the lyric stars
Chanted a birth-day ode, and angels lined
The silver battlements of Heaven above,
To see a masterpiece of human mould
In sinless purity from dust evoked,
And stamp'd with features from the Hand of God.
Then was the hour, if ever such might dawn,
When echoless a mortal heart might throb
And still be happy, in itself complete,
By woman's smile unwelcomed, and unwed.
But, not when paradise within made peace,
And paradise without, responsive joy,
Was human loneliness by Heaven approved:
"It was not good that man should be alone,"
And so, a female counterpart was framed
In oneness sacramentally* profound,
From his own being moulded, and educed;
And Woman thus to Adam's bower was brought;
There the first marriage by almighty hands
In stainless Eden was perform'd, and seal'd;
And the first miracle Messiah work'd
To Wedlock gave the glory of its power:
Hence, life-monastic came from man alone;
But life domestic is from God derived.

But she, the Murd'ress of emotions pure,
The vile Creatress of mistaken good,
Both law and love in nature contravened;
And dared, with hand of sacrilegious force,
From the young Bosom, where soft feeling dwells,
Expunge all instinct, and the soul uproot,
To plant, and place it in a coarser soil
Blighted and bare, with chills unmanly cursed.
But Nature proved an unmonastic Thing!
And when in light, the monk of God arose
To stay the famine of the soul for truth,
The heart was hung'ring for its food of love.
Pining, and pent, in passionless remorse
It wither'd, by a torturing fetter bound
To vow itself to suicidal gloom.
Yet, few had fester'd in o'er-righteous chains:
Though canons frown'd, and convent-law decreed
Death to each heart, by female hearts enticed!
And thus, in self-revenge, the blood o'erboil'd
In fires of feeling; ruffian passion raged;
And homes, which might have been like heavens of bliss,
Had holy Wedlock lit the vestal flame,
Grew hells impure, unmentionably vile,
Where powers of darkness turn'd to priests of lust
And Satan saw himself in Rome secure.

But he, who brought the buried Scripture forth
From tombs of silence, and monastic death,
The bright Restorer of domestic bliss
At length with dreadless vigour dares to be.
Affections are the food of hearts which feel:
For such pined Luther; and in Ketha met,
Fresh in her maidenhood of life and love,
That feeling sympathy fond nature sought.

---

* See Eph. v. 32.

For what, though all around grew black and drear,
And the wild echoes of the peasant-war
Rang loud in Europe's ear; while reek'd the blood
Of thousands, on Thuringa's hoof-worn plain:
Yet did the Word about him cast a shield,
While o'er him hung the canopy of heaven.
The God of marriage was the God of man;
Here, on this rock, the thunder-blasts of Rome
Sank powerless, as the lisp of summer-winds!
Better by far, that flesh and blood should quail,
Or, all creation be annull'd in gloom,
Than One majestic truth of God be harm'd!
In heresy our God Himself we lose;
And the big universe a bubble seems,
Weigh'd in the balance of a single word
Dropt from the lips of His almighty Love!
But *that* was with him, sealing woman's love
As heavenly-bright, and by the Saviour blest:
And therefore, not by this a Cause sublime
Was perill'd; nor the Reformation's ark
In danger, when the monk of Wittemberg
Rose, in the freedom of a fervid soul,
To rive the fetters of monastic vows
Asunder, from his heaven-instructed mind;
And, lifting his pure conscience in the light
Of scripture, up to majesty and truth,
Look'd on the world, a husband not ashamed!

And round that scene, where his devoted heart
The wedded Luther to his Ketha gave,
Eternal Wisdom cast approving smiles,
And heaven its hymeneal blessings shed.
For then was Private Life from priestly lust
Deliver'd; peace conjugal back restored,
And wedlock in its sainted charm enshrined;
While Rome another and a ruder shock
Experienced, from the soul of Luther sent;
For now, affections, nerved with sudden life,
Together with deep principle combined;
Till both concenter'd, back to Nature gave
A creed which conscience could avow, and act,—
To guide the faith, to guard emotion pure,
And brighten homes with honourable love
Where prison'd Feeling, passionless and pale,
Languish'd alone; or, lewd Corruption came
To look the Angel, with a demon's heart!

And thus, within the haven of a home
Luther, at length, his care-toss'd spirit found
Anchor'd in peace, and matrimonial joy
Secure. And where do Love's fond annals tell
A home of heart, more exquisite than his?
The once cowl'd Monk, who trod the cloisters dim,
And made his melancholy footsteps ring
With cadence long and lone, was now become
A glowing husband, and a gladden'd sire.
And, lovely was it, when his mind, unrobed
Of all its panoply of public state,
Reposed in sunshine, and, at home retired,
Sparkled and play'd around his infant boy;
Or else, in laughing sweetness echo'd back
The tones of glee, and truths of gay delight
Which Ketha from her glowing spirit sent;
Or smiled approval, when his portrait rose
Under the magic of embroid'ring Art
Featured, and form'd. And so, when sombre night
Mantled his dwelling with sabbatic peace,
Seldom have Angels, as they waft their flight
From home to home, on voiceless errands wing'd,
A fairer landscape of domestic love
And life beheld, than Martin Luther made
Around him, with his wife and infant smile.
Nor haply, upon heaven's memorial page
The meek hosannahs of more thankful minds
Have they recorded, than the chants they heard,
When sang the great restorer of the Truth
Hymns of the heart around his household-shrine.

LUTHER MARRIED.

A MONK was married! how the priesthood raved!
But God was with him; and His word approved
A deed that shook all Popedom to its base,
The convents oped, the Vatican alarm'd,
And push'd the world by matrimonial law
A century forward into fearless paths
Of light, of liberty, and spousal love.
And Scripture canonised the act: but, powers
In nature also with approval smiled;
For imaged wedlock, in the vital bonds,
The unions pure, the harmonies profound,
The loving sense and sympathy of things,—
His fancy by poetic vision saw.

And let the hard utilitarian smile,
Building religion on a sensual base.
A Faith there is, which, like to Luther's, loves
The adumbrations of a deeper life
Beyond the sense, in Matter's self to trace.
Christ and His Church,—for these the world was framed;
And thus to souls, with sight divine endow'd
The Spirit's Kingdom on this earth to see,
Creation glows with poetry for Christ,
Through forms of matter unto faith reveal'd.
All pangs, all pleasures, faculties, and powers,
The hearts of God's elected race can find,
Or feel, or suffer, may from Nature draw

Tones of respect, and touches of regard,
Or something which resembles sympathy.

Nor let the worshipper of venal gods
Pronounce this pure Imagination's dream;
Since, haply, thus the myst'ry may unwind,
And what the poet sings a saint admire.—
When this fair World to conscious being rose
With beauty, and with vernal radiance clad,
Why were her forms, her symmetries, and scenes
Touch'd by a spell which can the mind pourtray,
And by such true analogies reveal
An image dim, but exquisite and deep,
Of much the moral universe combines?
Such forms of nature with the facts of grace,
Why do they so responsively apply,
That each with each in harmony coheres?
Or in that region, where the feelings dwell,
Why does our spirit from the sounds and scenes
Of Nature, catch a mute intelligence,
As if with consciousness of man and mind
The speaking magic of her aspect smiled?
The festive jubilee of summer-winds;
Or soothing descant of a far-off sea;
The storm's loud wail; the ocean's sullen roar,
Noon with its sun, and midnight with the stars,
The Spring, with her sweet family of flowers,
Or, widow'd Autumn, with consumptive leaves,
And pale-faced Winter in a frozen vest,
Why do they all intelligibly bring
Hints to the heart, and harmonies for mind?
Is this reply, which all Creation gives
To human feeling, but the fancy's mock?
Or, is not earth a parable divine?
And poets, when their inward eyes discern
Meanings that flow from matter into mind,
Priests of creation, may they not be call'd?
For Thou, O Christ! art universal King:
By Thee, and *for* Thee, were not all things made?
So, when the Spirit on the mass new-born
Of nature brooded, then, with mystic Seal,
All matter for Thy Glory was impress'd
With types peculiar, with expressive laws,
Thy church to show, Thy symbols to expound,
And thus preach gospel to our very sense;
Till Nature act the orator for Grace,
And all creation one gigantic type
For Christ and Christianity becomes.

And such the creed Imagination holds,
When the vast glories of this earth appear
But shadows from the Saviour's beauty cast.
And seldom hath poetic Sense replied
To Loveliness, with more impassion'd glow
Than Luther's, when ideal moments reign'd,
And his full heart, with purified excess
Of sympathy for life's unbounded range,
O'erflow'd all nature in one gush of love!
Yet, moods of preternatural calm there came,
With might of thought, and majesty of dreams
And a deep awe beyond all words to voice,
Under the mute and melancholy heavens
As oft he worshipp'd, in his window-shade
At starry moonlight. Then, th' unpillar'd vault,
By viewless Energy for aye upheld,
Harangued him like a holy Sign,* which spake
How like that arch of glory God sustains
The Church elect, by bleeding merit won.
Or when the moon through some black cloud emerged
In radiant victory from a brief eclipse,
To him a symbol of refulgent grace
It seem'd, of how the Reformation's cause
From the cold darkness of imperial frowns,
At length, would glide to glory and to peace.

POWER OF PRAYER.

Yet, not from nature, solitude, or night,
Nor wedded life, with all its household-sweets,
The sober quiet or the sterling joy,
His force to grapple with infernal Arms,
Wisdom to guard or prudence to restrain
The lawless plunges of impassion'd will,—
The brave Reformer drew: below the skies
No charm was found which could have moulded him:
From One high Source both cause, and courage sprang.
And that, divine!—from spirit-breathing prayer
Hour after hour communing with His God.

He loved the Bible; and he lived it, too;
Till each bright promise to experience turn'd
By faith transmuted, or by love enjoy'd.
The source of Luther was a strength of Prayer
Frequent, and full, and fervidly inspired,
As oft the castled gloom of Coburg heard.
Though loud the Reformation-battle grew
And empires as with moral earthquake heaved,
Throned was his spirit in Elysian calm!
But, where man wonders, faith can all explain.
'Twas God within, made Luther great without;
Whether, against that triple-crown'd Pretence,
The mitred Antichrist of Rome, he hurl'd
His thunders; or, on sacerdotal crimes

* This alludes to a memorable passage in one of Luther's "Letters from the Wartburg."

Pour'd the just vengeance of his free-born words,
Prayer was his panoply; the shield and strength
That arm'd him for the fight, and kept him there.
With this, the World, the Arch-fiend and the Flesh
Combined, he nobly fought, and bravely fell'd.
And we inherit what his prayers procured:
For, light in conscience, liberty in creed,
And the pure freedom of our British faith,
How much to blessings drawn by Luther's voice
From the high sanctuary of heaven, they owe!
Yea, half the glory living Empires boast
Springs from that mercy which the monk procured,
When Godhead listen'd to a Luther's prayer!

And round a privilege august as this
Less than inspired no language can entwine
The wreath, how due! of evangelic praise.
Prayer from eternity true riches gains
To make the poverty of time less poor;
Heaven down to earth, and earth to heaven it brings,
While Love with Deity by faith confers:
And mark! through nature, providence, and grace
What miracles hath mighty prayer achieved!
The kingly Elements their thrones have left
To bow before it, and obey, though vast,
Its high dominion: Flood, and Sea, and Fire
Have soften'd their severity of force,
Suspended by it; Sun and Moon have paused
In wonder, on their cars of wheeling flame,
As if arrested by th' Almighty's touch;
And the wild brute, which not a world could bend,
Meek as a lamb, before a Saint has crouch'd
Harmless and mute, when it beheld him pray!
Heroes in heart, in principle, or power,
Hath prayer alone with high perfection crown'd:
While saints, and martyrs, and the men of old,
Giants in grace, who grappled with the Fiend
Or threw him bravely in the spirit's fight,
By valiant prayer their elevation reach'd:
And earth's Emmanuel, in His day of flesh
Outwatch'd the midnight with His mountain-prayer;
And from the deep abyss of Godhead drew
His faith intense, his fortitude divine:
And all, who love the cause eternal, must
Like their pure Master, fight the world with prayer,
And strike for God, by God himself inspired!

DOMESTIC LIFE, AND WEDDED LOVE.

From out the Bosom of paternal bliss
When came the Second of th' almighty Three,
And God, in human image bodied forth,
Alighted on man's world of sin and death
As Prince of peace, and Purchaser of life,
How lived, how spake, this Archetype of all?
E'en like his Person, did His life appear,
Divinely human, with coequal grace:
In Godhead,—never sunk the God beneath;
In Manhood,—never raised the man above;
To each extreme symmetrical and true,
Believer! there, thine own Emmanuel hail.

How awful was He! when the cloud of flesh
Gleam'd with the lustre of indwelling God.
Thy steadfastness, vast Nature! from the sleep
Of twice two thousand years, by Him was moved;
For all those laws, by Science so revered,
Their changeless glory to His changing will
Yielded, like vassals by their king o'erawed.
He look'd—Creation by his glance was thrill'd;
He spake—the Elements each word obey'd;
Earth, Sea, and Air their royal sceptres threw
Down at His feet, and fell before their Lord;
While shrinking, as with conscious dread commoved,
Back from his word the rushing Storm recoil'd,
Soothed its mad roar, and like an infant smiled
Itself to sunshine and soft peace again.
Blindness, at His command, the sun beheld;
And Deafness heard Him when the fiat came;
Disease was Health; and Lameness felt her Limbs
With miracles of energy to move,
While the dead body from the bier uprose
Beneath the resurrection of His word!

And, awful was He! when the curse was borne:
While His bow'd Head was crimson'd o'er with blood,
Then shook the Earth, and shudder'd as the groan
Of Christ appall'd her! while a deep eclipse
Dropt like an eyelid o'er the flaming Sun,
Dreading to gaze on God incarnadined!
But, in that syncopé of mortal hopes,
That pause tremendous in our human fate
When sepulchred Messiah, cold and pale,
Seal'd in the rock a dead Redeemer lay,
While Nature seem'd as if with stern revenge
To triumph o'er Her pallid victor there,—
How awful was He when His grave-clothes stirr'd!

When the rock trembled with an earthquake-pant,
Till the stone, radiant with angelic touch,
Roll'd from His sepulchre; and, rising up
In perfect majesty of might, behold
The Saviour gather'd to a God again,
Martyr at once, and Master of the tomb!

But, gentle was He! with all grace of man
Completely, as with charms of Godhead crown'd;
For He who came, by Love eterne inspired,
From heights celestial, with a pitying stoop
The low horizon of our world to meet,
Not in the costume of corporeal flesh
Alone was found; but, Fellowship with man
The life of Jesus bodied forth, and breathed;
The accent of created love He caught;
The sunshine of created joy He shared;
The sorrow of terrestrial sighs He heaved;
And with the tenderness of mortal tears
Moisten'd his eyelids, when a sister wept.
His form was human, and His feelings, too!
Thus, Manhood there in archetype may see
Each moral beauty which a life presents
When holy; where affections crowd the scene,
And heart and home a mingled Eden make,
While virtue follows where the Saviour went
Through haunts of love, and bowers of social bloom.

And thus religion, like her Master, glides
With touching glory, or with tender grace
O'er duteous walks of Life's diurnal round.
For, while on wing celestial faith can waft
Up to the Throne a meditative soul,
Down to the actual with a graceful love,
Where plain Humanity in humble guise
The man develops, can Religion stoop,
And o'er it cast her consecrating smile.
So, from the gaze of public life retired
'Mong shades domestic, where Affection blooms,
And feeling all its happy foliage sheds,
A Hero now, whom death nor dungeon awed,
Serene and simple as a peasant lives.
No lofty, loveless, and disdainful looks
Around him here, severest judgment finds.
But, frank and free, with apostolic mien,
And full-toned manhood in its perfect type,—
A husband in the great Reformer hail,
Like Martin Luther and like nothing more!
No stern pretension, borne with saintly pomp,
Mere actor made him. In the walks of home
Lord of himself, His individual mind
Free from the fetters of o'ermastering fame
He kept: his life was freedom to the last,
Stamp'd in the mould simplicity admires.
The Man was never in his Name absorb'd,
Chain'd like a captive to his own renown.
Framed in the homeliness of cottage-worth,
A racy humour, and a rough disdain
For mock supremacies for mean effect,
For little greatness and for large pretence,
Were his: and he who held all Rome at bay
And bulwark'd nations by his brave appeals,
Looks he less lofty, to those hearts which love
The sterling and the true, when playful seen
In the mild sunshine of a married state?
There, could he sparkle round the social board,
As romp'd the infant on his rocking knee;
While the glad mother, sat with glowing face
And sunn'd her feelings in the father's smile.

Yes! beautiful, behind the scenes to gaze,
And there no mock attempt, whose aping pride
Would play the Hero in ascetic gloom,
To witness; but that solid worth of sense,
And healthful sanctity, whose fervid power
The christian fulness of o'erflowing heart
Betoken. Lofty in his bosom beat
The pulse of principle, and great design:
But not alone, or frowningly aloof,
A frigid, stern and adamantine Thing
Whose life in passionless contempt retires
From warm reality's most welcome hour,—
Not thus, the avenger of the Bible lived.
In faith a hero, but in heart a man,
With him the simple and the great combined,
And both together made a blended charm
Beyond the drama of affected life
To feel, though play'd with Art's consummate guile.

COMMUNION WITH NATURE.

And Nature, through her world of types appears
Simplicity in grandeur thus to teach.
Expressive mountains! from whose massive forms
The dread Almighty speaks Himself to man
By eloquence, which hearing mind translates,
How often, underneath their shade august,
Or in the hollows of some green descent,
The tiny flowers in tenderness and bloom
Wave their young beauty! or, infantile plants
Bow to the breeze their unresisting heads,
While the faint lisp of dropping leaves returns
A murmur'd echo to the rippling stream
Which runs beside them, with loquacious play.
And thus, methinks, beneath that mental shade
The tow'ring giants of the mind produce,
Simplicity in loving calm delights
To watch the flowerets of affection bloom;
And see those lilies in the heart arise

Which make the garden of our spirit green,
Breathing mild fragrance o'er affection's world.

And hence, admire we with revering gaze
True Greatness, when it lays all thunder by,
Till the soft childhood of the heart returns;
And solemn wisdom, sparkling into wit,
Can gild the heights of intellect with smiles.
But chief from music came the master-spell
Which Luther, like a spirit's echo loved!
To him it seem'd a charm divinely framed,
An earthless magic, out of mystery born,
And so with heaven instinct, that Satan fled
When Harmony her spells began to breathe,
Or sank o'er passion, like a healing dew
Pure from the fount of freshness in the skies.

'Twas thus the poetry of private life
Around him, with an unresisted reign,
Gather'd and glow'd. But oh! ye quiet fields,
Where, lost in sunshine, sang the soaring birds
In wing'd delight and ever-warbling song,
How would he listen to your choral joy,
Till the gay summer of his spirit smiled
With loving answer to the scene it loved!
And often, when some fever hot and harsh
From human outrage, wither'd him with pangs
Of weary anguish till the spirit wept,
Didst thou, meek Nature! with maternal smile
Look through his soul and laugh the cloud away.
To him thy shrines, thy solitudes profound,
Thy hues and shades, and harmonies perceived
Brought more than feeling to his heart of faith.
And so, the very flowers seem silent hymns,
And, by their aspect of persuasive bloom,
Remind him oft of Eden long no more;
Or, bid him muse on what the world *may* be
When second paradise again shall dawn:
Since all which fell by Adam's guilty fall
From outward glory into penal gloom,
And all of kingship which the soul enjoy'd
When man, as Monarch of creation, ruled
And, as anointed Priest of paradise, became
The mouth of Nature and her mute delights,—
To pristine splendour shall once more arise,
Till crownless Manhood wear a crown again;
Or earth redeem'd, Messiah's palace be,
And shine, as round His central throne it rolls,
The loved metropolis of sumless worlds.

PARADISE RESTORED.

And who, amid some holy trance of thought
On destined man, as prophet, priest, and king,
Hath never vision'd how his primal soul
In the bright mould of innocence was stamp'd,
When lord and master of this living world
The Ancestor of human kind was crown'd?
Who hath not ponder'd, or profoundly sigh'd
In the deep hush of some diviner mood,
O'er the dead glories of that regal scene
When all Creation, by his lip baptised,*
Look'd in his face as King on nature's throne?
For what is Science, but a shadow cast
From the pure substance of primeval Mind?
A reflex dim, indefinite and deep,
Of light departed in the gloom of sin?
Or, what is Justice, but our priesthood felt,
The moral echo of supreme desire
That God and conscience may in one combine?
Or, what this appetite for boundless sway,
This hunger of the heart to rule, and reign,
But sense of kingship in our soul alive,
A royal longing for a vanish'd crown?

By law of mild association led
From nature's step-stones, to ethereal heights
Of Things that shall be, thus the heart ascends.
A mute theology all nature makes:
The very ground no vain religion breathes,
Where thorn and thistle, blent with fruit and flower,
Both cross and curse by intimation teach.
And, when from feeling unto faith we mount,
What fine accordance doth Redemption show
Between the ruin and the rise of man!
For, in thy Person and thy Spirit, Lord,
A re-production of those Trinal Powers,
Or threefold state of majesty entire
When priesthood, prophecy, and kingship crown'd
The Man consummate, Faith's adoring eye
In dim rehearsal, or in dawning grace
May witness. Hence our Being, at the best,
Is but an embryo of the life to be.
Philosophy a mere precursor looks;
All high attainments but its preludes are;
And science but presentiment appears
Of Power which Manhood, when redemption brings
The primal glories of our birthright back,
In full millennium shall at length enjoy.

Behold a Centre! for our yearnings form'd,
That oneness, where all aspirations blend
When o'er the ruin of ourselves we roam;
And not from nature *up* to nature's God,
But *down* from nature's God, look nature through.
'Tis here, the meaning of their mystic strife
Passion and Principle alone explain.
The hell we merit, or the heaven we make,

---

* "Whatsoever Adam called every living creature, *that* was the *name* thereof."—*Gen.* ii. 19.

The poet's Eden and the painter's dream,
With whatsoe'er creative Genius cites
By shaping vision from her scenic world;
Together, with all temples and all shrines
A ritual heart instinctively erects,
These, by their secret unison of aim,
In blind concurrence to one Centre tend,—
E'en to regain what Sin's vast forfeit took
From earth of beauty or from man of bliss.

And what an Eden to prophetic mind
Predestined Earth by sight and sound unveils!
Oh, wise, beyond the learning of all books,
And learn'd, beyond the learning of The Schools,
And rich, beyond creation's gold to give,
The man, who thus by deep communion binds
His heart with Nature's, in maternal bonds.
A great proprietor of glories he!
Monarch of inward happiness at home,
And with the Universe a sharer deep
In all the march and movement of a life
Without embodied, or within inspired.

And what though Age, with shaded brow and cheek,
Or eye made solemn by a sense of death,
No longer, in the wild and wildering glow
Of new-born passion, looks on nature's scene
As once impassion'd Boyhood loved to do,
Gay as the sunbeam gambolling at his side,
Or headlong as the breeze that round him play'd,—
Still, not the less, may life's autumnal dreams
Be touch'd with beauty; and, not seldom, find
Meanings which melt, and mysteries that thrill
The musing heart which Nature's lover owns.
Through earth, and ocean, sky, and breathing air,
The ever-ancient and the ever-young
Creation, by persuasive charm, appeals
To youth and age, when genially inspired;
And by her moveless laws a symbol gives
To fleeting life, of permanence and power;
Till haply, in the hush of higher moods,
We mount aloft on meditation's wing
To Him, the Changeless! in Whose present thought
Both past and present make perpetual now;
While all the ages of unreckon'd time
Are but the pulses of Eternity
Around Him throbbing, on his dateless Throne.

CATECHISM.

Far as Imagination's wing can roam
Or free conception take its daring flight,
We love to image an Almighty power
Unfolding boundlessness of life, and love
For ever. Throned in secrecies of awe,
Unfathomably within Himself retired,
We vision worlds, as creatures of His will
Around Him summon'd: but the stooping grace
Of Love creative, when it moulds a flower,
Or makes an insect happy, thrills the heart
Like tearful music, and attunes within
Anthems of silent wonder. While the great
In Godhead magnifies adoring mind,
In His minuteness how we greet His name!
Since in the circle of an atom's range
Dwell the same Attributes which made and move
A universe, with all its breathing worlds!
If God, in great things, be supremely great,
To feeling, looks He greater still, in small:
For, when the Worker and His work appear
To human sense in harmony combined,
Religion, then, is reason at its height:
And our imagined Infinite is graced
With attributes, where just proportion reigns.
But, when some particle, or pulse, infolds
A Mind which makes eternity its home,
And through the chambers of immensity
Moves to and fro, creatively divine,
Then, dazzled reason into faith absorb'd,
Worships the Mystery; and with wonder glows
To watch the working of our God complete,
In all things center'd—no where circumscribed!
Yes, while He wheels ten thousand worlds along,
In the same instant, lo! He stoops to count
The tiny populace a sunbeam holds,
Time the quick beating of an insect's heart,
Or close the eyelids of a babe for rest:
As if nought else eternal Thought embraced
Each atom feels the concentrated God;
While our protection, by its grandeur, proves
All mercies waft th' Almighty on their wings!

And thus, if bold Analogy may dare
The human with divine to parallel,
With touching grace a moral sight appeals
To saintly Virtue, in the heart enshrined,
When he, who storm'd with supernatural force
Round the vile Popedom, till its pillars shook,
Sank to the level of a simple child,
And won frail childhood to the creed he framed.
The son of thunder, soften'd to a breeze,
Behold him shroud the lightning of his soul
In shading meekness; while the hand which hurl'd
The false Decretals to devouring fire,
Plies o'er some little book, or teaching page
Where infancy may learn the name to lisp
Of Jesus; or its budding mind unfold
In faith and freshness, to the call of heaven.

His was the heart that glow'd with all the grace
Which pure compassion for the spirit breathes.
One living soul, from sin and hell redeem'd,
He weigh'd it in the balance of that Blood
Whose every drop with Deity was priced!
And thus, behold him, with paternal smile,
And graceful stoop of his gigantic mind
Bow to the task, a creed for youth condense,
In language artless as the lisping mouth
Of Childhood could pronounce, or read, or pray.
While reason's light through fancy's prism falls
In lines of error on the proud man's view,
Luther himself a child with children knew,
That Cross beneath, where nature must again
Be born. He felt, to know he nothing knew,
Was knowledge, passing what the world calls wise:
And so, if mysteries, like the mountains, cast
A shadow deep'ning as their truths advance
Nearer and nearer to the kindred heaven,
He left them, in the glory of their gloom,
Untouch'd by reason with its carnal gaze.

And like him, may we learn to pause, and pray;
Nor argue down the glory we deny.
If Grace hath spoken, 'tis for Guilt to hear
And learn by rev'rence more than mind can reach:
Since God unshrouded, would be God no more;
Remove the mystery, and the Almighty's gone!

HUMILITY WITHOUT FAITH.

There is religion in the reign of night,
When earth entranced, and heaven ethereal grows,
And planets orb'd with palpitating beams,
In radiant eloquence to man reveal
Their sacred beauty; while the loving Stars
Unseal their eyelids, and with vestal gaze
This world salute, till our attracted souls
Responsively their looks of love return.
'Tis then the energies of mind escape
From sordid fetters, and, like eagles, sweep
The dazzling firmament of Thought divine,
Sparkling with truths unnumber'd as unnamed;
Till, earthward dropping on exhausted plume,
Like the awed Psalmist of the night, they feel
A soft religion from the sky descend,
A charm'd humility, which preaches thus:—
"Say, what is Man, when paragon'd with Worlds?
How mean a speck, how miserably small.
Minute, beyond minuteness to pourtray,
The orbit where he walks, and weeps, and dies!
And He, the Architect, Whose fiat call'd
And will'd this universe of worlds abroad,
Where is the Temple that can hold His praise,
Or mind created, which can worship Him
From whose dread glory not one ray would melt,
Were all this bright magnificence to fade?
For if deep Ocean, with her sumless waves,
Not less in majesty of water rolls
If haply some expiring billow sink;
Or forest huge, whose patriarchal trees
Their wild luxuriance to the winds present,
Not less o'erawes us, though some leaflet die,
Then would no countless throng of worlds, though dead,
Or stricken by some everlasting blight,
One shade on His supernal glory cast
Who makes and unmakes, moulds, and masters all,
But in Himself consummate God abides!"

And may not thus our lesson'd being lie
Low at the footstool of this felt Immense,
To learn humility from all it finds?
A contrast wise, comparison profound,
Nocturnal splendours may they not inspire?
When from the fever of his day-worn life
At length escaping, pensive and alone,
Oft may some Mystic of the heart delight
To soothe excitement, in that sainted calm
Breathed from thy presence, oh, ambrosial Night
Of solitude, serenity, and stars!
Thine is the hour for poetry, and prayer;
Searchings how deep, and soarings how divine
Are then experienced! Time and earth depart;
The shadows of exterior life recede
Like cloud-mist from a morning vale uproll'd;
And on the Infinite we seem to gaze.
'Tis thus, beneath the overawing heavens
Man sinks to nothing; and his world becomes
An atom, twinkling in eternity,
And Life,—the scintillation of a soul
Radiant, but restless with its tiny gleam,
That sparkles into suff'ring, and expires!

But here, Perversion, by its with'ring breath,
Would blast humility with chills of doubt,
And Christ from his created world expel
By logic, from our littleness educed
And call'd transcendant: "Can this puny ball
Of Nature, this revolving speck of earth,
Seen like a glow-worm 'mid the gorgeous blaze
Of suns, and systems, be a proper world
For Deity in Flesh to seek, or save?"

And yet, this argument, so base and blind,
Philosophy and faith alike o'erthrow

With swift prostration. Sceptic! pause awhile,
Nor dream that thus from orphan'd earth recedes
Redemption, since in nature's volume lies
The principle of thy profound rebuke.
Bend to the dust a microscopic gaze,
There God in atoms, e'en as God in worlds,*
Witness! and worship with believing awe.
To Him no magnitude as great appears,
And no minuteness, as the small can be;
Gradations all in Godhead are absorb'd
And vanish; languor cannot Him relax,
Nor low, nor lofty, vast nor various, bring
Distraction o'er Him. Hence, we rev'rence God
When the frail wonders of an insect-wing
Or radiant orbits of revolving worlds,
The traces of consummate mind reveal.
Jehovah, while vast Heaven His word upholds,
And life and matter, motion, space and time
Form but the channel where His will evolves,
Can note and number all whom earth contains!
Observe the monad in minutest play,
Robe the soft leaf, the choral winds attune,
Direct a sunbeam to its shining toil,
Or guard frail infancy on tott'ring feet
From death or danger; or, at balmy night,
The silken eyelids of young Sleep bedew
With slumber, watching o'er unconscious breath!

Thus may Philosophy and Faith sincere
Their creed unite; and when on high we view
Yon great epiphany of glorious worlds,
And echo back with thought's devoutest tone
The starry hymns by Fancy heard to roll,
We sink not, by immensity appall'd;
But in the sacred glory of our creed
Can call our Lord, the Master of it all!

Moreover, God-reflecting Mind is ours
Though faint, and feeble; nor can Truth deny,
A single thought more deity involves
Than all the beauty of yon blazing orbs,
If mind be absent. Therefore, while we own
The sad Palmyra of our ruin'd state,
And what a Tadmor in the desert-soul
Humanity on this soil'd earth presents,
Yet hither, from the heavens all heavens above
Descended, by paternal Glory sent,
Divine Emmanuel! Here His feet have trod;
Around His awful head our sun hath shined;
This air His breath of purity inspired,
And here the music of His lips was pour'd
In speech, and doctrine; miracles illumed
His mission; and each element confess'd
The bleeding glory of that Saviour's wounds
Whose heart for sin on Calvary bled and broke!
And thus, not all unfelt, nor all unknown
This orb minute, by God in flesh redeem'd,
In time or in eternity can be.
Rather may reason, when by faith enlarged,
The charter'd empress of all worlds pronounce
An earth so ransom'd, with such Blood restored;
And in the form of God incarnate see
How human Flesh outsoars the Angels far,
And mounts, in Jesus, an almighty throne.

* St. Augustine touches on this deep subject, in his 52nd Sermon, thus—"Ubique invisibilis atque inseparabiliter adest, non in parte major, in parte minor, sed ubique tota, nusquam divisa," &c. &c.

ANGELIC CONTEST.

Hence, wisdom does not back with doubt recoil,
By reason's name made reasonlessly proud,
When told that Man a mystic platform proves
Where clashing angels, for contested souls,
With, or against, the dread Creator fight.
Here, Attributes eterne their cause have staked;
Here, Character divine itself unfolds;
And from it men and angels wisdom learn,
While all untouch'd by accident, or change,
Divinely perfect as their nature is,—
How love and Law in harmony prevail.

Thus from the Bible heaven-taught lore perceives
The true position to our earth assign'd.
For, though embedded in a brilliant mass
Of worlds on worlds beyond all number vast,
Like some mean province, where ephem'ral dust
Shaped into men to nothing hourly dies,
It hardly glimmers,—thinking Angels see
In pardon'd myriads of immortal souls
Glories which render heaven more glorious still!
Since for their adoration Christ reveal'd
A new Apocalypse of God to man.
Thus they who once unwither'd Eden walk'd
With man, a human paradise to share,
Now when the banner of a Fiend has waved
Defiance, yet on our dismantled earth
Of sin and treason cast a yearning gaze;
And watch, and wonder, worship and admire
Unfolded secrets of forgiving Love
Developed here. And when some lurid gleams
Lighted, perchance, the features of the lost
Archangel, with a hope that ruin'd Man
With God unreconciled must ever be,
And all His attributes to crisis brought,
How did their wings ecstatically wave,

And loud their endless gratulations sweep
The arches of eternity with praise,
God's masterpiece of perfect Grace to hail!
While he, the Anarch of temptation, sank,
To plot in darkness for his own despair.

Thus Fiends against, but Angels for, our souls
Are now contending: on the Cross sublime
Their fix'd and fascinated eyes they bend,
Which glisten o'er its glories; while they cry,
"Depth within depth, O God! how deep art Thou,
Ark'd in Thyself, unvision'd and unshared!"
The councils of divinity they scan
Nor fathom; yét such vast revealings flow
From our Emmanuel, that this world becomes
A focus, where redeeming Wisdom brought
The fulness infinite of Love to bear,
And taught the Seraphim a song, how new!

FALLEN ANGELS.

Yet while angelic bosoms heave with love,
And Watchers bright from heavenly mansions glide
Down to this earth, the prodigal of worlds,
And with the elder love of sinless Truth
Bend o'er our doom, with ever-breathing care
Of pure compassion, are we not beset
By fatal opposites? by fiendish Hosts
Curtain'd in secrecy of hate and hell?
Shapeless, and sightless, round all hearts and hours
Inaudibly they steal: in joy, or gloom,
Present alike to poison or pollute
Man's being. Sin their fascination forms,
And hell in man, for their lost heaven atones:
So deep the horrors of infernal hate!

And what experience have the fiendish band
Who haunt creation with their spells accursed,
From human mind and misery derived,
As, age on age, to murder souls they watch,
And dog them to the very gates of heaven!
Six thousand years of study and of sin
Have deeply, through the labyrinthine heart
Instructed Satan how to wend his way,
Unfelt, unfear'd, deceiving as he goes.

Him Luther imaged, with an awe-struck mind
As God of this world, howsoe'er disguised,
In moments shaded with satanic gloom
And hours of harrowing darkness, when the blood
Ran wildly, aud his heated brain was worn
By fev'rish over-task. And, is the Fiend
A power impersonal, by shapeless awe
Summon'd around us, when the soul is weak?
Not thus did Luther into names abstract
Reduce the Devil; but a Person own
The Archfiend, such as fearless Paul unveil'd,
And, like his pattern, made high reason bow
Before the majesties of truth inspired,
Believing firmly what his Bible spake.
As fact to thought, or law to will is framed,
So scripture to his faith a reason was:
And he who shrunk not from Satanic foes
Mitred, or sceptred, but by zeal inflamed,
High o'er the heavens could wing his dreadless flight
To scorch the angels with a scathing curse,
If other than the gospel-truth they preach'd!—
To fight the devil God's own armour took.
Mail'd with the Spirit's panoply of prayer
Thus was he taught with ghastly fiends to fight,
Weapon'd by grace to lead infernal war.

And was he feeble, while his faith was strong?
Or rather, from his creed heroic might
Derived he not? Simplicity was strength,
In that deep mystery, whose unfathom'd glooms
And paths untrod defy adventurous mind.
Here, God is reason to Himself alone;
To us, mere revelation, and no more,
He deigns to be. Still, o'er forbidden ways
By Him foreclosed, its undisturbèd flight
The pride of Reason in her pagan dreams
Presumes to wing; but drops abash'd, at length,
Down to th' horizon whence conceit arose.
Oh! for a heart as docile, and as deep
In things divine, as that Immortal show'd,
Whose genius round the sun, and mystic stars,
And through the cycles of immensity
The march and movement of eternal Laws
Interpreted; and track'd each orbèd maze,
And, like a Priest o'er planetary worlds
Presiding, taught us how the spheres revolve.
And yet that Solomon in starry lore
Unrivall'd, whose pervading spirit read
Creation's secrets, with untroubled eye,
The Light anatomised to separate hues
By clear dissection, and with steady hand
Felt the tide-heavings of great Ocean's heart
Throbbing for ever with a billowy pulse,—
Sat like a pupil down to Nature's page;
And from her canons all that creed educed
Which makes him seem an oracle of mind
Devout: who, like th' apocalyptic saint
Of Patmos, hath for earthly science shown,
What he for heavenly,—God behind the veil!

And let the worshippers of bright result
Forget not, thus impassion'd Luther won

The bloodless laurels his brave memory wears,—
E'en by adherence to substantial Faith.
Simple as Newton, who could soar and pray,
Building philosophy on fact alone,
Luther in faith could Luther's self renounce,
And, like the scholar of the Holy Ghost,
Learn hallow'd science from the lips of God.

And, deep the knowledge which his spirit drew
From Heaven's own page, of devils and of men.
A stern arena, where a sightless crowd
Of Fiends and Angels in dread conflict ranged;
Or battle-scene, where strangely-awful Powers
Muster and mingle, and their arms unsheath
For good or evil,—did our world become
To him, who saw it in eternal light.
For, just as when some Empire's outraged heart
Big with emotion, swells with surging zeal,
If but a subject by his slaughter'd life
For Her be fallen, and around his grave
Pours the rich life-blood of Her dearest sons,—
So is our earth, though dismal and depraved,
And darkly mean with vaster worlds compared,
A centre where the Chivalries of heaven
Marshal their forces, and with fiends engage.
The terror of their arms, eye cannot see;
The rushing of their plumes, we do not hear,
Nor view the motions of their mystic flight;
But yet, the contest is for countless Souls,
While for the royalties of heaven they strike!
And who, save those who fetter with the bonds
Of clay all faculties of finer scope,
In some rapt hour when mind is half unearth'd
Like Luther's, have not felt the fight unseen,
And through each dim transparency of sense
Vision'd a battle, which the soul surrounds?

GOD OF THIS WORLD.

So felt the man, whom Superstition fear'd,
And Satan ever with a savage watch
Haunted, and down to his own hell desired
By dark temptation of the soul, to bring.
And hence to him, thus tempted, tried, and torn,
No mere abstraction, impotent as vain;
No vile creation of monastic gloom
The arch-Fiend was; nor, to his hell confined:
But here, on earth, in dark unrest employ'd,
And round the axis of infernal guile
Revolving ceaselessly his cruel plans,
Luther beheld him; such as God asserts,
By will, and intellect, and power endow'd,
In living personality array'd
Of being actual; Lord of souls undone,
Maker of death, and monarch of despair;
Who would the universe to cinders blast,
Undo redemption, all our mercies blight,
And hear a jubilee in Earth's last groan!

And must we, to some lacerating dream
Such agonies as rent th' undreading heart
Of Luther, in our sceptic age refer?
Was it with Phantoms of a brain diseased,
Or Actions, out of gloomy thought evoked
Fanatical and false, that saints of old
Contended? Or, by dismal clouds o'erveil'd,
Did Prophets only with the air contend?
Were brave Apostles, when their spirits bled,
By Satans of the mind alone convulsed?
Or, did the God-man, in His day of flesh
Tempted like men, no thrilling combat face,
But simply, by internal vision tried,
Fight with black Nothing in the form of fiend?
Let dread Gethsemane to this reply!
There, while the bloody sweat from Christ was wrung,
As round Him, in His human weakness, rush'd
With eyes which hunger'd on his pangs to feed
And wings that flutter'd with a fiendish joy,
The Hosts of darkness,—let the sceptic ask
If *that* be air, which made Emmanuel shake!

They mock the Devil who obey him most:
But hearts made simple by a power divine,
Believe the combat, and partake it too.
The Friend of sinners was the Foe of sin,
And therefore, saints with Satan must contend
As did their Captain for His cross and crown.
Such was the creed our Saxon hero held.
Yes! that brave Spirit, who in public stood
And calmly watch'd the papal furnace heat,
Prepared to battle with its sevenfold fires,—
Prostrate and pale, with agonising tears
Bound in the blackness of temptation's night
Behold him, like a reed of sorrow, now!
And they, whose wisdom faith and fear produce,
Touch'd by no common awe, will come to view
A martyrdom, beyond what fire inflicts
In the torn depths of Luther's tortured breast
When Satan fell'd him; and the shades of Hell
Frown'd on his heart their horrible dismay!

Oh! there seemed moments when th' Almighty frown'd,
When Sinai over Calvary hung its cloud
Till legal thunders struck the Gospel dumb,
And Jesu vanish'd into viewless air!

Then, pardon'd sin unpardon'd aspect took;
While conscience like a scowling demon lour'd
Full on the past: and e'en the Bible lost
Its music; till the melody of truth
Turn'd to strange discord, where no tones of grace
Or God were found! Then, fiend on fiend began
Between the Saviour and his soul to rush,
In raging darkness; while at times he shook
In fancy o'er the flaming deep of Hell,
And hover'd, as by grasping demons held.

But he, who bled beneath satanic blows,
Hereafter kiss'd the rod his heart endured
And found it gilded with a Father's smile.
For need there was, of educating woes
To pierce him to the centre, till he pray'd,
And the great Luther grew a little child
Safe in the hands of his almighty Sire.
Since much of darkness in his light remain'd;
And much terrene with his celestial mix'd;
And much of Adam with his faith there blent,—
Oh, what but Wisdom, in divinest force,
Knew how to build a perill'd Luther up?
Hence, not a pang his inner being tore
Which was not needed, and by Heaven o'er-ruled
To tame that temper, whose volcanic fires
So often rent him with outbursting rage.
Luther was great, and God would keep him so,
By proving in Himself all greatness lay,
And there alone the Reformation stood.

LIFE A SPIRITUAL CONFLICT.

Reader! the combat rages darkly still
Around thee; though an unrent cloud of flesh
Shut from thy soul their movement and their march,
And the dread soldiery by Hell array'd,
Yet, in the midst of Satan's host art thou
Contending: were thy veiling flesh withdrawn,
Full on thy spirit what a battle-field
Where all the Chivalries of heaven contend,
And the dread Sympathies of darkness fight
For souls immortal—would at once outflame!
But not with garments roll'd in blood, or death;
And not with weapons which our eyes perceive;
But sightless, these unbodied Hosts engage;
And therefore, Satan is the sense's mock,
The sneer of science and the scorn of fools.
But thy revealings, Faith! are ever true
And most tremendous, when the most denied.
A Devil doubted ends in God disown'd,—
Till the first glance a disembodied Mind
Takes of the truth behind the veil disclosed,
Looks on the Fiend, who made himself a lie
To rock the sinner into damning rest.

Reader! believe, the combat rages still;
No pause, and no parenthesis of love
Or pity for our world the Fiend allows.
Darkness his throne, destruction his delight,
Ruin and ravage his dominion make,
And earthquakes seem the echoes of His tramp.
But chief to battle with the sainted host,
Fighting beneath the banner of their King
Crimson'd with blood, and blazon'd by his cross
Redemptive, does the Prince of Hell advance.
Thus Luther felt: and thus shall ever feel,
And like him in the spirit's fight, contend
E'en to the gasp and agony of faith,—
The heirs of Light and heroes of our God.

"The Serpent's head the woman's seed Shall bruise!"
So spake the Lip almighty; and to man
Revolted then the Incarnation preach'd
In promise, which by grasp prophetic spann'd
Ages of conflict in the church to come;
Till time's worn clock his closing hour shall strike,
And this phantasmal scene where Satan fights,
This whited sepulchre of sin and woe,
This prison-house where dungeon'd nature pines,—
A thousand years of hallow'd rest shall have
In one long sabbath of millennial peace!
But not till hurl'd by thunder-blasts divine
Down to his pit, in chaining darkness bound,
The mystic "Dragon" will from earth withdraw:
But fiercely to the last, a fight maintain
Implacable, against all truth array'd.
So from the first imperial Rome he fired
With Pagan fury; when that flame was quench'd
By blood of martyrs, lo! an Arian creed
Flooded the church with desolating tides;
And when they ceased, Platonic visions came
And round the Cross a dazzling falsehood wreathed;
Till papistry in full-blown horror rose,—
The last perfection of satanic guile.

Perpetual motion of a will depraved
He was, and is, and shall for ever be
As Prince of darkness, from his throne of death

Dispensing ruin. Who his sway can meet,
Or stretch the word to where his sceptre waves
O'er time, and scene, and universal man!
For every wheat, he sows a rival tare
In the vast field where faith and virtue thrive:
Each ward of sin and selfishness he knows,
And so, for each some fitting key he finds
Wherewith to enter, and the heart possess.
And let the mockers of the World unseen
The solemn findings of experienced hearts
In this believe,—that like the Saxon monk's,
A life of faith is one long battle now,
Beyond the passion of excited words
To utter, when the heat of conflict comes!
As conscience preaches, so temptation tries
By Him directed: hence, no mood is safe,
No scenes are shelter'd, and no hours secure
From art Infernal. Ask some thoughtful Mind
How often, when th' inflated world hath shrunk
With all its forms, its follies and its fears
Down to a shade, before the solid truths
And substance of eternity believed,
How often then, when resolution winds
Our being up, by tension most sublime,
To heaven's pursuit and love's majestic toils,
Back to the low and little we are lured!
Fever'd as ever, and with fretting pangs
And noisome cares inexorably mean
Again involved: as if this earth were home,
And immortality below the skies!

No height in grace, no depth in guilt forbids
Our dread assaulter. Attributes divine
How oft he covers with deforming shade,
Darkens for dread, or deepens for despair,
Or softens down to sin's presuming dream
Till God a Sentiment almighty grows,
For weak indulgence! Then, the Law he wields,
Fangs its dread curse with everlasting fire,
And on the gibbet of tormenting doubt
Racks frighten'd conscience in perpetual gloom.
For though in health, when light the blood appears
And all looks bland which in Jehovah dwells,
Sin like a trifle of the past becomes,
Or vacant nothing, with a sounding name;
Yet when the dampness of the tomb bechills
Our nature; when fierce retribution frowns
Black on the spirit, from the bar of God,
Then sin, which once a moral pigmy seem'd
But scarce apparent, like a giant swells
Upward to heaven, and with some horrid shade
Beclouds The Infinite, on Whom it falls.

And more than this, the arch-Deceiver dares!
For He eternity in time contracts
And time to false eternity dilates,
When cheated fancy to his wand replies;
And not one grace The Spirit's hand bestows,
For which no counterpart in passion finds
This dreadful Parodist of God to man!
But, chief that Book, where inspirations breathe
And God in language human guilt accosts,
He yearns to silence, contradict, or change.

Still, praise to God! His heroes do not fight
In this fell combat, by their faith alone.
The Lord The Spirit leads them to the field:
And none can perish, o'er whose shielded heads
Waves His pure banner of protecting grace.
Safely through Him they grapple with the Foe
By brave endurance, till the field be won;
When Angels, with a battle-shout of praise,
Welcome to glory those heroic saints
Who cut their way unwounded to the skies!
And thus, what girded Luther for his fight
Doth each bold Gideon in the cause of heaven
Apparel now,—an armour spirit-proof,
Burnish'd and bright like that our "Captain"* wore
When He and Satan for creation fought.

OMNIPRESENCE OF THE SPIRIT.

Omniscient Teacher of regen'rate mind!
Vicar of Christ! who art to men redeem'd
Soul of their souls, and Light of light within,
Vast in Thy sway but viewless in Thy strength,
Thou o'er the chaos of the earth new-born
Didst move, and print it with Thy plastic seal
And inspiration. Beauty hence began,
Order, and shape and symmetry arose;
For Thou of all the Consummator art,
In the green earth, or garnish'd heaven display'd:
Since Nature is Thine organ, and is moved
By secret impulse from Thyself inspired.
Her laws, her lineaments, and loveliness
Are but expressions of Thy shaping will,
The outward index to Thine inward Hand
Creative: beauty is Thy vest Terrene,
Grandeur and grace Thine intimations are,
And second causes form but stepping-stones
By which Thou marchest to Thy works, and ways.

---

* "The Captain of our salvation."—*Heb.* ii. 10.

And o'er those waters of our human world,
The ruder chaos of revolted hearts
Still art Thou brooding, with Thy halcyon calm.
For never, since pollution's blight commenced,
And man apostate to his Maker turn'd,
Hath sigh, or tear, or penitential groan
To heaven ascended and God's welcome sought,
But from Thy grace, pure Spirit! it proceeds.

Then, are we lonely in the war of life
Terrestrial? Strengthless, are we doom'd to strive
With foes of darkness and with fiends of death,
Who round the heart, and in the heart, contend?
Perish the thought! The grace which Luther felt,
Soldier of faith! is prompt to succour thee;
Here is the haven for tempestuous woes
And trials; port of sabbath peace to souls
When the loud billows of temptation rise,
And the heart trembles at their sullen roar.

Oh, for a language, out of sunbeams made,
In syllables of light Thy power to praise,
Helper, and Healer of the heart alone!
Sustainer truly of the sinking mind,
Sole Paraclete to all, for sin who weep!
Descend, and with the dewfall of Thy grace
Our world refresh, a wither'd Church revive,
And the hot fever of man's thirsting heart
With healing balm of blessedness, allay!
Without Thee, creeds become a barren sound,
The Truth is charmless, and the Bible mute
To conscience, though to mental power it speak;
While all in morals, or in motive, gives
But heathen polish with a purer name.

And, where that shrine, the palace, or a throne
From whence Thy secrets and Thy splendours flow!
Where shall our hearts those inspirations seek
Which make all Christians echoes of their Lord?
Wherever man and mind, and scene and space
May act or mingle, there, O Spirit! Thou
With solemn fellowship the soul canst meet.
What, though the herald-stars no longer glide
To light the Magi; though no mystic Bush
Burn with divinity in speaking fire;
And by no miracle made bare, or bright,
An Arm Eternal from the heaven is waved;
Though shut the Vision, and the Witness seal'd,
Nor Voice, nor Thunder out of glory rolls
This earth to waken,—still, Thy love abides;
And the hush'd presence of the Holy One
No bounds can limit, and no laws may bind
From Hearts who seek Him, in their tempted hour.
In cities loud, amid the hum of men
He walketh; or in loved and lonely haunts
Shaded and secret, where Reflection hies;
On mountain-heights, by musing poets traced,
In vales withdrawn, by melancholy shores
Lash'd by the billows in eternal beat,
In each and all God's whisper may be heard,
And still small Voice through listening conscience steal.
Thus, heaven with starry eloquence inspired;
Earth with her scenes of grandeur, or of grace;
Home's gentle magic, infant's guileless laugh
And mother's glowing smile, a charm may prove
Or channel, where His unction can descend
Through soft illapses to our spirit's depths.

But in Christ's temple, there Thy palace is,
Spirit of grace! from Whom our glories come;
Where symbols, signs, and sacramental powers,
Anthems august and hallelujahs deep
Attend Thee, and Thy ministries attest.
And Thine, too, is that living Word which breathes
Of truth celestial, when by prayer perused,
The Bible! there we hail Thee on Thy Throne,
The Urim and the Thummim of Thy power.

Reader! thyself a God is reading now
While thus this question of all questions peals,
Art thou, like Luther, by The Spirit led,
Or, art thou by some hidden Fiend seduced?
Whoe'er thou art, this truth take home, and think!
Two Spirits only for thy soul contend,
The Good, and Bad; but now, alone is Grace
Imparted; soon thy final sands will fall,
And thou in moral nakedness shalt be
To Devil, or to Deity, assign'd
Through endless ages! Oh, that truth immense.
This mortal immortality shall wear!
The pulse of Mind can never cease to play,
But throbs with immortality begun,
Eternal from eternity decreed!
Above the angels, or below the fiends,
To rise in glory or in shame descend
Mankind are destined, by resistless doom.
A soul may perish, but it cannot die:
Immortal essence, 'tis from Godhead drawn,
And, like that Source, unquenchable endures.
But thou, calm Spirit of celestial truth!
Thee may we supplicate our soul to save,
And so renew it, till, resembling Thee,
Our heaven commences ere the earth depart.

PAPAL ROME.

THREE hundred years of beatific life
Unbodied, Luther's living soul hath breathed,
Since the last thunder-bolt of truth he hurl'd
With hand, how fearless! at the heart of Rome.
There, in that world where ransom'd minds repose,
Where priests, and prophets, and the kings of faith
Are gather'd into glory, and await
A pealing life-blast which shall rouse the dead,
The monk of Wittemberg his Master sees
And worships, waiting for his destined crown.
But, hath the world from sacerdotal chains
Itself unfetter'd? Is our faith the free
And pure, and prompted by the Spirit's love
And guidance, soul and spring of saving truth,
Light of all churches, and the Bible's Lord?
Alas! we slumber; and a carnal rest
Calmly around us lets the chain of Rome
Wind its dark coil, with most consummate ease
And falsehood. Bloated with our self-esteem,
And panoplied with intellectual might,
At ease in Zion are we; while a Foe
Remorseless, dragon-eyed, and unappeased,
Wakeful as ever, watches for the prey
Apostate weakness for Her fang prepares.

We want a Luther, with a dreadless voice
To front our modern antichrist, and face
The Vatican, with all its veil'd array
Of marshall'd doctrines or of muster'd lies.
So might we bare the heart of blushless Rome,
And rouse brave England's execrating voice
Till back the priesthood to her dens recoil'd;
While pope, and pop'ry, with a palsy smit,
And scared by scripture, would for ever shrink
In coward gloom to convents, and to cells,
Hooted by nature, and by freemen hurl'd
At once from virtue's and from reason's throne.

Oh! that our protest were as brave and pure,
As saints and martyrs sent, in olden time,
From their deep hearts against the Man of Sin,
Oh, that in light from flames where Ridley died,
Or Cranmer suffer'd his immortal death,
The Church of England would her hist'ry read,
And ponder as she read, with eye of prayer;
Till in that light her lethargy awoke
And rising, like a giant from his sleep
Enchanted, back the Romish chain would fall
Dissever'd, from her limbs of glory dash'd
In horror! Then, again that trumpet-cry,
That battle-voice magnanimously bold,
The tocsin of a nation's truthful mind
By heaven excited, would once more be heard
Like moral thunder round the seven-hill'd Seat
Of Antichrist, in peals of dauntless power,—
No peace with Rome, till Rome make peace with God!

But that bold spirit, which in martyrs burn'd
For truth and freedom, and our British name
Laurell'd with ever-blooming praises, sleeps
In dormancy most fatal. Thus the Beast *
Apocalyptic, once again his head
Of treason, and his horn of vengeance lifts,
To smite the Nations, and our Church eclipse
With papal midnight. Yet, his outward mien
Is stern no longer; smooth'd by modern hands
To gentleness, his ruffled hairs relax;
No savag'ry his watching eye reveals,
And all his claws of cruelty are cut;
But still, the Beast is changeless! for his heart
Unsoften'd, throbs with blackest hate within
Deadly, and dire as in the days of blood.
Full well the Mother of deception suits
Her face, her features, and exterior form
Chameleon, as the atmosphere requires.
And now, when learning, science and the Mind
From dismal orthodoxy's Bulls of death,
And blasts of excommunicating ire
Shrink with disgust, sly Rome the hint receives!
Till, like the echo of all wants and wills,
Behold her! with the freeman talking free;
With tyrants, she at once can tyrant act;
And for idolaters gives idol-forms
In saint, or Virgin! Whatsoe'er the creed
Political, she finds appropriate tones
And flatters each with some obliging key.
Thus for opinion, passion, low desires,
All tempers, dreams, imaginations, thoughts,
All moods, and morals,—whatsoe'er the man
In learning, commerce, or in life be found,
For each and all can Romanistic craft
A seeming counterpart affect, or frame;
But, deep at centre, antichristian still!
So works the Myst'ry, and the world is won,
And aspect changed for principle reform'd
Is now mistaken. Hence, for time prepared,
Rome meets all pressure from without enforced,
By powers elastically prompt within;
Responsive always to each varied call
From creeds perverse, or crisis which demands
Her weapon'd skill, her wisdom and her guile.

* See Rev. xiii. &c.

"And, why hath God, the merciful and great,
Rome's vile burlesque of christian truth allow'd?"
Perchance that Contrast may the earth instruct:
And hence, when man and world have both been taught
Their impotence; when Art, and Lore, and Skill
Their powers have tried, all moral engines used
To lift our nature from the gulf of sin,
And tried in vain; when Reason thus hath learn'd
No remedy from mortal wisdom comes
The plaguing leprosy of sin to heal,
And hearts apostate all their vileness know,
Descending Thunders from the Lord Himself
On Rome will burst, and ruin bury all!

Hence from the first, eternal war prevails
Against "The Woman," and her seed elect;
And each high plan supernal Wisdom chose
Satan hath mimick'd with his aping guile,
Or art stupendous. But the master-piece,
The dread hyperbolé of daring skill,
That great conception where his glory shines
With blasting lustre, is the Roman mock!
There, falsehood in the garb of truth is found;
There, darkness in a dress of light appears;
And all the many-chamber'd mind can hold
Of lies which lull, or sophistries that please,
Is met, and answer'd by some prompt reply.
No! not a tone which Character can sound,
Without an echo from some chord of lies
Play'd by the master-hand of popish Art!
Till, that which blood and havoc could not do,
When heathen Rome, or Arian butchers tried
The Church to mangle and her creed to mar,
This arch defection in canonic guise
By Him erected, hath for cent'ries done!
No partial error, out of reason framed,
Nor falsehood, from licentious will begot,
Hath Satan, in the Man of Sin, achieved;
But one great bondage for essential Mind!—
A ritual net-work, where the soul is caught,
And co-extensive with its ev'ry power.
Thus, all of tendencies, or truths which rise
By man or time develop'd into sway,
These, by a process of absorbing guile,
Rome with herself in soft alliance blends;
Can with her cause incorporate, and mix,
And thus transmute them out of social forms
To fine activities, whose friendly sway
Is won, and wielded for her own at last.

A CHURCH BY INVERSION.

But, whence the model for this curse immense,
This boundless magic of a baseless creed
For ages, like an incubus of hell
O'er human spirit brooding? Whence the power
Bewitching, far beyond destruction's range?
Why, 'tis a counterpart; a church reversed,
A mock of Satan by a man inform'd,
A mimic Show of what in very life
And lustre, form and glory, should the Church
As ground and pillar of the truth, have been.
For, had she constant to her First Love proved,
Binding on earth what God in heaven has bound,
And witness'd boldly for her absent King
A true confession, then would hostile Earth
And Falsehood from her hallow'd mien have shrunk
Self-blasted! and this o'erawed world beheld
The Saviour's Body arm'd with regal powers,
Mitred, and crown'd, in majesty supreme
Anointed Priestess of all grace to man.

But Satan copies, where he cannot change;
And thus a parody in Popes contrived
The Lord forestalling. Hence, the Fiend has framed
A pageant hollow, where his plot can hide
And act Himself beneath the Saviour's name.
For more than haughty Rome assumes to be,
By Heaven empower'd in privilege and grace
Imperial, would the gospel Church have *been*,
If holiness with apostolic charm
Her shrines, her altars, and memorial rites,
Her ministers, and members, all had crown'd.

And here, (as ever) from the Plan Divine
The lost Archangel hath, with fiendish craft,
Directive elements of wisdom drawn.
His model was Judaic: thence he stole
Those adaptations for the sensuous mind
He view'd there, organised in typic forms;
Myst'ries and rites, or ceremonial laws,
And ritual pomps where Priesthood looks sublime,
He found prevailing: these he studied well,
Then caught the genius of the mighty whole,
And made a copy for the papal Church
Which pope and priest, levitically blind,
Transcribed for ages, and is using now.
Thus, the dead carcass of Mosaic forms
By God deserted when Emmanuel died,
Satan himself hath repossess'd, and fill'd
Or quicken'd. Here, the Roman witchcraft see!
While man travesties what Messiah did,
And writes "unfinish'd!" o'er His perfect Cross.

Nor can our Age, though clad with self-conceit,
And helmeted with intellectual powers,

Produce the David whose predestined hand,
With sling of scripture, and with stone of truth
Well-aimed, her brazen forehead might indent,
Blasting her glory, with a righteous blow.
And, where the signs, the symptoms of Her fall?
Whence come the weapons Christian arms can wield,
Wherewith the triple Crown to pluck, and dash
Her high pretensions into baseless dust?
Alas! our locks of strength are almost shorn;
Distracted counsels, or divided aims
Impede fair union; and that mystic Robe
Which all unrent in perfect glory hung
While on His cross the dying Saviour bled,
Is torn to tatters, underneath His throne,
By hands and hearts schismatical, and wild!
Is this an attitude for deeds sublime?
With Masters many, while our Lord is One,
Our cold negations can no Church evince
In act embodying what our creed affirms
Of Union vast, and visible, and true.
How can we thus, with uncompacted force,
And mere abstractions, depthless, dim, or faint,
Battle with Rome, or keep her priests at bay?

Alas! expediency our Moloch was,
And at Her feet our ancient glories fell
Dishonour'd. Mute that mighty Protest, now,
By martyrs thunder'd like a voice from Heaven,
"Come out from her, my people! quickly come:"
Since base concession legalised her guile,
And lo! the Land, whose soil with sainted blood
Is hallow'd, where burnt Hooper's ashes sleep,
And lived the lion-hearted men, whose tongues
Shook the roused Empire with their shout for God,
For faith, and freedom! *there*, the Papal "Beast"
Is lodged, and in his den of lies secure!

Yet, to and fro, behold! the many "run"
And knowledge, as by Seers foretold, increase.
Still, what though ocean, air, and matter seem
A university for Mind become,
Where Sense can study, Science take degrees,
And Comfort all her sensual dreams enjoy,
Is this protection from the spells of Rome?
Oh! not in culture where no sacred germs
Are planted; not by knowledge, where no peace,
No pardon and no purity abound
For conscience, not by these are empires great,
A people glorious, or their welfare sure.

VICTORY OF FAITH.

Knowledge brings power; but Faith beyond it works,
And out of heaven that promised aid procures
Of mercy, whence alone true wisdom springs;
Till, through the heart's regenerated depths
The mind it reach, and make that holy, too.
To catalogue Creation's works; the tides
To balance; all the stars peruse; or scan
The secrecies unveiling Science loves,
This may enlarge, but not ennoble, Man,
If man be measured by his noblest scale,
By will, by conscience, and by perfect love,
Love that is heavenly and by God begun;—
For so philosophy divine asserts:
We find the lovely, and that thing we love;
But what God loves He thereby lovely makes.

In these alone pre-eminently live
Those elements which make our being great.
But Things to master, abstract names to know,
Their use, their natures, and their powers to wield,
May serve the Body, not the Soul refine
Or chasten. Thus, in vain would mental Power
Self-deified, the world's redemption try.

And how can mind, at best, a bulwark frame
To fence corruption from the inner soul?
In central likeness all men meet, at last;
For there is conscience in the vilest left,
With immortality, in each presumed;
And this stern Guardian on his throne of truth
Wakens at times, to vindicate the Law,
And preaches on eternity and doom
Sermons, which sound like arguments from God,
Prophetic, deep, and terribly divine!
And then religion, forced, or felt, or feign'd,
The heart's convulsion and its craven guilt
Alike demand: and where can earth produce
A Creed so organised with subtle craft,
To soothe the guilty, but retain the guilt,
As the mock creed of pharisaic Rome?
And though at times, pure Reason may rebel,
Shock'd into anguish by imposture's lie,
Reason is bribed, and understanding bought
When Lust is flatter'd, or the conscience freed
From harrowing guilt, from darkness and despair.

THE MAGIC CITY.

And thus, no energies from culture drawn,
No arguments, by mental skill applied,

The Man of Sin can weaken, or o'erwhelm:
Rome laughs at these, and she has laugh'd before!
And ev'ry realm progressive science haunts
Pre-occupies, or masters at her will.
Hence, what a paradox of wondrous crime,
What miracle of permanence and power
To men and angels, must Her hist'ry be!
For though a slaughter-house for souls she made
The Church for ages, still, without a blush
She lifts Her forehead in the light of Heaven:
And though full often have the pent-up fires
Of wrath around her, fierce with ruin flamed;
And Power hath tried, and Policy assail'd
Her bulwarks; battles and rebellions leagued,
Tyrants and victors have besieged her walls
And daring Intellect opposed Her well
And wisely; Truth and Science both have hurl'd
The thunderbolts of their denouncing ban,
While righteous scorn her hidden cheats unveil'd;
And from the bosom of the soul hath burst,
Time after time, Humanity's appeal
Charged with the wrongs of ages, to condemn
The blackest outrage which can e'er abase
Morals and mind, and all which Man should be—
The mystic Harlot, on her seven-hill'd throne
In pomp and theocratic pride array'd,
Reigns like a Priestess of the spirit still
O'er crouching millions, in their souls struck blind!

And find we not a symbol in the fate
Of Rome the city, how the Romish creed
All time would master, where the Cæsars ruled
In blood, or baseness? Babylon hath sunk
Beneath the blast prophetic, and become
A den of ruin; Nineveh is nought;
The Persian perish'd in his pride of arms;
Assyria's dead, and Macedon no more;
The daughter-islands of the ancient Deep
Once free and faithful, in their noon of fame,
With Tyre and Sidon, and the classic isles
Of Greece and glory, are but sunken things;
And Palestine, th' Almighty's home, remains
E'en like a mother for her children dead,
Wasted, and weeping in mysterious woe;
But Rome is mighty in her magic still,
Like man's eternity by stone express'd
Behold Her! fated for a future doom,
When Deeds by prophets sung, shall there achieve
A destined ruin. Well may pilgrims trace
In wonder, how august She yet remains!
With fountains, baths, and famous aqueducts,
Arches, and catacombs, and hoary shrines;
While all the genius of dead Ages haunts
Her soil with shadows, and her scene with spells
That speak, though silent. Past and Present meet
In high communion, and historic dreams
Her tombs unlock, till colonnaded streets
Move with stern Heroes, whose creative minds
Yet bow the world with intellectual sway,
Reigning like monarchs on each mental throne,
Tyrants at once and teachers of the soul.

THE MAN OF SIN.

And as the City, so the creed endures
Deathless in might, immortally depraved.
Her aspect alters—when her power is weak;
Her plans are soften'd—when her foes are strong;
Her practice gentle—when the Age requires;
But Rome, in principle, is Roman still
The changeless ever! for her creed is one;
And that is, to absorb the blinded world,
And on *herself* a faith almighty found
As truth infallible, or God divine!

And what a miracle of matchless force
She wielded, when the craven soul had sunk
Down to that level, which her creed demands!
Like to some vision of unearthly gloom
Shaped in the midnight of a dreaming brain,
By horror featured, doth Her sway emerge
From the gone ages, when the Gothic mind
Bow'd at her footstool, as the throne of God!
Two Worlds she claim'd; o'er both presumed to cast
The priestly shadows of Her sceptred power,
Moulding eternity, and mast'ring time!
Till in the glory of Satanic crime
Her mitred autocrat almighty grew
And challenged worship, such as God demands!
Heaven's attributes in libell'd form a Man
Did thus array: and when his frown grew black,
It shaded all things with submissive awe
And silence! On his lip creation hung;
The elements from him their course derived,
And plague, and pestilence, his law obey'd:
His names were natures! and those natures all *
Ambition wanted, or his will decreed.
But when his excommunicating arm
Was lifted, Heaven that ireful threat revered!
And Hell, with all its agonies and glooms,
The motion watch'd: but when indeed it fell,

* Bellarmine gravely argues, that *if* the Pope *should* decree virtues to be vices, or vices virtues, that moral transformation would at once be achieved!

Empires turn'd pale, and palsied Kings recoil'd,
And sackcloth'd Nations trembled into tears!

Yet had this tyrant but the body cursed,
Made Cities mournful, or a province poor,
Or, tax'd the Passions for an income base,
Mankind were left some virtue, still, to save;
But Nature, in her sacred ark of strength
Where man is man when all besides decays,
The Pope, by impious sacrilege, profaned.
And dreader far than famine, fire, or sword,
Dungeons, and deaths, or all which martyr'd Flesh
Can suffer, is what outraged Conscience feels
When, like a moral suicide, the Man
Himself must abdicate, the will destroy,
And not a Person, but a Thing become!
Then rots the mind in servitude, and shame;
The faculty august of reason fades,
And blinded Nature grows a base machine
By craft inspired, to work a despot's will.

HOPE AND HARP OF PROPHECY.

But, sheathed for ever is th' avenging Sword
Of Godhead? Will it ne'er on Roman crimes
And cruelty with flashing ire descend,
Cleaving her bulwarks to their very base?
Oh, dare we think, that all the mangled host
On Alpine mountains hunted, spiked, or slain
By thousands, or by Marian hell-hounds torn
To bleeding fragments, have in *vain* their voice
Heroic peal'd along the heaven of heavens,
Startling the angels on their golden thrones
When the last anguish of their dying lips
Came up before them? Fruitless have they lived,
Or preach'd, or felt, or suffer'd, who of old
Gave to the world the glory of their death
By wheel, or gibbet, rack, or fiery stake
In vaulted cells of subterranean gloom
By death-lamps lighted, where the lurid beam
Faintly along some victim's quiv'ring flesh
Glimmer'd, and lit his harrow'd features up?
Far otherwise may thoughtful bosoms feel,
When grateful Hist'ry to their shrines of Death
Resorts, where deathless Inspirations glow.
The living dead ones are they! and their words
Ring round the heart like tones which never die.
Beyond their sermons, preach their sorrows, still!
Their anguish is our glory; for we feel,
Who died for principle, for God yet lives
To perish never! Where they bled, or burn'd,
Corded, or chain'd, or rent by racking fires,
Devils were taught how Man's enduring strength
Can suffer, when by prompting grace inspired.
And therefore, Martyrs! of Britannia's church,
That ancient plant of apostolic growth,
We laud, and love ye with no cold delight,
Who bled for conscience, and to Britain left
A creed untouch'd, like Cranmer's heart, entire!
E'en from your tombs an eloquence proceeds
Which champions Ages to repeat your worth:
And never from our venerating hearts
The deeds ye dared, the majesty ye show'd
In the dread anguish of a godlike hour,
Shall die! All time your holy debtor is:
And long as in our Church's veins endures
The precious life-blood of protesting truth,
Never can England from her mindful soul
Cancel the debt, her glories owe to *you!*
Your pangs have her inheritance become,
A wealth bestowing more than gold creates.
Ye gave the Bible! which your tortures won;
And shame terrific on our head alight,
If what the blood of martyrdom bequeath'd
In black ingratitude we basely yield.
Ye gave the Bible! and that priceless Book
Our blessings all in germ at once bestow'd.
For, what is Science in her purest flights,
With all those blending harmonies which rise
From social nature, but the man evolved?
But, both the moral and the mental roots
Of human nature, with transmuting sway
The scriptures reach; and thus with latent force
And vigour these the heart of Britain cleansed,
Making her land the paradise of isles.

Then, not in vain, though Rome be blushless still,
And round her creed a Trentine darkness casts
Cruel as ever, have the martyr'd hosts
And hecatombs of peerless saints, who bled
For truth, to God against their murd'ress cried.
Beneath the Altar rise their mystic wails
And enter, not unfelt, the ear of Heaven:*
Since ev'ry drop their costly veins effused,
With every pang their burning limbs endured,
Have bright memorial in the Lamb's own Book,
And shall be answer'd, when avenging Time
Brings the dread hour by Prophecy decreed.
Then shall The Lord in robe of fire descend,
And with the breathing of His mouth shall smite,
And with the brightness of His coming blast,
And into cinders by His curse consume
Earth's second Babel, antichristian Rome!

* See Revelations.

Meanwhile, presuming man would fain achieve
What scripture to The dread Eternal gives
In plan and purpose, for His crowning work.
Thus, all are prophets to themselves, at least,
And preach perfection possible below.
But can corruption to itself be cure?
If man be ruin, and rebuilt he rise,
'Tis not by rubbish from himself produced,
But by a means transcendant, as divine.
The creed within forms character without,
And God alone can educate the will;
But, will makes man, in all essential powers,
And therefore must he, by regen'rate grace
Beyond himself through heavenly love ascend,
Or still be changeless, in his moral core.
Thus, to the last, a leper will remain:
The skin may whiten, but the blood is black,
And burns in secret like a plague-spot, still.

ROME SHALL FALL.

And yet, 'tis written with a pen of light
That Rome shall wither, and this Earth rejoice
In the rich beauty of her bridal robes
Apparell'd; and beneath her reigning Lord
Keep the long Sabbath of a thousand years.
And hence, millennial is the heart of man,
As if 'twere haunted by some primal grace
Of vanish'd Eden, when the Earth was young,
Sinless, and bright, without one scalding tear
To wet her eyelids, or the cheek to stain.
Creation groans for her sabbatic peace;
And echoing mind, in every age of thought,
Repeats the longing. This the poet's lyre
Hath warbled, in prophetic strains of song,
Caught from the harp of Scripture; and the creed
Of Aspirations, as they rise, and reach
Their zenith, with this inward faith accords,
That Earth shall bloom with paradise regain'd,
And be unweeded of her thorny woes
And thistles; and our Age itself is big
With expectation of some golden dawn,
Or peaceful glories. But alas! for earth,
If no millennium save what science brings,
Await her! if those moral truths sublime,
That reach the Everlastingness of man's
Dread future, have no room for reigning here:
For, sooner may the hand of Science think
To bale the ocean from its boundless depths,
Than drain corruption from the soul of man!

'Tis here the worshippers of Mind, seduced
By science, in their dreams half pagan grow,
Politely bow apostles to the door,
Or gently hint the Bible may be wrong!
For carnal Knowledge to herself is true
And constant ever!—back from God recoils
Behind the tree, to eat forbidden fruit,
Lurking, like Adam, in a guilty shade.
But oh! Thou Spirit of celestial life
And wisdom, teach them first Thyself to know,
And, knowing Thee, themselves to feel, and find
That man unchristian is embodied sin;
And though embellish'd, and by art subdued,
But veil'd corruptions all his virtues form
Till faith can touch them with a spell divine.

But there are prophets, who for Rome predict
A downfall, not by arms of earthly might,
Nor yet by reason, though its powers expand.
Far humbler they: in things divine as deep,
Jehovah is their reason; and they bow
With faith compliant at that mental Shrine
Where Deity, in human words, unfolds
The future, and Himself to love expounds.
And thus convinced, and by the Spirit taught
That man with man can never right be made,
Till right with Godhead will and worship be,
Our true advancement by preventive grace
Alone they augur. Well their natures know,
That as the sun with his bright rays is view'd
The living God with His own love we love.

Hence in the organ-voice of Prophecy
And chanted hymns by rapt Isaiah pour'd,
They catch the music of Messiah's reign
That in them warbles! But a wail there is,
Or ever thus the gladden'd Earth shall lift
Her choral triumphs, yet from man to rise:
From seers august, from Enoch's olden time
To him of Patmos, all their voice unite
In diapason terribly distinct;
Denouncing woes, beyond what Time hath seen
Or this world suffer'd, ere apostate Rome
Be ruin'd, or millennial splendours reign.
And though, by ardency of hope inspired,
The distant future in fond dreams we scan,
Enraptured, and those sun-gilt peaks admire,
Deck'd by the radiance of a blissful dawn;
Just as the mountains of our world appear
In the blue distance, lined in lofty range
And harmonised by one unbroken swell,
With no dark gulf beneath them,—so may Hope
Too often on the heights prophetic gaze,
And merge, and melt them in soft unity;
Though black the gloom, and dreadful the abyss
Of wrath and judgment that between them frowns.

A bridge of ages in prophetic time
Our Dispensation is, by heaven decreed:

Inclusively between those seers 'tis rank'd
Who first Emmanuel in His veiling flesh
Predicted, stricken, cursed and crucified
For our acquittal; then,—the Christ enthroned
Crown'd with the royalties of reigning pomp
Millennial. Thus an intervening gulph
The second Advent from the Church divides.

And stern analogy this view confirms,
When teaching ages of th' historic Past
Instruct the Present, not for heaven to hope,
But rather, that our Gentile sun will sink
A bloody occident in wrath and gloom!

And what a warning, would our ears attend,
Nor deaf as adders from the charming voice
Avert them, do the unforgotten scenes
Where Churches, once which miracles endow'd,
Apostles water'd, and the Spirit's grace
Divinely freshen'd with celestial dews,
Preach to the haughty Age we honour now!
Where have they gone, those Daughters of the sea,
Smyrna and Sardis, and the Sisters five
Whose "Angels" oft the loved disciple taught?
And by the shores, where oriental waves
Chime their lone music to the Afric blast,
How perish'd all Tertullian's page unfolds
When Carthage made his apostolic crown,
And martyr'd Cyprian into glory died!
While Hippo, where sublime Augustine mused,
Hath melted down to miserable nought!

These give dread warning, if we wisely make
The Past a preacher to our Present be.
But, sick at heart, and in the head unsound,
And sleek, and satisfied with all we do,
The mountain of *our* majesty appears
Immoveable! our age, Augustan call'd,
Our arts advanced, our science most complete,
Our wealth enormous, and our wisdom vast,
On land victorious and by sea the same,
While on *our* Empire sinks no travell'd sun!—
Bloated with privilege, we thus predict
Perpetual glory for the worshipp'd Isle,
Above destruction, and beyond decay.

SEVENTH VIAL SOUNDED.

A Church elected, not a world renew'd,
Here is the Centre for united aims;
And faithful round it, touch'd by solemn awe
Meekly and firmly may we watch; and wait
Th' unfolding Drama of that hour decreed
For vengeance, when the scarlet "Beast" shall fall;
When He, in whom all types of terror blend
And blacken into one colossal Form,
The dread Fulfiller of prophetic woes
And wailings, shall at last Himself reveal!
The sin of ages into one condensed
Shall thus be acted; then the Church endure
That Fiend in flesh, of whom all Scripture shows
Faint Antichrists, who cast their shades before
The coming substance of infernal Might
By Daniel vision'd, and by David sung
In song terrific. Then, a Day of blood,
Of burning deaths, of blackness and despair,
All Creeds shall test, all living Churches try,
Purging the faithful, till their dross they lose,
And purified from out the flames arise
In radiant beauty, and by love bedeck'd
With bridal vesture to receive their Lord.

And signs abound, and symptoms which escape
All but the souls who see with Scripture's eye,
That dooming hour by prophecy unveil'd,
When Gentile churches shall dissolve, and end
Amid the crash of Kingdoms. Far and wide,
From Thames to Tiber throng the shadows thick
Of terrors, which predict those Latter Times
Ripe for the harvest of almighty wrath,
When God for glory reaps His vengeance due.
Look where he may, a watching Saint discerns
No sackcloth'd Empire on its knees at prayer;
No Kingdom bow'd in penitence, or tears;
But all is headstrong, haughty, and unchanged
As ever. Vainly have revolving Years
Dread sermons preach'd on anarchy and crime
To banded nations, or benighted men:
And though Earth rocks, and Nature's footsteps reel,
Full on the* buckler of Jehovah's wrath
The Age is rushing, 'gainst His bosses dread
To dash its forehead, and endure the death
Of Treason. Soon, perchance, may come
A dark catastrophe, which closeth all
That fearful Drama, which this fallen world
Is now enacting on the stage of Sin.
The ancient Dotard of the triple Crown
Is yet a mocker, and the Bible hoots
Madly as ever; while absorbing Rome
Beneath the banner of her witchcraft draws
All warring opposites in creeds which rise,
To swell her potency and aid her charms.
Discord, and crime, and brutal passions rage;
And Lust, and Rapine, in delirium steep'd,

---

* Job xv. 16.

Weaken all truths, and let their lies abroad
In lawless havoc over hearts and homes.

And thus there rally, from the regions where
Disturbing elements of mind can mix,
All Powers and Principles, to final war.
And by such phalanx, which a Fiend might lead
To battle, when the world is well prepared,
And leaven'd to the core with lying spells;
When Faith, the bond of all cementing bliss
'Tween man and man, Her social life withdraws;
And no religion to the Throne eterne
Binds with a golden chain this earth below,
Then may that Hour, by Luther's prescient eye
Foreshadow'd, and by tragic Seers foretold,
Come to a head, and Antichrist be scorch'd
To cinders, by the thunder-blast of God!
The Vials six have all been emptied now;
The Trumpets six their peals of woe have blown,
And of the Seals apocalyptic, six
Their fated truths unfolded and fulfill'd:
But when that Vial, for the seventh decreed,
Its curse shall empty; when the closing Trump
Hurtles its thunder through the mystic heaven,
Then may this world an Incarnation see
Infernal: such as never, from the deeps
Of utter Darkness hath permissive God
Allow'd upon our palsied earth to stand.

But whatsoe'er this shape of Hell appears,
As Wicked, Wilful, or the Lawless one,
Myst'ry in flesh, or Man with fiend combined,
Papist, or Heathen, Jew, or Pagan he,
If not in name, by nature he shall prove
Son of Perdition; who himself shall dare
To magnify beyond all worshipp'd gods,
Or Saint, or Angel, on his temple-throne;
And rob the Infinite of glory due
By lying wonders. Come whate'er He may
In form, or fashion, faith in this exults,
That in the wine-press of almighty wrath
Trampled and torn, beneath avenging Christ
The final Antichrist is doom'd to fall!
For when awhile, on Satan's seven-hill'd seat
The nameless Anarch hath his wine-cup drugg'd,
And crush'd his compeers, till beneath his flag
All Shapes of evil shall themselves enlist,
Dilated, darken'd, and by deep excess
Made terrible, beyond what terrors dream;
When thus, fell Antichrist himself proclaims
A new almighty on creation's throne!
Then shall that Fight, whose dismal pomp arrays
Full many a Vision with prophetic awe
And many a promise with its glory fills,
And many a verse with battle-music storms,
Be hasten'd. Lo! the bright Avenger comes
In panoply of dreadful glory sheathed,
And blasting; till the disenchanted Earth
Again shall smile, and with responsive joy
Partake millennium in the Church's peace.

ANTICHRIST.

Yet, who can gaze, with spirit unappall'd,
On the vast outlines of this coming Doom
When all, which now in prophecy looks dead,
Leaps into life and acts the part sublime!
And this great Battle of Almighty God
By visions pictured, lyric poets sung,
And with whose muffled roar the Bible rings,—
Who can presume its awfulness to paint?
Then the Last Head of desolated Rome
Under his banner, with his Kingdoms ten,
And rebel Nations rallied at his cry,
Shall, front to front, the God eternal meet
For battle; and beneath the blast Divine
Down the deep hell of darkness and dismay
Descend for ever to his doom accursed!

Dungeon'd in fetters, for a thousand years
There shall He writhe; and in the racking curse
Of judgment holy, shut and seal'd by wrath
Resistless, magnify the Son of God,
By this endurance of avenging doom.
But yon bright Angels, who did faithful stand
When He, the primest of their Splendours once,
Fell in proud treason, by confirming grace
In heaven to worship and on earth to wait
Are destined; and their golden harps shall ring
In unison with choral saints, who now
Circle The Lamb triumphant and enthroned.

MILLENNIAL VISIONS.

As some pale Bard from fever-dreams awakes,
Haunted by shades and shadows undefined
Yet fearful, making dark imagination shrink,
Once more to look upon a heaven of stars
Through the high lattice beaming, and to bathe
His wearied temples in the fresh-wing'd air
Exulting,—so from these stupendous glooms
And themes of awe, where Reason stands abash'd,
Back to the brightness and the bloom of earth
We hasten. Here, what living glories throng,
Prophetic numbers might indeed rehearse;
And vision scenes o'er which the harping Seers
Enchanted roll'd their richest strains of song;
And in some lulling dream of Latter Days
For this world destined, feel what Luther felt,
On Pisgah-heights of prophecy enrapt
As oft he mused, and hail'd millennial times.

But, now, expressionless the heart recoils!—
Under a weight of glory melt all words
To muteness, when that imaged Kingdom comes
On earth to be, what thus the Bible types,
And tells of Purity's celestial reign.
Then shall Redemption's perfect work respond,
And reach to all which revelation sings
In forms of Matter, or in facts of Mind,—
Yet to evolve. Creation's groan shall cease;
And life, and sense, and earth, and air, and sky
The vast enthronement of their Lord reveal,
By the felt magic of His reign inspired
And hallow'd. Glory in the sun will beam
With sevenfold brilliance; and the placid Moon
Glide through the mazes of her moving stars
With lustre deeper than rapt David saw
By midnight harping: not a fruit, or flower
Which bares its beauty to the prying breeze,
That will not in th' o'erflowing love and light
Of Earth's millennial consummation share.

And when Christ reigns, far more than Adam saw
The Earth shall witness in this bridal hour.
But oh! if Matter thus resplendent be,
Who can pourtray inaugurated Mind?
For if e'en now the Church our world instructs,
Though in her weakness,—when with Christ she reigns
Entire creation from That Church may learn
Perfect instruction, in the things profound
Of God. And as her Lord gradations knew,
And to the heights of His predestined rank
Ascended, so may God's elect advance
By faint reflections of His threefold sway,
As Prophets, Priests, and Kings of other worlds
And systems; and this inorganic earth
A palace of material splendours prove,
Where Beauty visible its throne shall set,
And o'er all worlds our *own* as model shine.

Thus, on the footing of God's Word inspired
Our hope we plant, and there this promise find,
That throned Emmanuel with avenging ire
Proud Antichrist shall blast, and then consume.
The Jew shall yet his bright Jerus'lem see,
And draw salvation from the Sides he pierced
When Christ on Calv'ry bore the bitter Cross;
While hymning Gentiles their hosannahs join
The Lamb around; and resurrection-saints
Call'd from the dust to greet their living Lord,
A thousand years of coronation-bliss
With Christ in glory shall on earth partake.
Till when at length, on sin, and Satan's host
And earth rebellious, final Judgment sets
That Seal tremendous, which for ever shuts
The perish'd in their prison-house of Woe
And wrath unutter'd, earth and heaven shall reach
A beauty endless, in baptismal fires
Recast, and shine with more celestial bloom
Than Sense can dream or Inspiration tells.

Hence all creation will Messiah bring
To full perfection, in its brightest form;
And back restore it to the heart of God
From whence it wander'd. There, his kingdom ends,
And Mediation down its sceptre lays*
When nought between us and the Godhead comes.
Then face to face adoring man will view
The infinite; nor means, nor modes be used,
Nor sacraments, nor teaching symbols cast
'Tween God and soul their intervening shade.
In Deity the Church will be enshrined,
His Attributes her perfect temple prove,
Till God in mind the mind of God beget,
And life eternal be Himself enjoy'd.

TIME AND ETERNITY.

BETWEEN the living and the dead our life
Throbs like a brief vibration; and how soon
This pendulum of anxious being stops!
E'en in a moment, by some touch or tone
Arrested, lo, the life of sense concludes,
And we are launch'd beyond the tracking eye
To follow; by the Infinite absorb'd,
And *in* the secret of Eternity!

And yet, as though Reality were here
Alone authentic, how the hollow show
Of things, which eye, or ear, can apprehend
O'ercomes, and with monopolizing charm
Our cheated mind attracts, and blunts the edge
Of fine perception, for the spirit-world
To come! And oh, how rarely hoping Youth
Turns to the future a prophetic gaze,
Beyond this earth of shadows! Tomb on tomb
O'er life's descending pathway throws a shade;
And many a heart-ache to some fever'd brain
Must pay sad homage, ere the mocks of time
Be scatter'd, and our nobler dreams of soul
Their reign commence, and teach the gay to think.

---

* "The Son also Himself shall be subject unto Him that put all things under Him, that God may be all in all."—1 *Cor.* xv. 28.

Then, throbs the immortality of thought
Within us! then, adown the gulf unknown
Of Life's hereafter prescient fancy looks,
By faith made holy; while we learn to feel
That body forms the prison-house of soul,
And, out of it the dead indeed are free!

And such are round us, in ethereal hours
When earth recedes, and through the rents of Time
Beyond the Visible we dare to gaze,
And gather wisdom from a world unseen,
Though not unshadow'd by foreboding mind.
Thus may all clouds of Sadducéan tinge
Dissolve, and placidly our dreams recall,
And the loved features of our dead, recast!
By lonely shores, by melancholy seas,
At moonlight's trance, or sunset's dreamy close,
Down vaulted aisles or churchyard's cypress-gloom
Slow-pacing; or, beneath pictorial forms
By Art's eternity of hues preserved,
How oft we ponder o'er some face beloved!
Till, by that resurrection which the heart
Rehearseth, we can bid their cherish'd tones
To wake, and hear their wonted footsteps glide.

But, deep the truth omniscient Scripture tells
And sanctions,—not one pulse of conscious Mind
The Will Divine hath ever caused to play
In human being, hath a single rest
Experienced, since the primal throb began!
The spirit-people of God's world Unseen,
Millions on millions though their number be,
Are conscious, more than when by flesh encased,
And clogg'd in action. Not a soul's extinct!
Still Adam thinks; still Alexander feels;
Cæsar hath being; Cleopatra lives;
And those crown'd butchers, whom the world calls brave,
Are feeling more than when they battles fought:
Yes, all who *have* been, great, or good, or vile,
Patriarchs, prophets, intellectual kings,
Heroes, or warriors, and those laurell'd priests
Of truth, the poets of Eternity,
All are a living, though a sightless, race;
Each in himself a hell, or heaven, become!
For Mind is everlasting; and the Man
Is there in essence, when contingents die.
Thus may the Dead a more than sermon preach
To awe the living, and this truth impress,
That *as* we die, for ever we endure!
The same in principle the heart abides:
Since Morals in their root continue one
And changeless, though the Soul hath taken wing.

Hence two Worlds claim us, by a sleepless law;
But one moves round us, palpably instinct
With life and passion; and, alas! absorbs
In the wild vortex of its vain delight,
What to the other, though unseen, we owe
Of faith and conscience. Thus, *for* time we live
As well as *in* it; thus, our hearts deny
The Infinite that waits behind the Veil;
And when the living from our gaze retire
We talk as though they lived not, and were quite
From Being parted, as to sight no more!
Yet this is madness in the garb of sense;
The blinding mock of necromantic dreams,
Dilating time into eternity
And which eternity to time contract.
For faith and reason in this truth conjoin,
The dead are living, but their life unheard,
Unfelt, unknown, beyond ideal thought
To image, seldom can that man inspire
Who walks by sense, and worships but the same.

PARADISE OF THE DEAD.

YET, thought has moments, when deep souls exclaim
"Where are the Dead? the Minds who once look'd forth
In light from eyes, in language from kind lips,
And by the daring of immortal deeds
Breathed on our own, like inspirations? Where
Where dwell the Spirits, who once felt, and fear'd,
Who dream'd, desired, or acted, like ourselves?
Where have they fled? In blank absorption, lost?
Merged in the Infinite, engulf'd, or gone?
Melted to nothingness? Is this their doom?"
Oh! wait awhile: for e'en as wintry earth
By the green outburst of some glorious spring
Secrets of heavenly power in Nature's breast
Developes, so may this material Scene
With hidden radiance of celestial life
Be clad hereafter; since the reign of Saints
Shall yet be witness'd, ruling over all
Conspicuous, with a glory undescribed.
The shell of Matter shall at once remove,
Like a strange dream the Visible depart,
And lo! at once the "quick" on earth will stand
By angels circled, and by saints enthrong'd,
And in the midst incarnate God appear!

Meanwhile, the Bodiless in secret live
Till all be rife, for this predestined form
Of sudden, swift, and strange Apocalypse.
Holy of Holies! in thy shrine august

High o'er all heavens, ethereal, and unreach'd
By man's conception, dwell the Dead redeem'd.
There, the saved myriads of the seal'd First-born *
Present with Christ, from Him perchance acquire
Truths which on earth Experience did not gain.
Patriarchs, who dimly on the distant Christ
Gazed in a promise, now with clearness look
On Him they long'd to worship. Prophets, too,
The meaning and the majesty of strains
Mysterious, can by perfect thought expound;
Types are resolved; and shadowy rites unveil'd;
The mystic Lamb, on typing altars laid,
And Gospel, by Aaronic priesthood taught,
Their great Original doth here unfold
And proves Himself sole archetype of all.
While they, who died in dimness or dismay,
Haunted by fears, and harrow'd to the last
By many a tremor, in restoring beams
Of comfort, look upon their Lord, and live.
And there, is Concord! those conflicting notes
Of human dissonance, which now destroy
The solemn harmony of sainted minds,
These can the Lord by melodizing grace
Attune to oneness, till all souls agree.
Hence, may that World where parted Spirits meet,
A school of saintship for the Church elect
Be found: there, The Lord His priesthood act,
And God's magnificence of truth unveil;
Or, more and more the merit of His Blood
Teach the bright Spirits, who around Him throng.
And thrill they not, from Christ Himself to learn
His wounds, how deep! His mercy, how divine!
Till round that Saviour rapt hosannahs rise,
And in the minstrelsy of heaven we hear
"Worthy the Lamb! for He was slain for us,"
Through the deep ages of eternity
Swell like a torrent of melodious praise.

FAREWELL.

And to this world, around whose vision'd scene
Our thoughts have trembled, Luther's wearied soul
Advances; soon will that tried heart repose
In peace, beyond the loudest blast of time
To ruffle. Twice some thirty years have delved
Deep on his open brow their wrinkling trace;
And often hath he died in thought, and pray'd
At home with Jesu in yon heavenly clime
To have his welcome! Hopes, beyond man's world
To wither, far above the earth have borne
His spirit; in the balance of the truth
Its visions and its vanities he weigh'd,
And found them wanting! Warn'd by heaven, he waits
A kind dismissal to his last long home.
For there, how many have before him fled,
And seem to hail him from their thrones of grace
Celestial! 'Tis not, that proud murmurs rise
From out his noble spirit; but the hue
Of Life's pale sunset, whose foreboding charm
O'ershades the present with prophetic gloom.
Youth with the living loves gay converse bright;
Age with the dead can high communion hold,
Nor calls it mournful, when the graves unclose
Their treasures, or departed friendships rise;
While votive Mem'ry drops the tear intense
By Feeling gather'd in some aged eye!

And such, perchance, within the pensive gaze
Of Luther glisten'd, when in hoary eld
That home he enters, where a foodless boy
Through Eisleben from house to house he sang
For bread! and dropt unseen the bitter tear
Which moisten'd it, when cast from churlish hands.
There, at his window, on the wintry heavens
Bleak with the blast, and white with flaking snow,
Dejectedly a thoughtful gaze he fix'd,
While heaved his spirit with a swell of prayer
By man unheard, but audible in heaven,
Where thought is utt'rance. On his frame o'erbow'd
Chill age was falling; and both languid nerves,
And feeble sense, a boding symptom gave
How soon with him the silver cord would loose,
And bowl be broken at the fountain-head!
But not for this repined he: for the Church
He sorrow'd; and her doom with tearful eye,
Foretold, as witness'd in the war of Creeds
Around him raging. Thus, an autumn-tinge
Sadden'd his future with prophetic shades
Of woe and weakness; till, at times, he long'd
Like Simeon, now in solemn peace to part,
And on the bosom of his Lord expire.
His work is done; his warfare is complete;
And from eternity there seem'd to sound

---

* See Revelations.

A bugle-note, that summon'd his retreat
Home to the heaven salvation's Captain won.

And what a world of undeveloped thoughts
That moment of mysterious calm contain'd!
As in the centre of all boyish dreams
And hours departed, there he mused, and pray'd;
Or the long windings of his wondrous life
Haply with tears retraced, with sighs renew'd,
And God in shade and sunshine equal saw,
Guardian, and Guide, and Glory of his days
Perpetual! Like a fated life had been
The vast experience of his varied course,
From lowly nothing to that Alpine height
Of fame and influence, where his manhood climb'd,
And age was resting: scarce had patriarch's dream
Or prophet's vision more of strange and stern
And awful, in the things of God beheld
Or suffer'd, than the Saxon monk endured,
From faithful Enoch down to fearless Paul!
For, when had God His imprimatur put
With brighter proof, than on the boundless Work
Which now o'er kings and kingdoms, Man and Mind,
Breathed of brave Luther, wheresoe'er it came?
Sinful, indeed, before That Eye he felt,
In Whose bright ray the heavens unclean appear;
But faithful to his Lord, and creed, and cause,
Mercy had kept him; and to Him he gave
The crowning merit of the mighty Whole.

'Twas thus a charm of retrospective peace
Besoothed him, when he felt no dread reproach
From craft, or compromise, o'erwhelm'd him now.
Firm had he lived, and faithful would he die,
In life unblemish'd and in death the same!

CHAMBER OF DEATH.

And if the chamber where the humblest yield
The burden of their being up to God,
Down to the roots of tenderness awakes
Affection's nature; if the feeblest Saint
Who hovers on the precipice of time,
When beetling o'er Infinity below
Takes to himself some attributes, which speak
Of awe and grandeur, can we gather round
The bed of glory where a Luther dies,
Nor feel an inspiration? Can we mark
That eagle-spirit, from its chain unbound,
In light and liberty o'er this dim world
Escaping, nor a solemn thrill partake
Speechless, but how expressive! There he lies!
Pale in the swoon of swift-approaching death:
But mind is yet majestic; and his eyes
From the dark lustre of their burning depths
Yet flash with meaning, and the soul express
Conscious, and clear as ever; while the lips
Move with that verse, which on Messiah's once
Quiver'd in peace, when David's words of faith
Wing'd His worn spirit to the Breast of God.

Deeper and deeper now the shades of death
Around him close, while drop the fainting lids
O'er his sunk eyeballs; thickly heave and fall
Those panting breath-gasps, while the ear of Love
Drinks with delight some shatter'd tones, or sighs
Of Bible-promise, or those falter'd notes
Of Faith, which tell the spirit-life within.
The strife is mortal, but the strength divine
That meets it! Death all stingless, and the Law
All dreadless,—neither can from Luther's heart
Hurl the high confidence a christian seats
There on its throne of evangelic truth.
Around him friends, and mourners, each with sob
Half-stifled, and with tears which hang unshed
On the still'd eyelids of revering love,
Are group'd; while bands of waiting Angels watch
That mighty Spirit into glory pass!
Cold is the damp which dews his whit'ning brow,
And pains convulse him with continuous rack;
But underneath that palpitating flesh
Calm lies the soul! in peace celestial bathed,
Though clay and spirit sunder. Hark! again
The last weak cry of ling'ring nature lifts
A dying homage to the Truth Divine,
And then, on yonder kneeling forms and friends
Before him, falls one faint and farewell gaze,
And,—all is over! while his features fix
Their pale expression into placid trance.
No sigh is heard; nor groan, nor shudder comes;
But wordless, and with hands devoutly lock'd,
And mute as monumental Prayer, he lies,
A dead Immortal deep in glory now!

How hush'd, how holy, how intensely rapt
As though the blood would listen as it flow'd,
Till the brain rocks, and check'd emotion reels,
That moment is, when first mysterious Death
In full development his form unshrouds,
Solemn and stern! And there, yon reft ones bend
Moveless, and pale, like shapes of sculptured Woe
O'er breathless Luther: each, by curb of thought,
The big sensation from outbursting cry
Restraining; not a tone of anguish breaks
The silence; speechless on his brow they gaze;
So still, that breath most audibly intrudes;
And each can hear the living heart-beats play
O'er his beneath them, pulseless, and at peace.

Behind our veiling drapery of Sense
Baffled we are from darting forth one glance
Of mental knowledge; or the heart, methinks,
Might dream, when Luther's disembodied Soul
Pass'd from the flesh to join the spirit-throng,
The inner-world some vast impression felt;
While the high Dead, by heaven-born instinct moved,
Rose from their thrones, to give him welcome due
When first He enter'd their elysian scene.

Tears are the litany of weeping hearts
When heroes vanish to their native heaven;
And let them consecrate an hour like this,
For there th' Elijah of the Gospel lies!
And rarely to the spirit-clime hath fled
From this low earth, a loftier soul than he,
The lion-hearted Luther! Never more
That princely mind with gen'rous pang shall bleed:
He sleeps in Jesus, but he wakes to God
Chanting in heaven the song on earth he sung,
"Worthy the Lamb! for he was slain for me!"
The race is o'er; the goal immortal reach'd;
Servant of Light, and vassal of its Lord,
Him hath the Master with the host above
United, call'd, rewarded, and resumed
Back to the Bosom whence his graces flow'd.

And let the pope and priest their victor scorn,
Each fault reveal, each imperfection scan,
And by some fell anatomy of hate
His life dissect, with satire's keenest edge;
But still may Luther with his mighty heart
Defy their malice, though it breathe of hell.
If soul majestic, and a dauntless mien;
If faith colossal, o'er all fiends and frowns
Erect; if energy, which never slack'd,
With all that galaxy of graces bright
Which stud the firmament of christian mind,
If these be noble, with a zeal conjoin'd
Which made his life one liturgy of love,
Then may the Saxon from his death-couch send
A dreadless answer that refutes all foes,
Who dwarf his merit or his creed revile
With falsehood. Far beyond them soars the Soul
They slander; from his tomb there still comes forth
A challenge, which rebukes them by its power;
And the brave monk who made the Popedom rock
Champions a World to show his equal yet!

"DEAD, YET SPEAKETH."

Luther is dead! and like the Church's knell
Sounds the sad tale in Europe's startled ear:
Princes are thrill'd with consternation's throe,
And trembles now the Reformation's ark!
But, turn we most to see Melancthon's tear
Sacred as ever dropp'd from friendship's eye.
Nations alone the great Reformer knew,
But he the Man had loved, and mourn'd him thus
As David over Jonathan bemoan'd,
Passing the grief of woman! 'Twas th' eclipse
Of earth's best sunshine, when his Luther died:
For years had tried them with severest test,
And at each close, more fervidly in faith
Had left them: therefore, what but soothing Heaven
The dismal tumult of his harrow'd mind
Can hush, and soften into sacred calm?
Theirs was a friendship, which no earthly soil
Can generate; from heavenly seed it sprang,
And bloom'd unwither'd, 'mid the blight and blast
Of cold earth's changes. Each to each a grace
Imparted, which, apart, they did not wield.
Their light was varied but their love was one;
And the mild discord of commingled souls
In friendship made the harmony more sweet:
While o'er the failings of their mutual hearts
A garment of sweet charity was thrown,

To hide them. Thus, harsh Luther in some mood
Tempestuous, when a lawless rage ran high,
From mild Melancthon forced no bitter tone;
For soon that tempest of a moment sank
To loving silence; forth the rainbow smiled!
And rich good humour cast its rosy gleam
O'er the brief gloom a frowning word begot.
And thus 'twill ever be, when hearts are true
As tender: frankly bold, and freely plain,
'Tis not in nature when by Christ endow'd,
A smile forgiving from a fault confest
To hide, since love is here our holy creed:
And kindness forms a talismanic key,
Opening the heart well-lock'd to all beside.

Luther is dead, and lone Melancthon weeps;*
And, reader! hast thou no responsive tear
With his to mingle? Is *thy* gone career
Tombless? And over no departed friend
Heaves the green turf? Or is thy present hung
With no sad cypress for a perish'd joy,

* Luther died early in the morning of the 18th of February, 1546, at Eisleben, his native place. The Counts of Mansfeldt wished to have him interred in their own territories; but by command of the Elector, the body was brought to Wittemberg, and buried with all public honours in the church of All Saints. His tomb has a brass plate with the following inscription on it:—

MARTINI · LUTHERI · S · THEOLO-
GIÆ · D · CORPUS · H · L · S · E · QUI
AN · CHRISTI · M · D · XLVI · XII.
CAL · MARTII · EYSLEBII · IN · PA-
TRIA · S · M · O. C. V · ANN · LXIII.
M · II. · D. X.

When Melancthon first received the intelligence of his friend's death, he exclaimed, "My Father! my Father! the chariot of Israel and the horsemen thereof." (2 Kings, xi. 12.) For the following translation of the funeral oration, as delivered by Melancthon at the funeral of Luther, we are indebted to Dr. Cox. —*Life of Melancthon*, 2nd ed., p. 439—452.

ORATION.

"Although amidst this general mourning my voice is so obstructed by deep affliction and tears, yet something I would attempt to say, not to eulogise the dead as the heathen do, but to admonish the living in this vast assembly, and especially to impress just sentiments upon the junior part of the auditory respecting the government of the church and its dangers, that they may learn what to desire, and by what examples to regulate their lives. Wicked and infidel men represent everything in the present apparent confusion of human affairs as the result of mere chance; but confiding in the numerous and explicit declarations of God himself, we distinguish the church from the promiscuous multitude of mankind, and affirm that it is under Divine superintendence and protection. To this we constantly look, obeying our lawful governors, and cherishing a pious reverence for those guides and instructors whom we choose.

"It will be necessary to advert to these considerations as often as the name of the Reverend Doctor Martin Luther, our most beloved father and teacher, is introduced, whom we love and honour, detestable as he appears in the eyes of many wicked men, and whom we know to have been raised up by heaven as a minister of the true gospel, by evidences which, notwithstanding the charges of our opponents, prove that his doctrines were neither seditious, nor dispersed abroad with a blind and impetuous zeal.

"In this place, and on these occasions, many things are usually said in a panegyrical strain respecting the personal endowments of the deceased; I propose, however, to omit these, and advert chiefly to his ecclesiastical function. Intelligent and pious persons will admit, if he were the means of promoting useful and necessary truth in the church, we ought to be grateful to the providence of God for raising up such a light, while his labours, faith, perseverance, and other virtues, ought to be duly acknowledged, and his memory tenderly cherished by all worthy men.

"The Apostle St. Paul represents Christ as 'having ascended on high to give gifts unto men'—that is, the preaching of the gospel and the Holy Spirit; for the purpose of communicating which, 'he gave some apostles, and some prophets, and some evangelists, and some pastors and teachers, selecting them from amongst those who read, study, and delight in the sacred writings. Nor are they only called into the Christian service who occupy the more ordinary stations, but others are frequently introduced, under the direction of learned men, into this holy warfare; and it is both pleasing and profitable to witness the care of God to his church throughout all ages, in sending a continued succession of useful men, that as some fall in the glorious field, others may instantly rush forward to take their places. The first of our race who nobly occupied the foremost ranks were Adam, Seth, Enoch, Methuselah, Noah, Shem and Lot. The latter, being yet alive, and dwelling in the neighbourhood of Sodom, when the inhabitants of the earth, forgetting the instructions of Noah and Shem, became addicted to idolatry, God raised up a coadjutor to Shem in the person of Abraham, to co-operate in the great work of propagating divine truth. To him succeeded Isaac, Jacob, and Joseph, who kindled the light of true religion in Egypt, at that period the most flourishing empire in the world; and to them, Moses, Joshua, Samuel, David, Elijah and Elisha, Isaiah, Jeremiah, Daniel, and Zachariah. After them arose Esdras, Onias, and the Maccabees; then Simeon, Zacharias, John the Baptist, Christ and his Apostles. I am delighted to contemplate this unbroken succession, which affords conspicuous evidence of the presence of God in his church. The apostles were succeeded by a troop, so to speak, of inferior warriors, but nevertheless distinguished of heaven—Polycarp, Irenæus, Gregory of Neocæsarea, Basil, Augustin, Prosper, Maximus, Hugo, Bernard, Talerus, and others; and although the latter ages present a more barren prospect, God has always preserved a proportion of his servants upon the earth, and now through Martin Luther, a more splendid period of light and truth has appeared.

"To this enumeration of the most eminent amongst the sons of men who gathered and reformed the church of God, may be added others who may be regarded as the flower of mankind. Solon, Themistocles, Scipio, Augustus, and others, who either established or ruled

Or faded dear ones, into dust relapsed?
Alas! the heart's Necroplis is filled
With many a tomb by Mem'ry's votive hand:
And, where is he, that prodigy of joy
In age partaking all his childhood had
Of household-blessing, or parental bliss?
Oh! long ere wintry years the head have
hoar'd,

over mighty empires, were indeed truly great men, but very far inferior to our illustrious leaders, Isaiah, John the Baptist, St. Paul, Augustin, and Luther, and it becomes us to study this distinction. What, then, are those great and important things which Luther has disclosed to our view, which render his life so remarkable, and for which many are exclaiming against him as a disturber of the church and a promoter of inexplicable controversies? I answer, that when the Holy Spirit, in his regulation of the church, reproves the world for sin, dissensions arise out of the pertinacity of wicked men, and they alone are culpable who refuse to listen to the proclamation of the eternal Father concerning his Son—'This is my beloved Son, hear him.' Luther explained the true and important doctrine of penitence, which was involved in the profoundest darkness. He showed in what it consists, and where refuge and consolation could be obtained under a sense of Divine displeasure. He illustrated the statements of St. Paul respecting justification by faith, and showed the distinction between the law and the gospel, civil and spiritual justification. He pointed out the true principle of prayer, and exterminated that heathenish absurdity of the church, that God was not to be invoked if the mind entertained the least doubt upon an academic question. He admonished men to pray, in the exercise of faith and a good conscience, to the only Mediator and Son of God, who is seated at the right hand of the Father, making intercession for us, and not to images or deceased saints, according to the shocking practice of the ignorant. He also pointed out other services acceptable to God, was singularly exemplary himself in all the duties of life, and separated the puerilities of human rites and ceremonies, which prevent, instead of promoting, genuine worship, from those services which are essential to obedience. In order that heavenly truth might be transmitted to posterity, he translated the prophetic and apostolic writings into the German language, and with so much accuracy, that his version of itself places Scripture in a more perspicuous light than most commentaries. But he published also various expositions upon the sacred writings, which, in the judgment of Erasmus, by far excelled all others; and as it is recorded respecting those who rebuilt Jerusalem, 'with one hand they laid the stones, and with the other they held the sword;' so while he composed annotations on Scripture, replete with heavenly instruction, and consoled afflicted consciences by his pious counsels, he was necessitated at the same time to wage incessant war with the adversaries of evangelical truth. When it is recollected that this truth, especially the doctrine of faith and the remission of sins, is not discoverable by the merely human eye, it must be acknowledged he was taught of God; and many of us have witnessed his anxious solicitude to impress the great principle of acceptance by faith. Multitudes of the saints will therefore praise God to all eternity, for the benefits which have accrued to the church by the labours of Luther. To God their gratitude is primarily due, and then they will own themselves much indebted to his labours, although infidels, who ridicule the church in general, will consider these noble performances as no better than empty trifling or absolute insanity. The true church does not, as some falsely affirm, promote intricate disputations, throw out the apple of contention, and propose the enigmas of the fabled Sphinx; for to those who judge seriously, and without prejudice, it is easy from a comparison of opposite opinions to perceive what are consonant to the statements of heavenly truth, and what are otherwise. Christians are no longer in a state of hesitation on the subject of existing controversies, for when God determined to reveal his will, and display his character in the sacred writings, it is not to be imagined that such a communication would be ambiguous, like the leaves of the ancient Sibyl.

"Some, by no means evil-minded persons, however, express a suspicion that Luther manifested too much asperity. I will not affirm the reverse, but only quote the language of Erasmus, 'God has sent in this latter age a violent physician, on account of the magnitude of the existing disorders;' fulfilling, by such a dispensation, the Divine message to Jeremiah—'Behold, I have put my words in thy mouth. See, I have this day set thee over the nations, and over the kingdoms, to root out and pull down, and to destroy and to throw down, to build and to plant.' Nor does God govern his church according to the counsels of men, nor choose to employ instruments like theirs to promote His purposes. But it is usual for inferior minds to dislike those of a more ardent character. When Aristides observed the mighty affairs which Themistocles, by the impulse of a superior genius, undertook and happily accomplished, although he congratulated the state on the advantage it possessed in such a man, he studied every means to divert his zealous mind from its pursuits. I do not deny that ardent spirits are sometimes betrayed into undue impetuosity, for no one is totally exempt from the weaknesses incident to human nature; but they often merit the praise assigned by the ancient proverb to Hercules, Cimon, and other illustrious characters, ἄκομψος μὲν ἀλλὰ τὰ μέγιστα ἀγαθὸς, 'rough, indeed, but distinguished by the best principles.' In the Christian church, the Apostle St. Paul mentions such as 'war a good warfare, holding faith and a good conscience,' and who are both pleasing to God and estimable amongst pious men. Such an one was Luther, who, while he constantly defended the pure doctrines of Christianity maintained a conscientious integrity of character. No vain licentiousness was ever detected in him, no seditious counsels; but, on the contrary, he often urged the most specific measures, and never, never did he blend political artifices, for the augmentation of power with ecclesiastical affairs. Such wisdom and such virtue, I am persuaded, do not result from mere human skill and diligence, but the mind must be divinely influenced, especially when it is of the more rough, elevated, and ardent cast like that of Luther.

"What shall I say of his other virtues? Often have I myself gone to him unawares, and found him dissolved in tears and prayers for the Church of Christ. He devoted a certain portion of almost every day to the solemn reading of some of the Psalms of David with which he mingled his own supplications amidst

Or thoughts their furrows in the forehead plough'd
Eternity with time at least divides
Our friendships. Heaven has oft the better half
Of hopes which brighten'd, or of hearts that blest

Our Life's fair morning! Soon the world grows strange;
And bleak and barren do our pathways grow
As more and more they wind us to the grave.
And well, if friendship only be the loss
We suffer; oft, our noblest feelings die;
The heart is bankrupt, though the head be rich,
While all those young simplicities of soul *

sighs and tears; and he has frequently declared how indignant he felt against those who hastened over devotional exercises through sloth, or the pretence of other occupations. On this account, said he, Divine wisdom has prescribed some formularies of prayer, that our minds may be inflamed with devotion by reading them; to which, in his opinion, reading aloud very much conduced. When a variety of great and important deliberations respecting public dangers have been pending, we have witnessed his prodigious vigour of mind, his fearless and unshaken courage. Faith was his sheet anchor, and by the help of God he was resolved never to be driven from it. Such was his penetration, that he perceived at once what was to be done in the most perplexing conjunctures; nor was he, as some supposed, negligent of the public good, or disregardful of the wishes of others; but he was well acquainted with the interests of the state, and pre-eminently sagacious in discovering the capacity and dispositions of all about him. And although he possessed such extraordinary acuteness of intellect, he read both ancient and modern ecclesiastical writings with the utmost avidity, and histories of every kind, applying the examples they furnished to existing circumstances with remarkable dexterity. The undecaying monuments of his eloquence remain, and, in my opinion, he equalled any of those who have been most celebrated for their resplendent oratorical powers.

"The removal of such a character from amongst us, of one who was endowed with the greatest intellectual capacity, well instructed, and long experienced in the knowledge of Christian truth, adorned with numerous excellences, and with virtues of the most heroic cast, chosen by Divine Providence to reform the church of God, cherishing for all of us a truly and paternal affection,—the removal, I say, of such a man demands and justifies our tears. We resemble orphans bereft of an excellent and faithful father; but while it is necessary to submit to the will of Heaven, let us not permit the memory of his virtues and his good offices to perish. He was an important instrument, in the hands of God, of public utility; let us diligently study the truth he taught, imitating in our humble situations his fear of God, his faith, the intensity of his devotions, the integrity of his ministerial character, his purity, his careful avoidance of seditious counsel, his ardent thirst of knowledge. And, as we frequently meditate upon the pious examples of those illustrious guides of the church, Jeremiah, John the Baptist, and St. Paul, whose histories are transmitted to us, so let us frequently reflect upon the doctrine and course of life which distinguished our departed friend. Let the present vast assembly now unite with me in grateful thanks and fervent supplications, saying, in the spirit of ardent devotion—'We give thanks to thee, Almighty God, the Eternal Father of our Lord Jesus Christ, the Author and Founder of thy church, together with thy co-eternal Son, and the Holy Spirit, wise, good, merciful, just, true, powerful, and sovereign, because thou dost gather for thy Son a heritage from amongst the human race, and dost maintain the ministry of the gospel, and hast reformed thy church by means of Luther; we present our ardent supplications that thou wouldst henceforth preserve, fix, and impress upon our hearts the doctrines of truth, as our Saviour prayed for his disciples; and that by thy Holy Spirit thou wouldst inflame our minds with a pure devotion, and direct our feet into the paths of holy obedience.'

"As the removal of illustrious men from the church is frequently a means of punishing their survivors, such of us as are entrusted with the office of tuition, myself personally, and all of us collectively, entreat you to reflect upon the present calamities that threaten the whole earth. Yonder, the Turks are advancing; here, civil discord threatens; and there, other adversaries, released at last from the apprehension of Luther's censures, will proceed with a perverse ingenuity, and with increased boldness, to corrupt the genuine truth. That God may avert these evils, let us be more diligent in the regulation of our lives and studies, always retaining a deep impression of this sentiment in our minds, that as long as we maintain, hear, obey, and love the pure doctrines of the gospel, God will always have a church and a dwelling-place among us. 'If,' said Jesus Christ, 'a man love me, he will keep my words; and my Father will love him, and we will come unto him, and make our abode with him.' Encouraged by this ample promise, let us be stimulated to inculcate the truth of heaven; knowing that the church will be the preservation of the human race and the security of established governments; and let us constantly elevate our minds to that future and eternal state of being, to which God himself calls our attention, who has not given so many witnesses, nor sent his Son into the world in vain, but delights in the communication of these magnificent blessings. Amen."

* It is the combination of simplicity of heart with grandeur of intellect, which awakens such profound sympathy, when we contemplate Luther, the Man, as well as the Reformer. The following extracts from his "Colloquia" are each delightful in their way. The one testifies his tenderness; the second, his simplicity; the third, the genuine humour of his character.

Epitaph of Magdalena, Martin Luther's daughter, who died anno 1542, aged fourteen years, written by the father himself:—

"Dormio cum sanctis hic Magdalena, Lutheri
Filia; et hoc strato tecta quiesco meo.
Filia mortis eram, peccati semine nata,
Sànguine sed vivo, Christe, redempta tuo."

"When his daughter was very ill, he said, 'I love her well, but, O my God, if it is thy will to take her hence, I must resign myself to thee.' She was lying in bed, and looking at her, he said, with tears in his eyes,

Which lay on character's expanding buds
Like drops of morning, in their freshness
bright,
Exhale, and leave an autumn-waste behind.

Not such were thine, Melancthon! Round
thy grief
A radiant hope of sweet re-union there,
In that high world of fearlessness and truth

'My dear little daughter,—my dear little Madaline! You will remain willingly with your father here, or you will go willingly hence to your other Father?' She replied, 'Yes, my dear father, as God pleases.' 'Dear little child,' said Luther, 'thy spirit is willing, but thy flesh is weak.' He walked a long time up and down the room, and at length said, 'Yes, I have loved her well; if the flesh is strong, in what state will the spirit be?' He said, among other things, 'God has not bestowed so many gifts upon any bishop for a thousand years as upon me, for we ought to glorify God for his gifts. Ah! I am enraged at myself that I do not rejoice from my heart and render thanks. I will sing from time to time a little song of praise to the Lord.'

"The night before the death of his daughter Madaline, the Doctor's wife dreamt that there appeared to her two beautiful boys, well clothed, who wished to guide her daughter and take her in marriage. Philip Melancthon asked her,—'What did you make of your daughter?' She told him her dream; at which he was greatly affected, and said to the others, 'The two boys are sacred angels, who have come to lead the virgin to the true wedlock of the celestial kingdom.' She died that very day.

"When little Madaline was in agony, and was nearly breathing her last, her father fell on his knees at her bedside, wept bitterly, and entreated God to save her. She expired in his arms. Her mother was happily in the same room, but at a little distance from her bed, on account of her affliction. Doctor Luther often exclaimed, 'God's will be done!—my daughter has still a Father in heaven.' Philip Melancthon observed to him, 'The love of parents is a divine image imprinted on the heart of man. God no less loves the human race than parents their children.' When they put her into the coffin, her father said, 'Poor dear little Madaline! behold thee now!' He looked at her, and said, 'Oh, dear infant! you will rise again; you will shine as a star; yes, as a sun. I am joyful in spirit, but I am sorrowful in the flesh. It is a marvellous thing to know that she is certainly in peace, and yet for me to be so sad.'

"During the Diet of Augsburg, Luther wrote the following letter to his son John, then about fourteen years of age. This letter is remarkable for its happy composition and its playful allusions. It is in itself a complete elucidation of Luther's domestic character.

"'Grace and peace to you in Jesus Christ, my dear little child. I perceive with pleasure that you are making good progress in your learning, and that you now give attention to your prayers. Continue to do so, my dear child, and when I return home I will give you beautiful things.

"'I know a lovely and smiling garden, full of children dressed in robes of gold, who play under the trees with beautiful apples, pears, cherries, nuts, and prunes. They sing, they leap, they are all joyful; there are also beautiful little ponies, with bridles of gold and saddles of silver. In passing through the garden, I asked a man what it meant, and who were the children. He replied, 'These are the children who love to pray and to learn, who are pious and good children.' I said to him, 'Dear friend, I have also a child, his name is little John Luther: might he not also come here and eat these beautiful apples and pears, ride on these beautiful ponies, and play with the other children?' The man replied to me, 'If your child, your dear little John Luther, is wise, if he says his prayers, and learns willingly, he may come, and he may bring little Philip and James* along with him. He will here find fifes, drums, and other fine instruments to produce music; they will dance and amuse themselves with the cross-bow.' While I was speaking, the man pointed out to me, in the middle of the garden, a beautiful grass park, where the children danced, and where the fifes, drums, and cross-bows were all lying. But it was morning; the children had not breakfasted, and I only waited till the dance commenced. I then said to the man, 'Dear sir, I intend to write immediately to my dear little John, and I will tell him to be a good boy, to pray, and learn well, that he may be permitted to come to this garden. He has a dear little sister, whom he loves much; her name is Madaline, may he bring her with him?' The man replied, 'Yes; tell him they may both come together.' Be wise, then, my dear little boy; tell Philip and James to be wise also, and you will be allowed to visit and play in the beautiful garden. I commend my dear child to the protection of God. Salute Madaline, and give her a kiss for me. Your father who loves you, 'MARTIN LUTHER.

"'*19th June*, 1530.'

"He wrote to his friends at Wittemberg the following exquisitely humorous and satirical letter, during the sitting of the Diet of Augsburg—

"'Grace and peace in Christ Jesus our Lord be with you; dear sirs and friends. I have received your letters, and understand from them how it fares with you all. That you may be aware how it fares with us, I hereby give you to know that we, namely, I, Master Veit, and Cyriac, do not go to the Diet at Augsburg; we are, however, here attending another diet.

"'For know, that just beneath our window is a rookery in a small wood, and there the rooks and jackdaws hold their diet. There is such a journeying to and fro, such a cry and clamour day and night, without any ceasing, as if they were all drunken, and old and young chatter all at once, that it is a marvel to me how voice and breath can so long hold it; and I would fain know whether in your parts you have any such like nobles and cavaliers. It seems to me that they are gathered together here from all the ends of the earth.

"'Their emperor I have not seen; but their nobles and their great merchants are for ever strutting before our eyes, not, in truth, in very costly garments, but rather simply clad in one colour; they are all dressed in black; all are gray eyed, and sing the same song, except with some pretty differences of old and young,

---

* The sons of Philip Melancthon. Little is known of them, and it is supposed that they died in early life.

Where all of heavenly which on earth we lose
Again shall greet us, and a glory wear
Perfect and bright, beyond our purest mind
Below to witness. There, shall friend with friend
And babe with mother, son with sire, renew
In blest revival, unforgotten love.
Partings below will soon to meetings turn,
And serve, as foils, to set their gladness off
Hereafter, when the soul's embraces blend.
And there are moments, mystical as deep,
When time anticipates eternity,
Making the Easter of our mem'ry bright
Rise on the heart, with resurrection-bloom.
Bodied and bodiless can thus converge
Whene'er to worship at The Throne we bow,
Or sigh, or speak some lonely prayer of love.
Soothed by soft dreams of well-remember'd times,
There round that Centre of our common Lord
The dear and dead ones of the heart revive;
Inhale together a surpassing peace,
And bathe their spirits in one blended joy
Supernal: friendships thus in soul remain,
When tombs have swallow'd all the senses clasp'd.
So can the living with the dead commune,
And rob the grave of half its vict'ry here,
While love in Christ by sainted hearts is proved
On earth the brightest, as in heaven the best.

---

great and small. They reck not of vast palace or stately hall, for their hall is roofed with the fair wide heaven. Their floor is the bare field, strewed with dainty green twigs, and its walls are as wide as the world's end. Nor do they require steed or harness; they have feathered wheels, wherewith they escape from the fire of their enemies, and avoid their rage. There are high and mighty lords amongst them; but what they resolve I know not. Thus much, however, have I gathered from an interpreter, that they have a mighty expedition in hand, and wage war against wheat, barley, oats, rye, and all manner of corn and grain; and herein will many win knighthood, and do great feats of arms. We also sit here in diet, and hear and see with great pleasure and delight how the princes and lords, together with the states of the empire, so joyously sing, and make good cheer. But especial joy have we when we see with how haughty an air they strut, clean their bills, and attack the defences, and how they gain conquest and glory against wheat and barley. We humbly salute them all, and wish that they were all well spitted on a hedge-stake together.

"'I hold, however, that they are most like to the sophists and papists with their preaching and writing; for I would fain have them all in a heap before me, that I may hear their sweet voices and preachings, and see how right useful a folk they are to consume all that the earth brings forth, and to while away the heavy time in chattering.

"'To-day we have heard the nightingale for the first time; for she would put no trust in April. It has been right glorious weather all day, nor has it rained, except yesterday a little. With you it is perchance otherwise. Herewith I commend you to God. Fare ye well. From the Diet of the Conturks.*—April 28, 1530.'

"'The latter part of Luther's life was chiefly occupied in completing his version of the Scriptures, preaching, and composing tracts in opposition to the papal superstitions, and doctrinal or practical errors among the Protestants. His incessant and unremitting zeal brought upon him premature old age; and during the last years of his life his health and constitution were completely broken and enfeebled. 'His compositions,' observes a writer, 'consisting chiefly of controversial tracts, commentaries on scripture, sermons, epistolary disquisitions, and narratives of the chief events of his life, are calculated by Seckendorf at the extraordinary number of eleven hundred and thirty-seven; and if to these be added the labours of his public duty, and the variety of his correspondence, some idea may be formed of his indefatigable application.' His sedentary occupations and mental excitement began now seriously to affect his health, which had hitherto been maintained by his remarkably temperate habits. His letters from this period are filled with statements of his ill health, feebleness, and desire for death."

---

* *Conturks*, a witty sobriquet which Luther gives to the crows, whose *Diet*, as he calls it, he humorously describes in the above letter.

JESUITS AND JESUITISM.

I.—MIND IS POWER.

Mind is the centre of our human power
And action: 'tis that throne of secret law
Where, like a monarch, reigns the regal Will
Supreme in orbit. As this living world
Of varied substance, through its moulded forms
And functions, hath each primal source of change
Not in the region of created strength,
But rather from the will Almighty takes
Each plastic motion, so that time-bound scene
Where man's embodied agencies unveil
His vice, or virtue, good or evil acts,
Not from brute matter, but from conscious mind
Derives mutation, destinies, and deeds.

II.—SENSUAL DOUBT.

Yet, blind in soul, with sensual chains begirt,
The fettered victims of the senses five
In Matter place reality, alone!
Effect remote, contingent and involved,
Their view confounds, and is for cause mistook:
As though the mind a passive myst'ry were

By words created, not in things contained.
But 'tis not thus! All motion, power, and change,
Materially in heaven, or earth, or air
Unfolded, seen, or heard, or felt, or scann'd,
Up to the Mind Eternal must be traced
As their last Root, and secret Law alone.

III.—WHENCE CONDUCT SPRINGS.

Thus Mind, not Matter, is that seat and spring
Whence nature, providence and grace evolve
Their vital actions, on our sense impinged
With frequent pressure. Thus in Science, too,
Where through the medium of material acts
Wonder on wonder to her Priests unfolds
Amazing products, and mechanic force
Unbounded, high o'er all a Power presides
In secret; graced with philosophic name,
Men call it law, but what is law but mind
In ruling action? 'Tis the Will Divine
That, self-enforced, invisible as God,
And shapeless as eternity to thought,
Masters all Nature, moulds her myriad forms
Of growth, or grandeur, and the world empowers.
And hence, what Wisdom learns when most her grasp
Into the oneness of a glorious whole
Hath organised all forms, and facts of Life
Material, is to know her ign'rance more.
For, laws in Nature are *our* modes of thought,
Our vast conceptions of the unreveal'd
In matter, on whose aid all Science rests
And reasons: but no explanation climbs
That altitude where Law in essence dwells.
What God to faith, that Principle to sense
Becomes,—unseen, but actual, vast and true,
And yet, from sense how infinitely hid
In depths unfathomed! like the modes of grace,
Those methods deep, whereby The Spirit wields
His inward spells o'er all the central life of Man.

IV.—REAL AND UNREAL.

Thus, matter is the instrument of mind,
And mind, as monarch, over matter reigns
With secret magic: thoughts are throneless kings,
Yet, thrones must wither, when their potent sway
Becomes imperial! Then, the slaves of sense
Unlearn the lesson brutal science taught
Mere flesh to credit,—that the True
Is what we witness, handle, taste, or hear;
While Unreality to *that* belongs
Which faith hath canonised, as law and life
Supreme, by reason loved, and conscience own'd.
But this, how baseless! Power to mind pertains:
Reality within the realm of thought
Abides; and (what from sense is far remote)
Those lone Abstractions, which a lofty Soul
Visions before it, ponders o'er and proves,
Are oft the Factors whence our work-day life
Derives expansion, and more blest is made.
And not more truly can some Bard adapt
Poetic language to melodious thought,
Than to the process of those laws mind-born
Within us sanction'd, God this outer-world
Hath framed, and fashioned. Thus, the most abstract
Creator, who from sensuous earth retires,
While from her watch-towers Speculation eyes
In stillness what ideal problems prove,
Is no fanatic: for, resulting products show
That what pure Thought conceived, creation-laws
Hereafter realise; and hence attest
How facts in mind to forms of matter fit
Their truth, and justify what Thought foretold.

V.—THE INNER WORLD.

The Student, thinking in his mental bower,
Pale, and apart from all our blinded World
Calls useful, what a mock such man beseems
To Mammon's host, or Belial's pamper'd slave!
His world is secret, soundless as the soul
Which doth create it; one of perfect mind.
There, Truths in transcendental glory reign
Harmonious, which are yet by words uncloth'd.
Weeks, months, and years, that Devotee of thought
Works like an Angel, with a perfect will
To his pure toil surrender'd. Time and scene
Affect him not; gain and pleasure pass
His heart unheeded; passionately wed
To some high Problem, life unliving seems
From that divorced: 'tis health, and food to him!
Thus the whole man, in body, soul, and strength
A sacrifice to this achievement made,
Now to the world-wise half a maniac grows!
Or dreaming martyr, whom the moon affects
With visions mad, or theories befool'd.
But Genius is a prophet, priestess, queen;
To speak, to sacrifice, and reign
Her glory is, while inspiration bears
Her being up; and so, the world she braves:
And in those solemn agonies of thought
When brain o'ertask'd becomes a thinking fire,

And flames the blood with fever, still endures
That strong resolve, which makes a Will sublime!
And lo, at length the goal of mind is won,
The problem work'd, the grand result obtain'd;
And deep abstractions, such as Newton seized,
Kepler embraced, or Galileo scann'd
Alone, prophetic Science thus can bring
Down from the heights where speculation soar'd,
To grounds material,—to that homely soil
Where life and commerce, man and income blend,
Or struggle. Now, some calculus is got,
A truth unveil'd, or principle applied
Which moves the World for more than centuries on!
And they, that scornful host of sceptic hearts
Who mock'd the thinker, while creative thought
Was all internal, when 'tis robed with fact,
And 'mid the homes and haunts of life appears
Embodied,—let them now that Lie abjure
Which makes unthinking sense the Lord of soul!
For mind, not matter, is the king of men,
That salient centre whence our human world
All change, and crisis, law and movement takes.

VI.—HISTORY IN MAN.

Coil'd in the secret folds of some vast Mind,
Working unwitness'd, save by God's own eye
Which views a thought as we survey the sun,
The moral Life of ages lies uproll'd.
History unread hath there a virtual root
And fountain: in that comprehensive Soul
Empires, and thrones, and revolutions lie
In principle! there, carnage, crowns and creeds,
Battle and peace, commotions, strife, and change,
Lurk seminally hid, for future sway
Or active function. But, the shallow pause
Oft at the outposts, where material Force
Comes into play, or palpably unfolds
Realities, to earth and space and time
Apparent; yet the secret motive-spring,
The life, the law, the impulse, and the power
Which vivifies what men for History read,
Is viewless thought, a state of will unscann'd.
For years conceal'd, in mental depths contain'd,
Some brooding impulse of the Spirit works,
And thence, as from a pregnant germ, proceed
Gigantic changes which a world upheave
To glory, or in guilt and ruin plunge
Its greatness. History is but man unroll'd,
And man himself, but what the will prefers,
By mental action, or in moral force
Determined. For awhile, 'tis secret all!
Unheard, unknown, the boundless Project forms
And ripens; through ideal worlds of thought
The lone enthusiast, day by day, pursues
His great conception, then departs, and dies.
But, having to some genial few his plan
Discover'd, soon the speculation swells
And strengthens; till, at length, by living force
Develop'd, forth from out the mind's recess
That viewless Energy moves self-revealed
In shape historic; clothes itself with forms
Material; into contact bravely comes
With men and empires; human Life confronts
In all its faculties and myriad spheres
Of influence, such as reach the vital power
Of Nations, creeds, and churches, oft recast;
And now,—the flurried World recoils, and fears!
A sudden palsy over kingdoms falls
Mysterious; truths and principles are touch'd
In essence; baffled Reason looks aghast:
Amid the turbulence and shock of things,
Chaos seems come! And mark! how blinded Sense
Amid the crash of churches, thrones, and states
Around it crumbled, learns at last to see
That by a single Thought, this giant-world
Is moved, as though a moral earthquake shook
Both Past and Present, from their thrones of sway
For ever! Yes, some vast conception lives,
Which *once* was mind impalpable, and hid.
Results material are but Thoughts array'd
With formal being,—Soul and Will become
Embodied, and for creed and conscience made
Apparent, by the deeds they dare, or do;
But still in essence what they ever were,
As seeds and germs within creative mind
Maturing, where the soul of History dwells.

VII.—LOYOLA.

But, did we crave a specimen, and type
Embodied, how a single Mind can move
Backward or forward, churches, thrones, and creeds,
And on the motion of one mighty will
History depends, when earth and hell are sway'd,
Turn we to him, in whom combine and meet
Passion and principle, which make a Soul
Though single, like omnipotence to act
On men and empires. Turn we unto thee,
Ignatius! with that rich Castilian blood

Rolling within thy veins its noble tide
Ancestral, dreaming, daring, all on fire
With mad devotion, from whose wondrous spell
The glories of the Reformation's power
Receded. Never to a Cause was chain'd
A devotee, more passionately raised
To heights enrapt of superhuman zeal
Than was that flaming heart, when first it felt
How Law, and Gospel, Heaven, and Earth and Hell,
Sin, grace and time, eternity and truth,
In one abysmal thought, The Church of Rome,
Might be absorbed! And thus, to thee, that church
A Christ impersonal on earth became
A dread abstraction, thine almighty all!

VIII.—BATTLE-SCENE.

Beside the radiant Arga's rolling stream
Rise Pampeluna's walls; around them group
Hills of expressive grandeur, huge and high,
Cleaving the crystal air of old Navarre
With pendant summits, while a wooded vale
Of soft extent beneath their umbrage smiles.
'Twas here, enflamed by chivalrous romance
For deeds and darings, such as storied Gaul
In Amadis for ever laurels, stood
Fronting the beach, amid the clanging shock,
And brunt and carnage of a siege prolong'd,
The bold Ignatius! Ne'er hath poet's god,
Or dream-shaped hero, show'd more daring mien
And desperate valour; fighting in the rush
And roaring tumult of a blood-stain'd host
Firm to the last, this lion of Navarre
Contended, till beneath a gory heap,
Shouting the war-song, fell his wounded form
O'erwhelm'd by numbers:—Pampeluna sank;
Then, Gaul's proud banners o'er the towers high waved,
And red with carnage streets and temples ran.

IX.—RELIGIOUS IDEALISM.

The castled walls of his ancestral sires
Shelter'd the Hero; thus, with nerves o'er-strung
Fever'd by pain, emaciate, worn, and rack'd
Through bone and sinew,on his couch he lay
In long confinement: but the soul unchill'd
Burn'd in his being, with a martyr's fire
Heroical and strong; and here the captive fed
With vision, and with reverie sublime
Caught from the legends of the sainted host,
His heated nature,—till a sacred knight
Sworn to the Cross and to the Virgin vow'd,
Ignatius grew! and then, Romance began,
Blent with disease, to madden and inspire
His soul with more than passion, and "The Cross"
Wielded a spell o'er his ignited heart
Transcending human valour. Hence by faith
Etherialised, from fields where Glory wins
Laurels of earth, to scenes where Heaven rewards
Her heroes of celestial temper, turns he now:
And lo! in battle for the church of God,
Founded on Peter, like a war-machine
Against all heretics whom earth and hell
Concentres, yearns Ignatius soon to fight!
Here was a chivalry, whose new-born spell
Beat like a pulse of preternatural force
Fiercely within him! Visions, vast and bright,
Surpassing all apocalyptic Seers beheld,
Daniel conceived, or Chebar's prophet view'd,
Hover'd and hung around him, night and day
With their entrancing glories! Blood and brain
Were fever'd; with such gorgeous fancies thrill'd.
The very poetry of madness seem'd
To shake stern Reason from her throne,
And conscience to its roots. Then, fast and prayer,
Penance, and vigils of enormous length,
Blent with erratic dreams, together work
E'en to pale death this champion of the church
Devoted;—him to Mary ever vow'd,
Mother of God, and Queen of grace-born Souls!

X.—A DEVOTEE.

While thus impassion'd, Salem's heaven-loved soil
Before him glimmers; to that Land of dreams,
Christ's home on earth, by His incarnate Life
Eternalised, the new crusader hies.
Alone, in all the flush of flame-eyed zeal,
Sandalled by rope, with staff and calabash,
Unarm'd, the wounded Pilgrim drags his way
Till old Manreza's gates, at length, unclose
Before him. Here, again before the throne
Of worshipp'd Mary, fast and penance prove
His knighthood, while he hangs his weapons up
Before the imaged Virgin, and his flesh
Devotes to torment in the monkish cell
Of Dominic, that patron of all pangs
Ascetic, which redeem the will to God
Through shirts of pain, and thongs for bloody scourge!
Never did Penance such a hero boast,
As now was witness'd! Round his wasted loins
Clank'd iron fetters; while some thrice a-day

Fell on his frame the blood-absorbing lash:
With bitter ashes was some barren crust
Commingled; prayer, not sleep, the night
Engaged; and on the stair of his damp cell
A kneeling trance of seven-hour length unbroke
He often kept, and starved his body down
Till foodless life look'd death itself begun!
Loathsome his garb, beyond what beggars wear;
While underneath his gaberdine there lay
Thorns, which might pierce with laceration slow
The flesh abhorr'd! But still, the deadly work
Of martyrdom in horrid climax fail'd!
For now to cavern'd darkness lo! he flies
A serried anchorite; there fasting, keeps
His awful vigils, till the pallid gleam
Which through some crevice of the rocky cave
Glimmer'd, on his ghastly features play'd
As though it trembled on such face of death
To glisten! But the peace divine he sought,
Was far as ever from his gasping soul.
Then came the conflict! the convulsion dread
Which, like a living earthquake, heaved and rock'd
The moral ground-work of the man within
Till mind was shatter'd, and the will no more!
Voices, which seem'd from out Damnation's gulph
To issue, yell'd around his inward ear;
While visions, black as fiendish Magic forms,
Floated within him, till he gasp'd and groan'd,
Throbbing, as though the arch-fiend wrestled oft
With his spent anguish! In that hour of hell
When madness, guilt, impiety and dread
Raged in the depths of his convulsèd soul,
Dread Suicide beheld him on the brink
Of lost eternity, about to dash
His headlong spirit down the pit of death:
When, lo! The Virgin, veil'd with robes of light,
Floats in the air, before his eyes entranced
Clasping her infant-God: and, thus recall'd
From murder, straight with bare and bleeding feet
To Salem must that wild ascetic come,
Beggar'd, but not subdued, a Grave to seek,
The Sepulchre most holy of The Lord!
But ere he went, our Lady, to reward
Her dreadless champion, back the heavens unroll'd
Above him; more than Paul unbodied saw
Ignatius witness'd,—what no words reveal!
The Trinity to *him* unclosed its shades
Of awful Wonder, whose mysterious depths
To sight were open'd! Ages next, retired;
And *how* Creation at God's bidding rose
From nothing, and the motive *whence* it came,
His awed imagination then beheld!
And more than this the rapt enthusiast seem'd
To image: an apocalypse of soul
Did to his thought that spell of spells unwind,—
How bread and wine are in the Host transform'd,
And changed to Christ, when priested lips command
A sacramental Incarnation there
God to enshrine, and Calvary repeat! *

XI.—MISSION.

By vision strengthen'd, and by faith sublimed
To that fierce boldness which all Earth defies,
And time, or torture, to absorb or tame,
Nerved like a martyr, with his crown in view,
Ignatius onward to the tomb of Christ
Fearless of Saracens, advanceth near.
When, Lo! again, a visionary Christ
Hovers on high, above the blest sepulchral stone
Featured with glory; calls him to convert
The Orient, and His word of burning truth
Thrills through the soul of this heroic man
Like magic, out of Heaven's own music breathed.
And now, the work is done; the dreamer ends!
The cavern'd eremite no more exists
Fever'd by fancies dark: all visions die,
While calm Reality his heart ascends
To reign in wisdom, and the world o'erawe.
The giant from imagination's sleep
Awaketh, what a wond'rous race to run!
Yes, from the cloud-land, where confusion form'd
Ideas, like a mental chaos wild,
Down to the cold the actual and the stern
Descends the dreamer, and is Man again!
Before the sepulchre of Christ is born
That future Jesuit, who the earth rechain'd
To Roman falsehood; glorified the Pope
Like God, and push'd the Reformation back
For centuries, as some fallen Angel might
Reverse by giant craft the Good abhorr'd.
Nor ended he, till over ruin'd minds
And reeling empires, through his master-spell,
A vile theocracy of priesthood rose
As if by miracle! where myriads bow'd
Under his sceptre, like single Will
By God struck prostrate through resistless law.

* See the authentic Biography of Ignatius, *passim*, which all alludes to these tremendous visions.

XII.—THE VOW.

The wings unfold of some three hundred years,
And lo! a vested group of gather'd priests
In mute procession, from beneath the towers
Of Notre Dame there winds its solemn way
On to the capital, which now reposed,
Under the stealing brightness of the dawn
Quiet, in square and street. But, hark! at times
Peels in high cadence with a chanted swell
Their orisons, as o'er the fame-crown'd heights
Of Martre, to that sacred Crypt they move,
Where France believes her first Apostle gain'd
His crown eternal of celestial praise.
Mark, in the front, with war-like mien, and gait
Most kingly, He who leads yon priestly band!
His countenance seems in itself a Church
And Council,—grave, profound, august,
Delved with the lines which deep reflection brings
Upon the brow of Thinkers. From those eyes
That blaze with intellectual fire, there dart
Imperial rays, beneath a godlike front
Which Painting loves to study. None could view
That martial figure, and a King of mind
Imagine not; for, look and step and air
Betray'd his mission. He was born to rule,
And in the world's great heart a crisis form
Of glory, or disaster. Such appear'd
That incarnation of religious guile
Ignatius was, on more than empire bent,
As on to St. Denys' memorial fane
Of martyrdom, he leads his band elect.
And now, when o'er yon sacrificial Bread
The necromantic words of priesthood work
That spell almighty, making God *to be!* *
Are duly mutter'd, hark, the direful Vow!—
A vow, which, had encircling nations been
Around them gather'd, might have palsied kings
And kingdoms! 'Twas an Oath sublime, and stern;
From each of that sworn brotherhood it rose
Significant, and low, and deep as dread,
Rising from man on earth to God in heaven,—
In witness, they in life in limb and thought,
In soul and body, reason, conscience, will,
Prostrate before the Pope, would ever crouch
Slaves of his will, in whom a Christ on earth
Is worshipp'd, as the source of churches all!

* Bourdaloue, the celebrated French preacher, says, in allusion to sacramental transubstantiation, "Though the priest be in this sacrifice only the substitute of Jesus Christ, it is, nevertheless, certain, that Jesus Christ submits to him; becomes his subject; *and renders him every day, upon our altars, the most prompt and exact obedience.* If faith did not teach us these truths, could we think that a man could ever attain to such an elevation, and be invested with a character that ennobles him, if we may say so, to command his sovereign Lord, and *make* him descend from heaven!!!"

XIII.—THE SYSTEM.

Such was the Man! and now, the System view
Reigning victorious, realising all
Its founder imaged, while He watch'd and wept
In cell, or cave, on Tabor's rocky height,
And grew a priest-god, by whose sceptre awed,
Nations and kingdoms, churches, creeds, and states,
All tribes and peoples, passive things became.
Ere twenty years had vanish'd, what a world
Ignatius wielded! more than Pompey dreamt,*
Cæsar acquired, or Alexander's heart
Encompass'd, ere he died the Jesuit ruled.
Luther and he were two embodied Types
Of that great Problem, which the earth convulsed
With doubt and danger,—how in one to blend
The rights divine of individual souls
By God created, and by Christ redeem'd,
With that consentient law of common-life
Incorporate, which a perfect Church demands.
Luther for souls, as single, lived and died
In battle; but Ignatius for the Church
Contended, striving to engulph the Man
As unit, in that Body of the whole
Communion, where each separate life expires.

XIV.—PRIESTLY TRIUMPH.

Behold his triumph! In the convent veil'd
By solitude austere, from men remote
Like regal Grandeur, forth his genius sent
A world-wide power, which Empires still obey!
Europe, and Asia, and the far Brazils,
With India's giant realms,—his sceptre touch'd
Them, each and all! Thus, colleges and schools
Rise at his wand, to regulate the homes
And hearts of myriads: cabinets are moved;
Kingdoms admonish'd: councils awed and sway'd:
Battles commenced or sudden peace restored
And strengthen'd,—all betray the master-soul
Of this fam'd Leader. On his royal lip
Law absolute depended; at his word
Obedience rose, and where it will'd, there went
His banded zealots,—brave and lion-hearts
Burning for martyrdom, through East and West

* This is the substance of Loyola's epitaph on his tomb, at Rome.

And North and South, the faith of Christ to plant;
Making the desert with the rose of truth
To blossom, and the wilds of sin to bloom
With those rich graces which his Church admires!
Nor did the magic of his subtle power
Pause at conversion; since, to Him applied
Monarchs for help, while queens for civic aid
Besought Him: thus, by law divine he seem'd
Lord absolute o'er thrones and kings to reign,
Whose crown was genius, and his sceptre, mind.

XV.—SERPENTINE WISDOM.

Behold a system deeper than the thoughts
Of ancient Despots, in their dreams of power,
Fathom'd or framed, which now the world o'ertook.
Luther and Calvin, when Ignatius rose,
Had like a storm-blast heaved the mind and heart
Of Empires; mental life and action spread
With speed miraculous; monkish night dispersed,
Like cowering demons by the gaze of Christ
Daunted, and dazzled. Novelty awoke;
The fountains of the spirit's deep were barr'd
Or broken up; creation was abroad
And active; while in science, creed and art
Inventive genius with irruptive force
Burst into sway:—and now, behold! the plan
Both wise and wondrous, by the Jesuits work'd.
Not to reverse by effort mad they tried
The onward rush of European life;
But through the prowess of exceeding mind
Master'd its move, and led the mighty van
Church-ward to Rome, while yet they seem'd to act
And mingle with it! To suspend, or chain
The giant impulse, had their skill surpass'd
However subtle: so the lead they took,
Absorb'd, embodied, gather'd in the whole,
And guided *that* which else had govern'd *them!*

XVI.—SPIRITUAL AGGRESSION.

Thus they resolved a problem, dread and deep;
How with pure faith philosophy can blend,
Reason and science with religion act
Their mental freedom. This they strove to show
When Church and College, as two symbols, rose
Together, and their union thus involved.
Here is the secret of that Jesuit-work,
Which won an awful triumph. Mark it well
Student of man! for History hath no page
More to arrest a Thinker, and his thoughts.
To battle with the Reformation-power
Forth to their work those weapon'd Jesuits came,
And ne'er did such Machines of mental war
And conflict, fight with their unearthly skill!
Aggressively, with Nation Creed and Church
They grappled; Science and mechanic Art,
Language and Commerce, Poetry and Lore,
How did they master each, and model all,
Or shape them down to their dread purpose fit!
Man and his motives, mind and heart they probed
And scann'd, they search'd, anatomised, and knew
Where to begin, progress, and how to pause
In each career they ventured. Thus empowered,
These champions of the Roman church became
Resistless, by their secrecy of strength
In action; back the Reformation quail'd
Before them! city after city bow'd
True Liberties beneath their wizard laws;
Princes and people, by such craft inspired,
Barter'd the conscience, till Germanic minds
Which Luther ransom'd, into bondage sank
Abased as ever! Rome again prevail'd;
Darken'd the soul, and dungeon'd half the world
Of free-born Europe in her creed and chains!

XVII.—UBIQUITY OF GUILE.

It looks romance, but solemn archives show
What miracles were by the Jesuits work'd
O'er man and mind, when first their princes waged
Heroic warfare for the Pontiff's throne.
Never was education * so profound
As their adapting genius, form'd, and plann'd,
And carried out. But while such home-born minds
Were foster'd, far and wide their missions spread
From China's wall to Paraguay the wild,
Or, where by Ganga's Stream the black Hindoo
Waited for truth to set his spirit free.
Nor paused they here!—in palaces and courts,
In cabinets and councils were they hid

* Lord Bacon says, (*De Augment. Scient.* lib. 5, c. 4,) "For education within fifty years of the institution of the order, consult the school of the Jesuits. Nothing hitherto tried surpasses it." Education, that excellent part of ancient discipline, has been, in some parts, revived of late times, in the colleges of the Jesuits, of whom, in regard of this, and some other points of human learning and moral matters, I may say, "talis cum sis, utinam noster esses."—*Advancement of Learning,* book i.

And harbour'd ; metamorphosed to all shapes,
Ignatius seem'd self-multiplied, and ruled
By their dark subtleties o'er plots and plans
Tremendous, bloody, dismal, deep, and dire
As Rome conceived, or policy preferr'd.
Thus do we find, at infamous Versailles,
The poison'd words of persecuting Hate
Into the ears of Royalty distill'd
With potency infernal, while true Hearts
In Britain's court were basely undermined
Or master'd ; everywhere they move,
And everything they touch, pervade and thrill;
All places reach; all powers affect, or change:
No person safe, no principle secure !
From cot to court, from king to subject down,
Their zeal can like an omnipresence act.
Equal for them, to whom the Pope is God,
All powers of State; all governments the same!
Each to his Church is creature, slave, or tool;
Crime is not criminal, when She commands
The deed enormous ! treason noble looks,
And murder from the decalogue departs
No more forbidden, should the Church require
A splendid victim for her crown and cause !
"A Jesuit!" well might childish dread conceive
That Name far more than mortal nature clothed!
Satanic wisdom seem'd almost surpass'd
By them who bore it; guile and darkness there
Concenter'd all which intellectual Fiends,
On earth embodied, might for falsehood wield
Were Pandemonium in the mind to reign.

XVIII.—MECHANISM FOR SOULS.

But if the ground-work of that guile intense
And spell, whereby the man unsoul'd becomes
Enslaved to priesthood, we desire to search,
A Book*, behold, by right "mysterious" call'd;
For here, mechanics for the Mind exist
Which, when by crafty discipline applied
And studied, render man a living corpse
In spirit,—an automaton for Priests
To mechanise, until The Church appears
A thinking substitute, a faith-machine,
And swathes† the Will with swaddling bands which bind
Men to obedience, passive, base, and blind
As absolute ! And now, de-natured man
Sinks from a Person, and a Thing becomes,
Depress'd and dwarf'd, a mass of featured clay
Whence mental faculty and moral force
Have been absorb'd ! Yet, libel not that God
From whom Humanity her birth derives,
When thus impersonal, by calling such
A "Man!" Spontaneous will and thoughts are dead,
Or, sunk and swallow'd in the church of priests;
Conscience expires; the mind can think no more;
A soulless thing, an accident, or show,
A mere Negation for a man mistook
Is all that such mechanics for the mind
Can boast of; but their ruling charm succeeds !
The Formula* of hideous falsehood works;
Conversion by mechanical result
In thirty days is certain, ere one moon
Can vanish ! Let the "Exercise" be used
Completely ; let each posture, gait, and groan
Be duly balanced : let the dismal curse
Of silence, solitude, and darken'd rooms
Be wreak'd, together with an imaged Hell
Shaped from imagination's horrid depths
Of blackness, where the howling Fiends are heard,—
Such let the neophyte of Priests enact,
And lo, conversion ! passive as a stick
Wielded by aged pilgrims when they walk,
Or helpless as a shrouded corpse, when moved
By living creatures,—view the Convert now ! †

* The "Spiritual Exercises of Loyola."

† As one swathes the limbs of a child, from his very cradle, to give it just proportion, even so from his early youth we must, so to speak, swaddle his will, in order that throughout his life, it may preserve a happy and salutary suppleness."—*The Jesuit Cerutio.*

* "Servatis ubique iisdem formulis," (*Spirit. Exerc.*, p. 180). Loyola undertakes to reduce a reasoning creature into a ritual machine, in thirty days; and this is the precise period the Inquisition used to occupy in dislocating the human body, when torturing its victims for confession! Among other rules for mechanising the soul into a state of Jesuitical conversion, we find the following in 'The Spiritual Exercises,'—First, to draw upon a paper lines of various lengths, answering to the magnitude of the sins. Secondly, to shut one's self up in a room, the windows of which are half closed, (januis ac fenestris clausis tantisper), now falling prostrate on one's face, now lying on one's back, now standing, now sitting, &c. &c. &c. Fifthly, to burst forth in exclamations. Sixthly, in the contemplation of hell, which comprises two preludes, five points, and a colloquy!—to see in spirit, vast fires, monsters, and souls plunged into a flaming ergastulum; to imagine one hears wailings and howlings; to fancy also a putrid stench of smoke, sulphur, and cadaverous filth; to taste the most bitter things, such as gall, tears, the worm of the conscience," &c. With reference to prayer, mechanics are also employed, *e. g.* "Third manner of praying, by measuring in a certain manner the words and pauses;"—"Let equal intervals be observed between the breathings and the words," &c. &c.

† A little before his dying hour, Ignatius said, "I desire that the Company should know my last

XIX.—PERSONALITY DESTROYED.

What God created thus a Priest destroys,—
Man with a Soul! for now, that Soul reduced
By such absorption, in the Church resolves
Its nature: 'tis no more a choosing Power
Or Person; stifled reason hath expired
In self-renouncement; what is left, the Shape,
But not the Substance, of a man remains.
'Tis but an Organ, made of sigh, and sob, and speech!
Now on bare knees: then, prostrate in the cell
Of anguish; now, for ritual drama garb'd
And spangled; then, engaged in mumbling rounds
Of words, where sense through repetition dies,
Or the tired breath monotonously tones
Ave Marias! till the lip-work dire
Achieves its penance. What a boast is here!
When thus a mechanising Priest can make
Persons turn Things, and Things like corpses lie·
Passive and powerless: such the Jesuit seeks
To govern, and despotic Rome demands.

XX.—OBEDIENCE.

Monster of systems is the Jesuit-school!
Police and treason, accusations dire
As dismal, each on each a dragon-watch
Keeping incessant, so that counter-spies
Thus exercised, a bosom-hell create.
Suspicion lowrs on ev'ry guarded brow
Of this dark Band, whose jealous eyes are keen,
Prompt to denounce each alter'd shade of mind
Assumed disloyal. Thus, the living pulse
Of pure Emotion is by terror chill'd
Or death-struck; social life exhales,
And all enacted, is obedience now
Under the yoke of thy cadaverous Rule,
Ignatius! Fiends o'er such a scheme exult;

thoughts concerning the virtue of obedience." And from the Constitutions, afterwards framed, this obedience resolves itself into this terrible abasement,—man is to become, in the hands of the priest, "Ut Cadaver," "Senis Baculus." The Constitutions say, "Let every one persuade himself, that they who live under obedience ought to allow themselves to be borne and carried by Divine Providence acting in the person of their superiors! that they ought to permit themselves to be moved about as if they were a corpse, which suffers itself to be carried and swayed in any way you please; or, as if they were a staff in the hand of an old man, which allows him to use it whensoever, and for whatsoever purpose, he pleases." In another place, the "Constitutions" tell the convert to "become like soft wax in the hands of the superiors, to take what form he pleases!!"

But Angels, could they our dejection know,
Might shudder, veil their eyes, and weep for Souls!

CONFESSION AND CONFESSIONAL.

XXI.—PRIEST IN OFFICE.

Rome for the spirit a gymnasium proves:
Her Priests are posture-masters for the soul
Deluded, who can twist and turn the mind
And morals, just as Superstition shapes
Her ritual, or Effect on man requires.
Seek we a proof for this satanic aim
Of sacrilege on souls? Behold it, there!
The wooden screen of yon confession-shrine
Behind whose shelter lurks a probing Priest,
Contains it. 'Twere enough to blot the sun
At noon-tide blaze, to horrify the blood,
Or make Humanity to blush and burn
With shame eternal, might plain Truth disclose
All which Confessional has heard, or done,
Or vilely dared within the bosom's depth.—
Laid on the rack of Rome's lascivious tongue
The mental victim of confession sobs
Tones which are torture, while the fiendish words
Pierce their exploring way with foul success
Or skill'd advantage, till the Heart is won
And all the sacredness of soul expires.

XXII.—DEATH OF PURITY.

How the crush'd modesties of Woman bleed
Under the hoof of man's inhuman speech
Down-trampled! Mark that serpent-priest,
Holding his ear, lasciviously inspired
With loathsome appetite for all that should
Be wordless, and in blushing silence sleep,—
Feed on confession with his vampire-taste;
While maid and mother, wife, and sister wring
Their secrets into language, till their souls
Are agonised at every modest pore
Of feeling; wrench'd, as though infernal screws
Tortured their silence to convulsive speech.
Each gasping word seems like an oral pang
Breathed into utterance, with a growing shame
Which burns, and blisters, almost frenzies mind
And reason. Hell itself might cry, enough!
When a foul priesthood thus satanic grows.
E'en as from flesh an Inquisition tore
The limbs asunder, till each artery writhed,
And gush'd the life-stream from the corded veins
In drops of anguish, so Confession tears

The spirit into torment, on a rack of words
When some strain'd Heart is by the priest outstretch'd.
Oh! how it quivers, till the soul half swoons
With dread; and as the hideous work proceeds,
Well may wring'd conscience tremble, start, and groan!

XXIII.—INWARD MARTYRDOM.

Nature hath no monopolist like man
Unprincipled, to conscientious brute
Transform'd by juggleries of Jesuit-guile.
Through Her foul science for confessing hearts,
Crafty as hell, and cruel as the grave,
A very Sodom for the souls hath Rome
Created; and, with criminal excess
All crime exceeding, hath on Nature laid
An incubus of everlasting wrong.
True personality in mind inheres,
Lives in our thought, and when that thought is gained
The moral Person to the priest belongs
Who holds it. Thus, Confession drains and draws
The secret life-blood of a Spirit out
By science; melts it with persuasive skill
Into the mind of some mechanic priest,
Who to his own assimilates the same
By progress gradual, stealthy, sly and deep.
Thus, mind confess'd is through the mouth transferr'd
Into the Priesthood, which in turn reacts
With fearful magic on that mental wreck,—
Some whisp'ring martyr at his feet, unsoul'd!

XXIV.—WOMAN AND HER DESTROYER.

The shaping genius of a priestly tongue
When so applied, can secretly impress
On the soft wax of Woman's yielded mind
Each vile impression, which a Jesuit loves
Or sanctions. What a rav'ning lust of power
Inhuman, must that papal Church corrode,
Who God would rival, by discerning soul,
And analyse its living essence down
To system! Well may Superstition, mad
As impious, dream the pausing Angels stand
Respectful, when such priest-gods pass or speak:*

* We are historically called to believe that one of the new priests, under the order of St. François de Sales, often saw his own guardian angel. One day, arriving at the church-door, St. Travers abruptly paused: on being requested to tell why he did so, with a sweet innocence and sublime humility, he replied—"He was accustomed to see his guardian angel walk before him, but that this Prince of Heaven had then stopped and stood aside, out of respect for his character, giving him the precedence!" —*Life of St. François de Sales.*

For, what *they* cannot, priested tyrants do,—
Master the will, and mechanise a soul!

XXV.—MORAL IMMOLATION.

But ah! with all his power, let Pity weep
For such a Being, by confession train'd.
Fell must the heart, and foul his conscience, be
By such a process! Enervate as vile
His faculties become, who, day by day,
And hour by hour, in study, thought, or scene,
Woman and Hell before him must evoke
For question, and for trial! Not for worlds
With all their glory, ought man to command
So foul a scrutiny, which scans and sees
What yon confessor by a loathsome skill
Must probe, and punish. Hark! 'mid choking sobs
And big slow tears, that with a burning trace
Scald the fair cheeks they moisten; or, with sighs
Heavy as deep, by agony intoned,
The Bride, the Mother, or a Sister kneels
Before her priest-god. Heart, and home, and love,
Secrets of thought and starts of young Desire,
Each throb of Passion, throe of feeling wild
By warm emotion in the blood or brain
Excited,—*all* must sternly be exposed
In language, by describing speech unveil'd!
Ay, word by word, before that priestly Ear
Be all paraded! When that fiendish work is done,
An immolation of the soul complete
Begins; for, moral suicide is wrought,
And all we reverence in wife or maid
By purity of sex, exists no more.
The Woman dies when modesty is dead;
Her heart is corpse-like, and the Priesthood reigns
Most absolute, a soul within a soul
Transplanted, ruling there with master-spell
For ever: He in her becomes an all!

XXVI.—EXISTING JESUITISM.

Such are the Jesuits, that banded Crew
Whom guile has disciplined, and genius arm'd.
With secresy of power environ'd safe
They war incessant on the souls of men:
Malignant, dark, and merciless as deep
In all their plans, their principles and aims
Mysterious; Egypt's plagues in them appear
Eternalised, by Rome's tremendous charms!
Twice twenty times, although by prince or Pope
Disbanded, such a mischief-power resides
In their black Institutes, while friend and foe

Repulse them, when some crisis rocks the
church
They show their treason in most damning
shape
Embodied; and, religiously depraved
As ever, still their plotting Host endures!
No crowns are safe, no kingdoms rest secure
From these marauders; through all Lands they
steal,
And nothing touch but what they blast, or
blight.
Ubiquities of guile! from whom no spot
Or scene, or time, or principle, or truth
Or creed, or constitution can escape.
Now, at the helpless populace they strike
In secret, grinding down the People's heart
To dust; and now, a King they serve, like
God!
All creeds, all changes, and all climes alike
They vanquish: so that Rome can reign,
Earth hell and heaven in their enchantment
grow
But names of sounding emptiness, to fear!

The Babylonian Lady of the hills
Who martyrs more hath made, and numbers
less
Than churches all, is their celestial Queen
Whose cause they worship, and whose crown
appears
Jewell'd by Jesuits as the brightest gems.
And, when the archives of a soul are read
Under the light of Judgment, 'twill be found
That home of heresy, the Devil's heart,
Prompted by which schismatic Angels fell,
Since time began, no hateful brood hath nursed
Of human serpents, more intensely fit
Infernal poison through seduced mankind
To circulate, than this dread crew have been!

XXVII.—ENGLAND'S PROTEST.

Now therefore, Church of Britain's ancient
growth
And grandeur, from the Jesuit guard thy
creed!
That anti-trinity of scheming hell,
The Beast, the Dragon, and the Prophet,—
rise
Around thee; lo! the final conflict draws
Nearer and nearer to that bloody close
Where crime and havoc, heresies and wars
Clash in the fray, and worse than chaos comes,
Till palsied Earth shall palpitate with dread
And downward ruin! Free-born Isle of saints
Heroical, whose dust hath been sublimed
By martyrs! peerless Home of loyal hearts
And high-breathed virtues, God on Thee
devolves
A vast prerogative, to utter, No!
When priested blasphemy this lie propounds,—
That Rome's Melchisedec is God's ordain'd
Vicar on earth for Christ in heaven to rule.

Sublime negation! let it never end
My country; far as pulse of man can beat
Utter it forth, unsilenced and unshamed.
Rooted in scripture, let thy Creed remain;
Protesting, therefore catholic and true,
And catholic, because protesting found.

MORAL RETROSPECT.

NATURE alone, is universal want;
Yet how to fill it, Man can never find
Till Heaven instruct him. Sin a gap hath
made,
Which all the glory that below the skies
Our dreams may image, or some vast desire
Adumbrate, cannot now conceal, or close.
The happy are the holy; none besides!
But, God in man plants holiness complete:
Life from The Spirit, by His Word inbreathed,
Like to a soul within a soul must reign
Or, at the best, Humanity corrupts;
Her lights are cold, her attributes eclipsed,
And all her high prerogatives a cheat.

Still, man himself a moral Crœsus thinks,
And by his power perfected being longs
To frame, or fashion. Hence the World has
tried
The hunger of his heart with food to feed,
Drawn from the depths of that presumed
supply
By Self created: but the effort fails;
And Time recorded yet repeats the tale
Of mutual wants, by mutual pride befool'd
With false supplies, which took the name of
Good,
But never reach'd its nature: till at length
Giants in faith, by God himself equipp'd,
Rise into action and the earth redeem!
And these, like moral incarnations prove
Of all that sighing Ages had invoked,
Or Truth predicted as the master-mould
In which to cast our virtues. What was once
An aimless yearning, or a blind desire
Haunting the heart with perturbation wild,
Is now personified by Form express
And open: Want hath now a Priest obtain'd
Whose genius gives each high abstraction
voice,
And bodies forth by energy sublime
Sorrows which pleading Centuries long deplored.

And such was Luther, when the clock of Time
Sounded the hour for his decreed approach.
He was the Mouthpiece of oppress'd mankind,
A great Interpreter of tongueless wants
And pains, which lack'd an intellectual Power
Their own profundity to tell, or prove.
Yet, Preludes dawn'd which oft a change foretold
And Heralds of divine relief began
More perfect morals and a purer creed
To sanction, from the deeps of Scripture drawn,
Ere the lone monk from out his convent pour'd
Those thunder-peals of theologic truth,
Which startled Leo from a sensual trance
And shook the Vatican with such a force,
Its chambers vibrate with th' impulsive blow,
They gave them! though three hundred years
Have swept their wings o'er Martin Luther's grave.
There was a ripple in the mental tide
Awaken'd; streams of holier thought began
Heavenward and onward through the heart to roll,
Till lo! at length, a master-Mind proceeds
Forth from the secrecies of convent-life,
In whom the Spirit of the age can find
Its true Embodiment, by grace inspired
The mind to utter and its motion wield.

And we, who now the Reformation scan
Mellow'd by time, and by experience tried,
No random impulse, no erratic move
Aimless and blind, in that achievement hail;
But rather a momentum, pure and deep,
From Deity Himself directly sent
To Nature, that her inmost heart might wake.
Reason and Man were agencies alone;
They acted nought but instrumental parts:
One Great Director did o'er all preside,
But yet, invisible; behind the veil
Of mortal drapery, His guiding hand
Arrested, moved, and modified the work
With sacred watch incessant. Hence the Cause
So often grew mysterious, and appear'd
Curtain'd by gloom infernal, which bemock'd
A timid gazer; but the high result
Proved far beyond what Romish annals feign,—
Mere anarchy from man's revolted mind
Heady and proud, by lawless will inspired.
Nor was it but the negative excess
Of haughty Reason, with disdainful ire
All ritual forms time-hallow'd and revered,
Trampling to dust: for then, the Work had died
E'en in its birth, as imposition blind
As baseless; founded in no faith, or law,
And tinged with nothing but sectarian hues
Petty, and partial. No, The Truth was there!
And from that centre, like a scriptural heart,
Recover'd Grace with throbs of doctrine sent
A gospel life-blood through the generous Whole.
And thus, th' Almighty did Himself inspire
The Reformation: all unheard, unseen
And unimagined, in the midst He moved,
While Luther was the mental Hand, which made
The outward Index of His secret will.
And what makes history, but that Will evolved,
In fact embodied, or in form contain'd!
When thus perused, the page historic glows
With life intelligent, and force divine:
But when apart from heaven's presumed Decree
The glooms or glories of this world we scan,
Our creed must be confusion: then the Church
Matter and mind alone can thus display
To faith, or feeling. History's life is God:
All second causes are the First disguised,
And great results, though Man sole master seem,
Produce mere echoes which His will repeat.

And oh, how thrilling! touch'd with solemn awe,
Or, pregnant with philosophy how deep,
Are Time's events, when, thus divinely read!
Here is the harmony of Things obtain'd,
When from the Cross pure explanations flow,
And one vast Principle itself reveals
That binds with concord, and embraces all,
Which else, looks chaos in the whirl of life.
Yea, such the homage to some Power believed
Empires and nation in His hand to hide,
That pagan Instinct canonised the creed
Ere God in gospel to the earth came down
His heart revealing. Never yet hath man
A wisdom high, or greatness holy sought,
But claim'd he kindred with celestial Law
And by Divinity himself explain'd.
Thus Truth in time shall magnify the Cross,
Until the hearts of God-revering men
Echo on earth, the chant by angels sung
In glory,—"King of Kings! and Lord of Lords!
In Thee and *for* Thee, do all things consist
In souls, or systems, by the world contain'd.

BRITISH CHURCH.

Vine of the Church! whose mystic branches are
The Host elect of sanctified and seal'd
Immortals, long as Christ is own'd supreme,
Our light is safe, our liberty secure.
But when to human from divine we turn
With homage baseless, and to mortal Breath
A blind Religion blinder incense pays,
Our brightest health is but consumption's bloom.
Faithful, or faithless to her Lord, as Head
And true Bestower of all living grace,
E'en thus, as our beleaguer'd Church hath stood,
Sublime in gifts or sunken into shame
The Bride of Jesus hath on earth display'd
Her face, and features. To a threefold spring
Religion must for sacramental life
Betake her: and that triple source all time
Illustrates,—Man, or God, or mortal Priest;
As is each Master, so her fate hath been.
But when the priest his sacerdotal chains,
Forged from the links of apostolic truth
Perverted, round about pale Conscience wove;
When Man, unsceptred of his kingly mind,
A mere automaton for ritual springs
To pull or play, as guile or gain inspired
Their priestly Mover; when to such
The Esaus of the soul their birthright gave
Of faith, and freedom in salvation's gift,
Religion proved the Jailer of mankind,
And bound their spirit in a rotting gloom
Of pagan error. But when God appears
Again refulgent on his Throne of grace,
Revival wakens! and the Truth reform'd
By monk or martyr, is but Christ unveil'd;
Prophet, and Priest, and King of souls redeem'd
The Church adores him. Then, Her powers expand,
Her Symbols preach, her Sacraments revive;
And in the glory of Her greatness seen
As Ground and Pillar of the truth She stands.
Angels admire, and friends cannot withdraw
One ray of beauty from Her righteous crown!
For thus, Ambassadress from heaven to earth,
Glad tidings brings she on her mitred brow,
And gives the full-toned Gospel: then erect
In high pre-eminence o'er heart and head
She holds the Saviour, crucified and crown'd.
Sinner and sin to each her creed presents
Befitting argument, for God and man.
There, one is pardon'd—Mercy be adored!
The other, punish'd,—Justice own the doom!
Thus, in twin glory, Love and Law complete
Their vast expression; hence alike, can Law
The dreadful sanctions of its verdict teach,
While Love o'er all celestial radiance pours,
And pardoning Mercy in meridian shines.

And art Thou not thus venerably graced,
Founded in Christ, and by apostles form'd,
Glory of England! oh, my mother-Church
Hoary with time but all untouch'd in creed?
Firm to thy Master, with as fond a grasp
Of faith, as Luther in his free-born mind
Clung to Emmanuel, doth thy soul remain.
But yet, around thee scowls a fierce array
Of foes and falsehoods, mustering each their powers,
And all prepared, their hallelujahs wild
Or wanton o'er thy fallen towers to lift
Triumphantly. And well may thoughtful Hearts
Heave with foreboding swell, and heavy fears,
To mark how mad Opinion doth infect
Thy children; how thine apostolic claims
And love maternal are regarded now
By creedless Vanity, or careless Vice.
For time there was, when peerless Hooker wrote,
And deep-soul'd Bacon taught the world to think,
When Thou wert paramount, Thy cause sublime!
And in thy life, all polity and powers
The Throne securing, or in law enshrined,
With all Estates our balanced realm contains,
In Thee supreme, a master-virtue own'd
And honour'd. Church and State could then co-work
Like soul and body, in one breathing form
Distinct, but undivided; each with rule
Essential to the Kingdom's healthful frame;
Yet both in unity august and good
Together, under Christ their living Head,
A hallow'd Commonwealth of powers possess'd.

But now, in evil times, sectarian Will
Would split The Body, and to sects reduce
Our sainted Mother of th' imperial Isles,
Which have for ages from Her bosom drank
Those truths immortal life and conscience need.
But never may th' indignities of Hearts
Self-blinded, or the autocratic pride
Of reason, by no hallowing faith subdued,
One lock of glory from Her reverend head
Succeed in tearing! Love and Awe and Truth
Her doctrines preach with apostolic force;
Her creed is Unity, her Head is Christ,

Her Forms primeval as her Creed divine,
And Catholic the crowning name she wears,

MATERIALISM AND ITS CREED.

And signs portend still more disastrous gloom,
Frowning destruction over faith and forms
That, once intact, by sanctity begirt,
O'erawed betrayal. For a fitful heave,
A restless panting for the Unattain'd
And Undescribed, both church and world reveal.
Knowledge alone, from Faith's protective law
Divorced, would now sole educatrix be;
While the dread Universe itself is tax'd
For sensual income, through its living range.
Down from yon palace, where the sun-King reigns,
Throng'd by his court of seasons, to the dust
Existence crumbles on her daily rounds,—
All is for Profit! money makes the man,
And man the money. Gold is England's God,
While brute sensation forms the people's Lord;
And men are mechanised to flesh-machines
For grinding incomes out of earth and stones;
Till glorious Nature, once by genius loved
As one vast Temple where creation-rites
Are acted, is a common work-shop now
Polluted and depraved. Thus by sense deceived,
Our Cains in creed, those deicides in mind,
Abhor Religion with a quenchless hate,
Scouting the future as the mock of fears,
A poet's fiction, or a priest-born lie
Venal, as groundless! Thus, can men conceive
Income may do, what creeds have never done;
Till conscience is at length by lust betray'd,
And man,—a moral ruin! base and blind,
Anarchic passion, and bereft despair.
Myriads are such, whom sensual knowledge cheats,
And depthless minds with most satanic guile
Seduce, and govern. But, amid this whirl
Of things, when all by ancient Worth admired
And call'd immortal, waxes dim, and pale;
When law is weak, and legislation blind;
When guess-work dares all principle decry,
And time-hoar'd Verities, by heaven approved
As props and pillars of a nation's weal,
Uprooted lie, by violation's grasp,
And earth-born Self our second bible grows,—
Lo! in the midst of this disastrous change
The Church of England, like a bastion fronts
The warring elements which round Her rise!
Secure, unbroken, unalarm'd, and calm;
And haply, if ordaining Heaven decree,
The Spirit's organ for restoring life
To Virtues dead, and Morals half extinct.

SOURCE AND RELIEF OF UNREST.

If language can articulate the Truth,
What is the spring, the primal and profound,
Of all commotion, strange, or deep, or strong?
What is it, but the hunger of our hearts,
A moral famine of the foodless mind
For Good? or, thirst beyond all worlds to soothe,
And all the cisterns of created joy
To quench? But, in God's Infinite of truth,
There may the intellect its rest attain!
And in God's Infinite of love, the Will
Responsive adequacy alone can find.
Yet save in Christ, creation's true Relief,
Where can unresting hearts repose enjoy?
For here, all aspirations may their echo meet,
Center in calm, and reach consummate bliss.
But if that Christ in England's Church be found,
In pulpit, sacrament and prayer enshrined
(Her Priesthood faithful, and its Power express'd
With order'd grace and discipline revered)
Then, in the hands of her o'erwatching Lord,
Yet may she bring to European hearts
And spirit, that supply of nurt'ring truth
They need, but cannot name. And signs exist
Which stamp her, with significant effect,
Teacher of nations, fated yet to draw
The future round her, as a central ark,
Where Light and Liberty and Law secrete
Their saving essence, to conserve the world.
For in her still, with all their force inspired
Live the vast truths protesting Luther voiced
Like battle-tones, before the ear of kings!
And what, if thus by fav'ring heaven endow'd,
The high deposit of the Faith she guard
Unweaken'd? Trial then may glory prove,
Safety and splendour may her conflicts crown;
And what to our prophetic sense appears
A Future charged with paralysing woe,—
A true arena where our Church may stand
Fighting the battles of primeval faith,
May be, and grateful Empires call her blest!

And lo! e'en now, prelusive shadows throng
Round perill'd nations; signs which preach with power
The sermons deep of providence to man.
See Population, with enormous swell,
Increase a thousand ere the sun decline,
Day after day; while Space and Time depart
Before the miracles by modern speed
Enacted! Elements our vassals make;
And, like a war-steed harness'd and controll'd,
Ruled by proud Science, mark the subject Deep

Commerce to all Her thousand ports convey,
Rapid as winds can waft, or waters roll!
Empires with empires thus new contact form,
Powers with fresh powers, and minds with minds embrace,
For vice, or virtue; all in fusion meet
And mingle,—ready to ignite, and blaze
Heavenward or hellward, as the truth prevails,
Or falters: while around this huge ferment,
See Legislation to the lowest brink
Of sad Humanity her code direct;
And Wisdom brood with speculation deep
O'er plans and prospects, where the mind may grow
And learn to build a moral Being up.

These form the portents, which a change predict,
Or solemn crisis; while the dormant East
(That home of apathy and ancient pride)
Wakes from Her torpor, with mysterious life
And motion. What shall then the issue be,
When the World labours with some big event
Radiant with bliss, or dark with dreadful crime?
To God we leave it! this may truth pronounce;
That hell is forming where His grace breathes not;
And let but once thy spark, Rebellion! fall
Down on the mass of unconverted minds
By treason moulded, or by anarchs led
To lawless triumph,—and the World must bear
Suff'rings untold, and horribly intense
Beyond what Hist'ry hath for thought portray'd.
Then Earth a pandemonium would present
Raging with lust, or reeking with revenge,
Till by her blood incarnadined, the World
Would be as godless as the Fiend requires!

ASPIRATIONS.

Yet this, in mercy, may our God forbid!
Nor leave the world a dungeon of despair,
But bid the Church, by gracious heaven revived,
Her apostolic rank in word and deed
Resume, and dignify; and thus uplift
Her mitred forehead, and Her saintly mien
Untarnish'd, unattainted, safe alike
From popish rancour, or schismatic rent.
For in her shrine eternal morals dwell,
And through her sacraments and creeds there flow
Streams of pure life, from fontal Grace derived.
But could the Mammons of our day succeed,
Unchurch the Nation, prayer and praise destroy,
Silence the Pulpit, and all means of grace
Baffle, or blight, soon would Hell on earth
A more than rival in debasement hail!
For soul itself in sin would putrify,
Or wither down to senselessness and shame;
While Manhood, which the eye of faith declares
A true shechinah * for indwelling God,
A mere contingency of breath and brain
Becomes,—a paradox in flesh array'd,
A baseless nothing, though baptised a man!

But in thy heart, heroic England! long
May Luther's voice, and Luther's spirit, live
Unsilenced and unshamed. Thou peerless Home
Of liberty and laws, of arts and arms,
Of learning, love, and eloquence divine,
Where Shakspeare dreamt, and sightless Milton soar'd,
Where heroes bled, and martyrs for the truth
Have died the burning death, without a groan,—
Land of the beautiful, the brave, the free!
Never, oh never! round thy yielded soul
May damning popery its rust-worn chain
Of darkness rivet; in the might of heaven
Awake, and back to Rome's vile dungeon hurl
Her shackles base of slavery abhorr'd!
Without the Bible, Britain's life-blood chills
And curdles; in that book, and by that book
Almighty, freedom can alone be kept
From age to age, in unison with heaven.
Without it, life is but a ling'ring death,
A false existence which begets decay,
Or fevers only into restless life
Whose blood is madness, and whose breath despair.
For not Philosophy, with Attic grace
Bedeck'd, and dazzling; nor can Science deep,
Sounding with searchful eye the vast abyss
Of things created; nor politic Weal
Transcending all which earthly patriot dreams
Of pure, and perfect, this vast empire guard:
And though our banners on the four winds waft
Defiance in the face of boundless foes,
Our swords flash vict'ry, and proud Commerce vie
With more than Tyre, upon her throne of waves
Once free and famous, till our country prove
The banking-center of all climes and creeds,—
Reft of her Bible, not a drop remains
Of holy life-blood in the Nation's heart!

* "In the *image of God* created He him."—*Gen.* i. 27.

APOSTROPHÉ TO ENGLAND.

Land of the Lord! my own maternal Isle!
Still in the noontide of celestial love
Basking, beneath the cross of Christ adored,
How bounds the heart with patriotic throb
Devoted, till each pulse a prayer becomes,
When oft upon thy sea-dash'd cliff we stand,
While ships by thousands haunt thy favour'd shores,
And in their bosom half the world discharge
Of riches and of splendour! God is thine,
My country! faithful unto death be thou;
For He has made and magnified thy strength,
E'en like a second Palestine, to prove
The Ark of Scripture, where a creedless world
The truth may find which makes her spirit free!
Thy bulwark is the Bible, in the heart
Of Britain, like a second heart enshrined
For inspiration, purity and power:
And while upon thine ocean-throne erect,
Scepter'd by prowess, Earth reveres thy reign,
O'er public virtue as in private life
May Scripture be sole paramount and test,
The source and standard of majestic faith,
Where morals form, and whence our motives flow.
And thus, brave Empire! if thy Church beloved
Firm to the truths a second Paul restored,
Tenaciously through blood and fire remain,
Then, long as guardian-waves begird
Thy shores, or sunbeams o'er thy cornfields play,
And thy large soul with liberty exults
And brightens, will the Church uninjured stand,
Saintly and solemn, by the wise revered,
By greatness honour'd, as by goodness blest.
And never may the touching sabbath-bells
No echo in thy children's heart awake;
When pealing softly with a pensive chime
Or deep-toned cadence o'er thy hills and dales,
Cities, and towns, and hamlets far away,—
They bid us feel what Luther's victory won,
Giving to myriads God's own Day of rest
Pure as the dawn my page shall vision now.

SABBATH MORN.

And see! from out the radiant east, which blooms
As if with blossoms of carnation'd light,
The rose of Morning blushes into hues
Of purpling splendour, till the arch of heaven
Serenely mantled with one glow immense
Of opal lustre, tells that Day is born,
And that, a sabbath: sacred be the morn!
To all who welcome with accorded rites
Its high mementoes and its claims august.
And oh, how numb'd by earth's torpedo-sway
Their souls who will not, in the saintly prime
Of this rapt morning, feel how God hath framed
The world without intelligibly true
By living concord to the world within.
Now, matter seems a paraphrase on mind:
We pour our spirit into sounds and scenes,
Greeting creation, like an echo'd Self
In forms repeated, for poetic eyes,
Or hearts of high-strain'd purity, to hail.

And now, from secret depths of faith within
Rise thoughts, which in their trepid beauty hang
Faintly and freshly on the virgin soul,
By words unechoed. Sacramental hour,
Hail to thy glories! from the Lord they come,
And all they image but His name reflect:
The very sunbeams their own sabbath keep,
So hush'd and holy is the bright-hair'd Morn,
While balm and beauty through creation's breast
Are now prevailing! Nature's holy type
To sabbath-keeping hearts it thus presents,
Who early at the grave of Jesu watch
Like Mary, to behold their rising Lord.
We call it fancy, but it rules like fact
O'er yielded spirits with seductive power,—
Nature herself sabbatical becomes
And greets that Day, which to the other six
Imparts a pure and consecrating spell.

But, mark the heavens! whose inspirations melt
Through the deep eye which loves to drink their hues
Like draughts of glory, till our flooded gaze
O'erflows with radiance, and grows dim with light.
The larks sing matins; while the humbler birds
Send hallelujahs to the King of morn,
Tiny and broken, but replete with praise;
Who now, uprising from a throne of clouds,
Bares his red forehead to the greeting World.
The viewless finger of the fairy wind
Wanders about, and with a dimpling touch
Ripples a stream; or tunes the air to song,
Till like an anthem by the breezes hymn'd
Fancy admires it: but for this,—all earth
Seems cover'd o'er with meditation's calm,

Solemn as in some hoary minster dwells;
And if the trees emotional were not
By air-breaths flutter'd; or the lisping talk
Of flowers, wind-ruffled; or the mellow tones
Of gliding waters in their graceful flow
Broke the blest calm,—'twere all a perfect trance
In sweetest emblem of this hallow'd morn.

But if from rustic solitude we look
To where, through parted hills old Ocean heaves
His breast of waters in the mantling sun,
Thou hast no sabbath, ever-rolling Sea!
Restless with glory: yet methinks, thy waves
Throb like the pulses of a heart enrapt,
When high emotions quiver into praise.

THE TEMPLE OPENED.

But, day advances: hark! from tower and spire
Pointing the soul, like principles, to heaven
And happiness, the many-voicèd bells
Peal their high summons, which invite the world
To meet her Maker, in His temple shrined
Waiting due worship. Oh! ethereal Day
Beyond the grossness of the belial-sense
Rightly to value, what a blighted scene,
Yea, what a prison-vault of petty cares,
Polluted dreams, and soul-degrading joys
Would earth, if sabbathless, at once become!
For since like angels, men should feel and act
By God approved, if glory such desire,
How priceless is the sabbath! when we hail
The soul of six days in the seventh divine.

To let th' eternal o'er the temp'ral cast
A shading awe, which bids this world away;
Low earth to heaven by aspiration's wing
To lift; by symbols and by signs to charm
Cold nature, and imagination feed
With rites which nourish for ennobling growth
Our being; then, by combination due
Of epochs high, traditions pure, and faith
Unblemish'd, from a gospel-fountain drawn,—
Here is the function which a Sabbath fills.
With these conjoin appliances devout
Of praise, confession, penitence, and prayer,
Bathing the conscience in the crimson Blood
Of Christ, and who can such a day blaspheme,
Thus propertied with those divinest powers
That to the secret roots of all which makes
A people holy, or an empire wise,
Send a live influence from Religion's heart?

'Tis chiefly through such institute sublime
Sanction'd by God, and by Himself first kept,
The soul's position in the truth appears
E'en as it is before omniscient Heaven.
Now are we taught by rites, and facts reveal'd,
Or by appeals, whose virtue is Thy pang,
Emmanuel! through a hidden grace applied,
A truth which humbles, yet with holy might
The heart attempers till it loves the law
Celestial; e'en this truth, the base of all
In moral code or creed religious found,—
That God made man, but man himself unmade;
And now is fallen from supernal heights
Of being, into cursed and carnal depths
Apostate, helpless, hopeless, and impure,
And, having nothing but a guilt,—his own!
Oh Verity! beyond our solving minds
To master, but by all things sign'd and seal'd;
Since nature providence and grace combine
Their witness, and authenticate the Fall:
Explaining much, itself is unexplain'd;
Remains a myst'ry, but all myst'ries lights
With radiance, pure as reason's eye approves.
Deny it,—what a libel on the Love
Almighty, does this blasted Earth become!
So much of grandeur in our grief abides,
So much of glory in our gloom appears,
And in the soil of each corrupted soul
So oft the foot-prints of departed God
Leave shining impress of their primal track,
That, if not fallen, but in form of mind
Man in his perfect God-created mould
Be yet apparent,—what a satire, then,
On Power Creative seems our anarch state!
Or rather, by such contradiction judged,
Incarnate angels, base and yet sublime,
Would men be christen'd, if no beam from heaven
Lighten'd the gloom of this chaotic world.

And therefore, glory to this Day benign!
For now, eternity and time will meet,
The heavenly on the earthly state shall dawn,
And Man, who in the mass and multitude
Of work-day powers, and worldly movements, makes
Too often but an item unobserved,
Here in the Temple, where a church becomes
A shrine of morals to regen'rate hearts,
Himself shall realise as full-orb'd Man!
Single and one, within him hiding depths
Of solemn, vast, and individual life
Beyond all utt'rance! life which few discern
Or ponder, yet beyond all speech august,
Since there alone our secresy of strength
And power of unpartaken being dwell.
For what is Action, but the spirit's garb,
The form and pressure of a Life unseen?

And *that*, more awful than the outer-sense
Can shape, or recognise by teaching words.
But life exterior, with its painted shows,
And all its multiplex array of scenes
By conduct acted or experience tried,
Is like the ripple marked on ocean's face,—
Hiding an unregarded deep below
And tempting gazers to discern no more.

Then, lift your heads, ye Everlasting Doors!
And be ye open, O Eternal Gates!
That in the chariot of descending grace
Borne by His Spirit down to hearts which pray,
The King of Glory with His train of truths
Begirt, may come, and find due welcome there.
England! be grateful; for a scene that fills
The soul with thoughts, whose dialect is tears,
Around us opens with expansive range.
Uncounted steeples now to heaven uplift
Their chimes, and swell the wafting air with tones
Which rise and fall, like undulating waves
In volumed cadence heaved upon the shore:
And touching are they!—for the tombs of Time
Open amid them, as they peal, or pause;
While buried hopes, and forms, and feelings dead
Quicken beneath their resurrection-tones
Mysterious. But far more than gazing sense
On earth can witness, will those gather'd souls
Who meet for worship with commingled awe,
The God Incarnate,—to the Angels bright
This morn discover, when the piercing truth
Enters their spirit with irradiant power,
And bares the bosom of the soul to light!
For hearts to them, are like transparent hives,
Whose hidden workings are conspicuous made
And watch'd for ever. Yes, the sabbath gives
Wisdom to Angels, while they bend to see
How nature struggles, as the Spirit acts,
Revives our graces, or a sin rebukes;
Or, drags the guilty to that secret bar,
That stern tribunal where dread conscience reigns,
And self by self is summon'd!—'Tis a day
When such bright Angels watch the soul redeem'd
Who love to think, where infidels would sneer,
And learn divinity by reading man.

DAY OF THE LORD.

But, though some emanated charms exist
Born of the sabbath, which no eye discerns
Profoundly as consummate Angels can,
Haunting our temples with their wings unheard
And eyes unwitness'd,—yet, enough remains
To prove a magic clothes this holy morn
Beyond all others, beautiful and deep.
And now, methinks that potency begins,
Open the heavens, and drop their sacred dews
Distilling balm, and blessedness, and love.
Whether to yon cathedral, with its form
August, and massive elegance of towers
Serenely rising in the radiant air,
Your fancy wander, and awhile enjoy
The wave-like rollings of the organ peals
Bursting, and booming down the archèd aisles
And hollow naves, while choir, and chanted rites,
And vested priesthood in their pure array,
With awful loveliness the scene inspire:
Or rather, if to some arcadian haunt
Where rustic manners in ancestral stamp
Are yet embalm'd, you turn the roving eye
To view the patriarchs of some village-plain
Throng to their minster, with its gothic porch
And ivied windows, 'mid encircling yews
Embosom'd dimly,—yet, in each alike
How much of all the Reformation won
For peace and purity, devotion finds!

E'en where yon palaces of Commerce lift
Their dusky, dim, and many-window'd piles,
'Mid roar of capitals, or cities vast,
How does the day, on which Messiah rose,
Check the loud wheels, and hush the grating jars
And vexing hum of avarice and gain,
That care-worn artizans, with pallid cheeks,
And all the wasted family of Toil,
Each with his little one, awhile may feel
That Men are more than rational machines
For shaping matter, or absorbing food!
And on this day, by Heaven's ordaining law
Rank'd in the rubric of perpetual Grace,
Their sacred brotherhood in God enjoy.
There, as they group beneath the Bible's wing,
And through the centralising love of Christ
The level glory of our nature reach
Together, who can tell what sweet content,
What calm submission to their clouded lot,
And wasting sorrows which their toil-worn lives
Experience ever,—from such moment flows!
Here all are equal by the bond of flesh,
The ties of nature, and in guilt, with God:
Here, crowns, and coronets, and sceptres drop
To nothing; king and subject share alike:
And in thy royalties, redeeming Love!
A prince may falter, where a peasant lifts
His plea; while in the poor man's eye may shine

A tear of rapture, kingdoms could not raise,
Nor all which earth's diameter contains
Purchase the peace a sainted conscience hath.

Glory! to think that on this morn mankind
Bow at the footstool of their Common Sire
In co-equality of dust, and sin,
To plead for mercy at Salvation's fount.
Ye mighty Hunters in the fields of truth,
Titans of thought! ye giants of renown!
Colossal wonders in the world of mind,
Who with the shadow of a soul immense
Cover creation! though your genius charm
Th' eternal Public of posterity,
Your names are nothing in the balance, now!
Bend the stiff mind, and bow that stubborn heart,
And in the pleadings of your helpless guilt
Go, take your station with yon cottage-girl,
Or, chant a verse with yonder hymning child,
And happy are ye! if like them, ye feel
True wisdom is our ignorance to know.
There, cast your anchors in the cloven Rock
Of Ages! for, behind the Veil it towers
Deep as eternity, and high as God.
Abhorr'd be therefore a satanic wish,—
That e'er by riot, lust, or lawless gain,
Or by some logic false as fiends inspire,
Our sabbaths in due sanctity should fail
Or falter. On two worlds, at once, they touch,
The Lights of this, the Landmarks of the next;
And reft of such, all anarchies commence
To madden: nor can praise itself o'erprize
The order'd notions of a sabbath-day,
When thou, maternal Church! whose head is hoar'd
With ages, but whose heart, like Jesu's, beats
With love for spirits,—art a blessing proved
By forms, by functions, and by ritual chants,
And sacraments of soul-exalting grace.
Thine is a work, beyond seraphic lyres
To celebrate; for now, by Thee allured,
The infant, with its lisping tongue may speak
More truths than prescient Socrates could tell,
Or Plato in his most unearthly dream
Embody. Yes, the Church is Reason's friend!
For, what is Reason but th' informing Word
By grace imparted? and as He begins
Our nature's law to regulate and rule,
So all the circles of our secret life
Concentrical with perfect reason act.
And though alike the humble and the high
In sermons, sacraments, and symbols meet
Depths of divinity they cannot wade,
And meanings never master'd, yet by such
Our mental energies are boldly train'd
With truths to wrestle, as the patriarch did
With God's own Angel, nor to let them go
Without a blessing. But the creed which aims
Both man and faith in horizontal lines
To level, proves a flatt'ring lie, that draws
A force *from* reason, which it feigns to give;
Like fawning ivy round some oak entwined
Eating the heart its verdure seems to brace.

Again then, be our lauding chants uplift
To Him most holy, to the sabbath's God!
Who when the Planets sang their lays of light
While young Earth from her liquid cradle rose
Rejoicing, from His Throne of love decreed
A sabbath endless, modell'd from his Own,—
A rest whose archetype Himself enjoy'd.
Long may our Church, with her organic powers
And rites ministrant, this pure Day revere:
For sabbaths make the morals of our land;
And by their litanies of sacred love,
By pulpit, priest, and all that past'ral sway
Which makes the meanest village in our land
Some moral hues of soft refinement take,
They form thermometers, whereby to mete
Our true advancement in the noblest weal:
Since, public virtue, monarchy, and law,
And Church with State together are espoused
By league of principle, and power of love.
Hence, if our sabbaths be from sway dethroned
The music of the Commonwealth is gone!
Soon into atoms will dissolve and drop
That Fabric eloquent, whose walls are mind,
And founded deep in immemorial laws
And liberties,—the Constitution falls!
Then guard them well, ye Senators and Priests,
For they are priceless; and to us preserve
All which in heart and home, in Temple, or in State
Is pure of worship, or of lore profound.
And he who robs them of their rightful sway
By pen, or speech, example, creed, or life,
On Heaven itself a sacrilege presumes;
Man's awful being to the center shocks
And plucks the apple from a Nation's eye!

EVENTIDE.

Now ere we part, let meditation look
Once more on nature. Lo! the day is done;
And like the radiance of a lovely dream
Poetic slumber visions, softly melts,
And sweetly mellows into parting hues
The hour of sunset. From the ruby west
A flashing glory o'er the firmament
Deepens along, and over earth reflects

Beauty, which touches flower, and field, and fruit,
And yellow corn-fields sloping o'er the vale,
With charms more exquisite than garish noon
Inspires. And if on yonder height we stand,
Beneath us what a British Arcady
In lustre qualified with coming shade
Is then unveil'd, by sunny calm serened!
There as we pause, around our temples throng
The fresh-wing'd airs, from waving branches sent;
The breeze makes music; while the cadence low
Of distant sheep-bell dyingly comes on,
Or sinks delightfully on Feeling's ear.
Here Nature thrones enchantment: far-off hills
Crown'd with a coronet of glitt'ring trees,
Paler and paler, to the west retire
'Mid wood and coppice, lane, and hedges green,
With sun-bright cots, and farms of mossy roof;
While here and there some rustic temple shews
That gothic beauty, whose mysterious power
Acts on the eye like poetry in stone
Embodied. These in blent expression woo
The gazer; mix'd with many a fairy gleam
From rivers flashing, as the sun-ray tips
Their current, cheering it with gay surprise.
But now, a mellow shade of mantling hue
Advances; villages and towns retire
Like pictured visions, save where yonder tower
In its tall symmetry with golden tinge
Retains the sunbeam; and as home you wend,
Hark! on the ear of balmy Evening comes
The faint far chime of some cathedral-bell,
Whose pensive cadence to the fancy sounds
A curfew for Creation's sabbath rest.

That hallow'd rest is deep'ning: daylight ebbs;
But yet, or ever sinks yon Priest of light,
Around Him like a burning shrine the heavens
Gather and glow, and with their beams infold
His dying pomp; while colours rich, and deep,
And dazzling, woven from th' Almighty's loom
Of nature, all the occident inlay.
Brighter and brighter His dilated orb
Is now becoming; till, at length, He sinks
In soft decline magnificently calm
Beneath th' horizon, leaving all above
Tinged with his radiance; as true saints derive
From God's own heroes, when their dying beds
In farewell glory give the christian out,—
Flashes of meaning which the face o'erspread
With lustre, and the gazer's cheek impress
With light, whose source is immortality.

Vistas of thought, and avenues of mind
Where Truth may roam in philosophic shade,
Or Fancy by her shaping dreams begirt,
Image beyond what pict'ring words describe,
Open before us; while this pensive lull
And balmy prelude to the twilight's reign
Come o'er the heart, till with sabbatic love
Nature and mind responsively confer.
Oh, how the sacredness of silence steals
O'er all things! just as if a spirit-glide,
Inaudible but felt, through earth and air
Were passing. Mute and motionless, the trees
Stand in the gloom like sentinels entranced;
Not e'en an insect through the stirless air
At times is waking: boughs and birds repose;
While the dark shadows of yon distant hills
Arrest the eye, portentous and profound,
As if with speaking vastness: but the flowers
Breathe double fragrance, now the heated air
Is cooling; and a thousand secret plants
Which in the sun-warm noon their scents retain
Inviolate, a rich aroma yield;
Like hearts whose finer sympathies are shut
When fortune brightens, but when sorrow's night
Blackens around you, let their sweetness forth:
Or, as those promises the Spirit's love
To faith applies, which seldom while the sun
Of joy shines golden, make their treasures known,
But in our glooms, how gloriously they breathe
Their buried meanings into living force
And comfort!—But more hush'd and holy still,
Grows the dim landscape round the muser's tread
Who walks it, till he dreams his very step
Profane intrusion on the soundless air.
And now methinks, Miltonic eyes would view
Angelic Watchers of our mystic world
Patrolling earth, with immaterial garb
And tread unseen; or by their Lord employ'd
The wheels of nature to redress; or guide
The comings-on of Night, who soon begins
To spread Her mantle o'er the sleeping world.

Now rules the hour, when dormant Conscience wakes
If rack'd, or guilty; when Religion looks
On truths unwitness'd on the garish day,
While awed Imagination lives, and feels
Th' unborn poetry of speechless mind
Within her quicken'd: loud the heart-throbs beat;
And in this syncopé of nature's voice
What muté theology a moment wields
O'er the strain'd fancy! now indeed, we prove
That worded speech to manhood appertains,
But silence the Almighty's language is;
And faith can hear it, by Himself entoned
With inspirations from eternity.

MOONLIT SCENE.

But that is o'er; and from the shrouding awe
That girds thee, with a gentle force awake.
E'en such a night, as now prepares to reign,
The captive Luther from his watch-tower loved
To witness, when by inward prayer becalm'd,
He roll'd his eye-glance round the vaulted heavens
Studded with stars, like Scripture gemm'd with truths;
And gave his spirit to the charm of night
With all a poet's rapture! Such begins
O'er the lull'd twilight to assert its reign
Of trancèd loveliness, and stellar noon.
Lo! one by one, with timid gleam, and slow,
Star after star comes trembling into life
And lustre; radiant, mild, and mournful oft
Like the half-tears in Childhood's pensive eye,
Faintly they shine; while planets, rich and round,
Like burning jewels dug from mines of light
Flash on the forehead of the mellow'd sky
Most brilliantly; or, cluster'd into groups,
The rest commingle their associate beams
Dazzling the concave. Still, the earth obscured
Lies dimly veil'd, with umbrage unrelieved,
Waiting the lamp which lights her beauties up.
And, yonder comes it! lo, her placid brow
O'er the dusk air yon queenly Moon uplifts;
And e'en as music, solemn, deep and slow,
Through the dark chambers of dejected mind
Where all is shapeless, oft to order cites
Thought after thought, successive and serene,
So her wan lustre, as it mildly steals
O'er the mute landscape, tree, and bough, and bank,
Each out of dimness and disorder draws
To shape and aspect; till the dew-drops gleam
Like Nature's diamonds on her night-garb thrown,
In countless sparkles: all the stars grow pale,
Like mortal graces near th' excessive blaze
Of Thine, Emmanuel! save th' undazzled brows
Of those large planets, eloquent with beams
Unrivall'd. What a witching spell the moon
O'er all things by her fairy radiance flings!
Like faith, arising in some nighted heart
And touching nature with redemption's light
Celestial. Wheresoe'er his roving eye
Darts a pleased glance, lo! hill, and brook and hedge,
Rivers and streams, and meadowy range far-off,
Cities and towers, and tall cathedral-spires,
And village-churchyards with their grassy tombs
Attract the gazer; till his glance is charm'd
With loveliness, beyond the moving lip
To mention. But above, how beautiful!
There, solemnly the climbing moon ascends,
And each thin cloud within her silver reach
She clothes with splendour; like a mortal pang
By hope regen'rate into radiant peace
Transmuted. But in this access divine
Of Nature's sabbath, solitude and night,
How like the fortunes of the Saviour's Bride
The Moon's high progress through the heaven appears!
Varied, and full, now crescent and complete,
Shaded, or dim, and then with radiance clad,
So hath the Church along time's clouded scene
Flourish'd, or faded, shined, or suffer'd gloom,
But yet doth travel through her fated round
Upward to glory! Or, may deeper eyes discern
In yon pale symbol of mysterious sky,
The moon-like radiance of imperfect man
By grace made holy, but how changeful too!
E'en to the last by shades of sin o'erhung
And hidden: while th' imperial Lord of day,
By His prerogative of light portrays
That sun-clear righteousness of state complete,
Which all the justified of God arrays
With faultless glory, fair as Jesus wore.

NATURE AND THE CROSS.

But *that* deep Name, beyond all nature loud,
Peals like the trumpet of Eternity
Through secret chambers of responsive faith,

Making them echo with the voice of Christ!
Nature was forfeit, when the first man fell
By sin; and whatsoe'er in nature lives,
In reason, morals, or in mind enacts
Dominion, from His vast atonement flows.
Creation once her own Creator saw
In Flesh embodied, when for sin He died!
And now from Him this hour of beauty takes
All that cloud, or star-encircled moon
Is lovely. Here indeed, material sights
Touch'd by the Cross, with sacred meaning glow,
Turning creation to a creed of forms
Significant and glorious. What a truth!
Through Him this orb of sentient being came
From nothing cited; by His ceaseless hand
The wheels of nature, and the wings of time
Circle their way, or waft their soundless flight;
While all those properties those creatures have
Are but the actings of atoning Love
By virtue present. Here is faith heaven-born!
When all the motions which in Nature rule,
Her laws, and lights, her harmonies and hues,
From the faint insect to the flaming sun
Apparent, preach the Saviour's kingly hand,
And to the senses mirror forth His heart
For ever. What the sinful Adam lost,
The Sinless by eternal heirship gain'd;
The curse unsting'd, then took th' attainder off
And back redeem'd th' inheritance of Man.

Oh, tell me not, poetic harps can sing,
That science loves, and sentiment perceives,
And calm philosophy, with musing eye
Beneath the stars enraptured,—all which heaven
And earth of God and goodness testify;
'Tis only when by David's key * unlock'd,
The Secrets and the Splendours of the world
Unfold their magic, and by grace reveal'd,
Electrify the soul of answ'ring love.
The merest elegance which Pagan mind
Imparted, upward to creative Power
And goodness, dimly groped its erring way:
But when the Christian His incarnate God
Owns to be Head of all creation is,
All life becomes one vast religion;
And faith and feeling in communion move
Divorceless ever. Then, at once, all laws
And movements, like cathedral-rites appear
By nature's liturgy of Love perform'd
In the vast temple of the universe,
Shrining Emmanuel: then, the Whole applies
To Him the watching, weeping, dying, Lord,
The source of nature and salvation too,
The priceless merit of Whose Blood preserves
The heavens in motion and our earth alive.

So may we learn, at this nocturnal hour,
Morning, or noon, whatever time we walk
The halls of Nature with a holy tread,
All bright and beautiful, all vast and fair,
In Him to love, Who, when creation sinn'd
And crime on earth began like hell to reign,
Personified eternity in time,
And clothed th' Infinite with human Flesh
For our remission!

* "He that hath the key of David."—*Rev.* iii. 7.

HUSH OF NIGHT.

But the night is come;
The Moon, with her pale hierarchy girt
Of stars, is gliding to the ocean's brim,
And listen! for the chime of far-off bells
O'er a dead Sabbath tolls their dying tone:
And now, the Day is buried; to thy tomb
Eternity! with all its hopes and fears,
Gather'd and gone. But oh, how thrill'd
The chords mysterious of our secret frame!
As if the stirrings of a life unborn,
Latent but lovely, this rapt hour inspired,
The Dead seem gazing on our hearts again!
Illapses deep, irradiations pure
Glide through our spirit from a source unknown;
Until, by awful loveliness subdued,
Above, the pilgrim lifts his eye of prayer
Expressive: youth, and home, and long-fled days
With soft revival touch him into tears
Unshed; and while yon arch of midnight rings
With the soft echoes of those sunken chimes
Around him, many a thoughtful sigh is heaved
O'er visions gone; and things that once becharm'd
His dazzled fancy, pale and cold appear,—
Weeds of the past on Mem'ry's lonely shore!

And now, amid thy hush, most holy Night!
Here let us stand beneath yon hanging cliff,
Closing our song beside the placid sea
Which now lies breezeless. Who that thus beholds
Her bosom, by the braiding moonlight deck'd,
And heaving only to attraction's orb,
As pant young hearts beneath the eye they love,
Could ere imagine, everlasting Sea!
Thy billows, like the roar of human wrongs,
Clamour on high and cleave the heavens with sound

So often! Such thy halcyon slumber now,
The stars are mirror'd on thy glassy wave,
With beam unbroken; while the feet which press
The pebbled margin of yon moonlit-wave,
Rudely and loudly on the hush intrude
Their faintest motion.

Here, then, be farewell
To this blent strain of meditative truth,
E'en by thy bulwark, O Britannic Isle!
Whom Ocean ramparts with her wall of waves.
Now in the trance of this untroubled night
While all seems holy, our adoring hearts
To that supernal Power of truth we lift,
Who guardeth Empires, and Who guideth thee,
My country! with a most peculiar love:
That once as out of Zion peal'd the trump
Of ancient Gospel, hence the battle-voice
Of Truth should never cease to challenge Rome;
But waken echoes, bold as Luther's cheer
Might welcome, deep as lofty Cranmer loved,
Or Ridley o'er his pangs of fire prolong'd.

FINAL APOSTROPHÉ.

Mysterious Spirit of the ceaseless mind!
Heart of the Church, as Christ the only Head;
Soul of our souls! in supernat'ral light
Unbounded, deathless and transforming Grace,
And Love, and Wisdom, Thee I now invoke;
And to Thyself presume to consecrate
Pages, that whatsoe'er of hallow'd power
They have, from Thee alone their truth receive
And virtue. Oh! thou Sempiternal Life,
Breathe o'er this effort, and with force array
Whate'er is feeble; and by heavenly touch
And tone their meaning so affect and fill,
That onward to the inner-mind of man,
Or central being, where high Conscience holds
Her seat august, and faith's dominion acts,
What truths they carry may be safely borne
Beyond the heartless, and above the vain
To warp or weaken. Here, beneath the arch
Of midnight, solemn, deep, intensely calm,
Thy Presence would I realise, and lift
Mine awe-struck nature to the heights unseen
Of Essence Uncreate, where Thou art Third
In Godhead, as the Fountain-Sire is first,
Second, the Filial Word, and All supreme
As One co-equal, co-eternal Three.

Descend pure Spirit! light and life and love
Without Thee, are not: poetry is Thine;
Reason and science, and majestic arts,
The heaven-born virtues, intellectual powers,
And all pre-eminence in grace or gift
Are but as glances from Thy glory cast,
And caught by mind. But, who Thy sway can tell?
For at the first, the Heavens and all their host,
Moon, star, and planets, from Thy hand derived
Their radiance, from Thy wisdom learn'd their paths.
And Earth is thine: Her elemental laws,
Her motions, harmonies, and living hues
Are but the efflux of Thy fontal powers;
While Man himself, that miracle of forms!
Into his mould was copied from Thy cast
Ethereal; and the whole of truths inspired,
Prophetic utterance, or miraculous deed,
Which was, or is, or shall be, are but rays
Sent from Thine Essence to created mind.

Without Thee, more than night Egyptian reigns;
Duty sublime would stern distraction be,
Commanding what our impotence alarms,—
To love the Holy, which our hearts abhor
By nature! But Thy promised aid attends,
Arches our being like the roof of heaven
Where'er we wander, and to Will perverse
Such power imparteth, that the precept takes
Thy presence with it, in each task assign'd.

Thou teachest God; and man himself abides
By thought unfathom'd, till Thy light reveal
The two eternities of coming truth
Within him folded, like a double germ
Soon to expand, in heaven or hell complete.
And hence, our Nature grows an awful thing:
We thrill eternity in touching Man;
Since from the deeps of his immortal soul
Outlooks The everlasting, whence he came!

Unerring Judge! to Whose omniscient gaze
All the seal'd fountains of shut motive lie
Unseal'd and open, richly deign to bless
Both church and state, our monarchy and crown;
Teaching the highest, that of Thee bereft
Reason itself irrational becomes,
And virtues vices, with a better name
And brighter seeming: while by Thee becalm'd,
The rudest chaos of corrupted hearts
At once is soften'd, till in love and awe
Embodied harmony the Man appears,
Lives in Thy life, and thus by grace becomes
A radiant Likeness of the Lord he loves.

And now, O Spirit! at the noon of night,
Under the shade of these expressive skies,
While all around the hush of heaven prevails,
Thee I invoke, a christian song to bless;
From Whom apart, 'tis vanity and voice,
Or mere vexation into language thrown:
But when Thy sanction hath the poet crown'd,
His harp-strings quiver with a breath divine
And all its tones with heaven-born music ring.
They in my soul of aspirations dwell
For truths beyond Philosophy to preach,
Or master; if one thought this perill'd mind
Inspire, where Thou, O God of grace, art seen,
Prevenient Spirit! 'tis from Thee derived.
And oh, if Life, with all its loneliness,
The glow of youth hath still in heart retain'd;
If the stern waste, the fever, and the fret
Of buried pangs beyond the world to know,
From boyhood in its bleakness, e'en till now,
Have not untuned me, but a tone have left
In concord with the beautiful and bright;
If nature thrill me, with as keen a joy
As in the poetry of pensive youth
It ever did; if such for bliss remain,
Blent with far deeper things, by suff'ring taught
And faith transmuted for the life within,
As onward through a bleak and heartless world
My pathway windeth to the waiting tomb,
Spirit of Glory! take my gratitude
And sanctify the closing strain I sing.
Bear with my soul; Thy blessing o'er it breathe
And all who love the Master whom I serve.
Emmanuel! peace within thy Church abide;
Till faith shall in sublime fruition end,
All symbols cease, all sacraments retire,
Our earthly sabbaths into heavenly rise
For men and angels, and the host redeem'd
In the one Temple * of pure Godhead keep
The sabbath endless of almighty love.

* "I saw no temple therein; for the Lord God Almighty and the Lamb are the temple of it."—*Rev.* xxi. 22.

As the spell of a remote but unreal antiquity is one of the most potent fascinations wielded by Rome over ardent minds and imaginative temperaments, a Catholic student of the religious past will appreciate the following tabular view of those distinct periods when *Papal Novelties* were substituted for ancient truths. The author is indebted to the Rev. Charles Stanford, Prebendary of Michan's, Dublin, for this valuable chart:—

CENT. II.*—First steps towards a Purgatory, taken from Platonism.
- Rise of Ascetics, or Christian Hermits.
- Sign of the cross upon the forehead, on the most common occasions.
- Consecrated elements begun to be carried to the sick or absent, strangers, heretics, &c., a custom ending in the grossest abuse.

CENT. III.—Over-estimation of the celibacy of the clergy.
- Gradual approach to monastic life in Egypt.
- Anniversaries of the death, commonly called the birth-day, of the martyrs. Collections for the poor on such occasions, supposed by Baronius to be an example of the sacrifice of the Mass! Gradual corruption of Christian morals; ambitious rivalry, &c., &c., of some of the bishops and clergy the occasion of much animadversion and grief.

* The dates as above have been collected from Mosheim's "Ecclesiastical History," (Murdoch and Soame's translation, &c., &c., London, 1846); Spanheim's "Ecclesiastical History," edited by Wright, and compared with the original; Greer's "Epitome of General Councils;" Horne's "Popery delineated," &c. &c.

CENT. IV.—Multiplication of rites and ceremonies.
- First indications of usurped authority of the Bishop of Rome.
- Rise of Monachism.
- Invention (finding) of the cross, by Helena, mother of Constantine.
- Rise of superstitious veneration of the cross.
- Collyridian worship of the Virgin Mary. [The Collyridianæ were women who came from Thrace and the more distant regions of Scythia, into Arabia. While they were Pagans they baked and presented to Venus, or Astarte (the moon), certain cakes, called *collyrides*. And when they became Christians they retained this custom in honour of the Virgin Mary.]
- Rise of superstitious regard for relics.
- Rise of pious frauds, &c., &c.
- First steps towards masses for the dead.
- Wax-lights, salt, oil, &c., used in baptism.
- Wax-lights used in public worship.
- Incense used in divine service.

CENT. V.—Celibacy of the clergy additionally important.
- Private confession ordained by Leo. I.
- The Apocrypha, with the exception of one or two books, added to the canonical books of the Old Testament, by the Council of Carthage, A.D. 419.
- Increased veneration for the cross and relics.
- Rise, amongst the Orientals, of the invocation of the Virgin Mary and the saints.
- Rise of prayers for the dead.
- Further tendency towards the doctrine of a Purgatory.
- An enormous increase of ceremonies in

CENT. V.—*continued.*
the celebration of the Eucharist, respecting the garments of the priests, consecration of wax-lights, erection of crucifixes, &c.

CENT. VI.—Prayers to the saints, dedication of temples, and consecration of festival days to them.
Public use of images.
Increased veneration of relics.
Further belief in a Purgatory.
The absolute necessity of baptism to salvation.
The title "Mother of God" given to the Virgin Mary.
The Canon of the Mass founded by Gregory I.
Increase of Monachism.

CENT. VII.—Purgatory sanctioned by Gregory I.
Title of "Universal Bishop" assumed by Boniface III.
The clerical tonsure appointed, and the vow of celibacy enjoined on the clergy by Martin I.
Civil jurisdiction granted to bishops by Eugenius I., with the power of imprisoning men.
The universal use of the Latin language in divine service commanded by Vitalianus.
The right of the investiture of bishops, and the sale of the pallium or pall (the mantle of a bishop or archbishop) usurped by Leo. II.
Increase of superstition concerning Purgatory, prayers for the dead, images, relics, statues, crosses, pilgrimages, fastings, &c.
The rise of Antichrist in the Roman Church.
The total alienation of the Oriental or Eastern from the Roman or Western Church, in consequence of the usurpation of the title of Universal Bishop, and the claim to Papal supremacy.

CENT. VIII.—Doctrines insisted on by Church of Rome:—worship of images; invocation of saints; pains of Purgatory; prayers and masses for the dead; virtue and worship of relics; necessity of celibacy; merit of Monachism; confession to a priest, &c., &c.
Public service of God consisted, for the most part, in the mass, consecrations, prayers to images, pictures, &c., observance of feasts, &c., &c.
Solitary, or private, masses instituted.
New pilgrimages appointed.
Number of saints, relics, monasteries, and monks, multiplied.
Avarice, libertinism, and gross ignorance of the clergy, a most striking characteristic of this century.
Controversy upon image-worship burst out with great acrimony, and the worship of images sanctioned by regal authority (that of Irene, Empress Regent during the minority of her son, Constantine VII.) in the second Council of Nice, in which the honour of the salutation, the kiss, religious

CENT. VIII.—*continued.*
veneration, burning of lights, &c., &c., were decreed to images.
This doctrine was opposed by Constantine when he came of age; but his mother in consequence deprived him of his eyes, and soon after of his life: an act applauded by Baronius!
The origin of the great controversy respecting the Eucharist may be traced, in some measure, to this century. In the seventh Synod of Constantinople, under Constantine, son of Leo Isaur., the bread of the Eucharist is called the "image of Christ;" the "only true image" of himself, which he left, by the sanctification of the *substance* of the bread. On the other hand, the Fathers of the Second Nicene Council, and also Johannes Damascenus, strenuously denied this position, asserting that the bread was the proper body of Christ, not indeed by *transubstantiation*, but by *union* and *corporeal assimilation*, according to the hypothesis of the Greeks.

CENT. IX.—Valentine (Pope) first required the Roman Senate to kiss his foot.
The character and conduct of Formosus VI. and his successors in this century, drew from the Roman Catholic historian, Baronius, the following complaint:—"Behold the most unhappy times of the Roman Church, and the most disastrous of all periods," &c., &c. (Ad A. C. 897, N. 4.) And again—"Let us return to Stephen VII., whom I should not dare to reckon amongst the Roman Pontiffs, unworthy as he is of so illustrious a title," &c., &c. And again—"We consider it necessary to premise somewhat, lest the weak-minded should be scandalised, if he should happen to behold the abomination of desolation in the Temple of God," &c., &c.
Every day brought accessions to the tyranny of the popedom; to corruption in doctrine; idolatry in worship; superstition in rites and ceremonies. The cement of the papal structure consisted in the worship of images, relics, belief in a Purgatory, in masses for the dead, in Ecclesiastical and Apostolical traditions, including those of St. Peter, the celibacy of the clergy, the corporeal presence in the Eucharist, Papal supremacy, the power of the will, &c. &c.
The festival of the Assumption of the Virgin Mary.
Paschasius Radbertus, a monk of Corbey, asserted the doctrine of Transubstantiation, as now held and taught by the Church of Rome, and insisted upon all the unscriptural and antiscriptural errors inseparable from this palpable untruth.
Many portents and prodigies said to have been sent from heaven.
Numerous miracles alleged to have been

IX.—*continued.*

wrought in confirmation of Papal supremacy.

Violent contentions between the Eastern and Roman Churches.

Two places distinguished for relics—Compostella, in France, for the body of St. James the Greater; and Venice, for the body of St. Mark, brought from Alexandria.

X.—See, for the judgment of a Roman Catholic historian upon the Church of Rome and her rulers at this crisis, p. 181. According to the Roman Catholic writers, Werner, in "Fasciculo Temporum," Platina, Sabellicus, Onuphrius, Belarmine, Gerbrardus, and others, the "bishops of Rome" were "monsters and not men," "false pontiffs," "invaders of the See," "simoniacal," "adulterers," "necromancers," "knaves," "infamous," and sometimes "mere boys." They are stated to have been "rapacious, flagitious, prone to libertinism, and inordinately desirous of dignity and wealth." Baronius speaks with "horror and shame" (auditu horrenda atque pudenda) of the appointment of Hugo, son of a Count of Aquitaine, to the archbishopric of Rheims, at the age of five years, under Pope John XI., or X., and of the election of Octavian, at the age of eighteen, to the Popedom, with the title of John XIII.

The canonisation of saints; a fanatical devotion to relics; the adoration of images, which were made to utter voices, decide controversies, and adjudge lawsuits, &c.; saint-worship; institution of festivals, also of fraternities or sodalities, who were bound by an oath, and under pain of anathema, to chaunt so many masses, at stated times, to help souls out of Purgatory; the baptism of bells; trials of accused parties by the tests of hot iron, cold and hot water, &c., &c.; all these, with the daily increase of idolatry, error, and fanaticism, and the inculcation of blind obedience to Papal authority, while the schools of theology, laws, philosophy, and languages, &c., &c., were neglected and closed, are the striking, prominent, and deplorable characteristics of this century.

Pope John XVII., the rival of Pope Gregory V., was deposed and put to death with most barbarous cruelty. His eyes were torn out, and his ears and nose amputated; thus mutilated he was placed upon an ass, with his face to the tail, and led through the streets of Rome.

But in these dark and barbarous times God did not leave himself without a witness. Even amongst the monks some dared to reject the Papal thraldom, to expose the vices of the clergy, and the gloomy superstitions and vain traditions of the times. (Magdeburgh Divines; Hollinger's Eccles. Hist.; Usher, de Success.)

Cent. X.—*continued.*

Accounts were rife in this century of earthquakes, inundations, volcanoes, human monsters, miracles, apparitions, voices from Purgatory, and other crafty impostures, by which the monks generally secured the support of the credulous, and imposed upon the ignorant and weak.

The Crown of the Virgin Mary, and other offices to her, took rise in this century.

Cent. XI.—The clergy grossly ignorant. Corrupt and flagitious crimes openly tolerated. Religion consisted in legends of false miracles, apparitions, &c., &c. The annals of the time record strange prodigies, bloody wars, monsters in human form, &c., &c. The people, too, were as ready to receive these "lying wonders" as the priest were to invent them.

Pilgrimages; the endowment of monasteries; the discovery and consecration of relics; and implicit deference to Papal authority, entered largely into the religious observances of this century.

Roman Catholic writers acknowledge to the dissolute lives, the avarice, the ambition, and the profligacy of the clerical order, who were generally debased, and practised the most open and shameless simony. Baronius (in Gregorio VII., A.D. 1075), speaks of the "great perversity of manners, particularly among the bishops, who ought to have been examples to the flock; and that this proceeded from the vice of simony, and the abominable luxury which prevailed, so that the clergy and the faithful were tainted with it."

Three of the Popes, Sylvester II., Benedict IX., and Gregory VI., are called by Platina "three most dreadful monsters." They are also described as "infamous Antichrists, flagitious in their lives, tyrants in their rule, and diabolical in their acts." Also, most of the Popes in these ages are said by all historians to have obtained the pontificate by money or violence, and are described as "indolent, adulterous, proud, ignorant, simoniacal, covetous, and bloody."

A further apostacy from the truth of God marks this century. The dogmas inculcated as essential to salvation were, Papal supremacy, even in temporal things; the virtue of indulgences; the celibacy of the clergy; the intercession, merits, virtues, and worship of saints; the service of the Virgin Mary; veneration and virtues of relics; adoration of images; transubstantiation; masses for souls in Purgatory, &c., &c.

The act of penance was commuted into a pecuniary fine, pilgrimages, or chaunting a set of psalms.

A Sabbath was consecrated to the Virgin Mary by Pope Urban II.

CENT. XI.—*continued.*

Strings of beads for prayers were invented by Peter the Hermit.

Consecration of chaplets, &c., &c.

Infallibility in doctrine claimed by Pope Hildebrand.

In Pope Hildebrand (Gregory VII.) Papal tyranny attained its summit of insolence and pride. He is accused, upon good evidence, of having removed some of his predecessors by poison, and of obtaining the pontificate by purchase. By the wars which he fomented, and the rebellions he instigated, he deluged Germany with bloodshed. His conduct to the Emperor Henry IV. has been already recorded in the body of this work. He is described by Cardinal Benno as "impious, perjured, perfidious, cruel, proud, superstitious, and hypocritical." He was guilty of illicit intimacy with Matilda, the Princess of Lombardy, from whom he extorted some of her possessions. To this intimacy Baronius gives a spiritual meaning! and says, that "in Gregory the grace of the Holy Spirit abundantly inhabited, so that, beyond all other men, he excelled in divine things, by the gift of the same Spirit!" He is highly extolled by Roman Catholics, who speak of his visions, miracles, prophecies, and cures, with wonderful reverence!!!

The controversy on Transubstantiation raged fiercely in this century. This doctrine was resolutely opposed by Berengarius and his followers, who had adopted the sentiment of Bertram, the opponent of Paschasius Radbert; decrees were multiplied, and severe punishments enacted against all who denied the doctrine of Transubstantiation.

Monachism increased, and, of course, all its attendant evils.

CENT. XII.—In this century religion consisted chiefly in the piety of engaging in the crusades; seclusion in monasteries; auricular confession and priestly absolution; corporal penances; abstinence from meat; extreme unction, &c., &c.

Plenary indulgences granted to crusaders.

Fierce and bloody competitions of rival Popes for the Pontificate.

The bishops and clergy, examples of superstition, avarice, and lust.

Shameful traffic in relics.

The doctrine of Papal supremacy carried to a scarcely credible extent. In respect of his names, attributes, omnipotence, infallibility, divine worship, prophetical office, his sacerdotal and regal power, the Pope is represented as equal with God, (Baronius on Pope Paschal II., Innocent III., Adrian IV., Alexander III., and Celestine III.)

Pope Innocent III. prohibited the translation of the Holy Scriptures, and the reading of them in any vernacular language.

An increased importance attached to the intercession and invocation of saints. The power of canonisation monopolised by the Pope; also the power of granting indulgences.

The main points insisted on by teachers of religion, in this age, were Purgatory; human satisfaction for sin; the merit of pilgrimages, crusades, and the monastic life: auricular confession; transubstantiation; the denial of the cup to the laity; the celibacy of the clergy; and the omnipotence of the Pope.

Mention made of the addition of the five pretended sacraments of the Church of Rome to the two real sacraments instituted by Jesus Christ.

The Waldenses and Albigenses separated themselves from the abominations of the Church of Rome.

Many new orders of monks were instituted; amongst them the Dominicans, founded by Dominic, a Spaniard, for the purpose of extirpating error and destroying heretics. This order had many offices, privileges, and inquisitorial power granted to it in the following century by Innocent III.

CENT. XIII.—To the accumulated vices which characterised the Roman Church in the preceding ages is to be added in this century the barbarous and bloody persecution of the Waldenses and Albigenses; in order to destroy whom and extirpate them utterly, Innocent III. instituted the office of the Inquisition. He was followed, and imitated in his career of blood, by Honorius III., Gregory IX., Innocent IV., and Alexander IV. Dominic and Francis, the monks, were active agents in stirring up this cruel persecution against people whose crime was—to hold the Scriptures to be a sufficient rule of faith, and to denounce the avarice, tyranny, and ambition of the Popes of Rome; the vices, corruption, and despotic manners of the cardinals and clergy; and the various errors and anti-Christian traditions of the Romish Church. For the almost indescribable sufferings of this people, their invincible steadfastness, and the diabolical agency which was exerted to crush them, we must refer to their histories, which, as is well known, are within general reach.

The Rosary of the Blessed Virgin instituted by Dominic.

A pestilential flood of moral poison spreads over Europe by the two orders of monks, Dominicans and Franciscans. Their mutual hatred and hostilities involved the whole of Europe in strife and debate for nearly 300 years. One of the princi-

CENT. XIII.—*continued.*

pal points of their disagreement was the doctrine of the immaculate conception, which was asserted by the Franciscans, and as resolutely denied by the Dominicans.

Of these two monks, Dominic and Francis, Innocent III. declared that in a vision he was informed that they were "the two pillars of the Church; the two lights of the world; two angels, two witnesses; two patriarchs; two evangelical trumpets; two standard-bearers of Christ; two scourges of heretics."

This age abounded with pretended miracles and new monastic orders. The worship of the Virgin Mary, and images of her, increased and multiplied. Unceasing efforts were made to support the credit of relics, &c. Images were said to have spoken, eaten, emitted oil, and sweated blood. The Host is said to have been turned into real flesh, moist with blood, and to have been adored even by beasts. This age also gave birth to the faith of the "wounds of St. Francis," which was commanded by the Popes to be believed, under the pain of incurring the guilt of heresy. To this age also is due the marvellous history of the "house of Loretto," which took place, according to the Romish legend, A.D. 1291. It is alleged to have been the original dwelling of Mary and Joseph; but when the Christians were expelled from Palestine, it was carried by angels through the air, over Asia Minor and the Archipelago, and placed in a part of Dalmatia, overlooking the Adriatic Sea! In 1294, it was removed again, across the Adriatic, to Picenum, to a wood belonging to a lady, named Lauretta. It afterwards removed itself to a station on a neighbouring hill, where it became remarkable, according to Romish authorities, for many signs and miracles. Pilgrimages were made to it by all classes and conditions, and most valuable offerings made to it. These offerings, however, were gradually lessened by the invasion of less superstitious Romanists; and the house was finally plundered by the French.

In the year 1300 Boniface VIII. commanded a jubilee to be held at Rome, at which a plenary indulgence, and pardon for every sin, was granted to all who should visit the churches of St. Peter and St. Paul, and observe other ceremonies. This jubilee was designed to substitute a pilgrimage to Rome for one to the Holy Land; and so, as Spondanus asserts, this Pope "opened heaven to mankind by a shorter route." (Breviori manu cœlum mortalibus aperuit.)

CENT. XIII.—*continued.*

The feast of Corpus Christi and the elevation of the Host may be traced to this century.

CENT. XIV.—Pope Boniface VIII. exercised a proud and austere tyranny over the kings of Europe and their subjects. Antichristian doctrine, idolatry, superstition, monachism, and inquisitorial cruelty and persecution were at their height. All these, with the barbarity of the scholastic philosophy, dimmed and defiled the feeble rays of sound doctrine and truth which yet lingered over Christendom.

The characters of the successive Popes, of this century are to the last degree shocking and offensive to religion and common humanity. They seem to have been actuated more by the animal passions of brutes than by the common sense and reason of men.

On the death of Pope Gregory XI., A.D. 1378, the Italian and French factions came into collision, and each appointed a Pope of their own—both of them alike infamous for their crimes; one of them had been supported by Catherine of Sienna, who was remarkable for her pretended visions, revelations, and prophecies, in the pontificate of Gregory XI. And the other, Clement VII., by Peter of Lombardy, said to have been remarkable for his miracles, and afterwards canonised! The schisms in the popedom during this century lasted fifty-one years.

Many Romish writers exposed the simony, corruptions, innovations, and vices of the Popes; the libertinism of the monks; and the ignorance and indolence of the clergy: particularly William Durand, "De Modo Celebrandi Generalis Concilii;" Nicholas de Clemangis, "De Corrupto Ecclesiæ Statu;" and Cardinal Alliacus, "De Emendandâ Ecclesiâ." Also Dante, and John de Rupescissâ, testified to the fact, that the inventions of men were preferred in the church to the oracles of God. Many other writers, undoubted witnesses for the truth, deplored the lamentable state of the Church, and expressed their indignation at the unsound doctrines and innovations which prevailed, respecting transubstantiation, saints, images, relics, the merits of works, &c., &c. Such were William Occam, Francis Petrarch, Oresmius, Nicholas Lyranus, Bradwardine, Gerson, Sagarelli, &c., &c.

A testimony for the truth of God appeared amidst the darkness of error and superstition in this century, in the person of John Wickliff, born at Wycliff, in Yorkshire, A.D. 1324, and first brought into notice by defending Edward III. against the Pope, who required homage from England. He demanded that every

CENT. XIV.—*continued.*
doctrine should be tested by the Word of God alone; and proved that not one of the accumulated errors of Romanism could abide this infallible test. In this century Mallaesius, or Militzius, a canon of Prague, contended with great zeal and ability for the unadulterated Gospel. He was soon followed by John Huss and Jerome of Prague, who imbibed the spirit of Wickliff, and were equally ardent in the cause of religion and truth. Of course, no other than a passing notice can be taken here of those illustrious men, and their ability and fidelity to the cause of God.

CENT. XV.—The beginning of this century witnessed two rival Popes. Soon after, three were found to claim each the pontificate for himself, and, by course, the infallibility alleged to accompany it!

In this century Pope Martin V. approved of the sentence by which John Huss and Jerome were burned alive—the former July 7, 1415, the latter July 29, 1416; and by a bull (Inter Cunctas) he delivered over to the secular power, for punishment, the Wickliffites, Bohemians, and Moravians. The better to effect this, he aroused the most dreadful persecutions against them, under the title of "sacred expeditions." His death was followed by new schisms, and by the deposition of Pope Eugenius IV., by the Council of Basil, 34th Session, in which the Pope was declared to be "notoriously and manifestly contumacious, disobedient to the universal Church, a rebel, simoniacal, perjured, heretical, useless, and damnable, unworthy of any rank, title, honour, or dignity, and therefore deprived of the papacy and Roman pontificate," &c., &c.

Pope Nicholas built several sumptuous palaces in Rome, and lived very luxuriously and expensively, supporting his extravagance by the sale of indulgences.

The characters of the Popes in this century equalled, if not surpassed, those of their predecessors. But it remained for Pope Alexander VI. to outdo all who came before him, and to have admitted no rival in his indescribable wickedness but his own son.

By a canon made at the Council of Constance, A.D. 1415, the laity were deprived of the cup in the Eucharist, upon the most wicked and at the same time ridiculous pretences.

The doctrine of the Immaculate Conception was asserted and decreed

CENT. XV.—*continued.*
by the Council of Basil. This did not terminate, however, the disputes on the subject. The Dominicans and Franciscan bishops, archbishops, cardinals, and universities, still contended on different sides of the question. Pope Sixtus IV. attempted to settle it, but could not succeed.

Several new festivals were instituted, the feast of the Immaculate Conception, &c., &c., and also new fraternities, which tended to promote idolatry. Amongst these was the Society of the Rosary, or Psaltery of the Virgin Mary in England; in which it was esteemed a singular mark of devotion to say 150 Ave Marias and fifteen Pater-nosters at one time; an original invention of Dominic, but which had fallen into disuse, and was revived.

Vast treasures of relics were said to have come to light in this century.

The disposal of indulgences for the remission of sins had now become a common traffic.

Miracles and apparitions multiplied. Visions and fables, and monkish legends; the wonderful virtues of images, relics, the form of the cross, &c., &c. all increased to uphold the credit of the false doctrines of the Romish Church. Unprofitable, and even impious, subjects of disputation occupied the pens and minds of the monks, schoolmen, and ecclesiastical writers of this period. Every species of crime and immorality was rife during this age. The darkness became every day, if possible, more dense, in order to impart a brighter lustre to the dawn of the approaching Reformation. The most relentless persecutions were instituted in England against the Lollards and followers of Wickliff; in France against the Picards and Waldenses; Louis XII. sent armed detachments against the Albigenses. In Bohemia the Hussites were persecuted. Amongst the chief and most active fomenters of bloodshed in this awful period was Pope Martin II.

The public auction of church preferments, and the sale of the pardon of sin, by which even the wickedness which one intended to commit might be commuted for money, proceeded to the most shameful extent.

CENT. XVI.—See a former page for a brief sketch of the Church of Rome at this period, and for the exigent necessity of that Reformation which it pleased God to effect, and in the light of which it is the glorious and inestimable privilege of our Reformed Church to walk.

WOMAN:

THE LIGHT OF HOME.

WOMAN.

CANTO I.

(In reference unto History).

"Without whom,—'le commencement de la vie est sans secours, le milieu sans plaisir, et la fin sans consolation.'"—*Miss Edgeworth.*

"The empire of women is not theirs because men have willed it, but because it is the will of nature. Miserable must be the age in which this empire is lost, and in which the judgments of women are counted as nothing by man."—*Rousseau.*

ANALYSIS OF CANTO I.

Commencing Apostrophe—Morning Scene at Elsinore—English Fleet passing the Sound—Cronburgh Castle—Queen Matilda a Captive there—Her dejection and dreams—Farewell Scene—Landscape changes—Moral analogy—Time—Ideal associations—Imaginary Sketches—City-portraiture—Human Life—Its trials ameliorated—Woman's Mission—Compared with Man's—Sexual characteristics—Degrading Theories—Moral Beauty—English Females are national glories—Prostituted Genius—Its unavailing Remorse—Design of the Poem—Grateful Retrospections.

EARTH, air, and ocean, glorious three! *
Inspired with living poesy,
More gladly than a bird regains
The freedom of unbounded plains,
And wanders on ecstatic wing
O'er meadow, lake, or laughing spring,
My spirit from the world retreats;
Again the bright Creation greets,
And learns how Nature's smile can bless
The hearts which love her loneliness.

How eloquent this silent hour!
Surrender'd to its lulling power,
The soul forgets that tears are shed,
That hopes are dim, and pleasures dead:
A hue of heaven on earth descends;
Th' immortal with the mortal blends;
And all we fancy, frame, or see,
Is found in faultless harmony.

Oh! ever thus, while bards can feel,
And celebrate with hymning zeal
The glories which for good combine,
The universe becomes divine:
Behind the veil of sense they dwell
Encinctured with a dazzling spell;
Where'er they tread, enchantment lives,
And Beauty all her magic gives
To hallow with poetic grace
Whatever dreaming eye would trace.
To them, the finished world is fraught
With fine appeals to glowing thought;
And meanings flow from all they view,
Of vast in form, or fair in hue;
And not a ray of sunshine gleams
But there the smile of Godhead seems
In token of paternal love
Reflected from His face above!

His torpid mind I envy not
Though crown and kingdom were his lot,
Who here, amid this morning balm
And conscious Nature's dream-like calm,
With tender sky and tranquil sea
Partook no inborn sympathy.
The canopy of heaven is hung
As blue as poet ever sung;
Though here and there serenely glide
Along the air's cerulean tide
Pale clouds, which seem too delicate
For breeze to touch their fairy state.
Beneath a window, far away
O Stranger, let thy fancy stray,
For seldom can thy dreams expand
Their wings o'er more delightful land:
The warble of yon distant waves,
As lightly oft the billow laves
The greenwood-bank and grassy shore
That bounds the sea of Elsinore;
The mountain's dim and dusky form,
Which, like a dying thunder-storm,
Glooms on the air with awful swell; [1]
The chiming of the castle-bell,
From frowning turret faintly heard;
The fruited boughs by breezes stirred,
With every sound that summer brings
From bird, and bee, and happy things,

* The first canto of this poem was written at Elsinore, Denmark, in the neighbourhood of Cronburgh Castle, which will explain the local allusion and historical illustrations by which the general subject is naturally introduced.

How exquisitely all combine
To make exulting morn divine!

And look, adown yon dimpled sea
As bright as liquid sun could be,
The tiny skiffs of Norway sail
And glitter, cloud-like, in the gale;
While frequent oars with flashing stroke
Appear, as oft the tide is broke
By fleet-wing'd bark, which gaily flies
To where the sand-girt Sweden lies.
In green extent of wood and hill,
With bowery hamlets, bright and still.
To him who loves a haunted scene
Where grief or glory once hath been,
Grey Cronburgh lifts her storied pile
And darkens o'er the Danish Isle: [2]
Whose vaulty depths and caves profound
Have echoed to the wizard sound
Of clanging shield, and shaken lance,
With each grim voice of old Romance.
And there on Fancy's spell-bound eyes
Behold! that royal spectre rise,
By Shakspeare summon'd, when the bell
Of midnight groan'd the hour's farewell.
But, ere thou leave the castled height,
Survey o'er all a patriot sight,
A scene that makes the life-blood start
And pictures England on his heart,
The banners Nelson thrill'd to see
Behold them wave!—how gallantly
They flout the wind with haughty threat,
And show the Deep her victor yet!
When bravely down yon beauteous tide
The monarchs of the ocean ride;
Or, tranced amid the drowsing air,
They whiten in the noontide glare
Those wings that wait the driving breeze
To waft them o'er a hundred seas!
Reflected on the wave is cast
The symmetry of sail and mast;
Or, booming o'er the startled deep,
Loud echoes of their cannon sweep,
Whose thunders in their dauntless tone
Can mock the Tempest on his throne!

Yet not on earth exists a scene
Where shades of sorrow have not been:
The softest verdure mead can spread
Is often paced by Misery's tread;
The magic of the clearest sky
Hath mock'd how many a clouded eye!
And, link'd with all that local grace
The wizard Fancy loves to trace
Wherever Nature weaves a spell
Round wood, or crag, or hoary dell,—
Live recollections sad as deep,
To bid Imagination weep.
And thus in this elysian hour
Oh! who can gaze on Cronburgh tower,
Nor dream of her, the young and gay,
Whose captive spirit pined away
The victim of a royal hate,[3]
In the vile gloom of dungeon-state!
Dejected queen! I view thee now
With pleading eye, and pensive brow
As pale as moonlight and as mild;
Or, watching o'er thy cradled child
While visions of regretted youth
Around thee float in fairy truth,
Till the full past o'ercrowds thy brain,
And thou art in thy home again!
But when at night a thund'ring sound
Of wave on wave, in deep rebound
Rang echoed o'er the castle-wall,
How wildly did that night appal!
How many a terror shook thy form,
As Midnight roused the yelling storm,
And, like the rush of demons, past
The pinions of the northern blast,
And through a grated window broke
The flashes of each lightning-stroke!—
Yet oft arose a sunny mood,
When gladness e'en an exile wooed,
As, gazing from a rampart's height,
Her eye might gather free delight,[4]
While slowly pealed the turret-bell,
And richly over Zealand fell
The flushes of retiring day,
Till earth one mass of glory lay!
Beneath her roam'd the Baltic wave,
Where oft an English banner gave
(While roll'd the gun's saluting roar,)
A dream of that remember'd shore
Her heart was doom'd to hail no more!
There, oft as gradual eve decayed
And glimmer'd o'er the beechen-shade,
How Denmark's bloom her smile would bless,
Laid forth in Eden loveliness,
Of bank and meadow, bush and stream
Like landscape in a painter's dream!
Or where the rocky Sweden lowers
She mark'd Landscrona's faded towers;
Or musing saw in verdant rest
The garden once by Hamlet prest,[5]
When haunted by majestic grief
The princely mourner scorn'd relief,
And dared to nurse in dreaming pain
The might and madness of his brain.

With many a gleam of pensive joy
Her captive-gloom could not destroy,
O'er sad Matilda ling'ring past
The lonely years, by fate o'ercast
With shadows of imputed crime,
Which deadened hope, and darkened time,

Till when, at Britain's high behest,
The exile found a foreign rest:
Entranced upon the deck she stood
And, while her straining vision could,
(As o'er the billows' bounding play
Her wafted vessel flew away)—
On Cronburgh's battlemented pile
Array'd by evening's rosy smile,
Matilda fixed her yearning eyes
While heaved her breast with broken sighs,
And on her cheek sat meek despair,
That mourn'd a child deserted there!—
There, in that tower where time had been
A sad, but still maternal scene;
How thrilling was that farewell-hour
Sublim'd by Pity's godlike power!
The mariner subdued his tone,
To make a mother's grief his own;
And souls who mock'd the lightning-flash,
Or dared the billows' wildest dash,
Felt more than milder bosoms fear
And soften'd down to woman's tear!

But, hark! the wind hath changed its tone;
The sun hath veil'd his burning throne;
And o'er the dazzling blue of heaven
Prophetic shades of storm are driven;
And fiercely shoots the slanting rain
On garden-bower, and window-pane,
While leaflets fall from branch and tree,
Like hopes from human vanity;
And like the moan of billows heard
From yon dim ocean, tempest-stirr'd,
With sounds that tell a dreary track
The waves of Life come rolling back,
That awful Life! whose endless roar
Breaks loud upon th' Eternal shore!

As one, when torture long hath tried
And rack'd his eye-lids, sleep-denied,
While bound in slumber's silken chain
And calm in heart and cool in brain,
Awakens on his midnight bed
To ghastly sense or gloomy dread,
And feels again each pang begin
To wrench the writhing soul within;
So wakes a heart that dreams awhile
All earth in sabbath-peace to smile
Around him like this lovely isle,
Till darkness on his dream descends
And in the world his vision ends.

A moment is a mighty Thing
Beyond the soul's imagining;
For in it, though we trace it not,
How much there crowds of varied lot!
How much of life, life cannot see,
Darts onward to eternity!
While vacant hours of beauty roll
Their magic o'er some yielded soul,
Ah! little can the happy guess
The sum of human wretchedness;
Or dream amid the soft farewell
  That Time of *them* is taking,
How frequent moans the funeral knell,
  What noble hearts are breaking,
While myriads to their tombs descend
Without a mourner, creed, or friend!

Could Fancy reach some throne of air
What vision would await Her there!
In tumult, agony, and strife,
Rolls the loud sea of human Life!
Before a despot's gilded throne
Hear Kingdoms weep, and Nations groan;
Yet tyrants in their slumber start
To feel the dagger at their heart;
And they can hear the murder'd call,
Can trace the hand upon the wall,
And not a slave who lays him down
Would change a dungeon for their crown!

Lo! yonder gleams a hoof-torn plain
Where moon-light shrouds th' unburied slain,
And bare against the naked sky
A thousand helmless foreheads lie!
On one is seen a parting trace
By torture graven on the face,
As dying Valour swoon'd away,
And blood congeal'd to breathless clay;
While others on their cheeks express
A smile from woman's tenderness,—
A ray of that remember'd scene
Where the bright heaven of home had been!
But, hark! from ocean heaves a cry
Deeper than when the tempests die,
As down men kneel upon the deck,
And listen to the crashing wreck!
A minute—and the murd'rous Storm
Hath mangled that colossal form,
Which floated o'er terrific seas,
Defied the blast, and faced the breeze,
But now, a fragment!—and the wave
Lies howling o'er the seaman's grave.

From these avert thy fear-struck view;
A vision, not so dark in hue,
But awful, with its deep array
Of all we suffer, do, or say,
The throne of Fancy may command,
While picturing with creative hand
The domes and temples, street and bath,
Whate'er a haughty City hath
Of sin and freedom, to decoy
The hearts whose pulse is tuned to joy.
And what a world of secret care
Lies wall'd within that compass there!

Where, Thought and Deed for ever toil,
And life is one permitted spoil
As each from cradle to the grave
Is half a tyrant, half a slave;
And shuts his breast, and steels the heart,
While Vice and Virtue act their part
And rarely lets the spirit speak,
But plays the courtier with his cheek;
Whose ready smile, like moon-light, when
It flutters o'er some noisome den,
Can bid the soul's corruption shine
And make its meanness look divine!

Yes! there in yonder city now
O'er which young Morning bends her brow,
On tower and temple smiling bright,
How weeping angels watch'd the night!
A captive tore his chain-worn limb,
And deem'd that God deserted him;
A felon heard the life-blood stream,
And saw the gallows in his dream;
The maniac's eye renew'd its glare
While his lip writhed with mocking pray'r:
The miser mutter'd in his sleep
And counted o'er and o'er his heap,
Then seem'd with restless hand to hold
And *taste* the touches of his gold!
And while in rooms of Revelry
Pleasure beheld bright moments flee,
A pillow for some dying head
With aching hand and heart was spread;
And who but sleepless Heaven can say
When Earth confronts the Judgment-Day,
The darkness of a thousand deeds
Dread Midnight in her shadow breeds!
For ever in the world there lies
What meets alone immortal Eyes;
While all man dreads that man should see
He dares unveil to Deity,
As though where guilty feet have trod
No power should track them, *but* his God!
And, pale Ambition! Sad wert thou,
As wanly on thy wasted brow
The feeble watch-light flung its ray,
While ebb'd thy pulse with dying play:—
But when thy filmy eyes uprose
Their glance untomb'd thy buried woes,
And round the room a meaning cast
Which told of time and truth o'ercast,
While fever'd blood and martyr'd frame
Avenged the toils that won a name!

And is it thus dark Life appears
A fountain of unfailing tears,
While to each minute's flight is given
The gloom of hell, or glance of heaven?
Lo! Nature speaks to all who look
And read aright Her glorious book,
How much there dawns to mitigate
The bleakness of our barren state.
Oh! who can hail the breeze-wing'd morn
When beauty in the heavens is born,
Or wander forth in sun or storm,
Nor love Creation's living form!
And life, though oft a wilderness
By passion made and wild distress,
Where like a leaf by autumn blown
The wither'd heart must fade alone,
To spirits nerved by glad desire
And pure from each debasing fire,
How much it yields of great and good
To make existence gratitude!
The wielding of colossal pow'rs
By which all earth is render'd ours;
The Arts that link'd with lovely grace
Form paradise round scene and place;
The pleasures proud as undefined
From fellowship with man and mind—
If bliss like this a world display
How weak to frown that world away!
But, ah! there is a brighter Charm
No shade can dim, no cloud disarm;
A Star enthroned o'er change and time,
Though meek, unmoved; though soft, sublime;
A spell beyond the world to break,
Which when our eyes this orb forsake
Will cling around the parting soul,
And gird it with a fond control,
For man design'd by Heav'n above,
And wafted down in woman's love!

That power without whose added spell,
So vast yet so invisible,
The lustre of our spirit wanes,
And pleasures are but smiling pains
Is holy Love, by hearts enjoy'd,
Unchill'd, unchanged, and unalloy'd!
And will the Stoic deem me wrong,
A martyr of mistaken song?
Without it, what are crowns and kings,
But barren toys and blighted things?
Art, Wit, and Genius, all we glow
To think cold earth contains below,
By woman's voice or woman's name
Have gather'd fortune, might, and fame.
And ask him whom the world hath worn,
Whose brain is rack'd, whose bosom torn
Amid the dust, the heat and strife
Around each day concenter'd,
How exquisite that purer life
At eve, when he hath enter'd
The garden-path where Peace can wind,
And cast the demon Care behind!
The tottering pace of infant feet
That haste a homeward sire to greet;
Each budding thought and broken word
So faintly seen, and softly heard;

The tones of air, the tender hues
Affection pours on all it views;
And, sweeter far, the eyes which live
Upon the rays his own can give,
Now kindled into fond excess
Of light that speaks, and looks that bless!—
To him who feels such blended power
They hallow Eve's domestic hour,
The Star of life, where'er he roam,
Is she whose ray attracts him home.

But, godlike is the creature, man!
The Past is glittering where he ran
Triumphantly his onward track,
With prints of glory!—trace them back;
Behold him stamp o'er land and sea
The might of immortality!
To him whom waves nor winds restrain
The Elements resign their reign;
While cowering Earth and Ocean meet
To lay their sceptres at his feet;
Whose hand the rock or mountain fells,
Or strews the globe with miracles
Of form and motion—wondrous Things!
Beyond a bard's imaginings;
And in his mind there dwells a sense
Of Adam's lost pre-eminence,
Which yearns for that ideal *more*
Than lip can speak, or thought explore.

Yet not because with bolder light
The traits of Manhood court the sight,
And Action with incessant claim
Can summon forth each high-born aim,
The softer tints of woman's soul
Pervade the world with less control.
The Thunder is the king of sound,
But ever may the breeze abound,
And quiver on melodious wing
Where beauty walks, or health can spring:
The forest wears inspiring gloom,
But yet we seek the flow'ret's bloom;
Stern Ocean hath terrific grace
Imprinted on his hoary face,
But oh! how dear some tranquil dream
Which haunts the bank of village stream!
And thus, methinks, doth woman's heart
A gentler, not less glorious part
In Life's dim tragedy fulfil,—
The feeblest, but the fairest still:
And as in nature charms may be
Which all enjoy, though none can see,
The light and love of female power
Have graced how many a graceless hour,
And round the spirit twined a zone
Too delicate for eyes to own!
Let Valour, Strength, and Wisdom, claim
Their summit on the throne of fame;
Yet shrinking heart and mind subdued
Become the charm of Womanhood;
And thoughts that might creation wield,
By man's dominion taught to yield,
Lie mute and dead in lonely rest
And leave the soul but half exprest!
For man, not nature, is the power
That darkens from its natal hour
The mind which decks the softer Race,
And dooms them to a second place.

But even thus, no formal chain
Can frighten, fetter, or restrain
That spirit-burst from time to time,
When, blazing forth with beam sublime,
The mind of Woman proves a spell
To make this truth shine visible—
That Genius of no sex can be,
When radiant with divinity!
And though in life her lovely sway
Fall dew-like o'er the parchèd day,
She rules that noiseless under-tide
Of happy thoughts by home supplied.
But, see! when peril claims her part,
The hero of a woman's heart!
Though weak in hand, and frail in form,
Her spirit strengthens with the storm;
In vain the warning thunders roll,—
They rally, not subdue, her soul!

Yet earth-born Passion soils her worth
With every shade of vulgar earth,
Nor dreams her highest glory can
Ascend beyond—a slave for man!
But vile that soul, however fraught,
If pride of sex be only taught:
The mind has lost its master-grace,
And thoughts demean their lofty race
When female love and virtue claim
No laurel in the wreath of Fame;
While all that Genius should adore
Is laugh'd away to live no more!
Not thus the bright and perfect One,
Whose Blood redeem'd a world undone,
Of woman spake, when Man had flown
And Mary watch'd and wept alone!

Another and a darker race
Whose doctrine might the brute disgrace,
So vilely from the dust of earth
It sprang, to prove its sullied birth!—
Oh, name it not, but let it be
Entomb'd in voiceless infamy!
If he who dares a Shrine deface
Where time has left a holy trace,
Is branded for his impious zeal
By all who ancient glory feel,
What damning tones can language find
For him who would profane the mind,

And dare, with sacrilegious smile,
The temple of the soul defile!—
Affection, deep as hearts desire,
Yet fed by intellectual fire;
Those graces felt, but undefined,
In gleams and glances of the mind,
Developed in a myriad ways,
By mien or manner, look or gaze;
The tones in dewy cadence heard
From lips that harmonise each word,
All, all the bright attraction bred,
From each fond smile a soul hath shed,
Oh! these transcend what Passion's might
Can raise to charm her maniac sight.

And when Disease's poison'd breath
Hath tainted life with hues of death;
When time has dimm'd that starry gaze
Whose magic thrill'd our younger days,
There is a love whose light remains
To warm the heart though passion wanes:
For beauty born within the mind
Admits no mean decay;
The Earth may shrink, the Sun grow blind,
Ere *that* dissolve away!

Alas! how oft since time began
Hath woman been abased by man;
To wisdom's rank denied a claim
Beyond the worst or weakest aim;
Or, doom'd by others, living toys
For brutal dreams, or selfish joys!
But thou, my England! first to be
In heart refined, in spirit free,
For ever may the virgin smile
Of Woman consecrate thine isle!
To guard thee, should fond ocean fail,
Thy banners cease to awe the gale,
Thy throne become a crushing weight
Of tyranny on rank and state,
Thy genius and thy glory fled,
With each high pulse of freedom dead—
E'en then, with female worth to throw
Its heavenliness round want and wo,
Ruled by the heart's unsullied reign
A Kingdom might revive again.
But trample once upon that shrine
Where Love hath sainted as divine
That Beauty which our dreams adore,
Religion, virtue, truth, are o'er!
And sooner shall Gomorrah rise
From out her grave to greet the skies,
Than Empires where no morals bloom
Awaken from their living tomb!

Oh! what a curse for them who can
Etherialise the world of man,
Yet prostitute a poet's line,
To render Woman less divine.
A tyrant, when his wrath is o'er,
Can break the chain, and back restore
The dungeon'd captive into day;
And tears may suffer'd wrong allay;
And scarce a pang the good endure
But some atoning sigh may cure.
But what is written—*that* is writ!
No soul-wrung tear may cancel it;
Like demons on dark errand sent
From out their fiendish element,
Polluting Thoughts, by passion fired,
Career the world, untamed, untired;
From heart to heart their plague is spread,
From soul to soul corruption bred,
Till myriads by their baneful spell
Are tempted to the brink of hell!

I envy not the unconfess'd
Remorse that gnaws his lonely breast,
Who weeps o'er that perverted mind,
Whose genius should have graced mankind,
Yet bow'd to be the mental slave
Of crimes which curse beyond the grave!
For when at noon of life he sees
His children circled round his knees;
Or triumphs in each dimpling grace
That dawns within a daughter's face,
What pangs with that proud moment cope,
What terror blights each blooming hope!
Perchance within his dying brain
Shall ring some recollected strain,
And gloomily those visions throng,
Corruption loved to shape in song;
And while they darken round his head
Portray the crimes their poison bred,
Till Fancy hears the parting groan
Of souls that shudder'd like his own!

Then, not for that unloving race
Who scorn each intellectual grace;
Or them, whose coarseness would destroy
The vestal-bloom of human joy,—
Be mine the lay. Yet should there be
A heart which loves true heart to see;
A father, who has felt how dear
The woman whom his thoughts revere;
A mother, in whose watchful eye
Affections deep and endless lie;
A maiden, who hath known how sweet
The sister of her soul to greet;
Or lover, who in lofty youth
Hath pleaded with impassion'd truth
To shape of Beauty, by whose light
The universe became so bright,—
If such the poet's page beguile
His guerdon be *their* grateful smile.

Oh! might he wake the richest tones
The harp of his enchantment owns,

For melody to waft along
The spirit of prevailing song,
And summon from the caves of Thought
Whatever shaping Dreams had wrought,—
A bard might think his visions rife
With rays of feelings, caught from life.
For, in such life what bliss he owed
To all that woman's reign bestowed!
The smoothest voice, the softest word
Delighted moments ever heard;
The dearest smile by pity shed
To quench the darkness sorrow bred;
The shadow of an Angel seen,
Where Goodness unobserved had been;
And, more than all, devoted truth
Whose years retain'd undying youth,—
If such a crowd of memory's charms
A poet's lyre too feebly warms,
It is because no words express
The light of Woman's loveliness;
And more than Poetry can speak
Is mirror'd on her brow and cheek;
While feelings oft the most sublime
Refuse to be portray'd in rhyme,
Though brightly round the heart they throng
And seem the archetypes of song:—
If doom like this attend my aim,
The song, but not the subject, blame!

CANTO II.

(In relation unto Sentiment).

"Yours was the nobler birth,
For you from man were made; man but of earth,
The son of dust!"—*Randolph.*

ANALYSIS OF CANTO II.

Man in Paradise—His sense of Loneliness—Creation of Woman—Social Instincts—Injustice of History to Female worth—Woman's gradual degradation—Greece and Rome—Their domestic wants—Civilising effects of feminine influence—Chivalry and its sway—Christianity the Social restorer of Woman—Heroism and benevolence of her nature—Blessings of her Empire—Her dominion in Home—Single Misery!—Poets and Poetry—How Woman has inspired both—Dante and Beatrice—Petrarch and Laura—Shakespeare and his Love—Tasso and Leonora—Milton and his affections—His History—Klopstock and Meta—Burns and Highland Mary—His mournful Fate—Byron—Harrow—Retrospective glance.

When first the wings of Light unfurl'd
Their radiance o'er a new-born World,
And choral music, faint and far,
Awoke in each melodious star,
Until the glowing Earth began
To thrill beneath the gaze of man,
Ah, who can paint the primal bliss
That charm'd an hour divine as this!

How beauteous in his dawn of birth
Without a shade of sullied earth,
Without one touch of deadly sin
To mar the perfect soul within,
The lord of Eden must have stood,
When God beheld, and call'd him, good!
Oh! to have heard his lips reveal
The first delight that dust could feel;
Have listen'd to each wild address
He paid to Nature's loveliness;
Or, flashing from his heaven-turn'd eye,
Have mark'd the spirit's majesty,
While round his heart religion stole
And mirror'd Him who made the whole!

A melody from leaf and flower,
Responding to the breeze's power
That warbled with exulting tone;
A blooming light on all things thrown,
On fruit, and foliage, grass, and lake;
The song that in sweet gushes brake
From birds which flew on fearless wing
And taught the very air to sing!—
The mute delight, majestic trance
Of things that shunn'd no mortal glance,
But gazed on man with love or glee
And felt that life was amity;
While stainless as a pall of light
The cope of heaven hung crystal bright,
And pour'd upon each perfect limb
A lustre which apparell'd him;
While ever, as he raised his eye,
A seraph, floating through the sky,
With gleams of glory track'd his way
Or arch'd his wings in beaming play,—
Though all like this composed a scene
To testify where God had been,
A soft disease of soul began
To prey upon the bliss of man:
A yearning which no language spoke
Within his clouded bosom woke;
A loneliness with awful weight
Lay brooding o'er his desert fate,
And darken'd with ideal shade
The countenance which heaven display'd;
Till sadly was each primal word
Upon the placid breezes heard?—
"Some other Form, oh! let there be,
To live, and love, and roam with me
This lone but gorgeous wilderness
Of sights that woo, and sounds that bless!
A Spirit whom my own can meet,
Some hand to hold, some eye to meet;
Creator! if thy wisdom can
Oh, let there be a mate for man!"

More lovely than a vision brought
From out the fairy realms of Thought;
Serene and silent, with a grace
Divinely breath'd o'er form and face,
In full array of love and light
Which dazzled his adoring sight,
By soul and sense to be revered
The Angel of the world appear'd.
Then, what a starry welcome rang!
Each orb an hymeneal sang;
While Shapes unutterably bright
From heaven gazed down with new delight,
When first the ground a woman trod
Just moulded by the hand of God!
Around her breast, in wreathy play
Her locks like braided sunbeams lay;
And limbs unveil'd a radiance cast
Of purity, as on she pass'd
Amid the bloom and balm of flowers
Which clustered round elysian bowers;
The bird and breeze together blent
Their lulling notes of languishment;
The Sun grew brighter as he shed
His glory round her living head,—
As if no conscious thing were free
From one fine spell of sympathy,
When woman rose upon the scene
Creation's fair and faultless Queen!

When Adam's trancèd eyelids woke,
Thus brightly on his vision broke
A living Shape for whom he pined,
To share his unpartaken mind.
Awhile they gazed in hush'd delight,
Each dazzled with the other's sight;
Then saw within their mutual eyes
Magnetic rays of soul arise,
And heard their lips fond tones repeat,
And heard their hearts in concert beat,
And felt within electric fire
Their spirit, blood, and brain, inspire:
Then Woman was espoused by Man!
The bridal dawn of Love began.
Oh! then was born of breathing truth
A feeling in ambrosial youth,
That soars above the vile decay
Of things which time and sense array,
And when the dying World departs
Still blooms within celestial hearts!

And thus, with all that forms a friend
The finer tints of love to blend;
To soothe the tempest, share the calm,
And pour on grief unfailing balm,
Did woman on the world appear.
And hath she fail'd in life's career?—
The Warrior wins a bright renown,
The Poet wears a peerless crown,
And History with heroic grace
Hath laurell'd their triumphant race;
But where, in what recording book
Can unforgetting Nature look,
To count, since first her ages ran,
What Woman hath endured for Man?
Alas! like dews which night hath felt
Within ungrateful earth to melt,
And freshen into living flowers
The grove that smiles at morning hours,
The virtues born of woman's soul,
(Though time has drunk their mild control
And had by them the heart supplied
With what the ruder sex denied)
In cold oblivion seem to fade,
Unknown, unsung, and undisplay'd!

But, might those Spirits who have been
Calm Watchers of our troubled scene,
Beholding with dejected eye
The throes of human agony,—
To earth repeat the tale of Life
Since first convulsed with gloom and strife,
How much, methinks, would Virtue prize
That never dazzled mortal eyes,
As Angels read the awful story
Of Empires dim, and ages hoary,
And, while they scorn'd a hero's crown
To Woman give the heart's renown![6]
For pangs endured with secret sway,
For tears by night, and toils by day;
For tortures by the world untraced
When love was wreck'd, and truth defaced:
For fondness in the fiercest hour
Of tyrant wrath, or ruin's power,
For every sad and silent wrong
That weakness suffer'd from the strong,—
For these, and all young Feeling bore
When misery made it love the more!
A chaplet of celestial light
Would Angels weave for Woman's right.
Oh! she is all that soul can be
In deep, undying sympathy!
When life is scarce a moving dream
'Tis like her spirit's native beam,
Which never from its fountain strays
But lives alone within her rays!
And round an infant how divine
The wreath a mother's arm can twine?
And when dark years of manhood bring
Their load of fated suffering,
As true as echo to the sound
Her blessings to his wants abound!
In sickness, ah! how smooth the bed
Her duteous hand alone can spread;
And, when the shades of Death advance,
What paradise within her glance,
Where all the yearning soul appears
Dissolved in sympathetic tears!

Yet scarce had Eden pass'd away
And sin begun its blighting sway,
Ere woman lost her mental rank
And in domestic thraldom sank
A Thing to be, whose witching power
Might serve to gild a wanton hour,
To feed a passion, soothe a frown,
Or magnify her lord's renown,
But ever, with unvalued heart,
In life to play the menial part!
And e'en in Greece, that land sublime
Whose glory lit the wings of time,
E'en there, where Beauty's faultless mould
Surpass'd what Sculpture's dreams behold,
In vain would truth a model see,—
Her love breathes no divinity!
From earth it sprung, on earth to live
On every charm mere Sense can give;
But all proud Sentiment could teach
Divine in thought, or pure in speech,
By Greece unfelt, or unadmired,
Hath scarce one classic page inspired.
And Rome, whose wizard banner waved
O'er half the isles far Ocean laved,
By conquest was not taught to school
The passions Heaven alone can rule;
But offer'd up each female Right
On altars of their stern delight,
Where rage might spend its haughty breath
And doom a guiltless heart to death.

But Rome and Greece, eternal two!
Have shown the world what mind can do;
And still from them the streams of mind
With living freshness charm mankind:
Their language in immortal notes
Around our list'ning spirit floats;
Their genius, throned in classic state,
Is haunted by the wise and great;
And high-born is the zeal that pays
True homage to heroic days
When valour woke the lyre of thought,
And poets sang the fields they fought!
Yet when prevail'd in Greece or Rome
The magic of a modern home?
There, lives the light our spirit hails!
There, beats the heart that never fails;
There, smiles beyond a realm to bring
Round calmest hours are clustering!
Where queens of mild affection reign;
The bloom of joy, the balm of pain;
And thus are more, when grey or young,
Than Homer dream'd, or Maro sung.

When first on Rome a tameless horde
From forest-depths their myriads pour'd,
And down to dust her empire broke,
Refinement's moral dawn awoke.[7]
The gloomy brow, the glaring eye,
The breast which never heaved a sigh,
But nurtured in its wild domain
The glory of surmounted pain,—
Amid them all there lived a sense
Of woman's meek pre-eminence;
While Chastity within the heart
Was shrined beyond pollution's art.
Thus, Nature! in thy darkest mood
How much remains of bright and good!
What Learning in her proudest day,
What Genius in her fiery sway,
With blended power might never reach,
These warriors of the wild could teach!
'Tis pleasant in the storm to see
The battle of some glorious tree,
Whose branches with resentful play
Can awe the beaten winds away;
But, beautiful! in calmer hours
To view it wave o'er meadow-flowers,
And hearken to its whisper mild
Like blessing murmur'd o'er a child:—
And thus, methinks, the contrast seen
When beauty reign'd where war had been;
When lion port and eagle eye
Had laid their horrid menace by,
And, resting in some oaken shade,
While round him laughing infants play'd,
The savage of the desert grew
Refined beneath a woman's view!

Next, Chivalry, heroic child,
With brow erect, and features wild,
Placed Love upon his matchless throne,
For Gallantry to guard alone.
Then, Woman! in that reign of heart
How peerless was thy magic part!
A word was more than human breath;
A smile dissolved the gloom of death;
And Beauty, while it awed the brave,
But made the mind a noble slave
To Honour, in the chastest light
That ruled the soul, or charm'd the sight.
And shall we, in a venal age
When love hath grown more coldly sage,
With frigid laugh and frown decry
The bright return of Chivalry?
The trumpet-music of the Past,
In tales of glory doom'd to last,
No longer must one echo stir
The pulse of English character?
Alas! our life is worldly lore;
The reign of heart-romance is o'er;
And all which fired heroic toil
Hath now become a meaner spoil
For time and circumstance to win,
While Self is throned secure within.—
Yet, valour in its fine excess;
A scorn that wither'd littleness;

Devotion in its grandest shape [8]
And love that sought no mean escape,—
Oh! darkly sunk, and vilely sway'd
The Clime that wills their might decay'd:
But ever prompts each servile art
To flourish in th' unweeded heart,
Till day by day we learn to see
False self is true philosophy!

But far beyond all forming powers
Which made expressive Beauty ours,
In that pure shape by God design'd
To soften, soothe, and sway mankind,—
Religion, voiced from Heaven, began
To rouse the fallen soul of man:
Then spirit, by the sense unbound,
Arose with grace immortal crown'd:
Emotions deep, unstain'd desires,
Serener hopes, and chaster fires,
Came flowing from a Fount above
All freshen'd with ethereal love!
'Twas then that Woman like a star,
Whose beam had flutter'd dim and far
And shed upon the troubled soul
A ray of undiscern'd control,—
Advanced above life's daily sphere,
Disclosed her radiance, full and near;
And kindled for beclouded man
The light a Christian woman can.
Restored to reign, as fair and good
As once in Eden's bower she stood,
Companion of the Soul to be
In love's avowed fidelity,
Religion, when its healing smile
First trembled o'er Britannia's isle,
By her assuasive meekness won
A way to visit hearts undone.
And, did her martyr'd spirit quake
To front the vengeance of the stake?—
E'en there Apostles might have known
A faith whose firmness match'd their own: [9]
Though limb by limb the fire devour'd,
She neither shook, nor shriek'd, nor cower'd,
But gloried in the murd'rous flame
To sing a martyr'd Saviour's name!

And view th' applauded domes which rise
In holy grandeur to the skies,
How much to female hands they owe
Their power to lessen human woe! [10]
But ah! how exquisite must be
Those charities that none can see,
In lovely darkness hid awhile
Surrounded with Jehovah's smile!
Till, stealing into holy light,
They glitter on the pilgrim's sight
When haply in some village-dale
His soul has drunk the secret tale,
How Saintliness a beauty shed
Around the dying mourner's bed:—
Thus oft upon some travell'd plain,
Where Winter holds his bleakest reign,
In sudden bloom young flow'rets rise,
And blush beneath our gazing eyes.
For, leaving oft the splendid home,
Unheeded will Compassion roam,
And where the roofs of Sorrow lie
Give tear for tear, and sigh for sigh;
To Famine deal the daily bread,
For Sickness hold the drooping head,
Be mother to some orphan boy,
Make widow'd hearts to sing for joy,
And should the parting Soul despair,
Points to bright heaven, and Jesu there!

And what were life, if woman's heart
Attemper'd with no guiding art
The household-morals of mankind,
Whereby the world is kept refined,
And each soft hue opinion wears
Its lovely origin declares?
Go, find a Land where female grace
Is honour'd by no gallant race,
And man's dominion deems it vile
To bend beneath a woman's smile,
But tramples with a brute delight
On mental rank and moral right,
How darkly do her people sink!
How meanly act, how basely think!
No loftiness that Clime reveals;
No purity her spirit feels;
Corruption cankers law and throne,
The language breathes a dungeon-tone;
And seldom there hath Virtue smiled;
But, wither'd, weaken'd, and defiled,
It moulders on from age to age
The scorn of hero, bard, and sage,
And seems on glorious Earth to be
A plague-spot, and an infamy!

But vain would Truth reflect in song
What nameless fascinations throng
Around that quiet hearth alone,
Where Tenderness hath rear'd its throne.
Oh! there are feelings rich but faint,
The hues of language cannot paint;
And pleasures, delicate as deep,
Which like the palaces of sleep
Melt into dimness, when the Light
Would look upon their fairy sight;
And there are chords of happiness
Whose spirit-tones our fancy bless,
And make the music of our joy
Complete, without one harsh alloy;
Yet ill can words one note reveal
Of melody which mind can feel!

But who hath left some calm domain
Where Home was charm'd by woman's reign,
And trifles through some magic wore
An air they never breathed before,
And enter'd where a proud abode
To ruder man its splendour owed,
Nor felt the contrast sternly cold,
Like winter o'er his spirit roll'd?
Still, there may garden, grove, and bower,
Attend on each retiring hour;
There Painting with impassion'd glow
The poetry of colours show,
While volumes rank'd in rich array
The heroes of the mind display:
But like a face when death has chill'd
The light that once each feature fill'd,
Contrasted with its living power
Beheld in some excited hour,
Are homes where single man is seen
With those where woman's spell hath been.

Alas! for them whose toil-worn days
Uncheer'd by Love's adorning rays,
In crawling loneliness depart,
Yet fret the bloom from out the heart.
Though Life, as lord of each desire,
To intellectual thrones aspire;
May win the laurel, wear the crown,
And madden envy with renown,
How much beyond what dreams bestow
Their loveless hours can never know!
With nothing but cold Self to please,
The waters of the spirit freeze;
And years but harden while they chill
A Bosom left unsocial still:
And like a tree by autumn shorn
Of all that summer-boughs had borne,
A leafless, bare, and blighted Thing
Where scarce a breeze will deign to sing,—
Is Man bereft of that control
That emanates from female soul.
For heart with heart was born to beat,
And soul with soul was made to meet,
And sex for sex design'd to be
The dawn of endless sympathy.

But ye! the laurell'd Host who live
A life beyond mere earth to give;
The deities of dazzled Thought,
To whom her incense aye is brought;
Ye Alexanders of the mind
Who conquer, but to charm mankind!
Enchanters! for the spirit's eyes
Remoulding ruin'd paradise;
Interpreters! whose tones declare
The dialogues of Sea and Air;
The priests of Nature taught to praise
And worship her mysterious ways;
Ye intellectual Kings of time!
Triumphant, matchless, and sublime,
How fervently your pages own
In music of transcendant tone,
That Woman in her lovely might
Drew worship, wonder, and delight
From Souls whose inward glance could see
Visions that crowd eternity!

Impassioned Lords of deathless song
To them the lips of Time belong,
As fired with their majestic fame
From age to age they sound their name,
And bid the world enshrine that scene
Where once a worshipp'd Bard hath been;—
For hallow'd seems *his* natal spot
Where thrones are crush'd, and kings forgot!
And they have earn'd that gorgeous debt
Of praise, that Time is paying yet,
Who taught us, though it bear the curse,
To love the heaven-born universe,
And trace wherever goodness trod
The lustre of a living God!

And glorious is it, when the base
Would frown upon Heaven's fairest race,
To echo into life again
The music of some master-strain;
And prove amid the ranks of fame
How each who won undying name,
In love's applauding eye could see
The ruling star of Poetry.

Then let me from the poet-throng
Who hymned on Earth unearthly song,
Select some all-surpassing few,
And as they rise in proud review
Let him whose spirit ever bow'd
Before the passion it avow'd,
Whose bosom hath been thrill'd or shaken
With dream fulfill'd or hope forsaken,—
Exult to find his soul hath felt
A charm which could the sternest melt;
That lent to genius half its glow,
Or taught eternal song to flow;
For fancy plumed the wing of fire,
And warm'd the soul of every lyre,
Whose language was the light of thought
From Love by consecration wrought!

With paleness on his awful brow
Who riseth like a spectre now
From darkness, where his fancy dared
To wander with an eye unscared,
And gaze on Visions such as roll
Around that blighted Angel's soul,
Who baffles in his dread domain
An immortality of pain
'Tis Dante!—whose terrific flight
Through caverns of Cimmerian night

Imagination vainly tries
To track with unappallèd eyes!
Severe, august, and sternly great,
The gloom of his remorseless fate[11]
Around him hung a dismal air
Which broodeth o'er intense despair;
Till frenzy half began to raise
A wildness in his fearful gaze,
As, roaming over crag and wood
He battled with bleak solitude!
For sooner might the maniac roar
Of ocean cease to awe the shore
When Starlight comes with fairy gleam,
Than Pity lull his tortured dream!—
Oh! 'tis not in poetic art
To paint the earthquake of his heart,
The storm of feeling's ghastly strife
When she, who form'd his life of life,
Had vanish'd like a twilight-ray
Too delicate on earth to stay.
For Love had heated blood and brain,
A fire in each electric vein,
A passion whose exceeding power
Was heaven or hell to each wild hour!

But from the wreck of ruin'd days
What gorgeous visions did he raise!
Since ne'er was Beauty so divine
Embodied in a breathing shrine,
As thronèd Beatrice on high
In the dark haze of Deity!
Her forehead wreath'd with starry light,
And she herself,—oh! what a sight
On Dante glitter'd, when afar
He listen'd to her mystic car,
As wafted in a cloud of flowers
And guarded by angelic powers
In veil of fire her spirit came,
And warbled his remember'd name!
He bow'd beneath her awful look;
Then gazed until his being shook
Like water, when the winds convulse
And stir it with a quivering pulse.
But when the wing'd enchantress soar'd
To where the Godhead was adored,
Without a shadow, speck, or bound,
Eternity lay imaged round!
There on some mysterious throne
Again he saw her, bright and lone.
Ineffably one look she cast
Angelic features ne'er surpass'd,
On him who knelt entranced awhile
Within the glory of her smile;
Till lo! in deep excess of light
She faded from his yearning sight!

As one who leaves a savage dell
Where day hath bid the sun farewell,
Comes forth to view autumnal beams
On bank, and wood, and dimpled streams,
Is he who turns from Dante's gloom
To see Parnassian flow'rets bloom,
As dreams of beauty dawn and glow
Along the page of Petrarch's wo.
How touching are those mental tears,
Delighted throbs and dazzled fears,—
The penance by his genius paid
Whenever recreant fancy stray'd
Beyond the path of pure desire!
'Twas Laura tuned his pensive lyre:
Madonna-like, and sweetly mild,
And pure as an untempted child,
Amid her white-robed virgin-throng
He saw her beauty glide along,
When lilies deck'd her sun-bright hair
Amid the walls of lone St. Claire.
That hour became a second birth!
Her lustre overveil'd the earth;
And never did a Ghebir kneel
Before his orb with truer zeal
Than Petrarch at that living shrine
Where dwelt the soul he knew divine!
To him she was a spotless Thing
Too bright for earthly lyre to sing;
A miracle of life and love,
A dream embodied from above,
A seraph whose unclouded eyes
Reflected back their native skies!

From *her* his inspiration came;
Each song enshrined her hidden name;
And not a shadow, tint, or sound
Creation could produce around,
But he beguiled with beauteous art
To typify her taintless heart.
How fervently his homage glows!
Pure from the mind it springs and flows,
Exhausting as his numbers roll
The life-blood of a feeling soul.
For Laura seem'd his spirit's breath,
And ruled it when she sunk in death;
Then, day and darkness, scene and hour
Were haunted with her holy power;
And when her smile illumed it not
The faded world was soon forgot;
Since only to embalm her name
He panted for eternal fame!

Adorner of the human race!
Great Nature's rival, who could trace
Her features with such perfect skill
That Time can but remould them still,
So matchless is that mighty One
Whom Fancy now would gaze upon.
Go, lend the skies a lovelier blue,
Or sunbeams o'er the sunshine strew;

Bid Horror to the tempest bring
A louder shriek and blacker wing:
Or dare suggest a deeper tone
To Thunder on his midnight-throne;
So powerless seems a poet's line
To sing what Shakspeare's works combine!
All tears and smiles to him belong;
All clouds that round the spirit throng;
All passions, principles, and powers
Which wring the heart, or rule its hours,
In language Nature's lip had taught
By him were into action wrought!
So truly with creative art
He paints the drama of the heart,
That long as tears haunt human eyes,
Or Pleasure laughs, or Sorrow sighs,
Whatever path his genius trod,
We hail him earth's poetic god.

And round him is a dimness thrown?
The colour of his life unknown?
While meaner names are chronicled,
And baseness in false light beheld,
That Masterpiece of mortal clay
Unhonour'd did he pass away?
Yes, like an orb whose affluent rays
Demand of earth no greeting praise,
He scatter'd intellectual light
Immortal in unconscious might;
Sublimely careless of renown
Then lay his awful spirit down,
Nor dreamt that Glory's arm would wave
Her brightest banner o'er his grave!

But yet there come faint shadows cast
From pining years which he had past,
That tell us how the soul could brook
Such pangs as once his bosom shook,
When dark-eyed Beauty rack'd and wrung
A heart round which the world had clung![12]
Her hair was like the sheen of night
When blackness seems to make it bright;
And melody her touch obey'd
When o'er the chords her fingers stray'd;
But sorrow dash'd her April years
With cold and melancholy tears;
And thus there grew a wild unrest
Within the gloom of Shakspere's breast,
Till he who sung what Romeo felt
Beneath like pangs was doom'd to melt,
And hide within his dreaming brain
The visions of a lover's pain.

And well may Woman proudly think
That he whose spirit thus could drink
Absorbing rays from beauty's eyes,
Hath sphered her sex amid the skies!
And none like him love's essence knew,
From hidden soul the lightning drew,
That subtile, secret, silent flame
For which the heart hath found no name.
There's not a throb that woman feels,
There's not a ray her mind reveals,
And scarce a blush on brow and cheek
When blood would rise and almost speak,—
But Shakspere hath the whole divined,
And held a mirror to the mind
That nature o'er his magic glass
Might view each play of feature pass.
And what a life-breath'd air there seems
To freshen those embodied dreams
Where character and grace arise,
To feast our unforgetting eyes
With all Affection can display,
When most we bow beneath her sway!
Bright, beautiful, and young, and warm,
With tears that melt and tongues that charm,
The creatures whom he call'd to birth
We pine to meet on mortal earth,
And trace by his revealing art
The windings of a woman's heart.

As moonlight weaves a varied spell
O'er rock and mountain, grove and dell,
So Love with his transforming beam
Hath colour'd each romantic dream,
As stern or mild the spirit lay
Beneath the spell-work of his ray.
A sense of beauty,—it was thine,
As deep, as burning, and divine
As ever fed with living fire
The passion of a poet's lyre,
Pale martyr! whom Alphonso's hate
Imprison'd for a madman's fate,
Because ere yet the lips could speak
Emotion had betray'd thy cheek,
To tell him how a bard could dare
To love a princess—and despair!
That love was like a blasting sun,
It sear'd the heart it shined upon!
But oh, how much of Tasso's strain
Was born of his devoted pain,
When feelings in their hopeless strife
Contended with those clouds of life
That 'tween him and his idol grew,
Till Death alone could break them through.

His youth was lonesome; and the light
Of half that won or woo'd the sight,
Enchantment from his spirit shed
Till earth was heaven beneath his tread!
And Nature like a mother smiled
On him her musing foster-child;
To whom her voice from wave or wind
Came with a magic more refined
Than echoes from the human soul:
And where a quiet stream did roll

While shade and sunshine blent their power,
He charm'd his own creative hour;
Till voiceless aspirations rose,
His bosom lost its young repose,
And round his heart a Syren came
Who murmur'd his immortal name!
Thus fancy set the soul on fire,
Till life itself he found aspire
To beauty, like that spirit bright;
When, tender as the touch of light,
Fair Leonora's vision stood
Before him, fresh in womanhood!
And all the heart's creation drew
At length his living eyes could view.
What heavenliness arrayed her form!
How exquisite the blushing storm
Of love's betray'd emotion rose!
When Tasso read his lyric woes,
And saw her eye's transparent blue
Bedimm'd with soul dissolving through!
Morn after morn, in youth's ripe age,
He read his own melodious page,
While Leonora's lips of love
The garland of his glory wove
In words whose magic seem'd to be
The tones of immortality!

And *could* they side by side remain
Nor feel the heart's delicious pain?
The might of that magnetic gaze
That each to each would softly raise?
Could Tasso in such perill'd hour
Be dead to passion's dawning power?
Alas for him!—Alphonso came
And bade a dungeon hide his flame!
They tore him to a hideous cell,
(Ferrara hath revered it well)
And left him, for a maniac's doom,
To rot in suffocating gloom!
Yet misery could not then decay
The dream that wore his mind away:[13]
Though frenzy might its faith destroy
Till life became a wretched toy,
Yet Passion round his wreck would smile,
Like Evening o'er a faded pile:
But when his Leonora died
And every bard a wreath supplied
To grace the glory of her bier,
Could Tasso's Muse deny a tear?
Yes! silence was the tomb of pain,
And grief was voiceless, when 'twas vain.
Let fancied wo prepare a sigh
To deck the fate of those who die;
And hypocrites their cheeks array
With gloom to serve a venal day,
The pangs which load a loftier breast
Lie deep, and dark, and unexprest;
Yet sternness in that blank despair
Hath buried more than anguish there!

Another of the wondous see!
Whose spirit talk'd with Deity,
And, blind on earth, beheld in heaven
The glory to archangels given,
When robed in light their garments blaze
And whiten in eternal Rays!
No cavern'd prophet while he felt
A trance almighty round him melt;
Or by some Babylonian stream
From darkness shaped his awful dream
Wherein there glided, vast and dim,
The cloud-apparell'd cherubim,
Hath scarce outsoar'd his epic flight
Who sang of Chaos, Death, and Night!
Had none, methinks, but Milton's song
Pour'd its grand tide the world along;
Had never page but *his* reveal'd
The miracles in mind conceal'd,
The hope immortal still would rest
Unblighted in our human breast;
For never could some narrow grave
Th' immeasurable soul enslave,
Which compass'd air, and heaven, and hell,
As lord of his creative spell!

With what a melody divine
The river of each noble line
Flows onward!—faint, or loud, or deep,
Accordant to the numbers' sweep.
Go, enter some majestic fane
And listen to the organ-strain,
When melting clouds of music float
Down the dim aisles with blending note;
Now with wild melodious thunder
The vaulted pavement echoes under,
Then, aloft in flights of sound
The winged harmonies abound,
Evanishing like birds that stray
And skyward sing their boundless way!—
E'en thus can Milton's numbers roll
Their cadence o'er a trancèd soul.

And can we deem that he who drew
In lines of love so brightly true
The Mother of our mortal race,
And made the lustre of her face
To dazzle back a Demon's guile,
When Eden laugh'd beneath her smile,
Reflected not through poet's art
The paradise of his pure heart?
The Lady-pilgrim of the wood
In star-like beauty, lone and good,
Was copied from a shape, perchance,
That kindled youth's adoring glance.

There is a tale—and let it live
Such life as fond romance can give,—
That once as slumb'ring Milton lay
In umbrage from the noon-warm day,

Beneath the twilight of a tree,
That arch'd its waving canopy,
A maiden saw his sleeping face
And, spell-bound with its beauteous grace,
Her wonder in sweet song express'd
And placed it on the poet's breast;—
"If eyes when *shut* the heart can take,
How bright their vict'ry when *awake!*"
Oh! who can tell what beauty flow'd
From feelings by such words bestow'd?
The Eve of his enchanted thought
From hues of nature's heaven was wrought,
And she of paradise the queen
Embodied what his soul had seen.

And could that Bard, whose mind was free
And boundless as eternity;
Who seem'd on earth to have the skies
Aye floating o'er his mental eyes;
To the low dust of life descend
And with the base its glory blend?
How nobly hath awarding Time
For Genius shaped the crown sublime,
And silenced in oblivion's shade
The war Opinion's fury made!
Till all the wounds and stabs of strife
Which agonised his bleeding life
Appear but like a mould'ring stain
That lingers on some marble fane,
But ere it rots one tint away
Hath vanish'd in some heavenly ray!

Oh! many are the pangs that wear
A spirit into proud despair;
And many are the tears which flow,
To swell the tide of human wo:
But seldom doth the sicken'd heart
From dreams of false perfection start
With pangs of such convulsive power
As when the great have ceased to tower,
Desert the sky, and fold their wings
To strive with earth's degraded things,
Like eagles when their flight is o'er
That wrangle on some weedy shore!

But one amid the poet-throng
To whom the wreaths of heaven belong,
From pride and coarser impulse free
Stands out, in solemn purity!—
His heart, by woman's power array'd,
The summons of high love obey'd,
And beautiful, beyond the light
Of language to reveal aright,
The passion of a deathless pair,
Who breathed on earth celestial air!
Before the dawn of being came
They dreamt their lot was doom'd the same,
And human love in heaven would be
A wedded immortality!

And when his Meta dying lay
And felt her spirit faint away,
Like music from a falt'ring wave
When sinking to its ocean grave,
Beside her Klopstock meekly stood,
And watch'd the pale and speaking blood
In awful changes come and go!
But never was such loving wo,
When Meta, to his fond request
That round him her bright wings should rest
While o'er the world his fate must rove,—
Responded with a burst of love,
"Who would not share that lot divine,
To be thine angel! thou art mine!"

A gentle stream which glides along
And tones the breeze with lovely song;
And that same stream, when torn at length
And arm'd with desolating strength
As down some rocky steep it pours,
And like a rival ocean roars,
May typify the tranquil soul
When calm'd by virtue's wise control,
And one by passion's whirlwind force
Compell'd to each disastrous course.
'Tis thus, when sad-eyed memory turns
From Klopstock to impassion'd Burns,
Two streams of life at once appear
In mild repose and mad career.

The Shakspeare of the woods and fields,
How wizard-like the sway he wields!
The heart-blood owns his lyric might
And ripples with confess'd delight
When Scottish valour fires the song,
Like clarion-music, stern and strong!
Excitement, that immortal pain,
The demon of a poet's brain,
On him it wreak'd its wildest rage!
And all that poverty could wage
Against a high and haughty mind
His trampled heart was doom'd to find.
Yet, cradled in dark misery's bed,
How nobly was his genius led!
What Man denied, great Nature gave:
His soul, no educated slave,
The Elements and Seasons taught,
Creation magnified his thought;
And when amid the foliage dim
The blackbird piped his vesper-hymn,
Or round him, like a lustrous pall
He felt the Day's bright curtain fall,
As tides th' attractive moon obey,
So throbb'd his pulse to Nature's play.
And Woman by her smile could throw
A sunbeam o'er his blackest wo,—
A ray whose beauty reach'd the soul
And bade his burning numbers roll!

Yet who can read the bitter fate
So darkly chill and desolate,
That brooded o'er the closing day
Of him who sang as proud a lay
As ever rose from Scottish lyre
On inspiration's breath of fire,
Nor weep to think that starless night
Should blacken round a soul of light!
Or, who can mark his mind's undress,[14]
The agony of lone distress,
The curse of want that crush'd his brain
To frenzy, with a fiercer pain!—
Can hear the groan of anguish'd hours
When Misery rallied all her powers,
And thoughts like hidden scorpions tore
The mind that could no longer soar,
But prostrate in its ruin lay
A blasted wreck and bleeding prey,—
Nor ask for Pity's brightest tear
To tremble on his early bier!
Yet warmly while around him shone
The worship that his genius won,
Prophetic truth beheld afar
The cloud that would conceal his star,
And leave him, long ere life should close,
To wither in degrading woes!
Yes, he whose lines are mottoes now,
Whose genius veils his Country's brow
With glory, when his stirring lays
Are greeted with exalting praise,
Was fated like an outcast thing
To moulder in dark suffering
Down to the grave, with scarce a bed
To pillow his immortal head!

Alas! how little can the great
Feel the dread curse of blighted fate;
Or think that they, whose spirits throw
Around the world a heavenly glow,
Whose bright imaginations seem
The fragments of a Seraph's dream,
Whose words imparadise the hours
And freshen earth with Eden-flowers,—
The martyrs of the mind have been
Or suffer'd more than eye hath seen!
For, while the theme of Glory's tongue,
Their homes were wreck'd, their hearts were wrung;
And songs which flow'd so gaily free
Gush'd from a fount of misery!

A noble Mind in sad decay
When baffled hope hath died away,
And life becomes one long distress
In bleak and barren loneliness,
Methinks 'tis like a ship on shore,
That once defied th' Atlantic roar,
And gallantly through gale and storm
Hath ventured her majestic form;
But now in stranded ruin laid
By winds and dashing seas decay'd,
Forgetful of her ocean-reign,
Must crumble into earth again!

To crown the lyric throng appears
Another,* whose poetic tears,
While a bruised spirit toils below
Shall consecrate Affection's wo;
And ever by their passion tell
The power of love's unfading spell,
Which beautified with lone despair
The visions that his lines declare.

The anguish of his riven heart
Hath ceased on earth to play its part,
And o'er his laurel-shaded brow
The damp of death lies coldly now!
The storm, the shadow, and the strife
That made and magnified his life,
Have sunk like winds along the deep
And left him to untroubled sleep:
But few, when Harold died, forget
The fulness of our fond regret,
As England echoed back the knell
Which toll'd from Greece his last farewell!
Oh! nought but some ignoble breast
Where feelings, iced in stony rest,
Can baffle with a stern disdain
The lightnings of each lofty strain,
That did not unto tears admire
The dirges of his gloomy lyre,
And speculate, if years had brought
A blessed store of brighter thought,
How much of all which mars his fame
Had vanish'd in some purer aim.—

* In common with the rest of those whose feelings offer homage to the beautiful, whether bodied forth in the breathing marble of the sculptor, the hues of the painter, or the burning language of the poet,—the writer of this *once* partook fully and dangerously of all that admiration which the genius of Lord Byron is so calculated to evoke. Both in this work, and elsewhere, he ventured to cast his votive wreath of eulogy on the grave of one, whose name was wont to be a spell-word to the lovers of impassioned song. But, although still retaining much of his admiration for the poetry of Byron, abstractedly considered, he cannot but feel that his language on this subject is by far too enthusiastic. As he advances in life, and learns to contemplate the vast responsibilities of mind, in reference to the Divine Tribunal, and to estimate the moral influence which popular verse must ever wield over the sentiments and ideas of the young and the romantic,—where is the Christian who is rash enough to rank Lord Byron among the real benefactors of mankind? In the spirit of the same love for that Truth which alone can make us free, the author must also regret, that in the allusions to other poets in this volume, the ethical tendency, as well as the poetical splendour of their writings, was not more discriminately viewed.—*Written in* 1841.

The earthquake that so rock'd his soul
With dread and undefined control,
Beneath some intellectual balm
Had soften'd to melodious calm:
Those feelings which were prompt to stray
Where all the weeds of vileness lay,
And linger with sarcastic stress
Round Nature's erring littleness,
As though in man no trait was true
But that which wore the meanest hue
And Goodness were a dream that dies
When dazzled by a poet's eyes,—
Yes, feelings dark as these, perchance
Had glorified by pure advance
The regions of exalted mind,
And loved the links of human-kind.
The spots upon Creation seen
For sorrow, not for scorn, had been,
And genius, from its darkness free,
Flash'd out in full divinity!

But, 'twas not so; and man must wait
The brightness of a better fate,
To tell him all which Grief would learn,
When back to dust the great return,
E'en in *that* hour when most they seem
To realise our noblest dream,
And purify the hopes of Earth
With promise of a second birth.

The sanctity of Virtue stands
Above the soil of human hands,
And Genius, though the world it awe,
Must bow to her corrective law:
Yet who, unless his mind can be
Transform'd to perfect Deity,
Can judge how terrible the sway
When Impulse leads the soul astray?
The meanest tongue can brand a sin,
But who can probe the heart within,—
The gloom of agonising strife
When Principle resigns its life,
Till Passion in her fiery reign
Pours madness over blood and brain!
A soul, that like Æolian lyre
Which faintest tones of air inspire,
Was thrill'd by sound, and hue, and scene,
As though its slumber ne'er had been;
A spirit, pining for the good
Till dreams became its daily food;
Or revelling in satiric gloom
Which mock'd at all above the tomb,—
Oh! these unite to arm a spell
That few below have wielded well!
And, blended with a slakeless thirst
To find the spot by crime uncursed,
In Byron lived a haunting dread
From moods of dark inquiry bred,
Of that Unknown beyond the grave
Where fancy's wings delight to wave:
Hence, doubt and scorn, with anguish rife,
Threw blackness on the stream of Life;
Till o'er each maze of erring man
The reckless eye of Satire ran,
Which finding nought but error free,
Call'd vice the sole reality!

But where the grave of Harold lies
May Virtue bend forgiving eyes!
The meek, whose time-worn spirits know
How much that Heart must brave below
When battling with the mystic gloom
Which haunts it from the spectral tomb,
No vengeance on his glory wreak
But softly of each error speak.
For who are they, if life had been,
Like Byron's, one uncurtain'd scene
Where every eye could point a gaze
And level all its envious rays,
Whose splendour would reveal no blot
Which now lies faded and forgot?
While some regard with bitter eyes
The tomb where buried Genius lies,
And bid the gates of Mercy close
On them whom Earth denied repose,—
The hearts that wisdom's humbling power
Has taught to fear the firmest hour,
In tender awe will bend and weep
Where Byron's noble ashes sleep,
Nor love o'er sorrow's wildering track
To trace the foot of Error back;
But thank him with a proud excess
For all the poet's mightiness!
Oh, there he lies! becalm'd in death,
Whose being was a tortured breath;
Whose years in whirlwind bore him on
To the dread gulf where time is gone!
And stirless as the travell'd lake
Whose waters down the mountain break
O'er wood and wild, and ridge and rock,
Convulsed and crash'd with many a shock,
The turbulence of trial now!—
The rest can God alone avow.

And was it nought to melt away
The frost that bound the spirit's play?
To summon into startling view
The deep, the daring, and the true,
Or light the chaos of the soul
And see its hidden waters roll!
Instead of polish'd rhyme, to raise
The stormy breath of wilder lays;
Or make us, in his milder hour,
Dissolve in dreams of beauty's power—
Such beauty as our thoughts create,
But never clad a mortal state!

There are who call the Poet's bliss
Too airy for a world like this:
Alas, for Wisdom ! if her voice
Can teach the heart no glorious choice;
If downward to the dust she try
For aye to fix our slavish eye,
And seldom bid one glance be given
Aloft to mind's unclouded heaven !
The freshness of poetic thought
From out the groves of Fancy brought,
And wafted o'er the soul's domain,
What is it, but a breezy strain
From winds of vanish'd Eden lent
To purify earth's element,
And summon forth those dream-born flowers
That grew in Milton's epic bowers!
'Mid all the waste of worldly arts
Oh! leave him yet some few fine hearts,
That still the Poet's wand may raise
A vision of unfallen days,
And rescue from the fangs of time
Some feelings that are yet sublime !

On Harrow, when the heaven of June
Was garmented with glowing noon
And not a cloud's minutest braid
Along its liquid sapphire stray'd,
I stood beneath that haunted tree,
And heard the leaf-toned melody
Which oft in Boyhood's dreaming years
Had warbled on the pensive ears
Of Byron,—when he loved to muse
Beneath the quiet churchyard-yews.
Oh! who in such an hour could stand
And look adown the sloping land
Where meadow, vale, and roving stream
So often charm'd his chequer'd dream;
And round him feel the fresh-wing'd air
That lifted oft his waving hair,
And press the same sepulchral stone
His pressure loved to make its own,
Nor feel a sense of fame and might
That shook the heart with strange delight?

'Twas here he mused in Fancy's bower;
And in the mind's prophetic hour
Would try with telescopic gaze
To read the brow of unborn Days,[15]
Hail the bright orb of future fame
And glory in a minstrel's name !:
Or dared with dreadless eye to see
A map of vision'd misery
In lines of awful length outspread,
Till darkness veil'd him with the dead !

And who with backward gaze can scan
The burning course his genius ran,
Nor feel how Woman's reigning star
With fervid eye he view'd afar,
And felt her beam of beauty cast
A light which heaven alone surpass'd !
His primal love—it never died,
But still within the soul supplied
The waters of affection pure
From fate and freezing time secure.
'Twas thence ideal sorrow drew
The pangs which pierce our nature through,
Till love became the breath of song,
And bore his inward life along.
But had his heart with *hers* entwined
Whose beauty struck his boyhood blind,
The starlight of whose cloudless eyes
Attracted his immortal sighs,
If happiness could reach the great
How bright had been his alter'd fate!
Instead of darkness, light would be
Around the soul's divinity !
Medora, Kaled, and Gulnare,
Each ruin'd maid and reckless fair,
Were vision'd from the shades of mind
Despair and passion leave behind.
But, once in home's attractive fane
Oh! had he worshipp'd woman's reign,
And seen her, not in mock romance,
Through daily paths of life advance
As angel of domestic hours,
How nobly might those lofty powers
He lavish'd on a Corsair's bride
Have been to *purer* love supplied !
While, feeling all which fancy drew,
His genius would have brighten'd too,
And Woman in his picture hail'd
A model that had never fail'd,
While love, by genius made divine,
Could sanctify a poet's line.

And such hath been fond Woman's sway
Since angels hymn'd her natal day,
By law of that instinctive love
Whose archetype is God above !
And while yon heaven is o'er us hung
For ever shall the brave and young,
The free, the fervid, fond and true,
Declare what female hearts can do !

And many a name as yet unknown,
Embalm'd in some immortal tone
Of genius, by a thrilling bard,
Shall Time exult to read and guard:
And Beauty, in domestic bowers
Now fameless as secluded flowers,
When buried queens forgotten lie
And royal tombs can raise no sigh,
In melody of deathless might
Shall live to be the World's delight,
While Love and Poetry can claim
To twine a wreath round Woman's name !

CANTO III.

(In connection with Domestic Life.)

——"The mild majesty of private life."
Akenside.

——"Show us how divine a thing
A Woman may be made." *Wordsworth.*

ANALYSIS OF CANTO III.

Introduction—Female Charms in all Climes—England paramount—Home-Scenery—Ideal Picture—Rural Landscape at Morning-Hour—Scenes, and Sights, and Sounds—Village-Cottages—Parsonage—The Hamlet-Queen—Her beauty and worth—An Angel of Social Mercy—Her little Sister—How trained and watched—The Brother—How remembered at Home—Village-reverence for the Pastor's Daughter—Dawning Emotions—Virgin Love—Its Depth and Delicacy—Transforming Power of the Affections—Courtship and its Charms—Progressive Love—Hopes and Anticipations—Tremors and Joys—Marriage-Bells—Social Preparations—Bridal Room—Wedding-Scene—Departure—Moral Effects—A Domestic Future—Farewell!

Angel of life! whose love hath been
The master-charm of time and scene,
Romance in her Elysian mood
Creating forms of fair and good,
Hath not outsoar'd thy virtue's height,
Nor imaged forth more purely bright
Those lineaments of perfect grace
Which yet adorn thy breathing race;
For Fiction, when her mould was cast,
On truth might gaze, and feel surpass'd.

But where is woman most array'd
With all that mind would see display'd?
O England! round thy chainless isle
How lavishly all blessings smile,
And crowd within thy little spot
A universe of glorious lot!
But never till the wind-rock'd sea
Have borne us far from home and thee,
Thy purer charms we learn to prize
And feel the patriot's glow arise.—
Though Nature with sublimer stress
Hath stamp'd her seal of loveliness
On climes of more colossal mould,
How much that travell'd eyes behold
Would sated wonder throw away
To take one look where England lay!—
To wander down some hawthorn-lane
And drink the lark's delightful strain;
Or floating from a pastured dell
To hear the sheep's romantic bell,
While valeward as the hills retire
Peeps greyly forth the hamlet-spire,
And all around it breathes a sense
Of weal, and worth, and competence.
But, far beyond all other dowers,
Thy daughters seem Earth's human flowers.—
The charm of young Castilian eyes
When lovingly their lashes rise,
And blended into one rich glance
The lightnings of the soul advance,—
Wild hearts may into wonder melt
And make expression's magic felt.
Or, girded by the dreams of old,
In Sappho's Lesbian isle behold
A shadow of primeval grace
Yet floating o'er some classic face:
But where, in what imperial land
Hath Nature with more faultless hand
Embodied all which Beauty shows
Than round us daily lives and glows?
Here, mingled with the featured might
Of charms that coldest gaze invite,
Th' enamel of the mind appears
Undimm'd by wo, unsoil'd by years!
To wedded hearts devoid of strife
Here Home becomes the heaven of life;
And household-virtues spring to birth
Beside the love-frequented hearth,
While feelings soft as angels know
Around them freshly twine and grow.

A landscape of domestic love
Which God's paternal eyes approve,
Reflected from a homely dream,
Shall form my lay's concluding theme:
If *there* one heart its home can see,
'Twill render more than fame to me!

A vale of beauty!—lo, the Morn
In clouds of crimson radiance born,
Hath risen from the couch of night
And fills the air with fresh delight;
While hues, like harmonies that range
The world of sound with lovely change,
In varied lustre o'er the sky
Awaken, mingle, melt, and die;
Till full-orb'd on his flaming throne
The sun-King is beheld alone!
And blue as Baltic waves asleep
Before him lies a dazzling sweep
Of azure,—in its deep excess
Of morn-created loveliness.

How exquisite this breathing hour!
As though awhile some choral bower
Where Cherubim partake repose,
Its crystal gates did half unclose,
Till fragments of delicious sound
Came wafted on the winds around,
And bloom and balm to nature given
Made earth a momentary heaven!
Hark! to the choir of yonder wood

Where life exults in solitude;
On each unrifled bough is heard
The lay of some melodious bird,
And young-wing'd breezes as they float
From brook and meadow learn a note;
And streams like tides of gladness, flow.
And in the earth there dwells a glow
Of elemental youth and joy
Unchill'd by one corrupt alloy.
How dazzlingly with rosy dyes
The fairies of the field arise!
And flutter on their insect-wings,
As each a song of matin sings;
And where around the glitt'ring blade
A liquid web of dew is laid,
As early peasants' footsteps pass,
How greenly shines the shaken grass!
While many a lark from out the ground
Is startled, like a magic sound
Which ere the sense be half aware
Comes trembling through the lyric air!

And list, from out yon village-dell,
Upon the breeze in broken swell,
The goings-on of life begin
To charm the ear with social din.
The creak of hill-ascending wain,
The shout of some exulting swain,
The watch-dog baying far behind,
The mill-sounds hoarse upon the wind,
With voices from the child or crone,
Are all in gay confusion thrown;
And murmur on the morning-breeze;
With notes whose human echoes please.
From the thatch'd chimney now have broke
The tinted wreaths of cottage smoke,
Ascending delicately bright,
And braided by a golden light,
Like air-wing'd hopes that glide away
Commingling with the boundless day.
And see! amid the straw-roof'd throng
Of homes that to yon dale belong,
As dwelt the patriarch on the plain
Surrounded by his pastoral train,
A mansion smiles; whose neater state
Though unallied to proud or great,
A central grace around it throws
And o'er each cot a charm bestows.
Embower'd in laurels, green and calm,
To view it yields the eye a balm:
But when at eve its garden hath
A lustre on each lilied path;
When bough, and branch, and grape-hung vine
In rays of pensive beauty shine,
While gladsome bee and quiring bird
And leafy song are faintly heard,
There often hath the worldling cast
A longing eye, ere on he past,
And while it wander'd o'er the scene,
Mused, Oh! that such my own had been!

But is it like gay hearts that hide
With sunny brow a bitter tide
Of anguish in their gloom below,
Which they who suffer only know?
Have venom'd passions, fierce or wild,
The pureness of its peace defiled,
While outwardly its walls declare
Life's inner-world most tranquil there?
No: war and famine, blood and crime
Have stain'd the ghastly scroll of time;
And tears, the rain of torture, flow'd,
And conscience borne its burning load
While twenty years o'er earth have roll'd,
The aged die, and youth grown old;
Yet still, in unalloy'd content
Remains yon blissful tenement!
And, save the shadows which o'ersteal
The brightest fate the good can feel,
Around its heaven-protected scene
A summer of the soul hath been!
And like a fount whose waters fling
A freshness with faint murmuring,
Perceived alone by desert-flowers
That bud beneath its nursing powers,
From thence hath Charity's sweet store
Been scatter'd for the sick and poor.
So noiseless were the feet that trod
Those lovely paths which led to God,
That Angels only heard their tread,
And track'd them to some dying bed.

But where the ivied gate expands,
Within it what a vision stands!
More exquisite in brow and limb
Than those aërial cherubim,
Which painting in some starry dress
Reveals on clouds of loveliness!
Around her like a viewless zone
A fascinating might is thrown:
Her brow is pure as thought can be
And whiter than the foam-clad sea,
Expanded with an arch of grace
Like heaven's above a heavenly face;
And on that polish'd cheek, behold
Her ringlets, by the breeze unroll'd,
In gleaming motion dance and shake
Like ripples on a restless lake.
Her years are on the verge of heaven,—
That period when to life is given
The freshness of elastic youth
Yet touch'd with woman's deeper truth,
Again, behold that virgin face!
'Tis beauty in the mould of grace;
Incarnate soul lies sculptured there;
A feeling so divinely fair

Is dwelling in those dark-fringed eyes,
That when they front congenial skies
Pure spirits well might deem that Earth
Had copied some celestial birth,
Or beauty in the world had grown
All spirit-like, to match their own !

Yet innocence with homely seal
Hath stamp'd the power her looks reveal;
And should her form the rustic meet
Amid some pent and crowded street,
So artlessly each lovely hue
Would dawn on his delighted view,
At once his mental eye would roam
To scenery round a village-home,
Till breeze and brook were heard again
Exulting o'er his native plain.

Companion of the morning hours
To tend her own infantine flowers,
Which grow beneath her guardian eyes,
And let their lids of bloom arise,
The garden-haunt she loves to pace:
And oft is seen, with bending grace,
And hand that scarcely wounds the air,
To nurse each bud unfolding there;
Till Fancy where her touch presides
Might dream the soul of flowers abides,
And wafts abroad their sweetest sigh
To greet her, as she glideth by.
Before her nought is forced to flee:
All undisturb'd, the rifling bee
When hived in bloom, may hum and sip
A banquet off the rose's lip:
The butterflies, bright gems of air!—
Can hover round her silken hair;
And not a bird that quells its song,
Or flutters when she moves along,
But sings as though a sunbeam came
Athwart the boughs with brighter aim.

'Twas here amid this haunt of dreams
Her childhood roved, and still it seems
Alive with voices heard of yore,
And breathes of them who breathe no more!
From out her casement's vine-clad height
She views it, when the veil of night
Lies dimly woven over all,
Or glitters like a dewy pall:
And here, when starry magic reigns
Amid the sky's nocturnal plains,
And moonlight with mysterious power
Hath mantled yonder grey church-tower;
The pensive maiden loves to stand
And let her night-born dreams expand.—
Nor is the scene bereft of charm:
The dusky roof of distant farm,
The meadows in their dim array,
The frowning coppice far away,
And cot that shows its twinkling pane
Adown the lone and green-bough'd lane,
While yonder where the cloven hill
Seems parted by a Tempest's will,
The billows wreathed with moonshine play
And warble forth an ocean-lay,—
To hearts that feel the hush of night
Enchanting is their mingled sight!

A daughter, beautiful and good,
On the fair brink of womanhood,
When all the debt of love-watch'd years,
Of buried pangs and bosom'd fears,
By filial worth can be repaid,
Is more than words have yet portray'd.
What links, which time nor death can part,
Have bound her to a parent's heart!
Oh, deep beyond description lies,
Pure as the ray of seraph-eyes,
The love within parental souls!
Whatever tide of anguish rolls,
Whatever wreck the world can make,
Till God himself the good forsake
Affection is the life of life,
A power with more than feeling rife
Above all base dominion free,
A passion for eternity!

O, blest! unutterably blest,
The visions to their fancy prest,
When sire and mother blend a prayer
For thee, young spirit! fond as fair.
Thy being sways their mortal breath,
And shouldst thou die,—'twere more than death:
For in thy tomb their thoughts would dwell,
And darkness be their brightest spell.
To think on all thine artless ways
Since childhood reap'd its golden days;
From year to year delighted trace
The magic dawn of mind and face;
To watch thee in Life's daily round
With every trait of heaven abound;
And when some friend, whom time endears,
Hath warbled in their tranced ears
Of noble acts in secret done,
And wreaths by silent virtue won,
Oh, then around their hearts to feel
A glow of admiration steal!—
Or haply, with prophetic truth
To picture for thy wedded youth
A Soul that shall be worthy thine,
With feelings from as pure a mine;
And when the church-yard yews shall wave
And darken o'er their cherish'd grave,
To feel, whatever time decree,
One Heaven their final home will be,
A bliss so pure no words unfold,
A joy so deep no eyes behold;

That language must be taught Above
Whose power reveals a parent's love!

And thou art worthy, on whose brow
The stainless mind lies mirror'd now,
Around their guardian hearts to twine
Those feelings that are so divine!
No wish, or want, or hope, or joy,
No dreams of time thy youth employ,
But blended with their meaning lies
Approval shed from parent eyes.
And as a ray from out the sun
Reveals its birth where'er it run,
Thy virgin thoughts, howe'er they stroll,
Retain the brightness of the soul.
And often in thy sleep is heard
The fragment of some duteous word,
When lips of imaged parents seem
To bless thee in thy girlish dream.
How winning are those myriad ways
By which a child fond homage pays,
Those ministries of heart and hand
Which none but parents understand!
When Morning reigns in dewy power,
To hie and cull the choicest flower;
Or pluck the fruit whose bloom appears
Bedeck'd with Night's refreshing tears;
Or else with magic pencil take
The likeness of some hill or lake,
Some haunted spot, whose beauty hung
Rich praises on her feeling tongue,
And these to place in proud surprise
Before a mother's greeting eyes!—
Affection, let thy voice declare
How tender-sweet such trifles are!
For what is kindness, but the heart
In action, without guile or art,
Imparting by some nameless power
A bloom to each attractive hour?

But when bleak winter bares the earth
And Comfort hails the wonted hearth,
Then, child of beauty! thou art found
The central star of bliss around.
Some book divine, or antique tale,
Or shipwreck, where the savage gale
Swells howling o'er the black-waved sea,
Perchance, the chosen page may be:
Or Bard eterne with visions bright
Shall charm the soul of taste to-night;
Or haply, Music's heaven-born spell
Whose spirit thou canst wake so well,
Shall melt fond memory into tears
Or votive sighs, for vanish'd years:
And then, adown the tides of song
While thou enrapt art borne along,
The throbbing chamber seems to glow
With Melody's rich overflow!
And full before his bick'ring fire,
Delighted sits a dreaming sire;
Nor blame the mother, if her gaze
Be fill'd with more than fondest praise,
And Nature whisper through the heart,
"My child, how exquisite thou art!"

But, 'tis not in the noon of joy
When Life endures no stern alloy,
A daughter from her mind can pour
The fulness of affection's store:
For let but once a pang prevail,
A limb be rack'd, or cheek grow pale;
Let the wild torture of disease
Deny to heart and hand their ease;
Let sorrow once her frown impress
On Earth's uncertain happiness,—
Then, scorner of the sex! advance,
And learn the power of Pity's glance,
The tender might of woman's gaze
Unweaken'd by tormented days.
Through hours of blackness, when the mind
Seems prostrate, wreck'd, and unresign'd,
What pathos in her pleading eye!
How gentle her devoted sigh!
One look speaks more than man could say,
And each word wafts a pang away.

And there are ties whose thrilling truth
Pervade her uncorrupted youth
With energies that breathe and move
In daily acts of duteous love.
Behold yon sister!—fairy thing
Whose forehead, like the brow of spring,
Is ever-bright and ever-young,
And with the glow of gladness hung;
So light in form, a breeze of life
Secure from earth's contagious strife,
Round her own orb of home and glee
On wing'd delight she seems to flee!
Each pulse within her fine-wrought frame
Is tuned to joy's unsleeping claim;
Whether a cloud-isle richly drest
Her wonder-beaming eye arrest,
Or magic from some household-word
Young laughter into life hath stirr'd.
And dear as Nature's dearest tie
She grows beneath a sister-eye,
Who watches with a star-like gaze
Around her pure but perill'd days.
And rather than the air might press
Too bleakly on her loveliness,
Or pain one fleeting pang awake,
Would let the blood her heart forsake,
And drop by drop dissolve away
To win her life one pangless day!

And what, though years now intervene
To veil her own from childhood's scene,

To robe an infant's face with smiles
And summon forth its mimic wiles,
As playmate she can stoop to be
Transform'd to frolic infancy!
Will echo back the bird-like sound
Of tiny laughs in merry round,
Nor coldly shun the meanest toy
That wings a moment's flight with joy.
And well those cherub-features play
In answer to her sister's sway,
Delighted, calm, or grief-array'd,
According as her words display'd
The tones which govern smiles and tears!
And often when some cloud appears,
By pain, or temper's gloom begot,
To shadow her infantine lot,
That sister can alone restore
The sunshine as it play'd before!
And duly as the car of Night
Returns, she bends with soft delight
Enamour'd o'er the precious sleep
Of lids too beautiful to weep!
No, never is the pillow prest
Before a parting gaze hath blest
That winning face!—so brightly warm,
So tinted with the rosy charm
Of slumber, that its beauty seems
The bloom of amaranthine dreams.

But ah! there is a dearer task
Whose toils a patient wisdom ask;
And who beyond a sister knows
Where best the germ of knowledge grows,
When Infancy begins to look
Abroad o'er Earth's unwritten book,
To read the world with curious eye,
And question truths beyond the Sky!
Fondly to aid the budding mind
When thought springs faint and undefined;
To teach her lips a word to frame
And prattle with some homely name;
Then day by day, as reason wakes
And mental twilight dimly breaks,
A delicate enchantment throw
Round each young truth the heart would know,
Thus nursing with a sweet control
The childhood of a cherish'd soul,—
O none but she can paint the joy
Of such divine and dear employ!
In wing'd delight thus years will speed,
And still in language, look, and deed,
Will sisterly affection be
A power of guardian purity,
And gently thus its magic wind
Around an infant's growing mind.

A brother!—oh, that thrilling name,
It vibrates through thy very frame
Thou queen of Boyhood's cloudless day!
In studious bower though far away,
Thy heart is haunted with a sense
Of all a brother's charms dispense.
His picture on thy bedroom-wall,
How frequently its lines recal
Th' imperial face, the manly brow,
The eyes which dared the soul avow
And smile that knew no mean eclipse
But ever round those graceful lips
In brightest welcome play'd for thee
In moods of unaffected glee!—
What tales of prowess, feats of mind
Around thy memory intertwined,
'Tis pure delight to oft unroll
In tones that touch parental soul!
Beside thee like a felt unseen
The shadow of his shape hath been,
Whene'er along some favour'd walk
Thy spirit dreams him smile and talk;
His voice is woven in the breeze
That carols round the garden-trees;
And fancy, when the moon gleams bright,
Can often on its mirror write
Emotions 'twas divine to share,
When *both* had fix'd their glances there!
Through weal and wo, through cloud and change,
Whatever clime or shore he range,
Till nature can itself deny
Undimm'd will shine affection's eye,
And stainless those deep waters prove
That well from out a sister's love!

And think'st thou, though thy smile afar
Hath vanish'd like a fairy star,
Companion of her girlish lot!
That thou art in thy home forgot,
Where memories like pulses play
Within the heart of each new day?
So long our early feelings last,
Affection owns no faded past!
For aye the glow of what was dear
Surrounds it like an atmosphere;
Eternal is the youth of thought,
Whatever outward change hath wrought,
And distance, though like death it seems,
Is conquer'd by creative dreams
Of fondness, acting o'er again
The brother in his spirit-reign!
For, all he fancied, felt, or did,
Her memory in fond silence hid,
And nought is trivial, wreck'd, or gone,
He cherish'd, loved, or gazed upon!
Like gems of earth *his* flowers abide,
With dew and tender rain supplied;
The birds are fed with fostering care,
His dog beneath the wonted chair

In unalarm'd repose may lie
And fawn to win her playful eye;
The glossy steed, whose bounding limb
O'er hill and mead had toil'd for him,
Beside it she will often stand
With greeting voice and gentle hand;
The page *he* read grows doubly sweet,
For there communing thoughts can meet:
Each melody whose magic sway
Could best dissolve his soul away,—
Delightful 'tis again to pour
Around the room its richest store
Of melting sounds, which ere they die
Seem blended with a brother's sigh!—
But holier far is memory made,
And deeper is its might display'd
Whene'er the poor he loved to feed,
The hearts he caused no more to bleed,
She welcomes in some rustic cot,
And finds his goodness unforgot!
And ye, whose locks with hoary truth
Betray the flight of faded youth;
Whose hands have rock'd the cradled boy,
Or ere he lisp'd his little joy,
Full proudly may your tongues prevail!
For dear is each domestic tale
The homely past untreasures now
To brighten on a sister's brow!
But when arrives his well-known seal,
What ecstacy young eyes reveal!
Warm on the page her lips impress
A kiss of perfect happiness;
And well in that entrancing hour
When feelings claim prophetic power,
Since all unworn his heart appears,
A sister may outwing the years,
And vision round a brother's head
The rays of future glory spread!

And wouldst thou trace her secret tide
Of goodness to the poor supplied,
Winding unknown its village-course
From charity's divinest source?
Angelic woman! if to be
On earth a child of Deity,
Surpasseth all we deem renown,
How peerless thine immortal crown!
For shipwreck'd hearts, sole haven thou;
With pity on thy pensive brow,
And mercy in thy healing hand,
And voice beyond all music bland,
From cot to cell, oh! thou hast been
Life's angel in its blackest scene,
And often with the dying good
On the bright verge of Heaven hast stood!

And such thou art; and many a dame
Delights to hear thy darling name;
And many a tatter'd widow glows
To bless the hand that heal'd her woes:
While orphan babes in lane and street
With bright'ning face thy welcome meet:
And many a tale of mercy lives
The life which grateful Memory gives,
When Feeling round a cottage-fire
Can pay the debt thy deeds inspire!
And they are such as cannot die
Though honour'd by no human eye;
Unchronicled in rolls of worth,
Ungreeted by applauding earth,
Silent and secret though they be,
Their tablet is eternity!
Where graven by the Hand Divine
The glories of the good will shine.

And thus in virgin solitude,
Unbroken by the waters rude
Of that rough world, whose waves afar
Billow with life's tempestuous war,
Queen of the hamlet! years have flown,
And still thou art unwoo'd and lone:
Yet time with magic unconfess'd
Has moulded feelings in thy breast,
Which now like buried music float
With soft and secret under-note;
So delicate, they scarce appear
To haunt thy spirit's maiden sphere,
But waken'd once,—and they shall be
A soul within a soul to thee!
Emotions, of themselves afraid,
A temple in thy heart have made,
Wherein they flutter, like a bird
That trembles when a voice is heard!
And fancy loves a Being now
Whom shaping words cannot avow;
A Form of fine imaginings
To which attracted nature clings.
At length he comes! that nameless one
The eye of Dreams had gazed upon;
The magic and the mystery
Of life have now begun for thee,
And thou the type of heaven wilt prove
In primal, deep, and deathless love!

Emotion that is most sublime
Of all which hallows earth and time;
That Principle from whence we draw
The light of each celestial law;
Pervading Sense, victorious Power
Whom death nor darkness can devour;
An omnipresent might and spell
Wherein all mind and matter dwell,
Is Love!—by that bright word alone
We vision forth The vast Unknown,
The Ruler of the seraphim,
Whose glory makes the glorious dim!

And not an element that glows
But breathes the life which love bestows.
So magical its wide command,
The sternest rock, the bleakest strand
Around an exiled wretch hath thrown
A charm that paradise might own!
And who, when form and face depart
Which seldom touch'd his deeper heart,
Or e'en in hours of marring strife
Disturb'd the pure serene of life,
That feels not, while he says, "Farewell!"
A love-born sense within him dwell?
A touch of heart, whose tenderness
Provokes him with a thrilling stress?
And hence the captive, when the light
Of freedom daunts his reeling sight,
With something of a mute regret
His gaze on dungeon-walls hath set,
Though Misery's hand had graven there
The words and weakness of despair!
There is but One who cannot love,
The Anarch of the thrones above;
Apostate, in whose sleepless eyes
A hell of burning hatred lies;
Whose torture is th' undying sense
Of unadored Omnipotence;
A wither'd, dark, defeated Mind,
That curses Heaven, and scorns mankind!

And will the loveless, stern, or grave,
Think human fancies wildly rave,
When young affection's meteors play
In dazzling falsehood round their way?
Oh! take him to some towering mind
Whose Orphic words entrance mankind,
And, when the mask is laid aside,
And backward rolls the blood-warm tide
Of feelings, rich with early truth,
And vital with the flush of youth,
How wither'd, wan, and leafless, grows
The laurel which Renown bestows,
To that bright wreath affection wove
Round the fair brow of youthful love!
That love, whose faintest impulse wrings
The bosom's agonised strings,
And even in its mildest reign
O'erpowers him with a yearning pain,
A feeling that is unforgot,
Which seems the core of life to rot
And deaden it with slow decay,
As water frets the rock away!—
Thus passion forms the bane or bliss
Of being, in a world like this;
The day or night of inward joy,
Which years may dim, but not destroy;
Love reigns but once, yet that will be
Affection's true eternity!
All future love mere echo seems
Of vanish'd hope's melodious dreams;
A dying tone of lost delight,
A fragment of those feelings bright
That once when youth and heart were whole
Excited, charm'd—and crush'd the soul!

But, maiden! in thy vernal bloom,
On thee attends a calmer doom;
No clouds along thy placid heaven
With heraldry of gloom are driven;
No! all is open, bright, and blest:
And hopes may wander unreprest,
Like birds of beauty when they fly
And wanton in their genial sky.
And not for thee are voiceless fears,
The rack of unrelieving tears,
The agonies which coil and wind
In secret round a wasted mind
Like vipers with envenom'd tooth,
To canker all the spirit's youth;
Nor Circumstance, with eye averse,
For thee hath framed a fearful curse!
That long as life's dull waters roll,
With broken heart and blighted soul
Thy feelings, on the rack of fate,
Shall live to mourn thy wedded state!
Serene as thy soft brow appears
The countenance of coming Years;
Consenting parents' blended voice
Hath sanction'd Love's ingenuous choice;
And nought descends from dreams above
More exquisite than woman's love,
When passion in its virgin morn
Within a soul like thine is born!
Thy love by self is undefiled
And foster'd like a spirit-child,
Revered and watch'd with heart and eyes;
To whom each thought would sacrifice,
Each hour devote its deepest care,
Each feeling give its fondest share;
And earth, and time, and joy, and youth
From hence derive their only truth.
Let *one* deceive, and dead would lie
The living world before thine eye!
And thus, when withered years depart,
They leave no wreck like woman's heart!
The ruin of her mind remains
Haunted by dim and dreary pains;
And pining thoughts each chamber throng
Where once arose the breath of song,
Till Sadness, link'd with cold Despair,
Unites to fix its dwelling there.

With man's compare her feelings fine,
How delicate, how half divine!
Torn by the slightest breeze of life
And shatter'd by each varied strife,
When wrong, or wo, or accident
Perturbs the spirit's element,

In fragile bloom they seem to be
Like leaves on some majestic tree,
That often when the boughs are still
Regardless of the breeze's will,
Are shaken by a touch or tone,
And perish, ere the blast hath blown!

But thou art loved, and unbetray'd;
And who can paint, enamour'd maid!
The paradise where dream and rove
Those moments dedicate to love?
For One there is, whose eye repays
The fervour of thy fondest gaze,
Whose language with its melting tone
Of tenderness can match thy own;
Whose visions of the beautiful
When most his yielded heart they rule,
Are woven out of thoughts of thee
Like rainbows from a lovely sea!

Has the world changed, more heavenly grown,
And every taint of darkness flown?
That brightness is the sudden birth
Of feelings which ennoble earth,
Of passion in its stainless prime
Just risen on the brink of time!
By these transform'd, creation glows
With each warm tint the mind bestows;
A deeper verdure decks the grass;
The clouds with richer glory pass,
The winds a sweeter welcome chant,
And wheresoe'er her footsteps plant
Their printless beauty, smile and sound
Of new enchantment hover round!
To *her* 'tis mystery;—but the mind
Grown exquisite and o'er-refined,
Can veil the universe with light
Till all is heaven that meets the sight,
And outward nature wears the dress
Of mind's internal loveliness.

Commingled souls! 'twere vain to tell,
Around them as rich evening fell
And clouds of calmest beauty lay
Like dreams of air along the way
Where wan and far th' horizon wound,
While nought but ocean breathed a sound,
How often on the placid shore
They rambled, till the light was o'er,
What rapture on each radiant cheek,
While softer than the billows speak
Responsive to the pleading wind,
The murmurs of each happy mind!
The waves beneath, the skies above,
All sights and sounds were born of love!
So all unstain'd by earth's alloy
Their very blood grew liquid joy;
So full their hearts, they fain would reel,
And make delight too deep to feel!
Th' aroma of all mortal bliss
Enrich'd an hour so charm'd as this;
Till soul-enrapt, they seem'd to be
Attracted nearer Deity;
While each to each immortal grew,
And saw the spirit beaming through
A glowing face, where Love had given
The features that were form'd for Heaven!

All hours are sweet, when love is there
A loveliness to make and share;
All scenes delight, when eyes adored
The magic of their gaze afford;
No rock is bleak, no desert rude,
When Beauty walks the solitude:
But moonlight charms the outward eye
Like music heard by memory;
And temptingly the moonbeams play
Around young lovers' lonely way,
As though fond Nature glow'd to meet
The pressure of their timing feet.
Belated, like a starry train
When loth to quit the azure plain,
Yon vision'd pair, behold them now
While Dian bares her crested brow,
And clouds of alabaster white
Float on the soundless breath of night.
How beautiful Creation's sleep!
So innocent, so calm, and deep:
The air is rock'd to voiceless rest;
The bird within his woven nest;
The dew upon unshaken leaves
A web of filmy lustre weaves;
And onward as the lovers steal,
You'd deem the fairy ground could feel
Their shadows o'er its silence fall,
So rapt a stillness veileth all!

But they have reach'd a woodland-shore,
Where billows, now the breeze is o'er,
Are blended into one broad mass
Of heaving glory,—like a glass
Reflecting forth with twinkling change
The heaven-lights, in their lofty range.
Magnificent, and mute, and bright,
To feel it, is to worship night!
And there they stand, absorb'd and blest,
In adoration unexprest;
Yet drinking in with eye and soul
Earth's beautiful and boundless whole.
And when that tranced delight is o'er,
They glide along yon glittering shore;
Where tones of whisper'd feeling take
The heart from each! as lips awake
In words which Love design'd to be
The heart's revealing masonry.

A past, in its undying truth
Still vocal with the vows of youth:
A future, with each promise rife
Of tranquil home and wedded life,
Of these they talk, and plan, and scheme,
Indulging hope's oracular dream:
So soft the hour, the future rolls
Obedient to prophetic souls
By banks of bliss, and meads of flowers,
As though from wishes came the hours!
But night hath deepen'd: now they roam
Enchanted to expecting home;
And see! where downward hills retire,
In dim repose the village-spire!
Around it smiles a yellow moon
Gilding the leafy flush of June.
But home is reach'd, the room is gain'd,
With many a blush the walk explain'd,
Whose length 'twas not for time to meet,
For *what* can weary lovers' feet!
And smiles on each parental face
Have risen with forgiving grace;
And on the mother's brow is read
A tale which truth might thus have said,
"How often when *my* age was thine,
Were walks as long and lonely mine!"

And say, can aught but death unbind
Affections round her soul entwined?
Though distance may bereave the eye
And o'er him hang a stranger sky,
The sun that brings her spirit's day
Is born of his illuming sway.
The ground he trod a glory wears;
The twilight-walk his step declares;
No melody so sweetly heard
As fancy's love-repeated word;
His picture on her heart portray'd,
(Soft mem'ry asks no other aid)
Bright o'er her face she oft can feel
His vision'd gaze of fondness steal!
The breathings of his soul begin
To thrill her echoing soul within;
And then, ere mind is half aware,
Her lips address the tongueless air
In words of unregarded tone,
As sunlight on a rock is thrown
Where flower nor herbage, fruit nor stream,
Exult to drink the offer'd beam.
Against him raise a slanderous breath,—
And blooming looks the cheek of Death,
Compared with that appall'd distress
That blights her features' loveliness!
Applaud him, and the heart will rise
Dissolved within her dewy eyes!
Lustrous, and fill'd with tearful light
Like rain-beads when the moon is bright.
Voiceless her tongue, but what a glow
Of spirit's grateful overflow,
In eloquent excess appears
To glitter through those dawning tears!
And ah! forgive, if fondly weak
Too soft of one her soul will speak;
And faintly interweave his name
With hours when love should hide its claim.
For thus chance-words will oft betray
How secret thoughts roam far away;
And hence by soft and sudden tone
The dreamings of the mind are shown,
Like rays of beauty when they dart
From out a cloud's divided heart,
And dazzle into gay surprise
The lids of unexpecting eyes.

Too much of pomp and aim is seen
Where'er the pen of man hath been;
But, lovely one! how sweet for thee
Within thy trellis'd room to be,
And there to language yield thy mind
As bends a flower before the wind!
And, aimless save the soul to show,
What magic will thy words bestow,
As bright they rush with fondest speed
To visit eyes which yearn to read
Each syllable that love can frame,
When hallow'd by so dear a name!
Between its banks as roams the stream
And murmurs like a liquid dream,
Surrender'd to the guiding force
Of nature in its beauteous course,—
So artlessly is woman's mind
To tones of untaught grace resign'd,
And wanders down the fairy tide
Of words whose sweetness love supplied!

* * * * *

Bells on the wind! hark! peal on peal
Comes wafted with melodious zeal,
Making the morn so bright and clear
To thrill like joy's own atmosphere!
A bird-song from each holly flows;
The bee hums loudly in the rose;
And like a soaring dew-drop seems
The butterfly to shed its gleams
Of hue and lustre, in wild play
Of rapture round its wingèd way.—
Creation, like a human soul,
Feels gladness through each fibre roll!

And mark ye, where yon churchyard shows
The tombs' and turfs' sepulchral rows,
And sunbeams o'er the graves advance
To touch them with as bright a glance
As once around each living head
The beauty of their joyance spread,—
A crowd of village forms attends;
Their lip with lip loud welcome blends;

And homeward by a rose-strewn track
The gay-eyed young are wending back,
To drink around a festive board
Such health as loving hearts afford.

But whence the joy?—behold yon room,
And there in hymeneal bloom
Array'd like clouds of fleecy mould
When round the moon their grace is roll'd,
And bending like a human flower,
With beauty for her matchless dower,—
The bride, the daughter, and the queen
Whose virtues crown our vision'd scene!

Poet and painter, each may bring,
Fresh from the spirit's fountain-spring
Full many a truth and many a tone
Which Nature shall confess her own.
But there, in yon bright room are met
Feelings which ne'er were mirror'd yet,
Save by the features when they start
To life from out the living heart!—
The old, the tried, whose years retain
The light of early friendship's reign,
From childhood holding firm and deep
The faith unworldly bosoms keep;
A sire, upon whose honour'd head
A silvery grace of time is spread,
Beholding like a priest of joy
The smiles which every face employ,
(Though mellow'd is the meeker smile
That slumbers on his own the while)
Again unite:—and *she* is there,
Whose heart becomes one voiceless prayer,
That life may round a daughter pour
Exhaustless mercy's heavenly store!

And thou! 'mid all the bridal star,
Thy bosom is one tender war
'Tween fond regret for faded hours,
And love whose fulness overpowers!
Deep tears within thy heart arise
Though scarcely yet they dim thine eyes,
Lest shades of grief should haply fall
Upon thy wedding-carnival,
And eyes parental catch from thee
A tear thy soul would shake to see!
But when the sad adieus are sigh'd
Thy spirit to its core is tried,
As garden, ground, and village-mead
From the wing'd chariot fast recede:
One look! so long it seems to cling
Around the spot of Life's dead spring!
One rapid glance at paths of yore,
Where roam'd the Days which breathe no more!
And nature, wrung beyond control,
In tears will then express thy soul!
And let them fall! for tears like thine
Might hang on eyelids half divine;
And love in their excess can see
How soft a woman's soul can be.

And she is gone! the wedded maid
Whose loveliness a home array'd
With lustre caught from every gaze,
Her look, her laugh, her winning ways,
How are they felt as unforgot
In each young scene and household-spot!
Dismal the once glad room appears;
And eyes are charged with coming tears,
When haply to their pensive sight
Some little gift is brought to light,
Some token of departed hours
For memory left, like waning flowers!
The fairy harp her fingers loved
In tomb-like calm stands unremoved;
And o'er her pictured face is sigh'd
A deeper thought than words supplied,
When silent, sad, unwatch'd, and lone,
A mother lets her grief be shown!
Yon garden, too, now reft and lorn,
Methinks its alter'd features mourn,
So droopingly the flowerets bend,
So dyingly their leaves depend,
To what they were, when dew-bright Dawn
Beheld her on the breathing lawn
The goddess of the matin hour,
Arraying each expectant flower
With life and beauty; while the bird
Sang in the laurel-boughs unstirr'd,
And each coy breeze which caught her hair
Enamour'd hung, and nestled there!
Her sister, she whose tiny feet
Were wing'd when one was there to meet,
Now prattles in her dream and walk,
As though the lisping mind could talk
Of nothing, save that dearest one
Her bosom yearns to rest upon!
And many a Home her hand relieved
For one so pure hath pined and grieved;
Whose presence to the cottage grew
Like heaven before a martyr's view,—
So bright the change her blessing made
When sorrow had the soul betray'd.

But what remains for Minstrel-art?
Aught further can his page impart
Of feelings whose domestic sway
Conducts the hours of life away?
Then picture for thy pensive mood
A tranquil home in solitude;
And there, behold! the maid we drew
In Nature's soft but sterling hue.
Those budding traits, when girlhood smiled,
Of heart and mind, which all beguiled,

Expanded now to full-blown grace,
Have alter'd not with time and place:
Each added year has hail'd the birth
Of some new charm and noble worth;
And, save that on her brow appears
A mellow tinge of matron years,
And in her eye serenely glows
The magic of the mind's repose,
A girl in spirit still is left
Without one ray of youth bereft.

She is a mother! what a bliss
Celestial fills a name like this
With meaning, whose concentred might
Is mock'd by that mean word—delight!
For sooner may cold earth describe
The glories of th' angelic tribe,
Than any save a mother tell
What mysteries in her being dwell.
How spirit-fill'd her loving face!
How beautiful! thereon to trace
The imagery of rising thought
By feeling's hidden sculpture wrought!
When infant-voices round her roll
Like echoes of maternal soul;
And words like shatter'd music rise
Faint on her ear, in fond replies
From lips that quiver lisp and play
Like blossoms on a breezy day.
But, ah! should malady destroy
Each fairy bud of infant joy,
And broken cries but half reveal
The buried pangs dark moments feel,
What wrung Despair in tragic stone,
What Misery in marble shown,
In eloquence of grief can vie
With all that speaks her loving eye!—
When bending o'er a tortured child
By fits 'tis fervent, sad, or wild,
And prompt, if pain might thus be quell'd,
To drink the anguish she beheld
Into her soul, with one deep gaze,
And bear it with immortal praise!

* * * * *

Home of my fancy, fare thee well!
Unbroken be thy guardian spell;
Though not unmarr'd may be thy fate,
Since darkness girds our brightest state,
And Life along each path of hours
With thorns hath intertwined the flowers:
Yet hearts where home and love unite
Share more than bleakest years can blight;
The sky may frown, the tempest fall,
But Woman can o'ercome them all,
While calm within affection's eyes
Endures that beaming paradise,
Where sorrow seeks a bright repose
And basks beyond the reach of woes.

Land of my soul! maternal Isle
Array'd by Freedom's holy smile;
Whose throne is founded on the cause
Of native worth and noble laws;
Oh, long may Private Life be found
The glory of our British ground,
And Woman on her stainless brow
Wear the bright soul we honour now!
For though thy fleets o'erawed the main
Till every billow felt thy reign;
And captive Empires drew the car
Of victory from triumphant war,
Thy strength is canker'd, if the core
Of private life be sound no more.
Consumption on the cheek can bloom,
When Beauty but declares a tomb;
And eyes their brightest meaning shed
While every ray foretells the dead;
And thus may fatal glory be
An Empire's garb of infamy,
If once that spring of manly pride,
True gallantry, be stain'd or dried:
Or Woman from her high domain
Must dwindle into meaner reign.

The touching grace, the tender glow
Of what our fondest moods bestow;
The hopes which keep the heart awake
And self from out the selfish take;
The softness and the spell of all
That bridal dreams elysium call,
Born of her magic, blend their sway
To charm the clouds of time away:
And if there be a home on earth
Where nature most unveils its worth
And earth and heaven can intertwine,
Angel of Life! that home is thine.

NOTES.

Note 1, Page 291, Column 2.

The mountain's dim and dusky form,
Which, like a dying thunder-storm,
Glooms on the air with awful swell.

A ROCKY elevation, that seems to rise from the bosom of the sea (well known to the mariners of the North), is here alluded to: it is termed the KOLL, whose aspect perpetually changes with the changing atmosphere.

Note 2, Page 292, Column 1.

Grey Cronburgh lifts her storied pile
And darkens o'er the Danish Isle.

The Castle of Cronenburgh, in the vicinity of Elsinore, was built by Frederick II. in the boldest style of Gothic architecture. Mr. Boeson, an honest old historian of the place, while describing the position, solidity, and magnificence of the castle, affirms that it may rank with the noblest castles, not only in the North, but in all Europe.

This venerable edifice is connected with subjects of traditional, dramatic, and historical interest. On descending into the casemates, the story of Holger Danske, (or Ogier the Dane, as he is called in the French romances,) will amuse the mind in these damp and dismal vaults. It is thus related by Mr. Thiele:—"For many ages the din of arms was now and then heard in the vaults beneath the Castle of Cronenburgh. No man knew the cause, and there was not in all the land a man bold enough to descend into the vaults. At last a slave, who had forfeited his life, was told that his crime should be forgiven if he could bring intelligence of what he found in the vaults. He went down, and came to a large, iron door, which opened of itself when he knocked. He found himself in a deep vault. In the centre of the ceiling hung a lamp, which was nearly burnt out; and below stood a huge stone table, round which some steel-clad warriors sat resting their heads on their arms, which they had laid cross-ways. He who sat at the head of the table then rose up. It was Holger the Dane. But when he raised his head from the arms, the stone table burst right in twain, for his beard had grown through it. 'Give me thy hand,' said he to the slave. The slave durst not give him the hand, but put forth an iron bar, which Holger indented with his fingers. At last he let go his hold, muttering, 'It is well: I am glad that there are yet men in Denmark.'"

Leaving the casemates, and ascending the ramparts, Englishmen will find themselves on classic ground. Here they may indulge the fancy of Mr. Matthison, the celebrated Swiss poet, who made the venerable ghost of Hamlet's father appear on the platform when he exclaimed,—

"There are more things in heaven and earth,
Horatio,
Than are dreamt of in your philosophy."

But a still deeper tragedy will awaken the sympathies of an Englishman on his visit to Cronenburgh Castle. For, (to use the words of a distinguished author, already quoted,) "here Matilda was confined, the victim of a foul and murderous court intrigue. Here, amid heart-breaking griefs, she found consolation in nursing her infant; when, by the interference of England, her own deliverance was obtained, and as the ship bore her away from a country where the venial indiscretions of youth and unsuspicious gaiety had been so cruelly punished, upon these towers she fixed her eyes, and stood upon the deck, obstinately gazing towards them till the last speck had disappeared."

During her imprisonment in the Castle of Cronenburgh, it was Queen Caroline Matilda's chief enjoyment to ascend the square tower, which commands one of the finest prospects in the world. No spot could better soothe the anguish of her mind. The animated appearance of the Sound, in which the English flag is so frequently displayed, would fill her mind with cheering images of the greatness and prosperity of her native land. And, in gazing on the beauties which nature has scattered with so lavish a hand over Denmark, her contemplations on the great First Cause of all good would create in her the best disposition to forgive her "enemies, persecutors, and slanderers."

Note 3, Page 292, Column 2.

The victim of a royal hate.

"Sacrificed in the bloom of life, being born the 22nd of July, 1751, and married the 1st of October, 1766, she was first sent an inexperienced victim to a court, in which, surrounded with spies and emissaries, who interpreted the most trifling levities of youth into enormous crimes, the young and unsuspecting queen could not long remain without giving her enemies too favourable an opportunity to effect her fall. They succeeded; and induced the wretched king to become the engine of their malevolence, by signing the order for her imprisonment. The interposition of the British Court saved her from further violence, and conducted her to an asylum in the Electoral dominions of Hanover. Here she appeared in her true and native character. Divested of the retinue and pomp which, on the throne of Denmark, veiled her in a great degree from the inspection of nice observers, the qualities of her heart displayed themselves in her little court at Zell, and gained her universal love. Her person was dignified and graceful; she excelled in all the exercises befitting her sex, birth, and station. She danced the finest minuet in the Danish court, and managed the horse with uncommon address and spirit. She had a taste in music, and devoted much of her time, while at Zell, to the harpsichord. The characteristic style of her dress was simplicity, not magnificence; that of her deportment, an affability which, in a personage of such high rank, might be termed extreme condescension. Her talents were liberal and diffusive, and, cultivated by reading, displayed themselves on all occasions. She conversed, with the most perfect facility, in French, English, German, and Danish; and to those extraordinary attainments she added a thorough knowledge of the Italian, which she studied and admired for its beauty and delicacy. Her manners were the most polished, soft, and ingratiating; and even the contracted state of her finances could not restrain that princely munificence of temper which made her purse ever open to distress or misery. Naturally cheerful and happy in her disposition, adored and beloved to the highest degree by the circle of her court, even the dark cloud of adversity could not alter the sweetness and serenity of her temper. Banished, with every circumstance of indignity, from the throne of Denmark, she yet retained no sentiment of revenge or resentment against the authors of her fall, or against the Danish people. Her heart was not tinctured with ambition; and she looked back to the diadem which had been torn from her brow with a calmness and superiority of soul which might have made a Charles the Fifth or a Victor Amadeus blush. It was not the crown she regretted; her children only employed her care; the feelings of the sovereign were absorbed in those of the mother; and, if she wept the day when she quitted the island of Zealand, it was because she was then bereft of those dear objects of her maternal fondness. Two or three months before her death, she showed, with transports of joy, to Madame D'O——, her first lady of the bedchamber, a little portrait of the prince-royal, her son, which she had just received. It happened that this lady, some few days after, entered the queen's apartment at an unusual hour. She was surprised at hearing her majesty talk, though quite alone. While she stood in this attitude of astonishment, unable to retire, the queen turned suddenly round, and addressing herself to her, with that charming smile which she alone could preserve at a moment when her heart was torn with the most acute and agonising sensations,—'What must you think,' said she, 'of a circumstance so extraordinary as that of hearing me talk, though you find me perfectly alone? But it was to this dear and cherished image I addressed my conversation; and what do you imagine I said to it? nearly the same verses which you sent not long ago to a child, sensible to the happiness of having found her father.' Madame D'O—— could not speak; she burst into tears, and overcome with her own emotion, retired hastily from the royal presence."

Note 4, Page 292, Column 2.

As, gazing from a rampart's height,
Her eye might gather free delight.

The note on Cronenburgh Castle will explain the above allusion.

Note 5, Page 292, Column 2.

Or, musing, saw in verdant rest
The garden once by Hamlet prest.

This is the spot which Danish tradition assigns for the scene where Hamlet was poisoned. Of the character of Hamlet, which has occasioned so much critical theory, Goethe (Meister's Apprenticeship, p. 4, c. 13,) says:—

"It is clear to me that Shakspere's intention was to exhibit the effects of a great action, imposed as a duty on a mind too feeble for its accomplishment. In this sense I find the character consistent throughout. Here is an oak-tree, planted in a China vase, proper only to receive the most delicate flowers. The roots strike out, and the vessel flies to pieces. A pure, noble, highly moral disposition, but without that energy of soul which constitutes the hero, sinks under a load which it can neither support nor resolve to abandon altogether."

Dr. Farmer, in his argumentative essay on the learning of Shakspere, refers the origin of the plot in Hamlet, not to Saxo Grammaticus, but to the "Hystorie of Hamlet," from which he quotes the following applicable fragment:—

"It was not without cause and juste occasion that my gesture, countenance, and words seeme to proceed from a madman, and that I desire to have all men esteeme me wholly deprived of sence and reasonable understanding: bycause I am well assured that he that hath made no conscience to kill his owne brother will not spare to saue himselfe, with the like crueltie, in the blood and flesh of the loyns of his brother; and therefore it is better for me to feigne madnesse than to use my right senses as Nature hath bestowed them upon me. The bright shining clearnes thereof I am forced to hide vnder this shadow of dissimulation, as the sun doth his beams vnder some great cloud when the weather in summer time ouercasteth; the face of a madman serveth to couer my gallant countenance, and the gestures of a fool are fit for me, to the end that, guiding myself wisely therein, I may preserue my life for the Dane's . . . . Neuerthelesse, I must stay the time, meanes, and occasion, lest, by making ouer great haste, I be now the cause of mine own sodain ruine and overthrow; for, seeing by force that I cannot effect my desire, reason alloweth me, by dissimulation, subtilitie, and secret praises, to proceed therein."

Note 6, Page 298, Column 2.

And, while they scorn'd a hero's crown,
To woman give the heart's renown.

"Il est une sorte de supériorité, que les femmes doivent conserver sur nous, et qui tient même à leur foiblesse, un respect qu'elles inspirent. Elle est plus facile à sentir qu'à exprimer. Il en est une autre qui tient à la dignité de l'homme, que non seulement sa compagne reconnoit, mais qu'elle ne lui pardonne même pas de lui sacrifier."—*Les Femmes*, by Ségur.

The same author remarks elsewhere that—"If we review the conduct of women in every country, we shall be convinced that, without exercising any particular office, they have rendered as great a service as men."—As examples of great intrepidity, we may adduce the characters of Marguerite of Anjou, Marguerite of Bethune, (wife of the Duke of Rohan,) Theresa, Countess of Montford, &c.

Note 7, Page 299, Column 2.

Refinement's moral dawn awoke.

Dr. Miller, ("History Philosophically Illustrated," vol. i. pp. 17, 18,) after alluding to the character of "the tribes of ancient Germany who acted a part so important in the modern system," says that Tacitus, "disgusted with the vices of a decaying government, seems to have sought a refuge for his feelings in the contemplation of the uncorrupted simplicity of its barbarous neighbours, and to have described their manners with the same enthusiasm which is experienced by the inhabitant of a crowded city when he beholds freedom and nature in some rural retreat." Another distinguishing quality of the Germans was "*the reverence which they appear to have entertained for the female character*, neither degrading their women into slaves, like other barbarians, nor into objects of merely sensual gratification, like those who called themselves civilised. The German woman was the companion of her husband, participating his cares without servile drudgery, and influencing his actions with the gentle sway of respect and affection. The countenance belonging to this character formed the most obvious contrast with the corrupted manners of the empire."

Note 8, Page 300, Column 1.

Devotion in its grandest shape.

Vide Kenelm Digby's delightful work, entitled "The Broad Stone of Honour," whose pages breathe the fine air of chivalry, and whose examples of heroism conjoined with piety are exquisitely described.

Note 9, Page 300, Column 1.

E'en there apostles might have known
A faith whose firmness match'd their own.

"Even women amongst us have sustained the most cruel and unrighteous suffering, and finished in patient faith their cause, and received, notwithstanding the weakness of their sex, the prize of Christian heroines."—*St. Clement's Epist. to Corinth.*

For a truly sublime instance of female magnanimity, read the account of the martyrdom of Blandina, as recorded by Eusebius.

Note 10, Page 300, Column 1.

How much to female hands they owe
Their power to lessen human wo!

If it were only to please the imagination, the character of a devout lady is essential to complete the personages of the drama of the world. If the knights in the field were brave and faithful, the ladies in the castle gave alms to the poor, and prayed to God in their chapel. To go back still further; it was Placidia, daughter of Theodosius the Great, whose influence upon Adolphus secured his favour to the Romans. It was Prisca and Valeria, empress and daughter of Diocletian, who protected the Christians of that era. It was Clotilda who converted Clovis, the King of France, to the Christian faith; it was the Princess of Olga who introduced Christianity into Russia. The history of the middle ages, romances, family portraits, records of public foundations, everything that is venerable in antiquity, are associated with the piety of our English ancestors. Eleonora commanded that there should be no other inscription on her tomb than this:—

"Eleonora, pauvre pecheresse."

The great Maria Theresa was in the habit of attending service daily in the church of the Capuchins, and of visiting the vault which contains the coffins of her family. There is also at Vienna an Institution to which none but ladies of the highest nobility belong, for the purpose of superintending and promoting public charities. *In our United Kingdom there is not one useful religious or charitable institution which does not derive support from the influence and munificence, and even personal exertion, of the female nobility.* Let us hope, then, that the successor of Mr. Gibbon may repeat his remark, that "Christianity must acknowledge important obligations to female devotion."

Note 11, Page 302, Column 1.

The gloom of his remorseless fate.

"The memory of his injuries pursued him into the immensity of eternal light; and, in the company of saints and angels, his unforgiving spirit darkens at the name of Florence."—*Hallam.*

Note 12, Page 303, Column 1.

When dark-eyed beauty rack'd and wrung
A heart round which the world had clung.

Shakspere alludes to this unfortunate attachment in several of his sonnets.

Note 13, Page 304, Column 1.

The dream that wore his mind away.

See Contemporary Histories.

Note 14' Page 306, Column 1.

Oh! who can mark his mind's undress,
The agony of lone distress.

The dark bursts of pathos continually occurring in Burns's letters must be well known to all who have read his correspondence.

Note 15, Page 308, Column 1.

And in the mind's prophetic hour
Would try, with telescopic gaze,
To read the brow of unborn days.

It has been said by the greatest of metaphysicians (Aristotle) that we all possess by nature a—*μαντευμα τι*—a kind of mental divination. In his letters, Lord Byron continually alludes to "a fear of what is to come, a doubt of what *is*, a retrospect of the past, leading to a prognostication of the future." In one of his darkest moods he writes:—"My friends fall around me, and I shall be left a lonely tree before I am nipped. Other men can always take repose in their families. I have no resource but my own reflections, and they present no prospect, here or hereafter, except the selfish satisfaction of surviving my betters. I am indeed very wretched. My days are listless, and my nights restless. I have very seldom any society, and when I have I run out of it. I don't know that I sha'n't end it with insanity."

How often must his bruised heart have translated that saddest of all sentences!—

Μη φυναι—τον ἅπαντα νικᾳ λογον!

That NOT TO BE, alone is bliss!

SATAN:

OR,

INTELLECT WITHOUT GOD.

SATAN:

OR,

INTELLECT WITHOUT GOD.

PREFACE

TO THE FIFTH EDITION.

(1838.)

"Thou sealest up the sun, full of wisdom, and perfect in beauty. Thou hast been in Eden the garden of God—thou art the anointed cherub that covereth; and I have set thee so: thou wast upon the holy mountain of God; thou hast walked up and down in the midst of the stones of fire. Thou wast perfect in thy ways from the day that thou wast created till iniquity was found in thee."—*Ezekiel*, xxviii. 12, 13, 14, 15.

In acceding to the demand for a new edition of his Poems, the author regrets that pastoral avocations will not allow him to effect that complete revision which these works may yet seem to require. So far, however, as limited opportunity will allow, he trusts the more prominent deficiencies will be found removed; and casts the remaining imperfections on the candour and indulgence of those who read with a desire to be gratified, rather than become censorious.

Having, in the preface which accompanied the fourth edition of this poem, ventured some observations on the consistency of the character there intended to be developed, it is unnecessary to fatigue the attention of the reader with additional argument. After all, on a subject around which the Bible itself has thrown a sacred darkness, beyond the light of present faith, much less of mere reason, entirely to remove,—there is room for variety of judgment and differing views, without the rashness of caricaturing folly on the one hand, or the sternness of adamantine dogmatism on the other. Previously, however, to concluding these transient remarks, the writer may perhaps be permitted to observe, that the tendency of our Age is to sensualise almost every subject with which its energies come in contact. Hence, any form of literature, whether in prose or verse, which helps to withdraw the mind from what is material and earthly, and to centre its regards on what is spiritual and unseen,—may contribute to purify the heart, and refine its moral susceptibilities. Supremely ours may be called the Age of Facts. Expediency is our authenticated Moloch; and every effort of the mind must pass through his idolatrous fire, before it can venture to be recommended for public service. All this while, the foundation-truth, that *utility* itself is a relative thing, and therefore a pregnant term capable of almost boundless application, is practically forgotten. In pronouncing our verdict on what is useful or useless to man, how much would it tend to lift us out of the blinding materialism in which we are so content to grovel, if utility and eternity were conjoined in our sympathies and principles, and we looked less to the gratification of temporal desire, and more to those elements of character, which are now in actual formation, and which are destined to expand themselves in everlasting illustration. It is *this mortal* which is to put on immortality; the Now and the Hereafter of the conscious spirit are destined to act and re-act on each other with never-ending relationship.

But if a proneness to degrading utilitarianism confined its exhibition to the arena of what is merely human, we might hope to surmount it by the speedy return of nobler taste and loftier sentiment. But the case is otherwise. The passion for analytical science and mathematical demonstration, not content with endeavouring to unshroud the secrets of the material universe, and expose to the scrutinising gaze of philosophy the venerable mysteries of Nature, is proceeding to desecrate the God-founded temple of Revelation itself; and by a bound of infidelity to leap at once from the dim guesses and half-discovered facts of physical truth, to a full and fearless denial of the great principle of moral truth. Hence the phrenologist presumes to talk of the "*hypothesis* of the fall!" And death itself, which Christians, who live *in* the light, and *on* the truths of the Bible, have ever considered as the penal result of transgression,* is now discovered to be one of the *original* organic laws of the human being!

From those who thus reject mysteries of revelation, the bare mention of Satan as a real, personal, and intellectual Agent, provokes a withering smile. In their view, such a Being can only find existence in the benighted brain of a priest, or the dreaming fancy of a poet; and thus, resolving the most express, vivid, and appalling announcements of the Bible into mere accommodation of language to the craving infirmity of our human Idea, they expunge the personality of Satan from the creed of every man worthy the name of a "Philosopher."

Meanwhile, the humble Christian, "taught of God" to submit, though not to sacrifice, his reason; and convinced, moreover, that the developments of physical science can never conduct the mind into an acquaintance with those *moral* purposes of the Almighty which pertain to Him as the offended legislator of a guilty creation,—clings to his Bible with as much holy confidence as ever. With him simplicity is strength; and in all the acquiescing docility of childhood he receives every announcement of truth which descends from a region round the Throne, where clouds and darkness dwell, but where also righteousness and judgment have their seat. *His texts are his philosophy;* and from the secure eminence of scriptural light, he can look down with the undisturbed eye of faith, and behold the storms of infidelity contending harmlessly at his feet.

> "His hand the good man fastens on the skies,
> And bids earth roll, nor feels her idle whirl."
>
> *Young.*

GLASGOW, *Nov. 12th*, 1838.

* "As by one man sin entered into the world, and death by sin; and so death passed upon all men."—*Rom.* v. 12.

PREFACE

TO THE FOURTH EDITION.

(1834.)

AMONG the high Mysteries which Scripture reveals, there is one which relates to the existence of a ruined Archangel; and the faint but awful notices which are imparted to us of his character and agency, are calculated to awaken the sublimest feelings of poetry. He withered the glory of paradise, and helped to darken the bright image of The Eternal in the soul of man. Our holy faith, also, teaches us to believe that he conditions the world by an invisible sway, and that till the dread consummation of men and things, this terrible Being is permitted, more or less, to reign as the "Prince of the Powers of the air."

There have been two ways in which the character of Satan has been illustrated:—as the active Antagonist of the Almighty, braving the thunders and lightnings of Jehovah, and seeking to avenge his exile from heaven in the "first disobedience" of created man; or as a dark Visiter from below, holding sarcastic colloquy and mysterious intercourse with the children of Earth. In the first light, the genius of Milton has portrayed him, and thereby achieved the grandest Epic which Poetry can boast; in the second, Goëthe's "Faust," and Lord Byron's dramatic "Mystery," introduce him as the Hero of their verse.

There remains another view in which a spiritual agent, like Satan, may be contemplated, —as reflecting on himself, his destiny, and deeds. Let the existence of Satan be granted, and there will appear no inconsistency in conceiving his monodramatic character to be such as the author has endeavoured to describe; not a caricature of monsters, nor the long-tailed spectre of nursery romance, but an intellectual Being who hates the good, but must, from his very nature, admire it. The eternal difference of things abides alike in heaven and hell; and to imagine a fallen archangel incapable of *whispering unto himself* his own perceptions of right and wrong, or of appreciating what is sublime, beautiful and fair, both in the moral and physical world, is neither a consistent nor religious view of the Truth. Though he is a Devil now, we should remember that he has been an Archangel once. To imagine him a Spirit who *loves* the good, would be absurd; but to describe him as one who *understands* it, harmonises both with reason and revelation.*

* The late Rev. S. Drew, the author of a sublime work on "The Immortality of the Soul," in his review of this poem, introduced the following pertinent remarks:—

"There can be no question that his infernal majesty may be exhibited in a variety of attitudes. Cloven feet, a long tail, and a frightful pair of horns, are not essential to the fidelity of the representation. He may transfer himself into an angel of light, visit the pulpit, the senate, or the bar, or admire the paintings at Somerset House, without displaying those terrific appendages to which fanatical superstition has given a monstrous birth. There are not many positions in which he can be placed, that will be wholly inconsistent with his real character. Satan is the only personage who either meditates or speaks. It (the poem) is a long soliloquy, which proceeds from beginning to end, without any interruption, containing observations on historical incidents, on passing occurrences, and on events which are as yet embosomed in futurity. To the dark workings of the infernal mind, no one is supposed to be privy; the poet has therefore a fair opportunity of representing Satan under the influence of feelings, and as uttering expressions which he can have no inducement to disguise. Thus circumstanced, we feel no astonishment that he should bear his testimony to the truths of Revelation, and half regret the miseries, as well as triumph, over the degraded condition of human nature.

Many of the strictures bestowed on the peculiar nature of this poem might have been avoided, if the author's aim had been more candidly reviewed. Satan, as the tempter of man, and as a reflecting spirit in relation to himself,—is a distinct character. The former we conceive to be the machinator of all that is evil; the latter we may suppose to look back, ever and anon, on visions of departed glory; and, as he watches the stream of time rolling into eternity, to believe and tremble!

. . . . . . diri conscia facti
Mens habet attonitos, et surdo verbere cædit,
Occultum quatiente animo tortore flagellum.*

"If 'the keen, keen vibration of bright truth be hell,' we may well allow Satan in solitude to become a genuine moralist, and even a preacher of righteousness, when there is no hearer to be benefitted by his discourse. In much of this character the poet represents him to our view."

To this discriminating review, the author begs to append another, from the pen of the lamented and accomplished Dr. Cooke Taylor, of Dublin. It appeared originally in an Irish periodical. His critical eulogies on the poem are, of course, omitted; and the extract is confined to Dr. Taylor's contemplations of the Evil Being, considered as a moral tempter in relation unto mankind:—

"The nature of Superior Intelligences must for ever remain a secret which the limited faculties of man cannot discover; but this very uncertainty more forcibly recommends them to the poet, since he is supplied with creatures possessing certain feelings with which men can sympathise, and yet so far raised above human nature as to render credible the 'speciosa miracula rerum' with which imagination invests their character and actions. That an Immortal Being, possessed of powers beyond conception, dared to rebel against the Omnipotent, that he hurled defiance at the 'Most Highest,' that he was punished by an eternity of anguish, but that sufferings have left unchanged his pride of soul—these are matters which, detailed in plain prose, fill the mind with that indistinct awe which is the very essence of sublimity. To embody these thoughts, to arrest the flitting dreams of power, grandeur, and feeling, which hurry through the soul, is the office of the poet—he giveth to these airy nothings 'a local habitation and a name.' But few are those who dare to venture on the delineation of superhuman energies,—there is danger in every step of their progress; genius shrinks from the encounter until it has mustered up all its energies, and concentrated all its vigour.

"The embodied principle of evil has been already made the subject of immortal verse by Milton and Byron; the Satan of the one and the Lucifer of the other are at bottom the same character, but, being described in different relations, assume a different aspect. The Satan of Milton is described in all the energies of rebellious ambition—a proud intelligence combating with the Almighty for the dominion of the universe. The Lucifer of Byron has given up the contest, and has substituted fraudful cunning for the 'pride, pomp, and circumstance of glorious war.' The former describes the relation of the Evil Being to Deity,—the latter, his relation to man. Another yet remained;—neither of these poets had described the relation of such a being to himself, and endeavoured to unfold the thoughts, the speculations, the intellectual. workings of a fallen spirit. There was in another respect also a gap in the poetical character of Satan—the time chosen by Milton was when the world had first started into life and beauty; the time selected by Byron was when sin and sorrow were just beginning to blight its moral loveliness; the period when ages had rolled over the history of the human race—when guilty passions and ferocious desires had written the annals of crime with indelible characters on the face of nature—when nations, and not individuals, were the subjects of the demon's observation, had been left untouched.

"This hitherto untouched field has now been occupied by Mr. Montgomery, in his poem of 'Satan:' he has chosen the present hour as the time in which the proud competitor for the dominion of the universe should revisit the earth and survey all its extremes of ennobling virtue and debasing crime; he has portrayed the thoughts of mingled scorn, sorrow, envy, and the maddening sense of degradation which such a spirit may be supposed to have felt from the view of such a spectacle. The world is shown to us as it may have appeared in his reflections, and the inmost workings of his soul are delineated with an intensity —with almost a profusion of power, rare at all times, and never more rare than in the present day.

* * * * * *

"The subject chosen by Mr. M. required much abstraction, much condensation of thought; it must, consequently, be read slowly and with care. To sum up the character in one word, the reader will find this a purely intellectual poem, in which the universe of matter is made subservient to the development of the universe of mind.

"A very foolish notion seems to prevail in the world, that Satan must possess a mind in which evil is constantly looked upon as good: this arises from the mistake of supposing that the object at which he aims in his fallen state is that which he believes would in any state have been the best; but it is perfectly absurd to imagine that the innate excellence and beauty of virtue could be hidden from any Superior Intelligence. The curse pronounced on the disappointed demons more probably included the bitter punishment which Persius prays may be inflicted on tyrants—

'Virtutem videant intabescantque relicta.'

Accordingly, we find Satan a very equitable judge of human nature—indeed, it would be hard to assign a reason why he should be a liar to himself—and yet there have been people who deem it inconsistent with demoniac nature that Satan should even whisper to himself his perceptions of moral loveliness, his contempt for the sensual slaves who are dragged bound to his chariot-wheels. They forget that 'the devils believe and tremble,' and that the greatest triumph of Milton's genius is when he describes Satan in the full consciousness of all he had lost, subduing by innate energies the intense agonies of hopeless despair. It is the fidelity with which Mr. M. has preserved in Satan the wisdom of his former high estate amid all the degradation of present misery, that gives the principal charm to his poem. Utterly depraved as a moral agent, Satan still maintains the dignity of superhuman intellect: though a devil, he is still an archangel."

* Juv. Sat. 13.

Briefly, then, let the writer be allowed to state the design of his work;—it is, to embody in a poetical form, the reflections of the dark Enemy of souls, while viewing the effect of his temptations on the world of Nature, and the world of Mind. As a Tempter, he must perceive the majesty of virtue, the power of beauty, and examine all the philosophy of religion and morals. Man, as the supposed heir to some of his lost glory, is not only hateful, but interesting to him; and therefore the magnificent scheme of his Redemption by Incarnate Deity excites his wonder, awe, and dread. Being the "god of this world," nothing which developes the character of the human soul can remain unregarded. The whole universe of man, character, and circumstance, demand his deepest attention; genius, art, science, and literature, as connected with the ultimate state cf an everlasting mind,—all are summoned before the eye of contemplation. Let the reader, then, distinguish between the character of Satan reflecting on himself, and when tempting man, and nothing will be found inconsistent, or improbable, in the doctrinal aspects of this poem. Admiration and hate often co-exist; and if Milton could make his sublime hero "sigh," * what may the Evil One not be conjectured to feel now! He was once the innocent Adorer of The Supreme; and as all that is glorious in creation, and divine in the soul, is a faint reflection of the Great Archetype of all,—he cannot but *admire* what is admirable, by virtue of his primeval nature; though he *detest* the dominion of the same over our hearts and affections.†

Hence, the warning lesson which is here attempted to be enforced, is one of the profoundest which can be impressed on the contemplative mind: namely,—The highest intellectual refinement may be associated with the greatest moral debasement. Religion, philosophy, and experience,—all may be cited to confirm the awful truths which such an assertion involves. But divine Scripture abbreviates the whole subject, when it thus addresses the mystic Babylonian,—"Thy wisdom and thy knowledge hath perverted thee: and thou hast said in thine heart, 'I am, and none else beside me.'"—(*Isaiah* xlvii. 10.)

INTRODUCTORY NOTE.

(1853.)

In addition to those views of the Evil One, propounded in the preface, which introduced the earlier editions of this poem, it may be useful to append the following extract which touches on the theology of the subject. It is derived from a Christian Essay * of the author's, which is now out of print.

ON THE PERSONALTY AND AGENCY OF THE EVIL ONE.

No one, we presume, can take even a rapid and superficial glance at the writings and letters of Luther, without being struck with the bold prominence and uncompromising simplicity of statement with which the Reformer introduces his allusions to the Evil One. For instance,

* "Tears, such as angels weep, burst forth; at last
Words, interwove with sighs, found out their way." *Par. Lost*, book i.

† The metaphysical divine, Jonathan Edwards, in discussing the text which appears on the title-page of this work, among other doctrinal illustrations, has the following remarks, which it is presumed will be neither uninteresting nor inapplicable on the present occasion:—

"The devil, before his fall, was among those bright and glorious angels of heaven which are represented as morning-stars, and flames of fire that excel in strength and wisdom—and though he be now become sinful, yet his sin has not abolished the faculties of the angelic nature; as when man fell, he did not lose the faculties of the human nature. Sin destroys spiritual principles, but not the natural faculties."——"As the devil has a faculty of understanding of a large capacity, so is he capable of a great speculative knowledge of the things of God, and the invisible and eternal world, as well as other things. Before his fall, he was one of those angels who continually beheld the face of the Father in heaven: and sin has no tendency to destroy the memory, and therefore has no tendency to blot out of it any speculative knowledge that was formerly there."——"Thus the devil has undoubtedly a great degree of speculative knowledge in divinity; having been, as it were, educated in the best divinity school in the universe,—viz. the heaven of heavens. He must have a very great knowledge of God's works of providence. He has been a spectator of the series of these works from the beginning. He must have a great degree of knowledge concerning Jesus Christ as the Saviour of men, and the nature and method of the work of redemption, and the wonderful wisdom of God in this contrivance. It is that work of God wherein, above all others, God has acted in opposition to him, and in which he has chiefly set himself in opposition to God. He must have a great knowledge of the holy scriptures, for it is evident he is not hindered from knowing what is written there, by the use he made of the words of scripture in his temptation of our Saviour. He must have a great knowledge of the nature of mankind, their capacity, their dispositions, and corruptions of their hearts. And it is evident that he has a great speculative knowledge of the nature of experimental religion, by his being able to imitate it so artfully, and in such a manner as to transform himself into an angel of light."——"The devils have a great sense of the vast importance of the things of another world. They have a great sense of the worth of salvation, and the worth of immortal souls, and the vast importance of those things that concern man's eternal welfare."——"Devils have a strong and most affecting sense of the awful greatness and majesty of God." And "some kind of conviction and sense of all the attributes of God; both natural and moral, that is strong and very affecting."

* "Christ our All in All." 4th ed. Hatchard & Co., London.

in his Patmos, on hearing of the dissenting tumults and disorganising heresies of Carolstadt, he writes thus to his Royal defender :—"Other agents besides merely human are at work. Don't be afraid, but be prepared for more events of this sort. This is only the beginning of the business : *Satan intends to carry matters much further yet.* Believe me in what I now say ; I am but a plain, simple man ; *however I know something of the arts*," &c. Almost countless indeed are the references made by Luther to Satanic temptation, guile, and dominion over the hearts and purposes of evil men. And here it is that the majority of those who have written on Luther, have thought it right to say a great many soft things, and utter many apologetic tones about the dreaminess of the German mind, superstitions of a barbarous age, heats of imaginations, relics of popish darkness, &c. ; all of which, if concentrated into a moral result, seem to amount to this—that though Luther was indeed a brave man and a great one, yet in all his ideas and creed concerning the devil there is much to be lamented as savouring of that religious imbecility which borders on fanaticism and superstition. Now with all deference to these writers, the question may fairly be asked, whether, on the whole, Luther be not justified by Scripture, as to his principal doctrines concerning the agency of Satan in the affairs of this fallen Creation ? Let it be allowed (as indeed all sober Christians readily grant) that in his ideas of visible and personal Manifestation of the Evil One, the Reformer was under the illusion of an over-heated brain : yet when we are assured by the infallible Spirit of God, "for this purpose the Son of God was manifested, that He might destroy the Works of the Devil :" when we call to mind that Christ Himself was humanly placed in a perpetual antagonism with Satan, and warned a disciple that "Satan" had "desired" to have him, that he might sift him "like wheat ;" and finally, when we recollect the inspired teachings of one who in many respects (when regarded in his individual experience) resembled Luther, both before and after his conversion,—even those of St. Paul : when we do this, and look fairly and honestly in the face of the matter, few Christians who take their entire theology from the revelation of God and not from the reasoning of man,—will hesitate to admit that Luther is not an object of pity for his belief in the constant agency and actual personality of Satan. On the contrary, he will rather admire and reverence the glorious simplicity of a great Mind, which was enabled by divine grace to "watch and pray," that it entered not into temptation ; and which was deeply convinced that if the Master was tempted, and tried, and wrung by the Evil One, it was not to be doubted that his disciples should be subjected to an experience like his own.

And who will deny (except those who consider God's solemnities to be man's frivolities) that a penetrating conviction that Satan is no theological Abstraction conjured up from the depths of superstition ; but an actual, living, intellectual Person, moving to and fro among the hearts and homes of mankind, curtained with Immateriality,—who will deny that such a conviction received into the public mind, would operate with power upon Christian vigilance and warfare ? Surely it appertains to the infidelity of a professing Church, that while in Scripture we are perpetually warned to "resist the devil,"—in the common experience of mankind, Satan is allegorised away into a Nonentity ; while (as might be expected) the entire subject of Hell is smiled down by the sneer of the sceptic, as the imbecility of a childish mind, or the bugbear of a weak and womanish heart. Yet amid all this, the truth of God touching Satanic agency remains unshaken ; and albeit that agency be inexplicable in the mystery of its principle, it is highly practicable in the doctrine of its application. Still is it a scriptural revelation, that this Creation *is* the haunt of Devils, and especially tried and tempted by a vast and immitigable Adversary, moving inaudibly around us with a sleepless desire for the ruin of souls, acting on us through sensible media, and in us, by moral and mental delusion. And would to God the Devil were more preached, proclaimed, and all his infernal wiles more scripturally and faithfully set before the people ! Then would our Christianity become not a mere nominal distinction, but a felt contest ; and instead of coolly resolving the doctrines of St. Paul, when speaking of the Evil One, into a metaphor, we should realise their counterpart in our own experience, and pronounce them—description.

We need hardly say, that the wish to resolve the statements of the Bible concerning a Personal Satan into mere Orientalisms or poetical impersonations, is to be traced to the native dislike of the unrenewed heart to admit into its experience any principle that calls for "reasoning pride" to submit itself, and be dumb before God. But beyond this, no thoughtful watcher over the times can hesitate to allow that for the last twenty years the habits, literature, science, and philosophy of this country have been gravitating with a fearful impetus towards the adoption of a Sensual Heresy ; or towards the practical belief that the *Real is bounded by the Visible ;* and that no evidence which does not convince our materialism (in some mode or other) can be admitted by a truly philosophic mind. Thus the hands, and eyes, and ears are lifted into a more than logical dominion over the intellect ; and Faith, or "the evidence of things not seen," ceases to be retained in the canons of our world's orthodoxy. For much of this infidel carnality we are indebted to that heartless libel on all that is spiritual in taste and pure in feeling, Utilitarianism :—a system that concentrates within its grasp the elements of a most debasing grossness ; adapted only to a world peopled with bodies out of which the soul has been evaporated ; and which, if carried out in all the fearless enormity of its principles, would speedily transform the Empire into a mere national shop, and Creation into a huge warehouse. There is, however, one encouragement derived even from the cultivation of the Physical Sciences themselves—viz., that true philosophy cannot receive a single principle into its system, without authenticating the reality of the Invisible. For, after all, what are electricity, chemical affinity, galvanism, and gravitation, but the expressions of Something Unseen, of which all the visible phenomena of matter and sensitive life are only the tokens and significances? Physical Science, therefore, if consistently faithful to the law of analogy, cannot reject the statements of Scripture with reference either to the Deity or the Devil, on the simple ground of invisibility; inasmuch as science itself cannot exist without a belief in the viewless agency of some Master Principle.

BOOK I.

"Earth's kingdoms and their glory."
Milton.

Awake, ye thunders!—and with gloomy roar
Deepen around me, while a darkness shrouds
The air, as once again this World I greet
Here on the haughty mountain, where of old
The God Incarnate, in the heavens re-throned,
Was tempted and withstood me.
Lo! the powers
Of Nature, by my dread command sublimed,
Mount into rage, and magnify the storm
To elemental grandeur; while as Prince
By whom the spirit-peopled air is bound
In bondage, from my viewless throne I gaze,
Prompting the Tempest; whose convulsive swell
Heaves like the echo of my spirit's war,
The moral earthquake that makes hell within!
Hark! to the crash of riven forest-boughs
In yonder waste, the home of Hurricanes,
That catch the howlings of the cavern'd brutes
And waft them onwards to Arabia's wild,
O'ercanopied with flying waves of sand
Like a dread ocean whirling through the skies.
But Thou alone, eternally sublime,
Thou rolling mystery of might and power!
Rocking the tempest on thy breast of waves
Or, spread in breezy rapture to the sun,
Thou daring Ocean! that couldst deluge worlds
And yet rush on,—I hear thy deep-toned wrath
In ceaseless thunder challenging the Winds
Resoundingly; and from afar behold
Thine armied billows, plunging in the blast,
And the wild sea-foam shiver on the gales!
Exult, ye waves! and, whirlwinds! sweep along
Like the full breathings of almighty ire,
Whose sound is desolation! Where the sail
Of yon lone vessel, like a shatter'd cloud,
Is moving, let the surges mount on high
Their huge magnificence, and lift their heads,
And like Titanic creatures tempest-born,
In life and fury march upon the main!
Rave on, thou Tempest! in thy fiercest roar;
To me thy reckless mood is fearful joy;
A faint memento of that direful scene
When proud rebellion shook the walls of heaven,
Till, girt with thunder, dread Messiah came,
And hurl'd us downward to the deep of hell.

The Tempest dies; the winds have tamed their ire;
The sea-birds hover on enchanted wing;
And save a throb of thunder, faintly heard,
And ebbing knell-like o'er yon western deep
Which now lies panting with a weary swell
Like a worn monster at his giant length
Gasping, with foam upon his troubled mane,—
The sounds of elemental wrath retire.
The Sun is up! look, where He proudly comes
In blazing triumph wheeling o'er the earth,
A victor in full glory! At his gaze
The heavens as with emotion smile, and beam
With many a sailing cloud-isle sprinkled o'er;
While forest-woodlands and enliven'd flowers
The central monarch of the skies salute.
Now hills are gleaming; rich the mountains glow;
The streams run gladness, yellow meads appear,
And palm-woods glitter on Judæan plains;
Beauty and brightness shed their soul abroad:—
Then let me, whom no mortal space can bound,
The Earth survey, and mark her mighty realms.

Why, what a stately Orb is this! how wide
In range! how wonderful in scene! the grace
And crown—the paragon of worlds!
And Thou, for whom all elements exist,
A second nature from thy soul hath sprung,
And made wide earth a new creation seem!

Deserted isles, with oceanic wastes,
Heaving and wild, monotonous and vast;
Terrific mountains, where the fire-floods dwell,
Or snows in iced eternity congeal;
And haggard rocks uplifted, huge, or bare,
The hoary frame-work of a ruin'd world:
And rivers deep, exulting as they glide,

And forests high, and dales by woods o'erhung,
With meadows greenly bright, and champaigns broad;
And flowers, whose beauty blush'd in Paradise,
By streams that murmur of their mountain-birth;
With high-domed cities, crown'd with misty clouds,
And shadow'd interchange of hamlets lone
Which deck the verdure of retreating vales,—
Before me, like a panorama, spread;
Far as the ice-clad North hath bared its brow,
To where the burning South extends, from East
To West this theatre of man I view.

Jerusalem, forlorn Judæan Queen!
Girt with the grandeur of prophetic hills,
How art thou fallen from thy sacred height
Of splendour and renown! Unhallow'd now,
Save by the tombs and memory of the past;
Hush'd are thy Trumpets, which enrapt the air
With Jubilee,* when Freedom burst the chain
Of captives, heart with heart embraced, and eye
To eye beam'd fellowship; while not an ear
But feasted on that soul-awakening sound!
Thy Temple vast, whose architect was God
Himself, when first the giant fabric grew,
That matchless Pile! on which Religion gazed
With haughty glance, where Glory dwelt enshrined;—
Where is it now? Dead as the Roman dust,
That erst, with living valour fired, uncrown'd
Thy queenly pride, and palsied thy vast walls,
Strewing the plains with atoms of thy strength.
And yet, where yonder marbled courts, and mosques
With sun-gilt minarets, like glitt'ring peaks
Of mountain-tops, are seen, a Prophet stood,
And in stern vision saw predestined Time
Advancing, with dark ruin on his wings,
To shatter thee, and sprinkle the wide earth
With orphans of thy race. How scornful rang
Thy laughter, when such vision was unroll'd!
But when thy rocks were echoed with the cry
Of Desolation, moaning her despair,
Many a Demon on the viewless winds
Exulted, shouting, with revengeful joy,
"Thus sink the glories of great Palestine!"

Alas, for human Grandeur! in the pomp
Of Temples, and the stony Wonders, rear'd
In rebel majesty against the might
Of ages, let Ambition learn her doom.
Bagdad, o'er famed Chaldea proudly raised
In tow'ring splendour by the Tigris' banks;

* The Jubilee was proclaimed by the sound of a trumpet throughout the whole land.—*Jenning's Jewish Antiquities.*

And hoary Smyrna of Mæonic fame,
All beautiful in ruins, where the fruits
And flowers yet flourish o'er deserted Art
And laughing streamlets run with liquid joy;
With Tyre and Sidon, where rich Commerce ruled
Showering her treasures o'er the sunny East;
And gay Damascus, whose delicious plains
Of verdure, striped with water's radiant flow,
Shine green as ever,—in your wrinkled piles
Are lessons for the loftiest eyes to read,
That mark ye now, and dream of vanish'd might
When merchants rivall'd Kings! But far o'er all,
Where yonder mountain mingles with the plain
Of billowy sand, gigantic, dread, and lone,
Great Heliopolis in ruin mourns.
And next, yon ancient desert-Queen behold,
The blasted Genius of the wilderness,
Palmyra! pillar'd yet in temple-pride,
Decayless arches show past glory still;
But wither'd down from her Zenobian pomp
When there the sun-idolatries were seen
And Grandeur call'd the streets her own,—but now,
Let Solomon arise, and read her fate!

But, sadder yet, beyond the Libyan wild
Sepulchral Egypt lies! Come royal heirs
Of Ptolemy, and patriarchal kings,
And see the shadow of your once sublime
And storied Egypt! True, her fostering Nile,
That flowing wand'rer of mysterious birth,
Her annual life-flood generously yields;
But where the soul of Science? where the fount
Of Wisdom, from whose deep and dateless spring
The Greek and Roman drank? Colossal Thebes,
How grimly sleep thy ruins! where of yore,
Like billows trooping at the whirlwind's call
Forth from thy hundred gates the battle-cars
Out-roll'd! Thy tombs and arches, Temples huge
As sculptured mountains, darkling yet remain,
But sadness broods o'er all. And ye august,
In blighted majesty of stone uprear'd,
Stern Pyramids! which point your heads to heaven
As pillars that could prop the spheres, a day
Is coming when ye moulder into dust,[1]
And melt like dew-dops by the wind annull'd!

So sink the monuments of ancient might,
So fade the gauds and splendours of the World.
Her empires brighten, blaze, and pass away,
And trophied Fanes, and adamantine Walls

Which challenged an eternity, depart
Amid the dying change, or lapse of things:
Enthroned o'er all, bleak Desolation frowns,
Save mind—omnipotent, surpassing Mind!
One scintillation of the soul inspired
Though kindled in an atmosphere of gloom
Or loneliness, will strengthen, glow, and live,
And burn from age to age, till it become
The sun and glory of a thinking world
When thrones are shatter'd, and their kings forgot!

The revolution and the wrath of Time,
Rolling his years with an avenging flow
Alike o'er all, hath been a thread-worn theme
Which tunes the sentiment of many an Age.
And thus, the musing lover of the past,
Romancing idly o'er the name of time,
Untombing empires, and re-crowning kings,
In sighing wonder ends his moral strain!
Thou fool! and martyr to a feeble word;
'Tis Thought and Action, those unslumb'ring two,
Which give to time solemnity and dread;
And he who marks mere havoc, not the war
Of passion, and inclining will, but prates
And lulls his moral in a dream of words.

Let him who muses on the awful wreck
Of Empires, wailing in the dust, and thrones
Reversed, or cities in their ruin vast,
Here History and her inspirations dwell,
Dive deeper, till he stretch a thought to *Me!*
Ere man was fashion'd from his fellow dust,
I was!—and since the sound of human voice
First trembled on the air, my darksome power
Hath compass'd him in mystery, and in might;
Upon the soul of sage Philosophy
And Wisdom, templed in the shrines of old,
Faint shadows of my Being fell;[2] a sense
Of me thus deepen'd through the onward flood
Of ages, till substantial thought it grew,
A certainty sublime, in that great soul,
The epic-god of ancient song, who down
The infinite abyss could dare to gaze,
And summon forth the imagery of Hell.

And in that Book, where heaven lies half reveal'd,
By words terrific as the herald-flash
That hints the lightning-vengeance of a storm,
Am *I* not vision'd? as the Prince of Air,
A Spirit that would crush the universe,
And battle with Infinity? Yet Truth,
So unrelenting in her solemn task,
A chilling welcome in the eyes of men
Hath found, denying what they dread to feel.
Kind Infidel! satanic praise accept;
Friend of the guilty, solace of the vile,
And teacher of the vain, mankind instruct
And make one world, my own. Oh, few believe
When condemnation awes the spirit back!
Save hearts, where all simplicities of faith
Abound, and warn each hell-born doubt away
Or men, self-tortured, who at midnight dream
Of oceans foaming with eternal fires,
Or ghastly air-fiends, writhing as they howl,—
Save unto these, and souls of kindred hue,
The Powers of Darkness are a cheat of words,
Framed by a Priest to juggle fools. Alas!
Yet oft they frown upon the mocker's path
And feel they *could*, did Nature not prevail,
Burst into life, and blast him with a gaze!

"What understanding cannot grasp, belief
Can never claim,"—a wisdom most divine!
Why, all around him, from the race of flowers
That woo his unadmiring gaze, to hosts
Of orbèd wonders which the sky pervade,
Is Mystery, robed in some material pomp;
Then why should mysteries of awe within,
Themselves resolve to charm a sceptic mind?
Religion acts, but unexplain'd abides;—
The beatings of the heart resemble this,
And men may wonder, but it still beats on!

But when the balance of sublunar Things
Is tried, amended, and for ever fix'd,
Belief for unbelief shall then atone
By sad conviction:—then shall it be proved,
The Sin that violated and deform'd
This World, and all true harmonies profaned,
(In dread similitude to mind o'erthrown)
Hath been the evil which my power hath fed,
By dark communion with this mortal Scene.
No! not a havoc Nature's kingdom feels;
No sound of Ocean when her wings rise plumed
With wrath; no frenzy of the tragic winds,
Those viewless pirates whom the pathless seas
Endure,—no terror in the darkest reign
Of Elements that lord it so sublime,
But images that dreadful curse I reap'd
For Nature and for Man! And ye, dead Climes!
Where high of old my bloody Altars blazed,
Where oracles from cave or temple breathed,
And Monsters, vision'd out of monstrous thought,
With stock and stone idolatries, were bred,
My hand was on ye, and your heathen soul!
And now, Ambition trampling out the heart
Of earth; the demi-gods of false renown;
And all the giants of heroic crime,
Are demons of my will; and by their doom
Shall testify the Genius whence they spring!

Might vanish'd ages be renew'd, and built
Again those daring Empires once renown'd,
From that huge one the haughty Ninus rear'd
And great Cambyses crush'd, to Rome and Greece
Of commonwealths the glory,—what a scene
Would time reveal! Who bow'd them into gloom?
They fear'd me not; but from the primal stone
Which mark'd the birthday of their city-queens
I mingled with them, and beheld them rise:
From dim obscurity my minions watch'd
Their growth to greatness, and imperial sway,
That over-shadow'd the far Isles. The Sea
Beneath them, like a suppliant crouch'd; the Winds
Sang victory! where exulting banners waved;
But now, uplifted to a fearful height,
They courted vilely-enervating Arts,
Unthroned the Virtues, let the Passions loose,
And pour'd corruption through their rank domain:
Then came the Nemesis!—that moral Curse
Whose ruin more than desolation brings.

But see, where Persia's beauteous clime extends,
How gloriously diluvian Ararat
Hath pinnacled his rocky peak in clouds!
Who thrones a winter on his heights untrod,
While summer laughs in roses at his feet!
Time cannot mar his glory: high he swells
As when that Ark was balanced on his brow,
Which saw the raging of the far-off floods
Beneath, and heard the Deluge die away!

But here, as in her day of olden might,
Ascendant Nature proves the God of souls
Who deify mere elements, and dream
Them symbols of their Maker. On the peak
Of mountains, the Chaldean hail'd the Sun
In the rich brightness of its morning-birth,
And bow'd his forehead to the flaming East;
The Night, ennobled with her stars, pour'd love
And worship into hearts, that from the fields
Beheld their throbbing radiance, as the face
Of Prophets, bright with their intelligence:—
And still upon the Gueber's fateful eye
The Fire darts gleaming magic; and his mind
Through nature darkly struggles on to God.*

A mightier scene upon the map of earth!—
Forests immense, and pine-wastes fiercely wild,
And ice-rocks, rear'd upon a dead-white sea,

* See Herodotus, Gibbon, &c. &c.

Far to the north where hoary deserts gleam
Dawn on my view in all their Arctic gloom.
But not Siberia, desolate and grand,
Nor Dneiper, thunder'd on by cataracts
That whiten o'er her howling waves, appear
So wondrous, as those battle-hosts that rush
Like rivers swelling from their deep abodes,
Precipitately o'er the regions round.
A King hath spoken! and the trump of War
Hath sounded like a herald through the land,
"Awake! great Peter is alive again."

A word of Kings, what potency it wields!
These delegates of God, yea, gods themselves,
Upon whose lips the fate of Empire hangs,
Tremendous is their charge: one speaks, and lo!
Up springs infernal War, and stalks abroad,
Unrolls his blood-red banner on the wind,
And in the groan of widow'd Nations hails
The music of his fame! Another speaks,
And Peace, with olive in her radiant hand,
Glides like an angel through the world, and prints
A trace of blessing wheresoe'er she treads.

And who could ponder on this war-doom'd scene,
Nor dream thy shadow swelling into life,
Napoleon! On the island-rock thou sleep'st;
But such a storm thy spirit raised, so full
The swell of feeling born of thee, that Time
Must lend his magic to allay the strife
And tempest of opinion into truth,
Which, taming wonder, stamps thee, as thou wert,
A tyrant![3] in whose passion for a power,
Above all liberty and law enthroned,
I hail, thee as a Paramount; thy pride
Of domination tow'ring far o'er heights
Of monarchy,—a shadow of mine own,
Which scorn'd an equal though He proved a God!

And therefore did I crown thee, Kingly One!
And those who worship thee, my thanks inspire!
Mean crimes are branded with avenging scorn,
While *great* ones, that should water earth with tears,
Can dazzle condemnation into praise,
And praise to pity, when false greatness fails!
The throneless, in the heart a throne acquires,
And Admiration in one sigh can drown
The wail of millions, haunting each red field
Of havoc, where some Desolator trod!

The wish is hated, but the deed caress'd,
Of mad Ambition; "glory" heals all wounds!

Yet, what a cloud on Liberty was thrown!
How deep a gash her dreadless form profaned,
When thine ambition march'd upon the world,
Till Europe quail'd beneath thy scepter'd arm!
Then, crumbled hopes which centuries will not build
Again; then god-like spirits felt a pang
That now, when canonading battles pause,
And Peace sits musing on the tomb of War,
Is felt,—an agony too deep for words
To fathom, too sublime for slaves to feel!

Lo! where the Tyrant felt a flood of wrath
From Heaven pour'd down upon his guilty head,
And first he knew himself a Man!—Yon spires
With golden pinnacles that pierce the clouds,
And river, winding by those pallid walls,
Proclaim where unforgotten Moscow stands:
There raged a scene* which ruin'd angels love
To witness, when the vaunting sons of Clay
Grow demon-like, and shudd'ring Time beholds
The fellest misery Despair can feel!
As when, all wildly through the unbarr'd gates
Like savage war-fiends his marauders swept,
And saw the city billow'd into flames,
Like some far ocean blazing through the storm!
Then Havoc started with a thrilling shout;
The shriek of violated maids, the curse
Of dying mothers, and despairing sires,
And dash of corpses, torn from royal tombs
And plunged amid devouring flames, were heard
Till hell in miniature wild Moscow seem'd.

But who, when Rapine could not pillage more,
While cannon-thunder chased the daunted winds,
Paused on a desert-heath, in speechless ire,
And mark'd the remnant of a ruin'd host
Flying, and pale as phantoms of Despair?
Napoleon! in the earthquake of thy soul,
The elements were reaping vengeance then!
While slaughter turn'd the tide of victory
And roll'd it back upon thy powerless host
Of famish'd warriors, freezing as they died!
That hour of agony, the crushing sense
Of danger and defeat, the broken spell
Which blasted all thy triumphs into shame,
Sublimed thy spirit with so proud a pang
It long'd to swell into a million souls,
And shake the universe to save a throne!

Thy race is o'er: and in the rocky isle
Of ocean, canopied with willow-shade,
In death's undreaming calm thou restest now.
But all the splendid infamy of War,
The fame of blood and bravery, is thine:
Thy name hath havoc in its sound! and Time
Shall read it when his ages roll:—'twill live
When time and nature are forgotten words!
For, as a noble fame can never die
But proudly soareth on from earth to heaven,
There to be hymn'd by Angels, and to crown
With bright pre-eminence the gifted mind
That won it gloriously; so evil fame
A fiery torment to the soul shall be
For ever:—let Ambition think of this!
Who murders kings, to make her heroes, gods.

In contrast wilder than the rude-faced globe,
Appear the workings of immortal mind.
Russia, through each great limb of empire, feels
Proud animation play; a panting wish
For high dominion, and sublimer rule
Than Nature's rugged vastness yields. But Thou,—
Of immemorial birth, whose massy wall
Of ages, with her thousand war-towers flank'd,
Majestic winds o'er many a savage hill
And mountain, China! thou art motionless,
Or like the Dead Sea, sullenly reposed
Amid the surging restlessness of Time.
Those burden'd waters, whereon breed and die
Thy generations; fancy-mountains, graced
With temples; or pagodas gaily deck'd,
And artful wonders, by the hand or tongue
Completed,—such are glories form'd for *thine*
Ascendancy! Thus bulwark'd in with pride
And baseness, virtues, arts, and vices act
From year to year, unchallenged and unchanged.
Antiquity, the childhood of the world,
Broods like a torpid vapour o'er thy clime,
And dulls its vigour into drowsy calm;
So let it sleep! till Revolution wake,
And summon spirits who shall cry,—Reform!

Lo! in the East, enormously uprear'd,
What ice-peak'd mountains point their roseate heads
Amid the richness of an Indian sky,
Soundless and solemn as cathedral-towers
Made dim and spectral by the wintry moon!
Hills of the North! not all your Greenland-pomp
Can more sublimely scale the clouds. And where
Bright Ganga! mountain-born, careers the flood
That matches thee? The vassal rivers mix

* See Relat. Comp. de la Campagne de Russie, en 1812; par E. Labaume. Paris, 8vo. Ségur, &c.

Their spirit with thine own; the rock-hewn caves
Shake as they hear thee sounding through their depths,
Then, upward springing with a glorious swell
And brightness on thy waves, to course green plain
And valley, like a charger in his pride
Let loose to lord it o'er surrounding meads!
Monarch of rivers! thy redeeming flow
Is life and beauty to the sun-brown lands
That border thy rich banks; but on thy stream
How Superstition glasses her dull creed!
Religion!—why, the undiscerning brute
Hath more divinity than vaunting slaves
Who, spirit-darken'd, oft blaspheme Her name:
For sun and shower by *him* are not unthank'd.
He bathes his forehead in the fresh'ning gale,
And, by enjoyment, pays the gift of life.
But how is reason carnalised and crush'd
When hell-rites are religion!—while it chants
Of mercy in the ways of heaven revealed
Can offer female holocausts to Hell
In burning widows, gasping forth their souls,
Or drowning babes, for sacrifice to God!
Oh, Wisdom! never thou the heart redeem,
Nor cast the cloud from Superstition's eye!

Another gaze, bright Hindostanic clime!
How beautifully wild, with horn-wreath'd heads,
Thy antelopes abound; and, thick as clouds
Paving the pathway of the western heav'n,
On wings enamell'd with a radiant dye
Thy birds expand their plumage to the breeze,
And glitter through air! Primeval woods,
And patriarchal trees, and forest-haunts,
And deserts spotted with their verdant isles,
And fruits, with showers of sunbeams on their heads,
Grow mingled there in magical excess;
The grand and beautiful, their glowing spell
Combine; Creation makes one mighty charm.

But let it pass: again the voice of waves!
Faint as the rush of rapid spirit-wings;
An Ocean, dreadful to the gazing eye
As dark eternity to human thought,—
Atlantic! where the whirlwinds are the scoff
Of billows, rocking with eternal roar,
Thou art a wonder e'en to me, whose eyes
Have fathom'd Chaos!
Thou astounding Main!
Time never felt so awful since his birth,
Angels and demons o'er thy terrors hung,
As when by hope prophetically wise,
On thine immensity Columbus launch'd.
Yet thou wert well avenged! for Storm and Doubt,
Despair and Madness on the billows rode,
And made deep Ocean one dark agony!—
Dismal as thunder-clouds, the fated hours
Toil'd on; a living solitude still howl'd
And heaved, in dread monotony around;
Yet hope was quenchless; and when daylight closed,
The ocean-wanderers, in the placid glow
Of sunset, soothing their despondent brows,
Hymn'd o'er the mellow wave their vesper-song;
Ave Maria! mingling with the choirs
Of billows, and the chant of evening-winds.

But he was destined! and his lightning-glance
Shot o'er the deep, and darted on thy world
America!—Then, lofty, long, and loud
From swelling hearts the hallelujahs rang,
And charm'd to music the Atlantic gales;
While, silent as the Sun above him throned,
Columbus *look'd* a rapture to the heavens
And gave his glory to the God they serve!

Thou fated Region of the varied globe
Where all the climates dwell, and Seasons rule
In majesty, hereafter when the tides
Of Circumstance have roll'd through changing years,
What Empires may be born of Thee!—thy ships
By thousands, voyaging the isle-strewn deep;
Thy banners waved in every land! E'en now
Defiance flashes from thy fearless eye,
While Nature tells thee greatness is thine own.—
Who on those dreadful giants of the South,
Those Pyramids by man's Creator rear'd,
Thine Andes, girdled with the storms, can gaze;
Or hear Niagara's unearthly flood
Rival the thunder with impassion'd roar,
Nor think the spirit of ambition rules
Thy moral nature. What a grandeur lives
Through each stern scene!—in yon Canadian woods,
Whose stately poplars clothe their heads with clouds,
And dignify creation as they stand;
Or in the rain-floods,—rivers where they fall!
Or hurricanes, which howl themselves along,
Like fierce-wing'd monsters, ravenously wild:—
Sublimity o'er all a soul hath breathed,
And yet my ban is on thee!—'tis the curse
Of havoc,[4] which the violators reap'd
For thy young destiny, when first amid
Thy wilds the cannon pour'd its thund'ring awe,
Shaking the trees which never yet had bow'd,
Save to the storminess of nature's ire.

Hath Gentleness thy guilt of old redeem'd?
Hath freedom heal'd the wounds of war, and paid
Her ransom to the nameless and unknown,
The unremember'd, but immortal still,
The Dead, whose birthright was sublime as kings'?
Approach, and answer me, dejected One!
Art *thou* the remnant of a free-born race,
Majestic lords of nature's majesty?
Of them, whose brows were bold as heaven, whose hands
Have tamed the woods, whose feet outfled the winds,
Who faced the lightning with undazzled gaze
And dream'd the thunder language of their god:
The earth and sky, 'twas Freedom's and their own!
But *thou*—the Sun hath written on thee, Slave![5]
A branded limb and a degraded mind
The tyrants give thee for infernal toil
And tears; or lash thy labour out in blood.

And *some* are Saxons, who enslave the free;
Then boast not, England! while a Briton links
The chain of thraldom, glory can be thine.
Vain are thy vows, thy temples, and the rites
Which hallow them, while yet a slave exists
Who curses thee: each curse in Heaven is heard;
'Tis seal'd, and answer'd in the depths Below!

From dungeon and from den there comes a voice
That supplicates for Freedom: from the tomb
Of martyrs her transcendency is told,
And dimm'd she may, but cannot be destroy'd.
Who bends the spirit from its high domain
On God himself a sacrilege commits;
For soul doth share in His supremacy;
To crush it, is to violate the power
And grasp the sceptre an Almighty wields!

For freedom, such as proud ambition call'd
A freedom, a Heaven I lost; and therefore slaves
On earth are victims whom I scorn to see.
No! let them in their liberty be mine;
Or, what if foul Oppression fill the cup
Of crime, that Hell may have a deeper draught?
My kingdom is of evil; and the crowns
Of many an earth-born Despot sparkle there!—
Then let the pangless hearts of Tyrants beat
Unblasted, till from deepest agony
With the proud wrath of ages in Her soul
Freedom arise, and vindicate her name!

BOOK II.

> "Porches and theatres, baths, aqueducts,
> Statues and trophies, and triumphal arcs,
> Gardens and groves, presented to his eyes
> Above the height of mountain interposed."
>
> *Paradise Regained.*

Sceptres are mighty wands, and few are found
With strength to wield them; yet how many dare!
And kingdoms are the agonies of Thrones,
Yet men will die to face them! thus the Heart
Exceeds itself, nor calls the madness vain.
But, were it mine from kingliness to take
The tyrant witchery, I'd bid some young
Idolater of throne-exalted power,
In the deep midnight when the World lies hush'd
In her humility of sleep, to gaze
Upon a prince's couch. The crimson pomp
And glare of palace-chambers round him lie;
But on his cheek the royal spirit stamps
A weariness which mocks this outward show
Of kings; a prison would have graced it more!
A sad rehearsal of unhonour'd youth
When years went reckless as the rolling waves,
Till passion grew satiety; a proud
Regret for trait'rous hearts; and that keen sense
Untold, which monarchs more than subjects feel,
Of slavery; (for servile is the pomp
Of kings, though gorgeously it dares the eye)
With a dim haunting of the dreary tomb,
That often through the banquet-splendour gapes
Like darkness that defies a sun!—such dream
From out his slumber that calm beauty steals
Which Innocence delights to wear. Then, watch
His features, when some trace of dreadful thought
Endows them with a spirit-eloquence,
That speaks of Judgment, with its thronging host
Of terrors; Monarchs cited, and the vast
Account of sceptred kingdoms render'd up;
Could Envy listen to his waking groan,
How poor, how perilous, the state of kings!

Away with this:—transcendently endow'd
And in her mass of mind concent'ring more
Of awfulness, than nature in its might
Of rock or mountain feels, proud Europe spreads
Her living map before me now! What hearts
And souls commune! what countless tides of thought
And feeling, in electric flow, from breast
To breast, from clime to clime, prevailing here;
Here is the throne of Mind; th' arena vast
Where principles and passions run their course
And pant and struggle with conflicting play,—

Where men and angels, heav'n and hell are met,
And Life flings shadows o'er eternity!

Region of wonders! who yon scenes can trace,
Or on thy many-featured visage mark
Each motion of thy spirit, in the glow
Of changing impulse, and creative power?
There, is an ocean, darken'd by the wings
Of vessels, leaping like the waves they front,
While thund'ring to and fro their country's wrath
They tell her glory to the list'ning skies!
And there, a river like a liquid sweep
Of light, where Commerce welcomed by the gale,
Sails onward in the sun; but here, a scene
Of battle, crimson'd o'er with clotting blood!
Banners are playing, rich as unroll'd clouds
Hung loose upon mid air; the gleam of arms
Incessant flashes through the misty fray
Fierce as the lightnings when they flutter wild;
While mute and sad, a City waits afar
With Doubt and Anguish in her desert-streets,
Who catch the war-notes from the travell'd wind
And answer them, with living echoes there.
In dream-like contrast, 'mid the hush of noon
How meekly yon romantic village lies
Beneath a canopy of cloudless blue!
With elm-trees twinkling as they wave, the meads
Made golden for their harvest, and yon spire
In peaceful beauty pointing to the heavens.

Sprinkled with mountains, and with cloud-capt hills,
Helvetia swells majestic on my view,
In her primeval glory. Free-soul'd Land!
Summer and Winter for thy smile contend,
Witching thy prospects into fairy pomp
With beautiful abruptness. Verdure-clad
And deck'd with flowers, these undulating vales
Extend, while vines the terraced hills embrace,
And Landscapes, laughing o'er the clouds, may hear
The Tempest-howl in cavern gloom below!—
But Winter hath his triumph; let the rush
And roar of cataracts; the darksome lakes,—
Convulsive rolling in the midnight-storm;
The glaciers, billow'd like a frozen sea
Iced in the plunging madness of the storm;
And, chief o'er all, the silent Alp-king rear'd
Like Grandeur risen from eternity,—
Let these declare thee for a land sublime.
Home of the dauntless! on thy patriot-soil
While sternness of simplicity can breathe
A Roman vigour, and the name of Tell
Haunts like a harrowing spirit every vale
And mountain-hollow, Time shall honour thee,
When many an Empire shall have pass'd away,
And forests wave where Capitals are seen!

Southward of thee, where shining rocks ascend,
Pointing their cannon to the broad blue main
Defyingly, what region of the sun
Is that, with green-dyed olive groves, and fruits
Whose ripeness glitters on the laden boughs?
'Tis Spain! the glowing clime of Luxury,
Of Chivalry, and dead Romance: her hills
Where aromatic odours scent the skies,
And bright-hued flowers, that in the mountain-breeze
Of wafted freshness dance their beauteous heads;
Her dark-eyed dames, and stately cavaliers
Whose brows are haughty with the dreams of eld;
Her pomp of palaces, her fountain-walks,
And many-templed Capitals,—betray
Her form'd for Pleasure's undisputed reign.
And yet, on History's most heroic page
Hath Andalusia an undying seal,
And Arragon a print of fame:—but deeds
Of blood, and Inquisition's torturing rack,
For vengeance when the world's arraignment sounds,
Will rise; and woe to Tyrants! they shall read
The chronicle stern Justice keeps in hell!

Here, too, the passions are despotic slaves
For me; and prove how features can reveal
The voiceless language of the varied mind.
The languor of luxurious eyes, for Love
Abounds; for Jealousy, the livid gaze
Which looks a murder where its meaning falls!
And for Revenge, an aspect darkly still
Like savage thunder sleeping in a cloud!—
And midnight is the mantle for them all.

Enchanting as thou art, romantic Spain,
The home of beauty and the queen of climes,
Loved Italy, whose oriental heavens
Are rich enough o'er Paradise to hang,
Outdazzles thee in splendour. 'Tis the hour
When noon-shine, dying into sunset-glow,
Suffuses, like a gorgeous wing outspread
In wanton glory, gleams of magic hue.
How radiantly adown those heaven-bright hills
The young streams tremble? Arno, mountain-born
With ling'ring progress writhes along the vale:
And groves and gardens on the cool wind shake
Their fragrance; while around vine-laden meads
Flush with their produce, and the playful breeze
Ruffles the golden corn-fields. Near yon lake
Mark sea-throned Venice in her island-pride,

Resentful dares the Adriatic-roar!
And o'er the river, where gondolas throng,
'Mid Palaces that frown with haggard Pomp
Out-arches her Rialto :—she hath reign'd
Her day; ducal tyrants are no more,
And blighted fabrics but reveal her fame.

And what is Venice to the wreck of Rome?
That Giantess of empire! blacken'd, bow'd,
And desolated on her seven-hill throne
Behold her seated by worn Tiber's banks!
Colossal ruin, like a noble mind
In desolation thou art haughty still!
Though Time hath conquer'd, can he equal thee?
Thy Temples huge where ages are enshrined;
The trophied porches, theatres august
Which heard the beating of ten thousand hearts;
And Fane sublime, on that Tarpeian rock,
Where Vengeance grasp'd eternity!—when Rome
Could trample kingdoms and o'erawe the world
What grandeur rivall'd these? Their very shades
Are solemn: but around them when the rush
Of life was heard; when chariots, bright as clouds
Which throne the morning sun, victorious came
Amid the tramp of war-steeds and the shout
Of millions swelling with their country's fame,—
Thy glory was a terror, and thine arm
Omnipotence to nations! Through all realms
The throbbing of thy faintest anger thrill'd,
And when thou frown'dst, what kingdom dared be free?

Men look on thee, as Seraphs gaze on Light,
With silent rapture solemnised to awe,
Till the dead Past in resurrection-pomp,
Arises, and the Roman lives again!
Heroes and sages start beneath their feet;
Their eyes are dazzled with a starry dream
Of old renown; and, like thy vassal-states,
They deify thy name. And I forgive
The weakness of their worship, when the sun's
Bright mockery plays along thy mould'ring piles;
Or when the moonbeam through some cypress-tree,
Sheds rays of sorrow on thy weed-tress'd walls
And gray-worn monuments; from thy young dawn
Of being, ere thy roofless huts were piled,
To the proud noon of greatness, thou hast proved
A theme of wonder to infernal hosts,
Half demons and half gods thy heroes were;
And Roman teachers,—are they not still felt
And follow'd? deities of mind, whose words
Are wings of knowledge to the daring.—Rome
Is dead; but mental Rome is reigning still
With vaster sway than Pompey's eagles won!

Long may it reign so! that a fiery love
Of fame and battle, which defeatures earth
With scars eternity shall fail to heal,
May live by inspiration fierce as Rome's.
Many a "hero" hath by Her been crazed;
And fancied "Cæsars" yet will come, to chain
The world, or fool it with disastrous fame!
Yea, at this moment, in tyrannic hearts
Ambition hath a mass of burning thought
In secret treasured, like volcanic ire:
Kindle it, Time! and rear thy second Rome.

Few years have fleeted o'er this tomb-like haunt
Of ruin, since a Spirit who appall'd
The world, by giving thoughts a thunder-tone,
And feeling, that terrific lightning-flash,
That show'd the storm-depths of the soul within;
Who pour'd himself in passion o'er mankind
Making each heart to quiver with delight,
Like water thrill'd by an electric sound,—
Amid thy canker'd fanes and crumbling halls
Mused in the deadness of the midnight-hour.

It was a haggard night; when mortals dream
That conscious Nature in dejection pines;
As though the elements were all diseased,
The moon hung rayless, and the few faint stars
Gleam'd pale and glassy as the eye of death.
Alone, the victim of his darkest mood,
In the stern shade of ruin'd Palaces
And pillar'd wrecks of desolated shrines
The wanderer roam'd; and when some sickly break
Of moonlight lit his features into play
With all their lines of passionate excess,
The haunting Genius of the spot he seem'd
Lost in the workings of a wilder'd mind.
He sigh'd, and mused; and then from earth to heav'n
His eye was raised, but moisten'd with a tear
Of tenderness, wherein the pride of years
Had melted out from his rebellious soul,
Most haughty in abasement:— blighted man!
His nature was a whirlpool of desires,
And mighty passions, perilously mix'd,
That with the darkness of the demon-world
Had something of the light of Heaven. He breathed
The sighs that after-ages will repeat,—
The selfish eloquence of tortured thought
In words that glow with agony! Yet far
From him that deeper sadness of the mind
Which, gather'd from the gloom of mortal things
In moments of mysterious sway, o'erclouds
A soul, yet sanctifies those thoughts which feel

Eternity a spirit's home to be,
And time mere exile, which the man endures.

So worshipp'd, and so sad!—Oh, were not hopes
Destroy'd, the moral landscape Devils love
To witness, idols of this world might win
My pity for their portion. How deceived
And how deceiving, is the race they run!
The King and Hero, Bard and Sage, with all
Who in the storehouse of departed time
Have heap'd such treasure, as great deeds and words
Beget, what bright delusions have they been!

To fancied Edens of poetic bloom
On wings of sentiment can Genius roam,
And meditate on worldless Things, whence comes
A glorious panting for a purer State,
Than Adam saw, when Earth's anointed Priest
In purity, his life was incense breath'd to God.
But, martyrs to unhealthy thought abound,
Who out of earthly elements have sought
A happiness to reap whose soil is heaven,
And, failing, sunk to profitless despair.
Thus Learning, Luxury, and laurell'd Fame,
Vain phantoms, what a worship have they won!
The first, a shallow excellence; the next,
A malady of brutish growth, debased
And most debasing, turning soul to sense
Till nature seems unspirited; the last,
Magnificent betrayer! while afar
Beheld, the crown of heaven itself seems thine;
But when attain'd, how oft a brilliant Lie
Whose lustre was but hollowness conceal'd!
Oh! many an eye that in the glow of youth
Hath brighten'd, as it gazed on pictured worth,
Or linger'd round those everlasting shrines
Where tombs have tongues, and monuments are speech,
Where great inheritors of Glory rest,—
Hath wept the laurels that it once adored!

The atmosphere which circleth gifted minds
Is from a deep intensity derived,—
An element of thought, where feelings shape
Themselves to fancies,—an electric world
Too exquisitely framed for common life,
Which they of coarser metal cannot dream.
And hence, those fascinating powers of soul
That robe the heavens with beauty, and create
Romance which makes reality untrue,
Upon the rack of quick excitement live;
Their joy the essence of an agony,
And *that*, the throbbing of the fires within!

And thus, while Fame's heart-echoing clarions ring,
The voice and visions of ideal renown
In one vile whisper may be overwhelm'd.
Made mighty by its littleness, a word
Of Envy drowns the thunder which delight
Hath voiced! so oft the phantom of a cloud
In single darkness cowering on the air,
Looks fiercer for the frownless heaven around!
So Fame is murder'd, that the dull may live;[1]
Or, to Herself grows false; then hideous dreams
And tomb-like shadows thicken round the mind,
Till, plunging into dread infinity,
It rides upon the billows which Despair
Hath summon'd from the stormy gloom of thought.
Dark victim! thus so ruinously famed,
What misery haunts thy smile of happiness!
Beneath the mountain of thy vast renown
There lives a mortal, unendow'd by aught
That Learning, Luxury, or Fame can yield,
And yet a Crœsus in his store of joy
With thine compared; the man whom sullied earth
Enslaves not, on whose soul the Truth hath smiled—
Truth which I loathe, but Hell cannot destroy!

A model first, and then the captive made
Of desolating Rome, the classic Isles
Of ancient Greece, beside yon full-waved sea
Laugh in the bright unbreathing air of noon.
Antiquity reigns here; see! on her throne
Of Athos, whence the giant-shadow sweeps,
As new alighted from a cloud she stands,
Waving her wand triumphant o'er her scenes;—
To hoar Parnassus, where the fabled spring
Of Castaly still flows; and time-awed wilds,
And mountain-pass, and Marathonian plain,
To every haunt heroic feet have trod
Her wand is pointed,—till the Past untombs
Her treasure; Athens is revived again;
The slave-isles hurl their shackles o'er the sea,
And Greece awakes to glorify the world!

Surpassing Clime! though man thy charms profane,
Nature bedecks thee with a bridal robe.
When moon-tints tremble on the Adrian-waves,
What sea so beautiful! what sun so bright,
So ravishingly deck'd with golden beams
As thine unequall'd orb!—And still yon skies
Are canopies of crystal; rich-leaf'd flowers
Ope radiant as the fairy wings of birds,
And fruit and tree wave luscious in the wind.

Again, thou upstart World, thy doom behold!
Where Valour with the sword of freedom fell'd
Her myriads down, like grass before the scythe;
Where Art and Science in perfection reign'd,

And Sculpture miracles of grace achieved;
Where Eloquence her spirit volley'd forth
In words that palsied Empires with their sound,
As shakes a forest in the deep-toned storm!
Where Poetry, by stirring passion bred,
From Feeling's heart responsive numbers drew,
While heavenly Wisdom to the soaring eye
Of sages half reveal'd her perfect form,—
There in that Land, surpassingly endow'd
With all that beauty wealth and art bestow,
Corruption in her darkest spirit dwells.
Then learn, Adorers of Athenian gods,
Learn, at the tomb of Glory laid in dust,
How human passions wither while they sway;
The Curse is living!—think of *my* revenge!

Northward of Greece, behold illustrious Gaul,
Britannia's rival, gaily doth outspread
Her scenery, and blooming flush of life.
She, too, hath beauty; and her sun-warm hills,
Which bare their bosoms to the mellowing sky,
With vine and fruitage, bountifully glow;
While rivers of romance, by wood and vale,
And bord'ring town, their sparkling waters lead.
Young, fresh, and gay, elastic as the breeze,
All spring and sunshine, her full spirit bounds;
Here vanity is virtue: out of hearts
Which seem to echo but what woman loves
Awaking valour, prompt to dare, and proud
To die. And yet, true nobleness of mind
Is faintly seen; sincerity, too harsh
To please, is polish'd into courtly lies,—
The frothy incense of a faithless soul.

Once France and Freedom were a mingled name;
And now, when all their wrathful clouds are roll'd
Away, the shadows which they cast endure,
Clothing the soul of memory with fear.
Her Revolution, who that saw forgets,
Or who that felt, and does not feel?—The storm
Which makes a midnight of affrighted day,
Is weak, to that rebellion of despair
When buried passions, like an earthquake burst
From out an injured Nation's heart. And such
Was thine, afflicted France! the far-off Thrones
Of tyrants stagger'd, distant Empires quail'd
When, like th' embodied spirit of thy wrongs,
Dread Revolution darken'd on the world,
Ringing a peal that echoed Europe round
And died in thunder o'er th' Atlantic deep!
But thou wert too unholy to be free,
Too grasping to be great; and when thy thirst
For havoc brutalised the scene of blood,
As though re-action for all human wrong
Were centred in it for *one* dire revenge,
A madness fired thee; and thy human fiends
Rivall'd their lord in blasphemy and blood!

Bounding with gladness, by yon castled banks
Roll the green waters of the glorious Rhine
In fullness and in freedom, swelling on
For ever. There, amid some minds which hold
Each hallow'd creed by dreading Hell abhorr'd,
While Men to "Ego" germanise their God
Dark Speculation does my brain-work well
In many a school, where reeling heads grow wild
And godless! Hence, all moral basis fails
Wherein the judgment can alone repose.
Secure and solid; while the eye of faith
Is darken'd, sacred conscience half extinct,
And doubts, refracting heaven's unbroken light
From Scripture, make the Man himself untrue,—
In reasoning pride irrationally lost!
Free though they look, my slaves all sceptics are;
Through mental fogs, or pantheistic gloom,
Blindly they grope their miserable way
And make confusion more confounded still:
Then, all is chaos, and the Spirit mine!—
Love, Faith and Law, a trinity of powers
Which shape the will, or sanctify the heart
For heaven, my human miniatures disdain:
Not grace for discipline, but truth for thought
Proud worshippers of Indecision love
Like mental antichrists: till God becomes
Impersonal, a Problem for the soul
To scan—mere Principle, and nothing more!
Hence, German thought a German Christ evokes
From misty depths, to speculation dear
Because unfathom'd. Now, my reign begins:
Let darkness be, where Deity said, light!
Till creedless mind call God an inward Myth
Of man's creation; and thus will sceptics prove
The incarnations of that Lie first-born
In Eden utter'd, when I whisper'd,—doubt,
Renounce Jehovah and *thyself* believe!

Fronting the wave-environ'd shore of France,
And bulwark'd with her everlasting main
O'er which the guardian-cliffs sublimely lower,
Like palaces of stern defence, behold
The Isle-queen!—every billow sounds her fame!
The Ocean is her proud triumphal car
Whereon she rideth; and the rolling waves
The vassals which secure her victory;
Alone, and matchless in her sceptred might
She dares the world. The spirit of the brave
Burns in her; laws are liberty; and kings
Wear crowns which glitter with a people's love;
And while the magna-charta of their rights
Is guarded, royalty is kept secure;
But let the cause of Liberty be wrong'd,—
The throne is shaken! patriot-voices rise,
And, prompt as billows by the tyrant-gale
Excited, loud and haughty is their roar!

Heaven-favour'd Land! where fitful climates reign,
And home-life from the ever-clouded skies
A bliss concenter'd more than France enjoys,—
Of mountain-pomp, and poetry of hills,
Though other climates boast, in thee supreme
A pastoral grace and gentleness abound;
Here all which quiet feeling love, or charms
The sweet sobriety of tender thought,
Is thine; a heaven whose beautiful, is change;
Or sunshine tinged by unreposing clouds,
That make bright landscapes when they blush abroad;
The dingle grey, and wooded copse; with hut
And hamlet, nestling in some bosky vale;
And spires brown-peeping o'er the ancient elms,
And steepled cities, faint and far away,
With all that bird and meadow, brook and gale
Impart,—commingle for romantic eyes
Which catch the sentiment thy scenes inspire.

But Ocean is thy glory: and methinks
Some musing wanderer by the shore I see,
Weaving his island-fancies.—Round him rock
And cliff, whose grey trees mutter to the wind,
And streams down-rushing with a torrent ire:
The sky seems craggy, with her cloud-piles hung,
Deep-mass'd, as though avenging thunder lay
And darken'd in its dream of havoc there.
Before him, Ocean, yelling in the blast,
Wild as the death-wail of a drowning host:
The surges,—let them each a tempest roll,
Or lash their fury into living foam,
Yon war-ship shall outbrave them all! her sails
Resent the winds, and their remorseless beat;
And when she ventures the abyss of waves,
Remounts, expands her wings, and then—away!
Proud as an eagle dashing through the clouds.

And well, brave scion of the empress-Isle,
Thy spirit mingles with the mighty scene,
Hailing thy Country on her ocean-throne.
But she hath dread atonements to complete,
And burning tears to shed. Thy lofty dreams
O England! may be humbled yet; behold!
Thy curse is coming;—mark! for in thine own
Great heart the darkness of rebellion breeds,
And frowns of Heaven hang awful o'er thy doom!

And now, the World before my view hath pass'd,
With multitudinous array of pomp
And power, of Kingdom, Plain, and Desert rude,
Of Oceans, garnish'd with their glitt'ring isles,
And the vast heaven which o'er-arches all!
How crime and havoc in dread union leagued
The fortunes of this fated earth have changed!
The present still is echo to the past;
Of both the future will an echo prove;
A rise and fall,—a fall and rise—the doom
Of men and empires thus gone ages tell.

And what of this proud Age, whose wings unfold
In bright expansion? Is she Wisdom's child?
From the dark catalogue of sin and shame
Is aught erased? Are passions more subdued,
The virtues laurell'd, and the vices dead?
The same in spirit doth the earth exist?
If so, then, Time, I hail thee! and the Curse
Shall multiply; new thrones and dynasties
May come, but Desolation shall foredoom
Their fate, though haughty be the aspect worn.
And as among the myriads who have lived
On earth, not many have our thrones regain'd,
So from the myriads yet to be reveal'd
In life and suff'rance, few shall face the heat
Of trial scathless; few shall overcome
The world, or win the crown apostles wear.

But lo! the day declines; and to his couch
The Sun is wheeling. What a world of pomp
The heavens put on in homage to his power!
Romance hath never hung a richer sky,—
Or sea of sunshine, o'er whose yellow deep
Triumphal barks of beauteous foam career,
As though the clouds held festival, to hail
Their god of glory to his western home.
And now the earth seems mirror'd on the skies!
While lakes and valleys, drown'd in dewy light,
And rich delusions, dazzlingly array'd,
Form, float, and die, in all their phantom-joy.
At length the Sun is throned; but from his face
A flush of beauty o'er creation flows,
Then faints to paleness, for the Day hath sunk
Beneath the waters, dash'd with ruby dyes,
And Twilight in her nun-like meekness comes:
The air is fragrant with the soul of flowers,
The breeze comes panting like a child at play,
While birds, day-worn, are couch'd in leafy rest,
And calm as clouds the sunken billows sleep:
The dimness of a dream o'er nature steals,
Yet hallows it; a hush'd enchantment reigns;
The mountains to a mass of mellowing shade
Are turn'd, and stand like temples of the Night:
While field and forest, fading into gloom,

Depart, and rivers whisper sounds of fear;
A dying pause, as if th' Almighty moved
In shadow o'er His works, hath solemnised
The world!

But that hath ceased; the herald-stars,
In timid lustre twinkling into life,
Advance; and, faint as music's rising swell,
The moon is rounding as she dawns. Fair orb!
The sentimental child of earth will say,
The sun glares like a warrior o'er his plain
Of morning sky; but thou, so wan and meek,
Appear'st a maiden of romance, who walks
In placid sorrow, beautifully pale.
Behold thy power! on tree and meadow falls
The loveliness of thine arraying smile.
How silverly the sleeping air is robed
Around me! Clouds above, like plats of snow
Which linger on the hills, and laugh the sun
Away with their white beauty, yet remain;
And now they vanish, and the soundless heaven
Forms one deep cope of azure, where the stars,
Bright pilgrims voyaging an unwaved sea,
Are strewn, and sparkle with incessant rays
Of mystery and meaning. Yet not heaven,
When islanded with all those lustrous worlds,
Nor cradled Ocean with the waves uproll'd,
Nor moonlight weaving forth its pallid shroud,
Is so enchanting as that stillness felt,
And living with luxurious spell, through all,—
Silent as though a sound had never been;
Or, angels o'er her slumber spread their wings,
And breathed a sabbath into Nature's soul.

No wonder moonlight made idolaters,
That their Creator in creation merged
As one surpassing Whole: for even I,
I who have look'd with archangelic love
On all the beauty and the blaze of heaven,—
E'en I, the burning of my soul can feel
Allay'd, when nature grows so near divine.
And man, when passionless and pure awhile
Amid the trances of unbreathing night
With adoration in his eye and heart,
He walks abroad, and measures at a gaze
The starr'd immensity above, becomes
Sublime; a shade of his primeval Soul
Returns upon him; chaste as e'er it fell
Heaven-ward the prayer-winged heart of faith ascends,
Beholding Angels in excess of light,
And joining in their chorus round The Throne!
Sublime, but impotent, he then appears:
The Fathomless, oh, who shall fathom? Time,
Eternity, and Truth,—those awful Three
That make the mystery God alone resolves.

BOOK III.

"On man, on nature, and on human life,
Musing in solitude." *Wordsworth.*

And such the nature of this noble world!
Magnificence and beauty, pomp and might
Supremely glorify God's earth for man,
The beatings of whose heart are heard in Heaven.
The chant of seas, the jubilee of winds
In forests heard, or playing their free wings
Till the glad air is one abounding swell
Of joy; Mortality's mysterious life
And motion; and the thrilling tones of mind
Which sound so awful on the sleepless ear
Of Angels, watching like pure sentinels
O'er human hearts,—such fearful stir of things
In viewless worlds might well an echo wake.
And may not he, the monarch of the scene,
Be crown'd with glory, when he champions Time,
Proclaiming what a vassal he hath been,
And how great Nature hath *his* charm obey'd!
The Elements—he made them servile powers,
Or mix'd their spirit with his own; the Rocks
Uprear'd—he scaled them to the clouds;
The Ocean, thunder'd with her dreadful waves,—
He braved them, and they bore him like a god!
Yea, more; in haunts where desolation nursed
The midnight Tempest howling for his prey,
There hath the City piled her myriad domes;
And Life her human scenery unroll'd.

So vast his triumph o'er the varied range
Of elemental being; but the soul
For its omnipotence is most revered;
How darkly-wild, how grandly undefined!
Now sunk in dreams of unethereal bliss,
Now glowing, gasping for infinity!
Of Senses, inlet to unnumber'd joys
And pains, all exquisitely toned and true;
Of Feelings, wrapp'd as life-nerves round the heart
Which throbs obedient to their lightning-call:
And Passions, gods or demons as they rule,—
Humanity may boast beyond decay:
While Thought,—eternity is not too deep
To fathom! she can sweep immensity,
Creating worlds, and soaring on the wings
Of awe, till, drooping like a weary bird,
She drop in wonder to the earth again.

With god-like attributes, ethereal powers
Developed as the living soul directs,
What grand perfections, then, hath Earth produced!
Proud of his being, hear some child of clay:—

"A Monarch holding empires in his grasp,
Is great; Philosophers who fathom depths
Of mystery, and plunge their minds in gloom,
That ages may grow brighter, are sublime:
And Genius, when by inspiration wing'd,
How gloriously the heaven of thought she mounts,
Fronting Jehovah with undaunted eye
As eagles gaze undazzled on the sun!—
Then, may She not the crowning laurel wear,
The purest of perfections?"—Further yet;
Methinks I'm challenged to admire a man
Adorn'd with meekness, graced by holy love,
And in the noiseless vale of humble life
Content, and charitably good; whose name
Is nobly register'd in realms divine,
Though unrenown'd below,—for men forget
Th' obscure in earth are oft the famed in heav'n.

These proud examples of terrestrial worth
Oft deify man's nature, and exalt
His dignity to such a seeming height
Of inward greatness, that it spurns away
The dimming memory of a primal fall,
And magnifies him to his first estate
Of glory. What am I, then, if this earth
By sin be all unblasted? Not a Shape
Of woe, the prey of agonising fires,
But Seraph, with his raiments roll'd in light
The hierarchal prince of heav'n!—If Man
Be undegraded, Hell is but a sound
Of falsehood, dwelling in the soul of fear.
Yet, judge them by their *greatness*, what are men?
Of imperfection is true wisdom born,
And vaunting knowledge, ignorance confess'd.[1]
The Unknown, when reveal'd, is not the new;
It *was*, before his mental vision saw,
And soar'd into a certainty; when seen,
The blindness of the past is proved, and Earth
May wonder, but she might be humble, too.

There are, who feel true glory but a ray
Of triumph over imperfection shed,—
Which looks the darker when the gleam is o'er—
When night hath deepen'd, and the massy earth
Lies cover'd with cathedral-gloom, abroad
Some starry Watcher roams, and 'mid the far
Array of planetary worlds, like Saints
In bright procession marching to the Throne
Of their Creator, spreads his wandering soul,
Till in the contemplated God absorb'd
The Man is nothing, and his wisdom, dust!

Nor dare he boast, as if perfection crown'd
His being, who can most himself unearth;
And from immortal beauty of the mind
Reflect the imagery of heav'n around;—
E'en he, whose gratitude in sunshine hails
The smiles from God's own countenance reveal'd,
Which flutter round his soul like fairy notes
Of music melting into magic there,—
Yes! he is boastless; though he soar aloft
Till Fancy, awe-struck, wait with folded wing
Before the blaze of Deity!—for dark
To him the meanness of this sin-worn earth,
When, breaking from a cloud of holy thought
Wherein he dreamt, and high communion held
With visions of a viewless world,—again
He hears the rolling waves of life, and sees
The gloom and turmoil of created things.

But if beneath the brightness of the soul
A shadow of degraded nature sleep,
To make it humble, then how far removed
From primal virtue are the men whom Vice
Imbrutes with her foul spirit! Well, indeed,
Hath Hell with Heaven divided empire won;
How widely, let the watching Angels[2] speak!
Who frequent shudder with regretful awe
When gazing down the wild abyss within
To view the passion-waves which billow there,
The gloom, the stir, and tempest of the mind!
To such, the blackness of the Past is known!—
Within whose bosom lies entomb'd a mass
Of crime, by sinful myriads heap'd:—the Curse
Lies buried with it, till the trumpet-blast
Be sounded and the sleep of Ages burst
For retribution; then will wrath awake,
And I, the doubted One, shall stand reveal'd!

And what a burden of unheeded sin
Upon the death of each departing hour
Is borne into eternity! the Past
Was roughen'd into storms of savage guilt:
The present, with a milder aspect tempts
The judgment; 'tis a most polluted calm!
Beneath it, in their soul-corrupting power
The fest'ring tides of passion act and live;
And when they burst o'er all prudential banks
To riot in the public view of man,
Then, Evil! thou indeed art god confess'd.
Oh! it is laughter which allays our pangs
To see these clay-born Upstarts, who were framed
To re-erect our fallen Thrones,—amerced
Of favour, all their glory dimm'd and marr'd,
And they, contented at the car of Vice
To follow, fetter'd by the chains of hell!

First in my train of ministers behold
Assuming Pride, who lifts her lofty eye
To Heaven, as though in scorn of its dread height;
And when She bends it to the earth, surveys
All creatures but to dwarf them in a glance
Of stern comparison. But nobler far,

Appears Ambition, whose prophetic voice
So fired my own proud nature, that it dared
Jehovah's thunders in full roar to face!
In all my tempters there is no such power,
Such mingling of the demon and the god
As that which in Ambition dwells. The soul
Of Virtue, by her hallowing spirit touch'd
May emulate bright seraphs, with a love
Divine, through this dark pilgrimage; but rare
On earth is such sublime ambition found,
Or seldom would she waft a soul to me!
She haunts the lowliness of life; there, shapes
Her phantoms wild, or glittering delights.
But oftener she assumes a warrior-mien
To make a hero; stirs him with the sight
Of banners flouting a defiance; plains
And battle-hills with throbbing echoes rung:
He rides a charger in victorious dreams
And wakes a Hero!—let him gash the World!

Ambition prompts that Genius in the mind,
Which mortals on a throne of Magic seat,
Most heavenly-bright, without a shade of earth,
Her nature a nobility! the great
She magnifies, the mean she can exalt,
Lend virtue majesty, on vice a veil,
The all-adored,—creation for Her charm!
Enrapt, and raised beyond the clouds of sense,
And all which coarse reality perceives,
She wanders forth, and views the budding morn
Freshen the pale sky, like that infantine glow
Which o'er the cheek of waking Beauty steals;
And night,—the paradise of dreams expands
Before her, when that sacred darkness smiles
Unutterably glorious!—not a sound
Abroad; the moon, an isle of loveliness;
The stars hung beautiful, as all new-born
And lavish of their lustre; She can dream
Her spirit roaming some elysian Orb
Deep in the luxury and bloom of heaven.
All sights and sounds bring meanings to Her mind;
The seas are mirrors of Almightiness;
And winds, like terrible magicians reign
And master ocean with a wizard spell.
Whate'er is vision'd, she can make her own,
Shaping the world to an enchanted sphere!

Yet Genius oft is mad ambition's wing
In shining motion flutter'd o'er mankind.
Alone, she cannot conquer Virtue's height,
Nor bask in her Elysium; for the Heart
One single virtue wins a prouder claim
Of eminence, than mighty Genius wears
In deepest glory:—while that peerless race,
Anointed demi-gods whom Fame adores,
Are blinded into self-idolatry,
Some unobtrusive child of Woe, through want
And anguish doom'd to meet his aidless lot,
Hath pour'd his spirit into fervent prayer,
And clung so faithful to the cross of Christ
That he is famous in the rolls of Heav'n,
Where lies a Mansion waiting for his soul;—
A withering, but eternal truth, to me!

Next Avarice and Envy, meaner powers
Of evil, aid me while I weave the chains
Which bind the captives of Corruption down.
The first, a boundless feeling: more or less
A second nature to the human mind
Whose self-love is the life of thought and deed;
But in some bosoms kindling all its fire,
And rendering man a hideous slave of self;
Till the bright universe and all it boasts
Becomes a Nothing, when apart survey'd
From what it ministers to gain and gold!
Mean wretch! the more he gets, the less he gives;
For ever greedy, as the hunger'd shark
Which scents the dead among the waves afar.
Nature is nought to him; the darken'd soul
Hath dimm'd his eye,—it glitters but for gold,
And *that* will gladden his departing hour!
For what so grateful to the clammy touch
Of dying fingers, as to feel his gold,
While, sighing o'er it with a farewell-gaze
He mourns the nothing of the wealthless tomb!

But though in such abasement I exult,
There is an excellence which daunts my gaze
With blighting glory; such is virtue's ray;
It trembles brightly through the gloom of hell
And though 'tis hated, must be *there* admired!—
How nobly different lives that Son of earth
Whose heart is large enough to hold the world!
Benevolence is life and breath to him;
He spreads it out like sunshine from the soul,
Itself its own reward. Whate'er he views
Can waken sympathy; the clouds and streams,
The meadows, trees, and family of flowers,
For each and all as livingly endow'd
He feels a beauteous love, but gives to Man
The throbs and throes of sympathy divine.
For buried grief, and those retiring pangs
Which prey unutter'd on the gentle mind,
He hath a healing word; and from the joys
That shoot and sparkle o'er the stream of life
Who fetches out the flash of bliss, like he?
A hoary parent clasping his brave boy,
With eyes all running o'er with ecstasy;
A sweet and fairy-featured Infant, sat
In laughing beauty on its mother's knee,
That rocks it into rapture; or a pair
Of lovers, looking in each other's eyes
As though the lustre of unclouded years
Were in them, beaming with prophetic glow,—

O'er these, and every sun-burst of delight,
Benevolence can wave her angel-wings
And find in sympathy the soul of joy.

To pay me for such pure excess of good
Why, who art Thou with eye of dead-like gaze
And care-worn aspect, on thy haggard cheek;
The seal of woe, and stamp of agony?—
Fiend of the heart, on man inflicting Hell,
And Envy is thy name! though often crown'd
For Emulation, by thy martyr'd slave;
But she, proud Spirit! walks a nobler sphere:
And when, amid the madness of the storm
When skies are rack'd asunder, and the sea
Lies rolling in the rapture of its strength,
She longs, to be the queen of Elements
Sublimely o'er a thousand tempests throned;
Or views, the starry natures, till her own
Seems panting to be bright and pure as they;
Or, fired by dreams of intellectual fame,
Hath gazed on Glory till her eyes are dim,—
A generous and god-like Thing appears.
But Thou art unredeem'd! a burning mass
Of self-made misery, tortured by the curse
Roll'd back in vengeance on thy horrid Self,
Though breathed for others with malignant scorn.
Merit is misery to envious eyes,
That look themselves to anguish, when they mark
Some high-born quality of soul or mind
They cannot rival;—yet their very hate
Most cruelly a false perfection gives
To that pure excellence they long to crush,
Conceal, or wither: thus the secret worm
Can gnaw the spirit to its vital core!
And hence, that scowling eloquence of eye:
While Beauty, with her fairiness of form,
And looks of light, like those by angels cast;
Or Wisdom, laurell'd with unfading wreath
Well earn'd, and woven round an aching head
Where thoughts have throbb'd like pulses in the brain,
Each beat a torture!—likewise Youth and Joy,
Two smiling phantoms on the wings of time,
Are blasting spectacles to envious hearts.

Thus envy images the pang of hell!
In secret preying with its vulture-tooth,
Or haply easing its infernal rage
In deeds of horror, whose unslumb'ring guilt
Is vengeance:*—how it haunts the craven wretch!
By writhing hell-flames o'er his tortured sleep,
And building oft the gallows which he dreads!
What though he shroud his spirit with a veil
Of outward gladness, artificial smiles
Are smiles of agony; and when alone
By some rude shore, where sullen waters roll
Like gloomy fancies through a guilty mind;
Or, doom'd to hear the sobbing of the wind,
The melancholy drip of midnight-rain,
And death-tales, faintly knell'd from far-off towers,
The calm is burst, the buried thoughts arise
With ghastly violence from their fell tomb;
The spirit storms with anguish, and Despair
Feels half the hell it shudders to foresee!

Far wider, and more deadly in his reign,
Is Lust; the malady of souls impure
That fills the senses with lascivious fire,
O'erheats the fancy, and to dalliant thought
Presents all beauty moulded but for shame.
And such is passion, when by truth survey'd,
Anatomised, and seen! Yet lewd-soul'd men
Romantically vile, decoy the hearts
Of virtue, and disease them by a word
Whose smoothness hides the shame its meaning hath.
Foul passion is the poetry of vice
And beautifies corruption. Hence the mind
That would have loath'd its undisguised attempt
Enchanted by delusion, locks its eyes
In fatal slumber, till the veil is torn,
And all the terrors of remorse begin!

Yet Hell cannot deny on earth there glows
A spirit scarcely weaken'd by the fall,—
The soul of feeling, and the sun of life,
Queen of the Passions, all-persuasive Love:—
And *could* they with the bliss of man commune
Fiends would be charm'd by pure affection's smile!

Ethereal essence, interfused through life,
Is Love. In orbs of Glory spirits live
On such perfection; and on earth it feeds
And quickens all things with a soul-like ray:
The beautiful in its most beauteous sense;
And symbolised by Nature, in her play
Of harmonies,—her forms, her hues, and sounds:
In each, connexion aptitude and grace
Reside. Thus, flow'rs in their infantile bloom
Of sympathy; the bend of trees and boughs;
The chime of waters, and caress of winds,—
Betoken that they all partake a sense
Of that sweet principle which rules the world.
And yet, though Love a human seraph be
When pure and blest, by circumstance deform'd
It turns a Demon, in the heart enthroned,
That drains the life-blood out of Virtue's breast!
For many, gentle as their wishes once,
When Love smiled round them with prophetic ray,
With hearts by disappointment torn and rent

* Φθονεϱο δ' ἀμύνοντ' ἄτα.—Pind. Pyth. xi. 83.

And spirits blasted with the blight of wrong,
Are driven onward through a wild'ring course,
Untemper'd and untamed. So flows the stream,
Which ever nurseth its delicious calm,
Till wrung by nature into torrent-force
And foaming reckless through the wild!

And Thou,
The Star of home, who in thy gentleness
On the harsh nature of usurping man
Benign enchantment beautifully shedd'st,
Soft as a dew-fall from the brow of eve
Or veiling moonlight on the tempest thrown,—
Woman! when love has wreck'd thy trusting heart,
What port remains to shelter *Thee!* Too fond
And o'er-intense thy truthful nature is,
Save for the heart's idolatry and dream;
And then, to virtue's path thy love allures:—
It dawns, and withering passions die away;
Low raptures fade, pure feelings blossom forth,
And that which Wisdom's philosophic beam
Could never from the wintry soul awake,
By love is smiled into celestial birth!
So love is wisdom with a sweeter name.

But love attracts not Me!—I *cannot* love;
For curses are the essence of each thought
As writhes my spirit on a rack of fire.
Oh, Vengeance! ere I heard thy thunders roll,
With what delight I roam'd Heaven's bowers among,
With kindred Angels, and elysian Shapes,
Amid revealings of seraphic love!—
But here, in low-sphered earth, a shadow dwells
Of its divinity. In virgin youth
When feelings are as foster'd buds of joy
And freshness, from the spring of soul within,
While the full gush of tenderness awakes
Like spirit-music in the mind,—the heart
For love is made, and owns its magic true.
And now, earth wears the attributes of heaven!
Two hearts are one, two natures are transform'd
Each into each by sympathy of soul;
What words in looks! what love in every tone!
Moonlight, and azure sleep of cloudless air,
Eve-walks, their mildness and romantic hush,
How beautiful for lovers' placid vows!
Then love, Enthusiast! ere the drossy world
Corrupt thee; soon shall sorrow dash thy lot
With bitterness; the spell shall then unwind,
And Evil woo thee to her envious arms.
Love is the revel of a summer-ray,
The shadow of a heaven-sent dream; once gone,
'Tis gone for ever! darkness shall invade
Thy spirit, and the green delights of youth
Drop witheringly into barren age,
When love remains a memory and a tear.[3]

Next, Jealousy, the curse of tainted love,
Or causeless agony, by selfish thought
Endured, a minister of Evil makes:
Who haunts unseen some haggard spot, to hear
The night-air panting with a rueful swell,
Like sadness from a loaded bosom heaved.
Her victim!—she hath blister'd his fond heart
And through his veins a fiery venom pour'd;
His mind is torture, and that torture, hell!
The world is changed, corrupted, false; and cold
As autumn when the bleakest rain-dews fall,
To his delightless gaze. For damning proof
All shades of accident cohere; he storms
And doubts,—despairs and doubts again,—then tames
His wild suspicion into sullen calm,
Dark as the stillness of a thunder-cloud.

And what of her, so fatally beloved?
Still beautiful and fair; but on each charm
The profanation of some fancied Eye
Hath dwelt, which haunts him like a hideous gaze!
Thus Jealousy the mind gangrenes, till thoughts
Feed on his soul like agonising fire
And wither him to madness!—oh, how oft
He wakes, and watches the suspected One,
When from her soul the light of slumber breaks,
As though it dreamt of sunshine and of flowers!
But dreams it thus for *him!*—To-morrow comes
And Jealousy renews her rack again.

"This world how fleeting and how vain! Our joys
Are blossoms torn by each tyrannic wind;
Our pleasures, but the painted dreams of air;
Our hopes, they light us onward to the tomb!"
Morality, how musical thy tones
Upon the lip of smooth Hypocrisy!

And such a strain, how sweetly does it lull
The idiot-ears of undiscerning men,
Who see in words a shadow of pure deeds
And think the tongue the heart translates. The world
Is rank with hypocrites!—a coward-race
Of such ignoble vileness, that they shame
Temptation, though they track its hellward path.
Who bravely dares the censure of mankind,
Pays dear for Vice, but reaps her value too,
In full and free enjoyment: but the Slave
Of hidden sin is ever Torture's fool,
Proving his own avenger. Many seem
The mantles which adorn your hypocrite!
Behold him now, a most unruffled man
Smoother than waters sleeping in the sun,

To common gazers,—now, a courteous Shape
All delicately civil! full of words
Well rounded into gracious compliments;
Or else, benevolently mad, with purse
In hand; Misfortune, dip thy finger there!
Neglected Want! for you it opens wide;
And, oh! ye soft-lipp'd dealers in applause,
Resound the dews of mercy as they fall,
And crown him famous, Charity's own child!
But why?—it pays a penalty for sin
And bribes the Conscience, while it gilds a name.

Then mark yon Hypocrite of pious mould,
For ever putting on unearthly moods
And looking lectures with his awful eyes.
A sun-like centre of religious zeal,
So pure, he would be better than the best!
True virtue is a heavenliness of mind
That, in the mercy of a mild reproof,
Sheds healing sympathy o'er human woe.
But he is cold, uncharitably good;
Dealing the thunder-bolts of sacred Wrath
With apostolic vengeance.—Mighty heaven,
What lip-work are his pharisaic prayers!
And like a sepulchre among the young
Or gay, when, clouded with an envious gloom
While death and judgment threaten from his brow,
He comes where youth and innocence embrace
To talk of Time and Change,—how gaping tombs
Their dead await to sleep in darkness here;
Or sternly paints some portraiture of sin,—
But feels *himself* the model whence he drew!

There is another and a fearful slave
I love to train—the glory of revenge;
A ruin which develops Me, and prints
The die of evil in its deepest hue
On erring souls,—The Atheist! with his creed
Of darkness, brooding o'er the sunken mind
Till Truth deny her nature; and the man
Live like a bubble dancing on the stream
Of time, which sparkles, and is seen no more,—
A Nothing with a name! But since the soul
Is effluence divine, the inward rays
Of Deity cannot be quench'd: the God
Is clouded, yet an indistinct and dread
Religion, in the cowering spirit dwells.[4]
Since Egypt worshipp'd her material gods
Through all the pantheistic gloom of Greek
And Roman ages, Deity hath reign'd,
Though hid in fabling wisdom. Where the mind
To pure conceptions of a perfect God
Ascended not, on wings of terror raised
To see Him as he is,—the Awful One,
Who wields eternity and portions time,
Commands a deluge, or dissolves a world!—
The Passions shadow'd forth fantastic gods,
As Fear, or Wonder, or the dreaming eye
Of Pagan Luxury sensualised the soul,
And fancied heaven the heaven of each desire!

An Atheist,—he hath never faced an hour,
And not belied the name he bore. His doubt[5]
Is darkness, from the unbelieving Will
Begot, and oft a parasite to sin
Too dear to be deserted;—for the truth
That unveils Heaven and its immortal thrones,
Uncovers Hell and awful duties, too!
Meanwhile, I flatter the surpassing fool,
And hear him challenge God to bare His brow,
Some Orb unsphere, and show Him all sublime.
He challenge Heaven! an atom against Worlds!
Why, angels and archangels, who have bow'd
Within the shadow of His Throne, and felt
The beams of an emitted glory burn
Around them, cannot comprehend His might,
Nor fathom his perfections:—*what* is Man!

If Nature fail, then Reason may despair.
The universe with God is stamp'd: who sees
Creation, and can no Creator view,—
To him philosophy will preach in vain:[6]
A blinded conscience and a blasted mind
Are his; Eternity shall teach the rest!
Yet who the Summer, that bright season-queen,
Hath hail'd, beheld the march of midnight-worlds,
The Sun in glory, or the realm of Sky
When kingly Thunders in sublime array
Ride the dark chariot of the rolling clouds;
Who that hath seen terrific Ocean frown,
Or moonshine ripple o'er the rocking waves
In smiles of beauty,—all this living might
And motion, grace, and majesty of things,
Nor caught some impulse which believing heart
Might share, and crown it with a creed sublime?
A soul so dark, so miserably vile,
Is form'd to grace a burning throne below,
And teach the Devils atheistic lore!

But there are others of unheavenly hue;
A mass of creatures, by the earth beloved,
Who bear a seemly fame; caress their limbs
And senses; smile on Nature, when they please,
And walk through life, as children by a shore
Who sport, and laugh, and pluck the sandy toys
Which glitter on their path—yet sometimes pause
With thinking eye, to mark the scene august
Of ocean, like a vision, heaving wild:—
Too mean for virtue, too polite for vice,
The happy medium which their spirits keep
Is fitly toned to temporal joys:—they live
As though Hereafter were *this* life prolong'd,
And drown all instincts of diviner growth

In plots and plans whereby the hours are wing'd.—
Lo! one is fearful of the traitorous Winds
Wafting a sailing palace o'er the deep;
What fancy-shipwreck overwhelms the soul!
What billows ever rocking in his brain!
Another hath some mountainous ascent
Of Life to vanquish, where a rival stands
And triumphs o'er him with a mocking gaze:
Though Angels whisper to his heart, return!
Still must he onward up to Glory climb.
Then comes your Zealot! weeping Country's wounds;
And yet, with what a yell of pleased delight,
As screams the vulture round his future prey
His fancy revels o'er a ruin'd land!
And thus, protected by his patriot name,
He lives on vileness which his tongue creates.

And such are these, who make the middle class
Of creatures, wedded to the dust they tread,
But doom'd to wrestle with contrasted lots
And Life's predestined woes. There droops a man,—
Poetic sadness in his pensive eye,
As haunting tombs, or scenes beyond the dead!
And here, a victim of tempestuous thought,
Wolf-eyed, and glaring out his wilder'd mind
In glances lit with torture!—while, to mock
Their meaner anguish, see a soulless Thing
Appear, whose spirit bubbles out in song:
And such is life,—a paradox at best!

Here dwells my power; in living things which grasp
The spirit, or that blind it with a glare
Reflected from bright scenes of earthly pomp
That curtain up eternity. No truths
Divine, no energies which pant for heaven,
In the cold depths of carnal spirit play;
But he who from his soul the sensual chain
Uncoils, and looks into Life's holier things,
Wears attributes beyond the reach of Hell.
Then, Time is no enchanter, though his cup
May sparkle, and with brimming sweets be crown'd:
The shadows of that far mysterious World
Faith images, o'er time and scene prevail,
And gather round him like a guardian-spell.

Not such the earth-adoring million prove.
When this world dies, the next begins to live!
With fearful sternness on the inward eye
It flashes, till the daunted mind start back
Aghast, like Fancy from a hideous dream!
At that deep hour, when dwindling to a blank
Dim Earth departs; and those dear sounds of life
Which once prevail'd so eloquently sweet,
Grow faint and dismal, as the dreary voice
Of waters gurgling round a drowning man,—
The solemn meanings of the past are known.
What prophet spake in every funeral knell!
How oft the hearse-train, stealing through the rush
Of sounding pathways with a spectral glide,
The vision of a dying moment gave!
And he, the victim of unvalued hours
As home he went from halls of festive glare,
The moon, night-weary, and the sallow dawn
In sickly lustre o'er the Orient spread—
How oft the nothingness of life he felt,
And dream'd the tragedy Death suffers now!

But these are moods unwelcomed and unloved,
The sad intrusion of a sober thought,
A cloud pass'd o'er the summer of his mind,
And laugh'd away in lightness, or in joy.—
The dead, the faded and forgotten dead!
The progeny of Ages, who have breathed
That breath of life which all the living breathe,
Have walk'd beneath the same blue sky, and hail'd
The Lord of brightness which illumes their path,
Inherited the same mysterious dust,
And form'd like them a link in nature's chain,—
Have shrunk away, like shadows into gloom,
And who laments them? They, the fair and young,
In the prime bloom of spousal years, who seem'd
Too beautiful to die; and Fame's proud race
Of Heroes, o'er whose bier a Nation wept;
With all that number multiplied can dream
Of mindless creatures dancing round their tombs,
And mocking at eternity!—are plunged
And buried in the unremember'd past,
Yet, few dare meditate their dying hour!
Oh! did the living but the dead recal,
As often as the dead the living do,[7]
The Sun would gaze upon a purer world
Than now;—but let the dead remain the dead!
Thus Pleasure teach thou *my* philosophy;
Thy truths are sweet, thy curses all conceal'd!

Never may Wisdom's heaven-communing eye
To these, the earthly and the low, reveal
That sounds of Folly pierce the gloom of hell;
That tongues of Torture syllable their names
In regions where inflamèd whirlwinds roar!
Back,—back to this forsaken Orb of life
Fain would a perish'd Father come, to dart
One glance upon an unbelieving child,
To breathe one sigh of warning round his soul!—
May never men of whisp'ring Angels learn
How heaven is brighten'd when the earth adores.

BOOK IV.

——"We gather honey from the weed,
And make a Moral of the devil himself."
Shakespere.

So weak and yet so wonderful; so frail
In act, and yet so splendidly endow'd
For action, are the race of Men abhorr'd,
That, view them in whatever rank they move,
Through fields of Glory which the warrior treads,
Or in proud realms of wisdom, fame, or power,
An awful distance from their primal State
Th' Inheritors of our scorn'd heaven have stray'd!
No longer now the bright and palmy Sons
Of God, but giants of iniquity,
Or Anakims of intellectual vice,
And helmeted with sin, the rebels stand,
Who fight against the Lord of life and death,
And make their crimes immortal as themselves!

That primal State!—had evil not prevail'd,
A heaven in miniature this world had been.
Her paradise! I see it as it rose
In youthful splendour on my savage eye!
A starry jubilee still rang; the wings
Angelical of many a hovering Shape
Still hung and glitter'd on the virgin air,
Which seem'd one atmosphere of melody!
As yet, no cloud was born; the sunshine fed
The flowers with beauty, till the twilight dew;
Birds exquisite, with dazzling plumage clad,
And butterflies, bright creatures, rich as they,
Like showers of blossoms from a tree upwhirl'd,
On starry wing hung trembling in the breeze,
More glorious yet!—from Eden's mount I gazed,
The emerald bloom of whose untrodden hills
Lay jewell'd o'er with amaranthine flowers,
And saw two Creatures of celestial mould.
Till these were made, companionless the World
Appear'd; and like a heart suspended lay,
All throbbing for the Vision that should dawn!
And they were fashion'd,—breathing shapes of life,
With radiant limbs, whose robes were innocence,
And eyes that spoke the birth-place of the Soul!
Again the star-chimed Hallelujahs rang
With wonder! while a gush of rapture thrill'd
Creation to her centre, till each breeze
Was gladness murmur'd out of Nature's heart!

And thus they rose,—that new-created Pair,
In loveliness complete, with forms of light,
Reflecting glory wheresoe'er they moved.
The one did mark the blue immensity
Above, with a majestic gaze, and eyed
The Sun, as though he felt himself akin
To his pre-eminence, and kingly state:
The other, in her fair perfection seem'd
A Shape apparell'd by her own pure smiles,—
Surpassing beauty, and subduing love!
While ever as she moved, the blush of flowers
O'erveil'd her, and a breezy host of sounds,
Like magic birds, embosom'd in the air
In sweet attendance caroll'd round her path:
Never hath young romance, or shaping dream,
Divined the vision which in Eden lay,—
Each sound was music, and each sight a heaven!

Oh! it was glory, that with blighting rays
Flash'd in fell triumph on these envious eyes,
Thus to behold the darlings bright of heaven,
Created, form'd to fill *our* Seats above!
Obedient, and they vanquish'd me; my doom
Of darkness would have set, without one gleam
Of vengeance for the living pangs I feel.
I plotted,—tempted,—and the earth-born sunk
From heaven's embrace into the arms of hell,
Henceforward to enclasp a world of souls!
Then, what a withering the Elements
Of life and being felt!—corruption pass'd
Through human into natural Things: the Earth
Was barren-struck; the guilt-abhorring Sun
His beams withdrew; the rivers howl'd with dread,
And deep the blast of desolation blew:
A curse came down, and Eden was no more!

And now, from his primeval state dethroned,
His very form o'ershadow'd by the sin
That, like a breath-stain on a mirror cast,
The beauty of his god-like mien eclipsed—
I look'd on Man, a remnant of despair,
But gloried as I gazed!—for then, the tongue,
That tameless member which o'ermastereth all,
E'en in an atmosphere of God himself
That grand deceit of erring souls began,—
Where guilt is flatter'd, and the heart secure!

Creation shudder'd! for mankind were lost,
Till God the seal of mystery should break
In him foredoom'd to bruise the Serpent's head,
And re-awake the hymns of Paradise.
Meanwhile, the Evil triumph'd o'er the Good:
And, exiled from their Eden-home, begirt
And guarded with an ever-living flame,
Two fallen Creatures on the race of life
In sorrowing loneliness appear'd. Time lash'd
His years along; but evil with them moved,

Till Death in fratricidal fury came!—
How Life hung shudd'ring o'er his glazing eye
When pale, and dash'd with many a bloody hue,
The prostrate Abel in the gasp of death
Lay stretch'd; while Cain, a maniac child of Hell
With lines of anguish working on his face,
Stood by, and knew himself th' embodied Curse!

Crime revell'd on, the peopled earth sank deep
In ruin, till the great Avenger woke;
Then came a Flood, a desolating tide,
Which deluged sixteen hundred years of sin!
Methinks I hear it now! so fiercely howl'd
The waves and whirlwinds of that dreadful hour.—
Dark prodigies, disasters in the sky,
Announced it; yet these heralds were contemn'd:
Still Blasphemy went hooting at the heavens,
And mock'd the Elements with impious joy.
The sun went down in sorrow; and the moon
Rose pale and icy, as an orb congeal'd;
While, ever and anon, there came a sigh
Of Air, so spiritually deep and sad,
It seem'd to issue from an Angel-heart
That ached to look upon a dying World,
Unconscious of her coming pangs:—thus Hell
Prevail'd, save o'er the sacred few. And one
The wicked counsell'd, glorious, and as good;
A hoary Patriarch, who would haunt the shore,
And hear a prophet speaking in the wind,
And prescient terror in the sound of waves,
Like mystery, mutter'd into Nature's ear;
Then darkly muse on some high-gazing rock,
And shape out Immortality!—But when
The skies were blacken'd to a cloudy sea,
Whose rage came down in cataracts, Despair!
The racking universe was all thine own.

And never were such horrid shadows frown'd
Upon the Waters, as thy victims threw,
When all aghast, in their avenging ire
They heard them ravenously sweep along,
As roaring for their human prey! Such sounds
Of wo, such shrieks of madness never rang,
Such eyes were never to a God upturn'd,
As mark'd this dread, unutterable hour!
A palpitation in the womb of Earth
Began, then upward burst a buried sea,*
That whirl'd the mountains on her waves, and heaved
The rocks, and shook the rooted hills abroad,
Till darkness and a deluge cover'd All!—

* See Burnett's chapter on the Deluge.

Save that which in the wilderness of waves
Triumphant o'er a weltering chaos rode,
And bore aloft the burden of the world!

Yes! these were dread catastrophes of old,
Loading with awfulness the tongue of Time;
Unparagon'd as yet: but 'tis decreed,
Another Day of unimagined doom
Shall come, a deluge of devouring fire
That now is redd'ning in the cavern-depths
Which eye hath pierced not, ravenous for the hour
When Earth shall wither into shapeless air!
And I,—no matter! mortal years remain,
And souls for ruin, ere *my* sun can set!

So fierce the sway of evil, and the power
Of will, o'er reason and religion's voice,
That though a thousand deluges had been,
Still the vile earth my sceptre should command.
The teeming volume of the Past unroll,
And from each page what lesson may be cull'd?
A moral justice sways the course of Things,[1]
Guiding them on to their eternal goal.
From evil, evil, and from good, a good
Is born, each one a payment in itself,
Its own avenger, or its own reward.
I thank thee, Passion! blinded by desire
Thou seest it not through every track which years
Have furrow'd on the travell'd sea of Time.
By tears of torture, wrung from out the soul
Of penitence; by arrows of remorse;
The inward hell in guilty bosoms found;
By retributions in the wrathful shape
Of elements, and dangers wing'd by death;
By frenzied Glory, that will venture on
Till dash'd to ruin by her own renown;
By each and all of such avengers Crime
Hath paid atonement to the Law of Life,
And agonised o'er that which is to come.

E'en Nature, in her elemental round
Of living wonders, a re-action shows,
In semblance to the moral law reveal'd
By human destinies. The poise of worlds
Which make infinity a beauteous thought;
The Ocean, panting as the tide-queen wills,
In ebb and flow of everlasting waves;
And that communion of the earth and sky
By heat exhaling water into clouds,
And clouds returning in the showery rain—
All teach a balance of prevailing power.
But thou, Reviver of departed days!
By whom, as beacon-light for time unborn
The past might well have risen, hast forgot
The law of retribution in thy love
Of fame, and adoration to the dead.

A War awakes!—what poetry is here
For History to picture into life
And splendour, making infamy sublime!
The armies rally,—vast machines of Mind
Half demonised, with one concent'ring heart
To animate and harmonise the whole;
The clarions ring, the banners chafe the breeze,
Earth trembles to the haughty-footed steeds,
And cannons thunder till the clouds are thrill'd!
Then comes your "Hero" sprinkled with a shower
Of blood,—how gloriously sublime he seems!
Yet Kingdoms mourn, and trodden myriads lie
All dead, and stiff'ning in the moonless air.

But, should re-action for heroic crime,
Or lavish conquest, smite a tyrant soul,
A human vengeance not a Hand Supreme,
Is traced; and retribution reason'd down,
As though life circled on the wheels of Chance!
Thus, when a Despot, weary of renown,
In sorrow to a throneless gloom descends,
How History flutters round his agonies!
And so the living, who the dead recall,
Are written into sympathy with shame;
While they, whose words are wisdom to the pure,
Rise dimly vision'd on th' historic page,
Where infamy in glowing language lives.[2]

Thus may it ever be! let ages gone,
Whence monuments, by sad experience piled,
Might o'er unheedful days a warning frown,
Like buried lumber in oblivion sleep;
Experience is the sternest foe of hell.
And though progression be the native soul
Of all things, human or divine, while Pride
Can hear no prophets breathing through the past,
Progression will be lame, and Nature slow
In her advancement to that heaven-like scene,
Prophetic rapture in its vision hail'd;
While frequently, an earthquake-shock will come,
Forcing the world a century back again
In vice and darkness, sucn as once o'erthrew
The Roman empire and her subject-isles.

Upon the forehead of these fearless times
I know the haughtiness which now exults:
But let the modern in his pride beware!
Corruption is the strongest in the best,
And knowledge wasted, worse than ignorance proved.
A moral, not an intellectual life
Alone, however rich with mental bloom,
God's Image in the human soul reveals:

And so taught He, that co-eternal One
On high, when leaving his Elysian throne,
He templed his bright Nature in the dust
Of dim Mortality, and unbarr'd heaven
Whose gates of glory now expanded shine.
Philosophy, benighted in the gloom
Of Pagan wisdom, fondly charming oft
The shade and silence of Athenian groves,
How failing in her eagle flights!—To clear
The clouded intellect was her prime aim:
The heart, that fountain-source of sacred life,
Rank'd second in the mental scheme for Man;
And thus, her wisdom in a weedy soil
Was sown; and perish'd in its mortal thirst
For feelings, which refresh the growing mind
As spring-dews foster the awaking flowers.

But Christianity, the child of Truth,
With searching light the inward nature clear'd,
And by a conscience, rooted in the soul,
And fears, from which unfading hopes are born,
And faculties of faith, which all possess,
Awoke the mind to wisdom, pure as heaven.
Spirit of Vengeance! would that I could hide
One living God, surpassingly supreme,
Parent of mighty worlds, pervading each,
The First and Last, Immortal, and the True;
The Son of his Eternity, from Heaven
Sent down, embodied in a human mould;
The Same upon the cross hung crucified,
Incarnadined with His redeeming blood
For fallen nature flowing, till the Earth
As in an agony did rock and heave,
While bowing angels worshipp'd in amaze,
And hell grew darker with despair!—a Life
Unending, shared by an existent soul;
A Resurrection, when the dead shall wake;
And, crowning all, the doomsday of the world;
When every eye must see Him in the clouds,
And time be swallow'd in eternity,—
Would that all this infernal hate could hide,
Which Devils own, and tremble to believe!

But thanks to man, man's most inveterate foe,
How oft, perverted, hath Religion proved
That curse she came to cancel and destroy!
By Bigotry, insatiate for the blood
Of martyrs; by the shadows and the clouds
That dream-eyed Innovation form'd and fed,—
The clash of Evil with the growth of Good
Hath half repaid me for the realm I lost,
When dawn'd salvation on the sinking world.

And now there is an animating throb,
An energy, and daringness of thought,
Awaken'd like one mighty pulse through lands
And isles, remotely set in ocean-gloom.[3]

But if the Heart uncultivated lie
Amid the reign of intellectual power,—
Though, basking in the sunshine of her hope,
Philosophy of perfect minds may dream,
She builds a vision, baseless, proud, and vain,
As ever revell'd on the eye of sleep!
For o'er the heart a vicious mind shall rule,
And poison each aspiring germ of thought,
Till Talent prove but wickedness inspired,
In baneful glory towering o'er mankind:
So be it!—Hell shall blaze a bright applause.

No, not till spirit over sense prevail,
And mortals to the awfulness of life
Advance, shall Earth a brighter visage wear.
And such, methinks, Creation might reveal.—
A Sea, for ever sounding with his voice
Of billows, "Might and majesty are here,
And in eternity my waves have roll'd;"
And Sky of living glory, when the storm
Lies back with fury on a sea of clouds,
Or, arch'd in beauty, shadowless and blue:
With all the wonders, swarming on each spot
Of being—hint they not an awful shade
Of Mystery unreveal'd, yet claiming thoughts
Of solemn hue?[4] And then, while hours depart,
(Myriads of spirits passing to and fro
From life and light, to darkness and the grave,
While feelings, words, and deeds, whatever mind
Betray of good or bad in ceaseless pulse
Of action, register'd above, remains
For judgment,)—bear they not, as on they roll,
A burden, and a meaning most sublime?
Yet who, in nature or in time, reveres
A sense and shadow of diviner Things?*

A spectacle to angels and to God
Is Man, while acting on the stage of time,—
Such truth the soul of inspiration breathed:
And what a meaning centred in the thought!
Around, above, beneath, where'er man lives
And moves, unvision'd Natures overhang
His path, and chronicle his history.
But o'er this pomp external, and the life
Of sense, such beautifying veils I throw,
That men become idolaters to sight,
Naming all else the nothingness of dreams:[5]
A wisdom worthy an infernal crown!
Why, if a bead of water in its orb
Of motion hath contain'd a countless host
Of beings, limb'd, and full of perfect life;
If not a leaf which flutters on the tree,
But is empeopled with an insect swarm;
If not a flower by fairy sunrise charm'd,
But in the palace of its dew-drop dwell
Unnumber'd beings, that in gladness live;*
Then why not, O ye self-adoring wise,
A world of spirit-natures, though unseen,
In number rivalling what creation yields?
And vacancy, that hueless void of air
Which men unanimated space define,
Be pregnant with aerial Shapes of life?

Yet better is such blindness for the cause
Of Evil; would it might eclipse the race
Entire, of all who have a soul to save!
For some can dare the prison'd mind unbar,
And view Reality behind the veil
Which mantles their mortality. And such
The pale enchantment of a moonlight-hour,
When the soft skies are fleck'd with silky clouds,
In veils of beauty floating on the breath
Of heaven, and stars in pensive light appear
The bright mementos of eternity,—
For high communion with celestial Things
Employ: such spirits never in *their* clay
Are dungeon'd; but in demi-paradise
Do wander, reaping holiness and love.—
And Guilt too hath her hour, when Spectres come
Array'd in fury, till the air grow dark
With demon-wings, and terror shrieks my name!

But this deep sense of something Unavow'd
Pervading nature, which the purer mind
May in some beauteous trance of holy thought
Perceive, and which the ghastliness of guilt
Oft tortures into life,—o'er few prevails:
In vain have heaven-taught Seers a coming World
Foreshadow'd: visions of unearthly blaze,
And princely Seraphs over empires throned,†
And Dreams which were the delegates of God,—
Of such vast wonders deep-voiced Prophets tell.
And now, in riper days, when men have crown'd
Themselves with false perfection, not an hour
But hints a spirit-nature to the soul,
Howe'er unhallow'd! Whence that prescient sense
Of peril doom'd to come? those guiding thoughts
Which helm the fancy with mysterious sway?
The heaven of feeling when a God descends?
Or mystic sorrow, which melodious strains
Wherein the spirits of the dead revive
And home and childhood have a pictured life,

* "For the invisible things of Him from the creation of the world, are clearly seen, being understood by the things that are made."—*Rom.* i. 20.

* See St. Pierre's "Studies of Nature," for some illustrations of this fact.

† See Daniel.

Oft o'er the heart of lone Bereavement brings?
Or, all which sound and scenery suggest
Of purity and grace?—The scoffer doubts!
And by that sneer his inner-light destroys.
Yet Angels are there, watching o'er mankind
With tenderness and eyes of heavenly love.
The same who, when the World-awakening trump
Is sounded, shall the buried dead untomb
For Judgment, and its awful throne sustain.

These Agencies divine, howe'er men veil
Their viewless presence mid the thrilling cares
Below, are often in their glorious range
Of wisdom, by the plotting Evil-powers
Encounter'd, with defiance and despair!
Visions of sunshine and of music made,
Where the bright soul, entranced with melody,
Communes with Seraph-watchers, are of heaven.
But whence that fancy-roll of billows, heard
In darkness, deluging the wilder'd brain
With hideous murmur? or those formless Things
Which hang and blacken o'er the shudd'ring frame?
Or whence that tongueless blasphemy of mind
Making the heart to shiver, and the eye
To gaze behind, as though a prompting Shape
Of Evil stood there, muttering hell-framed words?
The fire, the fury of appalling dreams,
Whence is it?—rend the veil, and ye would know
Proud victims of an unbelieving heart!
That such are demon-haunters of the earth,[6]
Who horrify the vision'd world of sleep,
And pall its midnight with infernal gloom.

Who wonders, the dark Mysteries of life
And hidden Beings of unearthly power
Are smiled away for superstitious creed,
When He, the Ransomer of lost mankind,
Whose Name a starry herald to the sage
Reveal'd, and at Whose birth the heavens were bowed,
To millions less than many a Hero seems,—
A Myth incarnate priests and fools adore!

A Saviour, Son of the Most High, enthroned
Amid the hallelujahs of the blest,
I saw Him ere the universe began;
When space was worldless, luminously fill'd
With emanations of vast Deity;
I saw Him when immensity His voice
Obey'd, and nothing startled into worlds.*
And did I not, be witness, Powers below!
Bear on my brow the lightnings which He wreak'd,
Because I would not to His Godhead bend?
Without Him, and this withered Earth had sunk
To hell, for ever blasted by that word
Of vengeance, which her frowning Maker spoke,
Who cannot His eternal nature change:
Immutable in majesty, in truth,
Or else His Infinite would finite be;
And therefore, by His attributes, the Law
When broken, should to violated heaven
Atonement offer;—where the Sacrifice?
Till God for God, and Man for Man, appear'd
In wondrous union of incarnate power,
Hung on the cross, and saved the guilty world!

I hate Him, and his everlasting cause,
The Church, upon the rock of ages rear'd,
His word, His truth, and heaven-directing sway;
And soul by soul, and heart by heart, through light
And gloom, by land and isle, through life and death,
'Mid all the legions of embattled Powers
Who on His Ministry attend, and war †
For holiness—my hate shall dare Him still;
Though Truth may vanquish, and the viewless thrones
Of Darkness tremble with their last despair!

Too deep the vengeance of atoning Blood
On me shall come, for *Him* to be forgot!
I hate Him, for the ruin'd world he saved:
And yet His glorious pilgrimage confess.
Sublime of Martyrs! in that dread career
What wonders hallow His remember'd way!
The blind awaken'd to the bliss of light,
The deaf and lame, the dying and the dead,
All yielding up infirmity to Him,
And putting on young attributes of life.
Vain mortals, read and tremble! Once the Sea,
That god and glory of the Elements,
Obey'd His fiat, when a tempest rose,
Till the huge waves like living mountains leapt
In the wild majesty of midnight-storm,
Mocking the haggard lightnings as they streak'd
The waters, in the fury of their flash.
Each billow was a tempest; and the ship

* "His Son, whom He hath appointed heir of all things; by whom also He made the worlds."—*Heb.* i. 2.

† Vide Chalmers' admirable "Discourse on the Contest for an Ascendancy over Man, amongst the Higher Orders of Intelligence."

Groan'd like a mariner at his last gasp;
Up rose He in almightiness! and bade
The whirlwinds into silence, and rebuked
The Ocean, calm'd by His resistless Eye!

And then, His Passion!—that tremendous scene
When God incarnate for the guilty bled,
While throbbing earth seem'd echo'd with His pangs
Almighty, and eclipsing horrors veil'd
The sun, which darken'd while its Maker died;
Or else, the midnight over Calv'ry's mount
Incumbent, coward fancy should have seen!
Have heard the cloven rock-piles as they burst,
The tombs unlock, and mark'd the solemn dead
In pallid stillness gliding through the town
As moon-clouds gleam along a midnight sky!

This grand array of miracles, this might
And majesty of preternatural things
Reveal'd in mercy, to arouse the world
To perfect sanctities of word and deed,
Have,—hear it, Demons! with exulting shout,
Fail'd! Long may Nature turn a slighting ear
To that true voice, which since Messiah bled,
By lips Divine and eloquence of life,
When, holiness the Christian heart inspires,
Hath testified that Virtue is the heaven
Begun, and vice the seed of Hell in man.

Delusion is the soul of young desire.
Behold a Vessel which has never braved
A sea: before her gallant bosom swells
A blue extent of ever-bounding waves,
All sunny-crested, glowing like the noon.
No stormy menace in the welkin frowns,
Sea, shore, and sky are in one mingled calm;
Loud, deep, and full the voice of welcome rings,
Away she flies in glory o'er the deep
Exulting in the wind!—And such is Youth,
So bright the promise of life's onward way;
Beneath the sunshine of fond hope awhile
The victim basks; drinks deep of every cup
Enchanted, feasts the faculty of sense,
And hails each hour the herald of new joy;
Thus on! as though unfading bliss were found,
Till weariness awake; the wing of joy
No longer o'er his soul a freshness waves,
And like the moody air he often breathes
A sigh of sullenness around his path.
And now, the verdure of delight no more,
The heart uneasy, and the soul unsaved,
With that dark fever of condemning thought,
Which conscience frets from out the sated mind,
As here the brute, and there the man, prevails,—
Behold your slave of pleasure rot from year
To year; obeying sin, yet feeling guilt;
His present, darkness, and his past, despair!

Of finer mould and far sublimer view,
Whate'er his lot, on Fortune's envied mount
High-throned, or lost in the secluded vales
Of lowliness,—is he whose hopes are built
In heaven; the hateful, but triumphant still!
Not all the pomp and pageantry of worlds
Such glory on the Eye Supreme reflect,
As the meek virtues of one holy man:
For ever doth his Angel from the face
Divine, beatitude and wisdom draw:
And in his prayer, what privilege enjoy'd!
Mounting the heavens, and claiming audience there,—
Yes! there, amid the sempiternal host
Of Seraphs, hymning in eternal choir,
A lip of clay its orisons can send,
In temple or in solitude outbreathed.

I loathe the bright, the beautiful, and good,
By man when mirror'd forth sublimely fair;
Yet how, the hero of the Cross deny
What Hell may hate,—but hating, still admire?
One universal love, the source and end
Of true philosophy, within such heart
Must dwell, and make the atmosphere of mind
All sympathy, wherein a good man breathes:—
A tear for sorrow, and a smile for joy,
Are ever his; and thus existence spans
A wider realm than the self-loving fill,
Who crawl about their own mean world. Not man
Alone, the empire of his heart contains
In its free compass of embracing thought;
E'en gentle nature wins a share of love;
From the frail being of a lonely flower
By earth forgot, in beautiful ascent
Up to the very clouds, which in the shine
Of heaven seem bathing with voluptuous joy,
And here I face the triumph of a soul
In such fine overflow of sympathy,—
However spread, 'tis unpolluted still:
As sunshine in its beaming intercourse
With earth, shines pure upon corrupted clay.

Then, Virtue hath a loveliness, a calm
So fresh and full, a blessing and a hope,
With such elysium of contented thought,—
Rejoice I may, but ever wonder more
To see her so forsaken. Her delights
Endure as rich above the hectic joys
The wicked and the worldly reap, as hues
Of nature on the rose-bright cheek of youth
Outbloom the artificial blush of age,
And blossom in the wintry gloom of life

Unfadingly sincere.—Another source
Of heaven, there opens on the virtuous mind,
Which daunts me with a deep excess of good,—
Pure sympathy, which makes the Past its own
By following where the great and glorious dead
Traced the true path which terminates in God.
Art, Love, and Wisdom, Nature and her scenes.
Each from association prompting force derives.
When in the coolness of declining day
As o'er autumnal woods brown evening falls,
In haunts where solitude hath breathed a soul,—
By Thought companion'd, oft the wanderer feels
Such sympathy, the while of good and great
He thinks, who loved like him the lonely hour,
Still walks, and dreams, and meditative joy.
And that prime bliss, perfection of delight,
Which is to ear what beauty is to thought,
Sweet melody,—methinks 'tis only framed
To nourish heavenliness, in hallow'd minds;*
There, how refreshingly must music flow,
And faint into the soul,—as dewy sleep
Melts o'er the eyelids of a weary man.

These holy yet another triumph crowns.
In woes which blacken o'er the brightest lot
How loftily above the bad they tower!
While those whom faith, nor resignation calms
Become a ruin, haunted by despair;
Save, when gay thoughts from gloomy moments spring,
As bright-leaved flowers that in the sunshine bloom,
From the chill damp of earth and darkness sprung.

And such the life which virtue seems to boast;
With gladness lighted, or by sorrow dimm'd,
Still wearing a contented smile, to meet
The great Approver: like a placid stream
That in its meadowy pilgrimage can wear
The aspect of a pure and gentle thing
Alike where sun-beams laugh, or shadows frown.—
And when the summons to a future State
Is heard, those hell-black phantoms of despair,
Those clouds of horror which the wicked dread,
Melt in the brightness of a better world:
Thus, arm'd with faith in Him who vanquish'd death,
A gentle summons from their Lord to meet
The angels bright and beatific souls
Who erst have battled in the war of life,—
Death comes, and wafts them to the waiting Skies.

And such is truth!—in heaven and hell the same.
And Hate herself in agony avows,
That Virtue *is* triumphant, and the best:
Her glories are my tortures; but they shine
Upon me, blasting with victorious light
The envy which I bear them, when I scan
The mazes of mortality.—How kind
In men, to aid the darkness which I bring
On fallen nature! lauding what I love,
And hating all which Fiends abhor. Thus vice
In splendour will appear, while virtue droops,
Like a long shadow pining in the sun.
And never shall the good the bad exceed,
While Sin can put enchantment in her smile,
And Passions are the tyrants of the soul!

Thou dread Avenger! ever-living One!
Lone Arbiter! Eternal, Vast, and True;
The Soul and Centre of created things,
In atoms or in worlds; before Whose Throne
The universe recoils; who look'st—and life
Appears; who frown'st—and life hath pass'd away!
Thou God!—I feel Thine everlasting curse,
Yet wither not: the lightnings of Thy wrath
Burn in my spirit, yet it shall endure
Unblasted, that which *cannot* be extinct!

Thou sole Transcendency, and deep Abyss
From whence the Infinite of Life was drawn!
Unutter'd is Thy nature; to Thyself
Alone the comprehended God Thou art.
Though once the steep of Thine almightiness
My tow'ring spirit would have dared to climb
And reign'd beside Thee, god with God enthroned,
And vanquish'd fell, Thy glories Fiends confess.
Immutable! omnipotence is Thine;
Perfections, Powers, and Attributes unnamed,
Attend Thee; Thou art All, and oh, how great
That Consummation! Worlds to listening worlds
Repeat it; angels and archangels veil
Their wings, and shine more glorious at the sound:
Thus, infinite and fathomless Thou wert,
And art, and wilt be. In Thine awful blaze
Of majesty, amid empyreal pomp
Chief Hierarch, I once irradiant knelt
Thy Throne before, terrifically bright,
And heard the hymning thunders voice thy name,
While bow'd the Heavens, and echoed Deity!

* Plato says that music accustoms the mind to order, and thereby allures it to the love of virtue, which is nothing but moral order.

Then heaved a dark and dreadless swell of pride
Within me! an ambition, huge and high
Enough to overshadow the Supreme,
In bright magnificence before me tower'd,
And fronted pride against Omnipotence!
Thus rose the anarchy of mystic war
The skies amid; then met embattled Hosts
In unimaginable arms divine:—
But why recount it? Spirits disarray'd
God hurl'd in flaming whirlwinds to the deep
Tartarean, where the Demons wait their doom.

And yet, divided empire have I won.
Behold! the havoc in Thy beauteous world:
And have I not, be witness, space and time!
Thy master-piece, creation's god of clay,
Dethroned from that high excellence he held
When first man walk'd a shadow of Thyself!
Prostration vile, an alienate from Thee
Man is;—and *shall* his fallen nature rise,
Enter bright heaven, and fill ethereal thrones?
Many a cloud of evil shall be burst
Ere that day come: severe and dread the strife
Of earth-born passion with the soul of man!
Wherever localised, whate'er his creed,
Fiends of temptation shall his soul beset,
Though every pang, by sin produced, increase
The agonised eternity I bear!
The blackest midnight to the brightest day
Is not more opposite, than I to Thee:
Thou art the Glorious, I the Evil one;
Thou reign'st above; my kingdom is below;
On earth, 'tis Thine to succour and adorn
The soul, through sacraments of secret grace,
By thoughts divine, and agencies direct;
To cheer the gentle, and reward the good,
And o'er the many waves and woes of life
To pour the sunshine of almighty love:
'Tis mine to darken, wither, and destroy,
And in destruction see the heaven of hell!

Then roll thee on, thou high and haughty World!
Still be thy sun as bright, thy sea as loud
In her sublimity, thy floods and winds
As potent, and thy lording Elements
As vast in their mysterious range of power,
As each and all have ever been: build thrones
And empires, heap the mountain of thy crimes,
Be mean or mighty, wise or worthless still,—
Yet I am with thee! and my power shall reign
Until the trumpet of thy doom be heard,
Thine ocean vanish'd, and thy heavens no more!
Till Thou be tenantless, a welt'ring mass
Of fire, a dying and dissolving World!
And then, Thy hidden lightnings are unsheath'd,
O God! the thunders of despair shall roll;
Mine hour is come, and I am wreck'd of all—
All save eternity, and *that* is mine!

BOOK V.

"This royal throne of Kings, this sceptred isle,
This earth of majesty, this seat of Mars—
England!"

How gloriously the festal chimes resound
Their pealing gladness through the azure night,
And thrill the air with jubilee and joy!—
As though the triumph of ten thousand hearts
In full-voiced chorus shook the starry heaven,
And made it conscious music! Now they swell
Aloft, in one excited wave of sound;
Then, faintly die, like war-notes on the wind,
Rousing the empire with a brave delight.

England hath laid her sceptre on the Deep,
And, with her thunder, chased her ocean-foes
Like leaves before the breathing of a blast!
England hath rear'd her banners on the plain
Of battle; victory waved them; and the world
Again shall echo with her haughty name.
And hence, a stormy rapture shakes the isle;
Hence the loud music of her steepled fanes,
Whether in cities emulously tower'd
Among the skies, or in lone hamlets seen,—
Still pouring out the language of the land;
With all those pageantries, and fiery pomps,
That hang and glitter from her window'd piles
Emblazed with mottoes, and triumphal scenes.

Not one, to whom the name of country sounds
Like heaven-born music, but this hour adores.
The old men feel the sunshine of far youth
Returning, fresh as when the hero glow'd.
The young,—lip, eye, and daring heart, are stirr'd;
Their very blood seems rippled with delight,
So deep the fulness of this warlike joy.
Yea, hollow cheeks of Sadness, and the brows
Of Poverty, and lean-faced Want itself,
Forget their nature in a share of fame!
And yet, most hideous are some human shapes
Which revel near me, by a tow'ring blaze
Of triumph;—as it flings its glaring life
Upon their faces, each one gleams beneath
The mockery, like a ruin'd shrine when noon
In bright derision dances o'er the walls.

Let Fancy to a distance wing her flight,
And learn the glory whence this scene is born.
How Sorrow treads upon the heels of Joy!

What puts a smile on some great Empire's cheek,
Hath wrung the life-blood from another's heart;
While one is revelling with impassion'd glee
Another moans like misery's bleakest child:
Thus seems the world a round of joy and wo,
Alike divided for the doom of things.

Hither, thou frantic Bacchanal! whose voice
Rings loudest, stand upon the hoof-scared heath,
And say if Heaven on *such* a scene can smile!
Here, deep as in thine own exulting land,
Night reigns; but not with noon-like azure crown'd,
While sympathetic stars, all gaily bright,
Look down on gladness: but with sullen calm
Where moans the conscious wind, and pensive stars
Seem pale-eyed watchers o'er those trodden dead,
In tombless havoc weltering on the plain.
Each heart now cold, to other hearts was chain'd,
Whose links were out of years of fondness framed;
Each eye now darken'd with eclipsing death
Once beam'd the sun of happiness and home;
Each of the dead hath flung a shade o'er life,
Henceforth to be a living agony.—
Mark! where the moon her icy lustre flings
What dead-romance! what visions of the slain!
One, calmly-brow'd, as though his native trees
Had waved their beauty o'er his dying head;
Another, marr'd with agonising lines
And dreams of home yet lingering in his face.—
Now go, and sing the splendour of the War!
Go, tell the Mother of the brave and free,
How beautiful this patriotic shout
Of Victory, when she counts the new-made dead,
Like Madness reeling with a murd'rous joy;
So shall a war-fame flourish ever-green,
And laurell'd History be trumpet-tongued,
To fire ambition with a bloody thirst,
Which makes the world a slaughter-house for man!

And this is "glory!" such as charms these days
When godly temples every street adorn;
While Tenderness, with its bewailing lip,
At ages of barbaric gloom affects
To wonder:—how the heart its flattery weaves!
Of proud deception, or intense desire,
The victim ever in its wariest mood.
To be the bulwark of a land beloved,
And drive aggression with avenging sword
From her indignant shore, commands renown:
But say, Thou Centre of created life,
Who charter'd man, and bade Thy heavens to mile
When from his eye outlook'd the living God!
What myriads upon myriads heap'd, to fill
The circle of ambitious thought, or please
Some royal dreamer who would dash a throne
To hear his trumpets pealing through the world,—
On hill and plain, and ocean's ravening waves,
The red libation of their hearts have pour'd!
But this is kingly:—so let tyrants dream;
Nor round their pillows may one death-cry ring:
The day, when dust shall give its monarchs back,—
Methinks I see it, and the fiery glance
Of Judgment scathing many a royal soul!

But night departs, the revelry is o'er,
And nature woos me. Through the orient heaven
A dawn advances with a beauteous glow;
And now, array'd in clouds of crimson pomp
The gradual Morn comes gliding o'er the waves
Which freshen under her reflected smiles,
And veils the world with glory. Rocks and hills
Are radiantly bedeck'd; the glimm'ring woods
And plains are mantled with their greenest robe,
And night-tears glisten in her rosy beam.
But in yon valleys, where from ivied cots
Like matin incense, wreathing smoke ascends,
How exquisite the flush of life! The birds
Are wing'd for heaven, and charm the air with song,
While in the gladness of the new-born breeze
The young leaves flutter, and the flow'rets sigh
Their blending odours out. And ye, bright streams,
Like happy pilgrims, how ye rove along
By mead and bank where violets love to dwell
In solitude and stillness: all is fresh,
And gaysome. Now the peasant, with an eye
Glad as the noon-ray sparkling through a shower,
Comes forth, and carols in thy waking beam
Thou sky-god! reigning on thy throne of light.
Sure airy painters have enrich'd thy sphere
With regal pageantry; such cloudy pomps
Adorn the heavens, a poet's eye would dream
His ancient gods had all return'd again
And hung their palaces around the sun!

And this is England, bathed in morning glow:
The isle where Freedom bears a lion-mien,
The Land whose echoes thrill the earth around,
The ocean-throned, the ancient battle-famed,
The Palestine of waters! O'er her realms

Enchantingly propitious Nature smiles;
Whose frowns and awfulness are seen afar,
Where snow-hills whiten in eternal glare,
Or soundless ocean, lock'd in icy sleep,
Deadens the polar world: but here alone
With summer hymning through the haunted vales,
'Tis beauty, bloom, and brightness all! How rich
The scented luxury of floral meads,
Reposing in the noon; where gentle winds
Exult, and many a choral brooklet sings:
Sure Admiration might be poet here!
Tall mansions, shadow'd by patrician trees,
Romantic farms, grey villages and cots,
With castled relics, and cathedral-piles
Where dreaming Solitude can muse and sigh,
Enchant dead Ages from their tombs, or hear
The dark soliloquy of ancient Time,—
Adorn the landscape and delight the view;
While haggard rocks, and heaven-aspiring hills
The sea o'ergazing, here and there create
A mountain-charm to solemnise the scene.

Or turn from Nature, in her fresh array
Of beauty, to behold the haunts of man,
In high-domed Capitals or cities huge
With varied grandeur round the island spread;
Here towers and temples overshade the streets
Where sound the life-floods in continuous roar,
And Commerce, whom the winds and waves revere,
To him whose veins are proud with English blood,
A scene suggests that bids the patriot glow.
Then Ocean,—listen, how th' intruding waves
With loud resentment trample on the shore,
Like pawing steeds, impatient for the war!

And such the magical array of things
By art and nature o'er this island strewn;
Than which, though envious clouds her sun
Conceal, and vapours curtain oft the sky,
Heaven canopies no lovelier clime. And they,
The children of her Freedom, with an air
Of kingliness they walk thy consecrated soil,
And thoughtful manhood, on their brows enthroned.
Though perfect beauty lost its moral grace
When Sin unmask'd her hideous front, and shades
Of hell rose frowning o'er this human scene,
It reigneth still; as mind though overthrown
And darken'd, yet hath gleams of glorious prime.
And here, methinks, a noble beauty dwells
These islanders among:—the daring eye,
Majestic brow, the gallant bloom of health
And dignity of their regardless mien
A power denote, which beautifies the free:
While they who move in loveliness and light,
Like memories of vanish'd paradise
Around the sternness of ungrateful man,
Have beauty such as perish'd Angels loved!

And yet, of myriads who this matchless isle
From day to day enjoy, from year to year
Environ'd with her fairest smiles, few dream
Or whence, or why, she hath the world surpass'd.
Thus hath it ever been, since time and truth
Have wrestled with that contradiction, Man!
Partaken mercies are forgotten things.
But Expectation hath a grateful heart,
Hailing the smile of promise from afar:
Enjoyment dies into ingratitude,
Till God is hidden by the boundless stores
Himself created; eyeless nature knows
Him not, for mighty Self absorbeth all!

That gulf descend where pristine ages sleep,
And lone, benighted in the savage gloom
Of her untravell'd woods and wilds, no light,
Save that of reason, struggling through a cloud
Intense,—lo! haughty-featured England lies;
An orphan region nursed amid the deep,
A fameless isle, imprison'd by the waves,
A speck upon the vasty globe. *Who* raised
Her littleness to lofty state? who bade
The daring majesty of Cæsar's mind
O'er her rude wilds a Roman spirit breathe,
Till, in the nursing shadow of his throne
She grew to youthful glory? Who hath been
Through perils, and volcanic bursts of war,
Earth-shaking tumult, and appalling strife
The guardian of her destinies till now,
When Ocean, wreathed around her rocky shore,
Hath lent his champion-billows to defend
Her fame, while storming at her daunted foes,
She spurns them with avenging roar?—Forth steps
The little greatness of a learned man,
And in the rapture of presuming thought
Through the dim valley of departed years
Sends down his spirit, and aloud proclaims,
The prince, the hero, and aspiring hearts
Which breathe omnipotence round mortal power,
Have made, and shall preserve us, as we stand,
The mighty and the free!—A proud response
Of hell-born feeling such as I would nurse;
And that which empires have of old indulged
Till, dizzy with renown, they reel'd away
Amid the havoc and the whirl of time.
For power and greatness are the awful twins

Of Destiny, whereby the earth is moved:
The first, a property of God Himself,
Which, when imparted to the soul, becomes
A curse, or blessing, in its moral sway:
The second will be judged by truthful Heaven
Convicted, or absolved. Of England's past,
When Time's dread chronicle shall be unroll'd
What glory then will clear-eyed Truth perceive?

Should I deny thee, angels would declare,
That spirits who enrich eternity
Have deck'd thine island-clay. Immortal kings,
Who sanctified their sceptres, and their thrones;
Patriots sublime, with whom hoar wisdom dwelt,
And tutor'd ages by advancing thought;
With saints and martyrs, heroes of the skies,
Approaching, shed their glory on thy name.
But paramount o'er all thy mental gods
Shakspeare and Milton, see those peerless two!
The one, a mind omnipotently dower'd,
Which multiplied itself through space and time,
Passing like nature through the soul of things!
Aloft, companion of the Sun he soars
Awhile, then travels with the moonless night,
Mounts on the wind, or marches with the sea,
And, god-like, gives the Elements a tone
Of grandeur, when his spirit walks abroad!
But Life! how well he tore thy mask away,—
The great Interpreter of man to man.
So royal are his kings, his maids so pure,
Such perfect heroes, and prudential knaves,
Such feeling smiles and unaffected tears,
So stern or sweet, so melting or sublime,—
Such life-warm substance in the vast array
Of Shapes, who live along his moving Scene,
Men deem the world were in him when he wrote,
And he the sum and soul of all mankind!

The last, who lived on earth, but thought in heaven,
Beyond compare the brightest who have scaled
The empyrean, and whose lyre might charm
The seraphim with its melodious spell,—
That sightless Bard, whose paradise of song
Hallows Britannia's isle, how deep he plunged
Into the infinite sublime of thought,
Flaming with visions of eternal glare!
How high amid the alienated Hosts
Of warring angels he could dare ascend,
Look on the lightnings of almighty wrath,
Array the thunders, and their God reveal!

These deities of earth, thy past sublime;
The birth of an immortal soul proclaim,
And show how far bright inspiration soars:
But thou, brave England! shalt for crimes be judged,
When they in awful resurrection rise
With thine own children, ere the world expires.
My Spirit hath encompass'd thee! Thy hosts
Who in the anarchy and ruffian stir
Of civil war, have won the sanguine wreath;
Thy lewd-soul'd princes, and voluptuous kings
Whose courtly halls were palaces of vice
That sensualised the land; the sins untold
Within thee nursed, and those remorseless deeds
Of vile aggression, haunting thy great name,—
Yet sully thee, and claim atoning tears.

And now reigns England in her noon of might
Secure; the future, with victorious eye
Prophetically dooming; distant Lands
Beneath her sceptre bow, and though her soul
Doth gather wisdom from her own domain,
In proud neglect of equal climes,—there spreads
No empire on the map of earth, where fame
Hath scatter'd not her mind's nobility.
Commerce,—the spirit of this guarded isle
Wherein the attributes supremely dwell
Of all which dignifies or nurtures power,—
Enthrones her on a peerless height, and works
Like inspiration through her mighty heart,
And yet, a poison at the core! To eyes,
Where avarice hath raised a blinding film
That flatters, while it bounds the view, her scenes
Array'd and glowing with commercial pomp,
More costly than the sun-enchanted skies
Appear. Triumphantly outspreads her show
Of trade and traffic round the sumptuous world!
See! from yon ports what merchant-vessels waft,
Daunting the winds, and dancing o'er the waves,
Rich wares and living burden, while the breeze
Toys with the flag, and fills the panting sail.
Others from many a tempest-haunted track
Return'd, in thunder beat their homeward way
And send their spirit wreathing on the gales.
Then hark! amid this wilderness of domes
Dark lanes, and smoke-roof'd streets, what mingled roar,
While Commerce, in her thousand shapes and moods
With eager hand and greedy eye, pursues
Her round of wonders and of gain! All arts,
All natures, and all elements are forced
To such obedience by transforming Power,
That matter quickens into living soul
And works harmonious to the will of man!

But here, methinks, had not one hideous thirst
For lucre parch'd all pity from the mind,
The hollow cheeks and livid brow of Toil
That, lean, and yellow'd by infectious gloom,
Droops o'er his hateful task—might thrill the heart
Of Selfishness, in her most griping hour.
And here amid the pestilential glow
Of heated chambers, where in sad revenge
Art flourishes o'er fading life, are pent
The infant young, and friendless orphan-poor;
They who should gambol on the golden meads,
While health the limbs, and beauty clad their cheeks,
Thus doom'd to anguish in degenerate toils!
Why, what a hell-slave will this Commerce prove,
When life and feeling perish for her cause!

Already hath an evil spell begun;
Though a proud Empire will not see, her heart
Is fever'd with a fest'ring mass of vice,
And lust of gain which rankles into lies
Deceptive, horrible, and base; while Truth
Integrity and Honour are diseased,
And die away in avaricious dreams
Of Mammon, that vile despot of the soul.
The happy meekness of contented minds
Is fretted with ambition; home and love,
The heart-links, and the brotherhood of joy
In life, and tomb-companionship in death,
Are nothing: money, God of England seems!

There is another and a nobler scene
Of triumph, for dark spirits to survey.
For knowledge,—true nobility of mind
When temper'd with a sanctifying tone,
Without it, but an ornamental curse,—
In full omnipotence is reigning now;
Yet haply, with a spirit and a power
Which breed an earthquake in the boastful heart
Of this free isle. A thunder-charged sky
When clouds float meaningly along the face
Of its dread stillness, not more threat'ning looks
Than England, bloated with ambitious minds
That dream in darkness, and await the hour
That like a storm-burst will the world arouse!
Sooner shall winds be caged, or billows hush'd,
Than pride be rooted from one human soul
By aught which man's corrective wisdom yields.
For dust with deity will dare contend,
The creature with his own Creator war
The most, where meek religion reigns the least.
To vanity a wildering charm, for vice
A weapon, to the fool a powerless gift
Is Learning.—Doth she lift her eyes to heaven,
Or downward gaze to idolise that world
Of promise, which around her seems to smile?

The soul of Intellect is spread abroad,
In whose gay flush men see flatt'ring bloom;
Yet, vain and unimpressive as the dance
Of leaf-shades, figured in the dreaming sun,
Are trivial fancies o'er a Nation's mind
For ever by inglorious spirits thrown.
As pictured Nature in the rich deceit
Of servile art, undignified appears
When with its glorious archetype compared,
So dim the genius of the living day
To that which brighten'd an heroic race
Of warriors, famous in the fields of mind;
High-soul'd and stern, they gave to time unborn
The heirship of their fame; but venal smiles
Which low accordance with the bounded view
Of spirits levell'd to the dust, procures,
Were spurn'd away in their immortal taste
For Truth, and her transcendent cause:—how few
Dare emulate these godlike of the past;
Renown immediate, from the vassal lip
Of smiling Dulness, is the dear reward
For which your intellectual pigmies grasp.
Hence, sickly woes, and sentimental lies
By passion woven to bewilder souls.—
Romantic panders! may your kingdom spread;
Let Beauty, Love, and Gentleness, and Thoughts
Which grasp eternity and heaven unveil,
Expire; but give to crime pathetic grace
And treat the world with new-made decalogues!

Creator! what a triumph can we boast
When oracles which fool, or flatter; dull
Expounders of a duller creed,—those mean
Arraigners, shrouded by a saving gloom
Which wraps them in false glory, as far scenes
In darkness magnify the truth of Day;
When such as these, in life and feeling, heart
And creed, and elements of thought, can win
A base surrender from a free-born soul
Cringing, or cowering, as their wands direct!—
Why, Hell may laugh, and liberty's no more.

So awful is the sway of human mind:
For good or evil an enduring charm,
Inweaved with ages, silently it works,
Reaping uncounted spoils from deeds and words,
And thoughts, which spring like blossoms from a ray
Of influence, by some ruling Spirit cast.—
There is a stormy greatness, by the sense

Of vulgar Apprehension hail'd, yet vain
When match'd against one all-prevailing mind.
A warrior's glory in his banner waves;
And ocean-heroes, when the tempest roars,
Outdare the winds; and echoes of renown
Roll mighty round the living head of each,
Yet ebb away to indistinct applause
By History echoed round memorial graves.

But he, who out of *mind* a fame erects,
In his eternity of thought will live
And flourish, till the Earth itself decays!
And what a tale would Time have told, had none
Burst through the thraldom of degrading sense,
And bade the spirit eloquently tell
Of Truth, of Beauty, and pervading Love!
The heavens they scale; the elements array
With glory; give the herb a greener hue,
The flower a fresher magic, and the stream
A melody which nature never sang;
Thus bright'ning all without by rays within
From light's great Source proceeding, they create
A second Eden, pure as sinless Adam saw.

The dark enchantment of corrupted mind
Not less prevailing in its secret course
Hath proved. For Havoc may be heal'd; and tears
And wrongs of desolated Kingdoms, cease;
But genius triumphs o'er decaying time
And taints a century with corrupting thought.
Ye prostituted Souls! when mind is judged,
How ghastly from your slumber will ye wake!
At that dread hour Perversion may not plead,
Nor Will deny, what Understanding own'd.
The wretched martyrs!—for a vain renown
From Unbelief, and her heart-blasted crew
Derived, they rouse the idiot-laugh, in clouds
Of falsehood clothe each attribute within,
Lend Infidelity a voice, the vile
Delude with flatteries such as impious ears delight,
And fashion doubts to mystify the world:
So be it! there is loud applause below!

For wealth too gasping, for a wise content
Too madly fever'd by ambitious thirst,
The moral greatness of this mighty Land
Thus charms me with a promise of decay.
Her heart is canker'd: I have roam'd unseen
Around her; lightly do her virtues weigh
Against the burden of her wickedness.—
By fortune moulded, what a countless herd
Who live to fascinate the palling hours
With pleasure, making life one masquerade!
Refinement is their heaven; and thus few crimes
Are nourish'd there; but lesser sins abound;
Revenge and spite, all vanities and hates,
The virgin whiteness of the soul deform:
Concealment is a virtue: virtue oft
Bare policy; religion but a form,
A taste most delicate for things divine!
The truth, convenience; and a lie,—the same.

And what a homage doth the tongue present
To evil! what alertness of delight
Attentive, comes it in whatever shape
The turn of accident assume; in blood,
Disaster, or some grand depravity
Where passions like heart-demons reign'd! But tears
Of charity, that language of the soul!
Some fine denial of a feeling mind,
Some noble act, or heaven-reflecting scene,
Let such be named, and weariness begins:
Nothing so dull as Virtues when admired!
Let Slander, with her false envenom'd lip,
Her aping mood, her sly assassin tone,
Appear,—and eye and ear and heart attend
To feed upon the foulness of her tongue;
Whether on crooked limb, or character
It fall; whether She waste it on a foe
Successful, or a rival far too good;
Or faintly drop it o'er a dying friend,—
Nothing so sweet as slander to the vile!

But deeper in society are bred
The vices ravening on a Nation's weal.
Philosophy! dar'st *Thou* confront me here?
Descend and look into degenerate life;
See deadly Vice, with brazen front, abroad,
And Murder, stalking through her savage round
Of midnight blood; see Theft her felon-hand
Uprear; and infamies of heart and tongue;
And Guilt, with godless triumph on her brow:
Mark Hell in miniature! wherever crime
Depraves, or poverty allures,—and pause;
Millennium is not come, nor Man reclaim'd!

Thus greedy, worldly, and defiled, how poor
The sum of happiness in England's heart!
Like other climes, her thousand children seek
A Shadow flying from their false embrace,
Still adding to the cheats of mocking time,
And with strange madness making life far worse
Than Adam left it. Earth indeed no more
Retains an Eden, and her richest hour
Yearns with deep longing for more glorious bliss,
Immortal as the mind itself;—yet joy
And hope, serenity without, and calm
Within, e'en here might visit gentle souls,
Who haunt the confines of a better world.
Like food to body, happiness to mind

Alone is healthful, when ingredients pure
Are mingled to create the charm they bring.

What numbers, on whose features the false smile
For ever plays; whose eyes, so brightly charged
With happy meaning, quicken envious fire
In other hearts; what wretches gaily-tongued,
And scattering words whence emulations spring,—
Have I beheld, whom Happiness is deem'd
With her full heaven to crown! yet where, oh where
Blind Mortals, is that priceless gem obtain'd
Which many seek, yet few in life have found?

The palace, and the parasitic host
Of minions, with that soft and sneaking race,
Who in the court of princes lie away
Existence, gasping for some golden lot,
I've mark'd:—the happy do not flourish *there!*
Then look'd I on a mightier Scene, where men
Draw glory from a Nation's heart, and voice
Their spirit round the listening World! How vain
And valueless this haunt of mind has proved
To all who battle for some cause adored!
Oh, England! such as Rome and Athens paid
Their architects of greatness, thou hast giv'n
To many who bequeath thee fame. There live
A host, who in the splendour of thy Great
Live, bask, and breed, like reptiles in the sun;
Who feast on venom, and infect the Land
With malice, and all miserable wounds.

Alas, Ambition! see yon gifted man
Awhile stand forth, surpassing and sublime:
His brow imperial; in his eye a blaze
Of meaning, pour'd from a majestic soul;
Borne on the whirlwind of triumphant thought
Through the wide universe his genius sweeps!
Thrones, Monarchies, and States,—he summons each
To strict accompt, their victories and kings
Arraigns, and bids Britannia front them all!
The Senate wonders, rapture finds a tongue,
And envy sinks abash'd to praise. But go,
Young Emulation! when this glowing scene
Hath cool'd to common life, and mark him well!
The hero is no hero here! the mean
Have tortured whom a Kingdom could not bend:
Around him, too regardful, scandal flies;
And words, like gnawing vipers, poison life
Away, or rankle in the spirit's core.—

From the proud Senate, to a sunnier realm,
Where Gaiety and her unseemly crew,
Like flowers of fancy in a hot-bed rear'd,
An artificial life enjoy,—I turn'd.
In such a sphere could happiness abide?
Where Fashion, that great harlequin of Life,
For ever plays the comedy of fools;
Where Luxury breathes a pamper'd air; where Love
Is venal; Wealth, a wearisome array;
And time, a curse,—the happy do not dwell.
A false delight, a snatch of feverish joy
And jading rounds of pleasure are supplied;
But oft the heart beats echoless to all
Though Custom wear its contradicting smile.

And the rank vileness of their pleasures vain
'Mid theatres of vice, I frequent view.
Music and Pomp their mingling spirit shed
Around me; Beauties in their cloudlike robes
Shine forth,—a scenic paradise, it glares
Intoxication through the reeling sense
Of flush'd Enjoyment. In the motley host
Three prime gradations may be rank'd; the first,
To mount upon the wings of Shakspeare's mind,
And view the flashes of Promèthean thought,
To smile and weep, to shudder, and admire,—
Attend; the second are a sensual tribe,
Convened to hear romantic harlots sing,
On forms to banquet a lascivious gaze
While the bright perfidy of wanton eyes
Through brain and spirit darts delicious fire:
The last,—a throng most pitiful! who seem
With their corroded figures, rayless glance,
And death-like struggle of decaying age,
Like painted skeletons in charnel-pomp
Set forth, to satirise the human Kind!—
How fine a prospect for demoniac view!
"Creatures, whose souls outbàlance worlds, awake!"
Methinks I hear some pitying Angel cry.

Another scene, where happiness is sought!
A festive chamber, with its golden hues,
Its dream-like sounds and languishing delights.—
Since the far hour when England lay begirt
With savage darkness, how divinely raised
Art thou, Society! The polish'd mode,
The princely mien, the acquiescing smile
Of tutor'd lips, with all that beauty, love,
Accomplishment and sumptuous Art, bestow,—
Are thine; but oh, the hollowness within!
One mingled heart society should be
Of glowing words and generous feelings made,
And hallow'd by sincerity; but hark,
The whisper'd venom of invidious tongues!
The shrug of falsehood, or the sly deceit

Of changing looks; the drama of the eyes,
And all the pantomime Refinement acts!
From simpering youth to unregarded age
'Tis vapour, vanity, and meanness all!
Where honest nature sickens with disgust;
While school'd hypocrisy, with glozing tongue,
Performs the social serpent of the night.

From Fashion moved I to the loftier scenes
Where hosts by Learning titled, for renown
And rank more elevate than kings bestow
Their inward toil pursue,—and yet how vain!
There is a craving for some higher gift,
A thirst which fame and wisdom fail to quench
Alone; the fountain hath a deeper well.
And what is Fame? When hope, the morning-star
Of life arose, Enthusiast! thou wouldst climb
Her envied rock, to hear the lauding tones
Of grateful myriads round thee, like the glee
Of waters wafted o'er a mountain-head.
Amid the dreams of some poetic shade
Where Fancy prophesies proud years to come;
Or by some gush of beauty, or the glow
Of emulation, or by spells of mind
Perchance her music whisper'd—be thou great!
No matter: midnight-watchings, gloom and tears,
Thy heart a fever, and thy brain on fire,—
The martyrdom of thought hath won the prize;
And midmost thou, among the laurell'd tribe
A Paramount art throned! And dear to thee,
Young hero of the mind, is first renown;
Fresh, warm, and pure, as early love, ere Time
Hath nipt it with a killing blight. Awhile
In paradise thou dream'st and seem'st to hear
The hailing worship of Posterity.
But now, come down from yon celestial height!
Descend, and struggle with the heartless crew
Who out of others' tears extract their joy.
The rocky nature of ignoble minds,
Ambitious Spite, or unrelenting Hate,
'Tis thine to wrestle with; the spell unwinds,
And Glory's hollowness appears at last!

And thou, religion, hell's appalling foe,
Yet least prevailing, on whose seraph-wing
Far, far away from this benighted orb,
A spirit mounts, though many Temples shrine
Thy sanctitude, and many tongues thy charm
Repeat, how few have found thee as Thou art,
The living Saviour of mankind! What hosts
Who boast my attributes, or ape my power,
Yet carry gospels in their saintly looks!
Ye hypocrites! how often have I torn
Your veils away! how often have I seen
A midnight where the world saw only day;
Beheld a Demon, where they dreamt a God!

'Tis not the vileness of hypocrisy
From which alone a hellish harvest springs;
But that contempt which on religion frowns
When hypocrites in unmask'd truth appear:
Then Vice is comforted, and lifts Her voice
Triumphant; pleased to have a broken step
However slippery, where to stand and cry,
Thank God! *my* soul religion never sway'd!
Delusion vain and exquisitely vile,
How gloriously thy cheating spells can work!
For thus might Painting and her fairy scenes
Be scouted, when a daubing mimic fails;
Or Music have her seraph-voice denied
When a poor screech-owl apes a melody;
As true Religion have her heaven disown'd
Because a false professor fools the world.

Nor dwells that happiness which mortals seek,
With them, fanatically crazed or wild:
Two Orders breathe there of this graceless crew:
The one, on ecstasy profanely soar
Full in the face of Deity, and sing
And shout, with more than archangelic joy!
And yet, so earthly is excessive love,
No heathen to a sensual god e'er raved
With more lip-service of degrading rant
Than dark Fanatics, when their roar is up!
The other, sink as deep as these ascend,
And so exult in self-accusing thought,
That nought's more proud than their humility.

And this is homage for the Dread Supreme!
Who comes—and Mountains from His glory flee;
Who speaketh—and a Universe begins;
Who frowneth—and Creation is no more!
So awful, that the dazzled Angels shrink
In veil'd humility His Throne beneath;
To such these holy maniacs cry, and bid
Him bow the heavens in thunder, and appear!
Or, in the vaunting of devotion's power
Can dare to humanise their Deity;
While others, with a superstitious cloud
Array His attributes, conceal His love,
And level Mercy to their own despair.

Nor let them boast, who in the vile content
Of worldly meanness, sepulchred in Self
And worm-like clinging to their genial clay,
The wisely good and only happy deem
Their narrow lot: to such earth-loving race
The seen and felt make all their paradise;
Should Hell be vision'd,—let it burn away!
If Heaven—bombast is thunder'd in their ears!

When yawns the tomb, then comes the hour to pray,
When death appears, the awe of future worlds.
Most glorious ! could I wither all men down
And tame them from their true immortal rank
To what *these* are, how demonised the earth
Would grow ! all feeling curdled into self,
All nobleness of thought a dream denounced,
All bright and beautiful sensations mock'd,
The world a vortex for engulphing heart
And soul,—one living curse this Life would prove !
Were I a mortal, with capacious mind
To grasp, and heart to feel, around me strewn
Such glory, pomp, magnificence, and might
In visible array,—I'd rather live
Some free-born creature of the stately woods,
Than with the form of Man a life of brutes
Embody, beathing but of earth and sin !

Glory and Pleasure, Learning, Power, and Fame,
All Idols of deceptive sway,—mankind
Have crown'd them for the master-spells of Life;
And yet, a mocking destiny they bear.
How often dwelleth gladness in the smile
They raise, or rapture in the heaven they dream ?
Unknown, unhonour'd, in the noiseless sphere
Of humbleness, one happy man I found.
It was not that the tears or toils of fate
Escaped him ; or that no tempestuous grief
The stream-like current of calm life perturb'd.
But in him dwelt that true philosophy
That flings a sunshine o'er the wintriest hour.
The proud he envied not ; no splendours craved,
Nor sigh'd to wear the laurels of Renown ;
But look'd on Greatness with contented eye,
Then, smilingly to his meek path retired :
Thus o'er the billows of a troublous world,
As o'er the anarchy of waters moves
The seaman's bark, in safety did he ride,
His woes forgot, and left his wants to Heaven.
I wove my spell, but could not once decoy
The eyes of that contented Soul. He look'd,
When Glory woo'd him with a traitorous glare,
On the calm luxuries of humble life ;
There was the Image of his own pure mind,
The peaceful sharer of his love and lot :
What beaming fulness in that tender eye,
What a bright overflow of spirit shone !
When by her cradled babe she mused, who lay
In beauty, still and warm as summer-air :
And what could camp, or court, or palace yield,
Of nobler, deeper, more exalted bliss,
Than when, as weary Daylight sunk to rest,
He shut his door upon the noisy world,
And, with no harrowing dream of guilty hue,
To stain the crystal hours of love and home,
Sat by his hearth, and bathed his soul in bliss ?

But more convulsive is the life I'd see ;
And few shall flourish in this homely sphere !
Excitement is my great enchanter, whence
The wisdom of the worldly fain would reap
That blissful nothing which delusion shapes ;
That onward, day by day, from year to year,
Through gloom and glory mocks them to the grave !—
I thank thee, Britain ! though religious call'd,
The perfect beauty of her living form
Thou hast not yet adored.—There is a sense,
A selfish, innate law of right and wrong,
Which makes a heathen moral : such is thine.

A loftier air the Christian breathes, who owns
The Alpha and the Omega of all
In life or destiny, is God alone.
Bid colour to enchant the blind ; or sounds
Of melody through deafen'd ears to glide,
Or dream of sensibility in stones ;
But think not, world-slaves ! to imagine all
That boundless yearning for ethereal bliss,
That more than rapture of a heart redeem'd
A Christian nurseth ; 'tis the heaven-wove charm
Which Devils hate, but cannot yet destroy.
Divinity is there ! Two thousand Years
In glorious witness gather round mankind
Attesting it divine ;—to conscience, peace ;
To Ignorance, beyond what sages teach,
It gives to poverty that wealth of heaven,—
The inward quiet of a grateful mind.

To such how welcome dawns this hallow'd day,
The Sabbath ! Hell perceives her darksome power
Confronted, when its smile salutes the earth ;
For, like a freshness out of Eden wing'd,
A sainted influence comes : the toils and woes,
The cankering wear of ever-busy life
In spiritual oblivion smooth'd away,
On such a dawn, celestial hearts by grace
Refined, can mingle in delicious calm
Like many clouds which into one dissolve.

How mildly beautiful this blessed morn !
Thy sky all azure ; not a cloud abroad ;
A sunny languor in the air ; the breeze
Gentle enough to fan an Angel's brow :
And thou, the Lord of beauty and of light
Enthroned, how oriently thy splendours shine
And make a loveliness where'er they fall !

Hark! on the stillness of the sabbath-air
From tower and steeple floats the mellow chime
Of matin-bells; and plaintively ascends
That pealing incense! up to heaven it glides,
As though it heralded creation's prayer.

And now, from England's countless homes and streets,
In motley garb, the trooping myriads come,
To kneel in Temples where their fathers knelt.
Among them, there are heaven-toned spirits found,
Hailing a sabbath as the blissful type
Of that which in eternity shall reign:
Others, whom Custom's all-resistless sway
Beguileth, in their pompous robes appear,
And use them for religion; many pine
For action, though a sacred mockery proved:—
While the loud wheels of common Life stand still,
And round it an unwholesome quiet reigns,
The show and music of the temple-pomp
May o'er the heart some fascination fling:
Yet what more weary than to worship God!

But now for Country, and her chaster scenes!
The melody of summer-winds; the wave
Of herbage in a verdant radiance clad;
And chant of trees, which languishingly bend
As gazing on their shadows, meet around
This haunt, where Loneliness and Nature smile.—
How meekly piled, how venerably graced
This hamlet-fane! by mellowing age imbrown'd,
And freckled like a rock of sea-worn hue.
No marble tombs of agonising Pomp
Are here; but turf-graves of unfading green,
Where loved and lowly generations sleep:
And o'er them many a votive sigh is heaved
From hearts which love the sacredness of tombs.

And such is thine, lone muser! by yon grave
Now lingering with a soul-expressive eye
Of sorrow. Corn-fields glowing brown, and bright
With promise, sumptuous in the noon-glare seen;
The meadows speckled with a homeward-tribe
Of village matrons, sons, and holy sires;
The hymning birds, all music as they soar;
And those loud streams so beautifully glad
With life and beauty all the landscape robe,
And yet,—one tomb-shade overclouds it all!

A churchyard! 'tis a homely word, yet full
Of feeling; and a sound which o'er the heart
Might shed religion. In the gloom of graves
I read the Curse primeval; and the Voice
That wreak'd it, seems to whisper by these tombs
Of village quiet, which around me lie,
Unmottoed, and unknown. Can Life the dead
Among be musing, nor to *Me* advance
The spirit of her thought? True, nature wears
No rustic mourning here: in golden play
Yon sprightly grass-flowers wave; the random breeze
Hums in the noon, or with yon froward boughs
A murmuring quarrel wakes: and yet how oft
In such a haunt the insuppressive sigh
Is heard, while feelings which may hallow years
With virtue, spring from out a minute's gloom!

Mind overcomes me here. Amid the pomp
Of monumental falsehoods, piled o'er men
Whose only worth is in their epitaphs,
I fear thee not, thou meditating One!
Infinity may blacken round thy dream
Perchance, and words inaudible thy soul
With dread prediction fill!—but worldly gauds
Entice thee; whisper'd vanities of thought
Arise, and though Life lose all glare awhile,
Ambition tints the moral of the tomb.—
'Tis not so here: pathetic eyes can dwell
On few distinctions, save of differing age;
The heart is free to ponder, and the mind
To be acquainted with itself alone.
And more development of Man is found
In such calm scene, than in the warring rush
Of life.—I watch him thus, and mark
How creed and conscience lift him up to God;
Or dark imaginings, from tombs derived,
O'erwhelm His spirit with a cold despair.

Nature begins; and in the white-roll'd shroud
The ghastly nothingness of Death appears.—
And then, a knell, Time's world-awaking tongue,
Rings in the soul, and by a new-turn'd grave
He paints a mourning vision; sees the tears
Telling of many a day's remember'd joy
Down cheeks of Anguish dropping; and can hear
The careless mutter of the broken clod
Upon his coffin echo.—Then, a dream!
The solemn dream! of *where* his spirit-home
May be, and what the everlasting World. .
Thou mortal! ask the overarching Heavens,
The mystic wind, the ever-murmuring Deep,
And all which night and day around thee dwells:
Doth nought reply? The elements all dumb?
Then ask thy soul, there God Himself replies!

I thank thee, Man! and all those mocking scenes
Wherein such vassalage of mind abounds,

That thoughts of death are exiled from the heart
Of many, till the sepulchre doth yawn.
Thus aid my black deception; and become
The sole omnipotent mere sense obeys!
And ever, when thou hear'st some true divine
Of nature's teaching, a Hereafter tell,
Then, brand Him as the martyr of mistake!
Oh, *think* not, Worldling!—or thy soul would say
The man who hangs on every smiling hour
A coward proves to questionings of thought;
While he, who dares with an undreading eye
To fathom his own nature, in the grave
Descend, eternity's deep gates unbar,—
Unblasted can the face of God behold
And grow familiar with the World to come.

England is bless'd in all which nature lends:
No fields spread greener magic to the gaze,
No streams of purer freshness flow, no winds
In richer harmony their wings unfold,
Than hers: and though invading grandeur frown
A heartless contrast o'er some ruin'd scenes;
Though petty tyrants and domestic lords
That elevating charm have long eclipsed
Of happy peasantry, with honest hearts
For country glowing, and for God prepared,
And wither'd much by pastoral poets sang,—
Enough for homage, or refreshing thought
Doth consecrate her yet. And thus, methinks,
Sweet Country might imparadise the soul,[1]
Where fine perceptions hold their placid sway.
Grey towers, and streets all surfeited with throngs
Of worldlings, greedy-eyed, and stale of heart,
As the dead air around them,—who should deem
Enchantment, when a lovelier world is free?
From dusky Cities, where forced nature grieves
To wear the meanness of surrounding men,
On wings of gladness might her lovers fly
To haunts divine as these. Lo! how She laughs
In sunshine, tinting with her bright romance
Hill, wood, and valley, rock, and wayward stream;—
What arch'd immensity of bending sky!
What flowery hues, what odorous delight
And, as her gales on wings of freshness come,
What ocean-mockery from th' excited trees
Is heard, in rapture echoing the winds!

Yet well for me, that Town's eventful sphere
Enchants the many more than nature can.
No sound melodious as the roar of streets;
No sky delightful as the smoke-dimm'd air
Above them, like a shrouding death-pall hung;
No joy prevailing as the selfish stir
Whilst interest, craft, or petty wants produce,
And on Life's stream those fleeting bubbles raise,
In bursting which their day-born wisdom lies.
Why, this is taste Corruption should enjoy!
She cannot fancy what she never felt.
There is an outward and an inward Eye,
Reciprocally moved; when that which sees
Within, is dimm'd, the eye of outward sense
Is darken'd too; creation wears a cloud,
And life a veil; when both are bright and free,
The world of nature and the world of man
A garment of celestial glory wear!

Both form and mind a fellow magic steal
Where the free visiting, of nature act:
As the fresh lustres of a cloudless morn
The languor of a dying eve excels,
So doth the beauty of yon country-girl
Surpass the city maiden in her charms;
The rich enamel of the rosy blood
Is painted on her cheek; and her glad eye,—
From the full joy and glory of the meads,
The freedom of the woods and waterfalls,
And the proud spirit of her village hills
Its glances come!—her step is like the breeze;
Her forehead arch'd, to face the skies; her form,
Perfection out of nature's hand; and words,
The native breathings of a happy soul.

Nor less in contrast to the bolder mien
Of city-manner, is thine artless air
Whom now a wanderer in the fields I view,
With sunshine lovingly around thee thrown.
A sweet unwillingness to be observed
Dwells in that maiden-glance; and oft away
From the bright homage of adoring eyes
In delicate timidity thou glid'st;
Like a coy stream which from fond daylight speeds
To hide its beauty in sequester'd dells.

Yet Fashion does, what Feeling would deny;
Making a charm where none is found: thus, hills
And lakes, the mountain-winds, and sea-fresh gales,
The idle from their town-retreats allure,
When fair-brow'd Spring appears. And some there live
Among them, of that undetermined race,
O'er whom the earthly and the heavenly sway
With fitful interchange, mere Epicenes
In mind. Worn by the hot and feverish stir
Of city-life, the many-mansion'd views,
Those pathways bleaching in the glare of noon,
And the fierce clatter of conflicting wheels,—
Some wearied heart romantically sighs
"O for the luxury of living gales,

And wafted music of ten thousand trees,
Whose young leaves dance like ringlets on the brow
Of Joy, and glitter gaily to the sun !
O for some deep-valed haunt, where all alone,
Saving the mute companionship of Hills,
My feet may wander, and mine eye exult ! "

So wish'd a Worldling; and behold him come,
And roused by new enchantment, thus exclaim:
" Again thine own, my heart, I give to thee
Sweet Nature ! once again thy fondling breath
Of music plays around my faded brow,
Pure as a father's blessing o'er a child
Forgiven, gently murmur'd. Let me look
With eyes impassion'd on this glorious scene.
Dilated, as with gladness, glows the blue
O'erhanging sky, untinctured with a cloud :
Around me, hills on hills are greenly piled,
Each crowning each in billowy ascent
And beautiful array : a breeze is up
In bird-like motion winging the bright air;
Or by the flow'rets, giddy with delight,
And dancing gaily o'er the golden meads.
Nor am I lonesome in this hour of bliss:
The grazing flocks which speckle the glad fields;
The larks; and butterflies that tint their path
With beauty, and yon group of laughing babes,
Fit company for sunbeams and for flowers,
So brightly innocent they seem,—partake
The heavenliness of this romantic hour :
And thou, beneath me in thy waveless mood
Luxuriant spread, with ripples twinkling gay
As insect-wings which flutter in the sun,
Calm Ocean ! often has thy phantom swell'd.
Upon me, in the rush of busy life,
With smile as glorious as thou wearest now."—
And canst thou, with a mind thus deeply toned
To all which nature for congenial heart
Provides, again be mingled in the mass
Of vulgar spirits, and their vain employ?—
Yes, Worldling ! earth is heaven enough for thee.

No marvel, when by moral rust decay'd
In each perception of ethereal growth,
That millions never know a joy sublime,
And call romance the sin of tender souls.—
How little do these menials of the mind
From their blind prison-house of earth perceive
That moods predictive of diviner scenes
Come oft inspired; and though morosely scorn'd,
Form inward foretaste of the Unreveal'd.[2]

But this enchantment of reposing thought,
When solitude falls heaven-like on the soul
Reflective, soars above thine aimless gloom,
Retirement ! When in fame or fortune wreck'd,
To make a winter where bright summer reigns
And sadden all things with sarcastic gloom,
The misanthrope to his dull haunt retires
For saturnine felicity ; 'tis vain.
For as the deep, unvisited by wind
And motion, tainted with pollution lies;
So turns the stagnant heart to foul conceits,
Unholy fancies, and unhealthful thoughts;
The world must wake it, as the angel stirr'd
The healing waters into glorious life
And motion,—making them to bless mankind.
Oh ! how I scorn false Eremites ! these mock
Philosophers, most elegantly sad,
Because outrageously befool'd. The man
Who battles nobly with his lot, and starves
Without a tear, hath more philosophy
In his true nature, than your Sages dream,
Who mope, for want of sterling misery !

But lo ! a vision fair as fancy sees.
Beside yon Deep, alive with laughing waves,
An infant stands, and views the billowy range
Of its immensity, with lips apart
Like a cleft rose hung radiant in the sun,—
Hush'd into sweetest wonder. How divine
The innocence of childhood ! Could it bloom
Unwither'd through the scorching waste of years,
Men would be angels, and my realm destroy'd:
With eyes whose blueness is a summer heaven;
And cheeks where Cherubim might print a kiss,
And forehead fair as moonlit snow,—thy form
Might be encradled in the rosy clouds
At twilight grouping amid the sun's farewell,
So gentle and so glowing thou appear'st.
And heavenly is it for maternal eyes
In their fond light to mark thee growing day
By day, with a warm atmosphere of Love
Around thee circled with unceasing watch;
While, like a ray from her own spirit shed
The lights of waking thought begin to gleam.
'Tis now the poetry of life to thee !
With fancies young, and innocent as flowers,
And manner sportive as the free-wing'd air,
Thou seest a friend in every smile; thy days
Like singing birds, in gladness speed along,
And not a tear which trembles on thy lids
But shines away, and sparkles into joy !

Yet Time shall envy such a dream as this;
And when I see thee in thine after-years,
As far as Virtue from her primal height
Is fallen, will thy tarnish'd nature be
From that which blasts me with its pureness now.

But need I travel into years unborn
To gather misery? Behold it here!
Here, where a childless mother by the tomb
Of her dead offspring, wan and wither'd, sits
In the dull stupor of despairing grief.
Her brow is bent; her visage thin and worn;
Her garments fading like neglected flowers,
And not a glance but speaks an agony.
Oh, Wretch! whose sorrow all thy virtue makes!
For she who perish'd in a timeless grave
Though beautiful as ever sunshine clad,
In love and truth most tenderly endow'd,
When living, was a curse to thee! Thy hate
Pursued her, and thy blighting envy frown'd
Like a dark hell-shade on her youthful path:
Oft in the midnight thou wouldst mutt'ring wake
And bid the grave to open on thy child.
Yet when her dwelling was the loathsome tomb,
And scowling Envy had no charms to dread,—
When that was dust which once an Angel look'd,
The mother's heart return'd again, and grief,
Too late, then rack'd thy being to remorse,
Making thee all which Demons could desire!
For hope, nor faith, one reconciling beam
Imparts, to brighten thy dark woes; unwatch'd,
Unseen, thou visitest the haunt and home
Of Death, and in the muteness of despair
Beneath a pining yew-tree lonely sitt'st,
In deep'ning anguish round a daughter's tomb.

And many, sad as thee, have I beheld
In my dark pilgrimage round Britain's isle.
A tree by lightning blasted to the ground,
And those proud branches which the seasons loved
To beautify, in leafless ruin laid;
A wreck upon the savage waters toss'd
And darkly hinting a terrific tale;
Or grey-wall'd castle, where of old were seen
The banner'd triumph and baronial pomp
But now the prey of melancholy winds,—
For each, how oft a meditative sigh
Or moral tear, awakes; yet what so sad
As creedless anguish in a guilty soul,
And human sorrow by no hope assuaged?
"My God! it is a miserable world,"
May'st thou, the wretched, cry. From faded years
No flower to rescue for remembering love,
Or blissful woe; the Future but a dread
Unknown; the Present all a blacken'd scene;
By friends unloved, or in the tomb, forgot,—
How desolate thy doom must be! Abroad,
The sunshine mocks thee with a cruel glare;
And in the smile of each unthinking crowd
No bright reflection for thy heart is found;
At home—blank weariness of soul awaits
Thee there, and turns it into dismal thought:
Or haply, when the sallow evening shrouds
Yon echoing city, at thy window placed,
With vacant eye thou view'st the yielding glow
Of day; or hear'st the moan of evening-bells,
Like elegies by air-born spirits sung.

But now a sunset, with impassion'd hues
Of splendour, deepens round yon curving bay;
'Tis Inspiration's hour, when heaven descends
In dream-like radiance on the earth becalm'd.
Hither! thou victim of luxurious halls,
The glory of these westering clouds behold
That rich as eastern fancies float the skies
Along: and hark!—the revelry of waves;
Now, like the whirling of unnumber'd wheels
In faint approach; then wild as battle-roar
In shatter'd echoes voyaging the wind;
And now, in foaming wildness they advance,
Dissolve, and mark the pebbled beach with foam.

Brief as a fancy, and as brightly vain,
The sky-pomp fades; and in his sumptuous robe
Of cloudy sheen, the great high-Priest of earth
Calmly descends beyond the ocean-bound.
Like weary eyelids, flowers are closing up
Their beauty; faint as rain-falls sound the leaves,
When ruffled by the dying breath of Day;
And twilight, that true hour for placid dreams
Or tender thoughts, now dimly o'er the wave
Its halcyon wing unfolds; in spectral gloom
The cloud-peak'd hills depart; and all the shore
Is lull'd, where nothing mars its deep repose,
Save when the step of yon lone wanderer moves,
Watching the boats in sailless pomp reposed;
Or, mournful listening to the curfew-sound
Of eve-bells, hymning from their distant spires.

And who art thou, of wither'd aspect there,
Whose slow faint footfalls sound of misery?
Consuming want thy lot hath never been:
But thou art one, from out whose bygone days
No memories breathe for retrospective moods
To welcome; the true dignity of life
Thy consecrated powers hath ne'er employ'd;
Thy past is blacker than the sunless tomb;
Reflection murders thy vain peace of mind!—
The moonlight, paving with a glassy shore
Of wrinkled lustre all yon desert-main;
The night's sad umbrage and her mystic hush
O'erwhelmingly becalm thee; thou wouldst fain
Again be flatter'd with the gorgeous Day,
And lose thy sadness in its fawning smile.

So terrible a speechless hour! when Thought
Banish'd by guilt, hath long an exile been
From Nature, dreading down herself to gaze.
In vengeance and convicting truth it comes
With the dread quickness of a lightning-glance,

Detecting all the danger of the soul,
Till conscience tremble, and the summon'd past
Is past no more!—but present, with a fire
And force concenter'd for terrific sway;
"I AM," which voices God's eternity,
Is heard, and fearful sounds the truth therein!

But oh, how bounded would my kingdom be
If what is life in common language deem'd,
Which unreflectively hath flow'd away,
Were *all* the law of Being did require!
Yet is there life, where no reflection acts?
Was Spirit with divinity endow'd,
Blindly to live by sense alone?—How well
For many, had they brute enjoyers been
Of homely nature; or, as trees and flowers,
Than charter'd with undying mind, to live
Mere breath and blood, without a spirit train'd
To pure advancement, by the hallow'd power
Of truths, which up to heaven and glory lead.
He lives the longest who has thought the most;
And by sublime anticipation felt
That what's immortal must progressive prove,
Or, retrograde in everlasting night!

BOOK VI.

"Divided by a river, of whose banks
On each side an imperial city stood,
With towers and temples proudly elevate."
Paradise Regained.

But, hail, thou city-Giant of the world!
Thou that dost scorn a canopy of clouds,
But in the dimness of eternal smoke
For ever rising like an ocean-steam
Dost mantle thine immensity; how vast
And wide thy wonderful array of towers
In dusky masses pointing to the skies!
Time was, and dreary solitude was here;
And night-black woods, unvisited by man,
In howling conflict wrestled with the winds,
But now, the tempest of perpetual life
Is heard, and like a roaring furnace fills
With living sound the airy reach of miles.
Thou more than Rome! for never from her heart
Of empire such disturbing passion roll'd,
As emanates from thine. The mighty globe
Is fever'd by thy name; a thousand years
And Silence hath not known thee! What a weight
Of awfulness will Doomsday from thy scene
Derive, and when the blasting Trumpet smites
All Cities to destruction, who will sink
Sublime, with such a thunder-crash as thou?
Myriads of spires, and temples huge or high,
And thickly wedded, like the ancient trees
Which darken forests with primeval gloom;
Myriads of streets, whose windings ever flow
With viewless billows from a sea of life;
Myriads of hearts in full commotion blent,
From morn to noon from noon to night again
Through the wide realm of whirling passion borne,—
And there is London! England's heart and soul:
By the proud flowing of her famous Thames
She circulates through countless lands and isles
Her tides of commerce; gloriously she rules,
At once the awe and sceptre of the world!

Angels and Demons! to your watching eyes
The rounded earth nought so tremendous shows
As this vast City, in whose roar I stand,
Unseen, yet seeing all. The solemn hush
Of everlasting hills; the solitudes
Untrod; the deep gaze of thy dazzling Orbs
Which decorate the purple noon of night
Oh, Nature! no such majesty supply.
Creation's queen, in sceptred grandeur, Thou
Upon the throne of Elements dost reign;
But in the beating of one single heart
There is that more than rivals thee! and here
The swellings of unnumber'd hearts abound;
And not a day but, ere it die, contains
A hist'ry, which unroll'd, will awe the Heavens
To wonder, and the listening Earth with fear!

In Capitals of such gigantic sweep,
And hence, involving for momentous sway
Materials, which by word or deed create
An impulse throbbing through th' excited world,
Spirits of Darkness! how hath vice prevail'd;
Though scornfully, as now your victims mock
The name of Satan with triumphant sneer.
Obliging creatures! did their race abhorr'd,
What blighting sense we have of Virtue's power
And all those living elements of love
And glory, which around them move and dwell
Imagine,—they would learn to guard them more.
But, no! so blindly fool'd and charm'd they seem
With the proud beauty of their own pure souls,
That when most fetter'd, they appear most free:—
How Devils laugh to see such wisdom bound!

Through what a range thy blended passions reach,
Thou second Babylon! The Book of Life
With records that have made the angels weep,
Each moment of thy fated hist'ry fills.
For, whatsoe'er a spirit can reveal

Of fallen nature, in its varied realm
Of Sin, thy demonstrations body forth.
Here, Fraud and Murder on their thrones erect
Infernal standards, and around them swarm
Such progenies as Vileness, Want, and Woe
Beget, to live, like cannibals, on blood;
Or, move as crawling vipers in the paths
Of infamy, foul lewdness, or despair.
Here, Misery her wildest form betrays,
And sheds her hottest tear. See! as they rush
Thy million sons, along yon clam'rous streets,
Upon them how she turns her haggard gaze,
Lifts her shrunk hand, and with heart-piercing wail
A boon in God's name asks:—but let Her die,
And be her death-couch those remorseless stones!
For when the hungry winter blast shall pause
To soothe the wailing of some lonely tree,
Thy crowds will stop, and pity her despair!
Here Pride, in her most vulgar glory struts;
And Envy all her vip'rous offspring breeds.
But Mammon! thou persuasive friend of Hell,
Sure London is thy ever-royal seat,
Thy chosen capital, thy matchless home!
Where rank idolaters, of every lot
And land, do bow them to the basest dust
Which Falsehood, Flattery, or Cunning treads
From dawn to eve; and serve thee with as true
A love as lauding Angels serve their God!
See! how the hard and greedy worldlings crowd,
With toiling motion, through the foot-worn ways;
The sour and sullen, wretched, rack'd and pale,—
The whole vile circle of uneasy slaves.
Mark one, with features of ferocious hue;
Another, carved by villany's own hand,
A visage wears, and through the trait'rous blood
The spirit works like venom from the soul.

What rush and roar unceasing! and how strange
A mass of objects, as I move along
Invisible, amid these floods of Life
I see;—a chaos of uncounted hearts
Beating and bounding, charged with great design,
And making Fate at every pulse to feel,
Before me acts its mighty tragedy!
Amid them rise those consecrated Shrines
Where ruins eloquent with history are;
Where Truth is worshipp'd, and the belfry-towers
Are frequent mutt'ring how the Hours depart,
With unregarded wisdom; or, with moan
Funereal, wailing for some vanish'd Soul.

But hail, thou monument to hell!—yon pile
Whose massiness a mournful shadow frowns,
Where felon captives, for their crimes, await
The vengeance due to violated Law.
A day restored, and in thy dungeon wept
A victim, whom a darker prison holds
Than ever prescient horror shaped! Had Youth
Beheld him, more than fun'ral sermons teach,
His glance of agony had taught! How oft
When gaily passing, ominously came
A chill of terror from those prison-walls!
And when he enter'd their sepulchral gloom
Like memory that chill return'd.—To die
A malefactor's death; to be the gaze,
The direful, hideous, and detested gaze
Of thousands, glutting their unsated eyes
With morbid wonder, while on tiptoe placed
To see the Spirit gasping from his throat,
And chronicle his agony;—to live
A ballad-hero, in the creaking rhymes
Of vagabonds, and have his felon-name
From lip to lip thus vilely bandied out
For vulgar warning,—oh, ye sinless days
Of childhood! oh, ye hours of love and home,
And summer-dreams by haunted wood or wild;
And blessings nightly murmur'd from the lip
Of parents,—Glory of remember'd days!
Is *this* your ending, and his ghastly fate
For whom old Age did prophesy renown
And Fondness built her palaces?—A sire,
Who dream'd the heroic grandeur of his race
In him revived, and in the youthful ear
Did oft unrol his ancestry high-born,
To thrill the blood and keep the spirit brave;
A mother made of tenderness, who watch'd
His cradle-slumber, and when manhood came
Still breathed her spirit round his onward way;
Oh! these would shudder in their sacred tombs,
And on his name the kindless world expend
The infamy which to a gallows clings,
If Law should wreak her vengeance. But, one drop
Of poison, and this ignominious doom
Was saved!—a tremor of despair, a tide
Of anguish, burning through his blood and brain,
With the fierce whirling of imagined fires,—
And shrunk and ghastly lay the Suicide!

Huge, high, and solemn, sanctified by time,
And gazing sky-ward in the tow'ry gloom
Of temple-majesty, another Pile
Behold! in mid-air ponderously rear'd.
How dread a power pervadeth Things, this mass
Of ancient glory tells. Whereon it stands
The vacant winds did trifle; and the laugh
Of sunshine sported in bright freedom there:
It rose, and lo! there is a spirit-awe
Around it dwelling; with suspended heart

'Tis enter'd; where a cold sepulchral hush,
The holiness of its immensity,
The heaven-like vastness of those vaulted aisles,
Banners and trophies and heraldic signs,
And tombs of monumental melancholy,—
All with commingling spell the minds o'ercloud
Of Mortals, as they walk the haunted gloom
Of arch and nave, immersed in dreams of death.

Methinks Ambition might grow humble here:
Though, blazon'd high, the mausoleums rise,
And from stain'd windows rosy light-shades fall
On armory, and crests of costly hue,
Funereal pride, and sculptured canopies
Which grace the dust of hero, sage, or king,—
The sense that rankling clay beneath such pomp
Alone remains, humiliates and chills
The passion for proud greatness. But Her eye
More frequent to yon lonely Transept turns,
Where the dead heroes of the heart repose,
And on it gazeth with a deeper awe
Than ever high-raised tomb of Monarchs won:—
No matter! bard or king, the Curse decrees
For all, re-union with their fellow-clay.

Echoes on echoes roll'd and reproduced!—
As though invisibly with rushing flame
O'erwhelm'd, the music-haunted Temple sounds:
Hark! peal on peal, and burst on burst, sublime
The prelude comes, ascendeth loud and deep,
And then in waves of melody departs:
But ere it died, a thousand faces shone
With ecstasy; as sunshine, in a sweep
Of gladness over hill and meadow shot,
Can summon tints of glory from the scene,—
So drew the music, in its sweeping flow
O'er mortal features, flashes from the soul,
Bright hues and meanings, passionate as true.

The heaven of Music! how it wafts and winds
Itself through all the poetry of sound!
Now, throbbing like a happy Thing of air,
Then, dying a voluptuous death, as lost
In its own lux'ry; now alive again
In sweetness, wafted like a vocal cloud
Mellifluously breaking—seems the strain.
And what a play of magic on each face
Of feeling! when the cadence dismal sounds,
All eyes look darken'd with memorial-dreams;
But when the Organ's deep-toned rapture swells
With harmonies which stir heroic mind,
Bright raptures revel in each glowing face!
Till slow at length, the dying Anthem breathes
A musing tone of melancholy power
And pathos, causing buried years to breathe,
While mem'ry saddens; and in thoughtful eyes
The dewy brightness of emotion dawns.

All music is the Mystery of sound,
Whose soul lies sleeping in the air, till roused,
And lo! it pulses into melody:
Deep, low, or wild, obedient to the throb
Of instrumental magic; on its wings
Are visions too, of tenderness and love,
Beatitude and joy. Thus, over waves
Of beauty, landscapes in their loveliest glow,
And the warm languish of their summer-streams,
A list'ning soul is borne; while Home renews
Its paradise, beneath the moon-light veil
That mantles o'er the past, till unshed tears
Gleam in the eye of memory. But when
Some harmony of preternatural swell
Begins, then, soaring on enchanted plumes,
A soul seems wafted through Eternity!

Such sorcery in music dwells;—if they,
Now doom'd awhile to walk this heaven-roof'd world,
Might hear the melodies which I have heard,
When heaven, complexion'd by almightiness
In glory, sounded with the choral hymn
Of Princedoms high, and Dominations grand,
Of thousand Saints, of thousand Cherubim,
And angel-numbers, who out-million far
Bright worlds, which in the blue and waveless deep
Of night, innumerable hang,—if men
Might hear it, 'twould absorb their souls away!
Yet such I heard; oh! what a sea of sound
Went billowing with ecstatical delight
Through fathomless immensity, when hosts
Divine, their Holy, Holy, Holy, sung,
While loud Hosannahs to the living God
Commingled, making heaven more heavenly glow!

Another triumph of exhaustless mind,
Which Love and Wisdom, Beauty and fair Truth,
Tempt as I may, enchantingly produce.—
Visions of holiness, and lofty dreams
Of lofty Spirits, glorify the walls
Of this vast room; revealings of the soul
Intense, and passions of pictorial spell.
Painters are silent poets; in their hues
A language glows, whose words are magic tints
Of meaning, which both eye and soul perceive.
How wonderful is deathless Art! for Time
Obeys her summons, and the Seasons wait
Her godlike call; while glory, love, and grace,

And the deep harmonies of human thought
Move at the waving of Her mighty wand!

Then let me look on this ethereal show
Wherein the painter hath a mind transfused,
Turning his thoughts to colours. What a thirst
For beauty in his longing soul must burn
Who vision'd this,—a landscape gods might tread!
The sky hangs glorious; and the yellow smiles
Of summer, on a brightly-wrinkled stream
Are flashing with a restless joy, 'mid trees
Unpruned, and bowing graceful as the wind
In melody its fairy wing expands
Among them: over rocks of cloudy shape
The green enchantment of declining boughs
Is flushing, whence a vein of water flows,
And frolics on in many a shining trail
Of stream-like revelry; till margin-flowers
Beside it bloom, and shadow the young waves.
But there, a beautiful Perfection smiles!
An Eve-like form beside a dimpled lake
Is standing;—in her eye, a heaven of soul,
And o'er her figure an expressive bloom
Of youth, and symmetry, divinely graced.
The moon-like glowing of her loveliness,
Those limbs of light, and that seraphic air,—
Whence sprung it all, but from ideal thirst
For Beauty, purer than mere Sense beholds?

Here is a sunset, in that golden calm
Appearing, when the lustrous King of day
Awhile in bright complacence views the world
Which he hath glorified,—as Wisdom look'd
On infant Nature, when she lay complete
Beneath the full reflection of His smile.
And near, a night is pictured in its dead
Of noon: the canopy of azure pomp
Hung starless,—but the queen of heaven is there
In placid glory, and her slumb'rous veil
Hath shadow'd earth, and on blue ocean lies
In rolls of silver:—by the sallow beach
Two maidens in their girlhood stand, and seem
Enrapt, to watch how delicately bright
The moon's pale fancies tint yon fleeting waves;
Or, listen to the faint sweet undersong
Of dream-like waters, dying on the shore.

But, what is this!—the Deluge which devour'd
A living World! a sunless, moonless waste,
The globe into a chaos of wild sea
Dissolved! Her hour of agony is o'er;
But yet, the fierceness of unnat'ral clouds,
Like dying monsters welt'ring on the deep,
Frowns awful in the gloom.—How dead and mute
Th' enormous ruin! Not a look of life
Dwells there,—the carcase of a guilty World!
Woods, trees and flowers, with all which landscapes wear
In spring-time's young magnificence of bloom
And promise, with the god-like shapes of men,
Have perish'd. By the rocky darkness, crags
And mountain-skeletons by billows wash'd,
The oozy branches, where lank serpents coil,
And in the deadness of two pallid forms
Hurl'd from the deep, and dash'd upon the shore
In solitude, a mortal may be awed,
And dream, until he hear the Deluge roar!

But let it pass: for lo! the dark sublime,
The midnight and immensity of Art
I see; as though his eye had seen the hour
When down in thunder through the yawning skies
A whirlwind of rebellious Angels came,—
The painter hath infernal pomp reveal'd.
A second Milton, whose creative soul
Doth shadow visions to such awful life,
That men behold them with suspended breath,
And grow ethereal at a gaze![1]—how high
And earthless hath his daring spirit soar'd,
To paint the hell which kindled up the skies,
And wield the lightnings that his Maker hurl'd!

These arts are revelations which unfold
How Mind, disdainful of material bounds,
In spiritual romance delights to dream;
Through heavens of her creation to expand
Her wings, and wanton in celestial light;
As soars the lark from her low nest of dew
To sing and revel in the boundless air.
The fallen Myriads in whose blighted gaze
A beam of ruin'd glory shines, may look
With something of ambitious sympathy
On this proud struggle of the soul with sense,—
This warfare of the Visible with Things
Of viewless Essence, yet prevailing power.
A haughty captive fetter'd in his clay,
Man's Nature, peering through her prison-house,
Doth catch a shadow, and a dim advance
Of Something purer, brighter, yet to be.
And what is genius?—but the glowing mind
Half disembodied, flutt'ring in a realm
Of magic, dreaming, dazzled, and inspired?

How dark a contrast hath a moment made
In this world's promise!—here, the shame of Art
Confronts me; and, might Pity deaden Hate,
My love for ruin should be lessen'd now.—

In a lone chamber, on a tatter'd couch
A dying Painter lies. His brow seems young
And noble; lines of beauty on his face
Yet linger; in his eye of passion gleams
A soul, and on his cheek a spirit-light
Is playing, with that proud sublimity
Of thought, which yields to death, but gives to time
A Fame that will avenge his wrongs, and write
Their hist'ry in her canonizèd roll
Of martyrs: be it for his epitaph,
He lived for genius, and for genius died!
So sad and lone! wall'd in by misery,
With none to smooth his couch, or shed the tear
Which softens pain, uncheer'd, unwept, unknown,
And famish'd by the want of many days,—
Hither, Ambition! wisdom breathes in woe.

There are, to whom Earth's elemental Frame
Of wonders seemeth but an outward show
To look upon, and form the life of things:
But some in more ethereal mould are cast,
Who from the imagery of nature cull
Fair meanings, and magnificent delights,
Extracting glory from whate'er they view;
Calling the common air a blessing, light
A joy, and hues and harmonies of earth
Enchanting ministers to sense and soul.
And such was he. An orphan of the woods,
With Nature in her ancientness of gloom
And cavern, dark-peak'd hill, and craggy wild
Whose boughs waved midnight in the eye of Day,—
He dwelt; until he hung the wizard sky
With fancies, and with nature one became
By deep communion with her scenes and sounds.
With all her moods, majestic, calm, or wild,
He sympathised. In glory did he hear
Ecstatic thunders antheming the storm!
And when the winds fled by him, he would take
Their dauntless wings, and travel in their roar!
He worshipp'd the great Sea;—when rocking wild,
Making the waters blossom into foam
With her loud wrath; or savagely reposed
Like a dark monster dreaming in his lair.

No wonder, then, by Nature thus sublimed,
With all her forms and features at his soul,
The brain should teem with visions, and his hand
A glorious mimicry of earth and heaven
Perform! till lakes and clouds, and famish'd woods
In wintry loneness, crags and eagle-haunts,
And torrents in their mountain-rapture seen,
All dread, all high, all melancholy Things,—
Full on his canvas started into life
And look'd creation! To the Capital
A parentless and unacquainted youth
He came, while many a prophecy still hung
About his heart, and made his bosom heave
With young expectancy. Romantic fool!
To fancy genius and success were twins
In *such* a sphere: how soon the dream was o'er!
Here Envy dogg'd him; Avarice trampled down
His worth, and in the gloom of aidless want
His spirit bow'd,—but never was enslaved.
There was that haughtiness of calm despair,
That forward looking to avenging years
Which plucks the thorn from present woe, and charms
Adversity from out her darkest mood,
To cheer him on, and buoy the spirit o'er
The indirection of opinion's tide.
He felt, as all the mighty ever feel,
True Greatness must o'erlook the living hour
And charge the Future with its fame alone!
Thus cherish'd he self-rev'rence; and the heart
Was faithful: from the hand or voice of men
No comfort came; but Nature was his own
As ever! When the jarring city-roar
Woke round him, he could hush it in the calm
Of memory, and natural solitude
Of pensive scenes: the dying thunder-tones
O'er his dark chamber mutter'd, bade him dream
Of deeper grandeur which pervaded night
Afar; and when a pilgrim sunset-ray
Came to his window, like a smile from Home,
He scorn'd the present, and would think, how once
He loved to watch the bright farewell of Day
Reflected o'er the roll of ocean-waves,
Like sea-clouds rising in a gorgeous swell:—
Thus lived the victim of an Art adored,
And perish'd in his passion!—On his name
A veil is hung, and his achievements lie
Forgotten; but a fame awaits them still!
Eternity will take a hue from time,
And life a shade of the immortal doom
Hereafter is. But even this false world
Shall round his honour'd tomb a death-wreath hang,
And on the eyelids of an Age unborn
Shall tears be trembling when his woes are read.—
Thus Merit starves, while pamper'd Folly struts
In mean presumption, with a golden lot
Endow'd, and smiled upon by vassal-eyes
Which hunt for favour. But the lofty Hearts,
Th' unbending pure, within whose natures lodge
All feelings that ennoble man and mind,
Are *they* by kingly fortune crown'd? Does Worth

Or Wisdom glorious exaltation win?
Look round the world, and answer! 'Tis the base,
The sly, insinuating, serpent-souls
Who wind about the meanest of mankind;
'Tis they, with lying blandness on the lip,
Whose tuneful flattery, that cloyless sweet!
Allays the gusty tempers of the proud
To fond subjection, and the vain enchant
To patrons blind, yet most benevolent,
Yes! *these* are they who glitter with the crown
Of fortune, sit upon the World's high thrones;
And on the toiling majesty of Worth
Beneath, look down, and laugh at virtuous Woe.

But there are other miracles of mind
In this Queen-city; whatsoe'er the Hand
Can shape, or pregnant Thought conceive; whate'er
Applying Art can from the soul translate
To sense or vision, for the World's free gaze,
Is here produced. Thus, London is a sun
Of inspiration to the parent-isle;
Within the circle of a minute act
Uncounted minds, of multiplying power
To times and generations.—But a trace
Of ME, humanity! thou dost not lose,
However lofty thy victorious march;
For in this region of the learn'd and wise,
The pettiness and pride of nature dwell.
Then what is Genius, with a heart unsound?
One noble action doth outweigh it all
With more than priceless value. Meek and pure,
Who lives in humble earnestness, partakes
His lot with cheerful eye, and loving heart,
And sees a Brotherhood in all mankind;
Whose Teachers are the Elements, whose lore,
A Bible on the soul impress'd,—that man,
Howe'er undignified his earthly doom
Appear, is far more glorious in the eye
Of Angels, than the spirit-ruling host
Of learning, who have never learnt the way
To virtue, and the heart's true nobleness.—
But this I would not that the earth believed;
Corruption is the rankling seed I sow,
And aye abundant may the harvest bloom!

That mighty lever which has moved the world,
The Press of England, from its dreadless source
Of living action, here begins to shake
The far-off Isles, and awe the utmost Globe!
The magic of its might no tongue can tell!
Dark, deep, and silent oft, but ever felt;
Mix'd with the mind, and feeding with a food
Of thought, the moral being of a Soul.
A trackless Agent, a terrific Power,
It *could* have half annihilated Hell
And her great Denizens, by glorious sway:
But oft, so false, so abject, and so foul
It grows,—no blasting pestilence e'er shed
Such ruin, as a tainted Press contrives
For thought and feeling, when its poison works:
This wrecks the body,—*that* can havoc souls;
And who shall heal them? Let thy Temples rise,
Britannia! they are but satiric piles
Of sanctity, while poison from thy Press
Is pour'd, and on its lying magic live
Thy thousand vulgar, who heart-famish'd seem,
When Slander feeds not with a foul excess
Their appetite for infamy. The sun
Not surer where his deadly rage extends
The fierceness of a burning nature proves,
Than pages of pollution, sent from hour
To hour, across an Empire's heart, awake
A tinge of sentiment and hue of thought
In many, till they *act* the crimes they read.

E'en now mine eye a dismal wretch beholds
By fate or fortune for a villain doom'd;
In whom is center'd all which can profane
The name of Man! ignoble as the dust,
And rocky-hearted as a wretch can be:
And him with what delight a Devil views
Heap lie on lie with such remorseless speed,
And so envenom with his viper-touch
The good and glorious, that all Virtue seems
To wither, and all Wisdom to be dead
Awhile, beneath the blackness of his taint!
Yea! such a Monster do I see destroy
The healthful nature of the noblest mind:
And yet live on his execrable life,
And like a plague-spot spread his soul abroad
Till millions turn as tainted as his own!

How false, and yet how fair, are scenes of man!
Between what is, and that which *seems* to be,
How dark a gap of untold diff'rence frowns!
There is a hollowness in human things
Of pride or pleasure born, which none confess
Yet all must ever feel. The moments tuned
To highest happiness, have strings which jar
Upon some inward sense; the sweetest cup
Enchanted Ecstasy can drink, will leave
A humbling dreg of bitterness behind.
But this sad vict'ry of unrestful thought,
This cloud-tint on the brightest firmament
Of Joy, this deep abyss of discontent
Beyond a universe to fill!—though felt
Is rarely own'd; for Pride steps in, and puts
A smile upon the cheek, and in the eye
Delusion; making Love, or Wealth, or Fame
The seeming aspect of Perfection wear;
And thus, deceiving each, and each deceived,
Men gild the hour, and call it happiness!

A proof is here: a chamber long and large,
Of regal air, and with o'erbranching lights,
From the high ceiling pouring down a noon
Of lustre, which doth goldenly bedeck
The costliness around. Amid it, group'd
For converse, meet a host of either sex;
And who are they?—the race Ambition bred,
And madden'd, till they won the envied wreath.
Oh! what a demon-fire, what parching heat
Through blood and spirit, is the lust of Fame!
No tiger-passion tearing at the soul,
So dreadful as the ever-gnawing wish
For reputation! How it burns the heart
Away, and blisters up the health of life!
Yet, such have many in this blended host
Endured; but now, as high and dominant
As Potentates and intellectual Lords
They reign upon their thrones of Mind, and live
The worshipp'd of the Land. But are they blest
With that deep fulness of supreme delight
Which young Imagination's eye portray'd?
Oh, Thou! bewilder'd with the mock of fame,
Come here, and prove what rottenness of heart,
What fev'rous envy, what corrosive sense
Of emulation, in these glorious dwell,
What under-currents in this scene of joy!
Smiles in the surface, but a coward-tide
Of jealousy beneath. Hark to the gibe
O Hate! the tart dissent, the damning sneer;
To such a littleness the mighty fall!
Behold it, Ignorance! thy blush recall,
And take a happier name. But what a feast
Of vengeance doth my gloomy nature find
In this false scene, where they whom Wisdom crowns,
And Praise exalts, whose spirits are abroad
In this great world, and so angelic seem,
Beneath the shadow of Almighty wings
The simple think they mused sublime!—betray
The more than weakness of unworthy man,
When nature's venom quickens at the heart,
Or stern reality some feeling tries.

And thou! just gilded with a public smile,
Thy mind is dancing on a sea of thoughts
Which revel onward with delirious joy:
For now, the hackney'd wonder of the Night
Thou art, and by the music of fair tongues
Enchanted; flatt'rers feed thine ears with praise,
And clog it into deafness. Hear'st thou not
How Envy whispers off thy bloom of fame,
Till Meanness in false robe arrayeth thee!
Thou fool of flatt'ry! *this* the glorious doom
Ambition sought! Is Greatness only great,
When flatter'd, known, and seen? Canst *thou* so bend,
And be thus derogate? Wilt thou, whose eye
The stars can read, with heaven and earth commune,
Who feel'st the fibres of Creation's heart
In trembling harmony with thine, descend
To lose thy loftiness in this dull scene?
Back to thy haunts! the Ocean and the Winds
Attend thee; Nature is thy temple; kneel,
And worship in her mighty solitude.
Look up! and learn a lesson of the Sun,
That bright Enchanter of the moving heavens!
Lonely and lofty in his orb sublime,
But acting ever;—such is noble fame.

Some gracious, grand, and most accomplish'd few,
Each with a little kingdom in his brain,
Who club together to recast the world
And love so many that they care for none,—
These have I witness'd, laughing at their realms,
Of airy texture, by ambition wove.
But here is madness, far outfooling this!
For lo! the den whence Oracles proceed
Like exhalations from the noisome earth
That, once inbreathed, are death! This wonderful
Perfection of the vile, surpasseth all
Temptation, in my darkest mood, employs!
Yes, here are Spirits, such as hell-thrones grace,
Convened to disinherit God of souls,
And on the blasphemous attempt of pride
Erect a dynasty of Sense supreme;
Each man a god unto himself, let loose
In all the blinding wantonness of will.
And this is "freedom," dignified for Man!
When, having fed the agonies of life
By years of being, weary, worn, and sad,
To close existence in the clay he treads,
A soulless, dreamless, unimagined Nought?

Where sleep the thunders of convicting Wrath?
Devils believe, and tremble; men deny
And laugh! How enviably endow'd they are!
We bow'd and blasted by opposeless heaven,
Abhor the Godhead, but his name confess;
But things of earth, infatuated, vile,
Too darken'd to dissect a flower, or tell
The meaning of an atom which they tread,
Would dare annihilate the living God
Above, and mock the pangs of Hell below!
Oh! all, and more than Satan could desire,
Blind Teachers of the blind! could this world dare
To wallow in the darkness that ye breed,
To such, the heathen would be heavenly-wise;

For they, by revelation unillumed,
Soar'd out of sense, and in the Skies their gods
Enthroned, or heard them on the haunted Deep,
Or in the howling of the homeless Winds.
A cloud was on them; but a Spark within
Yet lived, and saved them from eclipse of soul.
For admiration *must* be felt, while Power
Existeth; on it man will gaze, and learn
The vast dependence for his lot ordain'd;
Dread Shadows of an omnipresent ONE
Move round him; in the march of Elements
His steps are traced, and Truth is ever by,
To tread them deep, and track them on to God.

And hence, these murd'rers of the soul are weak
In process; *too* infernal is the Creed
They fashion; far too poor in its exchange
For that divineness of redeeming Love
They combat; since with freedom they are free,—
As billows toss'd upon the giant main,
As feathers on the travell'd whirlwind borne
Are free!—No, rather some corruptive arts
Of saintly mixture; or the glozing tongue
Of hypocrites, with innovating clouds
Of doctrine—would I at their work behold,
Than the rash vileness of blaspheming fools.
A few they poison, but re-action wakes!
For one they ruin, thousands are sublimed
To holy vengeance, which to hell may prove,
Excess of evil is the source of good.

* * * * *

But lo! again the calm-eyed Evening comes:
The heavens are flaming with a rosy sea
Of splendour, richly-deep; and, floating on,
It reddens round the dying sun, who glares
With fierce redundancy awhile, then sinks
Away, like glory from Ambition's eye.
Behind him, many a dream of old Romance
Will cry, "What rocks, and hills, and waves of light!
Magnificent confusion! such as beam'd
When the rash boy-god charioted the skies
And made a burning chaos of the clouds!"
But this hath ended: and a breathless calm,
As though eternity were closing round
The World, to let it faint in light away,
Creeps o'er the earth, like slumber shed on air.

And well, lone pilgrim, at the shaded hour
Of twilight, when a golden stillness reigns,
Like lustre from a far-off angel-host
Reflected, and the unoffending breeze
Hath music which the day-wind seldom brings,
May sadness oversteal thee; and thy heart
Unspeakably with yearning fancies glow.
Of life, a living Vision; and the hour
Which ends it, like a cloudy dream of Air
That vanisheth to some allotted world;
Of faded youth, and unforgotten friends
Whose tombstones over life a shadow fling
No sunshine can efface; of all which makes
The lone Heart wander to a dream-like home
Of sadness, mortal! thou didst ponder now.

Such will not ever be: thy death-gloom pierced,
And awful on the unimprison'd soul
A sun-burst of revealing Truth will blaze!
Wherein these mysteries of sight and sense
Shall all unravell'd lie.—The tender night
With tragic darkness robed; the lone sweet star,
Oft worshipp'd for a beatific Orb
Where bright Immortals dwell; the moon's romance;
The sun's enchantment, when He wakes to smile
The day abroad, or preach departing life
By his deep setting; with the spirit-tone
Of winds, the Ocean's ever-mutt'ring waves,
And all which thus predominantly awes
Or saddens feeling, shall itself resolve
In spiritual completion. Then, thy tear
Ecstatic, radiant with adoring thought;
Each thrill of rapture, like a viewless chain
From heaven let down and link'd around the soul,—
Shall be translated by unbodied Mind.
Meanwhile, be mine to veil thee with a show
Of outward Things; and sensualise the will,
Whose promptings, more than conscience, men obey.

Now hath dead Midnight hush'd the world: it lies
Suffused with freshness, like a meadow steep'd
In verdant quiet, when the flood hath pass'd.
All deeply pure, impalpably divine
A Something o'er this hour prevails, which men
Call Awe, which doth not in their day-life reign;
For then, a flush'd existence, and a false
Enchantment gathers round the rising Hours
To hue their destiny. But Midnight cools
The spirit into thinking calm; then sounds
Come o'er it with a deeper thrill; and scenes
Which in the day a common gladness wore,
Grow solemn; then the airy leaf-notes mourn:
And boughs, like hearse-plumes, wave their shadowy pomp.
By day the present, but at night the past
Prevails; a moonlight-tenderness o'er things
Departed, flings a fond and dream-like gloom;
And then, Life takes a feeling from the soul,
And in earth's tints of paradise can trace

A beauty which unkinder hours deny;—
The harp is shatter'd, but the sounds remain![2]

Yet, 'tis not that the tenderness of tears
Awakes; that Childhood smiles upon the thought
As looks an Angel through the veil of dreams;
It is not that the heart-remember'd rise
From early tombs, to be once more beloved
And featured, till the deadness of the dead
In mem'ry's vision-life is half forgot:
'Tis not such charm alone; nor that which frowns
From Temple, sky, or everlasting Hill
Which darkness hath enrobed. But that deep sense
Which he who pierces through the lonesome air
Far o'er the mute immeasurable sky
Where travel worlds, for adoration feels,
Making the midnight holy! Silent Orbs!
On *me* no mystic awfulness ye shed;
For when unblasted, I beheld ye rise
And glitter into being, bright and pure,
Like radiant echoes of Almighty will!
But mortals, dimly aided by their dreams,
Behold ye, nursing the unutter'd thought,
With pond'ring hope and apprehensive awe.
They wonder, *if* the unearth'd Spirit dwells
Among ye! *where* the seraph-mansions blaze,
And *who* amid them are the bright and blest!

And is there not a spirit-World? The blind
May question, and the mocking idiot laugh;
But in her, round her, wheresoe'er she move,
Mortality might reap immortal faith,
And feel what cannot in the flesh be known.
In the wild Mystery of earth and air,
Sun, moon, and star, and the unslumb'ring sea,
Science might learn far more than Sense adores,
And by thy panting for the unattain'd
On earth; by longings which no language speak;
By the dread torture of o'ermastering Doubt;
By thirst for Beauty, such as eye ne'er saw
And yet is ever mirror'd on the mind;
By Love, in her rich heavenliness array'd;
By Guilt and Conscience, that terrific Pair
Who make the Dead to mutter from their tombs
Or colour Nature with the hues of hell!
By all the fire and frenzy of a soul
Guilty with crime, or agonised by dread,
And by *that* voice where God the Speaker is,—
Thy doom, oh mortal! whatsoe'er thy wish
In the black deep of thine unfathom'd heart,
Is deathless, as the damnèd Angels are!

Now is mine hour, the hour of conflict, come,
When the dark Future over nature frowns
Like destiny; now spirit is itself
Again, and Thought, within her cell retired,
Doth hold dim converse with Eternal Things.
Many are musing now! and sighs are born,
In slow succession, like unwilling tears
Prophetic and profound. The worldling sees
In darkness, what the day could not reveal,—
Himself! and sorrows at the faithful view.
"Another day eternal made! O Time
And Destiny, how swift ye roll the world
Along, to which such eager myriads cling
In duty, fondness, or despair! Alas!
Too much we make, yet far too little think
Of time: but, oh, at this untroubled hour
How awfully mine inward visions rise!
Infinity is round me; and I feel
A dampness on my spirit, and a dark
Unearthliness of thought; the dead awake,
Unlock their tombs, and tell me I must die!"
What sadness here! and what a wounded soul;
And yet the World shall his physician be!

But, hark! the moaning voice of deep-tongued bells
Herald the midnight o'er the drowsy world.
Now Earth is one day older; time itself
More awful, and the dead to Hades gone.
Earth, Heaven, and Hell, have felt this fleeted day,
That now is chronicled for Judgment! Morn
Hath look'd on many with her radiant eye
Whose brows shall never meet Her beam again!
Another Sun, another System works
Around them; they who dwelt in distant climes,
And diff'rent aspect wore, the friend and foe,
The loveless and the loving, all who once
Through time, or circumstance, estranged and far
Existed,—now are met where nothing more
Is alien, but one Darkness, or one Light,
As vice or virtue doom'd them. Oh! ye sad
And discontented, weary, worn, and grey;
Thou martyr of the melancholy hour
Loving the silence for the dream it gave,
Sick of the world, and sighing for a tomb;
And ye, on whom this Life a burden lay,
Yet often loosed it when the dying bell
Of Midnight, like a warning from the grave
Went in its sadness through the soul,—your gaze
Doth witness what your nature never dreamt;
The Veil is torn, the Mystery unseal'd,
And ye are men no more! Methinks a Voice
From many, would revisit this far world!
But no:—the Dust is faithful to its dead,
And they are silent, till the Trumpet speak!

And now, my wand'rings dark though this free Isle
Are o'er; through town and village, house and street,
By virtue of my being, have I roam'd,
A sightless Presence, an unshadow'd Power,
An undream'd Watcher moving round the hearts
Of men, and looking into depths of soul
Where none but Hell, and the Immortals gaze.
The sights which none have seen; the voices none
Have heard, with all the agony and glow,
The longings, workings, and unrestful strife
Of passion, mingled in the sleepless mind,
And fever'd into what a life is named,—
These have I witness'd; and on what thou art,
And wert, and might'st have been, heaven-favour'd Land!
Reflected, weighing thee for future worlds.—
For future worlds! each day and hour, thy dead
Are there; each moment is a Hell or Heaven
To many of thy dust. Thou bear'st the awe
Of Destiny; as on the earth thy power
Hath stamp'd its mightiness on every realm,
Printing the roll of Time with many a track
Of gloom and glory, havoc or renown,
So, when the Universe is roll'd away
Beneath the shadow of Almighty frown,
Eternity shall chronicle thy name
For wonder; it will be a sign in heaven!

Then speed thee onward in thy vaunting course
Of empire; let no dream of Judgment shade
Thy soul, or touch thee with a solemn fear:
Plunge in the future! let the past be dead
To thee; for *when* shall England's sceptre fail?
Thus dare, and do, and perish in thy dream!
Ye buried Empires, which have braved the world,
Rise from your tombs, and speak! for once I mark'd
Your palmy greatness; sea-famed Tyre I saw
When ocean cower'd beneath her vassal-ships;
And hoar Chaldea's hundred-gated Queen
In high-wall'd glory! Tell me, what are they?
And she, earth's ancient tyranness, vast Rome,
The rolling of her battle-cars, the voice
Of Scipio, and the sound of Cæsar's march,
Did I not hear, when Kingdoms were her slaves?
And thou, the fairy-isled, forsaken Greece!
When Sage and Bard, and battle-wreaths, were thine,
When all which centuries glorified could yield
Was consecrated to thy vast renown,
I walk'd thy streets, and prophesied thy doom!
Thus fell the mighty;—shall not Britain fall?

But lo! the heavens are ominously black,
Methinks, as though they frown'd a dark response.
Erewhile, and star-troops in their island-glow
Around the wan Enchantress of the skies
Appear'd, while lovingly the azure lay
Between them, softer than the lid of sleep.
But now, all pregnant with portentous ire,
The clouds have muffled up the pomp of night:
There is a gasping in the heated air,
A wing-like flutter in the tim'rous boughs,
And sigh, and sound, from out the heart of Things
Invisible, breathed forth; the Storm awakes!
And tones of thunder thrill the heart of Earth;
The lightnings cleave the clouds, and north to south,
And east to west, a tale of Darkness tell!
Hark! as the wearied echoes howl themselves
Away, the clamours of the midnight-sea,
Beneath yon cliff in thund'ring chorus rise,
While she is waved with terror! billows heave
Their blackness in the wind, and, bounding on
In vaulting madness, beat the rocky shore
Incessant, till it whitens with their foam.

I love this passion of the Elements,
This mimicry of chaos, in their might
Of storm! And here, in my lone awfulness
While ev'ry cloud a thunder-hymn repeats,
Earth throbs, and Nature in convulsion reels,
Farewell to England! Into other climes
My flight I wing, but round her cast that spell
I weave for Nations till their doom arrive.
And come it shall! When on this guardian-cliff
Again I stand, the whirlwind and the wrath
Of Desolation will have swept all thrones
Away; a darkness, as of old, will reign,
The woods be standing where yon cities tower,
And Ocean wailing for a widow'd Isle!

NOTES.

BOOK I.

Note 1, Page 331, Column 2.

. . . . *a day*
Is coming when ye moulder into dust,
And melt like dew-drops by the wind annull'd!

"The sands of those deserts which lie to the westward of Egypt are encroaching on and narrowing, by a constant and irresistible inroad, the valley of the Nile of Egypt. We see the pyramids gradually diminishing in height, particularly on their western sides; and we read of towns and villages which have been buried in the desert, but which once stood in fertile soils, some of whose minarets were still visible a few years ago, attesting the powers of the invading sand; . . . . advancing, I repeat, to the annihilation of Egypt and all her glories, with the silence, but with the certainty, too, of all-devouring time."—SIR RUFANE DONKIN'S *Course &c. of the Niger.*

Note 2, Page 332, Column 1.

Upon the soul of sage Philosophy
And Wisdom, templed in the shrines of old,
Faint shadows of my Being fell.

"If we consult the most authentic monuments of antiquity, we find all nations under the sun, in the earliest ages, however differing in other points, agreeing in the belief of evil as well as good Spirits. The Persian Magi and the Chaldeans distinguished the Devil by the name of Arimanus; the Egyptians, under that of Typhon. The Greeks and Romans admitted both wicked and good demons."—SEED.

Note 3, Page 333, Column 2.

A tyrant! in whose passion for a power,
Above all liberty and law enthroned.

"We close our view of Bonaparte's character, by saying, that his original propensities, released from restraint, and pampered by indulgence, to a degree seldom allowed to mortals, grew up into a spirit of despotism as stern and absolute as ever usurped the human heart. The love of power and supremacy absorbed, consumed him. No other passion, no domestic attachment, no private friendship, no love of pleasure, no relish for letters or the arts, no human sympathy, no human weakness, divided his mind with the passion for dominion and for dazzling manifestations of his power. Before this, duty, honour, love, humanity, fell prostrate. Josephine, we are told, was dear to him; but the devoted wife, who had stood firm and faithful in the day of his doubtful fortunes, was cast off in his prosperity, to make room for a stranger, who might be more subservient to his power. He was affectionate, we are told, to his brothers and mother; but his brothers, the moment they ceased to be his tools, were disgraced; and his mother, it is said, was not allowed to sit in the presence of her imperial son. He was sometimes softened, we are told, by the sight of the field of battle strewn with the wounded and dead; but if the Moloch of his ambition claimed new heaps of slain to-morrow, it was never denied. With all his sensibility, he gave millions to the sword with as little compunction as he would have brushed away so many insects, which had infested his march."—CHANNING.

Note 4, Page 335, Column 2.

And yet my ban is on thee!—'tis the curse
Of havoc.

"The Spaniards conquered the islands, and a great part of the continent of America. Stimulated by the thirst of gold, which the New World offered to them in abundance, they committed crimes and barbarities which make humanity shudder. Millions of the unfortunates were either massacred or buried in the sea."—C. KOCH'S *Revolution, translated by Crichton.*

"In no period does human nature appear with more shocking features than in the Spanish conquest of South America."—MICKLE'S *Lusiad.*

Note 5, Page 336, Column 1.

But thou—*the Sun hath written on thee, Slave!*

"A SLAVE-MARKET.—A long table was placed in the middle of the street, upon which the negroes were exposed, not one by one, but in families at a time. From this conspicuous station, they were shown off by two auctioneers, one at each end of the table, who called out the biddings, and egged on the purchasers by chanting the praises of their bargains. The auctioneers having told the names of each, and described their qualifications, requested the surrounding gentlemen to bid. One hundred dollars for each member of the family, or five hundred for the whole party, was the first offer. This gradually rose to one hundred and fifty, at which sum they were knocked down!"—BASIL HALL'S *America.*

BOOK II.

Page 339, Column 2.

. . . . *so oft the phantom of a cloud*
In single darkness cowering on the air,
Looks fiercer for the frownless heaven around!
So Fame is murder'd, that the dull may live.

In the fourth edition of D'Israeli's "Literary Characters," (the most interesting work of its kind in the language,) there is a manuscript note quoted from Lord Byron, singularly illustrative of the sensibility of genius. D'Israeli records that "When Petrarch was passing by his native town, he was received with the honours of his fame; but when the heads of the town conducted Petrarch to the house where the poet was born, and informed him that the proprietor had often wished to make alterations, but that the town's-people had risen to insist that the house which was consecrated by the birth of Petrarch should be preserved unchanged; this was a triumph more affecting to Petrarch than his coronation at Rome."—Vol. ii. p. 286-7.

To this passage Lord Byron has added the following note:—"It would have pained me more that 'the proprietor' should have 'often' wished to make alterations, than it could give pleasure that the rest of Arezzo rose against his right (for right he had); the deprecation of the lowest of mankind is more painful than the applause of the highest is pleasing; the sting of a scorpion is more in torture than the possession of anything could be in rapture."

BOOK III.

Note 1, Page 343, Column 1.

Of imperfection is true wisdom born,
And vaunting knowledge, ignorance confess'd.

"It is to the imperfection of our faculties, then, as forcing us to guess and explore what is half concealed from us, that we owe our laborious experiments and reasoning, and consequently all the science which is the result of these and the proudest discoveries which we make; thus, in one point of view, whatever dignity they may give to a few moments of our life, may be considered as proofs and memorials of our general weakness."—BROWN'S *Philosophy*: Lecture XI.

Note 2, Page 343, Column 2.

How *widely,—let the watching Angels speak!*

Having, in several parts of this Poem, alluded to spiritual agencies and ministries, the author begs leave to offer the following body of evidence, which has been collected with some care and research, from the pages of our early divines, down to the most distinguished theologians of the present era. Considered of themselves,—without a reference to the scriptural authority for their active influence over human affairs,—a belief in Guardian and Evil Angels seems peculiarly adapted to adorn and solemnise a poetical creed.* But authorised by the relations of the inspired volume, the subject advances to something beyond the mere romance of poetry. And it is in this latter view the passages about to be quoted were written. And let it be remembered that they are the opinions of no shallow thinkers, but the solemn convictions of great minds and comprehensive understandings; and are drawn from the true and only authority for such matters—The Bible.

ON GOOD AND EVIL ANGELS.

"Millions of spiritual creatures walk the earth
Unseen, both when we wake and when we sleep."
MILTON, *Par. Lost*, B. 4, l. 677.

Extracts from the Fathers of the Christian Church.

"Let us consider the whole multitude of his angels, how ready they stand to minister unto his will, as saith the scripture. 'Thousands of thousands stood before him, and ten thousand times ten thousand ministered unto him—and they cried, saying, Holy! holy! holy! is the Lord of Sabaoth—the whole earth is full of his glory.'"—*Written about An. Dom.* 70, *by St. Clement, to the Corinthians.*

"For even I myself, though I am in bonds, yet am not therefore able to understand heavenly things, as to the places (orders) of the angels, and the several companies of them under their respective princes. Things visible and invisible—but I am in these yet a learner."—*St. Ignatius' Epistle to the Trallians.*

Ignatius was a disciple of St. John the Evangelist, and, by tradition, reported to have been the child our Saviour took into his arms, Matt. xviii. 3, and to have been thence called Theophorus.

"Take heed, therefore, lest, falling asleep in our sins, the wicked one, getting the dominion over us, stir us up, and shut us out of the kingdom of the Lord."—*Epistle of St. Barnabas, the Companion of St. Paul.*

"Stand fast therefore ye that work righteousness, and continue to do it, that your departure may be with the holy angels."

"There are two angels with man, one of righteousness, the other of iniquity."—*The Shepherd of Hermas.*

The following extract from Bishop Patrick includes many of the opinions of the ancient church:—

"I find it the constant opinion of the world, that these angels are assigned to several offices, and preside even over all creatures here below. There being some who are not only ἔφοροι τῶν ἐθνῶν, as Moses speaks, the guardians of the several nations of the world, but τῶν κοσμικῶν στοίχειων, conservators, and keepers of the elements of the world, as Arethas speaks and concludes, from Rev. xiv. 18, where you read of an angel that had power over the fire,—and from xvi. 5, where you read of an angel of the waters.

"Hence he thinks, we have sufficient ground to believe that some have the command over the air, others over the water, others over the earth, and others of the fire, and so proportionably, that some have the care of one species of creatures amongst us, and some of another, nothing doubting but that they have a more special superintendency over mankind, the chief of God's works in this inferior world—and more particularly take care of those who are good, and fear God as the most worthy of all men, and the nearest to the angelical world; and, whatsoever question we may make of the rest of their belief, we cannot doubt—if we believe the Holy Scriptures—of the truth of the last part of it, that there are some of those excellent beings who are ministers of God for the good of men, and especially of those who believe. This the Christian religion hath above all others assured us of: we have the word of the blessed apostles for it, that they are 'ministering spirits, sent forth to minister for them who shall be heirs of salvation.' Nay, the words of our Lord and Master, that the angels, even of the weakest Christians, behold the face of God in heaven.

"These high officers of Almighty God, Gregory Nazienzen calls λαμπρότητες δεύτεραι λειτουργοὶ τῆς πρώτης λαμπρότητος,—secondary splendours, the ministers and attendants of the First Brightness.

"They attend upon God to receive his commandments for the good of our outward man, being the most noble of all God's visible works upon this earth; but most especially for the good of our spirits, which are far more dear both to Him and to them, as nearer of kin to celestial beings."

"St. Basil declares that πάντι πεπιστευκότι εἰς τὸν κύριον ἄγγελος παρεδρεύει, &c. To every one who believeth on the Lord (that is, every Christian), there is an angel that is his companion, and as one may call him, his assistant genius.

"If thou hast any good works in thy soul worthy of angelical custody and security, God will give thee this guard and even wall thee round about with a great many angels, rather than it should be spoiled; and so he saith upon another Psalm, 'to every one

* See Dryden's "Discourse;" where this doctrine is elegantly and powerfully advocated.

of the faithful there is ἄγγελος παρεζευγμένος, an angel yoked together with him, who is worthy to behold the face of God in heaven;' nay, he quotes these very words in his third Book against Eunomius to prove it, that every faithful person hath an angel for his companion, who is, as it were, his governor, tutor, and keeper, directing and guiding his life, and adds, οὐδεὶς ἀντιλέγει, no man gainsays this, being mindful of the words of our Lord, saying, 'despise not one of these little ones, for their angels always behold the face of their father which is in heaven.' And therefore the author of questions and answers to the Orthodox (under the name of Justin Martyr) asserting this opinion, that every man is attended by a guardian angel, confidently adds, καθὼς ἡ θεία γραφὴ λέγει, according as the divine writing tells us: and St. Jerome, upon these words of our Saviour, cries out, Great is the dignity of souls, who have from their birth 'Angelum delegatum,' a delegate angel, commissioned from heaven for their custody.

"Now we meet with these two characters of the Devil in Holy Writ,—that he is a murderer, and that he is a liar. As he is a murderer, seeking the destruction of men, he doth all the mischief he can, both to men's bodies and to their minds. As he is a liar, he seeks only to deceive, abuse, and destroy the mind. For the hurt that this murderer doth to their bodies, it is either in men's private capacities, by troubling the air, bringing diseases and infections, when God permits him, raising storms and tempests, and such like things: or in their public capacity, stirring up the spirit of ambitious, haughty, covetous, and cruel men, to oppress and enslave others, to make unnecessary wars, to fill the world with rapine, slaughter, and blood, to overturn kingdoms, and to turn the world upside down. Then for their minds he doth them no small prejudice, even by those wars and tumults, in which one sin is wont to follow upon the neck of another. And besides, we may conceive that he instigates men to all sorts of villanies, according as he finds them inclined. He inflames their brutish desires, he pricks forward their pride and love of dominion, he stimulates their revenge, he heightens their choler and rage, and works upon all their other passions; so that he is the furtherer of adulteries and all filthiness, the great provoker to murders, thefts, robberies, violence, deceit, and fraud, and all other wickedness, that, if it were possible, there might be a hell above ground, and he might be the God of this world.

"Then for the other thing, as he is a liar, his business is to cheat and delude men's minds with false opinions, to propagate all the foolish conceits and lewd doctrines that he can invent, to lead men to epicurism and atheistical conclusions, or else to abuse and gull their minds with fancies and vain dreams which they shall glory in as the very revelation of Almighty God: from all which I think we may safely draw this inference, that as the Devil and his partakers seek whom, in this manner, they may devour, so the holy angels seek how they may save and deliver men from these mischiefs. And as I have shown you that they are the preservers of men's bodies, so I shall now make it appear that they are instruments of good to our souls, because they love their welfare, and they are the lovers of truth and piety, and seek the promotion of the faith of Jesus Christ in sincerity. This is one great commendation which St. Peter gives of the gospel revelation, 'that the angels desire to look into these things,' 1 Pet. i. 12. And St. Paul saith, 'It hath pleased God to gather together in one all things in Christ, both which are in heaven, and which are on earth.' Eph. i. 10. To make us all, that is, but one society, under one supreme governor, the Lord's Christ."—*Bishop Patrick's Sermons*, ed. 1719.

"La vue des bons Anges (disait St. Antoine à ses disciples) n'apporte aucun trouble, leur présence est douce et tranquille; elle comble l'ame de joie, et lui inspire de la confiance. Ils font concevoir un tel amour des choses divines, qu'on voudrait quitter la vie pour les suivre dans sa bienheureuse éternité. Au contraire, l'apparition des mauvais Anges remplit de trouble. Ils se présentent avec bruit; ils jettent l'ame dans une confusion de pensées, ou dans une frayeur qui la déconcerte. Ils dégoutent de la pratique des vertus, et rendent l'ame inconstante dans ses résolutions."—*Godescard, Vie de St. Antoine.*

"O how happy wouldst thou most justly think thyself, couldst thou but see with the eyes of thy mind those solemn rejoicings above, wherein the mystical and most magnificent sense of the Psalmist's description—'the princes go before, the instruments follow after, and in the midst are the damsels playing with their instruments.' Then wouldst thou plainly discover, and be abundantly convinced, that there are numbers of those bright spirits which do with wondrous watchfulness and satisfaction rejoice with the congregations of good Christians in their praises, and observe their behaviour, and their prayers, and are present with their pious meditations, and keep guard about them in their sleep and solitude, and direct and preserve the governors of our Church in the exercise of their spiritual authority. For this is sure, that the heavenly powers have a very tender regard for their fellow-citizens upon earth, and being 'all ministering spirits sent out to minister for them who shall be heirs of salvation,' we have no cause to doubt that they are very solicitously concerned for the good of their charge, that they conceive a sensible joy at it—that they strengthen, instruct, protect, and take all the care they can of them, in order to obtain it. In doing so, indeed, they study to promote, not our happiness only, but their own. For they long earnestly for our safe arrival in those blessed regions, as hoping to see the breaches made upon their glorious society repaired, and the numbers of their fallen brethren recruited by the succession of redeemed souls in their places. They delight to hear of good men. They fly upon despatches between God and us, and are the messengers and instruments by which our requests and holy sighs are carried up to God—and the graces and blessings he gives in return to those prayers and complaints conveyed down to us."—*St. Bernard's Book of the Soul*, chap. vi.

"The fall of angels, therefore, was pride. Since their fall their practices have been the clean contrary unto those before mentioned, for being dispersed, some in the air, some in the earth, some in the water, some among the minerals, dens, and caves that are under the earth, they have by all means laboured to effect an universal rebellion against the laws, and, as far as in them lieth, utter destruction of the works of God."—*Hooker's Ecc. Polity*, b. i.

"How often are men impelled by certain unaccountable persuasions either to do, or to forbear, a thing, upon which (as afterwards appeared by the event) the whole fortune of their lives has turned? Unaccountable, I say, must these persuasions be, unless we refer them to some higher cause; and to what cause can we better ascribe them than to the suggestions of angels?"—*Bishop Conybeare's Sermon.*

"The Scripture doctrine of Satan makes it probable,

that many of those horrible thoughts which sometimes come with an almost irresistible impetus into the minds of pious persons, are of diabolical origin, which is in some measure confirmed by what has been observed of the subtlety with which atheistical and sceptical arguments have sometimes been presented to the mind, even beyond the natural genius of the person assaulted by them.

"There is no greater evidence of the degeneracy which a rational mind, even with great degrees of sagacity and ability, is capable of, than the implacable malice of those wicked spirits, and the obstinate malignity with which they are opposing the course of God in the world, though they are sure that opposition will end in their own confusion and ruin."—*See Doddridge's Lectures.*

"As I am not a Sadducee, the account you give of the music which entertained you on the road, does not put my dependence upon your veracity or your judgment to any trial. We live upon the confines of the invisible world, or rather, perhaps in the midst of it. That unseen agents have a power of operating upon our minds, at least upon that mysterious faculty we call the imagination, is with me not merely a point of opinion, or even of faith, but of experience. That evil spirits can, when permitted, disturb, distress, and defile us, I know as well as I know that the fire can burn me; and though their interposition is perhaps more easily and certainly distinguishable, yet, from analogy, I conclude that good spirits are equally willing and equally able to employ their kind offices for our relief and comfort; nor have any a right to withhold their assent to what the Scriptures teach, and many sober persons declare, of this invisible agency, merely because we cannot answer the questions, How? or Why? The thing may be certain, though we cannot easily explain it, and there may be just and important reasons for it, though we should not be able to assign them."—*Rev. John Newton's Letters.*

"To the nature of their (angels') ministry, the testimonies are still more explicit and numerous. For greatly do these men wrong the zeal, and greatly do they undervalue the happiness of angels who dream that the first is suffered to evaporate in incense, and adoration, and never-ending minstrelsy—or that the second consists in luxurious ease alone amid the groves of Paradise, or the splendours of the empyrean. Heaven has, no less than earth, its active duties. The blessedness of heaven is an useful and energetic blessedness—and they who are sometimes painted as feasting in the kingdom, and enjoying the presence of their Maker, are at others described as engaged in battle with the great dragon and his adherents; as stopping, in the cause of the saints, the mouths of lions, and subduing the violence of fire; as keeping guard round the prophets of the Lord, and as bearers of his orders to them; as ministering to the Son of God after his temptation, and in the hour of his mortal agony consoling and sustaining him; as anxious and exulting witnesses of the progress of his kingdom upon earth—as calling the Gentile Cornelius to be the first-fruits of Christian adoption; as smiting with an invisible sword the arrogant and persecuting Herod, and breaking down before the apostle Peter the chains and gates of his captivity.

"Of some one or more celestial spirits (if our hearts be right with God), we are assured that we shall obtain the protection: and do not those hearts burn within us when we read of these mighty beings mingling in the converse, assuming the forms, and partaking of the hospitality of mortals? when we learn that not a sinner repents on earth, but the angels rejoice in heaven—that the celestial warriors encamp, not only round the houses of the prophets, but around the person and property of every servant of the Almighty—that even the weakest and humblest believer is an object of interest to those who are themselves privileged to behold the face of their Heavenly Father—and that, the death-bed struggle ended (and who knows how greatly their unseen presence may support us under it?)—it is they who carry the soul of the humblest saint to Paradise.

"All these things are written for our instruction.

"They are not the minority who devote themselves to the service, and submit themselves to the reproach of their Redeemer. His flock may seem in the world which now is 'a little one,' but 'other sheep there are which are not of this fold;' and when the seats are full in the marriage supper of the Lord, and when the new heaven and new earth, in which dwelleth righteousness, have received, in the day of his power, their holy and happy multitude, we shall understand how few, in comparison, have been the clamorous adversaries which in this life disturbed our repose;* how blind the cowardice which, with angels on our side, would have turned back in the day of battle."—*Bishop Heber's Sermon on Good Angels.*

An extract from Chalmers's Discourse, "On the Contest for an Ascendancy over Man, amongst the Higher Orders of Intelligence," will form an appropriate conclusion to this long, but, it is hoped, not unimportant or uninteresting note.—"To an Infidel ear, all this carries the sound of something wild and visionary along with it. But though only known through the medium of revelation, after it is known, who can fail to recognise its harmony with the great lineaments of human experience? Who has not felt the workings of rivalry within him, between the power of conscience and the power of temptation? Who does not remember those seasons of retirement, when the calculations of eternity had gotten a momentary command over the heart; and time, with all its interests and all its vexations, had dwindled into insignificancy before them; and who does not remember how, upon his actual engagement with the objects of time, they resumed a control as great and omnipotent as if all the importance of eternity adhered to them; how they emitted from them such an impression upon his feelings as to fix and to fascinate the whole man into a subserviency to their influence; how, in spite of every lesson of their worthlessness, brought home to him at every turn, by the rapidity of the seasons, and the vicissitudes of life, and the ever-moving progress of his own earthly career, and the visible ravages of death among his acquaintances around him, and the desolations of his family, and the constant breaking up of his system of friendships,

* "When we are speaking of the Devil, we are not to understand any one particular being, or any one particular evil spirit, but the whole aggregate or company of evil spirits, which inhabit round about us in the lower regions of the air. All these are, in the Scripture language, and common speech, called by the name of the Devil. That, nevertheless, there is one person, peculiarly, and by way of eminence, thus called, as the general of a hostile army is called 'the enemy,' is plain, from St. Matt. xxv. 41; Rev. ii. 9. 'Inter impuros spiritus unum esse qui præsideat et Judæorum et Apostolorum scripta nos docent.'—*Grotius.*"—*Note to Sermon IV.*

and the affecting spectacle of all that lives and is in motion withering and hasting to the grave; oh! how comes it that, in the face of all his experience, the whole elevation of purpose conceived in the hour of his better understanding should be dissipated and forgotten? Whence the might and whence the mystery of that spell which so binds and so infatuates us to the world? What prompts us so to embark the whole strength of our eagerness and of our desires, in pursuit of interests which we know a few little years will bring to utter annihilation? Who is it that imparts to them all the charm and all the colour of an unfailing durability? Who is it that throws such an air of stability over these earthly tabernacles, as makes them look to the fascinated eye of man like resting-places for eternity? Who is it that so pictures out the objects of sense, and so magnifies the range of their future enjoyment, and so dazzles the fond and deceived imagination, that in looking onward through our earthly career, it appears like the vista, or the perspective of innumerable ages? He who is called the God of this World!"

Note 3, Page 346, Column 1.

When love remains a memory and a tear.

"Il est une âge pour l'expérience; un autre pour le souvenir. Le sentiment s'éteint à la fin; mais l'ame sensible demeure toujours."—*Rousseau.*

Note 4, Page 347, Column 1.

Religion, in the cowering spirit dwells.

Witness Lucretius:—

"Usque adeo res humanas *vis abdita* quædam
Obterit; et pulchros fasceis, sævasque secures
Proculcare; ac ludibrio sibi habere videtur."
(Lib. 5, v. 1232.)

Note 2, Page 347, Column 2.

An Atheist,—he hath never faced an hour,
And not belied the name he bore. His doubt
Is darkness, from the unbelieving Will
Begot.

"Christianity is not a Theory, or a Speculation; but a Life. Not a Philosophy of Life, but a life and a living process. Try it. It has been eighteen hundred years in existence; and has one individual left a record like the following?—'I tried it, and it did not answer. I made the experiment faithfully, according to the directions; and the result has been, a conviction of my own credulity!' Have you, in your own experience met with any one in whose words you could place full confidence, and who seriously affirmed, 'I have given Christianity a fair trial. I was aware that its promises were made only conditionally; but my heart bears me witness, that I have, to the utmost of my power, complied with these conditions. Both outwardly and in the discipline of my inward acts and affections, I have performed the duties which it enjoins, and I have used the means which it prescribes. Yet my assurance of its truth has received no increase. Its promises have not been fulfilled; and I repent me of my delusion!' If neither your own experience, nor the history of almost two thousand years, has presented a single testimony to this purport; and if you have read and heard of many who have lived and died bearing witness to the contrary; and if you have yourself met with some one, in whom, on every other point, you would place unqualified trust, who has on his own experience made report to you, that 'he is faithful who promised, and what he has promised he has proved himself able to perform;' is it bigotry, if I fear that the Unbelief which prejudges and prevents the experiment, has its source elsewhere than in the corrupted judgment; that not the strong free mind, but the enslaved Will, is the true original Infidel in this instance? It would not be the first time that a treacherous Bosom-sin had suborned the Understandings of men to bear false-witness against its avowed Enemy, the right though unreceived Owner of the House, who had long warned it out, and waited only for its ejection, to enter and take possession of the same."—COLERIDGE'S *Aids to Reflection.*

Note 6, Page 347, Column 2.

To him philosophy will preach in vain.

"The arguments commonly termed Metaphysical, on this subject, I have always regarded as absolutely void of force, unless in as far as they proceed on a tacit assumption of the physical argument. . . . . . The universe is that which shows the existence of the Author of the universe. It exhibits a harmony of relations, to perceive which is to perceive design; that is to say, it is impossible for us to perceive them, without feeling, immediately, that the harmony of parts with parts, and of their results with each other, must have its origin in some designing mind."—BROUN'S *Philosophy,* Lecture xciii.

Note 7, Page 348, Column 2.

Oh! did the living but the dead recal,
As often as the dead the living do,
The Sun would gaze upon a purer world
Than now.

"It is reasonable to believe that the saints shall know that they had such and such a relation to one another when they were on earth. The father shall know that such a one was his child, the husband shall remember that such a one was his wife, &c. The ground of which assertion is this, that the soul of man is of that nature that it depends not on the body and sense; and, therefore, being separated, knows all that she knew in the body; and, for the same reason, it is not to be doubted that she arrives in the other world with the same designs and inclinations she had here. So that the delights of conversation are still continued in heaven. Friends and relations are familiar with one another, and call to mind their former circumstances and concerns in the world, so far as they may be serviceable to advance their happiness. The truth of what I say, concerning this knowledge and remembrance of things in a state of glory, may receive some confirmation from that history in Matt. xvii. 3, &c., where we read, that in that glorious interview, which was a glimpse of heaven, the Apostles knew Moses and Elias, and these knew them, though none of them had seen one another before. Much more, then, shall spirits who were intimately acquainted with one another on earth, retain their acquaintance and converse in heaven, and call to mind the passages of their lives. But there is irrefragable proof of this in Luke xvi. 25: 'Abraham said, Son, remember that thou in thy lifetime receivedst thy good things, and likewise Lazarus evil things.' And it is as true that Lazarus remembered him at the same time. Whence I gather that the knowledge and memory of things done here remain hereafter. And particularly that the damned, know and remember that they have relations on earth, is evident from the rich man's being concerned for his father's house and his five brethren, 27th and 28th verses. It is not to be questioned, then, that the blessed, likewise, call to mind those that were related to them, and that they are concerned for their good and welfare; and when they meet them in heaven, greet them most kindly, and hold commerce with them, and recal the passages of their former conversation. All the ancient and pious fathers agree in this. St. Cyprian owns that our parents, brethren, children, and near relations, expect us in heaven, and are solicitous for our good. St. Jerome comforts a lady on this account, that we shall see our friends and know them. St. Augustine endeavours to mitigate the sorrow of an Italian widow with this consideration, that she shall be restored to her husband, and behold, and know him. And this was an apprehension that thinking men among the Pagans had attained to. Socrates, a little before he drank his deadly draught, told his friends how valuable a thing it was to have conference in the other life with Orpheus, Musæus, Homer, Hesiod, and other brave men;—how happy he should be in their society;—and he often wished to depart out of this world, that he might enjoy the conversation of those excellent persons."—DR. JOHN EDWARDS' *Theologia Reformata.*

BOOK IV.

Note 1, Page 350, Column 2.

A moral justice sways the course of Things.

In a work* lately published, and which evidences an able mind, that has thought for itself, the momentous and deeply interesting doctrine of a moral balance is discussed with great clearness and originality. As few of his readers may have seen this Essay, the autnor ventures to submit the following paragraphs, and to recommend the whole volume to their perusal:—

"The greatest of all luxuries is that of faith, in what may be called a moral balance, even in the affairs of this world. If we add to this the other and still more important faith, as to eternity, we shall pass through life, with no more mental suffering, in our worst days, than may be necessary to wean us from it, and so to make the prospect of death endurable, and with a consciousness of luxury, at other times, far exceeding all other, as to permanence, security, and true elevation. This faith is, that evil produces evil, even in this world, in one shape or other, to those who practise it; and that good produces good; no other cases than those of instant dissolution, in either practice, being destined to the single retribution of a future state.

"To explain our meaning by an instance, let it be supposed, that a man, arriving in London from some distant country, finds his way into a room filled with gold coins, the owners of which have suddenly but entirely left the apartment; that he is aware of this, and also that no other person is so; that he has a certainty of being personally known to no one, within hundreds of miles; that his absence from his own home will be imputed to a visit, such as he has been accustomed to make, to some intermediate place; and that, after this and other considerations, he feels a perfect assurance of his being able to take away what sums he pleases, and to carry them home, without a possibility of discovery by any human being. What we call faith in the moral balance of human affairs, is, that this man, supposing him to forget for the moment his eternal interests, shall be fully confident of its being his wisest conduct, his best policy, even as far as regards this world only, to withdraw from the room, without touching the gold; being sure, that, after taking it, the retribution of some preponderating evil would reach him here, and that, not taking it, he will receive some far more than adequate recompense. Of the latter, indeed, he will instantly have some foretaste, in the state of his mind. This is our proposition, which we have endeavoured to make as comprehensive as possible, that we may not be encountered by questions as to its extent.

"The means by which the moral balance operates are, of course, not always visible. We should not be merely human, we should not be in a state of probation, if we could see them all; we should have no opportunity for faith. Yet, as if to guide us to this duty, some of these means are rendered perceptible. The intenacity of villany (that phrase being used in want of a better) is well known to be the main security of the worthy part of society; but is not always viewed in its true light, as a dispensation of Providence; in other words, as one part of the moral balance. The wicked are as incapable of a permanent union as some physical bodies of meeting without repelling each other. This is one of their long-known predicaments."

* "What is Luxury?" By a Lay Observer.

Note 2, Page 351, Column 1.

While they, whose words are wisdom to the pure,
Rise dimly vision'd on th' historic page,
Where infamy in glowing language lives.

Biography may too often apply to herself the speech of Bossola, in Webster's "Duchess of Malfi,"—"My trade is to flatter the dead." The "de mortuis nil nisi bonum" is a bad motto, and worse morality. Cowley's remarks might be advantageously remembered in historical analyses of human character—"When we fix any infamy on deceased persons, it should not be done out of any hatred to the dead, but out of love and charity to the living."—*Essays,* vol. i.

Note 3, Page 351, Column 2.

And now there is an animating throb,
An energy, and daringness of thought,
Awaken'd like one mighty pulse through lands
And isles, remotely set in ocean-gloom.

"A new state of mind and feeling is obviously coming upon mankind, the effects of which can scarcely yet be calculated. But they will far exceed what took place on the diffusion of the Reformation, and can only be compared with those which the introduction of Christianity produced."—SHARON TURNER.

Note 4, Page 352, Column 1.

————— hint they not an awful shade
Of Mystery unreveal'd, yet claiming thoughts
Of solemn hue?

"Horace looks upon it as the last effort of philosophical fortitude, to behold, without terror and amazement, this immense and glorious fabric of the Universe:—

'Hunc solem, et stellas et decedentia certis
Tempora momentis, sunt qui formidine nulla
Imbuti spectent'—

But the Scripture alone can supply ideas answerable to the majesty of this subject."—BURKE *on the Sublime and Beautiful,* sect 5, part ii.

Note 5, Page 352, Column 1.

———men become idolators to sight,
Naming all else the nothingness of dreams.

"We are conversant in the corporeal world from our infancy. Sensible objects make such early repeated, strong expressions, that it is sometimes difficult to let in, upon a mind already immersed in matter, one thought concerning immaterial Beings, through an immoderate fear of superstition. For men talk and write, as if that were the only evil to be dreaded at present. We run into Sadducism; and lest we should suppose any invisible Being immediately concerned, we assign visible causes, which are plainly unequal to the effect produced."—SEED.

Note 6, Page 353, Column 1.

——— such are demon-haunters of the earth,
Who horrify the vision'd world of sleep,
And pall its midnight with infernal gloom!

There is a sublime passage on this mysterious subject, in Jeremy Taylor's Funeral Sermon on the Countess of Carbery. After saying that "there are Sicknesses that walk in darkness," he adds, "there are exterminating Angels that fly, wrapt up in the curtains of immateriality and an uncommunicating nature, whom we cannot see; but we feel their force, and sink under their sword."

In beautiful contrast to the above may be quoted the eloquent Chalmers's passage in his discourse "On the Sympathy that is felt for Man in the distant places of Creation:"—

"I can say it of the humblest and unworthiest of you all, that the eye of angels is upon him, and that his repentance would, at this moment, send forth a wave of delighted sensibility throughout the mighty throng of their innumerable legions."

BOOK V.

Note 1, Page 366, Column 1.

Sweet Country might imparadise the soul.

Perhaps one of the most beautiful passages in Pope's Letters is on this subject. "I am growing fit, I hope, for a better world, of which the light of the sun is but a shadow: for I doubt not but God's works here are what come nearest to his works there; and that a true relish for the beauties of Nature is the most easy preparation and gentlest transition to an enjoyment of those in heaven; as, on the contrary, a true town life of hurry and confusion, noise, slander, and dissension, is a sort of apprenticeship to hell and its perils."

Note 2, Page 367, Column 1.

Form inward foretaste of the unreveal'd.

"The world is in general selfish, interested, and unthinking, and throws the imputation of romance or melancholy on every temper more susceptible than its own. I cannot think but in those regions which I contemplate, if there is anything of mortality left about us, that these feelings will subsist; they are called,—perhaps they are—weaknesses here; but there may be some better modifications of them in heaven, which may deserve the name of virtues."—MACKENZIE.

BOOK VI.

Note 1, Page 372, Column 2.

A second Milton, whose creative soul
Doth shadow visions to such awful life,
That men behold them with suspended breath,
And grow ethereal at a gaze!

To whom can this eulogium apply, but to the sublime painter of "Belshazzar's Feast," "The Deluge," "Fall of Nineveh," &c., &c.?—Long may he live to adorn his age and country.

Note 2, Page 377, Column 1.

The harp is shatter'd, but the sounds remain!

"I have been just taking a solitary walk by moonshine, full of reflections on the transitory nature of all human delights; and giving my thoughts a loose in the contemplation of those satisfactions which probably we may hereafter taste in the company of separate spirits, when we shall range the walks above, and perhaps gaze on this world at as vast a distance as we now do on those worlds. The pleasures we are to enjoy in that conversation must undoubtedly be of a nobler kind, and (not unlikely) may proceed from the discoveries each shall communicate to another, of God and of Nature; but the happiness of minds can surely be nothing but knowledge."—POPE'S *Letters.*

OXFORD:

OR,

Alma Mater.

WITH BIOGRAPHICAL NOTES.

(1830.)

TO THE

CHANCELLOR, MASTERS, AND SCHOLARS

OF

THE UNIVERSITY OF OXFORD,

This Poem

IS MOST RESPECTFULLY DEDICATED,

BY THEIR OBEDIENT SERVANT,

THE AUTHOR.

OXFORD:

OR,

Alma Mater.

PREFACE

TO

THE THIRD EDITION.

(1833.)

A THIRD edition of the present work having been required, the Author has endeavoured to correct some inaccuracies which prevailed in the first, and to remove those verbal innovations

> "quas aut incuriâ fudit
> Aut humana parum cavit natura."

The writer needs no censor to remind him of the many imperfections in this work which yet remain; or to convince him how unequal it is to the dignity and interest of his subject. Oxford is indeed a city of intellectual romance, and hallowed by memories of surpassing worth in every sphere which science, learning, and imagination command. Her venerable History is enriched with the proudest archives of genius; and you cannot unfold the great volume of mental Biography without finding its pages dignified and adorned with the almost countless names of men whose creative minds were cradled in her ancient University. If Cicero could feel a glow of classical enthusiasm on the eloquent ground of Athens, and say, "quacunque ingredimur in aliquam historiam vestigium ponimus;" surely *we* may look on Oxford with the triumph of patriots, and the sympathy of scholars; and imagine every grove to be peopled with the ideal forms of sages, poets, and philosophers,

> "And tread the sacred walks
> Where, at each step, imagination burns!"

For himself, without assuming a more than ordinary reverence for the mental Past, the Author cannot bid farewell to Oxford without deep and unaffected emotion. Though he entered College at an age when experience had chilled some of those local excitements which he might otherwise have felt; and though his days there, for the most part, have glided away in solitary thought and anxious toil, still he has to thank Her for many an hour of pure and elevated delight; and, above all, for the presence of those august Associations which hang like a spell round her walls. Oxford

> "Has many a worthier son than he;"

but none who entered on her scenes with more enthusiasm, or who will leave them with more regret. Often, from the loud turmoil of the world, will memory look back on the quiet of her sacred retreats, and hear

> "The many-mingled chimes
> Swell into birth, like sounds of other times!"

Long may her hoary spires point to heaven; long may she be the nursing Mother of the wise, the good, and the great; and still continue, from age to age, to irradiate the records of mind with the triumphs of those whose genius continues to enchant the world,

> "When thrones are crush'd, and kings forgot!"

LINCOLN COLLEGE,
December, 1833.

PART I.

ANALYSIS OF PART I.

Intellectual greatness—The homage due to any Establishment tending to promote it—Oxford—Feelings and associations awakened by its first appearance—Its mental quiet — Its literary Past — Studies — Ancient and Modern Learning—Classical Bigots—System of Study and Examination—The necessity of one General Standard—Reason why Men of Genius have often contemned it—Mind independent of Circumstance—The University—Present appearance—View from the Radcliffe—New College Chapel and Service—Biographical Associations—Illustrations of the same in Addison, Steele, Collins, Johnson, Sir Philip Sydney, Ben Jonson, and Locke—Origin of Locke's famous Essay—Intellectual Society—A Contrast—Canning—Davenant—Wesley — Hervey — Denham — Chatham — Thomas Warton—Lisle Bowles—Country Clergymen—Their seclusion, how fondly anticipated—A Scene suggesting such anticipation — Blenheim — Balliol — Ridley and Latimer—Their Martyrdom—Evelyn—

Southey—The wisdom of Literary Retirement, contrasted with the rivalries of the Literary World—Female Authorship—A characteristic Sketch—Return to Biographical Associations, which conclude with Heber—His early Life—Collegiate Course—Pastoral Character and Death in India.

Round the vast miracles achieved by Mind
Throng the deep raptures of entranced mankind:
For what though Empires spread their proud control
Far as the winds exult or waters roll;
Though Tyrian merchandise their ports bedeck
And navies thunder at their awful beck,
The pride of Commerce and the awe of Power
Melt into dreams, at desolation's hour:
Then, what remains of Kingdoms which have been?
Lo! deserts wave, where Capitals were seen!
The wild grass quivers o'er each mangled Pile,
And winter moans along the archless aisle;
Where once they flourished ruins grimly tell,
And shade the air with melancholy spell,
While from their wreck a tide of feeling rolls
In awful wisdom through reflective souls.

What then alone majestically reigns
When Empires grovel on deserted plains,
In morning lustre to illume the night
Which Time engenders o'er their vanish'd might?
'Tis Mind! an immortality below
That gilds the past and bids the future glow;
'Tis mind!—heroic, pure, devoted Mind
To God appealing for corrupt mankind,
Reflecting back the image that He gave
Ere sin began, or Earth became a slave!

If then from soaring intellect arise
Perennial triumphs, England's heart may prize,
In towery dimness, gothic, stern, or grand,
Behold her palaces of Learning stand!
When Day was dying into sunset glow
I first beheld them in their beauteous show,
The solemn turrets of each ancient pile,
And thought—How noble is our native Isle!
A silent worship o'er my spirit came,
While feelings far too exquisite for name
Exultingly began their rapt control,
And fluttered, like faint music, in the soul.
Where Greatness trod, is hallow'd ground to me;
There can I lift the heart, and bow the knee,
* The past awake to all its living might,
And charm my fancy with unearthly sight,
Restore the features of the famous dead,
Nor take a Kingdom for the tear I shed!

And how poetic is that haunted Spot
Where life is mental, and the world forgot!
A spirit wafted from collegiate bowers
And the dim shadow of her ancient towers
To Alma Mater holy calm impart,
And make her scene harmonious with the heart.
The very air seems eloquently fraught
With the deep fulness of devoted thought;
While all around her, famed as eye desires,
Each mind ennobles or some heart inspires.*
And here, how many a youthful Soul began
To sketch the drama of the future man;
How many an Eye o'er coming years hath smiled,
And sparkled, as incessant hope beguiled!
The star-like spirits, whose enduring light
Beams on the World, and turns its darkness bright,
In radiant promise here began to rise,
And glow ambitious for eternal Skies.
Oh! none whose souls have felt a mighty name
Thrill to their centre with its sound of fame;
Whose hearts have warm'd at wisdom, truth, or worth,
And half which makes the heaven we meet on earth,
Can tread the ground by Genius often trod,
Nor feel a nature more akin to God!
Here in their blended magic float along
Pindaric rapture and Virgilian song;
Still Homer charms as when he first prevail'd
And honour'd Greece her idol poet hail'd;
See Athens in her classic bloom revive,
Her sages worshipp'd, and her bards alive;
See Rome triumphant, with her banner furl'd,
Awaken genius to enchant a world!

There are, who see no intellectual rays
Flash from the spirit-light of other Days;
Who deem no Age transcendent as their own,
And high the Present o'er the Past enthrone.
Yet, not in vain the world hath aye adored
The treasured wisdom ages gone afford;
Or loved the freshness of that youthful Time
When Science woke, and Man became sublime!
For then, the Elements of mind were new,
And Fancy from their unworn magic drew;

* Sapiens nunquam solus esse potest; habet secum omnes qui sunt, quique unquam fuerunt boni; et animum liberum quocunque vult transfert: quod corpore non potest, cogitatione complectitur; et si hominum inops fuerit, loquitur cum Deo. Nunquam minus solus erit, quam cum solus fuerit.—*Hier. adv. Jovin.* I. 28.

* How admirably does a sentiment of the philosophical Reynolds ("Discourse at the Royal Academy") harmonise with what the scenery of Oxford suggests!—"Every seminary of learning is surrounded with an atmosphere of floating knowledge, where every mind may imbibe somewhat congenial to its own original conceptions."

Creation's self was one unrifled theme
To form the Poet, and enchant his dream:
As yet unhaunted by inquiring thought,
Each track of mind with mental bloom was fraught;
The first in nature were the first to feel
Impassion'd wonder and romantic zeal;
Hence matchless vigour nerved their living page,
That won the worship of a future age;—
From ancient Lore see modern Learning rise,
The last we honour, but the first we prize.

Then long enshrined in this august retreat
May Greece and Rome for high communion meet;
Long may their forceful page and free-born style
From year to year enamour'd Youth beguile;
The Judgment form, uncertain Taste direct,
Teach Truth to feel, and Fancy to reflect;
And Learning, hallow'd by immortal fame,
See England glory in her Oxford name!
Yet not forsaken be the proud career
Which circles through the realm of Thought severe;
The studies vast which measure earth and sky,
Or open worlds on the undaunted eye:
Which more offends,—the bigot who can read
No volume from the dust of Ages freed;
Or he who owns no intellectual grace,
But makes a cargo of the human race,
And values man like produce from the ground,—
'Tis hard to say, yet both, alas! are found.
The dark idolater of ancient Time,
And solemn Epicure in prose or rhyme,
The groping Pedant with a gloomy eye,
Who whines an elegy o'er days gone by,—
Oh! still from Oxford be such race removed,
And nobler far her gifted scions proved.

What soul so vacant, so profoundly dull,
What brain so wither'd in a barren skull,
As his who, dungeon'd in the gloom of Eld,
From all the light of living mind withheld,
Can deem it half an intellectual shame
To glow at Milton's worth, or Shakspere's name!

Farewell to Bigots!* whatso'er their hue,
Who darken Learning, and disgrace it too;
Another charge let Alma Mater own
By frequent Sages on her wisdom thrown:†
Alike one Standard for the great and small
Her Laws decree, by which she judges all;
Hence in *one* mould must oft confound at once
The daring thinker with the plodding dunce;

* Eruditum vulgus.—PLIN. *Nat. Hist.*, lib. 2.

† Since the second edition of this work, the Author has met with the "Oxford Spy," a poem in five dialogues, the first of which was published in 1818, and has been generally attributed to the pen of Mr. Boone. As the "Spy" touches on many local topics which the present writer has chosen not to introduce in the body of the poem, he will venture to enlarge on them in the more convenient form of a note. Mr. Boone's work is pregnant with poetical beauty, and exhibits great energy of expression, in unison with much fine sentiment and elevated thought, while here and there flashes forth a line of exquisite satire; but the writer was evidently charmed with an Utopian dream of some heaven-like University, where wisdom was to be perfect, education complete, prejudice annihilated,—youth just budding into manhood, philosophically sage,—and every trait of local bigotry extinct! Now, such a University as this may be founded in poetry, but, alas! for him who thinks that while human nature, human means, and human prejudices, remain unaltered, that reality will ever present us with the like. "Paulatim" is the motto to the Academy of Science at St. Petersburgh, and this may be considered as the one most applicable to the spirit and system of our University. The "Spy" seems to have forgotten that every man receives (or ought to receive) two educations, (*vide* Bolingbroke)—the first he receives from others, the second he must give himself. The course of study pursued at College is but preliminary, and if not followed up by future reflection, has effected little for the real expansion of the mind; and hence it is, that many who have tasked health and time to a most dangerous excess, in order to enjoy the brief laurels of a Class, after they have gained distinction, relapse into their original mediocrity, and gradually subside into oblivion. Now, let a right estimate of the aim and end of the collegiate studies and honours be duly made, and much unsound speculation would be avoided. The author of the "Spy" speaks of the time spent in the University as if it were the "be-all and end-all" of a man's life, and seems to hint that it might embrace the whole circle of the Sciences, and comprehend the acquisition of both ancient and modern Languages, in addition to the inductive philosophy of Bacon, and the metaphysics of Locke! Perhaps there may be some truth in his censure on the absurd devotion paid to classical literature, and the mechanical structure of verse and prose; but, since his work appeared, the system of examination has been much liberalised; more room is allowed the candidates for originality and reflection in their essays; while in divinity, history, ethics, poetry, and criticism, more profound analysis and bolder inquiry are allowed. The plan of introducing the study of living languages is very questionable; they are best acquired in their several countries, and would only tend to embarrass the mind, by overtasking its powers with a multitude of exercises and attainments. It is easy to libel the Classics, and pen severe remarks on the nothingness of mere verbal science; but no man who is capable of imbibing the true spirit of ancient Literature will ever lament that during his residence at Oxford it formed the prime and essence of his studies. That love for severe accuracy which scholarship promotes, becomes a valuable habit in after life; and a fine taste for ancient learning, acquired in youth, seldom fails to adorn the language and enrich the style of the future man, in whatever sphere of literature he may reveal his powers.—The "Spy," in a

The soaring Mind must sink into a plan,
Forget her wings, and crawl where Dulness can;
Those bolder traits, original and bright,
Fade into dimness when they lose the light
Of open, free, and self-created day
Where all the tints of Character can play.
Yet, what could Education's art provide
For countless Minds by varying standard tried?

---

dialogue which professes to examine, with an impartial eye, the imperfections and advantages of a University, ought not to have forgotten the generous spirit of emulation which a collegiate course awakens. "There is," says Johnson, in allusion to Oxford, "such a progressive emulation; the students are anxious to appear well to their tutors; the tutors are anxious to have their students appear well in the College; the Colleges are anxious to have their students appear well in the University; and there are excellent rules of discipline in every College. That the rules are sometimes ill observed, may be true, but is nothing against the system."

We shall now take the liberty of commenting on a few extracts from the "Spy," which allude to some "Oxford Abuses," which occasionally enliven the dulness of a Review, or awake the groans of a radical press, whose clamours so often remind us of the man who cried out "fire!" in Noah's flood.

The "Spy," it appears entered the shades of Oxford

——————— "To find
Peace for the soul and wisdom for the mind,"

yet found it not! and here he pours out his vial on the heads of those vehicles for a young man's laugh—the "Dons." We fear few of them darkened the High-street, and that some of them were confined to their beds after reading the following:

"What bade these feelings ebb, ye pedants say?
What broke the dream, and rent the veil away?
What dash'd these hopes to nothing?—'Twas to see
Such folly cloth'd in such solemnity;
To see, amid the foldings of the gown,
Lurk the same failings which disgrace the town;
Spleen, envy, meanness, pride but ill represt,
And all the meaner passions of the breast,
Mix'd with the calm, which leaves no trace behind,
The sullen, sad monotony of mind."

And then we are savagely informed—

"Oh! though remote from Isis, toil and strife,
And all the deeper interests of life,
Ye souls to feeling, and to nature true,
Who love retirement,—'tis no place for you."

And why, forsooth?—because the dull pomposity of some benighted Don annoys them! Really this is a complimentary allusion to the power of "brief authority!" What though a "Don" should cross them with arrogant strut and unmeaning stare; or a Proctor be inconveniently peremptory; or a Dean annoy them with the intrusiveness of his petty dominion; can these "souls to nature and to feeling true," when they breathe the intellectual air of Oxford, and commune with the shadows of her glorious Past, allow themselves to be deprived of all her local magic, because Bigotry and Dulness, robed in awful gowns, occasionally interrupt their delights?

Mr. "Spy" is no admirer of "Convocation," and verily he ought to have been knocked down with one of those golden maces we lately beheld in that sepulchral domain, for the impertinence of the following passage:

"Hail, Synod grave, which Heads of Houses keep,
To talk, and legislate,—'perchance to sleep!'
Hail, Heads of Houses, whom your stars have made
To seem philosophers in masquerade!
I hail you all, ye Dons of high degree,
Puff'd with the conscious pride of dignity;
Solemn, and sage, and portly, to a man,
The worthy semblance of the Turk's Divan!"

In reference to the magisterial powers of the Proctor, the "Spy" has introduced a description of a scene where the privacy of a sick-room were broken by the bear-like intrusion of those cloaked mysteries (as Mr. Galt would term them), yclept "bull-dogs." We do not deny the fact; but it was a solitary case; and we will venture to add, that no office in the University is generally executed with more urbanity than that of the Proctor. To arrest the progress of imposing young dandies, gownless and capless, who delight to brave authority, however wholesome, and to fumigate the High Street with the "spicy gales" of a cigar, is a task of responsibility, and not to be irreverently mocked.

In his fourth dialogue, Mr. "Spy" examines the course of study pursued at Oxford, and moans over the barren result, which he attributes to

"Dates, places, names, a valley, or a plain,"

and

"Little points, where still suspicions lurk,
That some old women must have been at work."

We have no space to analyse his sentiments, but they all tend to one point—viz., the necessity of introducing more science, history, and modern philosophy into the examinations for degrees; and then he adds

"For must we only Aristotle quote,
And all his treatises be learnt by rote?"

also

——————— "Can aught be found,
To strengthen reason, in itself more sound,
While Bacon, Paley, pour their flood of light,
To shame the doctrine of the Stagyrite?"

Now all this is very crabbed, and by no means philosophical. Aristotle was as great an original in his profound analysis of the mind, as Shakspeare was in his poetical interpretations of the heart; and surely no one who has accurately studied those matchless treatises, the "Ethics" and "Rhetoric," but has (though unconsciously, perhaps) strengthened and expanded his reasoning powers. It really is a noisome infliction to read the raw and ignorant remarks which appear in certain publications of the day, about the "gloom of the Stagyrite," the "fetters of Aristotle," &c., &c., as if the Mind that has reigned triumphantly over nearly two thousand years, were suddenly to be unthroned by the windy nonsense of a modern scribbler!—Neither Locke, nor Paley, underrated the vast intellect of Aristotle; and though we can now enjoy the cloudless noon of Gospel truth, yet may we not disdain to revert with grateful reverence unto the dawn of Reason, as emerging

For public Weal, not individual Mind *
As mental Nurse was Oxford first design'd;
And blindly wrong would be her guardian eye,
To love the great, but pass the lesser by;
From each due toil impassion'd Genius save,
And crown for merit what mere Nature gave.
Not all alike discerning Heaven endows,
Nor equal mind to equal heart allows:
Full oft th' ingenuous pang, the noble tear
Or modest Doubt, the phantom-child of fear,
To humble Worth a consecration lends,
Which proves for lost renown sublime amends;—
Let mind be nursed, though doom'd a narrow sphere,
And what his Maker gives, let man revere!

Allow that Genius feels a curbless soul,
Which chafes in fetters, and defies control;
And, haughty as the mountain eagle-chain'd,
Hath every empire but her own disdain'd:
Though customs old, like ancient roots, are found
With stubborn grasp to cling to native ground,
Fain would her boldness to Herself be rule,
And energy its own majestic school!
But when hath Mind such education lost,
However cabin'd, and however cross'd?
Alike triumphant over college-wall,
The mouldy cellar, and plebeian stall
We mark the Soul of Inspiration rise,
Expand her wings, and revel in the skies! *

Then vainly let the powerless sophist frown,
To hide one ray of Oxford's fair renown:
Or quote some verse to vindicate his cause,
Of scornful meaning at her ancient Laws.
Spirits have lived, who could not suffer chains;
The fire which fever'd their electric veins
Burn'd all too restless for obedient thought,[1]
And hence the solace indignation brought.
Yet when was Order known, or due Control,
To quench divinity within the soul?
Oh! little think they, how sublimely pure,
In godlike state above the World secure,
That earthless nature which they Genius call!
In vain the tides of circumstance appal;
Though clouds repress, and darksome woe detain,
The Soul remounts, and is Herself again.
Go, ask of Ages what made dungeons bright,
Vile Sufferance sweet, and Danger a delight?—
'Twas Spirit, independent as sublime,
The King of nature and the Lord of time!

The Sun is up! behold a genial day,
And all things glorious in its glorious ray;
Ascend the Radcliffe's darkly-winding coil

gradually into the glorious morn of Revelation. The fate of Aristotle has indeed been strange. In the early ages of the Church, the writings of Aristotle were condemned as allowing too much to reason and sense;[1] and now we are informed that they allow too little! Having tilted at the Stagyrite, the author proceeds to annihilate poor Aldrich! Now, if our Juvenal had told us that the Dean's Latin was by no means Ciceronian, and that "red-hot syllogisms" were frequently overrated, there would have been some truth, if no discovery, in his statement; but it is mistaken irony to satirise Logic as a science

"Where in the maze of subtle jargon lost,
The strongest reason could but err the most."

After the admirable defence accompanying Archbishop Whately's "Logic," it would be absurd presumption to offer any remarks on its tendency to promote argumentative accuracy, and arm the mind against the sophistry and dogmatism of opinion. So far from hoping that the sciences of Aristotle and Logic may cease to be prominent in the studies of Oxford, we ought to desire that every term should extend their legitimate sway over the intellectual character of the University.

And here, "candide lector!" we terminate a rambling note, for which you may conceive an apology, framed after your own delightful style; and furthermore, should you be in the amphibious state of an Under-graduate, we devoutly wish you may never personally explain that definition of Man, so quaintly given by a sapient wag:[2] in other words, may you never be "a two-legged animal without feathers!"—a species of zoological Curiosity occasionally issuing from the Schools!

* Il est bon de frotter et limer notre cervelle contre celle d'autrui.—MONTAIGNE.

[1] Herschell's "Preliminary Discourse," &c.

[2] In explanation of this definition, it is recorded that a rival sage plucked a cock bare, and placing it in a philosopher's school, observed,—"Behold a philosophic man!"

* It was in prison that Boëthius composed his excellent work on the "Consolations of Philosophy;" it was in prison that Goldsmith wrote his "Vicar of Wakefield;" it was in prison that Cervantes wrote "Don Quixote," which laughed chivalry out of Europe; it was in prison that Charles I. composed that excellent work, the "Portraiture of a Christian King;" it was in prison that Grotius wrote his "Commentary on St. Matthew;" it was in prison that Buchanan composed his excellent "Paraphrase on the Psalms of David;" it was in prison that Daniel De Foe wrote his "Robinson Crusoe;" (he offered it to a bookseller for ten pounds, which that liberal encourager of literature declined giving); it was in prison that Sir W. Raleigh wrote his "History of the World;" it was in prison that Voltaire sketched the plan and composed most of the poem of "The Henriade;" it was in prison that Howel wrote most of his "Familiar Letters;" it was in prison that Elizabeth of England and her victim, Mary Queen of Scots, wrote their best poems; it was in prison that Margaret of France (wife of Henry IV.) wrote an "Apology for the Irregularities of her Conduct;" it was in prison that Sir John Pettas wrote the book on metals, called "Fleta Minor;" it was in prison that Tasso wrote some of his most affecting poems. With the fear of a prison how many works have been written!

Of countless steps, nor murmur at the toil;
For lo! a Scene, when that ascension's o'er,
Which Painters love, when most their feelings soar.
There, from the base of her commanding Dome
O'er many a mile the spell-bound glance may roam,
While music-wing'd, the winds of freshness sound,
Like airy haunters of the region round.
Yon heavens are azured by one cloudless die;
Beneath—romance in stone to charm the eye!
Spire, tower, and steeple, roofs of radiant tile,
The costly Temple, and collegiate Pile,
In sumptuous mass of mingled form and hue,
Await the wonder of thy lingering view.
Far to the west, autumnal meadows wind
Whose fading tints fall tender on the mind;
And near, a hoary Tower with dial'd side,
And nearer still, in many-window'd pride,
All Souls', with central towers superbly grand;
But see! the clouds are rent,—they break,—expand,
And sunshine, welcomed by each ancient pile,
Like Past and Present when they meet to smile,
With tinting magic beautifully falls
On fretted pinnacles, and fresco'd walls,
Till dark St. Mary, with symmetric spire,
Swells into glory as her shades retire;
And Maudlin' trees, which wave o'er Cherwell-stream,
Flash on the view and flutter in the beam:
In yellow faintness, lo! that sun-burst dies,
The vision changes with the change of skies;
Again have Centuries their dominion won,
And shadows triumph o'er the failing Sun.

And every where time-hallow'd Temples rise,
Whose classic pomp corroding age defies.
What solemn beauty by the spirit felt!
While feelings into adoration melt,
As in their depth of Gothic gloom we tread
Amid the hush of Ages which are dead.
I well remember, when a stranger, first,
What stately Vision on my senses burst!
From towering lamps a noon-like radiance shone
O'er pavement mottled with mosaic stone,
And white-robed Choristers in due array,
Whose vestments glitter'd like the sheen of day.
There, silver-voiced, in many a heav'nward note,
I heard rich Music in soft billows float,
Now faintly ebb, then loudly swell again,
And grow resistless as the organ-strain
Came river-like, in one impassion'd roll
From the deep harmony of Handel's soul!

And tell me, thou whose wandering feet have trod
Like his who trembled on the ground of God,
The hallow'd soil where classic glories shine
Back on thy spirit with their beam divine,
Hath Oxford, haunted by her long array
Of Memories which cannot glide away,
No local Magic to entrance thy mind,
And make it prouder of thy Human Kind?
Whate'er of good and glorious, learn'd or grand,
Delighted ages and adorn'd the land,
Was foster'd here:—the Senate, Pulpit, Bar,
The scenes of Ocean, and the storms of War,
Wherever Mind hath high dominion shown
To counsel Kingdoms, or secure a Throne,—
There may Oxonia sons of glory hail,
And see the Spirit which she nursed, prevail! *
Forget awhile the fever of the hour,
And give the Past its resurrection-power;
Around thee Bards and Sages muse or stray,
And wind the garden that is walk'd to-day.
The pilgrim-clouds, those time-worn trees which wave
On banks whose beauty constant waters lave,
Their eyes beheld:—do burning thoughts begin?
Then dare to rival what you dream within!

Too vast Her list, might pen achieve it all,
Each form of memory into life to call;
Yet fain would fondness with some imaged few
Partake a moment, and believe it true.
Adown yon path, beside the grassy sweep
Of Maudlin' park, where light deer couch and leap,
And giant elms the haughty Winds delay,
There gentle Addison was wont to stray:
And where the mill-stream turns yon restless wheel,
As writhing on those broken waters steal,
His tree-lined walk of beauteous length began,
For ever hallow'd by that holy man!
In many a whirl hath Autumn's driving blast
From these fond trees their summer-foliage cast,
And leafy showers now mournfully abound,
In sallow redness scatter'd o'er the ground;
But here, full oft, the branches waving green,
And heaven's blue magic smiling in between,
The pensive Rambler dream'd an hour away,
Or wove the music of his Attic lay;
Saw[2] Cato's grandeur on his soul arise,
And Heaven half open to a heathen's eyes:
Or, happier themes, whose ethic pureness glows
With every tint that character bestows,
From ancient Lore his tender heart beguiled,
And lit his features when his fancy smiled,
Nor be forgot, who all his worth could feel,
The friend of Addison, delightful Steele!

---

* See "Biographical Summary" at the end of the poem.

Whose classic morn let Merton's annals claim,
Where first the Drama woo'd him on to fame:
More roughly hewn than his Athenian friend,
And venturing oft where Virtues never tend;
Yet warm of soul, and child-like to a tear,[3]
As when it dropp'd on Love's parental bier;
Now madly sunk in passion's deep excess,
Now high in wisdom which a saint might bless!
A mixture wild of all that man admires,
Whose faults may warn him, while his fame inspires.

Ere Steele began, what Addison pursued,
The path still trod with mental gratitude,
Those day-born graces, whose refinement blends
The charm of Manner with the soul of friends,
La Casa first in Italy awoke,
And sketch'd the Courtier with a master-stroke.
But next, a Gallic Theophrastus* threw
His playful archness o'er the scene he drew,
Dissected truth with Satire's keenest knife,
And mirror'd Nature on the glass of life.
Then rose on English ground the gifted pair,
Who taught to either Sex a softer air,
Proved Elegance to Virtue's self allied,
And laugh'd at Dulness, till her follies died!
O'er weeds and thorns which social life beset,
And tease their martyr into vain regret,
Their morning-smile satirically pass'd,
Till fools turn'd wise, and fops were cured at last!
Nor small the debt Society should pay
To him who flaps her buzzing Flies away;
Those noisesome Insects on eternal wing,
That hum at banquets, or in ball-rooms sting,
Which, though they cannot heart and mind o'erpower,
May fret the smoothness of the calmest hour.

Here Collins, too, whose perfect numbers roll[4]
Pathetic music o'er the dreaming soul,
In melancholy loneness pined and thought
'Mid the sad gloom by stricken genius wrought.
E'en now the curse was breeding in his brain,—
A nerveless spirit, and a soul insane;
While moon-born fairies would around him throng,
And genii haunt him in the hush of song:
Ill-fated bard! like Chatterton's thy doom,
To seek for fame, and find it in the tomb!

To Pembroke turn, and what undying charm,
Breathed from the Past, shall *there* thy spirit warm?

* La Bruyère.

There Johnson dwelt! the dignified and sage,
The noblest Honour of a noble age;
Whose mien and manners, though of graceless kind,
Were all apart from his heroic mind;
They were the bark around some royal tree
Whose branches towering in the heavens we see.
Here lived and mused that unforgotten Man![5]
Might Language speak, what only Feeling can,
As here I view these venerable walls
And slow as in some fane my footstep falls,
Young hearts would echo to a welcome strain,
And feel, as I do,—Johnson live again!
O'er Time's vast sea a century's waves have roll'd,
And many a knell hath unregarded knoll'd,
Since, fondly wrapt in meditative gloom,*
The sage of England sat in this lone room:
Yet, well may Fancy, at yon evening-fire
Behold him seated; and when moods inspire,
(As Sorrow droop'd, or Hope her wings unfurl'd)
His spirit hover through the varied world
Of life and conduct, fortune, truth, or fate,
His future glory, and his present state:
Or, when the noonshine reign'd in golden power
And dimly smiled some melancholy Tower,
Muse at his window with far-wandering eye,
And drink the freshness of the open sky;
Or round the gateway woo admiring Ears
To listen, while he charm'd beyond his years,
By spoken magic, or electric wit†
That flash'd severe, yet sparkled where it hit:—
A bright deception! far too often seen
To hide the heart where agony has been.
Oh! hideous mockery the mind endures,
To forge the smile whose merriment allures,
To gild a moment with fictitious ray
Yet feel a viper on the spirit prey!‡
Departed Soul! how oft when Laughter fed
On the bright frolic which thy fancy bred,
And happy natures, as they saw thee smile,
Seem'd mingling with thy sunny heart awhile,
Back to thy chamber didst thou darkly steal,
And there the blight of thine own bosom feel?

* Quis enim est cui non interdum obrepat mœror ac tædium quoddam intuenti mala quibus undique plena sunt omnia?—Erasmus.

† Johnson was a classical punster, and used to assert that his conversational rival, Burke, could not accomplish the enviable art of manufacturing puns: yet is not Burke's pun on Wilkes being carried on the shoulders of the mob, transcendent? e. g., "numeris que fertur Lege solutis"—i. e., a lawless mob!

‡ A plague of the sense, a convulsion of the soul, an epitome of hell—I say of the melancholy man, he is the cream and quintessence of human adversity!—Burton's *Anat.*

Then sink to slumber with a heated brain,
To-morrow wake, and wear that smile again ! [6]

I know not why, but since a dream of Fame,
My heart hath gloried in great Johnson's name,
And deeper worship to his Spirit vow'd
Than others have to loftier worth allow'd.
In what a mould was his high nature cast,
Who never ventured, but he all surpass'd !
And reign'd amid the realms of thought alone,
Nor left an equal to ascend his throne.
How truly deep, how tenderly divine;
The lofty meaning, the majestic line !
A moral sweetness, a persuasive flow
Of happy diction, whether joy or wo
Touch'd the deep springs of his devoted mind,
Where'er they muse, delighted myriads find;
And though the bleakness of his spirit threw
Round earth's rare sunshine too severe a hue,
How Life and Character before him stand,
Their mysteries open, and their scenes expand !
And well for wisdom, could the loud pretence
Of puny language with profoundest sense,
Such massy substance in the meaning show,
As that which ages to a Johnson owe !

Descend from learning to the nearer view,
Where Man appears in vital colours true;
And where was Piety more deeply shrined,
Than in the temple of that awful Mind
Whence day and night eternal incense rose
To Him from whom the tide of Being flows !
That self-respect, around whose constant sway
The purest beams of happiness must play,
He ever felt; the same proud dream it gave
To hours that wither'd in the toils of Cave,
And him, in aidless fortune high and free,
Who taught a Lord how mean a Lord could be ! *
And, mix'd with harshness, irritably loud,
Which came like thunder from the social cloud
Which pride or pertness round the moment threw,
His faith, how firm ! his tenderness, how true !
For Goldsmith's worth, or Garrick's lighter grace,
The tears of fondness trembled down his face;
And when did Want or Wo to him appeal,
Nor find a hand to give, a heart to feel ?
While Truth he worshipp'd with severest awe,
Of Fame the glory, and to life a law.[7]
So great he lived: yet round the greatest soul
How weakness hovers with its vile control !
As when some organ of the frame appears
In matchless strength beyond the mould of years,
A weakness balancing that strength is found;
So oft in mind where miracles abound,
The lying pettiness of nature seems
Revenged in mocking what perfection dreams.
In Johnson thus: the piety which trod
Each path of life, communing with his God,
In gloomy hours could childish phantoms see,
And give to Penance what was due to tea ! [8]
The mind that reason'd on the fate of Man,
And soar'd as high as wingless nature can,
Would oft descend, the petty bigot show,
And roll lip-thunders o'er some prostrate foe !
Or else, in whirlwind fury sweep along,
And risk the right, to prove a victor wrong.
The Soul which spake angelically wise
When Truth and he were throned amid the skies,
In human life his Rasselas forgot
To wear the meanness of our common lot,
By passion bow'd, each prejudice obey'd,
And grew ferocious o'er a smile betray'd !
Yet peace to such ! of all by men adored,
Than Johnson, who could better, faults afford ?
Let Time exult that such a man hath been,
And England follow where his steps are seen.

To swell the records of collegiate-fame
See Lincoln rise, and claim her Davenant's name; [9]
Within her walls the minstrel-student wove
Poetic dreams of melody and love.
On him, as yet a verse-enchanted child,
The prince of nature, Shakspeare's self, had smiled !
Oh ! to have listen'd to that glorious Tongue,
And seen the Man on whom a World has hung,*
Till admiration, too intensely wrought,
Becomes a worship, and adores in thought !
And, Wesley ! [10] often in thy room I see
A holy Shadow which resembles thee;
Let others laugh at that o'erheated mind
Which never gloried but to bless Mankind;
Be ours the tribute to as pure a soul
As Fame recordeth in her sacred roll.
A kindred line to pious Hervey [11] pay,
Whom Lincoln boasted in his morning-day:
When night begins, and starry wonders teem,
My fancy paints him in some mental dream,
With eye upturn'd to where th' Almighty shone
While vision'd angels warbled round His throne.

From Christ Church, lo ! a dazzling Host appears
Whom Time has hallow'd, and the World reveres,

* Lord Chesterfield.

* Τῆς φύσεως γραμματεὺς ἦν, τὸν κάλαμον ἀποβρέχων εἰς νοῦν.—(SUIDAS.)

Of prelates, orators, and statesmen high,
To be forgotten,—when the world shall die!
'Twas here the muse of Tragedy divine
Bade[12] Jonson rise, and picture Catiline;
Immortal Ben! to Selden dear, and fraught
With all that Homer loved, or Plato taught.
A later age, and Locke's eternal mind
Here soar'd to Reason, such as Heaven design'd;*
Help'd Understanding to redeem her sway,
And out of night call'd intellectual day.[13]

One evening, when delightful converse glow'd,
As friend on friend his gleam of thought bestow'd,
That spark was struck which set the soul on fire,[14]
Whence sprang the work fond ages shall admire.
Hours worthy Heaven! when cultured spirits meet
Within the chamber of divine retreat;
There Friendship lives; there mental Fondness reigns;
And hearts, oblivious of their lonely pains,
By feeling blended, one communion make,
To keep the brightness of the soul awake.

But who can languish through the leaden hour
When Heart is dead, and only Wine hath power?
That brainless meeting of congenial fools
Whose highest wisdom is to hate the Schools,
Discuss a Tandem, or describe a race,
And curse the Proctor with a solemn face;
Swear Nonsense wit, and Intellect a sin,
Loll o'er the wine, and asininely † grin,—
Hard is the doom when awkward chance decoys
A moment's homage to their brutal joys!
What fogs of dulness fill the heated room
Bedimm'd with smoke, and poison'd with perfume!
Where now and then some rattling tongue awakes
In oaths of thunder, till the chamber shakes.
Then Midnight comes, intoxicating maid!
What heroes snore, beneath the table laid!
But, still reserved to upright posture true,
Behold! how stately are yon sterling few:—
Soon o'er *their* sodden nature wine prevails,
Decanters triumph, and the drunkard fails;
As weary tapers at some wondrous rout
Their strength departed, winkingly go out,
Each spirit flickers till its light is o'er,
And all are darken'd who were drunk before!

* Were the author to write on Locke's Treatise now, his opinion would be *far otherwise* than the one here expressed (1853).

† That asinine feast of sow-thistles and brambles. —MILTON'S *Prose Works*.

Oh! thou, whose eloquence and wit combined
To make their throne the heart of all Mankind;
Whom Memory visions in his wonted place
Where passions lighten'd o'er a speaking face,
And sounds of feeling from the soul were heard,
While music hung on every magic word,—
Regretted CANNING! oft has Christ Church seen
Thy glance of lustre sparkle round her scene:
From[15] Eton famed, where dazzling merit shone
In each young theme thy Genius smiled upon,
Her walls received thee; where thy talents grew,
Bright in the welcome of her fostering view,
Till glowing Senates mark'd thy spirit rise,
And England hail'd it with applauding eyes.
Alas! that in thy Manhood's noble bloom,
The shades of death hung grimly o'er thy doom,
Thy frame, too weak, a fiery spirit wore,
Though Mind prevail'd till Life's last pulse was o'er!

Thy funeral knell, oh! when I heard it moan
Like the deep echo of a Nation's groan;
That Sky beheld, where sorrow loves to gaze
When mystery wraps us or the world betrays;
And thought how soon thy glorious sun had set!
I felt a sadness, which inspires me yet:
But had I, demon-like, e'er wing'd the dart
Whose poison fed upon thy feeling heart,
Inflicted pangs where only praise was due,
And vilely thwarted every soaring view,
A *more* than melancholy for him who died,
Slain by the weapons which Renown supplied,
My soul had borne; and, wrung with inward shame,
Cursed the dark hour that wounded Canning's fame!

The yew-tree'd walk, and wilderness of shade
Where rosily the twilight-hues have play'd,
By[16] Denham haunted, Trinity! revere;
There wander'd he, no step invasive near,
The world forgot, amid Parnassian skill,
And dream'd the melodies of "Cooper's Hill."
And haughty[17] Chatham, at whose humbling word
Proud Walpole trembled, when its sway was heard;
Who baffled Spain, America, and Gaul,
To throne his England like a Queen o'er all,—
Thy paths have echo'd his immortal feet,
Thy Shades enjoy'd him in sublime retreat.
Here[18] Warton's soul emparadised his hours,
And strew'd Antiquity with classic flowers;*

* Nor rude, nor barren, are the winding ways
Of hoar antiquity, but strewn with flowers.
WARTON.

Where'er he went, saw dim Cathedrals rise,
Or Gothic windows in their sunset-dyes.

And thou, whose ever-gentle page is fraught
With the sweet lore poetic sadness taught,
Not unremember'd let thy name be found [19]
Where Genius hallows an enchanted ground.
Upon that brow the seal of Time hath set
A mournful grace, but left no dark regret
For wither'd years, whose flowery bloom remains
In the pure freshness of Aonian strains.
Yet oft thy Memory in creative gloom
May fondly sigh o'er many a distant tomb,
Where moulder forms which brighten'd other Days
Whose eyes have glisten'd o'er thy youthful lays!
Thy noontide spent, serener twilight glows
Around thy spirit like a soft repose;
And oft I turn, when fancy wanders free,
Romantic Bowles! to meditate with thee:
Oh! long in Bremhill may the village-chime
Peal solemn anthems o'er departed Time;
And fairy echoes, while they float along,
Awaken visions which were born in song,
Of hope and fame, when first thy feeling Youth
Their beauty painted on a world of truth.[20]

Thy pleasing life, in pastoral quiet spent,
Where heaven and earth comminglingly are blent,
A prayer evokes, that England long may see
In wood-hung vales, from city-murmur free
That landscape-charm in varied shadow drest—
The village-steeple with its towery crest,
When dimly taper'd by romantic height,
Or grayly melted into morning-light.
Not Windsor vast, with battlemented towers,
With charm so deep a pensive gaze o'erpowers
As village-spires, in native valleys seen,
With nature all around them, hush'd and green:
How oft some eye, as o'er the wheel-track'd road
The whirling Coach conducts its motley load,
Hath wistful gazed where neat the parsonage rose,
With Church behind it in revered repose!

Ah! little know they, whom the harsh declaim
Of Folly leads to scorn a Curate's name,
* In hamlets lone what lofty minds abound
And spread the smiles of charity around!

It was not that a frowning Chance denied
An early wreath of honourable pride:
In College-rolls triumphantly they shine,
And proudly Alma Mater calls them, "mine!"

---

* "For about three quarters of a century, the public laboured under the delusion that Pope was a poet and, moreover, a man of tolerable morals, till an amiable clergyman took upon himself to disabuse the world of its errors."—Such is the lame sarcasm with which Dr. Madden, in his "Infirmities of Genius" (vol. i.), introduces the name of Bowles. Having some years ago been enabled to offer a few critical remarks on the "Pope controversy," in a periodical since defunct, we may be permitted, perhaps, to record our sentiments on the present occasion. Now, has Dr. Madden really perused Bowles' edition of Pope? or has he merely quoted the article which appeared in some hostile review on this subject? We suspect the latter; from the style in which he alludes to Mr. Bowles' edition, which in fact, so far from aiming to impress the reader with a dark idea of Pope's moral character, breathes throughout of generous appreciation, and candid inquiry. True, Pope is not imaged forth to our imagination as a sun without a spot; but there is no mean tendency in the occasional remarks on various and somewhat dubious passages in his life. It is a mock generosity, and a miserable desertion of the high and peerless cause of Truth, to deify the dead at the expense of the living; and we may recal to Dr. Madden a passage which he himself has quoted with singular complacency:—"Truth is to be sought only by slow and painful progress; but error is, in its nature, flippant and compendious; hops with airy and fastidious levity over proofs and arguments, and perches upon assertion, which it calls conclusion."

With reference to the question of Pope's rank and height on the debateable Mount of Parnassus, Dr. Madden luxuriates in the idea, that Lord Byron fired off one or two epistles to his publisher, which were intended to annihilate Mr. Bowles and his creed altogether. But, after the contrast exhibited between Lord Byron's private opinion of poets, as expressed in the correspondence edited by Moore, and his public sentiments on the same authors, men will estimate at its due worth the aristocracy of taste. For instance, in various parts of his "Letters," it appears that his lordship *did* think very highly of Southey and Wordsworth—and yet with what savage and ungenerous contempt does he ever allude to these men in his poetry? Yes, he could lavish unneeded eulogies on Pope, who was beyond his praise, and, from his peculiar style, utterly removed from rivalship with him—but for Wordsworth, at the fountain of whose intellect he had taken so many clandestine draughts,—there was no epithet too mean, and no ridicule too coarse, which he did not employ to underrate his worth! For our own part, we are free to confess, that the perversion of his popularity to blind the public against the genius of Wordsworth, Southey, &c., was an odious trait in Lord Byron's life. But these times are over; and in the increasing popularity of Wordsworth, is to be recognised the dawn of nobler taste, and higher appreciation for philosophic poetry.

As to the "Letters" to Murray, no one can read them without being amused by their animation, point, and drollery; but, we believe, it is generally allowed, the advantage of argument and solid criticism was on Bowles' side. Bowles considered Pope as the first in the second rank of poets, that is to say,

But heavenlier dreams than ever Fame inspired
Their spirit haunted, as the World retired.
The fameless quiet of parochial care
And sylvan home, their fancy stoop'd to share;

next to Shakspeare and Milton!—was this depreciation? Are we to place his exquisite but artificial verse beside the sublime revealings of Milton, or the dramatic creations of Shakspeare? We believe no man but Lord Byron would do so; if, indeed, he actually felt all he wrote about Pope, for there is much vanity in applause; and Lord Byron began to consider himself as the sole defence and support of Pope's immortality! But, had not the genius of Pope animated, as it were, the poetical life-blood of the country long before his lordship became illustrious? And though the heretics of Cockneyism presumed to invalidate the claims of the bard of Twickenham, and (as at the present) pale-faced young gentlemen, panting to be "Corsairs" enamoured of the "dark blue sea," and prating, in parrot-like tones, of "passion," "pride," and "discontent," uttered puerile nonsense, on the subject and sources of Pope's Inspiration,—still there was not a leaf withered in the laurel of his fame.

We shall not conclude without an allusion to one or two more passages in Dr. Madden's "Infirmities." He remarks, "There is a paradox in the conduct of literary men, which makes it necessary to draw a distinction between their actions and their sentiments, between the author with a pen in his hand, and the man without it." Is not the "paradox" the Doctor's own property? Does he expect a poet to come into drawing-rooms, and be the incarnation of his poetry? or wonder why the glow, the exultation, and purity of his mind, while composing, are so rarely visible in the intercourse and social morals of daily life? We suspect Dr. Johnson has unravelled the mystery in that pithy sentence, "It is easy to despise death when there is no danger, and to glow with benevolence when there is nothing to be given." Here is the difference between the abstract and concrete! "Poetry," says de Staël, "is the apotheosis of Sentiment!"—it is a love and a veneration for the ideal, a passion for the beautiful and unearthly—a consciousness and belief of the "immortal powers that lie folded up in man!" And surely it is no paradox, that a poet should be able to know, feel, and express all this, and, while surrounding himself with dreams of loveliness in the hush of retirement, picture forth the noblest specimens of man's mind—and yet, when the power of inspiration is past, come forth with all the imperfections of prose, and flesh, and blood.

Dr. Madden's work is not devoid of interest, and in its main tendency is benevolent; but he has attributed too much to the moral influence of malady. Indigestion has been admirably defined as "the remorse of the stomach;" and, doubtless, under its various inflictions, the most amiable hearts may for a while do injustice to their nature, and the most musical of tongues be out of tune; but this does not apply to all those cases cited by the author of the "Infirmities." He says (vol. ii.), "Who knows under what paroxysm of disease he (Pope) might have written those bitter sarcasms which he levelled against his literary opponents?" (he might have added, "and against his old friends and acquaintances.") And does Dr. Madden believe that poets compose under "paroxysms of disease!" Horace thought far differently, and so did Juvenal,[1] who was no mean judge in these matters. But, allowing that Pope did commit his poetical vengeance to verse under "paroxysms,"—was he obliged to publish it? The elaborations which his poems underwent are well known; they were not written by steam, nor published immediately after their production; consequently Pope had time to recover from his "paroxysms," and to soften down the maledictions of his rhyme—if he thought them unjust or undeserved. In regard to Lord Byron's physical "infirmities," whatever they may have been, the disposition of heart which would enable any man to compose such atrocious stanzas as those lately published on Rogers—for whom he professed the deepest regard, and on the Altar of whose Genius he had often laid the gift of his praise—is not to be explained by dyspepsia, or indigestion. Dr. Madden's practice must have taught him that Genius is not the only thing which undergoes infirmities; and though there are some mental "infirmities" which are peculiar to the temperament of literary men,—to refer a moral obliquity of mind and meanness of heart to such cause, is frail and imperfect philosophy.

And when arrived, no deeper bliss they sought
Than that which undenying heaven had brought.
On such, perchance, renown may never beam,
Though oft it glitter'd in some College-dream;
But *theirs* the fame no worldly scenes supply,
Who teach us how to live, and how to die!

In life so calm, unworldly, and refined,
What pictured loveliness allures the mind!
Hast thou forgot that balmy summer-noon
That glow'd so fair, and fled, alas! so soon,
My chosen Friend! in whose fond smile I see
A spirit noble, and a nature free,
When Blenheim woo'd us to that proud domain
Where History smiles, and Marlborough lives again.
And on the way how sweet retirement threw
A shade of promise o'er Life's distant view?
How softly-beautiful the bending sky,
Like heaven reveal'd, burst radiant on the eye!
A Spirit, bosom'd in the winds, appear'd
To chant noon-hymns, where'er a sound career'd;
While ev'ry leaf a living gladness wore
And bird-like flutter'd as the breeze pass'd o'er:
The lark made music in the golden air;
The green earth, yellow'd by a sunny glare,
In twinkling dyes beheld its flowery race
Dance to the wind and bloom with sparkling grace;
Faint, sweet, and far, we heard the sheep-bell sound,

[1] Sed vatem egregium, cui non sit publica vena,
Qui nihil expositum soleat deducere,—
Hunc ——————
Anxietate carens animus facit, omnis acerbi
Impatiens, cupidus silvarum, &c., &c.
Sat. vii., l. 5.

While insect-happiness prevail'd around:
And rich varieties of hill and glade,
Where viewless streams, by verdure oft betray'd,
(Like Charity, who walks the world unseen
Yet leaves a light where'er her hand hath been)
By bank and mead roll'd windingly away,—
'Twas ours to witness in adorn'd array.

Noon glided on, till day's declining glow
Beheld us sweeping o'er the verdant flow
Of meadow'd vales, to where the village-hill
In garden bloom we welcomed, bright and still.
That sunny eve in smiling converse fled
Around a banquet generously spread,
Beneath a roof where Elegance combined
The pure in Taste with Fancy the refined:—
The[21] Church antique, whose ivied turret won
The dream-like changes of departing sun
And glanced upon us at our parting hour,
I still remember in its beauteous power.
Then home we sped beside romantic trees
Whose leaf-pomp glitter'd to the starting breeze,
And fondly view'd in symmetry of shade
The mimic branches on the meadows laid.
In wave-like glory burn'd the sunset sky;
Where rosy billows seem'd to swell and lie
Gleaming and vast;—as if that haughty Day
Ere yet th' horizon saw him sink away,
His clouds and colours vassal-like would see
Once more awake, and own their deity!

Where Balliol frowns along yon ancient road,
By[22] Evelyn hallow'd, his endear'd abode
I never pass, nor think of them who died,
Heroic Martyrs, burning side by side!
Upon her walls there hung a crimson glare,
And red fires raven'd on the breezeless air;
But thou, false Bigot!* in that murderous hour
To heaven couldst look, and on thy victims lour,
Then feed thy gaze with agonies of fire,
As limb by limb the tortured Saints expire!
In serpent-writhings, lo! the flames awake,
Hiss as they whirl, and riot round the Stake;
While mitred fiends, as they behold them rise,
Glare on the martyrs with their wolfish eyes!
Yet firm they stand: behold! what Glories smile
Above the fury of that burning pile;
Ten thousand harps, ten thousand anthems swell,[23]
And heaven is worshipp'd in a scene of hell!

Here Southey,[24] in the spring-like morn of youth,
His feeling, conduct, and his fancy, truth,
Beheld the orb of Liberty arise
To gild the earth with glory from the skies:
What wonder, then, if his Chaldean gaze
With glowing worship met her morning-rays,
Beheld them bright as freedom's rays should be
And thought they darted from a deity?
Who did not feel, when *first* her shackles fell,
The truth sublime that France inspired so well,—
There is a freedom in the Soul of man
No Tyrant quenches, and no Torture can!
But when high Virtue from her throne was hurl'd
And Gaul became the dungeon of the World,
No mean deserter was that patriot proved
Whose Manhood censured what his Youth had loved.

In bloom of life he sought domestic shade,
Devoting hours a world had not betray'd
In deep affection to delightful lore,
Which Feeling loves, and Wisdom may adore.
While others linger'd in the restless Town
To wear the thorny wreath of young renown:
Or, spirit-worn, see rivals mount above,
With few to honour, and with none to love,—
Afar to Keswick's mountain-calm he hied,
And found the haven which a Home supplied.
There Nature pure to his pure soul appeals,
With Her he wanders, and with Her he feels,
While earth and sky for poesy unite,
And the hush'd mountains hallow morn and night.
Thus flowingly the fairy hours depart
And each day adds a virtue to the heart.
Ah, blissful Lot! which few have lived to share
Who haunt the world, and seek to find it *there*:
Forgetful that one day of Life is fraught
With years of meaning for inductive Thought,
In baffled hope the mind exhales away,
Their each to-morrow a renew'd to-day;
Too meanly anxious for some poor applause,
They burn for Glory, but betray her cause.
True fame is genius, in its earthless hour
Sent from the soul with world-subduing power,
From heart to heart electrically known
Till Realms admire, and Ages are its own!

Oh! blest resolve which consecrates a life
To leave for studious calm the noisome strife
Of London's everlasting round of self,
Pursued by Learning, or career'd for Pelf.
In wise seclusion heaven-ward thoughts incline
To form in Man the elements divine;
From day to day their semblance nearer grows,
Till kindred Mind a kindred Maker knows;

* Doctor Smith, the apostate, who recanted in King Edward's time. In perusing the dark volume of ecclesiastical history, how frequently is that sound maxim of Fenelon verified:—"La force ne peut jamais persuader les hommes; elle ne fait que des hypocrites!"

And then, what beautiful accordance seen
In all that Wisdom taught, or time hath been!
What once was dark becomes divinely clear,
And earth itself a heaven-reflecting sphere.
That living God enthron'd all worlds above
Whose Name and Nature are reveal'd by Love,
Our spirit feels within itself abide,
The Will direct, and o'er each thought preside;
In man or nature, whatso'er befal—
True faith can fathom and interpret all!

Turn from the calm secluded life bestows,
A life which Evelyn loved and Southey knows,
To London; where a world of anxious mind
In one dark fever of excess we find;
Where talent sparkles with incessant rays,
And authors* perish—for the want of praise!
Though minds abound, whose magical control,
Like truth from heaven, can elevate the soul,
Too rapidly our soaring authors teem
For each to fill the circle of his dream.
Though high the hope which Energy awakes,
And far the flight a free-wing'd Spirit takes,
A thousand hearts o'er disappointment bleed,
The many venture, but the few succeed.
Hence of all crimes, the last to be forgiven
Eternal barrier to some critic's heaven,
Success is proved;—that hour Her star appears
In daring brightness to outdazzle years,
The fogs of hate, the clouds of dulness rise,
To quench her lustre, and deface her skies;
Hence martial pens in pugilistic rage,
And venom oozing from each vulgar page,
Slander abroad on its exulting wings
To frighten fools, or flap the face of kings,
While faded authors, overcome with bile,
Turn into villains, and lampoon the Isle!†

But, hark! to sounds so musically dear,
By Flattery melted into Folly's ear;
Behold a "Lion" who must roar to-night,
And doubt if homage be not man's delight!
Amid the sweet, soft words, which come and go‡
From lord to lady, and from belle to beau,
There in thyself a night-throned Idol see,
'Tis all thou art, and all a fool should be!§

Enamour'd thus, nonsensically dream
Thy mental worth a supernat'ral theme;
Yet, look around thee ere the night be o'er,
Thy heart is free, and thou a fool no more!
Thy mien, thy manners, and thy person tend
To make no charm Politeness could commend;
And, lest they should not quite sufficient see,
The faults of others are bestow'd on thee;
Thus on, till all that once was "glory" thought
From tongue to tongue is whisper'd into nought;
While each is conscious, as thy fame's o'erthrown,
To wound another's, is to heal his own.*

Yet oft ambiguous Hate her truth beguiles,
And Envy wriggles into serpent-smiles!
Some cringing, cawing, sycophantic Sneak
With heart as hollow as his head is weak,
In smother'd voice will chance a rival sue
To feed the pages of a starved Review:
"Dear Sir! I think your genius quite divine,"—
To-morrow, turn, and lash it line by line!
And can it be, to such ignoble life
Of ceaseless longing and chicaning strife,
Where fever'd passion frets the hour along,
That woman's gentler soul would fain belong?
Oh! deem not the assuming pride of Man
Would claim a glory which no Woman can;
Nor think to her soft nature is not given
The flame of genius with the form of heaven.
Her tenderness hath made our harshness weep,
And hush'd our passions into child-like sleep;
Her dewy words fall freshly on the soul;
Her numbers sweet as seraph-music roll;
And beautiful the morn-like burst of mind
When first her spirit wakens o'er mankind!
Now painting clouds, now imaging the sea,
Bloom on the flower, and verdure on the tree!
But diff'rent far a genius thus display'd,
From mind corrupted into menial trade,
When reputation is the theme adored,
And pilfer'd learning† all its charms afford,
Those hues divine which delicately please,
The smile unfashion'd, and the soul at ease,
All, all that language is too frail to tell
Which forms in woman what we feel so well,

* "Stat contra, dicitque tibi tua pagina—fur est!" —MART.

"There came by chance into my company a fellow not very spruce to look on. I asked him what he was? He answered, a poet. I demanded why he was ragged? He told me this kind of learning never made any man rich!"—BURTON'S *Anat.*

† "Il n'y a point au monde un si pénible métier que celui de se faire un grand nom."—BRUYÈRE.

‡ The pregnant brevity of one of Montaigne's sayings is applicable to these artificial scenes—"Combien est le langage faux moins sociable que le silence!"

§ 'Tis all thou art, and all the proud shall be!—POPE.

* "The life of a celebrated man was more glorious in ancient times; but that of an obscure individual is more happy in this modern period."—DE STAËL. In allusion to the same subject this acute writer remarks in another place—"The most glorious triumph the Greeks could obtain excited much less hatred than the limited applause resulting from the niggard hand of modern criticism."

† One is almost tempted to suppose that human invention is limited, like a barrel-organ, to a specific number of tunes.—DUGALD STEWART.

In public life too often dies away
Like dreams forgotten in the flush of day.
There, taunting Pens dissect her dubious claim,
Or jeering coxcombs jest away her fame:—
Behold the beauty of yon garden-flower
In lovely bloom beside its native bower;
What winning freshness in its healthful dye,
Pure as the spring, and radiant as the sky!
Transplant it thence to some o'erheated room,
Where hands profane it,—and, alas, the bloom!

Let Man his intellectual sceptre wield;
To him have Ages in their march appeal'd
To shape the Elements of mind and power
Through the vast scene of Life's unrestful hour.
But thou, fond Woman! * on affection's throne,
Behold a kingdom of the Heart thine own!
Their feelings form the subjects of thy sway,
And all is Eden where thy glances play:
'Tis thine to brighten far from public strife
The daily windings of domestic life,
And by thy grace and gentleness of mien
Adorn and beautify Home's varied scene.[25]

. . . .

Pleasant is Morning, when her radiant eye
Opes on the world, enchanting all the sky;
And Ev'ning, with her balmy glow of light,
The beauteous herald of romantic night:
And pleasant oft to some poetic Mind
The sound of water, and the sweep of wind,
A friend renew'd in some heart-welcomed place,
With years of fondness rising in his face;
The tear which answers to a tale of woe,
And happy feelings in their heavenward flow:
But sweeter far proves his revengeful lot
Whom Fame hath slighted, or the World forgot,
When printed falsehood gratifies each bent,
And mangles volumes to the heart's content;
Corrupts what style, creates what fault you please,
Laughs o'er the truth, and lies with graceful ease!
Thus Envy lives; and Disappointment heals;
The gangrened wounds a tortured memory feels;
And wither'd hopes delightful vengeance wreak,
While pages witness more than scorn could speak.

And thus with one, whose life I now recal; *
When pens were daggers, he endured them all!
Each Reptile started from his snug review
To spit out poison,—as most reptiles do;
Oh, how they feasted on each faulty line,
And generously made *their* dulness thine!
From page to page they grinn'd a ghastly smile,
Yet seem'd to look so heaven-like all the while:
Then, talk'd of merit to the world unknown,
Ah! who could doubt them, for they meant their *own*.[26]

Religion, too! what right had Youth to scan
That scheme of Glory which Heaven unveils for man;
Or paint around him, wheresoe'er he trod,
The glowing fulness of eternal God?
Indeed, 'twas hinted,—hoped it was untrue!
His heart *had* worn an atheistic hue;
And still religion, though its hallow'd name
Imparted freshness to his early fame,
Had not alike both heart and head inspired;
In short, the World was sick, and they were tired;
And then to prove his verse was more than vile
They wrote bad prose with overflowing bile!
But venal Commerce hired a Serpent too
To sound his rattle in the Scotch review; †

* Bishop Newton's idea of a "substantial wife" would appear very prosaic to the super-sentimental ideas of a modern Miss: here it is, reader!—"Some clever, sensible woman, who would lay out his money to the best advantage, and be careful and tender of his health; a friend and companion at all hours, and who would be happier in staying at home than be perpetually gadding abroad!"—In Burnet's account of the unfortunate Queen Catherine ("Reformation," vol. i. p. 387), a touch of homely truth occurs, delightfully illustrative of her domestic character—"She was a devout and pious princess; in her greatness she wrought much with her own hands, and kept her women well employed about her, as appeared when the two legates came once to speak to her. She came out to them with a skein of silk about her neck, and told them she had been at work with her women."

* This passage, with others of a kindred tone, alludes to a *wounded state of feeling long passed away.* It is not the only record of past excitement in this volume over which, in all sincerity, the writer need exclaim—"σκιας οναρ!"—(1839.)

† As the note referred to in the text relates to his literary past, and contains the published vindication of a most estimable person, (SAMUEL MAUNDER, the author of the well-known "Treasuries," &c.) the author does not feel justified in cancelling it from his collected works. But he wishes the reader to understand it *was written some twenty years ago,* partly in badinage, and partly in seriousness; and refers to a style of popular criticism which has almost expired.

Were the author *now* to express his feelings on this and kindred subjects, the mellowing influence of experience would be visible in his strictures; he would speak in a calmer strain of critical injustice; and be reminded, while he wrote, that, after all, Criticism is but one of those exponents of our fallen, inconsistent, and fallible nature, which (like all we do, speak, write, and are) bears the impress of our common sin and selfishness. As far as his memory goes, he does not think that either Mr. Clarkson or himself, when the article in the "Edinburgh Review" appeared, was aware of the writer of that assault. But, as Mr. Macaulay, since then, has had the singular bad taste to republish and acknowledge himself to be the author of this article, without adding one word of explanation to alleviate its virtual untruth,—the matter assumes a different bearing; and few will deny

And yet, (alas! that such ignoble end
Should baffle those who injured Taste defend!)
Though perfect lies were most profoundly said
A Poet triumph'd and the Public read;
For truth is stronger than the envious know,
And gains new vigour from the vilest blow;
And when abusive falsehoods cease to pay,
Malice grows dumb, and slander dies away.

The faded past my fancy haunts again;
And lo! thine image shadow'd o'er my strain,
Thou lovely Spirit of celestial worth!
Whose saint-like pureness so adorn'd the earth,
And, when it vanish'd, thrill'd a world with woe,
And thoughts, which seldom into language flow,
But silently within the soul retire
And all the sacredness of grief inspire.

Yet, words and tears have minglingly adored,
Deep, warm, and true, as feeling Hearts afford,
Those angel-attributes which good men prize,
Lamented Heber! when they leave the skies,
Awhile some Spirit pure as thine array,
Smile on the World, and heaven-like pass away.

There is a shadow round the holy Dead:
A mystery, wherein we seem to tread,
As oft their lineaments of Life awake
And sorrowing Thoughts their hallow'd semblance take.

---

the "audi alteram partem" is a mere act of justice due alike to the dignity of truth and the cause of literature. It is, moreover, to be remembered, that occasionally one-sided references are made to Mr. Macaulay's attack; and therefore with the most perfect courtesy and good-humour, the present writer will venture some observations on the subject, and then dismiss it for ever.

1. In the honour of being misrepresented by Mr. Macaulay, the writer of this is not alone. Southey, Wordsworth, Gladstone, &c. &c., have been equally distinguished; indeed, it has not yet been discovered, that this gentleman has ever eulogised in public a *single contemporary*. His praise is for the dead, and those alone. 2. That a practised reviewer, like Mr. Macaulay, should be able to write an "Essay" on the first poem of an author, written in his nineteenth year, and by a mere selection of weak lines and verbal errors, and a determined concealment of all which might be rightly appreciated—produce a sarcastic article for a review, is neither surprising nor original. How far, indeed, a good man, who reverences truth, and scorns to be unjust in order to gratify his spleen, would condescend to write such a review, is a different question, not here to be investigated. 3. As regards critical eulogies, and the blinding effect of social attachment on the judgment, no man has received from personal or political friends, through the medium of criticism, more excessive adulation than Mr. Macaulay himself; or been more willing, on the eve of publication, in every way to secure them. 4. In opposition to Mr. Macaulay's criticism, the appreciation of such men as Professor Wilson, Southey, Wordsworth, Crabbe, and Bowles, &c. &c., can be adduced; and perhaps, Mr. Macaulay himself will admit that some of these distinguished men are, at least, his equals in genius, taste, and discrimination. 5. If the faults only of any production, either in prose or verse, are to be considered as the exclusive qualities of an author's mind, according to a crushing article in the "Quarterly Review," Mr. Macaulay himself is a paltry historian, full of prejudice, spleen, and partiality. 6. This reference to some galling strictures in the "Quarterly" on Mr. Macaulay's "History" suggests the following question. Is it not a violation of all literary decorum and critical truth, for Mr. Macaulay to head his article with,—"Writings of Mr. Robert Montgomery," seeing that *there is not one solitary verbal defect which he censures in the "Omnipresence," which has not been corrected many years since?* Let an analogous case be put. How would Mr. Macaulay, or his friends, like an "Essay" from the "Quarterly" to be published, headed, "Writings of Mr. Macaulay," which essay should be nothing more than a severe and searching exposure of blunders and incoherences long since removed? Yet this is the unchivalrous and splenetic wrong to which Mr. Macaulay condescends to put his name; and with perverse obstinacy continues to publish against an author who for more than five and twenty years, has done his best to proclaim Truth and Righteousness, and who would rather let the "flesh-fly blow in his mouth," than imitate such palpable injustice. And even this analogy does not meet the case. Mr. Macaulay's "History" was published in the full maturity of his powers; but the "Omnipresence of the Deity" was written *on the verge of boyhood;* and the specimens which he pretends to give of that poem in his "essay" have as much representative truth in them as Sydney Smith's question had of rational inquiry, when he begged to know "How far it was from the first of January to the top of St. Paul's?" Let Mr. Macaulay express and publish what opinions he pleases on his contemporaries; but let him remember spleen is not criticism: and that he who wilfully misrepresents the mind and Character of an author, has not only degraded the functions of Criticism, but inflicted a moral injury, which none but the meanest of mankind will approve. This was Southey's and Wordsworth's expressed opinion; and perhaps it will one day be Mr. Macaulay's also. 7. Lastly, if the continued appreciation of public Taste, be the ultimate source of an author's reputation, then is the victory, in the present case, altogether on the side of the young writer, and not on that of the old critic. When Mr. Babington Macaulay informed the world "*The Omnipresence of the Deity*" was a worthless production, and implied that such men as Wordsworth, Southey, and Professor Wilson, were fools for eulogising it, the twelfth edition of that poem was then in circulation. And as the public did not wait to know what Mr. Macaulay thought of that production *before* they purchased it, so, up to the present hour, with a strange infatuation, they have never ceased to welcome and peruse it. Surely *a quarter of a century* in an age like our own, is a sufficient period to test the real pretensions of any work, whether in prose or verse! Hence Mr. Macaulay's elaborate misrepresentation is as unjust towards his own name, as it is a miserable failure in respect to the object of his morbid dislike.

What once they dreamt, when mortal nature threw
Phantasmal dimness round each soaring view,
Now, all unearth'd, beatified, and free
From toil and tears,—their unscaled Eyes can see:
No more on them the fitful whirl of things
From joy to gloom, eternal trial brings;
In light array'd, before The Throne they shine,
And learn the mysteries of Love Divine:
Why tears were shed, why pangs of woe prevail'd,
Why Goodness mourn'd, and Virtue often fail'd,
No longer now a with'ring shadow throws
Like that which hovers round the World's repose.

The holy dead! of Earth and Heaven the dear!
Whene'er the darkness of our troubled sphere
'Twixt God and Man will demon-like arise,
The soul deject, and doubt away the skies,
Then Mem'ry points to where their feet have trod,
Redeems our nature, and recals her God.
Creation's debt to discontented Time
They help'd to cancel by a worth sublime,
And wisdom, which enthrones the good and great
High o'er the meanness of our mortal state;
The smile that withers in its cynic play
Each hope of earth when budding into day,
By merit awed, in forceless meaning falls,
Whenever mind exalted mind recals,
Since eras bright of holiness and love
Their spirits promise from a World above!

And such was he, whose toiling virtues won
A tomb of fame beneath a foreign sun.
In childhood, ev'ry dawning sweetness made
A tender magic which no truth betray'd;
While, fond as feeble, blendingly began
Those mental traits that ripen into man.
Romance and fairies, and Crusades inspired
The poesy which deeper Years admired:
Heaven's awful Book he loved to learn and read,
And mourn'd to see the great Redeemer bleed;
In all he did, benevolence prevail'd,
And from his frown no shrinking pauper quail'd;
Nor form of Woe, nor face of Grief, he pass'd,
But pitied all, and pitied to his last! [27]

From Neasden fresh, lo! Oxford hails him now,[28]
And fancies new are bright'ning o'er his brow:
Too warmly toned, too feelingly endow'd,
Companionless to linger in the crowd,
A brother's fame around him lives and blooms,
His mind awakes,—and magic fills his rooms!
Where souls have listen'd as he charm'd the hour,
And young eyes sparkled to confess his power.
Still, unentangled by the social net,
Though smile and banquet oft the heart beset,
Each dawn beheld him at his classic tome,
And pure, as in his unforgotten home.[29]

Scarce enter'd yet, and honours flower'd his way!
And soon the music of a master-lay
From circling thousands woke a thrill divine [30]
While England wept o'er weeping "Palestine!"
There are, that still in this cold world remain,
Whose ears are haunted by that holy strain,
Whose eyes dejected Salem still behold
As scene on scene the vision was unroll'd,
When invocation with her sweetest sound
Woo'd angel-forms, and angels watch'd around!
While grandly swelling into giant view,
"Like some tall palm the noiseless Fabric grew!"
Then Israel harping by her willow'd streams,
And Prophets bright with more than prophet-dreams,
The poet vision'd in his pictured strain
Amid the glory of Millennium's reign:
Then, bade his Thunders tell of time no more,
Till Nature shudder'd at their dooming roar!

Fond eyes were fix'd upon the Minstrel now;
A raptured sire beheld his laurell'd brow;
And blest his boy with all that tears bestow
When Heaven seems by, and human hearts o'erflow:
And where was *he?* escaped the glowing throng,
In the proud moment of triumphant song
He sought his chamber;—silent and alone
A Mother saw him at his Maker's throne! [31]

That hour hath pass'd: a village-curate made,
How nobly seen amid the pastoral shade!
Parochial cares his cultured mind employ,
Domestic life and intellectual joy.
The old men cry, a blessing on his head!
And Angels meet him at the dying bed;
Let fever rage; disease or famine roll
Tormenting clouds which madden o'er the soul,
Where life exists, there Heber's love is found,
And heaven created by its welcome sound!

None are *all* blest; without some mental strife
To ripple, not destroy, the calm of life:
That heart for ever open to the poor,
Who weeping came, but smiling left his door,
Was all unapt, when mean annoyments rose
From rustic fools or mercenary foes,
By happy lightness to o'erleap them all,
And melt the clouds which daily life befal.

More wisely oft, where common nature guides,
A pliant spirit of the world presides,
Than he, whose loftiness of feeling fails
To stoop or wind, as subtlety prevails.
Nor could that Soul, though high its lot had been,
Forget to paint a more expanded scene,
Or sphere of duty where his mind would sway
The wider realms of intellectual day.
They dawn'd at length! a not unclouded dream,
From golden climes by Ganga's idol-stream.
That Indian soil poetic Fancy knew,—
Her sculptured wrecks, and mountain's roseate view,
Her palmy meads by banks of radiant green,
And dusky cots where cooling plantains lean.
But when he felt a meek-eyed Mother's gaze,
And thought how soon might end her lonely days!
Beheld his child in cradled hush asleep,
Too frail to dare the thunders of the deep;
His books deserted, friendship's riven chain,
And he, a pilgrim on the boundless main,—
That strife of soul might well forbid him roam,
And softly hue the tenderness of home!

Those shading doubts a Providence dispell'd;
Each home-born fear aspiring goodness quell'd:
The parting o'er, behold! the billows sweep
In rushing music as he rides the Deep,
That wafts him onward to his Indian clime,
While mused his heart on future toil sublime,
Whereby Redemption and her God would smile
On heathen Lands, and many a lonely isle,
Where stinted Nature, in degraded gloom
From age to age had wither'd to the tomb!
And haply, too, when rose the twilight-star,
And billows flutter'd in a breezy war,
At that dim hour regretted England came,
Familiar walks, and sounds of early fame,
And village-steeple, with the lowly race,
Whose fondness brighten'd to behold his face!

The Land was reach'd; and oh! too fondly known
How Heber made that sunny Land his own,
Till pagan souls a Christian nature wore,
And feelings sprang which never bloom'd before,
As toil'd he there with apostolic truth,
Redeem'd the Aged, and reform'd her Youth,
For praise to honour with a powerless line
A heart so deep, a spirit so divine! [32]
He lived; he died: in life and death the same,
A Christian martyr! whose majestic fame
In beacon-glory o'er the world shall blaze,
And lighten Empires with celestial rays,
While Virtue throbs, or human hearts admire
A poet's feeling with a prophet's fire,
Or pure Religion hath a shrine to own
Where man can worship at his Maker's throne!

PART II.

"The still air of delightful studies."—MILTON.

"———— To range
Where silver Isis leads the stripling feet;
Pace the long Avenue, or glide adown
The stream-like windings of that glorious street!"
WORDSWORTH.

ANALYSIS OF PART II.

THE proud feelings arising from a Survey of the Past —Commencement of College Life—Entrance into Oxford—First Morning in the University—Chapel Service—A Walk through the Town—The New Clarendon—Circulation of the Scriptures—Sublime Hopes—Picture of the Indian reading his Bible—Return to Oxford Life—The Freshman—Acquaintances—Characters—Difficulty and danger of Selection—Importance of the First Step in College Life—The Pure Associations of Home—Advancement and Triumph—The Reprobate Tutors—Fellowships—Collegiate Retirement considered in reference to Happiness—Reflections on the same—Chime of Evening Bells—The Student—Fascinations of Midnight Study—Mental and Physical Effects—Nigh Scene—Moonlight—Its Splendours—Reflective con clusion—Time—Youth—Retrospections and Anticipations—Thirst for Fame and Struggles for renown —The Evanescent Nature of Human Glory—A Farewell View, and Apostrophe to Heaven.

AND thus, o'er visions of thy matchless few
Hath Fancy revell'd in her fleet review;
And, oh my country, glorious, brave, and free,
Heart of the world! what spirits hallow thee!
There is a magic in thy mighty name,
A swell of glory, and a sound of fame;
And myriads feel upon thy hills and plains
The patriot-blood rush warmer to their veins,
As all thou wert, and art, the mind surveys
With glowing wonder and enchanted gaze!

To this proud scene of architect'ral pride,
To all but Her, the ocean-famed, denied,
A parent sends, with many a voiceless fear,
His child, to arm him for the world's career.
Nor deem unawful that remember'd hour
When Fate and Fortune, with seductive power,
To Inexperience urge their blended claim,
And lead to honour, or allure to shame.
At length, young Novice! comes that hush'd farewell
Which words deny, but tears as truly tell;
The distance won, behold! at evening-hour
Thine eye's first wonder fix'd on Maudlin tower;
Then, Gothic Structures, as they swell to view
In steepled vastness, dark with ages' hue;
And on thine ear when first the morn-bells wake
As o'er the wind their wafted echoes break,
Delighted fancy will illume thy brow,
To feel thyself in ancient Oxford now!

Collegiate life * next opens on thy way,
Begins at morn, and mingles with the day;
The pillar'd-Cloister, in whose twilight gloom
Pale dreams arise, like shadows from the tomb,
Now hears thy step: and well at first I ween,
The stately Chapel, with its sculptured screen;
The windows dim, where Bible-dramas† live
For ages in the glow which colours give,
And golden beams of mellow'd radiance pass
Through vested figures on the tinted glass,

* A Sermon preached at "Poulis Cross, the xiii. day of December, 1550," contains the following description of University discipline at that period:—"There be diuers which rise dailie betwixt three and fyve of the clock in the mornyng, and from fyve until syxe of the clock use common prayer, with an exhortation of God's Word, in a common chapelle, and from syxe untoo tenne use euer eyther private studie or commune lectures. At tenne of the clock they go to dyner, where as they be contente with a feine piece of befe amongest iiii, having a few potage of the brothe made of the same befe, with salt and oatmeal, and nothing elles. After this slender dyner, they be eyther teachinge or learninge until fyve of the clocke in the euyning, when as they have a supper not much better than their dyner, immediately after which they go eyther to learninge in problems, or to some other studie, until the nyne or tenne of the clocke, and there being without fire, are faine to walk or runne up and down half a heure to get a hete on their fete when they go to bed."

† This expression recals the Mediæval Church, and the lover of ecclesiastical antiquity will thank us for the following curious details connected with the pulpits and preachers of the middle ages. The annexed is from the pages of a contemporary journal:—

"During the Middle Ages we find that the Pulpit-orators of that period delivered their discourses sometimes in the Latin language and sometimes in the vulgar tongue. Pierre de Limoges, a writer of the thirteenth century, relates that the festival of St. John the Baptist, falling on the fifth Sunday after Pentecost, a priest, by name Barthelemy, delivered in the Latin language the panegyric of the Saint, and on the Sunday following preached a sermon in vulgari. There are still extant some fragments of these pulpit addresses, in a manuscript bequeathed in the year 1260 to the Sorbonne by this same Pierre de Limoges. The mixture of Latin and French in the same sermon dates from about the year 1262; as for example: 'Demoniacum matrem sanavit, et tunc, *lo muz parle, lo poples s'en maravilhet* (the dumb spake, the people were astonished). Under the reign of Philip the Bold, and before the canonisation of Louis IX., Giles of Orleans, while preaching in the Chapel Royal, expressed himself in the following terms: 'Predicatores tenentur *ramentevoir* (to remember) statum Ecclesiæ.'

"The Abbé de la Rue, in the 13th volume of his 'Archæologia' relates that he was greatly surprised to find, in a sermon on the Virgin, composed by Stephen Langton, Archbishop of Canterbury, who died in the year 1228, the following stanza:—

'Bele Aliz matin leva,
Son cors vesti et para;
Enz un vergier s'en entra;
Cink flurettes y' truva.
Un chapelet fet en a
De bel rose flurie.
Pur Dieu trahez vus en la
Vus ki ne amez mie.'

"The orator applies each of these lines to the mother of the Saviour, and derives from thence a mystical explanation. 'The Virgin,' he says,—

'Ceste est la bele Alis
Ceste est la flur, ceste est le lis.'

"This fact of an English prelate employing the French language in a sermon delivered before an English congregation, is worthy of note; but more than one example of a similar kind may be met with. St. Bernard, in the year 1146, went to preach in Germany, and his reputation drew after him an immense concourse of hearers. Although he preached in the Latin tongue, the fire of his elocution and the eloquence of his gestures, made, according to the account of his companion Geoffroi de Clairvaux, so powerful an impression on his auditors, who could not understand his words, that they interrupted him with tears and sobs, and cried aloud as they smote on their breasts, '*Christ uns genade! Die Heiligen alle helfen uns!*' (Christ have mercy upon us! May all the saints aid us!)

"Jaques de Vitry, a French chronicler of the thirteenth century, has left us some very curious details respecting one of the most celebrated preachers of that day, named Foulques de Neuilly, by which we can form some idea of the immense influence the speech of an eloquent man exercised on the masses. 'He so inflamed all people,' says the historian of the Crusades, 'by his few and simple words, and not only the humblest classes but even kings and princes, that none dared or could resist him. They followed him in crowds to distant countries, both to hear his words and to witness the miracles which the Lord wrought by his hands. Those who could tear off and preserve the smallest portion of his garments esteemed themselves happy. Hence, as his vestments were in great request, and the multitude of the people tore them unceasingly, he was obliged almost every day to put on a new frock. As the crowd were accustomed to press upon him in an intolerable manner, he would frequently strike pretty smartly the most importunate with a stick which he carried in his hand, in order that he might get a little breathing room for himself, and not be stifled by those who desired to touch him. And although he sometimes wounded rather severely those whom he struck, the latter were not offended, and would not complain, but, in the excess of their devotion and the firmness of their faith, would kiss their own blood, as though it were sanctified by being drawn by the man of God. One day, as a certain individual made rather too free with the tail of his frock, he spoke to the crowd saying, 'Beware, lest you tear away portions of such of my garments which have not been blessed; but I shall bless this man's garment,' whereupon he made the sign of the cross, and instantly the poor man's coat was torn into a thousand pieces, and everyone that could obtain a fragment carefully preserved it.

"'The immodest priests and their concubines, whom he called the *Juments du Diable*, he harassed with severe reprimands and so many maledictions, that they were overwhelmed with shame and confusion, and were so pointed at, and even followed and hooted by all classes, that, in most cases, the servants of this description deserted their masters. A certain noble lady, dwelling in a village which she possessed, several times warned the companion of a priest of the

While Saints and Prophets, Priests and Prelates there,
And mitred Abbots, kneel in blended prayer;

neighbourhood to quit her master, but the latter refused. Whereupon Foulques, commanding the priest's concubine to be brought into his presence, performed on her the ceremony of the tonsure, saying: 'Since you will not quit the priest, I ordain you priestess."—*Histoire des Crusades*, liv. ii. c. 7—Collection Guizot, tome xxii.

"For the rest, those preachers, who, like Foulques, possessed the secret of assembling crowds around them, succeeded easily in amassing wealth, due in part to the collections which ordinarily accompanied each discourse. The most eloquent of the disciples of Foulques, Master Pierre de Roussi, 'who,' says Jacques de Vitry, 'preached poverty, gorged himself with wealth by the effect of his preaching, but from this cause he rendered his exhortations despicable.' Foulques himself having made numerous collections, under the pretext, real or feigned, of distributing the money among the poor crusaders, 'from this moment, by a secret judgment of God, his authority and the effect of his preaching began to diminish much among the people, and in measure as his wealth increased, so decreased visibly the fear and respect he had inspired in the breasts of men.'

"The ninth canon of a council held at Rouen in the year 1214 sought, and probably in vain, to remedy the abuses resulting from the habit which had crept in among the priests, of preaching for money; we find, also, that at this epoch laymen devoted themselves to a trade which most probably was highly lucrative, for many such were accustomed to travel about the country, offering their services in the various towns and villages at a certain fixed stipend, to those priests who, through ignorance, were incapable of pronouncing a discourse. Certain bands of lay preachers were thus established, who farmed by the year all the sermons of a parish, a diocese, or even a province, engaging by the terms of their articles either to preach themselves, or to furnish capable preachers whenever and wherever required.

"The bishops formerly were obliged to preach themselves, and there were for a length of time preserved in several churches in France traces of this ancient custom. The statutes of the diocese of Rouen directed that the bishop of that city should preach on certain days of the year, as, for instance, on the first Sunday in Lent, &c. In the seventeenth century, a bishop having required from the chapter the suppression of this statute, the chapter refused, alleging that if that custom was no longer followed, it at least ought to be followed, and that it was only right that the bishops should be kept in mind of their duty.

"Up to the seventeenth century nothing could be more grotesque and ridiculous than the style of the preachers of France. In order that the reader may judge of the materials of which these edifying discourses were concocted, we will lay before him a few extracts from some of the sermons of the most celebrated orators of the period.

"Gabriel Barletta, a Dominican of the fifteenth century, in a sermon preached on the day of the Resurrection, moves the question, to wit, who was the bearer of this great news to the Holy Virgin; whereupon he relates an imaginary conversation supposed to take place in heaven upon this subject, in which

The graven fretwork on the Gothic wall,
And flowery roof, which over-arches all,—

Adam, Abel, Noah, St. John the Baptist, and the good thief, in turn proffer their claims for the honour; but all are refused, each receiving an appropriate answer: Adam lest he should stop on the way to eat figs: Abel lest he should meet Cain; Noah lest he should be overcome with wine, &c. Finally, an angel is sent, who sings: '*Regina cœli lætare resurrexit sicut dixit*, alleluia.'

"Marini, bishop of Glandève, and confessor of King René, in his sermon upon the deadly sins, says, when speaking of sloth, that a demon is charged with the task of noting down all the verses, words, or syllables that professing Christians either entirely omit or pronounce indistinctly when saying their prayers. He calls this demon *Tintullus, quia tintillum de psalmis et horis non potest emitti quin ab hoc dæmone scribatur*; and he adds that he has been frequently seen, by several pious persons, carrying away whole sheets very well filled.

"In another sermon, preached on the Saturday in Passion Week, the same orator enlivens his congregation with a description of a pleasant method of catching monkeys.

"The 'Sermones Quadragesimales' (1519), in the macaronic style, of Menot, a French Cordelier surnamed the 'Golden-tongue,' are worthy of figuring beside those of Barletta. Preaching one day upon the parable of the Prodigal Son, he said:—

"'When this foolish and ill-advised child, *quando ille stultus puer et male consultus habuit suam partem de hæreditate, non erat quæstio de portando eam secum ideo statim:* he made ducks and drakes of it: he took it, he sold it, *et ponit* the cash *in suâ bursâ: quando vidit tot precias argenti simul, valde gavisus est dixit ad se: Oho! non manebitis sic semper! Incipit se respicere: Et quamodo? Vos estis de tam bonâ domo, et estis* dressed like a vagabond? *Super hoc habebitur provisio: mittit ad quærendum* the drapers, tailors, and silk-mercers, and had himself accoutred from head to foot: he had no fault to find with his equipment. *Quando vidit emit sibi pulchras caligas* of scarlet well fitted, the beautiful shirt with a frilled collar, the showy doublet adorned with velvet, the Florence cap,' &c. &c.

"In another sermon, upon the Magdalen, he expresses himself as follows:—'*Et ecce Magdelena* proceeds to strip herself, and takes so much in shifts *et cæteris indumentis*, the lewdest garments that any one *fecerat ab ætate septem annorum. Habebat suas domicellas juxta se in apparatu mundano: habebat* her perfumes, *aquas ad faciendum relucere faciem, ad attrahendum illum hominem* [*Jesum*], *et dicebat: Verè habebit cor durum, nisi eum attraham ad meum amorem. Et si deberem*, to mortgage, *omnes meas hæreditates, nunquam redibo Jerusalem nisi colloquio cum eo habito. Credatis quod visâ dominatione ejus, et comitivâ facta est sibi* place, the chair is decked *cum panno aureo; et venit se presentare* her pretty muzzle, face to face, *ante nostrum Redemptorem ad attrahendum eum*, at her ease.'

"His sermon for the Wednesday after the second Sunday in Lent, contains the following passages:—'*Est una maquerella quæ posuit multas puellas* at the trade; *ad malum ibit*, she will go full gallop *ad omnes diabolos. Est ne totum?* No, she will not have so good a bargain, *non habebit tam bonum forum; sed omnes quas incitavit ad malum, servient ei* with faggots and firewood to warm her thirty ribs.'

These in full action now, combine their charm,
And thrill young feelings, with devotion warm.

"A work entitled, '*Sermones Dominicales* dormi secure, *vulgo nuncupati.* Cologne, 1625,' affords some specimens of a similar kind.

"In the Gospel Narrative of the Temptation of Christ, the author introduces the devil, saying civilly to the Redeemer, 'Let us proceed to the desert, we will be alone there, and we will pray.' And after the Saviour's victory, the Holy Virgin sends him the dinner which she had prepared for herself; a cabbage, or a bowl of soup, or spinach, and perhaps sardines. *Virgo misit prandium quod pro se paraverat, ut caulas, vel brodium, ut spinachia, et fortè sardinetâ.*

"On Ash Wednesday he exempts from fasting those who travel on foot from necessity, but not so horsemen; he permits however the mule or horse, as the case may be, to eat its daily food without sinning: *Equitantes autem non excusantur; equus et mula potent cœnare, sed non vos sine peccato.*

"The first work in which mention is made of a species of pulpit eloquence, which may be styled, for want of a better term, *catarrhal eloquence,* is 'The Sermon preached on the fifth Sunday in Lent in the city of Bruges, Anno Domini 1500,' by the celebrated Olivier Maillard.[1] In this work we find marked in the margin, by the words, *Hem! hem!* the particular spots of the sermon where it was fitting for, or even the duty of, the preacher to cough! An edition of the Sermons of this preacher has been given by Crapelet.

"Musso, bishop of Bitonto, who died in 1574, at the commencement of a sermon upon the *Magnificat* invokes the Virgin by these words of Terence: "Lucina, Lucina, fer opem."

"'At this epoch in fact,' as has been well said by La Bruyère, 'the sacred and the profane were intimately allied; they had glided together even into the pulpit: St. Cyril, Horace, St. Cyprian, Lucretius spoke alternately. The poets were of the opinion of St. Augustine, and all the Fathers: they spoke Latin, and for a long time in the presence of women and churchwardens they spoke Greek. It was necessary to be prodigiously learned to preach badly. Other times, other customs; the text is still Latin, but the entire discourse is French, the Gospel even is not quoted; now-a-days we need to know very little in order to preach well.'

"The first sermon preached in the French language in Provence, where hitherto they had preached solely in Latin, was the funeral oration of Henri Quatre, delivered at Avignon in the year 1615 by Doni d'Attichi.

"Claude de Lingendes, one of the most celebrated preachers of the seventeenth century, was accustomed to compose in Latin the sermon he was afterwards to deliver in French. 'But,' says one of his contemporaries, 'he thought only of the strength of the argument, of the vehemence of the passions, and the grandeur and sublimity of the figures; and he was of the opinion of that ancient writer who considered that a discourse was composed when the words in which it was to be dressed only had to be found.'

"Tycho Brahé, perceiving the flights of the imagination, into which the preachers of his time permitted themselves to be enticed, was desirous that they should learn mathematics, in order to introduce more logic into their arguments, and to rid themselves of subtleties and vain discussions. Another geometrician, Father Mercennus, invited the sacred orators to adorn their discourses with illustrations and texts derived from the conic sections.

"Until the middle of the seventeenth century, the style of preaching criticised by La Bruyère found hosts of admirers, and people used to run in crowds to hear the sermons of the witty ecclesiastic André, commonly called *le petit père André,* of whose numerous bon-mots almost every collection of anecdotes is full. Here is the judgment pronounced by a serious critic upon Theophilus Raynaud, one of the most learned Jesuits of the seventeenth century. 'The fifth treatise of his volume entitled *Marialia,*' says Gallois, 'displays the vast erudition and fecundity of this author. For having to preach upon the seven solemn anthems which the Church chants before the festival of Christmas, each of which commences with the letter O, he took this single letter for the subject of his sermons, and in the sterility of this subject he found an infinity of beautiful things of which this treatise is composed.'

"The same preacher delivered one day a sermon upon noses, passing in review those of the Virgin, the Saviour, &c. &c.

"Fantastic as was the style of eloquence then in vogue, certain preachers produced nevertheless great effects at times upon their auditors.

"Jerom Mautin de Narni, a famous Capuchin preacher under the pontificate of Gregory XV., 'having,' relates Balzac in his tenth discourse, 'been appointed to preach before the Pope and Cardinals, he struck such terror into his hearers, by showing the sinfulness of a neglect of duty, that no less than thirty bishops posted the next day to their dioceses. The effects of his oratory upon the people were no less extraordinary, and many went from the church crying for mercy as they walked along the streets. On another occasion the conversion of an entire city was the fruit of one of his Lenten sermons; and it was computed that during the Holy Week there were sold cords for the purpose of discipline to the amount of two thousand crowns, though this article of commerce was by no means an expensive one. Narni, however, saw so little real fruit produced by his eloquence, that he resolved to give over the profession, and retired to his cell, where he employed himself in writing the history of his order.'

"Several authors, among others La Bruyère, have drawn a parallel between the advocate and the preacher; and Bayle, in the article "Accius" of his Dictionary, has written the following lines:—

"'I know,' he says, 'a man of sense and discrimination who made use of the following argument in order to deter his son from the study of jurisprudence, and to encourage him to pursue instead that of theology: 'What more agreeable,' said he, 'than the power of being able to speak before men who cannot contradict you? This is the advantage which preachers

[1] "Ollivier Maillard was an eccentric French ecclesiastic of the fifteenth century. His sermons were distinguished by their gross and ridiculous denunciations against those who might happen to offend him. Having glanced in one of them at some traits in the character of Louis XI. that king, who had just established the post in France, sent him word that he would have him thrown into the Seine. 'The king is master,' he replied, 'but tell him I shall get to Heaven by water, sooner than he will by his post-horses.' He died in 1502."

But, now the walk of wonder through the town
In the stiff foldings of a new-bought Gown!*
From cap and robe what awkward shyness steals!
How wild a truth the dazzled Novice feels!

Restless the eye, his voice a nervous sound,
While laughing echoes are evoked around;
Each look he faces *seems* on him to leer,
And fancied giggles are for ever near!
Through High-street then, the Town's majestic pride,
Array'd with palaces on either side,
He roams: him tradesmen's greedy eyes behold,
Each pocket gaping for a freshman's gold.
The Clarendon may next his look beguile,
Theatric dome, and Ashmolëan pile;
Or Bodley-chambers,* where in dusky rows,
The volumed wonders† of the Past repose;
Or, some bold thought his wayward fancy rules,
To take a freeze of horror from the Schools,‡
From lofty benches send a downward gaze,
Hear awful sounds, and dream of future Days!

But lo! in towering pride, with massy gate,
The Clarendon§ uprears its modern state;
There pause, and think; for then a sense sublime,
How proud a victor over Space and Time
When Mind hath wielded its undaunted power
Is man, both slave and monarch of an hour!—
Comes o'er thy spirit with unutter'd thought,
Life melody with years of feeling fraught.
Yet, not the miracles of England's Press,
(That mighty Oracle to curse or bless!)

possess: and what more disagreeable than that of being obliged to hear, the instant you have ceased speaking, a man who sentence by sentence refutes all your arguments, and who will pitilessly compel you to render an account of every word you have uttered: such is the position of an advocate.''[1]

"During the early age of Christianity, there was introduced into the Church a singular custom, which, derived from the stage, had crept from thence into the Christian assemblies: we allude to the custom of applauding the preacher. The congregation was accustomed to applaud the bishop when he preached with stamping of the feet and other sounds, but little suited to the sanctity of a place of worship. We find, from several passages in the writings of St. Chrysostom, that this father had conceived the idea of putting down the abuse, which, however, subsisted for a length of time.[2] In the year 1782, the Abbé Boulogne having delivered in the Church of the Oratory, the panegyric of St. Louis, the public interrupted him several times with bursts of applause, as though they were in a theatre.

"St. Chrysostom, however, while severely censuring the custom of applauding in churches, merely reproduces the arguments urged by the sages of antiquity against the same custom, which had, it appears, established itself in the schools of philosophy; for we find in the writings of Aulus Gellius these remarkable words:

"'When a philosopher,' said the philosopher Musonius, 'exhorts, warns, advises, blames, or gives a lesson in some branch of the moral sciences, if his auditors give vent with all the strength of their lungs to a host of empty and vulgar laudations; if, carried away by the graces of his style, by the harmony of his expressions, and the cadenced fall of his periods, they utter exclamations of admiration and delight, then be assured that both orator and auditors are losing their time—that we have not before us a philosopher instructing the mind, but rather a skilful flute-player tickling the ear.'"

* The scholars are supposed in their dress to have imitated the Benedictine monks, who were the chief restorers of literature. Their gowns at first reached not much lower than the knees. The shoulders were but a little, or not all gathered; neither were the sleeves much wider than those of an ordinary coat, but were afterwards enlarged. When degrees became more frequent in the reigns of Richard I. and John, other fashions were invented, both with respect to degrees and faculties. The wide sleeves are still worn by bachelors, and by those undergraduates who are on the foundation. The gowns were originally black; afterwards of different colours. In the chancellorship of Archbishop Laud, all were confined to black, except the sons of noblemen, who were permitted to select their colour. The present gown of the Masters of Arts is not ancient, and was not known before the time of John Calvin, who is recorded as the first who wore it. The primitive gown had the sleeve longways, and the facing lined with fur.

* The Bodleian.

† King James, in his visit to the magnificent library of Sir Thomas Bodley is recorded to have said:—"If I were doomed to be a prisoner, and the choice were given me of my prison, this library should be my dungeon; I would desire to be chained by no other bonds than the clasps which incarcerate these pages, and to have no other companions in my captivity than these volumes."

‡ In the statute, "De Exercitiis præstandis pro Gradu Baccalaurei in Artibus,' the exercises required are "Disputationes in Parvisiis." Chaucer, in the prologue to the Canterbury Tales, says,—

"A seargant at law, ware and wise,
That often had been at the Pervise."

And in the glossary at the end of an ancient edition, the word Pervise is explained, a church-porch, contracted from Paradisus—i. e., locus porticibus et de ambulationibus circumdatus; and Spelman says, that our lawyers formerly used to walk in such a place to meet their clients. Before the schools were erected, they held their disputations in Parvisiis in the porch of St. Mary's church. There they sat, vis-à-vis. This might, in the Norman-French of those times, perhaps be expressed by Par-vis, which, in barbarised Latin, would become Parvisiis.

§ This refers, of course, to the new building, denominated "The University Press."

[1] If we do not mistake, Sydney Smith, in one of his essays, makes use of a similar argument.

[2] See the Treatise of Ferrari, *De Veterum Acclamationibus et Plausu*, 1627. 4to.

Alone the worship of high thought demand;
Lo! earth-wide dreams around the soul expand,
As dwells thy gaze on yon enormous piles
Of hallow'd Books, for heathen Lands and Isles;*
A godlike present for benighted Man
Far as the soul can read Salvation's plan!

Transcendent thought! when changing Years have flown
Yon Bibles speak to every Clime and Zone!
The hut, the hovel, or the cottage wild
Where Sorrow shudders o'er her weeping child,
Their living words of holiness and love
Like angel-tones, shall warble from Above.
Omnipotence is there!—a power to be
God's voice on earth, inspired with Deity;
Thou Infidel! in tomb-like darkness laid,
By heaven deserted, and by sin betray'd;
And thou, pale mutt'rer in some midnight-cell,
Whose sad to-morrow is a dream of hell;
There is a Voice to wake, a Word to spread
Deep as the thunders which arouse the dead!
That Sound is heard; a Welcome from the skies!
Despair is vanquish'd, and Dejection flies;
Hope fills a heart where agonies have been,
The dungeon brightens, and a God is seen!

Immortal Pages! may your spirit pour
Celestial day, till heathen night be o'er.
In fiery lands, where roving Ganga reigns,
Eternal pilgrim of a thousand plains!
The tawny Indian, (when the Day is done
And basking waters redden in the sun,
Behold him seated, with his babes around,
To fathom mysteries where a God is found!
The Book is oped, some wondrous page began,
Where heaven is offered to forgiven man;
Lo! as he reads, what voiceless wonder steals
On all he fancies, and on all he feels!
Till o'er his mind, by mute devotion wrought,
The gleaming twilight of regen'rate thought
Begins, and heaven-eyed Faith salutes above
The God of glory, and a Lord of love!

"Thou dread Unknown! Thou unimagined Whole!
Thou vast Supreme, and Universal Soul,
Oft in the whirlwind have I shaped Thy form,
Or throned in thunder heard Thee sway the storm!
And when the ocean's heaving vastness grew
Black with Thy curse,—my spirit darken'd too!
But when the world beneath a sun-gaze smiled
And not a cloud the crystal air defiled,
Then I have loved Thee, Thou parental One,
Thy frown a tempest, and Thy smile a sun!*
But if there be, as heaven-breathed words relate,
A seraph-home in some hereafter-State,
Almighty Power! thy dark-soul'd Indian see
And grant the Mercy which has bled for me!" [33]

O'er Oxford thus the staring freshman roves†
By solemn Temples, or secluded Groves;

* What a glorious contrast does this immense collections of Bibles suggest, between the past and present state of Christian philosophy, when we read that—"So little were the Scriptures used in the time of Wickliff, that some secular priests of Armagh, who were sent by Archbishop Firzralph (the translator of the Bible into Irish) to study divinity at Oxford, about A.D. 1357, were obliged to return, because they could nowhere find a Latin Bible. The clergy were then seldom able to read Latin."—BISHOP GRAY.

* "In matters of faith and religion we raise our imagination above our reason, which is the cause why religion sought ever access to the mind by similitudes, types, parables, visions, dreams, &c."—BACON, *Adv. Learn.*, p. 128.

† "A Companion to the Guide, and a Guide to the Companion." A jeu d'esprit, under the above title, was attributed to Tom Warton; his account of the libraries and schools is thus humorously sketched:—"The prevailing notion is equally erroneous with regard to the number of our libraries. Besides those of Radcliffe, Bodley, and private colleges, there have of late years been many libraries founded in our coffee-houses, for the benefit of such academics as have neglected, or lost, their Latin and Greek. In these useful repositories grown gentlemen are accommodated with the 'Cyclopædia.' The 'Magazines' afford history, divinity, &c. The 'Reviews' form the complete critic, without consulting the dry rules of Aristotle, Quintilian, and Bossu, and enable the student to pass his judgment on volumes which he never read—[what a prophetic description of the railroad style of criticism that now prevails!] Novels supply the place of experience, and give lectures of intrigue and gallantry. Occasional Poems diffuse the itch of rhyming, and happily tempt away a young fellow to forsake logic, turn smart, and commence author either in the pastoral, lyric, or elegiac way. As there are here books suited to every taste, so are there liquors adapted to every species of reading. Amorous tales may be perused over arrak, punch, and jellies; insipid elegies over orgeat or capilaire; politics over coffee; divinity over port; and defence of bad generals and bad ministers over whipt syllabubs. In a word, we may pronounce that learning is no longer a *dry* pursuit. The schools of this university are more numerous than is commonly supposed, among which we must reckon three spacious and superb edifices, situated to the south of the High-street, one hundred feet long, by thirty in breadth, vulgarly called Tennis Courts, where exercise is regularly performed both morning and afternoon. Add to these certain schools, familiarly denominated Billiard Tables, where the laws of motion are exem-

Then, introduced, the social charms begin
By tongues which flatter, or by hearts that win;
Mien, mind, and manner,—all in varied style
Now woo his fortune, or reflect his smile.
For here, as in the World's unbounded sphere,
The countless traits of character appear.
In some proud youth, of feeling soul, we find
The winning magic of a noble mind;
Truth, taste, and sense whate'er he does pervade,
No virtue lost, no principle betray'd;
Another,—wildness marks his mien and tone!
His hand extends—and honours are his own;
Eternal plaudits in his ear resound;
He rides on wings, while others walk the ground!
A contrast see, whom hearts nor dreams inspire,
The booby offspring of a booby sire,
With leaden visage passionlessly cold
And ev'ry feeling round himself enroll'd.
Then, happy Pertness! how sincerely vain!
And, sour Perfection!—what sublime disdain!
For ever in detraction's art employ'd,
No virtue welcomed, and no look enjoy'd:
Then, pompous Learning! deeply read and skill'd
In pages which profoundest heads have fill'd,
Yet harsh and tasteless, and but rarely fraught
With knowledge sprung from self-excited thought.*
But, save me, Heav'n! from what no words can tell,
A human Nothing, made of strut and swell,
Who thinks no University contains
Sufficient wisdom to employ *his* brains:
Yet, frothy Creature! what a vacant skull!
In all but falsehood villanous and dull;
Big words and oaths in one wild volley roll,
And Nature blushes for so mean a soul!

By these begirt, how oft may heart-warm Youth
Grow blindly fond, and misinterpret Truth,
When feelings in their flush'd dominion lend
To fancied kindness what completes a friend!
Now dawns the moment, doom'd in future years
To waken triumph, or be born in tears;
When Morals sway, Religion lives or dies,
And cited Principles to action rise.
Oh! thou, o'er whom a Mother's eye has wept,
Or round thy cradle frequent vigils kept;
Whose infant-brow a father's love survey'd,
And oft for thee with Heav'n communion made;
Be thine the circle where true Friendship lives
In the pure light exalted spirit gives;[34]
And far from thee the infamous and vile
Who murder feeling with a Stoic smile,
Blaspheme the Innocence of early days,
Make virtue vice, impiety a praise,
Disease the health of unpolluted mind
And call it glory to disgrace mankind!
What though the eye may sparkle o'er the glass,
Or fondling words for fascination pass,
While flowers of friendship oft appear to bloom,
In the false sunshine of a festive room,
A day *will* come when sterner truths prevail
And* friendship dwindles into folly's tale!

But shouldst thou waver, when the awful hour
Of Pleasure tempteth with a demon-power,
And time and circumstance together seem
To dazzle nature with too bright a dream,
Let Home and Virtue, what thou wert and art,
A Mother's feeling, and a Father's heart,
Full on thy mem'ry rise with blended charm
And all the serpent in thy soul disarm!
For who shall say, when *first* temptations win
A yielded mind to some enchanting sin,
What future crime, that once appear'd too black
For life to wander o'er its hell-ward track,
May lead the heart to that tremendous doom,
Whose midnight hovers round an early tomb?
Let Home be vision'd where thy budding days
Their beauty open'd on parental gaze:
For there, what memories of thee abound!
Your chamber echoes with its wonted sound;

---

plified, and which may be considered as a necessary supplement to our courses of experimental philosophy. Nor must we omit the many Nine-pin and Skittle-alleys, open and dry, for the instruction of scholars in geometrical knowledge, and particularly for proving the centripetal principle. Other schools and places of academical discipline, not generally know as such, may be mentioned. The Peripatetics execute the courses proper to their system upon the parade; navigation is learnt on the Isis; gunnery on the adjacent hills; horsemanship on Port-Meadow, Ballingdon-Green, the Henley, Wyecombe, Woodstock, Abingdon, and Banbury roads. The Axis in Peritrochio is admirably illustrated by a scheme in a phaeton. The doctrine of the screw is practically explained most evenings in the private rooms, together with the motion of fluids."

* Gilbert Wakefield, in his correspondence with Fox, observes, that "his custom was 'multum potius quam multa legere;'" and Hobbes, with a pithy sarcasm, said, "if I had read as much as some others, I should have been as ignorant as they are."

* Hunc quem cœna tibi, quem mensa paravit amicum
Esse putas fidæ pectus amicitiæ?—
* * * * * * *
Jam bene si cœnem noster amicus erit!—MARTIAL.

"For a crowd is not company, and faces are but a gallery of pictures, and talk but a tinkling cymbal, where there is no love."—BACON'S *Essays*, 27th.

The flow'r you reared, a sister's nursing hand
Still fondly guards, and helps each leaf expand;
The page you ponder'd with delighted brow
Was ever dear,—but oh! far dearer now;
The walk you loved with her sweet smile to share
She oft repeats, and paints *your* image there;
And when bright meanings have adorn'd the sky,
Her fancy revels in your fav'rite dye;
While oft at evening when domestic bloom
Hath flung a freshness round a social room,
When hearts unfold, and Music's wingèd note
Can waft a feeling wheresoe'er it float,
Some chord is touch'd, whose melodies awake
The pang of fondness for a brother's sake;
And Eyes are conscious, as they gaze around,
That looks are falling where a son was found!

Let home begird thee like a guardian dream,
And time will wander an unsullied stream,
Whose wildest motion is the rippled play
Of rapid moments as they roll away!
Meanwhile, delightful studies, deep and strong,
To graduate-honours waft thy soul along;
They come at length! and high in listed fame
A College hails, a Country reads thy name;
And in that List when first thy name appears,
What triumph sparkles in those happy tears!
In after-life, when Oxford's ancient towers
Thy mem'ry visions in creative hours,
Or college-friends a college-scene restore,
Thy heart will banquet on the bliss of yore!

Now mark a contrast, in whose meanness lies
What purer thought should soaringly despise.
From careless boyhood to uncultured man
Indulged to act, ere principle began;
With just enough of spirit for excess,
And heart which nothing save a vice, can bless,
In Oxford see the reprobate appear!
Big with the promise of a mad career.
With cash and consequence to lead the way,
A fool by night, and more than fop by day,
What happy vileness does his lot reveal!
How Folly burns with imitative zeal
Whene'er the shadows of his greatness fall
In festive chamber, or collegiate-Hall!
Romantic lot! to vegetate secure
From all which might to mental paths allure;
To wake each morning with no deeper thought
Than that which yesterday's excess hath brought;
Then, wing'd by impulse, as the day proceeds,
To follow where coxcombic fashion leads.
Hark! Woodstock rattles with eternal wheels,
And hounds are ever barking at his heels,
The Chapel, voted a terrific "bore," *
The "Dons," head-pieces for the college door!
The Lecture scouted, the Degree reviled,
And Alma Mater all *save* alma styled!
Thus on; till Night advance, whose reign divine
Is chastely delicate to cards and wine,
Where modest themes amusive tongues excite
And faces redden with the soul's delight;
A Roman banquet! with Athenian flowers
Of festive wit, to charm such graceful hours!

Alas! that Truth must fling a doleful shade
On the bright portrait which her hand hath made:
Few years have fled,† and what doth now remain
Of him the haughty, who but smiled disdain

* When Hooker was at Corpus "enriching his quiet and capacious soul with the precious learning of the philosophers, casuists, and schoolmen," Izaak Walton thus describes his chapel conduct:—"In four years he was but twice absent from the chapel prayers; and his behaviour there was such as showed an awful reverence of that God which he then worshipped and prayed to, giving all outward testimonies that his affections were set on heavenly things."—Oh si sic omnes!

Before concluding this note, the reader will not find the following anecdote of Hooker tedious or uninteresting:—When, by his marriage with her "who brought to him neither beauty nor portion," the good man was drawn from the tranquillity of his college, into those corroding cares that attend a married priest and a country parsonage,—which was Drayton Beauchamp, in Bucks, not far from Aylesbury,—his two pupils, Edwin Sandys and George Cranmer, took a journey to see their tutor, where they found him with a book in his hand (the "Odes of Horace"), he being then, like humble and innocent Abel, tending his small allotment of sheep in a common field, which he told his pupils he was forced to do then, for that his servant was gone home to dine, and assist his wife to do some necessary household business. But when his servant returned and released him, then his two pupils attended him unto his house, where their best entertainment was his quiet company, which was presently denied them, for Richard was called to rock the cradle! Having paraphrased on many of the innocent recreations of their younger days, and other like diversions, and thereby given him as much comfort as they were able, they were forced to leave him to the company of his wife, Joan, and seek themselves a quieter lodging for the next night; but at their parting from him, Mr. Cranmer said, "Good tutor, I am sorry your lot is fallen in no better ground as to your parsonage, and more sorry that your wife proves not a more comfortable companion after you have wearied yourself in your restless studies." To whom the good man replied, "My dear George, if saints have usually a double share in the miseries of this life, I that am none ought not to repine at what my wise Creator hath appointed for me, but labour, as indeed I do daily, to submit mine to his will, and possess my soul in patience and peace."

† "In general, the foundations of a happy old age must be laid in youth: and, in particular, he who has

On all young Virtue in her meekness dared,
Ambition hoped, or Principle declared?
His friends are dead; his fortune sunk away
In midnight-Hells, where midnight-demons play;
A wither'd Skeleton of sin and shame
With nought but infamy to track his name
The wreck of Fortune, with despairing sighs,
Fades from the world, and like a felon dies! *

A nobler Theme! ere yet my strain conclude,—
The learn'd and gifted, dignified and good,
Those tasteful Guides, by whose directing hand
The seeds of learning ripen or expand;

not cultivated his reason young, will be utterly unable to improve it old."—BOLINGBROKE.

* The fate of the poet Churchill, a man gifted with genius, but not inspired by virtue, may be profitably studied by youthful ambition, when tempted by the seductions of circumstance to violate the sacredness of Conscience and Truth. His biography is summed up in the following narrative:—

He was educated at Westminster, but made so little use of the advantages afforded by that academy, that he was refused admission at Oxford on account of classical deficiency. A marriage, as early as it was imprudent, rendered a profession doubly desirable; and, after studying for some time in private, he was admitted to holy orders, and obtained a Welsh curacy of about thirty pounds a year. The death of his father, who was curate of St. John's, Westminster, brought him once more to London; and he obtained the vacant curacy. Still, his income was small, while his love of gay and expensive pursuits was unbounded; and he was on the verge of imprisonment, when Dr. Lloyd, of Westminster School, interfered, and effected a composition with the creditors. He now determined to exert the talents he had so long allowed to lie idle; and his first production was the "Rosciad," an energetic decription of the principal actors of that time. Public attention was fixed on this poem by the vehemence with which the players replied to it; and Churchill found it worth his while to give the town a new satire, under the title of an "Apology" for his former one. "Night," the "Ghost," in which he assailed Dr. Johnson, at that time all but omnipotent in the literary world, and the "Prophesy of Famine" followed; and he at length threw aside all regard for his profession, separated from his wife, and became a complete "man of wit about town," and a professional political satirist. He now rapidly produced an "Epistle to Hogarth," the "Conference," the "Duellist," the "Author," "Gotham," the "Candidate," the "Times," "Independence," and the "Journey." The vigour displayed in these makes it probable that he would in time have devoted himself to higher subjects than party politics, and have produced works calculated to give him higher and more lasting fame; but a fever hurried him to the grave at the early age of thirty-four, in 1764.

To this biographical record, let us append the following truthful and touching account of a visit to Churchill's neglected grave in the ancient church of St. Martin-le-Grand, Dover. We are indebted for the record to the "Home Friend," published by the "Society for promoting Christian Knowledge:"—

"We shall not easily forget the impression of dreariness produced on our mind by the first visit to the burial-ground of the old church of St. Martin-le-Grand. It was on a November afternoon, amid gloomy fogs and in a cold wind which swept over the neglected tombs like a wail for those whom men had long forgotten. As we could then trace more clearly the broken remains of the once magnificent church and priory, the words of Robert Nicholl came to the mind:—

'Decaying roofless walls! and is this all
That Desolation's blighting hand hath left
Of tower, and pinnacle, and gilded hall?
The everlasting rocks by time are cleft,
Within each crevice spiders weave their weft.
* * * * * *
Where are the glancing eyes that here have beam'd,
Where are the hearts which whilom here have beat,
Where are the shaven monks, so grim who seemed,
Where are the sitters on the abbot's seat?'

"The burial-place, though but recently disused, had the most melancholy aspect of desertion. Heaps of broken crockery and other refuse from the adjoining houses lay at one end. Scarcely a daisy would in spring look up to the sky from that mould, and now not a robin was there to chant a requiem for the departed summer. The graves were wet with the late rains, but neither rain nor sunshine brought greenness to the sods, for there was little grass in that dreary churchyard. We wandered on amid the gloom, searching for the spot where the last remains of the poet Charles Churchill found their resting-place in 1764. It was long ere we could discover the lowly grave; but at length an old headstone, green with slimy moss, was found, bearing the poet's name and time of decease, with the epitaph from his own poem of the 'Candidate,'—'Life to the last enjoyed, here Churchill lies.' One could have wished, certainly, that that life and its enjoyments had been more in accordance with the dictates of virtue and religion; yet it was impossible to look without sorrow on these last memorials of a man of genius—for a man of genius Churchill certainly was. 'Churchill,' says Cowper, 'is a careless writer for the most part; but where shall we find in any of those authors who finish their works with the exactness of a Flemish pencil, those bold and daring strokes of fancy, those numbers so hazardously ventured upon, and so happily finished; the matter so compressed, and yet so clear, and the colouring so sparingly laid on, and yet such a beautiful effect? In short, it is not his least praise that he is never guilty of those faults which he lays to the charge of others; a proof that he did not judge by a borrowed standard, or from rules laid down by critics, but that he was qualified to do it by his native powers and his great superiority of genius.'

"But neglected as was the poet's grave now, it had not been so always; there had been an interval when the last resting-place of genius had been honoured, and when the poet's own wish had in part been fulfilled:—

'Let one poor sprig of bay around my head
Bloom whilst I live, and point me out as dead;
Let it,—may Heaven indulgent grant my prayer!—
Be planted on my grave nor wither there:
And when on travel bound, some rhyming guest
Roams though the churchyard, while his dinner's drest,
Let it hold up this comment to his eyes,
Life to the last enjoyed, here Churchill lies!'

And if one task there be the Soul to try,
Whose with'ring toils a due reward defy,
On *them* it falls whom Merit ranks her own
And Talent seats on Education's throne.
Each mode of mind, the stubborn, wise, or stern,
The headstrong Wit that cannot stoop to learn,
The dunce or drone, the freshman or the fool
'Tis their's to counsel, teach, o'erawe, and rule!
Their daily meed, some execrating word
To blight the hour when first their voice was heard,
From prating coxcombs, whose foul tongues declare
In froth and flippancy, what fools they are!

Yet well may such a doom be nobly faced;
There comes a scene by no dark cloud disgraced,

"Between thirty and forty years since a bay was planted, and for some time carefully tended on the spot. A pilot from the neighbouring town of Deal, named Mowll, planted it there. Few who looked on the weather-beaten exterior of the brave sailor would have guessed that he should be the only one to fulfil a poet's wish; but the brave are often the gentle too, and he who had many times dared the raging ocean, had a thought of pity for neglected genius. Honoured be his name for this touching expression of sympathy! But the bay-tree did not thrive on the grave; evergreens are said not to flourish well on the soil of Dover; and the sheep browsed on its young leaves, and thoughtless persons broke away its shoots; and all the care of the planter could not save it. Those who looked upon it tell how it always seemed drooping. Long since it disappeared altogether, and when we stooped to the grave to gather a blade of grass to carry off as a remembrance of Churchill, nothing was there but a small nettle; and no raised sod marked a tomb, for the ground was trodden to a perfect level. It must have been in somewhat similar state in 1816, when Lord Byron, while his dinner was preparing at a neighbouring inn, literally fulfilled the poet's wish by visiting his grave, and who thus records his impressions:—

"I stood beside the grave of him who blazed
The comet of a season, and I saw
The humblest of all sepulchres, and gazed,
With not the less of sorrow and of awe,
On that neglected turf and quiet stone
With names no clearer than the names unknown
Which lay unread around it; and I asked
The gardener of that ground why it might be
That for this plant strangers his memory tasked
Through the thick deaths of half a century:
And thus he answered: 'Well, I do not know
Why frequent travellers turn to pilgrims so.
He died before my day of sextonship,
And I had not the digging of his grave.'
And is this all? I thought—and do we rip
The veil of Immortality, and crave
I know not what of honour and of light,
Through unborn ages, to endure this blight
So soon and so successless?"

An hour when Genius, borne aloft to fame,
On Oxford sheds the brightness of her name,
Whence first her wings those eagle-heights explored,
Where now She reigns, adoring and adored!
Then, he who taught her, shares with proud surprise
And dewy gladness of delighted eyes,
That hour triumphant, when a World repays
The toilful dulness of collegiate-days.
Ah! who forgets the Parents of the mind?*
What heart so dead, as no deep bliss to find
In thoughts which wander to their school-day scene,
Though years and distance darkly intervene?
The foot-worn mead; the playmate, wood, and walk
So sweetly shared in tenderness and talk;
The feats and pranks of undejected Youth
When Fancy wore the fairy mask of Truth,
Dull, drear, and worldly is the Soul that sees
No smile reflected from such joys as these!

And they who haunt, from year to year content,
That sacred home where studious hours are spent,
Does fancy think their stormless life *must* be
One still romance of mental liberty?
Yet Mind alone, whate'er the lot or state,
Her true delight must fancy or create;
From her the sunshine and the shadows fall,
Which brighten, tint, and oversway it all.
The daily clockwork of collegiate-life
Where nought is new, but Convocation-strife;
The bigotry which olden Times beget;
A sickly dulness, and a proud regret
For aught which seems of reformation sprung,
To let in light where ancient cobwebs hung,
If such combine, where weaker traits are found,
Who would not mourn that Fellowships abound?
The mighty brothers of the Sun and Moon,
Who tremble, lest a lip should smile too soon;
Nor treat their mouths except with college twang,
Where heavy words in heavy speeches hang;
Who hate the Present, but adore the Past,
And think *their* world the *only* one to last,—
How pitiful! should such a race be seen,
Where all the Monarchs of the mind have been.

Retirement, classic love, and studious ease,
A heart which deems it no disgrace to please,

* Di majorum umbris tenuem, et sine pondere terram,
Spirantesque crocos, et in urnâ perpetuum ver,
Qui præceptorum sancti voluere parentis
Esse loco.—*Juv. Sat.* 7, 207.

With retrospections fond of other Days
When minds were nursed, that now repeat their praise,—
A lot so calm no virtue will destroy,
But season life for solitary joy.
And yet, let shades of accident unite
In happy union for its best delight,
A life of Learning is a life forlorn :—
Be mine the world which social scenes adorn,
Where Woman's heart the central bliss is found,
And happiness, the smile it sheds around!'

But night is throned; and full before me frown
The dusky Steeples which o'ershade the town;
High in the midst, a dark-domed shadow see,—
The Radcliffe, pile of unworn majesty;
Around it, silver'd by some window-ray
Whirls many a smoke-wreath in ascending play:
Beneath, what massy roofs inmingled lie,
Misshaped by fancy, till they awe the eye!
Hush'd are the groves, in leafy dimness veil'd,
The winds unheard, as though they ne'er had rail'd.
But hark! the iron voice of Wolsey's bell [35]
Floats o'er the city like his last farewell,
While answ'ring Temples, with obedient sound,
Peal to the night, and moan sad music round;
But dread o'er all, like thunder heard in dreams,
The warning spirit of that Echo seems!
Now gates are barr'd; and, faithful to his stand,
The crusty Porter, with his key-worn hand.
Yet not with day, the day-born studies end;
Wan cheeks, and weary brows,—I see them bend
O'er haughty pages breathing ancient mind,
For Man and Immortality design'd:
The brain *may* burn, the martyr'd health may fail,
And sunken eyelids speak a mournful tale
Of days protracted into hideous length,
Till mind is dead, and limbs deny their strength:
Still, Honours woo!—and may they smile on thee,
Prophetic Youth! as bright as visions see;
Hours, days, and years severer far than thine,
In toil, and gloom, and loneliness, are mine.

The Day is earth, but holy Night is heav'n:*
To her a solitude of soul is given,
Within whose depth, how beautiful to dream,
And fondly be, what others vainly seem!
Oh! 'tis an hour of consecrated might,
For Earth's Immortals have adored the night;
In song or vision yielding up the soul
To the deep magic of Her still control.
My own loved Hour! there comes no hour like thee,
No world so glorious as thou form'st for me!
The fretful ocean of eventful day
To waveless nothing how it ebbs away!
As oft the chamber, where some haunted Page
Renews a Poet, or revives a Sage
In pensive Athens, or sublimer Rome,
To mental quiet woos the Spirit home.
There Stillness reigns, how eloquently deep!
And soundless air, more beautiful than sleep.
Let Winter sway,—her sounds the scene inspires:
The social murmur of a blazing fire;
The hail-drop, hissing as it melts away
In twinkling gleams of momentary play;
Or wave-like swell of some retreated wind,
In dying sadness echo'd o'er the mind,
But gently ruffle into varied thought
The calm of feeling blissful night has brought.
How eyes the spirit with contented gaze
The chamber mellow'd into social haze,
And smiling walls, where, rank'd in solemn rows,
The wizard Volumes of the Mind repose!
Thus, well may hours like fairy waters glide,
Till morning glimmers o'er their reckless tide;
While dreams, beyond the realm of day to view,
Around us hover in seraphic hue;
Till Nature pines for intellectual rest,
When home awakens, and the heart is blest;
Or, from the window reads our wand'ring eye
The starry language of Chaldean sky,
And gathers in that one vast gaze above,
A bright eternity of awe and love!

So heav'nly seems the visionary night:
But, ah! the danger in such deep delight.
The Mind, then beautified to fond excess,
With all things dare to brighten, or to bless:
A world of sense more spiritual is made
Than the stern eye of nature hath survey'd;
Some false perfection which hath never been,
By fancy imaged, lives through ev'ry scene;

* That ideal paradise in which imagination delights to roam, and gather hues of glory, wherewith to invest the bleak realities of life, beautiful as it is, has met with little respect from ethical writers.—Foster (vide "Essays") appears by no means enamoured of it, in the following passage:—"If a tenth part of the felicities that have been enjoyed, the great actions that have been performed, the beneficent institutions that have been established, and the beautiful objects that have been seen in that happy region, could have been imported into this terrestrial place, what a delightful thing it would have been to awake each morning to see such a world once more!" Abercrombie has also touched on the illusive danger of such dreams in his work on the "Intellectual Powers," p. 155, 3rd ed.

But morn awakes, and lo, the spells unwind,
As daylight melts light darkness o'er the mind!
The worldly coarseness of our common lot
Recals the shadows which the night forgot;
Each dream of loftiness then dies away,*
And heav'n-light withers in the frown of Day!
And then, the languor of each parching vein,
And the hot weariness of heart and brain,
That hideous shade of *Something* dread to be,—
Oh, fatal midnight! these are doom'd for thee.
Each breeze comes o'er us with tormenting wing,
Each pulse of Sound an agony can bring;†
Let Chatterton[36] Thy deathful charm reveal,
And mournful White, whose genius loved to steal
A placid sense of some angelic Pow'r
Around prevailing at thine earthless hour.[37]
And oft, methinks, in loneliness of heart
As noons of night in dreaming calm depart,
My room is sadden'd with the mingled gaze
Of Those who martyr'd their ambitious days;
The turf-grass o'er their tombs,—I see it wave
And visions waft me to a kindred grave!

But lo! the yielding Dark hath gently died,
And stars are sprinkled o'er yon azure tide
Of lustrous air, which high and far prevails,
Where now the queen-like moon in glory sails.
City of fame! when Morn's first wings of light
Wave their fresh beauty o'er thy mansions bright,
Have I beheld thee; but a moonrise seems,
Like hues that wander from a heaven of dreams,
To hallow thee, as there thy Temples stand
Sublimely tender, or serenely grand,—
Spire, tower, and pinnacle, a dim array,
Whose spectral features in the moonlight sway:
The stony muteness of thy massive piles
Now silver'd o'er by melancholy smiles,
With more than language, spirit-like appeals
To the high sense impassion'd Nature feels
Of all which gloriously in earth or sky
Exacts the worship of her gazing eye.

There is a magic in the moonlit-hour
Which Day hath never in its deepest pow'r
Of light and bloom, when bird and bee resound,
And new-born flow'rs imparadise the ground!
And ne'er hath City, since a moon began
To hallow nature for the eye of man,
Steep'd in the freshness of her fairy light,
More richly shone, than Oxford shines to-night.
No lines of harshness on her Temples frown,
But all in one soft magic melted down,
Sublimer grown, through mellow air they rise
And seem with vaster swell to awe the skies!
On archèd windows how intensely gleams
The glassy whiteness of reflected beams!
Whose radiant slumber on the marble-tomb
Of mitred Founders, in funereal gloom,
Extends; or else in pallid shyness falls
On Gothic casements, or collegiate-walls.
The groves in silver-leaf'd array repose;
And, Isis! how serene thy current flows
With tinted surface by the meadow'd way,
Without a ripple, or a breeze at play:
Yet, once again shall summer-barks be seen,
And furrow'd waters, where their flight has been;
While sounding Rapture, as her heroes speed
From Iffly locks, flies glorying o'er the mead,
Hails from the bank as up the river ride
In oary swiftness and exulting pride
Her barks triumphal:—let the flag be rear'd,
And thousands echo, when the Colour's cheer'd!

Again upon the wind a wafted swell
Of ebbing sound, proclaims a midnight-bell;
Lo, phantom-clouds come floating by the moon,
Then melt away, like happiness, too soon:*
And as they glide, an overshadowing smile
Of moving light is mirror'd on each pile.
Farewell the Scene! Farewell the fleeting song!
Wherein my spirit hath been borne along
In light and gloom through many a lonely hour,
With nought to gladden but its own weak pow'r.
In morning-youth far brighter dreams have play'd
Around a Heart which hope has oft betray'd,
Than those which hover o'er this dying strain;
But, faded once, they never form again?
"*Farewell*" to Oxford! soon will destined years
That word awaken which is spoke by tears:
When scheming Boyhood plann'd my future lot,
No scene arose by Oxford centred not;
And now, as oft her many-mingled chimes
Swell into birth, like sounds of other times,
Prophetic life a living mystery seems,
Unravell'd oft by consummated dreams!

* "The heroism of morals, the enthusiasm of eloquence, and the ambition of fame, are supernatural enjoyments necessary only to those minds which, at once exalted and melancholy, are weaned and disgusted with everything transitory."—DE STAEL.

† The wasting effect of excessive and protracted study did not escape the observation of Rousseau:—"Elle les rends délicats, affoiblit leur tempérament; et que l'ame garde difficilement sa vigueur, quand le corps a perdu la sienne; que l'étude use la machine, épuise les esprits, détruit les forces, énerve le courage, rend pusillanime, incapable de résister également à la peine et aux passions." In Lord King's "Life of Locke," there is an admirable "Essay on Study," which ought to be perused by every man who deems the martyrdom of health an interesting accompaniment to the acquirement of learning.

* So calm the waters, scarce they seem to stray,
And yet they glide, like happiness, away.
LARA.

Farewell! if when I cease to haunt her scene
Some gentle heart remember I have been,
As Oxford, with her palaces and spires,
The mind ennobles, or the fancy fires,
No vain reward his chosen theme attends
Howe'er the fate of him who sung it, ends!

Oh! fearful Time, the fathomless of thought,
With what a myst'ry are thine ages fraught!
Whose wings are noiseless in their rush sublime
O'er scenes of glory, as o'er years of crime;
Yet comes a moment when their speed is *felt*,
Till Past and Future through our being melt,
And boding shadows from a world unknown,
Deepen around us, and bedim our own.

A moment! well may that a moral be,
Whoe'er thou art, 'tis memory to thee:
A tomb it piled, a mother bore to heaven,
Or like a whirlwind o'er the ocean driven
Rush'd on thy fate with desolating sway,
And flung a desert o'er its darken'd way!
A moment!—Midnight wears a wonted hue,
And orbs of beauty speck yon skyward view;
Deep, hush'd, and holy is the world around,
But yet, what energies of Life abound!
In blended action through the realms of space
Where time and nature multiply their race
What crimes enacted, or what hearts awake
Which beat for glory or with anguish break!
And thou, dread spirit-World! to man unknown,
Where reigns Jehovah on His sightless throne,
Sense cannot view, but dreams would fain expand
Their wings ethereal o'er that mystic Land
Where Glory circles from the awful Three,
And Life is Love, and Love is Deity.

Who breathes, in good and ill must bear his part,
And each can tell a history of heart,
How Time hath tinged the moral of his years
Through gloom or glory, triumph, pangs, or tears.
And yet, howe'er Confession prove the right,
To give it voice is deem'd a vain delight;
And far too deeply is my mem'ry fraught
With the cold lesson blighted hours have taught,
To think a life so valueless as mine
With the stern feelings of a world may twine.
But words *will* rise from out perturbèd mind
As heave the waters to the helmless wind,
In some fond mood, when dreaming thoughts control
Departed years that slumber in the soul!

* * * * *

Life still is young, but not the world, with me;
For where the freshness I was wont to see?
A bloom hath vanish'd from the face of Things;
Nor more the Syren of enchantment sings
In sunny mead, or shady walk, or bower,
Like that which warbled o'er my youthful hour.
Let reason laugh, or elder wisdom smile
On the warm phantasies which youth beguile,
There *is* a pureness in that glorious prime
Which mingles not with our maturer time.
All earth is brighten'd from a sun within
As yet unshaded by a world of sin,
While mind and nature blendingly array
In light and love, whate'er our dreams survey:
Though perils darken from the distant years
They vanish'd, cloud-like, when a smile appears!
And the light woes that flutter o'er the mind
Are laugh'd away, as foam upon the wind.
Thou witching Spirit of a younger hour!
*Did I not feel thee in thy fullest pow'r,
As oft school-free I rambled, lone and still
Through the green twilight of some wooded hill;
Or oped my lattice, when the moonshine lay
In sleep-like beauty on the brow of Day,
To watch the mystery of moving stars
Through ether gliding on melodious cars;
Or musing wander'd, ere the hectic morn,
To see how beautiful the sun was born?

A reign of glory from my soul hath past,
And each Elysium proved mere Earth at last;
Yet mourn I not in mock or puling strain,
For joys are left which never beam in vain:
The voice of friends, the changeless eye of love,
And, oh! that bliss all other bliss above,
To know, if shadow frown, or sunshine fall,
There is One Spirit who pervadeth all!

And has that fame, for which pure feelings pine,
No motive sanction'd by a Creed divine?
To be remember'd,—is the hope for *this*,
A false ambition for unholy bliss?
Time, Man, and Nature speak a deeper truth
When hope predicts the fancies of our youth!
But, 'tis not fame to form the midnight-show,†
Where Vice and Vanity alike may go;

* Rousseau, when dying, ordered his attendant to place him before the window, that he might view the declining glow of day, and bid farewell to the worshipped countenance of Nature!

† Fame begets favour, and one talent, if it be rubbed a little bright by use and practice, will procure a man more friends than a thousand virtues.—COWPER'S *Letters*.

It is not fame, to hear the shallow prate
Of busy Fondness, or intriguing Hate,
To feast on sounds of patronising pride
And wring from dulness what the world denied.
A high-soul'd nature is its own renown,
And needs no jewels to begem the crown!
For 'mid the heat, the hurry and the strife,
Or daily nothings of distemper'd life,
Our spirit thirsteth for a purer World:
O'er this the wings of fancy are unfurl'd;
Hence painter's hue and poet's dream are brought,
And the rich paradise of blooming thought:
To quench that thirst, let heaven-born feelings flow,
Let genius wake! let inspiration glow!
Why thus we panted for a world like this
May form a knowledge in our future bliss.*

All are not framed alike: Love, Hope, and Truth,
Those three Inspirers which attend on youth,
To various minds a varied tone impart;
What this man freezes,—fires another's heart!
The words that waken melodies of soul,
In tuneless ears monotonously roll;
The Shapes and Shadows which creation forms
And Fancy moulds from seasons and from storms
To living beauty or to lovely hue,
And waves them phantom-like before our view,
Will rouse the life-blood into fresher play
Of him who visions what the words array:
Another, eyeless save to sterner things,
Will frown them back as false Imaginings!
And thus in nature, as her vales reply
To voices wafted where the echoes lie,
Our spirits answer to appeals alone
When tuned accordant with some inward tone.†
I've stood entranced beneath as bright a sun
As Poet's dream hath ever gazed upon,
In the warm stillness of that wooing hour
When skies are floating with seraphic power,
The gales expiring in melodious death,
The waters hush'd, the woods without a breath;
But when I look'd where lay immingled forms
Of fairy mountains or refulgent storms,
And cloud-born phantoms, delicately bright,
Laugh'd in the paleness of departing light,
Each fainting into each, a long array,
Like lovely echoes when they glide away,—
Another babbled in that beauteous hour,
Light as the leaf, and mindless as the flower!

Thou young Aspirer! darest thou dream of fame,
And hope another Age will read thy name?
The hidden stirrings of each voiceless pride,
The pangs unutter'd, by the soul supplied,
The ghastly dimness of dejected hope,
By dreams assail'd with which no pride can cope;
Those nameless thoughts of venom'd fierceness, sent
From the dark heavings of our discontent;
And, dreader still,—the clouds of daily life
That welter round us in disease or strife,
And the cold atmosphere of worldly sway
Where Life is self, and Self the life of day,
In mingled power will oft thy soul appal;
Too well I picture, for I felt them all!
Yet bear thou on! and when some breathing page
Of godlike poet, or divinest sage,
And secret energies of soul begin
To feed the passion that is form'd within,
Then let thy Spirit in her power arise
And dare to speak the language of the Skies!
Her voice may fail, in deathlike muteness lost,
Her hopes be visions, and those visions cross'd;
But, pure and noble if thy song began,
And pour'd high meanings through the heart of man,
Not echoless perchance a note hath been
In some lone heart, or unimagined scene.
How many a breeze that wings a noiseless way,
How many a streamlet unbeheld by Day,
How many a sunbeam lights a lonely flower,
Yet works unseen in its creative power!
Then highly soar, whene'er thy spirit feels
The vivid sway impassion'd thought reveals;
Unchill'd by scorn, undarken'd by despair,
So Martyrs lived, and such the Mighty were!

There is a pleasure in a praise denied;*
It feeds a folly, or protects a pride,

* There are some exquisite allusions to the philosophy of poetry in "Schiller's Lectures on Dramatic Poetry;" and Bacon has comprehended in one eloquent paragraph a world of criticism—e.g., Videtur Poësis hæc humanæ naturæ largiri, quæ Historia denegat; atque animo umbris rerum utcunque satisfacere. * * * Firmum ex Poësi sumitur argumentum, magnitudinem rerum magis illustrem, ordinem magis perfectum, et varietatem magis pulchram animæ humanæ complacere, quam in naturâ ipsâ post lapsum reperire ullô modô possit. * * * Adeo ut Poësis ista non solum ad delectationem, sed etiam ad animi magnitudinem et ad mores conferat."—*De Aug. Scient.*, lib. 2, cap. 13.

† The action of mind on mind is an unfathomable mystery, yet as beautiful as it is deep. It is recorded by Fontenelle,. that when Malebranche first read Descarte's "Treatise on Man," he was sometimes compelled to lay aside the work "till the palpitation of his heart had subsided!"

* Three endowments are required to constitute a noble critic of the genuine type. 1st. Intellectual competency. 2nd. Moral rectitude. 3rd. A spiritual faculty. As to the first, we understand by

It teaches Dulness what no Wit can say,
"I don't approve, let no one write to-day."
Thou narrow-minded, petty, pompous Thing!
What lent a feather to the boldest wing
Of soaring Fancy,—but a praise when due?
And wouldst thou hive it for the darling few?
Though Shakspere sang, and Milton's soul aspired,
Must Gray be scorn'd, nor Goldsmith be admired?
As well might Ocean of the Earth demand
To let no river roll, no stream expand;
As well might Mountains which embrace the skies
Entreat the heav'ns to let no hills arise!
Eternal Spirit! while thy day-beams smile
Around my path in many a sunny wile,
Their shining truth, oh, let my gaze deny
Ere merit sickens on mine envious eye:
As ocean kindles to her native sun,
As waters freshen when the wind's begun,
So brightening, quickening—let my spirit feel
Wisdom and genius in their just appeal!

Such dimming shades, thou young Aspirer! wait
On all who seek to glorify their state.

---

it the possession of a pure imagination, a refined judgment, an intense love of the beautiful, a discriminating taste, a talent for analysis and synthesis, mental intuition, and a profound reverence for the Intellect of Man. But on this subject let us hear the words of a master—A. W. SCHLEGEL. "No man can be a true critic or connoisseur who does not possess a universality of mind, who does not possess the flexibility, which throwing aside all personal predilections and blind habits, enables him to transport himself into the peculiarities of other ages and nations, to feel them, as it were, from their proper central point, and what ennobles human nature, and to recognise and respect whatever is beautiful and grand, under those external modifications which are necessary to their existence, and which sometimes even seem to disguise them."

As to the second qualification, how applicable are Tacitus' words, in his exquisite fragment on Oratory, "Nemo orator nisi bonus," so with a genuine critic. There must be a deep sympathy for truth in his nature; a free and unfettered love for humanity, under all its manifold utterances and complexions; a catholic regard for whatsoever things are lovely, pure, and of good report; together with a high disdain for the mean, the envious, and the malignant,—or else whatever may be the mental acuteness of a critic, he will want that severe rectitude which is the binding charm which harmonises into a generous whole both his censure and his praise. A man inspired by sentiments like these, writes "with the fear of God before his eyes," and looks beyond the poor applause of his fellow clay. His object is to widen the region of human happiness, and so to elevate the just, the beautiful, the true and the noble before the apprehensions of mankind, that art, science, and literature may become the handmaids of social virtue, and the sisters of genuine religion.

Finally, and perhaps chiefly, in the highest departments of criticism, where the theme is in alliance with the objects of faith, the perfections of Deity, the destinies of eternity, the glories of the Redeemer, and the actings of the Invisible Spirit through the organs of our human being—there we feel assured something beyond intellectual competency, and what surpasses even moral rectitude, is required before the critic can be worthy of this exalted office. He must, in truth, have that which nothing under the throne of God can give him; which genius inspires not; imagination conceives not; talent commands not; eloquence supplies not; nor education bestows, nor example begets, nor all the culture of the intellect, though carried to the summit of possible attainment, will ever procure him;—and that is, a Spiritual Faculty. This is that "secret of the Lord which is with them that fear Him," and with none else.

But let us endeavour to explain what may be understood by a Spiritual Faculty. There are three conceivable modes under which objects are manifested to human apprehension. The first is physical, whereby sensible forms are perceived; the second is intellectual, whereby reason looks into the system of things, and to some extent understands their mutual relation, adaptation, and position in the universe of God. But there is a third mode, and that is altogether a spiritual one. Now here is the grand distinction: while the majority of men are more or less adequately endowed for the two former modes of apprehension, no man by nature is competent to the third? And why? Because "that which is born of the flesh is flesh, and that which is born of the spirit is spirit." Precisely, therefore, as for the discernment of natural truth a sensible faculty is needed; for the discernment of mental truth, a reasonable faculty; so for the apprehending of spiritual truth, a spiritual faculty is required. Listen to the august announcement of Christ, "Except a man be born again, he cannot see the kingdom of God." Now the kingdom of God is a divine element, reigning for a divine purpose, and with a divine power, in and over the creation. And the Spirit which by grace is imparted to a believer, is that supernatural power in him which corresponds with the hidden divinity which constitutes "the kingdom of God" in the creature. In harmony with this the apostle of the Gentiles thus reasons—"The things of God knoweth no man (i.e., simply as such), but the Spirit of God." "But the natural man receiveth not the things of the Spirit of God: for they are foolishness unto him: neither can he know them, because they are spiritually discerned." "But," argues the inspired logician, "He that is spiritual judgeth all things (i.e., of a spiritual order), yet he himself is judged of no man." The application of this criticism is as follows:—There are, it will be granted, manifold kinds of literature; one species belongs to the World, another to the Flesh, and another to the Devil. But God also hath His literature, both in prose and verse; and our argument is this—that precisely in proportion as a writer hath the Divine Spirit inhabiting his being with a teaching light and transforming purity, and under the tuition of that Spirit prophecies for God, and His Christ, and glory—to that same extent both the man and his work must be repulsive, and half incomprehensible to critics who have not that same Spirit residing in them. (1848.)

But shouldst thou, wafted by a fearless gale,
Ascend a height no vulgar clouds assail;
Should Fame encrown thee, and thy mind suffuse
O'er other minds its vivifying hues;
Wake feeling, passion, and the pow'r sublime
That bids eternity o'ershadow time,
The sunny raptures of renown enjoy,
But deem, oh! deem them not without alloy.
The smile of Nations may illume thy fame,
The good repeat, the glorious love thy name,
Still, tongues of scorn, and words of venom'd pow'r
To be the vipers of a secret hour,
The petty tribute, and unfeeling phrase,
Which nought but iciness of soul betrays,—
Demand forgiveness in thy brightest reign;
On ev'ry pleasure frowns the demon, pain!

But deeper peril is the praise which gives
That very light in which young Genius lives:
A tyrant weakness is the worst to see,
Since men are vain, yet all hate vanity;*
When safely felt, most insecurely shown,
For who endures it, save it prove his *own?*
Yet should that energy, whose quenchless ray
Burns through the blackest and the brightest day,
Intensely pure within thy spirit glow
And colour dreams beyond the world to know;
If, eagle-like, thy Spirit dare to soar
On bolder wing than it had waved before;
If virtue love, and wisdom greet thy strain,
If *this* be vanity,—then still be vain!

Oh! for a nobler and a deeper sense
Of all which forms our true pre-eminence;
For high-born energies of heav'nly sway,
And flowers of charity to strew the way,
That Sin no longer may the world defile
And Nature glory in a good man's smile,
As on we hasten to that dreamless Shore
Where passion sleeps, and prejudice is o'er.

The days of fever, and the nights of fire
Felt in the blood, till health and hope expire;
An aching slumber, and a spectral tomb
For ever yawning in the spirit's gloom;
And that most agonising waste of soul
Where the deep currents of excitement roll
Morn, noon, and night, in one eternal play,
Are thine, Ambition!—till Thou wear'st away.
And, mix'd with agonies of outward state,
An inward torment which thy dreams create,
Thirsting within for some perfection made
By thought alone, or never yet display'd
Like that pure model which the mind surveys,—
'Tis thine to suffer through uncounted days.
Yet, welcome all! If ever thought of thine
Hath woo'd a spirit into calm divine,
Expanded feelings, purified their flow,
Or shed a sunbeam o'er the hour of wo,
Thy soul may triumph in exhaustless pain
And proudly think it has not lived in vain!

Ye midnight heavens, a Hand celestial hung,
In ev'ry age by ev'ry poet sung,
One parting glance, oh! let my spirit take
Ere dawn-light on your awful beauty break.
With what intensity the eye reveres
Your starry legions, when their pomp appears!
As though the glances Centuries have given
Since dreams first wander'd o'er the vast of heav'n,
Had left a magic where a myst'ry shone,
Enchanting more, the more 'tis gazed upon!
Stars, worlds, or wonders! whatsoe'er ye shine,
The home of Angels, or the haunts divine
Wherein the Bodiless from earth set free
Shine in the blaze of present Deity,
No eyes behold your ever-beaming ray
But think, while earthly visions roll away,
In placid immortality *ye* glow
Above this chaos of terrestrial wo!

Thy wings, Almighty! let them long o'ershade
A clime by Thee a matchless empire made;
Here in meek glory may Thy temples stand
While smiles from heav'n fall brightly o'er the land;
And those pure Worlds that have for ages roll'd
O'er Alma Mater, still her towers behold;
Till time be dead, eternity begun,
And darkness blacken round the dying Sun,
The toils of life, the pangs of being o'er,
Our doom completed, and the world no more.

* It has been said that Heaven, which gave great qualities only to a small number of its favourites, gave vanity to all, as a full compensation.—BROWN'S *Philosophy*.

NOTES.

PART I.

Note 1, Page 393, Column 2.

"Consider me very seriously here in a strange country, inhabited by things that call themselves Doctors and Masters of Arts; a country flowing with syllogisms and ale, where Horace and Virgil are equally unknown; consider me, I say, in this melancholy light; and then think if something be not due to yours," &c.

Christ Church, Nov. 14, 1735.

Such is the amusive pertness with which West, Gray's friend, alludes to this university. In another letter, he talks about "half a dozen new little proctorlings." This rebellious description of his Alma Mater is more than matched by the sarcasm of Gray, in speaking of Cambridge. "Surely it was of this place, now Cambridge, but formerly known by the name of Babylon, that the prophet spoke when he said, 'the wild beasts of the desert shall dwell there, and their houses shall be full of doleful creatures, and owls shall build there, and satyrs shall dance there; their forts and towers shall be a den for ever, a joy of wild asses,' &c. &c. You must know that I do not take degrees, and after this term shall have nothing more of college impertinences to undergo. I have endured lectures daily and hourly since I came last.—Must I plunge into metaphysics! Alas! I cannot see in the dark; nature has not furnished me with the optics of a cat. Must I pore upon mathematics? Alas! I cannot be in too much light; I am no eagle.—It is very possible that two and two make four, but I would not give four farthings to demonstrate this ever so clearly."—Letters.

"To Oxford," says Gibbon, "I brought a stock of erudition that might have puzzled a doctor, and a degree of ignorance of which a schoolboy might have been ashamed."

Lord King, in his "Life of Locke," remarks, "That Locke regretted his education at Oxford, is stated upon the authority of his friend Le Clerc." He adds, however, "Perhaps too much stress has been laid upon some accidental expressions; or rather, that the regrets expressed by Locke ought to have been understood by Le Clerc to apply to the plan of education then generally pursued at English universities; for to Oxford, even as Oxford was in the days of Locke, he must have been considerably indebted. If the system of education did not offer assistance, or afford those directions so useful to a young student, the residence at Oxford did no doubt confer ease, leisure, and the opportunity of other studies; it afforded also the means of intercourse with persons from whose society and conversation we know that the idea of his great work arose."

"Too much stress" has indeed been laid upon ebullitions of peevishness against the system pursued at our universities, which occur in the works and correspondence of a few celebrated men. With regard to Gray's opinion, it has been justly remarked, "At the time when he was admitted, Jacobitism and hard drinking prevailed still at Cambridge, much to the prejudice not only of good manners, but of good letters. But we see (as was natural enough to a young man) he laid the blame rather on the mode of education than the mode of the times." In allusion to Gibbon's taunts, a biographer observes; "By his course of desultory reading he seems unconsciously to have been led to that particular branch in which he was afterwards to excel. But whatsoever connection this had with his more distant life, he was exceedingly deficient in classical learning, and went to Oxford without either the taste or preparation which could enable him to reap the advantages of academical education. This may possibly account for the harshness with which he speaks of the universities. His fourteen months at Magdalen were idle and profitless; and he describes himself as 'gay, and disposed to late hours.' When he sat down to write his memoirs—the memoirs of an eminent and accomplished scholar—he found a blank which is seldom found in the biography of English scholars; the early display of genius, the laudable emulation, and the well-earned honours; he found that he owed no fame to his academical residence, and therefore determined that no fame should be derivable from an university education."—Ex uno disce omnes.

Note 2, Page 394, Column 2.

Addison was entered at Queen's, 1687.—In 1689, his Latin verses, "Inauguratio Regis Gulielmi," procured him the patronage of Dr. Lancaster, by whose recommendations he was elected a demy at Magdalen. While a student here, he wrote parts of "Cato," and forwarded them to Dryden, who admired them as poetry, but doubted their dramatical success.

Note 3, Page 395, Column 1.

Steele was removed in 1692 from the Charter-house to Merton. In 1695, his first production, a poem on Queen Mary, appeared. The Tatler was commenced on April 12th, 1709. Addison discovered its author by the insertion of a criticism on a passage in Virgil, which he had formerly communicated to him. The passage alluded to in the text is quoted by the elegant essayist, Dr. Drake, as a beautiful example of his pathetic powers:—"The first sense of sorrow I ever knew," says he, "was upon the death of my father, at which time I was not quite five years of age; but was rather amazed at what all the house meant, than possessed with a real understanding why nobody was willing to play with me. I remember I went into the room where his body lay, and my mother sat weeping alone by it. I had my battledore in my hand, and fell a beating the coffin, and calling 'Papa!' for, I know not how, I had some slight idea that he was locked up there. My mother catched me in her arms, and, transported beyond all patience of the silent grief she was before in, she almost smothered me in her embrace; and told me, in a flood of tears, 'Papa could not hear me, and would play with me no more, for they were going to put him under ground, whence he could never come to us again.'"

Note 4, Page 395, Column 1.

In 1740, Collins stood first in the list of Winchester scholars to be received in succession at New College; but there being no vacancy, he became a commoner of Queen's; from whence, in half a year, he was elected a demy of Magdalen. His early life appears to have been one continued scene of melancholy, want, and obscurity: and, contrasting his present fame with his once unnoticed merit, we may well recal an observation made by Goldsmith, in his Life of Parnell:—"A poet, while living, is seldom an object sufficiently great to attract much attention; his real merits are known but to a few, and these are generally sparing in their praises. When his fame is increased by time, it is then too late to investigate the peculiarities of his disposition; the dews of the morning are past, and we vainly try to continue the chase by the meridian splendour!"

The most touching anecdote in his life is thus related by Johnson:—"He had withdrawn from study, and travelled with no other book than an English Testament, such as children carry to the school: when his friend took it into his hand, out of curiosity, to see what companion a man of letters had chosen, 'I have but one book,' said Collins, 'but that is the best.'"

For biographical illustration of the morbid sensibilities and melancholies to which men of genius are peculiarly subject, the reader is referred to D'Israeli's interesting work on the "Literary Character." Allan Cunningham, in his Life of Sir Christopher Wren, has the following allusion:—"The wives of men of genius, in our earlier biographies, are treated with a sort of masculine indifference; but a gentler and a juster feeling has of late shewn itself. The man of genius and sensibility is pretty sure to have his moments of doubt and fear, when his noblest works seem weak or absurd; nay, even his days of despondency, when, exhausted by mental exertions, he can no longer think with clearness, and believes that his mental powers are forsaking him; and he is not unlikely, moreover, to be acquainted with those worldly miseries, sad enough to all hearts, but doubly so to his, whom a wise one of the tribe pronounces to be

'A thing unteachable in worldly skill.'"

Note 5, Page 395, Column 2.

Johnson's rooms, with some slight alteration in their division, and the substitution of a gothic window for the plainer one of his own time, remain as he left them. On entering them, who does not remember his own lofty sentence?—"To abstract the mind from all local emotion would be impossible, if endeavoured, and would be foolish, if it were possible! Whatever withdraws us from the power of our senses—whatever makes the past, the distant, or the future, predominate over the present, advances us in the dignity of thinking beings. Far from me, and from my friends, be such frigid philosophy as may conduct us indifferent and unmoved over any ground which has been dignified by wisdom, bravery, or virtue. That man is little to be envied, whose patriotism would not gain force upon the plain of Marathon, or whose piety would not grow warmer among the ruins of Iona."

There is nothing romantic in their appearance, distinct from other collegiate chambers; but the sombre hue which pervades them is not uncongenial with the associations which arise when we enter their hallowed precincts. Here, as the pensive shades of twilight closed around him, and the loneliness of his fate darkened on his mind, we can easily imagine him retired from the scene his gay hypocrisy had enlivened, to nurse those moods of feeling which afterwards revealed themselves in the melancholy wisdom of "Rasselas," and the moral gloom of the "Rambler."

Johnson was entered a commoner of Pembroke, on the 31st of October, 1728, in his nineteenth year. The following are the principal anecdotical allusions to his collegiate life, as recorded by his worshipper and biographer.

"The Rev. Dr. Adams, who afterwards presided over Pembroke college, gave me some account of what passed on the night of Johnson's arrival at Oxford. His father seemed very full of the merits of his son, and told the company he was a good scholar, and a poet, and wrote Latin verses. His figure and manner appeared strange to them; but he behaved modestly, and sat silent, till upon something which occurred in the course of conversation he suddenly struck in, and quoted Macrobius. Johnson gave the following account of his tutor, Mr. Jorden,—'He was a very worthy man, but a heavy man, and I did not profit much by his instructions. Indeed, I did not attend him much. The first day I came to college I waited on him, and then stayed away four. On the sixth, Mr. Jorden asked me why I had not attended. I answered, I had been sliding in Christ Church Meadow. And this I said with as much nonchalance as I am now talking to you. I had no notion that I was wrong or irreverent to my tutor.—'That, sir, was great fortitude of mind.' 'No, sir, stark insensibility.'

"What he read solidly at Oxford was Greek; not the Grecian historians, but Homer and Euripides, and now and then a little epigram. One day, while sitting in his apartment quite alone, Dr. Panting, then master of the college, overheard him uttering this soliloquy, in his strong emphatic voice. 'Well, I have a mind to see what is done in other places of learning; I'll go and visit the universities abroad; I'll go to France and Italy; I'll go to Padua; and I'll mind my own business. For an Athenian blockhead is the worst of all blockheads.'"

Note 6, Page 396, Column 1.

"Dr. Adams told me, that Johnson, while he was at Pembroke college, was caressed and loved by all about him, was a gay frolicksome fellow, and passed there the happiest time of his life. When I mentioned this account of Dr. Adams, he said, 'Ah, sir, I was mad and violent; it was bitterness which they mistook for frolic; I was miserably poor, and thought to fight my way by my literature and my wit; so I disregarded all power and authority.' The bishop of Dromore observes to me in a letter,—I have heard from some of his contemporaries, that he was generally seen lounging at the college gate with a circle of young students round him, whom he was entertaining with wit, and keeping from their studies, if not spiriting them up to rebellion against the college discipline, which in his maturer years he so much extolled."

"He contracted a love and regard for Pembroke, which he retained to the last. A short time before his death he sent to that college a present of all his works, to be deposited in their library. He took a pleasure in boasting of the many eminent men who had been educated at Pembroke." Dr. Johnson delighted in his own partiality for Oxford: and one day at her (Mrs. Thrale's) house, entertained five members of the other university with various instances of the superiority of Oxford, enumerating the gigantic names of many men whom it had produced, with apparent triumph. At last Mrs. Thrale said to him—"Why, there happen to be no less than five Cambridge men in the room now." "I did not," said he, "think of that till you told me; but the wolf don't count the sheep."—"Piozzi," p. 27, 28.

Johnson, it seems, (Hawkins' Life, p. 9,) would oftener risk the payment of a small fine than attend his tutor's (Mr. Jorden's) lectures. On receiving an imposition, he said,—"Sir, you have sconced me twopence for a lecture not worth a penny!" We should like to see the expressive ugliness of certain living faces undergoing a similar reply! Mrs. Piozzi (p. 27) remarks, that "when he made his first declamation, he wrote but one copy, and that coarsely; and having given it into the hand of the tutor, who stood to receive it as he passed, was obliged to begin by chance and go on how he could, for he had got but little of it by heart; so, fairly trusting to his present powers for immediate supply, he finished by adding astonishment to the applause of all who knew how little was owing to study."

The urbanity of the Rev. Dr. Hall, (now master of Pembroke college) has enabled Croker, in his annotated edition of Boswell's Life, to afford his readers a specimen of Johnson's college exercises, preserved in his college—e. g.,

EXERCISE.

——— "Mea nec Falernæ
Temperant vites, neque Formiani.
Pocula Colles.

"Quid mirum Maro quod digne canit arma virumque,
Quid quod putidulum nostra Camœna sonat?
Limosum nobis Promus dat callidus haustum,
Virgilio vires uva Falerna dedit.
Carmina vis nostri scribant meliora Poetæ?
Ingenium jubeas purior haustus alat!"
Pemb. MSS.

Note 7, Page 396, Column 1.

Mr. Tyers, who knew Johnson intimately, observed, "that he always talked as if he were talking upon oath."

Note 8, Page 396, Column 2.

A solitary cup of milkless tea was one of his domestic penances!

Note 9, Page 396, Column 2.

"William D'Avenant made his first entry on the stage of this vain world in the parish of St. Martin, in the month of February, and on the third of the following March, an. 1605-6, he received baptism in the church of that parish. His father, John D'Avenant, was a sufficient vintner, a very grave and discreet citizen, yet an admirer and lover of plays and play-makers, especially Shakspere, who frequented his house in his journies between Warwickshire and London. William, 'the sweet swan of Isis,' was educated in grammar learning under Edward Sylvester, and in academical, in Lincoln College, under the care of Mr. Daniel Hough, and obtained there some smattering in logic. But his geny, which was opposite to it, led him into the pleasant paths of poetry." —*Athenæ.*

Shakspere, in his frequent journeys between London and his native place, used to lie at Davenant's, the Crown, in Oxford. He was well acquainted with Mrs. Davenant, and her son was supposed to be more nearly related to him than a godson only! One day, when Shakspere was just arrived, and the boy sent for from school to him, a Head of one of the colleges met the child running home, and asked him whither he was going in so much haste?—The boy said, "To my godfather Shakspere." "Fie! child," says the old gentleman, "why are you so superfluous? Have you not learned yet not to use the name of God in vain?"—Pope—as related by Spence.

Note 10, Page 396, Column 2.

This wonderful man in the course of his itinerancy is supposed to have travelled nearly 300,000 miles, and to have preached above 40,000 sermons! Well, indeed, as Southey remarks, would it be for the world, if every man of equal celebrity had left a diary such as Wesley's! From the Charterhouse in 1720 he was removed to Christ Church, and from thence in 1726 he was elected fellow of Lincoln. "Though Wesley was not yet eccentric in the habits of his life, the strictness of his religious principles was sufficiently remarkable to afford subject for satire; and his opponents hoped to prevent his success by making him ridiculous. On this occasion his father told him it was a shallow virtue that could not bear being laughed at. His mother encouraged him in a different manner. 'If,' said she, 'it be a weak virtue that cannot bear being laughed at, I am sure it is a strong and well-confirmed virtue that can stand the test of a brisk buffoonery.' On his election, which was greatly indebted to the good-will of Dr. Norley, then rector, his father thus congratulates him:—'What will be my own fate before the summer is over, God knows! sed passi graviora.—Wherever I am, my Jack is Fellow of Lincoln.'

"While he was an undergraduate, his manners were free and easy; and that activity of disposition, which bore him afterwards through such uninterrupted labour, displayed itself in wit and vivacity."

The rise of methodism is thus traced by his able biographer:—"His disposition, his early education, the example of his parents, and of both his brethren, were in unison; not knowing how or when he woke out of his lethargy, he imputed the change to the efficacy of another's prayers, most likely, he said, his mother's; and meeting with two or three undergraduates, whose principles resembled his own, they associated together for the purpose of religious improvement, lived by rule, and received the sacrament. The greatest prudence would not have suffered to save men from ridicule, who, at such an age, and in such a scene, professed to make religion the great business of their lives; and prudence is rarely united with enthusiasm. They were called, in derision, Bible-bigots, Bible-moths, the Holy, or the Godly Club. One person, with less irreverence and more learning, observed, in reference to their methodical manner of life, that a new sect of methodists was sprung up, alluding to the ancient School of Physicians known by that name."

Note 11, Page 396, Column 2.

James Hervey, author of "Meditations among the Tombs," written while he held the curacy of

Bedford, in Devonshire. He was one of Wesley's earliest religious associates at Oxford.

Note 12, Page 397, Column 1.

"Benjamin Jonson, a poet as soon he was born, afterwards the father of our poetry, and most admirably well versed in classical authors, and therefore beloved of Camden, Selden, Hoskins, Martin, &c., made his first entry on the stage of this vain world within the city of Westminster, (being the son of a grave minister,) educated in the college school there, while Camden was master; thence his silly mother, who had married to her second husband, a bricklayer, took him home, and made him, as 'tis said, work at her husband's trade. At length, being pitied by some generous gentleman, Camden got him a better employment, which was to accompany a son of Sir Walter Raleigh in his adventures. After their return, they parted not, I think, in cold blood, and thereupon Ben went to Cambridge, and was statutably elected into St. John's College; but what continuance he made there, I find not; sure it is, that his geny being most poetical, he did afterwards recede to a nursery, or obscure playhouse, called the Green Curtain. Dr. Rich Corbet, of Christ Church, and other poets of the University, did, in reverence to his parts, invite him to Oxon, where, continuing for some time in Christ Church, writing and composing plays, he was, as a member thereof, actually created Master of Arts in 1619; and therefore I put him among the Oxford writers. At length, B. Jonson, after he had arrived at the sixty-third year of his age, marched off from the stage of this vain world, on the 16th of August, 1637."—*Athenæ.*

Note 13, Page 397, Column 1.

Locke was sent to Christ Church in 1651, and was speedily distinguished among his fellow collegians. He resided partly in Exeter House, and partly at Oxford.

Note 14, Page 397, Column 1.

"In 1670, his great work, the Essay on the Understanding, was sketched out. It arose from the meeting, as the author says, of five or six friends at his chambers."—LORD KING'S *Life of Locke.*

We may add to this, that in 1694, Mr. Wynne, fellow of Jesus, first recommended his Essay to the study of the University.

Note 15, Page 397, Column 2.

From Eton, Canning was removed to Christ Church, where he gained several prizes. From Oxford he went to the Temple, and studied the law; but being patronized by Sheridan, he was brought forward into political life, and returned member of Parliament for Newtown, in the Isle of Wight. Canning made his first speech, equally distinguished for its modesty and eloquence, on the treaty between his Majesty and the King of Sardinia, on the 31st of January, 1794.

As a statesman and a patriot, the world can do justice to Canning's fame; as the fascinating companion in private life, the memory of those who were honoured with his regard can alone enjoy him. They may truly apply to themselves, with a slight alteration, the words of a great historian, on the death of his revered friend,* "Finis vitæ ejus nobis luctuosus, patriæ tristis, extraneis etiam ignotisque non sine curâ fuit." "Quicquid ex Agricolâ amavimus, quidquid mirati sumus, manet mansurumque est in animis hominum, in æternitate temporum, famâ rerum."

* Tacit. in Agricol. c. 43, 46.

The following extracts are taken from a short account of the "Early Days of Canning," which was published by Mr. Newton.—

"Mr. Canning quitted Mr. Richard's school at Winchester in 1782, and in the same year, at about twelve years old, was sent to Eton. He is described to have made a considerable progress at Winchester, such as sufficiently to account for the distinguished rank which he had at Eton, where he was at once placed in the fourth form, and was never, therefore, in the lower school. He obtained the post of honour in the public speeches of 1787, by being made the last speaker, and he must consequently have been very high in the school, when he quitted it for the University. Mr. Robert Smith, the late representative in Parliament for Lincoln, who alone, of all the Etonians at that period, rivalled Mr. Canning in abilities, delivered, in 1788, a speech antecedently spoken by his friend, and this occasioned a warm discussion among the boys on their comparative merits. These two, together with Mr. Smith's brother, and Mr. John Hookham Frere, who was, during the late war, our envoy at Madrid, were the authors, while at school, of the Microcosm, to which periodical work a few other Etonians contributed papers occasionally. Dr. Pett, canon of Christ Church who lately declined a bishopric which was offered to him with circumstances of peculiar grace and favour, was Mr. Canning's tutor, as he was mine; and, in our various walks of life, we have seldom found a person who united, with literary acquirements, qualities more amiable, more considerate, and more estimable; he would have adorned the mitre. When I heard that Mr. Canning had only left behind him a small fortune, it did not at all surprise me, for he possessed from his youth a most liberal spirit in pecuniary matters. At college, his habits were uniformly studious. Enter his rooms in Peckwater when you would, you were almost sure to find him occupied with a pen or a book. Superior to all idle amusements, improvement was his continual object. He did not even keep a horse, and I have no recollection that he ever hired one.

"In the year 1787, a speaking society was established at Christ Church, the members of which were the Hon. Robert Banks Jenkinson, now Lord Liverpool, George Canning, Lord Henry Spencer, Sir William Drummond, sometime British ambassador at Constantinople, Charles Goddard, and myself. Most of these names are well known in the world, and are connected with the history of the country.

"Mr. Goddard, soon after he quitted Oxford, was the private secretary of Lord Grenville, at whose house in St. James's Square, Mr. Canning, Lord Liverpool, and myself, were in the habit of visiting him. I remember him with pleasure as a very instructive and agreeable companion. He is at present Archdeacon of Lincoln, and has been long distinguished for the active and zealous discharge of the arduous duties of his profession, and station in the church. This club, in which were heard the first speeches ever composed or delivered by Lord Liverpool and Mr. Canning, met every Thursday evening at the rooms of the members, who were, at its first establishment, limited to the number of six. Before our separation at night, or frequently at one or two o'clock in the morning, we voted and recorded the question which we were to debate on the ensuing Thursday. Sometimes we appeared at dinner in the hall, dressed in our uniform, which was a brown coat, of rather an uncommon shade, with velvet cuffs and collar. The buttons bore the initials of Demosthenes, Cicero, Pitt, and Fox.

"Thus habited, and much the object of notice to every passing observer, we pleased ourselves with the excessive curiosity which our dress excited. As secret were we as the grave on all that concerned our oratorical institution, and it would be difficult to give an idea of the anxiety evinced by our fellow collegians to discover the meaning of this brown coat and velvet cuffs.

"These, indeed, were boyish feelings, nor should I have entered so much into the particulars, were it not that, whether the questions debated by us were trivial or profound, this club cannot remain in obscurity, since it is the leading subject of Mr. Canning's letter, to which these remarks are introductory. Those who have been educated at public schools, which are the world in miniature, must have observed that boys are apt to exhibit themselves there very much in the same characters which they afterwards maintain on the more important theatre of life.

"I was the lowest boy in the list at Harrow, when I first went to that school, the only one at which I ever was placed; and having gradually ascended to the highest forms, many are the instances I could recollect in support of this observation. No example, however, of an early and decisive display of character could be more peculiarly striking than that which is exhibited in Mr. Canning's letter. Dr. Cyril Jackson, at that time dean of Christ Church, entertained the most favourable opinion of Mr. Canning's abilities, and foresaw his high destiny in those glances into futurity in which the dean was accustomed to indulge his contemplative and deeply penetrating mind, and frequently with an accuracy which was extraordinary: he had probably seated Mr. Canning on the woolsack.

"There was one member of our club at Christ Church, Lord Liverpool, whom it would be unbecoming in me to pass over without a more particular notice. When at the university, he was not only a first-rate scholar, but he had confessedly acquired a greater share of general knowledge than perhaps any undergraduate of that day. He was an excellent historian, and his attention had been directed so early, by his father, to the contending interests of the European nations, that intricate political questions were already familiar to his mind. Lord Liverpool's public career is now, alas! consummated. We have a complete view, and the world is able to make a full estimate of his transcendent abilities. These, we know, were extensively operative in the conduct of the last war, which was brought to its glorious termination by the prowess of our British hero, whose mode of warfare was marked in its superiority by so much of genius, that had his Grace continued to range his forces, from the year 1815 to the present hour, against the most celebrated captains in Europe, there is a moral certainty, or, to say the least, a strong conviction in those who had the best means of appreciating his talents in the East Indies, in the Peninsula, and in Flanders, that a succession of battles would have been to the Duke of Wellington a succession of victories. To return to Lord Liverpool. After dedicating himself for nearly forty years to the service of his king and country, his merit is universally acknowledged, and never did any man go through a long and arduous life less reproached, or more irreproachable. His temper was extremely conciliating, and all who reflect on the trying scenes in which he bore a distinguished part, and are happy enough to recollect the benignity of his personal intercourse, will feel the truth, and even the moderation, of this friendly testimony to his virtues. There was, perhaps, in all England, but one individual who was formed to compete successfully with Lord Liverpool, at that inexperienced age of academic life of which we have been speaking, and that was George Canning. He accidentally entered at Oxford about the same time with Lord Liverpool. The vivacity of Mr. Canning's conversation was invaluable to those of his fellow-collegians who enjoyed his intimacy. It sweetened the severity of our studies, just as the sallies of his vigorous imagination have since delighted the House of Commons, and cheered their midnight hours."

Brighton, Sept. 1st, 1788.

"My dear Newton,

"That the idleness of a long vacation should not have afforded you an answer to your two very deserving letters before this, to a mere contemplater of events might perhaps seem extraordinary; but to a philosopher, who is well convinced of the truth of the observation, that 'we are never more taken up than when we have nothing to do,' there will not be much room for surprise. Believe me, however, that I feel myself, very highly, very sincerely, obliged by your punctual performance of your kind promise, and that absence has not in the smallest degree weakened the desire I have always felt of proving to you in how high esteem I hold you, and how great a value I set upon your friendship. You will be a good deal surprised at the answer which your questions relative to our club will receive. That club, Newton, is no more. 'And by what dread event? what sacrilegious hand?' you will exclaim. Newton, mine! My reasons I never gave to any of the members, but I will open them to you. What my reasons for first becoming a part of the institution were, I protest I cannot at present call to mind. Perhaps I was influenced by the novelty of the plan; perhaps influenced by your example; perhaps I was not quite without an idea of trying my strength with Jenkinson. Connected with men of avowed enmity in the political world, professing opposite principles, and looking forward to some distant period when we might be ranged against each other on a larger field, we were perhaps neither of us without the vanity of wishing to obtain an early ascendancy over the other.

* * * * * *

"So long as the purport and usage of the club were a secret, I was very well contented to be of it: but when it became notoriously known—when the dean to me (and to *me* only), in private, recommended some reasons against its propriety to my serious consideration—(for had he presumed to interpose authoritatively, that single circumstance, 'albeit considerations infinite did make against it,' would have been sufficient to determine me upon its continuance)—when he represented it to me in a very strong light, as being almost an absolute avowal of parliamentary views—to a professional man an avowal the most dangerous—this representation made me resolve to abandon an undertaking which I saw evidently could neither promise eventual advantage, nor maintain a temporary respectability. Thus resolved, at my return after the Easter vacation, without any previous confidential communication of my reasons or intentions, I sent my resignation by Lord Henry on the first night of their meeting. William Spencer was now come, and was that night to take his seat. The message which Lord Henry brought occasioned, as it were, a combustion, which ended in the moving of some very violent resolutions. Among others, I was summoned to the bar; of course, refused to obey the summons. A deputation was then sent to interrogate me respecting the causes of my resignation, which, of course, I refused to reveal; and they were at last satisfied by my declaring that the reasons of my resignation did not affect them collectively or individually. I, of course, was anxious that everybody should know that I was no longer a member of the club; and, therefore, whenever it was a subject of conversation, disavowed any connexion with it. Lord Henry I with much difficulty prevented from resigning at the same time that I did. He however, attended but two more debates, and then formally 'accepted the Chiltern hundreds,' to use a parliamentary phrase. They all now unanimously gave out that there had been a complete dissolution, and that the thing was no longer in existence; altered their times and modes of meeting, abolished the uniform, and suspended their assemblies for a time. This, it seems, was intended to punish me, by carrying the face of a common, and not a particular secession. It was not long, however, before the truth came out; and their nightly debates are again renewed, not undiscovered, but with less pomp, regularity, numbers, and vociferation. This, then, is a full and true account of the decline and fall, and of the revival also, of the society. I do not think you can blame my conduct, when you recollect that the imputation of parliamentary prospects, already too much fixed upon me, is what of all others a person in my situation ought to avoid. I am already, God knows, too much inclined, both by my own sanguine wishes, and the connexions with whom I am most intimate, and whom I above all others revere, to aim at the House of Commons, as the only path to the only desirable thing in this world, the gratification of ambition;* while, at the same time, every tie of common sense, of fortune, and of duties, draws me to the study of a profession. The former propensity, I hope, reflection, necessity, and the friendly advice and very marked attentions of the dean, will enable me to overcome; and to the law I look as the profession which, in this country, holds out every enticement that can nerve the exertions and give vigour to the powers of a young man. The way, indeed, is long, toilsome, and rugged, but it leads to honours solid and lasting—to independence, without which no blessings of fortune, however profuse, no distinctions of station, however splendid, can afford a liberal mind true satisfaction—to power, for which no task can be too hard, no labours too trying. I look round the world, and even in the comparatively confined circle of my own acquaintance, I see an infinite number starting forward to the same goal; all fired with the same hopes, and animated with a like ardour. That your health may permit you to join us in our career—that the elasticity of your mind may spring from under that habitual indolence (pardon me for speaking in such a term) of philosophic pursuits, is very much my wish; though, with your heart and intentions, I do not doubt but you may be employed with equal, and, perhaps, better founded satisfaction to yourself, and with benefits to mankind, more real and more widely diffused, by putting into execution, where you have the will and the power, those systems which I have often admired you for forming, of useful beneficence and practical Christianity. Theories are easily formed, and plans easily laid down for the cultivation of the human mind, for the cure of those evils incident to a state of perpetual subjection, and the diffusion of those blessings of which every state is capable. Be it your work, as far as lies within the circle of your influence, to give life to the inactivity of philosophy, and energy and efficience to the idleness of speculation. I am much pleased with the idea of seeing you in England; for if in England you are, I trust you will not leave it without seeing me. The return you mention to me with you is a pleasing fairy scheme, but which, then at least, will not be put in execution. My plans for next summer are fixed, and I think will be improving and agreeable. You may know that I am shamefully ignorant of French, and though I have fifty times formed the intention of learning it, I never yet have brought my intention to the maturity of practical application. By this time twelvemonth, I intend to procure a smattering sufficient to call a coach, or swear at a waiter; and then to put in execution a plan formed long ago, in happier days, of going abroad with my three fellow scribes, the Microcosmopolitans. One of them you know and admire; the other two, though not equal to him in abilities, are not behind him in qualities to conciliate affection and secure esteem. Our idea is not that of scampering through France and ranting in Paris; but a sober sort of thing, to go and settle for some months in some provincial town, remarkable for the salubrity of its climate, the respectability of its inhabitants, and the purity of its language; there to improve our constitutions by the first, to extend our acquaintance with men and manners by the second, and to qualify ourselves for a further extension of it by perfecting ourselves in the third. I have taken it into my head that I shall receive * * * * into favour again. The truth about him is, that he is not without good points; his heart has some worth, his abilities very considerable eminence.

* * * * * *

"His character is far above that most nauseous of all things, insipidity, and negative good or evil. As a competitor, he was troublesome, and worth crushing; but that once done, and I can assure you it cost me some pains to accomplish it, 'his good now blazes; all his bad is in the grave,' as Zanga says. W. S. has again left Oxford, and I fancy for ever; he is, I hear, gone abroad, but whither I know not. Pity that abilities so great should be rendered useless to himself and to society, by such an eccentricity of temper, and unaccountableness of behaviour, as characterize him.

"Lord have mercy upon you, who have, in addition to the natural heat of the climate, such a letter as this to labour through! Grant you patience, good Heaven! with eyes to make out my scrawl; perseverance to unravel my meaning; comprehension to understand my allusions; good nature to be interested in my narrative; a heart to profit by my instructions; and, moreover, to believe me,

"With very great truth and affection, yours,

"G. CANNING.

"My direction is Oxford, of course."

* The child is father of the man!—WORDSWORTH.

D'Alembert, in his "Éloge de Montesquieu," has the following passage which appears so happily fraught with the social traits of Canning's character, that they may be quoted here without intrusion.

"Il étoit, dans le commerce, d'une douceur et d'une gaieté. Sa conversation étoit légère, agréable, et instructive, par le grand nombre d'hommes et de peuples qu'il avoit connus: elle étoit coupée, comme son style, pleine de sel et de saillies, sans amertume... Le feu de son esprit, le grand nombre d'idées dont il étoit plein, les faisoient naître. Il étoit sensible à la gloire; mais il ne vouloit y parvenir qu'en la méritant. Jamais il n'a cherché à augmenter la sienne par ces manœuvres sourdes, par ces voies obscures et honteuses, qui déshonorent la personne, sans ajouter au nom."

Note 16, Page 397, Column 2.

Denham became gentleman-commoner at Trinity in Michaelmas term, 1631, in the sixteenth year of his age. Anthony Wood, in the delightful quaintness of his usual style, observes,—"Being looked upon as a slow and dreaming young man by his seniors and contemporaries, they could never then in the least imagine that he could ever enrich the world with his fancy, or issue of his brain, as he afterwards did—'Cooper's Hill:' a poem, Oxon, 1643, in one sheet and a half, in quarto. A poem it is, which for the majesty of the style is, and ever will be, the exact standard of good writing. It was translated into Latin verse by Moses Pengrey, as I shall elsewhere tell you."

Of Denham's person, Aubrey gives the following account: "Denham was of the tallest, but a little incurvetting at the shoulders, not very robust. His haire was but thin and flaxen, with a moist curle His gate was slow, and was rather a stalking (he had long legges), which was wont to put me in mind of Horace, de Art. Poet.

'Hic, dum sublimes versus ructatur, et errat,
Si veluti merulis intentus decidit auceps
In puteum foveamque;'

His eie was a kind of light goose-gray, not bigge, but it had a kind of strange piercingness, not as to shining and glory, but (like a Momus) when he conversed with you he lookt into your very thoughts."

Note 17, Page 397, Column 2.

"William Pitt was born November 15th, 1708, and educated at Eton, whence, in January, 1726, he went as a gentleman commoner to Trinity college. When he quitted the university, Pitt was for a time in the army, and served as a cornet: but he quitted the life of a soldier for that of a statesman, and became member for the borough of Old Sarum, in February, 1735."—ALEX. CHALMERS.

Note 18, Page 397, Column 2.

"Thomas Warton became a scholar of Trinity in 1743, where in 1750 he took his master's degree, and the next year succeeded to a fellowship. In 1785 he was chosen Camden Professor of History. His 'Triumph of Isis,' written as a reply to Mason's 'Isis,' contains a spirited invocation to his beloved Alma Mater:

"Hail, Oxford, hail! of all that's good and great,
Of all that's fair, the guardian and the seat;
Nurse of each brave pursuit, each gen'rous aim,
By truth exalted to the throne of fame!
Like Greece in science and in liberty,
As Athens learn'd, as Lacedæmon free!"

Note 19, Page 398, Column 1.

No living writer must have a memory more delightfully stored with recollections of the past than Lisle Bowles. From youth to old age associating with the learned, the good, and the great of his country, devoted to literature, poetry, and criticism, and finally reposing in the calm seclusion of pastoral life, —to few is it permitted to say with greater truth, "Innocuas amo delicias, doctamque quietem." This quotation may be appropriately followed by his own beautiful sentence, in the "Life of Ken," which he has lately published. The contrast between the domestic quiet of Isaak Walton's home, and the Puritanic broils of the day, he compares to "passing through the tumult and din of the crowd at Hyde Park corner to Holland House, the seat of poetry and kindred taste, where, opening the garden door, in contrast to the noise through which you have passed, you hear only with intense delight the ancient pines murmuring in the still repose of a summer evening, and the nightingales contending in their solitary harmony."

Note 20, Page 398, Column 1.

It must be no slight gratification to Lisle Bowles, that Coleridge (see his Biog. Lit.) has recorded the inspiration his youthful mind caught from the perusal of some early sonnets by the reverend poet. The pure, the gentle, and the pathetic, abound in his poetry, and to no ear is "the dream of a village chime" more harmonious than his own. In his "History of Bremill" he gives an interesting account of church bells. "Bells, it has been said, were a late introduction into the Christian church; but respecting the common idea of their being introduced by Paulinus, Bishop of Nola, in Campania (from whence the words Noll and Campana), it is not entitled, I imagine, to much credit; nor can it be admitted that their introduction was of a very late period, when baptising them was so frequent in the eighth century, that Charlemagne, by a public ordinance, forbid 'ne clocos baptisent.' In Alet's ritual, the various mysterious applications to which they gave rise are minutely recorded. Their early introduction may be inferred from one circumstance. Epiphanius describing the Gnostic heresy, speaks expressly of the powers and princes of the air. Now, in the Roman church, one mystical use of bells was to keep 'these demoniacal powers of the air at a distance!' The ceremony of papal benediction is very curious. Holy water, salt, oil, incense, cotton, myrrh, and a crumb of bread are prepared: a procession is then made from the vestry, and the priest, instructing the people in the holiness of the art he is going to perform, sings a Miserere, blessing the holy water, &c. &c. After many ceremonies the bell-baptism is performed, by the finger dipt in oil, and the sign of the cross being made on its middle: it is then perfumed with incense, and another prayer to the Holy Spirit is read."

Note 21, Page 400, Column 1.

Combe Longa is in the patronage of Lincoln College. The curacy is held by the Rev. Charles Rose, B.D., fellow and tutor of Lincoln, whose delightful cottage residence adjoins the church.—(1830.)

Note 22, Page 400, Column 1.

John Evelyn became gentleman-commoner of Balliol College in January, 1637. By his interest, Lord Howard's ancient Marbles, the Arundeliana Marmora, were, in 1667, presented to Oxford, for which he received the "solemn thanks" of the university, and (1669) the degree of D.C.L. The famous old annalist thus sums up his character: "This Mr. Evelyn is an ingenious and polite person, and, most of all, affects a private and studious life; and was the first of those gentlemen who earliest met for the promotion and establishment of the Royal Society."

Note 23, Page 400, Column 1.

The following is the narrative of Foxe, in the third volume of his "Ecclesiastical History," respecting

"The behaviour of Dr. Ridley (bishop of London) and Master Latimer (bishop of Worcester) at the time of their death, which was the 16th of October, 1555.

"Upon the north side of the town (of Oxford) in the ditch over against Balliol College, the place of execution was appointed: and for fear of any tumult that might arise to hinder the burning of them, the Lord Williams (of Thame) was commanded by the Queen's letters, and the householders of the city, to be there assisting, sufficiently provided with guards; and, when everything was in readiness, the prisoners were brought forth by the mayor and bailiffs.

"Master Ridley had a fair black gown, furred, and faced with foins (fur of the ferret) such as he was wont to wear, being bishop, and a tippet of velvet furred likewise about his neck, a velvet nightcap upon his head, and a corner cap upon the same, going in a pair of slippers to the stake, and going between the mayor and an alderman, &c.

"After him came Master Latimer, in a poor Bristol frieze (coarse woollen) frock, all worn, with his buttoned cap, and a kerchief on his head, all ready for the fire; a new long shroud hanging over his hose, down to the feet; which at first stirred men's hearts to rue upon them (to repent of seeing them so, to be much concerned for them, or to pity them), beholding on the one side the honour they sometime had; on the other the calamity whereinto they were fallen.

"Master Dr. Ridley, as he passed (from the mayor's house where he had lodged) towards Bocardo, (a gateway of the city and a prison, over the street opposite to where now stands the Three Goats Inn), looked up where Master Cranmer (archbishop of Canterbury) did lie) hoping belike to have seen him at the glass window, and to have spoken unto him. But then Master Cranmer was busy with Friar Soto, and his fellows, disputing together, so that he could not see him through that occasion. Then Master Ridley, looking back, espied Master Latimer coming after; unto whom he said, 'Oh, be ye there?' 'Yea,' said Master Latimer, 'have after as fast as I can follow.' So he, following a pretty way off, at length they came both to the stake, the one after the other; where first Dr. Ridley, entering the place, marvellously earnestly holding up both his hands, looked towards heaven; then shortly after, espying Master Latimer, with a wondrous cheerful look he ran to him, embraced and kissed him, and, as they that stood near reported, comforted him, saying, 'Be of good heart, brother; for God will either assuage the fury of the flame, or else strengthen us to abide it.

"Then the smith took a chain of iron and brought the same about both Dr. Ridley's and Master Latimer's middles; and as he was knocking in a staple, Dr. Ridley took the chain in his hand, and shaked the same, for it did gird in his belly, and looking aside to the smith, said, 'Good fellow, knock it in hard, for the flesh will have its course.' Then his brother did bring him gunpowder in a bag, and would have tied the same about his neck. Master Ridley asked what it was. His brother said, 'Gunpowder!' 'Then,' said he, "I will take it to be sent of God, therefore I will receive it as sent of him. And have you any,' said he 'for my brother?' meaning Master Latimer. 'Yea, sir, that I have,' quoth his brother. 'Then give it unto him,' said he, 'betime, lest ye come too late.' So his brother went and carried off the samo gunpowder unto Master Latimer.

"Then they brought a faggot, kindled with fire, and laid the same down at Dr. Ridley's feet. To whom Master Latimer spake in this manner: 'Be of good comfort, Master Ridley, and play the man; we shall this day light such a candle, by God's grace, in England, as I trust shall never be put out.'

"And so the fire being given unto them, when Dr. Ridley saw the fire flaming up towards him, he cried with a wonderful loud voice, 'In manus tuas, Domine, commendo spiritum meum; Domine, recipe spiritum meum;' and after repeating this latter part often in English, 'Lord, Lord, receive my spirit.' Master Latimer crying as vehemently on the other side, 'Oh, Father of Heaven, receive my soul;' who received the flame as it were embracing of it. After that he had stroked his face with his hands, and, as it were, bathed them a little in the fire, he soon died, as it appeareth, with very little pain or none. And thus much concerning the end of this old and blessed servant of God, Master Latimer; for whose laborious travels, fruitful life, and constant death, the whole realm hath cause to give great thanks to Almighty God.

"But Master Ridley, by reason of the evil making of the fire unto him, because the wooden faggots were laid about the goss (furze) and over high built, the fire burned first underneath, being kept down by the wood. Which, when he felt, he desired them for Christ's sake to let the fire come unto him, which, when his brother-in-law heard, but not well understood, intending to rid him out of his pains (for the which cause he gave attendance), as one in such sorrow, not well-advised what he did, heaped faggots upon him, so that he clean covered him, which made the fire more vehement beneath, that it burned clean all his nether parts before it once touched the upper; and that made him leap up and down under the faggots, and often desire them to let the fire come unto him, saying, 'I cannot burn;' which, indeed, appeared well; for after his legs were consumed by reason of his struggling through the pain, (whereof he had no release, but only his contentation in God), he showed that side towards us, clean shirt and all, untouched with flame. Yet, in all this torment he forgot not to call unto God, still having in his mouth, 'Lord have mercy upon me;' intermingling his cry, 'Let the fire come unto me, I cannot burn.' In which pains he laboured, till one of the standers by with his bill pulled off the faggots above, and where he saw the fire flame up, he wrested himself unto that side. And when the flame touched the gunpowder, he was seen to stir no more; but burned on the other side, falling down at Master Latimer's feet."

Note 24, Page 400, Column 2.

In 1792, Southey became a student at Balliol; his political enthusiasm at this period has never been forgotten by his opponents. Yet, how happy may that man be deemed, whose retrospections discover no greater crime than a change of political principle! "The faults of great men are the consolation of dunces," a sentiment too often verified by Southey's foes. The late William Hazlitt has attempted a mental portrait of this distinguished writer, in his "Spirits of the Age;" and a more curious specimen of mingled bigotry, admiration, dislike, truth, and falsehood, as employed by one man in analysing the merits of another, was never, perhaps, exhibited than in his critical development of Southey's character.

Since the above remarks were written, Hazlitt himself is no more; "we could well have spared a better man." The obscure way in which he was carried to his last home was a melancholy comment on an unhappy life. There are those who think Voltaire's sarcasm on Dante not inapplicate to Hazlitt, "His reputation will now be growing greater and greater, because there is now nobody who reads him," and others who estimate him in a nobler way, and that, as Napoleon, with his code in his hand, so Hazlitt, with his life of that magnificent despot, will go down to posterity. Whatever may be said of his biography, none will deny the freshness, originality, and delightfulness, which often pervade his essays. With much wordy paradox, enormous conceit, and ineradicable bigotry, they reveal an intense love of the beautiful in the outward world, with an acute sympathy for all the mental workings of the mind within. Party and politics were his ruin; they tainted the pureness of his thoughts, distorted his views, and made hi believe himself a philanthropist, when most he became a bigot. To the oblique influence of politics, the constitutional infirmity of a bad temper must be added, and from these we may explain the unhealthy atmosphere in which his mind appears to have lived and breathed. To define Hazlitt's rank in contemporary literature is almost impossible; "Two voices are there;" the one, denying him all that learning can respect, or virtue admire; the other, a clamorous appeal for undying fame. Time, "the beautifier of the dead," will be Hazlitt's best historian. If he has been the mere effervescence of a frothy age, he will be forgotten; if, on the contrary, he has strengthened the Cause he affected to adore, there will be after memories to brighten round his fame, while

———————————— "springs
From the Castalian fountain of the heart,
The poetry of life, and all that art
Divine of words, quickening insensate things."
WORDSWORTH.

Note 25, Page 402, Column 1.

The early poets are allowed to be the most original: but whilst we admire the freshness with which their poetry is imbued, we must remember that the refinements of Life have multiplied since their day, and consequently, that what was then a single feeling, is now divided into a thousand shadowy modifications, too delicate for the sympathies of olden time to create. May we not, therefore, in some measure, console ourselves for absence of originality, by the fascinations which refined Sentiment has produced? It is to these that modern times are indebted for a galaxy of female writers—stars that never shone upon the ancient world. The social ascendancy of Woman has advanced with the progress of Christianity; and truly, when we compare the spirit of modern with ancient gallantry, we need not blush for the comparison. To the grossness of mere animal passion has succeeded an ethereality of sentiment, which, however perverted by sophism, or degraded by affectation, has, on the whole, exercised a purifying influence over modern life.

An ethical writer remarks, "The respect he feels for the virtues of woman may thus be considered almost as a test of the virtues of man." Judged by such a test, it is to be feared that both ancient and modern poets do not always appear to bright advantage. Amid a profusion of stately compliments and poetical gallantries, they have from time to time been most uncourteously inspired. Two lords of Grecian tragedy, Æschylus and Euripides, have profaned their dramas by some ugly passages which might well have been omitted. Mrs. Æchylus was evidently a virago; and the unmusical echoes of her voice must have murmured in her husband's ears, when he composed some lines in the "Agamemnon" and the "Septem;" both the Mistresses Euripides were addicted to flirtation; and hence the exaggerated vileness of female character in the "Medea" and "Hippolytus."

There are thousands who admire Horace's poetical style of love, and echo his bacchanalian sentiments on women. Others rejoice to feel themselves not amongst them. Horace, though a splendid lyrist, was a great sensualist, and, unlike Anacreon, has not always been very tasteful in his erotic allusions. A woman and a mistress are synonymous meanings in his poems; and whenever the "molle Calenum" affected his head, the "dulcium Mater sæva cupidinum" (lib. iv. ode 1,) invariably polluted his heart.

No man of humane disposition would willingly criminate the Sabine bard; but the truth must not be concealed,—he has fulminated many offensive remarks against old ladies, which have not been duly considered by those commentators who have indulged their tediousness in illustrating his style and meaning. That the ancient matrons of Rome were not so attractive as the mild old ladies in unassuming caps of the present day, it is easy to imagine. But there are some elementary principles from which we may form a judgment of a man's character in all ages and under all circumstances; it is to be regretted, therefore, that Horace has not evinced a proper respect for the venerable glory of a grey head. A wrinkle is anathematised as if it were an infamous defect, and a dim eye pronounced an odious mockery of nature. "May you live to be an old woman!" appears to have been his poetical curse towards offending damsels; and truly, if it were always fulfilled after his fashion, they must have become as luxuriantly ugly as his fertile fancy could have desired.

If we might venture to account for this unamiable obliquity in Horace's poetical creed, we should in some manner refer it to the voluptuous example of his patron Mæcenas. From the first time we read this person's name, to the present hour, a suspicion has haunted us, that he is indebted for his intellectual fame rather to the inflated adulation of poets than to the substantial truth of real character. Seneca has satirised his effeminacies; and if our memory do not fail us, Gibbon has ventured some observations which tend to demolish his "mountain" of greatness. In all probability he was the Bufo of his day, who gave good dinners, and therefore commanded the attendance of good poets to eat them.

"Proud as Apollo on his forked hill,
Sat full-blown Bufo, puff'd by every quill:
Fed with soft dedication all day long,
Horace and he went hand in hand in song."

We pass by the sarcasms against women, sprinkled over the pages of Virgil, Ovid, Catullus, Tibullus, Propertius, and others, to arrive at that ultima Thule of ferocious invective—the sixth satire of Juvenal. To us it appears neither more nor less than an obscene libel on Human Nature, utterly unworthy of the high spirit which produced the third, tenth, and thirteenth satires, in the latter of which the terrors of conscience are so sublimely depicted. That we may not be deemed arrogant in this opinion, we beg permission to quote the words of one who lived at a period of no outrageous delicacy. "This satire (sixth) is a bitter invective against the fair sex. 'Tis indeed a common place, from whence all the moderns have notoriously stolen their sharpest railleries. In his other satires, the poet has only glanced on some particular women, and generally scourged the men. But this he reserved wholly for the ladies. How they offended him I know not: but, upon the whole matter, he is not to be excused for imputing to all the vices of some few amongst them. Neither was it generously done of him, to attack the weakest as well as the fairest part of creation: neither do I know what moral he could reasonably draw from it. To bid us beware of their artifices is a kind of silent acknowledgment that they have more wit than men; which turns the satire upon us, and particularly upon the poet, who thereby makes a compliment where he meant a libel."—Dryden.

Indeed, so revolting a picture does this satire exhibit, that neither the world nor Juvenal's fame would suffer by its omission. It has all Swift's impurity, without any of his redeeming wit; and, as a moral corrective, is utterly useless. We might as reasonably expect health would be preserved by a nauseous exposition of every disease in the national hospital, as hope that Moral Beauty would be protected by parading the vilest of our depravities before the public view.

"Maxima debetur puero reverentia."—(xiv. 47.)

How did Juvenal reconcile this noble sentiment with his own practice?—The sentence may be profitably remembered by the instructors of youth in the present day.

It would be somewhat interesting to select the principal allusions to Female Character from our English poets, and endeavour to prove, that in most cases they have been tinged by the circumstances of each particular writer, whenever they tend to deterioration. In the present case, however, we can only presume on the reader's patience by quoting a few. Let us begin with Cowley, termed by Johnson "the last of the metaphysical race of poets." He has uttered but few direct impertinences against Women: but the cold indelicacy of his style and the amorous absurdity of his sentiments, almost amount to a want of gallantry. One can fancy mathematical Problems making love to each other, when we read the imaginary colloquies of Cowley and his mistress! He has compared her to every mystery above the earth, and every curiosity beneath the sun. Let the reader enjoy the following *morçeaux*. Here is a burning lover dried into Egyptian dust!

"The fate of Egypt I sustain,
And never feel the dew of rain
From clouds which in the head appear!"—

What a melancholy plight the lady alluded to in the following lines must have been:

"Her sacrifice is found without an heart,
For the last tempest of my death
Shall sigh out that too with my breath!"

"Once more upon the waters, yet once more." Confusion and fearful ruin are threatened; we should like to have seen his mistress perusing the passage below:

"Wo to her stubborn heart, if once mine come
Into the self-same room;
'Twill tear and blow up all within,
Like a grenado shot into a magazine!!"—

Mr. Galt's sublime description of Lord Byron's genius is in some measure applicable to Cowley;—"a mystery dressed in a winding-sheet, and crowned with a halo!!"

Who has equalled the heaven-like purity of Milton's description?—whether we approach the primeval loveliness of her, who

——"down to the slender waist
Her unadorned golden tresses wore;"

or the virgin majesty of "that aidless, innocent lady," whose voice came floating

——"upon the wings
Of silence through the empty-vaulted night,
At ev'ry fall smoothing the raven down
Of darkness, till it smiled!"

Yet there are many ladies in the world who denounce Milton, and allude unhandsomely to his wife, when they read that Eve was

——"all but a rib
Crooked by Nature, bent as now appears,
More to the part sinister,"—

and that Adam dared to ask,

——"*why* did God,
Creator wise, that peopled highest heaven
With spirits masculine, create at last
This novelty on earth, this fair defect
Of nature, and not fill the world at once
With men as angels, without feminine?"

We now arrive at the last of bye-gone English poets from whose works we shall select instances of ungallant poetry,—Alexander Pope. Many bitter ironies against the "fair sex" occur in Pope's writings; but the principal are contained in his celebrated "Epistle" on "the Characters of Women"—a title, by the way, in queer opposition to a line in the Poem,

"Most women have no characters at all."

In allusion to this piece, Johnson remarks, "The Characters of Men" are written with more, if not with deeper thought. In the women's part are some defects; the character of Atossa is not so neatly finished as that of Clodio; and some of the female characters may be found perhaps more frequently among men; what was said of Philomede was true of Prior. The sarcastic maxims which have offended the "ornaments of creation" are these—viz.

"Woman and fool are two hard things to hit.
In men we various[1] ruling passions find;
In women two almost divide the kind:
Those, only fix'd, they first or last obey,—
The love of pleasure, and the love of sway."

"And yet believe me, good as well as ill,
Woman's at best a contradiction still:
Heaven, when it strives to polish all it can,
Its last best work, but forms a softer man,"

We conclude with that pert blasphemy against the purity of woman which has enjoyed immortality on the lips of coxcombs and seducers:—

"Men—some to business, some to pleasure take,
But every woman is at heart a rake!"

These opinions are evidently imbued with sickliness and disappointment, and arose, perchance, from a slight on the part of Martha Blount, or from the colloquial tartness of Lady Mary Wortley, who sadly discomfited our poet at the table of their mutual friend, Lady Oxford.

"C'est que l'enfant toujours est homme,
C'est que l'homme est toujours enfant."

Lord Byron's admirers will, perhaps, admit that the general spirit of his poetry does not tend to elevate the female character. In nearly all his Heroines there is a pervading glow of sentimental wantonness, which, however attractive in the page of poetry, is by no means desirable in the intercourse of human life. His lordship evidently considered woman in no spiritual light. This view, however, was the necessary result of that misanthropic egotism which forms the soul of his poetical system. To him the world revealed no prospect of gradual progression to a better and brighter state of things: as it had ever been, so it would ever remain,—a blackened wilderness of selfish gloom. There are many who concur with him; for, as Shelley says,—

"Many heartless things are said and done,
And many brutes and men live on."

Yet are there, from time to time, glimpses of moral beauty, and loveliness, and lofty energies, and high-born hopes, and human charities, to be enjoyed by all who live and breathe the healthful air of existence. Croly has concentrated, in a few words, more than we have read elsewhere, in illustration of Lord Byron's mind:—"His moral system as a poet is founded on the double error that great crimes imply great qualities, and that virtue is a slavery. Both maxims palpably untrue; for crime is so much within human means, that the most stupendous crime may be committed by the most abject of human beings, while the man of the wildest licence is only so much the more fettered and bowed down.' This doctrine was anticipated nearly two thousand years ago by one who is called a heathen, but whose moral sentiments are often purer than those of the nominal Christian:

Nemo liber est, qui corpori servit.—SENEC. Epist. 92.

Those who think that to assume a Cain-like attitude, and wrestle with the Deity in words of doubt and defiance is freedom, will deny the sentiment. Let us hope, however, there are many who echo the words which Croly has breathed over the grave of Byron, "that living long enough for fame, he died too soon for his country."

It was our intention to have concluded this long, and, we fear, intrusive note, by a selection of passages relative to the minds and characters of women, from the works of Southey, Wordsworth, and Wilson—they whose fame

"Must share in Nature's immortality,
A venerable thing! and so their song
Should make all nature lovelier, and itself
Be loved like nature."—COLERIDGE.

Who teach us to

——————— "recognise
A grandeur in the beatings of the heart."

Whose genius surrounds us with

"A presence that disturbs us with the joy
Of elevated thoughts; a sense sublime
Of something far more deeply interfused,
Whose dwelling is the light of setting suns,
And the round ocean and the living air,
And the blue sky, and in the mind of man."

And whose philosophy illustrates the sublime words of St. Pierre, "Si l'Auteur de la nature est grand dans les grandes choses, il est très-grand dans les petites." But we will task the reader's kindness no farther, but conclude with

"Thanks to the human heart by which we live,
Thanks to its tenderness, its joys, and fears;
To me, the meanest flower that blows can give
Thoughts that do often lie too deep for tears!"

Note 26, Page 402, Column 2.

(Written in 1830.)

During the last year, some twelve or fifteen periodicals, beginning at the unambitious price of twopence, in graceful ascent to the lofty height of six shillings, have edified the public, and amused themselves, by discharging critical thunder at the head of the unfortunate transgressor alluded to in our text. Now, the first thing that must strike a reader in many of these reviews, is the sincerity of the writers! for who, when an author is glowingly depicted as "fool," and "ass," "knave," and hypocrite," "numskull," and sundry other pretty characters, can doubt a critic's earnestness? A few fastidious people, here and there scattered over the face of the literary globe, may, perchance, think these appellations a little uncourteous; and others compare the critics to those "grotesque faces in a gothic church, which grin and frown, and make such horrible distortions of visage, that you would think them the guardians of the whole building; whereas they are only excrescences, that add nothing to its strength, but disfigure it by their deformity." Still, sincerity is a rare virtue, and ought to be admitted into the very best society, however rudely apparelled.

To the noisy candour of this class of reviewers, succeeds the polite malignancy of more graceful criticism. By means of this, an author's poetry is anatomized into prose, meaning screwed into nonsense, words distorted into trash, sentiments conjured into

[1] In his "Essay on Man" he admits but one "ruling passion."

bombast, and the usual flippancies of "young gentleman," "bardling," "poetaster," &c. &c., are introduced with becoming effect. But as the subject as well as the style must be attacked, it is deemed proper to ruin the former, by blazoning forth the poetical impossibilities connected with it; or else by collecting its various parts into one ludicrous assemblage, after the manner of an auctioneer's catalogue. It cannot, however, be forgotten, that now and then a word of comfort and a line of eulogy escape the reviewer; but, ashamed of the weakness, he soon returns to a more pleasing task.

There are others connected with this laudable undertaking, acting in the double character of author and critic. Without resorting to any ungenerous surmise, their hostility may thus be explained,—a writer who had pleased the many could not of course delight "the few." Doubtless, these "few" are difficult personages to define; but as they are so frequently mentioned by their admirers, they must enjoy a respectable existence somewhere or other on the face of the earth. Happy authors! who, undegraded by a vulgar passion for present fame, fix their eyes on a bright futurity; happy posterity! that is destined to receive instruction which living times are unworthy to enjoy. Copies may remain in unsold obscurity on booksellers' shelves, and publishers' accounts prove inconvenient memorials, but *they* have that within that passeth show. A few years hence, when the false idols of the day are disenthroned and forgotten, "the few" will swell into the many, and then shall editions do justice to their fame. Thus, under the weight of unpurchased volumes, are they enabled to feel "that a thousand years after their death, the Indian on the banks of the Ganges, and the Laplander on his hills of snow, will read their works, and envy the happy clime that produced such extraordinary genius." *

Amid such distressful circumstances, a writer endowed with true delicacy would have faded into an elegant consumption, and died young, in order to be tenderly remembered. Such, however, was not the case; his health was audaciously good, and his pen as active as ever. To explain this tough pertinacity, we must suppose him to have been somewhat acquainted with the history of criticism, and to have found that from the days when Gray's Elegy was pronounced a "respectable piece of mediocrity," † to the time when Lord Byron was advised "forthwith to abandon poetry," ‡ and betake him to more profitable pursuits, similar afflictions had been constantly endured. Popularity was "vulgar fame;" praise, "absurd flattery," and religious feeling "mere cant" assumed for the occasion. Then, as now, did the great Unknown lament the decline of taste, the dearth of genius, and the nothingness of public opinion; while every author, imprudent enough to succeed, was described as the mere idol of the day, beneath the observation of the discerning "few."

May we not hope, then, that those gentlemen whose pens are prepared to demolish the present unfortunate production, seeing that they have as yet produced nothing new in critical warfare, will devise some other means for effecting an honourable purpose? For truly lamentable would it be, if, after exhausting such noble energies in the defence of true taste and feeling, a headstrong Public should decide for itself! Since mere critical blows, however violent and fierce, and constantly repeated, fail in effecting an author's annihilation, can they not contrive to invent a few immoralities, and phillipise against the hypocrisy, cant, and deceitfulness of the times? Success appears to smile on this plan; since, whatever may be the character of the critic himself, the morality of the author is indispensable. It is, doubtless, on the truth of this sentiment, that several religious periodicals have lately acted. Being a little puzzled with the Muse, they sneer at her morality; and according to the creed of *their* gospel, insinuate into the character of others what piety never admits in their own.

Let us conclude this discussion by a survey of the principal charges adduced against a writer whose volumes have sold. First in the list of offences appears—a portrait without a neckcloth! Assuredly this is a melancholy affair, inasmuch as it no more resembles the author than it does the face of Ali Pasha! And vanity, that fault which is only agreeable in ourselves, nothing but vanity, could have invented that upturned gaze! Here was a source of infinite martyrdom. One gentleman, remarkable for Byronic deficiency of cravat, considered the portrait a rivalrous attempt; while every reviewer who boasted an ugly face thought it a personal satire. It is but fair, however, to add, that any gentleman who has the misfortune to possess a copy of this portrait, by sending it to Mr. Hobday, the artist, may have his money returned, or a neckcloth supplied.

When we add to this circumstance that the author "gives no dinners," writes no critiques, corresponds with no magazine, haunts no coteries, and is subject to the weakness of being rather young,—can we wonder that he has been lampooned in periodicals, or slandered in reviews?" *

* See Gibbon's Essay on Polite Literature.

† See the London Magazine of that period.

‡ Vide Edinburgh Review.

* Lord Byron was fearfully alive to the annoyances of petty reviewers. Indignant sarcasm against the meanest Dennis who invaded his poetical renown is continually bursting forth in his correspondence. Speaking of critics in one of his letters to Murray, he says, after forbidding him to forward any more of the reviews, "These do not interrupt, but they soil the current of my mind. I am sensitive enough, but not until I am troubled." To this remark Moore has appended a note, evidently emanating from the smart which critical malignance produces:—"The petty but thwarting obstructions which are at present thrown across the path of men of real talent by that swarm of minor critics and pretenders, with whom the want of a seat in other professions has crowded all the walks in literature." Nor is it only the writers of the day who suffer from this multifarious rush into the mart; the readers, also, from having "the superficies of too many things presented to them at once, come to lose by degrees their powers of discrimination; and in the same manner as the palate becomes confused in trying various wines, so the public taste declines in proportion as the impressions to which it is exposed multiply."

To such sentiments Bruyère's remark applies:—"Quand une lecture vous élève l'esprit, et qu'elle vous inspire des sentimens nobles, ne cherchez pas une autre règle pour juger de l'ouvrage; il est bon et fait de l'ouvrage.. La Critique, après ça, peut s'exercer sur les petites choses, relever quelques expressions, corriger des phrases, parler de syntaxe," &c. &c.

Foot-note † 26, Page 402, Column 2.

(Written in 1830.)

A few months since an order issued from proprietary head-quarters, for a certain young writer to be immolated in the next number of the venerable "Blue and Yellow." In obedience to this command, several articles were prepared, all of which finally yielded to the one that was inserted, as combining a due quality of venom, with affectionate candour towards an ill-used public.

Majora canamus; let us, with modest gaze, approach the "bright excess" of this surpassing criticism. After a little uncomfortable wriggling, the reviewer works his way into the subject—Puffery. Here it is painful to add, that two or three pages are pilfered from "The Puffiad," * without any acknowledgment of the offence. After this follows a verbal analysis, rather clumsy, and by no means original. The plagiarisms are proved after the following learned manner:—A few lines, selected from various parts of the guilty production, are exhibited, in which the words "ocean," "dew," &c. &c. occur; some lines are also produced from Dryden and Lord Byron, in which similar expressions occur. Now, what is plainer, than that the former writer is convicted of plagiarism, since neither the ocean nor the dew was discerned, till Lord Byron and Dryden perceived them one day, and patronised them in their poems? This spirited hunt after plagiarisms extends through several pages, when, with a gracious smile at his own performance, the reviewer receives his pay, and bids us farewell. The hint to plagiarists, it is hoped, may prove serviceable. The advice given by a respectable old lady to her child of iniquity, in "Paul Clifford," ought not to be forgotten: "Never steal—'specially when anybody's nigh!" Yet may a question be put to this ingenious gentleman—If all *he has* pilfered from his predecessors, distilled from old magazines and encyclopædias, gathered from indices, and squeezed from the book itself under review, were combined, how much of any article he has composed, may be called his own? His critiques remind us of a circumstance in Armenia. When a poor man appears with a new coat, he is suspected to have stolen it; but if it be cleverly patched by contributions from old cloth, it is supposed to be his own!

The reviewer had evidently seen better days; though accustomed, from the blushing dawn of his talents, to perform the scrubwork of criticism, still he had occasionally spoken truth, and slept soundly after praising an author. Here, however, was a task of peculiar dirtiness, which threatened to soil even *his* hands, all accustomed as they were to menial offices. He had to grope his way through sixteen pages of lying print, and better men than he might be forgiven for not having accomplished this tiresome duty without some awkward grimaces on the road.

The critic's favourite metaphor is "a Turkey carpet:" from this it may be concluded that he is an upholsterer, haunted by the dreams of a shop; not but that an upholsterer may be a very excellent personage, though seldom, perhaps, a good critic; unless, indeed, after the manner of Addison's trunk-maker, who, it is recorded, could knock down an ox, or write a comment on the "Ars Poetica," with equal facility.

The article was a decided failure. There was, of course, a chuckle of delight among authorlings, and a yelp of applause from criticlings. Beyond this, nothing was effected. The public has a good memory on these occasions, and recollected that the same review, now employed in exposing the puff-system, had, from its infancy, invariably puffed its own coterie, from the budding statesman down to the full-blown versifier. It also appeared rather strange, that *no proofs* were produced to support an accusation; and that those who were notoriously addicted to the paragraphic vice, were suffered to remain "unknell'd, uncoffin'd, and unknown."

On a primary view of the matter, this treatment on the part of the public towards the patronising tenderness of a reviewer may appear unmerited; but when we remember that during the last fifteen years there is not a solitary instance in which the northern Review has guided public taste in conferring eminence on a writer, the matter is explained. With respect to poetry, this is especially true. All who have won reputation, it has endeavoured either to blast in their path to fame, or allowed them to be unmentioned till years had procured a popularity which required the aid of no reviewer to sustain it. Besides, there is a little impolicy in a critic's frontless assertion, that the public is a mighty Ass, easily led by the nose, wherever the popular impulse of an hour may conduct it: for, who is it but this same stultified public, that supports the very review which contemns it? In this the critic sees profound judgment and correct taste; in every other respect, the judgment of the many is altogether vain. Admirable logic! and urbane conclusion! No doubt, some literary bubbles have been puffed into popular favour, and that poetical unworthiness has been occasionally overrated. A few months, however, have redeemed the truth, and conducted Taste to her legitimate conclusions. He must, therefore, be a bigot of the very first water, and on tolerable good terms with himself, who condescends to patronise the public by assuming all judgment and taste as the inheritance of his own brains, while the many are catalogued as blockheads and dunces, never to be respected—except when they believe an oracular review!

The reviewer is, we believe, still alive, and from time to time employs himself in making mouths at distinguished men. His style is peculiarly his own:—

> For Appius reddens at each word you speak,
> And stares tremendous with a threat'ning eye
> Like some fierce tyrant in old tapestry.

His darling topic is the decline of poetry, which means, that some little abortion of his own not having sold, as a matter of course, true poetry has ceased to exist. On this subject he is known to crawl along in elegiac prose for several pages, till, suddenly pouncing on some hapless author, he grins himself into critical ecstasy:—

> All books he reads, and all he reads, assails,
> From Dryden's fables down to Durfey's tales:
> With him, most authors steal their works, or buy:
> Garth did not write his own Dispensary.

Let us, however, conclude this strange, eventful history; and let us likewise imitate the critic's atoning kindness, by expressing our regret, should any of these remarks be "painful to his feelings." Most heartily do we wish him a nobler office than

---

* A very unamiable production, concerning which the papers maintained a most disinterested silence.

that of being the hired assassin of a bigoted review.*

* The following extract from the second edition of Clarkson's pamphlet, entitled, "Robert Montgomery and his Reviewers," *London, Ridgway*, 1830, will unravel some allusions in the above note:—

"ADDRESS TO THE PUBLIC.

"The most illiberal attacks having of late been repeatedly made upon me as a publisher by certain reviewers, who, in their zeal to destroy the popularity, and with a view to account for the extensive sale of Mr. R. Montgomery's Poems, charged me with having unduly raised that author into public favour by a system of puffing, which they thus define:—1st, By the publisher having his own reviews; 2ndly, by his exchanging favours with other reviews; 3rdly, by his influencing the public opinion through the literary coteries; and, 4thly, by his bribing the periodical press; I feel myself called upon to declare (and I defy any man living to disprove the assertion), that this is a deliberate and malicious calumny. 1st, I have no review whatever; 2ndly, I have not the power of exchanging favours with other reviews, and should disdain so to use it if I had; 3rdly, I am not connected either directly or indirectly, with any of the coteries; and, 4thly, I never bribed, or paid, or offered to pay, any individual connected with the periodical press, to praise the works of Mr. Montgomery, or any other works in which I have an interest. What others may do, who notoriously possess the above means, and as notoriously use them, concerns not me. I shall, therefore, make no comment on the motives which influence these gentlemen, nor point to the corrupted source whence the venom flows; but I appeal to the public whether it is not a gross abuse of critical power, and a flagrant instance of critical injustice, thus to invade my property, and impugn my conduct on grounds which, I repeat, are at once malicious, scandalous, and false. SAMUEL MAUNDER."

"This is certainly manly and straightforward enough, and written in a tone of such honest indignation, that if the anonymous gentlemen, thus inscribed and branded, can feel anything lighter than a horsewhip, feel they must. That the shamefully dishonest practices resorted to by the junta—who, chiefly holding their brief from the Great Arch Puffer, audaciously stigmatise the whole town and country press with the charge of being bribed like themselves, called for some notice from the publisher and proprietor of Montgomery's Poems, I am quite ready to admit, nay, that a total silence on his part might have even been regarded by the 'miscellaneous rabble'—who, incompetent of comparative judgment, always consider the last and noisiest buffoon to be the victor—as amounting to an admission of the validity of these reiterated slanders. Otherwise, the whole clique are only fit to be laughed at. But I must say, he appears to me to have only half understood his case. I should really have given him credit for knowing the 'mysteries' of his profession better. He not only disclaims all connection with the reciprocally reviewing coteries, and the 'caw me, caw thee' system, but he adds with a naïveté quite amusing I should think to the gentlemen concerned (and concerned they really are), 'I never bribed, or paid, or offered to pay, any individual connected with the periodical press.' Ay, there's the rub! One of the secret motives of attack—perhaps 'the very head and front of his offending,' in the eyes of the Burlingtonians. I respect Mr. Maunder's feelings, but I am at a loss to conjecture how he could pen the sentence just quoted, and not be struck with the fact that his greatest sin was a sin of omission (i.e., 'he never bribed or paid,' &c.) Now, if he had been well read in the arcana of Burlington-street; if he had 'bribed or paid,' instead of expecting, 'good, easy man,' to reap honest fame or profit, in times like these, from honest practices, neither he nor his author would have been the objects of half the rabid abuse which has been lavished on them. Had he resorted to that golden system of puffing, befitting the present golden age of literary morals, there would have been no growling, no barking, no biting; the jealous watch-dogs of literature would have fawned and slavered on him like spaniels, and he might have plundered 'my public' with impunity. Ay, had he 'bribed or paid,' &c., he might have inundated the country with the veriest excrementitious trash that ever exuded in a fashionable novel, foamed in Millenarian delirium, or piped and snivelled in libellous and penny-trumpet imitation of the sonorous, enchanted horn of Walter Scott. He might then have been lauded to the skies for his 'public spirit and liberality,' instead of being lampooned and belied by the hungry descendants of Zoilus and Thersites."

* * * * * *

"With at least one half of the article in the 'Edinburgh Review'—all that relates to puffing—I the more cordially agree, since I was the first, or among the first, to earn the enmity of the publishing puffers, by exposing, so long back as 1822, the whole machinery of their nefarious practices in a series of papers published in a periodical, now extinct. A deep scorn of these knavish tricks is, indeed, one of the motives which determines my present stand by the side of Montgomery. All Englishmen like to see fair play. The young poet has been a bad politician with regard to the avowal of his politics; but he has been an equally bad politician with regard to puffers, of whose skill in the 'trade and mystery of picking pockets,' *he, in the 'Puffiad,' has been the most uncompromising and effectual exposer.* His frank avowal on these two points—politics and puffing—are certainly not those of a man trickily courting favour and panegyric from all quarters, as the 'Edinburgh Reviewer' insinuates. He must have strange notions, indeed, who thinks to win 'golden opinions from all sorts of people,' by knocking, right and left, all sorts of people down. But, is it not curious and suspicious, that the 'Edinburgh Review,' attacking Montgomery in an article professing to be an attack on puffing, should not advert to the circumstance, that Montgomery himself is the author of an attack on puffing, called the 'Puffiad?' There appear two reasons for this omission. *The Reviewer has borrowed the whole tenor and substance, nay, in some cases, the very words of his exposé, from the 'Puffiad,' without being so polite as to acknowledge the loan.* Whether Montgomery's publisher resorted, as warranted by the Reviewer's admitted case of exception—'self-defence,' to puff the poet's works, I have no means of knowing. I presume he adver-

Note 27, Page 404, Column 1.

See anecdotes of Heber's early life, as recorded by his widow.

Note 28, Page 404, Column 1.

"I am much amused with the preparation I see making for furnishing me with household stuff, such as table-cloths, sheets, &c. It is surely a luxurious age when a boy of seventeen requires so much fuss to fit him out. 'Sat de nugis, ad seria reverto.' My studies go on as usual. Machiavel I rather admire more than at first. My Greek studies will be soon, I fear, gravelled, if I continue at home. My brother

---

tised Montgomery as Murray advertised Byron; and Constable, Scott. Unadvised, no author of the truest genius could catch the long but shifty ear of the puff-ridden public; and his greatest luck, if even appreciated by the discerning few, would be glittering starvation—like him of old, who 'fregit subsellia versu' and 'esurit!' If, however, Montgomery's publisher did resort to puff, he deserved reproof. But my impression is otherwise.

"I have demonstrated (demonstrated here is not too strong a word), that I could not be actuated by the spirit of puff in criticising Montgomery's first works—nay, that I was in collision, rather than in collusion with it. During my wide connection with the press, I never wrote one word (for or against) on the subject of Montgomery's subsequent works. Had any unfair influence been in his favour been attempted, I think it must have come to my knowledge, either in town or provincial papers.

* * * * * *
* * * * * *

"The tenor of the criticism in the 'Edinburgh Review' might have been (as before hinted) anticipated. But it is pitiful that the great conductors of the 'Edinburgh Review' should either employ the stipendiary of a small magazine to make a collection of alleged faults, or copy his long-elaborated collectanea, with all their mistakes, mis-statements, and errata. I have admitted many of the faults imputed, and some others not imputed. But if I had only adduced those faults, and not exhibited the per contra of the account, in drawing the balance, I should feel that I deserved the reader's reproof for acting a dishonourable part. *No work of any age, could bear so unfair a test.* Could the 'Edinburgh Review?' Certainly not. Witness the reasoning of the critique before us, in which the idea is stolen from Montgomery's 'Puffiad,' and disfigured with gipsy-like ingenuity to prevent detection. The Reviewer's thus disfigured reasoning, like every other instance of integrity, consists of two halves; but one of them contradicts the other. Puffing, he says, defeats itself—this is one half. Puffing thus self-defeated, does immense injury, i.e., does not defeat itself; this is the other half. Now for his diction. While accusing Mr. Montgomery of loose expression, he says, 'Many intolerable lines of Mr. Montgomery's own.' What model of style is this? Again, after quoting nearly the worst passage in 'Satan,' he says,

"'Here we conclude. If our remarks give pain to Mr. Robert Montgomery, we are sorry for it. But at whatever cost of pain to individuals, literature must be purified from this taint.'

"What taint? This is sad slip-slop for an 'Edinburgh Reviewer.' The writer here forgets that nicety of relative grammatical construction, of a lapse in which he accuses another. These felicities may be found in the limited comments of one article, in which the critic, expecting perhaps to be criticised, is instinctively on his guard . . . . .

"Finally, as Montgomery (with unjustifiable temerity, as I have always thought) first attacked most of the gentlemen understood or admitted to be 'Edinburgh Reviewers,' their critical article can only be deemed a political rejoinder. If it be true, as confidently alleged, that the minor magazine collector of Montgomery's errors—from whom the 'Edinburgh Reviewer' has seriatim, and sometimes literatim, borrowed his examples—is the same individual, who, by a similar elaborate process, attempted to pluck, one by one, the leaves from the bay-wreath of Byron, it is a curious reminiscence, that the 'Edinburgh Review' attempted to crush in its bud that fame which the magazine writer attempted to canker in maturity.

"The 'Edinburgh Review' will permit me to wish it joy on this sympathetic uniformity of its fortune. It was its lot before to be united in the same sacred, though bruised and lacerated, fellowship of attack and defeat. Poetical critics are an obstinate tribe; too apt to be mistaken for drones in their 'Idle Hours,' they are easily teased to vindicate their character as wasps, and assert the honour of their sting. Their venomous tooth, like that of some serpents, is generally sheathed on common occasions—but, 'castigati, remordent.' It has been noticed, that the elaborately collected charges against Montgomery's poetical reputation are copied seriatim from a new periodical; the (probably deceived) proprietor and editor of which I shall not injure by naming it; the picked and garbled extracts are as unworthy of copy as reply; but among the above-named consecutive copies of alleged faults, one is curious, as it would seem to offer presumptive proof of collusive motives. In the magazine here noticed there is a perverted passage from the 'Omnipresence,' on the death of a war-horse, whose rider falls on the 'bleeding breast' of his horse, while the dying horse 'stares ghastly and grimly on the skies.' Will it be believed, that the 'Edinburgh Reviewer,' copying the garbled passage of the magazine, ask how the slain warrior, 'lying on his bleeding breast,' contrives to 'stare ghastly and grimly on the skies?' Fie! fie! this perversion is unworthy, and ungentlemanlike; and some writers, preferring the rough sincerity of truth to that bienséance, which I shall not lose sight of, would be tempted to call it mendacity and fraud, not criticism, as some readers, I lament to say, have already termed it.

"Enough has been advanced to show the quò animò of the last attacks on Montgomery. He, and all who come before the public, are 'fair game;' an anonymous rejoinder to an anonymous attack is fair; an anonymous attack on anonymous writers, though less equal, if frankly conducted, is also fair, but the fair public will never approve of any individual stabbing a long-marked victim, under the appearance of fair duello,—like that personification of devilish malice, Goethe's Mephistophiles,—beneath the arm of a deceived ally. The unfairness of quoting none but garbled passages, picked out by an ambushed enemy with leisurely malice, might irritate little minds, but it can only excite a pitying smile in 'les gens comme il faut.' Alas! for the littleness of all human pretence! It is well for real genius, that it is calm, patiently contemptuous of wilful misappre-

particularly recommends me to attend to the public lectures on astronomy and mathematics at Oxford, as he says they are at present very clever."—*Life*, by Mrs. HEBER, vol. i. pp. 22, 23.

Note 29, Page 404, Column 2.

"Notwithstanding the miseries of Fellowships on which you descant, I should like very well to have one. I cannot, indeed, conceive how an excellent society, good rooms, and the finest situation for study in the world, can have that effect in benumbing the faculties which you ascribe to it. There will, no doubt, be many illiberal men in these sort of societies; but I fear those men would have been still less gentlemen than they are at present, had it not been for the advantages of a college society. I was much entertained, my dear friend, with the account you gave of time-passing at Cambridge. 'The beef of yesterday is succeeded by the mutton of to-day,' are your words; when you show me the manner in which the Cantabs pass their time. You, indeed, who are clothed in purple, and fare sumptuously every day at the Fellows' table, would have more reason to reckon by meals than I should; for the dinners we get here, at least the commoners (for the gentlemen commoners have a table to themselves, and fare very well,) are the most beastly things that ever graced the table of a poor-house, or house of correction. (Ohe!) I write this letter in a very ill-humour at some circumstances I happen to be engaged in, which are as follows:—It is thought expedient that as I principally feel myself deficient in mathematics, I should stay in Oxford during this next vacation, in order to go through a course of lectures with the mathematical professor. This is certainly very much for a man's interest, but it will be very dull, I fear, as few Brazen-Nose men with whom I am acquainted will stay. If you could contrive to take the opportunity of this vacation at once to see Oxford, and make an old schoolfellow perfectly happy by your company for a day or two, I need not say how glad I should be. If you conveniently can, pray do come. Per hoc inane purpuræ decus precor.

"I have fagged pretty hard since I have been here, on a perfectly different plan, however, from my Neasden studies. I was very closely engaged last week with a copy of verses, as you will believe, when I tell you that I had literally no time to shave, insomuch that my beard was as long and hoary as that of the celebrated bearded king. I succeeded tolerably well in my verses, and had to read them in the hall, the most nervous ceremony I ever went through.

"I agree with you on the subject of the fabled academical leisure. We are, at Cambridge and Oxford, in the economy of time, perfect Cartesians—we admit of no vacuum. I have been through my Cheshire connections, and, through the long residence of my brother introduced to a great many people, and this has, of course, produced very numerous parties; but, I assure you, I shall preserve my character for sobriety: no man is obliged to drink more than he pleases, nor have I seen any of that spirit of playing tricks on freshmen, which we are told were usual forty or fifty years ago at the universities. Vale; si possis, veni. You seem not much to like the concerts at Cambridge; I very much approve of ours here, both as it is a rational scholarlike amusement, and as it affords a retreat, if necessary, from the bottle."—*Life*, vol. i. pp. 26—28.

Heber's first university distinction was the prize for Latin verse, gained by his "Carmen Seculare." This was followed, in 1803, by "Palestine," to which the following notices interestingly refer:—

"I know not whether I told you in my last, it is a sort of prize extraordinary for English verses—the subject, 'Palestine.' I was not aware till yesterday that the same subject had been some time since given for the Seatonian prize. I think it, on the whole, a fine one, as it will admit of much fancy, and many sublime ideas. I know not whether it ought to have been made exclusively sacred or not. Many men, whom I have talked with, seem inclined to have made it so; but I have an utter dislike to clothing sacred subjects in verse, unless it be done as nearly as possible in scriptural language, and introduced with great delicacy. I could not, however, refrain from mentioning and rather enlarging on the Messiah and the last triumphs of Judea. The historical facts of Scripture I of course made great use of, as well as of the crusades, siege of Acre, and other pieces of modern story. My brother, my tutor, and Mr. Walter Scott, the author of the 'Border Minstrels,' whom I have no doubt you know by name, if not personally, give me strong hopes; and I am, on the other hand, I hope, pretty well prepared for a disappointment. Whether the event be favourable or otherwise, I shall know in about two days, and will not fail to communicate my victory or defeat."—LIFE, vol. i. pp. 29, 30.

"In the course of its composition, Sir Walter Scott happened to breakfast with him one morning, together with his brother and one or two friends, previous to their joining a party of pleasure to Blenheim; 'Palestine' became the subject of conversation, and the poem was produced and read. Sir Walter, to whom the editor is indebted for the anecdote, said, 'You have omitted one striking circumstance in your account of the building of the temple, that no tools were used in its erection.' Reginald retired from the breakfast-table to a corner of the room, and before the party separated, produced the beautiful lines which now form part of the poem, and which were at a subsequent period, and alas! on a far different occasion, quoted by Sir Charles Edward Grey, as illustrative of the manner in which he trusted the church of Asia would arise, and in which the friend he then mourned was so admirably qualified to hasten its growth. On mounting the rostrum to recite the poem, Reginald Heber was struck by seeing two young ladies of Jewish extraction sitting in a conspicuous part of the theatre. The recollection of some lines* which reflect severely on their nation flashed across his mind, and he determined to spare their feelings by softening the passage, which he feared would give them pain, as he proceeded; but it was impossible to communicate this intention to his brother, who was sitting behind him as prompter,

ciation, and self-confiding as to ultimate results; that though prompt in proper season, it is not easily discomposed; and that it is only to the small talent of the smallest witlings, that the proverbial fallacy of talented irritability can justly apply."—CLARKSON'S *Pamphlet*, p. 156—60.

* "Oh, lives there one who mocks his heartless zeal!
Too proud to worship, and too wise to feel?
Be his the soul with wintry reason blest,
The dull, lethargic sovereign of the breast!
Be his the life that creeps in dead repose,
No joy that sparkles, and no tear that flows."

and who, on the attempt being made, immediately checked him, so that he was forced to recite the lines as they were originally written.—*Life*, pp. 30, 31.

Note 30, Page 404, Column 2.

An eloquent article on Heber's Hymns in "Blackwood's Magazine," and from the beautiful diction that pervades it, apparently written by Wilson, contains an affecting allusion to the recitation of "Palestine."

"None who heard Reginald Heber recite his 'Palestine' in that magnificent theatre, will ever forget his appearance, so interesting and impressive. It was known that his old father was somewhere sitting among the crowded audience, when his universally admired son ascended the rostrum; and we have heard that the sudden thunder of applause that then arose so shook his frame, weak and wasted by long illness, that he never recovered it, and may be said to have died of the joy dearest to a parent's heart. Reginald Heber's recitation, like that of all poets we have heard recite, was altogether untrammelled by the critical laws of elocution, which were not set at defiance, but either by the poet unknown or forgotten; and there was a charm in his somewhat melancholy voice, that occasionally faltered, less from a feeling of solemnity, and even grandeur of the scene of which he was himself the conspicuous object, though that feeling did suffuse his pale and ingenuous countenance, than from the deeply felt sanctity of his subject, comprehending the most awful mysteries of God's revelations to man."

(Written in 1830.)

A Magazine,

"That grins immensely at its own sagacity,"

some time since informed its readers, that the present writer had "written for the Newdigate and failed." It would be needless to contradict this and similar atrocious absurdities, were there not an imbecile race in the world of letters always prompt to believe what is absurd, and to quote what is malicious. For their benefit, be it remarked,—without the faintest sneer at a poem which Heber consecrated, and Milman has adorned,—that the glorious uncertainty of the "Newdigate" has not been endured by the present author; nor is it probable that it ever will.

In the course of this volume incidental allusions have been made to contemporary criticism; no candid reader will mistake or misapply them. It would be a censorious foppery for any man, whatever his rank in literature, to express unlimited contempt for an art in which many of the most accomplished and profound scholars of the day are engaged; and laughable bigotry to deny the wit, eloquence, and brilliancy, from time to time exhibited in our modern reviews. But while we allow the excellences of criticism, we cannot be blind to the theoretic dulness, flimsy sarcasm, and monotonous twaddle, which distinguish a great part of it. Of late, a new class of critics has arisen, composed chiefly of bankrupt prosers, and miscellaneous rhymers, whom Pope has christened, "Grub-street poets run to seed."* At present they are trying an experiment with public taste,—whether "criticism," diseased with prejudice, and bloated with vulgarity, will be popularly relished, and meet with success. Their whole power consists in noise and nonsense, and with these they make a most industrious rattle from week to week and month to month.

But let no reader consider these remarks as intended to excite indignation against a mournful race of men, who are too often compelled to eat the bread of infamy, and, under the name of critics, unite the double character of poltroons and maligners. Rather let him change contempt into the Christian feeling of pity. For are they not to be pitied, who are born—wretched—and die? He may indeed, on observing the swagger of their style, and the mock-heroism exhibited in their "defence of public taste,"—imagine them to be the happiest fellows alive. Yet were he to single one out of the herd for minute observation, how often would he discover him to be a shrivelled unfortunate, gnawed by disappointment, or jaundiced by despair!—one who has indeed been a writer of all work—the Helot of literature. Tragedies that were never acted, poems that were never read, and novels that were never sold, are his to claim. He has murdered for morning papers, and set houses on fire for evening journals, and yet remains unknown. Amid such disasters, let a generous mind pause ere it condemn him whom circumstances have twisted into a degenerate hireling. When the petty rivalries of the hour are forgotten, and truth alone is remembered, the retrospections of such a character are by no means enviable. To him belongs not the smile of the good, nor the friendship of the great: as he has lived to be degraded, so will he die to be forgotten.

——————— "be one poet's praise,
That not in fancy's maze he wander'd long,
But stoop'd to truth, and moralised his song,
Laugh'd at the loss of friends he never had,
The dull, the proud, the wicked, and the mad;
The tale revived, the lie so oft o'erthrown,
Th' imputed trash, and dulness not his own."

Note 31, Page 404, Column 2.

"When Reginald Heber returned from the theatre, surrounded by his friends, with every hand stretched out to congratulate, and every voice raised to praise him, he withdrew from the circle; and his mother, who, impatient of his absence, went to look for him, found him in his room, on his knees, giving thanks to God, not so much for the talents which had, on that day, raised him to honour, but that those talents had enabled him to bestow unmixed happiness on his parents."—*Life*, vol. i. p. 33.

The following sketch of Heber by a contemporary, while residing in the university, after his political triumph, will be read with deep interest.

"At a time when, with the enthusiasm of the place I had rather caught by heart than learnt "Palestine," and when it was a privilege of any one of any age to know Heber, I had the delight of forming his acquaintance. I cannot forget the feeling of admiration with which, in the autumn of 1803, I approached his presence, or the surprise with which I contrasted my abstract image of him with his own simple, social, every-day manner. He talked and laughed like those around him, and entered into the pleasures of the day with them, and with their relish; but when any higher subject was introduced, (and he was never slow to introduce literature at least, and to draw from his exhaustless memory riches of every kind,) his manner became his own. He never looked up at

* Bad poets become malevolent critics, just as weak wine turns to vinegar.—SOUTHEY.

his hearers, but with his eyes downcast and fixed, poured forth in a measured intonation, which from him became fashionable, stores of every age; the old romances; Spenser; some of our early prose writers; of Scott's published works; or verses of his own. I speak not of one day only, but of my general recollection of his habits as after that day witnessed often. Even at this time, however, he was a very severe student, and made up in hard reading at night, the time given to society and lighter pursuits in the evening."—*Life*, pp. 345—348.

Note 32, Page 405, Column 1.

A beautiful letter, descriptive of Heber's character in India, must not be omitted in these biographical illustrations:—

"My Lord,—I know not how to refrain from venturing in some allusion to the general sentiments of deep interest and lively gratification excited by your lordship's visit to this place (Benares), and the very sincere regrets which have followed your departure. Of all the pleasing impressions which your lordship has left to commemorate your brief sojourn amongst us, I will not here presume to speak; but I may hope your lordship will not be displeased with the brief assurance that your visit has been productive of much good in this community, in points essentially connected with those high and sacred interests which are so peculiarly under your charge, and even so near to all the movements of your heart. For the mention of my own individual share in the grateful impressions your lordship has diffused amongst us, I will hope to have found an admissible excuse with your lordship, while I ascribe some portions of it to associations awakened by your presence, recalling to my mind the days of other times, the scenes of my youth, and of my native land; and many a recollection of no light or ordinary interest, to one who has wandered so far and so long from the dulce domum of his early life. Your lordship will readily conceive how this might be; and thus it will hardly seem strange to you, that the strains of pious and holy instruction, which fixed so impressive a record of our first visitation by a protestant prelate on the minds of us all, should have spoken with peculiar emphasis to one, who, after many a year of toil and exile in a foreign clime, recognised in the accents which now preached the word of the living God, amid the favourite abodes of heathen idolatry, that self-same voice, which in the days of youthful enthusiasm, and ardent and undamped fancy, had poured on his delighted ear the lay that sung the sacred theme of the Redeemer's hand, amid the long-loved haunts of his Alma Mater; amid the venerated temples of the religion of our fathers. But let me not give a licence to my pen, which may seem to bespeak me forgetful of the high value of your lordship's time. Permit me, my lord, to conclude with unfeigned and most fervent wishes for your long enjoyment of health and vigour, for the gratification of all the hopes with which you contemplate the interesting journey before you, and for the success of every plan which you may form for the advancement of those concerns of eternal moment which have been so happily entrusted to your lordship's care.

"I remain, my lord,
"Most respectfully and sincerely yours,
"Norman Macleod."

(*Life*, pp. 242—244.)

PART II.

Note 33, Page 410, Column 2.

The sublime hopes which are awakened by the circulation of the Scriptures suggest the name of one, whose pure spirit now brightens in the presence of his Maker, but whose memory lives in the hearts of all who revere the faith of an apostle, and the devotion of a martyr,—Henry Martyn, late fellow of St. John's College, Cambridge. He who can peruse the biography of his glorious mind—as exhibited amid fearful toils and Christian labours, in a far and deathful clime—without emotion, must be "more or less than man."

"By him, and by his means, part of the Liturgy of the Church of England, the Parables, and the whole of the New Testament, were translated into Hindoostanee! By him, and by his means, also, the Psalms of David and the New Testament were rendered into Persian! By him also the prophet of Mecca was daringly exposed, and the truths of Christianity openly vindicated, in the very heart and centre of a Mahometan empire!—Surely, as long as England shall be celebrated for that pure and apostolical church, of which he was so great an ornament, the name of the subject of this memoir will not wholly be forgotten; and whilst some shall delight to gaze on the splendid sepulchre of Xavier, and others choose rather to ponder over the granite stone which covers all that is mortal of Schwartz; there will not be wanting those who will think of the humble and unfrequented grave of Henry Martyn." —*Memoir* by Sargent.

Note 34, Page 411, Column 2.

To atone for the jealousies which too often disgrace the annals of mind, a delightful train of literary friendships may be adduced. Those familiar with intellectual biography will recall the names of Scipio and Lælius, Erasmus and Sir Thomas More, Montaigne and Charron, Petrarch and Boccaccio, Beaumont and Fletcher, Addison and Steele, West and Gray. Cowley has a beautiful allusion to a literary friendship:—

"Say, for ye saw us, ye immortal lights!
How oft unwearied have we spent the nights,
Till the Ledean stars, so famed for love,
Wonder'd at us from above.—

"We spent them not in toys, in lust, or wine,
But search of deep philosophy,
Wit, eloquence, and poetry;
Arts which I loved, for they, my friend, were thine."

This passage is matched by one in Persius:

"Tecum etenim longos memini consumere soles,
Et tecum primas epulis decerpere noctes.
Unum opus, et requiem pariter disponimus ambo,
Atque verecunda laxamus seria mensa."
Sat. v. 40—44.

Note 35, Page 415, Column 1.

"At the dissolution, the great bell at Christ's Church, commonly called 'Tom,' was taken from the tower of the monastery of Osney; it was then placed in the campanile of the tower of Christ Church Cathedral, whence it was removed to its present situation, after the completion of the tower by Sir Christopher Wren. Prior to its being recast, it bore the following inscription: 'In Thomæ laude resona Bim Bom sine fraude;' its present inscription is, 'Magnus Thomas Oxoniensis.'"—*Vide* SKELTON'S *Oxonia Antiqua Restaurata.*

Note 36, Page 416, Column 1.

Chatterton,

———— "The marvellous boy,
The sleepless soul that perish'd in its pride."

Midnight studies and midnight agonies were not unknown to him. Poor, proud, and persecuted, alone in the wilderness of London, with a genius restless as it was extraordinary,—how often did the daylight shine upon his sunken brow and shattered frame! Kirke White was equally a victim to the fascinations of midnight study. Several pathetic allusions to this fatal luxury are sprinkled over his productions. In a poem entitled "Time," he exclaims—

"The night's my own; they cannot steal my night!
When ev'ning lights her folding star on high
I live and breathe: and in the sacred hours
Of quiet and repose, my spirit flies,
Free as the morning, o'er the realms of space."

While on the subject of Chatterton and Kirke White, may we venture to add, that the mind of the former was of far more original grasp than that of the latter; yet how different have been their poetical destinies! The beauty of White's moral has reflected a brightness over his intellectual character; and it is well for mankind that it has done so; for virtue is worth a thousand talents.

Lord Orford has thus appreciated the genius of Chatterton:

"His life should be compared with the powers of his mind, the perfection of his poetry, his knowledge of the world, which, though in some respects erroneous, spoke quick intuition; his humour, his vein of satire, and, above all, the amazing number of books he must have looked into, though chained down to a laborious and almost incessant service, and confined to Bristol, except at most for the last five months of his life; the rapidity with which he seized all the topics of conversation then in vogue, whether of politics, literature, or fashion; and when, added to all this mass of reflection, it is remembered that his youthful passions were indulged to excess, faith in such a prodigy may be well suspended; and we should look for some secret agent behind the curtain, if it were not as difficult to believe that any man who possessed such a vein of genuine poetry would have submitted to lie concealed, while he actuated a puppet; or would have stooped to prostitute his muse to so many unworthy functions. But nothing in Chatterton can be separated from Chatterton. His ablest flight, his sweetest strains, his grossest ribaldry, and his most commonplace imitations of the productions of magazines, were all the effervescences of the same ungovernable impulse, which, chameleon-like, imbibed the colours of all it looked on. It was Ossian, or a Saxon monk, or Gray, or Smollett, or Junius; and if it failed most in what it most affected to be, a poet of the fifteenth century, it was because it could not imitate what had not existed."

Note 37, Page 416, Column 1.

"Solitude and society may be illustrated by a lake and a river. In the one, indeed, we can view the heavens more calmly and distinctly; but we can also see our image more clearly, and are in danger of the sin of Narcissus; while in the river, the view both of the heavens and ourselves is more broken and disturbed; but health and fertility is scattered round."—*From* WOLFE'S *Juvenile Papers.* "Removed from the soft intercourse of domestic life, our feelings are not mellowed into that tendency which is so congenial to the spirit of Christian love. Living in solitude, the undisputed lords of our dwelling, and with no inclinations to consult but our own, the harshness of our tempers is not worn down by collision, nor the selfishness of our dispositions subdued by the habit of our yielding to the wishes of others."—BENSON'S *Hulsean Lectures.*—20th.

A BIOGRAPHICAL SUMMARY OF EMINENT CHARACTERS CONNECTED WITH THE UNIVERSITY.

IN compiling the following summary, which it is presumed will not be found useless as a literary reference, the author was greatly indebted to Chalmers' list, extracted from the "Athenæ," and other collegiate records. His acknowledgments are also due to Mr. Skelton, whose magnificent work, "Pietas Oxoniensis," is alike honourable to his genius and his country.

MERTON COLLEGE.*

FOUNDED IN 1264.

Duns Scotus; John Wickliffe; Sir Thomas Bodley; Sir Henry Savile; the pious John Hales; William Harvey (discoverer of the circulation of the blood); Bradwardine and Islip, Archbishops of Canterbury;

* Wood, in his "Athenæ," mentions the following curious customs as existing at this college in his time:—

"There are various fires of charcole made in the common Hall, on All Saints' Eve, &c. &c. At all these fires every night, which began to be made a little after five of the clock, the senior under-graduates would bring into the Hall the juniors, or freshmen, and make them sit down on a forme in the middle of the Hall, joining to the declaimer's desk; which done, every one in order was to speak some pretty apothegme, or make a jest, or bull, or speak some eloquent nonsense, to make the

Hooper, the martyred Bishop of Gloucester; Dr. Jewell, of Salisbury; Dr. Carleton, of Chichester; and Grimoald, poet; Heywood, ditto; Dr. Goulston; Sir Isaac Wake; Dr. Bainbridge; Devereux, Earl of Essex; Farnaby; Francis Cheynell; Samuel Clarke, the orientalist; Hugh Cressy, the Roman-catholic historian; Anthony Wood, the Oxford historian; Sir Richard Steele, at one time postmaster here; Beresford, the author of that amusing work, "The Miseries of Human Life;" and Dr. Edward Nares, the Burghley historian, &c.

UNIVERSITY COLLEGE.

FOUNDED IN 1280.

Prelates.—Walter Skirlaw, Bishop of Durham, ob. 1405; Richard Flemming, Bishop of Lincoln, and founder of Lincoln College; John Sherwood, Bishop of Durham; Ridley, the martyr, sometime fellow here, afterwards of Cambridge; Dr. Tobie Matthew, Archbishop of York; Bancroft, Bishop of Oxford; Potter, Archbishop of Canterbury, and author of "Grecian Antiquities," &c. &c.; Dr. C. Littleton, Bishop of Carlisle, and President of the Society of Antiquaries; Bishop Jeremy Taylor.

Richard Stannyhurst, poet and critic; the learned family of the Digges; Leonard and Thomas, mathematicians; Sir George Croke, chief-justice of England; Lord Herbert of Cherbury; General Langbaine, the first biographer of dramatic writers; Dr. Dudley Loftus, the oriental scholar; Dr. John Hudson, keeper of the Bodleian library; Flavel, the nonconformist; Dr. Radcliffe, afterwards of Lincoln; Rev. Joseph Bingham, author of "Origines Ecclesiasticæ;" William Elstob; Carte, the historian, took his first degree here, previously to his removing to Cambridge; Jago, the poet, and friend of Shenstone; Sir Robert Chambers, Vinerian Professor in 1777; Sir William Jones, whose monument by Flaxman was presented to his college by Lady Flaxman; Sir Roger Newdigate, the founder of the "Newdigate Prize;" Lord Eldon, the late Lord High Chancellor of England; Lord Stowell; and Shelley.

---

company laugh; but if any of the freshmen came off dull, or not cleverly, some of the forward or pragmatical seniors would tuck them—that is, set the nail of their thumb to their chin, just under their lip, and, by the help of their other fingers under the chin, would give them a mark, which would sometimes produce blood!"—On Shrove Tuesday, Feb. 15, (1647), we are told that "brass pots full of caudle, at the freshmen's charge, after the Hall was free from the fellowes, was brought up and set before the fire. Afterwards, every freshman, according to seniority, was to pluck off his gowne and band, and, if possible, to make himself look like a scoundrell. This done, they were conducted, each after the other, to the high table, and there made to stand on a form placed thereon; from whence they were to speak their speech with an audible voice, to the company; which, if well done, the person that spoke it was to have a cup of caudle, and no salted drinke; but if dull, nothing was given him but salted drinke, or salt put in college beer, with tucks to boot. Afterward, when they were to be admitted into the fraternity, the senior fellow was to administer to them an oath, over an old shoe, part of which runs thus:—Item tu juratis quod Penniless," &c. &c.

(1830.)

[*Note.*—Moore says that Shelley's life was "a bright but erroneous dream." Bright, indeed, as to what it hoped, but dark and dismal in all that it experienced! The writer of this has obtained some biographical recollections relative to Shelley's character and conduct at Oxford; and to the conclusion of this note is appended a sketch by his accomplished friend and relative, Medwin, and also a record from the pen of one thoroughly acquainted with Shelley's life while at college. Those who admire genius, but lament its desecration, will be gratified by a fact alluded to in Medwin's remarks—viz., that Shelley never intended the publication of "Queen Mab," and that his maturer years regretted the deadly spirit of scepticism which polluted the notes of the first edition. A late biographer (vide the memoir attached to the "Beauties of Shelley") talks of his attacking "the commonly received notions of the being of a God." This may be charity, but is by no means truth. The pamphlet here alluded to was entitled, "The Necessity of Atheism," and, in harmony with some of the doctrines in the notes to "Queen Mab," was imbued with odious and horrible sentiments. The university has been unwisely and unjustly censured by certain writers, for its expulsion of Shelley on the appearance of his pamphlet. They have talked about liberality, but have shown none. Strange and unnatural as it may appear to their views, there are many in Oxford who think that a university, based on the immortal truths of the Gospel, ought not to license and encourage blasphemy, however gilded by genius. Had Shelley privately consulted with his seniors, he might not have escaped censure, yet he certainly would have received advice and warning; but when he openly dared the university, and violated the whole spirit of her discipline, by the publication of an atheistic pamphlet, there remained but one course to be promptly and peremptorily pursued.

With regard, however, to the reviews which afterwards appeared on Shelley's poems, there can be but one opinion with an honest mind.

Periodicals were then in their mid-noon glory; they held a kind of papal dominion over the taste and poetical creed of their readers; they could shout nonsense into fame, or hiss genius into obscurity, when and where they pleased. Shelley was a fine subject for their abuse. Under the mask of saintly enthusiasm, they could attack the man, and, by a mean and merciless style of criticism, they could contrive to dissect his poems into trash and absurdity. Shelley's poetry has no flesh and blood in it; it is all ethereality and disembodied mind: his utterances are those of a lone, lofty, and melancholy spirit, too sublime for the many, and too obscure for the worshippers of homely truth and external realities. It was easy, therefore, to distort his language, to cloud his meaning, and to present the author of "The Cenci" to the public eye as a mass of poetical deformity, only to be seen in order to be shunned.

This was not the way to reclaim a great but erring soul—the malice and envy of these writers were too palpable—yet the effect on the public was prodigious. Shelley was exiled, and his after works fell dead from the press.

But the time of re-action has come, and the venal tyranny of reviews is over, It is no longer deemed requisite that in order to be read, an author must be a member of a clique which directs a review; in short, it has been discovered that critics, like the popes, are not infallible; and the proscribed Shelley has been brought back to the admiration of his country, in glory and triumph. Lamenting, as all do, who think that one ray of genuine Christianity will do more to enlighten the hopes and destiny of man than all the blaze of genius apart from this, they will peruse the pages of Shelley with mixed and mournful thought; yet a benevolent spirit will delight to gaze on the brightness rather than the darkness of a genius, whose works are too far removed from the toil and turbulence of daily life ever to be popular, or hold a Shaksperian sway over the feelings of the general mind.

"Like hues and harmonies of evening,
Like clouds in starlight widely spread,
Like memory of music fled,
Like aught that for its grace may be
Dear, and yet dearer for its mystery."

These lines, from his "Hymn to Intellectual Beauty," might be said to describe the evanescent magic of Shelley's poetry. His soul dwelt apart from the coarseness and sternness of actual life, amid the bright and exquisite conceptions of an imagined world. Never was there a mind more enamoured of the beautiful, or a heart more attuned to sympathy with all that is sublime in nature, or profound in man. His odes rouse the dead feelings into a glorious life, and many of his dramatic passages reveal to us the gloom, the glory, and the agony of human destiny, with a startling apocalypse, and with an awful truth. Milton himself scarcely surpassed him in the full and faultless harmony of his numbers, and the magical richness of his language. But "Adonais" is

——— "fled!
Like some frail exhalation, which the dawn
Robes in its golden beams!"—

and it were vain to speculate to what an exaltation and holy change of sentiment a spirit like his might have arrived; many of his doubts might have been dispelled; many of the harsh thoughts which occasionally jangled the melodious chords of his mind might have vanished, and Shelley might have stood forth in the unclouded majesty of genius, had it pleased Him, to whom the fiat of life and death belongs, to have spared him. As it is, we can only say, peace to the young, the gifted, and the dead!]

The following is Medwin's brief recollection of Shelley:—

"Shelley was sent to University College because his father, Sir Timothy, had been at that college, and Sir Philip Sidney a benefactor of it. He was only seventeen when he went there, and kept very few terms—not more than three, I think. His studies were anything but academical—German, chemistry, electricity. He used to charge the lock of the door, to give the scout a shock, laughing immoderately thereat. Though a tolerably good Latin scholar, he knew at that time little Greek, reading Plato (afterwards his constant companion) through a French translation. Although there were many Etonians of his standing at Oxford, he sought the acquaintance of none. The only one of his fellow collegiates with whom he was intimate was Hogg, who entertained congenial opinions with him on metaphysical subjects, and was expelled with him, for having been partly the author of a treatise called the "Necessity of Atheism." This silly work was enclosed by Shelley to the heads of colleges, the examining masters, and, I believe, the bench of bishops; the letter containing a challenge to argue the non-existence of a God in the schools. The consequence of such a step was obvious; he was called before his tutor, and, refusing to retract, was expelled.

"At Oxford he printed (I think at Parker's) a volume of poems, called the "Posthumous Works of my Aunt Peg Nicholson,"* and wrote a Romance, entitled, 'St. Irvyn, or the Rosicrucian,' of which no copy, I imagine, exists. There are several short poems interspersed in the volume; I send you one as a specimen. The first lines are imitated from Byron's lines, beginning 'Shades of the dead,' &c., in the 'Hours of Idleness.'

"Shelley also began 'Queen Mab' at Oxford.

"He never sanctioned the publication of this extraordinary poem. It was, in fact, printed from the manuscript that fell accidentally into the hands of the publisher; and there exists a copy of the first edition, corrected by the hand of Shelley himself, containing most important alterations and corrections, and additions, which would show how materially he had modified his opinions. This revision was made at Marlow.

"Shelley's character has been much misunderstood. His whole life was one aspiration for the good of his species. Whether his writings have such a tendency is another question; but they are too sublimated and noble to make many proselytes—they escape common understandings—however the glittering veil of his poetry may render attraction to a few of his abstractions.

"I remember, as though I saw him yesterday, even at this time, the fearlessness of his nature contrasted strangely with his slight, boyish, almost feminine appearance. Shelley more resembled Rousseau than any other writer. But Rousseau's object was to excite wonder by paradox. Not so Shelley. However mistaken might be his philosophy, he was sincere in it!

"I copy the lines, as promised:—

'Ghosts of the dead! have I not heard your yelling
Rise on the night-rolling breath of the blast
When o'er the dark ether the tempest is swelling,
And on eddying whirlwind the thunder-peal past?

'For oft have I stood on the dark height of Jura,
Which frowns on the valley that opens beneath;
Oft have I braved the chill night tempest's fury,
Whilst around me, I thought, echo'd murmurs of death.

'And now, whilst the winds of the mountain are howling,
O father! thy voice seems to strike on mine ear;
In air, whilst the tide of the night-storm is rolling,
It breaks on the pause of the element's jar.

'On the wing of the whirlwind which roars o'er the mountain,
Perhaps rides the ghost of my sire who is dead;
On the mist of the tempest which hangs o'er the fountain,
Whilst a wreath of dark vapour encircles his head!

"T. Medwin."

* "Posthumous Fragments of Margaret Nicholson." Printed and published by Munday & Slatter.

"OXFORD, *Dec.* 18, 1833.

"DEAR SIR,—I at last sit down to give my long promised sketch of Shelley at Oxford. The present is perhaps the most fitting time, as it may serve to illustrate your third edition of 'Oxford.'

"Mr. Percy Bysshe Shelley was brought to Oxford by his father, now Sir Timothy Shelley, at a very tender age, 'tis true, but with a highly cultivated understanding. He placed him at his own college (University), and Sir Timothy himself, not liking the accommodations of an inn, went to his old quarters, and remained a few days at the house he had formerly lodged at, when himself at the university, and near the Angel inn. It was a house rendered remarkable from its having a leaden horse,* and two large leaden ornaments, or flower-pots, on the balcony, emblematical of the trade of a plumber, and the last remnants of the sort in Oxford. While lodging there with the son of his former host, he made anxious inquiries respecting the family of his departed old friend, as he was pleased to style him, and learned that one of the sons was about embarking as partner with a bookseller and printer. Thither Sir Timothy repaired with his son, and gave him a particular injunction to buy whatever he required in books and stationery of the aforesaid parties. Sir Timothy, moreover, said, 'My son here,' pointing to him, 'has a literary turn; he is already an author, and do pray indulge him in his printing freaks.' One of the works alluded to was his Romance of 'St. Irvyn; or, the Rosicrucian.' He soon put the parties to the test, by writing some fugitive poetry, entitled, 'Posthumous Fragments of Margaret Nicholson,' a work almost still-born, and directing the profits to be applied to Peter Finnerty. The ease with which he composed many of the stanzas therein contained, is truly astonishing. When surprised with a proof from the printers in the morning, he would frequently start off his sofa, exclaiming, that that had been his only bed, and on being informed that the men were waiting for more copy, he would sit down and write off a few stanzas, and send them to the press, without even revising or reading them. This I have myself witnessed.†

* * * * * *

"About this same period he wrote a novel (in conjunction, I have since learned, with Mr. Hogg, of the same college), entitled, 'Leonora,' which was commenced at the same press, but the printers refused to proceed with it, in consequence of discovering that he had interwoven his free notions throughout the work, and at the same time strongly endeavoured to dissuade him from its publication altogether; but this was disregarded, and he afterwards took the copy to Mr. King, the printer at Abingdon, who had nearly completed the work, but was stopped in its further progress, by the circumstance of Mr. Shelley's expulsion from Oxford, with his friend and associate, Mr. Hogg.

"Mr. Shelley's various publications caused him frequently to call on his printers, with whom he entered freely into conversation; they therefore felt a most anxious solicitude for his welfare, and used more than ordinary endeavours to reclaim the waywardness of his imagination; and, on one occasion in particular, they applied to a literary friend,* then residing in Oxford, to meet him, in order to canvass and combat his extraordinary opinions. They appeared to make a strong impression at the time; but, as a well known writer expresses,—

> 'He that's convinced against his will,
> Is of the same opinion still.'

The same gentleman also undertook to analyse his arguments, and endeavour to refute them philosophically, which he afterwards did at considerable length; but Mr. Shelley said, 'that he would rather meet any or all the dignitaries of the church, than one philosopher,' and ultimately refused to reply in writing to the philosophical arguments adduced by this writer.

"The pamphlet for which Mr. Shelley was expelled his college was entitled, 'The Necessity of Atheism,'† and he himself strewed the shop windows and counters of his bookseller in Oxford, unknown to them, but gave instructions to their shopman to sell them as fast as he could, and at the charge of sixpence each. Shortly afterwards, a judicious friend of the booksellers, a fellow of a college,‡ dropped in, and was attracted, by the novelty of the title, to examine the contents of the pamphlet. He immediately desired to see one or both the principals, and at once inveighed against the dangerous tendency of such a pamphlet, and advised the destruction of them forthwith. This was immediately complied with, and they proceeded into a back kitchen and burned them, in this gentleman's presence. At the same time, these booksellers sent a request to Mr. Shelley, to be allowed a few minutes' conversation with him at their house; he came instanter, and it so happened that Councillor Clifford, of O.P. notoriety, was in the house, and being made acquainted with the subject, and at the earnest request of the booksellers, undertook, in conjunction with the parties above named, to use his best endeavours by entreaties, till entreaty seemed of no avail, and next by threats, to dissuade him from the error of his ways, for the sake of himself, his friends, and connections. All seemed of no avail; he appeared to glory in the course he had adopted, and said that he had sent a copy of his pamphlet to every bishop in the kingdom, to the vice-chancellor, and the other heads of houses in Oxford, and other dignitaries, addressing them under the fictitious signature of 'Jeremiah Stukeley.'

"I am, Sir, your obedient servant,

"HENRY SLATTER."

* This said horse has been the subject of frequent hoaxes to unwary *freshmen*, many of whom have applied, booted and spurred, anxious to ride a horse that has been so much extolled for its beauty and gentleness.

† The asterisks here are intended to denote certain remarks, which, as they related to pecuniary matters, may be wisely omitted.

* Mr. Hobbes, author of "The Widower," a poem.

† Printed at Worthing, by C. & W. Phillips, to whom a friendly hint was sent by Munday & Slatter, warning them of the dangerous tendency of disseminating such vile principles, and the liability they ran of a prosecution by the attorney-general, at the same time advising the destruction of every remaining copy, together with the MS. copy, types, &c.

‡ The Rev. John Walker, B.C.L., Fellow of New College, and afterwards Vicar of Hornchurch, Essex, editor of the "Oxoniana," 4 vols.; "A Selection of curious Articles from the Gentleman's Magazine;" 4 vols.; and some other valuable works, also, the author of a pamphlet, entitled, "Curia Oxoniensis."

BALIOL COLLEGE.

FOUNDED IN 1282.

Prelates.—Morton, Archbishop of Canterbury, and second perpetual chancellor of the university; Dr. John Douglas, Bishop of Salisbury, who detected the impostures of Lauder and Bower, and ably advocated the miracles of the Christian faith.

Humphrey, Duke of Gloucester, founder of the Bodleian; John Tiptoft, Earl of Worcester, who presented some valuable MSS. to the university; the celebrated lawyers, Sir John Popham, Lord Coventry, Sir Humphrey Davenport, and Sir Robert Atkyns; Dr. Thomas Holland; Tobias Crisp, founder of the Antinomian sect; John Evelyn; Dr. Charles Davenant, son of the poet; Dr. David Gregory; Keil and Bradley, the Astronomers; Dr. William King; Hutchins, the historian of Dorsetshire; James West, President of the Royal Society; Robert Southey, Poet Laureate, &c. &c.; Lockhart, editor of the Quarterly, &c. &c.; C. Girdlestone; C. T. Collins; J. Campbell, &c.

EXETER COLLEGE.

FOUNDED IN 1314.

Prelates.—Dr. Bayley, Bishop of Bangor, author of "The Practice of Piety;" Dr. Prideaux, Bishop of Worcester; Dr. Bull, Bishop of St. David's, one of the ablest champions of our church; and Archbishop Secker.

John de Trevisa, translator of Higden's "Polychronicon;" Sir John Fortescue, the eminent lawyer; Sir George More; Browne, the poet, author of "Britannia's Pastorals;" Robert Hayman, a poet of less renown; Lord Falkland; Sir John Doddridge; Sir William Noy, attorney-general; Sir Anthony, Nicholas, and Thomas Fitzherbert; Diggory Wheare, first Camden Professor; James, Duke of Hamilton, beheaded for his attachment to Charles I.; Dr. Arthur Duck; Lord Chief Justice Rolle; Sir Simon Baskerville; Joseph Caryll, the commentator on the book of Job; John Poulett, Marquis of Winchester, whose epitaph Dryden writ, as Milton did that of the Marchioness; Thomas Brancker, mathematician; Lord Shaftesbury; Quick, the ecclesiastical historian; Dr. Gideon Harvey; Anstis, the heraldist; Dr. Walker, historian of the loyal clergy; Maundrell, the traveller; Samuel Wesley, father of the founder of Methodism; Dr. Borlase; Sir Michael Foster; Mr. Lewis, of Margate, the biographer; Norris, the Platonist; Upton, the editor of Epictetus; Toup, of classic fame; Tindal, the continuator of Rapin; Hoole, the poet; and Dr. Kennicot.

ORIEL COLLEGE.

FOUNDED IN 1326.

Prelates.—Arundel, Archbishop of Canterbury; Dr. Butler, Bishop of Durham, author of the celebrated "Analogy;" Bishop Mant; Dr. Whately, Archbishop of Dublin; and Dr. Edward Copleston, Bishop of Llandaff.

Robert Langlande, supposed author of "Pierce Plowman;" Alexander Barclay, translator of the "Ship of Fools"—Warton thinks his five eclogues the first which appeared in the English language; Dr. Edgeworth, a Popish writer; Morgan Philips, the sophister; Peter White, ejected Dean of Waterford; Sir Walter Raleigh; Prynne, the republicanist and antiquary; Richard Brathwaite, a poet and wit; Sir William Scroggs, and Sir John Holt, Lord Chief-Justices of the King's Bench; Dr. William Berriman; Dr. Edward Bentham, originally of Corpus; Joseph Warton; Keble, author of a beautiful collection of poems, deservedly popular, entitled the "Christian Year;" Drs. Hawkins, Arnold, and Hampden; Baden Powell, Davison, Heberden, Berens, and Newman.

QUEEN'S COLLEGE.*

FOUNDED IN 1340.

Prelates.—Cardinal Beaufort, brother to Henry IV.; Bishops Bainbridge, Robinson, Potter, and Barlow; Dr. Guy Carleton, Bishop of Bristol, afterwards of Cirencester; Dr. Compton, Bishop of London; Dr. William Nicholson, author of the "Historical Library;" Dr. Gibson, Bishop of London, founder of the preacherships at Whitehall; Dr. Tanner, Bishop of St. Asaph, author of "Notitia" and "Bibliotheca;" Dr. Van Mildert, Bishop of Llandaff, and of Durham in 1826.

Henry V., whose character was over the great gate of the old college, opposite to Edmund Hall; Bernard Gilpin; Sir Thomas Overbury; Wingate, an eminent lawyer and arithmetician; Burton, the commentator on Antoninus; Dr. Holyoake, lexicographer; Sir John Davies, poet; Sir John Banks; Sir Edward Turnour, chief baron; Dr. Samuel Annesley, an eminent nonconformist; Dr. Lancelot Addison, dean

* There is a custom at Queen's College to serve up every year a boar's head, provided by the manciple, against Christmas-day. This boar's head, being boiled or roasted, is laid in a great charger, covered with a garland of bays or laurel, as broad at bottom as the brims of the charger. When the first course is served up in the refectory on Christmas-day, in the said College, the manciple brings the said boar's head from the kitchen up to the high table, accompanied with one of the tabarders, who lays his head on the charger. The tabarder sings a song, and when he comes to the chorus, all the scholars that are in the refectory join together and sing it:—

The boar's head in hand bear I,
Bedeck'd with bays and rosemary,
And, I pray you, masters, merry be.
[CHORUS.—Quotquot estis in convivio,
Caput Apri defero,
Reddens laudes Domino.

The boar's head, as I understand,
Is the bravest dish in the land,
Being thus bedeck'd with a gay garland.
Let us Servire convivio,
Caput Apri, &c.

Our steward has provided this,
In honour of the King of bliss,
Which on this day to be served is.
In Reginensi Atrio
Caput Apri, &c.[1]

[1] From a MS. in the Bodleian. Tradition refers this ceremony to a deliverance of a scholar of Queen's from the attack of a wild boar, which had rushed out of Shotover forest, and which he stifled by thrusting a volume of Aristotle down his throat!

of Lichfield; Dr. Thomas Hyde; Wycherley, the poet; Dr. John Mill, editor of the Greek Testament; Sir John Floyer; Dr. Edmund Halley, an eminent philosopher, and Savilian professor; Addison, and his friend Tickell; Dr. Hugh Todd, antiquary; Dr. Thomas Smith, biographer; Dr. John Hudson; Christopher Rawlinson and Edward Thwaites, Saxon scholars; Rev. Jeremiah Seed; Dr. Shaw, the traveller; Collins, the poet; Dr. John Dalton, the reviver of Milton's 'Comus;' Edward Row Mores, antiquary; Thomas Tyrwhitt, Editor of Chaucer, afterwards fellow of Merton; Dr. Richard Burn, author of the 'Justice of Peace;' Dr. George Fothergill; Mitford, the historian; Jeremy Bentham; Ireland, dean of Westminster; Dr. Meyrick, author of works on "Arms and Armour;" Lancaster, author of the "Harmony of the Law and Gospel."

NEW COLLEGE.

FOUNDED IN 1386.

Prelates.—Cranley, Archbishop of Dublin; Chichele, of Canterbury; Thomas Beckington, Bishop of Bath and Wells; John Russel, Bishop of Rochester and Lincoln, chancellor of England; William Warham, archbishop of Canterbury, patron of Erasmus; Sherborne, Bishop of Chichester; Bilson, of Winchester; Lake, of Bath and Wells; Gunning of Ely; Turner, of Ely; Kenn, of Bath and Wells; Bisse, of Hereford; Lavington, of Exeter; and the illustrious Dr. Robert Lowth,* of St. David's, Oxford, and London; George Isaac Huntingford, Bishop of Hereford; Hon. Henry Bathurst, of Norwich; and William Howley, Archbishop of Canterbury.

Grocyn, one of the revivers of learning; Stanbridge, the grammarian; Philpot, civilian and linguist; Talbot, antiquarian; Pullaine, poet and translator; Harding, opposer of Bishop Jewell; Fowler, the learned printer; Nicholas Saunders; Sir Henry Sydney, father of Sir Philip; Thomas Neale; Dr. Baley; Turberville, the poet; Christopher Johnson, Latin poet; Thomas Stapleton Lloyd, master of Winchester school; Pits, one of our early biographers; Bastard and Owen, the epigrammatists; John Bond, the commentator; Dr. Thomas James, first librarian at the Bodleian; Herbert, the poet; Sir Henry Wotton; Sir Henry Martin; Dr. Zouch; Thomas Lydiat; Sir Thomas Ryves; Dr. Bruno Ryves, dean of Windsor, and writer of the first newspapers published in England; Dr. Edward Young, father of the poet; Sir Edward Herbert; Wood, author of the "Institutes of the Laws of England;" Dr. William Musgrave; Somerville and Pitt, poets; Rev. Joseph Spence; Dr. Gloster Ridley, the biographer of his great ancestor, the martyr; Dr. William Smith, translator of Thucydides and Longinus; Dr. Robert Holmes, the learned collator of the Septuagint; Rev. Sydney Smith; Rev. Philip Smyth, collector and translator of the "French Anas;" Rev. John Walker, editor of "Oxoniana," "Selection of curious Articles from the Gentleman's Magazine," author of "Curia Oxoniensis," &c.; Dr. Crotch, the celebrated composer of "Palestine," &c. &c.; Dr. Bandinel, editor of Dugdale's "Monasticon," &c. &c.; Dr. Shuttleworth, the learned head of this society, &c.; John Shute Duncan, and Philip Bury Duncan.

LINCOLN COLLEGE.*

FOUNDED IN 1427.

Prelates.—Dr. Edward Wetenhall, Bishop of Cork and Ross, of Kilmore and Kildare; Dr. Clavering,

* At one period of his life, this eloquent divine and exquisite scholar came under the critical fangs of the controversial Warburton; but the author of the "Divine Legation," in Lowth, met with an antagonist who was not to be silenced by sarcasm, or appalled by a sneer. In a pamphlet, entitled "A Letter to the Right Rev. Author of the 'Divine Legation,' demonstrated by a late Professor in the University of Oxford, 2nd Edition, London, 1766," Lowth thus defends himself and his University against the attack of Warburton:—"But the abuse is not merely personal: it goes farther; it extends even to the place of my education,—'But the learned professor, who has been hardly brought up in the keen atmosphere of wholesome severities, and early taught to distinguish between de facto and de jure,'—Pray, my lord, what is it to the purpose where I have been brought up? You charge me with principles of intolerance, adding a gentle insinuation also of disaffection to the present royal family and government; you infer these principles, it seems, from the place of my education. Is this a necessary consequence? Is it even a fair conclusion? Had I not your lordship's example to justify me, I should think it a piece of extreme impertinence to inquire, where you were bred; though we might justly plead, in excuse for it, a natural curiosity to know where and how such a phenomenon was produced. It is commonly said that your lordship's education was of that particular kind, concerning which, it is a remark of that great judge of men and manners, Lord Clarendon, (on whom you have conferred the unrivalled title of 'Chancellor of Human Nature'), that it peculiarly disposes men to be proud, insolent, and pragmatical. Now, my lord, as you have, in your whole behaviour, remarkably distinguished yourself by your humility, meekness, &c. &c., this unpromising circumstance of your education is so far from being a disgrace to you, that it highly redounds to your praise. But I am wholly precluded from all such merit: for, my lord, I was educated in the University of Oxford, I enjoyed all the advantages, both public and private, which that famous seat of learning so largely affords; I spent many happy years in that illustrious society, in a well-regulated course of useful discipline and studies, and in the agreeable and improving commerce of gentlemen and scholars; in a society where emulation without envy, ambition without jealousy, contention without animosity, incited industry, and awakened genius. I breathed the same atmosphere that the Hookers, the Chillingworths, and the Lockes had breathed before me, who did not amuse their readers with empty declamations and fine-spun theories of toleration, while they were themselves agitated with a furious and inquisitorial spirit, seizing every one they could lay hold on, for presuming to dissent from them in matters the most indifferent, and dragging them through the fiery ordeal of abusive controversy," &c. &c.

The last paragraph of this rejoinder contains a painful truth; and yet, amid all the harshness, petulance, and dogmatic severity of Warburton, there was much that was often tender, noble, and magnanimous; and even now, his paradoxes seem more fascinating than other men's truths!

* "'He looks as the Devil over Lincoln.'—Some

Bishop of Llandaff and Peterborough, many years Hebrew professor; Dr. Robert Sanderson, Bishop of Lincoln, the famous casuist. Archbishop Potter was also a fellow of this college.

Robert Flemyng, nephew of the founder, author of an elegant poem, entitled "Lucubrationes Tiburtinæ." On his return from the Continent, he deposited in the College library some finely illuminated MSS., and a Greek and Latin dictionary of his own writing, extant in Leland's time, by whom it is mentioned; Sir Edmund Anderson, chief-justice of the king's bench; Bolton, the puritan divine, afterwards of Brazen-Nose; Dr. Kelbye, one of the translators of the Bible; Edward Weston, champion of the Roman Catholic cause; Richard Brett, one of the translators of the Bible; Dr. John Davies, an eminent linguist and antiquary; Thomas Heyne, the grammarian; Dr. Christopher Bennet, physician and medical writer; Arthur Hopton; Sir William Davenant, poet; Cornelius Burges, a distinguished parliamentary divine; Henry Foulis, ecclesiastical historian; John Kettlewell and Dr. George Hickes, nonjurors; Sir George Wheeler, traveller and botanist; Tindal, the Deist, afterwards of Exeter and All Souls'; Dr. Richard Grey, and the pious James Hervey; John Wesley, founder of Methodism; Dr. John Sibthorp, author of the "Flora Oxoniensis," and the "Flora Græca." The two greatest modern benefactors to this university were fellows of this college, Lord Crewe and Dr. Radcliffe; Dr. Tatham, rector, author of Bampton Lectures entitled "A Chart and Scale of Truth," "Oxonia Purgata," and many political pamphlets of celebrity.

ALL SOULS' COLLEGE.

FOUNDED IN 1437.

Prelates.—Among the most celebrated are, Goldwell, Bishop of Norwich, and Bullingham, Bishop of Lincoln and Worcester. Duppa, of Winchester, and Archbishop Sheldon, were elected fellows here, but educated, the first at Christ Church, the second at Trinity: Jeremy Taylor, the illustrious divine, Bishop of Down and Connor, became a fellow here in 1636, by the nomination of Archbishop Laud.

Linacre, the first person who taught Greek at Oxford; he was one of the founders of the College of Physicians; Leland; Recorde; Andrew Kingsmill, linguist and divine, formerly of Corpus; Dr. Key or Cay, one of the earliest Oxford historians; Sir Anthony Sherley; Sir John Mason, privy councillor; Sir William Petre; Robert Herrick, poet; Marchmont Needham, one of the earliest newspaper hacks, who supported the Oliverian cause; Joseph Keble, first of Jesus, a law writer of incredible industry, so diseased with fondness for reporting, that he reported all the cases in the King's Bench from 1661 to 1710, and all the sermons preached in Gray's Inn Chapel, amounting to above 4000. Dr. Matthew Tindal, equally famous for gluttony and deism; John Norris, rector of Bemerton; Dr. Sydenham, improver of medical science; Sir William Trumbull, the friend of Pope; Lord Chancellor Talbot, first of Oriel; Sir Christopher Wren; and Dr. Young, author of "Night Thoughts."

In the departments of Law and Politics—Sir Robert Weston, Lord Chancellor of Ireland, in Elizabeth's time; Sir Clement Edmonds; Sir Daniel Dunn; Henry Coventry, Secretary of State to Charles II.; Sir William Blackstone, formerly of Pembroke.

MAGDALEN COLLEGE.

FOUNDED IN 1456.

Prelates.—Fuller remarks that there is scarcely a bishopric in England to which this college has not afforded a prelate. Cardinals Wolsey and Pole were both educated here; Pole entered as a nobleman, and resided in the president's lodgings; Lee and Frewin, Archbishops of York; Boulter, Archbishop of Armagh; Longland, Bishop of Lincoln; Cooper, of Winchester; Warner, of Rochester; Nicholson, of Gloucester; Hopkins, of Raphoe and Derry; Hough, of Worcester; Smalbroke, of Lichfield and Coventry; Horne, of Norwich; Philpotts, of Exeter.

Many of the scholars who studied here during the first half century from the foundation, contributed greatly to the revival of literature, which aided the advancement of the Reformation. Of these, Dean Colet, and Lily, the grammarian, Linacre, and Latimer, may be mentioned. It could afterwards boast of Dr. John Roper, the famous theologist; Dr. Wotton, physician to Henry VIII.; Robertson, one of the compilers of the Liturgy, 1549; Fox, the celebrated author of "Acts and Monuments of the Church;" Sir Francis Knollis, statesman; Lily, dramatic poet; Dr. Field; Dr. Thomas Godwyn, Hebrew antiquary; Sir Thomas Roe, the ambassador; Hampden, the patriot; John Digby, Earl of Bristol; Chilmead, critic and philologist; Theophilus Gale, nonconformist; the pious Dr. Hammond; Dr. Peter Heylin, ecclesiastical historian; George Withers, poet; Harman, the Greek professor; Elisha Coles, Latin lexicographer; Sir Robert Howard, dramatic poet; Dr. Thomas Smith, the traveller; the illustrious Addison; Dr. Sacheverell, the associate of Addison; Colins, Yalden, and Holdsworth, poets; Horbery and Waldgrave, divines; Gibbon, the historian Dr. Townson and Dr. Chandler; John Wilson,* the

fetch the original of this proverb from a stone picture of the devil, which doth (or lately did) overlook Lincoln Coledge. Surely, the architect intended no farther than an ordinary antick, though beholders have since applied those ugly looks to envious persons repining at the prosperity of their neighbours, and jealous to be over-topt by their vicinity. The devil is the map of malice, and his envy (as God's mercy) is over all his works; on which account he is supposed to have overlooked this church (viz., the cathedral at Lincoln), when first finished, with a savage countenance, as maligning men's costly devotion, and that they should be so expensive in God's service; but it is suspicious, that some who account themselves saints, behold such fabrics with little better looks!"—FULLER'S *Worthies.*

* To say nothing of the beauty of Wilson's poetry, he has exerted more influence over the periodical literature of the day than any living writer. But, like all original minds, he has been mimicked by small reviewers, who contrive to ape the eccentricities of his style, but are utterly destitute of the merit and fervour of his thoughts. Similar was the fate of Lord Byron. His lordship felt, or fancied himself, an unhappy being, and vented his feelings accordingly. Forthwith a sentimental paleness overspread the land, and poetical "Werterism" became the fashion of the hour! Such vulgar mimicry recals to our mind a saying of Allan Cunningham, in reference to a certain writer's Napoleon, when compared to Sir Walter Scott's—"The braying of an ass after the sound of a trumpet."

distinguished poet, and Professor of Moral Philosophy in the University of Edinburgh; Dr. Hurdis, the poet; Dr. Routh, president, author of "Reliquiæ Sacræ;" Dr. Faussett; Dr. Daubeny; Richard

The following note, relative to Wilson's career at the University, is from the pen of the celebrated "Opium Eater,"—De Quincey, himself an Oxford man. At a time when the surly ignorance of mistaken writers is wont to sneer at our Universities, it is gratifying to see an author of acknowledged genius like De Quincey, looking back on the scenes of Alma Mater with respectful love, and speaking of her greatness as becomes his theme.

"——— Vos, dulcissima mundi
Nomina, vos musæ, libertas, lætitia, libri,
Hortique sylvæque, anima remanente relinquam?

"From the latter end of 1803 to the spring of 1808, Mr. Wilson had studied at the University of Oxford. He had previously studied as a mere boy, according to the Scotch fashion, at the University of Glasgow, chiefly under the tuition of the late Mr. Jardine (the professor, I believe, of logic, and Dr. or Mr. Young, the professor of Greek). At both universities he had greatly distinguished himself; but at Oxford, where the distribution of prizes and honours of every kind is to the last degree parsimonious and select, naturally it follows, that such academical distinctions are really significant distinctions, and proclaim an unequivocal merit in him who has carried them off from a crowd of 1600 to 2000 co-rivals, to whom the contest was open; whereas, in the Scotch Universities, as I am told by Scotchmen, the multiplication of prizes and medals, and the almost indiscriminate profusion with which they are showered abroad, neutralises their whole effect and value. At least, this was the case in Mr. Wilson's time; but lately, some conspicuous changes have been introduced by a royal commission (not yet, I believe, dissolved) into one, at least, of the Scotch Universities, which have greatly improved it in this respect, by bringing it much nearer to the English model. When Mr. Wilson gained a prize of fifty guineas for fifty lines of English verse, without farther inquiry it becomes evident, from the mere rarity of the distinction, which, for a University of now nearly five thousand members, occurs but once a year, and from the great over-proportion of that peculiar class (the under-graduates) to whom the contest is open, that such a victory was an indisputable criterion of very conspicuous merit. In fact, never in any place did Mr. Wilson play off his Proteus variety of character and talent with so much brilliant effect as at Oxford. In this great University, the most ancient, and, by many degrees, the most magnificent in the world, he found a stage for display perfectly congenial with the native elevation of his own character. Perhaps you are not fully aware of the characteristic differences which separate our two English Universities of Oxford and Cambridge from those of Scotland and the Continent; for I have always observed that the best-informed foreigners, even after a week's personal acquaintance with the Oxford system, still adhere to the inveterate preconceptions which they had brought with them from the Continent. For instance, they continue obstinately to speak of the professors as the persons to whom the students are indebted for tuition; whereas, the majority of these hold their offices as the most absolute sinecures; and the task of tuition devolves upon the tutors appointed in each particular college. These tutors are called public tutors; meaning that they do not confine their instructions to any one individual, but distribute them amongst all the under-graduates of the college to which they belong; and, in addition to these, private tutors are allowed to any student who chooses to increase his expenditure in that particular. But the main distinction, which applies to our immediate subject, is the more than regal provision for the lodging and accommodation of the students, by the system of colleges. Of these there are in Oxford, neglecting the technical subdivision of halls, five and twenty; and the main use of all, both colleges and halls, is not, as in Scotland and on the Continent, to lodge the head of the University with suitable dignity, and to provide rooms for the library and public business of the University. These purposes are met by a separate provision, distinct from the colleges: and the colleges are applied as follows—1st, and mainly, to the reception of the fellows, and of the undergraduate students; 2ndly, to the accommodation of the head (known in different colleges by the several designations of provost, principal, dean, rector, warden, &c.); 3rdly, to the accommodation of the private library attached to that college, and to the chapel, which is used at least twice every day for public prayers; 4thly, to the hall, and the whole establishment of kitchen, wine-vaults, buttery, &c. &c., which may be supposed necessary for the liberal accommodation at the public meals of dinner (and in some colleges supper) of gentlemen and visitors from the country, or from the Continent; varying (we will suppose) from twenty-five to five hundred heads. Everywhere else the great mass of the students are lodged in obscure nooks and corners, which may or may not be respectable, but are at all events withdrawn from the surveillance of the University. I shall state both the ground and the effect (or tendency rather) of this difference. Out of England, universities are not meant exclusively for professional men: the sons of great landholders, and a large proportion of the sons of noblemen, either go through the same academic course as others, or a shorter course, adapted to their particular circumstances. In England, again, the church is supplied from the rank of gentry—not exclusively, it is true, but in a much larger proportion than anywhere else, except in Ireland. The corresponding ranks in Scotland, from their old connection with France, have adopted (I believe) much more of the continental plans for disposing of their sons at this period. At any rate, it will not be contended by any man, that Scotland throws anything like the same proportion with England of her gentry and her peerage into her universities. Hence a higher standard of manners and of habits presides at Oxford and Cambridge; and, consequently, a demand for much higher accommodations would even otherwise have arisen, had not such a demand already been supplied by the munificence of our English princes and peers, both male and female; and, in one instance at least, of a Scottish prince (Baliol). The extent of these vast caravanseras enables the governors of the various colleges to furnish every student with a set of two rooms at the least, often with a suite of three—[I, who lived at Oxford on no more than my school allowance, had that number]—or in many cases with far more. In the superior colleges, indeed (superior, I mean as to their purse and landed endowments), all these accommodations keep pace with the refinements of the age; and

Walker, author of "Flora Oxoniensis," &c.; and Sir Charles Wetherell, the Chancery barrister.

BRAZEN-NOSE COLLEGE.

FOUNDED IN 1509.

Prelates.—Hugh Curwen, or Coren, Archbishop of Dublin; Barnes, Bishop of Durham; Wolton of Exeter; Miles Smith, of Gloucester, one of the greatest scholars of his day, and principal translator of the Bible; Reginald Heber, Bishop of Calcutta.

Robert Nowell, attorney-general, and Lawrence Nowell, Dean of Lichfield, an eminent antiquary, who revived the study of the Saxon language; Caldwell, president of the College of Physicians; William Whittingham, poetical coadjutor of Sternhold and Hopkins in the translation of the Psalms; Fox, the martyrologist; Sir John Savile, and his younger brother, provost of Eton, where he printed his edition of St. Chrysostom; Barnaby Barnes, dramatic poet; Ferdinand Pulton, law-writer; Jeremiah Stephens, coadjutor of Sir Henry Spelman in the publication of the Councils; Sir John Spelman, author of the "Life of Alfred the Great;" Brerewood, mathematician; Ralph Radcliffe; Humphery Lluyd, or Lloyd, the Welsh historian; Sir John Stradling, poet; Sampson Erdeswick, the Staffordshire antiquary; Sir Peter Leycester, the Cheshire antiquary; Lord Chancellor Egerton, Baron Ellesmere, and Viscount Brackley; Burton, author of the "Anatomy of Melancholy;" Sir William Petty; Elias Ashmole, founder of the museum; John Prince, author of the "Worthies of Devon;" Dr. W. Assheton; Thomas Beconsall, defender of revealed religion; Thomas Church, D.D., whose degree was presented to him by diploma, Feb. 23, 1749, for answering Bolingbroke; the Rev. John Watson, author of the "History of Halifax, &c. &c.; Whitaker, the Manchester historian, afterwards elected a scholar of Corpus; Milman, the late professor of poetry; Dr. Cardwell, since Principal of St. Alban Hall; and Lord Nugent, author of "Memorials of John Hampden, &c.

CORPUS CHRISTI COLLEGE.

FOUNDED IN 1516.

Prelates.—Cardinal Pole, first of Magdalen; Jewell, Bishop of Salisbury; Webb, Bishop of Limerick, some time of University College; Dr. Fowler, of Gloucester; and Dr. Richard Pococke, Bishop of Meath, the celebrated orientalist; Burgess, Bishop of Salisbury.

John Shepreve; Redman, or Redmayne, afterwards first master of Trinity College, Cambridge, one of the compilers of the Liturgy; Morwen; Nicholas Udal and Richard Edwards, poets, the latter one of our earliest dramatists, whose "Palæmon and Arcite" was acted before Queen Elizabeth, in Christ Church Hall, on her visit here in 1566; Miles Windsor, the first Oxford historian; Hooker; Sir Edward Sandys, statesman; Dr. Sebastian Benefield; Gill, master of St. Paul's School; Dr. Daniel Featly; the illustrious Hales; Sir John Menis, traveller, seaman, and poet; Edmund Chishul, divine and antiquary; Dr. Richard Fiddes, the biographer of Cardinal Wolsey; John Anstis, the herald; Henry Hare; Lord Coleraine; Dr. Nathaniel Forster; Dr. John Rogers; Dr. John Burton; Dr. Jeremiah Milles, Dean of Exeter; Sir Ashton Lever, the collector of an immense museum of natural history, dispersed by auction a few years ago; Thomas Day, an eccentric fellow, who never obtained a degree: Lord Chief Justice Tenterden; Coleridge, the poet; Professor Buckland, since Canon of Christ Church, author of "Geological Evidences of the Deluge," one of the Bridgwater Treatises, &c.; Vaughan Thomas, the distinguished divine; and Edward Greswell, author of "Harmonia Evangelica."

CHRIST CHURCH.

FOUNDED IN 1532.

Prelates.—The archbishops and bishops educated here are too numerous to be noticed. Among the most eminent we find Bancroft, Prideaux, Sanderson, Blanford, Dolben, Compton, Gastrell, Synge, Potter, Tanner, Benson, Robinson, and Shipley. Among the

---

thus a connection is maintained between the University and the landed noblesse—upper and lower—of England, which must be reciprocally beneficial, and which, under other circumstances, could scarcely have taken place.

"Of these advantages you may be sure that Mr. Wilson availed himself to the utmost extent. Instead of going to Baliol College, he entered himself at Magdalen, in the class of what are called 'Gentlemen Commoners.' All of us (you know) in Oxford and Cambridge wear an academic dress, which tells at once our academic rank, with all its modifications. And the term, 'Gentleman Commoner' implies that he has more splendid costumes, and more in number; that he is expected to spend a good deal more money; that he enjoys a few trifling immunities; and that he has, in particular instances, something like a king's right of pre-emption, as in the choice of rooms, &c.

"Once launched in this orbit, Mr. Wilson continued to blaze away for the four successive years, 1804-5-6-7, I believe, without any intermission. Possibly I myself was the one sole gownsman who had not then found my attention fixed by his most heterogeneous reputation. In a similar case, Cicero tells a man that ignorance, so unaccountable, of another man's pretensions, argued himself to be a 'homo ignorabilis;' or, in the language of the Miltonic Satan,

'Not to know me argues thyself unknown.'

And that is true; a homo ignorabilis most certainly I was. And even with that admission it is still difficult to account for the extent and duration of my ignorance. The fact is, that the case well expresses both our positions: that he should be so conspicuous as to challenge knowledge from the most sequestered of anchorites, expresses his life; that I should have right to absolute ignorance of him who was familiar as daylight to all the rest of Oxford, expresses mine. Never, indeed, before, to judge from what I have since heard upon inquiry, did a man, by variety of talents and variety of humours, contrive to place himself as the connecting link between orders of men so essentially repulsive of each other—as Mr. Wilson in this instance.

'Omnis Aristippum decuit color, et status, et res.'

"From the learned president of his college, Dr. Routh, the editor of parts of Plato, and of some Theological Selections, with whom Wilson enjoyed an unlimited favour—from this learned academic doctor, and many others of the same class, Wilson had an infinite gamut of friends and associates, running through every key."

names eminent in ecclesiastical history, we find the Reformer, Peter Martyr; M. Heton, Bishop of Ely; Richard Edes, Dean of Worcester; Leonard Hutten; John Wall, Prebendary of Salisbury; Thomas Lockey, public librarian; Dr. Edward Pocock; Dr. Robert South; Dr. Richard Allestree; Dr. Roger Altham; Archbishop Wake; Dr. Robert Friend; Dr. Newton, founder of Hertford College; Van Mildert, Bishop of Durham; Dr. Richard Laurence, Archbishop of Cashel.

"The scholars," observes Chalmers, "of other ranks, who have added to the reputation of this college, are so numerous, that a few only can be noticed. The literary history of Christ Church might be extended to many volumes."

In the list of statesmen and lawyers occur the names of Sir Dudley Carleton; Sir William Godolphin; Sir W. Ellis; Edward Sackville, Earl of Dorset; Sir Gilbert Dolben: Henry Mordaunt; Heneage Finch and Daniel Finch, Earls of Nottingham; Henry Bennet, Earl of Arlington: Sir J. Vaughan; Thomas Lutwyche; Trevor; Viscount Chetwynd; Wainwright; Skinner; Trelawny; Henry Villiers; Sir William Wyndham; Earl Granville; Sir Thomas Hanmer; Andrew Stone; Lord Littleton; Earl Mansfield; Lord Holland; John Mostyn; Sir Francis Bernard; Baron Mendip; Amyand; Devisme; Sir John Skinner; Sir Gould Morgan; Richard Leveson Gower, &c. &c.

Poets and Orators.—Dr. James Calfhill; Sir Philip Sidney; Stephen Gosson; George Peele; Thomas Storer; William Gager; Thomas Goffe; Ben Jonson; Gomersal; Strode; Warmstrey; Hemmings; Holyday; Cartwright; Randolph; Waring Maplet; Rhodes; Owen; Allestree; Nicolas Brady; Otway; Villiers; King; Harrington; Alsop; Samuel Wesley; Phillips; Edmund Smith; Gilbert West; Bramston; Thornton; George Colman; Dr. Butt.

During the sixteenth century, among the scholars of this house were Hackluyt, the traveller; Mulcaster, master of Merchant Taylors' School; Carew, the historian of Cornwall; Camden; Torporley; Caleb Willis; Sir Humphrey Lynd; Sir Thomas Aylesbury; Edmund Gunter; Dr. John Owen, dean and eminent divine, in the time of the Commonwealth.

Of the seventeenth century are, Nicholas Grey: John Gregory, astronomer; the learned Meric Casaubon; James Heath, the historian; Dr. Willis; Penn, the founder of Pennsylvania; Stubbe, second keeper of the Bodleian; Lower; Locke;* Francis Vernon, traveller and poet; Sparke, Prebendary of Lichfield, editor of "Lactantius" and "Zosimus;" Dr. Hooke, architect; Sir Edward Hannes, professor of chemistry; Daniel Man; Dr. Freind; Sir Andrew Fontaine, Anglo-Saxon scholar; Temple Stanyan; Ivie, translator of "Epictetus;" Frewen, professor of chemistry.

In the eighteenth century, Richard Ince, a writer in the "Spectator;" Eustace Budgell, a more considerable contributor to that work; George Wigan; Robert Leybourne, Principal of Alban Hall; Lord Bolingbroke; Desaguliers; Charles Boyle, Bentley's antagonist; John Wigan, editor of "Aristæus;" Charles Wesley; Browne Willis, antiquary; Dr. William Drake, the historian, of York: Dr. W. Sharpe, Greek professor; the Rev. Clayton Mordaunt Cracherode, who left his valuable library to the British Museum, books estimated at 30,000*l.*; Dr. W. Burton, historian of Yorkshire; the late Sir Robert Peel, Bart.; Conybeare, professor of poetry; the illustrious Canning; William Wyndham, Lord Grenville, the late Chancellor of the University; Dr. Cyril Jackson; Dr. Gaisford, Greek professor, and dean; Dr. Henry Cotton; Lord Henley; Lord Dover; Fynes Clinton, author of "Fasti Hellenici;" Thomas Vowler Short; Sir D. K. Sandford, Greek Professor at Glasgow; Dr. John Anthony Cramer, since Principal of New Inn Hall, author of works on Asia Minor, Ancient Italy,

* The following is Dr. Gell's letter to the Earl of Sunderland, respecting Locke's expulsion:—

November 8th, 1684.

"Right Honourable,—I received the honour of your lordship's letter, wherein you are pleased to inquire concerning Mr. Locke's being a student of this house, of which I have this account to render:—That he being, as your lordship is truly informed, a person who was much trusted by the late Earl of Shaftesbury, and who is suspected to be ill affected to the government, I have for divers years had an eye upon him; but so close has his guard been on himself, that after several strict inquiries, I may confidently affirm, that there is not a man in the college, however familiar with him, who has heard him speak either a word against, or so much as concerning the government. And although very frequently, both in public and private, discourses have been purposely introduced to the disparagement of his master, the Earl of Shaftesbury, his party, and his designs, he could never be provoked to take any notice, or discover, in word or look, the least concern; so that I believe there is not in the world such a masterpiece of taciturnity and passion. He has a physician's place, which frees him from the exercises of the college, and the obligations which others have to residence in it; and he is now abroad in want of health. But notwithstanding that, I have summoned him to return home, which is done with this prospect, that if he comes not back, he will be liable to expulsion for contumacy; and if he do, he will be answerable to the law for that which he shall be found to have done amiss, &c. &c. But if this method seems not effectual or speedy enough, and his Majesty, our founder and visitor, shall please to command his immediate remove, upon the receipt thereof, directed to the dean and chapter, it shall accordingly be executed by, my lord, yours, &c.

"Joh. Oxon."

The revolting meanness and servility of character which the above letter exhibits need no remark! It seems that it had the desired effect, for, in a few days afterwards, the following letter from his dictatorial Majesty was received:—

"To the Right Reverend, &c. &c.—Right Reverend Father in God, and trusty and well-beloved, we greet you well. Whereas we have received information of the factious and disloyal behaviour of Locke, one of the students of that our college, we have sought thereby to signify our will and pleasure to you, that you forthwith remove him from the student's place, and deprive him of all rights and advantages thereunto belonging, for which this shall be your warrant, and so we bid you heartily farewell.

"Given at our Court, at Whitehall, the 11th of November, 1684, by his Majesty's command,

"Sunderland."

We need not state the result; it stands on record, as a specimen of royal baseness and episcopal servility.

and Ancient Greece; James Shergold Boone, formerly one of the masters of the Charter House, &c.; Professor Burton; Dr. Buckland; Professor Pusey; Dr. Kidd; Rev. John Jones (Tegid), M.A., precentor, translator of the book of Isaiah from the Hebrew text of Vander Hooght, also author of Prize Poems and Essays in Welsh, &c.

TRINITY COLLEGE.*

FOUNDED IN 1554.

Prelates.—Warton gives the following list of bishops and other eminent men, either educated at Trinity College, or living in it, while Dr. Bathurst was fellow or President:—Ironside, Bishop of Bristol; Lucy, Bishop of St. David's; Skinner, of Worcester; Glemham, of St. Asaph; Stafford, of Chester; Parker, of Oxford; Archbishop Sheldon; Selden; Chillingworth; Gellibrand, mathematician; Aubrey, antiquary; Arthur Wilson, author of the "Life of James I." Sir John Denham, poet; Sir Henry Blount; Sir James Harrington, author of the "Oceana;" Dr. Derham, author of "Physico-theology;" Dr. D. Whitby; John Evelyn; Sir Edward Bysche, the heraldist; Potter, mathematician; Dr. Warton, physician; Anthony Farringdon, author of some learned sermons. To these may be added the first Lord Baltimore; Charles Montague, Earl of Halifax; Lord Somers; Earl of Chatham; and the second Earl of Guildford, Lord North; the poets Lodge, Settle, Glanville, Manning, Merrick, and Headley; Allen, mathematician; Gill, master of St. Paul's School; Ludlow, the republican chief; Sir John Ford, hydraulist; Henry Birkenhead, founder of the lecture on poetry in the University; Chamberlaine; Dr. Cobden; Coxeter, the miscellanist; Lethieullier, antiquary; F. Wise, ditto; Thomas Warton; Lisle Bowles, poet; Ingram, the president; Kinsey, author of "Portugal," &c. &c.; Medwin, the biographer of Byron, translator of "Æschylus," &c. (In the opinion of some of our first classical scholars, Medwin's translation is the finest which the English language contains.) Walter Savage Landor, author of "Gebir," a poem, "Imaginary Conversations," &c.; Henry Kett, author of "Elements of General Knowledge;" Richard Duppa, author of "Life of Michael Angelo," and numerous botanical works; James Ford.

ST. JOHN'S COLLEGE.

FOUNDED IN 1557.

Prelates.—Tobie Matthew, Archbishop of York; Archbishop Laud, elected the ninth president of this college; in 1603 he was one of the proctors; Dr. William Juxon, Bishop of London; Peter Mews, Bishop of Winchester; Sir William Dawes, Archbishop of York.

Among the scholars are Campion, the celebrated Jesuit; Dr. Case, the Aristotle commentator; Blagrave, mathematician; Sir James Whitelock, chief-justice; How, the botanist; Shirley, the dramatic poet; Gayton, poet; Whitelocke, the annalist, one of Cromwell's lords; Marsham, the chronologist; Bernard, Savilian Professor; William Lowth, the learned divine; Sherard or Sherwood, botanist; Dillenius, ditto; Bevil Higgons, poet and historian; Bonwicke, master of Merchant Taylors' School; Sir William Trumbull, the correspondent of Pope; Dr. Robert James, discoverer of the febrifuge powder; Ducarel, antiquary; Dr. Munro, one of Radcliffe's travelling fellows; Whalley, commentator on Shakspeare and Jonson; Samuel Bishop, poet; Dean Tucker, author of sundry tracts on politics and commerce; Dr. Bliss, editor of "Wood's Athenæ;" Dr. Dibdin, author of "Bibliomania," "Bibliotheca Spenceriana," "Bibliographical Decameron," "Bibliographical Tour in France and Germany," "The Library Companion," "Introduction to the Classics," &c. &c.

JESUS COLLEGE.

FOUNDED IN 1571.

Prelates.—Rider, Bishop of Killaloe; Lloyd, of St. Asaph; Wynne, of ditto, father of Sir William Wynne. Archbishop Usher was on the books, and resided here.

David Powel, the celebrated antiquary; John Davies, lexicographer; Rees Prichard, a popular Welch poet; James Howell, the leading miscellanist of his time; Sir Thomas Herbert, an eminent traveller, and benefactor to the University; Sir William Williams, lawyer; Sir Leoline Jenkyns; Dr. Jonathan Edwards, Principal, an eminent controversial divine; the pious Dr. Richard Lucas; Edward Lloyd, antiquary and botanist, afterwards keeper of the Ashmolean Museum; and the learned divines and theological writers, Dr. William Worthington, Dr. Henry Owen, and Dr. James Bandinel, the first Bampton Lecturer.

WADHAM COLLEGE.

FOUNDED IN 1613.

Prelates.—Among the principal are the names of Gauden, Bishop of Worcester; Seth Ward, of Salisbury; Thomas Sprat, of Rochester; and Samuel Parker, of Oxford.

Creech, editor and translator of "Lucretius;" Walsh, the poet; Dr. J. Trapp, Professor of Poetry; Thomas Baker, mathematician; Sir C. Sedley; Earl of Rochester; Admiral Blake; Mayow, physician; Dr. Hody; Sir Christopher Wren;* Arthur Onslow,

* In the "Computus" of the bursars of Trinity College for the year 1631, the following article occurs:—"Solut pro fumigandis *chirothecis*." Gloves make a constant and considerable article of expense in the earlier accompt books of the college here mentioned, and, without doubt, in those of many other societies. They were annually given (a custom still subsisting) to the college tenants, and often presented to guests of distinction. But it appears (at least from accompts of the college in preceding years) that the practice of perfuming gloves for this purpose was fallen into disuse soon after the reign of Charles I.—T. WARTON.

These perfumed gloves are mentioned by Shakspeare. Autolycus, in the "Winter's Tale," has among his wares,

"Gloves as sweet as damask roses."

* "In his fourteenth year, Christopher was admitted as a gentleman-commoner at Wadham College, Oxford. These were tender years for acquiring any sort of notice in a learned university, and still more so for gaining the friendship of such men as John Wilkins, Warden of Wadham, and Seth Ward, Savilian Professor of Astronomy, two of the most distinguished mathematicians of their day; yet nothing is more certain than that he obtained both. His talents, if their fame had not gone before him, were soon discovered at Oxford. He loved, what was fashionable in those

for many parliaments Speaker of the House of Commons; Chief-Justice Pratt; Costard, linguist; Harris, the philosopher, of Salisbury; Floyer Sydenham, the translator of "Plato;" Kennicott, collater of the Hebrew MSS.; Richardson, author of the "Persian Dictionary;" Anderson, who translated the "Arenarius" of Archimedes; Dr. Austen. The famous Bentley, of Cambridge, became a member of Wadham College in 1689.

PEMBROKE COLLEGE.

FOUNDED IN 1624.

Prelates.—Repingdon, Bishop of Lincoln in 1405, and cardinal, 1408; Bonner, of London, surnamed the Bloody; Dr. William Newcome, Archbishop of Armagh, the Biblical critic; Dr. John Moore, Archbishop of Canterbury.

Camden, the illustrious historian and antiquary; Sir Thomas Browne; Carew, Earl of Totness; Sir James Dyer; David Baker, ecclesiastical historian; Pym, the noted patriot. In more recent times we find the celebrated names of Judge Blackstone, who was first educated here; Philip Morant, historian of Essex; Whitfield; Dr. Durell, principal of Hertford College; the eccentric Henderson; the poets Southern,* Shenstone, Graves, and Hawkins, the Professor of Poetry; Dr. Samuel Johnson, who was entered a commoner, Oct. 31, 1728. His apartment was the second-floor over the gateway.

WORCESTER COLLEGE.

FOUNDED IN 1714.

Gloucester Hall, afterwards St. John Baptist's Hall, and now Worcester College, was one of the most ancient houses belonging to the Benedictines at the time of the dissolution.

Prelates.—Before the Reformation, occur the names of three bishops, educated in Gloucester Hall; John Langdon, Bishop of Rochester, 1422; Mylling, of Hereford; Dunstan, of Llandaff, 1545, who had been prior, but lived to the reign of Elizabeth, and acknowledged her supremacy.

In the same hall were educated, and some time resided, the celebrated traveller, Thomas Coryate; Dr. Budden; Thomas Allen, the mathematician; Richard Lovelace, poet and linguist; the learned Sir Kenelm Digby; De Quincey, the "Opium Eater."

HERTFORD COLLEGE.*

FOUNDED IN 1725.

Prelates.—James Cranlegh, Archbishop of Dublin; and Morgan Owen, Bishop of Llandaff; Dickson, Bishop of Down and Connor; and Archbishop Newcome, already noticed as belonging to Pembroke, are claimed by Hertford College.

Nicholas Brigham, and Lord Buckhurst, poets; the illustrious Selden; Sir John Glynn, an eminent lawyer; Dr. Donne, afterwards of Cambridge; Nicholas Fuller, the greatest Hebrew critic of his time; Sir William Waller, the parliamentary general; Sir Richard Baker, author of the popular "Chronicler;" Edward Lye, the Saxon lexicographer; Thomas Hutchinson, the editor of "Xenophon;" Dr. Hunt, Arabic Professor; Dr. Benjamin Blayney; and the illustrious Charles James Fox, educated here under the tuition of Dr. Newcome.

THE HALLS.

Before the foundation of colleges, all education in the University was carried on in certain houses, and sets of buildings, called halls, inns, or hostels, which were the property of the citizens of Oxford, who let them, partially to individuals, or generally to societies, connected under one roof, in which case they were denominated halls.

ST. ALBAN'S HALL.

FOUNDED IN THE REIGN OF JOHN.

Prelates.—Hooper, Bishop of Gloucester, and martyr; Lamplugh, Archbishop of York; and Narcissus Marsh, Primate of Ireland, were of this hall; which also enumerates among its scholars, Massinger, the dramatic poet; William Lenthall, Speaker of the House of Commons during the Long Parliament; and Sir Thomas Higgons, an English writer of some note, and ambassador at Vienna; the distinguished scholar

---

days, to write Latin descriptions of his studies and designs, in verse as well as prose."

A proud memory is connected with Wren's fame, from his share in the original plan of the Royal Society. "A young gentleman," says Allan Cunningham, "thus remarkable for talents and diligence, was a welcome addition to that little band of scientific scholars, who, says Sprat, resorted, 'soon after the civil wars, to the chamber of Dr. Wilkins, and laid the foundation of the Royal Society for improving natural knowledge.' Amid the unsettled days of the Commonwealth, these scholars pursued their inquiries with all the zeal which genius brings to the aid of speculation; drew up descriptions, and made models and drawings of their inventions and discoveries; formed connexions with learned societies and individuals abroad; and looking forward to more settled or fortunate times, prepared a draught of the present charter of the Royal Society."

None who have seen that majestic pile, the Theatre at Oxford, will think the following reference devoid of interest:—"This, at all events, was the first of his designs, which he saw realised; for it was opened on the 9th of July, 1669, with great solemnity, and followed," says the author of "Parentalia," "by a most splendid act, such as had not been equalled in the memory of man. The munificent founder (Gilbert Sheldon, Archbishop of Canterbury) honoured the architect, on this first essay of his skill, with the present of a golden cup, and by his statutes appointed him, jointly with the vice-chancellor, perpetual curator of the fabric." The finished work, splendid as it is, cannot, however, be compared to the original design. Wren planned a structure bearing no small resemblance to the theatre of Marcellus, yet exceedingly bold and original. Nevertheless, the building is famous for a roof constructed out of small pieces of timber on the truest geometrical principles.

* Johnson delighted to mention the names of poets educated at his own college; adding, (says that agreeable twaddler, Boswell), with a smile of sportive triumph, "Sir, we are a nest of singing birds."

* Dissolved in 1816, and its site now occupied by Magdelen Hall.

and critic, Elmsley; Dr. Richard Whately, Archbishop of Dublin; and Dr. Cardwell, the present learned Principal.

EDMUND HALL.

FOUNDED IN THE SIXTEENTH CENTURY.

Carleton, Bishop of Chichester; Kennet, of Peterborough; and Dr. Daniel Wilson, the fourth Bishop of Calcutta; occur among the prelates who were educated or resided some time in Edmund Hall. Among its eminent scholars are Sir W. Jones, the law writer; Judge Jenkins; Dr. Bate; Dr. Newton, mathematician; John Oldham, the poet; Kettlewell, the nonjuror, afterwards of Lincoln; Blackmore, the poet; Chamberlaine, author of "Anglia Notitia;" Humphrey Wanley, librarian; Hearne, the antiquary; Dr. Kennet; Felton, author of a "Dissertation on the Classics," &c.; Mill, editor of the Greek Testament; and Dr. Grabe.

ST. MARY HALL.

FOUNDED IN 1325.

The illustrious Sir Thomas More; Sir Christopher Hatton, George Sandys, and Fulwell, poets; Hariot, an eminent mathematician; Marchmont Needham, the political writer; Dr. Phineas Pett, the tutor of Canning, principal, &c., afterwards canon of Christ Church; and Dr. Renn Dickson Hampden, Bampton Lecturer, &c.

NEW INN HALL.

FOUNDED IN 1391.

Twyne, the antiquary, and the Rev. Dr. Scott, author of the "Christian Life," &c., were members of this hall. Dr. John Antony Cramer is the present Principal, and the author of works on Asia Minor, Ancient Italy, and Ancient Greece, together with accurate maps of those countries.

ST. MARY MAGDELEN HALL.

FOUNDED IN 1480.

Among its *Prelates*, Magdelen Hall enumerates John Longland, Bishop of Lincoln; Stokesley, Bishop of London; and Wilkins, of Chester. Among its scholars are, Warner and Daniel, poets; Sir Harry Vane, the republican; Sir Julius Cæsar, a learned civilian; Leigh, theologian; Lord Clarendon, the historian, who entered here in 1622; Tombes, whom Wood calls the Coryphæus of the Anabaptists; Sir Matthew Hale; Dr. Godwin; Theophilus Gale, author of the "Court of the Gentiles;" Dr. Sydenham; Pococke, afterwards of Corpus; Dr. Hickes, afterwards of Lincoln; Dr. Charleton; Edward Phillips, Milton's nephew; Dr. Plot, naturalist; Dr. Tyson; Sir George Wheeler; Dr. William Nichols, commentator on the Liturgy; Thomas Hobbes, the philosopher of Malmesbury.

As an appendix to this Biographical Summary, may be added, "An exact account of the whole number of scholars and students in the University of Oxford, taken anno 1612, in the long vacation."*

	Totals.		Totals.
Ædes Christi	240	Trinitatis Coll.	116
Magdal. Coll.	246	Jesu Coll.	91
Novum Coll.	130	Corpus Christi Coll.	94
Ænenasense Coll.	227	Auld S. Maria	48
Universit. Coll.	72	Auld Magdal.	161
Merton Coll.	93	Auld Edmundi	47
Reginense Coll.	267	Auld Laturum Port.	141
Omnium Anim. Coll.	93	Auld Glocteri	62
Eton Coll.	206	Auld Albani	52
S. Joannis Coll.	128	Auld Cervini	71
Lincoln Coll.	109	Novum Hospitium	30
Balliolense Coll.	127		
Oriel Coll.	79	Sum. Totalis	2920

The author is fully aware that omissions may be discovered in the preceding summary, and that additions might be conferred on it by many ornaments of later times. Should a future occasion offer itself, together with the adequate records, those additions will not be neglected.

* From Tanner's MSS., in the Bodleian, quoted in "Oxoniana."

THE MESSIAH.

(1832.)

TENTH EDITION.

"If I have done well, it is that which I desired; but, if slenderly and meanly, it is that which I could attain unto."—2 *Maccabees* xv. 38.

TO

QUEEN ADELAIDE,

(BY GRACIOUS PERMISSION,)

THE FOLLOWING POEM

Is most respectfully inscribed,

BY

HER MAJESTY'S

VERY DUTIFUL AND OBLIGED SERVANT,

THE AUTHOR.

THE MESSIAH.

PREFACE.

(1832.)

THE following Poem is submitted to the public with great deference. The religious grandeur of his theme increases the responsibility of an Author, and renders him anything but sanguine as to the result.

To those who may accuse him of arrogance, he can only reply, that he approached his subject with no irreverent thought, or careless speed; nor is he aware of any instructive source, whereby light could be thrown on doctrine, scene, or character, which has been left unconsulted. What the delay of years might have effected, to render this attempt more worthy the reader's attention, he will not venture to suggest. The Horatian advice, though often the critic's precept, has rarely been the poet's example: time and circumstance are to be duly estimated; and, in the present instance, it is hoped, allowance will be made for the vivid impression produced on the mind from our earliest years, by the awful scenery of the Redeemer's human life, which

> "—— might demand a seraph's tongue,
> Were it not equal to its own support,
> And therefore no incompetence of mine
> Can do it wrong."

"To inbreed and cherish in a people the seeds of virtue and public civility, to allay the perturbations of the mind, and set the affections in right tune; to celebrate in glorious and lofty hymns the throne and equipage of God's almightiness, to sing victorious agonies of saints and martyrs, the deeds and triumphs of just and pious nations, doing valiantly against the enemies of Christ; lastly, whatsoever in religion is holy and sublime, in virtue amiable or grave; whatever hath passion or admiration in all the changes of that which is called fortune from without; or the wily subtleties or refluxes of man's thoughts from within,—all these things with a solid and tractable smoothness to point out and describe," —is the true aim of poetry, as described and realised by the loftiest of epic poets. To aspire after this, even at the remotest distance, can form no man's disgrace: he may not secure fame, but assuredly he partakes a higher reward than mere reputation can bestow, while he endeavours to promote that spiritual elevation of character which constitutes the true enjoyment of a Being whose destiny survives the world.

LINCOLN COLLEGE, *Oxon*, 1832.

BOOK I.

> "Floriferis ut apes in saltibus omnia libant,
> Sic nos scripturæ depascimur aurea dicta,
> Aurea, perpetuâ semper dignissima vitâ!"
> LUCRET. lib. iii.

"Prophecy is of prodigious extent.—It commenced from the fall of man, and reaches to the consummation of all things.—The declared purpose for which the Messiah, prefigured by so long a train of prophecy, came into the world, corresponds with all the rest of the representation,—it was to deliver a world from ruin, to abolish sin and death, to purify and immortalise human nature. We have no words to denote greater ideas than these; the mind of man cannot elevate itself to nobler conceptions."—HURD.

ANALYSIS OF BOOK I.

Apostrophe to the Divine Spirit—Creation, the Offspring of Almighty Love—Sketch of Man's primal state and fall—The fathomless Mystery of Evil—The Curse, and its attendant awfulness—Necessity of Atonement.—The Majesty of Christ's Redemption—He is the Soul and Centre of all Revelation and Rites—Was present at the delivery of the Law from Sinai—Picture of the Camp of Israel in the Wilderness—The Gloom of Death as it must have appeared to our first Parents—Their Retrospections—Birth of Eve's first Child, and her triumphant Exclamation—Abraham—Isaac—The offering of the latter, a type of that Heavenly Sacrifice hereafter to be offered up for the whole World—Beauty and Simplicity of the Patriarchal State—Balak—Prophecy—Grandeur of the Prophetical Character—The Announcement of Messiah, a leading Characteristic of the Sacred Predictions—Job, the Doctrine derived from his Sufferings—His sublime expression of Faith in a Redeemer—David, his magnificentc haracter as a Poet and Prophet—Prophecies relative to Christ—Isaiah, his Style, and Predictions—Ezekiel, Daniel, and Malachi—Each considered as Prophetical Announcers of Christ and His Kingdom—Reflections on the Saviour, as they may arise to a contemplative Mind in Solitude—The Glory and Felicity of Spirits who worship, love, and obey Him.

Of Man's redemption by almighty Blood,
When God incarnate on the earth became
Apparent, and in bleeding glory died,
I sing: O Thou! for Whom the worlds were made,
Instruct me in this high attempt, and theme
August of all-surpassing Love divine;
That with no daring eye or step profane
The Muse may wander where the Saviour trod:
If e'er at morning, noon, or solemn night,
Thy shadow on my soul hath been, or prayer
Or praise before Thy hymnĕd Throne prevail'd,
Priest of the Universe! my song inspire.

Ere Matter out of nothingness arose,
Or, Time his destined march of years began,
Himself was All! the unapparent God:[1]
But, Life the symbol of His Love appeared;
He will'd a universe, and lo, it was!

With Nature in her young excess of bloom
Array'd, and with a living sense of joy
Abroad upon the verdant face of things,
How exquisite must earth's primeval state
Have been, how tinted with the hues of heaven!
And when amid it, from unbreathing dust
A living Shape of godlike beauty rose,
Alas! that e'er on such transcendent scene
A shade of guilt could fall! that clouds advanced
In wrath and darkness o'er offending Earth,
No longer bright with angel-steps, but sad
And stricken, trembling at her God!

When Man as monarch of the globe was placed
Where lavish Eden waved and smiled, erect
He stood; but to his Maker homage due
By test of one supreme command was tried.
"Of every tree which in the garden grows
All freely eat, save *that*, wherein of Good
And Evil the forbidden knowledge lies;
Whereof the day thou eatest,—thou shalt die!"[2]
A Tempter came, the interdicted Fruit
Man dared to eat, and from his high estate
Of sinless glory into darkness fell!

In this black hour when evil Doom prevails,
Shall finite teach the Infinite his ways
Or shape the path Omnipotence shall tread?
Shall man, in dreams of wild presumption, dare
His Maker criticise, or blindly call
Our fate unjust? Shall fancy, in her flight
Insane, beyond the Empyrĕan soar,
The God unthrone, His attributes affect,
And fashion worlds to prove his wisdom wrong?

Let Nature hope; and while her blessings thrive,
To secret Heaven resign the dark unknown![3]

A deathless soul, as imaging its God,
In preciousness the jewell'd earth transcends;
And when 'twas darken'd, vast Creation felt
Its value, since the righteous Curse which came
On ruin'd manhood, thrill'd all nature through,
And round the world its dread vibration ran!
Cited for judgment, then the Creature saw
The Face Almighty robed in frowning ire
Bent o'er him; and with sinking brow and frame
While reel'd the ground whereon the trembler trod,
Heard the dread fiat, which all time confirms,—
"Dust since thou wert, to dust return and die!"

Pale in the gloom of that departed Cloud,*
Whose shadow, like a lightning-track had scathed
The bowers of Paradise, when Adam stood
With eyes aghast, and view'd the forfeit-world
Wither around him, while his fancy heard
The Curse still rolling on the awe-struck wind,
The dimness and the agony of doubt
How terribly his fallen soul endured!
For what forbade, but in the hour he sinn'd,
By one annihilating word consumed
That earth should perish in the pangs of hell?
Oh! ye, who in the choir of Cherubim
Divinely shaped, upon your sapphire-thrones
Which in the palace of Jehovah blaze,
One anthem of seraphic bliss prolong,
My lyre attune, triumphantly to sing,
Who sun-like dawn'd upon the gloom of death,
Justice and mercy in His cross combined,
And roll'd away God's thunders from the world!

But say, hath ever hymn by Angel sung,
Hath thought divined, or human voice express'd
This miracle of miracles profound,
A world redeem'd, and Christ redemption's Lord?
I've seen the Sun, creation's paramount,
Rise o'er the waves and lead the march of Day;
Alone have mused, when tempest roof'd the heavens
With blackness, and the quiring Ocean heard,
When choral billows, as with conscious swell,
Chanted loud anthems in the hush of night;
The dark sublimity of deepest storms
Hath girdled, and the glories of the sky

* The cloud of glory, which betokened the Divine Presence.

O'erwhelm'd me : in humbleness and awe
Before the majesty of human Worth
I've bow'd, and felt how lovely Virtue is ;
But poor and powerless, dim and undefined,
The adoration born of scenes or hours
Below, to *that* which o'er the spirit comes,
When silent, Lord ! it thinks alone of Thee.

In Christ all Revelation lives. His voice
With man in Eden dread communion held,[4]
To teach him morning-vow, or evening-prayer,
Or sacrifice divine : the shadowy Type,
The mystic Law, and sacramental Powers,
To Him relate : and when thy desert rang
O Sinai ! with the battle-hymns of old,
While Judah's banners in victorious play
Flouted the vassal wind, the Lord o'erhung
The travell'd wilderness ; a signal-Cloud
By day and night His awful guidance led :
And Horeb heard Him ; when, in lightning veil'd,
Her giant form beneath His thunder bow'd,
As high o'er all the dreadful trumpet clang'd
With heaven-toned music, till the Desert shook.

That Wilderness ! oh, when hath mind conceived
Magnificence beyond a midnight there,
When Israel paused, and o'er her tented host
The moonlight lay ? On yonder palmy mount,
Lo, sleeping myriads in the dewy hush
Of night repose : around, in squared array,
The camps are set ; and in the midst, apart,
That curtain'd Shrine where mystically dwells
Jehovah's presence : through the soundless air
A cloudy pillar, robed in burning light,
Appears ; concentered as one mighty heart
A million* lie, in mutest slumber bound,
Or, panting like the Ocean when a dream
Of storm awakes her. Heaven and Earth are still :
In radiant loveliness the Stars pursue
Their pilgrimage, while moonlight's wizard hand
Throws beauty, like a spectre-light, on all.
At Judah's tent the lion-banner stands
Upfolded, and the pacing sentinels,—
What awe pervades them, when the dusky groves,
The rocks Titanian, by the moonshine made
Unearthly, or yon mountains vast,† they view !
But soon as morning bids the sky exult,
As earth from nothing, so that countless host
From slumber and from silence will awake

* Lamey's Account of the Hosts and Camps of Israel. † Horeb and Sinai.

To mighty being : while the forest-birds
Rush into song, the matin-breezes play,
And streamlets flash where roving sunbeams fall.
Like clouds in lustre, banners will unroll,
The trumpet shout, the warlike tramp resound,
And hymns of valour from the marching Tribes
Ascend, to gratulate the risen Morn.

Though Mercy, when a malediction fell
On Life and Matter from the lips of God,
That Woman's seed should bruise the Serpent's head
Predicted, still, in ghastly vision came
The shadows of thy then unenter'd world
O Death ! but time hath half thy gloom unveil'd.
Though yet invisible, no more thy realm
A desert seems where nothing human dwells :
By ages peopled, 'tis the haunt of Dreams
Forsaking earth, to roam and muse awhile
With Shapes of being, who did once imbibe
The vital breath. There, ancient Seers exist,
Whose words were mightier than thunder-tones
When Nature trembles; there, the Good abide,
The glorious, gifted, and immortal are.
And who of death would all oblivious be
When friends are tomb'd, and parents smile no more ?
To loved eternity where *they* repose
The orphan wanders in parental dreams
How often, and the widow calls it, Home !

Yet 'twas not thus, when new-created Earth
From chaos rose, with deepest verdure clad :
Flower, fruit, and tree, in primal beauty waved ;
No tint of death, no touch of sad decay
Then marr'd the freshness of the lovely scene.
Hence, the dread fiat, " Perish ! dust thou art,
And unto dust shalt thou again return,"
To Adam sounded like Creation's knell !

Upon the wide and voiceless world, alone
The guilty wanderers, whom fair Eden once
Embower'd, in fond remembrance often mourn'd
The bloom of Paradise, and pure estate
For ever lost. The Morning rose, and light
Around them in its warm luxuriance fell ;
But ah ! it could not through the spirit beam
As once, when Day and Heaven together rose,
While harping angels on the breezes sang :
And Evening, with her tenderness of shade
O'ercame them, like a cloud of solemn grief ;
For then, of Paradise and dewy calm
They thought, as there they watch'd the vesper-hues
In beautiful consumption fade and die,
All innocently blest. Thus pass'd the day

In wo; and dreams of sworded Cherubim
Glared on their slumber! still, their God was near;
And when the pangs which only mothers feel
Dejected Eve endured, and lo! a child
Was born, th' unclouded spring of hope began.
And who can fathom that deep hour of love
When *first* an infant on its mother smiled,
And in the bright enchantment of that bliss
Her babe she clasp'd, and to Jehovah cried,
"The promised Seed! Almighty! *now* 'tis born!"

Thus dimly on the world's primeval state
Messiah dawn'd; till God himself declared
To sainted Abram, as the countless orbs
Of midnight glitter'd over Hebron's plain,
That like yon stars a glorious race should rise
Unnumber'd, till the earth's Deliverer came,
And crown'd all nations blest. Then, Isaac rose,
The child of promise, the Redeemer's type
On the stern altar by his parent laid!
The son, the only son, whom Abram loved
Yet did not spare, when Heaven commanded, "Slay!"

Ere the rich morning on the mountains flung
A robe of beauty; in that vestal hour
When birds are darting from the dewy ground,
And nature, soft as sleeping life, begins
To waken, and the spell of day to wear,
Unseen the patriarch and his cherish'd boy
Uprose, the sacrificial wood prepared,
And thus, companion'd by his household-youths,
They onward journey'd with the laden ass.
Through piny glens, and green acacia-vales
The pilgrims wound their undulating way.
Oft as he went, upon his child beloved
The Sire of nations look'd, and inly pray'd;
And felt the father in his bosom rise,
As bound and bloody, on the altar stretch'd
He vision'd him!—the long-hoped, destined son
Who fond and dutiful had ever been,
And guiltless of a parent's tear. But, faith
Triumphant in the power of mercy proved.
Twice had the Sun around the pilgrims drawn
His evening-veil, when o'er a distant mount,
Upon Moriah's steep and rocky clime
A Vision of the Lord reposed, and shone,—
A cloudy signal, shaped for Abram's eye
Alone to see, and there his altar raise.
The patriarch bow'd; and o'er the mountain-path
Both child and parent took their solemn way,
But each was silent, for they thought of Heaven.

Thus on they went, till at the mount ordain'd
Arriving, with enamour'd gaze they saw
Green heights, and forest-crested hills afar,
And willow'd plains; and drank the balmy air,
And cool'd their foreheads in the breeze, which play'd
Like the soft tremor of an angel-wing;
So hush'd the hour, the spot so calm, that God
Himself seem'd waiting there to welcome man!
Then Isaac, as the stony altar-pile
Beneath the shadow of a mountain-tree
Was reared, and sacramental fire prepared,
In words of unsuspecting sweetness cried,
"My father!"—Abram answer'd, "Here, my son!"
"The wood and fire behold! but where the lamb
Of sacrifice, to crown yon flaming pyre?"
Then heaved his bosom with the love of years
Departed; and a tear paternal rose
As gazed he fondly on that only child,
And far away a childless mother saw
Whose heart had echoed every infant-cry!
But soon the strife, and soon the tear was o'er:
To Heaven he look'd, and thus to Isaac spake:
"My son! in *thee* a sacrifice the Lord
Hath found, and—thou to God art dedicate!"[5]
He answer'd not; but meekly knelt him down
And on the altar lay, a willing Lamb.
But God descended; and the hand uplift
In glorious faith to sacrifice a child,
Was holden, while angelic tones proclaim'd
"O Abram! spare thy son! thine only spare,
And let him live, for thou art faithful found."
With thrilling wonder and ecstatic awe
Up look'd the Patriarch, and behold! a ram
Beside him, in a woody thicket caught:
And while it bled, again the Voice sublime
Repeated, like the sound of golden waves,
"In blessing I will bless thee; and thy seed
The sand of ocean shall outnumber far,
And from it spring the Glory of the World!"

But next, on Jacob, in symbolic dream
The Incarnation dawn'd, as lone and sad,
His couch the earth, his canopy the skies,
The exiled patriarch from wild Esau fled.
When night had deepen'd, homeless, pale, and worn,
The wanderer, pillow'd on a stone-built couch,
For slumber stretch'd him on the dreary plain.
Companionless he was, 'mid forests dark
With midnight-umbrage, torn by wolfish winds,
And echoed by the frequent lion-roar
Howl'd from the hills; but God he ever felt;
And round his heart parental blessings twined,
Till sleep came o'er him, like a smile from Heaven.
Rude was the couch, but oh! his angel-dream

To witness, Saints would now a ruder share!
He dreamt; and lo! a Ladder, based on earth,
And buried in the sky, before him rose;
Adown it Shapes of awful beauty stole,
While others clad with archangelic beams
Did solemnly from step to step ascend:
Above, a formless Apparition shone,
Ineffable! from Whom a voice divine
In accent richer than the full-toned sea,
Proclaim'd, "Thy father's God! and thine, behold!
Wide o'er the world thy destined seed will spread,
And, numberless, empeople lands and isles,
Till ONE arise, and make all kingdoms blest."
"How dreadful! 'tis the gate of heaven!" he cried:
'Mid solemn breathings of melodious air
Aloft then moved the hierarchal Pomp;
And ere the lark to hymn the Day began
The exile rose, a rocky pillar raised,
Shed o'er its top the consecrating oil,
And in the hush of morning hied away.

"From Judah's hand the sceptre shall not fall,
Till Shiloh come; to Him shall Empires bow!"
So spake a patriarch from his couch of death;
And thus, through all the realm of holy Writ,
Messiah is the Morning Star of Hope
Who beams for ever on the soul of truth.

But, ere deep Prophecy its organ-strain
Its full magnificence of tone begin,
A vision of that unforgotten prime
The patriarchal age, when Earth was young,
Awhile, oh! let it linger. On the soul
It breaketh, like a lovely burst of spring
On gazing captives, when the open skies
Again are floating over Freedom's head.
Though sin had wither'd with a charnel-breath
Creation's morning-bloom, there still remain'd
Elysian hues of that angelic scene
When the Sun gloried o'er a sinless world,
And with each ray produced a flower. From dells
Untrodden, hark! the breezy carol comes
Upwafted, with the chant of radiant birds;
While meadows, bathed in greenest light, and woods
Gigantic, towering from the skiey hills,
And odorous trees in prodigal array,
With all the elements divinely calm,
Our fancy pictures on the infant globe.
And ah, how godlike, with imperial brow
Benignly grave, yon patriarchal Forms
Tread the free earth, and eye the naked heavens!
In nature's stamp of unassisted grace
Each limb is moulded; simple as the mind
The vest they wear; and not a hand but works,
Or, tills the ground with honourable toil.
By youth revered, their sons around them grow
And flourish; monarch of his pastoral tribe,
A Patriarch's throne is each devoted heart;
And when he slumbers on the tented plain
Beneath the vigil-stars, a living wall
Is round him, in the might of love's defence.
And he is worthy: sacrifice and song
By him are ruled; and oft at shut of flowers
When queenly virgins in the sunset go
Water to carry from the crystal wells,
In beautiful content, beneath a tree
Whose shadows hung o'er many a hallow'd sire,
He sits; recording how Creation rose
From nothing, of the Word almighty born;
How man had fallen, and where Eden-boughs
Had waved their beauty on the breeze of morn;
Or, how the Angels still at twilight love
To visit Earth with errands from the Sky.

But like a river that its course renews,
Again my song to its high Theme returns.
When Balak, frighted by the banner'd hosts
Of Israel, camping on unbounded plains,
For Balaam sent, upon his trancèd eye
Prophetic visions from th' Almighty fell.

There, when the monarch on the mountain stood,
Seven altars,[6] oxen, and seven rams prepared,
And sacrifice of mystic numbers paid,—
The Seer his oracle of light unroll'd.
He look'd, and lo! along that river'd vale
Where Arnon glitter'd, shone the myriad tents
Of Judah, whitening in the lustrous air,
Like clouds which congregate on summer-sky
In ranks of infinite and fresh array:
Then, all the chords of Heaven's predictive lyre
Quiver'd, with more than melody intoned,
And superhuman Poetry began!
His curse was buried in the bliss foretold;
While glory, blessing, and mysterious joy
The tents of Jacob from the prophet drew:
Till Ecstacy this higher strain attuned
In—"I shall see Him, but not now! a Star
From Jacob, and from Israel shall arise
A Sceptre, in whose shadow will depart
Thy race and region, O deserted king!"

Thus Prophecy to man from heaven was breathed
A miracle beyond all utterance deep,
Immeasurably vast; outmarching Time,
Subduing Space, and with colossal might
Erecting Thrones; or crushing city-walls
With curses, like the winds when desert-born,
Terrific, loud, with desolation wing'd![7]

And they, elected to be Mouths for God,
Dread Oracles! whose dooming words have blanch'd
The cheek of Empires in their godless pride
And palsied high-domed Capitals with fear,
August and lonely, sad, yet all sublime
They lived, in sackcloth robed, in deserts housed
Or mountain cavern; fated, and apart
From blinding shadows of terrestrial sway,
They dwelt, communing with almighty Thought.
The gloom, the glory, and the Vision came,
The Future rendered voiceless secrets up,
And then, like phantoms, from eternity,
Dim Ages rose, and answered to their Spell!

And he, whose sorrow was sublimely borne,
Whose grief was glory, for it made the soul
A witness how the Everlasting thinks,—
Behold him! on the ashy ground reclined.
Seven days and nights have o'er his throbbing head
Departed, still, in mutest wo he bows
With three beside him. Oft when darkness rose,
A groan sank dreary on the midnight-air;
But, soon his agony again retired
Back to the gulph of unlamenting gloom!
Nor lip, nor limb his inward strife reveals;
Despair in stone was not more dumb than he!
Prometheus, chain'd on Scythia's burning rock,
When lightning, tempest, and Tartarean ire
With thund'ring earthquake round his martyr'd frame
The tragedy of Nature's wreck begun,
In full sublimity of godlike wo
Was less exalted than the silent Job.

And, what a lesson of undying truth
The torture of the Scene supplies! Array'd
In whirlwind, did the vocal God declare
Secrets of glory, or mysterious depths
Of Essence Infinite to man unshroud?
No! sea and mountain, thunder-storm and cloud,
The glorious miracles of life and form
Which float the waters, or the earth command,
These are but types of Trinitarian power,
Yet, who the mystery of *their* being knows?
Lost in the march of God's material ways,
If Reason wander, how could thought abstract
His moral Kingdom perfectly conceive?
To question deeply what we darkly know,
Our boding fancies in their raven flight
Cross and re-cross a universe of gloom,
And yet, in *this* appall'd conviction ends,—
That God is good, and infinite, and wise,
But Man a daring antichrist, who dreams
Himself the measure of Eternal Mind!

When Nature, in her awful doubt, creates
Mystery and madness for the heart and brain,
From all which life endures, let mortals feel
That man, the infant of eternity,
By wo is nursed, and strengthen'd for the skies;[8]
And a brave soul, though Earth and Hell combine
To scatter tempest round its blighted way,
Beholds a God in all things but despair!
In hours of sadness, when Oppression rules,
And each pale sunburst of unwonted joy
Breaks o'er the spirit, like derisive beams
Of summer playing round a wintry realm,
Let Grief remember how the patriarch cried
With voice that travell'd o'er the sea of Time,
"Oh! that the graven rock my words imprest,
And iron stamp'd them with eternal truth!
For though in dust my body be dissolved,
That my Redemer liveth, and shall stand
When time is ended, on this mortal earth,
I surely know: on Him mine eye shall gaze,
And in my flesh shall I The Lord behold!"

God's Incarnation is the focal truth[9]
Where prophecy's converging beams unite.
And Thou! the shepherd-king, of Jesse born,
Of Heaven beloved, similitude express
Of Christ, the Lord of everlasting worlds,
Whether on Zion hill thy holy strain
Be harped, or by the brook of Kedron hymn'd;
Or nightly warbled, when unnumber'd orbs
To thee their origin divine declared,—
Thy words are breathings by the soul attuned;
For aye thou seem'st a Singer from above
Who chants the glory of remember'd skies.

Wouldst thou in meekest adoration bend,
Or mount the heavens, and with bright myriads swell
The chorus of eternity? Does Grief
Around thee blacken in her stormy ire,
Or sad dejection on thy eyelids weigh?
The royal minstrel hath a mood for thee
And in his heart deep echoes for thine own!
But when the frame of this majestic World
The mind o'erawes, then! who like him appeals
To clouds and whirlwinds, with the Thunder talks,
Partakes the tempest, and of Ocean learns
Such mimicry sublime, that Fancy hears
In God's own orchestra of waves and winds
The billows, echoed by his heaven-strung lyre.
But Nature in her gentleness, alike
From David woos a sympathy divine.
The lull of night, the language of the stars,

And all that beautiful, serene, or blest
Is deemed, his harp melodiously inspires.

Bard of the Spirit! thine heroic song,
Whose hallelujahs in Engeddi's cave,
Or forest glens, and palmy grove, prevail'd
O'er every pang his exiled bosom felt,—
Attunes Religion's universal voice.
Canadian forests, or the parchèd wilds
Of Afric, ocean-rocks, and cavern-gloom,
Wherever Man to God in prayer ascends,
Thy melodies the yearning heart relieve.
And oh! what blessings have thy hymns evoked
From Heaven's vast treasury of light and love
Since first they sounded on a shepherd's lyre!
For they are all Imagination dreams
Angelic lips might warble:—on the Cross
Of Calvary, ere the Son of Man dismiss'd
His martyr'd spirit, *thine* was His farewell!

But chief o'er all in David's glorious strain,
The homage wafted to that destined Throne
Whereon would reign a universal King
From him descended:—in his darksome wo
The Martyr and the Maker of our world
Was symbolised, beneath a veiling gloom.
And when exalted, his far-reaching eye
By heaven unscaled, in emblematic light
Foreshadowed Him, the Triumpher o'er death,
And Victor of the grave. Thus, vision-blest,
The prophet-minstrel all divinely sung;
Thus rose from mortal to immortal themes,
Above his nature tower'd, and hail'd on high
Christ from eternity by God decreed
The earth to ransom and mankind restore.

And how he imageth the Lord of souls
Before us, when he mounteth on the wings
Of rapture, soaring through the heaven of heavens!
"From Zion shall He wither in His wrath
Rebellious kings! to me hath He declared,
My Son thou art! this day Jehovah hath
Begotten Thee; the heathen are Thine own,
And vanquish'd worlds beneath Thy sceptre bow!"

But when the starry hush and pomp of night
O'erawed him, and the moon her Maker's hand
Confess'd, the spirit of prophetic Truth
Again was vocal: thus the minstrel sang:
"When I consider how the balanced heavens
Almightiness in moving pomp reveal,
Lord! what is man? yet Him hast thou encrown'd;
Upon the deep his vast dominion walks,
And subject earth beneath his sceptre bows.

"Ever before me lives the Lord of Hosts!
His hand o'ershades me, and my heart exults:
And soaring hope, by inspiration plumed,
Wings o'er the sepulchre its flight,—for there
A Soul shall triumph; and thy Holy One
No dark corruption of the dead shall stain!"

"How beauteous Thou, above the sons of men!
Upon Thy lips what loveliness diffused!
Array Thee in thy glory! gird Thy sword
Upon thy thigh; majestically ride!
Hark! Earth is quaking; her foundations rock,
Thine arrows thicken; terrible Thy sway!
For ever and for ever is Thy Throne,
And righteously Thy boundless sceptre rules,
And over all Thy God anoints Thee great.

"Through dateless ages are Thy years unroll'd;
The earth was founded, and the heavens were arch'd
By Thee; Creation felt Thy forming hand;
But while they perish, Thou shalt aye endure:
When, like a vesture, they are changed and gone
Still, Thou art One, Eternal and the True!"

And thus did Zion's royal minstrel chant,
And through the cloud of unaccomplish'd time
His glance direct, to that transcendent reign
Of Mercy, when the veil would be uproll'd
And brightly dawn th' Incarnate Sun of Worlds.

Next in the train of these immortal Seers
Another of the heaven-directed hail;
Who, like the clarion that shall rouse the dead,
Might quicken dust,—such life his song inspires!
Amid a temple, bright as Syrian noon,
Upon a Throne unutterably high
O'er which the six-wing'd Seraphim appear'd,
The Lord was seated; and the awful cry
Of "Holy, Holy, Holy, is the Lord!"
Melodious came from each seraphic lip:
And in that Vision, as a centre stood
Appall'd Isaiah, seeing, hearing all.

Terrific Bard, and mighty! in thy strain
The passion and the poetry of truth
And deep-toned storms of inspiration roll,
Whether for cities by th' Almighty cursed
Thy wail arose; or, on enormous crimes
Which darken'd heaven with supernatural gloom,
Thy flash of indignation fell, alike
The feelings quiver when thy Voice awakes!
Borne in the whirlwind of a dreadful song
Our spirit travels round the destined globe,

While shadows, cast from solemn years to come,
Fall round us, and we feel a God is nigh!

But when a gladness from thy music flows,
Creation brightens; glory decks the sky,
The Sun is mantled with millennial smiles
And green earth temper'd for immortal spring:
The lion smoothes his ruffled mane, the lamb!—
And wolf together feed, and by the den
Of serpents, see the rosy infant play!

There is a Day, the darkness of whose scene
In visitings of dread might well subdue
The world's false brightness, foreordained to come,
When the huge fabric of this stately Globe
Shall bow with terror in the storm of doom.
Then, in that hour of chaos, while the earth
And heaven shall fade like elemental dreams,
High on some rocky eminence enthroned
Methinks Isaiah might *his* voice awake
In bursts of wo magnificently wild,—
The last that lingers round a dying World!

But, Prince of Prophets! in thy page eterne,
How visibly the Son of God appears!
"Behold, a Virgin shall conceive, and bear
A son; Immanuel shall his name be call'd."
Again;—"For unto us a Child is born,
To us a Son is given; and his name
Is, Wonderful, the Everlasting Prince
Of Peace! the Counsellor, and mighty God!

"A Voice comes wafted through the Wilderness!
Prepare the way, and be the Desert smooth:
Arise, ye valleys! and ye mountains, sink
Before Him! for the Lord Jehovah comes!

"Despised, rejected, and a Man with grief
Acquainted, surely He our woes hath borne,
And in His bosom all our sorrows ta'en!
Our chastisement is on Him: we are heal'd,
But He is wounded! and on Him alone
The Lord hath laid th' iniquity of all!"

Nor, when captivity by Chebar mourn'd,
And Israel wore the Babylonian chain
Beside the willow-shaded streams, was dumb
The Voice prophetic: but where Belus rose
In her stupendous prodigy of towers,
Ezekiel pour'd his passionate lament;
Or shaped for time the Destinies he saw
From heaven prefigured:—what colossal shades
As though reflected from the scenes immense
Around him, crowd upon his fated world!
But high o'er all the visionary Pomp
To us the Cedar of the Gospel rears
Its allegoric boughs, beneath whose shade
Birds of all clime, and wing, and beauty dwell.

So Daniel, when his midnight-trance began
On the dim bosom of that mystic Sea
Whose waters quiver'd in the tempest-grasp,
Beheld him, coming with the clouds of heaven,—
The Son of Man; then, throned in flaming pomp
With myriads of Angelic Forms begirt,
Perpetual empire to the Son was given
O'er land and language, kingdom, sea, and isle.

And thus, wherever bright prediction beams,
The glories of the Incarnation dawn.
At last, with healing on his wings, arose
The Sun of Righteousness, to him* who cried,
"Before the splendour of that dreadful day
A Herald of the Lord, Elijah comes,
To turn thy heart, O guilty world! to me,
Or thou shalt wither in My blast of ire!"

So Prophecy, with time begun, with time
Shall end; and when in some empyreal Sphere
The mind expands with far sublimer reach
Than prescient faith, or fancy can extend,
In proud fulfilment Prophecy will reign.
For, having grasp'd the glory of the world
Redeem'd, and taught us how Millennium smiles,
Beyond the Universe of sense it wings
An awful flight, and in mysterious depths
Of Being unexplored, for man foredooms,
A state unspeakably divine and pure,—
Eternity, O God! and shared with Thee.

Almighty Priest! Thou angel-worshipp'd Lord
In secrecies of uncreated Light
Though now enthron'd, Thy sympathies retain
Their human oneness with Thy People still;
And, for the Church, thy Mystic Body call'd,
Plead and prevail with eloquence divine.
As oft in chamber dim, or lonesome walk
By leafy twilight arch'd, the Mind foreviews
Its own eternity, and dreams Thy Form
To life again,—how wonderful, apart,
By time unsoil'd, by accident, or sin
Immaculate as Love and Law required
Thy Being riseth in irradiant truth,
Before us, purer than the light of light,
Of all Transcendencies the sum and soul![10]
And when did Earth Thine attribute display,—
One vast Benevolence, which girt a world
Of hearts by catholic embrace of love?
All time and truth, all empires and all powers

* Malachi.

That were, or would be, in the march of fate,
By Thee were compass'd for Redemption's plan!

When o'er the grandeur of unclouded heaven
Our vision travels with a free delight,
As though the boundless and the pure were made
For speculation, so the towering mind
By inward oracle inspired and taught,
The Lofty and the Excellent in mind reveres;
And thus, the Incarnation of divinest love,
God's perfect Image, humanised for Man,
As Finite loved, as Infinite adored,
Messiah is; and hence to faith presents
A Model for the Universe.—Though God
Be round us, by the shadow of His might
For aye reflected; and with plastic Hand
Prints on the earth the character of Things;
Yet He Himself,—how awfully retired
Depth within depth, unutterably deep!
His Glory brighter than the brightest thought
Can image, holier than our holiest awe
Can worship—utter'd only in, I AM![11]

But Thou! apparell'd in a robe of true
Mortality; meek Sharer of our low
Estate, in all except compliant sin,
To Thee can sacrificial Awe devote
A living holocaust of sense and soul
By love enkindled. Thou hast lived and breathed;
Our wants and woes partaken; all that charms
Regenerate hearts to Thine unspotted truth
May plead for sanction;[12] Virtue but reflects
Thine image; Wisdom is a voice attuned
To consonance with Thine; and all which yields
To Thought a pureness, or to Life a peace,
From Thee descends; whose spirit-ruling sway,
Invisible as thought, around us brings
A balm almighty for Affliction's hour.
Once felt, in all the fulness of Thy grace
The mystic essence of our moral life
To form,—and heaven by holiness begins!
Which purifies the base, the dark illumes,
And binds our being with that holy spell
Whereby each function, faculty, and thought
Surrenders meekly to the central Guide
Of hope and action, by a God empower'd.[13]

Until the eyelids of the Dead unclose
Though Christ has vanish'd into viewless light,
High o'er the world, beyond heroic state,
To reach or rival, is Man's inner-life
Securely founded on the Rock of faith!
All the wide glories which the eye commands,
Or air and ocean, earth and heaven supply,
Of Him report, whose potency begat
Them all. The ground is hallow'd, for 'twas trod
By Him; all Earth is radiant with a sense
Ethereal, born of His remember'd sway:
Nor pang, nor trial, torture, grief, nor care
Communion high and mystic interchange
With Him destroys; in solitude alike,
As in the roaring capital, a Saint
Embodies into human Form again
That living Saviour, Whom the Past perceived
And worshipp'd, angels gloried to announce,
And Whose perfections so harmonious are
That o'er them God's eternal sabbath smiles.*

BOOK II.

"The intellectual Power, through words and things,
Went sounding on, a dim and perilous way."
WORDSWORTH.

"Melior origo nos expectat, alius rerum status. Dies iste, quem tanquam extremum reformidas, æterni natalis est."—SENECA, *Epist.* 102.

ANALYSIS OF BOOK II.

Having shown that the gradual announcement of an Incarnate Redeemer was the primary object of the Prophetic Scheme, the Second Book is principally devoted to a consideration of the necessity and probability of a Revelation from God, by an argument drawn from the nature of the human mind and the destinies of man.

Natural and Revealed Religion—The total inadequacy of the former is endeavoured to be shown by exhibiting a mind most exquisitely attuned to the glories and harmonies of the Universe, yet averse to the truth and character of Christ's atonement; till, finally convinced, by the utter helplessness of human philosophy, it reposes in the Faith which is from Heaven—The probability of a Revelation from God, induced from the weakness, obscurity, and impotence of ancient systems, and the frequent longing of their founders for some certain Lawgiver from above—The Doctrine of Pagan and Christian Philosophy—Sublime superiority of the latter—Its triumphant effects—This Revelation was gradually made, in analogy with the progressive tendencies of the human mind, and the Divine arrangements from the commencement of the World—Belief by compulsion would violate the freedom of the will, and reduce the character of man to an irresponsible nature—Christ—Revelation extends through all ages—Apostrophe to England as a country gloriously distinguished by the ameliorating influence of Christianity—Her Sabbaths—Prayers for the diffusion of the Gospel—And our Country's efforts in this holy toil—Concluding thoughts, sentiments, and descriptive associations.

THERE is a God, the Universe exclaims:
There is a God, Man's echoing heart replies,
And round the world that heaven-born answer rolls!
And thus Creation, while the spirit throbs

* "*This* is my beloved Son, *in whom I am well pleased.*"

In full response to her sublime appeal,
Hath canonised Imagination's creed,
Till all her splendours to the soul become
The faint reflections of a Vast Unseen ! [14]

Yet, vainly beautiful this god of earth
Whom Nature's worship for the soul creates :
Our homage is material ; and the mind,
While in the light of elemental pomp
It lives and moves, may still its darkness keep ;
Unvisited by that perpetual ray
Of Truth divine, from revelation born,
Where God a Person, not Abstraction is,
And His high Attributes to faith become
That inward Decalogue the will obeys.

There is a haunt whose quietude of scene
Accordeth well with hours of solemn hue,—
A church-yard, bosomed in a beauteous vale
Besprinkled o'er with green and countless graves,
And mossy tombs of unambitious pomp
Decaying into dust again. No step
Of mirth, no laughter of unfeeling life
Amid the calm of death that spot profanes.
The skies o'er-arch it with serenest love ;
The winds, when visiting the dark-bough'd elms,
An airy anthem sing ; and birds and bees
That in their innocence of summer joy
Exult, and carol with commingling glee,
But add to solitude the lull of sound.
By sea environ'd, yet the choral waves
By noon entranced, in dreaming slumber lie ;
And when roused Ocean at the roaring blast
Foams in loud fury, still, the deep-toned storm
Mellow'd by distance, into music dies
Like that which echoes from the world afar,
Or lingers round the path of perish'd Years.

And here, companion'd by his soul alone,
A Being, whose unfathom'd spirit fought
With Loneliness, did wander oft and muse
His hours away ; while dream-wove spells entwined
Their mystery round him :—if the Tomb its dead
Surrender'd, well might he arise and prove
How frail the creed which erring Nature moulds
When darkness rushes on the doom of Man !

In vain the witchery of words would tell
How fondly, by impassion'd dreams inspired,
His fancy wed the Universe with love.
The hues and harmonies of blended Things
Were beauty to the magic of his mind ;
And all the thousand wheels of moving life
The intellectual melodies, which played
For ever on the mystic harp of Thought.
Such warm imaginings, where'er he came,
A glittering falseness on the true and stern
Suffused ; and through the light of feeling shone
The scene of earth, and countenance of heaven.
The young enchantment of angelic Spring
Flow'd in his veins, voluptuously deep ;
The budding infancy of flowers was dear
To him, nor would he tread their life away ;
Nor wander in the soundless gloom of dell
Or grove, without a sympathetic hush.
And oh ! to view him when the balmy night
Breathed o'er this quiet world, and from her throne
The lustrous Moon on tree and temple pour'd
The pallid radiance of her peaceful smile,—
In second paradise he seem'd to muse,
Priested by Sentiment, to worship there !

So lived, so felt he ; making all without
Enchantment for responsive thought within ;
But that Eternity which girdles time,
Majestic Faith, and everlasting Hope,
Commoved not him : *Hereafter* drown'd his soul
In seas of darkness, billowing with doubt
And fear !—That this divine, all-beauteous Orb
Whose faintest impulse, sent from breeze or star,
So thrillingly his heart confess'd, was framed,
Upheld, and circled through the void profound
By Power apart, invisibly enthroned,
His innate majesty of mind declared.
But such a god, of dreams and shadows born,
No bended knee, no voice nor vow adored :
He was—a Spirit, or pervading Sense,
A sightless Agent, an almighty Self
Articulated by the tones of Earth
And gloriously by nature's pomp reveal'd,—
So fancy dreamt ; and Feeling taught no more.
And hence did Pride and Passion, which imbue
Mortality with taints of sin and wo
And colour all the atmosphere of life
With clouds of awful gloom, work unrestrain'd,
And rule or sanction the decrees of Thought.

At length Affliction, in whose teaching gloom
The keen-eyed jealousy of Guilt beholds
Truths which our mental Cains deny, or dread,
Blighted his home with desolating blast !
And One, the beatings of whose heart were *his*
Re-echo'd, she who walk'd with angel-step,
Her looks the living sunshine of his soul,
Her tones the music of his memory,
Whose printless foot made consecrated ground,
The hope and heaven of all,—lay still in death !
Then came that worldless, dread, eclipse of mind,
The agony which curdles soul and sense
As though annihilation had begun,
Or man were mouldering into dust again !

One beam of heaven had brought salvation now;
But Darkness girt him with its deepest shroud,
Wherein he stood, nor wept, nor spoke, nor sigh'd,
But, mute and stone-like, turn'd to cold despair!

With tender rudeness to his couch they bore
The widow'd martyr; day by day, and hour
By hour, Affection with her heavenly eye
Attended, faintly smooth'd his pallid brow,
Then touch'd his hand, and with a yearning gaze
Woo'd his dumb anguish into speaking life,
Which came at last; and then, alone he nursed
His sorrow;—in the breathless noon of night;
All unperceived, the lovely dead he found;
There stood, and gazed, enamour'd of the grief
That, now unfrozen, from his spirit pour'd
Tears fast and free, in all the storm of wo!
On that cold form, so spiritually pale,
Where the lone night-watch flung a spectral gleam,
He look'd, as though a life were in that look
Absorb'd, and felt that never more would flash
From pulseless clay revealings of the soul!
The mystery of Being was fulfill'd,
The seal of Nature set, the vision gone,
Or vanish'd in some universe of gloom!
And yet, from dreams a Light immortal soothed
The mourner, when from out the grave he saw
An Apparition, bright as golden air,
Ascend, assume her own appealing smile
And point with waving hand to better worlds!

But Life no longer seem'd the living sense
Of mortal nature; but a ghastly dream
Wherein he moved, by Destiny compell'd.
A dismal trance of dull satiety
This lone world grew; a dampness of despair,
The sullen winter of a broken heart
Was all he felt,—was all he wish'd to feel!
A demon-shadow, by his anguish bred,
O'er all things brooded: in the light no light
Appear'd; e'en melody no music brought,
And earth emaciate as an orb of death
To him became; his thoughts alone did live;
And these, like pulses from a tortured brain,
Throbb'd in the spirit with eternal pang!

And now, the poison of dejection work'd;
His cheeks were blighted; o'er his thin-worn hands
The veins meander'd with a dying hue;
The mournful hair that arch'd his manly brow
Droop'd like decaying locks; his bright eye lost
The boldness of expressive fire, and grew
Unearthly, from its depth of lifeless gaze:
And oft did mothers heave maternal sighs,
And children cease their revel, when he pass'd
Unheedful by them, like a Shape from tombs.

At length, the unbeliever sought the Night
To tell him secrets of eternity.
And then, how terrible the spirit-throes
Of doubting agony a Deist felt!
Above him,—the majestic sea of heaven
Where island-orbs of beauty sail'd and shone;
Around him, dimness and the calm of death
By nothing marr'd, but when some moving branch
Of cypress, like a dying billow shed
A faint sound on the feeble wind.—Intense
And deep, and passionate the gaze he sent
Far in the blue infinity of night!
Oh, let some Angel on his wings of love
Be wafted, and the burning doubt which preys
On sorrow with permitted voice subdue!
He listen'd!—on the air a faded leaf
Fell slowly, with a sad and ling'ring sound
Whose tone seem'd not of earth; but soon it still'd:
And then, the midnight of despair return'd,
And in the blackness of his heart he wish'd
Eternal nothingness his tomb to be!

An hour there came from heaven at last, when Faith
Look'd up, and view'd her God.—As evening smiled
On ocean's western brim, where molten waves
A restless glory of rich waters made,
A pensive wanderer, on the pebbled beach
He stood, communing with the conscious Scene.
Where'er his feeling glance reposed, a charm
There glow'd, which told Almightiness had touch'd
The world; and when the folding clouds enwreath'd
The Day-god on his sunset-throne, and cool
And calm the unimpassion'd Twilight rose,
That purity of second childhood came
Whose tenderness is truth.—In such meek hour
When darkness from the soul dissolves away,
With gentle step and gentler mien approach'd
A hoary Sage, by hallow'd wisdom blest.
The balmy light, the beauty and romance
Of scene, well harmonised with heavenly thought.
And hence, the solemn Teacher on his soul
The dews of immortality distill'd:—
Not hiding Mercy in dogmatic gloom,
Or, led by light presumingly inspired,
Outvent'ring on the mystic waves which roll
Between us, and the shore of worlds unseen;
But, meekly firm, of everlasting Love,
Creative power, and providential Truth

That Christian spake; and leaf by leaf the Book
Of Man's redemption from primeval wo
Unroll'd, and challenged wide Creation's law
To prove, how Nature visioneth the plan [15]
Which God himself descended to reveal.

With soften'd eye, and brow intently sad,
Such theme of glory did the sceptic hear,
Yet answer'd not; but look'd to heaven, and sigh'd.
Now twilight into solemn gloom retired;
The pomp of clouds was o'er; and ocean lay
In floating darkness round the rock-hewn beach;
But here and there prevailing starlight gleam'd
On some excited billow: deep the hour
And holier the scene, as each, immersed
In contemplation, track'd his homeward way;
Unvoiced their feelings, and their thoughts unknown:
But Heaven had watch'd them; and ere shrouding night
Mantled the earth, an unbeliever pray'd!—
When years had vanish'd, and converted mind
Lived in the light of Deity, and knew
The depths of God's redeeming love, how look'd
The Infidel on what his heart had been?
Go! ask some martyr of a dungeon-gloom,
How fresh the light, how beautiful the airs
Of heaven which visit his reviving frame,
And he shall tell thee, what the mourner felt
When broke the clouds from his benighted soul
And Morn, eternal Morn, began to smile!

So weak is all unaided Nature lends
To educate the restless soul of man,
Or solace wo, or subjugate the will
To Conscience, on whose throne dread Justice reigns.
Became it not, then, that almighty Love
From Whom did emanate this wondrous world,
The silence of eternity to break,
Become apparent, and His Name divulge
That mortals might draw near Him, and adore?
Could He, to whom the universe of life
From wave and wind a hymn of worship sends,
Let Man *alone* be ignorantly dumb,
Or mock by Superstition's jarring creed
The awful witness of the God within?
And, did not Man himself, of old, secure
By feign'd communion with celestial Pow'rs,
Profound dominion for the sacred rites
That reach us from the past? In wood, or grove,
And cave orac'lar, Legislation knew
From Heaven to find a sanction and a strength
Reveal'd; and long'd for Deity by truth
Declared, and by celestial faith adored.
Thus Plato,[16] in his pure ambition, nursed
A glorious longing for supremer Mind,
The soul to tune, and teach him perfect Law.

The past survey, and what hath Reason done?
Passion and Doubt her waning light withstood:
And stubborn ages, as they swept along,
But mock'd her impotence with blind misrule,
Of creed, or crime begot.[17] Man look'd abroad,
And on his spirit rush'd one vast belief!
From life and matter, from the sun and moon
And the deep waters did a power appeal,
Attesting God, and teaching His domain;
But *how* to worship, how His law obey,
In vain would philosophic Reason find
In pensive shade, or Academic bower.
The World was deified; terrestrial gods
In all that pantheistic Sense believed,
A mystic reign for adoration held:
Thus, Neptune on his ocean-car appear'd,
Apollo gloried in the realm of light,
And Dian, with her starry nymphs begirt,
The virgin Moon inspired. No wind there breathed,
There waved no grove, no fountain-music play'd,
No River roll'd in liquid joy along,
But Superstition lent a listening ear
To hail her fancied god; each City claim'd
Presiding deities, and built her fanes
For monsters imaged out of monstrous thought,
Where dark Pollution fed her secret fires.
At length, Idolatry the mind subdued;
From tombs evoked the undeserving Dead,
Or, round the statues of her living great
In sycophantic homage knelt, and pray'd.

Religion thus in clouds of error lost,
Morality no saving charm possess'd
To harmonise the wheels of social life.
The world without, to that far mightier world
Within, a secondary station held,
And action was alone the source of law;
While thought and impulse, those creative springs
On which the conduct of our being turns,
In secret wildness kept unholy sway.
Men learn'd to live, but were not taught to die;
Each hour proclaim'd its own peculiar heaven;
The heart might covet what the hand revered;
And in the soul, a thousand years of sin
Lie floating, on a sea of fancy toss'd,
And be unblamed! No inward law prevail'd,
Like that which ever to the Christian speaks;
Prejudging thought, ere yet by deed express'd,
And throning conscience in the heart of man.

Thus, who can wonder that a darkness hung
Round heathen ages, by no hand unveil'd?
Magnificent and mighty was the Past,
In learning, prowess, and devoted arts:
Yet ne'er was hero, in his sun-bright car,
With all his panoply of gorgeous hues
And lauding thunders from a nation's lip
To tell his conquest,—so sublimely great
As dying Stephen, when that martyr quench'd
By glorious faith the agonies of death,
The sky beheld, and for his murd'rers pray'd!

Bright as the morning of primeval day
Burst on the waters of chaotic gloom,
Came revelation on the darksome world.*
Then error vanish'd in celestial truth;
Hush'd were false Oracles, and quench'd the fires
Which savage bigotry for ages fed:
New light, new order, new existence rose!
The pangs of Wo, the wrongs of patient Worth,
Were now no more, as once their truth had been:
Eternity the debt of Time would pay,
The soul redeem, and justify its God.

Yet was not this transcendent scheme of love
To Earth unfolded, till maturing age
Had nerved the spirit for its high display.
But just as nature, by apparent means
And fine gradations of effective power,
The miracle of life and form achieves,
So Mind, in her advance to heavenly things,
Progressively to full redemption came.
In the calm innocence of youthful Time
When Earth undeluged lay, the vocal WORD
By deep communion did Himself impart
To his frail creature, Man: and Spirits bright,
And loving Angels by their Lord empower'd
Brought inward messages from God on high.
When darkly sunk in Amoritish guilt
The patriarchal purity was o'er,
Religion hallow'd with Mosaic law,
And special covenant, and ritual pomp
Of ark and fane and sacrificial blood,
The chosen People;[18] thus in types began
Sublime Theocracy; and when it sunk
To kingly sway, prophetic Bards reveal'd
The One Jehovah, and the promised Seed:
Thus moved the destinies of Earth along
In light and darkness, as career the waves
Through sun and tempest, till Messiah rose.

There are, who deem no revelation true
Which doth not, by divine compulsion, awe
The universal mind to one belief.
But, where the freedom of inviolate will,
If, dazzled into reasonless assent,
Belief is passive, and conviction blind?
The lines of human character are lost,
No principle can act, no feeling sway,
No Passion on the altar of pure Faith
Can nobly die, in sacrifice to Heaven:
As heave the waters to a reinless wind,
So, led by impulse, would the spirit yield
To Fate's high will, without one virtue blest.
For what is virtue, but a vice withstood,
Or sanctity, but daring sin o'ercome?
Life is a warfare, which the soul confronts,
While good and evil, truth and error clash,
Or rally round it in confused array;
And he who conquers, wins the crown of Light
Which Heaven has woven for her warrior-saint.

A God incarnate, with His glory veil'd,
Altar, and priest, and sacrifice combined
In mystic oneness of almighty Love,
Behold Him bleeding! on His awful brow
The mingled sorrows of a world repose:
"'Tis finish'd!"—at those words Creation throbs;
Round Hell's dark universe the echo rolls;
All nature is unthroned; the mountains quake
Like human beings when their death-pang comes;
The sun has wither'd from the frighted air,
And with a tomb-burst, hark! the Dead arise,
And gaze upon the living, as they glide
With soundless motion through the darken'd streets
Most awfully!—the world's Redeemer dies!

That hour of Blood, that scene of Death, is past,
And quench'd the savage eyes that mock'd and smiled
On Calv'ry, when the direful Cross upbore
A martyr'd Saviour: but there comes a mood,
When Fancy wanders to that fated hill,
And from His pleading face, to heaven upturn'd
In godlike pity for the murd'rous Jew,
A look celestial for the soul derives
When faints it oft in penitential gloom.

And thou, my Country! foremost in the van
Of glory found, no Empire which bedecks
The globe, exalted mercies can record
Like those that crown, and still encircle Thee,
Eden of isles! whom ocean loves to guard.
From the foul darkness of engulphing sin
Celestial Mercy bade thy spirit rise
Victorious, and in Christ regen'rate be.

* In Europe alone, at the early periods of Christianity, the number of idols known to be worshipped amounted to thirty thousand.

And, thus environ'd by elective grace,
E'en like a fortress for the faith art thou:
And though not spotless be thy past career,
Religion from thy thousand Temples calls
Aloud on Deity, and walks unseen
The paths of goodness, musing holy joy.

But ah! that day of spiritual delight
Of old revered, and by our fathers blest,
Thy Sabbath, England! is that halcyon morn
Of holiness, when Heaven remembers thee
With sanctifying love, and sheds abroad
A balm that beautifies the face of things.
Redemption won the boon; and long may sounds
From steeple-towers of venerable gloom
Or Minsters brown which deck the hawthorn-vales,
Of sabbbath-music on the breezy wings
Of matin rise, and soft emotions crowd
The soul that listens to their tender chime.
And thus, while unpolluted Altars stand
O'er time secure, and christian ardour keeps
The virtues of our glorious Land alive,
Jehovah! still for us Thine arm will rule;
And Ocean, faithful to her island-born,
Bulwark the clime whose sceptre bows to Thee.

And may the glories of Thy gospel shine
From zone to zone, till earth one Temple prove,
And lauding angels, as they gird the Throne
With choral raptures, hear from saints below
Perpetual anthems which to Christ ascend.
For Thou hast promised, and Thy word shall reign.!
Let earth be riven, sun and system die,
Or nature into nothing be recall'd,
Ere *this* be doubted,—the decree of God!
Oft in the hush of meditative hours
When fancy wanders on mysterious wing
Far into chaos, greets the dawning world,
And down the surging tides of ages floats
E'en to the living hour,—I glow to trace
Omniscient wisdom and perennial love.
E'en now, as here in solitary mood
My spirit warbles in a dream of song,
What destinies are weaving for the race
Of man! what energies of heart and soul
In mingled yet harmonious play, for time
That doom complete Eternity has plann'd?

And, if our wingèd aspirations dare
The hour outfly, and future glory meet,
My brother Man! wherever doom'd thou art,
In dark isles bosom'd on the dusky main
A savage found, magnificently free;
Or, in some icy wilderness of waves,
Soon on thy soul may Revelation dawn
And bid lost nature recognise its God.

That prayer is heard: for with it richly blend
Approving echoes from Britannia's heart.
E'en now, her Genius on some native cliff
Let Fancy view, in speculation rapt.
To rocky isles, and dreadful island-wastes
That spot the billows, her dejected eye
Is turn'd, and what a vision of despair
The savage dwellers on the sea create,
Who round their dying captive dance and howl;
Or, prostrate at some tow'ring idol's car,
In bloody rapture limb and life destroy.
To Heaven she looks, and lo! a sudden burst
Of morning-brightness o'er the midnight-scene;
For woods of horror, laughing corn-fields wave;
For cavern'd homes, and huts of wildest gloom
What sylvan cots and glitt'ring mansions rise,
While sun-clad spires in every woodland gleam!
And ships are riding in securest bays
Of Commerce, where of old untravell'd sea
Lay in grim slumber, or by whirlwinds lash'd.
All things have glided into beauteous change,[19]
And Man, at whose creation God rejoiced,
Not in the gloom and guilt of nature pines,
But beaming with recover'd soul, appears,
A true Schechinah* where the Spirit dwells.
The Genius of my Country!—on her brow
What apostolic smiles of love and light
Begin; for *her* the vision hath unroll'd
Its promise; and to *her* hath God appeal'd.
For Earth, and bade from His divinest source
The spirit of immortal truth proceed
In heavenly conquest, till the knell of Time
Be sounded, and the church in heaven complete.

And here awhile, on this majestic hope
Of brighter ages let the Lyre repose.
But pardon, ye who feel how Nature makes
Her priesthood vocal, if in fond delay
A poet gaze upon the gorgeous eve,
And watch the shadows of a waning sky.

A sunset! what a host of beaming clouds
In mingled lustre multiplied and flash'd,
And flung their beauty in reflected tints
On golden waters, lull'd in gleaming rest,
And then, concenter'd in one pomp of light
Like that which girds th' apocalyptic throne! †
But, ere the sun behind yon sea withdrew,
A thunder-gloom in silent threat advanced;
And the loud hiss of unexpected rain
Rang through the air with its rejoicing fall,
The verdure sparkled, and the sun retired
On waves of glory like an ocean god:
From out the billows beam'd a rainbow-form

* "God hath said, I will dwell in them."—2 *Cor.* vi. 16.
† Vide the Apocalypse.

Which died in azure o'er the distant hills;
The sea-gull flutter'd on his foam-like wing,
And, like a seraph in the air conceal'd,
The wind-tone warbled with unearthly joy.

An hour with nature is an hour with heav'n,
When feeling hallows what the fancy views:
And thus, O Twilight! may a soul discern
In thy meek stillness what harsh day obscures.
Now Mem'ry too with mournful love recalls
Some heart-romance, till years of verdant joy
Revive, and bloom within affection's world.
Bright Forms, by greeting childhood so beloved!
Maternal tones, and features, of whose smile
In blissful rivalry our own was born,
And voices, echoed in our dreams of heaven,
Around us throng, until th' unliving past
Our being enters, and seems life again.

In no false weakness heaves the votive sigh
Of fond remembrance o'er man's fleeting youth;
The poetry of pure regret is there!
To love the past but makes the present dear;
The mournful wisdom of our discontent
Can then unteach what young Delusion taught
Alone; since who that lives, and living, thinks,
But adds another to an endless train
Of sad Confessors since the world began?—
A life of glory is a dream fulfill'd,
That fades in acting, as the gorgeous cloud
E'en as it dazzles is but dying air![20]

If I too, ere autumnal age my brow
Has wrinkled, or the twilight of chill days
Begun, the barrenness of earth perceive,
And feel mortality's most aching wear
Fever and fret the soul; if all which bloom'd
Like Eden once, hath grown a desert now
Of dying hope, and faded joy; if Life be lone,
And sad, and bleak, while aspirations droop
Unwatch'd within me, and delightless earth
More tomb-like grows, as death's absorbing dream
Haunts the worn spirit wheresoe'er it fly
For refuge, may I not existence mourn?
No! let me fall, and worship at the Fount
Of promise; life is Heaven's surpassing gift,
And what his Maker wills, should man revere.

To cover earth with shades of hell; accuse
The sun of darkness, and the world blaspheme;
All hope deny, coequal man disdain,
And mar the heavenliness of human joy,
Betrays a tempest of unholy thought
Raised by the Demon of our darker hours!
But, nobly true, inexplicably deep
That mournfulness by solitude inspired,
When mild dejection ends in musing bliss.
Like a mute pilgrim, on some distant shore
At twilight shaping in the skiey air
The towers and temples of his native land,
While on his ear the sounds of home renew
The sweetness of their social melody,—
Oft may some Dreamer in a spirit-trance
Fancy existence to be exile *now;*
See visions of departed heaven, and hear
The muffled language of mysterious Worlds.
And oh! how oft beneath the bluest sky
In summer arching over lake or wood,
When round and round, with antic motion sport
The insect-populace of beams and flowers;
When herb is bright, and breeze is gay, the Mind
A mystic shadow of dejection feels,
While voiceless omens and prophetic fears
Haunt the deep heart with their undying spell.
For ever on the solemn verge we seem
Of gloom unknown, or glory unreveal'd;
And who shall say, that life does *not* preserve
A faint reflection of some vanish'd State
By man forgot, as oft the sea retains
A dim resemblance of departed storm?

'Tis night; the holiness and heaven of time!
And censure me, mild Elements, whose sway
Of loveliness hath now serened the world,
If by your charm my soul is unsubdued
By prayer, while Nature in devotion seems.
Mysterious hour! when most self-knowledge reigns.
And minutes are soft Teachers, whom the heart
Obeys: and, art Thou not more deeply fill'd
With inspiration from thy Maker sent,
O Earth! than in the day's tyrannic roar?
And if there be, as saintly minds allow,
Some god-like moment, when pure Spirits walk
This lower world,[21] where man is doom'd to strive,
Tranquillity enshrines their presence now.
In pale omnipotence of light the moon
Presides, too brilliantly for meeker stars
To venture forth, save one bright watcher, seen
O'er yon lone hill to let his beauty smile:
The clouds are dead; and scarce a breeze profanes
The blissful calm, save when some rebel dares
On fitful wing to wander into life
Awhile, and make unwilling branches wave,
Or moonlight flutter through the boughs, and fall
In broken radiance on the grass beneath.
The earth grows soundless; and yon giant elms
Hush'd into leafy trance their shade project
Before them: Night and Stillness are enthroned.

Now may the spirit on religious wing
Expatiate; soaring where no science can,
Yet haply, hover round some truth unknown.
And be this earth all reverently trod,
Since out of it did human Dust proceed!
Let all we look upon religion make
For inmost thought, or meditative love.[22]
On choral winds aye let there float a voice
Of God; and Ocean with his organ-waves
Eternal anthems to Jehovah peal.
And oh! may I, when pangful life is o'er,
In some pure region of almighty bliss
A harping strain from those bright Singers learn,
Who in the orchestra of Glory waft
Divine Emmanuel! to Thy merit due,
From golden lyres an everlasting praise.

BOOK III.

"Prepare the way! a God, a God appears!
A God! a God! the echoing vales reply."
POPE.

"A venerable and sacred tradition relates, that by the rising of a certain uncommon star was foretold, not diseases or death, but the descent of an adorable God for the salvation of the human race, and the melioration of human affairs; which star, they say, was observed by the Chaldeans, who came to present their offerings to the new-born God."—*From* CHALCIDIUS, *an ancient Commentator on the Timæus of Plato.*

ANALYSIS OF BOOK III.

The fulness of Time—Probable Sympathy of distant and unknown Worlds—Despair of the Evil One—State of the World—Gabriel commanded to Earth—The Annunciation—Mary's holy raptures—Her Visit to her Cousin at Hebron—Her Journey described—The subject naturally suggests an allusion to the hallowed associations which the beauty and scenery of Palestine awake—The Virgin's arrival—Congratulations—Cæsar's Order for a General Census—Birth of the Messiah—Appearance of the Angels to the Shepherds in Bethlehem Vale—Their Hymn—Visit of the Shepherds to the Cradle of Jesus—Reflections on the humility of Christ's entrance into this World—How contrary to the martial ideas of the Jews—Their doubt, rejection of Christ, and consequent dispersion, when compared with their former high estate, kindle our deepest thoughts of fear and faith—Their future Restoration—Return to the order of the Gospel—Day of Circumcision—Presentation of the Divine Babe in the Temple—Simeon's Ecstacy—Return of the Holy Family to the Vale of Nazareth—Arrival of the Magi—The Craft and Cruelty of Herod—Massacre of the Innocents—Childhood of Jesus—His appearance among the Rabbis at twelve years of age in the Temple—Second Return to Nazareth—The Meditations of the Saviour as He contemplated the Redemption of Man, amid the seclusion and silence of his lowly lot—John the Baptist—His Dwelling in the Desert—Obeys the Holy Spirit—Announces the coming of Christ—Preaches Repentance, which is true wisdom. The Book ends with a view of the consolation of the Scriptures, and the beauty of the outward Universe, when enjoyed in connexion with the Divine Creator.

Now was the fulness of predestined time
Complete, when councils of the God Triune
In Christ embodied, should at length evolve;
And not ungreeted did Redemption's hour
Arrive: before the Throne new radiance burn'd;
And emanations of intenser bliss
Than that which kindled o'er creation's birth,
Angelic myriads felt, as peal'd their chants
Of hymning wonder!—yea, in spirit-worlds
From whence no living Shape to earth has come,
Round these, perchance, a sympathetic thrill
Of worship ran, when first Salvation dawn'd.[23]

And thou! the demon-King of darkness throned
In thine eternity of tort'ring fires,
Thou dread Apostate! who didst shake the skies
For vict'ry, vanquish'd, but rebellious still;
On thee the glories of Messiah's reign
Beam'd terrible: within thy dark abyss
When ruin'd angels to the summons throng'd,
With dreadful beauty, like a dying sun
Amid the tempest sinking, each adorn'd,
No triumph on thy thunder-blasted brow,
But deeper vengeance, more despairing wo
Than yet the realms of agony endured,
Was visible; that hour, so long foredoom'd,
Is coming, when a world shall be unbound
From chains infernal, and the Powers of Hell
Disarm'd for ever on their crumbling thrones!

Meanwhile, on earth mute Expectation sat
And listen'd; for a rumour, echoed down
From dateless time, of two surpassing Kings
Predestined on the globe to rule, prevail'd;
Whose powers, though blended in Virgilian song,
Sublimely differ'd.[24] In Augustan peace
The world reposed; and grateful Rome beheld
Her Janus shut, her crimson banners furl'd.[25]
No more Dodona, from the oaken shade,
Or Delphi, from exhaling cavern, sent
Vain oracles in mystic verse enweaved.
The Temples mourn'd; Idolatry was dumb,
Or mutter'd faintly from her glimmering shrines;
While Art and Science, in their palmy state,
Triumphantly advanced. Thus, all matured,
And apt to question with profoundest thought

Each creed or doctrine of diviner sway,
The World awaited her Messiah's dawn:
From realm to realm a vast tradition reign'd
Of sibyl-words, which sang the coming God;
While many a heart, prophetically deep,
Mused in the silence of majestic hope,
Or, heaven-inspired, the Earth's Redeemer hail'd.

Thus all below; when Gabriel heard a voice
Of thunder from the Throne proceed, which bade
To Galilee a wingèd flight convey
His presence, where in rocky Naz'reth dwelt
A Maiden pure, to Joseph then betroth'd.
And lo, an Angel brighten'd into view
Before her, like a lovely burst of morn!
And while she trembled, dazzled into dread,
A Salutation of entrancing sound
Fell on her ear:—"Divinely favoured Thou!
Of women blest! The Lord is with thee, hail!
A Son, behold, thy virgin womb shall bear;
Son of the Highest! Jesus let His name
Be called; upon the throne of David fix'd,
O'er Jacob's house for ever shall he reign,
And endless his predestined kingdom prove."
"But how?" cried Mary, "Since I know not man."
Again the Angel: "Overshadowing thee
The Holy Spirit will in power descend,
And That thou bearest, Son of God be call'd."
Then answer'd she, "Behold thy handmaid, Lord!
And be thy word fulfill'd," as brightly fled
The glowing Angel to his native skies.

Let Silence think, for how can words reveal
Her full devotion of ecstatic thought,
When Mary ponder'd on that promised Child?
Let mothers tell! to whose enchanted ears
Earth brings no music like the helpless cry
Of new-born life, from lips which know not guile.
Oh! Maid elect! with more than gladness wing'd,
In the young beauty of thy spousal bloom
To Hebron didst thou o'er the mountains pass,
And visit one, by Heav'n's bright herald warn'd.

'Mid the faint crimson of a flushing dawn
That Pilgrim started, when the breeze was up,
And, like a wing, invisibly career'd
O'er woods and waters: from the grey ravines
The oak and olive sent a leafy sound,
And with her multitude of orient flow'rs
The blooming Sharon glitter'd from afar;
Or, gazing from some terraced rock or hill,
The herding goats from villages and vales,
And wild onagras,* free as desert-wind,
Her eye discern'd; while veil'd Arabians sought
A distant well, like Midian girls of old;
And others to empurpled vineyards hied,
'Mid the soft radiance of unshrouding morn.

By Heaven secured, o'er lone and lofty heights
She glided on; and trod with eager foot
Each verdant slope, each rocky change of scene,
Where olive waved, or cypress-shadow fell.
But oft she paused, and bless'd the vital breeze
From lake upborne; or, when some hill or plain
Of green magnificence, or glorious view
Of nature's wonders, to her eye appeal'd,—
How beautiful! to hear the Maiden chant
Hymns to Jehovah, while her soul recall'd
Those hallow'd memories which ever cling
To ground immortal as great Palestine!

Oh, tell me not of trophied Greece, and groves
Where Plato wander'd; or poetic streams
That wind through Homer's page, or Pindar's song;
For Palestine by God Himself was loved,
Inhabited, and blest! His Spirit there
Hath walk'd, the shadow of His glory been,
His miracles prevail'd,—the mountains blazed
With His descending lustre! all her vales,
Her fountains, rivers, and delicious plains,
Of patriarchs and prophets speak; beneath the shade
Of her ancestral trees have Angels sat,
And holy Abram smiled: her meanest spot
Is mighty, and her dust a sacred charm,
For in it sleep the World's primeval sires!

Unbounded Fancy! on whose fairy wings
The spirit voyageth o'er realms and isles,
Oh, waft me now to Tabor's solemn height,
Where Barak and his heaven-arm'd thousands hid,
And there the Drama of the world renew!
Let Eden rise, her boughs and branches wave,
And Shapes aerial from the clouds descend,
To view her lovely bowers. The Flood react,—
Earth, sea, and sky in billowy chaos lost!
Revive the Patriarchs; mark their rev'rent forms,
Or hear the Prophets when the people rage.
Or, wouldst thou from the sacred past retire

* The wild ass, or pard.—"He scorneth the multitude of the city, neither regardeth he the crying of the driver. The range of the mountain is his pasture, and he searcheth after every green thing."—*Job*, xxxix. 7, 8.

To scenes which live,—from haunted Tabor view
The greenness of a hundred glorious plains!
Lo, vast Esdraelon, like a verdant sea,
By dew-famed Hermon bound; there, Endor lies.
Where dwelt the night-hag in unholy gloom
And Saul seem'd wither'd as the spectre rose,
Wrapp'd in a mantle, out of Hades call'd.
But northward, lock'd in azure calm of noon,
Thy lake, Tiberias! on *that* blue extent
Of shining waters oft the Saviour look'd;
And near yon mountain, iced with dazzling snow,
The sacred hill whereon He sat, and taught
The wisdom of eternity to man.

But, see! o'er Judah's aromatic clime
The sun is west'ring: long ere twilight rose
With dewy welcome to her second night
Of mountain-pilgrimage, the Virgin stood
Beneath the shelter of a rustic cot,
In Hebron, and her holy cousin hail'd,
Enraptured! What sublime emotion clad
Each feature, what a radiance fill'd her eyes,
And touch'd her form, when that saluting voice
Was heard, as thrilling with celestial truth
Elizabeth on Mary gazed, and cried,
"Of Women blest! divinely blest, art thou!"
While leapt the babe within her womb, for joy.
And thus did Mary in her chant respond,
"My soul the gracious Lord doth magnify!
The proud He scatters, but the meek regards;
For thus to Abram and our fathers spake
The God of Israel; glorious be His name!
For me, his lowly Handmaid, ever-blest
Shall ages deem, and generations call."

But now, from Cæsar came a high command
For Judah's offspring to enroll their birth.
Then Joseph, by angelic dream forewarn'd
How vestal Mary had from God conceived,
To Bethlehem went; and there the infant Christ
His Virgin-Mother in a manger laid:
All pure and holy, as the promise spake.—
And say! what hour so awefully instinct
With Secrets from eternity ordain'd,
As when th' Incarnate met the placid gaze
Of His unspotted Mother! what enshrined
A scene, where Deity the mortal shape
Of feeble infant took,[26] and, rudely wrapt,
In new-born meekness smiling forth the God,
Deliver'd earth and thrill'd the Heavens with joy!

That night were shepherds at their watches due
Around unfolded sheep, in that soft vale
Whose fountain warbled to the dreaming ear
Of David, when he sought Adullam's cave.
A calm so deep, that silence seem'd a soul,
Pervaded all things; dew-light on the ground
Was glist'ring, and the vigil-shepherds watch'd
Contentedly their breathing charge recline
On pastures, where the morning flock had fed.*
No cloud the heaven defiled; but, clear and large,
The planets in their throbbing lustre shone.
'Twas then, while Nature mute as dreaming air
Reposed, a melody in wafted flow
Advanced; and when it reach'd the starry plain,
An earthless Form, seraphically robed,
Evolved, and glitter'd like a noontide-sea.

Awe-smote, and blinded with excessive blaze
Of archangelic lustre, on the ground
Each shepherd sank, nor dared with lifted eye
The Glory face, till words of music came:
"Ye pious watchers; tremble not; behold
The tidings of eternal joy I bring:
This night the Saviour of the World is born!
Within a manger, lo! the Babe is found!"
He said; and as the lull of golden streams
When soft-toned winds melodiously awake,
The radiant quiver of angelic plumes
The air attuned, which trembled into song,
While, robed with brightness, thus the choir began:

"Thou Lord of Lords, and Light of Light!
Who, with empyreal glory bright,
Art seated on th' Eternal Throne
Invisibly, the vast Alone,
Ten thousand worlds around Thee blaze,
Ten thousand harps repeat Thy praise,
Yet hymn, nor harp, nor song divine,
Nor myriad orbs created Thine,
This measureless display of love
To earth below and heaven above
With blending eloquence can tell
That ends the Curse, and conquers Hell;
For lo! the manger where He lies,
A world-redeeming Sacrifice:
Peace on earth, to Man good will,
Let the skies our anthem fill!

"Hail, Virgin-born! transcendent Child
In mortal semblance, undefiled,
By ages vision'd, doom'd to be
The Star of Immortality;
Hail! Prince of Peace, and Lord of Light!
Around thy path the world is bright;
Where'er Thou tread'st an Eden blooms,
And Earth forgets her myriad tombs:

---

* Vide the Abbé Fleury's account of the agriculture &c. &c. of the ancient Jews.

Thy voice is heard—and Anguish dies,
The dead awake and greet the skies;
Lo! Blindness melts in healing rays,
And mute Lips ope in hymns of praise;
The famish'd on Thy bounty feed,
While myriads at Thy summons speed
Redeem'd from woe, and sin, and pain
To see the lost restored again:
Peace on earth, to Man good will,
Let the skies our anthem fill!

"Awake, awake, thou ransom'd Earth!
And, blooming with a second birth,
In loveliness awake and shine,
Thy King is come, Salvation thine!
The winds are rock'd in holy rest,
The waves asleep on Ocean's breast,
And beautiful the boundless calm
O'er nature spread, like midnight balm;
For lo! the manger where He lies,
A world-redeeming Sacrifice;
The Promised, since the world began,
To live and die for guilty Man.

"Again, again, the anthem swell!
For Heaven *shall* burst the gates of Hell!
A vision of uncounted years
Which travel on through toil and tears,
Is all unroll'd in wild extent
Like ocean's surging element:
But soon that darken'd scene hath past
And rules the Lord in light, at last!
The sunbeams of a sabbath-day
Around adoring myriads play:
From north to south, from east to west,
All pangs are hush'd, all hearts at rest:
Pacific homes, Atlantic isles,
Far as the vast creation smiles,
The rudest spot which man can own,
Shall hail Messiah on His throne;
And lauding souls by land and sea,
One Altar build, O God! to Thee;
While men and angels round it throng
To chant the sempiternal song,
Peace on earth, to Man good will,
Let the skies our anthem fill!"

Hush'd the deep chant, the choral Train ascends,
And then commingles in one pomp of light,
While all entranced th' adoring shepherds kneel:
But when the bright ascent was o'er, up rose
They all in ravishment; to Bethlehem sped,
And there Messiah wrapp'd in swaddling-clothes
They found, and sang with reverential joy
A hymn of worship to the Babe divine;
While Mary, meekly silent, heard the tale
Of wonder, musing with prophetic soul.

O World! and was it thus thy Saviour came?
Rich as the chorus of Creation's morn
From every region should thy lips have pour'd
A loud hosannah to proclaim the Lord!
The skies have bent, the mountains clapp'd their hands,
The cedars waved from every conscious hill,
And Sun and Moon, and each melodious Star,
And Ocean, with his jubilee of waves
Have thrill'd the universe with natal joy!
But all was silent, unobserved and still;
No Empire sung, when man's Redeemer came;
The peasant-mother in her Alpine cot,
At dreadful midnight, no desertion feels,
Like that rude manger where the Virgin lay,
And scarce a solitary taper shone!

Is this the Wonderful? the Prince of Light,
The King of kings, o'er countless worlds enthroned.
Oh! Language cannot with its brightest words
Adumbrate, or by epithets express
The imagined splendors which proud Judah dreamt
Would crown Messiah, when He came to give
Her ransom'd myriads all Isaiah sung!

Empires have sunk, and waning kingdoms died,
But still, apart, sublime in mis'ry stands
The wreck of Israel! Christ hath come, and bled,
And miracles and ages round the Cross
A holy splendour of undying truth
Preserve; yet still their pining spirit looks
For that unrisen Sun which prophets hail'd!
Where once the Temple, bathed in golden hues,
Immense as glorious, with her matchless spires
On mount Moriah stood, a race exist
In darkness,—still to Zion turn, and weep![27]
And when I view him in his garb of wo,
A wand'ring outcast, by the world disown'd,
The haggard, lost, and long-oppressèd Jew,
"His blood be on us," through remembrance rolls
In fearful echo from a nation's lip!

Then widow'd Zion! still for thee awaits
A future, teeming with triumphal sounds
And Shapes of glory; still a remnant lives,
Who once again thy banner shall unroll
And plant it on thine everlasting walls.
The Cities huge which overaw'd the world
Rot in a gloom, irrevocably seal'd,
Of desolation; Time shall never rear
The towers, nor crowd *their* weed-grown walks again.
But Judah, like some Babylonian wreck

Which age nor elemental wrath subdues,
In mournful grandeur that outlives decay
There as it lies on yon deserted plain,—
Shall yet endure, till Restoration's voice
Her orphan'd race to Salem's clime recall.[28]

Exult, O Zion! for thy God is king,
And lift thy banner on the mountain-tops;
From Egypt, Pathros, and Assyria call'd,
From Shinar, Hamath, and the sea-born isles,
From the vast regions of the utmost orb
Returning Israel for dominion comes!
A voice of Weeping, it is heard no more;
The timbrels sound, her glad-eyed maidens dance,
Her young men shout, the aged meekly smile,
Rememb'ring all the pleasant things of old!
The lea of Sharon, and the pastured glen
Of Achre, beautiful in verdure shine;
While planted vineyards with a costly bloom
Wave on her hills, and court the rip'ning sun.
The lamb, the lion, and the infant play
Together; Righteousness thy gate adorns,
And peace divine, by purity bestow'd
From God incarnate, in thy sacred walls,
Recover'd Palestine! for ever dwells.

As when a mother for an absent child
Laments, till beauty on her cheek decays,
Yet haply in declining loveliness
More exquisite than in her glowing prime
Appeareth, so doth thine afflicted Land
Touch the deep spirit with diviner thought.
Now in thy wo, than when a bridal pomp
Bedeck'd thee. For the homeless race afar
Thou yearnest with a soft maternal grief;
To hill and mountain the devouring Curse
Hath clung; and rivers down unpeopled vales
Like mournful pilgrims glide; while fruit nor tree
Bear to the tyrant what thy children took
From thy fond bosom: yet, a latent power
Of life and glory in thy wither'd soil
Is buried, that shall rise when Judah comes;
Like music sleeping in a haughty lyre,
Whose muteness only to the master-touch
Breaks into sound which ravishes a world!

Now, o'er the infant God a day decreed
For circumcision rose, in wonted light,
And "Jesus" (let the heavens and earth revere
That word almighty!) was the name he bore.
And then, each light of due lustration done,
The lowly Virgin to the Temple brings
The young Redeemer; thus had God ordain'd.*
No lamb had she; but in her meekness brought
Two turtle-doves of pure and spotless wing,
And solemnly within the outer-court
Awaited, while a Priest the Lord approach'd:
And haply, on the Temple's wondrous mass
Of finish'd beauty and effulgent pomp
Oft gazed, and gloried in her ancient creed
That there the God of Israel loved to dwell!
But when th' oblation of unspotted doves
Was paid, an inner court's wide precincts ope,
And Mary enters with her bosom'd child;
Then silently, with glance of tend'rest love,
For presentation yields the Babe divine.

But who is he, with beard of flowing white,
Who onward moves amid the ritual pomp?
Led by the Spirit, lo! a bending Form
Approaches, kindles as with sudden youth,
Her Babe enclasps, and to his Maker cries,
"In peace, O Lord! now let Thy servant go;
These eyes have seen, these wither'd arms embrace
Thy promised One, a Child of Glory, sent
To lighten Israel, and the world restore!"
Yes, morning, noon, and night, in dream or prayer,
In temple-worship, and mysterious hours,
For this he long'd, to see Messiah born!—
The Saviour came, and Simeon died in joy.

Each rite complete, the Holy Fam'ly sought
In Bethlehem-vale their consecrated home;
There, scarce arrived, when lo! as Magi bow'd
In nightly worship to unnumber'd worlds
Of starry name, an orbèd Meteor shone
With mystic beams oracularly bright!
But well they knew, those star-adoring Seers,
That revelation high, and sped on wings
Of holy speed to Zion's stately haunt;
There wond'ringly around old Salem's walls
Exclaim'd, "The new-born great! Judean King,
His dwelling say, for Him would we adore!"

And souls there lived, which drank, as thirsty ground
A summer-rain absorbs, refreshing hope,
When orient Sages of a mighty birth
For Israel spake: for Judah long had pined,
And on the willows hung her captive harp:
But he, whom Mariamne's murder'd form
For ever haunted like a dream of hell,
The guilty, pamper'd, pale Herodian king!
Heard this, and trembled: yet in bloody calm
His purpose lay, and thus that king address'd
Those eastern Magi: "Swift to Bethlehem, haste!
The infant find, around his cradle kneel,
And tell, where I may come and worship, too?"

* See Exod. xiii. 2; Lev. xii. 6. Also, Lightfoot on the Temple Service.

They went; and lo! yon beauteous Star,
In loveliness beyond all radiant orbs
Which decorate the night, a guidance lent,
Till o'er that roof where lay the Lord of Worlds
It paused, and quiver'd as with conscious beams;
There sped the Magi, earth's Redeemer found
Encradled; and with bending awe they kneel,
His Form adore, and solemn worship pay
With myrrh and frankincense; while Mary stands
In wonder; with her eye to heaven upturn'd,
Her bosom swelling with a silent hymn,
And in her spirit more than mother's joy!

Their homage done, and earth's Messiah seen,
By God forewarn'd, the orient pilgrims wend
Afar from Herod, to their destined home.
That night, in visionary trance, appear'd
The Shape angelic Joseph once beheld:
"Arise! to Egypt with the Virgin speed,
And holy Infant; Him would Herod slay!"
To that high word obedient, ere the blush
Of morning crimson'd Horeb's sainted brow
Or Jordan's waters in the sunshine wound,
By Heaven environ'd, as a viewless guard,
To Egypt went he, till the monarch died:
"For out of Egypt have I call'd my Son!"
So spake the Seer, whose word our God fulfill'd.

Then passion, like a kindled hurricane
Burst from the tyrant with terrific sway,
And cruel havoc, dark as Hell desired;
Oh! then were shrieks maternal, sounds which came
From riven souls, and childless Rachel wept.
In Rama was the voice of mourning heard,
And red with blood the streams of Israel ran,
'Twas Murder's banquet on a thousand babes!—
Sweet flowers of Life, whose fragile beauty made
The living Eden of parental hearts;
Asleep in cradled stillness, with the light
Of infant slumber on their lovely cheeks,
Or prattling gaily at the cottage-door,
Slaughter o'ertook them, and with murderous yell
Mock'd the sad mothers, shrieking for their God!
That cry was answer'd when the monster-king,
By pain corrupted, turn'd a loathsome mass,
And died! Then, heralded by Gabriel's wings,
The infant-Saviour into Nazareth came;
For Archelaus o'er Judah's empire ruled,
And, Herod-like, had bathed his throne in blood.

Mysterious Time! o'er many realms and lands
Thy shadow broods, which man cannot dispel,
Or brighten; but o'er that most hallow'd scene
Where dwelt unknown, in human meekness veil'd,
Incarnate Glory, lies thy thickest gloom.
For ever hidden, by no voice reveal'd,
The holy childhood of the Saviour-God.
Yet, wafted back on no irrev'rent wing,
Imagination oft her eye would fix
On that green vale, where first The Morning-Star
With mildest beauty rose. By earth unfelt,
Celestial watchers! did ye not descend
And hover round, while grew that awful Child
In the pure light of Mary's pensive gaze?
Maiden and mother! whom all ages bless
When lock'd in slumber the Redeemer lay,
How on His features did thine homage dwell!

But years departed; and Messiah grew
Strong in the spirit, wisdom, grace and power;[29]
Then oft at eve, when sultry day was o'er,
The holy Infant, by parental knee,
The Book of Life with tender awe perused,
And question'd; while in love's delightful dream
Each parent mused; recalling oft the Shapes
Angelic, or that vision Bethlehem saw;
Or, sounding all the dim and mighty depths
Of prophecy, where solemn meanings lay.
And ah, how beautiful! in cradled sleep
While slept her Child, to mark the wedded Maid
On His pure brow a gentle kiss implant,
And then to Joseph, with a speaking look
This truth convey—"How wonderful is Heaven,
If *there* the Hope of fallen Israel lies!"
When twelve years thus the Son of God had spent,
To celebrate a high and solemn feast,
Begun when over Egypt's first-born flew
The direful Angel on his wings of death,
All came; and with excited myriads went
Christ's holy parents up to Salem's walls,
As true adorers. When the seventh day saw
Each rite concluded, back to Nazareth vale
They speed, but where is He, the sacred Boy?
With friends beloved, or in Jerusalem lost?
There hasten'd they, and sorrowingly roam'd
The Virgin-mother, garden, grove, and field;
And as she hurried through becrowded paths
Her eye's fond question moved each passing face
With feeling:—such as thoughts untold betray
When look is language, and that language read
By hearts which sympathise with pangs unknown.
And thus she sought Him with unwearied step,

Till tears had gather'd, and her gaze was dim,
Yet found Him not: when hark! a burst of joy
Maternal; in the temple, lo, He stands;
With priest and sage, and vested rabbis mix'd,
The lost One lingers:—on His brow the light
Of Godhead! from His lips a stream of words
Is flowing, fraught with spirit-moving power
That shook all hearts, the ear of Age entranced,
And through dark conscience pour'd celestial rays
Which had not shone before. Each look'd on each,
Astounded; wisdom seem'd a thing unwise
By man announced; Divinity was *there!*
But, garb'd in lowliness, that peasant-Child
His temple left, a mother's smile renew'd,
And gently her inquiring wonder check'd
With words unfathom'd, yet, in Mary's heart
Embalm'd for ever with revering love!
Then, homeward once again the pilgrims haste
United; musing on the festal pomp,
And crowded worship, such as Salem loved.
And long before the pallid star of Eve
Had heralded the hush of twilight-hour,
A cot was round them, in their quiet vale.

By Nazareth are green and silent dells,
Secluded groves, and rocky shades profound;
And here Messiah dwelt:—those eighteen years
Of fameless calm, wherein the Lord of Light
Reposed, and suffer'd like a human Child,
But sinless, all our burden, toil, and tears,
With what a mystery of voiceless awe
They sink upon the inmost heart of man!
Whether on thee, O Virgin blest! we muse,
Thy soul by reverence and awe subdued
To something holier than mother's love;
Or that all-glorious all-majestic Form
In Whom was center'd man's eternal hope,
Survey, amid the still and solemn vale,—
Our thoughts are thrilling as the tears which rise
When Angels warble round a soul forgiven:
That wondrous Being! in those mountain-dells
As lone He wander'd, did He not forecast
The awful drama of His life to come?
On this He ponder'd; this the mind perceived;
From Cana's miracle to Calv'ry's mount,
The crown and cross, the agony of death
He view'd; nor dash'd the bitter Cup away
The Curse had fill'd, and Man was doom'd to drink
Had Christ not come, and drank the cup, and died!

But now the hour decretive Heaven ordain'd
For Jesus to unfold th' Almighty will,
Approach'd. Tiberius o'er imperial Rome
Was reigning, and in subject Judah ruled
The savage Pilate; when the Word of God
To John amid the wilderness was sent;
For thus the Seer prophetically sang:
"A voice comes wafted through the wilderness!
From Him who crieth, 'Let the mountains sink,
The valleys rise, and be the deserts smooth!
A God approaches! be His way prepared!'"

That great Precursor, whose proclaiming voice,
"Repent ye!" pierced the wilderness with dread,
Was robed in hairy sackcloth; round his loins
A leathern girdle wound; the mountain-spring,
Which bubbled through the vale, his drink supplied;
His meat was honey and the locust wild.
Alone, but angel-watch'd, that Orphan grew
To manhood; nursed amid the elements,
A son of Nature, where the Desert waved
Her wildest boughs, or flung the blackest gloom
That cavern'd Eremite with God communed,
In storm or stillness, when the thunder voiced
His anger, or a sunshine wore His smile.
One awful loneliness his life became,
In thought and prayer mysteriously it pass'd;
And oft, sublime!—as when at sunset-hour,
A fierce magnificence of crimson hues
Redden'd the mountains, while each rocky crest
Of Judah with volcanic lustre blazed,
And slept the sultry air, the prophet knelt;
And the wild glory of his dreaming eye
To heaven was turn'd, in meditative awe.
The hush of woods, the hymn of waters faint,
And azure prospect of yon midland-sea
Beyond the desert, glimmering and vast,
And dying cadence of some distant bird
Whose song was fading like a silver cloud,—
'Mid sights and sounds, commingled like to these,
Earth had no grander scene, than when the hour
Of Syrian twilight heard the Baptist pray!

Beside the waters of th' unliving Sea
Where buried cities lift their ghastly wreck
In tomb-like waste,[30] the Prophet chanced to muse,
Dreaming of dark Gomorrah, and the loud
Despair of millions, when the thunder knell'd
And rapidly a burning deluge came.
An airy stillness, solitude intense
Was there: no bird upon enchanted wing;
No murmur, but the reedy moan of banks
Of sickly herbage; or the creeping sound
Of Jordan, dragging its sepulchral way;
Sea, sky, and air in one unearthly calm
Reposed! In such a scene of lifeless gloom

While mused the Baptist on the guilt of Man,
A mighty impulse, an inbreathing power
Of Inspiration on his spirit came!
He felt the God; and, fill'd with sacred fire,
To Jordan hasten'd; soon that region round
"Repent ye!" heard each hill and vale repeat.
Where ran the holiest of holy Streams
That wind and glitter through green Palestine,
His cry awoke, from whence a warning rung
With tones of terror, till before them fled
The sinful passions of a sensual crowd,
Like waves before the wind! From Judah's realm
To Alexandria's clime, his solemn threat
Was echoed; till around the Baptist throng'd
All sects and nations, to repent, and live
By laving waters of Baptismal power.
There stood the Sadducee! with eye unscaled,
To see the darkness of the grave illumed
By Words immortal; there the glozing tribe
Of Pharisees, with frighted soul appeal'd
For mercy, cowering as the prophet cried,
"Ye vipers! who hath warn'd you from the wrath
To come? Repentance! let thy fruits appear;
The axe is laid, and every fruitless tree
Shall wither! lo, the fire of vengeance falls!"

Divine Repentance! in thy sacred tear
Alone is wisdom for the erring heart.
That infancy of soul, that stainless hour
When the stern chaos of our spirit sleeps
In passionless repose, how oft it woos
Our feelings back to purity and heaven!
Alas! that in our solitude we soar
To perfect goodness, but in life descend
To dust again!—our aspirations quench'd,
Till all which purer moments wisely taught,
And conscience sanction'd, is a dream forgot!

Yet all we ponder, fancy, feel, or view,
Hath something for the soul's mysterious chords
Attuned, to thrill them with religious tones.
But, far above each sight or sound of earth,
Or mind of man, that heaven-revealing Book
In whose dread tones of everlasting truth
The inspirations of Jehovah dwell!
There find we visions of transcendent blaze,
And heralds bright, embassadors divine,
And voices from the Throne and Seat of bliss,
And hallelujahs from angelic choirs,
And God Eternal, with His Thunder girt,
And Radiance, speaking like the ocean vast!
And you, blest Oracles! whose words relate
The story of Redemption, all sublime,
With what a simple rectitude severe
Your page immortal moves from change to change!
Nor turn'd, nor daunted, whatsoe'er the gloom
Or brightness of the awful Scene, it paints:
So rolls a river through a wide domain;
Whate'er the colour which the clouds reflect,
Or bank, or verdure, on its beauty flings,
It travels onward with the stately course
Of sound and motion, to the fated sea.

By these alone, can mortal Life unweave
Her web of mystic lines, and many hues,
And man's eternity before him rise
In dreams of light, or shadows of despair.
At evening once, beside a circling shore
Of sandy wildness, where the billows loved
Their foaming solitude, my fancy stray'd:
Dark crags, and summits, fit for tempest-thrones,
Hung near: but mid-way, on a lofty mount,
By the green splendour of tumultuous grass
Made beautiful, there mused a wither'd Shape
By sorrow featured: on his wasted cheek
Sat wan decline; but still the quenchless eye
Was glorious, — there, undying radiance gleam'd!
A Book, an ancient Book of faded leaves
Was open'd, which, with bended brow, he read
Intently: nearer still my footstep crept,
And by the breeze from his pale lip was brought
Soft under-tones of some almighty speech;
Till, quaking with excess of thought divine,
Down on the herb adoringly he sank
And fix'd his eyes upon the awful heavens,
As though enthroned there God himself appear'd!
And then, while rolling tears ran bright and large,
Exultingly his gasping spirit cried,
"For ever and for ever is Thy Throne
Transcendent, Lord, and everlasting King!"

True Adoration, what a voice is thine!
From earth it wanders through the heaven of heavens,
There from the mercy-seat in light evokes
An answer, thrilling the seraphic Host
With new additions of adoring song! *
For prayer is man's omnipotence below,
A soul's companionship with Christ and God,
Communion with eternity begun.

Oh, love celestial! earth can heaven-like grow,
If man profane it not by savage tread
And sordid gaze. E'en now, the sun appears
A king of glory: and this breathing world,
Like some vast instrument of varied sound
The conscious melodies of life awakes:

* "There is joy in heaven," &c.—*Matthew's Gospel.*

Yon sky is covered with soft isles of cloud,
Which flash or float as sun and wind command;
The air is balm, the breeze a living joy;
My heart is dumb with an exceeding bliss
Of light and beauty, pouring in from Day's
Enchantment; while beneath yon vernal hill
Whose sunny greenness mirrors all the clouds,
Poetic murmurs from a distant sea
In lulling falls come faintly on the mind.

But now, the wearied Elements prepare
For slumber; modulated breezes swell;
The sky, with ocean-mimicry adorn'd,
Grows pale and paler; soon will stars advance
And seem to palpitate, as there they shine,
With throbbing beauty! Thus will night begin
And earth lie cradled in a dim repose,
Till the pure heaven comes down upon the soul
And all is hush'd beneath a holy spell.
So ends a sabbath; so may sabbaths end
Devoutly sacred, till the wings of Time
Be folded, and eternal sabbath reigns.
For all Thy ministries begin and end
In Love, that glorious synonyme of Thee,
Both in the heavens, and in the heart enshrined!
From the first tear which roll'd down Adam's cheek
To the last pang of living bosoms now,
In light and darkness, still our God is Love!

BOOK IV.

> "Oh, Goodness Infinite! Goodness immense!
> That all this good of evil shall produce
> And evil turn to good; more wonderful
> Than that which by creation first brought forth
> Light out of darkness!"—*Paradise Lost*, book xii.

ANALYSIS OF BOOK IV.

The glorious manifestation of Truth in the Appeal of the Baptist—Approach of Christ to be Baptised—Jesus led by the Spirit into the Wilderness—The Temptation described—Angels sent to console Him—Thus proved, He commences his Ministry as the Redeemer of the World—Purity and Majesty of His Life and Doctrines—First Miracle—The Marriage in Cana—Jesus goes to Jerusalem—The Modern State of Jerusalem, compared with her Ancient Glories—The Passover described, at the celebration of which Christ arrived—His entrance to the Temple—Miraculous expulsion of its Defilers—Nicodemus, his Character, and Visit to the Saviour by Night—Jesus, on the Death of the Baptist, hastens to Galilee to avoid the Jews—His Journey through Samaria—Scenery—Well of Sychem—Interview with the Woman of Samaria—He travels to Cana—The Nobleman's Son healed by a Word of Christ—His appearance in the Synagogue—Is expelled from thence by his offended Countrymen—Led to the brow of a hill—Delivers Himself from instant destruction.—Capernaum—Lake of Tiberias, described—Miraculous Draught of Fishes—Confession of Peter—Exultation of the Crowd who witnessed the miracle—To this was added an innumerable number of Divine Deeds and Mercies—Doctrine adduced from Miracles—The Power they exhibit cannot be fathomed; but the Principle which they inculcate is to be imitated—for it teaches boundless Love to the whole family of Man.

"Repent ye!" was the dreadless sermon preach'd
In Judah's Desert, by the Baptist now;
And who can measure the exalted might
Of truth, deliver'd by such daring Soul
Till conscience quiver'd, like the world's great sire
At that "Where art thou?" earth's Creator spake!
A brow irradiate with impassion'd zeal,
An eye majestic, and a voice intoned
With vocal energy from heaven inspired,
Were his, who usher'd in th' expected God!
From cot to palace rose his high reproof;
Wherever wander'd in the realm of vice
The heart of man, "Repent ye!" sounded there.

What marvel, then, Messiah's self appear'd
In John embodied, till the people cried,
With loud impatience, "Art thou Christ, the True?"
"With water I indeed baptise and bless;
But One shall come, transcendently sublime
O'er me, the very latchet of Whose shoes
I am not worthy to unbind! with fire,
And with the Holy Ghost shall He baptise;
Behold, the fan is in His fearful hands!
The wheat He gathers, but the wicked chaff
Ungarner'd, burneth with a quenchless flame!"
Thus answer'd he; and shaded Israel's heart
With wonder, dreaming on the dark unknown.

While thus by Jordan's hallow'd wave, the Rite
Of Waters, sanction'd by mysterious sway,
The Baptist to repenting souls perform'd,
The Lord of Life, in human weakness veil'd,
Himself presented. Round His awful head
No glory play'd; nor dread effulgence beam'd
As on He came: yet, sacredly o'erpower'd
By some deep impulse, vast and undefined,
The Crowd stood parted; and a solemn hush,
Like stillness o'er a forest when the winds
Lull'd into soundless trance their wings upfold,
The murm'ring host subdued: but on thy face

Great Harbinger! a recognition glow'd,
And spirit-bright thy gladden'd mien became;
For He, whom prescient heaven to earth foretold,
Before Thee stood; Salvation's Prince appear'd!
And this, thy greeting: "Lo! at length He comes;
Behold the Lamb of God! Oh! pure above
All Beings pure, from *me* this rite forego;
For need I have of Thy baptising grace,
And comest Thou to mine?" "Refuse me not,
Since thus all righteousness must be fulfill'd:"
So speaking, down the bank Messiah moved,
Stood in the waters, there the Rite received,
And thence arose, with voiceless prayer becalm'd.
When lo! the heavens miraculously oped,
The dazzling concave God himself reveal'd
Descending, lustrous with ethereal light:
While dove-like hover'd o'er the Saviour's head
Th' Eternal Spirit, and a Voice declared
Like sea and thunder when their music blends,
"Adore Him! This is My beloved Son!"

But now advanced temptation's demon-power
To crush the Saviour! By the Holy Ghost
Compell'd, within a desert's trackless wild
Alone He wander'd, unperceived by eyes
Of mortal; there to meditate and pray,
And scan the secrets of almighty grace
Himself embodied by redeeming love.
A noontide o'er his contemplation sped
Away, and still the awful Thinker roved
With foot unwearied: sunset, fierce and red,
Succeeded: never hung a savage glare
Upon the wilderness, like that which tinged
This fated hour! the trees and herbless rock
Wore angry lustre, and the dying Sun
Sank downward like a deity of wrath,
Behind him leaving clouds of burning wreck.
And then rose Twilight: not with tender hues,
Or choral breezes, but with shade as dim
And cold, as Death on youthful spirit throws:
Sad grew the air; and soon th' affrighted leaves
And branches from the crouching forest sent
A wizard moaning, till the wild-bird shriek'd,
Or flutter'd, and in dens of deepest gloom
The lion shook, and dreadful monsters glared.

Tremendous are ye, ever-potent Storms
In wild magnificence of sound and scene!
Watch'd on the mountains in convulsive play,
Or from the ocean-margin when the sea
Foams in the fiercest of her billow'd ire.
But when hath Tempest, since a deluge roar'd,
The pale Earth shaken, like that frenzied storm
Which tore the desert, while Messiah mused?
Then God to hands infernal seem'd to trust
The helm of nature, while a chaos drove
The Elements to combat, 'mid the rushing gloom
Of rain and whirlwind, in commingled wrath
Triumphant, while aloft unnat'ral clouds
Hung o'er the sky the imagery of Hell!
Not hence alone tempestuous horror sprung:
To aid the Tempter, shapes of ghastly light,
With Phantoms, grim beyond a maniac's dream,
To thunder darkness and dread midnight gave
A power unearthly:—round Thy sleepless head
Adored Redeemer! did their voices chant,
Or wildly mutter some unhallow'd spell;
Yet all serene Thy godlike virtue stood,
Unshaken, though the universe might fall.

Thus, forty days of dire Temptation leagued
Their might hell-born, with hunger, thirst, and pain.
Meanwhile, in thankless calm the World reposed:
Life went her rounds, and busy hearts maintain'd
Their action: still uprose the parent Orb,
And all the dewy ravishment of flowers
Enkindled; Day and Ocean mingled smiles;
And then, meek Night with starr'd enchantment rose,
While moonlight wander'd o'er the palmy hills
Of terraced Palestine: and thus unmark'd
By aught portentous, save demonian wiles,
His fasting period in the desert-gloom
Messiah braved. At length, by hunger rack'd,
And drooping, deaden'd by the scorching thirst
Of deep exhaustion, round Him nothing stood
But rocky bleakness, mountains dusk and huge,
Or riven crags which seem'd the wreck of worlds.
And there, amid a vale's profoundest calm,
Where hung no leaf, nor lived one cheering tone
Of waters, with an unappallèd soul
The Saviour paused, while arid stillness reign'd,
And the dead air, as if by magic quench'd
Brooded and thicken'd o'er the lifeless dale.
When lo! from out the earth's unfathom'd deep
The semblance of a mighty cloud arose;
From whence a Shape of awful stature moved,—
A vast, a dim, a melancholy Form;
Upon his brow the gloom of thunder sat,
And in the darkness of his dreadful eye
Lay the sheath'd lightnings of immortal ire!
In ruin'd glory thus the Demon faced
Messiah, cent'ring in that one still glance
The hate of Heaven, the agony of Hell,
Defiance and despair!—and then, with voice
Sepulchral, deep as when a tempest dies,

Him thus address'd: "If Son of God Thou be,
These stones, command them into living bread!"
"'Tis written," answer'd the most holy Christ,
"Not bread alone, but every word of God
Is life!" Scarce utter'd that sublime reply,
When each ascended, and on noiseless wings
Invisibly both God and Demon soar'd.
Together, rapid as th' almighty glance
Enspheres infinity, on Herod's towers
From whose dread altitude the very sky
Seems nearer[31] while below a hush'd abyss
Extendeth,—dark with supernatural depth,—
They soon alighted; where with impious wile
Again the Tempter Second Adam tried.
"If Son of God Thou be, Thyself cast down!
'Tis written, 'Thee protecting Angels watch
For ever, lest a stone Thy feet may dash.'"
"The Lord thy God thou shalt not tempt!" replied
The Saviour: awed by such divine repulse,
The baffled Demon for his last design
Prepared; and swiftly by an airy flight,
To Quarantania's unascended top
That crowns the wilderness with savage pomp,[32]
Messiah next he bore; from thence, a world
In visionary pomp lay all reveal'd,
By airy portraiture of magic drawn
With luring splendour: regions, thrones, and climes
Of bloom and fragrance, meadows, lakes, and groves:
And there seem'd Cities, capp'd with haughty towers,
And Piles, and Palaces of marble sheen,
And Domes colossal, with exulting flags
Of royal conquest on their gilded spires:
And there were Armies, thick as trooping clouds,
On plains assembled,—chariot, smoke, and steed,
The pomp of death, and thunder-gloom of war:
Nor absent, fleets within the silver bay
Reposed, or riding o'er a gallant sea:
All this, the world's Inspirer thus evoked,—
One vast Enchantment, one enormous Scene
Of splendour, deluging the dazzled eye
With mingled radiance till the fancy reel'd!
And then, outstretching with imperial sway
A shadowy hand, Hell's crafty monarch spake,
"This pomp and glory, this surpassing World
Is Thine! if Thou wilt kneel, and worship Me!"
Then bright as Deity, with truth erect,
Victoriously Messiah thus rebuked
That Prince of Hell: "Behind me, Satan, get!
'Tis written, thou shalt worship God *alone*;"
And thus responding, rays of awful truth
His Eye emitted; from Whose dreaded glance
The Devil shrunk, and wither'd into air!
When, light as breezes, lovely as the morn
Descended, blooming with celestial grace,
Angelic Creatures, in whose hands upborne,
By man unseen, the wafted Jesus sank
To earth again; and there, a squadron bright
Of heaven-born Spirits round Him knelt, and sang.

His trial o'er, by men and angels proved
Consummate Lord; by John again confess'd
Amid the Sanhedrim, as Christ foretold
Since time began, by five disciples found
And follow'd, Jesus on His glorious task
Now enters; fallen Earth shall be restored!

Will Kings array him? Shall the Palace ope
Its gorgeous portals to admit His train?
Alas! the bird his nest, the beast his lair
Inhabits, but the homeless Son of Man
Forsaken, hath not where His head to lay!
And He, Whose fiat was the birth of Things,
Whose frown had made the Universe no more,
The pangs and woes of meanest want endured;
For others wept, and toil'd through tearful gloom,
But stood Himself, unaided and alone,
A God who suffer'd, while the World he saved.

And who can paint him? Oh! the sweetest tone
That ever trembled on the harps of Heaven,
Melt into muteness, or like discord seem
Ere on the summits of celestial love
Incarnate, they can reach the Lord of worlds!
Be mine, with solemn step and reverent gaze
From miracle to miracle to roam,
Through paths of glory, tracks of peaceful light;
And on the way, devout accession cull
Of thought or meaning, from the Book divine
Translated: pleased beyond ambition's joy
If thus, companion'd by consenting mind,
My theme advances, till on Calv'ry's mount
Arriving, Faith behold her Saviour die.

In mercy, miracles from Christ began.
To Cana, peering o'er a woody crest
Of green ascent, beside Capernaum raised,
Messiah with his Virgin-mother went;
And there, by one expressive deed of Love
Sanction'd for ever hymeneal Bliss.
Unknown the bride, or whom the wedding throng
A bridegroom hail'd; but Nature has not seal'd
That fountain up, from whence all feeling flows,—
The Heart, whose current is by time unchanged.
And thus, in garlanded array behold
Two happy creatures, 'mid rejoicing friends
In white apparel gemm'd by nuptial-flowers.

What beautiful emotion, born of dreams
Which make the future paradise, abounds!
Yet, in thy gaze a gleam of vanish'd years
Is mirror'd, maiden! round whose virgin brow
A bridal wreath consenting parents wove.
The home of love, the haunts where infant feet
Have roam'd, with mingled and o'ermastering sense
Of truth and tenderness the past awakes,
And on thee like returning childhood come.
A cloud melts o'er thy summer-noon of joy,
Serenely dark, and exquisitely sad:
For haply, on the old familiar walls
And chamber where thy lispèd vows began
Thine eye hath look'd farewell: or down the paths
Of garden-loveliness, where tiny hands
So often labour'd with delightful toil,
How mutely hast thou wander'd!—blessing flowers
Whose fairy magic woo'd thy frequent touch
When dew and sunshine call'd thy fancy forth
To drink their beauty with absorbing gaze;
And that green haunt by fragrant trellis hung,
Yes! there thy soul hath dream'd of days no more
When twilight redden'd o'er thy girlish bowers.

But now the banquet: such as lowly roof
Demanded, and which simple manners claim'd.
O'er milk and honey, rice and kneaded flour,
And water, cool as mountain-well contain'd,
When consecrating prayer arose for Heaven's
High blessing, then the marriage-feast began.
But soon to Jesus, Mary's asking eye
Was turn'd, and meekly for the aidless want
Of friends beloved, a miracle she hoped;
But thus was answer'd: "Woman! unarrived
My dawn of glory; what have I to do
With thee?" Oh! think not from *That* sinless mouth
A mere denial in cold sternness came:
The pity, not the anger, of rebuke
Was there! Six stony water-pots antique,
For pure lavation, such as holy Rite
Demanded, in the nuptial chamber stood;
And each, obedient to Messiah's voice,
With gushing water to the brim was fill'd;
When lo! the Element, by power subdued,
Blush'd into wine and glow'd beneath its God!
And when the ruler of the rustic feast
Admiring drank this new-created wine,
A miracle stood forth! as shines a star
Clear, round, and large, the only one in heaven:
Each heart beat louder; on the lifted brow
Of mute-struck guests, o'erawed amazement sat;
And from the eyes of new disciples flash'd
That beaming eloquence all speech beyond,
When ecstacy is dumb. And when at night
By torch and timbrel home the vested train
Return'd, amid the hymenèal songs
Of sweetest rapture, while each bridal robe
Like snow in moonlight glitteringly shone,
The holy mildness of thy deep-toned voice
Redeemer! still in hearts its echo rang.
Though vaster miracles Thy Name enthrone,
In this omnipotently-tender shine
The rays of Love; concenter'd, calm, and clear,
They dazzle not, but still Thy power declare.

With fame before Him, now for Judah's feast
Of sacrifice, to Zion's city-queen
The Saviour went.—In moods of high romance
'Tis pleasant down the depths of Ages past,
To venture, re-erect huge Capitals,
And hear the noise of Cities now no more!
But Egypt, with her pyramids august,
Titanian Thebes, or Athens temple-famed,
Or Rome, the once metropolis of earth,
And whatsoe'er historic fancy dreams
In visions of the vast and gone, dissolve
To shadows, when Remembrance pictures thee,
Jerusalem! Alas, thy wailing harps
Have truly mourn'd; a throneless captive thou!
In dust thy robes of beautiful array
Have wither'd; tears are on thy faded cheek,
And nothing, save a deathless past, is thine!
Those Mountains, branded by th' almighty curse,
Ascend, and look down yon sepulchral vales,
Where silence by the tramp of desert steeds
Alone is echo'd: paths of lifeless length,
Dim walls, and dusky fanes, barbaric homes
And Arab-huts,—how eloquently sad
Their ruin, how sublime the tale it tells!
Jerusalem! the clank of heathen chains
In iron wrath hath sounded o'er thy doom
For ages: sword and savage on thy blood
Have feasted; fatal martyrdom was thine
From Roman, Frank, and fiery Mameluke;
E'en now, thy wreck is made an impious prey,
And minarets their flashing spires uplift
Where once the palace of Jehovah blazed!

But round thy desolation lives a dream
Of what thou wert, when Heaven o'ershadow'd thee.
Religion, fame, and glory—all endow'd
With mingled light thy once celestial home.
There, 'tween thy Cherubim, Th' Eternal dwelt!
From out the Cloud His utter'd meanings came;
The hymns of David, and the voice of seers
By vision raptured, through thy streets have roll'd;
And He, who spake as never mortal did,
In temple, home, and synagogue proclaim'd

His awful mission:—well might Warriors pause,
The Poet chant, and pure Apostles bend
Before thee, casting down their sacred wreaths,
Queen of the desert! once by angels walk'd,
And still where murmurs of Jehovah's lip
In dreams of melody thy vales entrance!

To such high city came Salvation's Prince,
When all was loud, on that religious eve
That marks a feast, by whose unblemish'd lamb
Was typified the Lamb of God eterne.
But, hark! the clang of trumpets on the wind!
Down hill and mountain, red with lustrous sky
The banner'd Tribes of shouting Israel come:
And how magnificently full and deep
Their choral anthems! reaching from the heart
Through heaven's infinity, where angels list,
And waft their echoes round the throne of God.
Beneath them, beautiful, and bright, and vast,
Jerusalem with all her dazzling towers
Reposing; Zion the beloved is there!
And midmost, pinnacled in golden pomp
O'er all uplift, the gorgeous Temple stands,
And glitters, like the sheen of Alpine snow.*
While downward, jubilant with holy glee,
Enamour'd thousands to the city rush:
Each window, roof, and balcony, alive
With gazers, scattering o'er the marching Tribes
A spring of flowers, and wreaths of rosy bloom.†

While thus, from every region which the heavens
O'er-canopy, the host of Israel came
In troop and tribe, as though the Archangel's trump
Had sounded, Jesus to the Temple pass'd.
Nine gates enormous, folding back like clouds
Of splendour, when the prince of Morning comes,
Round Herod's temple blazed: without, were Courts;
And one, the Gentiles', circling with a range
Of gleaming columns of colossal height
The rest within; and here alone, the Jew
To proselytes an entrance gave; nor deem'd
That where a Gentile vow'd, Jehovah was!
And thus, with unconcern, and loud contempt
Of holiness, convened a merchant-throng
Of money-changers, in that outer-court,
Whose tongue and tread the House of God defiled.
Then rose He! like a Hierarch array'd
With might celestial; or a fervid seer
In the deep passion of prophetic truth
On realms and vices warring,—the unknown
Redeemer; driving with a wielded scourge
The vile profaners, whom His visage awed
With sudden brightness of appalling power!
"'Tis written," cried a soul-commanding Voice,
"*My* House the solemn House of prayer shall be,
But ye profane it like a den of thieves?"
While fled the crowd, a mutt'ring wonder rose,
Till one, perusing with an eye of wrath
The face of Christ, thus haughtily inquired:
"For this high daring, what miraculous sign
Or what omnipotence from Heaven hast Thou?"
"This Temple scatter, and ere three days end,
Command it rise again!"—Then spake the Jew,
While o'er the vastness of Jehovah's pile
His eye-glance roll'd, and thence with flashing pride
On Jesu fell: "Through six-and-forty years
This Temple rose, and widen'd! canst Thou crush
Its Glory, and in three days bid it rise?"
But Christ of His corporeal Temple spake
In resurrection-power. Yet words that rung
A knell of ruin o'er the noblest Fane
Which earth had borne, or gazing awe beheld,
Such fatal warning could not be forgiven
E'en in that hour of agony divine
When shook the World, as pass'd her God away!

Eternity! there is a sound and sense
Of terror, dwelling in thy dim abyss
Of meaning, whether by a Spirit named
When lips are whitening in the gasp of Death,
Or utter'd by the pensive voice of Life.
In vain immunity and calm we seek,
Dark intimations of thy state will rise,
Though time be mock'd, and tombs unheeded stand.—
There was a man whom meditation charm'd
And counsell'd, by the Sanhedrim beloved
For wisdom; hiving in his inmost heart
Prophetic truths, and hopes of regal pride
For Judah destined, when her king appear'd.
All gloomy, lone, and melancholy things
To him were genial: on the face of Death
His eye would fasten a devouring gaze,
For some confession! down unpeopled haunts
At midnight, when the fainting moon retired,
Or planets sicken'd, by sepulchral caves
Where prince and prophet slumber'd,—he would stray
And ponder, dreaming of immortal doom.
No spot or scene, where past Religion shed
A glory, but to him entrancement gave.

* Vide Josephus' Description of the Temple.
† See Lightfoot and the ancient Commentators.

On Horeb he had mused, and heard the choir
Of Sinai's thunders, heralding their God:
On dewy Hermon, loved by David's lyre,
And Carmel's oaken top, where trembling stood
Elijah, when the cloudy Answer came,
He wander'd; and the eagle-haunted heights
Of cedar'd Lebanon by him were trod,—
That mountain chill'd by everlasting snow,
When all the firmament lies bathed in fire.

For high revealings of immortal truth
His soul was thus attuned; and when the light
Of miracles, by Jesu's hand perform'd,
His heart illumined, as the risen day
Oft suddenly with living splendour cheers
The gloom and hollow of deserted vales,—
A sudden radiance on his darkness stream'd.
Goodness and glory, both in Christ he saw;
But in delusions of terrestrial hope
Still blindly yearn'd a carnal Throne to see,
And scepter'd Judah queen of earth admired!
And thus, by ebbing moods of doubt and faith,
The Pharisee was sway'd, till Mercy came
And led him safely to the Lord, at last.
'Twas on a night of meditative calm,
Devoutly while his musing spirit read
The story of creation, sin and fall,
And second Eden by atoning grace
Procured, that impulses of sacred power
Moved Nicodemus to consult the Lord.
And what an interview that night reveals
'Tween sinful Earth and condescending Heaven!
Go, read it, where Eternal Life is found.
The second birth of renovated souls
Commenced; the Holy Spirit, how He comes
The world to sanctify, unseen departs,
And worketh like an unbeholden wind,
The Lord explain'd; till Nicodemus bow'd
In wonder, doubted, trembled, and believed!
Since light was born, and condemnation found
For deeds of evil, which in darkness lurk
And blacken, hating light that brings a God.
Then ask not, how the doubter home return'd,
Or how his dreams to slumber's Paradise
That night was wafted on melodious wing:
From this deep hour his heaven of faith began.
A Saviour living and a Saviour dead,—
For *both* he pleaded, when the bravest shook,
And they who loved Him were the first to flee!

When John was prison'd, from those hating Jews
Whom miracles confounded, Jesus fled
To Galilee; that haunt supremely loved!
Where sprung Apostles, where His childhood grew,
And where He hasten'd, when from death unbound.
Through dells of beauty, hushed and shaded haunts,
Or meadows, whiten'd by the olive-boughs
That waved and flashed amid the swelling breeze,
Through each and all, as Nature's fancy tinged
And character'd her glowing realm, He roam'd
Till day advanced; and burning, breathless noon,
When earth was heated to her inmost core,
And light and languishment the brain oppress'd,
At Sichem[33] glitter'd round the Saviour's form.

Alone, beside a patriarchal well
He rested, wearied by the toil intense
Of travel; while his fond disciples sought
The city, bosom'd in Gerizim's vale.
Majestic calm and mournfulness divine
Around Him incommunicably reign'd,
Like stillness breathed from His eternity:
So 'tranced the air, that each minutest sound
By wing, or breeze, or basking insect made,
Was audible, and seem'd profanely loud:
At that deep moment Nature knew her God,
And bade the silent Elements adore!

While thus, immersed in some immortal dream
Of bright salvation, man's Redeemer sat,
There came a woman to that haunted well
Where holy Jacob, in the dawn of time,
Cool'd his hot thirst beneath a zenith sun.
A Jew!—of that abhorrent nation sprung,
Who, ever since on Dan and Bethel stood
Samaria's Idol, bade her miscreant race
Of heaven despair, and scorn'd her rival fane,
How spake He aught to one of Sichem born!
With touching beauty and with tender grace
Messiah answer'd, "Had she *known* the Gift
Of God, and who he was, that fain would drink,
A living water had divinely flow'd!"
His heaven-like mien, and voice augustly toned
With spirit-searching power, the woman awed;
And nearer still, with eye intently raised,
She wond'ring stole, and mortal-like replied;
That from the well, o'erhung by solemn boughs
Whose shadows oft on patriarchal heads
Had play'd, He had not now wherewith to draw,
And was He greater than their primal Sire?
Alas! the dimness which our being shrouds,
To keep us mortal in immortal hours!
Of Water springing with eternal Life
Whose fountain is the awful soul within,
Th' Incarnate spoke; but when the letter still
And not the spirit of His words prevail'd,
Back from her heart prophetic wisdom roll'd

Clouds of dark guilt which there concealment spread,
And bare before it laid her life of sin!
Then, Conscience! like a voice from other worlds,
Sudden and piercing, did thy power appeal
To yon frail woman! on her cheek's array
Of paleness, in her eyes' dissolving shame
It witness'd; and her loudly-beating heart
By every throb a pang to memory paid!
Then, pointing to Samaria's mountain-fane,
Whose massy pomp of pinnacles and towers
Rose black and solemn in the cloudless air,
She call'd Him, Prophet! and in meekness ask'd
Where heaven from earth the purest essence hail'd?
From Zion's hill, or where the Fathers knelt,—
Gerizim? whence of old from Joshua's lip
The full-voiced Blessing by a myriad tongues
Was echoed, while from Ebal's blanchèd height
A Curse came down, like thunder from the skies.[34]

Oh, ye who narrow to the dungeon-walls
Of bigotry, the limitless design of Heaven,
Approach and tremble!—God a spirit is!
And they who worship, must in spirit bend
His Throne before! The universal Heart
Of Man by revelation's light redeem'd,
Jehovah! *this* Thy purest temple forms.
So heard the woman; and a hope confess'd
Of coming Glory, in whose morning-beams
The night of error would dissolve away.
But when Messiah, "I who speak am He!"
Responded, mute, and statue-like, she stood,—
Embodied wonder! till disciples came
And marvell'd, how His purity could speak
To one so branded, that her blood was crime!
But awe withheld them; and on raptured wings
Of speed, to Sychar back the woman rush'd,
And, like a prophetess when new-inspired
To holy madness, gloryingly cried,
Through street and dwelling, "Lo! Messiah comes!
A Man who told me all I ever did,
The Saviour, by yon well of Jacob sits!"
At once, to see the heaven-descended Christ,
Up the green valley troop ecstatic throngs,
Till thick and fast the mingling shadows fell
From young Samaritans, on herbs and flowers,
As on they sprang, like birds to meet the morn!
While slow behind, the hoary-headed forms
Of Age were gliding, pale with wordless joy.
"The harvest, say ye not, four months will bring?
Behold! the meadows are already white,
And he who gathers, reaps immortal fruit!"
Thus spake the Saviour, and His welcome high
The crowd attracted; dumb with deepest awe
They linger'd; not a heart but quaked with bliss
Divine, or dreamt it immortality begun:
Then lovingly that simple-hearted race
The mighty Stranger to their dwellings brought,
And fell before Him, in sublime belief
Exclaiming, "Thou alone art Christ the Lord!"

From Sychar, hence to Cana Christ advanced,
And there again shone forth, incarnate God!
A Nobleman, around whose only child
The shades of death were deepening, at His feet,
With all the father mirror'd in his eyes,
Sank prostrate; and in tones which tore the heart
With dreadful truth, His healing power besought
To soothe the madness of parental wo,
And back to life a dying son recall.
"Thy son is living!" so Emmanuel spake,
And he who trusted found his faith's reward!
And thus for ever His unwearied Arm
Is present, guiding worlds along their paths,
Or waved in mercy round the fate of man.

But His it was, though all divinely meek
Each virtue shone, to drink the bitter Cup!
As in the synagogue when call'd, as won't,
From out th' assembly, to unroll and read
The Haphtoroth,[35] a deaden'd language rose
To life upon His lips! there, all in vain
The saving wisdom of Messiah spoke:
Their eyes were dark, they saw but Joseph's son!
But when of miracles for Gentiles work'd
Alone, while famish'd Israel droop'd in dust,
And on the heavens immitigably seal'd
From dawn to midnight turn'd her mournful gaze,
When such He mention'd, to convict the soul,—
The living frame of that Assembly shook
With passion! not an eye but glared revenge!
And, fell as tigers, savagely they sprung,
And bore Him upward to the rocky hill
Where hung their city, down whose awful depth
To atoms they would hurl the Saviour-God!
But in a moment, by its dizzy brink
Each eye was dazzled, and a Power unknown
Invisibly that human chaos quell'd!
In the full whirlwind of their fiercest ire
They soften'd to a breezelike calm, which died
To utter stillness, when the crowd beheld
Their Victim, passing through the parted throng
Unhurt; as he who faced a fiery death
And walk'd the furnace with the Son of Man.

To thee, Capernaum! by Messiah bless'd
And haunted, turn we now our solemn gaze.
There, mead and hamlet, mountain, shore, and plain
His presence felt, His mighty works enjoyed;
While Nature to each theme of glory lent
Her own sweet magic, imagery, and power.
And seest thou, girdled in by barren wilds,
Yon blue expanse? Gennesareth is there!
Quiescent now as meditation's hour
Yon lake of beauty in the noontide gleams;
But when a hurricane with Syrian roar
Descends the mountain, and its calm defies,
Then, Chinnereth! thy sleeping might awakes;
And yon deep billows with disastrous swell
In hollow thunder to the winds respond.

By the bright waters, on that lovely beach
Of famed Tiberias, where a wondering crowd
Around Him panted for immortal truth,
Was Jesus standing; while the fisher wash'd
His net, and dried it on the pebbled shore.
Two silent vessels on the lake reposed;
The one He enter'd, and the people taught;
But ere the music of His mighty words
Was still'd, "Launch forth! and let your nets descend,"
The Lord commanded: worn by fruitless toil,
All doubtingly did Peter's hand obey:
But when at once, with its enormous load
The net uprose, till e'en the laden ship
Beneath her living burden sank, and reel'd,
Silence adored! the tongueless air was hush'd,
As though Creation wonder'd! till, a cry
Yon multitude from off the shore awoke,
Which scatter'd silence like a broken dream!
While Peter, quivering with unearthly dread,
Fell in amazement at Messiah's feet
And utter'd, "Leave me, Lord! for I am vile!"
That moment his Apostleship began
For ever: death and darkness, time and wo,
From Faith's high throne he overlook'd them all!
Then James and John at once that Power revered
To Whom the Elements their laws resign'd,
And laid their sceptres down. Of old prevail'd
The Prayer of prophets, for the sick and dead
Arising; but a Word that ruled the waves
And master'd ocean with creative might,
Had ne'er till *now* a lip on Earth inspired!

To this high deed, an unrecorded mass
Of miracles, in one successive throng
Was added: when the sun's expiring gleam
Paled o'er Capernaum, round Messiah's door
Disease assembled all her ghastly troop
Of martyrs: in an instant, ere a sound
Could perish, Health's untainted blood return'd!
The lame and sightless, palsied, deaf, and dumb
Recover'd, fleet as resurrection's change;
And thus, by deed embodying all Isaiah sung,
Through town and village the Redeemer went
And rested never from His glorious toil;
Except when God th' incarnate Son adored,
As oft He did in melancholy wilds,
Where, all unseen, the Man of Sorrows knelt
And sanctified His human will by prayer.

And must we sink, in lifeless wonder lost
'Mid the pure radiance of such perfect deeds?
The power, but not the principle sublime
Is hidden, whence creation's ruling Lord
Each miracle derived;—and that is Love,
Which link by link connects a thousand worlds,
And chains them all to one Almighty Throne!

For true example, not inactive awe,
Messiah lived; and he who soars to Him
That living Orb of Righteousness beholds,
Whose beams are catholic with boundless grace
And sunlike fall on universal Man.

BOOK V.

. . . . . "All the stars
Thou knew'st by name, and all th' ethereal powers,
All secrets of the deep, all Nature's works,
Or works of God in heaven, air, earth, or sea."

MILTON.

ANALYSIS OF BOOK V.

Solitude—How exaltedly employed when devoted to a contemplation of the glorious plan of Redemption—The Sermon on the Mount—Scenery—A Summary of its Doctrines—The measureless good they have effected in the world since first promulgated—Christ at Capernaum—A Leper cleansed—Escapes from the Multitude who would force Him to be their King—Passage over the Lake—Storm—Peril and affright of the Disciples—Jesus rebukes the Elements to perfect calm—The Demoniac—A description of his horrid sufferings—the Demons are expelled, and their Victim cured—How utterly impossible for Human Pen to paint or express the Divine loveliness of the Redeemer's actions and character—The Daughter of Jairus—Her youth, education, sickness, and death—The Father's despair—Arrival of the Saviour—His Miraculous Display of Power in recalling the Spirit to Life—From hence Messiah goes to Galilee, passes a Night in Prayer, and on the morrow elects His Disciples—Then passes in Retrospective View their Triumphs and Toils, as they are recalled by the associations and scenes of Nazareth—Jesus goes to Nain—Calls to life the Widow's Son—Description of the Miracle—Reflections on the tenderness of Christ in his conduct to Women—The Magdalene—Christ again at Jerusalem—Cures a Man at the Pool of Siloam—The Jews mock observance of the Sabbath—Observed best by imitation of Christ—Messiah enters the Desert of Bethsaida—Feeds a Multitude—Reflections on this surpassing Miracle—Our strange neglect of the wonderful Love daily exhibited by God to Man—The Disciples embark on the Lake—Storm—Appearance of Christ walking on the Waters—Peter's Faith and Despair—Lesson taught by his presumption—The Transfiguration—Pride still the dominant principle in the Disciples' souls—Christ blesses little Children, and proposes them as examples of what his Followers should be—The Woman taken in Adultery—Her accusers how appalled and subdued by conscience—The Feast of Lights—Raising of Lazarus—Christ's triumphant entry through Jericho to Jerusalem—The Widow's mite—The Saviour's last farewell to the Holy City—His prediction of its terrible fate—A vision of its fall.

How beautiful the soul's religious calm
When thought is heavenward, and the chainless mind
Like soaring Enoch, to our God ascends!
And oh! how glorious, by deep vision led,
Six thousand years to travel back and view
How from the cradle of eternity
The infant-world at God's command arose.
The new-born winds, the ocean's young delight
Heard in a rhapsody of rolling waves;
With every tint and motion, gleam or glance
Of life and matter, from the lyric host
Of Stars, with quiring gratulation loud,
To fairy insect and minutest flower,—
On each and all Imagination dreams,
When Earth lay basking in Jehovah's smile!

But what is this, or all th' amazing stream
Of glories, terrors, and supernal acts
Of truth and judgment, down the mighty page
Devolved, to thine all-wondrous Plan,
Redemption? Vast beyond the vastest dream
That circles round the comprehending soul,
Thy range extendeth! Nature's utmost bounds,
From earth to heaven, from heaven to higher worlds,
And higher still, beyond the furthest reach
Of finite thought to mention or conceive,
Immensity, and all Eternal Power
Created, forms, or may hereafter free,—
Redeemer! over all Thy glories reign!

But lo! the Mount, whereon Messiah sat
And taught; while multitudes with lifted gaze
And soul that listen'd with suspended breath,
Beneath Him swarm'd, to drink eternal Life
Whose fountain issued from the Throne of God.
The Spring was forth: young loveliness and bloom
Her reign attested; trees and meadows flash'd
With verdant lustre, while the shaken flowers
Their scent and beauty to the breeze resign'd
With playful murmur. From its sacred top
A bright extent of ever-changing view*
The beatific Mount o'ergazed: from thence,
Gilboa, where amid the chariot-rush
Of Philistines, the dying Saul despair'd,
Was seen to lift her Pyrenèan crags
And cloud-like spires; Gennesareth's azure mass
Of waters, and the snow-clad Hermon's height
Conspicuous beam'd; and all which gave
To hallow'd words an instantaneous glow
Of life and feeling, full before Him lay.
Bethuliah to a thousand eyes appear'd,
When Jesus of the hill-throned City spake;
The lily-flowers, which neither toil nor spin,
Yet, beautiful beyond arrayèd Solomon!
In golden freshness on the meadows waved;
And when on providential Care alone
He bade terrestrial Want repose, and cried,
"Behold the fowls your heavenly Father feeds!"
Their wings exulted on the air around
And nerved the precept with example's force.

Oh, what a scene of heart-affecting power
Was there beheld!—That consecrated Mount
On whose green summit sat the Son of Man;
The words he utter'd; deep and awful tones,
Yet tender in their might, as mellow'd-sounds
From Ocean's lip; with all unclouded spring
Of fresh and fair commandeth; and the crowds
Which hung like bees upon the mountain-side,
As thick and numberless, yet hush'd and chain'd
To utter calm, as though their living mass
Together breathed but one absorbing soul,—
Religion! thou wert throned in godlike pomp
Amid a scene transcendently endow'd
Like this, with attributes of holy might
Beyond the Temple in its costliest hour.

And what a doctrine of almighty depth
Messiah founded, when His truth declared,
In meekness lies the majesty of Man!
At once the Wisdom of the world was dumb,
And Mammon blighted on his throne of bliss.
The ways of pleasantness, the paths of peace
Are dim and narrow, tracks of noiseless gloom
Which Glory flies, and Grandeur seldom walks:
The poor in spirit, and the meek in heart
Who thirst and hunger for Thy righteous Word,
Oh! these are blest, for Thine unerring Voice
Hath call'd them so, and crown'd their lowly Lot,
And sanctified its unrebellious tear.
To them divinely was the blessing given;

* Vide Wilson's Travels; and Maundrell's Journey, p. 155, eighth edition.

And while in shed or cottage, swamp or wild,
The sacred pangs of Poverty endure,
There Goodness and her Lord may constant meet,
And Charity, with soft and silent foot,
Move like an Angel to a deed of heaven.

And vaster Truths, unspeakably divine,
Which live before the Throne, and light effuse
O'er all who worship their immortal Source,
Did Christ reveal:—of uncomplaining Love,
Forgiving, as it hopes to be forgiven;
Of Sanctity, within the spirit shrined;
Of Passion, rooted from terrestrial ties
And trampled as the soul's unhallow'd weed;
Of alms in secret,—temples in the mind
Where God in dedicated moments comes
To earth unknown,[26] and needs no trumpet-voice
To tell the world a conscious sinner prays;
Of Providence, life's angel, ever nigh,
Who feeds the bird, and robes the meadow-flower;
Of lofty hope, of meditative peace,
And feeling, touch'd with man's infirmity,
O'ercoming wrong with mercy's tender gaze
That looks aside when human error falls,
But loves a virtue in its frailest hours,—
Of these He spake, and taught believing Man
A worship, which eternal Wisdom loves.

E'en Him, whom yonder choir of worlds
Adores, *our* faltering tongues may Father call!—
Glory of glories! can archangels boast
A voice, or language of mysterious love
Surpassing this, which bids "our Father" sound
From lip of mortals, when a soul renews
Her solemn intercourse with God on high?
Give ear, O Heaven! thou wondering Earth, be still,
For here is love so measureless and deep,
That Feeling staggers, and Expression fails,
Or ventures only, "let Thy will be done!"
Oh! long as man upon creation moves,
In solemn aisles of monumental gloom
Ascending with a loud melodious swell,
In rustic fane, or tranquil home beloved,
By hoary age, or lisping childhood breathed,
From cave or desert, dungeon, rock, or sea,—
That mighty Prayer upon the mountain taught
To Heaven and Jesus may it ever rise,
And win the Mercy it was framed to woo.

His task is o'er, the sacred Teacher gone,
And the last murmur of descending feet
Dies on the hill; where now a breeze awakes
The spring-born flowers, till livingly they stir
And tremble into low sweet song again.
But all the host who heard immortal Truth
Upon the beatific Mount declared
Are vanished, like the dew of yesterday!
And thrones and states and Babylonian piles
Have wither'd; Dust has claim'd its dead
For ever, quenching in sepulchral sleep
The Earth's unquiet generations gone;
Yet, pure as perfect, Christ's majestic Law
High o'er the wreck of Men and Things endures,
And will,—till heaven and earth dissolve away!

What toils and agonies, what glorious tears
And blessed pangs by penitence sublimed,
The earth has known, though unrecorded left!
O History, thou hast done the world a wrong
Immense and mournful; on the alpine heights
Of human Greatness, thine enamour'd gaze
Has linger'd; mindless in that partial mood
Of meek-eyed Virtue, in the vale below!
And robed thy themes of darkness with a veil
Of bright attraction, as the Thunder wraps
His ruin oft in clouds of gorgeous spell.
Yet better far, had thy pervading glance
From earthly pomp to scenes of heavenly truth
Descended; marking how the Saviour's word
Had triumph'd, how it lived in lonely hearts
And aching bosoms, weeded daily life
Of sin and wo, and dried the widow's tear.—
Sublime of Sermons! atheistic tongues
Have bless'd thee, and the worldling's rocky soul
Gush'd into tears beneath thy tender sway:
When life is gladness, or when sorrow flings
A sudden autumn o'er the leaves of joy,
The purest homily of peace and love
Wisdom has utter'd since the world began!

But thou, Capernaum! once again the Arm
Almighty bares itself for thee, and thine
Oh, misbelieving Land! to heaven upraised
And hell cast down.—A grim and ghastly wreck,
Upon his face beneath Messiah's feet
A Leper falls, there, lifts his bloodshot gaze,
And with a voice of choked and dying tone
His help implores:—From Egypt's fiery realm
The dread corruption came, when burning noon
Flamed o'er the limbs of Pharaoh's toil-worn slaves;
And now, a victim of its direst rage
The Son of Man beheld. Each sign accursed
Disease had printed on his mouldering form;
Till fruit had wither'd in the hot embrace
Of each infected hand!—let Fancy shrink,
But still a martyrdom of nature see,
Then, picture how the Lord of Being look'd,
When graciously His godlike hand approach'd,

The Leper touch'd, and with a word divine
Commanded, "Be thou clean!" and lo! he sprang
To earth again, a free and perfect man
And pure as childhood in its glowing prime!
For, health with instantaneous gush o'erflow'd
His being; like the world's untainted Sire
He stood in glory, eyeing earth and heaven
As though his spirit would encircle all!

And well might gratitude obedience quench;
On wings, that seem'd round every limb to play,
O'er mount and vale th' ecstatic Creature fled,
A living miracle: and cried aloud
"A God! a God! His mighty cure behold!"
Roused into motion, like autumnal leaves
By wind invoked, a rushing Host that cry
Re-echoed: onward with exulting speed
To fall in worship round th' Almighty Priest
They came: but not in Him, the loud uproar
Of shouting numbers, nor the false delight
Of glory flashing over envious eyes,
Nor crown, nor throne upon the dying breath
Of sudden wonder raised,—acceptance found.
The shady desert, and the dark-bough'd wild
Again He haunted; there, amid the calm
Of Nature, hush'd by some instinctive awe,
Alone The Everlasting pray'd, and thought.
But, vain seclusion! through the verdant depth
Of solemn woods the rush of thronging feet
Advanced; and voices, with a sea-like roar
Confused and clashing, round the Saviour roll'd:
'Twas then, escaping from the countless herd,
Upon the Lake His prompt disciples launch'd
Their bark, and bore the great Redeemer on.
Far o'er the blue and rippled waters sail'd
The boat; serene as yonder twilight-cloud
It moved, whose haven was the ruddy west.
In pillow'd slumber on the silent deck
The Son of Man reposed: sublimely calm
His features in the light of evening shone;
And oft entranced, some fond disciples stood
To gaze upon His holy sleep, and draw
Transcendent meanings from that Face Divine!

But ere the Twilight, and her fairy crowd
Of splendours, melted in the dark embrace
Of night, with soul intent the seamen heard
The incantations of a Storm begin!
The air was toned with sadness, like a sigh
Of broken hearts, or moan of guilty dreams
When Midnight is confessor: o'er the Lake
A breezy and a sudden life arose,
Till ripples flash'd, and bubbling foam began
To whiten o'er the waters. In the sky
No mercy dawns; for all is scowling there,
And savage clouds are in funereal march
Benighting heaven with one enormous gloom.
But hark! with ominous array it comes,—
Creation's tyrant! list the Tempest howls;
The South-East sends her hurricane, and back
The Jordan in affrighted motion rolls:
The Lake is heaving with convulsive throes
And billows writhe in agonising play
Loud o'er the surface, till like living Shapes
Of water battling with the Winds they seem
In liquid thunder, wheresoe'er they move!
In that wild hour, while star nor moon reveal'd
A solace, and the only light which gleam'd,
Shone when red lightning with a wizard flash
Call'd the dun mountains into dreary form
And station,—then the pale disciples ran
And cried, "We perish! save us, Lord! arise!"
He heard; He rose; and while the vessel creak'd,
And cordage rattled in the roaring gale
Like wither'd branches in a forest-wind,
Till o'er the deck the climbing billows rush'd
And darken'd round her with devouring yell,
His hand He waved, the rolling storm rebuked,
The Tempest knew her God,—and still'd!
Then o'er Tiberias, calm as cradled sleep,
The Moon uprose; and in her silver hue
Each cloud dissolved, as angry feeling dies
By music overcome; and once again
The doubting crew their wingèd bark beheld,
With stars above, and star-lit waves beneath,
Serenely gliding on to Gadarene:
Oh! then, amid that elemental trance
The meek reproach of their forgiving Lord
Was felt; each gazed on each with holy fear;
The calm of Nature grew a fearful charm;
For Sea and Air with more than language cried
"The waters hear Him, and the Winds obey!"

The shore is reach'd; but what unearthly Shape,
What Thing accurst, in human semblance clothed,
Foaming and wild, with eyeballs sternly fix'd,
Glares on them, like a cavern'd brute aroused
By errant footsteps, when her whelps are nigh?
O Prince of Darkness! and ye Powers of Air
By Heaven permitted, from the fiery doom
Of Hell's abyss, to roam the peopled earth
Awhile, and enter in the breathing frame
Of mortals, maddening with demonian rage
Both blood and spirit,—there, *your* victim stands!
Thou dreaded martyr! words and feelings fly
Aghast, or shudder round thy gloomy pangs:
Thy limbs are bare, and down their wither'd length
The blood has track'd the lacerating stone
Tormented Madness from the hills hath wrung
To glut her agony! Among the tombs

Thy dwelling is; from human face apart,
The dead around thee in sepulchral caves
Of rocky darkness,*—there thy spirit moans,
Or mutters, till the very mountains seem
Appall'd to echo with thy blasphemy!
But, dreader far, when night's dominion came
To hear thy howlings! e'en the desert-beast
Hath trembled, when the horrid echoes rang;
While, pillow'd on a sleeping mother's breast,
The infant shook to think thy shadow nigh!

Thus stood the foaming maniac, while there glared
The terror of his demon-haunted eyes
Through each disciple's heart!—but, ere a limb
Could move, that dreadless Voice, which made
The roaring Tempest mute, and never spake
But Heaven was raptured, and profoundest Hell
With agonies of coming doom convulsed
Or shaken,—like omnipotence arose:
"Come forth, defiler!" and the spirit fell
In kneeling torture at Messiah's feet!
There, "By the living God!" dark Legion cried,
"Thou Jesus! Son of the Most High! adjured,
Before our time torment us not! nor plunge
Our spirits in th' Infernal Deep again,
But let us enter in yon mountain-prey."
When thus permitted, like a gentle dawn
His soul emerged, and spread each vital hue
Of nature o'er the freed demoniac's frame.
And when the crowding Gadarenes advanced
In gazing terror round Messiah's form
No bleeding maniac from the rocky tombs
They witness'd, but a man renew'd and mild,
From Hell deliver'd, at the feet of Christ
Reposing, with his native vesture clad:
And as he sat, how superhuman seem'd
The great Restorer! thanks in wonder died;
But what a language in his lifted eye,
Whose words were tears, the eloquence of joy!

Divine perfection of embodied Love,
Supremely fair, insufferably bright,
By Thee, the Muse is dazzled! all is deep
August, and holy, where Thy presence rules;
The bigot tamed, the hypocrite unmask'd,
The Law illumed, and blinded Israel taught
The darkness of exclusive faith was o'er,[37]
And light celestial, from the depths of God
Would soon irradiate universal Man.
Him, Son of Alpheus! though the luring world
Had long enchain'd thee, thou didst not refuse,
When, "Follow me" fell sudden on thine ear,
And thou wert his, by deathless grace redeem'd.

* See Maundrell's Account of the Ancient Tombs, &c. &c.

But what awaits us? Let maternal Hearts
Whose pulse beats love, approach and tell,
Oh life! how beautiful thy maiden-bloom
In that bright morn, when youth's unfolded years
Like rising veils before enchantment spread,
Recede, and down a fairy vista roams
The glancing joy of Expectation's eye!
Then day by day, as some meek violet rear'd
By fondling sunshine, grows the virgin Mind
In home's retreat, till childhood melts away,
And dawning Womanhood her smile begins.
Then all is fair; affection's graceful smile
From out a purity of spirit plays,
And life and motions, inspirations are
Which tone the voice, or teach the step delight;
And frowning Sorrow, though it shade the cheek,
The soul can darken not, whose placid tears
Melt as they rise, like tender dews of wo.
Romance is true, reality a dream,
And cares,—oh! what are *they*, but minute-clouds
That speck the ether of our calmest life!

And canst thou, Death! congenial dungeons quit
Where thou art woo'd by dark and wretched men,
To come where Youth and Loveliness unite
Their magic, and the breath of life is joy?
Alas! the knells, that with diurnal grief
The wind intone; alas! the frequent pall,
The church-yard tales on tomb and stone rehearsed,
A blinded chamber, or that weeping Home
Where round some coffin drooping parents bend,
Like marble shapes of monumental Wo,
Thy victims tell, thy savage choice reveal!

Then think, if in bereavement's blackest hour,
When flooding agonies the brain o'erwhelm,
And a last gaze seems looking life away,
The parted spirit of the Dead return'd!—
For such the scene, by Revelation drawn.
On Jairus Heaven an only child bestow'd;
A lovely scion, round whose being twined
The clinging fondness of parental fear.
For beautiful as Syria's lonely flowers,
That wave and murmur on the shady top
Of wooded Lebanon, her form had grown
From infancy, till now revealing time
Had written woman on her vestal cheek.

Born in that Land where summer's pregnant beam
Was brightest, where the fruits of Eden hung,
And the rich mulberry spread a snowy bloom,

While grapes empurpled every terraced hill,
Her shape and spirit magic influence caught
From Syria's clime of glory. Nature's grace
By power of exquisite attraction seem'd
Reflected from it; light and beauty fill'd
Her soul, and flash'd from those irradiate eyes;
And walk'd she not, as Israel's daughter would,
The mighty scenes where patriarchal feet
Had trodden, where the God of Zion spake!
Lake, fount, and river, and those Mountains three
Which camp'd her warriors, and that still o'erlook
Esdraelon's plain, where tented Arabs dwell,
Around whose home, when dewy nightfall comes,
The gamb'ling flocks to reedy murmurs play,—
From each and all pure inspiration sprung,*
And told, how beautiful religion look'd
By youth entempled in a spotless heart!

And yet on her, with vestal radiance clad,
Infection breathed, and poison'd blood and brain,
Till the rich bloom of animation died.
Her form was blighted; and her faded cheek
The pallid certainty of coming doom
Betray'd: oh, hear it, Heaven!—a father's prayer
The sky ascends to claim a brighter hope:
Away, with agonising speed he flies,
Nor treads the ground, nor hears the city-roar,
Nor feels the motion of his moving limbs!
Condensed, and darken'd into wild despair
His soul became, till Nature's functions fail'd,
And earth was reeling from his dazzled gaze,
When full amid the pharisaic throng
He rush'd, and prostrate with a burst of wo,
Voiced his dread agony with this deep cry,
"My daughter, Lord! her deathful pangs approach,
But hasten! touch her with Thy healing hand
And yet my child shall live:" ere Jesus came
Her spirit vanish'd, like a lovely sound!

The house of mourning!—hark, the funeral-dirge,
The doleful flutes, and dying melodies
Of instrumental tone, or wailing yells
Of frantic Grief, and mercenary Wo.†
But, enter! there in yon sepulchral room,
Alone a childless mother comes to seal
The lids of Death, and on that marble lip
Imprint a long and last—the parting kiss!
And *shall* the worm of putrefaction feed
On that young form, of Beauty's finest mould?
The light and life of twelve enchanted years,
All sunk and shaded in remorseless dust!
Oh agony! could thawing tears the soul
Dissolve, let suffering Nature shed them now.
While o'er thy cheek, so eloquently pale,
Once full of rosy life, her bending eye
With dreadful speculation broods, beloved
And blessed! all thy winning ways and smiles,
Thy look and laugh, in one sweet throng, return
Upon her, till thy warm and living breath
Again is playing round Affection's heart!
But ah! her martyr'd frame's convulsive heave,
As if in that chaotic gloom of mind
When feeling is our only faith, the soul
Would rive the body and at once be free,—
Betokens *thou* art death, and *she* despair!

Believe, and fear not: in the blackest cloud
A sunbeam hides; and from the deepest pang
Some hidden mercy may a God declare.
There as she stood, delirous, rack'd, and wild,
The Saviour enter'd, and his soothing glance
Fell on the mother's torn and troubled heart
As moonlight on the ocean's haggard scene.
The wailing minstrel, and the dirge of death,
He bade them cease; "The maiden is not dead,
But sleepeth!" Then around her vestal couch
The mourning parents, with His chosen Three,
Advanced, and in the midst, divinely calm,
The son of Man! In lifeless beauty laid,
A loveliness and not the gloom of death
The virgin wore; and on her placid cheek
The light of dreams reposed: oh, ne'er could dust
A purer sacrifice from Death receive!
But when He stoop'd, and held her icy hand,
And utter'd, "Maid, arise!" the beating heart
Of wonder, doubt, delight, and awful fear
Was hush'd; for, swift as echo to the voice
Replies, the spirit of the dead awoke
At His high summons! whether from the arm
Of Angels, lock'd in some oblivious trance;
Or from the bloom and breath of Paradise
Amid beatitude to earth recall'd,
To us untold; enough for man to know
That *when* the Lord of resurrection spake
The soul return'd! And mark its dawning glow;
Soft o'er each deaden'd cheek the rosy light
Of cherub slumber steals; the eyes unfold
And lift their veiny lids, as matin-flowers
When dew and sunshine fascinate their gaze;
In red and smiling play the lips relax,
And, delicate as music's dying fall,
The throb of life begins; she moves! she breathes!

* See Malte Brun on Palestine.

† Abbé Fleury's Account of Jewish Ceremonies, &c. &c.

The dead hath risen, and a living child
Sinks on the bosom of maternal Love!

From hence, to Galilee the Prince of Life
Again retreated; there His Own beloved
Received Him not, but savagely repell'd
The Nazarene; alas! they little dreamt
Of shrouded glory ark'd in Mary's Son!
But from the vain, whom pomp alone allured,
To multitudes of meek and aidless men
Who, faint and scatter'd, for instruction pined,
And tractable, the mild Redeemer turn'd.
Upon the mountain, when a night of prayer
Had pass'd, and awful Invocation knelt,
The Twelve were chosen, seal'd and heaven-inspired,
And yet, how poor!—a Galilēan tribe
By man untaught, to Science all unknown.
But not as ours, are Thine unfathom'd ways
Jehovah! in the mean Thy might display'd
Its vastness; on the low Thy lofty truth
Descended; out of weakness wisdom sprung,
As light from darkness, worlds from nothing, came!

And these were living Oracles, whose voice
Was power, whose doctrine breathed eternal life!
To them was portion'd this almighty Task,
"Advance! though Hell's dark legions rise, advance!
And preach the kingdom of approaching Heaven.
Nor gold, nor silver, raiment, staff, nor scrip,
Provide, but enter ye the city-gates;
The lame restore, the dead recal, the blind
Illumine, cleanse the leper, heal the sick,
And hurl the Demon from the haunted soul.
Be wise as serpents, innocent as doves;
Beware of all, but flatter none; for Thrones
Shall tremble, and the cheek of Kings
Look blasted, and your words of lightning cleave
The spirits which appal ye, when the lash
Is loudest, and the blood of trial flows.
Advance, and fear not! for your very hairs
Are number'd; viewless, God your Guardian is,
And he who offers to the parchēd lip
A cup of water, him will I repay!"

And did they not, by living grace empower'd,
The Earth evangelise, till idols shook
Before them, and the gates of hell were storm'd?
Its truthful witness let the solemn Past
Uplift, and there, along the boundless scene
Of time departed, shines the glorious track
Of true Apostles! On their heads the curse
Was wreak'd, and fires of persecution rain'd;
Their limbs were torn, around them dungeons gaped,
And yet, they ceased not; still the cry was heard,
"Redemption! on the Cross a Saviour hung;
Repent, believe, and be for ever blest!"

Transcendent martyrs! round your awful brows
Seraphic wreaths are twined, and ye adore,
In throned array, the Co-Eternal Three!
But with your presence, not your *power* sublime
Departed; still around us in their might,
Recorded mercies miracles and truths
Divine, are breathing: by whose vital sway
Are sanction'd all which daily Life enjoys
Of charity, protection, faith, and peace;
The light of Laws, the Liberty of home,
Content, and all that makes a Country dear.

From what high armory, celestial Band!
Were your bright weapons taken? Was your creed
A pliant courtier, bending to the will
Tyrannic, culling from each varied clime,
Or doctrine, some accordant hue to please
A passion, flatter doubt, or soothe despair?
Or, did ye, by undaunted truth sublimed,
Like second Daniels and Elijahs prove
And brand the vices of corrupted man?
Against the Passions, wheresoe'er they ruled,
Ye march'd, and fought them in their fiercest shape
Of Lust and Pride, and dark Ambition's dreams,
And Hopes which make eternity a lie
By moulding heaven to each infirm desire.[38]

O traveller! far from England's elmy dales
To Syria wafted, in the trance of noon
When thou art seated on some rocky cliff
Of Nazareth, and think'st that *there*, unknown,
In meek subjection lived the Son of Man,
Till came the hour when like a buried stream
Of glory bursting into sudden day,
That mighty Doctrine which embraced a world
Rose into light, and ran its vast career,—
What visions o'er thy musing spirit roll?[39]
The flood of centuries, in their fancied roar
Thou hears't them sweeping! but amid the tides
Of desolation over king and kingdom pour'd,
The "Rock of Ages," based on earth indeed
But towering to the skies,—unshaken stands,
Deep as eternity and high as heaven!

But now, from everlasting triumph fresh
And ardent, met the apostolic Band

Once more around Him; then to lovely Nain
By Hermon shaded, o'er whose dazzling snow
A mid-noon burn'd, the godlike Jesus went.
Whoe'er thou art, a scene of touching might
And tender beauty waits thy spirit there.
And yet, how simple! such as link mankind
Together by unbroken ties of soul,—
The glories of the Gospel! from the heart
They spring, and to the heart alone appeal
With eloquence divine.

Behold, as noon
Was calming down from its meridian heat,
And Tabor o'er Esdraelon's verdure threw
A longer shade, where cooling Kishon ran
His midway course, the Lord of mercy reach'd
That mountain-dell where Nain of Hermon stands:
But ere He enter'd, came a mournful troop
In dark procession from the city-gates.
The air was rung with anguish; and the dirge
Fell sad and frequent on Messiah's ear:
While midmost, on a mantled bier upborne,
A youth was carried to an early grave,
An only child, the Star of widow'd home
In whose fond ray a mother's spirit smiled!
With what a sense of beautiful delight
Her ear drank in the father's fancied voice,
Still in her son triumphant o'er the tomb!
How tenderly her soul's creative eye
Gazed on the meanings of his manly face
And made each feature all the sire restore
In proud resemblance! while a sacred hope
Survived, that when her widow'd race was done,
His hand would smoothe, his gentle voice attend
Her dying bed; and tears of filial truth
Fall on the flowers which graced a mother's tomb!
But Heaven had frown'd, her living star was set,
In the bright morning of its beauty gone
For ever. Pity! thine are barren tears,
And unrefreshing as the thunder-drops
On burning sands, to wo intense as this!
For life and feeling in the grave descend;
And sounds of comfort, like the clamorous waves
In heedless revel o'er the ocean-dead,
Awake no echoes in her spirit now.

But on they come, the sad funereal crowd,
And deep o'er all the blended tones of grief
A heart-wrung widow's lamentations rise
Distinctive of the Mother! Not a gaze
By feeling unbedewed; the young men weep,
As fancy pictures, on yon cover'd bier
Their pale companion, from whose mirthful brow
So many a gleam of young enjoyment flash'd
Like daily sunshine over kindred hours:
The aged bow their heads, to dreams of death
Surrender'd; parents muse on buried hopes,
Or clasp the living with a fearful joy!
And e'en the children, as the mourning-train
Advances, from unthinking revel cease
And sadden down the innocence of glee.
'Twas then the Lord of Life and Death approach'd
The long procession, and a widow's tear
Was mighty, for it thrill'd Emmanuel's soul!
At once, majestic through the yielding crowd
Beside the corse He came, the bier He touch'd,
Then, moveless as the dead that living host
Stood silent; every throbbing breeze grew loud,
And motions of the human heart were heard
In the deep hush of this portentous hour!
The awful coming of some dread Display
Each soul awaited: then was heard, "Arise!"
The spirit answer'd, and that youth arose;
And to his mother took Messiah's hand
Her only child!

Oh, ask not, what excess
Of rapture, what ecstatic shriek of joy,
What thrilling fires of new affection rose
When heart to heart the beat of life return'd,
As there they stood, unutterably blest,
Each twined round each, affection's holy pair!
The mountain-top, though daring clouds retreat
Below it, oft victorious feet ascend;
And down the ocean have undaunted eyes
Descended; but the height and depth of Love
Maternal, who shall meet its boundless sway?
But, rather witness how one eager gaze
From the vast multitude's concentred awe
Is bent on Jesus! dreadful light enrobes
His Form, divinity His features wear,
And as He moves, in loud hosannahs rise,
"Our God hath visited His people now!"

And thus, whene'er the tears of Woman fall,
Compassion! in the Lord of pity view
Thy godlike Semblance. Never from His lip
The crushing heartlessness of cold rebuke
Descended, when the soul of woman cried!
And was not this example? Ere the tongue
Can utter, or the eye a wo reveal,
Her smile is round us, like a guardian-spell
Which nothing scatters, save the tyrant-gloom
Of death; and then, *whose* unforsaking glance,
Till the last hue of being fade, from dawn
To midnight keeps angelic watch beside
The ebbing spirit, lighting it to heaven?
'Tis Action makes the world of man; but life
Is feeling, such as gentler woman bears;
The fairy people of her inward world
Are true affections; when the blight hath touch'd

Or wrong'd their beauty, darkly cold this earth
Becomes, the elements of being fade,
And silence is the sepulchre of thought
Wherein the anguish of her spirit dwells.

But should there yet some icy soul remain
Which never melted at a woman's tear,
Let such advance, and meet The Saviour's eye!
Behold a chamber; round a simple board,
On circling couches, with unsandal'd feet
Reclined, a pharisaic throng convened;
Amid them, the Redeemer: as He lay,
Behind him crept a penitential form
Of faded beauty; years had fiercely traced,
And chronicled with Time's disastrous pen
The countless agonies of guilty wo
On her pale visage, from whose haggard eyes
The tears gush'd big and bright, while down her neck
In flowing ringlets fell unheeded hair
Of blackest lustre:—in her hand appear'd
An alabaster box of rich perfume.
But when her flood of anguish on the feet
Of Christ intruded, with her flowing hair
The tears she dried, and costly unction pour'd:
Divinely humbled, *That* mysterious Head
She would not dare profane! but, sin-abash'd,
Upon his feet alone an ointment due
She pour'd, the sad and silent Magdalene!

On her, as some mute parent's pensive gaze
The home-returning child of Error greets,
Messiah look'd; but from the scorner's eye
A scornful flash of indignation broke,
To think a vile corruption, frail as she,
Might touch a Prophet, or communion hold
With mortal Sanctity! Yet, ere contempt
Grew vocal, He whose comprehensive glance
Both heaven and earth and time and space commands,
And from the dungeon of the darkest soul
The craven thought with sudden light expels,
The brooding rancour of self-righteous man
Perceived, and thus the hidden soul unmask'd:
"Two debtors once a creditor forgave;
Five hundred one, the other fifty pence.
Which loved him *most?*" "The one forgiven most,"
The cowering Pharisee at once replied,
With curling lip, and brow which blacker grew!
"Behold yon woman! *she* hath loved the most,
And is the most forgiven!" Deadly rage
At those high words, which to Jehovah's lip
Belong'd, and character'd almighty power,
How fiercely did that proud assembly feel!
They spake not; but the blood's resentful ire
Flow'd on each visage with a fiery rush
Of inward passion, while derisive tones
Around the table murmuringly ran,—
That He, a throneless Heir of mortal clay,
The sanction of tremendous God assumed,
And pardon'd one by pharisaic creed
Accursed, whose presence was defiling breath,
Than whom, for their celestial robe to touch
To hug the Pestilence were purer far!
In deep soliloquy of hate and dread
So mutter'd each dark soul; but, mildly firm,
Emmanuel then to weeping Mary cried
"By faith forgiven, in thy peace depart!"

Again Jerusalem's Mosaic feast
Return'd, and Christ within her hoary walls
Hath enter'd, and beside Bethesda's pool
Unknown amid the lazar-crowd appears,
Beneath the porches lying. Round the bath
A pillared shade, five towering cloisters threw
Where each with ravenous impatience eyed
The blood-stain'd waters! panting for the hour
Medicinal, when some high Angel stirr'd
That healing Pool: as oft a summer-lake
Convulsively a thrilling breeze attests,
Bethesda rippled into mystic life
Beneath the wave of His unshadow'd wings.

Amid the martyrs, pale o'er all the rest,
And ghastly, bearing on his palsied frame
The loathsome curse of eight-and-thirty years'
Dread malady, an aidless Victim met
Divine compassion, when his Lord approach'd.
"Wilt thou be whole?" the Great Physician cried:
"My limbs are moveless! lo, the crowd advance
Down in the waters ere my weakness come."
As man to man, that pining creature spake;
But when, "Arise, thy bed uplift, and walk,"
Commanded Jesus, limb and life renew'd
Their freshness! free as Samson in his hour
Of glory, with his couch the man uprose,
While magic blood like streaming rapture ran
From vein to vein, how exquisitely felt!
He walk'd, but not unenvied; savage frowns
Were seen, and stern the loud resentment rose:
"A broken Sabbath! did it not condemn
The cure? That burden, was it not profane!"
The rebel heart of Jewish envy cried.
Thou hypocrite! let days and seasons quench
Thy soul, and narrow down the lofty creed
Of true Religion: vital worth ascends
Beyond them; goodness is a godlike power
And active; it can lead an angel-life,
But keeps a holy calendar in heaven.

Celestial Founder of the Christian faith,
Saviour of spirits! Thy denouncing words
Have been fulfill'd: the race who mock'd Thy deeds

And darken'd all Thy bright perfection did
Of good and wond'rous for afflicted Man,
The cup of wrath have drench'd, and are become
The scoff and vileness of our peopled globe!
But have *we* not Thy sacred Word defiled,
Thy Law profaned, the light of Truth repell'd,
And often crucified Thee o'er again
Lamb of the World! Descend, O Lord! descend
And lighten, as Thou didst the Jews of old,
The dimness of our nature! Still remain
The curse of Sect, the bigotry of hate,
And Doctrines impious whose exclusive lie
Would limit God, and shut the gates of heaven!
The pure and open, the unbounded scheme
Of Earth's redemption, let not man presume
To shape or alter; but submissive faith
The grand relationship of human Souls
Confess; and while external Sense reveres
Each hallow'd Rite, let inward love abound,
And centre all its paradise in Thee:
So will religion spread, and time record
The days of Eden, sabbaths of the mind
When dream and doctrine, hope and faith unite
To make the heart anticipated heaven.

Where Jordan mingled his melodious wave
With the blue waters of that famous Sea
Which often mirror'd the Redeemer's form,
The grassy desert of Bethsaida lay.
To this deep wild the Lord of Glory went
Dejected, for the murder'd Baptist's fate
A veiling sadness o'er His spirit threw.
But such a halo of pure light begirt
His Person; wisdom so surpassing flow'd
From perfect lips, that sooner might the sun
At flaming noontide from the eye recede,
Than Christ in unregarded loneness rest.
And lo! around Him, like a wilder'd flock
Of mountain-sheep, unshepherded and lost,
The poor have gather'd; and their pleading eyes
Were overpower'd, when Incarnate Wisdom spake
Of Time and Nature, man's undying soul,
And Blood mysterious that would cleanse the world:
Till deep entrancement on each spirit came,
Serene as starlight o'er a dusky lake
Of troubled water:—hunger, want, and toil
Were unremember'd in th' absorbing bliss
Of vast instruction; on the Bread of Life
They feasted, mindless of all other food!
But day was dying; and the mellow light
Of evening slanted through the desert-boughs,
Whose leafy motion, like a refluent tide
The pebbles chafing, made a restless sound.
And when Messiah in the pallid gleam
Of western sunlight mark'd the wearied host
Before Him, and a thousand faces turn'd
Full on His gaze, all famish'd, feeble, worn!—
Compassion for their uncomplaining want
Awoke; at once a miracle sublime
His soul conceived, His mighty hand perform'd.

Among the multitude a lad was found;
Five barley loaves and two small fishes made
His poor possession; but that scanty meal
Became abundance to creative Power!
By fifties rank'd, along the verdant ground
The people sat, with expectation dumb,
And trembling with profoundest awe! Then took
The bread, and lifted His majestic Eyes
To heaven, the Saviour; blessing, as He gazed,
The food from whence a miracle would rise
Magnificent, beyond those dreams of love
Celestial, such as sainted Prophets saw.
Oh! when His eye immensity o'ercame
And travell'd through yon infinite expanse
Of worlds on worlds, His own almighty Seat
It witness'd! There, pavilion'd round about
With clouds and waters,* in array'd excess
Of unimagined Glory, it beheld
Jehovah!—then the mortal bread He brake,
And bade Disciples to the awe-struck crowd
The food bestow, till that enormous host
Were fill'd; and fragments of abundance lay
Around them scatter'd from the glorious feast!
As though a seed of earth's minutest growth
Rose from the ground, and like a forest spread,
From that mean food miraculously sprung
The glory of a great increase, which grew
And multiplied beneath Messiah's hand,
Till famish'd thousands were profusely fed.

Was ever banquet so sublime as this?
No canopy of regal pomp was there,
But the bright vastness of unclouded heaven;
The turf, a table, and the meanest food
A mountain-peasant knows, the sole supply,—
But God to serve, a Miracle, the meal!
The hour of beauty; Syria's matchless sky
Of floating crimson; like Genesareth stretch'd
In molten slumber, and her distant flash
Of waters gleaming through the forest-boughs,
And the deep moral of the mighty scene,—
What fancy yearns not, to have witness'd all?

But He who fed five thousand, feeds a world
And makes all earth miraculous by love!
Creation's undiminish'd banquet, spread
For ever by the elemental Laws

* 18th Psalm.

And Seasons ministrant to growth and good,
How mindless we by Whose stupendous gift
It fosters being as a boundless whole!
Enjoyment makes the world's ingratitude;
Above, around, beneath, th' almighty Hand
Itself avows; at morn, conducting forth
The Lord of Brightness; and when day concludes,
And dews descend, the fairies of the night,
Arraying yonder firmamental arch
With moon and planet, and uncounted orbs,
Too beautiful for sullied lips to name!
But, constant good proves mercy unadored;
And while dumb Glories of creation give
Their daily witness, Man alone is mute.[40]

But night commenceth: hark! a shouting cry,
A Multitude's delighted spirit speaks,—
And woods are shaken with exulting sound!
Like mingling torrents, loud and far ascend
Their many voices, blending into one,
That hails him Monarch! who had blest the poor.—
Then Jesus to Bethsaida bade depart
His own Disciples, from the crowd withdrew,
And sought his mountain-solitude again.

Meanwhile, obedient to a high command,
Beloved disciples in their boat embark'd
Upon the lake are rocking: Darkness weaves
Her veil; and, like a tempest-demon yells
The howling wind, and tears the rising sea
To billowy madness, o'er whose heave and surge
Th' affrighted vessel like a weary bird
Advances, hung with flakes of whitest foam.
At starless midnight, on the yawning deep
The mariners with death and gloom contend,
Till in the sound of each remorseless wave
Each Heart has heard a funeral anthem howl'd!
But ere the redness of reviving dawn
Approach'd, when nature wore that spectral hue
In which the shadows of the dead arise,
A living Shape along the billows stalk'd!
God of the Waters, on the waves He moved
Sublimely calm! behind Him, like a cloud
His garments floated on the gloomy air,
And where He trod, the conscious billow sank!
At that dim sight each pale Disciple cower'd
And trembled, holding in the gasping breath,
Yet gazing, till their icy blood congeal'd,
Each limb was marble, and the palsied heart
Throbb'd loud and quick with supernatural play!
A Spectre from the unapparent World
He seem'd; or, Spirit of the tempest born,
Who walk'd the waters terribly divine!
But when in answer to a shriek of dread
Heard o'er the billows in its wildest tone,
Upon the winds in solemn murmur roll'd
"'Tis I!"—the frenzy of affright was calm'd;
And he, whose feeling human faith surpass'd,
Entreated like a God to tread the deep!
"Then come," the Saviour like a God replied.
And he descended; on the deep he walk'd
O'erawed by dreadful wonder! wave on wave
And wind on wind, in elemental roar
Like chaos, how can mortal faith defy?
His soul hath doubted, and th' Apostle sinks,
Till, "Save me, Lord!" the drowning Peter cries;
And him the affable Redeemer caught
From out the billows, in their fierce array,
Rebuking thus, "O thou of little faith!"
His fond disciple: when the toiling bark
They both had enter'd, on the waves He look'd,—
The Lake was silent, and the Tempest gone!

Appalling grandeur! sea and midnight, God
And Man, angelic Faith and mortal Fear,—
All imaging with allegoric truth
A storm of trial on the world's great Sea!
Thus, Heaven is round us in the dreadest hour.
Her radiant mercies, like the mystic stars
Through darkness glitter on the trembling soul:
And from that shriek, 'mid whelming billows sent
By human frailness, let Presumption learn
How Nature falters when she feels secure!
Oh! could our actions overtake Resolve,
That oft in solitude so highly soars
To perfect regions of primeval Good,
What noble vengeance would the spirit wreak
On baser qualities, which clog the soul!
Alas! perfection is our moral dream,
And error, nature's true reality:
We *would* be angels, but we *must* be men!

Yet marvel not, that frail delusion hung
And hover'd o'er his apostolic mind
Who loved the Saviour with impassion'd truth,
But oft out-soar'd himself, when feeling dared
To mount where Faith alone her flight commands.
To him, as all, Messiah's kingdom seem'd
Dominion sceptred with terrestrial might;
The spell of earth was on them, and they rear'd
On words whose meaning look'd *this* world, beyond
Imperial thrones whereon The Twelve would sit
Holding the keys of heaven! But Jesus tore
That veil of darkness; as rejected Christ
By malefactor's death foredoom'd to die,
Himself described; and when the shrinking mind
Of Peter started with rebellious doubt,

How quiver'd it at that august rebuke !
"Avaunt thee, Satan ! not the Things of God,
But those of men, thy blinded heart adores."

And then, at once from out this fading world
To heaven, and heaven's unutterable scene
Whence throned in glory the Redeemer comes,
He led the Conscience, and of Judgment spake,—
A shout of Angels ! and a trumpet-Voice,—
Hark ! how it thunders round the shaken earth
Till space becomes a universal sound;
The graves are riven, and the Sea aghast
Unsepulchres her dead ! then, all is still,
And every eye the Judge of Doom beholds !

Ere the dim shadow of this dreaded hour
Predicted, from the mind has been dispell'd,
His three disciples holy Jesus took
From out the plain, to where the balmy hush
Of aromatic Tabor breathed. And there
While Christ paternal Deity adored,
A languor like a cloud of music wrapt
The yielding Sense, till wearily o'ercome,
Their eyelids closed in slumber's soft eclipse,
And slept the mortal three. While such repose
Entranced them, into awful glory grew
The Form of Jesus ! dazzlingly His face
That lustrous Mien which Seraphim behold
With eyes wing-veil'd, assumed; His raiment shone
Like robes that whiten in immortal beams
Emitted from the throned Eternal ! Bright
Beyond imagined brightness, He became
Transfigured; God of God, and Light of Light
Apparent, round Him earth's surpassing two,
In type of law and prophecy fulfill'd
By Jesus, Moses and Elias, knelt,
Communing; like the roll of thunder-clouds,
Their melody of voice the air inspired
With deeper magic than expressive sound,
That woke the sleepers, whose awe-stricken eyes
Reel'd in the blaze as though in heaven unclosed !
The Cross, and Resurrection of the Dead
Appallingly distinct they heard reveal'd:
And Peter, burning with sublime dismay,
"Three tabernacles let us rear," exclaim'd,—
"For Thee, for Moses, and Elias, one !"
But while he spake, an overshadowing Cloud
Descended, such as o'er the golden wings
Of Cherubim the Ark's shechinah made;
And from its depth a vocal Presence cried,
"My Son of Glory ! hear His voice ! adore !"
Like riven trees th' affrighted mortals fell
Beneath that sound almighty, till, "Arise,"
Messiah utter'd;—they arose, and view'd
Nor Cloud, nor Vision, but the lovely green
Of Tabor; Jesus in His wonted garb
Of meekness; and the soft luxurious sky
With azure canopy o'erarching all.

The passion that confounded heaven, unthroned
Archangels, and the spotless earth defiled;
Not Christ himself could overawe ! In vain
Of agony and blood Messiah spake,
To be His direful portion: still prevail'd
In each frail mind Ambition's royal dream
Of Thrones to come; and *whose* imperial rank
Was most exalted, each with rival hope
Disputed. Fathoming their inmost heart,
Amid them all the mild Redeemer placed
A little child; then, gently with His arm
Encompassing that infant, thus began:
"Except man be converted, and become
As little children, humbled, meek, and pure,
My kingdom he cannot partake, nor feel;
For childlike is the greatest *there!*"—How quail'd
The pride, how shook the domineering thoughts
Of that Assembly, when they thus beheld
A passive meekness in the Form august
Of Christ embodied; and an artless child
The type of man's eternal glory made?
Thou happy mother! at whose nursing breast
That infant fed; still happier child wert thou,
Whose eyelids fell beneath Emmanuel's gaze,
Whose brow was hung with innocent alarm,
Before that holy Presence !—Fairy Things !
Incarnate poetry of human life,
Oh, teach us, as around ye lisp and play,
Nor heed the clouds, nor hear the muttering wind
Which heralds what to-Morrow's doom may be,
Like you content in uncomplaining hope
To rest resign'd; and innocently wear
The smile which universal Love bestows.

Pride blasted Eden; and the world has crouch'd
Beneath her sceptre, which to break in dust
God bow'd the heavens, and every meekness wore.
Yet, what are *we*, that our Titanic dreams
Assault the skies with their incessant aim?
Oh, could we read Creation's book aright
Our nothingness by each vast page would be
Convicted ! Atoms mock our deepest ken;
The winds invisible as angel-wings
Attend our path, and tell not whence they come;
The Dust derides us ! from the floating Orbs
Of night's dim world an overwhelming ray
Of mystery pierces the distracted mind;
And Ocean thunders with resounding scorn
When monarchs dare him, and our fleets like foam

From wave to wave are darted! Gaze within,
And what is there?—a tempest in repose
Of passions wild, dark energies, and powers
Which storm and madden at the Demon's call!

But evil is eternal war with heaven;
And Pride, how dauntless! E'en that hallow'd fane
Where sacramental Deity is shrined,
She enters, balancing with haughty brow
The merits which opinion, rank, or sect
Assumes, before the Throne of that Supreme
From Whose dread gaze the Universe recoils!—
When Jesus, from the triple-crested mount*
Where midnight heard His orison arise,
At morn descended, as the rosy flush
Of daylight slanted over Kedron's vale
And pilgrim-waters, in the Temple throng'd
A pharisaic crowd, whose sleepless ire
With blood-hound fury track'd His glorious way.
Before Him now, as there the people stood
And drank His words like inspiration's breath,
A poor adulteress they rudely dragg'd
For judgment; should He dare condemn
Her frailty, Rome would see rebellion rise,
And dungeon him for slaughter; should He blot
Her guilt, upon His soul her crime devolved!
But Christ their black attempt at once unveil'd
And answer'd not; and, bending to the ground
In mute abstraction, with His finger wrote;
Till once again That awful Soul they tried
For judgment; then with look divinely-stern
He rose, and in a voice of withering tone,
"Let him among you who is sinless, cast
A stone the *first*," the Son of Man replied:
Then, Conscience! (Thou that in the deadly night
The soul canst wring, and rack the murderer's sleep,
Or people solitude with shapes of hell,)
The vile accusers Thy terrific power
O'erawed; till one by one, as though unseen
A Hand compell'd their motion, dumb like Death,
And slow, each follow'd each till all were gone!
But on the hush of that deserted room
A sigh, as though some heart had heaved, and broke,
Distinctly fell:—the Saviour's solemn eye
Was lifted, and beheld the guilty shape
Of woman! on whose burning cheek the blood
Confess'd her spirit, and the crime which drew
Those tear-drops, running like a liquid fire
From agony within. Her downcast head was hung

With locks dishevell'd, wild as her despair;
Her lips were moveless; but the buried pang
Which heaved her bosom with convulsive throes,
And frequent shudder of her bending frame,
Were language; all which Penitence employ'd
To tell the damning shame!—"Hath none condemn'd
Thee, woman? Where are thine accusers?" "None,"
She answer'd: "Neither then," the Saviour cried,
"Do I condemn thee; go, and sin no more?"

The Feast of Lights, when dedicated lamps
Flash o'er the walls of Israel's echoing homes,
December brings: Jerusalem is loud
With chanted song, and melodies from harp
And timbrel, dulcimer and tabret pour'd;
From towering Altars an unwearied blaze
Ascendeth, rolling up with spiral glee
And gladness, crimsoning the sultry air.
The hearths are heap'd, and silver-headed Age
Delightedly to Youth's enamour'd ear
The Festival unfolds;[41] while maidens twine
The holy Dance, or tune the patriot-lyre
To measures, floating like the silky clouds
The west along, so meltingly they die!
The street-ways, dappled with reflected gleams
From many a lattice, like a forest sound
When every leaf is motion.—But apart,
Beneath yon shadow of the Temple-porch
Messiah walk'd, till thence the scowling Jew
Compell'd Him, thirsting for His righteous blood,
To seek a shelter where Baptising John
Had lived, when first by Jordan's laving stream
He heralded Redemption. There He taught
Believing thousands, till from Mary came
A sudden messenger of wo, who said,
That Lazarus, whom Messiah loved, was sick.
But from that sickness sprang a glorious power
The sisters dream'd not! Both did Jesus love;
Yet still He rested, till the night of death
Advanced, and Lazarus in the tomb reclined.
Then slowly went to where in mourning gloom
The fond and brotherless with mingled tears
His presence waited! Ere the olive-trees
Of Bethany o'erhung His meadow'd way,
Rush'd Martha forth, to meet her mighty Lord!
"Hadst Thou been here, my brother had not died,"
Was her sad greeting. "He shall rise again!"
Responded Jesus: "When the dead awake
And time is ended," sadly she replied.
"I am the Resurrection and the Life!
And whoso liveth, and in Me believes,
Shall never die!" "The Son of God Thou art

* Olivet.

The Christ to come, the Everlasting Lord!"
In one deep burst of lofty faith she cried,
And then withdrew, to where her sister mourn'd,—
To Mary, who the better Part preferr'd.
At once she rose, the distant meadow sought
And prostrate at the feet of Jesus fell;
"Hadst Thou been here, my brother had not died"
She utter'd; tears alone the rest could tell,
And not a lid was dry! Around He gazed,
Their tears beheld, their voiceless anguish view'd,
Then, meekly bowing His majestic Head,
He sigh'd and groan'd in spirit:—Jesus wept!

A mournful beauty, a sepulchral grace
Doth hallow nature, when the dead are tomb'd
In garden-quiet, 'mid the wave of boughs,
Which often murmur in our living ears
Like tones ancestral by the heart revived.
Beneath the twilight of o'erhanging trees
A cave was hollow'd, in whose rocky depth
Affection to the arms of Earth resign'd
Her dead; in mute companionship, there lay
The babe and mother, sister, son, and sire,
A household, though in dust! A sad delight
More exquisite than loud-tongued pleasure feels,
Serened the spirit of surviving Love
Whene'er it rambled in the pensive gloom
Of such a garden. If the summer-air
Breathed gladness, heaven was flaked with fleecy clouds,
And playsome leaves hung prattling to the wind,
While hue and sound made life immortal seem,—
A shade of sadness mellow'd, not destroy'd
The mirth and beauty of surrounding day.[42]
Oft would the eye of some fond mourner rest
On the green rock, whose cavern'd silence made
The home of Death, where generations slept.
And haply, as the wild flowers meekly grew
From the dim verdure of sepulchral stone,
Delightful thoughts from sad mementos sprung.

'Mid such a scene departed Lazarus lay:
And lo! Messiah by the rock-hewn grave
Arrived: around him with unspeaking awe
Disciples, mourners, and the sisters meek
Collect. "The tomb unbar!"—when thus exclaim'd
The Lord of Resurrection, from the tomb
They roll'd the stone; then Martha's doubting soul
Full solemnly He chided! Time had seen
Four suns upon her brother's grave reflect
Their brightness: on his frame corruption fed
E'en now she deem'd, and buried in her doubt
That faith whose glory soon its God reveal'd.
The stone removed, apart Messiah stood,
To heaven uplifted His appealing gaze;
Divine communion with the Vast Unseen
Awhile He mutely held, and then arose
The intonations of His prayer divine.
But when a soundless answer from the Throne
Descended, more than mortal radiance clothed
Each feature! on His brow mysterious calm
Was mirror'd; like a Deity he stood,
And spake the fiat,—"Lazarus, come forth!"
And Lazarus came! as once Creation did
From darkness, by His forming Word produced.
Bound hand and foot, amid the living breathed
The dead, new risen! But his presence cast
A terror round it, awe without a name!
Entranced, as if another world begun,
Dumb with amaze, the whole assembly stood,
Till Jesus bade the grave's funereal robes
To be unwound, and breathing Lazarus spake.
As though a tree by blasting time destroy'd
Bloom'd into life, and suddenly display'd
The perfect glory of its forest-prime,
So did the freshness of reviving blood
At once the lividness of death dispel;
And Lazarus, pure as Man's primeval form
Appear'd when first creation call'd him, Lord.

Such power immense, in open day reveal'd,
Through town and village, plain and hamlet woke
A grateful wonder. At the school of Seers
The sage consulted; street and dwelling heard
One mingled clamour of admiring tongues;
And in the Synagogues a muttering crowd
Would linger, to peruse each other's face,
And chronicle, as Rumour told its tale,
The words of age, or wisdom. But the blaze
Miraculous, which round the risen dead
Concentred, fell like pestilential fire
Upon the soul of that dark Sect, whose reign
Was clouded, and whose mouldering sceptre shook.
Their fancy gloated on His bleeding form;
Their dreams were haunted with His dying pangs,
And every heart some malediction framed
To mock His agony! Amid the wilds
Of Ephraim, hence the Lord of grace withdrew,
Till came the moment for the final Scene
Of Man's redemption, to unroll its gloom:
Amid the Capital with dreadless foot
Then march'd He forth to meet that blood-red Hour!

To Jericho, along whose plain immense
In greenest lustre rose unnumber'd palms
That waved their beauty on balsamic winds,

Amid the breath of roses, flush'd and bright
As clouds of damask when they drink the hues
Of sunset, Jesus and disciples went.
But soon from out her walls, and stately crowd
Of palaces, and domes of marble sheen,
He passed to Bethany, where Lazarus rose,
And shouting hosts with palms had come to meet
The Son of David. From the verdant top
Of Olivet, to where a hamlet smiled
Before them, bosom'd in a mountain-vale,
The two Disciples, at the word divine,
Departed. There, as Christ's prophetic eye
Fore-shadow'd, at the village-gate they found
A colt, which never mortal burden bore,
Then led it to the Lord; devoutly hung
Their garments o'er its sacred back, and placed
The Christ thereon. Thus Zechariah sang,
When Centuries, in their darkest slumber bound,
To him like animated Creatures rose,
And utter'd visions!—Wonderful Thy ways,
Jehovah! in the whirlwind, Thou art there!
The tempest is Thy language; sea, Thy path;
And Glory, but the shadow of Thy shade!
Yet human actions, by completing words
Which drew aside the veil of Time, and roll'd
Their meaning down the depth of Years unborn,
With voice as mighty as creation speaks,
Thy power attest, Thy ruling hand portray.

But oh! what jubilant hosannahs rose
As Him they sung, magnificent, and great,
And good, and glorious, Israel's promised King,
The Prince of Peace! Beneath His path their robes
They strew'd, and round Him waved triumphant palms,
And scatter'd branches; while a choral shout
Deeper and deeper like colossal waves
Of sound ascended! till the Air partook
The rapture, and the sympathetic leaves
As with a breezy joy of summer-noon
Were shaken! Then a sudden silence came
On the loud Host; as when the pausing storm
In elemental muteness dies away,
The clamour ceased; a multitude was dumb.
On vast Jerusalem's devoted towers
The gaze of Christ prophetically fell,
And tears from out His mournful spirit rose
While He beheld them, and their doom pronounced:
"If Thou hadst known, at least in this Thy day,—
But peace hath vanish'd ever from Thine eyes!
Thine hour is coming; round Thee shall a trench
Be cast, and compass Thee on every side,
Till tomb'd in dust Thy towers and children fall,
Nor leave a stone to tell where Thou hast been!
Jerusalem! Jerusalem! whose hand
Hath stoned the prophets, and the holy slain,
How often, as the hen beneath her wings
Her brood protecteth, would My shielding hand
Have shelter'd Thee!—Thy children would not come!
Thine House is desolate, thy Kingdom gone,
And never till the clouds of Judgment waft
His Glory, will thine eyes again behold
The Son of Man. But magnify, O God,
My Father! magnify Thine awful Name:"
The heavens grew vocal, and an angel-voice
Came forth,—"I have, and will," whose thunder spake.

Thus saying, in the portico He sat,
Where ever and anon, within a chest
Beside the pillars chain'd, an offering fell
From worshippers. Amid the pompous crowd
Of rich adorers, came a humble form,
A widow, meek as Poverty doth make
Her children; with a look of sad content
Her mite within the treasure-heap she cast:
Then, timidly as bashful twilight stole
From out the Temple. But her lowly gift
Was witness'd by an Eye, whose mercy views
In motive all which consecrates a deed
To goodness: so He bless'd the widow's mite,
Beyond the gifts abounding Wealth bestow'd.
Thus is it, Lord! with Thee: the heart is Thine,
And all the world of hidden action there
Works in Thy sight like waves beneath the sun
Conspicuous; and a thousand nameless acts
That lurk in lovely secrecy, and die
Unnoticed like the trodden flowers which fall
Beneath a proud man's foot, to Thee are known;
And written with a sunbeam in *that* Book
Of Life, where mercy fills the brightest page.

Front of the Temple, whose enormous wall *
Outlived the fury of Chaldean fires,
And while around chaotic ruins fell
Stood, like a master-spirit when the world
Is rocking,—Olivet's green summit rose:
And there Messiah, with his few elect,
Ascended; thence He took a last farewell!
Beneath them, in a wilderness of homes,
The thousand-streeted City lay, and roll'd
The hum and murmur of her myriad sounds
High in the air; while far around her stood
The guardian-mountains, bathed in ruddy hues

* Josephus' Account of the Foundation and Form of the Temple, &c.

Of sunlight, while the peaks of countless spires
Flash'd from the midst like pinnacles of flame.
But, lone in glory, pillar'd, proud, and huge,
Colossal as some architectural dream
Embodied, Israel's massy Temple blazed;
And seem'd, in her immensity of shape,
A Shrine that would endure eternally!
When each disciple had around him gazed,
And feasted with magnificent delight
On such a miracle of pomp and scene,
"It all shall wither! not a stone endure"
Messiah cried; and, like a dying knell
That murmur sank upon their listening souls!

That dread prediction! was it not fulfill'd
Beyond Imagination's blackest dream
Of horror, when the hell of earth began,
And men were Demons with a robe of flesh
Enveloped, banqueting on human blood?[43]
Ere forty years had swept the scene of time,
On that same Mount where spake the awful Seer
And drew from darkness the almighty Curse
To come, the fierce-eyed Romans had encamp'd
Their Legions; while the roll of martial drums,
And a loud music from the brazen lips
Of trump and clarion, with a sound of death
Frighted the hills and dales of Palestine.

Distress of nations! Sun and Moon withdrawn
Enshrouded, that their gaze might not behold
The World's disaster. From the howling sea
Hark to the tempest! on the earth are crime
And famine, fear and pestilence combined;
While Havoc, on the wings of fury borne,
Scatters fell ruin like a burning wind
Which hurries round the universal orb
To wither up creation! Far and near,
Whatever Light can face, or Darkness feel,
Is terrible:—and list! amid the gloom
Of midnight, like a guilty creature shakes
A giant-City, as the earthquake-pant
With fitful heavings moves her mighty heart!
Jehovah is abroad! the heavens appall'd,
Forget their seasons; cloud-like visions, fill'd
With fiery battle, and a myriad Shapes
Of warriors charioted by burning steeds
That vanish in commotion, throng the air
With omens! Then, a starry Weapon cleaves
The sky, and flashes with descending might
As though 'twere wielded by Eternal Hands!
While day and night, Jerusalem's ghastly eye
Looks up, and sees a blood-red Comet blaze,
Fix'd like a Curse of fire above the scene
To agonise whate'er its flashes meet!
And once at midnight,* with appalling burst

* Vide Tacitus' Hist. book v.; Josephus, &c.

The massive portals of God's inner Shrine
Expanded, and the shuddering Fabric heard
A Voice that issued with a dread farewell,
Whose thunder was departing Deity!

The hour of Judgment! lo, at length it comes,
And God is in it with devouring wrath
That deepens, till the stricken Earth despairs.
The Queen of Zion, beautiful and vast,
Glory of nations! who shall paint thee now?
Enwrapp'd with horrors, famish'd, weeping, faint,
And fallen, round thee like a circling flood
Rears a huge wall of Babylonian height,
And thou a captive in the centre art
For martyrdom. But, hark! in whirlwind-rush
A roaring flame around the Temple sweeps!
Moriah like a seething furnace glows
And reddens; as a cloudy palace built
By sunset, there it dwindles, melts, and dies,—
The fabric of Jehovah! Palsied, wild, and pale,
In solemn agony hush'd myriads stand,
Scorch as they gaze,* but still yon gorgeous wreck
Beholding, on their ghastly features plays
A light of ruin, ere the Temple falls,
Like funeral glory! then, in tombs of fire,
While the last pillar of expiring flame
Mounts o'er yon wreck, they shriek, despair, and die!

BOOK VI.

"But who is He with tortured brow,
Degraded, bleeding, dying, now;
His Visage marr'd beyond despair?
Thou quaking earth! thy God is there!
The Sun appall'd hath slunk away,
And darkness hides the guilty Day;
Avert, O World! thine impious eyes;
The curse is o'er,—but Jesus dies!"—*MS.*

ANALYSIS OF BOOK VI.

The Book commences with an apostrophe connected with the sad and mighty events which the conclusion of the Saviour's Life unrolls; but, previous to detailing them, a retrospective view of His Character, Actions, and Doctrine, is attempted; the order of time is then preserved to the Ascension—The Sanhedrim take council against Christ—Judas agrees to betray Him—The Last Supper—Description of the same—Terror and sadness of the Disciples when Christ announced that He was about to be betrayed—The Rite of Sacrament founded—The Redeemer's Farewell—The Garden of Gethsemane

* See Josephus for historical verifications.

—Jesus in His Agony—Is traduced—The Dawn of the Day of Crucifixion—Jesus brought up for trial—Peter's Denial—Reflections on his Faith and Weakness—Jesus is condemned—Led to Caiaphas—Pronounced guiltless—Pilate makes his final attempt to acquit the Redeemer—Barabbas preferred to Jesus—At last is led forth on the judgment-seat in sight of the multitude—The repentance, horror, and destruction of Iscariot—The Crucifixion and its attendant scenes—The Miracles which attested His Godhead at His Death—The Burial of Christ—Night Scene—Moonlight on the Tomb of Jesus—The Roman watch, &c. &c.—The Resurrection—Affright of the Soldiers—Vision of the Angels—Jesus reveals Himself to Mary—Journey of the two Disciples to Emmaus—Appearance of Christ—Discovered by the breaking of Bread—His Second Appearance to the Eleven—Miraculous Draught of Fishes—Peter thrice questioned—Previous to His Ascension, Christ takes the Eleven with Him to a Mountain—Explains the Scriptures, gives His Final Charge, and ascends to Heaven.

Here, as far as the Life of the Messiah is included, the Poem ends; but the Second Advent is the Hope, Faith, and Glory of a Christian, and could not be omitted. Previously to this, however, some reflections on the subject of the Poem, state of the human mind, the destinies of man, and the spirit of Poetry, viewed in connection with the advancement of Christianity, are offered: these naturally conclude in a contemplation of the immortality which was brought to light through the Redeemer—His Second Advent—Resurrection of the Dead—Last Judgment of Men and Angels—Conclusion.

Prepare, O Earth! with solemn gloom invest
Thy glories; bid the rayless Sun retire,
The Sky be sad, the Winds be tongues of wo,
And deep-toned litanies from Ocean swell:
Let time and nature, scene and conscious man
In one vast fellowship of grief unite;—
An hour is coming, charged with dreadful fate,
Whose darkness palls a Saviour's agony!

But, ere the crisis of creation dawn
And palsied Earth her bleeding God proclaims,
Behold the beauty of His matchless life
In deed and thought connecting earth with heaven!
Cull every virtue which the Mind conceives,
Or view Perfection's archetypal Form
And what can emulate the Prince of Peace?

Where once the Seasons, in luxuriant strife,
Reign'd on the shore of that immortal Lake
*Whose wave is purple as the heaven it loves,
In that blest clime where fruit and verdure bathed
Their tinted beauty in the richest sun,
Where all is dreary now—Messiah dwelt,
And bodied forth God's everlasting Will
In life and love, by Incarnation there.

Born in a manger,—yet by guardians bright
And wing'd adorers, heralded and hymn'd;
The Heir of all things—yet possessing none;
Surrender'd now to tears of mortal truth,
Or ministrant at some disciple's feet,
Then,—thunder-greeted by the glorious Sky!
Here from the flower a lovely doctrine flows,
And now,—a Tempest from His frown recoils;
Hung on the cross, a malefactor's doom
He suffer'd,—yet a paradise was there
By Him accorded to the felon-soul!
Though bleeding clay,—incarnate God confess'd
Whose pangs an aching Universe partook;
While from those agonies which man beheld
And mock'd the terror-blighted Sun withdrew![44]

Man never spake, in words divinely-toned
With tenderness beyond a tear to move,
Like Him, to Whom unutter'd feelings lay
Free as the clouds before a sun, exposed.
The Heart,—He knew it best, and proved it most,
And touch'd the master-chords of human mind.
And oh! what exquisite discernment mark'd
Each high discourse, to creed or sect applied.
Some true analogy in scenes, or sounds,
And palpably by outward sense perceived,
From mead and plough, the summer-task or toil,
From storm and season, fruit and flower,—enlived
Each sacred lesson which Emmanuel taught.
And when hath Poet from his airy world
To shape or action summon'd such express
And touching images of graceful power,
As Parables,[45] where conscience is instinctive judge
And to the mind celestial truth commends?
Pathetic loveliness in all abounds;
And as the eloquent Creation oft
By moonlight more than storm the soul subdues,
When language by severest wrath sustain'd,
No passion quell'd, the parable prevail'd;
Whose soft dominion, like an angel-smile
Moved o'er the heart, and seemed reflected there.

A Being thus surpassingly endow'd,
Whose life was goodness in perpetual act;
By pure magnificence of spirit raised
Above whate'er Platonic vision[46] shaped
Of high and holy, in the perfect Man,
What hymnèd worship *should* all Earth have paid
To such embodied Glory! Yet a doom
Of torture hover'd o'er His righteous Head:
The Sinless for the sinful World must die!

---

* Vide Josephus' description of the shore of Tiberias.

E'en now, the plotting Sanhedrim convened;
When suddenly, disorder'd, pale, and rack'd
With guilty terror, which on brow and cheek
Imprinted, villain ! lo, the traitor comes,
And thirty pieces for his Lord betray'd
Demandeth : then with unappall'd delight
The Priesthood revels o'er His dying form !

There, as the traitor in the twilight-gloom
Is homeward skulking with a stealthy pace
While every breeze like condemnation sounds,
By Nature mutter'd with mysterious scorn,
A Spirit, dark as demons love, behold!
He, ever when the proffer'd crown approach'd
The head of Christ, in worldly vision hail'd
The sceptred honours of some high domain
About to dawn: but when the Saviour's lip
Blest the meek hands which typically pour'd
Balsamic odours to anoint His head,
Rebuke was felt, and disappointment raged;
Till Satan enter'd with a rush of guilt
The soul of Judas, and the traitor rose
A dark apostate in his dream of blood !

Meanwhile Messiah, whose omniscient word
A room appointed for the paschal Feast,
To eat the Lamb of covenant prepared.
His pangs approach, His agonies begin
To throng around Him ! and that hour, foretold,
Prefigured, and so oft in gloom unveil'd
To His mistaken Twelve, is come at last
The Man of Wo to meet ! A feast is set
Of wine and water, as Mosaic law
Ordain'd; where each with due thanksgiving drinks
The Cup whose seal and sanction typified
The Blood of Jesus, by symbolic power;
And then, the taintless Lamb, the ritual Herb,
And Bread unleaven'd, psalm and prayer succeed,
Each serving each with ceremonious awe.
But in the midst, again rebellious pride,
Like Satan when he darken'd Paradise
By curst intrusion, mars the lovely scene
And mournful beauty of our Lord's farewell.
But, princes, thrones, and dominations bow,
Lie mute and dead, ye arrogant desires !
Ambition ! dooming life one long despair,
Quench the wild fever of thy fire-struck brain,
Heaven stoops to earth, a Deity to dust,
A God is kneeling at the foot of Man !—
Humility which makes the heart to reel,
Our blood to quiver, and the brow of pride
Prostrates beneath the scathing light of shame !
Oh, when was meekness so almighty found,
As when the Saviour dwarfs degree and state
And dims the splendour of all outward things,
Till, like the radiance of a dying eve,
The waning glories of the World depart !

But why hath sadness with a sudden gloom
On each descended ? What hath blanch'd the cheek
With terror, in the eye dejection pour'd,
And stirr'd the calm of countenance with lines
Of feeling, working into restless play
Like breeze-moved water ? Eye to eye, and brow
To brow, in horrible dismay upturn'd,
Each reads the other with unspoken dread
Of something buried in the soul's abyss,
Which now must be untomb'd, and stand condemn'd
In the full light of God's omniscient gaze !
And yet, though terror-struck, with sad exclaim
Each utters, "Is it I?" Eleven are pure;
Their souls are ramparted with sacred truth,
They tremble deeply, but with guiltless fear.
And one there was, o'er all the rest beloved;
Whose tender mildness and devoted faith
With childlike fervour to the Lord endear'd
A guileless nature,—him whom "Jesus loved,"
The meek St. John ! Beyond expressive wo,
The tearful language of his eye reveal'd
A yearning spirit; while his drooping head
Lay fondly pillow'd on the breast of Christ.
By Peter urged, with look of saddest depth
On Christ he gazed, and whisperingly ask'd,
"Who is it, Lord?" Then Jesus, "He who takes
The bread I give, the Son of Man betrays :
But, wo the traitor ! well for him, had light
And being never an Iscariot known !"
Betrayer ! thou whose spirit coil'd and sunk
Within thee, as a serpent when the day
Shines on the darkness of his den retires
To deeper gloom ! upon thy face appears
A pale confession, which thy tongue denies :
Yes ! thou art he,—a traitor to thy Lord !
And driven by the whirlwind of despair,
Forth from the chamber of discover'd guilt
Thou speedest; darkness is a heaven to thee;
And thou hast night, sepulchrally array'd,
And starless, fit to cloak a traitor's deed
Or give to earth the gloominess of hell !

As the dim spell-work of some awful dream
Can people slumber with a ghastly host
Of shapes and sounds, till lo ! the morning-smile
Dissolves it, so hath this phantasmal scene
Of doubt and dread, of agonising sway,
At once receded; and quiescent joy
Again upon the true disciples came,
When Judas from the paschal-chamber went,

Convicted traitor! Then, with mien august,
The mild Redeemer took the Bread, and blest
And brake it; and the cup of Wine He took,
And then of both made each disciple take:—
A holy Sacrament, whose typic shade
The great Passover was; but mightier far
The rite of Jesus, whose remembrance speaks
No single nation, but a boundless World
Deliver'd, saved, and free! As bread and wine
The body nourish, so the soul is fed
By faith in this symbolic meal of Love,
Wherein is shadow'd the Redeemer's death.

"Do This, and thou wilt then remember Me!"
Remember Thee! the Way, the Truth, and Life,
On Whose pure eyelids hung our mortal tears;
Who wert so inaccessibly supreme
In the bright plenitude of awe and power,
And yet, so veil'd by condescending love
That Childhood gazed upon Thy glorious smile,
And deem'd it heavenlier than mothers wear;
Refuge and Rest 'mid all the woes of time!
Almighty Anchor for a sin-toss'd world!
Incarnate Saviour, and co-equal God,
Remember Thee!—oh, if some dying words
Of honour'd parent round the memory cling
With aye unweaken'd charm, shall man forget
That dear and solemn, Thy divine command
Beyond all parents'? Till Thy Kingdom come
When the great Banquet of perpetual bliss
With Thee in glory Thine elected sons
Partake, O Saviour! be this Sacrifice
And Sacrament with awful love revered:
For in it pardon and preserving grace
Abound, and by it Earth with Heaven communes;
And when o'erwearied by this anxious world,
Or toss'd in the tempestuous gloom of sin
The soul repenteth, yet in doubt appears
Like Hagar in the wilderness, to weep and die
Forsaken, there in this all-heavenly Feast
Redeemer! Thine incarnate Presence dwells:
And gently as the arkless dove was ta'en
Back to a shelter from the dreary wild
Of waters, welcomed by a meeting smile,
The soul is bosom'd on Thy holy rest.

But listen! for the Lord's farewell begins,
And deeply-solemn, His mysterious tones
Fall on the silence of the sacred room,
Till tears have gather'd in their gazing eyes
From whence He parteth, to ascend and reign
Where man beholds not. Yet, in dreadless faith,
The fervent Peter, with erected brow
And voice triumphant over hell, replied,
"Though all desert Thee, still will Peter stand
A rock unshaken! death nor dungeon frights
His spirit; life itself but lives in Thee!"
"I tell thee, Peter, ere the cock shall crow
This very night wilt thou deny Me thrice!"
Then, more impassion'd with a louder voice
And lip that quiver'd with exulting throb,
"Deny Thee! unto death my soul is fix'd!"
The fond one answer'd, and on Jesus gazed
With mild reproach, like one who *feels* his wrong,
But pleaded only by a look which spake!

A sadness, deep and holy as the heart
E'er felt, came o'er that mute assembly now,
When the meek Saviour with angelic truth
Began: "Believe in God, in Me believe,
For in My Father's everlasting House
Are many Mansions, and your Lord departs,
That ye may follow to a place prepared.
The Comforter, the Holy Ghost, shall come,
And all I utter'd, memory shall teach,
By Him instructed; peace, immortal Peace!
Beyond the world to give, with you I leave:
Abide in Me, as branches in the Vine
Endure, and ye shall bear celestial Fruit!"
And then, as o'er Him, in its dark array
A vision of their sad desertion swept,
Messiah added, "Do ye now believe?
Behold! it cometh, yea, the hour *is* come!
When all are scatter'd, and the Son of Man
Is left,—yet not alone, for God is there:
The world is trouble, but in Me a peace
Unfading; let your souls in that confide
Nor tremble; I have overcome the World!"
Then, lifting his omniscient eyes to Heaven,
"My Father, glorify Thy Son!" He cried;
"Thy work is finish'd, and Thy faith is taught,
And Light and Immortality declared;
And now The Glory, Mine before this earth
Was founded, I ascend with Thee to share!"

Thus ended, Lord! thy first and last farewell.
When rose the parting hymn Devotion sang,
And all o'er Kedron to the Olive Mount
Departing, wait upon Thy steps divine.*

But, veil thyself, Imagination! veil
And worship; put thy shoes from off thy feet,
Thou mortal Gazer! for on hallow'd ground
More consecrate than he of Horeb saw
When the bush burn'd with sacramental fire,

* The hymn that they sung was Ps. 110, 117, 118, which was the last part of the *great Hallal*, as they called it, which was constantly sung at the Passover and their other great solemnities; and with this latter part was this solemnity concluded.—LIGHTFOOT'S *Harmony*.

Thou tread'st,—the garden of Gethsemane!
The Moon, pale hermitress of heaven, hath found
With no bright fellowship of starry orb
Her midway-sphere; and now with conscious dread
Shrined in a cloudy haze, she disappears,
While motionless yon patriarchal trees
Of towering olive lift their spectral gloom.
But listen! groan on groan, with awful swell
Heaves on the air, as though a God bewail'd
His creatures!—Christ in agony is bow'd,
And prostrate; while from each denuded pore
A litany of Blood to Heaven appeals!
Convulsed within Him, hark, the *Human* cries,[47]
"My Father! if it *can* be, let this Cup
Be taken from Me, from this hour removed:
And yet not Mine, but let Thy Will, be done!"

Dark agonies, ineffable as deep
That moment knew, whose merit countervail'd
All which Eternity's remorse could pay,
Wrung from the torment of a punish'd World!*
As once on Tabor His transfigured Form
A shadow of celestial Glory threw
On Man's perception, so in this doom'd hour
Gethsemane's most awful Scene declares
The dreadful Infinite of sin, and guilt.
His Manhood suffer'd all that Flesh could feel:—
God unappeased, and Satan unsubdued,
Darkness, and death, and unrepented crimes
Still brooding o'er the world, and He fore-doom'd
Upon the Cross of agony to die
That Heaven might open on forgiven man,—
These were combined in *one* almighty pang!
Exceeding sorrowful His soul became
E'en unto death; till from the Throne His cry
Of anguish brought a soothing Angel down.
But in the passion of this fateful hour,
Oh! where are they, whose eyes so oft beheld
His wonders, in whose hearts His voice had pour'd
The balm and blessing of immortal Truth?
Alas! one hour they could not watch, nor pray;
And they were sleeping, when the Saviour thrice
From prayer arose, and thrice their sleep forgave!

Yet now sleep on; and take unthinking rest;
The Son of Man, Emmanuel is betray'd,
The traitor hath his treason-work fulfill'd!
For, hear ye not the sound of rushing feet
And ruder voices, through the moonless air
Advancing? Stirr'd, as by a tempest-wing,
Around the olive-branches creak and bend,
And light comes flashing with a fierce intent,
Till on the countenance of Christ it falls
And lights His features: marr'd and pale they shone
Beneath it, as He met a midnight-band
With torch and lantern, sword and stave em-power'd
Their impious hands on His pure Form to lay.
When "I am He!" was spoken, back they fell
Like life before a sudden blast of death
By miracle emitted!—"I am He"
Again was utter'd, and again they fell
Confounded, till the traitor with a kiss
Betoken'd Jesus; then the troop approach'd
And bound Him. Legions! from your thrones of Light
Descend, and wither that unhallow'd throng!
No: meekly as a lamb to slaughter goes
The Lord hath yielded; fetter'd, silent, sad,
Deserted, and betray'd, alone He meets
The Powers of darkness in their deepest might.

The break of morning with a dim uprise!
Pale as a Prophet, when his eye foresees
Unutter'd woes upon the future throng,
The Sun awaketh from his cloudy sleep
To usher in this all-tremendous Day.
Already in yon judgment-chamber meet
The fell accusers; there, aloft upraised,
Their holy Victim in the upper-hall[48]
His trial waiteth:—not a shade of fear
The innocence of that calm Brow defiles!
In shape a Man, in dignity a God
He seemeth. But around the palace-fire
Beneath Him, from the council-seat apart,
What curses, loud with wrathful meaning, roll?
A damsel, when the Galilean-voice
Of Peter sounded with betrayful tones,
His true discipleship at once declared
Then, he who hail'd Him "Son of living God!"
Adored His Person, saw His glory shine,
And vow'd eternally with changeless love
Through life and death unswerving faith to hold,
The sacred knowledge of his Lord denied!
But when with horrid malediction rang
The fierce denial of his furious lip,
Till his eye glitter'd with a ghastly fire,
And falsehood, cowardice, and guilty fear
All met and mingled with terrific clash
Within, a second time the Cock then crew!
And Jesus,—who shall paint the *glance* He gave,
Where pity, pardon, and subdued reproach

* Vide Barrow's remark on the agony of Christ.

Concenter'd in such look of loving power
That Peter shrank, and trembled into tears!

Impassion'd, bold, beyond thy strength sincere,
Sublime apostle but a sinful man,
As in thy faith, so in thy fall we find,
A truth which bids the yearning bosom feel,
E'en as thou wert, how half the world has been!
Forgiven mourner! while with mantled face
In groaning penitence without the porch
Thou weepest, and from unforgotten scenes
A radiant vision of the Past returns
With blighting splendour to condemn thy soul,
Thou art a Moral for mankind to read
And heart to study, long as Earth remains!

While thus in penance sad St. Peter wept,
Amid a council of encircling priests
And scribes and elders, lone Emmanuel stood
For judgment. Witness after witness rose,
Suborn'd and savage; yet a war of words
Where lie to lie and truth to truth opposed
A meaning, all their accusation grew;
But when His doctrine the Archpriest assail'd;
"The temple, synagogue, the open world,
Let these My doctrine testify, and tell,
For nought in secret have I said or done!"
Thus answer'd the Redeemer; then uprose
Accusers, who with dreadless voice declared
"The gorgeous Fabric which our eyes adore,
He thus blasphemed; 'This temple built with hands,
Will I destroy; in three days shall arise
Another, built by no terrestrial hands!'"
Majestic silence was the sole reply.
Then Caiaphas, with fierce emotion shook
And darken'd; from his council-throne up sprang
And with a voice like far-off thunder cried,
"Now by the living and tremendous God
Thee I adjure! art *Thou* The Christ?"—"I am!
Hereafter, coming with the clouds of heaven
Girt like Jehovah, see the Son of Man!"
Then, "Let Him die!" throughout th' assembly rung.

The morning comes; and with unfolding day
The tragedy a deeper die assumes.
Again did Pilate, with proclaiming voice
To elder, priest, and multitude pronounce
The Saviour guiltless: "Let Him be released!"
In vain he cried; for hark the savage yell,
"A prisoner! be our wonted right perform'd,
A captive freed!" 'Twas in that stormy hour
The dark confession of a hideous dream
The wife of Pilate in her slumber saw,
Was then reported: but His hour had come![49]

"Barabbas!" was the universal shout
By thousands echoed, when their judge preferr'd
To free Messiah, "Let Barabbas loose!"
But "Christ, what deadly evil hath he done?"
Again did "Crucify!" in one fell war
Rise on the air so murderous and loud,
That Pilate quiver'd on his judgment-throne.

Then Jesus, by the soldiers dragg'd, endured
The mockery of reed, and robe, and crown
Of platted thorns, upon His temples press'd;[50]
There as He bled, before Him bow the knees
Of scoffing worshippers, who shout and hail
"King of the Jews!" then smite His awful head
And crush the crown upon His aching brows!

Thus bleeding, marr'd and mock'd, the Saviour comes:
Unmoved He stands, insuperably calm.
But wilder grew the clamour; hand, and eye,
And voice were raging with terrific signs
Of vengeance; till the name of "Cæsar" rang
Loud on the soul of Pilate, like the knell
Of his destruction! Cæsar's foe must die;
And Hate shall crucify whom Justice spared.
Then took he water, laved his hands, and cried,
"That I am innocent of blood, behold,
Of this just Person; be it yours to bear."
"His blood be on us! on our children be!"
In mingled answer from that murderous crowd
Ascended; dreary as the dying swell
Of ocean, up to heaven this awful breath
Of imprecation roll'd, and drew from God
The answer, Judah's myriads suffer *now!*

Earth never parallel'd a scene like this,
When list'ning Worlds were overawed to hear
A creature his incarnate God condemn![51]
A paved tribunal by the Palace rose
Of pictured marble, and mosaic sheen,
Whereon was Pilate as in kingly state
Enthroned; before him stood a bleeding Form
Of solemn aspect, in Whose mild regret
A sanctitude beyond expression spake.
Below a raving multitude was seen
Upgazing, all athirst for righteous blood;
And who, with features harrow'd by the strife
And scorn of passion, from their God invoked
Eternal vengeance for eternal Blood!

But where the vile traducer? While the doom
Of death was pass'd, and Jesus like a Lamb
To slaughter by the savage crowd decreed,
Then, Conscience, thy tremendous power began!
The beauty, glory, and sublime display
Of virtues godlike by the sinless Christ

Embodied, back upon his memory came;
And in the light of that immaculate Lord
From all He did reflected, dark and deep
The perfidy of His betrayer frown'd!
Lash'd by remorse, the council-Chief he sought,
The crime of Innocence by him betray'd
Confess'd; but when in vain his pleading guilt
Repented, in the Temple down he hurl'd
The wages of Iniquity, and fled
On wings of horror!—like a maniac, wild
And blasted into solitude he ran.
The ground grew fire beneath his guilty tread;
The heavens hung o'er him like a vast reproach;
And groans which make the jubilee of hell
Heaved from his soul with terrible excess!
Where rose a precipice, whose rocky gloom
The plunging billows of a torrent fill'd
With mimic thunder in chaotic roar,
At length he stood, and on the black abyss
Stared wildly—then a pace withdrew,
Look'd o'er the heavens his horrible despair!
Till Nature with a ghastly dimness seem'd
Enshrouded; round him the horizon reel'd,
The earth was waning, and with hideous yell
He seized the branches of a rock-grown tree,
Swung from its height, and down the dizzy steep
Sunk into darkness, and was seen no more![52]

But come, thou Spirit of believing Awe
Whom nothing boundeth, and a scene behold
More wond'rous than eternity conceals,—
A crucified Redeemer! With His cross[53]
To Calvary the lacerated Christ
Is now ascending; famish'd, faint, and pale,
Beneath the burden of a tree accursed
He falters; yet the goading throng
His limbs profane, and trample when He falls
Their silent Martyr!. Lest at once He die
And cheat the tortures of intended doom,
To bear it, from Cyrene is compell'd
A pilgrim; and again with murd'rous glee
The rabble round about Him dance and hoot.
Thus, all are merciless, while Mercy bleeds,
Save thou, fond Woman! in thy faithful eyes
Are tears; and from thine unforsaking love
The language of sublimest pity flows.
Yet not for Him, but for yourselves lament;
Ye daughters of Jerusalem! who wail;
The days are coming when the soul will cry
"The wombs how blessèd which have never
borne!"
But lo; the hill of Golgotha appears;
The Cross is planted; with convulsive shake
Each limb unloosen'd; and the starting blood
In liquid torment from the flesh distill'd;
In vain, a potion to benumb His pangs
Is proffer'd; dying God, He suffers all.
"Forgive them; for they know not what they
do!"

And thus they crucify the Son of Man!
Those Hands are bleeding, which have bless'd
a world;
Those Feet are tortured, which have never
moved
Except on errands of celestial Love;
Those Brows are throbbing, and those Eyes
bedimm'd
Where light and immortality were throned;
And ah! that pure, unspotted, perfect Soul,
Divine as Deity on earth could be,
Doth agonise beneath th' imputed Curse
Whereby a ransom for the World is paid:
And silently He all endures! Around His
Cross
The soldiers wrangle for the parted vest;
And when His eye in lifted torment gazed
O'er Calvary, by crowding myriads trod,
How few the faces where compassion dwelt,
Or tears were trickling, did that look behold!
The scowl of Pharisees, the hate of Scribes,
And the fierce glance of hypocrites rebuked,
Were turn'd upon Him, to translate His
pangs,
And drink the fulness of a deep revenge!
While others underneath the Cross advanced
To read His title with reviling scorn,
"King of the Jews!"

Two thieves beside Him hung
In kindred torture to increase the shame.
The one did rail, the other's soften'd heart
Repented; sudden faith his soul illumed,
And, "Lord! when in Thy kingdom Thou art
throned
Remember me!" the dying creature said;
And lo! a paradise was his reward.

Then look'd Messiah where His mother
stood,
The Virgin Mary, with His Own beloved
Disciple; agony could not subdue
His tenderness; compassion fill'd His gaze
With heavenly lustre, while in filial love
He bent on Mary the divinest look
That ever Child on weeping parent cast,
And murmur'd, "Woman! there a Son behold;
Disciple! there a future Mother see."
O Maiden! purest of all pure, who felt
A love maternal, when thy bosom throbb'd
Beneath the pangs of thine almighty Son,
The sword of anguish, then thy soul it pierced,
As hoary Simeon in the Temple sang.

Thus in the light, 'tween heaven and earth
upraised,
Upon the malefactor's cross was nail'd,
Was crucified, the Lord of living Worlds!
Till came the sixth hour, when the noontide-sun

Waned from his throne; and sudden darkness fell
O'er all Judea, till creation seem'd
By God forsaken, Whose averted face
Bade darkness emblematically type
The gloom internal God in Flesh endured.
Jerusalem, her temples, domes, and towers,
Were shaded; Lebanon and Tabor shrunk
And wither'd; Carmel, Gilead, and the rocks
By ocean towering, shadow cover'd all
With night's terrific semblance. In the gloom
The mutter of a multitude uprose
Like sounds infernal; while their features wore
A fell expression of unearthly hue,—
Each fearing what his impious tongue denied,
As ever and anon some coward took
A shuddering glance, where Man's Redeemer hung,
While the blood quiver'd in his guilty veins
Till blasphemy in hollow murmur died!
Heart cannot dream, imagination dare
By words to image th' almighty pangs
That in His darkness and distress of soul
Th' Ineffable upon the Cross endured!
Who held His spirit as the Prince of Life,
To torment subject, till the Curse was paid.
The ninth hour came; and then, with loud appeal,
From the deep midnight of atoning Blood,
He utter'd, "Why hast Thou forsaken Me!
My God! My God!"—then came an awful hush
In which they deem'd Elias would descend
To save Him: but, a second time, a Voice
More audible the souls of myriads shook:
"'Tis finish'd! Father, to Thy hands divine
My Spirit I commend," the Saviour cried,
And bow'd His head, and breathed* His soul away!

"'Tis finish'd!" let seraphic mind these words
Translate, for immortality is there!
Which heaven re-echoed, while the regions dark
Where Christ descended in a shape of Light
Triumphant over Powers and Thrones of Hell,[54]
Groan'd at the sound which deepen'd their despair!
The Universe a ghastly signal gave,
And Nature, as in agony, confess'd
The Lord of Glory as His Spirit fled.
The earth was palsied; and the mountains rent
Like garments; tomb and sepulchre their dead
Released, and out of dust the saints arose
And look'd upon the living; while the Veil,
As 'mid the Temple of the Holies stood
A robed High Priest, in sacerdotal pomp,
Was riven, from the top to bottom torn;
And full at once the Oracle reveal'd.
Now, in the tremor of created things
While rock and earthquake, tomb and temple, speak
With dread conviction, "'tis a God that dies!"
The pale centurion and the crowd aghast
Lift their wild looks, and smite their breasts, and cry,
With lips that shudder, "'Tis the Son of God!"

A Tragedy which made the sun eclipse
His beams, and sympathising Earth to cast
Her waken'd dead from out their riven tombs,
Is ended! and the oriental Night
O'er Palestine her dewy wings unfolds.
On Calvary the solemn moonbeams lie
All chill and lovely, like those trancèd smiles
Which light the features, when the pangs of death
Have ceased to flutter, and the face is still.
The stars are trooping; and the wintry air
Is mellow'd with a soft mysterious glow
Caught from their beauty; not a vapour mars
The stainless welkin, where the moon aloft
One blue immensity of sky commands,
Save where the fringe of some minutest cloud
Hangs like an eyelid on a brilliant Orb,
Then vanishes, in quenching lustre hid.
Few hours have fleeted, and yon trampled hill
Was shaken with a multitude, who foam'd
And raged beneath their agonising God!
But Nature hath her calm resumed; and night,
As if to spread oblivion o'er the day
And give creation a sabbatic rest,
In balm and beauty on the world descends.
The crowds have disappear'd like waves that melt
And leave a shore to quietude again:
Some in their dreams, perchance, the day renew;
But thou! upon a kingly couch reposed,
The Judge of Jesus, could thy soul conceive
That long as Time's recorded truths endure
Thy name, united to this awful scene,
Would live, when all the Cæsars are forgot?

The hum and murmur of a distant town
How faintly on the breeze they roll, and die
In soft confusion! Turn thy gaze, and see,
Encircled with a huge Titanian wall,
Where tower and turret, and Herodian piles,
And battlements of dusky gloom uprear
Their vastness, there the Holy City stands!
Augustly beautiful, in moonlight bathed,
Jehovah's palace awes the midnight-air
Around it; while her mountain-bulwarks veil'd

* ἐξέπνευσεν—*Luke* xxiii. 46.

With dimmer lustre, far and near preside
Like guardians planted by almighty hands,
To watch the city, where a million breathe.
From plain and desert, isles and regions call'd,
Wherever son of Abram was, they throng
For worship, and their Paschal Feast enjoy.
And there, in some unnoticed chamber lurk
The panic-struck apostles ! When the gloom
Of earthquake on the hill of Calvary hung,
That God was coming from the Cross to take
Messiah, or, that Christ Himself would free
And shake the universe to show the God,—
Ambition blindly dreamt. As Lord of Worlds
Him they conceived too wonderful to die !
A veil was on them ; though the truthful Lord
His future resurrection oft declared,
'Twas unremember'd, while the sudden pangs
Of terror crucified the faith of all.

But north of Zion, on a mountain-slope
That garden where the tomb of Jesus lies
Behold ! impressively by vestal beams
Of moonlight touch'd, his rocky grave appears ;
Before it, with a frequent play, the flash
Of steely armour, as the Roman watch
Changes and moves in circular array,
Is seen ; yet, save the night's uncertain sound,
The fitful motion of a rambling breeze
That stirs the olive, or the towering palm,
And timid murmur of a garden-brook,
The scene is voiceless ; while on high enthroned
Yon firmamental Orbs are fixed and bright,
As though in wonder, that their glory falls
On the dread tomb where buried Godhead lies !

Still Calvary sleeps ; and nothing harsh or wild
The holy slumber of the Night arrests.
The sentries in their panoply are ranged ;
Some on the gleaming worlds of air a glance
Upturn, and with inaudible delight
Adore their beauty ; some on fairy wings
Of fondness to the haunt of childhood flee
Among the hills of unforgotten Rome ;
Or vaguely round yon high-wall'd city view
The shadowy watch-towers on the vineyards raised,
Or mountain dim, or Maccabean pile ;
While others, haply, to the tomb devote
A gaze of sorrow, for that righteous Form
They helped to rivet on the Cursed Tree !

But in that syncope,* that solemn trance,
When darkness as a fading thought decays
Amid the glimmer of increasing dawn,
Like God in thunder, hark ! an earthquake-throb
While the rock quivers as a shaken reed !
In rushing glory down the sky advanced
A giant Angel ; from the tomb he roll'd
The barrier-stone, and on it sat, and blazed.
His face was lightning ! and as dazzling snow
His vestment glitter'd : with a clang of arms
Prone on the earth affrighted soldiers fell !
And as Eliphaz, when the vision spake,
Upon the Formless turn'd a fearful gaze,
They look'd—were blasted—like the dead they lay !
And then Emmanuel from the grave arose
Invisible ; all paramount and pure
The Resurrection and the Life He stood,
Lord of the tomb, victorious and sublime !
Oh, then Captivity was captive led ;
Satan unthroned ; His domination spoil'd ;
Hell-gates were sunder'd, and from earthy sleep
The dead awaking, as they lived and moved
Felt on their brows a beam immortal play !

But He who moved invisible to man,
To guardian woman did Himself reveal.
As weeping Mary by the tomb remain'd
And bow'd within its rocky depth to gaze,
Two angel-watchers, robed in dazzling white,
Were seated, where the vanish'd body lay :
"Why weepest thou ?" with gentlest tone they cried :
"Because I know not where my stolen Lord
Be taken ;" back she turn'd her eye of tears,
And there stood Jesus ! but to her unknown.
"Why weepest thou ?" again was mildly heard ;
Then Mary, with mistaking love, replied,
"If thou hast borne Him from this garden-tomb,
Oh ! tell me where ; these hands will take Him thence."
But Jesus, vocal with His wonted voice,
Responded, "Mary !" and the mourner fell
Down at His feet ! Rabboni she adored !
Let one at midnight, when the cradling sea
Hath rock'd his slumber, and a dream of Home
In murmuring faintness to the soul renews
Parental language, till his ocean-sleep
Is harrow'd by that heart-entrancing sound,
Her feeling image ! such may faintly tell
When Mary worshipp'd *how* her spirit thrill'd !

'Twas on the evening of this hallow'd day
That two disciples, down a western vale
To where Emmaus in the sunset show'd
Her whitening cots, with pensive step approach'd.
O dying hour of beautiful delight !
The painter's worship and the poet's song,
How few embrace thee with a purer thought

* A syncope, a solemn pause.—COWPER.

Than one, whose dreaming Boyhood loved to form
Romantic visions of the unreveal'd
From thine own hues; when like those fairy clouds
Which float and perish, yearning Fancy shaped
Bright unrealities long roll'd away!
Divinest evening! when thy Syrian glow
On verdurous olive, sycamore, and palm
Descended, not unfelt thy magic woo'd
These holy pilgrims. Homeward flocks and herds
Were wending; while around them richly-soft
The lingering decadence of light began.
But more than Nature on their brows has hung
A solemn meaning! of the Day they talk,
Of Death, and Resurrection; such their theme,
When, silent as the shadow of their forms,
Another came! and mingled word with word,
In deep communion. Then of Christ He spake;
From prophecy to prophecy unroll'd
Each revelation, till the shade of doubt
Fell from their spirit like a film removed
From Blindness, letting in the light of heaven.
But when, abiding to partake their meal,
He sat before them, and the Blessing gave,
That Eye, so eloquent with awe devout,
That voice heaven-toned, that superhuman Mien
Declared Messiah! Now at once He gazed
Upon them, featured like that living Christ
So often follow'd, worshipp'd,—and forsook!
Within them how each wondering heart had burn'd
To hear Him as an Oracle reveal
The Word of Life, God's Everlasting Will!
But like a vision of the soul He fled.
Then back they speeded, to th' Eleven rehearsed
Their tale of wonder: when again behold!
Th' Incarnate Saviour! "Peace be with you! hail!"
Becalming thus with salutation mild
Th' appall'd Assembly, on them all He breathed
His Holy Spirit, and to each bestow'd
O'er sin a power, to pardon or retain.
But Thomas doubted, till his hand could touch
The living Jesus! lo! again He came
Inaudibly, within a chamber barr'd;[55]
So like a Spirit of the shapeless air
He enter'd, that o'erawed disciples quaked!
"Thy finger hither reach, These hands behold,
And thrust thine own within My wounded side,
Not faithless, but believing!" Thus He spoke
To him who answer'd "Saviour, Lord, and God!"

Once more upon the lake Messiah view,
Whose azure waters at His word o'erfill'd
With countless fish the Galilean bark,
Which night had baffled; then was Peter ask'd
That threefold question, threefold wisdom fill'd
With memory of his denial thrice!
And yet, so toned with tenderness divine,
The soul of Peter in his fond reply,
"Thou knowest I love thee!" spake with answering tears.

And now, the Counsel of eternal Love,
Mysterious, vast, omniscient as profound,
Wrapt in the folds of Heaven's decretive Will
Before the universe was shaped or born,
Concludeth! Man's Redemption is complete,
And sanction'd; all the archetypal Plan
Of Deity, for reconciling grace
With justice, by the mediating Blood
Of covenant, in Christ has been fulfill'd.
The Woman's Seed hath bruised the Serpent's Head;
For Man hath lived, for Man hath bled, and died,
Soar'd from the grave, and His true Person shown
Not in the midnight, when the spirit shapes
An earthless phantom; but by living day
Was risen Jesus handled, seen and heard.*

But, ere ascending to His seat on high,
Again the apostolic Band He taught
The true Salvation, in its glorious light.
From age to age prophetically sung,
By type and shadow heralded or seen,
Begotten Son of Co-Eternal Sire,
His goings forth from Everlasting were! †
Before the works of Old, ere earth began,
When God His compass on the waters set
And gave the sea commandment,—He was there!
The Star; the Prophet, like to Moses raised;
The Priest for ever, on the Right Hand placed
Of glory, while the sun and moon endure,—
Dominion o'er all nations, kings, and isles,
To Him was given, whom the Gentiles sought;
Born of a Virgin; perfect God and Man;
Desire of nations; He whom Daniel saw,
Ancient of Days; by king and kingdoms served;
The Heritor of Heathens and the Throne
Of David: higher than the Heaven of Heavens,
Expressive Semblance of the bright Unseen!
And Morning-Star of Immortality;
The Light of Light, unspotted Lamb of God,
For sin an Offering, and for sinners slain,

* There are eleven distinct appearances of Christ, after His Resurrection, recorded in the New Testament.

† For this summary of Christ's magnificent titles and offices, vide Scriptures, *passim*.

But now arisen from the tomb to soar
Eternal Saviour of forgiven man! *—
Thus in the beams of revelation shone
The great Messiah: thus the cloudy veil
Of error from their souls He took, and cried,
"Go forth! repentance and remission teach,
Baptising Nations in the Name triune
Of Father, Son, and Holy Ghost![56] Behold
All living Unction from the Spirit's grace
From Me shall clothe you, as the promise spake;
Within the City tarry till they come,
Lo! I am with you to the ended world."

My soul is shaken with a mighty Dream!
Dominion, Majesty, and Truth proceed
In blended union from the deeps of Heaven.
I hear the gates of second Eden ope,
And balm and freshness on the blighted world
Come flowing forth with universal love
And Earth regenerate with redemption's smile.
And hark! the echoes of a choral strain
Above; a new and Everlasting Song†
Is chanted, for the seven-seal'd Book unroll'd
The Lamb hath open'd; and symphonious hymns
Of thousand times ten thousand Saints ascend
The Throne around: "Hosannah to the Lamb!"
For He is worthy! shout, ye Angels! shout
Till Earth re-echoes that unwearied strain!
Let sun, let moon, and each melodious star,
The winds, the rivers, mountains, floods, and hills,
The diapason deepen, and the loud
Eternal hallelujah of the Sea
Wake into sound; while regions, zones, and isles,
The glory of our great Redeemer sing!
And thus with angels and archangels laud
The Lamb Almighty, in the skies adored!

But, lo! upon Mount Olivet appears
With hands uplifted in their last farewell,
The parting Saviour; on His God-like brow
The radiance of eternity begins:
Disciples kneeling for His blessing ask,
And, hark! 'tis given; on their souls He breathes
The breath of sanctity, of love sublime
And endless: then His mighty hand is lift,
But while it blesseth the beloved of earth,
The Air is waiting to upwaft its Lord.
And see, He riseth! solemnly and slow,
Array'd in brightness, such as God invests,
In soaring grandeur from the baffled gaze
Of His adorers, through the pathless air
In the full lustre of unclouded day
He riseth! leaving, like th' Atlantic sun
On ocean when he dies a gorgeous death,
A beaming track magnificently bright
Behind Him; till a radiant star He seems,
And then, is trackless., in celestial depths
Evanish'd, soaring back to God again![57]

But, oh, if Angels at His birth did sing,
What pæans now through heaven's wide concave roll!
Who welcome there the sempiternal Lord,
The Son incarnate, into glory come,
O'er Sin and Death victorious, with a World
Recover'd, ransom'd, and for ever saved,
To speak his triumph in the state of Man.
The skies are kindled! from the opal walls
And battlements of uncreated Light,
Lo! seraphim and cherubim appear,
With angel and archangel,—rank on rank
In wing'd array of infinite extent
And brightness, to conduct the Lord of heaven.
Now lift your heads, ye Everlasting Doors,
Receive the King of Glory! Hark! the choir
With jubilant Hosannas shout and sing,
"For ever and for ever is Thy Throne,
Thou Holy, Holy, Holy, Lord of Hosts!
By Thee of old the heaven and earth were framed,
Were founded: but they all shall fade and die
And as a vesture shalt Thou fold them up,
And they shall perish! still art *Thou* the same
Unchanging, Holy, Holy, Lord of Hosts!
Thy Throne eternal in the heavens resume
Almighty Saviour, and triumphant King!"

My theme is o'er, the great Messiah sung;
And this attempt, whose vast persuasion fill'd
My being with o'erawed delight, concludes.
How often, in some pause of holy fear
Hath Fancy folded her adventurous wing,
And my soul bow'd with this unutter'd thought,
That He, whose mediatorial love I sang,
Beheld me, fathoming my spirit's depth!
And now, as girt with glory, in the Heaven
Of Heavens the Son of Man His Throne resumes,
A dread comes round me, like a shadow cast
From waning tempest o'er a tranced sea.

Thou Land sublime, of miracles and men,
Where Poetry from God on earth came down
In warbled echoes of celestial song!
Where Hebron, Tabor, and Mount Carmel, lift
Their speaking vastness in the sultry air

* Then opened He their understanding, that they might understand the Scriptures, and said unto them, Thus it is written, and thus it behoved Christ to suffer, and to rise from the dead.—*Luke* xxiv. 45, 46.

† Rev. chap. v.

Divinely-haunted; where the Jordan rolls,
Where rock, and cavern, grotto, cell and cave
Are mighty; where the curse of Heaven has graved
Terrific warning on thy blasted trees
And haggard vales, all fountainless and dry,
The stately vision of thy mingled Scene
Departeth! He whose spirit oft has heard
The thunder-music of thy tempest roll,
Beheld thy sun-blaze, seen thine eagles mount
And dream-led roved beside that mournful Lake
Where man's Redeemer in His days of earth
Hath wander'd,—bids thee now a long farewell!

Autumnal morning round my chamber threw
The gleaming wanness of its gentle smile,
When tremblingly, as though omniscient Eyes
Look'd on my soul, I struck the sacred Lyre
And bade it warble this surpassing Theme.
But ever, as the waves of moving life
From England's capital, with heave and swell
Came surging from afar, my soul partook
A deep communion with the fate of Man
Amid a sea of wide Existence toss'd,
Whose billows only the Redeemer trod
Secure; but left along the stormy wild
A track of glory for terrestrial feet
To follow, guided by the star of Heaven.

But now, the Spirit of mysterious Night
Comes forth, and, like a ruin'd Angel, seems
All dimly-glorious, and divinely-sad:
And Earth, forgetful of her primal fall,
Lies in the beauty of reflected heaven.
Oh! night creates the paradise of thought,
Enchanting back whatever Time has wrong'd
Or exiled, touch'd with that celestial hue
Which faith and fancy on the Dead bestow.
Emotions which the tyrant Day destroys
Can now awaken, like reviving flowers;
And e'en the darkness of unheavenly souls
Must feel illumined, as the Eye receives
From all its views, a loveliness which comes
To light the dimness of the spirit's depth.
As when at morning, oft a sunrise pours
A stream of splendour through the window-panes
Of Temple vast, to cheer its barren aisles,
And on the gloom of monumental Sleep
To glisten, like a resurrection-morn.

Thus, life is charter'd for a nobler fate
Than glory, by the breath of man bestow'd:
A living world a living God reflects,
Morn, noon, and night, with everlasting change!
And who can hide the universe; o'erawe
The Elements; the sun unseat; or mar
That mighty Poem which the heavens and earth
Exhibit, written by Eternal Hands?
A sense of beauty, which is so divine,
Haunts human nature with undying spell;
And while the wonders of creation teem,
To love and worship their majestic power,
Can lift the spirit into purer light
Than ever canopied the throne of Fame.

And cold the heart, whose aspirations wing'd
Their flight from thee, my own inviolate Land!
Whom night and beauty have apparell'd now.
Thy heavens are stainless, as the molten blue
Of ocean, in the noontide's dazzling sleep;
Thy starry multitudes their thrones have set;
And the young Moon gazeth on yon quiet sea
Tranced like a mother, with her doating eye
Intently fix'd upon a cradled child.
While, round, and full, and ravishingly bright,
A planet here and there the sky adorns.
A path of lustre has o'erlaid the Deep,
Which heaves and glitters, like a wizard shore
For sea-enchanters, when they rise and walk
The waves in glory: voice nor foot profanes
This dreaming silence; but the mellow lisp
Of dying waters on the beach dissolved,
Makes ocean-language for the heart and hour.

Now thought is heaven-like; and our earthly frame
Of Purity beyond the day to bring,
Is conscious. From the uncreated Fount
Of Glory, may not emanations steal,
By night absorbed, and mystically felt?
Or creatures, such as once the mental eye
Of seraph-haunted Milton[58] saw descend
Like sunbeams darted from a riven cloud
On Eden's mount, with viewless wing career
Around us, charming with a gaze unseen
Whate'er the beauty of their glances touch?

But oh! dark Spirit,[59] whose unquiet shade
Our fancy visions in reflected gloom,
Again thou comest! and thy frown declares
What penal agonies, what groans and pangs,
In this calm hour a bleeding World contains!
E'en now, the curtains of Futurity
Are shaken, by the blasts of coming doom!
For Self[60] has overshadow'd Love divine
With dread oblivion; till our daring thoughts
To helm the Universe, and guide the wheels
Of human Fate, have awfully presumed!

A Mind which glories in the world of Man
And graves, immortal! on the meanest brow,
Oh! how it loves the universe, and longs
To see the spirits whom Redemption won
Annihilate the hopes of Hell! Shall souls,

So highly destined, that a swell of joy
Heaves o'er the harp of Heaven's resounding choir
When Sin repents, be perfected and lost?
No! let us, as the prince of morning quells
A cloudy tempest with imperial rays,
So learn to vanquish with celestial light
Our Sin and Darkness, till, as demons shrunk
To shapeless nothing at Messiah's look,
Our Vices wither from our Virtues' gaze.

Amid deep Energies which now unfold
Like harmonies from some awaking lyre,
Wilt Thou, divinest of all Arts divine!
Last in the train of renovating Truths
Advance, poetical Enchantress? Muse,
Who art the Angel of the soul, whose voice
The primal loveliness of vanish'd Things
Renews; or haply, thou in pure perfection art
A Priestess, who behind the veil of sense
Conducts the Spirit to the holy shrine
Where Beauty, Love, and Everlasting Light
Are shrouded; or, a Prophetess, whose lip
Their power interprets with a vocal spell.

Thou beautiful Magician! be thy name
Whate'er Thou wilt: Creatress of delight
Expression paints not! though the World affright
Thy radiant visit, still art Thou revered;
And the soft wave of Thy descending wings
Is token'd by the pulse's quivering joy.
Beneath the play of thy melodious smiles
Our spirit quickens into thrills of heaven,
And Feeling worships at thy faintest sound!
All hours are thine; all climes and seasons drink
Thine effluence bright, and immaterial power.
Thou with the Universe twin-born didst rise!
And Thou alone, when tempted Nature fell,
Unfallen wert: and thus Thy glorious aim
Like true religion's, is to lead us back
From recreant darkness to primeval bliss.[61]

All moods are Thine; all maladies of thought
By thee are visited with healing sway.
In those dread moments, when a hideous veil
Of darkness, woven by some demon-hand,
Lies on the world; when Love itself is cold
Or earthly; and the tone Affection breathes
Falls fruitless on the mind, as ocean-spray
Which dies unheeded on the savage rock;
When Nature is untuned, and all things wear
The coarse reality Derision loves,
E'en then, how often thine assuasive balm
Spirit of beauty! intellectual queen!
Descendeth, melting over heart and brain
Like dew upon the desert, till the soul
Revives, and this bad World seems exorcised!
And Thou canst hallow with ennobling power
High impulses, of superhuman sway,
Which come like shades of pre-existent Life
Athwart the mind, when dream-eyed Fancy rules.*
For is not Man mysteriously begirt
By something dread, imagination feels,
Yet fathoms not? Dare human Creed deny
That mortal feeling, in its finest mood,
May be some thrill of sympathetic chords
Which link our nature to a world unknown!

And since the spirit with the flesh doth war,[62]
And Life is oft an agonising thirst
Which nothing visible can tame, or cool,
That Beauty, which the hues of thought create,
By thee enchanted, slakes the mental fire
That parches us within: and yearning dreams
And hopes which breathe of immortality
Thy power ennobles with mysterious aid.
Then, long as Earth is round us, and the wings
Of Fancy by the light of faith ascend,
May Poetry her sibyl-language weave,
Enlighten, charm, and elevate the world.

Creation's hope! our universal All!
From Thee alone believing spirits learn
That man is deathless, an immortal heir
Of Being yet to be. Stupendous thought!
Though frail as dew thy fleeting life departs,
The Soul is godlike! world on world may rise
And wither, quench'd in everlasting gloom;
And surging ages into silence roll
Like haughty billows which have heaved and died;
But still unfading, bright with awful bliss,
Or pale with agony, the Soul shall live
And like Jehovah, utter its "*I am!*"

We shall not sleep, but we shall all arise
For judgment;—with an instantaneous frame
Of being, Dust shall look on God, and live!
An hour is coming when the grave will hear
And answer to a tomb-awakening trump
Which thunders o'er the icy trance of Death:
The waning universe, the earth and heaven
Shall vanish in th' immeasurable Deep;
But Thine own promise shall not pass away.
And though that hour, for resurrection doom'd,[63]
Be hidden, shrouded from angelic mind
A secret buried in Eternal Thought,—

* Man can never altogether turn aside his thoughts from Infinity; and some obscure recollections will always remind him of his original home.—M. SCHLEGEL.

As certain as the blood of Christ hath flow'd,
Messiah risen, and the heavens received
And throned His Presence, He shall come
again!

And then, the funeral of Creation see!
Sun, moon, and star dissolve, and wane, and
die;
The earth is riven; with appalling roar
The Sea departeth, as her dead ascend;
And wing'd Archangels on the winds unroll
Their summons; not an atom but is thrill'd
With life or feeling, at that dreadful sound!
And now look up! behold, He cometh! clouds
And splendours, with seraphic armies, throng
Before Him, cleaving the prophetic sky
With vanward glory, to announce The God.
And lo! the semblance of His far-off Throne
Advances; as embodied lustre bright
The Judge of Earth, the Son Almighty, comes!
And all who have been, since creation was,
Moveless and countless, on their features wear
A solemn radiance, from His Form Divine
Reflected; every eye is fix'd and still,
To Him upraised, whose eye discerneth all!

Again the trumpet! and this dread array,
The multitudinous and living mass
At once is sever'd; right and left they stand
Divided, as of old the fated sea
Was cloven when the wand of Moses waved;
And in each soul there is a judgment-throne
Erected, where eternal Conscience reigns.

But listen!—far behind this breathing host
Of mortals, myriads of colossal Shapes,
Unearthly, wild, and dim with ghastly wo,
Rise in the glare!—the ruin'd Angels * come
From darkness, and a clank of chain resounds
Appallingly, above the world distinct!
But One, who, vast above the vastest there
In towering majesty the sky confronts,
As though the fabric of the heavens would
shrink
From the dark light of his unfathom'd gaze,
Behold him! how magnificently dread!
From the huge mountain into embers sunk
To the last billow of expiring sea,—
O'er all the terror of his ruin frowns,
Who battled with omnipotence in heaven
And will be fearless in the fires of hell!

Another gaze! e'er Earth and Nature die;
The Spirit of eternity descends,
Seven thunders speak,† to heaven his arm He
lifts,
And utters, "Time and earth shall be no more:"
Creation withers at that dread command,
And like a shade, the Universe departs!

Oh! in this agony of Nature's death
May he, who dared from erring fancy's gloom
To lift his spirit to the Light of Light,
And shadow forth some lineaments divine
Of God Incarnate, by redemption seen,
Unblasted look upon the Lord he sang:
And in yon world unutterably bright
Where thought is holy as the heaven it breathes,
By Angels taught, around The Throne renew
The song eternal hymning Time began.

* Epistle of Jude, 6. † See Revelation.

NOTES.

Note 1, Page 456, Column 1.

Himself was all! the unapparent God.

Since the above line was written, the author has perused an emphatic comment on its meaning, in a sermon of South's, on the Divine Mercy:—"His goodness was so vastly, so infinitely full, that He seemed unquiet and unsatisfied till He had, as it were, disburdened Himself by some communications of it. One would have thought that these perfections had been too rare to be communicated, so much as in resemblance, and that God would have folded them up within His own essence for ever; so that He who now contents Himself with the prerogative of being the best and greatest Being, might have been the only Being; but He chose rather to draw out, than only to possess, His own fulness; to scatter something of His image upon the creature, and to see Himself in effigy."—*Works*, vol. viii. p. 81.

Note 2, Page 456, Column 1.

Whereof the day thou eatest,—thou shalt die!

It was fit to lay upon Adam this small restraint, to make him sensible that, though he had dominion over all things, yet he was not their lord, but a servant of the Most High. But still, some ask, why should his obedience be tried in such an instance as this?—not considering that a trial of it could scarcely have been made in any of the usual precepts, which there was no opportunity of violating. For what should tempt him to idolatry, or to take God's name in vain, or to murder his wife? How was it possible to commit adultery, when there was nobody but he and she in the world? How could he steal, or what room was there for coveting, when God had put him in possession of all things? It had been in vain to forbid that which could not be done; and it had been virtue to abstain, not from that to which there was no temptation, but from that which invited them to transgress.—Bishop Patrick.

In Vitringa, on the "Tree of the Knowledge of Good and Evil," the reader will find some profound and vigorous reasoning. He says that "the tree of the knowledge of good and evil was so called, because, from the divine institution, it was a moral cause of that knowledge,—i.e. it was a visible, familiar, and permanent lesson, by which man was not only admonished of the eternal distinction between good and evil, but was put upon his guard as to the quarter from which alone evil could assail him." Concerning the command itself, it is observed, "the prohibition answered the threefold purpose of trial, instruction, and of a sacramental pledge." We will venture to extract his eloquent comment on the second of these purposes:—"Placed in the midst of the garden, and often meeting the eyes of our first parents, it (viz., the 'Tree of Knowledge,') could hardly fail to teach them such truths as these: That God is the Lord of all things; and, consequently, that man's dominion was neither absolute nor independent; that in the enjoyment of God alone is the satisfying good of man; that, in judging of good and evil, man is not to be directed by his own reason or pleasure, but by the revealed will of God; that man had not yet arrived at his highest happiness, but was bound to expect and desire a more perfect state, yet in that way alone which God had appointed; that if he would escape death, he must avoid the cause of it,—i.e., sin. How much further the unclouded mind of the first man might have carried his reflections on the forbidden tree, to what sublime conceptions of the Divine Nature and works of Providence it might have led him, we, in our shattered state, with our discordant affections and obscure lights, are poorly qualified to judge. Yet, disabled as we are by the Fall from taking such rapid, capacious, and elevating views of whatever is fair, and good, and magnificent, in the creature and Creator, as were competent to a sinless being, we can discern enough to persuade us, that the tree of knowledge of good and evil must have been to an innocent man a rich source of intellectual improvement and moral joy."—*Observ. Sacr.*, tome ii., lib. iv., c. 12.

Note 3, Page 456, Column 2.

Let Nature hope; and while her blessings thrive,
To secret Heaven resign the vast unknown!

A beautiful illustration of our limited apprehension relative to the origin and destiny of things occurs in one of Paley's Sermons, for which he is indebted to Tucker's "Light of Nature:"—"All such partial knowledge must be encumbered with many difficulties,—it is like viewing the map of a district, or small tract of territory, by itself, and separated from the adjacent country; we see rivers marked out, without any source to flow from, and running where there is nothing to receive them. In like manner we observe events in the world, of which we trace not either cause or origin, and tending to no design or purpose that we can discover."

Note 4, Page 457, Column 1.

In Christ all Revelation lives. His voice
With man in Eden dread communion held,

It is perhaps deserving of observation, that, in the account of the production of the world, in the first chapter of Genesis, the absolute term "God," is constantly used; but when the account of the administration of the new-created world begins, the term, "the Lord God," is introduced. And in all the intercourse and converse between the Deity and the first inhabitants of the world, this appellation is constantly given to the Divine Person, whom we find administering the affairs of the new creation, and seems to denote a distinct person and character. And in the several conversations between this Divine Personage and Adam, Eve, Cain, &c., as recorded in the third and fourth chapters of Genesis, it seems plain that he presented himself in some personal form or visible appearance. And whether or not this might have any relation to the assumption of Humanity in the Mediator, there is, I think, no doubt but it is to be referred to the same Person, and relates to His mediatorial character, being part of the administration of that important government, which was from eternity ordained to be laid upon His shoulders; and which comprehends, not only as the Jews fondly believed, the protection and restoration of their nation, but of all the race of mankind.

Note 5, Page 458, Column 2.

My son! in thee *a sacrifice the Lord*
Hath found, and—thou to God art dedicate!

Bishop Warburton supposes that the command of sacrificing Isaac was a mode of information by action, instead of words, concerning the great sacrifice of Christ, given to Abraham at his own request; which is well illustrated by Mr. Gilbook ("Script. Hist.") and might receive perhaps some confirmation, by observing that this scene was placed, most probably, upon the very spot where Christ actually suffered.

Note 6, Page 459, Column 2.

Seven altars,

It is well known that, in the Oriental style, the perfection of any quality is expressed by the application of the number Seven; a figure, probably, derived from the history of the Creation, the division of time into weeks, and the primeval honour of the Sabbath day. But whatever was its origin, seven came to be regarded as a most dignified and sacred number. It occupied a marked place in the religious and political institutions of the ancient Persians, who had derived many principles of primitive revealed truth from undoubtedly a patriarchal source: and it was adopted into the sacred phraseology of the Jews. Thus the extremity of distress is denoted by seven troubles: the most complete refining of metals is called a being purified seven times; a character of consummate wickedness is represented by an enumeration of seven vices, or the habitation of seven evil spirits; the highest measure of accomplishments is signified by seven men that can render a reason; the perfect excellence of wisdom, by a palace of seven pillars; and the omniscience of God, by seven eyes and seven lamps. So also, still more remarkably, in this book of mystical visions, the perfection of the Divine government, in different parts of its administration, is described by the symbolical agency of seven angels, seven thunders, seven phials, seven plagues; and the perfection, and power, and wisdom of Christ, as exercised in the protection and government of His Church, is represented by seven horns and seven eyes. —PYE SMITH'S *Scrip. Test.* vol. iii. 153—4.

Επτα με φωνηεντα θεον αφθιτον αινει
Γραμματα των παντων, ακαματον πατερα,
Ειμι δ' εγω παντων χελυς αφθιτος η τα λυρωδη
Ηρμασαμην δινης ουρανιοιο μελη.

"Seven sounding letters sing the praise of me,
Th' immortal God, th' Almighty Deity,
Father of All, that cannot weary be.
I am th' Eternal Viol of all things,
Whereby the melody so sweetly rings
Of Heaven's music which so sweetly sings."

What these seven letters are, that do thus express God is easie to guess that they be the letters of the name of Jehovah.—LIGHTFOOT'S *Miscell.*, fol. edition.

Note 7, Page 459, Column 2.

With curses, like the winds, when desert-born,
Terrific, loud, with desolation wing'd!

As the storm darkened over the Hebrew kingdom, the voices of the prophets became louder and more wild. In their magnificent lyric odes, we have a poetical history of these momentous times. They were like the great tragic chorus to the awful drama which was unfolding itself in the eastern world.—MILMAN.

Note 8, Page 460, Column 2.

The infant of eternity
By wo is nursed, and strengthen'd for the skies.

The existence of misery and evil in the world has ever been, and continues to be, the grand question in theological and sceptical controversy. But on such a subject we may say, with Young,—"Those things which our hands can grasp, our understanding cannot comprehend: why then deny to the Deity himself the privilege of being one, amidst that multitude of mysteries which he has made.—*Essay on Infidelity.*

How noble is the sentiment of Seneca with reference to the trials and afflictions of this present scene! "Magnus es vir; sed unde scio, si tibi fortuna non dat facultatem exhibendæ virtutis. Descendisti ad Olympia; si nemo præter te, coronam habes, victoriam non habes."

The sentiments of a great modern metaphysician are in perfect unison with those of the Roman philosopher: "If virtue be excellent, the capacity of suffering, by which virtue is formed or perfected, must, when this great relation of it is considered, be allowed to have itself an excellence that is relative to the excellence produced by it. Without it we might indeed have been what the world terms happy—the passive subjects of a series of agreeable sensations; but we could not have had the delights of conscience; we could not have felt what it is to be magnanimous, to have the toil, the combat, and the victory; to exult that we have something within us which is superior, not to danger only, but which can vanquish even pleasure itself."—BROWN *on the Philosophy of the Human Mind,* Lect. 95.

Note 9, Page 460, Column 2.

God's Incarnation is the focal truth
Where prophecy's converging beams unite.

Instead of loading the text with prophetical references, the author has thought it more convenient to introduce, by way of note, a table of prophecies relative to the kingdom, office, and character of Christ. This summary was originally collected by Hartwell Horne, to whose invaluable Introduction the writer begs to acknowledge infinite obligations.

TABLE OF PROPHECIES RELATIVE TO THE MESSIAH AND HIS KINGDOM.

I.

PROPHECIES CONCERNING THE LIFE, DEATH, RESURRECTION AND ASCENSION OF THE MESSIAH.

1. *That a Messiah should come.*

PROPHECY.	FULFILMENT.
Gen. iii. 15, xii. 3, xxii. 18. xxvi. 4, xxviii. 14. Ps. lxxii. 17. Isa. xl. 5, 9, 10. Hag. ii. 7.	Gal. iv. 4. Romans xvi. 20. 1 John iii. 8. Rev. xii. 9. Heb. ii. 14. Luke ii. 1—16.

2. *When he should come.*

PROPHECY.	FULFILMENT.
Gen. xlix. 10. Hag. ii. 6—9. Dan. ix. 24, 25. Mal. iii. 1.	Luke ii. 1—3, 5. Mat. xxii. 20, 21. John xix. xx. 10—15. Mat. ii. 1—10. Mark xv. 43. Luke ii. 25—38. John i. 19, 45.

3. *That the Messiah should be God and man together.*

Ps. ii. 7, cx. 1. Isaiah ix. 6. Micah v. 2.	Heb. i. 8. Mat. xxii. 42—45. 1 Cor. xv. 25. Heb. i. 13. Mat. i. 23. John i. 1—14. Rom. ix. 5. Col. ii. 9. 1 John v. 20.

4. *From whom he was to be descended.*

From the first woman, Gen. iii. 15; from Abraham, Gen. xii. 3, xviii. 18; from Isaac, Gen. xxvi. 4; Jacob, Gen. xxviii. 14; Judah, Gen. xlix. 10; Jesse, Isa. xi. 1; David, Psa. cxxxii. 11, lxxxix. 4, 27; Isa. vii. 13, 14, ix. 7; Jer. xxiii. 5, xxxiii. 20, 21.	Gal. iv. 4. Acts iii. 25. Mat. i. 1. Heb. vii. 14. Rom. xv. 12. John vii. 42. Acts ii. 30; xiii. 23. Luke i. 32.

5. *That the Messiah should be born of a Virgin.*

Isa. vii. 14. Jer. xxxi. 22.	Matt. i. 24, 25. Luke i. 26—35. Matt. i. 22, 23.

6. *Where the Messiah was to be born.*

Micah v. 2.	Luke ii. 4—6, 10, 11, 15. Matt. ii. 1, 4—6, 8, 11. John vii. 42.

7. *That a Prophet in the spirit and power of Elias or Elijah should be the Messiah's forerunner.*

Mal. iii. 1. Isa. xl. 3. Luke i. 17.	Matt. iii. 1—3; xi. 14, Luke vii. 27, 28.

8. *That the Messiah was to be a Prophet.*

Deut. xviii. 15, 18.	John iv. 19; ix. 17. Matt. xxi. 46. Mark vi. 15. Luke vii. 16. John vi. 14; vii. 40. Luke xxiv. 19. Matt. xxi. 11.

9. *That he should begin to preach in Galilee.*

Isa. ix. 1, 2.	Matt. iv. 12—17. Luke iv. 14, 15.

10. *That he should confirm his Doctrine by Miracles.*

Isa. xxxv. 5, 6; xlii. 7; xxxii. 3, 4; xxix. 18.	Matt. xi. 4, 5. Luke vii. 21. Matt. iv. 23, 24; xv. 30, 31. Acts ii. 22, and many other passages.

11. *In what manner he should enter Jerusalem.*

Zech. ix. 9.	Matt. xxi. 4, 5, 7, 10.

12. *That the Messiah should be poor and despised, and that he should be betrayed and sold by one of his disciples for thirty pieces of silver, with which the potter's field should be purchased.*

Isa. liii. 3. Ps. xli. 9; lv. 12—14. Zech. xi. 12, 13.	Luke ix. 58. 2 Cor. viii. 9. John xi. 35. Luke xxii. 3, 4. Matt. xxvi. 14; xxvii. 3—10.

13. *That the Messiah should suffer pain and death for the sins of the world.*

Ps. xxii. 14, 15. Isa. i. 6; liii. 5, 8, 12.	John xix. 1, 2. Matt. xxvii. 29—31. Mark xv. 19, 25. 1 Pet. ii. 23, 24.

14. *That the Messiah should be cruelly mocked and derided.*

Ps. xxii. 7, 8; 12, 13.	Matt. xxvii. 39—44. Mark xv. 31, 32. Luke xxiii. 35, 36.

15. *That vinegar and gall should be offered to the Messiah on the cross, and lots cast for his vesture.*

Ps. lxix. 21 xxii. 18.	John xix. 29. Matt. xxvii. 34, 35. Mark xv. 36. John xix. 23, 24.

16. *That not a bone of him should be broken, but that his side should be pierced.*

Ps. xxxiv. 20. Zech. xii. 10.	John xix. 32—34.

17. *That the Messiah should die with malefactors, but be buried honourably.*

PROPHECY.	FULFILMENT.
Isa. liii. 9, 12.	Matt. xxvii. 38, 57—60.

18. *That the Messiah should rise from the dead, and ascend into Heaven.*

Ps. xvi. 9, 10. Isa. liii. 10; lxviii. 18.	Acts ii. 32, 33; xiii. 35, 37. Matt. xxviii. 5, 6. Luke xxiv. 5, 6. 1 Cor. xv. 4.

19. *That the Messiah should send the Holy Ghost the Comforter.*

Ps. lxviii. 18. Joel ii. 28.	Acts ii. 1—4, 16—21; iv. 31; viii. 17; x. 44; xi. 15.

II.

PROPHECIES RELATING TO THE OFFICES OF THE MESSIAH.

1. *That the Messiah was to be a Prophet and Lawgiver like unto Moses, but superior to him; who should change the law of Moses into a new and more perfect law, common to both Jews and Gentiles, which should last for ever.*

Deut. xviii. 15, 18, 19; also, Acts iii. 22; vii. 37.	John vi. 14. Luke xxiv. 19. Heb. iii. 5, 6; vii. 18, 19. Isa. ii. 3. Matt. xxviii. 19, 20. Heb. ii. 20; ix. 24. John xiv. ii. 3. 1 John ii. 1. Heb. vii. 25. John i. 45.

2. *That the Messiah was to be a Teacher.*

Isa. lxi. 1; liv. 13, l. 4. Ps. lxxvii. 2.	Mark i. 14. Luke viii. 1. Mark vi. 6. Luke iv. 15, 44. Matt. v. 1, 2; xiii. 34. Mark iv. 33. John iii. 2; i. 49.

3. *That the Messiah was to instruct and enlighten men.*

Isa. ix. 2.	John xii. 46; viii. 12; ix. 5. Luke ii. 32. John i. 4, 5. Acts xxvi. 18. Ephes. v. 8.

4. *That the Messiah was to be the Christ or anointed of God.*

Isa. lx. i. Dan. ix. 24, 25. Ps. cxxxii. 17; lxxxix. 20, 51; ii. 2.	John iv. 25, 42; vi. 69; xi. 27. Matt. xvi. 16; xxvi. 63, 64. Mark xiv. 61, 62. Acts xviii. 28.

5. *That the Messiah was to be a Priest.*

Ps. cx. 4 (cited in Heb. v. 6; vii. 21.) Zech. vi. 13.	Heb. iv. 14; viii. 1; iii. 1; x. 21; ii. 17; vii. 24.

6. *The Messiah was, by the offering of himself as a sacrifice for sin, to make an end of sin; to make reconciliation for iniquity; to make men holy; and to destroy the power of the Devil.*

Isa. liii. 6, 10, 12. Dan. ix. 24. Gen. iii. 16.	Eph. v. 2. 2 Cor. v. 21. Rom. viii. 3. 1 John ii. 2. Heb. ix. 14. 1 Pet. i. 19; iii. 18. Heb. x. 12; ix. 12; vii. 27; ix. 25, 26. John i. 29. Acts v. 5. 1 John i. 7. Rom. v. 10. 2 Cor. v. 18. Col. i. 20. Heb. v. 8, 9. 2 Cor. v. 15. Rom. vi. 10—12. 1 Thes. v. 10. 1 Pet. ii. 24. Tit. ii. 14. 1 Cor. vi. 20. 1 Pet. iv. 1, 2.

7. *The Messiah was to be a Saviour.*

Isa. lix. 20; lxxii. 11.	1 John iv. 14. Luke ii. 11. Matt. i. 21. Acts xiii. 26. John iv. 42. Acts v. 31. 2 Pet. ii. 20; iii. 18. Tit. iii. 6. 2 Pet. i. 1. Phil. iii. 20. Tit. ii. 18.

8. *The Saviour was to be a Mediator.*

Ps. cx. 1. Dan. ix. 17, 19. Isa. viii. 14. Ps. lxxx. 17.	John xiv. 6. 1 Tim. ii. 5. Heb. xii. 24. Eph. ii. 13, 18. Heb. vii. 22; viii. 6; ix. 15. John xv. 16; xvi. 23, 24; xiv. 14.

9. *The Messiah was to be an Intercessor.*

PROPHECY.	FULFILMENT.
Isa. liii. 12.	Luke xxiii. 34; xxii. 32. John xvii. Heb. ix. 24. 1 John ii. 1. Rom. viii. 34. Heb. vii. 25.

10. *Messiah was to be a Shepherd.*

Isa. xl. 11. Ezek. xxxiv. 23; xxxvii. 24.	John x. 11, 14. Heb. xiii. 20. 1 Pet. ii. 25; v. 2, 4.

11. *Messiah was to be a King.*

Ps. ii. 6; cxxxii. 11. Isa. ix. 6; lv. 4. Zec. vi. 13. Jer. xxiii. 5, 6. Isa. xxxii. 1. Ezek. xxxvii. 24, 25; xxxiv. 23, 24. Jer. xxx. 9. Hos. iii. 5. Zech. ix. 9. Mic. v. 2.	Matt, ii. 2, 6; xxi. 5. John xii. 15. Luke xix. 38; i. 32, 33. John i. 49; xviii. 33, 36, 37. Matt. xxvii. 11. Acts v. 31.

12. *Messiah as a King was to be above all others, and Head of his Church.*

Ps. lxxxix. 27, 36. Dan. vii. 13, 14, 27; ii. 44.	Rev. i. v. 1 Tim. vi. 15. Rev. xvii. 14; xix. 16; Eph. i. 21—23. Phil. ii. 9. Col. i. 18. Eph. iv. 15, 16. 1 Cor. xii. 27.

13. *Messiah the King was to be exalted more particularly after his sufferings and resurrection.*

Ps. ii. 6, 8; viii. 5. Isa. liii. 10, 12.	1 Pet. i. 11. Luke xxiv. 26. John xvii. 1. Rom. i. 4. 1 Pet. i. 21; iii. 22. Acts ii. 32, 33. Phil. ii. 8—10. Heb. ii. 9; xii. 2.

14. *That there is salvation only in Christ.*

Isa. xlv. 21. Zec. xiii. 1. Mal. iv. 2. Isa. liii. 11; lix. 20 (see also Rom. xi. 26). Ps. cxxxviii. 22. Isa. xxviii. 16. Mark xii. 10.	John iii. 16. 1 Thess. v. 9. John xvii. 3. Luke xxiv. 47. Acts x. 43; xiii. 38, 39; iv. 11, 12.

15. *Of the necessity of believing in Christ, and the danger of rejecting him.*

Deut. xviii. 15, 19 (see Acts iii. 23. Num. xv. 30, 31. Ps. ii. 12.	John iii. 18. Heb. ii. 3; x. 26—29. 2 Thess. i. 7, 8.

NEW TESTAMENT PREDICTIONS, WITH THEIR FULFILMENT.

I.

PREDICTION THAT THEY WOULD FIND THINGS ACCORDING TO HIS WORD.

Matt. xxi. 1—3. Mark xi. 2. Luke xix. 30, 31. Mark xiv. 13—15. Matt. xxvi, 18.	Mark xi. 4—6. Luke xix. 32; xxii. Mark xiv. 16.

II.

PREDICTIONS OF JESUS CHRIST, RELATIVE TO HIS SUFFERINGS, DEATH, RESURRECTION, AND ASCENSION.

1. *That he was to be betrayed by one of his disciples, Judas.*

John vi. 70, 71. Matt. xx. 18; xvii. 22. Mark x. 33. Luke ix. 44. Matt, xxvi. 2. John xiii. 10, 11, 18; xvii. 12. Mark xiv. 18. Matt. xxvi. 21. John xiii. 21, 26. Luke xxii. 21. Mark xiv. 20, 42. Matt. xxvi. 46.	Matt. xxvi. 14—16. Mark xiv. 10. Luke xxii. 34. John xiii. 2. Matt. xxvi. 47, 49.

2. *That his other disciples would forsake him.*

Mark xiv. 27. Matt. xxvi. 31. John xvi. 32; xviii. 8, 9.	Matt, xxvi. 56. Mark xiv. 50.

3. *That Peter would deny him.*

Luke xxii. 31—34. John xiii. 38. Matt. xxvi. 34. Mark xiv. 30.	Luke xxii. 60—62. Matt. xxvi. 75. John xviii. 27. Mark xiv. 72.

4. *That he should suffer.*

PROPHECY.	FULFILMENT.
Matt. xvi. 21. Mark viii. 31. Luke ix. 22. Mark ix. 31. Matt. xvii. 22, 23. Mark x. 33, 34. Matt. xx. 18, 19. Luke xviii. 31—33.	John xi. 53. Matt. xxvi. 4. Mark xiv. 1. Luke xxii. 2. Matt. xxvi. 66. Mark xiv. 64. Luke xxii. 71. Matt. xxvii. 26. Luke xxiii. 24. John xix. 16, 18. Matt. xxvii. 35. Luke xxiii. 33; xxiv. 6, 7, 26, 46. Acts ii. 23; xiii. 27; xvii. 3. Gal. iii. 1.

5. *That he should suffer in Jerusalem.*

Matt. xvi. 21. Luke ix. 31; xiii. 31, 33; xviii. 31. Matt. xx. 18.	Luke xxiv. 18. Matt. xxvii. Mark xv. Luke xxiii. John xix. Acts xiii. 27. Heb. xiii. 12.

6. *That he should suffer by the Chief Priest.*

Matt. xvi. 21. Mark viii. 31. Luke ix. 22. Matt. xvii. 12. Mark x. 33.	Matt. xxvi. 3, 4. John xi. 53; xviii. 13, 24. Matt. xxvi. 57, 65, 66. Mark xiv. 63. Matt. xxvii. 20. Luke xxiii. 13, 18; xxiv. 20. Acts xiii. 28.

7. *That he should suffer by the Gentiles.*

Luke xviii. 31, 32. Mark x. 33. Matt. xx. 18, 19.	Acts xiii. 28. Matt. xxvii. 1. Mark xv. 1. John xviii. 31, 32. Mark xv. 15. Luke xxiii. 24. Acts iv. 27.

8. *That he should be mocked.*

Mark ix. 12. Luke xvii. 32. Mark x. 34.	Matt. xxvi. 67, 68. Mark xiv. 65. Luke xxiii. 11. Mark xv. 17—19. Matt. xxvii. 29. John xix. 2. Mark xv. 29—32.

9. *Jesus foretold that he should be crucified.*

John iii. 14; xii. 32; viii. 28. Matt. xx. 19.	Matt. xxvii. 31. John xix. 16. Luke xxiii. 33. Mark xv. 24, 25. Luke xxiv. 6, 7, 20. Acts ii. 23; iv. 10. 1 Cor. i. 23. Gal. iii. 1.

10. *Jesus Christ foretold his resurrection.*

John ii. 19, 21; x. 17. Mark x. 34; viii. 31. Luke ix. 22. Matt. xxvii. 62, 63.	Luke xxiv. 5, 6—15. Matt. xxviii. 6, 9, 11. Luke xxiv. 15, 23, 34, 36. John xx. 14, 19, 27; xxi. 4. Acts i. 3; x. 40, 41; ii. 32; iv. 33. 1 Cor. xv. 20. Acts xvii. 3; xxvi. 23. Rom. i. 4.

11. *Jesus Christ foretold that he would appear again to his disciples.*

John xvi. 16, 22. Matt. xxvi. 32. Mark xiv. 28. Matt. xxviii. 10. Mark xvi. 7.	Mark xvi. 14. John xx. 19. Luke xxiv. 36. Matt. xxviii. 16, 17. John xxi. 1. 1 Cor. xv. 5, 6.

12. *Jesus Christ foretold his ascension into heaven.*

John vi. 62; xvi. 28; xx. 17; vii. 33; xiv. 19; xvii. 13.	Mark xvi. 19. Luke xxiv. 51. Acts i. 9, 10. Eph. iv. 10. 1 Pet. iii. 22. Heb. ix. 24; iv. 14; vi. 20. 1 Tim. iii. 16.

13. *Jesus Christ foretold the descent of the Holy Ghost after his ascension.*

Matt. x. 20. Luke xi. 13; xii. 12. John vii. 39; xiv. 16, 17, 26; xv. 26; xvi. 7—15; xx. 22. Luke xxiv. 49. Acts i. 8.	Acts ii. 1—4, 33; iv. 8. 31; v. 31, 32; vii. 55; viii. 15—17; ix. 17; x. 44; xiii. 9; xv. 8, 28; xix. 6; xx. 22, 23, 28; xxi. 4, 11. Rom. viii. throughout; xv. 13. 1 Cor. ii. 10—16; iii. 16, 17; vi. 11, 19; xii. 3—13. 2 Cor. v. 5. Gal. iii. 3; v. 16—18, 22—25. Eph. ii. 18, 22; iv. 4, 30. 1 Thess. i. 5, 6. 1 Tim. iv. 1. 2 Tim. i. 14. Titus iii. 5, 6. Heb. vi. 4. Rev. i. 10; ii. 7; xvi. 13; xxii. 17.

To this prophetical scheme, the masterly comment of the Rev. W. Lancaster ("Harmony of the Law and Gospel." p. 326) may with much propriety be appended. "Redemption is the great centre-point of scriptural instruction; every other divine ordinance either meets in this point, or diverges from it. The doctrine of the Atonement is the great and leading doctrine of the Bible from beginning to end. This was darkly intimated to fallen man before he was expelled from the abode of innocence and bliss. The sacrifices offered by the faithful immediately after the fall, were in unison with this intimation. Abraham rejoiced in it, when he saw the day of Christ afar off. The bloody ordinances of the Levitical law shadowed out the same truth in emblem and mystery. The sweet psalmist of Israel spoke a congenial language when he painted the sufferings of Him who was to be the Saviour of Men. In strains of mingled sadness and triumph, the prophetic son announced the Man of Sorrows and acquainted with grief; and it bore, also, in different ages of the Jewish church a varied yet harmonious testimony to the great Personage in whom truth was substantially verified. The latest prophet under the law, and the immediate harbinger of the Messiah, proclaims the same truth, when he announces Christ as the Lamb of God which taketh away the sin of the world. Christ himself declares the doctrine he verifies, and bears witness to it in his death. The apostles proclaim our Redeemer as him whom God hath set forth to be a sacrifice and propitiation for the sins of the whole world. The holy martyrs under the agonies of death testify the same; nor does the attestation stop here. After the Church militant hath maintained it throughout every stage of its warfare, the Church triumphant takes up the heavenly theme, resounding it in hymns of exaltation and praise to the end of time. It was first heard in the terrestrial Eden, and it ceases not to be heard in the songs of the blessed Spirits who inhabit the celestial Paradise."

Note 10, Page 462, Column 2.

purer than the light of light,
Of all Transcendencies the sum and soul!

On the same principle that prophecy, when proved by the admissions of Volney, and similar writers of the French school, affects the mind with a more convincing power than when illustrated by orthodox divines, the testimony of Rousseau to the glorious perfection of Christ's character is extremely valuable. It forms one of his most eloquent passages, and cannot be deemed intrusive on the present occasion.

"The majesty of the Scriptures strikes me with admiration, as the purity of the Gospel has its influence on my heart. Peruse the works of our philosophers, with all their pomp of diction; how mean, how contemptible are they when compared with the Scripture! Is it possible that a book, at once so simple and sublime, should merely be the work of man? What prepossession, what blindness must it be to compare the son of Sophroniscus to the Son of Mary! What an infinite disproportion is there between them! Socrates, dying without pain or ignominy, easily supported his character to the last: and if his death, however easy, had not crowned his life, it might have been doubted whether Socrates, with all his wisdom, was anything more than a vain sophist. He invented, it is said, the theory of morals. Others, however, had before put them in practice; he had, therefore, only to say what they had done, and to reduce their examples to precept. But where could Jesus learn, among his competitors, that pure and sublime morality of which he only has given us both precept and example? The death of Socrates, peaceably philosophising with his friends, appears the most agreeable that could be wished for; that of Jesus, expiring in the midst of agonising pains, abused, insulted, and accused by a whole nation, is the most horrible that could be feared. Socrates, in receiving the cup of poison, blessed the weeping executioner who administered it; but Jesus, in the midst of excruciating tortures, prayed for his merciless tormentors. Yes, if the life and death of Socrates were those of a sage, the life and death of Jesus were those of a God."—*Emil.*, vol. ii. p. 215.

The following testimony of Publius Lentulus (who was Governor of Judea during the period of Christ's ministry), as transmitted by him to the Roman senate, though deemed spurious by many writers, is too interesting to be omitted:—

"There appeared in these our days a man of great virtue, named Jesus Christ, yet living amongst us, and of the Gentiles is accepted as a Prophet of the Truth, but by his own disciples called the Son of God. He raiseth the dead and cureth all manner of diseases. A man of stature somewhat tall and comely, and a very reverend countenance, such as beholders may may both love and fear.* His hair is of the colour of

* "Irenæus, who was born as early as the year 130, says, that the Carpocratians exhibited both statues and pictures of our Saviour, and that Pilate had caused a likeness to be painted of him. Tertullian speaks of the intention of Tiberius to assign a place to our Saviour among the deities of Rome, as a thing publicly and commonly known. Eusebius relates, that there was, in his time, in the city of Cæsarea Philippi, a group of bronze figures, representing Christ and the woman whom he had cured, and proceeds,—'We are not to be surprised that the Gentiles should raise a monument to those who were cured by our Saviour;' and further, 'that he had seen pictures of the apostles, as of St. Peter and St. Paul, and of Christ himself, kept and preserved; for it was an ancient custom among the heathens,' he continues, 'to honour those after this manner who had benefited their country.' Zozomen, too, reports that Julian, who lived at the same time, took down the statue of Christ, to withdraw the people from idolatry, and in order to substitute his own. It is not essential to my purpose that these details should be literally true; but we cannot deny the existence of what men like these declare that they have seen. The same gratitude and veneration which prompted the early Christians to preserve a resemblance of their Lord would operate equally in making them hand down his features to posterity. The impulse is natural, and has been observed from remote antiquity; and the heads of Socrates and Plato, for instance, are as well known to us now, as they were to their contemporaries. If, therefore, we can produce a portrait of Christ of the time of Zozomen, the latest of the four writers above quoted, may we not fairly conclude it to be a faithful resemblance? One of these was, within these few years, to be seen in the Basilica of St. Paul, in the Via Ostinese, before that structure was destroyed by fire. The situation of it was over the Arcus Triumphalis; and it possessed traits of benign majesty beyond what we observe in common mortals. It was executed in mosaic, an art practised through every period at Rome, and which is almost as indestructible as the building it adorned. The date of the edifice was verified by an inscription, by which we learn that it was dedicated to Placidia, the mother of Valentinian the Third, A.D. 441. When at Rome, I was very careful in collecting the opinions of persons best qualified to judge concerning this portrait. I have viewed it with our own Flaxman—'himself a host;' and every one whom I consulted concurred in the belief of its being a genuine remain. A question will instantly suggest itself to the reader, 'Why was not the portrait

a filbert full ripe, and plain almost down to his ears, but from his ears downwards somewhat curled, more orient in colour, and waving about his shoulders. In the midst of his head goeth a seam or partition of his hair, after the manner of the Nazarites: his forehead very plain and smooth; his face without spot or wrinkle, beautified with comely red; his nose and mouth so formed as nothing can be reprehended; his beard somewhat thick, agreeable in colour to the hair of his head, not of any great length, but full in the midst; of an innocent, mature look; his eyes, grey, clear, and quick. In reproving, he is terrible; in admonishing, courteous and fair spoken; pleasant in speech, mixed with gravity. It cannot be remembered that any have seen him laugh, but many have seen him weep; of proportion of body well shaped and straight; his hands and arms right delectable to behold; in speaking, very temperate, modest, and wise. A man, for singular beauty, surpassing the children of men."

---

of Christ uniformly continued among the faithful, with the same accuracy as those of Socrates and Plato?' One reason might be found in the wide diffusion of the Christian religion through so many countries of different manners, habits, and ideas; each of whom would naturally represent the countenance of the Redeemer under the similitude most congenial to their own minds and feelings, although the true effigy might still be preserved in the capital of the western church, such as we presume to be the portrait once existing in the church of St. Paul. Another cause might be, that in the early periods of the Christian faith, the cross was represented simply as it was in imagination seen by Constantine. This sacred symbol was at times rendered significant by the accompaniment of a gemmed or laurelled crown, held over it by a hand from the clouds with A and Ω. The body of Christ was not represented on the cross till the seventh century. It was first so admitted in the western church, with the head bowed down; whereas inthe eastern (though not without some exceptions) the face was lifted up. In the latter, the effigy of Christ is first seen on a Byzantine coin, struck in the reign of Justinian the Second, 685—695; previous to which time we find only crosses and anagrams. The Greeks, indeed, reluctantly yielded to an innovation which they deemed degrading to the Divine character, and rarely, if ever, exposed the Saviour of mankind (and how barbarous the exposure!) to open view, nailed to the cross, crowned with thorns, exhausted with suffering, and devoid of grace and majesty. To the Latins, among whom the rudiments of ancient art are not so evident as among the Greeks, and whose ideas were therefore more on a level with common life, this mournful character of the 'Man of Sorrows' was more congenial. Anxious to render the subject in the highest degree affecting, and to bring it home to the feelings of every one, under national configuration, attempts to be pathetic degenerated into low life; and a system of worship was inculcated which addressed itself more to the passions than to the understanding of its votaries. In the aspect of the Author of my redemption, let me not contemplate a mortal sinking under infirmities like those to which I feel myself exposed, but a being who animates me with hope, and inspires me with a confidence which enables me to exult in the consciousness that 'my Redeemer liveth!'"—Gunn's *Cartonensia.*

Note 11, Page 463, Column 1.

holier than our holiest awe
Can worship,—imaged only in, I AM!

Nothing is, in fact, more difficult, for such a creature as man, surrounded as he is by gross material objects, and necessarily occupied in worldly pursuits, than to lift up his thoughts and affections to God. A being whose nature is so incomprehensible that our knowledge of him is chiefly negative,—of whom we know not so much what he is as what he is not,—it is difficult even to make a steady object of thought. Now we believe that God is a spirit; but we have a very faint notion of the nature of a spirit, except that it is not a body; God is eternal; but we are bewildered with the very idea of eternity, of which we only know that it is without beginning and without end: we say, that the divine attributes are infinite; i. e., not bounded, unlimited. And even where our knowledge of God extends beyond mere negatives, we cannot but perceive, on attentive reflection, that the attributes assigned to the Deity must in reality be such in Him, as the ordinary sense of those same terms, when applied to men, can but very faintly shadow out.—Archbishop Whately *on Declaration of God in his Son*, pp. 130, 131.

Note 12, Page 463, Column 1.

all that charms
Regenerate heart, to thine unspotted truth
May plead for sanction.

We may consider that our Lord, as partaker of our nature, and in all things (bating sin) like unto us, had a natural human will, attended with senses, appetites, and affections, apt from objects incident to receive congruous impressions of pleasure and pain; so that whatever is innocently grateful and pleasant to us, that he relished with delight, and thence did incline to embrace; whatever is distasteful and afflictive to us, that he resented with grief, and thence was moved to eschew. To this, probably, he was liable in a degree beyond our ordinary rate; for that in him nature was most perfect, his complexion very delicate, his temper exquisitely sound and fine.—Barrow's *Works*, vol. ii. p. 308.

Note 13, Page 463, Column 1.

Surrenders meekly to the central Guide
Of hope and action, by a God empower'd.

Jeremy Taylor, "the Shakspeare of divines," thus illustrates the mysterious operations of the Holy Spirit over the human heart.—Vide *Sermon preached to the University of Dublin*:—

"God, who designed the heavens to be the causes and changes of all motions here below, hath placed his angels in their houses of light, and given to every one of his appointed officers a portion of that fiery matter to circum-agitate and roll; and now the wonder ceases: for if it be inquired why this part of the fire runs eastwards, and the other to the south, they being both indifferent to either, it is because an angel of God sits in the centre: and so it is in the understandings of men; when they all receive the same notions, and are taught by the same master, and give full consent to all the propositions, and can, of themselves, have nothing to distinguish them in the events, it is because God hath sent his Divine Spirit, and kindles a new fire, and creates a braver capacity, and applies the actives to the passives, and blesses their operation. For there is in the heart of man such a dead sea, and an indisposition to holy flame, like as in the cold rivers in the north, so as the fire will not burn them, and the sun itself will never warm them, till God's Holy Spirit does, from the Temple of the New Jerusalem, bring a holy flame, and make it shine and burn."

BOOK II.

Note 14, Page 464, Column 1.

The faint reflections of a vast Unseen!

If Phidias could so contrive a piece of his own work as in it to preserve the memory of himself, never to be obliterated without the destruction of the work, well may we read the Great Architect of the World in the works of his own hands, and by the existence of one thing demonstrate the First Cause of all things. * * * No age so distant, no country so remote, no people so barbarous, but gives a sufficient testimony to this truth. When the Roman eagle flew over most parts of the habitable world, they met with atheism nowhere; but rather by their miscellaneous deities at Rome, which grew together with their victories, showed no nation was without its God.—PEARSON, fol. 10th edit., pp. 19—21.

One of the finest thinkers of modern times (the author of "Natural History of Enthusiasm"), in alluding to the revelations of a Deity, as exhibited by the material universe, in his last work, presents us with a noble passage:—"The nocturnal heavens at once symbolise and demonstrate the concealed existence and attributes of God, just as the presence and symmetry of a man are made known to a distant spectator, when the shadow of his person, in sharp outline, falls upon a brightly illuminated surface: we see not indeed the man, nor, in strictness of argument, is it more than his exterior form of which we have direct evidence: nevertheless we do not scruple to fill up in idea what is wanting in formal proof; and we think almost as distinctly of the person, as if he stood, without a screen, fronting us in the blaze of light. Thus is it that, both in the vastness and in the richness of the visible universe, the invisible God is adumbrated. If the eye be but clear, we can never gaze upon the expanse of stars without descrying, as it were, filling all the bright abyss of worlds, the great lines, or contour, of the Supreme Majesty."—*Saturday Evening*, p. 171.

Note 15, Page 466, Column 1.

. . . . how Nature visioneth the plan
That God himself descended to reveal.

The whole analogy of nature removes all imagined presumption against the general notion of a "Mediator between God and man;" for we find all living creatures are brought into the world, and their life in infancy is preserved by the instrumentality of others; and every satisfaction of it, somehow or other, is bestowed by the like means. So that the invisible government which God exercises over the world is by the instrumentality and mediation of others. And how far his invisible be, or be not so, it is impossible to determine at all by reason. And the supposition that part of it is so, appears, to say the least, altogether as credible as the contrary. There is, then, no sort of objection, from the light of nature, against the notion of a Mediator between God and man considered as a doctrine of Christianity, or as an appointment in this dispensation; since we find by experience that God does appoint mediators to be the instrument of good and evil to us, the instruments of his justice and mercy.—BUTLER'S *Anal.*, part. ii. p. 176.

Note 16, Page 466, Column 1.

Thus Plato, in his pure ambition, nursed
A glorious longing for supremer Mind.

"Socrates, in a conversation with his friends, from the present visibly perverted state of the world, infers the apparent necessity of a Divine mediator and restorer, and from hence that we have reason to hope for and expect one. And on another occasion, he says something very remarkable, and then thought very mysterious, concerning a Divine Person to be sent from heaven, to instruct mankind and restore them to virtue and happiness. And Plato, either in his own person or in that of Socrates, makes mention of the divine *Logos* as of a personal existence, and seems to have had an idea of his distinct operation in the economy of the world. And when Orpheus (if he is really the author of the fragments that are ascribed to him), admonishes the person to whom he addreses himself, 'that the thing which he had been revolving in his mind should not rob him of his much-desired futurity,' and directs him to 'look to the Divine *Logos*, and adhere to that;'* whether by the word (*Logos*) he means a person, or a precept, law, or instruction, it is clear that he recognises some Divine aid to which men might have recourse when human reason fails them. And whether he derived it from the writings of Moses, of which he certainly had some knowledge,† or from a still more ancient source, he seems to have had a clear persuasion of the Deity's being to appear personally on earth at a certain period;‡ as also an idea of the Only-begotten, who alone was capable of beholding the Divinity, and of personal approach unto him. And if his describing him as of Chaldean extraction§ refers to the promise

---

* ——— ἐξερέω γαρ ἀληθέα; μηδε σε τα πρὶν
'Εν στήθεσσι φανενται φίλης αἰῶνος ἀμέρση.
Εις δὲ λόγον θεῖον βλέψας, τούτῳ προσέδρευε.[1]

† 'Ως λογος αρχαιων ὡς ὑδρογενὴς[2] διέταξεν,
'Εκ θέοθεν γνώμαισι λαβων κατὰ δίπλακα θεσμόν.[3]

‡ Ουδὲ τις ἔσθ' ἕτερος· συ δὲ κενρεα παντ' ἐσορήσαις ιων
Αἴ κεν ἴδης αὐτον πριν δὴ ποτε δεῦρ ἐπι γαιάν.[4]

§ Οὐ γάρ κέν τις ἴδοι θνητων μεροπων κραίνοντα,
Ει μη μουνογενης τις ἀπορρωξ φύλου ἄνωθεν
Χαλδαιων.[5]

---

[1] I will declare truth. Neither shall those things which you have been considering in your mind rob you of desired futurity; but looking to the Divine word (Logos), hold to that.

[2] And she called his name Moses: And she said, because I drew him out of the water.—*Exod.* ii. 10.

[3] As the doctrine of the ancients, as he that rose from the water hath taught: who divinely received precepts according to a twofold law.

[4] Neither is there any beside him. But you would clearly discern all this, could you see him before the time when he shall at last appear here on the earth.

[5] None can see the Supreme Ruler of mortals except a certain Only-begotten, whose descent is from an ancient race of the Chaldeans.

made to Abraham, he must have had a much clearer conception of that promise than ever the Jews themselves had."

Note 17, Page 466, Column 2.

And stubborn ages, as they swept along,
But mock'd her impotence with blind misrule,
Of creed, or crime begot.

"Let us turn our eyes to those remote regions of the globe to which this supernatural assistance has never yet extended, and we shall there see men endued with sense and reason not inferior to our own, so far from being capable of forming systems of religion and morality, that they are at this day totally unable to make a nail or a hatchet! These have uniformly flowed from that great fountain of divine communication opened in the last, in the earliest ages, and hence been gradually diffused in salubrious streams throughout the various regions of the earth. And as Reason in her natural state is thus incapable of making any progress in knowledge; so when furnished with materials by supernatural aid, if left to the guidance of her own wild imagination, she falls into more numerous and gross errors than her own native ignorance could ever have suggested. There is then no absurdity which she is not ready to adopt: she has persuaded some that there is no God: others that there can be no future state: she has taught some that there is no difference between vice and virtue, and that to cut a man's throat and to relieve his necessities are equally meritorious; she has convinced many that they have no free-will in opposition to their own experience; some that there can be no such thing as soul or spirit, contrary to their own perceptions; and others, no such thing as matter or body, in contradiction to their senses. By analyzing all things, she can show there is nothing in anything; by perpetual shifting, she can reduce all things to the dust of scepticism, and by returning to first principles, prove to the satisfaction of her followers, that there are no principles at all."—JENYN'S *View*, &c.

Note 18, Page 467, Column 1.

and ritual pomp
Of ark and fane and sacrificial blood,
The chosen People.

"A splendid ceremonial dazzled their senses, perpetual sacrifices enlivened their faith, frequent commemorative festivals not only let loose their gay and joyous spirits, but reminded them of all the surprising and marvellous events of their national history. The tabernacles preserve the form of the more solid and gigantic structures of Egypt; their priesthood were attired in dresses as costly, in many respects similar; their oblations were as frequent;—the exclusions of daylight probably originated in subterranean temples, hewn out of the solid rock, like those of Ipsambul, and the cave-temples of India: the use of incense seems to have been common in every kind of religious worship."—MILMAN.

Note 19, Page 468, Column 2.

All things have glided into beauteous change.

Those who, from doubt or indifference, are apt to regard the efforts of Missionaries as fruitless and vain, will do well to peruse the highly interesting volumes of Mr. W. Ellis, Missionary, entitled "Polynesian Researches." Speaking of converted isles, he remarks, "Aged chiefs and priests, and hardy warriors, with their spelling-books in their hands, might be seen sitting hour after hour on the benches in the schools, by the side, perhaps, of some smiling little boy or girl, by whom they were now thankful to be taught the use of letters. Others might be seen pulling down the houses of their idols, and erecting temples for the Prince of Peace. Their sabbaths must have presented spectacles on which angels might look down with joy. Crowds who had never before attended any worship but that of their demon-gods, might now be seen repairing to their rustic and lowly temple erected for Jehovah's praise; amidst their throng, mothers, wives, sisters, and daughters, who were never before allowed to join the other sex in any act of worship. Few remained behind; all the inhabitants of the district or village who were able, attended public worship."—vol. i. pp. 262, 3.

Note 20, Page 469, Column 1.

as the gorgeous cloud,
E'en as it dazzles, is but dying air!

There is a severe truth in a remark of Wollaston on the unreality of human fame. "A man is not known ever the more to posterity, because his name is transmitted to them; he does not live because his name does. When it is said Julius Cæsar subdued Gaul, beat Pompey, changed the Roman commonwealth into a monarchy, &c., it is the same thing as to say, the conqueror of Pompey was Cæsar; that is, Cæsar and the conqueror of Pompey are the same thing; and Cæsar is as much known by one distinction as the other. The amount then is only this: that the conqueror of Pompey conquered Pompey; or, somebody conquered Pompey. Such a poor business is this boasted immortality; and such as has been here described is the thing called glory among us."—*Relig. of Nat. Del.*

In consolatory opposition to this, may be added the sentiments of the elegant and philosophic Gray:—"One principal character of vice in the present age is the contempt of fame. Many are the uses of good fame to a generous mind: it extends our existence and example into future ages; continues and propagates virtue, which otherwise would be as short-lived as our frame; and prevents the prevalence of vice in a generation more corrupt even than our own."*

Note 21, Page 469, Column 2.

And if there be, as saintly minds allow,
Some god-like moment, when pure Spirits walk
This lower world.

The idea of some mystic communion between the living and the dead has been a beautiful source of

* The above passage is taken from the notes which Gray had collected for a poem entitled "The Alliance of Education and Government." The fragment we possess vies with anything the poet has written. In what ode has he surpassed, or equalled, the following image?—

"Where Nile redundant o'er the summer bed
From his broad bosom life and verdure flings,
And broods o'er Egypt with his watery wings."

Of this poem well might Gibbon exclaim—"Why did not Mr. Gray apply the powers of his genius to finish the philosophic poem, of which he has left us such an exquisite specimen?"—*Decline and Fall*, vol. ii. p. 248.

religious consolation in all ages. Klopstock was constantly dwelling on this. In one of his letters to his departed wife (Meta), he remarks:

"All the ideas that man can form of the ways of Providence, and of the employment of angels and of spirits, must ever fall short of reality; but still it is right to think of them. What can have a more exalting influence on the earthly life, than in these first days of our existence to make ourselves conversant with the lives of the blessed, with the happy spirits whose society we shall hereafter enjoy? We should accustom ourselves to consider the spirits of heaven always around us; observing all our steps, and witnessing our most secret actions. Whoever has become familiar with these ideas, will find the most solitary place peopled with the best society."

Of a mind breathing such elevated sentiments, well may his excellent wife say—"It will be a delightful occupation for me to make you more acquainted with my husband's poem. Nobody can do it better than I, being the person who knows the most of that which is not published, being always present at the birth of the young verses, which begin by fragments here and there of a subject of which his soul is just then filled. He has many great fragments of the whole work ready. You may think that persons who love as we do, have no need of two chambers; we are always in the same; I with my little work, still, still only regarding sometimes my husband's sweet face, which is so venerable with tears of devotion and all the sublimity of the subject." —*From Letters to Richardson.*

Note 22, Page 470, Column 1.

Let all we look upon religion make
For inmost thought, or meditation's love.

"Why is this the order of Nature, that there is such a difference in the duration and destruction of her works? If the mere stone decay, it is to produce a soil which is capable of nourishing the moss and the lichen; when the moss and the lichen die and decompose, they produce a mould which becomes the bed of life to grass, and to a more exalted species of vegetables. Vegetables are the food of animals,—the less perfect animals of the more perfect; but in man, the faculties and intellect are perfected —he rises, exists for a little while in disease and misery, and then would seem to disappear, without an end, and without producing any effect.

We are deceived, if we suppose that the human being who has formed himself for action, but who has been unable to act, is lost in the mass of being; there is some arrangement of things which we can never comprehend, but in which his faculties will be applied.

The caterpillar, on being converted into an inert scaly mass, does not appear to be fitting itself for an inhabitant of air, and can have no consciousness of the brilliancy of its future being. We are masters of the earth, but perhaps we are the slaves of some great and unknown beings. The fly that we crush with our finger, or feed with our viands, has no knowledge of man, and no consciousness of his superiority. We suppose that we are acquainted with matter, and with all its elements, and yet we cannot even guess at the cause of electricity, or explain the laws of the formation of the stones which fall from meteors. There may be beings, thinking beings, near us, surrounding us, which we do not perceive, which we can never imagine. We know very little; but, in my opinion, we know enough to hope for the immortality, the individual immortality of the better part of man."—Dr. PARIS'S *Life of Sir Humphrey Davy*, vol. i. p. 198.

BOOK III.

Note 23, Page 470, Column 2.

Round these, perchance, a sympathetic thrill
Of worship ran, when first Salvation dawn'd!

Though we can trace particularly the designs and effects of the Redeemer's undertaking only in that part of the system of Nature which, in some degree, falls under our knowledge and observation, yet there is ground from Revelation, as well as from analogy of things, to suppose that it extends to beings that lie entirely beyond the reach of our conception. For whoever adverts to the boundless beneficence of the Universal Parent, and the ways and degrees in which an Infinite Operator may confer being and enjoyment, cannot doubt for a moment that there are more things and more beings in Nature than either our reason or religion gives us any notice of. But all these, whatever they may be, are the subjects of the Mediator's government, and the objects of his redemption; as being the Universal Operator of Omnipotence, He by whom the Almighty executes all his purposes, carries on, and shall bring to perfection, all his works: for it is a doctrine laid down in the most pointed and express terms in Scripture,—"That God hath purposed in himself, in the dispensation of the fulness of time, to gather together in one all things in Christ,— and having made peace by the blood of his cross, by him to reconcile all things to himself; by him, I say, whether they be things in earth or things in heaven."

Note 24, Page 470, Column 2.

Whose powers, though blended in Virgilian song,
Sublimely differ'd.

Vide "Tacitus Hist.," b. v. c. 13. "Suetonius Vespas.," c. 4.—The Sibylline books were an assemblage of rumours, accounted sacred, that circulated in different regions of the ancient world.* Part of

---

* Bishop Horsley says, the Sibyl oracles "were composed of adulterated fragments of the patriarchal prophecies and records, and that put it out of doubt that of much of the prophetic part the Messiah was the specific subject."

The origin of the Barbaric and Grecian philosophy may incontestably be traced to fragmental records derived from patriarchal ages, which were adopted into various systems, together with all the pollutions and extravagances of each successive founder. This is briefly but comprehensively proved by Clement of Alexandria.

"With regard to the wise men and philosophers of Greece, it is hardly necessary to remark, that the greater part of the most ancient of them were either barbarians by birth, or instructed by barbarians; since it has been shown that Pythagoras was either a Tyrrhenian, or a Tyrian; Antisthenes was a Phrygian; Orpheus an Odrysian, or a Thracian; and Homer is, for the most part, thought to have been an

these were Judean—i.e., relative to the Messiah; and hence confusion of the prophecies relative to a Temporal King and a Spiritual One. Virgil, in his "Pollio," has blended them, and thereby puzzled the commentators. The Judean oracles had foretold, for several ages, two great kings,—Augustus was one (the last of the four monarchs alluded to by Daniel), and Jesus Christ the other.

The following extracts are quoted by Sandys, as genuine specimens of the Sibyl Oracle:—

" Sed manibus passis cum mensus cuncta coronam
De spinis tulerit, nec non latus ejus arundo
Fixerit acta manu, cujus causâ tribus horis
Nox tenebrosa die medio monstrosaque fiet.

Tunc hominum generi magnum Salomonia signum
Templa dabunt, Ditis cum tecta profunda subibit,
Nunciet in vitam reditum quo morte peremptis."
Orac. 1, 5.

His Name.

———— " vocales quatuor autem
Fert, non vocalesque; duas binum geniorum:
Sed quæ sit numeri totius summa docebo,
Namque octo monadas, totidem decadas super ista
Atque hecatonradas octa, infidis significabat
Humanis nomen."—L. 1.

Thus explained:

I	H	Σ	O	Υ	Σ
10 .	8 .	200 .	70 .	400 .	200

8 . 8 . 300.

Egyptian. Thales was a Phœnician by birth, and is moreover recorded to have conversed with the prophets of Egypt. Pythagoras did the same, and was likewise circumcised by those prophets, in order that he might be admitted to the most sacred recesses of their temples, and thus become instructed in the mystical philosophy of the Egyptians. He also conversed with the most ancient of the Chaldeans and the Magi. As for Plato, he does not deny that he brought home from the barbarians the noblest parts of his philosophy, and confesses that he visited Egypt. Indeed, it is manifest that he takes every occasion to magnify the barbarians, since he speaks of both himself and Pythagoras as having learned the largest and the best part of their doctrines among them. In one of his dialogues he discloses his acquaintance with the Egyptian king, speaks of Thoyth, an eminently wise man, whom he knew to be the same with Mercury; and in another he appears to have known certain Thracians who held the immortality of the soul. Pythagoras is recorded to have been the scholar of Sonches, the Egyptian chief prophet; Plato, of Sechnuphis, the Heliopolitan; and Eudoxus the Cnidian, of Cenuphis, who was also an Egyptian. With regard to Democritus, we find him in his writings magnifying his own learning after the following manner:—'I have travelled over a greater part of the earth than any of my contemporaries, carrying my inquiries into the most remote points of human knowledge; I have also witnessed a greater variety of climates and soils; I have conversed with a greater number of learned men. No man, not even those who are called Aspedonaftæ, among the Egyptians, ever surpassed me in the construction of lines, together with the demonstration of their properties. With these learned men I have maintained an intercourse, in the whole, for eighty years in foreign countries.' For he visited Babylon, and Persia, and Egypt, and was a scholar of both the Magi and the Priests. Pythagoras first made mention of Zoroaster, the Persian Magus, of whose secret books the followers of Prodicus boast themselves in possession. Alexander, in his 'Treatise on the Pythagoric Symbols,' records that Pythagoras was a scholar of Zasoratus, the Assyrian, and that he was moreover a hearer of the Gauls and Brachmans. It appears, then, philosophy flourished in ancient times among the barbarians, and diffused its light among the nations; and that it was afterwards introduced into Greece. And those who taught it, the prophets of Egypt, the Chaldeans of Syria, the Druids of Gaul, the Samarians of Bactria, those who philosophised among the Celts, the Magi of Paris, the Gymnosophistæ of India, and other barbarian philosophers."—Clement, *Alex. Strom.*, i. 15.

Note 25, Page 470, Column 2.

The world reposed; and grateful Rome beheld
Her Janus shut, her crimson banners furl'd.

"Augustus Cæsar, having united all nations in peace, from east to west, from north to south, closed for the third time the gates of the temple of Janus; and at that particular period, in the same year, in which, by the ordinance of God, he had established a universal peace, Christ was born into the world; to whose advent that peace was made preparatory."—Orosius, a native of Spain, 4th cent., *Hist.*, vii. c. 22.

Note 26, Page 472, Column 1.

where Deity the mortal shape
Of feeble infant took.

"The world's salvation was, without the incarnation of the Son of God, a thing impossible; not simply impossible, but impossible, it being presupposed that the will of God was no otherwise to have it saved than by the death of his own Son. Wherefore taking to himself our flesh, He had none of his own, although from us, what to offer unto God for us. And as Christ took manhood, that by it He might be capable of death, whereunto He humbled himself; so because manhood is the proper subject of compassion, and feeling pity, which maketh the sceptre of Christ's regency even in the kingdom of heaven, be affixable, He which without our nature could not on earth suffer for the sins of the world, doth now also, by means thereof, both make intercession to God for sinners, and exercise dominion over all men with a true, a natural, and a sensible touch of mercy."—Hooker, *Eccl. Pol.*, vol. ii. p. 202.

Note 27, Page 473, Column 2.

In darkness,—still to Zion turn, and weep!

"Amid this extraordinary desolation, you must pause a moment to contemplate two circumstances still more extraordinary. Among the ruins of Jerusalem, two classes of independent people find in their religion sufficient fortitude to enable them to surmount such complicated terrors and wretchedness. Here reside communities of monks, whom nothing can compel to forsake the tomb of Christ. Night and day they chant their hymns around the holy sepulchre. Cast your eyes between the Temple and Mount Sion; behold another petty tribe, cut off from the rest of the inhabitants of this city. The particular objects of every species of degradation, they bow their heads without murmuring; if their head be required, they present it to the scimitar. Enter the abodes of the people—you will find them, amid the most abject wretchedness, instructing their children to read a mysterious book, which they in their turn teach their offspring to read. What they did five thousand years ago, these people still continue to do. Seventeen times have they witnessed the destruction of Jerusalem. Nothing can prevent them from turning their faces toward Zion."—CHATEAUBRIAND.

Note 28, Page 474, Column 1.

till Restoration's voice
Her orphan'd race to Salem's clime recall.

From the melancholy grandeur of prophecy fulfilled, it is delightful to turn to the bright futurity that is promised to afflicted Israel. The restoration of the Jewish kingdom is as clearly revealed as its destruction was. In Keith's invaluable work on Prophecy, the reader will find the various prophecies relative to this assembled. The author remarks:—

"Not naturalised to the isles of the Gentiles, either by law or affection, nor bound to any soil by the possession of fixed property, which would be of no easy transference; but ever looking with undiminished love to the land of their fathers, even after an expatriation uninterrupted for nearly eighteen centuries, they are ready—whenever the time shall be fulfilled—to fly thither, like a cloud, and like doves to their windows. But to what degree, and in what manner, the present convulsions in the Turkish empire, combined with the peculiar, and, in many instances, novel condition of the Jews throughout Europe and America, shall be the means of facilitating their eventual restoration to their own land, no mortal can determine. It is enough for Christians to know, that two thousand of years, through nearly which it has been dormant, can neither render extinct the title, nor proscribe the heaven-chartered rite of the Seed of Abraham to the final and everlasting possession of the land of Canaan; that God will remember the land, and gather together unto it his ancient people; and that his word concerning Zion, which he hath neither forgotten nor forsaken, is, 'I have graven thee upon the palms of my hands, thy walls are continually before me—thy children shall make haste; thy destroyers, and they that made thee waste, shall go forth of thee.' And that, through all the changes which have happened in the kingdoms of the earth, from the days of Moses to the present time, which is more than three thousand two hundred and sixty years, nothing should have happened to prevent the possibility of the accomplishment of these prophecies; but, on the contrary, that the state of the Jewish and Christian nations at this day should be such as renders them capable, not only of a figurative, but even a literal completion, in every particular, if the will of God be so. This is a miracle which hath nothing parallel to it in the phenomena of Nature."—KEITH'S *Work*, p. 410, 7th ed.

Note 29, Page 475, Column 2.

And Messiah grew
Strong in the spirit, wisdom, grace, and power.

"The act of the Son of God, in becoming a Mediator and Saviour to mankind, is considered as that which involved a temporary cessation or diminution of the developments, or manifestations, ab extra, of the essential divine glories. It is, therefore, according to our apprehension of those phrases, described as coming forth from the Father, coming down from heaven, being sent into the world, becoming flesh, and making his tabernacle among men, being sent in the likeness of sinful flesh, divesting himself, taking the form of a servant and humbling himself. It cannot be but immensely difficult, and probably, to human powers, impossible to form perfect conceptions of all that is included in the fact which these expressions designate; yet it seems undeniable, that they all contain the idea of degradation, humiliation, and submission to a subordinate capacity. Such a state we may, with reverence and sacred modesty, conceive to be congruous with the supposition, that the habitual consciousness and feelings of the Man Christ Jesus were not those of unspeakable delight, in the enjoyment of intimate communications from the unexistent Deity; but that, on the contrary, they were the feelings of a mental depression which no words could describe, or imagination represent."—SMITH'S *Scripture Testimony*.

Note 30, Page 476, Column 2.

Where buried cities lift their ghastly wreck
In tomb-like waste.

"Several travellers, and among others, Troilo and D'Arvieux, assert that they remarked fragments of walls and palaces in the Dead Sea. This statement seems to be confirmed by Maundrell and Father Frau. The ancients speak more positively on this subject. Josephus, employing a poetic expression, says he perceived on the banks of the lake the shades of the overwhelmed cities. Strabo gives a circumference of sixty stadii to the ruins of Sodom, which are mentioned also by Tacitus. I know not whether they still exist; but as the lake rises and falls at certain seasons, it is possible that it may alternately cover and expose the skeletons of the reprobate cities."—CHATEAUBRIAND, quoted by CONDER in his *Palestine*.

BOOK IV.

Note 31, Page 480, Column 1.

On Herod's towers,
From whose dread altitude the very sky
Seems nearer.

"The city lay over against the Temple, in the manner of a theatre, and was encompassed with a deep valley along the entire south quarter; but the finest part of the Temple, which was southward had indeed gates in its middle, as also it had the royal cloisters with three walks, which reached at length from the east valley unto that in the west, for it was impossible it should reach any farther: and this cloister deserves to be mentioned better than any under the sun; for while the valley was very deep, and its bottom could not be seen if you looked from above into the depth, this farther vastly high elevation of the cloister stood upon that height, insomuch, if any one looked down from the top of the battlements, or down both those altitudes, he would be giddy, while his sight could not reach to such an immense depth."—JOSEPH. *Antiq.*, lib. xv. c. ix. sect. 5.

Note 32, Page 480, Column 1.

To Quarantania's unascended top
That crowns the wilderness with savage pomp.

"After some hours' travel, you arrive at the mountainous desert into which our Saviour was led by the Spirit to be tempted by the Devil: a most miserable, dry, barren place it is, consisting of high rocky mountains, so torn and disordered, as if the earth had here suffered some great convulsion, in which its very bowels had been turned outward. Certainly there could not be found in the whole earth a more comfortless and abandoned place for that purpose. As soon as we entered the plain, we turned up on the left hand, and going about one hour that way, came to the foot of Quarantania, which, they say, is the mountain into which the Devil took our blessed Saviour, when he tempted Him with that visionary scene of all the kingdoms and glories of the world." —MAUNDRELL'S *Journey*, &c., pp. 106, 7. Eighth Edition.

Note 33, Page 483, Column 2.

At Sichem glitter'd round the Saviour's form.

"Naplosa is the ancient Sychem, or Sychar, as it is termed in the New Testament. It stands in a narrow valley between Mount Gerizim on the south, and Ebal on the north, being built at the foot of the former. From Mount Gerizim it was that God commanded the blessings to be pronounced on the children of Israel, and from Mount Ebal, the curses."—MAUNDRELL.

Note 34, Page 484, Column 1.

while from Ebal's blanchèd height
A Curse came down, like thunder from the skies.

"Never did human imagination conceive a scene so imposing, so solemn, so likely to impress the whole people with deep and enduring awe, as the final ratification of their polity, commanded by the dying lawgiver. In the territory afterwards assigned to the tribe of Ephraim, a central region, stand two remarkable mountains, separated by a deep and narrow ravine, in which the ancient Sechem—the modern Naplus—stands. Here all Israel was to be assembled, six tribes on one height, six on the other. In the open day, and in a theatre, as it were, created by the God of Nature for the express purpose, after a sacrifice offered on an altar of stones, the people of Israel testified their free and deliberate acceptance of that constitution which their God had enacted. They accepted it with its inseparable condition, maledictions the most awful, which they imprecated on their own heads, in case they should apostatise from its statutes,—blessings equally ample and perpetual, if they should adhere to its holy and salutary provisions. The type of either destiny lay before them: Mount Ebal was a barren, stony, wild, and desolate crag; Gerizim, a lovely and fertile height, with luxuriant verdure, streams of running water, and cool, shady groves. As God has blasted Ebal, so he would smite the disobedient with barrenness, hunger, and misery; as he crowned Gerizim with beauty and fruitfulness, so he would bless the faithful Israelites with abundance, with peace, with happiness."—MILMAN.

Note 35, Page 484, Column 2.

to unrol and read
The Haphtoroth.

"The 'Haptoroth' was the section or lesson from the prophets for that day. The one alluded to in the text commenced with the first verse of the forty-first chapter of Isaiah. In the synagogues of the Hellenists, or Greek Jews, the law was always read in the Greek version; but in those of the native Jews, the law was always read in the Hebrew; whence it became necessary, as soon as that language ceased to be vernacular among the Jews, to establish an interpreter, by whom the Jewish Scriptures were expounded in the Chaldee dialect, which was spoken by them after the return from the Babylonian captivity. The doctor, or reader, therefore, having the interpreter always by him, softly whispered in his ears what he said, and this interpreter repeated aloud to the people what had thus been communicated to him. To this custom our Saviour is supposed to have alluded, when he said to his disciples, 'What ye hear in the ear, that preach ye on the house-tops.' Matt. x. 27."—HORNE.

In the midst of the synagogue was a desk or pulpit, on which the book or roll of the law was read very solemnly. There, likewise, he stood who intended to harangue the people. At the highest part of the synagogue, towards the east, and over against the door, which is always west, as far as can well be, is the chest, or press, wherein the book or roll of the law is kept, wrapped up in fine embroidered cloth. The women are distinct from the men, and seated in a gallery inclosed with lattices, so that they may see and hear, and not be seen.—PRIDEAUX, *Connect.*, and JENNINGS' *Jew. Antiq.*

BOOK V.

Note 36, Page 487, Column 1.

temples in the mind,
Where God in dedicated moments comes
To earth unknown.

The following quotation is pronounced by Wordsworth to be "one of the finest passages in modern English prose:"

"A man is supposed to improve by going out into the world, by visiting London. Artificial man does; he extends with his sphere; but, alas that sphere is microscopic: it is formed of minutiæ, and he surrenders his genuine vision to the artist, in order to embrace it in his ken. His bodily senses grow acute, even to barren and inhuman pruriency; while his mental become proportionally obtuse. The reverse is the Man of Mind: he who is placed in the sphere of Nature and of God might be a mock at Tattersall's and Brookes's, and a sneer at St. James's: he would certainly be swallowed alive by the first Pizarro that crossed him;—but when he walks along the river of Amazons; when he rests his eye on the unrivalled Andes; when he measures the long and watered Savannah; or contemplates from a sudden promontory the distant vast Pacific, and feels himself a freeman in this vast theatre, and commanding each ready-produced fruit of this wilderness, and each progeny of this stream—his exultation is not less than imperial. He is as gentle, too, as he is great: his emotions of tenderness keep pace with his elevation of sentiment; for he says, 'These were made by a good Being, who, unsought by me, placed me here to enjoy them.' He becomes at once a child and a king: his mind is in himself; from hence he argues, and from hence he acts, and he argues unerringly, and acts magisterially: his mind in himself is also in his God; and therefore he loves, and therefore he soars."—From the Notes upon the *Hurricane*, a Poem by William Gilbert.

Note 37, Page 487, Column 1.

The Law illumed, and blinded Israel taught
The darkness of exclusive faith was o'er.

Without a correct acquaintance with the doctrinal character of the Jews at the time of our Saviour, it is utterly impossible to understand or duly feel the solemnity of his rebukes when the Pharisees attempted to shape religion into a mechanical observance of rites and ceremonies. A few passages from uncommon sources are therefore submitted to the reader's perusal.

"Whoever shall sincerely keep even any one of the six hundred and thirteen precepts [of the Law], behold he, by fulfilling that precept, shall merit eternal life."—Obadias de Bartenora.

"This is also one of the fundamental principles of our law, that all the good which God has done, or will do, to us, is done on account of the merit of Abraham, Isaac, and Jacob, because they kept the way of the Lord, by doing justice and judgment."—Maimonides.

"Every Israelite will have his portion in a future life."—Mishna.

"Abraham sits near the gates of hell, and suffers not any wicked Israelite to go down to hell."—Talmud.

"The resurrection will be peculiar to the Israelites, and that the Gentiles will not partake in it, for the whole world was created for the sole benefit of Israel! Our wise men have said, 'To Him who spake the word, and the world was made, it was well known that Adam would sin; why, then, did he create Adam? Because a nation in whom he found refreshment would come from him. From the Israelites who stood at the foot of Mount Sinai, that is, who received the law, which is the tree of life, defilement was taken away, and they were thus made fit for eternal life: the Gentiles who were not present there, were not cleansed from this defilement, and therefore are unfit for life. The resurrection is therefore wholly confined to the Israelites!'"—Judah Zabarah, Pocock, *Notæ Misc.*, p. 194.

The extreme repugnance between these doctrines and the boundless glory of Redemption will account for the rejection of Christ by the Jews. The following is a curious and valuable summary of the popular notions which the Jews had formed of the Saviour of Israel:—

"As to the days of the Messiah, that is, the time when the kingdom will be restored to Israel, and the Israelites will return to Palestine—The Messiah will be a powerful king: Zion will be the metropolis of his kingdom: his name will be illustrious, and fill the uttermost parts of the earth with its renown: he will be greater and richer than Solomon: the nations will enter into peace with him, and the provinces will yield obedience unto him, on account of his distinguished righteousness, and of the miracles which he will perform. If any man shall rise up in rebellion against him, God will destroy that man, and deliver him into his hand. Moreover, all the texts of Scripture declare both the felicity of the Messiah himself, and that which we shall obtain through him. But there will be no change in the nature of things from the state which now prevails, except that the kingdom will be with Israel. So our wise men have said, 'There is no difference between the present age and the days of the Messiah, except only the subjugation of the kingdoms.' And under his dominion, some will be stronger and some weaker than others. But in those days men will enjoy a remarkable facility of obtaining food, so that a man will be able to obtain riches with the least possible trouble. This is the meaning of the saying, 'It will be that the land of Israel will bring forth cakes and silk garments.' The sons of the alien shall be your ploughmen and vinedressers. But the great facility of that time will be, that we shall then be liberated from that yoke of evil dominion, which keeps us back from the pursuit of every virtue; and that knowledge will then be multiplied, as God hath said, 'For the earth shall be filled with the knowledge of the Lord:' and that then contentions and wars shall be done away, as He also hath said, 'Nation shall not lift up a sword against nation.' For to them who live at that time shall be granted every advantage by which they may attain to the life of a future world. But the Messiah will die, and his son and his posterity will reign after him. For that he will die, God declares: 'He shall not fail nor be discouraged, till he set judgment in the earth.' But his reign will be of very long duration, and men will then attain great length of life; for life is prolonged by the removal of grief and sorrow. And it is certainly true that his reign will last for some thousands of years. For it is said the coalition of society among the good cannot be dissolved. But the days of the Messiah are not so much to be desired, either that our corn or wealth may be multiplied, or that we may ride on horses, or drink together to the sound of musical instruments; but the prophets have wished for, and excellent men have eagerly expected, those days, on account of that society of good men, that virtuous conversation and knowledge which will then prevail, and on account of the righteousness of the king and his distinguished knowledge, and the near degree in which he is related to his Creator, as God hath said to him, 'Thou art My Son:' and because the whole Law of Moses will then be fulfilled without reluctance, perturbation, or constraint."—Maimonides, *Porta Mosis*, p. 60.

Note 38, Page 491, Column 2.

And Hopes which make eternity a lie,
By moulding heaven to each infirm desire.

According to the author of the Koran, there will "not only be marriage, but also servitude in the next world. The very meanest in Paradise will have eighty thousand servants and seventy-two wives. He will also have a tent erected for him of pearls, hyacinths, and emeralds!" In a catechism printed at Constantinople are the following principal articles to which a Mussulman is required to assent:—"I believe in the books which have been delivered from heaven to the prophets. In this manner was the Koran given to Mahomet, the Pentateuch to Moses, the Psalter to David, and the Gospel to Jesus. I believe in the prophets, and the miracles which they have performed. Adam was the first prophet and Mahomet was the last. I believe that, for the space of fifty thousand years, the righteous shall repose under the shade of the terrestrial Paradise; and the wicked shall be exposed naked to the burning rays of the sun. I believe in the bridge Sirat, which passes over the bottomless pit of hell. It is as fine as a hair, and as sharp as a sabre. All must pass over it, and the wicked shall be thrown off. I believe in the water-pools of Paradise. Each of the Prophets has, in Paradise, a basin for his own use: the water is whiter than milk, and sweeter than honey. On the ridges of the pools are vessels to drink out of, and they are bordered with stars. I believe in heaven and hell. The inhabitants of the former know no want, and the houris who attend them are never afflicted with sickness. The floor of Paradise is musk, the stones are silver, and the cement gold. The damned are, on the contrary, tormented with fire, and by voracious and poisonous animals."

Note 39, Page 491, Column 2.

What visions o'er thy musing spirit roll?

"The pilgrim need not trouble himself about the authenticity of the tradition which gives to every cave in Palestine a sacred name. In Nazareth, at least, there is a religion in the place, which needs not the adventitious aid of superstition to excite enthusiasm. The peaceful valley of Nazareth, hemmed in from the noisy world by an amphitheatre of verdant hills, is the spot which one might imagine the meek and lowly Jesus would have chosen for his earliest abode. The silent paths, the deep ravines in the eastern hill, might well have served for meditation; every morning during my stay in Nazareth I visited these solitudes, calling to my mind the miracle of morality and philosophy which came from the little town before me, and reflecting on the revolution in religion which every country had undergone since Jesus of Nazareth first broached his doctrines in the village synagogue, the site of which was then before me. The feelings these reflections inspired were intense."—*Travels in the East.*

Note 40, Page 495, Column 1.

And while dumb Glories of creation give
Their daily witness, man alone is mute.

"The miracles of Nature are exposed to our eyes long before we have reason enough to derive any light from them. If we entered the world with the same reason which we carry with us to an opera, the first time we enter a theatre,—and if the curtain of the universe were to be rapidly drawn up,—struck with the grandeur of everything which we saw, and all the obvious contrivances exhibited, we should not be capable of refusing our homage to the Eternal Power which had prepared for us such a spectacle. But who thinks of marvelling at what he has seen for fifty years? What multitudes are there, who, wholly occupied with the care of obtaining subsistence, have no time for speculation! The rise of the sun is only that which calls them to toil, and the finest night, in all its softness, is mute to them, or tells them only that it is the hour of repose."—*Diderot*, tome i. p. 100.

How deeply did Foster feel this deadness of human mind to those fine appeals coming from a glorious universe, when he penned the following passage:—"It is unfortunate, I have thought within these few minutes, while looking out on one of the most enchanting nights of the most interesting season of the year, and hearing the voices of a company of persons, to whom I can perceive that this soft, solemn shade over the earth, the calm sky, the beautiful stripes of cloud, the stars, and waning moon just risen, are things not in the least more interesting than the walls, ceiling, and candle-light of a room."—FOSTER'S *Essays*, vol. i. pp. 26, 27.

Note 41, Page 497, Column 2.

Delightedly to Youth's enamour'd ear
The Festival unfolds.

"Now Judas celebrated the festival of the restoration of the sacrifices of the temple for eight days, and omitted no sort of pleasure thereon; but he feasted them on very rich and splendid sacrifices; and he honoured God, and delighted them by hymns and psalms. Nay, they were so very glad at the revival of their customs, that they made it a law for their posterity that they should keep a festival, on account of the restoration of their temple-worship, for eight days. And from that time to this, we celebrate this festival, and call it Lights."—JOSEPHUS, *Antiq.*, lib. xii. c. viii. s. vii.

Note 42, Page 498, Column 1.

A shade of sadness mellow'd not destroy'd
The mirth and beauty of surrounding day.

The poet Young was devotedly attached to the quiet loveliness of a garden-walk, and its attendant associations. In his "Essay on Pleasure" occurs the following passage:—

"A garden has ever had the praise and affection of the wise. What is requisite to make a wise and happy man, but reflection and peace? And both are the natural growth of a garden. Nor is a garden a promoter only of a good man's happiness, but a picture of it; and in some sort shows him to himself. Its culture, order, fruitfulness, and seclusion from the world, compared to the weeds, wildness, and exposure of a common field, is no bad emblem of a good man compared to the multitude. A garden weeds the mind; it weeds it of worldly thoughts, and sows celestial seed in their stead.—Who cannot look on a flower, till he frightens himself out of infidelity?"

Note 43, Page 500, Column 1.

And men were Demons with a robe of flesh
Enveloped, banqueting on human blood?

The capture of Jerusalem forms the most terrific tale which the records of history unfold. Human nature seems to have gone out of itself, and to have become a demonised and savage thing, amid the horrors and devastations of a besieged capital. Yet everything that was done, suffered, or displayed, in this dreadful scene, had been predicted by the Saviour; and those who will compare the descriptions of Josephus with the prophetic denunciation delivered nearly forty years before the event, cannot escape the conviction, that "never man spake like this Man!" A few of the most fearful and illustrative passages from the Jewish historian are here selected. The classical reader will not fail to detect in them an occasional resemblance to the condensed and vehement style that distinguishes the pages of Tacitus, who was contemporary with Josephus.

"Famine was too hard for all other passions; children pulled the very morsels their fathers were eating out of their very mouths, and what was still more to be pitied, so did the mothers do as to their infants: the old men who held their food were beaten, and if the women hid what they had within their hands, their hair was torn for so doing; nor was there any commiseration showed either to the aged or to infants, but they lifted up children from the ground, as they hung upon the morsels they had gotten, and shook them down upon the floor.

"All hope of escaping was now cut off, together with their liberty of going out of the city. Then did the famine widen its progress, and devoured the people by whole houses and families: the upper rooms were full of women and children that were dying by famine, and the lanes of the city were full of the dead bodies of the aged; the children also and the young men wandered about the market-place like shadows, all swelled with the famine, and fell down dead wheresoever their misery seized them! Many died as they were burying others, and many went to their coffins before that fatal hour was come! Nor was there any lamentation made under these calamities, nor were heard any mournful complaints; those who were just going to die looked upon those who were gone to their rest before them with dry eyes and open mouths. A deep silence also, and a kind of deadly night, had seized upon the city; while the robbers were yet more terrible than these miseries were themselves, for those who entreated them their sword to dispatch them, they were too froward to grant their requests, and left them to be consumed by their famine. Now every one of these died with their eyes fixed upon the temple, and left the seditious alive behind them. When Titus, on going his rounds along those valleys, saw them full of dead bodies, he gave a groan, and spreading out his hands to heaven, called God to witness that this was not his doing.

"The multitude of carcasses that lay in heaps, one upon another, was a horrible sight; but as those were to go in battle-array, who had been already to ten thousand murders, and must tread on those dead bodies as they marched along, so were they not terrified, nor did they pity men as they marched over them."

Then succeeds the more than horrible description of a woman who fed on her own infant, and when the seditious came, uncovered what was left of her son, and exclaimed, "This is mine own son, and what hath been done is mine own doing. Come, eat of this food; for I have eaten of it myself. Do not you pretend to be either more tender than a woman, or compassionate than a mother!"

A description of the temple on fire shall conclude these extracts. Pindar and Æschylus, with a volcano to inspire the fury of their verse, are vapid, compared with the calm terror of the following passage:—

"While the house was on fire, everything was plundered that came to hand, and ten thousand of those that were caught were slain; nor was there a commiseration of any age or any reverence of gravity, but children, and old men, and priests, were all slain in the same manner. The flame was also carried a long way, and made an echo together with the groans of those that were slain; and because the hill was high, and the works at the temple were very great, one would have thought that the whole city had been on fire. Nor can we imagine or conceive any greater or more terrible than this noise, for there was at once a shout of the Roman legions, who were marching all together, and a sad clamour of the seditious who were now surrounded by fire and sword. The people made sad moans, at the calamity they were under; the multitude also that were in the city joined in this outcry with those that were on the hill; and besides many of those that were almost worn away by famine, and their mouths almost closed, when they saw the fire of the Holy House, they exerted their utmost strength, and brake out into groans and outcries again. Perea did also return the echo as well as the mountains round about the city, and augmented the force of the entire noise! yet was the misery itself more terrible than this disorder; for one would have thought the hill itself on which the temple stood was seething hot, as full of fire in every part of it, that the blood was larger in quantity than the fire, and those that were slain more in number than those who slew them; for the ground did nowhere appear visible, for the dead bodies that lay on it; but the soldiers went over heaps of these bodies, as they ran upon such as fled from them! As for the priests, some of them plucked up from the holy house the spikes that were upon it, with their bases, which were made of lead, and shot them at the Romans instead of darts. But then, as they gained nothing by so doing, and as the fire burst out upon them, they retired to the wall that was eight cubits broad, and there they tarried. The soldiers were in such a rage, that they set the cloister on fire, by which means it came to pass that some of these were destroyed by throwing themselves down headlong, and some were burnt in the cloisters themselves. Nor did any one of them escape with his life."

BOOK VI.

Note 45, Page 501, Column 2.

As Parables, where conscience is instinctive judge,
And to the mind celestial truth commends?

"Our Saviour, in all his parables, puts the case on the charitable side, and makes the most favourable representation of things which the matter will bear. In the parable of the ten virgins, he supposes the number of the wise to be equal to that of the foolish. In the parable of the lost sheep, he supposes but one in a hundred to go astray; and yet the Good Shepherd is content to leave all the rest, and go in quest of the single straggler. In the third place, there is an exact decorum observed in all Christ's parables, and everything that is spoken is fitted to the character of the person who speaks it,—a beauty which the critics look upon as the greatest ornament of a poem, and which of itself is sufficient to make it heard or read with delight and admiration; and therefore I hope it may recommend our Saviour's parables to the nice and delicate taste of our modern wits, who are apt to think everything in Scripture so mean and flat, as not to be worth their reading."—LOWTH, *Div.*, p. 185.

Note 46, Page 501, Column 1.

By pure magnificence of spirit raised
Above whate'er Platonic vision shaped.

"When Plato described his imaginary good man with all the shame of guilt, yet meriting the high reward of virtue, he describes exactly the character of Jesus Christ. The resemblance is so striking that all the Christian Fathers describe it."—ROUS.

Note 47, Page 504, Column 1.

Convulsed within Him, hark, the Human *cries.*

"There was present before his eyes in that fearful hour, on the one side, God's heavy indignation and wrath towards mankind—as yet unappeased, death as yet in full strength, hell as yet never mastered by any that came within the confines and bounds thereof, somewhat also, peradventure, more than is either possible or needful for the wit of man to find out; finally, himself, flesh and blood, left alone to enter into conflict with all these. Secondly, on the other side, a world to be saved by One, a pacification of wrath through the dignity of that sacrifice which should be offered, a conquest over death, through the power of that Deity which would not suffer the tabernacle thereof to see corruption, and an utter disappointment of all the forces of infernal powers, through the purity of that soul which they should have in their hands, and not be able to touch." —HOOKER, *Eccles. Pol.* vol. ii. p. 187.

Note 48, Page 504, Column 2.

there, aloft upraised,
Their holy Victim in the upper hall
His trial waiteth.

"St. Luke is the only Evangelist who has preserved this beautiful circumstance of Christ's turning and looking on Peter. The members of the council, who sat in judgment on Jesus, were placed at the upper end of the hall; in the other were the servants with Peter, at the fire; so that Jesus, being probably placed on some eminence, that his judges, who were numerous, might see and hear him, could easily look towards Peter, and observe him denying Him, and in passionate terms, loud enough to be heard, perhaps, over all the place."—MILNER'S *Life and History of Christ*, p. 294.

Note 49, Page 505, Column 1.

But His hour had come!

"In all this we observe a remarkable display of a particular providence. It had been foretold that the Messiah should be crucified; but this could never have happened, if he had died by the hands of the Jews, or for any offence against their law; for crucifixion was a mode of punishment customary with the Romans, but not with the Jews."—DEAN STANHOPE.

Note 50, Page 505, Column 2.

and crown
Of platted thorns, upon His temples press'd.

"There still exists a plant in Palestine, known among botanists by the name of the 'spina Christi,' or thorn of Christ, and supposed to be the shrub which afforded the crown worn by our Saviour before his crucifixion. It must have been very fit for the purpose, for it has many sharp prickles, well adapted to give pain; and as the leaves greatly resemble those of ivy, it is not improbable that the enemies of the Messiah chose it from its similarity to the plant with which emperors and generals are accustomed to be crowned; and hence that there might be calumny, insult, and derision meditated in the very act of punishment."—RUSSELL'S *Palestine*, p. 448.

Note 51, Page 505, Column 2.

When list'ning worlds were over-awed to hear
A creature his incarnate God condemn!

"A kind of structure was erected, adjoining the palace, which served instead of a tribunal or judgment-seat. This building, called in the Hebrew 'Gabbatha,' was finely paved with small pieces of marble, of different colours; being always exposed to the weather; perhaps it resembled a stage, but larger, open on all sides, and on one part of it a throne was placed, whereon the governor sat to hear causes. One side of this structure joined to the palace, and a door was made in the wall, through which the governor passed to the tribunal. By this contrivance the people might stand around the tribunal, in the open air, hear and see the governor when he spoke to them from the pavement, and observed the administration of justice without the danger of being defiled."—MILNER.

Note 52, Page 506, Column 1.

and down the dizzy steep
Sunk into darkness, and was seen no more!

"After he had thus returned the wages of iniquity, he retired to some lonely place, not far, perhaps, from the scene of Peter's repentance, and in the frenzy of despair, and at the instigation of the devil, hanged himself; crowning with suicide the murder of his master and his friend; rejecting his compassionate Saviour, and plunging his own soul into perdition! In another place it is said, that 'falling headlong, he burst asunder, and all his bowels gushed out.' —(Acts i. 18.) Both these accounts might be true; he might first have hanged himself from some tree on the edge of a precipice, and the rope or branch breaking, he might be dashed to pieces by the fall." —HALE'S *New Analysis of Chronology*, vol. ii. book ii. p. 878.

Lightfoot's surmise is very eccentric on the manner of Judas's death:—"The devil, who dwelt in him, caught him up on high, strangled him, and threw him down headlong, so that, dashing upon the ground, he burst in the midst."—*Talmudical Exercitation on St. Matthew.*

Note 53, Page 506, Column 1.

With His cross
To Calvary the lacerated Christ
Is now ascending.

"The form, then, of the cross on which our Saviour suffered, was not a simple but a compound figure, according to the custom of the Romans, by whose procurator he was condemned to die; in which there was not only a straight and erected piece of wood fixed in the earth, but also a transverse beam fastened into that towards the top thereof; and besides these two, cutting each other transversely at right angles, there was also another piece of wood infixed into, and standing out from, that which was erected, and stood straight up. To that erected piece was His body, being lifted up, applied, as Moses' serpent to the pole; and to the transverse beam his hands were nailed; upon the lower part, coming out from the erected piece, his sacred body rested, and his feet were transfixed and fastened with nails; his head, being pressed with a crown of thorns, was applied to that part of the erect which stood above the transverse beam; and above his head, to that was fastened the table, on which was written, in Hebrew, Greek, and Latin characters, the accusation, according to the Roman custom. The writing was—'Jesus of Nazareth, the King of the Jews.'"—PEARSON *on the Creed*, fol. ed., pp. 203, 4.

Note 54, Page 507, Column 1.

in a shape of Light
Triumphant over Powers and Thrones of Hell.

"As the souls at the hour of death are really separated from the bodies, so the place where they are at rest or misery after death is certainly distinct from the place in which they lived. They continue not where they were at that instant when the body was left without life; they do not go together with the body to the grave; but as the sepulchre is appointed for our flesh, so there is another receptacle, or habitation, or mansion, for our spirits. From whence it followeth, that the soul doth certainly pass by a real motion from that place in which it did inform the body, and is translated to that place, and unto that society, which God of his mercy or justice allotted it. And, not at present to inquire into the difference and distance of these several habitations, it will appear to have been the general judgment of the Church, that the soul of Christ, contradistinguished from his body, that better and more noble part of his humanity, his rational and intellectual soul, after a true and proper separation from his flesh, was really and truly carried into those parts below where the souls of men before departed were detained; and that by such a real translation of his soul, he was truly said to have descended into hell. Many have been the interpretations of the opinions of the fathers made of late. The persons to whom, and end for which, He descended, they differ in; 'but as to a local descent into the infernal parts, they all agree.' And this leads me to the end which I conceive most conformable to the words of the prophet, and least liable to question or objection—that He might undergo the condition of a dead man as well as of a living. He appeared here, that we might never come into those torments, which are these:—By his descent he freed us from our fears, and by his ascension he secured us of our hopes. He passed to those habitations where Satan hath taken up possession, and exerciseth his dominion; that, having no power over him, we might be assured that he should never exercise any over our souls departed, as belonging unto them."—PEARSON.

Note 55, Page 509, Column 1.

Lo! again He came
Inaudibly, within a chamber barr'd.

"The circumstance of the doors being shut is very happily mentioned by St. John; because it suggests a reason why the disciples took their Master for a spirit, notwithstanding many of them were convinced he was really risen from the dead."—MILNER.

Note 56, Page 510, Column 1.

Baptising Nations in the Name triune
Of Father, Son, and Holy Ghost!

"Among the Jews, the controversy was about the true Messiah; among the Gentiles, about the true God: it was, therefore, proper among the Jews to baptise in the name of Jesus, that he might be vindicated to be the true Messias: among the Gentiles, in the name of the Father, Son, and Holy Ghost, that they might be hereby instructed in the doctrine of the true God."—LIGHTFOOT'S *Talmudical Exercit.*

In the earlier part of his life, the sublime Milton thus apostrophises the Trinity:—

"Thou, therefore, that sittest in light and glory unapproachable, Parent of angels and men! Next Thee I implore, Omnipotent King, Redeemer of that lost remnant, whose nature thou didst assume, ineffable and everlasting Love! And Thou, the third subsistence of Divine infinitude, illumining Spirit, the joy and solace of created things! one Tripersonal Godhead, look upon this thy poor and almost spent and expiring Church."—MILTON, *Prose Works*, vol. i. p. 57.

Note 57, Page 510, Column 2.

And then, is trackless,—in celestial depths
Evanish'd, soaring back to God again!

"Ascension into heaven is a plain local translation of Christ, according to his manhood, from the lower to the higher parts of the world. Session at the right hand of God is the actual exercise of that regency and dominion, wherein the manhood of Christ is joined and matched with the deity of the Son of God. Not that his manhood was before without the possession of the same power, but because the full use thereof was suspended till that humility, which had been before as a veil to hide and conceal majesty, were laid aside."—HOOKER'S *Eccl. Pol.* vol. ii. p. 225.

Note 58, Page 511, Column 2.

Or creatures, such as once the mental eye
Of seraph-haunted Milton saw descend.

Symmons has finely remarked of Milton (Vide Life, p. 526), that he was "a man who, if he had been delegated as the representative of his species to one of the superior worlds, would have suggested a grand idea of the human race." In tracing the history of his mighty spirit, we cannot but observe the majestic view which he entertained of the poetical character. With him poetry was something more than amusement or pleasure,—it was a high and consecrated energy, to be devoted to the mental elevation of mankind. From dawning manhood, through all the progressive years of his life, the master-dream within was that which prefigured poetical greatness. In a "Vacation Exercise," he confesses a desire to

——————— "soar
Above the wheeling poles, and at heaven's door
Look in, and see each blissful deity,
How he before the thund'rous throne doth lie."

And in a letter to Deodati, he says:—"For a moment let me talk proudly to you;—Do you ask me what is in my thought—So may God prosper me, as it is nothing less than immortality!"—And how often, in the barren wilds of political controversy, do paragraphs of surpassing beauty and loveliness flower forth, and evince the ruling purpose of the soul.—Never did he forget the "destiny divine" which awaited him in the completion of a work. "Not to be obtained by the invocation of Dame Memory and her stern daughters, but by devout prayer to that Eternal Spirit, who can enrich with all utterance and knowledge, and sends out His Seraphim with the hallowed fire of His altar, to touch and purify the lips of whom He pleases:—then, amidst the hymns and hallelujahs of saints, some one, perhaps, may be heard offering at high strains, in new and lofty measures, to sing and celebrate the divine mercies and marvellous judgments in this land throughout all ages."*

Note 59, Page 511, Column 2.

But oh! dark Spirit, whose unquiet shade
Our fancy visions in reflected gloom.

The reader is referred to one of Chalmers's sermons for some noble remarks on the sadness and darkness of the human soul; and the gloomy atmosphere in which our spirits so often delight to shape their fancies, and converse with futurity. Was not Young sincere when he penned the following passage, that resembles the mighty and mysterious anguish which the Greek choruses develop?—"The numberless pains of body and mind; the dark solemn approaches to, or dismal vestibules of the grave, as well as opening graves themselves, are so thickly scattered over the face of the earth, that an unpetrified heart cannot look round without feeling an inevitable damp, and general disconsolation; and venting a sigh universal for the whole family of Adam. Nothing but strong faith in eternal life could hinder tears from bursting over it: nor are tears too much, for sympathy is the chief duty of human life."

Schlegel has philosophically analysed this propensity to sadness in the human mind, which neither the brightness of the world nor the scorn of affected stoicism can entirely overcome.

"To man alone, of all animals with which we are acquainted, is it permitted to look back towards the past, and forward into futurity; and he has purchased this noble privilege at a dear rate.—The desire for what is infinite which dwells in our being, is thwarted by the limits of the finite by which we are fettered. All that we do, all that we effect, is vain and perishable; death stands everywhere in the background, and every good or ill spent moment brings us in closer contact with him. There is no bond of love without repentance, no enjoyment without grief for its loss! When we contemplate, however, the relations of our existence to the extreme limit of possibilities; when we consider that we are exposed, in our weak, helpless state, to struggle with the immeasurable powers of Nature, with conflicting desires on the shores of an unknown world, and in danger of shipwreck at our very birth:—that in our passions we carry our enemy in our bosom; that every moment demands from us the sacrifice of our dearest inclinations, in the name of our most sacred duties;—then every mind which is not dead to feeling must be overpowered by an inexpressible melancholy, against which there is no other protection than the consciousness of a destiny soaring above this earthly life."—W. SCHLEGEL'S *Lectures*, p. 42.

Note 60, Page 511, Column 2.

For Self has overshadow'd Love divine
With dread oblivion.

"What is wanting at the present era is, an insurrection against egotism; for the moral virtue of each individual is found to centre in his own personal interest."—DE STAEL.

May we not subscribe also to the truth of another observation by the same illustrious thinker—"Tous les vices se coalisent, tous les talens devraient se rapprocher!"

Note 61, Page 512, Column 1.

Thy glorious aim
Like true religion's, is to lead us back
From recreant darkness to primeval bliss.

Lord Bacon relates, that a noble somebody, on being asked his opinion of poets, replied, that "next to prose writers, they were the best going!"—But the philosopher himself took a high view of poetry, and has thus recorded it:—"The use of this feigned history* hath been to give some satisfaction to the mind of man in those points wherein the nature of things doth deny it, the world being, in proportion, inferior to the soul; by reason whereof there is, agreeable to the spirit of man, a more ample greatness, a more exact goodness, and a more absolute variety, than can be found in the nature of things. Therefore, because the acts or events of true history have not that magnitude which satisfieth the mind of man, poesy feigneth acts and events greater and more heroical:—so it appeareth that poesy serveth to and conferreth to magnanimity, morality, and delectation. And, therefore, it was ever thought to have some participation of divineness, because it doth raise and erect the mind, by submitting the shows of things to the desires of the mind, whereas reason doth buckle and bow the mind unto the nature of things; to ascribe unto it that which is due for the expression of affections, passions, corruptions, and customs, we are beholden to poets' more than to philosophers' works; and for wit and eloquence, not much less than to orators' harangues."—*Advancement of Learning*, p. 88—91.

* How minute are the links in that chain of events which compose a life, and yet how important!—If the act of oblivion (on the accession of Charles II.) had excepted Milton, or if he had not been concealed in St. Bartholomew's Close, we could not have boasted a "Paradise Lost." Sir W. Davenant was the means of saving Milton by his interposition.

* Il y a toujours dans les fictions poétiques une sorte de logique cachée: elles doivent être en accord avec elles-mêmes; le beau est l'image du vrai; la coördination des idées précède et prépare leur analyse. Les conceptions poétiques exercent au plus haut degré les forces actives de l'esprit; elles le dirigent à la recherche de cet idéal qui est aussi à plusieurs égards le type des spéculations philosophiques.—DEGERANDO'S *Systèmes de Philosophie*, vol. i. p. 380, 2nd edit.

Note 62, Page 512, Column 2.

And since the spirit with the flesh doth war,
And Life is oft an agonising thirst
Which nothing visible can tame, or cool.

"Among the Greeks, human nature was in itself all-sufficient; they were conscious of no wants, and aspired at no higher perfection than that which they could actually obtain by the exercise of their own faculties. We, however, are taught by superior wisdom, that man, through a high offence, forfeited the place for which he was originally destined. The religion of the senses had only in view the possession of outward and perishable blessings. The very reverse of all this is the case with the Christian; every finite and mortal object is lost in the contemplation of infinity; life has become shadow and darkness, and the first dawning of our real existence opens in a world beyond the grave. The soul, resting, as it were, under the willows of exile, breathes out its longing for its distant home. Hence, the poetry of the ancients was the poetry of enjoyment, and ours that of desire; the former has its foundation in the scene which is present, while the latter hovers betwixt recollection and hope."—W. SCHLEGEL.

Note 63, Page 512, Column 2.

And though that hour, for resurrection doom'd,
Be hidden, shrouded from angelic mind.

"For aught we know, the soul may remain combined with a portion of matter less than the ten-thousandth part of the minutest particle that was ever perceived by our senses; since great or small is only relative. All that we can be sure of is, that if the soul be wholly disengaged from matter, and yet shall enjoy consciousness and activity, it must be in some quite different manner from that in which we now enjoy them; if, on the other hand, the soul remains inert and unconscious (as it does with respect to the seeing faculty—for instance, when the eyes are closed, or blinded), till its re-union with matter, the moment of our sinking into this state of unconsciousness will appear to us to be instantly succeeded by that of our awaking from it, even though twenty centuries may have intervened—of which one may convince himself by a few moments' reflection."—WHATELEY'S *Essay on a Future State*, Note B, page 29.

MINOR POEMS.

WELLINGTON:

OR,

THE HERO'S FUNERAL.

TO HER

WHO NUMBERS MORE

THAN TWENTY RELATIONS

THAT HAVE FOUGHT AND SERVED

UNDER

ARTHUR, DUKE OF WELLINGTON,

THE FOLLOWING ATTEMPT

IS AFFECTIONATELY INSCRIBED BY

HER HUSBAND.

"The mighty Man, and the Man of War,
The Judge and the Prophet, and the Prudent
And the Ancient and the Honourable Man."
Is. iii. 2, 3.

"The King lifted up his voice and wept at the grave of Abner, and all the people wept. And the King said unto his servants, Know ye not that there is a Prince and a great man fallen this day in Israel."—2 *Sam.* iii. 32—38.

"SATIS DIU VIXISSE DIGITO."

I.

INTRODUCTION.

THROUGH England's capital no rest to-night!
Where sleepless myriads watch for morning light,
Whose hearts concentre in one vast regret
To feel the fullness of that awful debt
A shielded Empire to her saviour owes,
When grey-hair'd Glory finds its last repose
Under the crypt, where storied banners wave
Their drooping pageant o'er some public grave.

With a fev'rish awe opprest,
And a something in the breast
Neither tones nor tears explain,
Like a mute and mighty pain,
Or a pulse of voiceless grief
Too august for word-relief,
Millions now are slumberless;
And in thinking loneliness
Are brooding o'er the unbreath'd thought,—
To-morrow down to dust is brought
That hoary Chief, whose high career
Will range half Europe round his bier;
Who fifteen battles fought and won
Nor left nor lost a British gun,
But took three thousand cannon from the foe
The thunder of his charge had laid in battle low!

A COMPARISON.

But while the riband, star, and coronet
With mingled radiance in one warrior met,
Austerely simple to the last he stood,
A hero great by being good!
In unity of heart and mind
Thus he and Nelson are combined
For prowess, deeds, and all we prize
When perils round a nation rise:
The first became the Nelson of all lands,
The second proved our Wellington by sea;
And both were weapon'd by Almighty hands
To guard the island-fortress of the free:
Nor when the bomb-shell blazed, and roll'd the culverin
From iron lips of death its thunder and its din,
From Tagus to the Thames
From Sambre to the Seine
Is there a brand that shames
The spot where he hath been!—
The Man was never in the Hero lost
Nor Valour glorified at Virtue's cost.

II.

NIGHT-SCENES ON NOVEMBER 17.

November's night is harsh and cold;
Like banners seem the clouds up-roll'd
Sable and dusk, in starless heaven,
And, here and there, by night-gales driven;

Fiercely and fast the loud-toned rain
Rattles against the window-pane;
But neither wet nor winter's chill
The mingled rush becalm of myriads coming still:—
Through dusky lane, and street, or lighted square
London is moved, and motion ev'rywhere!

MIDNIGHT.

But at last, there seems a lull
Making night more beautiful.
Chariot, steed, and rapid car
With fainter cadence roll afar;
Till a deeper hush is come,
And the wide and wakeful hum
Ebbs and falls, and dies away
Like a dream-tone's melting play.
Through their rent and riven shrouds
Planets beam from yonder clouds;
Pallid stars patrol the sky,
And arrest some musing eye,
While yon weak and wat'ry moon,
Like a soft and silver noon
On the turret gleams awhile
With a pale and placid smile.

Soon o'er the varied City's vast extent
A deep'ning stillness from the night is sent;
And the calmer few who can
Master all the scenes of man,
Keeping down the pulse of life
When it throbs in storm or strife,—
Feel the balm of slumber now
Brooding over cheek and brow;
Those that work, and they who weep,
Woo the mercy of mild sleep;
And in soft innocence of sacred rest
The babe lies pillow'd on maternal breast.

III.

DAWN.

But the cloudy dawn is waking
And the day-blush dimly breaking:
Again the fevers of excitement roll
Tides of emotion through that public soul
Which heaves vast London, while 'mid hearts that mourn,
A dead Immortal to his tomb is borne.
A thrilling freshness in the bracing air
Gives sudden token that the wind is fair;
Or the blue forehead of the Sky afar
Glows like a gem of lustre one lone star,
Whose quiv'ring radiance, exquisitely bright,
Throbs through the air, and fascinates the sight.
Relenting Winter hath subdued her rain,
And, lo! the clearing heavens are calm again:—
A beaming change of blessed weather
To welcome hearts convened together,
As though the conscious Atmosphere would pay
Some genial homage to this glorious day.

IV.

MORNING.

And now go forth!—a spectacle to see
Eternalized in mind and memory.
Yet, when the Muse of History records
The pomp we celebrate, in deathless words,
She will not pause o'er car and cavalcade,
Or mailéd hosts in banner'd pomp array'd;
But *this* will be the truth, to tell,—
That Empires loved one Man so well,
A million and a half of mourners came
Whose hearts were motto'd with his cherish'd name!
The People make the pageant then;
His monument is living men;
And never in the past of hero-crowded time
Look'd Hannibal so great, or Pompey so sublime!
And why? because the Chief of Waterloo
Teaches all ages what firm Will can do
When, all intol'rant of the mean and low,
Virtue his friend, and Vice his only foe,
Each baser passion from the bosom hurl'd,—
The vanquisher of Self is victor of the World!
Career and character, where thus combined,
Both make and move the hist'ry of mankind,
When perill'd Crisis and o'erwhelming Power
Need more than strategy to front the hour.

V.

On window, roof, and balcony,
Where foot can stand, or eye can see;
By churchyard-gate, or garden-wall,
Near porch and palace, hut and hall
Crowd human forms, like clust'ring bees
That swarm at noon on summer-trees;
While, clashing with incessant jar,
Rush chariot-wheels and rolling car;
Horse and horsemen then combine,
Clear the way, and close the line:—
Still, the trooping thousands come!
Deeper yet the distant hum;
Ev'ry form and ev'ry face
Apparell'd with emotion's trace;
Each for each, and all on all
For succour in loud chorus call,
Till the whirling air around
Surges like a sea of sound!

VI.

THE PROCESSION FORMS.

'Tis eight o'clock by matin-chime;
And signal-guns announce the time,

While countless numbers, mute with breathless
trance,
Seem melted into one, to view the Pomp
advance.

With ling'ring preludes, long and low,
Comes marching on, serene and slow,
'Mid symphonies of solemn woe
Yon Cavalcade of Death!
With mourning trump and muffled drum
Behold the vast procession come,
And hold your pausing breath!

Cornet, flute, and clarion pour
Mingled death-wails more and more;
Bannerets and blazonry
With plumes of tow'ring pageantry,
Mingled with the harness'd gun,
Streaming Flag and Gonfalon,
Colours out of carnage won,
Rifles, Horse, and Fusileer,
Dragoon, Marine, and Grenadier,
And scar-worn Pensioners, with sable wands
That faintly quiver'd in their feeble hands,
Steed and soldiers' measured pace,
Wearing each some mourning-trace,
While sob and sigh intensely show
The heavings of the heart below,
All this, with heavy tramp, and hollow
tread,
To symbolise they mourn the dead,—
Concentre, if thou can, the harmonising
whole,
And treasure it with tears of sympathy and
soul!

VII.

THE CHARGER.

But yet awaits a tearful Sight,
Though not with martial splendour dight.
As some lone bugle, when the fight is done,
That wails a death-note, while the dying sun
Goes down on carnage-cover'd fields;
O'er sad imagination wields
A spell more potent than the cannon-roar,
So, yon last steed which bears its Chief no more,
Pierces the heart with pathos all its own
And moves each chord with some responsive
tone;
Where now, the last to close the cavalcade
That through three miles its winding pomp
display'd,
A groom-led Charger riderless
Comes drooping in its loneliness,
As though the meek-eyed Creature felt
Funereal sorrow through it melt.
And, who that saw the boot and spur,
And did not feel his life-blood stir,
When that denuded Steed a type was made to be
That glory is the garb earth puts on vanity!

VIII.

MILITARY SCENE.

Hark! again the muffled drum,
While the plumed Battalions come
Timing deep their measured tread
To the March surnamed the Dead,
Six in file, in single rank,
Ringing out a hollow clank:—
Mingle with the martial scene
Mailéd Guard and red Marine,
Foot and Horse-Artillery,
And brigades of Infantry:
For thus, each Regiment sent its type to show
Some fitting token of funereal woe;
And when, to end the vast array,
Hussar and Lancer lined the way,
The wailing Piper, next, a pibroch blew
And coronach that thrill'd the soul of Feeling
through!

IX.

FUNERAL-CAR.

But lo! with gloomy scutcheons glorious
Each telling of the Past victorious,
Engraved by heraldry of war,
Comes rolling on the laurell'd Car
Under the shade of whose triumphant pall
Imagination dreams the earthly all
Of Arthur, Duke of Wellington!—
The greatest Hero Time has gazed upon.
And never since bereavèd patriots met
In solemn anguish and sublime regret
Round the mourn'd bier of warrior, saint or
king,
Could grateful Mem'ry into action bring
Such impulses of thrilling awe
As sanctified the scene I saw,
Drawn by twelve steeds of sable hue
When first the Death-car roll'd in view.

X.

A LIVING SPECTACLE.

'Twas not the pomp, the banner, nor the
plume,
Nor all which glorifies a Warrior's tomb,
That touch'd with superhuman power
The awful pathos of that deathless hour.
'Twas moral Grandeur! 'twas the true
sublime
Of sacred Nature soaring out of time,
And drinking in from worlds which faith
can see
The inspirations of eternity.

And one such moment grasps an age of life,
With more than poetry and passion rife;
Making us feel immortal instincts rise
And claim celestial kinship with the Skies.

XI.

Round that high Car though countless hosts assembled,
And under pawing steeds the pathways trembled,
You might have heard your heart-pulse beat,
So hush'd became the o'eraw'd Street!
And pale, as if with inward prayer,
The living Mass stood gazing there,
With heads uncover'd and with moisten'd eyes,
Whose silence utter'd, "There a Hero lies!
From whom, when call'd to bid the earth farewell,
The truncheons of eight laurell'd Armies fell;
The pillar of our Church and State,
By self-renouncement nobly great;
Who in the storm of public danger stood
Bold as the rock that baffles ocean's flood,
And when the lion-flag of warfare was unfurl'd
Bade Vict'ry rear it high, and wave it round the world!"

XII.

EUROPEAN HOMAGE.

Upon his honour'd Bier, attendant,
With nodding plume and waving pendant,
Alone not Britain sent the bearers of his pall;
But, moved by gallant chivalry
That breathed of heart-nobility,
Seven Marshals graced with Heraldry,
From foreign lands, spontaneously from all,
Have come to tell of his career
Whose prowess friend and foe revere,
Each bearing in the crape-bound hand
Some bâton of extinct command
Monarchs or princes had in life bestow'd
On that brave Chief, to whom their Kingdoms owed
A vaster debt than peerless Rank can pay,
Or golden Orders in their gemm'd array.
Belgium and Prussia, Portugal and Spain,
And distant Russia, from her ice-bound plain,
With Hanover, and England too,
Remember'd mighty Waterloo!
But Austria sent no warrior-chief
Her own to blend with British grief;
Coldly apart from those united kings
Who each their homage to a Hero brings,
Preferr'd to stand, and gracelessly forget
The Past she burdens with an unpaid debt,
Because a woman-scourger in his body felt
A Nemesis for that vile blow he dealt;*
Alas! that in an hour like this, the pride
Of less than Littleness was gratified!
And caused a Kingdom thus to stand alone,
Nor honour Him who saved her shaken throne.

XIII.

VETERANS AND MOURNERS.

But turn we to a nobler theme.
How mournful, then, their martial dream
Who, while around them tramp and stir
The Herald, Troop, and Trumpeter,
Were haunted with a blent array
Of scenes which ne'er dissolve away;
And imaged forth with mind's creative eye
The Man who taught them how to dare, and die,
As, trench'd with many a battle-scar,
The white-hair'd Veterans of war
Gather and group beside yon bier,
And scarce can hide the welling tear!

Past sharers in dread fields of blood
Full oft with him these comrades stood,
When valour beam'd from that victorious brow
Which cold in coffin'd death lay plumeless now!
And *could* they view those guns, whose dauntless roar
Thunder'd proud Albion's name from shore to shore,
Or on the steed, array'd in boot and spur,
Fix their sad eyes, nor feel the dead Past stir
Within them, like a living thought
With years of resurrection fraught?
On Torres Vedras' bulwark'd lines
Again the flag of England shines!
Vimiera's field, and Salamanca's fight,
And Talavera's, when it roused the night,
Sebastian's siege, and Badajos' return,
And Albuera, with its conflict stern:
Visions of battle and campaign arise
And flash before their unforgetting eyes!—
From the first laurel gain'd at dread Assaye,
To the red carnage on that thrilling day

* These lines allude to a summary act of popular vengeance executed by an English mob on an Austrian, who had disgraced himself by cruelty to women.

Embalm'd for ever in sublime renown,
When England struck the Gallic Eagle down,
And the War-Fiend,* who half a world had won,
Sank wither'd by the blast of Wellington!

Thus, round the coffin of th' heroic Dead
A living atmosphere of love is spread
That glows with hist'ry, till the plumèd bier
Is almost hidden by a warrior's tear.
The shock of Armies, and the battle-shout
Of charging Valour, when it put to rout
Column and cavalry in fierce attack,
Ring through his brain, and bring the dead Years back:
Till fancy hears the loud "Hurrah!"
That Picton raised at Quatre-Bras
Where royal Brunswick closed his eye,
While, bivouack'd beneath the sky,
Some bleeding sentinel who watch'd the night
Heard the last bugle that bewail'd the fight.

XIV.

PROCESSION TO THE CATHEDRAL.

Again we listen! for the cornet's wail
Pours on the wind its melancholy tale.
Upward, o'er the troop-lined way
Flank'd in full and firm array,
Still the banner'd Pomp proceedeth,
Horse and horseman onward leadeth;
Mourning hearts with inward chime
To the Dead March beating time;
Near and nearer still they come
To the Hero's burial-home,
Under the arching shade of yon cathedral-dome.

XV.

FAREWELL.

Ere between the church-yard gate
Car and cavalcade have enter'd,
Still for thoughtful eyes await
Such a scene and sight concenter'd,
As all the pomps which fascinate the gaze,
The wreaths of conquest, and the palms of praise
Can rival not,
But sink forgot,

* Have you forgotten that the bones of our children, of our brothers, everywhere attest our fidelity—in the sands of Africa, on the shores of the Guadalquivir and the Tagus, on the banks of the Vistula, and in the frozen deserts of Muscovy?—During more than ten years, three millions of Frenchmen have perished for a man who wishes still to struggle against all Europe.—LA FAYETTE.

When England's sworded Prince appears;
And, marching by him, touch'd with manly tears,
Saluting warriors slowly move,
And shadow forth the signs of love
On face and feature, which betoken
What quiv'ring words could *not* have spoken,
But now with tearful eloquence they tell,—
The British army bid their Chief farewell!

XVI.

ST. PAUL'S.

'Mid radiant masses of reposing light
Yon Temple seems dilated to the sight,
While vast perspectives of cathedral-gloom
Whose drap'ry serves to symbolise the tomb,
Entrance the gazer with absorbing spell
As though some Vision on the spirit fell.
Thoughts of earth and thrills from heaven
Thus to each and all are given,
And accost the inner-sense
With a dumb, deep eloquence,
Such as Faith and Conscience hear
When they bend around the bier.

Now enter there! survey that vaulted Dome
Encircled o'er with beads of golden light,
As though a supernat'ral noon had come
To glorify the realms of night.
Round the curved base a wreath of lustre glances,
High o'er its many-pictured roof advances,
And lights, as if with living play,
Gigantic forms in war-array:
From capital to capital
Through transept and pilaster'd wall
Down nave and aisle the line of lustre streams
O'er circled tiers of dome-ascending seats,
Till the last row some closing pillar meets,
Where soft effulgence tremulously gleams.

But not by picture-words of poetry
Yon mass of concentrated human kind
In hues of language can reflected be,
As e'er to fascinate and fill the mind,
And realise what *they* beheld,
With voiceless wonder inly quell'd,
Whose spell-bound eyes o'ergazed the mighty Whole,
And caught the magic of the mind and soul

Which beam'd from ev'ry face in that funereal throng,
Beyond the painter's hue, above the poet's song!
Throne and Altar, Bench and State,
Brave and wise, and good and great,
All Britain welcomes with revering eye,
Fill'd the hush'd Fane where buried heroes lie,
And ocean's warrior, in his tomb sublime,
Waits the last trump which rings the knell of Time.*
Another gaze! while amber'd sunbeams fall
And through the lofty dome-light streaming,
Come slanting downward on the concave wall
With more than earth-born radiance gleaming,—
On tinted robes in tremulous array
Pulses of painted lustre seem to play.
But, hark! before the western-gate
A solemn Dead-March sounds;
And, moving in sepulchral state,
Approaches to its hallow'd bounds
The last Procession; while the booming knell
Blends its deep cadence with the organ-swell.
Planted by each bearer's hand,
Flag and Guidon take their stand;
In glitt'ring column, robed with gorgeous vest,
A double file of grouping warriors rest
Around yon hidden burial-place;
While Choir and Clergy up the nave
Marshal and move, and gleam and wave
Their priestly robes, as on they pace.
And mark, along the living mass
Electrical emotions pass!—
Profound, unreason'd, an instinctive awe
Of something deeper than mere Vision saw,
Thrills the mute concourse, till they meekly rise
With all the patriot glist'ning in their eyes;
And feelings not of this world clothe each brow,
As on, with measured tread, advances now
The choir-procession, while the burial-chant
With resurrection-tones so jubilant,
Peals the dead Warrior on his plumêd bier,
'Mid sigh, and sob, and many a martial tear,
Onward to his long, last home
Underneath th' illumined Dome!
But as the wind-bow'd plumes were bending
High o'er his coffin-lid depending,

* Nelson is buried in St. Paul's.

How life and death together seem'd to be
And awed the gazer like a Mystery!

. . . .

XVII.

Thus amidst the boom of bells
Tolling their funereal-knells,
The organ-peal, and cannon-roar
Re-echoed round the temple-door,
With all due pomp of heraldry,
With each befitting pageantry,
'Mid waving banners to his tomb is borne
Great Wellington!—and soon shall wailing horn
And cadence of the muffled drum
Tell the awed Soul the last is come!
For, ducal crown and scutcheon'd bier
Will be engulph'd, and disappear;
Down the chasm, dark and deep
Yearning eyes will strain and weep;
Then, the staff of office broken
Will reveal its sign and token;
And the Garter-King proclaim
More than ever earth-wide fame
Gave heroic Man before,
Or the brightest patriot bore.

THE BURIAL.

Like dream-heard music when it melts away
Serenely dying, sad and slow,
Thus from the living air and light of day
Adown the vaulted crypt below
The coffin'd frame of Wellington
Descends,—recedes,—and all is gone!
And o'er it deepens with expressive gloom
The yawning darkness of that open Tomb,
Where Nelson sleeps, but now, where two are laid
In death's cold slumber, side by side;
Of whom hereafter 'twill be nobly said,
Millions were mourners when they died!

And in the Temple, where he lies
Entomb'd with martial obsequies,
Oh! never since that Shrine of prayer
Lifted its cross in sun and air,
Or choral praise with chanted swell
Upon the ears of Godhead fell,*
Have quiring voices breathed an anthem-tone,
From sixteen thousand melted into one,
The diapason of whose deep Amen
To earth seem echo'd back from glory-realms again!

* "Thou that hearest prayer."—*Ps.* lxv. 2.

XVIII.

CONCLUSION.

The booming echoes of the minute-gun
Hark! how they roll from London's castle-towers,
Proclaiming the sepulchral rites are done:
Yet, ere the World resume its wonted powers,
While dying notes from many a distant knell
Sink into silence with a sad farewell,
A moralising gloom on man descends
And not unfitly with the Pageant blends.

NATURE'S ANALOGY.

In red magnificence of evening-dyes,
Oft like a paradise of cloud there lies
A pomp aërial, such as poets love,
When beauty consecrates the heavens above.
There, musing on some breezy height,
Enthroned in loveliness and light,
A lone spectator stands to view
The day-god wear his parting hue,
When gliding down the crimson'd west
He wraps him in his regal vest.—
How exquisite awhile to be
Surrender'd up to Sky and Sea!
As drinking in the splendid whole
He mingles with Creation's soul,
While lisping waves, with pensive lull,
And cadence faintly-beautiful,
Chime with the hour, till earth and air
An elemental magic wear,
And so entrance impassion'd Hearts,
The soul forgets, the Scene departs.—
But while they dream, the cloud-pomp dies
A beauteous death along the skies;
The pallid dews of night descend,
And dimness and dejection end
Those witching spells of sunset-hour
Which give to poesy its power.

XIX.

MORAL CONTRAST.

So would it be when this great Day shall close
Which bore the Warrior to his dead repose,
If tinsell'd pageantry or painted scene
Gave the *true* witness which the day hath been.
But when the blazonry of public Woe
Fades from our vision, like an air-born show,
The deep significance which underlies
All outer-forms is one that never dies,
But melts into the moral life within
And prompts that spirit where those Aims begin
Which soar beyond a passion for renown,
And learn from Duty how to win the crown.
For England's people, from the humblest clan
Of working poor and toil-worn artisan,
From town, from hamlet, and the hawthorn-side
Where the lone cotters in contentment bide,
Have each received within responsive mind
Ennobling thoughts which elevate mankind.
And thus, perchance, when other palms are won,
Time will reveal how much this day hath done
To form the patriot in the public heart;
Or, teach the warrior his predestined part,
And sow, as far as pure Example can,
Those seeds, whose harvest is—heroic Man!

Mere vulgar Heroes of the vicious stamp
Whose names suggest a carnage, or a camp,
Meteors of Crime, the monsters of the past
Who sweep the world with desolating blast,
And when they perish in their dread career
Leave Time to track them by the widow's tear,—
May point the moral of some future page:
But, when the Warrior, Senator, and Sage
Meet in one man, like Him we mourn to-day,
Conscience predicts, what unborn years will say,—
That he had pass'd into the Nation's heart
Of which he grew a principal and part;
And when he died, far more than boundless Grief
Sought in the burial-pomp a fit relief,—
Each for himself put fun'ral raiment on,
And wept a friend in mourning Wellington.

XX.

PATRIOTISM.

And Thou, environ'd with thy zone of waves,
Nursling of waters! whom old Ocean laves
As though He loved to hear his billow-roar
Champion the rocks which sentinel thy shore;
Intrepid Isle! whose amaranthine bays
Bloom in the light of Heaven's approving gaze;
Defender of the Faith in Christendom's great heart!
Well may we proudly think on this day what Thou art,
And, pond'ring o'er th' imperishable past,
See Glory's halo round thy hist'ry cast!

Let Patriots boast of thine and thee,
Of Commerce, Arms, and Chivalry,

Of princely homes, of palace-halls,
Of Culture, and whate'er recals
How lofty Will can dare, and lion-heart can do,
When Trafalgar became an ocean-Waterloo:
'Tis right to let such feeling reign,
And when dead Ages breathe again,
O'er the harp-string of the soul
Like a lyric rapture roll.

And their proud boast is purer still
If Thou thy mission-work fulfil,
As dauntless champion of the Truth to stand
And brighten Europe like a beacon-land,
By teaching tyrants who would crush the mind,
'Tis sacrilege!—for God is there enshrined.
Thus sacred law and liberty unite
A Prince's sceptre with the People's right,
And in the thunder of a bold-voiced Press
Nations can utter forth their nobleness,
Who find in scripture, when it frees the soul,
A Magna Charta which sublimes the whole!

THE PEOPLE.

Yet bounds the heart with patriotic bliss
Through all excitements of a morn like this,
To think, how nobly have the People proved
They well can honour whom they wisely loved!
For while they paid to peerless Wellington
A homage Alexander never won,
The lofty and the low, our peasants and our peers
Have met and mingled here, unchill'd by frowns or fears,
In this metropolis of varied Man
Where Nature musters every type she can;
And yet, no impious Wrong hath once profaned
The sabbath-peace of sentiment which reign'd;
But all was just, magnanimous, sincere;
And, heralded by many a votive tear,
The sun went down with no recorded crime
And left the British character sublime!

XXI.

THE HERO.

With parting homage let these lines conclude,
And consecrate a poet's gratitude
To him, the paragon of English praise,
In whom Posterity's admiring gaze
Will mark a Hero, who adorn'd the Earth
And made the World a debtor to his worth:
Best of the best, and greatest of the great
In all which guards a throne, or guides a state;
The massive grandeur of whose balanced mind
Was so adjusted, that the Will inclined
Where Conscience led, and not where Fortune threw
Her fleeting radiance o'er some distant view.—
His frame was iron; and with sleepless force
Through half a cent'ry traced his hero-course:
Abroad, at home, in Senate-house, or Field,
Friendship and Hate alike to his firm counsels yield,
Whose glance, by mental intuition, ran
Through each dark maze of policy and plan,
And reached conclusions whose results contain
Maxims and morals, which will rule and reign
As long as Treason, Stratagem, and War
Endanger thrones, or threaten from afar.

Just as the Law, inflexible as Truth,
Thus lived great Wellington in age and youth;
And when hoar'd years had bow'd that classic head
With silver-locks so venerably spread,
How did we greet him in the public Square
And rouse the stranger with re-echo'd "There!
"There comes The Duke! whose very shadow throws
A light on England, wheresoe'er he goes;"
While pausing Childhood with entrancéd eye
Beheld him in his glory moving by:
And though the winter of declining age
Touch'd form and feature with a sad presage,
In list'ning reverence how the Senate hung
On the plain Saxon of that pithy tongue!—
The smiting earnestness of honest speech
Which taught more wisdom than mere words can reach.

And hence, the Arbiter of Empires, he
Reign'd on his throne of true simplicity,
And by the firmness of unflinching will
Rallied around him trusting Empires still:—
A Kingly Subject, whose unscepter'd hand
Was more than Armies, when it waved command.
And this, by virtue of that noble Creed
That helm'd each movement in the hour of need,
The master-spell which rein'd emotion down—
That danger must be met by duty to The Crown!

XXII.

FINAL APOSTROPHÈ.

Since God descends through history to Man
Whose dark vicissitudes but veil His plan,
And mortal Agents, while they do and dare
Are but the Organs of His purpose there,
Oh, Thou ! to whom the shields* of earth belong,
The everlasting Stronger than the Strong;†
Divine Upholder of heroic souls
Whom prowess arms, or purity controls,
Bulwark'd with blessings which reveal Thy Hand
Long may the charter'd State of England stand;
That peerless growth of patriotic mind,
The great, eternal Wonder of mankind!
Lodge in our British hearts true love of Thee
And cause Thine Image on this earth to be,
Whose varied destinies of weal and woe
Preach the vast truth a creedless world should know,—

The life of Nations is a god-like thing
Beyond mere Laureates of the world to sing;
Nursed and ennobled not by wealth and power
Nor all the pageants which bemock the hour,
But ruled by reason, and by faith sublimed
To loftier heights than Glory ever climb'd.

Celestial Lord of uncreated Love!
Waft to our souls pure wisdom from above,
And teach the secret of Thy moral plan,—
The source of freedom is God's will in man,
When sainted hearts have meekly understood
That perfect greatness is a power for good;
Typing the Godhead, Who Himself is great
Not by the thunders of enthronéd state;
Yet in the majesty of boundless might
Wills what is law, but in that law wills right;
That Saints and Seraphim alike may see
Their archetypes in His eternity,
And while they anthem an almighty Throne
Reflect His glories, and increase their own.‡

* Ps. xlvii. 90. † Luke xi. 22.

‡ Every reader who can appreciate the homage of intellect to the illustrious dead, will be gratified by the perusal of two masterpieces of eulogy which appeared when the great Duke died. The first is an article from "The Times," and the second, Mr. D'Israeli's speech, delivered in the House of Commons.

"If aught can lessen this day the grief of England upon the death of her greatest son, it is the recollection that the life which has just closed leaves no duty incomplete, and no honour unbestowed. The Duke of Wellington had exhausted nature and exhausted glory. His career was one unclouded longest day, filled from dawn to nightfal with renowned actions, animated by unfailing energy in the public service, guided by unswerving principles of conduct and of statesmanship. He rose by a rapid series of achievements which none had surpassed to a position which no other man in this nation ever enjoyed. The place occupied by the Duke of Wellington in the councils of the country and in the life of England can no more be filled. There is none left in the army or the Senate to act and speak with like authority. There is none with whom the valour and the worth of this nation were so incorporate. Yet, when we consider the fulness of his years and the abundance of his incessant services, we may learn to say with the Roman orator, '*Satis diu vixisse dicito,*' since, being mortal, nothing could be added either to our veneration or to his fame. Nature herself had seemed for a time to expand her inexorable limits, and the infirmities of age to lay a lighter burden on that honoured head. Generations of men had passed away between the first exploits of his arms and the last counsels of his age, until, by a lot unexampled in history, the man who had played the most conspicuous part in the annals of more than half a century became the last survivor of his contemporaries, and carries with him to the grave all living memory of his own achievements. To what a century, to what a country, to what achievements was that life successfully dedicated! For its prodigious duration—for the multiplicity of contemporary changes and events, far outnumbering the course of its days and years—for the invariable and unbroken stream of success which attended it from its commencement to its close, from the first flash of triumphant valour in Indian war to that senatorial wisdom on which the Sovereign and the nation hung for counsel to its latest hour—for the unbending firmness of character which bore alike all labour and all prosperity—and for unalterable attachment to the same objects, the same principles, the same duties, undisturbed by the passions of youth and unrelaxed by the honours and enjoyments of peace and of age—the life of the Duke of Wellington stands alone in history. In him, at least, posterity will trace a character superior to the highest and most abundant gifts of fortune. If the word 'heroism' can be not unfairly applied to him, it is because he remained greater than his own prosperity, and rose above the temptations by which other men of equal genius, but less self-government, have fallen below their destinies. His life has nothing to gain from the language of panegyric, which would compare his military exploits or his civil statesmanship with the prowess of an Alexander or a Cæsar, or with the astonishing career of him who saw his empire overthrown by the British General at Waterloo. They were the offspring of passion and of genius, flung from the volcanic depths of revolutions and of civil war to sweep with meteoric splendour across the earth, and to collapse in darkness before half the work of life was done. Their violence, their ambition, their romantic existence, their reverses, and their crimes will for ever fascinate the interest of mankind, and constitute the secret of their fame, if not of their greatness. To such attractions the life and character of the Duke of Wellington present no analogy. If he rose to scarce inferior renown, it was by none of the passions or the arts which they indulged or employed. Unvanquished in the field, his sword was never drawn for territorial conquest, but for the independence of Europe and the salvation of his country. Raised by the universal gratitude of Europe and of this nation to the highest point of rank and power which a subject of the British monarchy could attain, he wore those dignities and he used that influence within the strictest limits of a subject's duty. No law was ever twisted to his will, no right was ever sacrificed by one hair's breadth for his aggrandizement. There lived not a man either among his countrymen or his antagonists who could say that this great Duke had wronged him; for his entire existence was devoted to the cause of legal authority and regulated power. You seek in it in vain for those strokes of audacious enterprise which in other great captains, his rivals in fame, have sometimes won the prize of crowns or turned the fate of nations. But his whole career shines with the steady light of day. It has nothing to conceal, it has nothing to interpret by the flexible organs of history. Everything in it is manly, compact, and clear; shaped to one rule of public duty, animated by one passion—the love of England, and the service of the Crown.

"The Duke of Wellington lived, commanded, and governed in unconscious indifference or disdainful aversion to those common incentives of human action which are derived from the powers of imagination and of sentiment. He held them cheap, both in their weakness and in their strength. The force and weight of his character stooped to no such adventitious influences. He might have kindled more enthusiasm, especially in the early and doubtful days of his Peninsular career; but in his successful and triumphant pursuit of glory her name never passed his lips even in his addresses to his soldiers. His entire nature and character were moulded on reality. He lived to see things as they were. His acute glance and cool judgment pierced at once through the surface which entangles the imagination or kindles the sympathy of the feelings. Truth, as he loved her, is to be reached by a rougher path and by sterner minds. In war, in politics, and in the common transactions of life, the Duke of Wellington adhered inflexibly to the most precise correctness in word and deed. His temperament abhorred disguises and despised exaggerations. The fearlessness of his actions was never the result of speculative confidence or foolhardy presumption, but it lay mainly in a just perception of the true relation in which he stood to his great antagonists in the field or in the Senate. The greatest exploits of his life, such as the passage of the Douro, followed by the march on Madrid, the battle of Waterloo, and the passing the Catholic Relief Bill, were performed under no circumstances that could inspire enthusiasm. Nothing but the coolness of the player could have won the mighty stakes upon a [cast apparently so adverse to his success. Other commanders have attained the highest pitch of glory when they disposed of the colossal resources of empires, and headed armies already flushed with the conquest of the world. The Duke of Wellington found no such encouragement in any part of his career. At no time were the means at his disposal adequate to the ready and certain execution of his designs. His steady progress in the Peninsular campaigns went on against the current of fortune, till that current was itself turned by perseverance and resolution. He had a clear and complete perception of the dangers he encountered, but he saw and grasped the latent power which baffled those dangers and surmounted resistances apparently invincible. That is precisely the highest degree of courage, for it is courage conscious, enlightened, and determined.

"Clearness of discernment, correctness of judgment, and rectitude in action were, without doubt, the principal elements of the Duke's brilliant achievements in war, and of his vast authority in the councils of his country, as well as in the conferences of Europe. They gave to his determinations an originality and vigour akin to that of genius, and sometimes imparted to his language in debate a pith and significance at which more brilliant orators failed to arrive. His mind, equally careless of obstacles and of effect, travelled by the shortest road to its end; and he retained, even in his latest years, all the precision with which he was wont to handle the subjects that came before him, or had at any time engrossed his attention. This was the secret of that untaught manliness and simplicity of style that pervades the vast collection of his despatches, written as they were amidst the varied cares and emotions of war; and of that lucid and appropriate mode of exposition which never failed to leave a clear impression on the minds of those whom he addressed. Other men have enjoyed, even in this age, more vivid faculties of invention and contrivance, a more extended range of foresight, a more subtle comprehension of the changing laws of society and the world. But the value of these finer perceptions, and of the policy founded upon them, has never been more assured than when it was tried and admitted by the wisdom and patriotism of that venerable mind. His superiority over other men consisted rather in the perfection of those qualities which he pre-eminently possessed, than in the variety or extent of his other faculties.

"These powers, which were unerring when applied to definite and certain facts, sometimes failed in the appreciation of causes which had not hitherto come under their observation. It is, perhaps, less to be wondered at that the soldier and the statesman of 1815, born and bred in the highest school of Tory politics, should have miscarried in his opinion of those eventful times which followed the accession of William IV., than that the defeated opponent of Reform in 1831 should have risen into the patriot senator of 1846 and 1851. Yet the Administration of 1828, in which the Duke of Wellington occupied the first and most responsible place, passed the Catholic Emancipation Act, and thereby gave the signal of a rupture in the Tory party, never afterwards entirely healed, and struck the heaviest blow on a system which the growing energies of the nation resented and condemned. Resolute to oppose what he conceived to be popular clamour, no man ever recognised with more fidelity the claims of a free nation to the gradual development of its interest and its rights; nor were his services to the cause of liberty and improvement the less great because they usually consisted in bending the will or disarming the prejudices of their fiercest opponents. Attached by birth, by character, and by opinion to the order and the cause of the British aristocracy, the Duke of Wellington knew that the true power of that race of nobles lies, in this age of the world, in their inviolable attachment to constitutional principles, and their honest recognition of popular rights. Although his personal resolution and his military experience qualified him better than other men to be the champion of resistance to popular turbulence and sedition, as he showed by his preparations in May, 1832, and in April, 1848, yet wisdom and forbearance were ever the handmaidens of his courage, and, while most firmly determined to defend, if necessary, the authority of the State, he was the first to set an example of conciliatory sacrifice to the reasonable claims of the nation. He was the Catulus of our Senate, after having been our Cæsar in the field; and, if the commonwealth of England had ever saluted one of her citizens with the Roman title of Parens Patriæ, that touching honour would have been added to the peerage and the baton of Arthur Wellesley by the respectful gratitude and faith of the people.

"Though singularly free from every trace of cant, his mind was no stranger to the sublime influence of religious truth, and he was assiduous in the observances of the public ritual of the church of England. At times, even in the extreme period of his age, some accident would betray the deep current of feeling which he never ceased to entertain towards all that was chivalrous and benevolent. His charities were unostentatious but extensive, and he bestowed his interest throughout life upon an incredible number of persons and things which claimed his notice and solicited his aid. Every social duty, every solemnity, every ceremony, every merry-making, found him ready to take his part in it. He had a smile for the youngest child, a compliment for the prettiest face, an answer to the readiest tongue, and a lively interest in every incident of life, which it seemed beyond the power of age to chill. When time had somewhat relaxed the sterner mould of his manhood, its effects were chiefly indicated by an unabated taste for the amusements of fashionable society, incongruous at times with the dignity of extreme old age, and the recollections of so virile a career. But it seemed a part of the Duke's character that everything that presented itself was equally welcome, for he had become a part of everything, and it was foreign to his nature to stand aloof from any occurrence to which his presence could contribute. He seems never to have felt the flagging spirit or the reluctant step of indolence or *ennui*, or to have recoiled from anything that remained to be done; and this complete performance of every duty, however small, as long as life remained, was the same quality which had carried him in triumph through his campaigns, and raised him to be one of the chief Ministers of England and an arbiter of the fate of Europe. It has been said that in the most active and illustrious lives there comes at last some inevitable hour of melancholy and of satiety. Upon the Duke of Wellington that hour left no impression, and probably it never shed its influence over him; for he never rested on his former achievements or his length of days, but marched onwards to the end, still heading the youthful generations which had sprung into life around him, and scarcely less intent on their pursuits than they are themselves. It was a finely balanced mind to have worn so bravely and so well. When men in after times shall look back to the annals of England for examples of energy and public virtue among those who have raised this country to her station on the earth, no name will remain more conspicuous or more unsullied than that of Arthur Wellesley, the Great Duke of Wellington. The actions of his life were extraordinary, but his character was equal to his actions. He was the very type and model of an Englishman; and, though men are prone to invest the worthies of former ages with a dignity and merit they commonly withhold from their contemporaries, we can select none from the long array of our captains and our nobles who, taken for all in all, can claim a rivalry with him who is gone from amongst us, an inheritor of imperishable fame."

DISRAELI'S SPEECH.

"The House of Commons is called upon to-night to fulfil a sorrowful, but a noble duty. It has to recognise, in the face of the country and the civilised world, the loss of the most illustrious of our citizens, and to offer to the ashes of the great departed the solemn anguish of a bereaved nation. The princely personage who has left us was born in an age more fertile of great events than any period of recorded time. Of those vast incidents the most conspicuous were his own deeds, and those were performed with the smallest means, and in defiance of the greatest obstacles. He was therefore not only a great man, but the greatest man of a great age. Amid the chaos and conflagration which attended the end of the last century there rose one of those beings who seem born to master mankind. It is not too much to say that Napoleon combined the imperial ardour of Alexander with the strategy of Hannibal. The kings of the earth fell before his fiery and subtle genius, and at the head of all the power of Europe he denounced destruction to the only land which dared to be free. The Providential superintendence of this world seems seldom more manifest than in the dispensation which ordained that the French Emperor and Wellesley should be born in the same year; that in the same year they should have embraced the same profession; and that, natives of distant islands, they should both have sought their military education in that illustrious land which each in his turn was destined to subjugate. During the long struggle for our freedom, our glory, I may say our existence, Wellesley fought and won fifteen pitched battles, all of the highest class, concluding with one of those crowning victories which give a colour and aspect to history. During this period that can be said of him which can be said of no other captain—that he captured 3,000 cannon from the enemy, and never lost a single gun. The greatness of his exploits was only equalled by the difficulties he overcame. He had to encounter at the same time a feeble government, a factious opposition, and a distrustful people, scandalous allies, and the most powerful enemy in the world. He gained victories with starving troops, and carried on sieges without tools; and, as if to complete the fatality which in this sense always awaited him, when he had succeeded in creating an army worthy of Roman legions and of himself, this invincible host was broken up on the eve of the greatest conjuncture of his life, and he entered the field of Waterloo with raw levies and discomfited allies. But the star of Wellesley never failed. He has been called fortunate, for Fortune is a divinity that ever favours those who are alike sagacious and intrepid, inventive and patient. It was his character that created his career. This alike achieved his exploits and guarded him from vicissitudes. It was his sublime self-control that regulated his lofty fate. It has been the fashion of late years to disparage the military character. Forty years of peace have hardly qualified us to be aware how considerable and how complex are the qualities which are necessary for the formation of a great general. It is not enough to say that he must be an engineer, a geographer, learned in human nature, adroit in managing mankind; that he must be able to perform the highest duties of a Minister of State, and sink to the humblest offices of a commissary and a clerk; but he has to display all his knowledge, and he must do all these things at the same time and under extraordinary circumstances. At the same moment he must think of the eve and the morrow—of his flanks and of his reserve; he must carry with him ammunition, provisions, hospitals; he must calculate at the same time the state of the weather and the moral qualities of man; and all these elements which are perpetually changing, he must combine amid overwhelming cold or overpowering heat; sometimes amid famine, often amid the thunder of artillery. Behind all this, too, is the ever-present image of his country, and the dreadful alternative whether that country is to receive him with cypress or with laurel. But all these conflicting ideas must be driven from the mind of the military leader, for he must think—and not only think—he must think with the rapidity of lightning, for on a moment more or less depends the fate of the finest combination, and on a moment more or less depends glory or shame. Doubtless all this may be done in an ordinary manner by an ordinary man; as we see every day of our lives ordinary men making successful ministers of state, successful speakers, successful authors. But to do all this with genius is sublime. Doubtless, to think deeply and clearly in the recess of a cabinet is a fine intellectual demonstration, but to think with equal depth and equal clearness amid bullets is the most complete exercise of the human faculties. Although the military career of the Duke of Wellington fills so large a space in history, it was only a comparatively small section of his prolonged and illustrious life. Only eight years elapsed from Vimiera to Waterloo, and from the date of his first commission to the last cannon-shot on the field of battle scarcely twenty years can be counted. After all his triumphs, he was destined for another career; and, if not in the prime, certainly in the perfection of manhood, he commenced a civil career scarcely less eminent than those military achievements which will live for ever in history. Thrice was he ambassador of his sovereign to those great historic congresses that settled the affairs of Europe; twice was he Secretary of State; twice was he Commander-in-Chief; and once he was Prime Minister of England. His labours for his country lasted to the end. A few months ago he favoured the present advisers of the Crown with his thoughts on the Burmese war, expressed in a State paper, characterised by all his sagacity and experience; and he died the active chieftain of that famous army to which he has left the tradition of his glory. There was one passage in the life of the Duke of Wellington which should hardly be passed unnoticed on such an occasion, and in such a scene, as this. It is our pride that he was one of ourselves; it is our pride that Sir Arthur Wellesley sat upon these benches. Tested by the ambition and the success of ordinary men, his career, though brief was distinguished. He entered royal councils and held a high ministerial post. But his House of Commons must not be measured by his seat at the Privy Council and his Irish Secretaryship. He achieved a success here which the greatest Ministers and the most brilliant orators can never hope to rival. That was a parliamentary success unequalled when he rose in his seat to receive the thanks of Mr. Speaker for a glorious victory; or, later still, when he appeared at the bar of this House and received, Sir, from one of your predecessors, in memorable language, the thanks of a grateful country for accumulated triumphs. There is one consolation which all Englishmen must feel under this bereavement. It is, that they were so well and so completely acquainted with this great man. Never did a person of such mark live so long, and so much in the public eye. I would be bound to say that there is not a gentleman in this House who has not seen him; many there are who have conversed with him; some there are who have touched his hand. His countenance, his form, his manner, his voice are impressed on every memory, and sound almost in every ear. In the golden saloon, and in the busy market-place, he might be alike observed. The rising generation will often recal his words of kindness, and the people followed him in the streets with a lingering gaze of reverent admiration. Who indeed, can ever forget that classic and venerable head, white with time, and radiant, as it were, with glory?—

—— "Stilichonis apex, et cognita fulsit.
Canities."

"To complete all, that we might have a perfect idea of this sovereign master of duty in all his manifold offices, he himself gave us a collection of administrative and military literature which no age and no country can rival; and, fortunate in all things, Wellesley found in his lifetime an historian whose immortal page already ranks with the classics of that land which Wellesley saved. The Duke of Wellington left to his countrymen a great legacy—greater even than his glory. He left them the contemplation of his character. I will not say his conduct revived the sense of duty in England. I would not say that of our country. But that his conduct inspired public life with a purer and more masculine tone I cannot doubt. His career rebukes restless vanity, and reprimands the irregular ebullitions of a morbid egotism. I doubt not that, among all orders of Englishmen, from those with the highest responsibilities of our society to those who perform the humblest duties, I dare say there is not a man who in his toil and his perplexity has not sometimes thought of the Duke, and found in his example support and solace. Though he lived so much in the hearts and minds of his countrymen—though he occupied such eminent posts and fulfilled such august duties—it was not till he died that we felt what a space he filled in the feelings and thoughts of the people of England. Never was the influence of real greatness more completely asserted than on his decease. In an age whose boast of intellectual equality flatters all our self-complacencies, the world suddenly acknowledged that it had lost the greatest of men; in an age of utility the most industrious and common-sense people in the world could find no vent for their woe and no representative for their sorrow but the solemnity of a pageant; and we—we who have met here for such different purposes—to investigate the sources of the wealth of nations, to enter into statistical research, and to encounter each other in fiscal controversy—we present the world the most sublime and touching spectacle that human circumstances can well produce—the spectacle of a Senate mourning a hero!"

SHADOWS OF DEATH.

(1829.)

"Darest thou die."—SHAKSPEARE.

VISION-SCENES.

THRONED in a vault where sleep departed kings
Behold the Tyrant of the world! Around
His shadowy head he waves a sceptre, made
Of monumental dust; and as it moves,
Before him glide a visionary throng
Of ministers, that do his deadly will.

First, Murder, with an eye of wolfish glare,
And brow of adamantine sternness, frowns,
His brooding visage blanch'd with guilt, and cold
As dead revenge; then Madness, with her locks
Of graceless beauty, crowding o'er a face
Terrifically wild: her cheeks are shrunk
As wither'd flowers, and in her fixèd eye
A lustre, meaningless yet mournful, dwells;
Like a pale cloud she glides along, and looks
Upon her lean-worn palms, before her spread
As tablets, where her idiot thoughts are traced!

Next Melancholy, with a downward brow,
Slow-paced, and solemn in her aspect, comes;
Behind, Intemperance, with degraded face,
Complexion'd like the redden'd clouds, which clasp
The dying sun; then Anger, with a storm
Of meaning hung upon her blacken'd front,
And Terror, eloquently dumb, appear.

With step as noiseless as the slumbering air,
Who comes, in beautiful decay?—her eyes
Dissolving with a feverish glow of light,
Her pallid nostrils delicately closed,
Her ringlets gathered in a languid wreath,
And on that cheek, once round with health's rich bloom,
A hectic tinge, as if the fairy tip
Of Beauty's finger faintly press'd it there:
Alas! Consumption is her fatal name.
But lo, a contrast! fierce with shining mail,
Sublime in aspect and supreme in gait,
Waving a crimson banner o'er his head,
With giant pace, stalks by terrific War!
His task?—To shatter thrones, and sully kings.

To these sad ministers of Death, succeed
Of Maladies a hideous crew; not least
Appalling, Pestilence, with eyes aghast,
And Famine, withered to a woful form.

Next, Phantoms round the Lord of human dust
In pallid indistinctness rise and move
For mental slaughter fearfully predoom'd!
Despair, with hollow, dim, sepulchral eyes;
And Love, the martyr of his own fix'd stake:
Ambition, with a canker-eaten soul;
And Genius, proud and pale, the self-consumed,
Whose gaze Infinity with spirit-light
Hath kindled, while the pining form decays
Like colour from a fainting cloud of eve!

CONTRASTS.

Such are thy delegates, disastrous Power!
Which make the martyr'd world thy prey, and seize
Their victims when and where they please. Alike
To thee the palace or the hut, the hall
Of Pleasure or the house of Wo.—A king
Mounts his high throne, with starry robes begirt;
Each look commands, and bright that royal brow
Beneath the burden of his jewell'd crown;
Before him princely courtiers bow their heads,
And on their fawning cheeks his smiles reflect,
And hover round him like a human god!
Thy bow is bent, thy dooming arrow shot,
And like a cloud-shade by the sun destroyed
Melts the great monarch from his pride and power!
The pale companion of the speechless earth,
A vault his palace, like his brother clay
Corrupted—bid his Court adore him now!

ANTICIPATIONS.

To die!—this gorgeous world of life and love
Forsake, and fleet beyond the bounds of thought;
To feel the death-dews creeping o'er each limb,
Our life-stream curdle, and the heart grow cold;
To be the flesh-worm's feast; to mould away
And blend our being with embracing dust;
All this, together with imagined wails
Of friends, whose tearful eyes attend our bier,—
Calls a chill horror round the name of death,
Which daunts the good, and makes the bad despair.

ANALOGIES.

All that we love and feel in nature's world
Bears dim relations to our common doom.
The clouds that blush, and die an airy death,
Or melt in weeping showers; the pensive streams
Whose tones are dying music; leaves new-born,
Which fade unpitied in the frosty arms
Of Winter, there to mingle with dead flowers,
Are all prophetic of our own decay.
And who, when hung enchanted o'er some page
Where genius flashes from each living line—
Hath never wander'd to the tomb, to see
The hand that penn'd it or the head that thought?

Dark feelings, coloured by the cloud of death,
With grand oppression thus the mind o'erflow,
As when some warm adorer of the dead
Who live, along the dim and banner'd aisle
Of arch'd cathedral, frames a dream sublime,
And learns how eloquent a tomb can be:
Or roams at twilight, where the Deep resounds,
To watch the ever-rolling waves converge
To where faint ocean weds the sky, and think,
Thus roll the restless hours of time along!

ASSOCIATIONS.

In banquet-halls, where queenly pleasures bloom,
And bright-faced Joy and young-eyed Beauty meet,
To them the shadows of the grave extend.
How oft, as unregarded on a throng
Of lovely creatures, in whose liquid eyes
The heart-warm feelings bathe, I've fondly look'd
With all a Poet's passion, and have wish'd
That years might never mar those perfect smiles,—
How often Death, as with a viewless wand
Has touched the scene, and witch'd it to a tomb,
Where beauty dwindled to a ghastly wreck
While moaning spirits of the Future cried,
Thus will it be when Time has work'd revenge!

LIFE A GRADUAL DEATH.

Our Yesterday is dead; our Morrow dies;
This hour is pining, and the breath we draw
So carelessly, our souls may waft—to where?
Our ages are but periodic tombs
Of those that went before: for childhood seems
The death of infancy; and childhood dies
When youth commences, which itself departs
In daring manhood; then old age begins,
Whose wrinkle deepens into manhood's grave:
Thus death is imaged by our very life!
And hope and pleasure, feeling, action, fame,
Have each their sepulchre: our visions melt
To dimness in Reality's chill tomb;
Creation's self a burning death must die,
And in eternity shall Time expire!

STREET FUNERAL.

And o'er the laughing holiday of life
When men are cheerful as the dancing beam
How often death's terrific darkness frowns!
See! where they come, the black-robed funeral train,
Solemn as silent thunder-clouds athwart
The noon-day sky: from heaven a radiance dies
The flowing pall with hues of mocking light;
Around Life moves his mighty throng, and deep
The death-bells wail along the ebbing air:
But one poor week hath vanish'd,—and that form,
Now clay-cold in the narrow coffin stretch'd,
Stalk'd o'er the street which takes him to his tomb!
On with the mourning train!—the crowd divide
Before them with a busy hum, then close
Behind, like billows by a prow dispersed
That sever but to clash and roar again!

ANGEL OF DEATH.

Angel of Darkness! out of hell evoked,
With dread the bosom of Creation thrill'd
When fell thy shadow over Eden's bower,
Whose beauty wither'd like the spirit's bloom
When the rich breath of young affection dies.
Look back! appall'd Imagination! gaze
Thine eye to dimness, o'er the track of time

Scathed by his fury! mark the demon-wing'd,
'Tis Death! the Uncontrollable! *his* flight
Begins, whose path wears Desolation's smile!
And how eternity its gate unbars
To let them in, those fleet and countless dead,
While myriads melt and vanish, like the gleams
That flash from fever's eye!————

HIS TRIUMPH.

Thy spell hath work'd,
Thou King of woes! thy wand hath been obey'd;
Destruction saw it, and Her deeds reply!
The sea hath buried in her floating tomb,
The fire devour'd, the blighting pest consumed,
The rocking earthquake into atoms crush'd,
And conflagration, havoc, siege, and war,
And malady which like a fiend-breath acts,
Have martyr'd,—what an unimagined host
Since the first grave for Adam's corpse unclosed!
And, oh, let mother, maid, and orphan tell,
Let parent, friend, whate'er affection clasps
Or sweet relationship of soul implies,—
How tears have rain'd from lids that watch'd and wept
As each beloved one, like a featured Shade
Melted in mute eternity! For Death
Hath cull'd his victims from the choicest bowers
And gardens of Existence: fair as bright
And pure as paradise before the Fall
Have babes departed, ere one smiling look
Hath travers'd earth, or seen the life of things:
And voiceless as the uncomplaining dews
That wither on the dusky cheek of Night,
The silent victims of the heart's decay
Have perish'd! while within the dart was fix'd
And rankling; not a sigh their secret told:
For pure and proud, and delicate as light
Their being faded: 'twas the blight of soul,
The mildew of the mind, that check'd and chill'd
Their health of spirit: friend and parent yearn'd
Around them, wondering *where* the venom lurk'd
Which thus with cruel stealth defaced and marr'd
That earth-born seraph, Beauty robed for heaven!
But still they faded with a calm decline
Serene as twilight; leaving early death
A lovely secret, by th' Almighty known.

DEATH'S PROGRESS.

What is the Past?—The sepulchre of time
Where lies the dust which once form'd living man.
By thousands oft, or one by one, decay
Hath reap'd mankind for thy dread harvest, Death!
Thus in the forest, where a leafy host
Hangs on the mercy of autumnal winds
In withering tremor, when a howling gust
Havocs the branches, throngs of leaves descend
Countless and quick as human glances fall;
But when the air is tranced, with thrilling tone
A leaflet drops,—how awfully distinct!
To him whose moralising dream surveys
A hue of death on each consumptive bough.

DEATH HAS NO HISTORIAN.

And Thou! pale Chronicler of perish'd years,
Whose page is studded with the dyes of sin
And blood, or brighten'd with deceptive gleams
Of miscall'd glory, what can thy dark book
Of History teach?—but half what Truth has been!
The heat, the struggle, the majestic toils
Of high contention, which colossal Minds
Exhibit on the stage of human dreams,
By thee are traced with emulative glow;
But hadst Thou, by omniscient aid inspired,
The dread instruction from each dying lip
Recorded,—what a page for conscience thine!
A thrilling sermon for the soul to read
Whose text would be, eternity unveil'd!
* * * *

IDEAL VIEWS.

Around thee, for awhile, the den recal,
The shore, the blood, the battle-wasted fields,
The dungeon, rock, or sickly chamber dim
Where nature gasp'd or groan'd its last farewell!
From death-beds back the curtain draw, and see
How Clay and Spirit to the last contend.
Advance, and view a haughty sinner die!
Behold the brow where thought satanic reign'd,
The glance which threaten'd to appal the tomb,
The hand whose motion made a tempest rise
In hearts and empires!—hark! the voice
That once created valour by its sound,
How fruitless all, how infantile and vain!
He dies, as underneath our foot the dews,

Gone at a touch of death! Or mark the bed
Where he whose spirit had his God unthroned,
Annihilated Heaven, Hereafter mock'd,
And call'd the world a fatherless Unknown,
Lies wild and restless as the moaning wave;
His guilt hath set eternity on fire
And shuddering, like a shrivell'd leaf,—he dies!

DYING SAINTS.

But Death has often been by faith uncrown'd
And daunted, till his dim and icy gaze
Forewent its terror; and his summons rang
Like fairy preludes from seraphic lyres
Heaven-wafted, on the parting Spirit's ear.
And if that Volume, where pure Angels keep
A soul's bright history, could unfolded be,
Pilgrims of earth! who seek the better land,
How would ye burn with apostolic love
And in the ashes of the tomb discern
A Spark immortal, kindling for the skies
What adorations, warm as incense-fire,
What bursts of faith, what notes of speechless joy,
What gleams of Christ in glorified array,
What tones and tears of overwhelming love
Around the couch of dying virtue throng'd
Ere rushed the spirit from its house of clay!

Oh! beautiful beyond depicting words
To paint, the hour that wafts to heaven a soul!
The world grows dim; the scenes of time depart;
The hour of peace, the walk of social joy,
The mild companion, and the deep-soul'd friend,
The loved and lovely, see his face no more:
The mingling spell of sun, of sea, and air,
Is broken; voice, and gaze, and smiles which speak,
Must perish; parents take their hush'd adieu;
A wife, a child, a daughter half divine
Or son which never drew a father's tear,
Approach him, and his dying tones receive
In God's own language!—'tis an hour of awe
Yet terrorless, when revelations flow
From faith immortal; view that pale-worn Brow,
It gleams with glory! in his eye there dawns
A dazzling earnest of unutter'd joy:
Each pang subdued, his longing soul respires
The gales of glorified eternity;
And round him, hues ethereal, harps of light,
And lineaments of earthless beauty throng,
As, wing'd on melody, the saint departs
While Heaven in miniature before him shines.

DEATH NEVER PAUSES.

The thought[1] how dread, that not a moment fleets
But with it many a soul hath sunk away
To that untraced Abyss, within whose womb
Six thousand Years have buried all they bore!
Yes, while around unvalued pleasures throng
In the soft atmosphere of human smiles
We play with time, as infants do with toys,
And rarely think, how Death is heaping fast
The new-dug graves; exulting o'er a wreck;
Or counting victims from the corpse-strewn sea,
Or laughing where the thunder-bolt has dash'd
Some lord of earth to nothing! Then the flood
And blast, the conflagration dire, disease
And danger, death-bed horrors, broken hearts,
And exiles in their damp-wall'd dungeons chain'd,—
Oh! each and all would melt a moral tear
If known or felt, from Pleasure's sated eye.

Then come, poetic Spirit! plume thy strength,
Thy wings expand, Imagination, wake!
Traverse the troubled world from shore to shore,
That with a panoramic glance my soul
May vision forth dark tragedies of Death![2]

STORM.

Listen! for, hear ye not the startled Winds
Invisibly are coming from their caves?
Fierce as avenging fiends from hell evoked,
They march, and madden with a mingled howl;
Creation shudders at the waking Storm,
Or darkens, by prophetic tremors thrill'd.
Again, again, the congregated Winds
Unroll their voices! they have roused the Sea,
And on her back ten thousand thousand waves
Like wings of wrath are swelling as they rise!

Above, the rocky clouds are wildly clash'd,
Till darkness quickens into light! and fierce
And far, as though the universe obey'd,
Monarch of sound, the Thunder's mandate rings
Rattling the heavens with long-repeated roar!
While ever and anon pale lightnings gleam
And flash like armoury of waving fire:

SHIPWRECK.

Alone upon the leaping billows, lo!
What fearful Image works its way? A ship,
Shapeless and wild, as by the Storm begot;
Her sails dishevell'd, and her massy form
Disfigured, yet tremendously sublime:
Prowless and helmless through the waves she rocks,
And writhes, as if in drowning agony:
Like valour when amid o'erwhelming foes
The vessel combats with the battling waves,
Then fiercely dives below:—the Thunders roll
A requiem, and the Whirlwinds howl for joy.

THE CREW.

And where are they, who from the breezy deck
Beheld the sun in orient glory rise
Like a divinity, and breathed a prayer
O'er the fresh promise of a placid sea?
Float they in lifeless masses through the deep?
Look! where a flash of lightning stripes the sea,
Like straw upon the wind a bark is whirl'd
From wave to wave: within, a pale-faced crew
Sit dumb as phantoms; with their eyes bedimm'd,
Their locks foam-sprinkled, and their lips unclosed;
And when the clouds their fires unsheath, against
The wizard glare their upturn'd faces gleam
In one despairing row! Their doom is seal'd
Above: Death howls in every wolfish blast
And rides on each gigantic wave: the sea
Their sepulchre shall make; their coffins be
Her caves, until the summon'd Ocean hear
The death-trump, and her tombless dead arise.

CALM AND LANDSCAPE.

Wave, wind, and thunder have departed: shrunk
The vision'd ocean from our mental view,
And lo! a landscape, green as Painting loves,
Or sunshine veil'd when Milton's spirit-gaze
Saw Paradise around him wave her flowers
While glorious Adam with his Maker walk'd,
Or Eve her shadow on the lake admired.
On yonder vernal mead, a cherub boy
Is bounding, playful as a breeze new-born,
Light as the beam which dances by his side.
Phantom of Beauty! with his golden locks
Gleaming like water-wreaths,—a flower of Life
To whom the fairy world is fresh, the sky
A glory, and the Earth one huge delight!
His brow makes joy; his eyes are Pleasure's own;
While Innocence, from out the budding lip
Darts her young smiles along his rounded cheek:
Grief hath not dimm'd the brightness of his form;
Love and affection o'er him spread their wings,
And Nature, like a nurse, with sweetest look
Her child attends. The humming bee will bound
From out the flower, nor sting his baby-hand;
The birds address him from the blossom'd trees,
And suppliantly the fierce-eyed mastiff fawn,
Come when he may, to court his playful touch.

INFANCY.

To rise all rosy from the arms of Sleep,
And, like the sky-bird, hail the bright-cheek'd Morn
With trills of song; then o'er the cowslipp'd mead
The blue-wing'd butterfly to chase, or play
With curly streams; or, led by watchful Love,
Admire the chorus of the trooping waves,
When the young breezes laugh them into life;
Or listen to the mimic ocean-roar
That waves have buried in a sea-shell's depth;
From sight and sound to catch intense delight
And frolic meaning from each happy face,—
Make his fond round of infantile romance.
And when at length dejected Evening comes
Joy-worn he nestles in the welcome couch
With kisses warm upon his cheek, of heaven
To dream, till morning wakes him to the world.

THE DEAD INFANT.

Into a curtain'd room the Scene hath changed,
Where a wan semblance of the mournful sun
Lies dreaming on the walls. Dim-eyed and sad,
And dumb with agony, two parents bend
O'er a pale Image in a coffin laid,
More exquisite than Death in marble looks,—
Their infant once, the laughing, leaping boy,
The bud of life, the nursling of their souls!
Pain touch'd him, and the life-glow fled away
Swift as a gay hour's fancy: fresh and cold
As Winter's shadow, with his eyelids seal'd
Like violet-lips at eve, he lies enrobed
An offering for the Grave; but, bright and pure
The infant martyr hath to heaven been call'd,

Lisping soft hallelujahs with the choir
Of sinless babes, imparadised above.

CHURCHYARD.

A glimmering churchyard, heap'd with countless graves
Like hosts of billows couch'd upon the deep,
Dawns into vision now. The dormant air
Is hush'd, and on that rich-leaf'd file of elms,
The choral wind hath sung itself to sleep.

And here, where Meditation loves to dream
While noon a burning stillness breathes around,
From out yon mouldering cells let Fancy cite
A heart-wreck'd Being, whom the savage world
Deserted, and repentance wore to death.

BETRAYED AFFECTION.

In beauty moulded like a shape of love
From the damp earth behold her meekly rise,
As delicate as when the worshipp'd form
Bade Envy stand abash'd, while youth and grace
Round her fair mien a faultless magic threw.
Light of her home, impassion'd forth she came
And where she moved a thousand Hearts were drawn!
But he who won her warm in virgin-truth,
Belied his homage and betray'd her trust;
Then, like a haunted tomb the erring maid
By the cold World was shunn'd, nor found one spot
Of shelter, from th' accusing eye of Scorn:
Till far away, from all her scene of wo
The unlamented mourner came, with griefs
Like thunder-scars upon her soul engraved!

SECLUSION AND DEJECTION.

In a lone hamlet all retired she dwelt
In meekness and remorse: but Sorrow taught
Her kindliness to bloom; and by the Poor
A heaven-born Lady was she rightly deem'd,
Whose smile made every peasant-cottage bright
And took from Poverty the sting of shame.
Among the hermit-walks, and ancient woods
When mantled with the melancholy glow
Of eve, she wander'd oft; and when the wind
Like a stray infant down autumnal dales
Roam'd wailingly, she loved to mourn and muse;
To commune with the lonely orphan-flowers
And through sweet nature's ruin trace her own.

PARTING HOUR.

But through the quiet churchyard's elmy range
Unwatch'd she loved to roam; and there was seen
Like a pale Statue o'er some weed-grown tomb
To bend, and look as if she wept the dead;
And when the day-gleam faded o'er far hills
She gazed with such deep look, as Love would mark
Some parting smile, to treasure it when gone!
But when the yellow moonlight clad the air,
How from the window she the heavens would watch,
Till in her eye an adoration shone:
Sad Lady! then her thoughts in tears arose
And every tear ran burning from her heart!

Thus day by day her unpartaken grief
Was nursed, till sorrow grew a sleepless fire
That parch'd her soul. One evening while she mused,
And from her lattice read that starry lore
Which mourning Fancy half believes, her face
Grew lily-white; a languid murmur came;
Her head hung drooping like a laden flower,
And soft as sound her spirit fled to heaven!

YOUTHFUL GENIUS.

Upon the mountain, with Thy hectic cheek
And soul outlooking from the lifted eye
As if the beauty of some thought were seen,
Why, who art Thou, undaunted by the storm
In rolling anthems round thee gather'd? Clouds
Swell back; and underneath wild Ocean roars
As though her waves were all to whirlpools lash'd:
Yet canopied with thunder, there thou stand'st
Till feeling like a storm of music wakes
And trembles through thy being! Art thou there
A Spirit tempest-born, and on the rock
Enthroned, to parley with the thunder-peals?

INSPIRATIONS.

Thou wert not moulded for the selfish world;
Too lofty and too full of heavenly fire
E'er to be measured by ungifted minds
Whom Glory hath not raised. Ambition rock'd
Thy cradle; Genius all thine infant soul
Etherealised, and in the rich-orb'd eye
The rays of thought and inspiration pour'd:
Before the tongue a budding thought reveal'd

Imagination dallied with thy mind,
And sent it playing through her airy realms:
But when the man upon thy forehead beam'd,
Impassioned Creature! then thy race began:
Feelings of beauty and of rich delight
Flow'd from the countenance of this fair Earth
Full on thy soul, wherein a second world
Was shrined: for thee inspiring Nature glow'd,
And warm'd thy fancy like a dream from heaven.
Thou lov'st her mightiness, her glorious mien!
Whether she loose her ocean-zone, and let
The waves abroad, or hang the sky with storms,
Or hail thee in her thunders; or at eve
When sunshine like a beauteous memory dies
And the breeze anthems like a bird of air,
Call thee to witness, how in deck'd array
The marshall'd clouds attend th' imperial Sun
Before his throne of waves,—alike divine
She seems. And not alone does Nature charm
Thy senses into wondering awe; but all
Which men admire, by genius or by art
Created, bids thy soul with homage swells;
Rich music, like a warbling seraph, flings
Entrancement round thee, till emotions melt
As yielding darkness when by light subdued;
A living picture, like a passion pours
Delight into thine eye; and Poesy,—
Is stamp'd thy mind, and colours all thy thoughts!

To have thy glory on the chart of Time
Recorded, mapp'd in deep and dazzling lines,
And thus be deathless in the fame the power
And offspring of creative soul; to build
A monument of Mind, on which the good
May gaze, while future Ages round it bend
With homage nobler than a king commands,—
Desire so godlike is for ever warm
And panting in thy breast; and oft, methinks,
When darkness like the death of light begins
Beneath the lone magnificence of heaven,
While planets glow oracularly bright,
Ambition dreams, and Hope the charmer smiles!

PENALTIES AND PAINS.

But, oh! thou Victim of a mental curse,
The fire and fever of the soul are thine
Which burn within, like Desolation's breath!
Body and mind, before they bloom, decay;
And ere upon the rock of high renown
The banner of thy fame exulting waves
Lost in the tomb thy buried hopes will lie
And o'er thy name Oblivion's pall descend!
The path to glory is a path of death
To feeling hearts, all gifted though they be
And martyrs to the Genius they adore:
The wear of passion, and the waste of thought,
The glow of inspiration, and the gloom
That like a night-shade mars the brightest hour,
And that fierce rack on which a faithless World
Will make thee writhe—all these ennerving pangs,
With agonies which mock the might of words,
Thou canst not bear: thy temple is a tomb!

PESTILENCE.

The Scene hath vanish'd! swelling like a mist
From out a marshy vale at morn, behold!
A City, dimly-vision'd: on the view
It grows, till full in vast perfection seen.
There all is mute and motionless; no spires
Hallow the air with heavenly chime; no flags
Or banners shiver in the suppling breeze;
No eager steps sound pattering through the streets;
No life seems in it,—silent as a shade!
Look up! the sickly clouds like corpses lie
Along the heavens; and yonder dark canal
Flags like a monstrous serpent stretch'd in death;
The houses shed a monumental gloom:
The Pestilence is there!

CITY OF THE PLAGUE.

Young Morn beheld
A beauteous City, with the floods of life
Billowing loudly through her million paths:
Her Temples bathed their heads in azure sheen;
Her rivers spread themselves along in joy;
The spirit of the world within her walls
Inspiring walk'd; by noon the sun grew red
And glared his fierceness through the sky, till forth
From out the lurid deeps of heaven, the Plague
Her breath exhaled, that with a viewless spread
Itself suffused through all the living town,
Which, sudden as an ocean chained, grew dumb!

The old man faded like a blasted tree,
And dropp'd into the dust! and he whose cheeks
Were round and fair, with eyes of lustrous youth,
From beauty wither'd to a yellow wreck
Distorted and decay'd, till Madness came,
And shrieking, shuddering, writhed herself to death!

Along each river crept the Plague; then hush'd
The grinding cables! and the barges lay
Like dead sea-monsters on the ocean stretch'd;
E'en on the mead with emerald verdure clad,
Where the gay urchin drove the whirling ball
Fleet as a bird along the sunny air,
The Pestilence her burning vapour breathed;
Each limb relax'd, upturn'd his darken'd lids,
And from his ghastly eyeballs glared the Pest!

From house to house the hot infection stole;
To gloom all gladness changed, and not a smile
In the whole city lived! Within the fane
Amid the pillar'd aisle, while lowly knelt
In all the holiness of virgin love
The fair-zoned bride of Beauty, came the Pest!
She coil'd, and shiver'd like a wounded dove;
Her form grew wild; and as the bridegroom watch'd
The heaven reflected from her face depart,
Contagion clasp'd him in her fiery arms,
His spirit whirl'd within him, and he fell
And o'er his loved one yelled his life away!

But in the tomb-fill'd churchyard, what a howl
From the parch'd throats of mourners came! for there
The graves were brimm'd with corses; and around
Unburied dead lay blackening in the air,
While Shades of being stagger'd by the heaps
Of friends and relatives together piled:
Such was the revelry of horrid Death;
And when at last by God himself recall'd,
The Sun of health arose, his eye beheld
Yon City hush'd as one enormous tomb!

MOONLIGHT SCENE.

Turn to a vision of contrasted joy:
Ne'er since creation out of chaos roll'd
With the mild bloom of young existence fresh
Around it, hath more glorious night bedecked
The World, than that which beautifies her now.
The stars like ruminating spirits walk
The mellow sky, from whence the queenly moon
With a maternal aspect eyes the earth,
Tranced into dreamy stillness by her smile.
No! not a breeze, nor bird is on the wing;
The shy sweet flowers have shut their dewy lids,
And distant trees, upon the dark-brow'd hills,
Like shadowy sentinels are ranged. And now
The reign of heart-romance! the lulling hour
When aspirations from the mystic heaven
Effused, the high-toned mind awake with thoughts
Which angels love: but see! beneath
Yon hill, down where the wrinkled brooklets flash
In liquid revelry, the silver'd Deep
Lies bare unto the moon; and on her breast,
In swan-like glory, glides a white-wing'd boat
Calm as a cloud along its blue career.

LOVERS.

Within, like Beings from a purer sphere
A youth and his confiding maiden sit,
Her yielding waist environ'd with his arm:
Above them, beautiful the starry dome!
Beneath, the sighing of romantic waves
Woke from their slumber, or melodious heave
Of tide, the panting of the World's great heart—
Breaks on the pleasing calm: oh, lovely pair!
Warm is the gush of young affection; sweet
The overflowing of affianced hearts
Each into each with holy rapture pour'd;
Now is the spring-time of the soul, whose bloom
Is love, but once ne'er felt, and ne'er but once
Enjoy'd! On would ye float for ever thus
O'er moonlight seas, in one immortal bliss—
Silence! the language of delighted hearts.

CONSUMPTION.

And hast thou, Curse of the primeval crime!
On one of these Thy vulture-glances fixed?
Shall knells of death moan heavy on the wind
When marriage peals should merrily resound
In tuneful rapture o'er the village spire?
Alas! for every age Death finds a grave,
And youthful forms as oft as hoary heads
Are pillow'd there. Thou loved and loving One!
From the dark languish of thy liquid eye
So exquisitely rounded, darts a ray
Of truth, prophetic of thine early doom;
And on thy placid cheek there is a flush
Of Death,—the beauty of Consumption there!

Few note that fatal bloom; for bless'd by all
Thou movest through thy noiseless sphere, the life
Of one,—the darling of a myriad hearts!
Yet in thy chamber, o'er some graceful task
When delicately bending, oft unseen
Thy mother looks with telescopic glance
Down the dim world of Time, and sees thee robed
A pallid martyr, shrouded for the tomb!

THE LOVED ONE DIES.

A year hath travell'd to eternity;
And now, the shadows of the grave grow dark
Upon the maiden; yet no fruitless wish
Or word abrupt, unlovely thoughts betrays
Of gloom and discontent within; she fades
As gently as the flower declines,—not false
To living claims, and yet for death prepared.
Beautiful resignation, and the hopes
From the rich fountain of her faith derived,
Around her a seraphic air have breathed
Of wither'd loveliness. The gloss of life
And worldly dreams are o'er; but dewy Morn,
And dim-eyed Eve, and all the mental gleams
Of rapture, darted from regretted joys,
Delight her still; and oft when Twilight comes,
She gazes on the damask glow of heaven
With all the truth of happier days, until
A sunny fancy wreathes her faded cheek;
'Tis but a pleasing echo of the Past,
A music rolling from remember'd hours!
The day is come, by Death led gently on;
With pillow'd head all gracefully reclined
And glossy curls in languid clusters wreath'd,
Within a cottage-room she sits to die:
Where from the window, in a western view,
Majestic Ocean rolls. A summer-eve
Veils the calm earth, and all the glowing air
Stirs faintly, like a pulse; against the shore
The waves advance with undulating joy,
While o'er the midway-deep her eye-glance roams,
Where like a sea-god glares the travell'd Sun
O'er troops of billows marching in his beam.
From earth to heaven, from heaven to earth her eyes
Are lifted, bright with wonder and with awe,
Till through each vein reanimation rolls!—
'Tis past; and now her filmy glance is fix'd
On the rich heavens, as though her spirit *gazed*
On that immortal World, to which 'tis bound:
But sunset, like a burning palace fades,
In hues of visionary pomp destroy'd;
And Day and Beauty have together died:
For there like sculptured Death the maiden lies,
More exquisite than Love's embodied dream!

WAR.

The smoke, the thunder, and the din of War!
Loud as an ocean leaping into life
I hear the storm of battle swell. Advance;
And listen to the cloud-ascending peals
Of Cannon, from whose lips a lightning glares!
Hark! how the bugle-echoes beat the air,
And how the deep-roll'd drums their wrath resound,
While on the throbbing Earth the Sun looks down
Like a dread war-fiend, with a fierce delight.
Death! here thou art; and here the flashing swords
Shall reap thy harvest, and devoted souls
By thousands rush into the hands of God!

FIELD OF DEATH.

Noon into eve, and eve to night hath roll'd;
The heavens with starry eyes are set: but, see!
No wafted banners, flapping like the wings
Of eagles in their glorious strength; no steeds
Pawing and prancing with erected manes;
No warriors hand to hand; no sword to sword
Confronted, till from out some bloody gap
Their spirits bound into eternity!—
But heaps of corses, lines of dead laid out,
Unhelmeted, or gash'd and gory; men
Whose morning-beauty shamed the risen sun,
With glassy eyeballs gleaming on the moon!
A living host hath deaden'd into clay:—
No more! away, O Death! and count thy dead.

THE CAPTIVE.

Now from the hoof-worn plains of war, where blood
Makes glory, to a scene of stagnant gloom
Avert thy fancy. Lo, a dungeon, roof'd
By one erected arch of blacken'd stone;
'Tis Freedom's tomb! The all-reviving air
Of heaven those mildew'd walls has never fann'd,
The light hath shed no lustrous beauty there;
But shade, and damp night-breath, and noisome slime
Traced o'er its rocky vault, the clank of chains,
With groans from wasted lungs exhaled, the laugh
Of lean-faced Madness, and the fitful moan
Of iron'd captives,—these have horrified
This den of Darkness. Look! a ray of eve
Hath wander'd to it through a narrow chink,
And stealthily it creeps along the wall
Then quivers, like a smile upon the cheek
Of what has *been*,—a miniature of God!
A free-born, free-bred spirit, bright and brave,
Who loved the mountains and the sea adored,
And call'd the wind a song of Liberty
As loud it warbled o'er his fearless head!
By Pagans captured, here the chains have gall'd,
And rusted on his limbs; long years roll'd by
And yet he gnash'd in fetters, till the flame
Of anguish burn'd his being up; he died,—
With home and country pictured on his heart!

That den within he was not tomb'd alone:
For twice ten years another captive wretch
Had withered there; but long ere that, the soul
Was quench'd, and Madness in her mightier wo
Forgot to weep o'er thraldom! Mark them both;
The one like marble on the earth reposed
In rigid silence, coffinless and cold;
The other madly glaring o'er him: see!
How oft he twines the matted locks, and hoots
With idiotic joy, then grinds his teeth
And leers around him with a dumb delight,
And babbles to the corse, till on his face
A ray of pity dawns; then down he kneels
And howls a dirge, till voice within him dies;
His head droops o'er him; dimly rolls the eye,
And the last life-breath gurgles in his throat;
'Tis o'er: and Heaven hath open'd on his soul!

THE METROPOLIS AND DEATH.

The grand arena, where insatiate Death
Drags every day his hundreds to the tomb,
London the huge, earth's capital and queen,
In dim array magnificently spread
Towers into vision now! not sending forth
The hum and clamour of her myriad streets,
Made awful by the roar of life; but stretch'd
In mute immensity beneath a sky
Of midnight, breathless with the summer glow.
And now, within their curtain'd chambers lie
What hosts of beings, of all age and clime!
Some laugh in dreams; and some with laden hearts
Mutter strange secrets; others quake and groan,
And kindle darkness with a torch of hell!
Now steals the murderer from his den; now hies
The robber to his haunt; and from their lanes
And unfrequented walks the haggard Shapes
Of Poverty and Crime come creeping forth
Like Spectres, crawling out of dusky tombs.

The heavens are visor'd; hark! the dreary howl
Of Thunder challenging the Night; or like
An unseen monster, moaning as he prowls:
Awhile 'tis hush'd; then flash the riven clouds
Asunder, and a lake of lightning gleams
Like shining water through the cloven dark,
While rain-drops hiss along the sultry air.

THE DESERTED ONE.

Wo to the houseless wanderer! doom'd to walk
Through the drench'd street barefooted, or bereft
Of life's sweet charities, at such an hour:
And yet, e'en such a martyr Anguish owns!
For down yon lane of gloom, upon the cold
And dripping steps, with garments moistly clung
Round her shrunk form, a lifeless woman lies
With face upturn'd unto the flooding shower.
The chain of life despair hath just unlink'd;
And on her cheek an agonising trace
Of parting spirit, as it work'd and writhed
And with the body wrestled, still remains.
Approach! and with the lamp-beam learn her fate,
In mournful lines upon her visage mapp'd:
A chronicle of sorrow and of sin
And shame whose fountain is a brain of fire;
A heart for ever on the rack of care;
Oppression from without, and pangs within;
Despair, then death, the master-cure of wo,
Survey her features, and you read them all!

Unhappy maiden! round whose days of bloom
A father's prayers their holy influence cast,
And from whose eyes a mother reap'd delight,
Death should have torn thee earlier to the tomb,
And in thy native churchyard heap'd thy grave
Of grassy mould: for once, along the mead
Fleet as the fawn thou boundest; bright and fair
The beauty of the valleys o'er thy form
And features breathed, while in each glance there shone
The magic of an uncorrupted mind:
And this is all that now of thee remains!—
In Heaven's dread book thy sorrow hath a page,
And when 'tis open'd, *who* shall quail the most,
The man who tempted, or the maid who fell?

* * * *

THE UNDESCRIBED.

These fearful visions of thy varied power
Appalling Death! with dreader ones compared,
Reflect a shadow of thy murderous sway,—
Thy ceaseless havoc through the realms of Life.
Let others paint thee on the desert-heath
Where, melting into blood, with lukewarm limbs
A gory wretch lies gasping and alone;
Or in the roofless and deserted homes,
Where fires have blacken'd on the blister'd walls;
Or in the Suicide,—lo! where he stands

With visage colourless, with look aghast
And spirit shivering through his guilty frame!

DEATH'S UNIVERSAL REIGN.

Yes! far or near, where'er the life-blood flows,
By ruin, violence, or calm decay
Death's ravages are felt: the very dust
That in our daily walks we tread, hath once
Some breathing mould of Beauty been. O earth!
Thou grave, and mother! in thy hollow breast
What faded myriads are entomb'd! Your dead
Give back, departed Ages, and arise
Ye spirits of the Past!—they come, they come!
From mountain and from cave, from vault and tomb
The Dead are darting into life again!
The generations that have been, from Earth's
Young dawn, to moments on their very wing
Behold them! sumless as the ocean sand;
A world of Life walks o'er a world of Death;
Till all are buried in one deep Abyss,
The tomb of passion, prejudice, and time!

WHAT ALL HAVE FELT.

To die, is Nature's universal doom;
The Past hath braved it, and the Future shall;
Though little deem we, as we laugh the hours
Along like echoes dandled by the wind,
How swift our path is verging to the grave.
Terrific Power! how often in the hush
Of midnight, when the thoughtless learn to think,[3]
The gay grow solemn, and the foolish wise,
Visions of thee come floating o'er the mind
Like exhalations from a grave! How oft
We feel an awfulness the soul o'ershade
As if 'twere soaring to the throne of God,
Till in one thought of heaven we bury all
The breathing universe of life and man!

HUMAN FATE.

A death-cloud rises with the star of Life;
And ere upon the world our hearts expand,
Like flower-buds opening to the kiss of Morn,
With gay and guiltless love, the voice of doom
Awakes; this sermon from the grave is preach'd;
We live to die, and die again to live
A spirit-life in unimagined worlds!
First, Infancy, whose days are prattling dreams;
Next, Childhood, crown'd with beauty, health, and joy,—
Those wizard three, which make the mind like spring,
The breath, the bloom and sunshine of the soul;—
Then, Manhood, most majestic; through the heavens
Piercing with haughty eye, and printing earth
With kingly steps; ambition, love, and care,
And energy, in wild and restless play
For ever heaving like a wave of fire;
And then comes passionless and feeble Age
That droops and drops into the silent grave!
Here ends the scene of life; one moment wept,
The next forgotten; let the curtain fall,
Oblivion has our tale,—we lived, and died!

PAST AND FUTURE.

Thousands of years beneath thy sway have groan'd
Unwearied Death! *how many* more shall bear
The burden of the curse, no human tongue
Can tell, for they are chronicled above;
Though ofttimes number'd by a guilty mind
When thunders, like dread oracles, the world
Awake. Yet, come it will, however late,
That day foretold when Death himself shall die![4]
And generations, now but dust and worms,
Rise into being with an angel-shout
And on the winds of glory soar to heaven!

PREPARATION.

And yet, though Life enchant, and Death appal,
How gently does the hand of Time unloose
Those many links which chain us to the world!
The passions which inspirit youthful hearts
And spread a lustre o'er the brow of life
And bid the hopes of young Ambition bound,
Decay and cool, as further down the vale
Of twilight-years we wend, till, all resign'd,
The time-worn spirit ponders o'er the tomb
With elevating sadness; and the night
Of death is lit with those immortal stars
By Revelation sphered in heaven.

How pure
The grace, the gentleness, of virtuous Age!
Though solemn, not austere; though wisely dead
To passion, and the wildering dreams of hope,
Not un-alive to tenderness and truth,
The good old Man is honour'd and revered,
And breathes upon the young-limb'd race around
A grey and venerable charm of years.

ALLEVIATIONS.

And, glory to the Power which brings the heart
In sympathy with Time! how much remains
In the pure freshness of ideal life,
For him who loves the bloom of Days no more!
A meditative walk by wood or mead,
The lull of streams, and language of the stars
Heard in the heart alone; an inward view
Of all which beautified or graced his youth,
Is yet enjoy'd; and with that bliss are found
The feelings flowing from a better World.

SPIRITUAL TRIUMPH.

Then, melt, ye horrors! which the grave begets,
And turn to glory, by the spell of faith
Transform'd; for Christ hath overcome the tomb.—
What though 'tis awful, when the pulse of Life
Is bounding, and the blood seems liquid joy;
To look Corruption in its ghastly face,
The mind is Man! no sepulchre for souls
Can dust and darkness frame; like God apart
In calm eternity they act and think:
The shroud, the hearse, the life-alarming knell;
The grave's cold silence, and the vision'd friends
Whose dreams will hover round our chill decay,
Harrow our living dust, and give to Death
A sting that dwells not in his own dark power.
We die in body, but in soul we live,
When flesh and spirit sunder; *then* our chains
Are riven, and celestial freedom dawns!
The fetter'd eagle whom a narrow cage
Imprison'd, where so oft his haughty wings
In wild unrest have beat his hated walls
With blood-stain'd plumage, while his eyeballs glared
Proudly along the blue and boundless sky
Above him,—free and fetterless at last
On plumes of ecstasy can soar away
And mount, and mingle with the heaven he loves!

RETROSPECTIONS.

Of Death I sing; yet soon may darkly sleep
And press the pillow of the dreamless grave
Forgetting and forgot! But twenty years
Have wither'd, since my pilgrimage began,
And I look back upon my boyish days
With mournful joy; as musing wanderers do
With eye reverted from some lofty hill
Upon the bright and peaceful vale below.
Oh! let me live, until the fires which feed
My soul, have work'd themselves away, and then
Eternal Spirit! take me to Thy home
For when a child, inspiring dreams I shaped,
And nourish'd aspirations that awoke
Beautiful feelings, flowing from the face
Of Nature; from a child I learn'd to reap
A harvest of sweet thoughts for future years.

How oft, be witness, Guardian of our days!
In noons of young delight, while o'er the down
Humming like bees my happy playmates fled,
I loved on high and hoary crag to muse
And thread the landscape with delighted eye:
The sky besprinkled o'er with rainbow-hues,
As if angelic wings had wanton'd there;
The distant City capp'd with hazy towers;
And river, shyly roaming by its banks
Of green repose, together with the play
Of elfin-music on the fresh-wing'd air,—
With these entranced, how often have I glow'd
With thoughts which panted to be eloquent,
Yet only ventured forth in tears!

PARTING THOUGHTS.

And now
Though haply mellow'd by correcting time,
I thank thee, Heaven! that this bereaving World
Hath not diminish'd the undaunted hopes
Of youth, in manhood's more imposing cares.
Nor titled pomp, nor princely mansions swell
The cloud of envy o'er my heart; for these
Are oft delusive, though adored: but when
The Holy and the Beautiful from God
Descend into my being; when I hear
The oracles which from Creation-shrines,
Roll their deep melody round listening hearts;
Or gaze on Virtue, till her glory seems
Emmanuel's shadow by a Saint expressed;
Then feel I envy for immortal words,
And the full pulse of Poetry begins
To waken in me, with exulting throb
No language echoes! then the spirit yearns
To dash my feelings into deathless verse
Which may administer to Time unborn,
And tell some lofty Soul, how I have lived
A worshipper of Nature, and of Thee.

NOTES.

Note 1, Page 550, Column 2.

The thought how dread, &c.

Note 2, same page and column.

Dark tragedies of Death.

The difference between the history of action and the history of mind is finely developed in the following extract from Jones's Preface to his Life of Bishop Horne:—"I have heard it said that Dr. Horne was a person whose life was not productive of events considerable enough to furnish matter for a history. But they who judge thus have taken but a superficial view of human life, and do not rightly measure the importance of the different events which happen to different men. Dr. Horne was no circumnavigator; he neither sailed with Anson, Drake, nor Cook; but he was a man whose mind surveyed the intellectual world, and brought home from thence many excellent observations for the benefit of his native country. He was no military commander: he took no cities; he conquered no countries; but he spent his life in subduing his passions, and teaching us how to do the same. He fought no battles by land or by sea; but he opposed the enemies of God and his truth, and obtained some victories which are worthy to be recorded. He was no prime minister to any earthly potentate; but he was a Minister to the King of heaven and earth—an office at least as useful to mankind, and in the administration of which no minister to any earthly king ever exceeded him in zeal and fidelity. He made no splendid discoveries in natural history; but he did what was better; he applied universal nature to the improvement of the mind, and the illustration of heavenly doctrines. I call these events; not such as make a great noise and signify little, but such as are little celebrated and of great signification."—*Epistle to William Steevens, Esq.*, p. 22.

Note 3, Page 557, Column 1.

How often in the hush
Of midnight, when the thoughtless learn to think.

"L'éclat du jour peut convenir à la joyeuse doctrine du paganisme; mais le ciel étoilé paroît le veritable temple du culte le plus pur. C'est dans l'obscurité des nuits, dit un poète Allemande, que l'immortalité s'est révélée à l'homme."—De Stael.

Note 4, Page 557, Column 2.

Death himself shall die!

In revising the poem entitled "Death," the author has not neglected a remark made by a critical friend, on the necessity of brightening his picture of the grave by allusions to the light which emanates from the hope of our immortality. "Futuri contemplatione jam vivimus," is a deep truth, whether morally or religiously considered. Annihilate the doctrine of a hereafter, and the whole universe of things is involved in a mystery of darkness; both man and mind are at once reduced to an inexplicable and unutterable despair. But conscience—reason—revelation—all blend their voices into the solemn harmony of truth on this point; even the visible creation is an emblematical witness of what religion asserts; and while the pale leaves of autumn fall witheringly round us, Hope has connected with every naked tree and desolated flower a dream of the future spring, sunshine, and bloom. There is indeed an exquisite analogy existing between the material and intellectual world; and from this philosophical source, Poetry in all ages has drunk some of her richest draughs of inspiration. And where is the visionary madness in this creed of the imagination? Both mind and matter are the productions of the Almighty, and therefore their mutual adaptation illustrates His wisdom.

"How often we forget all time when lone,
Admiring nature's universal throne:
Her woods, her wilds, her waters—the intense
Reply of hers to our intelligence!"

St. Clement, in his apostolical address to the Corinthians, alludes to the symbolical nature of day and night, as imaging forth the doctrine of man's resurrection.—Ἴδωμεν, ἀγαπητοὶ, τὴν κατὰ καιρὸν γινομένην ἀνάστασιν: ἡμέρα καὶ νύξ ἀνάστασιν ἡμῖν δηλουσιν. Κοιμᾶται ἡ νὺξ, ἀνίσταται ἡμέρα, ἡ ἡμέρα ἄπεισιν, νὺξ ἐπέρχεται.—*Clem. Epist. ad Corinth. Prim.* The same ideal illustration of our renovated being is beautifully sketched in the following passage from Minutius Felix:—"Vide adeo quam in solatium nostri resurrectionem futuram omnis natura meditetur. Sol demergit, et nascitur; astra labuntur et redeunt; flores occidunt et reviviscunt; post senium arbusta frondescunt; semina non nisi corrupta revirescunt; ita corpus."—κ. τ. λ. *De Idolor. Vanitate.*

A VISION OF HEAVEN.

A FRAGMENT.—1829.

"The heavens were opened, and I saw visions."
Ezekiel i. 1.

"Juvat, quandoque in animo, tanquam in tabula, majoris et melioris mundi imaginem contemplari: ne mens assuefacta hodiernæ vitæ minutiis se contrahat nimis, et tota subsidat in pusillas cogitationes."—*T. Burnet.*

One summer-evening, from the molten sky
When radiance came to beautify the world,
By Fancy led, along a noiseless vale
I roam'd, and trod the earth with deep delight,
Felt in the soul, and in the eye reveal'd.
'Twas one of those immortal hours, when man
Unheedful of the jarring world, feels thoughts
Within him too sublime for words; a sense
Of that divinity o'er all which breathes,
Making creation one vast temple seem,
Where shadows of His glory are enshrined.

Thus felt I at this balmy hour: Above
Magnificently hung the dome of heaven;
Along the concave floated fairy isles;
And where the sun stood burning on the brim
Of ocean, the horizon wound its curve
Festoon'd with clouds of beauty, fresh and white
As sea-foam in the sun.

Beneath the span
Of heaven, the Earth lay languishing in light;
Her streamlets with a bee-like murmur ran,
And while the trees, like living creatures waved
Their plumage on the wind, the bird and breeze
Together hymn'd, and harmonised the air.

Pensive, awhile along the placid vale
I roam'd, then sat delighted on a mound
Green-tress'd, and glittering in the dizzy rays
Of eve, and heavenward turn'd my musing eye.
Who ever gazed on heaven, nor dream'd of God,
Of human destiny, and things divine?
Oh that mine eye could pierce yon azure cope!—
Thus stirr'd the daring thought; and while it warm'd
Within, a trance like heavenly music stole
Round my hush'd spirit, weaning earthly sense,
Till in a vision up the airy deep
It darted, as a sky-bird to the clouds!

Thus disembodied, through the air it rose
Till earth beneath me in a glassy depth
Lay twinkling, like a star; but all around
Those burning mysteries which mortals view
With wonder, floating o'er the face of night,
Not gems of fire, but full and perfect orbs
In congregations vast, as glorious,—beam'd.
Aloft! aloft! still soared my spirit on
Through hosts of worlds, self-balanced and secure,
Till the bright atmosphere appear'd to bloom
With rich suffusion, like a topaz-glow;
And here, enchanted by a spell divine
My Spirit paused, became all eye and ear,
And Heaven, the palace of the mighty God,
Expanded into view:—Unbodied soul!
With o'erawed feeling enter where He dwells.

An arch'd immensity of crystal sheen
Rich with the glory of all glories rare *
Before me lay: beneath this dazzling vault
Splendour beyond the dreamings of the heart
To vision, round interminably blazed:
I *felt*, but cannot paint the magic there!

While, with permitted glance, the scene I mark'd,
A thrilling tide of rich-toned music roll'd,
Waking delicious echoes as it wound
From Melody's divinest fount. All Heaven
In glorious fascination heard, and drank
The tones elysian:—Silence breathed again;
And where I gazed, a Throne of awful Fire
Flamed ceaselessly: before it Thunders roll'd
And veiling Darkness round about it hung.
And here alone, in uncreated Bliss
And Glory, reigns The One Eternal Power,

* Vide the symbolic imagery of Heaven as unfolded in the Apocalypse, *passim*.

Creator, Lord, and Life of All. Again
Stillness ethereal reign'd; and forth appear'd
Ecstatic Creatures, clad in robes of light,
Together flocking from celestial haunts
And mansions of purpureal mould; the Host
Of heaven assembled, to adore with harp
And hymn the First and Last, The Living God:
They knelt,—an immaterial Choir, and glow'd
More beauteous, while they breathed the chant divine;
And Hallelujah! Hallelujah! peal'd,
And thrill'd the concave with harmonious joy.

The melody was hush'd; and I beheld
Cherubic Forms of unimagined grace
And beauty walk o'er amaranthine meads,
And soar on shining pinions: as they rose,
A radiance quiver'd forth, and from each plume
Soft as the breeze and silky as a cloud,
A gleam play'd liquidly around their path.

Of archangelic mien, upon the wing
Two Shapes I watch'd, careering to the bound
Of vision; lighting there, they welcomed in
Three happy Spirits, by The Lamb redeem'd:
And Heaven they enter'd with triumphal shout;
Transfigured, into glory grew, and were
Beatified for ever!
In a bower
Remote, whose em'rald leaves with liquid drops
Of light were gemm'd, two Angels next I mark'd,
In sympathetic converse sat. Amid
Life's wilderness below, they had o'erwatch'd
The errant beings just arrived: through dark
And light, through sin and toil, their guardian power
Presided, until Mercy came to crown
Their doom, and they were saved and seal'd for Heaven.
Seraphic sweetness from their lips exhaled
As, rapt with angel love, th' immortal pair
Their tale of heavenly triumph told. Oh, joy!
Dream'd I, around us viewless Spirits dwell;
Our minds to tune, or consecrate our thoughts,
And guard, relieve, and hallow souls for God.

From these I turn'd, and saw a sumless host
Of Cherubim, and bright pavilions rank'd
In endless files; and then, Remembrance warm'd
Within me; heavenly Intuition woke,
And myriads who on earth erewhile had run
The grand career of Life, were all reveal'd.

I saw the Sages, whose immortal words
Are truthful Oracles to man and mind;
I saw the pure, the patriotic bands
Of Heroes, whose avenging swords had cut
The fetters from their Land and bade the brave
Be free! the renovated forms I saw
Of Martyrs, robed with glory, on their heads
Inwreathèd crowns of life; and they of old
Whose names more eloquent than thunder sound
On young Ambition's ear,—the good and great
Of every cast and clime, were now reveal'd;
The Past was in the Present born again.

For sainted Bards of earth I look'd; a breath
Of hymnèd music through the mellow air
Came wafted, from beside a crystal fount
That glitter'd like a living gush of light,—
There sat our own Mæonides! Around
A throng of listening Angels stood, and glow'd
Till rapture trembled o'er their sunny wings,
While from his lyre the epic minstrel struck
Pure inspiration,—sounds replete with soul!

Among the myriads of celestial Shapes
Which mused and wander'd by the springs of Life,
I mark'd the humble, the dejected sons
Of Want and Wo, apparell'd bright as morn.
On earth deem'd vile, their trampled hearts had bled
With sorrows, never told; their joyless eyes
With tears had melted dim; at wintry night
They roam'd, and shiver'd in the bleak-wing'd wind,
And often writhed beneath the glance of scorn,
Yet fainted not: and now, unfading joys
Beatitude and thrones in Heaven, were theirs!

Fairest of all fair Visions seen above,
Remember'd Thrones and unforgotten Friends
Were recognised again! Along a mead
Of bright immensity I saw them stray;
Not anguish-worn, nor rack'd with inward fears,
But shining in the beauty of the blest.—
Oh! ye in life so loved, in death so mourn'd,
How oft Affection through the desert-world
Delights to track ye, where your feet have trod,
Through fav'rite walks or fancy-haunted bowers!
Blend your calm voices with the twilight breeze
In fairy music, fraught with infant years?
Are echoes woven from your hymns above?
In solemn days and melancholy hours
Of you we think! Love shrines ye in the stars,
And recreates ye in celestial robes.
But while at eve's poetic hour we watch
The golden isles that glitter from the west,

In lovelier climes *ye* live, and chaster skies;
By choral streams and aromatic walks
Ye roam, rememb'ring heaven-like bowers on earth,
And friends, whose mansions ye survey above.

And such was *Fancy's* vision-moulded heaven
Around me miniatured. Here God, enthroned
In measureless perfection, truth, and power,
His unimaginable Glory wields:
And thus Eternal Love, from Him the fount
Of Love, enlightens, lives, and flows through All.
No tears, no trials, and no perils known,
No sin-worn hearts, and shatter'd feelings here,
But calm fruition of unfailing bliss:
All which the beauty of creative Thought
Hath pictured to Devotion's eye, is felt
Ineffably more beauteous by the Blest:
Wisdom and Virtue breathe their native air
And Pleasures smiling on their steps attend.

Nor is the vanish'd World forgot; for oft
In bowers of everlasting bloom retired,
The Ransom'd, by the blood of Jesu bought,
Think of the Fight their spirits fought below,
Or sweetly muse o'er some terrestrial hour,
While heart to heart with holy truth responds;
Still Sages feed on ever-fruitful thought;
And Poets sing and raptured Knowledge * mounts,
From step to step for ever climbing up
Yet never on the radiant summit throned!
Here, bliss and love Eternity embrace,
And perfect Mind its perfect God adores.

* A sentiment in harmony with that illustrated in the above lines occurs in an Essay on "Novelty," by Grove, which was pronounced by Dr. Johnson one of the finest which the English language contains—"I cannot think he detracts from the state of the blessed, who conceives them to be perpetually employed in fresh researches into nature and eternity, advancing into the fathomless depths of the divine perfections. In this thought there is nothing but what does honour to these glorified spirits; provided still it be remembered that their desire for more proceeds not from their disrelishing what they possess, and that the pleasure of a new enjoyment is not with them measured by its novelty (which is a thing merely foreign and accidental), but by its real intrinsic value. After an acquaintance of many thousand years with the works of God, the beauty and magnificence of the creation fills them with the same pleasing wonder and profound awe which Adam felt himself seized with, as he first opened his eyes upon this glorious scene."—*Spectator*, No. 626.

A VISION OF HELL.

A FRAGMENT.—1829.*

"Where peace
And rest can never dwell, hope never comes
That comes to all, but torture without end."—Milton.

No longer Death and Time remain'd: the doom
Revokeless, by prophetic lips foretold,
Was past; the universe had disappear'd,
And Chaos revell'd o'er demolish'd worlds.

Apart, upon a throne of lurid fire
The Fiend was seated; in his eye there shone
The look that dared Omnipotence; the light
Of sateless vengeance, and sublime despair!
Amid a burning world he sat, and saw
Tormented myriads, whose blaspheming shrieks
Were mingled with the howl of hidden floods
And Acherontine groans; of all the host
The only dauntless he. As o'er the wild
He gazed, the pride of agony endured
Awoke, and writhed through all his giant frame,
That redden'd, and dilated like a sun!

And then, as ever-vanish'd hours awoke
The torment of wild memory, to feed
The cravings of infernal wrath, he bade
The roar of Hell be hush'd,—and Silence came;
He call'd the cursèd, and they flash'd from cave
And cell; from dungeon and from den they rose,
And stood an unimaginable mass
Of Spirits, agonised with burning pangs!
In silence stood they, while the Demon gazed
On all, and ponder'd on dead Earth and Time,
From whence his vengeance such a harvest reap'd.

Before him, what a congregated host
Of perish'd creatures!—sumless as the waves
Lash'd into life from out the wind-swept seas;
Long ages gone, and they were breathing airs
Of heaven, with noble attributes endow'd,
Sharing the beauty of the world, and led
By Mercy through the round of being; bliss
And endless wo before them lay;—the doom
Of guilt they braved, and barter'd Heaven for Hell!

Famed Idols of the earth, around whose paths
The blinding light of admiration blazed;
Despots, who bathed the battle-field in blood,
And many, whose immortal names had fired

* As it has been said that in the "Vision of Hell" I have drawn the portraits of some individuals recently dead, I take the earliest opportunity of giving this assertion an unqualified denial.

I do not think that any mortal is warranted in determining the final state of any fellow-creature, nor have I presumed to do so. But my purpose was, both for the moral and for the poetical effect, to sketch imaginary pictures of those classes of human characters, whose actions or works may be supposed to have been pernicious to mankind, and who therefore might be considered as having by their misconduct subjected themselves to be residents in the future kingdom of the Evil and of the Unhappy. Writing in modern times, it was necessary to invest these in modern drapery. On these principles, my first sketch was drawn as that of a great, ambitious Conqueror, desolating the world for his own gratification. I had not Napoleon more in my intention than Alexander, Cæsar, or Ghengis Khan; but as it was necessary to dress the imaginary being in modern costume, in some features he may appear to resemble the late French Emperor, because my visionary portrait is represented in modern imagery. The same remark is applicable to all the rest, and especially to my second, which has also received a specific application; though Lucretius, Lord Rochester, and some French atheists, may with equal consistency be applied.

The reader will therefore be pleased to consider all the portraits as imaginary characters, presenting only a collective assemblage of features which, if applicable to any one person that has lived, are also applicable to many others,—and are exhibited by me as general pictures of those classes and characters of mind and conduct, which having been detrimental to human welfare, might be allowably placed in the region to which the "Vision" consigns them.

1829. R. M.

The page of history with a fearful glow,
Were here, commingled with a nameless host.

And one, among the legions of the lost,
The wonder and the curse of Time! there was;
The vial of almighty wrath, he held
And pour'd it on the world; or, with a frown
O'erclouded nations, while his fearless sword
Flash'd in defiance o'er th' astounded globe!
His word roll'd thunder to the haunted ear
Of Kings; and Empires quail'd, as from afar
The darkness of his coming deeper grew!
Ambition was his God; and to o'ersway
Or chain the world to his triumphal car,
The demon-passion of his soul. Though Man
And Nature wail'd; though Ocean storm'd,
And mountains threaten'd an eternal bar,
Still went he on, and battled with them all!
Nor paused, till on the tower of Conquest waved
The planted banner which proclaim'd him lord.
No wail of widows o'er the tombless dead;
No groan of orphans; nor the hideous cry
Of Havoc, through the vanquish'd city howl'd,
E'er deafen'd him; dominion was his heaven,
Rebellion hail'd him with applausive roar,
And slaughter'd millions swell'd his fame!

Beside
This reprobate, another ruin'd Soul
Stood haughty: one of those surpassing Minds
It takes a century to create! a man
Whom Genius fill'd with her electric fires.—
Oh! genius is a great, but fearful gift,
A double portion of the God within,
A talent not our own; but to entrance
And elevate mankind with lofty thoughts,
To shadow forth the Spirit that surrounds,
Protects, adorns, and glorifies the world.—
And Genius, nursed in Nature's mighty lap,
For him work'd marvels. On his matchless page
The vast creation lived; both when the voice
Of thunder with his music roll'd; or war
Of Ocean, when the deep-toned winds arose
And whirl'd her into storms; or when he bade
The heavens be sprinkled o'er with starry isles,
Or damask'd with the crimson clouds of eve,
His verse array,—magnificent the Muse
Appear'd: around Her glowing form the light
And breath of nature play'd. But, not to Him
The Architect of all, was incense breathed;
An atheistic shade his lines eclipsed:
High o'er each haughty page a spirit moved
More changeful than a cloud; now beaming forth
Bright in the summer beauty of the soul;
Then, veil'd with darkness, and infernal gloom
From whence the luridness of passion glared!
Yet, had he pleased, he *might* have hallow'd earth
And human nature with immortal lines,
Pure in their radiance, like prophetic gleams
From heaven: but in his breast a storm there was,
An anarchy of impious thoughts: he loved
With minds to play, as whirlwinds do with waves.
No God his genius own'd; and man was deem'd
A chance-begotten shape of dust,—his doom
Annihilation! Principles which nursed
The soul of Ages, he would mine away,
And laugh Religion from her hoary shrine.
Thus sang a prostituted Muse, and taught
The tongue of fools to be profanely wise:
Till lo, a summons from th' Almighty came,
And he was dust!—his Mind the earth appall'd;
And men gazed upward on the burning sweep
His genius circled o'er the heaven of fame,
As though some meteor through the sky had whirl'd,
And summon'd them to trace its dread career!

Another of the lost, who might have lived
In joy's unclouded atmosphere, was he,
The Suicide—the darkest of them all!
The lonely scion of an ancient line,
A princely mansion, when his manhood bloom'd,
Beheld him master. How augustly peer'd
The turrets from the wooded park! how proud
The young fawn bounded o'er the breezy knolls,
And down the vales, where interwinding streams
Ran musical; yet, what to him were trees
With sun-smiles sparkling o'er their boughs, or song
Of birds, and streams, and all the glory shed
By morn and eve his hill-girt home around?
No natal ties he own'd; benignant Heaven
Had bless'd an ingrate; soon the stranger held
His ancient halls,—the City-queen for him!

Full in the prime of youth, to England's Rome
He came, the meteor of his day to shine.
What wonder, Admiration woo'd his eye
Where'er the idol shone? Devoted friends,
Delightful women and officious hearts
Were his; the Capital beneath him crouch'd;
And when the glorious sun of noon beheld
The city roaring like a sea of life,
Who shot through street and square so fiercely swift
As he? How paused the many-headed Crowd,
When, rolling like a distant thunder-car,
His chariot darted through the smoking dust
And shook the glitt'ring windows! In the park
When proudly throned upon his warlike steed

What eyes devour'd him with adoring looks!
Thus pass'd the day; then came the midnight Mask
And ball, with every splendid thief of time:
To crown his course, he blighted trusting hearts,
Jeer'd Honour to her face, and out of tears,
The father's curse, and desolated home,
A pleasure, such as Demons fancy, quaff'd.

Soon fled the glories of a fatal year,
And left him an unpitied wreck of pride
And dissipated hours. No more the smile,
Shot from the heart, flash'd o'er his happy face;
No more the soul-dear friend, and sumptuous dome,
Where beauty, or the banquet, witch'd the hour
With languishment and love; the sun of wealth
Had set, and darken'd into joyless gloom!

One hope, the hope of Desperation left,
He sought it, where the secret gamblers met
And, madden'd o'er their midnight-game. Amid
The sickly glimmer of a silent room,
Like Spectres, there they sat, and ventured all;
Till Ruin scared them, and some faded cheek
Flinch'd from the gripe of agony within!
Night after night, from this infernal haunt
He came, and felt the voice of Conscience rise
Like hell-words sounding through his guilty soul!
One night, as homeward he return'd, and heard
The death-knell of another buried Day,
While far o'er street and lane the waning moon
A wintry radiance shed, the past arose;
The frowning spectre of his murder'd Hours
Appall'd the conscience! then Despair began,
And in him like a living hell-spark burn'd.
Awhile, in chamber'd solitude he sat,
Where through the riven wall the cold blast whined
And mourn'd, and rioted in rueful dreams;
Till, with a laugh, deliriously he snapp'd
The thread of life! and sent his spirit—where?
Where are they all, who, cowards to themselves,
Rob their Creator, cut existence short,
And hurl their spirits back again to God,
Of life disdainful, by His wisdom lent?

Th' antipodes to this self-murder'd Wretch
Stood by, in fellow-torment: once a man
In face so meek, so honied in his tongue,
A martyr to a sinful world he seem'd!
What holy passion work'd his eye, as oft
With woful voice, and words of heavenly tune,
He sermonised, and shook his head, and sigh'd!
But God unmask'd him; and he stood condemn'd,
A hypocrite,—a saint without a soul!
While others braved the censure of their crimes
And to the world their sinful bosoms bared
And sallied heedlessly to Hell, he plied
His guilty pleasures in the dark, and did
Unknown what millions dare, and die condemn'd:
And yet, a living Sermon he appear'd;
Far nearer heaven than unassuming minds
Where God was templed, and his truth adored.
Such was the hypocrite! and when his tomb
Was piled, his epitaph Devotion read,
And glow'd to think that such a man had been!
By saints anointed,—yet with devils leagued.

And who, among the myriads of the cursed,
Was yon red Shape of unconsuming fire?
A blighted Angel! Never round a soul
Did fairer prospects shine: before her moved
The majesty of birth, the graces breathed
From polish'd mode and princely scenes. And oh!
Who ever look'd upon that lovely face
Where the soul sunn'd itself in smiles, or heard
The prattled music of her tongue, nor dreamt
She was a Seraph, born in heaven to beam!

Time roll'd her years along; but with them came
No saintly thoughts, which beautify the soul
And tune the passions to their heavenly tone.
Ne'er did the voice of pure Instruction charm
Her willing ear; nor meek-eyed Wisdom stoop
With fond attention to each budding word
And sweet demand. Unto the dew-bright stars
Her finger pointed oft; the sun and moon
Were radiant wonders; and the ocean-roar
Like hidden rapture, ran through every vein
Until her being throbb'd with joy!—yet none
Were by, to warm her wonder into praise,
And stamp God's image brighter on the soul;
In prayer none lock'd her little hands, or spoke
Of Angels, who the growing child o'erwatch.

But when, at length, the peerless woman dawn'd,
Never did Mind a lovelier form create:
She was a paragon, a poet's queen!
The starry lustre of her speaking eyes,
Her brow, her hair of fascinating curl,
And neck of swan-like grace,—all seem'd divine,
When with the lightness of a cloud she walk'd
Her chamber, or amid the ball-room shone:
The *form* was heavenly, but the *mind* of earth,

A shrine for vain-born hopes, and sensual dreams,
Without a thought, a sigh, or wish for Heaven!
E'en to the last, when on her pain-worn cheek
Approach'd the tints of death, no tender lip
The coming hour reveal'd; nor in her heart
Did Faith's sweet music roll: so mildly-good,
In form so fair, and so adored below,
Sure God would take her to his bowers of light!
So dream'd Compassion's unreflecting heart
And form'd a heaven, how beautifully vain!

Not least deserveless of a nobler lot,
Among the legions of assembled Souls
Was he, the self-idolater: who made
His mind a vortex for ingulphing all
That worldly craft and sordid dreams inspire.
To self unlink'd,—and earth a desert seem'd,
A vacancy, where nothing glorious dwelt;
But, to administer to mean-bred pride,
His wealth augment, and lend ambition wings,—
For this mankind were fool'd with base applause!
For such a soul the very Devils long'd,
So loveless, and with selfish dross defiled:
And yet, no law he broke, no crime he dared,
But in his pew devoutly pray'd; and felt
The pulse of reputation, with the pride
Of specious virtue: Yet, tremendous God!
Before Thee, never could *that* Spirit stand
And live; a worldling could not breathe in Heaven!
When did he look upon the lofty sky
Or round his temples hear the breezes hymn,
And glory in his Being? When did Morn
The world to re-awake arise; or Night
Descend to beautify her brow with stars,
And *he* admire them? Though the wrathful Deep
Should thunder all her waves to foam; or Plagues,
Like noiseless whirlwinds sweep half earth away,
Still, tomb'd within himself, he would not weep,
Or wonder; what to *him* were Nature's pranks?
Not Genius, crown'd with her celestial light;
Not glorious Art; nor Beauty darting out
The mental radiance of her meaning eye,
One noble passion in his soul could plant:
No renegade was he! for when the beam
Of life in death was languishing, and hell
Before him sounding like a furnace-blast,
A Thought look'd back, and wept the world behind!

Such were a few of all the dark undone.
Among them, millions who were crowned, when Time
Stalk'd o'er the earth, as demigods of fame,
Were seen: Philosophers, whose rebel doubts
Would, Titan-like, have disenthroned The God
In heaven, were here; and hosts of every shade
Of sin, from visor'd Crime, to daring Vice;
And those, whose coward-virtues only shone
Untried, when happiness around them smiled;
Unlike the truly good, whose virtues were
As stars,—unnoticed in the haughty glare
Of day, but in their full effulgence seen
And felt, when darkness overshrouds the world.
Not least in number were of middle-stamp,
Nor good, nor bad, and yet for heaven too base;
Triflers, who gaily pass'd from life to death
Like full-wing'd vessels o'er a gallant sea!

And did not meek-eyed Mercy stoop to save?—
To Heaven she beckon'd every breathing soul!
By day, by night, she whisper'd to the heart,
"A God! Eternity! A Day of Doom!"
By funeral-knells, and swiftly-dying friends;
In solemn hours, and serious moods; by pangs
Within, and perils from without; by all
The eloquence of love and truth divine
She summon'd man to glory, and be saved.
In vain!—the tides of joy unebbing flow'd,
And lightly tript the fairy Hours along:
Eternity was all a cheat! and Heaven,
Some bright creation of a poet's dream;
And Hell, but burning in a priestly brain!

Men died; and could they have their breath resumed,
With one terrific shriek they would have thrill'd
Creation round,—"There is, there *is* a Hell!"
But now, for ever dungeon'd must they groan
Where minutes hold eternities of pain!

The crowns in happier realms they *might* have worn
In mocking dreams now only view'd, which make
Damnation more severe; their wasted hours,
Corrupting pleasures and degraded joys,
The sabbaths broken, and the God blasphemed,—
All, in one blended, burning mass of sin
And mem'ry, round each guilty Soul revolve,
Where self-conviction forms the deepest Hell.

* * * * *

UNIVERSAL PRAYER.

ALMIGHTY, True, Eternal, and Supreme,
By Person Threefold and in Nature One,
Jehovah dread, adorable I AM!
Through Christ alone accessibly reveal'd,
In whom Thine attributes and counsels meet
Become incarnate and the World redeem,—
Look on our hearts, and lift them up to Thee,
By prayer and praise for due ascension wing'd.
Illume, expand, and purify the Soul
With inward radiance, from Thyself derived;
The springs of mind unlock, and let them gush
Heavenward to Thee in one commingled stream
Of adoration, duteous as divine.

Thou Infinite! since first creation roll'd
Of heaven thy mercy hath a shade reveal'd
To Nature's heart; in ev'ry age or clime,
Heard in the wind, or by the tempest robed,
Or in the parent-sun presumed to shine,
Still has immortal soul been stamp'd with Thee!

Oh, all which thought can span, or eye perceive,
Is but a part, a shadow of Thy Power
Creating, filling, and upholding All!
The arch'd immensity above us spread,
Where mystic worlds their silent march perform,
And Seasons live, and act; the chainless Deep
Belting the earth with majesty and might;
The mountains pinnacled with storms; the floods
And streams, the meadows beautified with flowers,
A God declare! and in the thunder-peals
Rattling from cloud to cloud their voices dire,
Like Sinai, when the awe of sound convulsed
Her cavern'd height,—a Deity is there!
But when dark whirlwinds o'er creation sweep
Like rebel Spirits plunging from the sky,
We dread Thee, wing'd upon each awful blast!

Fountain of Light and Love! while Nature hymns
Thy praise in wave or wind, from shore to shore,
Thy miniature, immortal Man, the grace
And glory of the earth, with brow erect
Was made the world to walk in joy; to share
Thy goodness; and adore the Hand divine.
Then look, Thou Universal One! Whose eye
Alike on all is fix'd, with mercy view
This wide and peopled World; from east to west
From north to south Thy guardian care extend:
In Polar climes, in lands refined or rude,
In isles remote, or deserts grimly vast,
Where beats a heart within a human breast
There be Thou present, and Thy power adored!
And oh, since all one common race are doom'd
To run, and one Eternal Goal to reach,
May Thy prime Attribute each bosom warm
With tender sympathy and truth; may Man
To man be link'd, in fellowship of soul,
Till one vast chain of Love the world embrace.

Unsearchable! before whose boundless gaze
The Past the Present and the Future stand
Submissive, we implore Thee to unshroud
The Sun of truth; His heavenly beam advance
From pole to pole, till on His perfect face
All earth shall gaze, one glorious Altar rise,
And every soul unite to hail thee, God!

And, ah! may those who fight the war of faith
With weapons such as brave Apostles wore,
In climes where Sin and Satan darkly rage
Feel holy valour, from Thy shield derived:
Defend them, Thou! Whose cross their banner decks,
When bleak with ice or burnt with torrid glow
Deserts of gloom and death their eyes appal;
Or when at midnight, round their flapping tent
The hurricane like a demon howls,
Let Hope descend, their falt'ring hearts confirm,
And free as morning let their faith arise
Again for conquest, o'er the host of Hell;
While round them, daily may Redemption see
Idolatry from thrones of darkness fall
For ever, by the sword of Truth destroy'd.

As o'er the treach'rous sea of human life
We wander, till our anchor'd spirits rest

In the calm haven of eternity,
Without a heart-deep sense, a wakeful dread
Of Thee, felt in the mind, and by the act
Reveal'd, we perish on the rock of sin:
Lord of the Universe! impress, we pray,
Upon our minds Thy majesty, that breathes
A holy freshness through the heart; and raise
And animate the soul to things sublime;
O'erawe the passions, and each thought arrest
Which on the fiery wing of impulse roams
Unheedful of the Voice within, where dwells
The chronicler of virtue and of crime.
Omnipotent! in every Soul be shrined:
So shall our deeds be echoes of good thoughts,
And at Thy dreadful summons we shall stand
Unharm'd, secure amid the shock of worlds!

And since to Thee the unveil'd heart be known,
Nor voiceless thought, nor wish can rise, but Thou
Record'st it in Thine awful Book of Life,
The tempted mind oh! may we ever watch
And keep it pure from each unhallow'd wish,
From each depraved desire: so shall our days
In beautiful declension fade; and Hope
And Faith triumphant o'er the world exult;
Till back recall'd, the renovated Soul
Shall reap beatitude in realms of light.

On each degree of men, benignant God!
Thy sleepless care we pray Thee to bestow;
Grave it on each adoring mind, that Heaven's
Bright portals are to all unbarr'd, that high
Nor mean, nor rich nor poor with Thee prevail
By aught peculiar, save a perfect heart:
The meanest orphan of the world may win
A wreath in heaven; the humblest wear a crown
Of life. And oh! may those, the gifted few,
Archangels of the earth, before whose thrones
Mortality will bend, and half adore,
Remember what to Thee and Man they owe:
May Genius never stoop to pander vice,
But fix her eye on heaven, and walk the earth
A Spirit conscious of her native sphere.

Prime Source of being! let the richly-dower'd
Forget not Him from whom their riches flow,
And heaven-born Charity exult to be
A bright reflection of Thy glorious self!
Her office 'tis, sweet Harbinger of love,
To light the burden from oppressed hearts,
To pluck the arrow from Affliction's breast,
Nor leave a pang behind; and where the sad
And unobtrusive Virtues toil, to shed
The balm of joy, and wreathe their cup of wo
With smiles accorded by approving Heaven.

To Thee, to Thee alone, pervading God,
The sum of human agonies is known!
But wheresoe'er the race of sorrow dwell
There may Thy dews of mercy fall; refresh
The wither'd heart, the languid eye of Want
Relume, and bid Misfortune smile again:
And since from Thee the breath of Life began
And on each brow the seal of God is set,
Oh, hear the bitter sighs of Thraldom, breathed
Morn, noon, and night, from out ten thousands hearts
Of agony, to Thee: Awake, arise,
God of the slave and free!* and disenthral
The World; bid freedom shine, and like thy sun
Illume and animate Creation round.

And let the young, on whose delighted gaze
In hopeful beauty dawns the dream of life,
In their unspotted bosoms treasure thoughts
Of Thee, to guide them through the cloudy years;
And may the Old, upon whose gray-worn heads
An honourable crown past Time has placed,
When earth grows dim, and worldly joys decay,
Find heaven advancing as the world retires.

Oh! Thou that fathomest the guilty mind
And canst interpret each debasing thought
Untold, the erring soul arouse, by Sin
From Thee withdrawn; the form of Vice unveil,
And bare her hideous aspect to the eye
Of Truth; then, bid return the rebel heart,
And blot its error with repentant tears.

On him, whom Hope and Faith exalt, what dreams,
What joys, and what diviner moods attend!
The world He walks, as Jesus walk'd the waves,
Triumphant and secure. In every scene
A love for Thee prevails; Creation breathes
Of heaven: the vaulted sky with stars bedropt;
The Ocean roll'd to rest, or sending up
Tremendous pæans to her mighty Lord;
The field and flower; whate'er in noontide walk
Is sweet, to Him his wondering heart allure,
The source and spirit of the moving Whole.
All order, beauty, and perfection here
Form but the shadows of more perfect Bliss
Cast from a purer world; he dwells in Thee,

* See Note, p. 570.

And Thou in him; Heaven seems his native home
And Immortality embowers him there.

Not for the fleeting joys of Life alone
We pray, and those by blood or truth allied:
When Life'sfierce storms are hush'd, and Death that veil
Undraws, beyond which never human glance
Hath seen, oh, then be present, viewless Power!
And calm the pangs of Nature's closing scene:
Let haunting fears, nor fiery dreams the past
Recall; but may the grave a future bed
Of glory be; around the dying couch
May bands of sympathetic Angels watch,
And waft the wingèd Spirit to its home.

Omnipotent! at Whose creative word
Eternity a shining host sent forth
Of worlds, to balance in the beauteous air,
Still may the Sun upon his dazzling brow
Thy smile of mercy o'er mankind reflect;
Still let abundance crown the year; still roll
The seasons o'er a prosperous land, and breeze
And blast, and all the treasure of the clouds
The pregnant earth enrich, and heap the load
Of human gratitude to gracious heaven!

Incarnate King of kings, and Lord of lords!
Since at thy fiat empires rise and fall
And melt like palaces of painted cloud,
Mantle our cherish'd Country with Thy wings
Of glory: may she prosper in the pride
Of liberty; Her ancient throne around
Let all the kingly virtues throng; and bid
Thy delegate, the Monarch of our Land,
Be graced with wisdom, and his sceptre wield
The majesty of Justice and of Truth;
May he be great and good, and ever find
A loving bulwark in the People's heart!

But with the prayer let boundless praise ascend
On wings that never droop. We praise Thee, God!
For life and limb; we praise Thee, God! for health
And wisdom, hope divine, and deathless truth;
For each vast symbol of Thy power portray'd
By this dread Universe, where Thou art seen,
As ocean mirrors an imperial sun.
In feeble infancy, when on the breast
We hang in slumber, Thy protecting Hand
O'ershades us; on our steps Thine angels wait;
And day by day, Thou shap'st the formless mind,
Teaching the thought to bud, the tongue to speak,
And on the heart reflecting grace and truth,
Which are the flashes that Thyself reveal.
And thus, through all the ravell'd maze of life
With viewless guidance Thou direct'st our feet,
Till, lo! upon *that* awful Brink we stand
Where shines the light which leads to Heaven the soul.

But Thine infinity of awful love
Oh who can fathom, when th' Incarnate came
And bade the moral resurrection dawn?
He look'd,—and in His glance grew bright the Earth!
Her slavish eye Idolatry unscaled,
While Superstition from her gloom arose
Burst from her bonds, and with an angel-shout
From east to west the Hallelujah rang!

Victor of Death! mysterious God and Man,
Who bore the vial of almighty Wrath
Upon His head outpour'd, the tomb unlock'd,
Trampled on Hell, and oped the gates of Heaven
To banish'd Man, hail Prince of Peace! enthroned
In glory, with Thy co-eternal Sire,
Our prayer accept, the incense of the soul,
And hallow it with Thy perfecting grace.

Thou Light of Light! by ancient seers foretold,
And by prophetic minstrels hymn'd, the sun
And centre of our faith, redeeming Christ!
Look down, and consecrate thy Church below:
Around it rally all thy faithful hearts,
Pillars beyond the power of Hell to shake!
Reluctant time roll on; and spread from land
To land, from isle to isle, the Word of Truth
Till Earth shall seem one universal soul.

But all is fruitless, save Thy Spirit teach,
Console, attract, illumine and adorn
The penitential Mind. Can deaf men feel
How Music wakens her enchanted might;
Or blind ones, when the lids of Morning ope,
Greet the proud radiance of commencing day?
So dull, and eyeless to the words and beams
Of truth heaven-sanction'd, is the rocky heart,
Before an unction of converting grace
Descend, and bid the glorious change begin.
Or, mark the body, when the soul is fled,
How pale and powerless, how corrupt and cold
It lies, and withers like a Dream of clay!
So dead to things transcendently divine
In carnal trance the soul itself abides,
Till comes Thy Spirit with celestial breath,

The faded lineaments of God revives
And quickens nature with transforming power:
Then, Thou art all, and all in Thee resides.
Eternity upon the Book of Life
Reflected, how sublime the means of Grace!
In Christ what love immeasurably deep
Embodied! what a glory robes the Cross!
Each word, each promise, each divine appeal
By Thee brought home, how vast redemption grows!
Vile passions sink; and low affections raised,
No longer worm-like creep in dust and gloom,
But, wing'd by faith, beyond the world ascend,
Exulting round The Throne, and hearing oft
Faint echoes of some archangelic hymn
To Jesu chanted; Who, as Lord of deed
And life of thought, o'er all our being reigns;
And oft, by sacred fascination led,
To Calvary our yearning Hearts retire,
Kneel at the Cross, and see the Saviour die!

Be with us, Lord, till years of fadeless bloom
Act the bright wonders which Isaiah sung,
And Eden, lovelier far than Adam saw,
Lit by the Sun of Righteousness, appear!
And when at length Thy gospel-Kingdom comes,
When the last Trumpet wakes the trance of time
And thunders roll creation's knell, Thine eye
Shall beam with mercy; and Thy voice will sound
A welcome to the Skies; while, angel-wing'd,
Myriads ascend to shine immortal there.

LONDON, 1829.

Note to Page 568, Column 2.

God of the slave and free! and disenthral

* As the awful question of human slavery is once more exciting the deepest sympathies of Christian men, the author ventures to subjoin, in a note, a speech which he happens to retain, which refers to this subject. It was delivered by him, "AT THE FIRST PUBLIC MEETING OF THE GLASGOW SOCIETY FOR THE CIVILIZATION OF AFRICA, HELD IN HOPE STREET, ON THURSDAY, 24TH SEPTEMBER, 1840." He need scarcely preface it by the remark that his righteous abhorrence for this impious outrage on the body and soul of man, remains in all its unweakened intensity. (1853.)

"My Lord, Ladies, and Gentlemen,—Although an introduction to a speech, like a preface to a book, is, for the most part, a gratuitous infliction which might well be avoided, I shall venture to brave the encounter of your taste, by assuring your Lordship that my appearance here to-day has originated in no desire for prominence on my part; on the contrary, I was most anxious to commit the subject to abler hands and to more practised intellects. And, in addition to this felt incompetency, I was fully conscious that various professional engagements left me little time to consolidate my thoughts, to collect facts, or to embrace those scattered principles in alliance with the subject in that symmetric order, and that condensed harmony of expression, which alone could render them suitable to be offered to an assembly like this. But, overcome by the Christian urgency of my Rev. Friend, the highly-respected Secretary of this Society, I yielded to his wish: and now, with a profound sense of my incompetencies in the unwonted atmosphere of a platform, I shall proceed to the high and holy cause before us.

"And here, at the very outset, my Lord, allow me to congratulate this great assemblage that we have so far realised the cheering idea, which, we presume, all present indulged at the commencement of our proceedings, viz., that whatever might be the politic bias of specific mind on this occasion—however varied might be our views on certain questions touching other departments and interests of human nature—we should be found united to a man here; and, though arithmetically numerous, morally one. And thus, my Lord, we have imitated the noble concord and graceful unity which inspired the first meeting of this Society, at which the illustrious Consort of our Queen presided; and by placing himself in the front of freedom's sacred cause, added an additional throb of loyalty to the beating of that Empire's heart, in whose affections he had already begun to be enshrined. And here, my Lord, perchance it will not be presumptuous should I venture to congratulate yourself also on this deeply interesting occasion. For justly as your Lordship may have endeared your memory to the minds of those distinguished[1] strangers whose presence has adorned, and whose genius has irradiated, our city during the past week, by presiding with dignified courtesy over their association of science; you have now added a richer charm to your name, and a more abiding motive to our gratitude, by taking the chair at this great meeting of humanity. For without the remotest depreciation of the lofty claims and enduring trophies of science, may we not assert, that associations of a sublimer cast than ever encircled the cause of mere earthly science combine themselves around us now? Our object, my Lord, in its upward aspect, connects itself with the moral perfections of the Almighty; while in its downward reference, it applies to the most costly interests of humanity. In a word, we have to wing our thoughts to that far Continent of whirlwind and of gloom—to the sun-burnt soil of deserts and of slaves, where man is bartered by his brother man—where sacrilege is attempted on the Divine glory through the inalienable prerogatives of the reasonable spirit;—in fact, ours is the sad and solemn duty to surround the terrific altar of human suffering, heaped with the hecatomb of some four hundred years of outrage and wrong, and to offer there the sacrifice of noble sympathy and indignant remonstrance!

And here, let us ask, what is the nature of this tremendous curse against which we now meet to lift our righteous testimony?—That curse is Slavery!—

[1] An allusion to the meeting of the British Association, held in Glasgow.

and what is that? Let us answer this by considering what is freedom. Is it not the spring of thought, the source of conduct, the fountain of character—at once the centre of nearly all that is good, and, at the same time, the circumference of all that is great, in man? And if so, then Slavery is the infernal opposite to all this!—a system of stern and absolute vassalage, whereby one man becomes a mere excrescence to the existence of another—a mere appendix to his master's pleasure,—in fact, the slave is dwarfed down from the high majesty of being a person, to the low prostration of becoming a thing—a mere negation of humanity—a living machine of flesh and blood, to be worked and used at the mercy of his master. But after all, my Lord, I feel the inadequacy of my language here; for, however deeply seated among the complexities of our nature, nothing, in fact, is more difficult to anatomise than moral instinct; and, however big the impression of our horror, we cannot always break it up into luminous fragments, so as to explain in detail what in the compound our entire being feels to be just. But even as on beholding some masterpiece in art, we instinctively exclaim—beautiful!—so must every rightly-constituted heart, on considering the Slave Trade, burst into the moral interjection, and say,—abominable! And here, again, my Lord, we realise a blessed concord: for not more completely are all the warring varieties of Protestantism united into doctrinal fellowship when they meet round the harmony of the Everlasting Intellect, even the Bible, and pronounce it to be the standard of truth; than are all the discords of political interest harmonised into one expressive indignation when they contemplate together the system of slavery, and declare it to be—the summit of their common detestation! And here, my Lord, had not the day so far advanced upon us, we might have attempted to analyse these elements of human corruption out of which the fell injustice of slavery has morally originated; and appended to this view some remarks on the more immediate sources to which it owes its modern birth,—such as war, conquest and crime. But leaving this, and omitting also the dark traces of slavery as occurring in ancient history down to its milder form in feudal times—we would remind this assembly that it is in Africa, where slavery has been concentrated into the climax of all conceivable horrors! There it is that, from the fifteenth century (when the West Indies first began to be possessed by Europeans), more than tongue can speak has been endured and done! But, my Lord, I shrink from the ghastly detail—I recoil into mute helplessness before the abominations that mark the traffic in human flesh—I have no language sufficiently tragic to personate the woes—I have no epithets sufficiently scathing in their fire and force to brand the atrocities connected with Afric's children; and, therefore, leave them to the expressive silence of imagination to conceive. If described, at all (I say it with awful reverence), the description must come from more than mortal lip; for as God, in the mystery of His sovereignty, has permitted slavery to exist, so, I solemnly believe, He alone has language adequate to describe it! And yet,—(can the powers of perversity exceed this?)—something like an apology has been feigned for this masterpiece of iniquity!—from the whips and branding-iron, even down to that floating hell—the slave-ship—the excuse has dared to proceed! And what is worse, not content with bringing all the vile urgencies of mere venality to bear on the subject, the Bible itself—that great Magna Charta of the soul!—has been violated for arguments wherewith to defend the system of slavery! Yes, my Lord, our ears have heard with dismay the assertion that slavery may be defended on the principles of Scripture!—and thus has the ark of the Divine mystery been blasphemed by the touch of the infidel; even thus has the cold-blooded worldling attempted to transmute that almighty volume—which was intended to quicken, to purify, and exalt the world,—into the hemlock of falsehood, which would terminate in the death of moral truth, and the destruction of all social principle. But, my Lord, we will not fatigue this assembly by details unrequired in order to prove what the majority of all sincere Christians already know—namely, that the endeavour to adduce scriptural authority for Slavery derives all its strength from confounding the permissive with the preceptive economy of God in the Old Testament; and from an infidel determination to mistake what is barely recognised, regulated, and restrained in the judicial facts of the Mosaic dispensation, for that which has been actually ordained and directly approved by the moral Governor of the universe. Let us, however, turn from abstract argument to one fact, which includes more than mere logic can achieve—we allude to a circumstance in the history of that hero of the Apostles, St. Paul. Now while he, beyond all men, knew how to borrow from the splendours of eternity, in order to irradiate the darkness of time; and, therefore, how to overcome the powers and persecutions of this evil word—whether he were fettered or free; yet even he, when summoned to plead before the proud king and his pampered court, uttered these memorable words—'I would to God, that not only thou, but all that hear me this day, were both almost and altogether such as I am'—but here, my Lord, the chain clanked in his ear—the iron entered his soul—there was a parenthesis in his grief—for he added, with uplifted arm, 'except these bonds!'

"And now, my Lord, permit me to direct the attention of this assembly to consider two points, most interestingly allied to the cause of this noble Society:—1st, Let us ask what has been already accomplished towards the Abolition of Slavery? To answer this, completely and correctly, would lead us far too extensively into the history of the abolitionists; we must, therefore, content ourselves, by reminding your Lordship that those who have befriended the Slaves may be divided into three classes. The first comprehends all those who opposed the principle of Slavery; 2nd, those who assailed the system; and 3rd, those who attacked the thing. Among the first of these philanthropists are found a series of writers, poetical, moral, philosophic, and historical—reaching from the time of Cardinal Ximenes (who composed the Polyglott Bible early in the sixteenth century), down to the times of Granville Sharp. Selection here is impossible; but amongst these moral pioneers to a great result, we cannot resist hearing the illustrious Montesquieu, who, in allusion to the negro, utters this pithy and profound sarcasm—'We must take heed that the negroes do not discover they are men—or assuredly they will at the same time find out that we are no Christians!' In reference to the second class, those who assailed the system, we presume we may consider Granville Sharp in the present rank; for it was owing to his righteous zeal and intrepid humanity that the judges, in 1772, gave their immortal decision, viz.:—'That as soon as any slave set his foot upon English territory he became free!' A decision over which every attribute in Godhead smiled, and for which angels round the throne might have given a cheer! It was in allusion to this result that Cowper wrote those lines which concentrate as much of piety, poetry, and philanthropy as can be well condensed into a few syllables:—

'Slaves cannot breathe in England: if their lungs
Receive our air, that moment they are free!
They touch our country, and their shackles fall.
That's noble, and bespeaks a nation proud
And jealous of the blessing. Spread it then,
And let it circulate through every vein
Of all your empire—that, where Britain's power
Is felt, mankind may feel her mercy too.'

. . . .

"In connexion with this period, however, we cannot forget the name of Thomas Clarkson. And here, my Lord, how deeply interesting it is to mark the ways in which the God of wonders often connects moral influences together. At the time to which we now allude, Clarkson carried off the Chancellor's Prize Essay, for that year in Cambridge; the subject of which was connected with Slavery. It was after reading this essay in the Senate House, while on his way to London, that the awful statements and appalling facts contained in his essay returned on his mind with double force; and in one of those mournful reveries, in which the high mysteries of our nature come so strangely into action, he sat down on the green turf by the roadside, and pondered deeply and sadly on the wrongs of Africa!—and there was formed, my Lord, that magnificent resolution, which, as a germ, contained all the energies and principles which he hereafter brought to bear on the cause of abolition. It occurred to him that if the essay were true, the case must be tremendous, and called for instant aid; and to connect with this reverie the fact that, in a few years after this, the cause of slavery was rolled off from myriads of the human race! But, my Lord, we now hasten, with many apologies for this protracted harangue, to introduce the venerated name of Clarkson's great coadjutor, even that of William Wilberforce. And is it too imaginative, or rather is it not becoming this temple, dedicated to the sublime impressions of eternity, to think, that if the holy dead can recognise the conduct of the living, that patriarch of liberty, whose spirit now brightens before the throne, may be permitted to gaze on this assembly, and waft a blessing on that cause on earth, the trophies of which he remembers in heaven!—But here, my Lord, we need not linger; the character and conduct of Wilberforce require neither eulogy nor history; they form part and parcel of our national sympathies. We would simply remind the meeting that although associated with Wilberforce were those giants of intellect, Pitt, Fox, and Burke,—it was only after innumerable delays, cabals, and conspiracies, that Wilberforce succeeded in carrying his glorious measure; and that as the chime struck midnight in May, 1807, the last act of the Grenville administration was to sign and seal the 'Magna Charta for Africa in Britain.'

"And now, my Lord, from this hurried retrospect of past exertions, we turn to the future, and ask, What remains to be done?—and what is our corresponding duty? Our reply is, let the past instruct the present, and from the triumphs of what has been effected, let us reason hopefully to what may be achieved. And this suggests an allusion to Wilberforce in the way of encouragement. Now, what is it that demands our chief admiration in contemplating the career of this eminent man? Why, my Lord, we do not hesitate to remark that while the result of his labours has been duly lauded, the moral process whereby that consummation was reached has scarcely yet been sufficiently admired. Here, just as in the history of struggling intellect, when the palms are won, and the laurel binds the fevered brow of triumphant genius, the voice of fame is loud and long; yet all the solitude and sorrows, all the waste of heart and wear of mind, all the toilsome days and sleepless nights, are seldom estimated. So in the career of Wilberforce's philanthropy—his success has been nobly congratulated; but the heroic self-denial and all the high elements of patience, zeal, and fortitude, which he evinced throughout his arduous and protracted fight against the world's antagonism, are too often unremembered in an estimate of what is great and good in his history. With this great man, indeed, we may assert, that the energy of opposing circumstance only served to draw forth the energy of victorious principle. So, my Lord, from some green eminence in this romantic land have I oft beheld with delighted gaze some gallant bark, contending nobly with the winds and waves around it—at times, amid the darkening heavens and the uprising billows, the bark would seem to sink and disappear,—but when the sunbeam came through the riven cloud, and flashed along the deep, there was the little bark,—bearing on to the harbour, where at length it arrived, and dried its dripping sails in the sun. So, amid all the clashing waves and contending winds of opposition, did Wilberforce, with never-failing heroism, carry forward the sacred cause of human freedom, and bear it finally unwrecked and uninjured into the haven of a nation's welcoming smiles! My Lord, be it for us now, who are on the eve of following out his glorious precedent, to remember, that with Wilberforce success was neither the motive nor standard of duty; and that (under the Divine blessing) he was indebted for his costly triumph in the cause of humanity to a fine combination of unquailing principles, set in motion by indomitable resolution. Be a spirit like this our inspiration now! By combining prayer to God with exertion towards man, let us march forward to meet the holy cause that now demands all our energy, prudence and zeal. And, so may the period soon arrive, when the spirit of divinest freedom shall inspire the hearts, purify the homes, and exalt the characters of Africa's now degraded offspring: when not a limb that moves within her vast domain but shall be found as fetterless as MAN was made to be! And then, my Lord, visions fairer than Christian patriot ever conceived, nobler than painting ever sketched, and richer than poetry ever drew, shall be realised and seen; and the land where Tertullian penned his burning page, and Cyprian died the martyr's death, shall awake from the dark slumber of a thousand years of ignorance, slavery and crime, and more than rival what it once possessed, when Egypt was the cradle of science, the seminary of art, and the birth-place of literature. And why? Because, my Lord, Africa may have that which imparts to science its ennobling strength, to art its presiding beauty, and to literature its sanctifying life and glory—even that which heightens the moral lustre round the throne, being,—'glory to God in the highest,'—while at the same time it awakens 'peace on earth, and good-will to men'—even the Gospel of our Lord and Saviour Jesus Christ. Yes, my Lord, it is because this Society recognises that great verity, for which we should all be ready to bleed on the block, and to burn in the flame—viz., that Christianity, and Christianity alone is the conservatrix of liberty, and the true reformer of the world,—it is on this account, my Lord, pre-eminently, I would give this Society my very cordial, though insignificant, support. For if the Son shall make the Africans free, they shall be free indeed! And now, where savage waters wind their lonely course—unwhitened by a single sail—there may Commerce lift her thousand signals, streaming in the gale; instead of forest depths, where the tiger preys, and the lion howls,—there may the thronged city, the busy wharf, the crowded street, be hereafter seen, with all the glow of commercial life, and the grace of social advancement; and instead of the war-whoop of contending tribes, the tyrant's lash, the clank of chains, and thraldom's bitter sigh—there may be heard the voice of prayer, the sound of praise, and the sweet music of the 'church-going' bell. My Lord, the cold head and the calculating heart may pronounce this to be mere poetry—but He who ruleth on high may in mercy render it prediction! And therefore, in conclusion, I most warmly anticipate the time when the energies of Scotland, England, and Ireland will be found condensed into one high, magnificent, and holy enterprise, for carrying out the principles of this Society, and for putting down that consummate treason against God and man—human slavery. Yes! soon may that vessel be launched, from whose deck the voice of this united empire will proclaim the commencing jubilee of Afric's glorious freedom, and the termination of her shameful wrongs—for

'Thus saith Britannia, empress of the sea,
Thy chains are broken—Africa! be free.'"

THE STAGE COACH.

(1827.)

———Jumenta vocant——eundum est;
Nam mihi commota jam dudum mulio virga
Adnuit. Juv. *Sat.* 3.

ADVERTISEMENT TO FIRST EDITION.

The following Poem was written when the writer was on the brink of boyhood, some two years before the "Omnipresence of the Deity" appeared. The reader will, of course, be eandid enough to estimate it by a right standard; nor expect a homely subject not to be treated in a homely style: "parvum parva decent." There is something peculiarly national in the neatness, comfort, and rapidity of our Stage-coaches; and the Author thought many of the feeling reflections which a journey in England suggests, might not be inappropriately described in a poetical form. With this brief preface, he leaves this poetical trifle to the indulgence of his readers;—happy will he be, if, when steam has rendered our present style of travelling almost extinct, an occasional passenger will be old-fashioned enough to patronise him, by taking a place in his "Stage-Coach."

April 25th, 1834.

ANALYSIS.

Sunrise in an obscure Village—Woodland described—Curate's abode—Breakfast scene before the journey—Coach arrives—Its influence on the Villagers, &c.—A respectful apostrophe to the subject—Pleasure of a journey from town on a fine day, or of a visit to a secluded Friend—Schoolboy's love of travel—A Coachman sketched—a farewell at the Parsonage—Journey recommenced—Landscape Scenery—Park Mansions—Country Gentlemen—A homely Man's feelings on surveying their comforts—Moral scenery on the Road—Instruction often derived from a casual acquaintance with Passengers—Characters—Politician—Pleasure of a social Temper—The quiet demeanour of the Curate contrasted with his loquacious Friend—A retrospect of the Author's—A sad but interesting Passenger is next described—then, two Schoolboys, and their pleasant glee—Its effect on a Sailor and an old Soldier, who each relate the story of their Lives—Arrival at a Town where the Coach stops for Dinner—Comforts of an Inn—Scene described—Journey recommenced—Evening Scenery—Delight of revisiting the Place of our Boyish days—Sailor's joy on his return Home after a long absence—Journey concluded—The Passengers part—And the Poem concludes with a moral comparison.

The morn is up; on Woodland's eastern sky
Masses of cloud in rich confusion lie;
Awhile they mingle, then apart they glide
Like painted isles upon a far-off tide:
Till, orb'd with glory, see! the sun appear
To light the world, and lead the Day's career.
Now from yon hamlet's moss-grown chimneys rise
Wreaths of blue smoke which curl along the skies,
And far the stir of village-life resounds
And rings the morning air with merry sounds.

Ask ye of Woodland, site of boyish days?
A village, such as Goldsmith's verse might praise:
The grey church glimm'ring through the dark elm-trees,
Whose pealing chimes oft harmonise the breeze;
A Gothic mansion on the green withdrawn,
With freckled steps and smoothly-levell'd lawn,
Where priest and parish sages oft retire
And bow obsequious to the ruddy squire;
An ocher'd inn behind a bench-girt tree,
Where chatt'ring statesmen kindly disagree,—
These are the noblest piles on Woodland's plain,
To charm the pilgrim, or delight the swain.

Though barren now, not so when summer-bloom
Spreads a bright magic over winter's gloom,
Fair Woodland looks, and every garden greets
The way-worn traveller with exulting sweets.
The gravel winding to the lilac-bower
Where shaded friends beguile their sultry hour;
The guarded hive where humming bees abound,
The well-rope creaking forth its homely sound,
The fairy babble of a road-side stream
Where the brown urchin shapes his infant dream,

With many a charm awake the wand'rer's smile,
Tempting his eye to pause, and dream awhile.

But to our scene!—Beside yon beaten road
Behold the village Curate's neat abode;
Time-worn, it stands in unobtrusive state
Behind the circling pales and ivied gate,
With pointed windows based by massy beams,
Where orient Morn delights to shed her gleams:
No fruits, or flower-parterres in spruce array!
The night-beads glisten on the leafless spray,
And, safely housed within his pendent cote,
The plaintiff pigeon coos his winter-note.

But in yon parlor, where a window-blaze
Now flickers redly o'er the white-frost haze,
And the bold robin, fed by infant-zeal,
Pecks from the scatter'd crumbs his morning meal,
How merrily resounds the mingled din
Of social love and life, awake within!
Bright on the pictured wall the fire-beams play;
There the loud tea-urn sings its bubbling lay,
And on the glossy table-cloth are spread
The glitt'ring china and the cottage-bread:
The parting hour, like death itself to meet,
Is come!—the curate from his calm retreat,
Doom'd by domestic care, awhile must roam
And leave the heaven which Virtue forms at home.

Around him now a darling group is met
With faithful looks of fondness and regret;
Yon fair-brow'd child, the gentle, loving, good,
And budding sweetly into womanhood,
Presidingly the breakfast-rite surveys
While a meek sorrow dims her pensive gaze;
One prattling cherub, with infantine grace,
Leaps on his knee, and pats his smiling face,
While elder boys within their hearts receive
The counsel pious fathers care to give.
But, ah! what lovely dews of feeling rise,
Melt from the soul, and glitter in *her* eyes,
As moves the mother with a placid mien
And fondly hovers round this parting-scene!
Full well yon tender sire perceives the care,
And smiles it off with many a winning air;
Talks of his quick return, the news he'll tell,
And *looks*, what language could not speak so well!

But, hark! the merry bugle peals a sound
Till the roused echoes ring the hills around!
From doors half open'd peeps out many a face,
The grandam hobbles from her wonted place,
While noisy urchins scour the village through,
To hail the Stage-coach wheeling into view!—
That Thing of glory to a rustic throng
Who shout and gambol as it whirls along;
Or, idly vent'rous, balance at its back
Braving the guard, and whip's repeated smack;
While at the blacksmith's murky door preside,
With solemn eyes, and mouths all gaping wide,
A prying group—that pertinacious class
Who quiz profoundly as the coaches pass!

Triumph of Art! extemporaneous home!
For pain or pleasure unto all who roam;
Compactly fashion'd to a useful form,
To poise the burden, and defy the storm,
Let Life and Commerce, Love and Duty show
What daily blessings to thy speed we owe:
Sure of thy succour, see the Friend depart,
To press the absent to his faithful heart;
Swift as thy speed, behold the Lover fly
On Love's warm breast to breathe his welcome sigh;
The proud and mean, the hapless and the gay,
Thou waft'st them all, along their varied way!

And pleasant 'tis when Winter's flooding rains
Flash on the pools, and beat the rattling panes,
Snug in a Coach's padded nook to lie,
Stretch the free limb, and close the languid eye:
But sweeter far, on some auspicious day
When lovely clouds the crystal sky inlay,
And choral breezes o'er the meadow spring
Like uncaged birds exultant on the wing,
Throned on a coach to leave the smoke-dimm'd town,
And view the vernal mead and sloping down,
The wood-crown'd hills, and laughing streams that glide
While sunbeams gambol on their gurgling tide.
How warms the spirit into young delight
As views romantic greet the gladden'd sight!
While lip and brow partake the fresh-wing'd breeze,
Till fancy echoes to the warbling trees;
'Tis now, as slow and soft some distant bell
Dies on the air with solemnising spell,
That worldly feelings faint off, one by one,
Like ice-drops melted by the noontide sun;
Till, soften'd all, they mix in one soft sigh,
Or bask delighted in the beaming eye!

On morn like this, to quiet hearts how sweet
To leave the noise of life for some retreat,
Where haply dwells in his Arcadian cot
Far from the world and by the world forgot,

The friend of virtue, gentle, wise and good,
In mental ease and classic solitude;
There, warm at heart, within his social room
Where fragrant woodbines waft their mild perfume,
At eve's soft hour, behold the vesper-star
And talk of vanish'd scenes and friends afar;
Renew the hours of rapture and of pain,
The past create, and be the boy again!

By moonlight, too, when vale and coppice gleam
Like landscapes pictured in a poet's dream,
How charming from the coach, with half-closed eye
To mark the glimm'ring meadows gliding by:
The spectral valley, or the dark-brow'd hill,
The woods in dewy slumber, dark and still,
Or taper twinkling from some far abode,
Or waggon winding up the lonesome road,
While the meek night-bird's melancholy lay
Melts like a wreath of woven sound away.
Not least the coach's charm let schoolboys tell,
When to their prison-walls they shout, farewell!
Then through the joy-wing'd night glib tongues display
The fairy visions of their homeward way;
And oft the ceaseless tongue would fain relate
What coach-wheels rattle at the school-yard gate!

But who, emburied in his coat's broad fold,
With triple kerchief round his neck enroll'd,
Stalks forth, with brindled waistcoat, full and free,
And glossy boots, braced o'er his giant knee?
Our Coachman! who, with smiling pomp and mien,
Full-blown and square, directs the road-machine.
Alike when winter wraps the world in snow,
Or o'er it summer sheds her sleepy glow;
Not unimportant is his busy post,
Or on the road, or parleying with my Host,
Or when, with merry eye and mottled face,
The whip he twirls, whose ev'ry turn is grace!

Happy the trav'ller who on coachey's throne
May sit, and make the country round his own;
Well pleased to hear him, with official pride,
To asking strangers act the courteous guide;
Point with his whip to each patrician house,
Portray the owner, or depict his spouse;
Or, fraught with whisper'd tales of sly import,
Presume to paint a Baron for his sport!
Then, too, what puns and proverbs quaint he knows!
What ruddy humour on each feature glows,
When, gazing round him with theatric leer,
He tells the freaks of many a by-gone year!

But see, the fond farewells are said and o'er,
And, lo! the Curate, at the coach's door,
Smiles on the red-cloak'd dames and hoary men
Who humbly wish him *safe* return'd again:
Up roll the steps,—the echoes of the horn
Far on the breeze from hill to hill are borne;
And see, along the road's extended sweep,
Loud as the billows lording o'er the deep,
Again the bick'ring wheels their course renew,
And Woodland fades amid the distant view.

And now, while languid mists dissolve away
And golden sun-tints o'er the landscape play,
Look round! the unpretending view admire;
From shady dingles peeps the taper spire,
While far around yon richly-wooded green
What still romance o'erveils the rural scene.

But most the pilgrim eye delights to see
My Country! monarch of th' imperial Sea!
Those ancient mansions where thy Gentles dwell,
And grace the homes their fathers built so well.
Far on the lawn, amid the leafy shade,
Behold the porch and pillar'd walls display'd:
Hark! round the Park, begirt with olden trees,
The sheep-bells shake their echoes on the breeze;
Fleet on his fairy foot, the timid deer,
With glancing eye pursues his wild career;
While browsing cattle crop the stunted food,
And snuff the wind with conscious gratitude.

And long, fair England! may *such* homes be seen,
In modest grandeur shadow'd o'er the green;
Long may the country-Gentleman be found
The grateful lord of his paternal ground:
Far from suburban toil, and meaner care,
No midnight-brawls, no masquerading there,
A bounteous fortune, and a feeling breast,
Loved by the good, and by the humble blest,—
How calm he marks the bloom of life decay,
How breeze-like float the fleeting hours away!

And ah! forgive the wand'rer, doom'd to roam
O'er life's autumnal waste, without a home,
If chance an unforbidden wish should swell
For some dear haunt, where Love and Truth might dwell:
How blithely would he hail the welcome dawn
And stroll enamour'd round his dew-bright lawn!

Or when pale twilight hued the garden-trees
And the boughs twinkled in their vesper-breeze,
Delighted stray, with heavenward feeling fraught,
And wind the mazes of immortal thought!

But from the road unnumber'd scenes transfuse
O'er the quick mind, reflection's moral hues;
Each, as it passes, claims a sigh or tear
For Want, or Wo, and all their offspring, here.
There, the blind beggar, led by faithful Tray,
Bareheaded moans along his mournful way;
Here, a lean pedlar winds his wintry track
With wallet strapp'd upon his weary back;
And far withdrawn on yonder coppice-green,
Like wood-born regents of the lonely scene,
The sun-brown gipsies o'er their caldron gaze
And watch the faggots crackle as they blaze.
But lo! a livelier scene: beside the wheel,
Wild urchins whirling round from head to heel;
Around and round, and still around they turn,
Till lip and eye with bright suffusion burn,
Then mildly beg, with upward-looking face,
Some poor reward to crown their wheel-side race.
And oft to him, whose moral Eye hath been
A quaint observer of Life's comic scene,
Hath social Travel true instruction brought,
Which form'd a theme for many an after thought.
Abroad, our lines of character appear;
For who would crouch to affectation here,
Where all are free, unknown, and unrestrain'd,
And fashion profitless, however feign'd?
A rapid meeting (like the glad surprise
Of nature, when a sun-burst brings the dyes
Of verdure wood and water into life
Each with a sudden power of freshness rife)
Calls traits of mind and tones of feeling forth
And bold opinion in its native worth!
Within the compass of a hundred miles,
How vast a subject for our frowns, or smiles!
How much that opens like a scenic view
Of Nature's drama, such as Shakspere drew!
The selfish, vain, the volatile, or proud,
The pert, the spruce, the silent, and the loud,
All, in their turn, some living truth impart
Which threads the labyrinth that conceals the heart.

Meanwhile, our rumbling Coach pursues its way,
Adorn'd with passengers—and who are they?
Inside, and warm'd with sympathy, recline
A Politician and a plain Divine;
The first can lay the cabinet quite bare,
And fathom all the well of wisdom there!
A smile of candour clothes his merry cheek,
And his eyes twinkle what his heart would speak:
Genteely plain in periwig and vest,—
Let buckled shoes and snuff-box speak the rest!

Within a coach, perchance we oft may find
Some choice companion with a kindred mind;
Here, unsubdued by ceremonious fear,
The sterling traits of Character appear;
And thoughts unmanacled by mean control
Flash bright and clear, like sparkles from the soul.
Shame on the Man who drones himself away,
When conversation should have turn to play!
A Soul so bare, companionless, and cold,
Can scarce be stamp'd in nature's kindly mould,
Who bids the social flame to kindle, when
We meet, though strangers, with our fellow men.

Commend me him who with colloquial art
His tongue can loose, and let out half the heart;
Above suspicion, conscious of no end,
He turns the stranger to a passing friend,—
Refined or rude, no matter, if the mind
Be meet for converse, and for truth inclined.
With him a journey yields delightful ease,
His wit may gladden, and his wisdom please;
Long miles escape amid such talking charms,
The temper brightens, and acquaintance warms.

And such is he, whose glowing tongue hath sped
As if a parliament were in his head;
How well he weaves each patriotic plan,
And, like a Minister, selects his man!
A war condemns, or conquers distant climes,
And paints the leading wonder of the times;
With fond remembrance turns to scenes of yore,
And mourns that mind will be revived no more,
As when, with eagle-glance, great Chatham rose,
And flash'd defiance to his country's foes;
As when, enrapt, immortal Burke he saw
The House inspire, and give the world a law!

Meanwhile, the pensive Curate, pleased to learn,
But ventures half an answer in his turn;
Remotely blest, *his* humble lot has been
Through life to move unvalued and unseen;
To watch and weep beside the couch of Woe
And bid the tear of blest contrition flow;
Or woo immortal mercy from the Throne,
The poor protect, and make their griefs his *own*:—
His heart replete with heavenly love and truth,
The prop of age, and hallow'd guide of youth,

His home the bosom-spring of tranquil joy,—
Ah! who would mar him with the world's alloy?

And here, oh! let one dreaming line renew
That hour when Life's far ocean dawn'd in view,
And, fired by young Ambition's inward flame,
To battle with its stormy scenes I came.
As o'er the winding street our coach-wheels roll'd
And from the Abbey-dome the town-clock toll'd,
How lingeringly my parting glance was cast
On each loved spot that hail'd me as we past!
Till far behind old Bladud's hills were seen,
And glittering uplands clad by forest-green,
And rocky woods enrapt in sunset-glow,
With beechen valleys bathed in light below,
Till dim and faint the city-mansions grew,
Like cloud-shaped temples of aerial hue:
Then all the heart seem'd melting into tears
While fancy hover'd o'er my future years!

That time hath fled; and Truth might well relate
The toiling woes of life's eventful state;
The tinge of circumstance that hued my hours,
Not gently lost in academic bowers,
But roll'd away in energetic toil,
With friends to gather, and with foes to foil:
But these are past; and that Great Power alone
To Whom the history of hearts is known,
Those chronicles of inward-life can tell
Where truth and conscience in communion dwell.

Night roll'd away; and when, with weary eye,
I watch'd the dawn awaken in the sky,
London, the vast, the wonder of mankind,
The mart of Commerce, and the fount of Mind,
Like an immortal Vision rose in view,
Dim vast and distant in the morning-hue!
How did the startled feelings rush and roll
In pleasing tumult o'er my prostrate soul,
When timidly, as on enchanted ground,
I mark'd the peopled desert spread around;
And heard the waves of Life around me roar
Like echoes wafted from a distant shore,
While bands of glorious Spirits that have been
Rose from the dead, and stalk'd the mighty scene!

* * * * *

Still wheels the coach along the hoof-worn road,
Whose windings tell of many a mingled load;
The golden sun pours forth his noontide glare,
And cheeks catch beauty from the bracing air,
While talking glee and social voices sound,
And pleasure quickens as the tongues abound.

Amid the tumult of a crowded street
In pensive walk who has not chanced to meet
Some unregarded wretch who seems alone,
Sad as an exile in a land unknown,—
A form of Woe upon whose mournful face
Compassion loves the line of thought to trace?
And such yon aged man, with haggard mien
Who, all unconscious of the present scene,
His every feature with dejection fraught,
Sits in a shroud of melancholy thought:
Upon that wintry brow and blighted cheek
Departed years their doleful history speak!
For him no welcome by a cheering hearth,
No home of comfort and no song of mirth;
No gentle heart to mingle with his own
Pilgrim of life, he roams the world alone!
On such a wither'd face and dim-worn eye,
The gay might look, and learn for once, to sigh!

Merriest of all whose bounding gladness feels
The flush of joy a laughing eye reveals,
Two schoolboys from the coach's roof resound
Triumphantly, and hail the woods around;
Glad as the sunbeams when the storm is o'er,
That gild the wave, and gambol on the shore.

Oh, could the horses like their wishes speed,
Then short the road, and travelling swift indeed!
And mark yon blue-eyed rogue with daring brow,
Round his young heart what visions revel now!
Restless and wild, all gaze and wonder he;
Sky, coach, and road, he fills them all with glee!
How dark a mystery to his infant mind,—
The wheels advance, the bushes glide behind!
Full oft a school-room dream hath pictured this,
A journey home, the paragon of bliss!
This heal'd up many a birch-awaken'd smart,
Cut short the lesson, and relieved the heart:
It comes at last! adieu to "*Propria quæ*,"
Long-rooted verbs, and puzzling prosody,
The tame sky-blue, the task-recalling bell,
The stern infliction, and the piteous yell;
A month of joy each parted woe repays.
With nights of fun and frolic-loaded days.
Not he who cross'd the Rubicon for Rome,
Plann'd more immensely than these rogues for home;
What feats immortal on the frozen lake!
What tittering mirth around the twelfth-night cake!
Then snugly nestled by the parlour-fire,
Hobgoblin-tales shall Christmas-eve inspire;

Or, hand in hand by Love parental led,
They'll see the showman smooth the lion's head!

A glad spectator of these roguish two
Garb'd in a time-worn suit of woollen blue,
A plump-faced Tar sits by, and joys to see
The heart-warm flow of boyish revelry;
His tiny hat of weather-beaten straw,
His twinkling eye, and look so fresh and raw,
The winning bluntness of a seaman's guise,—
Allure the urchins' archly-smiling eyes;
Looks grow to words; and kind, without delay,
With ocean-tales he charms the travell'd way;
Of howling wolves that haunt the ice-bound Cape,
And surges which surpass the mountain-shape,
Or billows thundering by the vessel-side
While mariners in swinging hammocks ride,
Of these he tells; till one, with wonder grave,
His hand uplifts to meet a mountain-wave,
And in dread vision, eyes the shatter'd sail,
And starts and shivers at the seaman's tale!

A veteran Soldier, in his faded lace,
One-legg'd, with plumeless cap, and scar-worn face,
Upon whose sunken features, rough and plain,
Is mapp'd out many a fierce and far campaign!
Smiling, obeys the elder boy's behest,
To read the medal on his martial breast:
Though battle-roar, and moonlit-bivouac,
And mounted breach, and city's dreadful sack,
Return no more, his eye illumes to tell
Of foe and fight he loved to brave so well;
Once more in heart he marches to the sound
Of deep-roll'd drums and clarion's echoing sound;
Front in the rank again he seems to be,
And inly shouts the song of Victory!

And well the eager boy his rapture feels,
To hear of clarion-voice, and cannon peals;
Or how the Battle raged till setting sun,
Retreat and charge, who vanquish'd, and who won;
Till his heart triumphs with a warrior-glow,
Pants for a sword, a charger, and a foe!
But hark! the watchful guard, in champion state,
Twangs his shrill summons to the turnpike-gate:
And promptly coming from his spruce abode,
A grey-beard opes the barrier of the road:
'Tis pass'd; and, lo! beside yon sun-bright down,
The giant-shadows of the distant town;
Till, brightly-towering in the noontide-blaze,
A City flashes on the eager gaze!

Brick walls and temples, domes, and mansions dun,
And steeples whitening in the welcome sun,
And banners shivering in the smoke-dimm'd air,
And lofty house-roofs, slanting, broad, and bare,
With the faint windings of a clear canal
Like a lone pilgrim roaming far from all,—
Majestic spread beneath a cloudless sky
In one full mass arrest the traveller's eye.

Though sweet awhile the noisy world to leave,
Forsake its follies, and forget to grieve,
Pleasant the city-roar renew'd again,
When impulse flags, and solitude is pain!
List to the clamour of the clattering street,
The bickering car, and hoof, and pattering feet;
The rush, the stir, the deafening, struggling din
Of moving life!—but, lo, a stately Inn!

Hail to the timely welcome of an Inn;
Hail to the room where home and cheer begin;
Where all the frost-bound feelings melt away,
And soul-warm sympathies begin to play,
While Independence shows her careless mien,
And unforced traits of human life are seen.
The crackling blaze which dyes the chimney red,
The gracious substance on the table spread,
The glowing wine-cup and the rich ale's foam,—
Partake them all, and dream thyself at home!

As round the festive board our travellers sit
With appetites far sharper than their wit,
What busy knives and gracious meats abound,
What hissing corks and tinkling glasses sound!
Some, fiercely-rapid, sheathe the gleaming blade
In joints that seem for hungry pilgrims made;
Some by the glittering hearth-side sit and gaze
And bathe their features in its welcome blaze;
Nor still the Host, who waddles here and there
Like a live Barrel come to take the air!
The time is past; the feast partaken, o'er;
Again they journey over hill and moor;
Fresh at the rein, behold yon rapid steed
Roll his large eyes, and cleave the wind with speed;
Thus, unimpeded with its plenteous load,
The eager Coach pursues the varying road,
Save when Relays from local barns are led,
And horses tired move steaming to their shed.

Now shadowy eve the fading woods hath crown'd,
And dew and darkness shed their spirit round;

Hark! o'er the hills what bugle-echoes play,
And die in many an ebbing note away;
Behold! the Mail in glimmering pomp appears,
And, as it onward speeds, what smiles and tears,
What shades of time, or accident, or scene,
And memories for all which life has been
It brings,—to sadden, sweeten, or beguile
The myriad hearts within our crowded isle!
Perchance the morrow will an orphan hail,
A wife be weeping o'er some funeral-tale,
A friend be doom'd in distant isles to roam,
And music cease in many a happy Home!

Where is the heart unmoved by more than glee,
Where is the eye which kindles not to see
That spot where first our beam of Life began,
And Youth put on the energies of Man?
When far remote from youth's regretted scene,
Imagination sped the way between,
And, hovering round each well-known spot, restored
All which young memory loved, and heart adored!
A Sabbath-bell recall'd the street we trod
Each holy morn, to hymn the name of God;
A ballad-singer in his homely strain
Would thrill the bosom with delicious pain,
As oft beneath the moon's romantic ray
We mused on home and friendship far away:
At length return'd, again we glow to greet
Each favorite spot and unforgotten street;
Once more on haunted wood and stream to gaze,
And clasp the shadow of departed Days.

And lo! upon yon Sailor's swarthy brow
What home-born feeling is enkindled now?
What tear-drops gush from out his happy soul
As up familiar lanes the coach-wheels roll,
Joy flies from lip to brow, through heart and limb,
The very houses seem to welcome him!
Though doom'd awhile a foreign Deep to roam,
Each breeze and blast had wing'd a blessing home;
Where Hope and Memory bade him oft retire
And tell sea-tales around his winter fire.

But list! the Schoolboys' mingled shouts of glee
Round a fond parent dancing merrily!
Such bliss to come, such pain and peril past,
Can their glib tongues unload the heart too fast?
The old man smiles, and mingles with their joy,
Pleased to remember he was *once* a boy;
And blandly paints the joyous scenes to come
As hand in hand he leads the prattlers home.

Reader! a pensive Moral ere we part
And be its tablet thy persuaded heart;
Our vanish'd day like human Life hath been,
An onward-view of many a varied scene,
A changeful path, where faces come and go,
Friends meet and part,—like all we love below!
Thus on, till Life's eventful journey's o'er,
And meeting Souls embrace, to part no more.

SCARBOROUGH.

A DESCRIPTIVE SKETCH.—1846.

Farewell the scene, but not farewell the charm
Of ancient Scarbro'! Long as mem'ry lives
And for my past a secret mansion builds
Within me, like a sacred Thing I prize,
Her touching beauties shall be unforgot
And treasured there, with no affected love.

The spirit of the olden time's romance
Haunts her loved scenes, where each abiding grace,
By Nature hallow'd, blooms unwither'd still;
And beautiful are all her wooded bays,
Her winding creeks of loveliness and calm
And mounts of woodland-green, as when the Saxon gazed
In dreaming sternness, or with soften'd brow,
At twilight on them, while the rosy tinge
Of vesper-clouds o'erveil'd the ocean-rocks
Before him. History, too, may yet perceive,
Where the helm'd Roman in his banner'd pride
Lifted those eagles which o'erswept the world,
Invincible in valour. Lone and sad,
Wrapt in a shroud of melancholy thought,
With heart unecho'd, and with mind unnerved,
I thank thee, God! that often I have won
From scenes that here are eloquent of Thee,
Feelings divine, and hopes from heaven new-born,
Grandeur and Beauty, with a bliss serene
That o'er my future like a dew will steal
Hereafter, when the feverish world may fret
My soul, and shore and sea lie far away.

Where rise the hills, and rolls the sacred Deep
Her minstrelsy of many-voicèd waves,
There, is the Poet's haunt, and home of song!
If true to Nature, his responsive heart
Replies in music to those myriad calls
Which still accost him from Her shrines august,
Or lone, or lovely; then, the lyre of thought
Is thrill'd with magic, and each pensive chord
Vibrates at once in poetry and praise.
For, aye between the mountains and the mind,
Infinite Soul and God's unfathom'd Sea,
A poetry of pure attraction dwells
For ever. Ye have felt it! who the Lyre
Have struck, by intellectual beauty charm'd,
In answer to a living harp of song
Within you, Poets! that our mystic world
Alone interpret, and to thought create
A richer Paradise than Adam saw,
Ere ruin fell on Eden's forfeit-bowers.
Is it that mountains are our kindred types
And, in their soaring majesty of shape
Between two worlds thus gloriously uplift,
Instruct us, heavenward how the heart ascends
When man with his high Maker most communes?
Does Ocean, in her measureless profound
Deep within deep interminably sunk,
E'en like an echo of the soul's abyss,
With dread eternity appear instinct?
We cannot tell; enough for Truth to feel
That Man and Nature are responsive works,
Shaped into concord by a Hand divine.

Here while I muse, what inspirations throng
Full on my sense, and through the mind o'erflow,
Till fancy kindles, and a fervent rush
Of bright emotions, blent with deeper thoughts,
Pour inwards: like an intellectual flood
From some heart-fountain, suddenly unseal'd
As if by magic, and with radiant speed
Rolling at once through all the spirit-depths!

Look where you can, the Beautiful is there,
Touch'd with that boldness rock-bound waters lend
To each loved region on our island-coast.
Look where you please! some answering grace responds
To your charm'd glance; as if with conscious power
Rich Nature in her prodigal supply
Of blent attractions, tender, green, or wild,
Echo'd the spirit of your wish, and gave
Her all of lovely in one view combined;
That so, elysian fancy might be lull'd
With landscapes Eden-like, and full of God.

In azure brightness, lo! that billow'd Sea
Rolling in rapture, and alive with beams
Of sun-made glory, with a living joy
Oh, how it heaves its bounding way along,
Cheer'd by young breezes! like a poet's heart
Panting with visions, which before him rise,
And bear him onward with a swelling pulse
Of passion, dreaming, daring, and sublime!

This cliff below, in green remoteness raised,
I mark the outlines of the curvèd shore
Upward receding with a gradual rise
Of roofs, and mansions, blendingly array'd;
While to the left a grassy mount appears
O'er which, mid benchèd walks, and shaded bowers,
In stream-like windings artificial paths
Ascend, and glitter in the glow of eve.
But, near the brink of yon impending height,
The proud Marine its modern piles erects
On high; and full before its window'd front
The surging vastness of the German sea
For ever rolls, and still for ever charms
How many a land-sick Heart, that often sigh'd
To look once more upon the leaping waves
Of laughing ocean! But, again behold
How the brave skill of architectural man
Both height and depth can subject and reduce
To his proud service! There, the high-poised Bridge
O'erarches with magnificent effect
The cloven hills, and both in one combines:
Beneath the circle of each ponderous arch
The fascinating blue of ocean breaks
Softly, and sweetly on arrested eyes,
That downward from the cresting hills o'ergaze
The sea-girt landscape. Freshly shines the Main,
Rippled with breezes, and with sun-beams clothed
Which make her waves like liquid diamonds flash,
Dazzling the eye with over-bright excess
Hither and thither, where no shade intrudes.
How gently, o'er the beach the swelling tide
Rolls inward! falling with melodious plunge,
It murmurs to the Town's contiguous walls
And garden trees, which round the shore descend,—
As if the Sea were conscious that her waves
Were loved, or look'd upon with greeting eyes,
And hearts which echo those poetic strains
Each breezy stanza to the billow sings!

Behind me, in their yellow ripeness spread,
The upland cornfields, o'er whose bladed stalks
Bending with produce, play the choral airs
From ocean wafted, till the meadows breathe
A fitful undersong, and wild-flowers laugh
In waving gladness. List! the larks are poised
High in the air, and trill their lyric strains
Above me, in an ecstasy of sound,
And seem to quiver forth their vesper hymns.
But lo, the magic of yon peerless Main!
How graceful in majestic strength she heaves
Her breast of waters, tinged with gorgeous hues
From heaven reflected, while her boundless spread
Of billows gently to the breeze upcurls!
Far as our straining eyes can stretch the view,
Rolls that vast ocean the horizon round
Her volumed waters, till both sea and sky
Look wedded in the distance. Near the shore
Or sanded beach, the gambolling children bathe,
And in the foam and freshness of the wave
Plunge their delighted heads, and disappear
A moment, then, again their dripping frames
Lift into light, all innocently clad.
While many a bark, symmetrical and small,
Opes its white sail, and on the azure calm
Mirrors its beauty; like a bird it moves
Born of the sea, and on the waters bred;
With such a vital grace it seems to glide
O'er the light wavelets, which around it curl
Amid those taller vessels. O'er the strand
Rising within the bay's prolong'd recess,
Bold Scarbro' with her slanting roofs appears,
That redden dimly, now the pallid beam
Of sunset strikes them. Hark! her busy hum
In broken cadence to the ear is brought,
And not unpleasing; while beneath this cliff
Where now I watch, the pulsing billows play
In languid motion, while its pebbled base
They moisten; or, in lulling tones dissolve
Of sea-born music, exquisitely sad.

But stranger! high o'er all the Town behold,
Breathing stern history from its haunted walls
And mangled towers, yon warlike Castle frowns:
Sublime in ruins, like Romance in stone,
Still to the present does it preach the past
With more than language! There, a moral sigh
O'er the gone splendour of heroic times
May well be heaved, when Chivalry prevail'd,
And knightly bosoms with heroic pulse
Were beating nobly, as the brave became!
Now turn from man, for God himself is nigh
Whene'er His Temple to the heart appeals,
Like mute religion!—Thus, St. Mary's shrine,
Dim with dead ages, lifts her hoary pile,
And almost touches into pensive tears
The hearts who view her, bow'd and bent with time:
Conventual mother of Cistercian monks,
Once in the pride and pomp of Romish art

Her structure tower'd, and o'er this ancient Burgh
Ruled like a queen; but now, both damp and dust
Feed on her walls, and waste her mouldering form.
And can Wealth look upon a wreck like this,
Nor feel the blush of self-rebuke to burn
Into her conscience? Is the Christ we serve
To Mammon given, while with hoarding grasp
A hideous worship unto heartless Gold
We proffer, gripe our bloated incomes back,
And grudge to God the boon we well might give,
From Faith how due, to feeling how divine!

But in her widowhood St. Mary's pile
Affectingly to pious hearts appeals:
From this far mount I view her churchyard-slopes
With tombstones populous, whose pallid fronts
In the slant brightness of the sunset gleam,
And glisten o'er the humbler graves which lie
Beneath them, nameless as the grass that mourns
Of death unconscious, when the night-airs wake.
Methinks, that in her mournfulness august
E'en like a Mother, does that hallow'd Fane
Gaze on the tombs which round about her seem
To nestle; while to living Souls she pleads,
That once again the pious and the pure
Her ruin'd Shrine may raise, till Gothic arch
And roof majestic o'er rapt thousands bend
Within Her gather'd, full of praise and prayer.

Yet, ere we part from such ideal bliss
This hour of beauty and this heaven of scene
Embosom, yonder local charm survey;
That Light-house, in its guardian pride erect,
Gilded by sunshine, when it haply gleams
Full on its whited column, points afar
Through storm and gale, to mariners at Sea
Rock'd on rude surges; or, at misty night
Becalm'd, when Darkness and the Deep embrace
In black confusion, like a spectral gloom,
To them it beckons with its beacon-ray
For ever welcome to their wave-toss'd view;
And often, when the glassy ocean sleeps,
Projects its shadow with unbroken trace
Of imaged portraiture, the tide along.

There is a nobleness in nature's gifts;
A free enchantment; and a bold delight
Flow from her vital scenes of grace, or power,
Or beauty, did but man his bosom yield
To fine impressions, breathed from sylvan haunts.
Oh! none but hearts sectarian, shut, and cold,
Contracted into smallness, vain as vile,
Which do not in the cheering thought exult,
How catholic entire Creation looks
And glorious! loving all whose souls reply
To grace, or grandeur, clothing hills and dales.
If to loud Cities men contraction owe,
'Tis from the Country minds a largeness gain
Healthful and hallow'd, open as the skies
Above them, nobly breathing freedom's air!
'Tis from her landscapes our loved England takes
A moral freshness, and romantic tinge
That hues her heart with beauty: Commerce dries
The soul of Cities into venal dust,
Or, sanctions false refinement; but from shores
Embay'd in quiet, or from rock-girt waves,
Where on the beach with loud pulsation swells
The billowy heart of God's mysterious sea
For ever, may the town-worn race derive
Emotions, which immortalise their play
In that deep inwardness where feeling dwells.
Thus, let them wander by the sanded beach
O'er rocks, and crags familiar with the clouds
Where the red morning throws her radiant blush,
By meadows, lakes, or lanes of twilight green
Devious and far, to view those rustic charms
Which clothe our hamlets with an English grace
Unrivall'd. Nature is no dull effect,
No dead appearance of an outward show
To sense confined; but, oft in secret wields
A bosom-influence, when the gazer's eye
Hath long departed from the scene it saw.
Many a tone of tenderness and truth
Comes to a heart, in city-prisons pent,
Where joyless Labour plies her feverish task
Incessant,—not from streets of noise, and strife,
But from the stillness of remember'd fields,
From inland-quiet, landscapes hush'd and lone,
Or, from the magic of poetic waves
In breezy chorus, such as now resounds
Time-honour'd Scarbro'! o'er thy sweeping bay.

Ideal landscapes beautify sad minds
Immersed in cities, worn and wasted down
Into a wreck of carking wo, and care
Emaciate; or, amid some crowded mart
Of commerce, where in rooms of airless toil
Britannia's helots drudge, for Mammon's lords,
Through tedious rounds of everlasting toil
Healthless as hopeless, day by day, and year
By year, like work-Machines, unsoul'd for hire!
Hence, may the Country man's remembrance haunt
With freshening beauty, and the fever cool
Of pent-up weariness, and unvoiced woe.

And thus will Hearts benignant, wise and meek,
Of Christian tone and temper, e'er rejoice
In the chance-visit, which the o'erlabour'd poor
And pale mechanic to some rustic mead,
Or ocean, pays; and trust they there imbibe
Beautiful thoughts, or spells of inward power
To charm remembrance, when hereafter-toil
Hangs on each life-pulse, like a choking weight
Which burdens health, or blasts it to decay!

With man in sympathy all Nature moves,
And human Destiny: her forms his doom
Embody: featured for his primal good
By Hands celestial, when from God he fell
And glory, Nature felt the awful shock
Of his disaster! and, alike she waits
That hour millennial, when regenerate Earth
From the dark curse deliver'd, shall exult
In beauty, richer far than Eden wore,
And hush the groan* which twice three thousand Years
Have ever breathed for purity and heaven!

But lo! the Day has died, and o'er the waves
Shadow and silence like two spirits creep;
Rock, hill, and radiant shore and castled fort
Melt into dimness; while the plaintive chime
Of lone St. Mary's o'er the landscape wafts
A sound of sadness, which the hour beseems.

Here ends my strain, imperfect but sincere;
Such passing tribute from a pilgrim Bard,
Stranger, accept; and with him, gently cry,
Farewell the scene! but *not* farewell the charm
Of ancient Scarbro': Beauty and Romance
Are thine, thou region of the rock and wave!
And priests of Nature, such as poets are,
May well enshrine thee in their songs, and make
Thy scene immortal to melodious hearts.

* "The whole creation groaneth and travaileth in pain until now . . . waiting for the adoption, to wit, the redemption of our body."—*Rom.* viii. 22, 23.

MISCELLANEOUS POEMS.

WRITTEN, FOR THE MOST PART, IN EARLY YEARS.

MISCELLANEOUS POEMS.

INFANTS AND THEIR GLORY.

(1840.)

"Of such," the kingdom in the skies prepared.
Alas! how rarely do such words impress
An awe most vital, on the Souls which read
The letter only, but the life forego.
For here Philosophy and Reason stand
Rebuked, and silent; learning, language, art,
The palms of Mind, the laurels of Renown,
The shout of Senates, and the world's applause,
How weak, and worthless, absolutely nought
When rank'd beside the destiny of babes!
And yet, to souls of earth, who measure truth
By sight, organic flesh *alone* they seem
Scarce by a spark of intellect inspired!
A mother's plaything, or a father's toy,
Incarnate trifles, fit for woman's smile
To gild and welcome, or her lulling voice
To soothe and soften when the temper cries,
Such *may* they look, to undiscerning mind!
But, since Emmanuel hath the skies unveil'd
And taught Religion to behold them there,
As true inheritors of conscious bliss
In yon bright kingdom,—let our Faith a child
Revere; and look upon its pleading form
With love, by venerating awe subdued;
As well we ponder, how beneath that frame,
Though fragile as the web of dew, there lies
A spirit with eternity instinct!
Nor doubt, that He whose hallow'd unction gave
Prophets their light and brave Apostles zeal,
Through all its faculties can so diffuse
Enlarging grace, that what on earth appear'd
Little beyond a mindless form of clay,
At the first bound which into light it makes
When disembodied,—may at once eclipse
Archangels in their knowledge; and from God
A coronet beyond the Cherubim to match
In splendour, on its infant-brow receive!

But dare we, by some earth-born pride betray'd,
Presume to question, why a sinless babe
In this bleak world of wo and crime, should live?
If but a moment on this earth it breathe,
Untaught, untried, untempted and unskill'd,
Neither by reason proved, nor faith inform'd,
What is it, but a blank of being lost,
In life all mystery, and in death no more?

Yet who are *we*, but stammering babes of dust,
When upward as to God's untold designs
Fancy attempts to soar on fearless wing?
But thou, fond mother! o'er thy pallid child
In coffin'd beauty for the tomb array'd,
Cold as the flowers which on it calmly lie,
Hush the wild language of thy heart's despair!
For in the twilight of our doom there flash
Gleams of instruction through the cloud of death
By wisdom darted on believing souls.
See, how the Fall when infants die, is proved,
Stung by that fatal sting, which stingeth all!
Mute sermons preach they upon primal Sin
Beyond all pulpits, in their palmiest hour
Of eloquence and truth! O who that feels
The wear and waste of this soul-trying world
Where life is one long martyrdom to most,
However gilded, back would e'er recall
The child of mercy, unto heaven resumed?
The crown it wears, but has not fought the fight,
Reaches the goal, but has not won the race;
Balm to bereavement let this thought inspire!
But with it, may this added comfort blend,—
That as eternity the dead absorbs
Youthful, or aged, our affections seek
That mystic Home with more familiar sway.
'Tis not a solitude which awed Amaze
Dreads to encounter; but a peopled clime
Fill'd with the loved and lost, we long to meet
And once more welcome! And beyond this bright
Assurance may consoled Reflection press
Inquiry: for when shuddering Reason starts
To think on millions of unpitied babes
Mangled, and massacred in heathen climes,
How do those words, so tenderly profound
Of Jesus, light the path of Providence,

Which tell us, Heaven the murder'd child receives,
Whose death-pangs lift a stainless heart to God,
Through early martyrdom to glory rapt.

And hence, true mothers! ye, at least, are bound
To Jesus; in His words an echo dwells
To each inquiry, which beyond the grave
Longs to pursue an infant's parted soul.
Love to Emmanuel! let your motto be;
And so on Childhood's brow of beauty gaze,
As that whereon the Sacrament shall print
A sealing import; then, your child devote
Like Anna, early to the Lord of love,
And from the cradle guide it to the Cross!

NOBLENESS OF FAITH.

DEISTIC Thomas, with his doubting mind,
I envy not that most exacting man
Though eye to eye and face to face he stood
Before Messiah; and, with hand outstretch'd
And daring finger to his wounds applied,
Answer'd his doubt, and silenced unbelief
By evidence, which drew his adoration forth
With over-awed amazement. He to sight
And sense appeal'd; and well were both assured
When the mild Saviour to his eye appear'd,
Thrilling that doubter with resistless proof,—
E'en by the print, and pressure of those wounds
Whence gush'd salvation o'er a guilty world!
But rather let me, with a glance of faith
All time pervade, by Christ Himself inspired;
And in the glass of His describing Word
His life and lineaments of beauty trace.
Child of the Church, and by Her creed sustain'd,
By prayer, and praise, and Her memorial rites,
Doctrines and duties and the hallow'd round
Of fasts and festivals, oh! let me learn
The sense to crucify; and walk by faith
As prophets, patriarchs, and priests have done;
By grace empower'd beyond mere sight to live,
And earth-born feelings, in their finest mood.
For not to Thomas did *that* blessing come,
Which round the weakest who can now adore
And clasp Emmanuel with the mind's embrace,
Hovers like music,—from the lenient mouth
Of Christ descending on the souls of all
Who though they see not, yet the Lord believe
In risen glory. Thus can Faith exalt
Man out of self, and unto God reduce
His errant nature, as its proper home.
Sense but the shadow, Faith the substance holds;
And while the pageantries of Earth and Time
Like golden clouds which line the glowing west
In airy nothingness have died away,
That glorious Infinite of truth will beam
Brighter and brighter, which pure faith pursues:
Till what in weakness now we dimly scan,
By open vision future heaven shall prove,
And God unveil'd our spirit's glory be.

WORDSWORTH.

A THOUGHT the universe in worth outweighs
View'd as dead Matter, meaningless and dumb:
Hence, on some Form where intellect is shrined,
And genius dwells, in purity of power
To God and wisdom dedicate, we gaze
With no cold glance, by common love inspired.
And thus, on Him, that venerable Bard!
A laurell'd Priest of poetry and truth,
August with years, by mournful calm subdued,*
With filial reverence my spirit look'd
When first I heard him, in his mountain-home,
My entrance welcome. Boyhood's pensive dawn
Ideal magic from his mental springs
So oft had drunk, that when their breathing Source
Before me stood embodied, all the spells
His numbers wielded seem'd in one combined
And round my soul in high remembrance drawn,
Till like a Seer, or Hierarch of mind
And melody, immortal Wordsworth thrill'd
My heart, and made it vibrate into tears!
For tones there are in his creative verse
By childhood not unecho'd: but when age
Deepens the character, and powers awake
To more majestic strains attuned, his thoughts
The hidden lyre of consciousness within
Electrically move, and mental chords
By him are touch'd, which prove the soul divine.

When thus indebted to his wealth of mind,
How could I gaze on that capacious brow
Open and high, and like an arch of thought

* An allusion to the Poet's late bereavement in the death of his beloved daughter.

O'er eyes of intellectual blandness curved,
Or scan the lines, or view those silver'd locks
Which o'er his countenance a hoary grace
Suffused, and not ennobling homage pay.
What! shall mere Nature's majesty of forms
The eye entrance, where admiration glows,
Because, though mute, those forms to fancy hint
A soul in matter and a speech in things,—
And earth's own laureates be unreverenced
By mind? The human Race their debtor is;
Sea, air, and mountain, lake and lonely shore,
Forests and woods, and fields where freshness blooms
All are immortalised by radiance cast
From *their* high meanings, who the world transform,
And cast a beauty round the common lot
By making loveliness more lovely still.

A mental prophet and a priest of song
The bard of Rydal is to Souls who see
How heaven-born genius, like a mouth of God,
Opens some new apocalypse of Power
Which faith reveres, and meditation loves.
For have not Nature, Providence, and Man
Of both the centre, from his thoughtful muse
A sympathy of mild and mournful tone
Partaken, till Association's law
Have each invested with a beauteous charm?
Thus, mountain-grandeur and the grace of hills
Like thine, Helvellyn! in their hollow sweep;
Or forked Skiddaw with his famous brow;
Parnassean groves and glades of blissful calm
Where trees their twilight cast,—to him were dear
And with his being half incorporate grew.
The thorn had meanings; and a thistle spoke
Its own stern language; while each meadow-flower
A glow of beauty on creation's brow
In blooming radiance, seem'd by Angels dropt:
Nature to him was one almighty Speech
Significant, and deep, and full of God.
Nothing was lost, but all to love appeal'd,
The linnet's chaunt, a homeless cuckoo-song;
An eagle's majesty, or insect-mirth
To him were welcome, and some feeling touch'd.
All voices, visions, all of sense and sound
Home to his heart a deep impression sent
Which gave him partnership in nature's All,
As though 'twere *conscious*. Hence the landscapes were
An outward-token of the inward mind,
Loved in his life, and from the Spirit's lyre
Drew melodies of thought, which shall not die
While throbs the heart with poetry or prayer!

Not mere description, pensive, deep or grand,
His verse unfolds: but he the Mind has taught
How nature's sacraments and symbols speak
To mental reverence with a language mute
But mighty; how Her moods and motions are
Responsively to Man's more hidden world
With such accordance shaped, that heaven-born minds
See God and Angels, where a sensuous heart
Is charm'd by nothing but material show.

And human Life, and Providential love
To man reveal'd by Omnipresent acts
Of watching tenderness, from heaven at work,
His numbers prove with philosophic grace
And wisdom most benign. To him the scene
Of dark Existence was divinely touch'd
With sacredness and awe; whence prayer and praise
Were due, and godless Pride should learn to think,
And none seem orphan'd from the Father-God!
For as in nature, nothing is by Heaven
Forgotten, from the vaster forms of Life
And Being, down to each minutest speck,
But in the beam of God's parental eye
Remains for ever,—so that social World
Where Mind and Will their awfulness unfold
And character is moulded, to *his* gaze
An order'd scene of theocratic Law
Presented, where enthroned, the Godhead reign'd
And all were precious, who His cause maintain,—
Possible Angels, whom The Christ redeem'd.

All Nature thus made spiritually deep
By her significance of conscious life
To Soul responsive, and the moral World,
Where Providence to human will conjoins
Each plan and purpose, being hence enlink'd
With Glories uncreate,—no wonder Man
A true schekinah of transcendant powers
To Wordsworth seem'd; a Soul of priceless cost,
Whose incarnation, in its meanest guise,
Involves more grandeur than the "Worlds" contain!
Earth, space, and time, and all which tinsell'd pride
Amid the pageantries of wealth pursues
Or mere Convention by dull creed exacts
Before it vanish'd!—Individual *mind* *

* See "The Excursion," *passim.*

To him became the summit of his song:
And, how he trembled into wordless prayer
And grew religious, when unfathom'd depths
Of man's capacity for bliss or woe
Were open'd, and on Faith's predictive eye
The soul's hereafter like a vision rose
Self-realised, for heaven, or hell prepared! *

FORTY LINES ON WELLINGTON.

I.

Though shaded by death, yet his glory remains
Like beams on the billow when day-light is set;
And deeper than language the sorrow that pains
The heart of a Nation, enshrining him yet.

II.

Oh! *his* was a greatness the good can admire,
Which Virtue may laurel, and Vice only dread;
And pure as the principles Truth can inspire
The wreath of renown which encircles his head.

III.

From peasant to peer, from the cot to the throne
The thrills of dejection pervadingly ran,
When the myriad-wing'd Press to Europe made known
The death of a leader in Liberty's van.

IV.

The soar of an eagle when sweeping its flight,
The heart of a lion which throbs o'er his prey,
But weakly can image the worth and the might
Of Wellington marching in battle-array.

V.

Resistless in conflict, but simple and stern,
Serene in the tempest, and calm in the shock,
Let the valour of Youth thus patiently learn
When the whirlwind is raving,—to rival the rock!

VI.

A Cæsar in battle, and Cato at home,
Protecting our Altars from infidel-hate,
We challenge the records of haughty old Rome
To boast of a Hero so gallant and great.

VII.

When the war-hounds of France in horrors of blood
Had raven'd on Freedom, and outraged her laws,
The bulwark of Empires, brave Wellington stood,
And stifled Rebellion by quenching her cause.

VIII.

Thus, onward he triumphs in prowess and pride,
A king of all subjects, yet subject to kings;
Till the banners of England wave out far and wide
And Earth o'er her ransom with jubilee rings.

IX.

A pillar of Patriots, the foremost and first,
Erect in his grandeur of spirit and zeal
Ambition ne'er saw him, by self-aims accurst,
Pursue the bad triumphs we blush to reveal.

X.

Then, deepen for ever the homage and praise
From past and from present, to Wellington due,
And hallow the glory which brightens the bays
He won for Mankind, when he gain'd Waterloo.

"BETTER DAYS."

"All our pleasant things are laid waste."
Isa. lxiv. 11.

"Remember the days of old."—*Deut.* xxxii. 7.

How eloquent the ruin'd shrine
August, or sad, or lowly!
'Tis haunted with a spell divine
Deeper than melancholy:
For still it breathes of poetry and prayer,
And mild dejection woos Religion there.

Temples, and tombs, and cities vast,
The roofless cot, or home
O'er which Destruction's wings have past,
And where pale memories roam,
How are we moved by their mysterious sway
And lulling sadness of severe decay?

Strange though it seem, not royal state,
Nor brilliant pomp and pride
Encircled round the earth-born great
To rank and wealth allied,
Attract the spirit with so true a power
As wreck and ruins in some pensive hour.

---

* This poem is extracted from the 2nd vol. (pp. 483—486), "Memoirs of William Wordsworth," by Christopher Wordsworth, DD. Lond., Moxon, 1851.

Engirdled are they by a spell,
A wordless charm of mind,
And something more than tones can tell
Sinks o'er the soul refined,
When the dead glories of departed Years
Moisten the eye with meditation's tears.

But, what are *we*, but wrecks of man,
A fallen race of sin,
Creatures who marr'd the Almighty plan
And let rebellion in,
Through that pure Will which Heaven created free,
Whose law was Love, and that was Deity.*

And thus, perchance, for ruin'd Things
Our moral instinct wakes,
And o'er the heart's electric strings
A breath from Eden breaks,—
A mournful sense of forfeit-bloom and bowers
When Eve was perfect as the vestal flowers.

But if o'er what is dumb and dead,
A palace, shrine, or cot,
The tears of History are shed
And sanctify the spot
Where genius wept, or wisdom thrill'd and thought,
The martyr burn'd, or heroes bled and fought,

Shall not a living wreck of love,
An orphan sad and lone,—
Children whose angels stand above
So near the Glory-throne,
Soften the heart when sounds the touching phrase,
Heard in some homely tale of "Better Days?"

It is, indeed, a moving sight!
A pale and pensive child
Whose brow enthrones no young delight;
As though it ne'er had smiled;
Friendless and homeless, with dejected face
Too early touch'd with sorrow's withering trace.

Around it *once* fond parents hung
With love's enamour'd eye;
And Age itself again grew young
With that bright creature nigh!
Pangless the heart, the step was like the breeze
In bounding gladness borne above the seas.

Wealth, home and peace were there combined
To make that child secure;
And all which moulded heart and mind
Was radiant, sweet and pure:
Soft Innocence unveil'd her beauteous smile
And childhood flourish'd free from want and guile.

Prophetic dreams must oft have play'd
Around its virgin morn,
Ere baffled circumstance betray'd
A lot now bleak and lorn:
The future seem'd the poesy of life
Read by a heart with golden fancies rife.

But all is wither'd, changed and gone,
Friend, home and fortune o'er!
And hard-eyed worldlings cease to own
The wreck of wealth no more;
That once gay child is now a gloomy Thing
Wan with disease, or worn by suffering.

Blessings divine, then, hallow those
Who sheltering mansions build
To anchor from tempestuous woes
Children, whose hearts are fill'd
By past remembrance, blent with present grief,
Where life seems darkness, waiting death's relief!

Never till Christ unveils His throne
Whose heart beats human there,
And echoes to each plaintive tone
Breathed in the sigh, a prayer,—
Will the vast mercy these Asylums prove
Be understood, except by boundless love.

Long may they flourish! like the shrine,
St. Ann's of regal name;
Where better days, with love combine
To form a noble claim
For pleading orphans, and the helpless poor
In whom Christ owns His lot * repeated o'er.

* "God is Love."—1 *John* iv. 16.

* "Inasmuch as ye have done it unto one of the least of these, my brethren, ye have done it unto me." —*Matt.* xx. 40.

ENGLISH PEASANTRY.

(1826.)

Behold our peasantry! Britannia's pride
While baleful Luxury her boon denied;
The tyrant grasp of Desolation spoils
Each homely shelter for the labourer's toils;
While sad and far the houseless peasant flies
And mansions o'er his ruin'd hamlet rise:
For him no more shall bloom the garden flower,
No sabbath guest shall greet his hazel bower,
No winter's evening bring domestic bliss,
No laughing infants leap to share the kiss.

Inhuman Tyrants! whose destructive hand,
To grasp domain would desolate the Land;
Can barren pomp one joyous hour bestow
While Famine fills a thousand hearts with wo?
Can palisadoed lawns of wide extent
Please like the rural homes of calm Content?
Sweeter by far, methinks, were Wealth to pour
Diffusive blessings from her ample door;
And if the sick man pined, to visit there
And with the smile of Mercy, hush despair.
And dear the scene that charm'd the pilgrim's eye
Ere Luxury rose, or Avarice peal'd her cry,
Where cottage-homes, upon the green domain
Gave health and shelter to the toiling swain:
There many a way-worn traveller sighing stay'd,
And ask'd of heaven some equal hamlet-shade
Where humble life flow'd undisturb'd away,
And happiness led on each new-born Day.
The smoke enwreathing with the playful breeze,
A glowing produce ripening on the trees,
The laden bee low-humming in some flower,
Or pigeon cooing from his shaded tower,
With all the nameless charms that nestle round
The cottage-garden and the pasture-ground,—
Made every passing stranger stop awhile
And lit his lingering eye with many a smile!
Here was the home, where toil-worn age, at last
Might rest secure, and muse on labours past;
Here was the welcome round of rustic mirth,
The family-supper, and the blazing hearth,
The happy converse, and the cheerful gaze,
With all that Gratitude to Mercy pays!
Rare *now* a scene so simply pure as this,—
The quiet plenty and the cottage-bliss!
Oppressive Wealth usurps each lawny spot
Where bloom'd the garden and where rose the cot;
Mansions, and groves, and princely parks abound,
Stretch o'er the plain, and seize each rood of ground,
While Pomp frowns every meaner home away
And leaves the peasant but a scanty pay;
Doom'd through the day to bear the summer-blaze,
Or mend, 'mid ice and snow, the public ways;
Or else, beneath the bleak autumnal-showers,
In damp and pain to pass the tedious hours,
A pittance from the tyrant of the soil
Is all which pays him for his dismal toil:
Then, home he wanders to a cheerless shed
With discontented heart, and aching head:
Here shall no rosy babes, nor smiling wife,
Attend to make the sweetnesses of life;
No social ease to keep the mind in tune
And shed delight around life's waning noon;
But starving infants with imploring eyes
Raising their pallid hands and piteous cries,
Till agony distract the parent's brain,
Flame the wild thought, or rack the soul with pain;
Till Want burst every tie of virtue free;
And Crime conducts him to the gallows-tree!

STARLIGHT ON MARATHON.

No vesper-breeze is floating now,
No murmurs shake the air;
A gloom hath veil'd yon mountain-brow
And quietude is there;
While night-beads on the dew-white grass
Drop brilliant as my footsteps pass.

No hum of life disturbs the scene,
The clouds are roll'd to rest;
'Tis like a calm where grief hath been,—
So welcome to the breast!
The warring tones of Day are gone
And starlight gleams on Marathon.

I look around from earth to sky
And gaze from star to star;
Till Grecian hosts seem gliding by
Triumphant from the war:
Like deathless spirits from the dead
Revisiting where once they bled.

What though the mounds which mark'd each name
Beneath the wings of time
Have worn away,—*theirs* is the fame
Immortal and sublime:
For who can tread on Freedom's plain
Nor wake Her dead to life again!

Oh! to have seen the marching Bands,
And heard the battle-clash,
Have seen their weapon-clenching hands
And eyes' defiant flash,
Their radiant shields and dancing crests
And corslets on their swelling breasts!

Then said the mother to her son
And pointed to his shield,
"Come *with* it, when the battle's done
Or *on* it, from the field!"
Then mute she fix'd her dreadless eye
That spoke of ages vanish'd by.

'Twas here they fought: and martial peals
Once thunder'd o'er the ground,
While gash and wound from plunging steels
Bedew'd the battle-mound;
Here Grecians trod the Persian dead,
And Freedom shouted while she bled!

But, gone the day of Freedom's sword
And cold the patriot brave,
Whose valour crush'd the servile horde
Like victims for the grave;
While Greece arose sublimely free
And dauntless as her own dark sea!

Yet, starlight sheds a pallid beam
For aye upon the plain;
And musing breasts might fondly dream
The Grecian free again;
For empires fall, and freedom dies,
But changeless beauty robes the skies.

May He whose glory veils yon sky,
God of the slave and free!
Hear every patriot's burning sigh
Hope dedicates to thee;
For thee, sad Greece! and every son
Who braves a Turk on Marathon.

LONDON BY MIDNIGHT.

(1828.)

The fret and fever of the day subside,
And London slumbers; but with murmurs faint
Like Ocean, when she folds her waves to sleep:
'Tis the pure hour for poetry and thought,
When passions sink, and Faith the heaven beholds,
As yearns an exile for his father-land.

O'er all a dim sublimity is spread,—
The garniture of night; amid the air
Darkly and drear yon airy steeples rise,
Like shadows of the past; the houses lie
In dismal clusters, moveless as in sleep;
And, towering far above the rest, yon Dome*
Appears, as if self-balanced in the gloom,—
A spectre cowering o'er the dusky piles.

And, see! on ground I stand whose glorious name
Might turn the coward brave; on thy huge bridge
Triumphant Waterloo! Above,—how calm!
There moon and star commingling radiance shed
And bathe the skies in beauty. Smooth and pale
The pearly-bosom'd clouds recline, enlink'd
Like wave-festoons upon the furrow'd deep.
Below, the Thames outspread, serene and cold;
And as I gaze, a cooling breath ascends
And melts upon my brow: like the worn heart
When harrowing cares have slept, the river seems
Peaceful and still; save when a wind-sigh wakes
The brooding slumbers of its breast; like dreams
That quiver on the marble face of Sleep.

Along each side the darkling mansions frown
Funereal in their gloom. Afar and faint,
The bridge-lamps glimmer o'er the tranquil stream,
As if enchain'd upon the air; beneath,
Gleams of pale lustre tremble through the gloom;
And, here and there, a tower and shadowy spire
Are imaged on the water; sad and shrunk
Like flower-leaves wither'd by the summer-blaze.

Yonder, in dim magnificence, behold
The many window'd Pile;* apart and stern,
In lowering grandeur, like a lofty mind
Unmingling with the baser crowd. One half
Is clothed with moonlight's pallid veil;
Beneath, a darkness broods, whence portals yawn
In cavern-gloom upon the drowsy tide,
Like tombs unbarr'd.

But hark! from yonder Dome
Into Eternity the Day is toll'd:

How hollow, dread, and dismal is the peal
To heaven its vast account now rolling up!
Awhile it undulates, then dies away
In mutter'd echoes, like the ebbing groans
Of drowning men; and see! the lustrous Moon
Veils her white brow, and leaves me in night-shade,
Unseen, but by the sleepless One: O God!
I *feel* thine eye upon me, I shrink
Awe-smote beneath its gaze, like melting snow
By moon-beams touch'd, when golden radiance smiles.

How noiseless are the streets! A few hours gone,
And all was fierce commotion; car and hoof,
And bickering wheel, and chariot-rush, and crowds
Which rang with revelry and woe, were here,
Immingled with the stir of life; but now
A deadness mantles round the midnight scene;
Time with his awful wand the world has touch'd,
And soothed her myriads into sleep!—'Tis hush'd!
Save when a distant drowsy watch-call breaks
Intrusive on the calm; or rapid cars
That roll them into silence. Beauteous look
The train of houses yellow'd by the moon,
Whose tile-roofs, slanting down amid the light,
Gleam like an azure track of waveless sea!

* St. Paul's.

* Somerset House.

But who was she, that with a fairy step
And lip of wreathing smiles, came floating by
Buoyant as April's breeze? Alas! alas!
Let nights of laughing agony, and crimes
Which burn their torture through the sullied heart,
Let sated passion and the form consumed,
Let these betray the orphan of the night!
As on her guilt-worn face a lamp-beam fell,
Reluctantly methought, her eye reveal'd
That curse of misery—gladness in disguise!

The squares, how haughtily reposed they stand
At this deep hour, with massy piles erect
And stately! where the windows broad and bright,
Like molten water shine; and freckled walls
In light are steep'd, which ripples on the stone;
Beneath, amid the laurel boughs that bend
Responsive to the breeze, the lamp-rays flit
In twinkling playfulness, like infant-eyes.

Once more upon the climbing moon, ere yet
Cloud-shaded she withdraw, a moment glance!
There, as we gaze, what undefinèd awe,
What thoughts ethereal flutter round the heart!
On Her fair brow we seem to write and read
The mind's quick fancies; all the Past awakes
Begirt with sweet creations, till the source
Of sympathy unlocks; and then a tear
Will venture brightly from the manliest eye,—
A precious tear, whose fountain is the soul.

The past,—Oh! who through London-streets can pace,
Nor vision forth the spirits which have *been?*
An atmosphere of genius quickens here
Remembrance of the dead! The storied nurse,
The ancient mother of the mighty, thou
Unrivall'd London! Sages, poets, kings,
And all the giant-race of glorious fame
Whose world-illuming minds, like quenchless stars
Burn through the night of ages,—triumph'd here,
Or martyrdom of mind endured! And now
Those Kings of mind, by death immortal made,
Forth from their tombs Imagination cites!

And who the midnight-scenes of life shall paint,
In this vast city, mart of human-kind!
In sleep some living wrecks of wo, are lapp'd,
And bless'd in dreams, whose daylight was a curse!
Some, heart-rack'd, on the sleepless couch recline,
And from the heated brain create a hell
Of agonising thoughts or ghastly fears;
While Pleasure's moths amid the golden sheen
Of princely halls, dance off the dull-wing'd hours;
And oh! perchance, in some infectious cell
Far from his home, unaided and unsoothed,
The famish'd wand'rer dies;—no voice to breathe
Mild comfort to his heart; no hand to smooth
His bed of death; no sainted eye to bless
The spirit hovering o'er another world!

But list! a laugh of Pleasure thrills the wind;
'Tis Folly's soulless idols sauntering home,
Faced with a mask of smiles. And One there is,
Upon whose haggard cheek a glance may read
A tale of blighted years and buried woes!
His home is reach'd; and where yon window-gleams
Dart o'er the street a dizzy chain of light
Awhile he gazes on his mirror'd face,
And sighs to mark what havoc Pleasure makes!
Then drops upon his couch, while round him float
In visionary throng, the glowing forms
Which beautified the night; and where are they?—
At home, heart-wearied, wilder'd as their dreams
And glad that Time another day has kill'd!

Turn to a nobler victim of the night:
Where yonder casement sheds a pallid gleam
Upon the breezeless air, aloft and lone
An unregarded wreck of Genius toils,
With throbbing brain and dewy brow. The Day
To rest hath gone: but slumber visits not
His sunken eyes! The gnawing fires of thought
Upon his youthful cheek have fed, and parch'd
His tongue, and from his lip drawn the life-stream;
The lightnings of the soul his form have seared.
But Fame stands beckoning; and he battles on
Through want and wo, until he win the goal,—
A welcome one, though Death should drag him there!

And shall this City-queen, this peerless mass
Of pillar'd fanes, and grey-worn towers sublime,
Be blotted from the world, and forests wave
Where once a second Rome was seen? Oh! say,

Shall rude grass cover England's royal streets,
And wild beasts howl where Commerce reign'd supreme?
Alas! her moral glance let Memory dart
Down vanish'd time, till summon'd Ages rise
With ruin'd empires on their wings! Thought weeps
With patriot-truth, to own a funeral day
Heart of the universe! may visit thee,
When round thy wreck some lonely man shall roam,
And, musing, say,—"'Twas *here* vast London stood!"

But hark! again the heavy bell has peal'd
Its doleful thunder; on their watch the Stars
Grow pale; the Moon seems wearied of her course;
And morn begins to blossom in the east;
Then, let me home; and Heaven my thoughts protect!

PAINS OF GENIUS.

Envy not the Poet's name,
Darken not his dawn of fame;
'Tis the guerdon of a mind
Free from thralls of earthly kind;
'Tis the fascinating Star
Brighter than the brightest far;
It often glitters o'er his doom,
A halo round an early tomb!

The whirling brain and heated brow,
The dreams which torture while they grow
The soaring fancy over-fraught;
The burning agonies of thought;
The sleepless eye and racking head,
The haunting terrors round him spread:
Or freezing smile of Apathy;
Or scowl of green-eyed Jealousy;
Or haggard Want, whose lean hands wave
Unto a cold uncover'd grave!—
Oh! these must win a Poet's name;
Then darken not his dawn of fame.

THE CATARACT.*

In slumber, when some dream of daring night
Transcends creation, or out-dazzles earth,
Man's wither'd paradise may seem revived;
And oft when Poesy and young Romance
Imagination's throne together mount,—
What landscapes, fit for Seraphim to walk,
In the green loveliness of Nature's youth
Beneath their fascinating smile have bloom'd!
And yet, no dreaming pomp nor bardic spell
Can rival thee, by God himself array'd
With glory terrible, and beauty wild,
Thou earth-adorning Cataract!—once seen,
And seen for ever: heard by sense for once,
And in the spirit heard for evermore!

When, like some vision of a ruin'd world,
In foaming majesty I saw thee fall
From crag to crag terrifically swift,
My soul was hush'd, in trance of wonder bound;
A word was outrage! mute as thought, I gazed
Upon thee, vanquish'd by the dread sublime:
As in the presence of Almighty spells,
My being trembled: language was extinct!

Aloft, aloft, precipitate and loud,
The plunging torrent like a war-horse leaps
Adown the black ravine! and white with rage
And thunderingly hoarse, the headlong-wave
From rock to rock in froth and foam careers,
In tameless terrible, unwearied ire
For ever raving! Hark! the mountain thrills
And throbs, the leaflets palpitate with awe;
The branches quiver like the limbs of fear
On each grey elm; while, floating like the breath
Of conscious being, lo! the mist ascends
In tremor from yon panting surge below,
Lingers awhile, in airy balance hung,
Then trembles downward with a quavering fall
In rain-drops delicate as tears unshed.

King of stern waterfalls! thine awe pervades
And like the genius of romance creates
A spirit of enchantment round thy home:
The valley, hush'd as Desolation, loves;
The gloom chaotic of thine ancient hills
Torn by the tempest's savage wing, and deck'd
With foliage, touch'd by autumn's pale decay;
And drip of water, from the rocks dissolved
In feeble music, faint as dream-heard sighs,—
All these in one vast sentiment unite
Around thee, making sight and sound appeal
Like poetry, from Nature's heart evoked.

And while, with contemplation's spell-bound eyes,
Amid the spray, the thunder and the din,
Monarch of Waters! upon thee I gazed,
The witchery of deep association rose.—
On myriads, now in earth and darkness mute,
I ponder'd, who, like me, had feasted soul
And sense, and drank emotions rich as mine
From thine enchantment. Here the worldling came

* This poem relates to a celebrated torrent in North Wales, called "The Pistyll Rhaiadr."

And left, perchance, his worldliness behind;
Here Pride, Ambition, Avarice, and Hate,
Those Demons of the mind, their sceptres broke,
And shrunk, like Satan from the Saviour's
word,
By thee o'erawed! and here the Poet dreamt
While sentiment and thought his heart o'er-
whelm'd
With magic potency, till he became
Sublime in thy sublimity of scene!
And from the centre of his spirit felt
Warm inspiration, like a sunrise, break,
And meanings, full of worldless beauty, flow.

Farewell! thou roaring flood of Scynfa* born,
In loud monotony of roaring ire
Rage on for ever! rule all hearts and eyes
Which bow before thee: Teacher of the wild
And wondrous! may thy voice eternal be,
And speak of HIM Whose Shadow is the sun,
Whom torrent, sea, and tempest loudly praise;
Whose Love by every breeze is syllabled
While, seated on Eternity's vast throne,
He wields His sceptre o'er ten thousand
worlds!

Farewell! thou glory of a glorious Clime,
Farewell, the sight, but *not* farewell the sense
Of thee:—since in the core of memory's heart
The true dominion of thy scene will dwell;
And oft amid the dust of daily Life,
Or prose of dry existence, will beget
Sensations high, and feelings nobly-pure:
Or, wafted back on fancy's sun-bright wing,
My soul will visit thee, and hear again
The thundering harmonies of thy dread stream,
Like a huge wave in endless plunge and roar,
And own the Almighty by His work revealed!

VALE OF CLWYD.

Majestic Land of liberty and song,
And bardic fame and soul-exciting tales,
Of feudal glory! clime of old romance,
Whose records make the heart of History
bound,
A stranger greets thee with exulting pride,
And grows a Cambrian; while thy woods and
waves
Rouse the full voice of unaffected song.—
Poets are Nature's patriots; sea and sky,
Mountain and rock, and wood-hung vales and
hills,
Deep glens, or lakes, and thunder-mocking
cataracts
Round them appear like Inspiration's home.

* * * * * *

Thy tower, St. Asaph! when the noon-bright
heaven
With crystal arch o'er-canopied thy walls
And the breeze caroll'd like a bird of air,
I trod; beneath me, Arcady revived
Burst on the wonder of my ravish'd eye!
Painting ne'er form'd, nor poetry conceived
A paradise of more bewitching scene:
Leftward the river'd Vale of Cluid lay
Magnificent, with woods and trees adorn'd;
Where castled halls and princely mansions
stood,
And towns remote, and cots, and hamlet-spires,
With white-faced homes in blossom'd trees
embower'd,
'Mid meadows greenly-bright, and mountain-
forms
Whose wavy outline on the sky was mapp'd,—
All on the gaze a mass of beauty pour'd
Beyond what Poussin in Italian dreams de-
scribed!
In calm sublimity of conscious strength
The Hills reposed; but when some cloudy
shade
Form'd into life, a floating semblance fell
With dim surprisal on their meadow'd sides,
And chequer'd them with ever-changing hue.
Bright ran the river, with melodious speed
Contented; fit for fairy barks to sail,
Or Infancy beside its banks to roam
And gaily prattle to the new-blown flowers,—
So timidly the modest waters flow'd:
And yet, when rains and mountain-floods
descend,
The demon-spirit of the water frowns!
In roaring swiftness o'er the prostrate fields
The exaggerated river foams along,
And ruins as it rolls! like some proud mind
That when unwrong'd in meek retirement
dwells,
But, injured,—how the buried fire outbreaks,
And maddens round it withering and fierce!
Upon my right, in ivy-tress'd array,
Sublime in ruin, Rhyddlan Castle frown'd;
And, gazing there, the heart religious grew,
To think how glory, pomp, and all the world
adores,
A dream becomes for moralist to scan!
Home of the Warrior! where the banner waved,
And Towers! where Cambrian kings and chief-
tains reign'd,
Whose halls within, the harp of Cymru rang,
While melodies, from Freedom's soul evoked

* The name of the mountain whence the Rhaiadr rises.

Pour'd tides of feeling over Princes' hearts,
In thy decay how eloquent thou stand'st!
Gigantic Emblem for the mind to read
How perishing is glory! while the Sea
In loud eternity of water beats
Grandly as ever on thy throbbing shore.

From thee, dread Monument of vanish'd days,
Baronial relic of the fierce and free,
Mine eye retreated; far as sight could roam,
Pictured on clouds, in outlined magic lay
The Peaks of Snowdon; silver-bright they shone,
And seem'd the very walls of Heaven! so fair,
So dazzling-white their towering beauty rose,
Like sculpture out of snow by sunshine carved.

Stranger! if ever pent in cities loud,
For many a month thy yearning eye has dream'd
Of Nature, throned amid the green romance
Of woods and waterfalls, thy heart might beat
In thrilling answer to the strain I sing,
Hadst thou beside me, from the sacred tower
This beauteous Vale beheld:—or ere I left,
One long, enamour'd, and delicious gaze
It bade me fasten on the faultless scene;
The sunshine in its golden lull reposed
On tree and mountain: cot and castle gleam'd,
And field and flower their blending graces show'd;
But when the breeze, in wingèd life arose,
How richly all the stirring Landscape flamed!
'Till the glad meads like emerald-sunshine flash'd,
So lustrously that living verdure play'd!

Soft be the winds that visit thy domain
And fair the flowers which gem thy matchless vale
St. Asaph! long may yon cathedral-tower
A sanctity around thy region shed!
For never, while a pulse of memory beats,
Can I that hour of thrilling awe forget
When first amid the gazing crowd I knelt,
A white-robed Novice; while with trembling lip
And soul that to its centre shook, and pray'd,
I vow'd to feed and watch the fold of Christ! *

* * * * * *

Vale of calm beauty! peace be ever thine
And plenteousness within thy cottage-homes,
Thy castled halls: when fateful years have fled
And worn the furrow deeper on my brow,
Vision'd by fancy, thou wilt yet remain
And help to form imagination's heaven!

* An allusion to the Ordination held at St. Asaph, on Sunday, May 3rd, 1835.

ELLESMERE LAKE.*

(1836.)

Calm as the beauty upon childhood's brow
On whose fair arch young tenderness is throned,
The Lake reposes; not a ripple mars
Its cloud-reflecting face; where hues of heaven
In soft variety of liquid smiles
Float o'er the water, in successive play
Of light and motion, exquisitely wild.
Oh! Nature, art thou not a spirit now,
While the rich poetry of silence reigns
Heard by the soul, which feels almost unearth'd
And girded round by inspiration's spell?

Pale Martyr of the feverish thought and care!
Sad Victim of a spirit-crushing world!
And Thou, who, dungeon'd in the gloom of self,
To thine imprison'd view art dwarfing down

* The town of Ellesmere, situated in the northern part of the county of Salop, takes its name from an adjoining lake, or mere, which being more extensive than some others in the neighbourhood, was by pre-eminence called Al, or Aelsmere (i. e. the greatest mere). It is of Saxon origin; *ael*, excellence or fulness, and *mère*, a little sea. This beautiful and picturesque lake comprises about 120 acres, and is bordered on one side by the town, and on the other by Oteley Park, the residence of Charles Kynaston Mainwaring, Esq. On the town side of the lake is the elevated site of an ancient castle (none of the ruins of which are now visible), that retains the name of the Castle Hill; on the most elevated spot, formerly, the keep, is a fine bowling-green, commanding an extensive and pleasing view, nine different counties (some say thirteen) having been discovered from it in clear weather—Ellesmere having been a frontier fortress of considerable note, during the unsettled period which preceded the final subjugation of Wales. The castle and government of the town were alternately in the possession of the princes of North Wales and of the English monarch. King John, in the sixth year of his reign, gave the castle and manor of Ellesmere in frank marriage with his daughter Joan, to Llewellyn, Prince of Wales; and four years afterwards revoked his grant, and placed his brother William, Earl of Salisbury, in possession. In the 25th Hen. III., David, son of Llewelyn, late Prince of Wales, surrendered up Ellesmere to the crown of England; after that we have no record of its being again in the hands of the Welsh, although the continual skirmishes between the English and Welsh made its tenure very uncertain. The castle was probably destroyed in the seventeenth century, during the parliamentary wars.

All grand conceptions, all august desires,
Hither! and while the dreaming water basks
Beneath the play of noon's attemper'd smile,
Lull'd in a trance of thought, the Lake admire.

Above, the curved immensity of heaven
Attracts thee, making eye and heart ascend
To wander in those palaces of cloud,
Or fairy-chambers, by the sunbeams paved.
And ye! vast Hills, that in your towering pomp
Touch the bow'd sky, and belt the horizon
round
With guardian might, how lofty and alone,
In stern supremacy of height and shape
Ye stand! And, gazing on your giant-forms,
The charm'd beholder grows exalted too,
Till wing'd emotions waft the mind aloft
And, mountain-like, from earth to heaven he
soars!
But, hark! in gushes of unwearied song
From yon green isle the hidden birds outpour
Their ecstasy of voice; and round them flows
An atmosphere of melody and praise;
While here and there, some fairy insect-form
Floats on the air, and fans its playful wing;
Or butterflies, like soaring gems, abound,
And scatter forth their gleams of dazzling
joy!

But, see! where Oteley with its terraced
pomp
And sun-bright aspect through the foliage
smiles
Imposingly serene; Oh! long around
That Home of hospitality and peace
May all the social graces throng and bloom!
And you, that gently on the lake encroach
Or round the shore a verdant twilight cast,
Majestic Trees! by summer-grace bedeck'd,
How lovingly your green array invites
The pausing Eye, while many-coloured leaves
Flash in the sun with fascinating hue.

And list, in undulating cadence rolls
The peal of bells from yonder gothic Shrine
Most venerably grey, as broad and dim
Through the bright air its dusky tower
ascends;
While soft vibrations of the sacred chime
Ebb on the breeze;—and tenderly, of days
Now sepulchred in memory's tomb, they speak,
Till the fine chords of quick reflection thrill
And waken to the tones. That fane beneath
The dust of immemorial thousands sleeps,
Who once along the churchyard's haunted
ground
Did ramble oft, and hear with soul unmoved
The very hymn that like a funeral dirge
The passing hour bemoans; or saw, perchance,
The sunbeams gambolling round *their* destined
grave!

But now, mild eve advances, and the Lake
More winning tenderness of hue and sound
Begins to gather: beautiful delight
Art Thou, fair Scene of water! in thy calm,
As thus reclining; yet in sterner mood
There are who love thine eloquent harangue
Of tempest-voices, when the black-wing'd
Storms
Revel above thee; and in sea-like rage
Thy tossing billows whiten, heave, and roar
Beneath the glances of uncertain light,
That downward in their arrowy fleetness dart
From the torn clouds, which let the sun-flash
through.

Adieu, loved scene of meditative joy;
Yet, oh! how lingeringly the eye retires
From beauty fresh as thine! The world
forgot,
And all its crowd of pale-faced cares repell'd,
In heavenliness of thought my heart has roam'd
Beside thy magic, drinking in awhile
The balm and freshness of a better world;
While Nature on the throne of feeling sits,
And reigns, accorded queen of heart and
soul!

Farewell! to *outward* gaze a long farewell,
Perchance, for ever: yet the dreaming eye
Of Fancy, when the landscapes of the soul
Are imaged, often o'er thy charms will bend;
And pure sensations into life will flow
Of loveliness and verdure; while the tones
Of rippling water throb on Memory's ear,
Like those that warble round thy grassy shore.

Oh! that the heart of man would more and
more
Hold converse with the Beautiful and Bright,
And hear those oracles of truth and love
Which come from Nature's everlasting shrine
To all who seek Her, and with filial awe
Her sanctities admire. And who can tell
How often, while along yon wheel-track'd road
The hard-eyed worldling in some dream of Self
Hath hurried, thou didst breathe a moment's
balm
On that dry wilderness,—an earthly heart!
And thus, amid the blank of common things
Thou seemest, in the contrast of thy charm,
A page of sentiment by Nature spread
In the coarse volume of man's daily Life,
The eye to soothe,—or satisfy the heart
Which hungers for imagination's feast!

But lo ! upon the placid brow of Eve
A star of glory like a gem is set,
And round the air a dreaming quiet broods ;
While tree and lake in glimmering beauty lie,
And the rich shadows of a summer's night
Begin to deepen ; once again, farewell
Thou ancient Water !—centuries o'er thy face
Have fleeted, and unnumber'd millions sunk
Back into breathless clay, but Thou, unworn,
Unwrinkled, and unchanged, art still preserved
In youthful glory : thus, while men decay
And generations toil, and weep, and die,
Some other bard in moralising dream
Will muse, perchance, along thy lovely shore,
And learn how nature, when the soul responds
To fine appeals, can into song awake
The music of the heart's mysterious lyre.

ELLESMERE, *June 14th*, 1836.

ORGAN BOY.

HE hath a spirit bright in its content
And playful in its poverty ; the rain
Of English clouds and atmospheric gloom
Of this brave island-clime have not destroy'd
The mirthfulness of his brown cheek ; nor quench'd
The lustre of those deeply-laughing eyes
Which sparkle forth the sunbeams of the soul !

Then breathe no pity on the organ-boy ;
From *his* gay Land a stock of sterling bliss
And proud young feelings that can well outwear
Each frown of Fate, the stripling wanderer brings.
Maternal smiles his heart still brighten round ;
A father's blessing, when he climb'd his knee
At night, still sounds upon love's inward ear ;
And when the streets are wintry, and the tones
His organ weaves fall fruitless on the air,
He dreams of home deep-bosom'd in bright vales
Of beauty ; hill-spread vines, and fairy streams
That trifled sweetly as a sister's voice
Who prattled in her slumber : days will dawn
When he *again* those glowing vales shall thread,
And tell his travels with unwearied tongue
To fond ones, nestling round his own fireside.

Nor think his errant life too mean to sing :
Albeit no music tuned to courtly ears,
Which seem regardless of those native sounds
That raise sweet echoes in romantic souls,
From him is heard ; there are of meeker taste
And simpler mind, who bid the roving boy
A welcome ; and enchanted hear the notes
His organ wakes, of tenderness and truth.
As through the City's ever-busy streets
And darkly-winding lanes he roams and plays,
Many an ear drinks musical delight ;
Many an eye with beams of vanish'd years
Is brightly charged ; and from her window haunt,
Who makes the street to tingle with the sound
Of halfpence, thrown with no ungentle hand,
By some fair listener ? Haply he woke dreams
Of childhood ; thoughts which cannot breathe in words,
But live and fade in sighs of fond regret !

And round him what a throng of urchins group,
And dream his music sweet as Orpheus made !
The laughter hush'd, the noisy tongue asleep,
The hoop, as weary, on his shoulder hung,
A Schoolboy stands to listen, and admire
Those melodies which dance along his soul
Like ripples fleeting o'er a ruffled stream !

Then let the streets still waken to the sound
Of such boy-minstrels ; when afar they roam
Through villages, where Music breathes a spell
Of magic in her meanest tone, may smiles
Of welcome flash along the rough-worn face
Of age, and ruddy offspring of the fields :
May gentle skies and glowing days attend,
And feelings toned to every tuneful hour !

There are who deem a Ballad-singer brings
No music which rewards harmonious ears ;
To whom an Organ-boy but grating notes
Of discord scatters on the homeless wind ;
Their sympathies are season'd high, and scorn
The gentle : envy not the ungenial souls !
For, hallow'd Nature ! thou art ever true ;
And he who wanders with an eye of love
And feeling wide among thy many haunts,
Through mountain-walks, or unambitious vales,
Where stream and meadow mingle their romance
Around, in storm and sunshine finds thee still
The same and magical ! and so, in Life ;
Her sweet humilities have grace and power
Beyond her loftiness and pomp : the Muse
Can never play the courtier ; from the halls
And palaces of Kings she flies to glades
Of lowliness, where Faculties are found,
And Will and Action can their sway reveal :
Where beats a heart, there Poetry may breathe
Her spirit round it ; beautifying look
And word, extracting all the soul of things,
And veiling Nature with a hue divine.

BALLAD-SINGER.

(1829.)

> "As if the streets were consecrated ground,
> The city one vast temple—dedicate
> To mutual respect in thought and deed."
>
> WORDSWORTH.

THE dewy spirit of a summer-rain
Falls not with fresher magic on the flower
Than flows sweet music through the soul of man:
In melody the heavens were hung;* the Sea
Weaves music when she rolls her full-voiced waves:
The cloud-born Thunders sound an organ-peal;
And every breeze hath music in its breath!
What, wonder, then, while Nature hymns around,
That music is a sympathy to souls,
The power of exquisite delight? From lips
Of beauty, like aroma from the mind
Exhaling forth; or in the hoary aisle
Of dim Cathedrals dying slow away;
Or in some dream-built palace of the night,
Where angel-whispers make the spirit glow,
How sweet is Music!—with the Light twin-born.

And thy sad voice, poor Minstrel of the street!
Hath sweetness in its sorrow: wild thine air
And dim the meaning of that mournful eye;
For, blighting Poverty hath made thee droop
And worn the health-bloom of thy once fair cheek:
Pale-lipp'd thou art; and charity may read
Upon thy face the story of thy life;
The damp night-gush, the stony bed, the gripe
Of famine, and that fever of a soul
Whom not a smile hath visited through years
Of deep despair, hast thou not felt them, maid
Of many sorrows! yet so sweetly flows
The tide of music in thy homely song
Of tenderness, that when I hear thee sing,
As in a vision thou art beautified above
Thy lot; and tripping o'er the dew-clad hills
When young birds pipe their anthem to the Morn,
Like some bright Creature whom the wood-gods love
I see thee, in thy youth's elysian prime!

That voice, of misery, oh! was it born;
Or; breathed by Happiness into thy soul
When hand in hand o'er childhood's vanish'd fields
Down hawthorn-lanes, by margins of clear brooks
And laughing streams, she led thee in her love?
With cottage-hymn hast thou not hallow'd oft
The sacred hour of eve, and called the smile
Of holiness upon thy father's cheek,
As flowed his kindled feelings in thy song
Of adoration? Minstrel of the street!
Whate'er has been thy lot, thy ballads breathe
Of summer-days to me; and from each strain
My heart can gather echoes, which have wings
To bear it downward into Years, where lie
The buried Joys that will not bloom again!

LONDON, *February* 14*th*, 1829.

* "Προῆλθε τὸ μέτρον ἐκ Θεοῦ. ἁρμονία γάρ τις ἐστι καὶ τοις ἐπουρανίοις καὶ ἐπιγείοις."—*Longin. Frag.*

STANZAS FOR MUSIC.

WHEN the hush of Twilight deepens
Wake, music! then;
Or when the star of Hesper glows
And flings a beam of pale repose
Where yonder tide in beauty flows,
Wake, music! then.

When the yearning heart is melted
Wake, music! then;
As oft some dream of perish'd days
Comes floating o'er the spirit's gaze
'Till every pulse of memory plays,
Wake, music! then.

When the cloud of sorrow blackens
Wake, music! then;
Or, like the hymn of moonlight-bird,
Or rain-dew in the desert heard;
Or leaflet by a night-breeze stirr'd,
Wake, music! then.

When the storm of pain arises
Wake, music! then;
Like glory from an angel-eye,
Like pity in a parent-sigh,
In feeling softness tenderly
Wake, music! then.

SUMMER WAVES.

EXULTING waters! how ye leap and laugh,
Instinct with rapture; while the restless beams
Of sunlight flash in sympathetic glee
O'er your glad bosom: hark! the hurried tones
Of sea-born music thrill the Air with mirth,
Till all around me, like a viewless swarm
Of bees, the humming atmosphere resounds.

Strand on Green, Kew, Sept. 1834.

MARIUS.*

(1827.)

SAD on the echoing shore great Mărius mused,
Deserted and alone; his harass'd eye
The crested waves cast sullenly athwart,
Where rode the traitor's bark. How fallen now
Since that proud day when triumph fired his eye,
And Rome beheld her valorous saviour there!
To brighter days his dreams went back. He thought
Of that high morn, when, fronting Scipio's view,
With firm-paced step, and unretreating arm,
The foe he dash'd, and dragg'd him in the dust:
Of Rome's acclaim, when, throned upon his car,
Jugurtha's fetters clanking on his ear,
He moved triumphant, 'mid the banner'd throng
Who hail'd his Afric conquest: prouder still,
His memory hover'd round the laurell'd pile
Heap'd from the spoil'd Ambrones;—torch in hand,
And purple-clad, as veterans round him stood
He waved and whirl'd the blazing light to heaven,
While shields, and clashing spears, rang martial joy.
Of these he thought, and then Despair awoke,
And delved a frown upon his war-worn brow,
That bent with recollections dark and deep.

Thus Marius sat; and mused before the sea;
Till, bursting from his shroud of grief and gloom,
O'er bogs and wilds dejectedly he sought
A shelter from his foes. Unto the fens
With wild and weary step the wanderer came,
And found compassion in a cotter's hut:
Roused thence, he couch'd within a narrow cave,
Beside the river; there was Marius ta'en,
And naked dragg'd unto Minturnæ's walls!

Within a cell, whose dungeon-wall shed round
A dreadful gloom, the imprison'd Warrior lay,
Stern, fierce, and frowning, dubious of his fate
Like a chain'd eagle glaring at the skies!
The door burst open; and with clattering teeth,
And hand which trembled like a dizzy flame,
Stalk'd in a savage Gaul; but, ere he sheath'd
His gleaming dagger in a Roman breast,
From his fierce eyes a living flame there flash'd,
Like lightning from a cloud! Th' assassin shook
And reel'd, and shrunk affrighted from dread eyes
Whose flashes fell like phantom-darts of fire,
On that pale coward's face. Then Mărius rose
And, with a voice of thunder, loud and deep,
"*Darest* thou do the murderous deed!" exclaim'd.

* See Plutarch's Life of Marius.

VIVE L'EMPEREUR!*

(1827.)

BY Wilid's banks the headlong river swept
Like whirlwind for its havoc! white with foam,
And plunging on in many a gurgled roar
Of furious rage! So fiercely flies the steed,
Unmanacled, that with his upshot ears,
And limbs vein-swelling in their wrathful glow,
Undaunted gallops over hill and dale
With name dishevell'd and his eyes on fire.
Each massy bridge was ruin'd; and afar
The giddy wrecks were battling with the flood
Till whirl'd below. 'Twas then Napoleon came
With his embattled hosts. That wondrous Man!
Whose daring spirit, with volcanic rage,
Breathed flame and ruin on the affrighted world.
His eyes the universe could span! His soul
Had fire enough to vanquish all! In vain
Wild Nature barr'd his progress with her crags
O'er-crested by the clouds; in vain the rocks
His path to block, their icy heads uprear'd
Or hurl'd their torrents at him! With a glance
Fierce as the eagle's, when his piercing eye
Gleams through the darkening air, he look'd beyond
Them all: Nature and He were giants twin,
And her impediments but forced the flames
Of genius from his soul; as thunder-clouds
Together clash'd, their lightning-gleams dart forth.

* The river Wilid being swollen with rain, and the bridges destroyed, the emperor (Napoleon) commanded a body of Polish cavalry to cross by swimming: they did not hesitate to dash into the river; but ere they reached the middle of the stream, an irresistible torrent broke their ranks, and they were lost almost to a man before the eyes of Napoleon, to whom some of them, in the last struggle turned their faces, exclaiming "Vive L'Empereur!"—SIR WALTER SCOTT'S *Life of Napoleon.*

Upon the howling flood a glance he threw,
Such as the tiger darts, ere on his prey
He springs, to gnash it in his ravening ire;
Then fiercely cried "On! on! my valiant
Poles!"
They answered not; but with a clanging stir
Goaded their pawing battle-steeds, and plunged
Amid the torrent's rush. Like loosen'd crags
Down-rushing on the sea, the warriors sank
Emburied in the stream; then buoy'd again,
And panting, cleaved their roaring track.
Beneath
Their gallant burdens, bravely paw'd the steeds,
With blowing nostrils and dilated eyes,
And many a furious snort; against their breasts
The cloven waters foam'd, and flash'd behind
Their darting hoofs; and roar'd, and raged
around
The dripping foemen, like a startled den
Of lions in the wood:—but vain the rush;
Midway the maddening torrent overwhelm'd
The struggling files; like a tremendous blast
Among autumnal leaves, it scatter'd all!
Rank after rank was buried in the flood,
Their steeds upon; while round their sinking
heads
The waters yell'd, as victors o'er their foes:
But in that gasp, while yet their spirits hung
'Tween life and death, as feathers in the air,
Backward they gazed, and with triumphant
shrieks
Of valour, fiercely sounded, "Vive l'Empereur!"

He heard their death-cries rolling on the blast;
And, as a lake just rippled into life,
His features flutter'd with terrific throes
Of suffering; then, his grinding teeth he
gnash'd,
And dug the nails into his palms; and groan'd
In more than agony, whose deeps were dumb!

DEATH OF CORINNE.

(1828.)

All pale, and pillow'd on a chair she lay,
The beautiful, the passionate Corinne!
The brilliant language of her eyes no more
Darted around such eloquence of soul,
As when, amid the crowd, her feelings flash'd
The bright expression forth; while she herself
Was *living* poetry! Deep pensiveness,
And looks intense which tell the blighted heart,
Of coming death prophetically spake!

Ere yet her spirit breathed itself to heaven,
She yearn'd, upon the shrouded moon to gaze,
Silvering the mellow skies. Athwart her face
Floated *that* fatal cloud! the same she saw
When Melville woo'd her by the winding shore:
On him, enamour'd, kneeling at her feet,
She look'd, and in one look condensed
The buried anguish of a broken heart;
Her white lips feebly parted, then reclosed
For ever! Gazing then upon the sky,
She faintly beckon'd to the gleaming moon,
While down her neck her streaming ringlets
fell
Like dropping sunbeams on the pallid air.

And now a change came on; back the blood
retired
Her radiant cheek beneath; her eyelids moved
Like melting snow-flakes in the noontide-
glow,
And all her beauty quite empyreal turn'd,
As if refining, ere to heaven it went;
Her hand fell downward with her farewell
sigh,
And with eternity her spirit was!

CÆSAR ON THE BANKS OF THE RUBICON.

(1829.)

Amid the roar of revelry
Within Alesian's home,
He moved with glad but musing eye,
The vanquisher of Rome;
His spirit mingled with the gay,
And smiled the gloom of war away.

He tarried there till darkling Night
Threw round her dewy veil,
And shadows pall'd each Alpine-height
That beetled o'er the dale;
Then Cæsar rose, his bosom fraught
With incommunicable thought!

And swiftly sped the Hero on
Along his shadowy road;
And reach'd where roll'd the Rubicon,
That from the mountain flow'd;
And there,—prophetic thought's control
Becalm'd the dauntless Cæsar's soul!

Before him heaved the river-bound
Between great Rome and Gaul;
If cross'd—what trumpet-clangs would sound!
How many a foeman fall!
The vision'd future wild with woes
Before him, like a Spectre, rose!

He mused on battle, war, and blood,
On plunder'd cities' storm;
The impatient daggers of the good
Against a tyrant's form;
On all the mountain-perils thrown
'Tween Rome and triumph,—for his own.

Of what the unborn Times would say
At Rubicon's grand name,
Of Him who track'd with blood his way,
And with it built his fame:
Would he not seem a demon *then*,
Who ravish'd all the rights of men?

And thus reflecting Cæsar stood
And battled with his mind;
Then, gazed upon the fatal flood,
And dash'd his doubts behind!
Like a bent bow, his pride return'd,
And all the Roman in him burn'd.

"The die is cast! the die is cast!"
With reckless shout he cried;
Then swift the Rubicon was pass'd
And reach'd the Roman side;
Ere day had dawn'd he drew the sword,
And vassal Cities hail'd him lord!

A THOUGHT.

Dreams of our Youth! like birds of beauteous wing
Which haunt the paradise of morn and sing,
How have ye vanish'd into viewless air
And left the mind a Temple for despair!

July, 1833.

MORNING.

(1829.)

The Sun is seated on his ocean-throne,
Attended by a court of clouds. Around
And midway, rosy phantoms form and swell,
Advance, and, like battalions in array,
Mingle their pomp, and make a shining plain
Of crimson on the skies.

Beneath, the waves
In gleaming motion lie, like ruffled scales
Of liquid steel: and, lo! awaking now
With the white dew of slumber on her breast,
The Earth, all fragrant, fresh in living green,
And beautiful, as if this moment sprung
From out her Maker's hand. Athwart the trees
A verdant lustre shines; where matin-beads
With gems of light have jewell'd all the boughs;
While here and there, some gently-vocal stream
Touch'd by a sun-ray, laughs with conscious light.

The Flowers are waking, too, and ope their eyes
To greet the prying sun, while meads and dales
With hoary incense steam: and list! there floats
A buzz of life; myriads of insects now
Creep from their green-wood caves and mossy homes,
And wind their way to glitter in the sun;
While from yon wooded green the sheep-bells send
Their tinkling echoes down the forest-dale.

And is creation's heir, in slumberous calm
Unmindful of the morn? Ah, no: its beams
On the lone cotter's straw-roof'd hut hath smiled,
And call'd him forth. And see! the lattice oped,
Far o'er the landscape's freshen'd view His eye
Expatiates; while the choral breezes wake
Like matins from the harp of Air produced:
And then deep sentiments, by purity evoked,
Thrill the true heart; instructively it owns
The gloriousness of God; while faith ascends
On wings of prayer and praise the Mercy-seat,
And Him adores, Whom day and night reveal.

NOON.

The Sun is burning with his noontide-beams
Inflamed to fierceness. Cooling winds are dead;
The shallow lakes are film'd; and fetid pools
Gleam darkly from the arid ground, while hosts
Of swarming insects on the creviced soil
Basking and buzzing creep. The trees are tranced
In breezeless air; and at their matted trunks
The ploughman lies, his head upon his palms,
Watching between the leaves heaven's cloudless arch
Smile on him beauteously. The flowers decline,
As if they languish'd for a breezy draught;
And e'en the flirting bee, now honey-cloy'd,
Is humming languid on the rose's brim.
The world grows faint; and all is stirless, save
Yon sky-bird travelling to the sun; and hark!
Wing-poised, he peers undazzled at the blaze,
Hymning his heart-full of aërial strains.
Beneath this towering cliff behold the sea

Magnificently spread! The billows pant
And revel in the beams, which crest and crown
Their heads with golden brightness; or adorn
The dimpling bosom of the calmer deep,
And gambol to the shore.

But, far beyond,
Behold a rock majestically rear'd;
Upon whose brow the eagle sits at noon,
Rolling his eye-balls at the blazing run;
High on the yellow beach, its hoary side
Is bared unto the ocean, and the breeze
Upwafted, like a tight and stately sail
When whitening in the glow of heaven. And look!
The feathery shapes of far-off sails are seen
Alone upon the billows; and like clouds
Which glance and tremble on the ocean-brim,
Their motion gleams upon the water's breast.

NIGHT.

Another day is added to the mass
Of buried Ages. Lo, the beauteous Moon,
Like a fair shepherdess now comes abroad
With her full flock of stars, which roam around
The azure mead of heaven. And oh, how charm'd
Beneath her loveliness creation looks!
Far-gleaming hills, and light-inweaving streams,
And fragrant boughs with dewy lustre clothed,
And green-hair'd valleys, all in glory dress'd,
The pageantries of Night compose. One glance
Upon old Ocean, where the woven beams
Have braided her dark waves!—Their roar is hush'd;
Her billowy wings are folded up to rest;
Till once again infuriate winds shall yell,
And tear them into strife.

A lone owl's hoot;
The waterfall's faint drip; or insect-stir
Among the emerald leaves; or infant-wind
Rifling the pearly lips of sleeping flowers,—
The stillness of the scene alone disturb:

Spirit of All! as up yon star-hung deep
Of air, the eye and heart together mount,
Man's Immortality within him speaks;
That Thou art all around! Thy Beauty walks
In dream-heard music o'er the midnight heavens;
Thy glory garmenteth the slumbering world.

SPIRIT OF TIME.

1830.

"Horæ quidem cedunt et dies, et menses, et anni: nec præteritum tempus unquam revertitur; nec quid sequatur, sciri potest."—Cicero.

Another Year, methought a Spirit cried,
Another Year is dead! Still rolls the world
Magnificent as ever; bright the Sun,
And beautiful his native heaven; the Earth
Around looks fresh as on her birth-day morn;
And Man, as gay as if no knell had rung,
No heart been broken, and no tears been shed!
Where, then, the history of the buried Year,
Of weal and woe, of glory and of shame?
Eternal! not a minute fleets away
That to Thy throne a record doth not waft;
Time *cannot* die; the unapparent Years
Again will rise; and cited Ages come,
And in our human resurrection share.

A Year hath perish'd, who can tell his tale?
Ye Thunders! kings of cloudy wrath sublime,
With herald-lightnings to announce your power,
Say from your sleep shall ye be summon'd forth,
And tell your havoc, in the blaze of noon
And in the night-wing'd tempest darkly made?
Or, shall I bid unbosom'd Ocean yield
Her dead; or let the unfrequented graves
Expand, and show their ghastly inmates, there?

No moral is there loud enough and deep
The laugh of Life to hush above the tomb;
Time, accident, and change,—they melt forgot
Like clouds of feeling: not the dread alarm,
Of Nature can arouse the world to think.—
An earthquake was there in a far-off isle:
The heavens were blacken'd; and the grim waves yell'd,
While Ocean, heaving like a human breast
In agony, groan'd wildly from her depths:
All Earth seem'd fear-struck; on their bowing trees
The leaves hung shuddering; through the heated air
The dull wind mutter'd with a spirit-tone,
And fitfully the island-cities rock'd;
At midnight, came the Earthquake in his ire
And gloom, which made the world's foundations reel!
Temples and towers were shatter'd: shrieks and prayers
Rang in wild tumult through the riven skies;
And, crush'd to dust, a thousand corpses lay

Gulph'd in the ground and sepulchred by night!
Cold morning came; each brow a sadness cloak'd;
Yet none of *Judgment* in their doom could dream,
And in the Earthquake hear the Voice of God!

A Year hath vanish'd, and how many eyes
Are film'd, how many lovely cheeks are cold!
What lips, which let out music from the soul,
Are death-seal'd, now! Bend, human Pride, and see
The desolation and the curse of Time.
Monarch of millions! at whose royal feet
The treasures of the ransack'd earth were laid,
And on whose brow the pride of Ages sat,
Where slumberest Thou? the sleep of death is thine;
And worms will revel on thy pulseless clay
As on the meanest of forgotten dust.

What hast thou lost, unheedful World? Thy great
Have died; Spirits amid whose radiant track
In bright eclipse the common herd are lost:
Thy Kings, thy Warriors, and thy Statesmen too
Have perish'd: hast Thou mourn'd thy mighty dead?
Go, weep for *One*, the wonder of his day,
A mental Titan of amazing grasp,
A man whom England may exult to hail
Her own; a Patriot, round whose dying lips
Her name of glory like enchantment, clung.
His chief inheritance, a lofty soul,
He battled through the darkness of his lot
And shone aloft,—the brightest of them all
Who wrestled with the tempest of renown!
What genius glow'd that gifted mind within,
What eloquence came flowing from the fount
Of salient fulness there,—of Hearts demand
Which each word felt, like new-born feeling, pour
Warm inspiration round them, when with eye
That kindled with the kindling truth, he stretch'd
His mind o'er Empires; and round captive-isles
Bade Liberty her wings of light expand!

But, when the mighty die, the mean begin
To live; and thus with thee, departed One!
Scarce on the wind thy death-knell ceased to moan,
Ere darkly rose the pestilential breath
Of slander's venal lip, thy name to blight,
And turn thy soul as tainted as her own.
Yes! they the thunders of thy voice who fear'd
In Retribution's high revenge, arose,
And on thy memory heap'd the hoarded wrath
Of envy;—let them riot in their shame!
What though some error cast a doubtful shade
Upon thy glories, shall we laud them less?
Are skies less beautiful, because the clouds
Sail o'er them? shines the morning sun less bright
Because a passing shade his brow profanes?—
A monument in noble minds thou hast,
That will not moulder; Time shall guard it there!

But not alone the glorious and the great
Hast thou entomb'd, thou unreturning Year!
'Tis in the noiseless sphere of common life,
In placid homes, by quiet evening-hearths
Where once the social hearts were gather'd round,
We trace a fearful havoc in thy flight.
Alas! how many whom the infant Year
Beheld in beauty, looking on through life
As through a vista of eternal Joy,
Have vanish'd, like the bloom of early hope!
What blue-eyed babes, the parent knee beside
Reflecting smile for smile, have flown away
Like birds of Paradise, to their own home!
What Creatures, budding into womanhood,
The silent walk who loved, and made the flowers
Companions of their virgin-thoughts, have gone
To graves, with all a mother's treasured hope!
Go, see the mournful chamber, where of yore
When Winter howl'd his dirge, the gush of song
And heart-warm fellowship of feeling hours
Was heard, now mute, as if the tones of Joy
Had *never* scatter'd echoes there! Alas!
For him, who in the green young spring had wed
The Heart he echo'd; brightly laugh'd the Sun
Upon that morn of love complete; long days
Of bliss, and all the warm romance of youth
In radiant vision gather'd round his heart,
And now, to him a tomb the world becomes!

And thou, dread Fashion, at thy gilded shrine
What victims have been offer'd up! From haunts
Where all the young Emotions bloom and dwell,
And Nature is the holy nurse of Thought,
What maiden victims have been brought to thee!
And saddening 'twas to see their piteous change
From innocence to each corrupting joy:
At home they wander'd in ancestral woods,
Follow'd the brooks, and felt a kindred ray
Flash from their surface o'er the sunny heart;
Yes, beautiful that magic reign of soul,

When air seem'd haunted with the vocal wings
Of spirits, who beatify the winds;
Or when, with looks expanded in delight,
The heavens they mark'd besprinkled o'er with clouds
And beams, and bless'd The Hand which hung them there:
Then life was holy, full of heavenward joy,
And all their thoughts, like sunbeams, where they fell
Shed brightness and a beauty round: oh! ill
Exchanged for gilded rooms and crowded halls,
For heartless pride and unromantic hours!
Then work'd the havoc of the mind within;
The fount of generous feeling frozen up,
The heart-laugh tamed to an obsequious smile,
And young affection slowly wither'd down
To bleak and barren pomp,—they died;
And heavy knells were rung, when marriage-peals
Like merry prophets, should have loudly hail'd
The coming years;—'twas Fashion stopt their course!

E'en thou, pale Genius! whose unearthly tones
The world intrance, within the grave art sunk,
Since her dim gates Eternity unbarr'd
To let the dead Year in. Yet, one there lived
On whom Oblivion's pall should not have dropt
Her gloom; he never heard a great Man's name
Without a thrill, electric as divine;
He never saw a monument to Mind
But Glory came, and sat him on her throne.
The haughty light I saw, which lit his brow,
The emulation from his soul reveal'd
And mantling all his features with the mind,
When *first* that ever-haunting dream of Youth,
The goal to which ambitious thoughts would run,
The City-queen of England,—met his gaze
Of wonder. Round him flow'd her streams of life;
Temples, and Towers familiar with the clouds,
And Streets gigantic, in their glittering flow
Branching away like rivers in the sun,
Claim'd tributary awe; but soon grew dim:
From ancient times a mental shadow came,
And *in* it, his enthusiastic eye
Saw Heroes, Lords and Lights of man and mind!

But genius to itself a martyr is;
And that immortal lava of the soul,
That fire he felt for which there is no name,
Consumed him, while it glorified each thought:
One midnight, when, deserted and untrod,
The Capital had lock'd her thousand limbs
In slumber, and a silence shrouded all
With a cathedral-awe, alone he stood
Some mute vast square amid; and deeply watch'd
The heavens, and spread his spirit to the stars,
That seem'd to brighten as his fancy glow'd!
The mystery of Being; and the might
Of Him, whose fiat moulded sumless worlds;
And Life; and Death; the silence of the grave,
That dark Unknown we all are doom'd to know!—
Assail'd him now; 'twas his last hour of *dreams;*
The orbs of heaven on him ne'er look'd again,
The Morrow saw him shrouded for the grave!

No more of sorrow for the fleeted year:
No tears can cancel, or recal it now:
Hereafter, when before the throne of God
Dead Ages shall revive, all its crimes
And Virtues will be summon'd to their doom.—
Hark! from a host of dimly-vision'd Spires
The midnight-hour is rolling to the skies,
While doubtful echoes undulate the air,
Then glide away, like shadows, into gloom.
A solemn peal, a farewell-voice of Time,
It leaves a lingering tone in many a heart
Where merriment a home had made! The young
Who hear it in the festive chamber, sigh,
And send their thoughts, sad pilgrims to a tomb;
The aged hear it, and the Dead revive!

A Year hath vanish'd, and another Year
Is born; what awful changes will arise,
What dark events lie hidden in the womb
Of Time, imagination cannot dream.
Ye Heavens! upon whose brow a stillness lies,
Deep as the silence of a thinking Heart
In its most holy hour, the world hath changed,
But *ye* are changeless; and your midnight-race
Of starry Watchers view our glorious isle,—
Beaming, as when amidst her forest-depths
The savage roam'd, and chanted to the moon.

O England! beautiful, and brave, and free,
With Ocean, like a bulwark round thee thrown,
Thoughts of Thy destiny the heart awake
To fearful wonder; from the wildest state
Of darkness, raised and magnified by Heaven!
What though a troubled Spirit walk the earth
And Fancy hear the distant war-drums roll,
Long may thy sceptre proudly awe the waves;
Still o'er the world enthroned as Island-Queen
While each new year adds glory to thy name,
May Time be vanquish'd, ere he conquer Thee.

HYMN.

Thy temple, Lord! creation stands,
Magnificently vast;
And o'er it Thine adorning hands
A roof of heaven have cast.

And there, all sights and sounds proclaim
The glory of Thy power,
And preach Thine everlasting name
To every conscious hour!

But though Thy temple be all space,
The heaven of heavens Thy throne,
Yet deign with condescending grace
This earthly fane to own.

O here may vocal incense rise,
And songs of Zion sound;
And lowly hearts and lifted eyes
Thy Presence feel around.

Salvation through the Blood of Him
Who conquer'd Death and Hell,
Assist us, O ye seraphim!
In strains like yours to tell.

And may thy living Gospel reign
Till sin and darkness flee,
And ransom'd Earth be pure again
As when it came from thee!

HYMN.

How sacred is that chosen spot
Where praise and prayer arise,
And earth and time seem half forgot,
While Faith unveils the skies,
And visions bright in beauty roll
Around the tranced believer's soul!

One hour within Thy Temple, Lord,
When blending hearts can meet,
And banquet on Thy blessed word
Before the Mercy-seat,
The antepast of heaven may prove,
And teach us how Thine angels love.

And ever in this calm abode
May Thy pure Spirit be,
And guide us on the narrow road
That terminates in Thee;
While dews of Thine absolving grace
Descend upon our fallen race.

Before the Cross where Jesu bled
On Calvary's fated hill,
With bended knee, and bowing head,
And soul devoutly still,
May each adoring sinner find
Salvation awe and soothe his mind.

And by Thy Blood, and by Thy Tears,
By all Thy pangs unknown!
Allay, O Lord, our rising fears,
And make these hearts Thine own;
Till each with loud hosannah sings,
Hail! Lord of lords, and King of kings!

A DREAM OF WORLDS.

(1839.)

Those starry Wonders, everlasting Worlds
Of light and loveliness, I saw them all,
As on the magic wings of mystery borne
Methought my unembodied spirit swept
Immensity. Vast multitudes there shone
Of beauteous Orbs, whose brightness was intense,
Beyond the noon in its most sunny reign.
Majestic, o'er a measureless extent
Of azure, moved those high immortal spheres,
Less terrible in beauty, but more shaped
To mortal vision; as they onward roll'd,
Each sounded as instinct with melody.

'Twas but an eye-glance that such pomp reveal'd;
And yet, before it pass'd a heaven-like host
Of Forms, and Phantoms which can never die
While memory lives. Who hath not charm'd the air
To rapturous delusion? Who hath lived
And yet not loved? and loved, and hath not shaped
His angel? Who a paradise not dream'd,
When from within a glorious longing woke
For *that* which earth and earthliness to none
Supply? Let Nature answer; she will tell
What shapes of beauty throng'd a dream of Worlds.

The Midnight!—how we gaze upon its pomp
Of orbs, and waft ourselves among their host,
As though they were bright Palaces for Souls
When clay doth not corrupt them. Who shall prove,
That such are *not* bright Eden's of pure bliss
Where myriads reap eternity? On high
The Seer* of old mysteriously was rapt

---

* Enoch.

To blessedness; aloft Elijah soar'd,
Rapt in dread thunder through the riven
skies
'Mid fiery chariots and emblazon'd clouds!
And He, the sanctifying Lord of Life,
Through air ascended to His throne eterne...
Ever have awe and glory, love and hope
Divine, the gaze of rapture skyward turn'd.
And oh! the cold *may* laugh, the worldly
jeer,
Mocking whate'er their miserable clay
Partakes not of the mind's celestial dream—
Yet are there spells of beautifying power
And passion, which a stern Reality
Can never reach. Go, ask the widow'd heart
Of young Affection, when she walks the night
As in a vision of departed hours,
If all which day-charms yield, her love
transforms
To such a blissful heaven of memory,
As that sweet lonely Star, whose angel-gaze
Like Mercy looks upon her lifted eye!
Or, ask a friend, of some bright Soul
bereaved,
When stars expressively the sky adorn,
What radiant solace from their beam is caught,
While Fancy sighing thinks, "My friend is
there!"

Ye holy Watchers! who this earth have
view'd
In darkness rolling on to destiny
Through countless ages, and are glorious still,
With no feign'd worship sing I your romance.
My boyhood was Chaldean; and your beams
Like rays of feeling quiver'd round my heart:
Yes, I remember, when becalm'd and still
My school-companions on their couches slept,
With moonlight on their beautiful young brows
Like holiness arraying them for heaven,—
Unhinder'd, to my casement I would steal,
And muse; and gaze upon the midnight-orbs
Until my spirit *seem'd* the skies to float.

Such homage for the heavens is not extinct:
For now, when weary of the heartless stir
Around me, and sad nothings which o'erwhelm
The daylight, and our nobler mind disease;
When darken'd by unkindness, or deceived
By finding clouds where sunshine should
prevail:
In such dark mood, upon those peaceful worlds
That shame us with their bright sublimity,
I gaze, and woo unheavenly fancy off
By visioning eternity.—Mere time
Too great a burden on our spirit lays;
We bow before our idols, and adore
The glittering falsehood of some fading scene;
Forgetful of yon glorious Sky, where, day
And night, Divinity is marching forth,
In sun or darkness, thunder or in worlds!

We know not *what* these heaven-illuming
orbs
May be; to us—but Mysteries, that roll
And shine. Yet, none upon them ever gazed,
Whose eye could gather beauty which the soul
Can image, nor within him felt a spell
Of admiration, spreading o'er the mind
Till it became a mirror of delight
Reflecting back the glory that it hail'd.
And oft have I some heaven-born influence
caught,
When sick of human Festival, where smiles
Are tutor'd till the heart forget to reign,
And eyes are beaming with hypocrisy;
While that soft tongue, whose angel-accents
fall
In honey'd accents on the flatter'd ear
Can play the dagger, when the moment comes!—
How often, tired with such delightless pomp,
I've hail'd the homeward solitary way:
Here, once again, the immeasurable sky
Around me, and a starry wilderness
Open and free, for spirit to expand,
With what a worship hath my soul return'd
To night and nature, to itself and heaven!

A FADING SCENE.

A FADING scene, a fading scene
Is this false world below;
And not a heart has ever been
Which hath not proved it so.

The clouds are dying while we gaze
Upon them, young and warm;
And sweet flowers in the summer-rays
But perish while they charm.

The trees that woo'd us as we pass'd
With many a leafy strain,
Bow, wither'd by autumnal blast,
When visited again.

The music which the soul doth melt
Like magic from the skies,
Though sweetly-heard, and softly-felt,
In swiftest echo flies.

Our pleasures are but fainting hues
Reflected o'er the waves;
Our glories,—*they* are phantom-views
Which lure us to our graves!

And Beauty,—see her 'mid the crowd
A night-queen in her bloom!
To-morrow, in her maiden shroud
A martyr for the tomb!

And Love,—how frequent does it mourn
For some remember'd scene;
Or, doom'd in darkness reft or lorn
To live on what hath been.

And Friends,—alas, how few we find
That consecrate the name,
With glowing heart and generous mind,
To feed their hallow'd flame:

But should there be some blessed one,
However sad or lone,
Whom dearly we can look upon
And feel such friend our own,

The iron wings of Fate unfold
And bear him far away:
Or else, we mourn him dead and cold
Companion of the clay.

Oh, no! there's nothing on this earth
We fashion, or we feel,
But death is mingled with its birth
And sorrow with its weal.

Then, hail the hour of glorious doom!
That wafts my soul away
To regions radiant with the bloom
Of everlasting day.

THE DEPARTED YEAR.

"In silent night the vision of the dead passed by—
I saw our friends all pass,—
And oh! in silent night I saw the open graves—
I saw th' immortal host!"
KLOPSTOCK'S *Odes*.

A VISION, by eternity unveil'd,
When midnight in a trance of darkness lay,
My soul beheld. Methought that time and earth
Had vanish'd, while the unforgotten Dead
In glory bright and bodiless appear'd.
How deep their gaze! oh, how divine their smile!
A pensive mildness, an immortal grace
Each Semblance wore; the father had not lost
That light paternal which his living eyes
To greet his children, loved to have express'd;
Still on the mother's placid brow was throned
A tenderness, which triumph'd o'er decay;
And perish'd babes, whose beauty dazzled time,
In the young bloom of resurrection rose
Serenely glad, and innocently-bright.

And thus, by dreams of never-dying soul,
The Dead around us, with a voiceless power
Are present, mentally distinct and known;
As though some chain, whose links are unbeheld,
The living and the dead conjoin'd, that love,
E'en in the grave, no gloomy trance might bear,
But throb immortal in the spirit's core!

Thought flies the banquet, to embrace the tomb:
And, oh! if joy-wing'd hours awhile seduce
A faithful mourner from his fond regret;
If the dull prose of daily life contract
And dry his feelings into worldly dust,
Or selfish duty,—how divinely-pure
The calm of intellectual grief again!
Thus can creative fondness from the world
Of parted spirits, all it loved evoke:
And he whose years are chronicles of wo,
From the strange earth, where few companions dwell,
Can wander where the hopes of youth repose,
And make eternity his mighty home.—

* * * * *

A hollow knell heaves mournful on the air,
And my dark song in solemn echo rolls
To that dread music. From this orb of time
Another in the noon of manhood call'd
To lie and fester with unfeeling clay!—
Oh, God! the terror of Thy rising frown
Mantles the universe with more than night:
Each Kingdom, like a childless Rachel, mourns;
A Power of darkness, on the wings of death,
Hath travell'd earth with pestilential speed,
And left but havoc to declare his flight.
How many tombs this Year hath dug! what homes
Are fill'd with desolation's fearful calm!
The chairs are vacant where the Forms we loved
So oft reposed, where still their semblance chains
Our fix'd and fond delusion! In the streets,
Like silent mourners in a talking crowd,
Cold mansions tenantless and still remain,
From whose glad chambers rush'd the household-tones
That made sweet music to a social mind;
And many a garden, whose luxuriant green
And laurell'd bowers the sunbeams loved to grace,
In weedy ruin is decaying now:

The hands it welcomed with rewarding bloom,
Are iced by death, and ne'er can tend it more.
'Twas exquisite for him, whose town-worn life
Was fever'd by the hot and fretful day,
When evening, like an angel-wing, could waft
His spirit home, to greet yon tranquil cot
Again, and bid the vexing world depart.
How dear the beauty of each dawning flower,
How rich the melody of choral leaves,
To him, whose wisdom was a feeling mind!

And thou, lone sharer of a widow'd lot!
Where is the language, though a Seraph hymn'd
The poetry of heaven, to picture thee,
Doom'd to remain on Desolation's rock
And look for ever where the Past lies dead!
What is the world to thy benighted soul?
A dungeon! save that there thy children's tones
Can ring with gladness its sepulchral gloom.
Placid, and cold, and spiritually-pale,
Art thou; the lustre of thy youth is dimm'd,
The verdure of thy spirit o'er: in vain
The beaming eloquence of day attracts
Thy heart's communion with Creation's joy;
Like twilight imaged on a bank of snow
The smile that waneth o'er thy marble cheek!

Oh, when shall trial, tears, and torture cease?
Despair, and frenzy, and remorseless gloom,
Defiance, and the Thoughts which crouch before
The bright severity of Virtue's eye,
When shall their mystery lie unweaved, and bare?
When shall the lips of Agony be dumb,
And the dark wail of wounded Nature hush'd?

* * * * *

A Tragedy of twice three thousand years
Hath almost ended; soon perchance, may fall
A Curtain, whose unfolding darkness brings
Oblivion o'er the universe decay'd.
Already looks Earth's final scene begun:
The elements, like human limbs unnerved,
Forego their function; seasons out of tune
Creation's harmony of change destroy;
And in their wildness of unwonted act
Reflective eyes an awful omen read,
By Nature given to prophetic man
Of Time's conclusion. Sea and Air confess
A strange excitement; through the trackless heaven's
Immensity the unheard Comet rolls;
No vision'd eye his path may comprehend,
Nor dread imagination dream, what orbs
May crumble, or what blighted planets shrink
As on the burning Desolator sweeps
And blazes o'er annihilated worlds!

Spoiler of hearts and empires! vanish'd Year,
Ere for eternity thy wings were spread
Alone I listen'd to thy dark farewell.—
The moon was center'd in the cloudless heaven
Pallid as beauty on the brow of death;
And round about her, with attracted beams,
Group'd the mild stars; the anarchy of day
Was hush'd, the turbulence of life becalm'd.
From where I stood, a vast and voiceless plain,
A City garmented with mellow light
Lay visible; and, like romance in stone,
Shone gloriously serene. All sounds were dead:
The dew-drop, stirless as a frozen tear
Gleam'd on the verdure; not an air-tone rang;
The leaves hung trancèd as the lids of Sleep;
Around me Nature in devotion seem'd,
The Elements in adoration knelt,
Till all grew worship,—from the heart of Things
Material, to the conscious soul of man!
'Twas then, sepulchral, hollow, deep, and loud,
The bell of Midnight on the stillness burst
And made the air one atmosphere of awe.

Sublime of hours! I thought on all the grave
Had buried, since the infant Year began:
What dreams, what agonies untold
Dead as the hearts whose depth they once turmoil'd,
Lay motionless, and mute! Of pomp in dust,
Of wither'd pride, of wealth from glory hurl'd,
Of lull'd ambition and appeased despair,—
Of each I dreamt: and then, in sad array,
Pale visions of the Kings of thought arose,
The wise, the wondrous, the adored, whose deaths
Enrich'd eternity with added mind,
Sleep with the Patriarchs now! and *one* how great!
For whom the costly tears of genius fell;—
The wand is broken, and the Wizard gone!

Many and mighty are the stars of Fame;
But his deep splendour has outdazzled all
Since Shakspeare, that unrivall'd planet! rose,
Whose radiance clad the intellectual heaven.
Yes, he hath vanish'd; but his country wears
A veil of glory that shall garb her clime
For ever. How we hung upon his parting hour!
And when it summon'd the transcendant Mind
From earth to heaven, the souls of myriads felt
O'ershadow'd; Europe bow'd in dim eclipse,
And Kingdoms mourn'd round his imagined tomb.

Monarchs of time, and ministers of thought,
Felt in the frame of intellectual life
As rolls the blood-tide through our breathing form,
Where is the palace of your spirits *now?*
In what immensity are ye enshrined,
Imperishably pure? Was quiet earth
In beauty, but an archetype of heaven?
Your dreams, your towering aspirations high,
The far-off shadows of each Truth divine,—
Are all absorb'd in beatific light,
And *this* world like a rain-drop in the deep
Of time, for ever from the soul dissolved?
Our craving passion for the Unreveal'd
Fain would it know, to what vast height removed,
To what perfection of sublimest powers
Ye are ascended: but, the baffled Wish
Is driven earthward, and cold Nature cries
In tones as thrilling as the touch of Death,
"Back to thy clay, Mortality! and bend
Like Faith, before the infinite Unknown."

* * * * *

As water copies a portentous cloud
By stern reflection, so the spirit's gloom
Lies darkly mirror'd on the mimic page.
And if some features of a faded Past
Be thus recall'd, they bring no aimless grief
To deaden song, by female worth inspired.
For seldom, since the groan of earth began,
Hath Woman shone more visibly-divine
Than in the gloom of this remember'd year!
When Forms all spirit, moulded by the touch
Of Nature in her most ethereal power,
Whose beauty, delicate as painted air
At the light breeze seem'd ready to dissolve,
Transform'd by feeling, have at once become
Heroical, for superhuman aid!
Behold that chamber, where a feeble lamp
Is quivering, pulse-like, with a dying flame;
There, by yon couch, a soft-eyed mourner fades
Night after night, with uncomplaining brow:
While a soul flutters in *that* Form revered
From whence her being,—though her brain should parch
Till the flush'd eyelids hang like drooping flowers
About to wither, still, her watch endures!
The bough may blossom from the tree removed,
Ere young affection, from its parent torn,
Can live and flourish, while one ebbing pulse
Articulates within those precious veins!

And thus, calamity with glory comes:
From out its gloom, as streams from caverns pour,
The tides of human tenderness proceed.
And virtues, which the noon-bright hour of joy
May dazzle, when a cloud of anguish breaks,
Dawn into birth, and decorate the soul
With heaven-born lustre; like the pale-eyed stars
That shut their lids when gaudy daylight rules,
But ope them on the sun-forsaken night.

Then let the scorner, whom the vernal glee
Or laughing wildness of delighted youth
Hath taught, that pleasure would to pain deny
The sacrifice of one exalted tear,
His creed forego: the fount of Woman's heart
Lies deeper than his shallow gaze detects!
For Beauty, that a soulless idol seem'd
Rear'd on the breath of some adoring night,
Oh, let one pang a cherish'd mind convulse,
The mist is scatter'd! and the unblemish'd heart
Free from the world, like day from darkness comes,
And acts at once the ministry of heaven.

Then look at Woman, when by love sublimed:
Misfortune moulds her by a graceful power
To fit the cast of fate; and in her wo
Each mental attribute can bloom as bright
As when the home was costly, and her smile
Fell like a glory on attracted eyes.
As stoops an eagle from his lordly height
Where once he soar'd, companion of the cloud
And storm, so sinks, with a triumphant fall,
Her spirit down to some domestic vale;
There, looks more beauteous in each act and thought
Through the meek round her cottage-virtues run,
Than when it reign'd amid the hall of kings.
A mortal Weakness by the world admired
Let others paint her; and, in Woman find
The uncertain heart by light-wing'd impulse led,
The mind which fruitless admiration feeds,
The tottering purpose, and the tameless will:
There *is* a passion, that with fine eclipse
O'ershadows all such failing hours present,
When the soul falters,—'tis maternal love!
Unbounded feeling! Space, and Scene and Time
Succumb before thee: infinite in power
As fathomless in depth; no rack affrights,
No dungeon quells, no agony impedes
Thy wondrous action; in the horrid grave
Thou darest to cherish the unconscious Dead,
And heaven admits Thee, when thou soarest there!

Lo, how that feeling with transforming might
Shapes a wild spirit to its tender will!

Gay as the breeze and dainty as the flower
To-night behold her, on whose jewell'd head
Fashion hath set an ever-fading crown:
Again regard her!—and the trace of God
Is character'd on that ethereal change
Mien, mind, and manner all have undergone;
As broods a Poet o'er some wordless thought
Affection gazes on her unborn child;
And, ere its being into life expands
Love, like a seraph when the soul departs
For glory, waiting to receive its charge,
Stands on the threshold of commencing Life
Bright with the welcome of a mother's bliss!

Charm of the world! whose light makes human love,
If I apparel with too rich a robe
The fascinations which around thee float,
And on thy beauty let no dimness fall
To mar its radiance, 'tis an error blest,
Though blind: for Thou, in thy transcendent worth,
Art lifted to the highest sphere of Song,
When, like a human providence below,
Thy days are consecrate to deeds of heaven.

LINCOLN COLLEGE, OXON, 1833.

REFLECTIVE STANZAS.*

THERE is a sadness in my soul,
But whence, and why, I cannot tell;
As though a Spirit's dark control
Had bound it with a deadening spell.

The sun wears not that glorious brow
Poetic morns were wont to bring;
And many a wind which mourneth now,
A song of rapture used to sing.

For all my summer-glow of thought
Hath sadden'd into wintry gloom;
And much that Fancy shaped or sought
Lies buried in oblivion's tomb.

Yet, dream not that I nurse the grief
Which discontented moments bring;
Or sullen gloom, whose sole relief
Comes flowing from a bitter spring.

For human hearts, where'er they breathe,
Have still their human charm for me:
I would not bind a selfish wreath
Without one bud of sympathy!

Then let me not a mournfulness
From clouds of hidden sorrow steal;
Nor wring from thee a vain distress
A bosom soft as thine would feel.

A scene of sunshine and of gloom,
Like human life my page will be;
And, mutter'd o'er our mortal doom,
Will sound a dark Soliloquy!

Thou wilt not deem such verse supplied
By superstition's haggard gaze;
Nor think that Fancy's wing hath tried
To wander in forbidden ways.

Who paints His beauty on the cloud,
Or smileth on the breezy shore,
Or wraps Him in a whirlwind-shroud
Or speaketh in the thunder-roar,

That Power, the visionless and dread,
In words where inspirations dwell,
By His almightiness hath said,
Earth wears a shadow cast from Hell!

The Spirits and the Powers of air
In mystery and in might they roam;
Unseen they act, unknown they dare,
And make the evil heart their home.

And One, their centre and their soul
There is; the demon-god of sin
Who o'er the wicked hath control
And fires the hell we feel within.

And such a Wanderer o'er the earth
The viewless Power I've dared to draw;
And mentally have given birth
To all he felt, and all he saw:

To each avenging throe of thought
That *might* so dread a Spirit thrill,
With hateful ruin ever fraught,—
Yet blasted and believing still!

Thus Virtues are as Heaven reveal'd,
And Love and Truth eternal shown;
While whatsoe'er the Tempter wield,
Is darkly hued, and stamp'd his own.

Nor marvel thou, if scenery bright
And beautiful by Nature made,
If sight and sound that yield delight,
Are in elysian charm array'd:

For who can bliss or beauty know
Like him, a Rebel from the skies,
Who, though his doom be endless wo,
Hath witness'd all pure Angels prize?

---

* The stanzas which follow, were originally prefixed (as an explanatory introduction) to the author's poem of "Satan." For adequate reasons they are now presented in a detached form.

And such the matter of my verse
Whate'er its fate or force may be,—
Inwoven with the primal curse,
But, hailing immortality.

An awful maze for human Mind!
And enter'd with a holy fear;
God of my sires! where I am blind,
Descend, and make Thy glory clear.

How darkly-bound this scene of life,
How dread the mysteries of time,
And all our being's passion-strife
With things unholy and sublime,

I ever felt:—and deeply now,
As o'er the page my fancies steal,
My spirit seems in awe to bow
Beneath a Sense the bravest feel.

The wings of Darkness are unfurl'd,
The Earth lies hush'd, as in her grave;
And all the sound that thrills the world
The rocking of yon midnight-wave!

Who hath not own'd such tragic hour,
The sadness, and the dream it brings,
Solemnity and spirit-power
Reflected from Eternal Things?

O'er time and destiny we weave
Our inward-fancies, thick and fast;
And start to see, how moments leave
The present, to begin the past!

And we, my friend, howe'er our doom
Of life and years may varied be,
Must pierce the dampness of the tomb
And mingle with eternity.

And what art Thou?—The dark Unknown
Thy name to mortals bound and blind;
Yet like a faint-heard mystic tone
Thy meaning hovers o'er my mind.

I see Thee in the vigil-star,
I hear Thee in the muttering Deep;
And, like a feeling from afar,
Thy Shadow riseth o'er my sleep:

Thou comest where the witching power
Of festive hearts alone should be,
Till life itself appears an hour
That flutters o'er eternity!

Away with this! and may I feel
Whatever cloud o'erhang my lot
There *is* a joy Time cannot steal,
There blooms a flower which fadeth not.

And might I doom my future days,
Like thee, I'd seek some calm retreat
Unhaunted by the public gaze,
And only to the pensive sweet.

For nobler far thy noiseless life
Than all the gayer World can give;
Whose best reward's a wretched strife
'Tween fear to die, and hate to live!

I see thee oft, my guardian friend,
Companion of the mead and bower,—
What glories from the hills descend,
What meekness flows from every flower!

To thee, the hymn of winds and brooks,
The waving joy of wood and field,
With all fresh Nature's thousand looks,
A love and holy feeling yield.

And long be thine the unruffled hour
That leaves thee guiltless as thou art;
And never may one evil power
Profane the heaven within thy heart.

Thus, blooming shall thy pleasures last,
And leave thee grateful, calm, and sage;
While Memory, smiling o'er the past,
Shall be the vesper-star of age.

And when mysterious time is o'er
And round my soul are scenes divine,
Oh, may it reach th' Eternal Shore
As placid and as pure as thine!

BEAUTY.

(1827.)

Oh, Beauty is the master charm,
The syren of the soul,
Whose magic zone encompasseth
Creation with control;
The love and light of human Kind,
And foster-flame of ev'ry mind.

'Twas Beauty hung the blue-robed heavens,
She glitters in each star;
Or trippeth on the twilight-breeze
In melody afar;
She danceth on the dimpled stream,
And gambols in the ripple's gleam,

She couches on the coral wave,
And garlandeth the sea;
Or weaves a music in the wind
Which murmurs from the lea;
She paints the clouds, and points the ray,
And basketh in the blush of day.

She sits among the blossom'd trees
And streaks the bud and flower;
Becharms the air, and drops the dew
Upon the moonlit-bower:
'Tis she unwreaths the locks of Night,
And freshens nature with delight.

And Woman!—Beauty was the power
That with angelic grace
Breathed love around her glowing form,
And magic in her face;
She twined the tendrils of her hair,
And on that brow—Her throne is *there!*

Oh! Beauty is the master-charm,
The syren of the soul,
Whose magic zone encompasseth
Creation with control:
The love and light of human Kind,
And foster-flame of ev'ry mind.

A DAUGHTER'S APOSTROPHE TO A DEPARTED MOTHER.

(1827.)

If gentle spirits wing'd away
To some elysian sphere,
Can hear Affection meekly pray,
Or mark a mourner's tear;

Pure Spirit! shrined in realms of love
Beyond this earthly wild,
Oh! breathe calm influence from above
To bless thine orphan-child.

As oft at pensive eve I roam
Thine image visits me;
While Fancy paints the radiant home
Once so adorn'd by thee!

The smile which rambled o'er thy cheek
And shamed the pang of art;
The mellow tones I heard thee speak,
Still linger round my heart.

That glowing welcome of thine eye,
The fondness in thy fear;
The meek borne anguish in thy sigh,
The pity in thy tear;

The mild reluctance in each frown
That won me ere it changed;
The glance which charm'd my spirit down,
When giddily it ranged;

Those lips that lull'd each maiden wo
And bade the smile to play,
Nor left the scalding tears to flow
But kiss'd them all away,

Yes! these, and all the spells of love
That charm'd my childhood's hour,
Oft bear me to yon home above
To thy seraphic bower.

Oh, if thou hear my orphan-prayer
And yearning fondness see,
Thou know'st I sigh to enter there
And be at rest with thee!

STANZAS.

(1825.)

Oh! rest thee in thy green-turf grave,
There is no sorrow *there;*
For tomb'd within, the wretched have
A freedom from despair.

No more shall come the hour of wo,
Nor hope's delusive light;
Untroubled is thy sleep below,
Upon the bed of night.

The dews of anguish damp'd thy brow,
Thine was the wither'd heart;
No stormy woes can scare thee now,
So dreamless as thou art!

Then rest thee in thine early tomb
Beneath the dewy sod,
Till Mercy shall unshroud the gloom
And summon thee to God.

THE CRUCIFIXION.

(1827.)

Rock of the Church, and Rest of wearied souls!
Thou that wert bosom'd in the searchless depths
Of uncreated Light, before the world
Roll'd fresh and glittering from almighty
Hands,
The hymning Choristers, who harp on high,
Alone the sorrows of Thy love can sing;
Of love, that snatch'd a universe from hell
And oped for man the starry gates of heaven!

Lo! in yon pillar'd hall, amid the hum
Of fierce-tongued soldiers, God incarnate stands
All quivering from the scourge! around they
rave,

And tear His lowly dress with tiger-hands,
Then robe Him in an azure vest, and crown
His godlike temples with entwinèd thorns:
At last, as from His pierced and flesh-torn brow
The heavy blood-drops ooze, with impious jeer
Within His hand the sceptre-reed they place,
And kneel, and bow, and smite His awful head,
And spit upon His grief-worn face, and cry,
"Hail, Monarch of the Jews!"

That mockery's o'er;
And now, to crucifixion see Him led
His cross in front by some Cyrenian borne.
Oh, never yet was such an Altar rear'd!
Oh, never yet was such an Offering slain!
His agony is dumb; they scoff, and taunt,
And grind their murderous teeth, but not a throe
Of ire can ripple His Almighty calm!
Forgiveness is His prayer: The undying souls
Of those long swallow'd in the eternal gulph,
And they who are, and they that *shall* be born
To battle with the Flesh; the Throne of God,
And all the bright-wing'd Choirs, whose harps shall ring
"Salvation!" through the star-roof'd halls of heaven
To welcome back the Heir of Glory,—these
Are imaged round His heart: and deadly pangs
Force no resentful frown.

At Golgotha
The blessed Christ behold! Upon the Cross,
Upon the cross His holy limbs are stretch'd;
And every nerve and vein is rack'd, and wrench'd;
By agonies unspeakable; and look!
How through His palms the hammer'd nails have pierced,
And through His bare and unresisting feet
The red wounds gape, and bleed! Stupendous hour
Of awful pain,—the martyr'd Son of God
On yon dread Tree uprear'd, the World to save!
Approach! and gaze; and wonder till ye weep!
Convulsive lines of torture grave His face,
And flutter o'er His breast; the veins unroll
In loose and languid stretch, and from His brow
The lukewarm life-stream trickles slowly down,
And clots beneath His feet. His head is bent
Blood-matted o'er His shoulder: while His eyes
Dim-grown, and hollow with the rack, look meek
Upon His butchers round the Cross, who scoff,
And o'er His riven garment cast their lots.

And, lo, with eye upturn'd in voiceless wo,
His Virgin-mother! all a mother's pangs
Of pity for her tortured Son upheave
Her bosom, and array her bloodless cheek;
Nor can the deadly riot of His pains
Chill the warm current of celestial love:
Adown, with tender gaze of truth, He looks,
And to the bosom-partner of his toils
Confides the weeping Mary, to a Son!

And sad, but ignominious Sight! two thieves
In bloody fellowship with Christ are hung:
One turns around, with sidelong-glance of scorn,
To rail, and mutters from his parchèd throat
A hideous jeer: the other, meek and faint,
Dejected cries, "Remember me, O Christ!
When Thou art in the palace of Thy love!"
Divine, and glorious answer! "Ere the Day
Shall die, in Paradise with Me thou'lt walk."

But, see, in clouds the Sun hath sunk away
As if aghast! A pall of darkness shrouds
The land of Palestine; a speechless gloom
More ghastly than Tartarean night. The hills
Grow dim; the Rivers moan as if in dread;
And men, with quailing limbs and ashy lips
Come forth, and stare, tongue-tied, upon the skies!
And hark: from off the Cross, is loudly heard,
In piercing tones of death, "My God! My God!
Oh, *why* hast Thou forsaken me?—Again!
"My God! My God! oh, *why* dost Thou forsake?"
'Tis o'er! the blood-red Eye is film'd, and shut
Within its socket; 'gainst His weary breast
The last heart-pulse hath beat; and now, behold
In death's pale slumber, while His tender lips
Have sweet compassion printed on their curve,
The Christ! a Sacrifice for lost mankind.

Oh, never since the infant beam of Time
Glanced on the new-born world, was such an hour!
To symbol it, the Temple's veil was rent;
The Sun of Israel set; the God-breathed curse
With holy Blood was blotted out; Earth quail'd
As though some impulse out of Hell had come
To heave her huge foundations! Every rock
And mountain throbb'd, while o'er the muttering Deep
The dismal waters coil'd, as if they fear'd!
And last, the graves themselves unlock'd, and Shades
Stalk'd out, and glided through the quaking Town,
And floated by the living, like faint-gleams
Of pallid moonlight o'er some haunted Shrine.

Hell heard; and shudder'd as it heard the wail
And dying words of Christ; while Satan howl'd
And gnash'd his teeth, amid the furnace-glow
Of everlasting Fires, to know his wrath
Should ne'er be glutted on the World; that Heaven
Was won, and to rebellious Man unbarr'd.
Unbarr'd!—oh, if Imagination *may*
Plume her young wings, and wander faith-born, there,
A peal more joyous than the choral Stars,
Upon the birth-day of created Worlds,
Re-echoed round her crystal domes; while all
The countless Seraphs wreathed their lustrous wings
In awe, before the lightning-shrouded Throne
Of God invisible; then, woke their harps
To melodies divine, and hail'd The Lamb
Triumphant from His martyrdom below!

Two thousand Years have almost floated down
The gulph of time, since on the glorious Cross
Divinest Martyr! Thou wert nail'd: the world
With all its pageantry and pride prevails;
Men smile and struggle, labour, sin, and die
As if Thy Blood had never blotted out
The crimes of earth; as if, at last, Thy might
And majesty should *not* appear! Still, Thou
Hast prophesied, again the Incarnate God
This earth will visit and her dead restore.—
But, not as homeless orphan of the world,
To wander on in pain and wo, and weep,
And perish on the Tree; but on Thy car
Of lightning, rolling from unfathom'd depths
Of heaven, while seraphs robed in radiant light,
Brandish their glitt'ring banners o'er Thy throne,
And all the clouds like burning billows flash
And bound beneath Thy feet!—The Trump shall peal
That dead-awakening blast, more full and loud
Than thunder in its deepest roar: the Sea
Shall yawn, and all her buried hosts arise;
The graves burst open, and the dust unite
Into a living Form; and then, shall come
The Judgment, and our Everlasting Doom!

STANZAS WRITTEN IN DEJECTION.

I.

THE pining leaf, the perish'd flower,
The tints of autumn thrown
In pensive ruin o'er some bower
Where gay spring-buds had grown;

The faltering wave, the feeble cloud
Which faints like thought away,
With Nature's warning unavow'd
Predict our own decay.

And who can look down Life's dim vale
Where buried hours repose,
Or listen to the rueful tale
Of man's recurring woes,

Nor feel within the spirit-core
A pang of mute regret,
For feelings that exist no more,
For joys whose sun is set!

Yes, Lady! in this life of dreams
My heart has had its share;
And still around wild fancy beams
The wreck of visions fair;

But hollow laugh, and heartless smile,
And tones of mirth untrue,
Can barely mock the soul awhile
And veil it from thy view.

Another to the countless mass
Of Spirits who have fled,
I add my sigh, as on I pass
To regions of the dead!

II.

Yon sunbeams in their brightest mirth
Are dancing o'er the sea,
And hues and harmonies of earth
Betoken summer's glee.

I watch the clouds with fairy glide
Athwart the blue air gleam,
And view them mirror'd on the tide
Like features in a dream:

The very leaves are toned with joy
And carol to the wind,
Gaily as when, a pangless boy,
They echo'd back my mind:

Gladness and glory blend their sway
Around this ocean scene;
And yet, to me the brightest day
Is dark, to what hath been!

The flowers of hope, the young and fair,
Are dewless, cold, or dead;
The lip may laugh, but where, oh, where
The inward sunshine fled?

I hear the voice of vanish'd Hours,
And mourn the buried Past;
Oh, why should feeling e'er be ours,
And nought but memory last!

OYSTERMOUTH, *July*, 1833.

THE DREADFUL PRAYER.*

(1827.)

No priestly vows avail'd: gaunt Famine stalk'd
Through Cairo's streets by day and night, and suck'd
The life-blood from her hungry thousands there.
From wall to wall, from house to house, were heard
The gasping yells of famish'd men, and wail
Of mothers, with dead infants at their breasts,
Whose bakèd lips, and eyelids curling up
Like wither'd violet-leaves, and fleshless hands,
Were blasted by the pest of Famine's touch!
In agony some gnaw'd their nails; some groan'd
And with a horrid glare their eyeballs work'd,
Rooted their tresses,—and expired! And here
Pale groups, with bony cheek and beamless stare,
Stagger'd abroad, and choked themselves with cries
For death; while others, 'neath funereal-palls
Moved slowly on, like sable thunder-clouds;
Then sat, and howl'd upon the new-dug graves!
So ghastly look'd the bloodless Shapes around,
That Cairo seem'd a charnel-house revived
Whose dregs were crawling into life again!

In vain the Priests with agonising prayer
Storm'd the mute Heavens; no Mercy smiled
An answer to their vows. Still, Famine swept
Her thousands into dust; still, every wind
Wing'd to the skies the howlings of Despair!
At length, unspotted babes, whose milk-white robes
Gleam'd pure as dove-wings on the radiant air,
By Imans led, the Minaret-spires up climb'd
For pestilence to pray, the Famine's cure!
There, on the gilded peaks their hands were raised
In adoration clasp'd, as if with prayer instinct;
And while their cherub-mouths in lisping tones
The plague besought, a pale-eyed Crowd below
Stirr'd like a moaning Wind upon the deep;
Their lean lips moved, and mutter'd, "Let it be!"

That prayer Heaven heard: a Pestilence came down,
And made an atmosphere for death! Men dropp'd
Into corruption, thick as winter blights
Upon the poison'd bushes. Hill and dale,
Hamlet and city, groan'd with ghastly piles
Of green-eyed dead: the houses turn'd to tombs;
And they who roam'd the Desert's dewless wilds
Were plague-smit by the way, and moulder'd there
Like riven branches from a forest-tree:
And thus was Cairo cursed, till by the dead
The Plague, itself corrupted, died away!

INFANCY.

"The smile of childhood on the cheek of age."

A CHILD beside a mother kneels
With lips of holy love;
And fain would lisp the vow it feels,
To Him enthroned above.

That cherub gaze, that stainless brow
So exquisitely fair!
Who would not be an infant now,
To breathe an infant-prayer?

No crime hath shaded its young heart,
The eye scarce knows a tear;
'Tis bright enough from earth to part
And grace another sphere!

And I was once a happy Thing
Like that which now I see;
No May-bird on ecstatic wing
More beautifully-free:

The cloud which bask'd in noontide-glow,
The flower that danced and shone,
All hues and sounds, above, below
Were joys to feast upon!

Let Wisdom smile, I oft forget
The colder haunts of men,
To hie where infant hearts are met,
And be a child again:

To look into their laughing eyes
And see the wild thoughts play,
While o'er each cheek a thousand dyes
Of mirth and meaning stray:

---

* See Anastasius, vol. i. p. 101.

O Manhood ! could thy spirit kneel
Beside that sunny child,
As fondly pray, and purely feel
With soul as undefiled,

That moment would encircle thee
With light and love divine;
Thy gaze might dwell on Deity
And heaven itself be thine !

BEAUTIFUL INFLUENCES.

"Suppose the singing birds musicians;
The flowers fair ladies; and thy steps no more
Than a delightful measure, or a dance."
SHAKSPEARE.

(1829.)

Oh for a summer-noon, when light and breeze
Sport on the grass like ripples o'er a lake
Alive with freshness; when the regal Sun,
With God's own smile upon his forehead seen,
Walks in his golden radiance through the path
Cerulean.—Vast and overhanging heaven !
Arching the earth with thy majestic sweep,
At such an hour, with what unsated eye
We look upon thee, till the mind seems lost
In thine immensity, and we appear
O'erwhelm'd by such a vision.
Care-worn man !
Whom Duty chains within the city-walls
Amid the toiling crowd, how grateful plays
The fresh wind o'er thy sickly brow, when free
To tread the elastic turf; and hear the trees
Wave music on the gales; to catch the voice
Of waters, gushing from their fount unseen,
And singing as they wander :—How sublime
Upon a time-blanch'd cliff to muse, and while
The eagle glories in a sea of air,
To mingle with the scene around ! survey
The sun-warm heaven, or at the cavern'd base
Of yon wood-crested mount, the ocean view
With radiant billows ruffled by the breeze:
Then, dawns the resurrection of thy youth
In dewy freshness o'er thy wither'd heart !

Nor is the scene, though unbeheld, forgot;
The eye is faithful to a feeling heart:
When torn from some Arcadian haunt, we thread
The crowded city's unromantic streets,
The spot we love refreshing influence yields;
Beneath our feet a fairy pathway flows;
The grass still flutters in the summer-winds,
The dusky wood and distant copse appear,
And that lone stream, upon whose chequer'd face
We mused, when noon-rays made the pebbles gleam
With gem-like dazzle through the wrinkled tide,
Is mirror'd to the mind: though all around
Be rattling hoofs and roaring wheels, the eye
Seems wandering where the *heart* delights to dwell.

Are there not hours of an immortal birth,
Bright visitations from a purer Sphere,—
A trance of glory, when the Mind to heaven
Attuned, can out of dreams her worlds create?
Oh ! none are *so* absorb'd, as not to feel
Those calming thoughts which harmonise the mind.
When prayer, the purest incense of a soul,
Hath risen to the Throne of heaven, the heart
Is mellow'd; and the shadows which becloud
Our state of darken'd being, glide away;
The heavens are open'd; and the eye of Faith
Looks in, and hath a mystic glance of God !

And, Genius, undisputed gift of heaven,
From Thee what feelings flow ! the passions own
Thy sway, and waken at thy quickening power
Like flowers expanding to the breath of morn.
Then bind his temples with a fadeless wreath;
Give him the proudest seat, a princely rank
And all the deeper homage of the mind,
Who like a god among mankind is felt,
And, from the purest sunshine of his soul
Sends forth the rays which glorify the world !

Who hath not felt the might of genius rise,
And stir his spirit to a storm of thought?
Oh ! had I kingdoms, I would yield them all
To him, whose thoughts like angel-wings exalt
The fancy, and a thousand springs unlock
Of feeling, that have never gush'd before.
So noble is such joy, that I have blush'd
For all dark thoughts, for all demeaning cares.
In such rapt mood our solitude is fill'd
With bright creations; and elysian scenes
Ope in a vision on the eye of Thought.
Thus charm'd by Genius, hie thee to the haunts
Where Nature shows her blooming face ! how bright
The sun, how beautiful the liquid air,—
Like floating music ! and the soft-toned wind
Around thee warbling like a conscious joy.
A veil of beauty o'er the world is drawn,
Till thy heart seems to beat for all mankind,
And, full of glorious feeling, thou wouldst fain

Become an Angel to adore thy God,—
A more than mortal to complete His praise.

And will not Mind a beauteous influence yield?
Oh, glorious 'tis, amid some room antique
To study, all alone, those pictured Shapes
From the soul's Eden call'd! where genius sheds
Spells of entrancement round you; and while the eye
Banquets on beauty, from a painter's soul.
Whether a landscape, whose ethereal lights
Like gleams upon the water, glow o'er tree
And bower, and sky luxuriantly bespread,
Or love-shaped forms, or features angel-bright
Float o'er the enamour'd gaze,—a rich
Excess, a harmony of feeling rules
The fancy, when again the world we greet;
The mind with loveliness is bathed, which yearns
Enchantment over common scenes to throw,
And make dull earth draw nearer heaven, at last!

Who hath not felt the *spirit* of a Voice,
Its echo haunt him in romantic hours?
From Melody's own lip who hath not heard
Sounds which become a music to his *mind?*
Music is heaven-born! In the festal home
When throbs a lyre, as if instinct with life,
And some sweet mouth is full of song, how soon
From eye to eye a rapture flows, from heart
To heart! while, floating from the past, the Forms
We love, are re-created; and the smile
Which lights the cheek is mirror'd on the heart.
So beautiful the potency of sound,
There is a magic in the homely chime
Of village-bells; I love to hear them roll
Upon the breeze; like voices from the Dead
They seem to hail us from a viewless World!

And yet, nor music, nor the painter's mind
Upon the canvas breathed, a charm imprints
So deeply-faithful, as the piercing glance
Of young-eyed Beauty. Beauty!—she hath been
The witching tyrant of the universe
Since her young blush in Paradise began;
Her throne Time cannot shake; stern Wisdom bows
Before her; warriors are her slaves; and half
The vassal world hath worshipp'd at her feet!
Her glance is conquest; and the Mind is moved
Like air by music haunted, when her name
Melts on the ear, and makes the heart serene.
Then, cursed be he that with unhallow'd eye
Can look on Beauty; which for heaven is born,
The boast of nature, and the spell of souls!

LOST FEELINGS.

"But yet we stand
In a lone land,
Like tombs to mark the memory
Of hopes and joys which fade and flee
In the light of life's dim morning."

Oh! weep not, if our beauty wears
Beneath the wings of time;
That age conceals the brow with cares
That once appear'd sublime.

Oh! weep not if the clouded eye
No sunny thought can speak;
And fresh and fair no longer lie
Joy-tints upon the cheek;

And weep not, if the ruin-trace
Of wasting years is seen
Around the form, and in the face
Where youthful lines have been:

But mourn the *inward* wreck we feel
As blighted hours depart,
And Time's corroding fingers steal
Young feelings from the heart!

Those bounding thoughts which rise and spring
From out the buoyant mind,
Like summer-bees upon the wing
Or echoes on the wind;

The hopes that sparkle every hour,
Like blossoms from a soul
Where sorrow sheds no blighting power,
And care has no control,

With all the rich enchantment thrown
On Life's fair scene around,
As if the world within a zone
Of happiness were bound,—

Oh, these endure a mournful doom
As day by day we die;
Till age becomes a barren tomb
Where perish'd Feelings lie!

March, 1828.

THE TRANCE.

A FRAGMENT.

(1827.)

————One faint and lingering glance I took,
And then, all vanish'd in the sickly light
That swam around the bed; all seem'd to melt,
Shaded by indistinctness, like the shore
From those who wander far on ocean-waves:

A dazzling giddiness my brain dissolved;
The eye-balls sunk; and coldly press'd like lead,
While creeping chills my pallid form bedew'd,
That shrank as if it shudder'd at itself,
Or would condense, like water ere it freeze!
My life-fount curdled into clotted blood;
Then, cold and nerveless lay each marble limb,
And moisten'd with the mystic dews of death.

Sightless, and breathless, thus entranced I lay;
Though motionless, with *feeling* so acute
As if it doubled, to make up for sight:
Thus, like a solitary cloud, I seem'd
Self-balanced in a universe of gloom!

And, oh! how sad it was, to hear and feel
Fond friends around me, dreaming Death had closed
All sense of life; their blood-warm lips to feel
Upon mine ice-cold face, and then to hear
Their heart-swell'd groans, and choking sobs and sighs
While gazing on my hush'd and breathless form!

When midnight-bells had toll'd the World to sleep,
A young, but unforgetting sister, came
To meditate, and sorrow o'er my doom:
Her printless steps I knew, as on they stole
Like twilight o'er the flowers. And, when she took
My pulseless fingers in her pale-worn hand,
And kiss'd the marble brow, and talk'd so sweet,
And lisp'd her mournful love,—how horrible
That Language could not speak my conscious mind!

Two days departed; then, the wonted shroud
Enwrapp'd me, and around my body clung
Like ruffling waters: last, the coffin came,
And well I knew, as with a fear-like touch
Of trembling hands, my dead-cold form they lay
In funeral vest enveloped. But more drear
Than all, was that long, sad, and silent hour
When, one by one, the speechless mourners took
Their last and lingering glance; their sighs I felt,
And tears which burn'd my cheek,—but yet, was *still!*

And, oh, most horrible!—The nails I heard
Pierce the crush'd wood and seal my coffin-lid;
And then, the rattling hearse, the grave-side prayers,
The thick and careless clods, which patter'd down
Upon my bier, till bedded with the dust;
And then——

TO * * * *

Oh, Lady! in my boyish hour
Perchance thou seest me gay as young,
The dazzled slave of pleasure's power,
With rapture in the heart and tongue.

Yet, think not thus I ever seem,
As though *beyond* the world's alloy;
For darkness girds our brightest dream,
And sorrow tones our deepest joy!

I never knew a moment yet
Which did not wear *some* withering stain,—
An outline of a dim regret,
Or shadow of some coming Pain!

Alone amid the world I move,
With scarce a smile, or tear, for me,
And not a heart to share the love
That springs from bosom-sympathy:

Without it, what can realms bestow
Of all harmonious natures feel?
It is to kindred mind we owe
The magic Time delights to seal.

But, may no winter-shade intrude
Upon the spring-time of thy lot,
And all which mars my gayest mood
In thy young freshness be forgot:

May heaven attend thee, wheresoe'er
The bright-wing'd years may waft thee on;
And nothing cloud that blissful air
All eyes have loved to look upon!

September 4th, 1829.

LONELINESS.

"We are not happy, sweet; our state
Is strange, and full of doubt and fear;
* * * *
Hiding from many a careless eye
The scorned load of agony."

Lost in the peopled desert of the world,
Cheer'd by no heart which echoes back our own,
How feverish all the pomp and play of Life!
A solitude there is which lifts the mind

To lofty things,—seclusion from the rush
And stir of that unfeeling Crowd, whose days
Reap scarce a thought to sanctify their flight.
Far from the city-din, may Wisdom haunt
Her veil'd retreats, and yet not live *alone;*
For, is there not the fellowship of books
Divine, a company of gracious thoughts,
And all which Nature yields a grateful mind?
Such is not loneliness!—Around to look
Life's crowded world, and 'mong its myriad-hearts
No sympathies to find, our own to nurse,
Oh, this makes loneliness! that solitude
Of mind, which bids the world a desert seem.
What is the guerdon of ambition worth,
Of common lips the cold applause, the crown
Of genius, or the envied wreath of Fame,
Graced by no smile from some congenial soul?
For, when the heart is full, an overflow
Of bliss, by being shared, is sweeter still:
The bashful flowers which in the May-breeze shake,
Bloom out together: and belated Stars
Of night walk not yon pathless heavens alone,
But twinkle, though unseen, in blissful play
Of sympathetic beams; all beauteous Things
Hold mystic fellowship; and fine-toned hearts
Without responding hearts,—how bleak and bare!
In sorrow lone, in happiness the same.

A man I knew, in mind and fame supreme
And yet, not happy, though by happiest ones
Admired. A loftiness of feeling sprung
From centuries dead and ancestors unknown,
Together with a soul-born pride, which soar'd
Far o'er the varied scene of vulgar life,
In childhood fill'd him with a thirst of fame.
High fancies, from the hills and mountains caught;
And inspiration born of lovely streams,
And silence-loving woods; and all the rays
Of beauty which creative mind attracts
From scenes by Contemplation sought,—awoke
His genius into glorious play; the lyre
He struck; a World admired, and wreathed his brow
With the green laurels of a lofty fame;
For him a thousand tongues grew eloquent!
A thousand eyes would sparkle forth his praise;
And, when amid the brilliant throng he sat
A gay-tongued hypocrite, the hour to charm,
And not obstruct the flow of joy, the dreams
Of young Ambition brighten'd at his praise;
Alas, how often his unecho'd mind
Clothed its mute anguish with concealing smiles!
That soul within a secret blank remain'd
Which admiration could not fill. Alone;
No trusting heart, no gentle voice of love,
No happy faces round his evening-hearth
Were his to love; and what was brief renown?
A shade! and he?—a soul in solitude.

EPSOM, *October*, 18*th*, 1828.

STANZAS.

"The flower that smiles to-day,
To-morrow dies;
All that we wish to stay,
Tempts and then flies;
What is this world's delight?"

THE hour is past, the pleasure o'er,
And dumb the heart of glee;
Young feet no longer trip the floor
Alive with melody.

Those fairy brows, those forms of love
That wake the dreamer's sigh,
Like Shapes who leave their bowers above
To charm a human eye:

All, all are gone! the lights have fled
From yon deserted room;
Dim as a chamber of the dead
And voiceless as the tomb:

And now I am alone again,
With feelings undefined;
A pilgrim in a world of pain,
An unpartaken Mind.

The silent walk, the sickly moon,
And melancholy sky
Unite to make me feel how soon
These hours of beauty fly.

Oh, pleasure! brief as bright thou art,
A momentary ray,
A dream roll'd o'er a vacant heart
To charm, and melt away!

June, 1828.

STANZAS.

(1825.)

WHO hath not watch'd the heaven of eve,
When round the horizon seems to weave
A sea of clouds, whose bosoms heave
In floating beauty, there?

Those lovely phantoms, how they glide
In all their calm and airy pride,
Moved by the breath of eventide
Along the dew-lipp'd flowers!

Some, crimson-wove, voluptuous sail;
Some, girdled with a ruby veil;
And others, beaming brightly-pale
As Beauty's pensive brow.

And thus smiles now this rose-wreathed room,
Where float along in braid and plume
All blushing with their virgin bloom
The maidens of the night.

Lo, yonder trips a blue-eyed troop,
Who bend their glowing heads and droop,
As graceful as a lily-group
All languid with perfume.

And near them glides a gentle pair
That dance their grape-like clustering hair,
As if their very ringlets were
Communing with their joy!

On each fair cheek a life-blush warms,
While, radiant with expressive charms,
The virgins twine their ivory arms
And circle through the dance.

Like moon-gleams shivering on the lake
Their feet with dizzy motion shake,
As down the dance their steps they take
With love-beams in each eye.

Then, why, amid this heaven of joy
Should dreams of darkening woe annoy,
Or thoughts of blighting gloom destroy
The elysium of the hour?

Alas! the scene will swiftly fade;
The music cease; depart the maid,
And cold-eyed Day the room invade,
With uncongenial smile!

Some hearts will pine, and some will weep,
And many in the grave will sleep,
And every eye shall sorrow steep
Ere we unite again!

Yes, many a Shape of love and light
Whose eyes are glittering with delight
Like starry Dreams that visit night,
Shall wither into clay!

A SAD THOUGHT.

I LOVE the present; but the past
Hath such a spell around it cast,
That oft from all I hear or see
I turn, dead Time! to gaze on Thee;
And o'er the grave of buried hours
Bid Memory strew her pallid flowers!

THE TOMB OF GRAY.

(1836.)

THE poetry of dreams that spot surrounds
Where Genius ponder'd; when oblivion's pall
In mocking darkness on the tomb of kings
Descendeth, memories bright and deep pervade
The quiet scene where once a Bard has been.
For him the laurel deathless! when the wreath
Dyed by the blood of Victory's crowning hand
Withers to nothing on the warrior's brow,
How many a foot, where pensive Gray hath roved,
Will love to linger! 'Tis the spell of mind
Which consecrates the ground a Poet trod;
With living thoughts the air is eloquent,
And fine impressions of his favour'd muse;
While Inspiration, like a god of song,
Wakes the deep echoes of his deathless lyre.

In the calm glory of declining eve
'Twas mine to wander where the tomb* of Gray
In green seclusion stands. Around me smiled
A Landscape, veil'd with sunlight's pallid robe
Of beauty, over tree and landscape drawn.
On such, (by contemplation's dream enticed
Like Isaac, oft at eventide to muse)
The Bard had gazed; and drew from Nature's heart
How many a touch of grace, and tone of song!
While Eton, with her turrets grey, her towers
Antique, in azure distance frown'd;
Or round him, in their rich confusion, throng'd
The sounds that wait on sunset's balmy hour:—
The lay of birds; the sheep-bell's lowly chime;
The chirping insect in the grass conceal'd;
The bough made vocal by the exciting breeze;
Or shout of home-returning shepherd boy,
And city-hum,—all charm'd his dreaming ear.

But, lo, the churchyard! Mark those "rugged elms,"
That "yew-tree shade," yon "ivy-mantled tower,"
And thread the path where heaves the "mouldering heap;"
Then, Stranger! thou art soulless earth indeed,
If the lone Bard beside thee does not stand
Form'd into life by Fancy's moulding spell!
'Twas *here* he mused; here Poetry and Thought,
And Silence, their enamour'd Sister, came;
And Taste and Truth their kindred magic blent,

* In the romantic churchyard of Stoke Pogis, near Eton.

And proud Attempt, and pure Conception rose,
While Melody each chord of mind attuned;
Till soft Religion, like an Angel, smiled,
And bade his genius make the grave sublime.

Sweet Bard! whose mild and meditative lays,
Or lyric numbers, warm with classic fire,
Heal the torn mind, or thrill young Memory's heart
With deathless pleasure, Time hath not despoil'd
Thy crown poetic of one glorious leaf:
Yet many, since thine eyes in death were veil'd,
Have grasp'd the laurel; harps of witching tone,
And thrilling strains of more impassion'd swell,
Round the rich world of Poesy have flung
Enchantment,—yet thy page is precious still.
And *wherefore?* 'Tis because the moral heaven
Remains unsullied by thy words, and dreams:
And hence, amid the Babel-voice of song,
In such pre-eminence to thy calm powers
Accorded. Thus, when lays corruptly-sweet,
The flash and fire of o'er-excited verse
And mock intensity, have ceased to charm,
Back to thy page, by purity inspired,
The Heart returns; and finds a magic there
Of thoughts which bloom beyond the earth's decay:
And hence, when Stars of more ambitious light
Shine dimly through the hazy depths of Time,
Bard of the Soul! for ever wilt thou reign
An Orb of beauty in the heaven of song.

WHITTINGTON, NEAR OSWESTRY,
SHROPSHIRE.

THE MINSTREL'S FUNERAL.

"Thou shalt go to thy fathers in peace; thou shalt be buried in a good old age."—*Gen.* xv. 15.
"The hoary head is a crown of glory, if it be found in the way of righteousness."—*Prov.* xvi. 31.
"Even to your old age I am He; and even to hoar hairs will I carry you."—*Is.* xlvi. 4.

A Christian never dies; in coffin'd dust
What though he slumber, and the speechless grave
With cold embrace his pallid form receives,
Religion, like the shade of Christ, appears
To heaven-eyed Faith beside the tomb to smile;
And from her lips, seraphically fired,
Rolls the rich strain, "O Death! where now thy sting?
O Grave! thy victory, where?"—extinguish'd both,
And baffled; stingless Death, and strengthless Law*
Together round the Cross like trophies hung
Self-vanquish'd; *Death* himself in Jesus died!

The Christian never dies; his dying hour
To him a birth-day into glory proves:
For then, emerging fetterless and free
From this dark prison-house of earth and sin,
(All sensual dimness like a veil withdrawn)
In mystic radiance soars the seraph-mind
To regions high and holy; where the Truth
Essential, Beauty's uncreated form,
And Wisdom pure, in archetypal state
To souls unearth'd their trinal blaze reveal.—
Unchain the eagle, break his iron bars,
And when aloft, on wings exultant poised,
Sunward he sweeps through clouds of rolling sheen
And makes the blue immensity his home,
Go, mark him! while the flash of freedom breaks
Forth from each eye-ball, in its burning glee;
And there, the imaged rapture of a mounting Soul
When prisonless, from out the body pure,
May fancy witness!— far away it flies,
And where the Sun of Righteousness enthroned,
Eternal noon-tide round His ransom'd pours,
Basks in the smile of glory, and of God!

And thus of thee, the venerably-good,
The mild old Man with apostolic mien,
Let memory in some heavenward moment, think;
Thou art not dead, but from thy bondage free!
Alive, as in the sunbeam lives the mote,
Art thou, encinctured with the blaze of heaven
In that Assembly, where the crown'd ones chant,
With robes blood-whiten'd by the wondrous Lamb.†
Oh, what a sunburst of immortal truth
In keen effulgence on thy spirit broke
When forth, from out the fettering walls of flesh
It soar'd!—the dull eclipse of death no more,
The daylight of eternity begun!
Thy bed around, while children knelt and pray'd,
And sorrow trembled into tears and sighs,
Thine was the song ecstatically-loud
From harping Angels, and from hymning Saints
In concord, round the throne of Jesu raised!
And who, when gospel-music charm'd thine ear,
Or promises with preciousness divine
Deep-laden, lighted up thine aged eyes

* 1 Cor. xv. 55, 56.
† Vide the Apocalypse, *passim*.

With more than youth's glad lustre,—who that heard
Thy holy breathings for the better Land,
And did not from his eyelids dash the tear
Of mourning, when he thought, that thou wert *there!*
In that pure Home of perfect light and peace
At length arrived! to that bright City brought,
Whose silver-turrets oft thy faith beheld,*
When down the streets Imagination walk'd,
By angels, and the Church's first-born lined!

Around that tomb, where thy cold ashes sleep,
The unbought homage which a good man wins
'Twas mine to witness, when the gather'd crowd
Attended, with a train of weeping Hearts
Who knew thee best, and therefore mourn'd thee most.
And well that Scene thy pure and placid life
Betoken'd; Feeling deck'd thy funeral;
The moral blazonry of Christian grief
Was there, and touchingly the whole array'd
With more than splendour,—with the truth of tears!

The hoary Minster, eloquent as vast,
Lifting its forehead with cathedral-grace,
Whose form revered some twice three hundred years
Have girt with grandeur, like a zoning spell
That binds bewitchingly; the tombs antique
By jagged walls, in sculptured ruin bent;
The graves of myriads, like a sea of mounds
In swells of grass on all sides rank'd, and ranged
In death's confusion,—till their cited dust
Leaps into life beneath the trumpet blast
Of Time's archangel, striding Earth and Sea!†
The rock-hewn church-yard, with its green uprise
Of monumental landscape, where the grief
Of Nature, and the grace of Sculpture vie
In soft contention, each expressing each,
And hiding death between them, by the spell
That o'er the grimness of the grave is thrown;
All this, while high in front, severely-calm,
The fearless Knox in stony grandeur frown'd,—
Together met, a scene of soul combined,
And made one Sentiment the whole become
Of sacredness and silence! Childhood hush'd
Its laugh; and Youth each lawless smile forewent;
And the mute Crowd a single mourner seem'd,
When slowly, to its last long home was borne
Thine earthly portion! Heaven the better took;
Thy tomb within, one farewell-gaze we had,—
The heart out-speaking with a tongue of tears,
While friend on friend a look of meaning turn'd,
And said no more! The *soul* must speak above;
No language learns it in this world of graves
And gloom; for silence forms a spirit-voice,
When Faith and Feeling by the tomb embrace.

Pure on the bosom of almighty Love
From sin and sorrow thou art resting now:
And who would bring thee, might availing tears
Be answer'd, back to this cold earth again!
To peace and glory, to perfections high
Around thee smiling, rather may we mount
On these sure wings of faith that carried thee;
And o'er the track thy saintly virtues trod
Her way let holy Imitation wend,
Her eye on Him intently fix'd, and firm,—
Our bright Precursor to the Cross and crown!

And now, farewell! If age's hoary charm;
If gentleness, with solid worth combined;
If faith and truth, by patriarchal grace
Bedeck'd; if boundless love, that god-like smiles
Serenely, over Sects and Names enthroned;
If these were thine; with all the enriching spell
Of temper, cloudless as the crystal noon,
And feelings, tuned by every tender call;
While round about thee hung the glow
Of youth's gay morning, by the eve of age
Subdued, like spring and autumn's blended smile,—
Then, o'er thy grave recording Truth may bend;
And drop, not undeserved, the simple wreath
Of memory, a Muse has ventured now.

F arewell! A few more rolling suns and years
Will yon dark Minster from his turret speak
Of Time's departure, with an iron-voice*

* In allusion to Heb. xii. 22, 23,—verses which Dr. Burns pre-eminently loved to quote.

† See Apocalypse.

* The bell to which a passing allusion is here made, acts as a curfew to the inhabitants at the hour of ten each night. On the outside is the following inscription: "In the year of Grace, 1594, Marcus Knox, a merchant in Glasgow, zealous for the interest of the reformed religion, caused me to be fabricated in Holland, for the use of his fellow-citizens of Glasgow, and placed me with solemnity in the tower of their cathedral. My function was announced by the impress

Wailing a hollow dirge o'er life's dead Hours,
And the roused Earth at ev'ry pore will heave
Around thee! Myriads from their pulseless clay
In throbbing consciousness shall rise, and bound
Warm into being!—What a mass of life
Under the trumpet's dead-awaking call
Will stand, and tremble in the gaze of God!
And thou wilt rise; nor rock, nor mountain seek
To crush thee, from the piercing eye of Him
Array'd in lightnings of resistless glare,—
Immanuel! on the Judgment's burning throne
Of glory, wheeling through the heaven of heavens.
And when creation in a tomb of fire
Shall welter, and the wicked lift a cry
Of quenchless agony, beneath the frown
Of truth's Avenger, undismay'd thine eyes
Will greet Him; thou shalt look on God, and live!

PROVIDENCE.

FRAIL king of dust, Man loves to look around,
And think,—"for *me* the elements abound
With life and motion; shade and sunshine wait
In mixt attendance on my human state;
Light, sea, and air, their glorious spell maintain
That I alone, as Lord of Earth, may reign!"
And yet, what art thou?—but a fleeting breath,
A pulse of life which throbs away in death!
Myriads of creatures round thee move and die,
Minute beyond the ken of mortal eye;
Perfect as *thine*, their bright existence teems
With beauty, in a paradise of beams;
Or in some crystal-world of water play
A floating populace of insects gay;
And He who bade exalted Man to be
An Image of His own eternity,
Alike to them a form and feature gives,
And not a mote but in His mem'ry lives!

---

in my bosom. Me auditô venias, Doctrinam Sanctam ut Discas. And I was taught to proclaim the hours of unheeded time. 195 years had I sounded these awful warnings, when I was taken by the hands of inconsiderate and unskilful men. In the year 1790 I was cast into the furnace, refounded at London, and returned to my sacred vocation. Reader, thou also shalt know a resurrection,—may it be unto eternal life. Thomas Mears, fecit, London, 1790."

GLASGOW, 21*st February*, 1840.

IN MEMORIAM

C. H. E. M.

VANISH'D Infant! years have fled
Since thou wert coffin'd, pale and cold;
Yet, to me thou art not dead,
But still mine inward eyes behold
The fairy brow, and form, and cherub feature
Perfect as when they graced the living creature.

Little dream unloving Hearts
Which never thrill'd with parent-gladness,
Seldom from the soul departs
A shade of unpartaken sadness,
Cast by the death of some sweet babe who died,
As though this World its young soul terrified.

Coil'd within man's secret mind
Mysterious chords of feeling dwell;
But they ne'er their charms unwind
Till something wakes their dormant spell,
When lo! at once with magic life they move
Deeper than passion, but divine as love.

Ever thus, in casual street
A nursling pillow'd on the breast
If alone I chance to meet,
How oft it brings a fond unrest!—
The aching flutter of a wordless thought
With more than mem'ry in full action fraught.

Almost in my hand I feel
The cling and clasp of baby-fingers,
And a life-breath o'er me steal
Which faintly ebbs, and fondly lingers;
Till once again a cradled form I see,
And breathe, dead Flower! a father's prayer for thee.

Like a dove-wing in the sky
Melted and mingled with soft light,
Hast thou faded from an eye
That when it saw thee, grew more bright;
But still, in love's eternity thou art
A *living* infant to thy father's heart.

DIVINE OMNISCIENCE.

MERE chance exists not; 'tis a libel dread
On Providence, which those unblest of mind,
Poets of Vice, and laureates of Despair,
Often pronounce,—who into merest fate
The motions of our moral world resolve.
For, God o'er all eternally presides;

And, from the quiver of the bladed grass,
To wheeling Systems, hung in starry space
Enormous as unnumber'd,—all occurs
How, when, and where, His guiding will decrees.
And we, who now with backward-gaze revolve
The hoary annals of Mosaic time,
Behind the curtain of that outer-scene
Where man was acting, view His prompting Hand
At work for ever: Hist'ry's moving form
Points like an index to that secret God;
E'en as the timepiece, which the hour reveals,
The hidden motion of a main-spring shows.

SOVEREIGNTY OF DIVINE GRACE.

Goodness to all may infinitely come,
But pard'ning Grace for sinners *only*, acts.
And thus, o'er evil triumphs endless good
Beyond all words (save what in Heaven they speak)
Rightly to equal with o'ertaking praise,
Or rapture. Yet, in this a Will Supreme
Itself must glorify, by calling whom
The counsel of the Holy One decreed
To make a monument of grace divine
Ere Time to count his awful hours began.
Yes, though in justice no election acts,
But each award to character applies
With truth unerring; yet, when Mercy smiles,
Prerogative alone the Godhead shows
Unquestion'd, such as men, nor angels, scan,
Nor measure.—Motive God hath none;
For that, from His completeness steals a ray,
And on the orb of true Perfection casts
A veiling shadow: Motive, End, and Aim,
All in Himself eternally abide.
His reasons are His attributes alone;
And each vast grace the Trinity unfolds
In mercy's fulness, acts divinely-free.

THEOLOGY FOR MOTHERS.

And, oh, fond mothers! whose mysterious hearts
Are finely-strung with such electric chords
Of feeling, that a single touch, a tone
From those ye fondle, some responsive thrill
Awakens, when at night, a last long look
Which almost clings around the form it eyes,
Ye take of slumb'ring Infancy, whose cheeks
Lie softly pillow'd on the rounded arm,
Rosy, and radiant with their dimpling sleep,—
Well may ye waft upon some wingèd prayer
A grateful anthem to your Lord enthroned,
Who, once an Infant on His mother's knee,
Not in His glory childhood's life forgets!
For He, while systems, suns, and countless worlds
Hang on His will, and by His arm perform
Their functions, in all matter, space, and time,
Can hear the patter of an infant-foot,
List to the beating of a mother's heart,
Or, seal the eyelid of some babe at rest.

A MOURNFUL TRUTH.

But, like the lustre of a broken dream,
How soon the fairy grace of morning-life
Melts from the growing child! Corruptive airs
Breathed from an atmosphere where sin is bred,
Around them their contaminating spell
Exhale; and Custom, with its hateful load
Of mean observances, and petty rites,
Bends into dust those Instincts of the skies
In the pure heart of genuine Childhood seen,
And, so enchanting! Then, comes artful Trick,
With forced Appearance, and the feeling veil'd,
When Fashion's creed or Folly's plea forbids
A free expression. These, with blending force
The sweet integrities of Youth assail
For ever: mar the delicacy of mind,
And from the power intact of conscience take
Its holy edge; and soon the Child impress
With the coarse features of corrupted Man.
And, add to this, how omnipresent sin,
That from the womb of being to our grave
Infects our nature with a fiendish blight,
Will act on passions earthly, and desires
Malignant, base, or mutinously warp'd
From virtue,—and, alas, how quick we find
The vestal-bloom of Innocence depart!
Then, what remains of all that blessèd prime,
That blooming promise, which the fair-brow'd Child
Of beauty gave in home's domestic bowers?—
Lisping God's love beside parental knees,
And seeming oft, as if the Saviour's arms
Had compass'd them, and left a circling spell
Round his soft being! Where, oh! where is gone
The unworn freshness of that fairy Child?

GOD'S INFANTS.

Yes! eloquent, and touching more than tears,
Those incarnations of maternal dreams,—
Infants, by Beauty's plastic finger shaped,
Have ever been: in all their ways and moods
A winning power of unaffected grace

Poetic faith, or pious fancy, views.
Wild as the charter'd waves, which leap, and laugh
By sun and breeze rejoicingly inspired,
Till the air gladdens with the glowing life
They shed around them,—who their happy frame
Can mark; or listen to their laughing tones;
Behold their gambols, and the fairy gleams
Of mirth which sparkle from their restless eyes,
Nor feel his fondness to the centre moved
Beyond a mere emotion? But, to watch
The tendrils of the dawning mind come forth,
The buds and petals of the soul expand
Day after day, beneath a fost'ring care
And love devoted,—*this* Religion deeply loves!
How the Great Parent of the universe
The outward to the inner-world hath framed,
With finest harmony; and for each sense
Some region of appropriate joy secured,
Philosophy may there, with reverence, learn,
As grows the virgin-intellect of youth
Familiar with all forms, effects, and moods
Of Nature, in her majesty or might.
And, what a text on Providence we read
In the safe life of shielded Infancy!
For, who can count the multitude of Babes
That look more fragile than the silken clouds
Which bask upon the bosom of the Air
They brighten,—God's o'ershading Hand secures!
And number, if Arithmetic can reach
The total, what a host of tiny feet
Totter in safety o'er this troubled world!
Though all around them throng, and rage
Destructive Elements, whose faintest shock
Would strike an infant into pulseless clay.

HEAVEN POPULOUS WITH INFANT SOULS.

Then, look not lightly on a pensive child
Lest God be in it, gloriously at work!
And blind Irrev'rence touch on truths, and powers
And principles which round the Throne are dear
As holy. Never may our hearts forget
That Heaven with infancy redeem'd is full;
Crowded with babes, beyond the sunbeams bright
And countless. Forms of life that scarcely breathed
Earth's blighting air, and things of lovely mould
Which, ere they prattled, or with flowers could play,
Or to the lullaby of watching Love
Could hearken, back to God's own world were call'd:
And myriads, too, who learnt a prayer to lisp,
Bend the soft knee, and heave Devotion's sigh,
Or caroll'd with a bird-like chant the psalms
Of David, with the Church in Heaven are found.

THE HEART'S SANCTUARY.

And thus, there is a loneliness of heart,
In all deep souls a never-enter'd shrine;
Where neither love, nor friendship takes a part,
Which no eyes witness, but, Jehovah! Thine.

But, shall we mourn, that each is circled round
With veiling mystery from the ken of man?
That waters deep within the soul abound
No word has fathom'd, and no wisdom can?

No, rather let such merciful disguise
Move the just thinker unto grateful prayer;
For, who could live beneath terrestrial eyes
If such could witness *all* secreted there!

And if no mantle by our God were thrown
Round fallen souls, to hide man's world within,
How should we hate, what now we love to own,
And cry for darkness to conceal our sin!

"THE HOLY CHILD JESUS."

How beautiful the brow of Jesus was,
Methinks Imagination's hallow'd dreams
Would fain adumbrate. Virgin-born was He!
Not shaped by sin, but, through o'ershading power
Divinely-perfect, His conception took
Human Reality in flesh and form
Embodied. Never did one taint of earth,
A touch of sensual feeling, or a tone
Of temper, harshly-loud, or rudely-quick,
Assail the soul of that mysterious "Child."
And therefore, Beauty's most ethereal power
Haply upon His forehead's arching grace
Was throned; and from His eye's divine appeal
Broke a soft radiance, exquisite and deep;
Or, on His lips pure Inspiration sat;
While from the glory of His heaven-born face
There beam'd expression on the gazer's mind,
Awfully mild, and full of melancholy;
And, like the cadence of an Angel's sigh,
Could such be sadden'd, moving more than tears.

REASON AND FAITH.

By Unbelief our primal nature fell
From light to darkness; and by Faith it mounts
Back to the glory whence its pureness sank:
But still, that fatal tyranny of Sense,
Which Adam first around the virgin-soul
Allow'd to cast its paralysing chain,
Abides; and needs a disenchanting spell
Beyond mere Reason, in its brightest noon,
To shame or silence.—Yes, the Felt, the Seen,
And Tangible, alone appears the True!
Our touch must regulate the law of truth,
And to the Body must our high-born Soul
Stoop like a slave, before the mind admits
Motives divine, and miracles of grace,
Or myst'ries, where the Infinite Unknown
Enshrines His nature, and His love reveals.
Yet, 'tis the madness of outrageous pride,
The dismal lunacy of self-esteem;
And Reason here a suicide becomes,
When god o'er God it thus presumes to be,
And dwarfs the Everlasting down to Man!
But, faith is reason in its noblest form;
And boasts an evidence most heavenly-bright,
Sublimely-equal to our Spirit's need,
In whatsoe'er submissive Love believes
From Deity derived, our world to save.
For, breathe we not the Church's sainted air
Where all is fragrant of the truths of old?
And ritual Forms, and ceremonial Types,
With each high record of auxiliar sway,
Historic truths, traditionary lore,
And monuments of sacramental Grace,—
These have we not? And, though rejecting pride
Back on the blaze of this commingled orb
Of evidence, a sneer presume to cast,
Yet, have the wise and wondrous to such light
Their hearts submitted, and repose enjoy'd.
And, more than this, a clear-eyed wisdom finds:
For if unrisen were our spirit's King,
Then long ere this the Galiléan Lie
Had vanish'd!—for the Creed its claims involve,
Binds on the world offensive purity
Which flesh endures not: and if Christ were dead,
Tomb'd in the darkness of sepulchral clay,
How could His promise with our souls to be
Present for ever,—*still* on earth be proved
Infallible, through faith's unbounded world?
A living Christian *proves* a living Christ
As firmly to the soul, as if the heavens
Were now uncurtain'd, and our eyes entranced
Look'd through the Veil and saw Him shining there
In glory, bright as what the Martyr view'd,
When Stephen mounted from his mangled clay
In bleeding triumph, to his Master's breast.

GOD IN MATERIALISM.

God in creation is a glorious thought;
Making the Matter, which we touch, or see,
Like mute religion on our senses act;
And to all forms and faculties of Things
A power imparting, more than mere delight.
'Tis thus, in nature God alone we hail
The ground of Being, and the grace of all
That in this temple of Creation stands.
No dead Abstraction, no almighty Law
To faith suffices:—Life itself is God
In will, and wisdom, actively employ'd:
It spurns the idol, Second Cause, and springs
On to the Infinite and only First!
Creation a Theocracy becomes,
When thus perceived; intelligibly ruled
By that Great King, Whose hidden sceptre sways
Alike the dew-drop, and the host of worlds.
And, blest is he, who thus through nature walks
Companion'd by its Author! Scenes and sounds
Are unto him as Tokens of His power,
Perpetual Teachers of mysterious love.

Feeling the work, but Faith the worker views
Devoutly: and the pomp of heaven's display,
The floor of ocean, the green face of earth,
And each variety which Objects wear,
With more than language to his mind appeals,
Proclaiming Him, Whose Power no sabbath keeps
But quickens nature with incessant laws.
And how this acts where'er we walk, or muse!
Freshens the grass, and beautifies the flower,
Gives to the canopy of heaven a grace
Beyond the symmetry of clouds to form;
And so with reverence the soul attunes,
The very air-song seems to warble truths
Celestial; syllables by Angels toned,
Haunt the pure breathings of the balmy wind
Around us heard: and when along the shore
Haply we roam, in some reflective dream
When life hangs heavy on the grief-worn heart,
The billows make a litany of sound
Which half interprets what sad Thought suggests.

God in creation!—'tis a Creed sublime
Which makes all nature solemn; and the mind
With such desire for veneration fills,
The universe one vast Shechinah grows
Whence Piety, creation's priestess, draws
Prophetic glimpses, as the tribes of old
Drew from the Breastplate, where the Urim gave
Responsive radiance and unerring law.

THE CHURCH IN CANADA.

(INSCRIBED TO THE BISHOP OF TORONTO.)

RECORDS of Grace divinely move
  The Church's heart with hymnèd praise,
When the deep thought, how guardian Love
  Has camp'd around her peril'd ways,
In some high mood of heaven-born calm
O'er mem'ry breathes a solemn balm;
Till Christ Himself in shadows seems
To rise upon Her ancient dreams.

"For ever with you, I shall be,"—
  Here is Faith's charter, strong as heaven!
Framed by incarnate Deity
  And to His mystic Body given,
When, for Her mission-work on earth,
The sacrament of second Birth
Her Lord imparted; and the grace
To spread it o'er earth's boundless race.

Though manacled in murd'rous flame,
  The martyr'd herald of The Cross
Hath gloried in Messiah's name
  And counted life, not death, a loss:—
That Charter, like a living power
Sustain'd him in some tortured hour;
While viewless Angels, hov'ring nigh,
Wafted to heaven his farewell-sigh.

Yes, fire and sword, and dungeon-gloom,
  And all which Hell and Hate have done
To bury truth in falsehood's tomb,
  And blast the triumphs Faith has won,
The heroes of the Church have braved:
And never left Her cause enslaved,
Since all they suffer'd, fann'd the zeal
Her sacramental Warriors feel.

Thus Canada! thy church and creed
  Pure as our own, from England bred,*
When Loyalty was doom'd to bleed
  And banner'd Treason myriads led,
A sworn allegiance nobly kept
While havoc round thee raged, and swept,—
Ark'd in the promise of thy Lord,
And safe within His shelt'ring Word.

By Lake Ontario's rocky shore
  Where creedless pagans once abounded,
And exiles heard the torrent roar
  By wood and wilderness surrounded,
Churches arise; and saintly Bands
Have come from far and famous lands;
And apostolic Symbols reign
O'er rescued swamp and ransom'd plain.

But never, till that Day of light
  When God shall grief and guilt disclose,
Will thankless myriads learn *aright*
  What to her Church Canadia owes:
For, social worth, and moral grace,
Freedom divine, and all we trace
Of present heaven in heart and home
From Faith, and not from Culture, come.

The churchless, soon, are godless, too!
  The unbaptised grow base and blind;
And where no sacraments renew
  The sin-worn heart and earth-toned mind,
All virtues die; all vices bloom;
The soul becomes a sensual tomb,
And men the Saviour yearn'd to cherish,
Eternalise their guilt, and perish!

Hence, laurell'd with a wreath of love
  Be Stuart's * patriarchal name;
While Langhorn, in the Church above
  With Addison, of kindred fame,
May oft, perchance, the Past revive,
And view salvation's harvest thrive
From germs divine 'twas theirs to sow
Through scorching years of toil and woe.

* See the Rev. Ernest Hawkins' valuable work, entitled "Annals of the Diocese of Toronto." At page 3 he says: "Canada was the asylum of suffering loyalty; some of its earliest settlers were refugees from the United States."

* For interesting records of these Apostles in the Church of Canada, consult Mr. Ernest Hawkins' "Annals," &c.

THE INSPIRATION OF DREAMS.

No incantation which the outer-sense
In the full glow of waking life perceives,
Rivals the magic by mysterious Night
Evoked, when Dreams, like messengers from heaven
Rise from eternity, and round the soul
Hover and hang, ineffably-sublime;
But mocking language, when it tries to catch
The true expression of their awful power.

  And, how religious is the sway of Dreams,
Which are the movers of that secret-world
Where most we suffer, learn, and love,
Building our Being up to moral heights,
Stone after stone, by rising truths advanced
To full experience, and to noble aims.
The tombs of time they open, till the forms,
The faces and the features of our Dead
Lighten with life, and speech, and wonted smiles!

While mem'ry beautifies the Thing it mourns,
And to the Dead a deeper charm imparts
Than their gone life in fullest glory had.
And thus, in visions of the voiceless night,
Apparel'd with that beauty which the mind
Gives to the loved and lovely, when no more,
Rise from their tombs the Forms of fleeted days,
Friends of bright Youth, the fascinating-dear!
Till back returns life's unpolluted dawn;
And down the garden-walk, or cowslipp'd field
Where once he prattled, full of game and glee,
The man, transfigured back to childhood, roves
Tender as tears. So, on the wind-bow'd mast
The sailor-boy in dreams a mother hails,
And hears her blessing o'er his pathway breathed;
Or, pale and gasping, ere his life-drops ebb
For ever, how the Soldier thus depicts
In the soft dream of some remember'd day,
The hands which rear'd him; or the hearts that heaved
With omens, when the charm of tented fields
Seduced him from the sweets of sainted home
And virtue. Dreams are thus half-miracles;
All time they master; and all truths embrace
Which melt the hardest, and our minds affect
With things profounder than our Creed asserts.

SACREDNESS OF INFANCY.

A dew-drop, trembling on the stem of Life;
A rose-bud peeping into fairy bloom;
A billow on the Sea's maternal breast
Leaping, amid some jubilee of airs
By glad winds caroll'd; or, a dancing beam
Of sunlight, laughing in its brightest joy;
In truth, whate'er is delicate and soft,
Minute and fragile, innocent or gay,
Oft to the mirror of the mind presents
Types of that beauty which a tender babe
To feeling Manhood's fascinated eye
Affordeth; touch'd at times with solemn hues,
Which Hearts prophetic cannot fail to cast
Round a frail Heritor of life unknown!

But, when o'er Revelation's book we bend,
There do we find, with more than love confirm'd,
Whatever Nature by her mute appeals
Hath prompted: for the Bible e'en to babes
Lends the sweet mercy of its soft regard
And bland protection. Other creeds may scorn
Such aidless Being; and the gibing laugh
Of Science o'er their frailness may uplift
Its godless pēan; but in this we boast,—
That Christianity the cradle seeks,
Stoops to a babe with condescending brow;
And while the Pagan, by her creed transform'd
From yearning softness into heartless stone,
Commits her infant to broad Ganga's stream
Foodless to perish, Christ in Spirit comes,
Commands the Priesthood on its forehead plant
The sealing water, and the mystic sign,
And bids it welcome to His Ark of grace.

CHRIST IN THE HEART'S CLOUD.

He stood before her, but she could not *see*
That Holy One: and oh! how often, thus,
The sad experience of a stricken mind
Like Mary, cannot view the Lord it loves,
Though in the mercy of our ev'ry breath,
And in the promise of His perfect Word,
In prayer, and praise, and sacramental life,
Together with that unbreathed thought which tells
Home to the heart acceptance in the skies,
When the free spirit of assuring grace
Glows in our bosom,—though in each and all
Christ to the conscience doth himself present,
Yet, Mary-like, the soul mistakes Him, still!
Some carnal shade, or clouding sin prevents;
And the high faculty of seeing Faith
Grows undiscerning; or, in nature's eye
The tear of sorrow doth so thickly stand,
That *through* it, God himself grows unbeheld
A moment: nothing but dark grief is seen!

WORLDLINGS.

How much Anxiety the heart corrodes
Wasting the moral health of man away,—
We seldom ponder, till too late perceived!
When, under burdens, which ourselves inflict,
The Intellect of half its glorious life
Is sapp'd, while conscience turns a crippled thing;
The heart gets agèd ere the head grows old,
And those bright virtues, which might nobly shine
In that clear firmament of thought and power
Where lofty Manhood would exult to act,
Rarely, if ever, into influence dawn.
For else the grandeurs, graces, charms, and scenes,
The smiles of matin, and the shades of night,
Sun, moon, and star, wild mountains and glad seas,
Meadows and woods, and winds and lulling streams,

With fruits, and flowers like hues of paradise
Amid us scatter'd,—would so well impress
The moral being, that responsive Mind
Upon the Beautiful would back reflect
An answer, most intelligibly pure,
To each appeal of Beauty. But the World
Can so infect the myriads of mankind,
That all those latent harmonies, which link
Nature to man by loveliness and might,
Lie undiscern'd; and though a spirit deep,
A living sentiment of love and truth,
In all Creation cultured souls may find,
How few perceive it! but, on objects gaze
With eye unmoved; as if by God unmade
Their beauties, and by Him unform'd their powers!
Nature to them in all her shrines is mute;
Nor to Her mystic oracles, which yield
Such music to Imagination's ear,
Can the cold worldling condescend to list.

THE PEOPLE AND PRAYER BOOK.

Nor be forgot, that England's Prayer Book gives
Pure, full and plain, The Word by which she lives;
Not dungeon'd in some dead and alien tone,
But where the peasant-boy perceives his own.

There, lisping Childhood, when it longs to learn
Truths for which Prophets bled, and Martyrs burn,
In such pure liturgy of grace may find
All which can feed the heart, and form the mind.

For, Common Prayer, if catholic and true,
Must not be tinged with individual hue,
But be proportion'd to the soul of Man,
In deep accordance with Redemption's plan.

INDIVIDUAL PROVIDENCE.

And, there are moments, when mysterious Life
Is so attended with a train of Facts
Sudden and strange, through which a mercy glares
With such intensity of sacred light
Full on the conscience,—that Paternal care
To us revealing God's elective will,
Runs through the heart with overwhelming proof!
And bids it, like ecstatic Hagar, cry,
By Heaven when mercy-struck to more than prayer.
And He, the Infinite by Form array'd,
Who took our Nature in all sinless truth
Into His Own, as Man embodied loved,
In modes and shapes of individual cast.
For, while in Providence th' unblemish'd Lord
Moved on the lines of Justice and of Truth,
Boundless, beyond respect of single homes
Or spirits; He, in walks of social life
Loved like a Man, and chose the friend He will'd:
And hence, the winning might Emmanuel wields
By His example! for, on Person, Place,
And Time, His pure affections deign'd to shed
Their fullness. He who wept a City's doom,
As if the crashing of its crumbled walls
Rang in his ear, while Roman butchers bathed
Their swords in slaughter, also, by a grave
Wept o'er the dead, most humanly perturb'd,
And to His bosom took the mild St. John!

A PRODIGAL'S RETURN.

And now, behold him, wither'd, tatter'd, bow'd;
Pale with long famine, wearily he drags
His homeward-track; but, so by suff'ring worn,
That through the village, where his boyhood dwelt,
Unknown he steals, disguised in haggard woe.
Oh, what a tide of memory there rolls,
And what a gush of agony and grief
Runs through his being, when *that* hill he gains,
Climb'd in calm hours of vanish'd innocence,
And underneath him in the sunset pale
Looks on the landmarks of paternal home!
Mute with remorse, amid the tranquil scene
Awhile he ponders; till the silent forms
Of Things grow eloquent with meek reproach:
Meadow, and tree, and each familiar nook
Instinct with meaning, to his mind appeals
With more than language from Rebuke's harsh lip,
For, Nature yet her old expressions wore,
And each loved haunt remain'd familiar still.
There, was the olive he had loved to watch;
There, was the vine his infant hand had pluck'd;
And there, a field-path, where he often paced
As bright in spirit as the joyous beam
Beside him, and with step as gaily-swift
As the wild breeze which hurried o'er his head;
Nothing look'd alter'd:—for, the fig-tree stood,
And caught the day-gleam in its dying glow
As oft his boyhood watch'd it, when he sat

Under the twilight of its laden boughs
And fondly wove his fancies; and, how sweet
The lulling cadence of yon well-loved stream!
E'en as of old, so wound its waters still
In stainless beauty, down their pebbled way:—
Nothing has changed; but, oh, how changed is *He!*

MORAL INFLUENCE.

Our moral centre is a point minute:
But our circumference, oh! who can grasp,
In action, suff'ring, or involved Result?
A smile, a glance, a single breath, a tone,
A look of meaning, or a laugh of scorn,
The mere expression of the hectic mind
Clothing our features,—each may, haply, thrill
Some chord which touches by effectual ties
Events unborn; and make th' eternity
We dread, to vibrate with the deed we do!

Oh! for a sense of Duty more sublimed,
In all our ways, our wishes, and our words:
A sense that we are links in that long Chain
Of Consequence, which e'en from Adam's sin
To our last error, its unbroken length
So reaches, that we *cannot* act alone!
But rather, each with each is so inwove
By past connection, or by future power,
That Conduct grows immortal; and the act
From soul to soul with multiplying power,
Itself repeateth, when the Agent sleeps
In cold oblivion, by the world forgot.
The blemish'd morals and the blotted mind
How often thus our Rev'rence would escape!
And 'stead of reckless pride, religious care
The paths would purify where Virtue walks,
And solemnize existence. Action, then,
Inward, or bodied forth in social form,
Of sacredness in every sphere would breathe;
Till the whole Earth a mystic Temple grew
Hallow'd by God, by angels overwatch'd,
And by Humanity in all its moods
Devoutly-trodden: then would Duty spread
Its canopy above our ways and walks,
E'en as the heaven o'ervaults the varied earth
For ever: Faith would be our Law supreme,
And guarded Life one long religion prove.

THE LAKE OF BEAUTY.

A MORNING SCENE AT VEVAY.

Lake Leman! in the hush of this deep hour
The poetry of waters is thy power;
And o'er my spirit steals that lulling calm
Which bathes the earth in some celestial balm.

Here from my window, with a spell-bound gaze,
I view yon shore beneath a silver-haze
Unshroud its glories; till, with dim uprise
The Alpine summits cleave the sun-lit skies.

Far to the east, those mountain-kings enthrone
Their rocky grandeurs o'er the ice-born Rhone,
Whose foreheads, pure as angel-brows, present
Their dazzling whiteness to the Firmament.

And who can mark thine awful Mountains gleam,
When faintly-hued with morn's seraphic beam;
Or, crimson'd o'er with magical array
Caught from the rosy death of ling'ring day,

Nor feel them, like an infinite Control,—
Embodied hymns, where Silence to the soul
Speaks more of God, than thunder, wave, or wind,
With dark-wing'd Terrors, from the storm combined?

Thus may true Poets from their presence gain
Fresh purities, which o'er the conscience reign;
Till thoughts grow vaster than the lyre can own,
And Man seems lifted to his Maker's throne.

But, Leman! once again to thee I turn,
And from thine everlasting beauty learn
Profounder Wisdom than a sage can teach,
Whose words are bounded by the sense's reach.

While soft, yet stern, though mild, majestic too,
Serenely-bright, and exquisitely-blue,—
Almighty Taste around thy scene hath cast
What makes thy loveliness the unsurpass'd!

For ever varied!—rock, and terrace, field,
Vineyards and turrets, tower and village yield
A concentrated Spell, which thus imparts
A more than landscape to melodious hearts.

And seldom, since the bend of beauteous skies
Enrich'd thy waters with reflected dies,
Hast thou, fair Leman! more ideal bliss
For mind created, than on morns like this.

The grace, the gentleness, and glow of heaven
Now to thy charms are so intensely given,
That on thy waveless sea of fairy sound
The Heart seems floating, as we gaze around.

And hark! the drip of yon descending oar
In wafted grace as glides the boat ashore,
With what a cadence it enchants the ear,
And drops in radiance, like a dazzling tear,

Down on the waters !—where a breezy strife
Makes Leman palpitate with rippling life,
And liquid glances, as the broken sun
Laughs on the dimpled stream it lights upon.

Earth, air, and sky, and range of rocky pass,
Glaciers, and crags, and sternly-wild morass,
The bird, and foliage, field and distant towers,
Vine-mantled hills, and fancy-haunted bowers,

Blent with the mellow chimes of matin-bell
Heaved o'er the Lake with deep and dying swell,—
Oh! how can words such pictured Whole combine,
Or Leman roll through this imperfect line?

E'en like a Consciousness of sound and scene
Nature doth now her master-spells convene;
And lovingly this hour for man array
As though She treasured what *his* eyes survey;

While leafy murmurs from yon flutt'ring trees
Quiver abroad like new-born ecstasies,
And gleams come dancing down the golden air,
As though bright angels hover'd everywhere.

Yet, in mine incapacity of speech
This lulling paradise of Lakes to reach,
Still can I feel, that even thus the soul
Bows in its unbreathed thought to *that* Control

Which God intended, Who to scene imparts
Predestined magic, framed for deathless hearts,
Whose pulse with His eternity shall glow—
When Earth has vanish'd like an air-born show.

A purifying calm of central power
Attunes high feeling to this chasten'd hour;
And from the World's more artificial scene,
Oft shall it woo me to this Lake, I ween.

Meanings divine endow a Morn like this
With magic that outsoars an earth-made bliss;
The very soil grows sanctified and fair,
And deepens poetry to silent prayer.

Beauty is hallow'd, when on mind it leaves
An impress grander than mere Sense conceives;
Till all without, within, below, above,
Becomes transfigured to almighty Love.

And thus, that God from Whom vast nature flows
Inspires religion through the heart's repose;
And so connects it with creation's plan
That heaven seems throbbing through the earth on Man!

INDEX.

THE END.

LONDON:
BRADBURY AND EVANS, PRINTERS, WHITEFRIARS.

Lightning Source UK Ltd.
Milton Keynes UK
UKHW020730191218
334233UK00007B/627/P

9 780656 347988